Lecture Notes in Computer Science   6582

Commenced Publication in 1973
Founding and Former Series Editors:
Gerhard Goos, Juris Hartmanis, and Jan van Leeuwen

T0181032

Martin Wirsing   Matthias Hölzl (Eds.)

Rigorous Software Engineering for Service-Oriented Systems

Results of the SENSORIA Project
on Software Engineering
for Service-Oriented Computing

 Springer

Volume Editors

Martin Wirsing
Ludwig-Maximilians-Universität München
Institut für Informatik
Oettingenstraße 67
80538 München, Germany
E-mail: wirsing@pst.ifi.lmu.de

Matthias Hölzl
Ludwig-Maximilians-Universität München
Institut für Informatik
Oettingenstraße 67
80538 München, Germany
E-mail: matthias.hoelzl@pst.ifi.lmu.de

ISSN 0302-9743   e-ISSN 1611-3349
ISBN 978-3-642-20400-5   e-ISBN 978-3-642-20401-2
DOI 10.1007/978-3-642-20401-2
Springer Heidelberg Dordrecht London New York

Library of Congress Control Number: 2011925495

CR Subject Classification (1998): D.2, D.3

LNCS Sublibrary: SL 2 – Programming and Software Engineering

Typesetting: Camera-ready by author, data conversion by Scientific Publishing Services, Chennai, India

Printed on acid-free paper

Springer is part of Springer Science+Business Media (www.springer.com)

Preface

Service-oriented computing (SOC) is a paradigm for developing and providing software that can address many IT challenges, ranging from integrating legacy systems to building new, massively distributed, interoperable, evolvable systems and applications. Government agencies and enterprises from many economic sectors have already adopted service-oriented architectures (SOAs) as the basis of their IT infrastructure. The widespread use of SOAs demonstrates the practical benefits of this approach, but it also raises the bar for reliability, security and performance for IT providers, system integrators and software developers.

The initial implementations of SOA in industry and practice were performed without a clear understanding of the theoretical foundations of SOC. Many challenges, such as dynamic automated composition, compensation of long-running transactions, performance prediction, and security guarantees were not taken into account; little support was available for using formal methods to validate or verify SOA-based systems.

The SENSORIA project has addressed these problems from first-principles, building novel theories, methods and tools to support the engineering of service-oriented computing systems. SENSORIA, an Integrated Project funded by the European Commission in the period of 2005–2010, was one of three Integrated Projects of the Global Computing Initiative of FET-IST, the Future and Emerging Technologies action of the European Commission.

The SENSORIA Consortium consisted of 13 universities, one research institute and four companies (two SMEs) from seven countries[1]; the project was coordinated by Ludwig-Maximilians-Universität München. The scientific output as well as the practical impact of SENSORIA are impressive: more than 650 scientific articles were published, three start-up companies were founded, more than 25 students obtained their PhD thesis for research within the project; SENSORIA methods and techniques are taught in many university courses and several summer schools were organized around the SENSORIA topics.

This book presents the main results of the SENSORIA project. It shows a novel comprehensive approach to the design, formal analysis, automated deployment, and reengineering of service-oriented applications. The SENSORIA techniques

---

[1] Ludwig-Maximilians-Universität München, Università di Trento, University of Leicester, Warsaw University, Technical University of Denmark at Lyngby, Università di Pisa, Università di Firenze, Università di Bologna, Istituto di Scienza e Tecnologie della Informazione "A. Faedo", University of Lisbon, University of Edinburgh, ATX Software SA, Telecom Italia S.p.A., FAST GmbH, Budapest University of Technology and Economics, S&N AG, Imperial College London (London Software Systems), University College London (London Software Systems), School of Management Politecnico di Milano (MIP), ATX Technologies SA, Cirquent GmbH.

enable service engineers to model their applications on a high level of abstraction using service-oriented modeling languages; automated model transformations convert between these notations and formal calculi. This enables the principle of "hidden formal methods": Tools based on formal methods developed as part of the project, e.g., for checking the functional correctness of services, early performance analysis, prediction of quantitative bottlenecks in collaborating services, and verification of service level agreements, can be used by developers without detailed knowledge of the underlying mathematical formalisms. Thereby SENSORIA integrates foundational theories, techniques and methods with pragmatic software engineering for service-oriented architectures.

This book starts with short introductions to SENSORIA and the SENSORIA case studies in the areas of e-finance, automotive engineering, telecommunications and e-university. The remainder of the book is divided into seven parts corresponding to the research areas of SENSORIA: modeling in service-oriented architectures, calculi for service-oriented computing, service discovery, negotiations and reconfiguration, qualitative analysis techniques for service-oriented computing, quantitative techniques for quality of service and service level agreements, model-driven development and reverse-engineering for service-oriented systems, as well as case studies and patterns.

Many people contributed to the success of the SENSORIA project. We offer sincere thanks to all of them. We are particularly grateful to the EC project officer Wide Hogenhout for his continuing encouragement, patience and support. We thank the project reviewers Jim Davis, Frantisek Plasil, Mathilde Romberg, Wolfgang Schreiner and Carles Sierra for their always constructive and helpful criticism and suggestions. We are also grateful to Springer for their helpful collaboration and assistance in producing this book. Our sincere thanks go to all authors for the high quality of their scientific contributions and to the paper reviewers for careful reading and many suggestions for improvements. Finally, we thank all SENSORIA members for their excellent work, their inexhaustible effort and never-ending enthusiasm for achieving the goals of the project.

November 2010

Martin Wirsing
Matthias Hölzl

Table of Contents

IV   Negotiations, Planning, and Reconfiguration

V   Qualitative Analysis Techniques for Service-Oriented Computing

VI   Quantitative Analysis Techniques for Service-Oriented Computing

VII   Model-Driven Development and Reverse-Engineering for Service-Oriented Systems

VIII   Case Studies and Patterns

Sensoria – Software Engineering for Service-Oriented Overlay Computers*

Martin Wirsing, Matthias Hölzl, Nora Koch, and Philip Mayer

Ludwig-Maximilians-Universität München, Germany
{wirsing,hoelzl,koch,mayer}@pst.ifi.lmu.de

Abstract. Service-Oriented Computing is a paradigm where services are understood as autonomous, platform-independent computational entities that can be described, published, categorized, discovered, and dynamically assembled for developing massively distributed, interoperable, evolvable systems and applications. These characteristics have pushed service-oriented computing towards nowadays widespread success, demonstrated by the fact that many large companies invested a lot of efforts and resources to promote service delivery on a variety of computing platforms, mostly through the Internet in the form of Web services. In the past, service-oriented computing and development has been done in a pragmatic, mostly ad-hoc way. Theoretical foundations were missing that are needed for trusted interoperability, predictable compositionality, and quality issues like security, correctness, or resource usage. The IST-FET integrated project Sensoria has addressed these issues by developing a novel comprehensive approach to the engineering of service-oriented software systems where foundational theories, techniques and methods are fully integrated in a pragmatic software engineering approach, supporting semi-automatic development and deployment of self-adaptable (composite) services.

1   Introduction

Selling services rather than hardware or software has become the biggest growth business in the computing industry. Business in this area has already evolved from relatively simple (customer) services to global complex (business) solutions. Computing is becoming a utility and software a service. This trend is changing the economics of IT industry and influences the e-Society as a whole.

In the service-oriented computing (SOC) paradigm, services are understood as autonomous, platform independent computational entities that can be described, published, discovered, and dynamically assembled for developing massively distributed, interoperable, evolvable systems. Today, services are being delivered on a variety of computing platforms, mostly through the Web, Personal Digital Assistants, and mobile phones. Tomorrow, they will be delivered on all kinds of global computers and a plethora of new services will be required

---

* This work has been partially sponsored by the project Sensoria, IST-2005-016004.

M. Wirsing and M. Hölzl (Eds.): Sensoria Project, LNCS 6582, pp. 1–14, 2011.

for e-government, e-health, and e-science, just to name a few of the areas that are already taking shape within the Information Society. Thanks to their ability to be dynamically assembled, services can provide a much required layer of integration between the different global computers that are being studied and proposed by industry and academia for supporting the operation of the future Information Society. As a result, service-oriented computing is bound to play the role of an ideal overlay computer for Global Computing.

In the past, service-oriented computing and development has been done in a mostly ad-hoc way. Theoretical foundations for trusted interoperability, predictable compositionality, and quality issues like security, correctness, or resource usage were not well-established and service-oriented software development was not integrated in a controllable process based on powerful analysis and verification tools. Furthermore, it was not clear whether formal approaches to service-oriented software development would scale up to the development of large, complex systems.

In order to answer these questions, SENSORIA has developed a novel comprehensive approach to the engineering of software systems for service-oriented overlay computers where foundational theories, techniques and methods are fully integrated in a pragmatic software engineering approach. This approach is focused on global services that are context-adaptive, personalizable, and may require hard and soft constraints on resources and performance; it takes into account the fact that services have to be deployed on different, possibly interoperating global computers to provide novel and reusable service-oriented overlay computers.

The results of SENSORIA include a new generalized concept of service for global overlay computers, new semantically well-defined modeling and programming primitives for services, new powerful mathematical analysis and verification techniques, tools for system behavior and quality of service properties, and novel model-based transformation and development techniques. The innovative methods of SENSORIA are demonstrated by application in the service-intensive areas of e-business, automotive systems, and e-university.

This chapter is structured as follows: In section 2, we introduce the SENSORIA project with its aims and contributions to the field of service-oriented computing. Sections 3 to 5 outline the three main research themes of SENSORIA and provide pointers to the remaining parts of the book. We conclude in section 6.

2   SENSORIA – Well-Founded SOC Development

The core aim of the SENSORIA EU project was the production of new knowledge for systematic and scientifically well-founded methods of service-oriented software development. SENSORIA provides a comprehensive approach to design, formal analysis, automated deployment, and reengineering of service-oriented applications. The research themes of SENSORIA therefore range across the whole life-cycle of software development. SENSORIA methods and tools rely on mathematical theories and methods that allow rigorous verification of SOA artifacts.

Realistic case studies for different important application areas including telecommunications, automotive, e-learning, and e-business are defined by the industrial partners have been used to verify the applicability of SENSORIA methods to industrial domains.

In SENSORIA a model-driven approach to service development was chosen, as it enables developers to control the variety of specific distributed, global computing platforms, and to ensure a strict separation of concerns that can break the complexity of service composition and evolution. In this approach, services are first modeled in a platform-independent architectural design layer; these models are then analyzed using formal methods and refined; afterwards, they can be used for generating implementations over different global computing platforms in a (semi-)automated way. This is shown in Fig. 1.

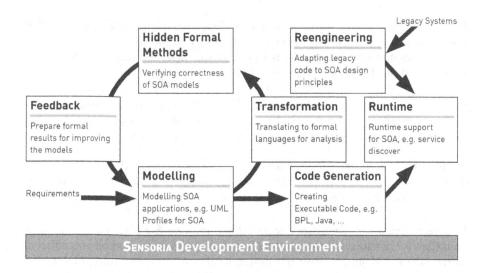

Fig. 1. SENSORIA support for the model-driven development process

In more detail, the main technical ingredients that SENSORIA provides to the service engineer are:

Modeling. Service-oriented applications are designed using high-level visual formalisms such as the industry standard UML or domain-specific modeling languages to precisely capture domain-specific requirements.

Transformation and Feedback. Formal representations are generated by automated model transformations from engineering models.

Hidden Formal Methods. Back-end mathematical model analysis is used to reveal performance bottlenecks, or interactions leading to errors or violation of service contracts. For critical services, the developers can perform deep semantic analysis for certification.

Feedback. Feedback from the formal analysis is presented to the developer in a way that is easy to understand and used to improve the engineering models.

Code Generation. The high-level models are used to generate executable code, e.g., in Java or BPEL, and configuration data for deploying the resulting services to various standards-compliant service platforms.

Runtime. The generated code can utilize advanced run-time infrastructure that was developed as part of the SENSORIA project, e.g., dynamic service brokering, as well as standard service platforms.

Reengineering of legacy services. Many existing systems are built as monolithic non-extensible applications which cannot be easily adapted to new business processes. SENSORIA develops methods to transform these applications into layered systems with well-defined service interfaces.

SENSORIA *Development Environment.* The SENSORIA Development Environment supports the above activities by providing an Eclipse-based, fully-customizable tool chain for the entire model-driven workflow.

These individual development activities have been grouped into three major themes that served as drivers for the scientific research of the SENSORIA project; they also provide the structure for the remainder of this book:

Linguistic Primitives for Modeling and Programming SOA systems. Language primitives for services and their interactions have been developed on two different abstraction levels, an architectural design level and a programming abstraction level for service overlay computing. The scientific tools used are category theory and process calculi, defining software architectures and programming languages for mobile global computing systems. To make these formal approaches available for practitioners, appropriate UML extensions have been devised which provide a visual representation of the declarative modeling primitives. In addition, the process algebraic programming primitives and their mathematical theory serve for simulating and analyzing UML models.

Qualitative and Quantitative Analysis Methods for Services. Mathematical models for service computing formalize different aspects of overlay computers: at this level, services are seen as abstract computational entities, modeled in a platform-independent architectural layer. The mathematical models, hidden from the developer, enable qualitative and quantitative analysis supporting the service development process and providing the means for reasoning about functional and non-functional properties of services and service aggregates. SENSORIA results include powerful mathematical analysis techniques; in particular program analysis techniques, type systems, logics, and process calculi for investigating the behavior and the quality of service of properties of global services. These techniques are then tailored to several specific purposes: Firstly, they can be used to reveal performance bottlenecks or interactions leading to errors or violation of service contracts. Secondly, they are used to deal with security issues like confidentiality, integrity, non-interference, access control, and trust management. Finally, for critical services, deep semantic analysis may be used for certification.

Model Driven Development, Tools, and Validation. SENSORIA techniques may be integrated into several software process models. Specific emphasis is placed on Model-Driven Development (MDD). SENSORIA introduces automated model transformations to allow generation of formal representations from engineering models, back-translation from formal results to user-level models, and generation of code. All techniques and methods developed within SENSORIA are accompanied by tools, which are integrated into a common tooling platform (the SENSORIA Development Environment). To prove that the developed methods are applicable in industrial contexts, SENSORIA includes several case studies from various application domains of software engineering, whose scenarios have been rigorously tested.

Summarizing, the added value of SENSORIA comes from the availability of sound engineering techniques supported by mathematical foundations, languages with formal semantics and associated analysis methods, and the ability to automate many of the development steps currently done by hand in the design of service-oriented software. The next three sections describe the above three points in more detail.

3   Part I: Linguistic Primitives for Modeling and Programming SOA Systems

The first theme of SENSORIA has been focused on the definition of adequate linguistic primitives for modeling and programming service-oriented systems, enabling model-driven development for implementing services on different global computers. The primitives introduced in SENSORIA allow both high-level system modeling as well as detailed, rigorous specifications of SOA systems using mathematical notations. Automated model transformations allow switching between these two levels, and in addition enable generation of executable code.

SENSORIA has first established foundations for service description, interaction and composition, at the level of architectural specification. Based on this, core calculi for service-oriented computing have been developed, accounting for different interaction and composition architectures, like message-driven or data-driven. Finally, the core calculi have been extended to establish a solid mathematical basis for quality of service, service level agreements, workflow-like transactions with compensation, and dynamic reconfiguration.

3.1 Modeling in Service-Oriented Architectures

Modeling of Service-Oriented Architectures has been investigated on different abstraction levels and with different aims in SENSORIA, which has led to four main outcomes.

Firstly, SOA systems can be modeled on a high level of abstraction with the help of the Unified Modeling Language (UML). The UML is accepted as the *lingua franca* in the development of software systems. It is the most mature language used for modeling. However, plain UML is not expressive enough for the specification of structural and behavioral aspects of services. SENSORIA therefore provides individual UML extensions which form a SENSORIA *family of profiles* for SOA development, which are jointly used to model the different aspects of service-oriented software. The SENSORIA family of profiles comprise a profile for service orchestration (*UML4SOA*), for non-functional properties of services, business policies, for implementation modes of SOAs, and service deployment. The UML extensions are further detailed in Chapter 1-1 (UML Extensions for Service-Oriented Systems).

Secondly, one can also take a more formal approach to SOA system specification with the help of the SENSORIA *Reference Modeling Language (SRML)*. SRML is inspired by the Service Component Architecture (SCA). It makes available a general assembly model and binding mechanisms for service components and clients that may have been programmed in possibly many different languages, e.g. Java, C++, BPEL, or PHP. However, where SCA supports bottom-up low-level design, SRML instead addresses top-down high-level design. More specifically, the aim was to develop models and mechanisms that support the design of complex services, and analysis techniques through which designers can verify or validate their properties. These composite services can then be put together from (heterogeneous) service components using assembly and binding techniques such as the ones provided by SCA. SRML will be discussed in detail in Chapter 1-2 (The SENSORIA Reference Modelling Language).

Business processes typically structure their activities with workflows, which are often implemented in a rather static fashion in their IT systems. Nowadays, system requirements change rapidly as business activities try to maintain their competitive edge, and hence a predominant need arises for the IT systems to present the same agility. This problem has been investigated in SENSORIA and has lead to a new approach, *StPowla*, which marries service-oriented architecture, policies and workflows to provide businesses with this agility at execution time of their workflows. In StPowla the business is modeled as a workflow and is ultimately carried out by services. Indeed, policies provide the necessary adaptation to the varied expectations of the various business stakeholders. A key idea is that the stakeholders can define policies to adapt the core work by modifying the service to be invoked or the QoS levels. StPowla is further discussed in Chapter 1-3 (Model-Driven Development of Adaptable Service-Oriented Business Processes).

Finally, another important aspect of service-oriented computing systems lies in their architecture, which must match the global structure required by the business processes they are intended to support. SENSORIA provides a solution for this problem with *Architectural Design Rewriting (ADR)*, which can be used as a formal model for architectural and business design and helps in formalizing crucial aspects of the UML4SOA and SRML modeling languages mentioned above. The key features that make ADR a suitable and expressive framework are the algebraic presentation of graph-based structures, which can improve the automated support for specification, analysis and verification of service-oriented architectures and applications. ADR is discussed in Chapter 1-4 (A Formal Support to Business and Architectural Design for Service-Oriented Systems).

3.2 Calculi for Service-Oriented Computing

SENSORIA has investigated a foundational methodology for describing service specifications and for developing a discipline for their composition. This methodology relies on services as the fundamental elements for developing applications, thus conforming to the Service-Oriented Computing (SOC) paradigm. The fundamental vehicle used in this respect has been the theory of process calculi and their operational modeling as labeled transition systems, intended as the collections of linguistic constructs, tools, models, and prototype implementations that have been developed for designing, analyzing, and experimenting with open components interactions.

Core calculi have been adopted in the SENSORIA project with three main aims. First of all, they have been used to clarify and formally define the basic concepts that characterize the SENSORIA approach to the modeling of service-oriented applications. In second place, they are formal models on which the SENSORIA analysis techniques have been developed. Finally, they have been used to drive the implementation of the prototypes of the SENSORIA languages for programming actual service-based systems. The SENSORIA core calculi are described in Chapter 2-1 (Core Calculi for Service-Oriented Computing).

In a formal language, it is common to have several terms denoting the same process. To understand when different terms refer to the same process, the language needs to be equipped with a notion of *equivalence*. SENSORIA has investigated bisimilarity notions applied to some of the SENSORIA core calculi. The aim was to develop algebraic reasoning on processes by finding useful axioms (correct with respect to bisimilarity). Two different applications for this are program transformations and spatial characterizations of systems. The former is used to show how to transform object-oriented diagrams to session oriented ones, how to break sessions into smaller pieces that can be implemented using current technologies, and to show that an implementation of a service is compliant to a more abstract specification. The latter proves that bisimilarity is a congruence and shows behavioral identities that illuminate the spatial nature of processes and pave the way for establishing a normal form result. This is further discussed in Chapter 2-2 (Behavioral Theory for Session-Oriented Calculi).

An important tool for verifying system correctness are *static analysis techniques*. Within SENSORIA, such techniques have been developed for CaSPiS (Calculus of Sessions and Pipes) and CC (Conversation Calculus), two session oriented calculi developed within the project. Each technique aims at guaranteeing a specific property one would expect from service-oriented applications. These models and techniques may be complementary used and combined in order to provide as many guarantees as possible on the correctness of services' behavior. Chapter 2-3 (Static Analysis Techniques for Session-Oriented Calculi) contains more information on static analysis.

A key issue of the service approach is given by its compositional nature. For example, existing services can be combined (a process which is called *orchestration*) to create a more complex business process. This yields the problem of properly selecting and configuring services to guarantee that their orchestration enjoys some desirable properties. These properties may involve functional aspects, and also non-functional aspects, like e.g. security, availability, performance, transactionality, etc. SENSORIA includes a framework for designing and composing services in a *"call-by-contract" fashion*, i.e. according to their behavior. For a discussion on how to plan compositions of services so that the resulting choreography satisfies the desired functional and non-functional properties see Chapter 2-4 (Call-by-Contract for Service Discovery, Orchestration and Recovery).

3.3 Negotiations, Planning, and Reconfiguration

The SOC paradigm has to face several challenges like service discovery, Service Level Agreements (SLA) and Quality of Service (QoS), workflow-like transactions and compensations, monitoring and dynamic reconfiguration. SENSORIA has addressed these aspects, namely SLA/QoS, transactions with compensations, and dynamic reconfiguration, to a) establish a solid mathematical basis that can serve to formalize crucial aspects of SLAs, b) distill service aggregation patterns, and c) provide a sound architectural basis for dynamic reconfigurations.

One of the ultimate goals of service-oriented computing (SOC) is to provide support for the automatic on-demand discovery of basic functionalities that, once combined, correctly compute a user defined task. To this aim, it is necessary for services to come equipped with a computer-understandable interface that exposes enough information in order to match the provided functionalities with the user needs.

Services may expose both functional properties and non-functional properties. Non-functional properties focus on the Quality of Service (QoS) and typically include performance, availability, and cost. QoS parameters play an important role in service composition and, specifically, in dynamic discovery and binding. Indeed, a service requester may have minimal QoS requirements below which a service is not considered useful. Moreover, multiple services that meet the functional requirements of a requester can still be differentiated according to their non-functional properties. In SENSORIA, this challenge is addressed with a simple calculus, called *cc-pi calculus*, for modeling processes able to specify QoS requirements and to conclude QoS contracts. See Chapter 3-1 (CC-Pi: A Constraint Language for Service Negotiation and Composition) for more information.

Another prominent issue in the automated combination of services concerns the compliance between the operations invoked by the client – the client protocol – and the receive operations executed by the service – the service protocol. Among other things, this requires a) actually extracting a manageable description of the service interface (contract) from a reasonably detailed service specification, and b) guaranteeing that the services retrieved from a repository behave correctly according to the user and the other retrieved services needs. Such techniques have been investigated in SENSORIA and are detailed in Chapter 3-2 (Advanced Mechanisms for Service Composition, Query and Discovery).

In enterprise computing, services are used to model business processes, which may potentially take a large amount of time. Such activities, known as *long-running transactions*, are often supported by specialized language primitives and constructs such as exception and compensation handling. Exception handling is used to react to unexpected events, while compensation handling is used to undo previously completed activities. The impact of adding exception- and compensation handling to a language is detailed in Chapter 3-3 (Advanced Mechanisms for Service Combination and Transactions). Furthermore, specification and refactoring of long-running transactions is discussed in Chapter 3-4 (Model-Driven Development of Long-Running Transactions).

Finally, SOA systems should offer the ability to dynamically reconfigure SOA architectures to adapt to changing requirements. The SENSORIA *Architectural Design Rewriting* approach introduced above can also be used as a foundational model for reconfigurable service-oriented systems. This is detailed in Chapter 3-5 (A Formal Support to Reconfiguration of Service-Oriented Systems).

4 Part II: Formal Analysis of Service-Oriented Systems

The previous section has introduced language primitives and in particular core calculi for the rigorous specification of service-oriented systems. These mathematical models, hidden from the developer, enable qualitative and quantitative analysis supporting the service development process and providing the means for reasoning about functional and non-functional properties of services and service aggregates.

In SENSORIA, a full spectrum of qualitative analysis techniques has been developed, thus allowing service engineers to guarantee a high level of security and trust for the location transparent delivery of services while allowing mobility of resources. Furthermore, SENSORIA has investigated means for coping with the quantitative aspects of service-oriented systems. The focus lay on stochastic methods for developing analysis techniques and tools to study and verify quantitative properties such as resource usage and quality of service.

4.1 Qualitative Analysis Techniques for Service-Oriented Computing

Quality of service is becoming a key parameter in determining the success or failure of information systems offering their services using overlay computers;

techniques are needed for validating the performance of systems with respect to their specifications (in particular as regards security and trust). Sensoria has investigated analysis techniques for ensuring quality of service properties in SOC systems.

In the service-oriented environment, the view of a system can be divided into different levels; at the abstract level (as is usually the view found in academia), the system is independent of the underlying communication protocols, and at the concrete level (as is usually the view found in industry), the system must be understood in connection with how it makes use of established communication protocols. Motivated by this separation of concerns, Sensoria has devised a specification approach called *CaPiTo* to facilitate modeling systems at both the abstract and the concrete level. To bridge the gap between the two levels, an intermediary level has been defined that connects them. Chapter 4-1 (Analysing the Protocol Stack for Services) discusses CaPiTo.

Early validation of system requirements and early detection of design errors is an important cornerstone of creating high-quality software systems. Sensoria supports such validation by a common logical framework for verifying functional properties of service-oriented systems, which has been instantiated in the *CMC* and *UMC* model checkers. The design principles used in these tools are detailed in Chapter 4-2 (An Abstract, On-The-Fly Framework for the Verification of Service Oriented Systems).

Service architectures should be dynamic, where service bindings and contexts change with the environment. The task of designing and analyzing such architectures becomes very complex. As a remedy, Sensoria has developed a specification profile and analysis framework for so-called *service modes*. A service mode provides an encapsulation of both specification and adaptation in different service scenarios. The modes approach is described in Chapter 4-4 (Specification and Analysis of Dynamically-Reconfigurable Service Architectures).

Finally, Sensoria also provides various tools which accompany the formal methods laid out in the previous sections for analysis and verification of service-oriented systems. Four of these tools (CMC, UMC, ChorSLMC, and LocUsT) are described in Chapter 4-3 (Tools and Verification).

4.2 Quantitative Analysis Techniques for Service-Oriented Computing

Service-oriented computing is made up of many activities that are quantity driven (service level agreement, quality of service, negotiation, orchestration, resource usage are only some of them). As a consequence, the issue of quantitative description and analysis of such systems in the global computing setting needs to be addressed in all the phases of SOA software development.

Service-oriented computing goes beyond the usual problems encountered in network based systems by its focus on open-endedness. Addressing key functional aspects of network aware programming such as distribution awareness, mobility and security, and guaranteeing their integration with performance and dependability guarantees is complemented in Sensoria by specific features intended for service-oriented architectures. Chapter 5-1 (SoSL: Service Oriented Stochastic Logics) introduces the temporal logic *SoSL* and shows how SoSL formulae can be model-checked against systems descriptions expressed with *MarCaSPiS*, a process calculus designed for addressing quantitative aspects of SOC.

Service Level Agreements (SLAs) underpin the expectation of the performance of a system as seen by a particular client of a service. Most often an SLA will speak about the response-time of the system. In general, a qualitative analysis of a service-oriented system requires abstracting the parts of the system which are relevant to the analysis into an abstract model which is generally defined in some modeling formalism. In SENSORIA, the process algebra *PEPA* was used for this purpose, along with *eXtended Stochastic Probes (XSP)* for the specification of the passage of interest within the defined model. Both are detailed in Chapter 5-2 (Evaluating Service Level Agreements using Observational Probes).

The quantitative analysis of large-scale applications using discrete-state models is fundamentally hampered by the rapid growth of the state space as a function of the number of components in the system (state-space explosion). However, service-oriented architectures often lie in the large-scale section of the application landscape. Here, the fluid-flow interpretation of the stochastic process calculus PEPA provides a very useful tool for the performance evaluation of large-scale systems because the tractability of the numerical solution does not depend upon the population levels of the system under study. Scaling performance analysis using fluid-flow approximation is discussed in Chapter 5-3 (Scaling Performance Analysis using Fluid-Flow Approximation); a related method called *passage-end calculations* is discussed in Chapter 5-4 (Passage-End Analysis for Analysing Robot Movement).

Finally, as in the previous section, SENSORIA provides various tools performing quantitative analysis accompanying the methods and techniques laid out in above. Chapter 5-5 (Quantitative Analysis of Services) shows instances of exact model checking of MarCaSPiS against the both state-aware and action-aware logic SoSL, exact and statistical model checking of sCOWS against the state-aware logic CSL, and querying of PEPA models by terms of the XSP language that expresses both state-aware and action-aware stochastic probes.

5 Part III: Model-Driven Development, Tools, and Validation

The third theme of the SENSORIA project deals with the engineering aspects of service-oriented system construction. It builds on both previous themes and introduces the glue with brings all SENSORIA methods and tools together and wraps them in a validation cocoon.

The theme includes new model-based development techniques for refining and transforming service specifications, novel techniques for deploying service descriptions on different global computers, and methods for reengineering legacy systems into service-oriented ones. These results form the cornerstone for the practical usability of the SENSORIA approach, and are complemented by realistic case studies from industrial partners.

5.1 Model-Driven Development and Reverse-Engineering for Service-Oriented Systems

In order to allow developers to use the qualitative and quantitative analysis of services discussed in previous sections, SENSORIA has created model transformation tools and concrete transformations for a) strengthening and streamlining the connections between formal languages and high-level systems models, b) orchestrating the experimentation and analysis process, and c) deploying well-managed analysis on systems of increasing scale and complexity. Due to their complexity, SOA systems also require advanced and diverse mechanisms for deployment and runtime management. SENSORIA has investigated such mechanisms and provides a suite of tools and techniques for transforming SOA artifacts, deploying service-oriented systems on global computers and for reengineering legacy systems into services.

Model transformation serves as a key technology for the model-driven service engineering approach suggested by SENSORIA. To be effective for a day-by-day use in the engineering process, SENSORIA had to solve some common problems (traceability, back-annotation, intuitive requirement definition, etc.) with model transformation techniques. These problems, and the solutions provided by SENSORIA, are introduced in Chapter 6-1 (Methodologies for Model-Driven Development and Deployment: an Overview), along with an end-to-end example for using model-driven techniques for analyzing services, and the tool support provided by the project. Going into more detail, SENSORIA has employed model transformation techniques which make use of precise mathematical foundations provided by the paradigm of graph transformation. The unique challenges and solutions provided by the graph transformation paradigm are discussed in Chapter 6-2 (Advances in Model Transformations by Graph Transformation: Specification, Analysis and Execution).

The ability to dynamically compose autonomous services for meeting the requirements of different applications is one of the major advantages offered by the service-oriented computing paradigm. A dynamic service composition implies that services requesters can be dynamically bound to most appropriate service providers that are currently available, in order to optimally satisfy the service requirements. At the same time, the autonomy of services involved in a composition means that the resulting composition may need to be adapted in response to changes in the service capabilities or requirements. Naturally, the infrastructure and technologies for providing runtime support for dynamic and adaptive composition of services form the backbone of the above process. Within SENSORIA, the *Dino* approach has been developed, which provides comprehensive support for all stages of a service composition life-cycle, namely: service discovery, selection, binding, delivery, monitoring and adaptation. More on Dino can be found in Chapter 6-3 (Runtime Support for Dynamic and Adaptive Service Composition).

Many companies and organizations have already invested heavily in their IT infrastructure in the past. The migration of such legacy systems towards service-oriented architectures is therefore of particular importance. SENSORIA has developed a general methodology for *software reengineering*. This method has been instantiated to allow service components to be extracted from legacy applications. Chapter 6-4 (Legacy Transformations for Extracting Service Components) describes a systematic way of addressing such reengineering projects with a high degree of automation while being largely independent of the programming language.

Developing service-oriented software involves dealing with multiple languages, platforms, artifacts, and tools. The tasks carried out during development are varied, ranging from modeling to implementation, from analysis to testing. For many of these tasks, the SENSORIA project has provided tools aiding developers in their work. To enable developers to find, use, and combine these tools, SENSORIA provides a tool integration platform, the SENSORIA *Development Environment (SDE)*, which a) gives an overview of available tools and their area of application, b) allows developers to use tools in a homogeneous way, re-arranging tool functionality as required, and c) enables users to stay on a chosen level of abstraction, hiding formal details as much as possible. The SDE is described in detail in Chapter 6-5 (The SENSORIA Development Environment).

5.2   Case Studies and Patterns

The research in the SENSORIA project has been based on a series of realistic case studies, which have been used for feeding and steering the research process, discussing and communicating ideas among partners, and finally disseminating research results to and getting feedback from the research community at large, both in industry and academia.

The immediately following Chapter 0-3 (Introduction to the SENSORIA Case Studies) will introduce the *case studies* used within the project. Having in mind the relevance that these areas have in society and the economy, three case studies have been extensively used in SENSORIA during the whole project. Two of the case studies come from industrial applications in automotive, telecommunication and finance domains, and one comes from an academic application for distributed e-learning and course management. After the SENSORIA notations have been introduced, Chapter 7-1 (Specification and Implementation of Demonstrators for the Case Studies) goes into more detail about the case studies.

Chapter 7-2 (SENSORIA Results Applied to the Case Studies) provides a *concise overview* of the exploitation of SENSORIA results in all of our case studies. In addition to this overview, Chapter 7-3 (Analysing Robot Movement Using the SENSORIA Methods) provides an in-depth review of SENSORIA methods applied to the *robot case study*, while Chapter 7-4 (The SENSORIA Approach Applied to the Finance Case Study) provides an in-depth view of the SENSORIA approach applied to the *finance case study*.

Finally, the SENSORIA project contributes to existing software development processes and methodologies by providing *patterns* for common tasks and problems encountered when developing service-oriented software systems. Chapter 7-5 (SENSORIA Development Patterns) discusses a pattern language for augmenting service engineering with formal analysis, transformation and dynamicity. The pattern language is designed to help software developers choose appropriate tools and techniques to develop service-oriented systems with support from formal methods; the full pattern catalog spans the whole development process, from the modeling stage to deployment activities. Chapter 7-6 (Organizational Patterns for Security and Dependability: From Design to Application) specifically discusses security and dependability (S&D) patterns, which are of great help to designers when developing service-oriented software systems.

6   Conclusion

In today's networked world, service-oriented computing and service-oriented architectures are an accepted architectural style for creating massively distributed network-based applications. The SENSORIA project has contributed to this field by addressing the foundations of modeling, transforming, analyzing, and deploying service-oriented artifacts as well as reengineering legacy systems. SENSORIA has thereby created a novel comprehensive approach to the engineering of service-oriented software systems where foundational theories, techniques and methods are fully integrated in a pragmatic software engineering approach.

SENSORIA has brought mathematically well-founded modeling technology within the reach of service-oriented software designers and developers. By using these techniques and tools, IT-dependent organizations can move to a higher and more mature level of SOA software development. In particular, using the SENSORIA techniques can increase the quality of SOA applications, measured both in qualitative and quantitative terms. As SENSORIA methods are portable to existing platforms, application of these methods is possible while keeping existing investments.

A Unifying Formal Basis for the
SENSORIA Approach: A White Paper*

Ugo Montanari

Dipartimento di Informatica, University of Pisa, Italy
ugo@di.unipi.it

1 Introduction

SENSORIA is an IST project funded by the EU as Integrated Project (IP) in the 6th Framework Programme (FP6) as part of the Global Computing Initiative (GC). It started on September 2005 and ended on February 2010.

Project SENSORIA has developed a novel comprehensive approach to deal with Service-Oriented Computing (SOC), where foundational theories, techniques and methods are fully integrated in a pragmatic tool-supported software engineering approach.

In the paper we focus on the foundations of the formal methods employed in SENSORIA. We try to give evidence that, while spanning over a variety of theories and employing diverse mathematical results, the formal methods of SENSORIA are coherent and refer to a well understood kernel of theoretical computer science.

2 The SENSORIA Approach

The SENSORIA development process is illustrated in Fig. 1. The *Code Generation* phase is preceded by a *Modelling* phase, where specific modeling languages and tools, like suitable UML profiles, are employed to specify various aspects of the design. The models are then transformed into *formal* models, typically (but not necessarily) process calculi agents, which are analyzed for verification and validation using *Formal Methods*. Analysis may involve animation and execution, or model checking, or other ways of assessing relevant properties. A *Feedback* phase takes into account the results of the formal analysis for improving the design. Finally, after the code generation phase, the runtime versions are deployed, possibly combined with existing legacy code. The latter often goes through a *Reengineering* phase, where innovative design steps are taken to make reuse easier.

In Fig. 2 we see a more detailed description of the formal methods employed within SENSORIA. Suitable process description languages are defined using

---

* Research supported by the EU, FET integrated project IST-2005-016004 SENSORIA.

M. Wirsing and M. Hölzl (Eds.): SENSORIA Project, LNCS 6582, pp. 15–25, 2011.

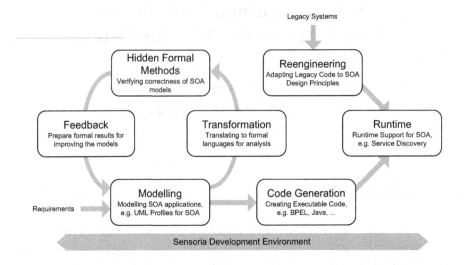

Fig. 1. The SENSORIA development process

well-founded mathematical models. Their soundness is proved with standard assessment techniques (e.g. compositionality of the semantics) and their usability is shown via case study developments particularly relevant for Global Computing. Qualitative (typically functional) and quantitative (e.g. quality of service) properties are then stated/proved for the agents using state-of-the-art methods and tools.

Additional formal developments concern the ability of coordinating the execution of several agents guaranteeing certain properties, like session progress, transaction commit or compensation. In general three phases are distinguished occurring in every cooperation: (i) negotiation, (ii) commit, and (iii) execution (*NCE* approach). In (i) the prospective participants negotiate some guarantees in order to define a sort of contract. In (ii) each participant can either accept or reject the contract. If they accept, the contract will bind their behaviours in (iii) to guarantee a globally correct execution.

Finally, modeling languages and software architectures themselves can be formally defined, typically using graph transformation techniques. This development is quite useful, since it builds a link between models and agents, which is needed for assessing the correctness of the transformation from the former to the latter formalism.

In conclusion, in SENSORIA a large body of formal contributions involve: (i) service oriented calculi, (ii) service oriented process coordination, (iii) qualitative & quantitative analysis, and (iv) modeling languages and service oriented architectures.

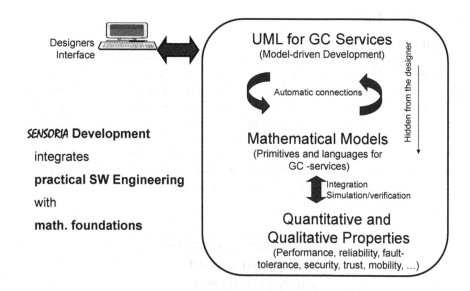

Fig. 2. The SENSORIA formal approach

3 The Formal Basis

3.1 Labelled Transition Systems and Their Properties

The starting point of almost every formal development in the area of interactive communication systems are labelled transition systems (LTS), see Fig. 3. Their abstract semantics is most often defined in terms of bisimilarity [27,31]. The simplest logic for expressing properties of LTSs is Hennessy-Milner modal logic [16], which is *adequate* for bisimilarity, i.e. there is a property expressible in Hennessy-Milner logic which distinguishes between two agents iff they are not bisimilar. Bisimilarity and Hennessy-Milner logic can be conveniently expressed and generalized using the theory of *coalgebras* [30], where every LTS can be mapped to its minimal representative, which is the final object in a category of coalgebras. A model checker for a temporal logic extending Hennessy-Milner logic has been developed in SENSORIA [32]. The work is described in Chapter 4-2 of this book.

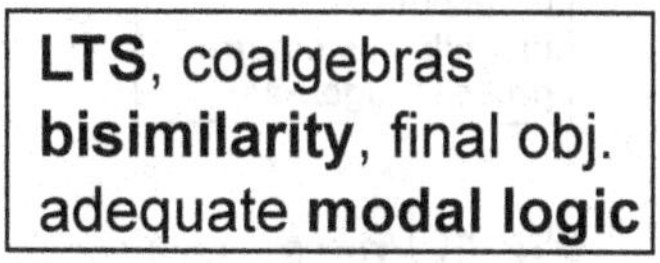

LTS, coalgebras
bisimilarity, final obj.
adequate modal logic

Fig. 3. State-transition systems

3.2 Design Algebras

When dealing with large, distributed systems the key properties are compositionality, reconfigurability and open endness. The simplest way to achieve them is to define a design algebra where terms can be composed, rewritten, contextualized and refined (see Fig. 4). A good example of a general formal system for algebraic specification is *Rewriting Logic* and *Membership Equational Logic* [24], which is supported by the popular tool *Maude*[1], successfully employed for the work described in Chapter 1-4 of this book. Particular formats of *conditional* term rewriting rules (*Structural Operational Semantics* [28], SOS; De Simone format; GSOS) have been used with extreme success for defining the operational semantics of process calculi and programming languages.

```
algebraic specifications
typing, refinement
(conditional) rewr.
SOS, De Simone
```

Fig. 4. Compositional systems

3.3 Process Description Calculi

Labelled transition systems defined in the SOS style are the definition method used for most, if not all, process calculi.

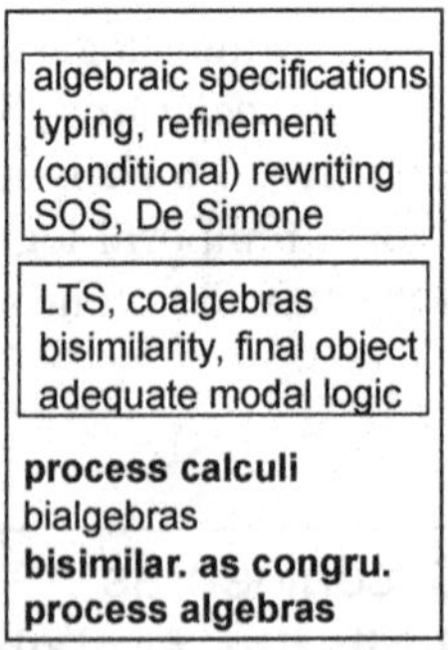

```
algebraic specifications
typing, refinement
(conditional) rewriting
SOS, De Simone

LTS, coalgebras
bisimilarity, final object
adequate modal logic

process calculi
bialgebras
bisimilar. as congru.
process algebras
```

Fig. 5. Process calculi

---

[1] See [12], http://maude.cs.uiuc.edu/download/

The coexistence of the bisimilarity relation and of the algebraic operations asks for a proof of congruence and gives the opportunity of defining bisimilarity axiomatically (process *algebras*). In terms of categorical foundations, the coexistence of the coalgebraic and the algebraic structure is possible in *bialgebras* [34]. The construction automatically guarantees that bisimilary is a congruence and provides an algebraic structure for the minimal representative (see Fig. 5). Several process calculi have been specifically designed to model continuous client service interactions in Service Oriented Computing by resorting to a notion of implicit or explicit session: here we mention CaSPiS [4] and COWS [23]. This work is described in Chapter 2-1 of this book.

3.4   Process Combination

The next step (see Fig. 6) is coordinating the execution of several agents guaranteeing session progress, transaction commit or compensation and, in general, a smooth NCE approach. A key concept along this line are behavioral types [19,21,20], which express and prove/type check important behavioral properties of agents. Several results have been obtained in this line within SENSORIA concerning secure, contract-based composition of services [2,5], client-server sessions [22,8,1,36], multiparty sessions [10] and transactions [11]. This work is described in Chapters 2-4, 3-2, 2-2, 2-3, 3-3 and 3-4 of this book respectively.

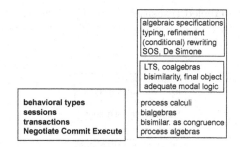

Fig. 6. Guaranteed process combination

3.5   Graphs and Diagrams

Graphs and diagrams are suggestive modeling media and are supported by well-developed theories (e.g. *Double Push Out* rewriting, DPO; *Synchronized Hyper-edge Replacement*, SHR).

Graphs themselves should be structured, and the interesting case is when the terms are in one-to-one correspondence with the graphs, where the terms are taken up to some intuitive structural axioms and the graphs are considered up to isomorphism. In SENSORIA (see Fig. 7), the specific case of hierarchical graphs

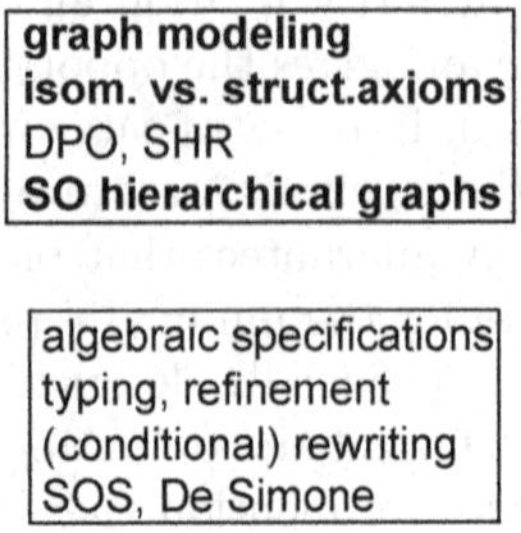

| graph modeling |
| **isom. vs. struct.axioms** |
| DPO, SHR |
| **SO hierarchical graphs** |

| algebraic specifications |
| typing, refinement |
| (conditional) rewriting |
| SOS, De Simone |

Fig. 7. Graph-based modeling

for modeling service-oriented computing systems has been tackled [7], and it has been applied to a service-oriented UML profile [6]. This work is described in Chapters 1-4 and 3-5 of this book. In the SENSORIA approach, a relevant role have also graph and model *transformations*. They have been used in many ways, e.g. for producing transformations from UML to process calculi, for extracting service from legacy code, and for deploying service designs. This work is described in Chapters 6-1, 6-2, and 6-4 of this book.

3.6   Graph-Based Calculi

When considering the labeled transition system generated by a graph transformation system, the concepts of process calculi apply (see Fig. 8).

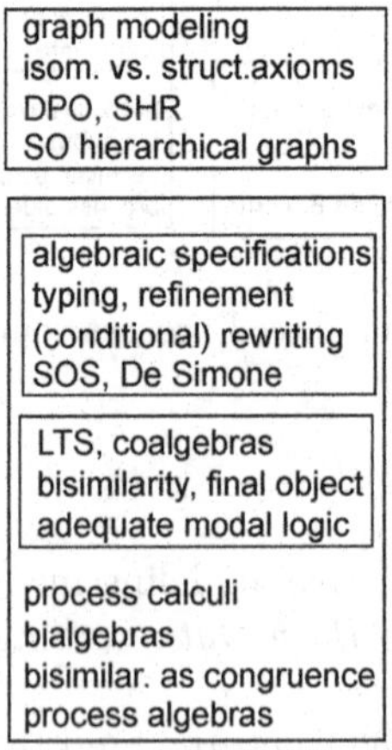

| graph modeling |
| isom. vs. struct.axioms |
| DPO, SHR |
| SO hierarchical graphs |

| algebraic specifications |
| typing, refinement |
| (conditional) rewriting |
| SOS, De Simone |

| LTS, coalgebras |
| bisimilarity, final object |
| adequate modal logic |

| process calculi |
| bialgebras |
| bisimilar. as congruence |
| process algebras |

Fig. 8. Graph calculi

The SHR approach [14] can then be compared successfully with SOS definitions, with the advantage of allowing more general synchronization capabilities and of yielding a concurrent semantics.

3.7 Calculi with Names

A key extension of process calculi took place with the introduction of π-calculus names. *Nominal calculi* use names to represent channels, ports, sites, keys, sessions, etc. Names are resources, which can be allocated, communicated and, sometimes, deallocated [25]. States of labelled transition systems can be indexed by their resources. Correspondingly, coalgebras can be defined on presheaves categories rather than on **Set** [15]. Most of the core calculi of SENSORIA (see Fig. 9), like CaSPiS, COWS, etc. use names, typically to denote sessions. Also, in SENSORIA, states of π-like calculi have been equipped with soft constraints to handle *Quality of Service* negotiations [9]. Here names subject to constraints can be considered as general kinds of resources. This work is described in Chapter 3-1 of this book.

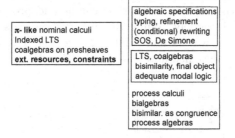

Fig. 9. Nominal calculi

3.8 Probabilistic and Quantitative LTS

Transition labels of LTSs can carry quantitative information about the transition, which can refer to cost, access rights or probability distributions.

If the LTS is timed and the probability distribution is exponential, a rate can be exposed which indicates the probability of occurrence of the transition in the next time unit (stochastic LTS). In SENSORIA (see Fig. 10) some of the existing process calculi (CaSPiS [26], COWS [29]) have been extended with stochastic and probabilistic features, in the style of CSP-based PEPA process algebra [17]. Tools like the PEPA Eclipse Plug-in tool [33] and PRISM [18] have been employed for the analysis of case studies. This work is described in the chapters in Part 4 of this book. From the foundational point of view, quantitative models make a big change for LTS theory. For instance, idempotency does not hold any more, namely process algebra axiom $x = x + x$ is not valid, since two transitions with the same behavior are heavier than one. In general, classical bisimilarity is not expressive enough, since two transitions with a small difference in probability would be distinguishable, while in practice one might not want it. Recent results extend the colagebraic approach defining coalgebras on a category of metric spaces rather than on **Set** [35], recovering in a systematic ways most of the classical results.

```
┌─────────────────────┐
│ LTS, coalgebras     │ ┌───────────────────────────────┐
│ bisimilarity, final │ │ quantitative LTS              │
│ object              │ │ probabilistic/stochastic LTS  │
│ adequate modal logic│ │ Markov chains, processes      │
└─────────────────────┘ │ non idempotency               │
                        │ coalgebras on metric spaces   │
                        └───────────────────────────────┘
```

Fig. 10. Quantitative LTS

3.9 Probabilistic Calculi

Extending LTS theory to the probabilistic/stochastic case is relatively easy, recapturing well known notions like Markov chains and processes. Making such models compositional, namely adding the algebraic aspects typical of process calculi in a convincing way is more difficult (see Fig. 11). The extensions of CaSPiS and COWS mentioned above are in this direction.

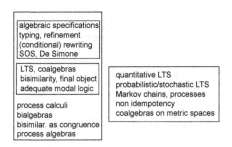

Fig. 11. Quantitative calculi

3.10 Everything Together

In Fig. 12 we see the full picture. Notice however that it is convenient to understand the various extensions as separate, since it is not realistic (and probably uninteresting in most cases from the scientific point of view) to build large, very complicated models. It is the role of specification language designers to extract from the general picture those items which are needed for a particular applications and combine them.

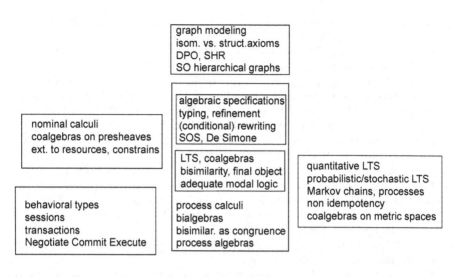

Fig. 12. The full picture

Acknowledgements

I would like to thank Roberto Bruni, Rocco De Nicola and Martin Wirsing for their comments and suggestions on earlier versions of the manuscript.

References

1. Acciai, L., Boreale, M.: A type system for client progress in a service-oriented calculus. In: Degano, P., De Nicola, R., Bevilacqua, V. (eds.) Concurrency, Graphs and Models. LNCS, vol. 5065, pp. 642–658. Springer, Heidelberg (2008)
2. Bartoletti, M., Degano, P., Ferrari, G.L., Zunino, R.: Semantics-based design for secure web services. IEEE Trans. Software Eng. 34(1), 33–49 (2008)
3. Bernardo, M., Padovani, L., Zavattaro, G. (eds.): SFM 2009. LNCS, vol. 5569. Springer, Heidelberg (2009)
4. Boreale, M., Bruni, R., De Nicola, R., Loreti, M.: Sessions and pipelines for structured service programming. In: Barthe, G., de Boer, F.S. (eds.) FMOODS 2008. LNCS, vol. 5051, pp. 19–38. Springer, Heidelberg (2008)
5. Bravetti, M., Zavattaro, G.: Contract-based discovery and composition of web services. In: Bernardo, et al. [3], pp. 261–295
6. Bruni, R., Hölzl, M.M., Koch, N., Lluch-Lafuente, A., Mayer, P., Montanari, U., Schroeder, A., Wirsing, M.: A service-oriented UML profile with formal support. In: Baresi, L., Chi, C.-H., Suzuki, J. (eds.) ICSOC-ServiceWave 2009. LNCS, vol. 5900, pp. 455–469. Springer, Heidelberg (2009)
7. Bruni, R., Lluch-Lafuente, A., Montanari, U.: Hierarchical design rewriting with maude. Electr. Notes Theor. Comput. Sci. 238(3), 45–62 (2009)
8. Bruni, R., Mezzina, L.G.: Types and deadlock freedom in a calculus of services, sessions and pipelines. In: Bevilacqua, V., Roşu, G. (eds.) AMAST 2008. LNCS, vol. 5140, pp. 100–115. Springer, Heidelberg (2008)

9. Buscemi, M.G., Montanari, U.: Cc-pi: A constraint-based language for specifying service level agreements. In: De Nicola (ed.) [13], pp. 18–32.
10. Caires, L., Vieira, H.T.: Conversation types. In: Castagna, G. (ed.) ESOP 2009. LNCS, vol. 5502, pp. 285–300. Springer, Heidelberg (2009)
11. Ciancia, V., Ferrari, G.L., Guanciale, R., Strollo, D.: Checking correctness of transactional behaviors. In: Suzuki, K., Higashino, T., Yasumoto, K., El-Fakih, K. (eds.) FORTE 2008. LNCS, vol. 5048, pp. 134–148. Springer, Heidelberg (2008)
12. Clavel, M., Durán, F., Eker, S., Lincoln, P., Martí-Oliet, N., Bevilacqua, V., Talcott, C.: All About Maude - A High-Performance Logical Framework. LNCS, vol. 4350. Springer, Heidelberg (2007)
13. De Nicola, R. (ed.): ESOP 2007. LNCS, vol. 4421. Springer, Heidelberg (2007)
14. Ferrari, G.L., Hirsch, D., Lanese, I., Montanari, U., Tuosto, E.: Synchronised hyperedge replacement as a model for service oriented computing. In: de Boer, F.S., Bonsangue, M.M., Graf, S., de Roever, W.-P. (eds.) FMCO 2005. LNCS, vol. 4111, pp. 22–43. Springer, Heidelberg (2006)
15. Fiore, M.P., Staton, S.: Comparing operational models of name-passing process calculi. Inf. Comput. 204(4), 524–560 (2006)
16. Hennessy, M., Milner, R.: On observing nondeterminism and concurrency. In: de Bakker, J.W., van Leeuwen, J. (eds.) ICALP 1980. LNCS, vol. 85, pp. 299–309. Springer, Heidelberg (1980)
17. Hillston, J.: Process algebras for quantitative analysis. In: LICS, pp. 239–248. IEEE Computer Society, Los Alamitos (2005)
18. Hinton, A., Kwiatkowska, M.Z., Norman, G., Parker, D.: PRISM: A tool for automatic verification of probabilistic systems. In: Hermanns, H., Palsberg, J. (eds.) TACAS 2006. LNCS, vol. 3920, pp. 441–444. Springer, Heidelberg (2006)
19. Honda, K., Vasconcelos, V.T., Kubo, M.: Language primitives and type discipline for structured communication-based programming. In: Hankin, C. (ed.) ESOP 1998. LNCS, vol. 1381, pp. 122–138. Springer, Heidelberg (1998)
20. Honda, K., Yoshida, N., Carbone, M.: Multiparty asynchronous session types. In: Necula, G.C., Wadler, P. (eds.) POPL, pp. 273–284. ACM, New York (2008)
21. Igarashi, A., Kobayashi, N.: A generic type system for the π-calculus. Theor. Comput. Sci. 311(1-3), 121–163 (2004)
22. Lanese, I., Martins, F., Vasconcelos, V.T., Ravara, A.: Disciplining orchestration and conversation in service-oriented computing. In: SEFM, pp. 305–314. IEEE Computer Society, Los Alamitos (2007)
23. Lapadula, A., Pugliese, R., Tiezzi, F.: A calculus for orchestration of web services. In: De Nicola [13], pp. 33–47
24. Martí-Oliet, N., Meseguer, J.: Rewriting logic: roadmap and bibliography. Theor. Comput. Sci. 285(2), 121–154 (2002)
25. Montanari, U., Pistore, M.: Structured coalgebras and minimal hd-automata for the i-calculus. Theor. Comput. Sci. 340(3), 539–576 (2005)
26. De Nicola, R., Latella, D., Loreti, M., Massink, M.: Rate-based transition systems for stochastic process calculi. In: Albers, S., Marchetti-Spaccamela, A., Matias, Y., Nikoletseas, S., Thomas, W. (eds.) ICALP 2009. LNCS, vol. 5556, pp. 435–446. Springer, Heidelberg (2009)
27. Park, D.M.R.: Concurrency and automata on infinite sequences. In: Deussen, P. (ed.) GI-TCS 1981. LNCS, vol. 104, pp. 167–183. Springer, Heidelberg (1981)
28. Plotkin, G.D.: A structural approach to operational semantics. J. Log. Algebr. Program. 60-61, 17–139 (2004)

29. Prandi, D., Quaglia, P.: Stochastic COWS. In: Krämer, B.J., Lin, K.-J., Narasimhan, P. (eds.) ICSOC 2007. LNCS, vol. 4749, pp. 245–256. Springer, Heidelberg (2007)
30. Rutten, J.J.M.M.: Universal coalgebra: a theory of systems. Theor. Comput. Sci. 249(1), 3–80 (2000)
31. Sangiorgi, D.: On the origins of bisimulation and coinduction. ACM Trans. Program. Lang. Syst. 31(4) (2009)
32. ter Beek, M.H., Mazzanti, F., Gnesi, S.: CMC-UMC: a framework for the verification of abstract service-oriented properties. In: Shin, S.Y., Ossowski, S. (eds.) SAC, pp. 2111–2117. ACM, New York (2009)
33. Tribastone, M., Gilmore, S.: Automatic translation of UML sequence diagrams into PEPA models. In: QEST, pp. 205–214. IEEE Computer Society, Los Alamitos (2008)
34. Turi, D., Plotkin, G.D.: Towards a mathematical operational semantics. In: LICS, pp. 280–291 (1997)
35. van Breugel, F., Worrell, J.: Approximating and computing behavioural distances in probabilistic transition systems. Theor. Comput. Sci. 360(1-3), 373–385 (2006)
36. Vasconcelos, V.T.: Fundamentals of session types. In: Bernardo, et al. [3], pp. 158–186

Introduction to the Sensoria Case Studies[*]

Jannis Elgner[1], Stefania Gnesi[2], Nora Koch[3,4], and Philip Mayer[3]

[1] S & N AG, Germany
jelgner@s-und-n.de
[2] Istituto di Scienza e Tecnologie dell'Informazione "A. Faedo"
ISTI–CNR, Pisa, Italy
gnesi@isti.cnr.it
[3] Ludwig-Maximilians-Universität München, Germany
{kochn,mayer}@pst.ifi.lmu.de
[4] Cirquent GmbH, Germany

Abstract. The foundational research carried out in Sensoria has been steered by a number of case studies for ensuring applicability of Sensoria methods and meeting expectations of society and the economy. In this chapter, we introduce these case studies. Three of the case studies came from industrial applications in automotive, finance and telecommunication domains; one came from an academic application for distributed e-learning and course management. Having in mind the relevance that these areas have in society and the economy, the above case studies have been extensively used in Sensoria during the whole project.

1 Introduction

One of the challenging characteristics of Sensoria has been the use of realistic case studies in order to assess the applicability of the insights, methodologies and tools developed within the project to service applications on top of Internet-based Global Computing environments. Sensoria has used four case studies: three from the industrial domains of automotive, finance and telecommunication; the fourth from the academic domain of distributed e-learning and course management. These case studies have been extensively used during the whole project for developing intuitions that could feed and challenge the research process according to the expectations of society and its economy, discussing and communicating ideas among partners, communicating research results to and getting feedback from the research community at large, and for dissemination and training activities.

The development activities related to the case studies have been carried out in parallel with the foundational activities of technical Sensoria work packages. In this way, the case studies have driven the results produced in those work packages, giving feedback that has been considered in the refinement of the methodologies and tools developed in the project.

[*] This work has been partially sponsored by the project Sensoria, IST-2005-016004.

M. Wirsing and M. Hölzl (Eds.): Sensoria Project, LNCS 6582, pp. 26–34, 2011.

In the following sections, we introduce the four case studies, presenting their main characteristics that have been investigated during the project together with some scenario descriptions for each of them. More detailed descriptions of some of scenarios will be presented later (see Chapter 7-1).

2   Finance Case Study

The finance domain plays an important role in the worldwide economy and wrong decisions have a great influence on nearly all aspects of our society, even when they seem not to be directly connected. So, any wrong decisions and simple individual mistakes can be a disaster for the economy, as the world wide financial crisis has shown in the recent past. A bank has to handle critical information of customers and has a deep impact of their progression, e.g. when they need to borrow money from the bank. The finance case study is set in this context. In particular, we investigated the process of credit approval [1] as an example of a typical finance application.

Credit Request. This scenario, also known as *Credit Portal*, models a loan work-flow including interaction with customers and employees. Normally, several employees with different authorisations facilities are involved in the communication process with the customer. The credit approval process is error prone and time consuming due its complexity in information collecting, customer and employee interaction, and risk management. Thus, the aim of IT in this context is to create a software system for simplifying and automating the credit request process in order to minimize mistakes and speed up the approval process.

In our scenario, the credit request workflow is implemented using a SOA-based system: Several specialized services are orchestrated to realize the process. SENSORIA tools and methods have been used to verify properties of this system.

A web-based system is employed to handle the tasks involved for approving a credit request. This system is available to and used by both the customers of the bank as well as employees, the latter of which additionally may have different access rights.

The overall workflow in the credit request scenario works as follows:

- The customer logs in to the *Credit Portal* website. In order to start the process, the customer enters the necessary data like the amount of money and intended use. Furthermore, the customer has to enter his securities and balances data.
- This information is used for the calculation of a rating which is automatically started after the information is provided. The rating is based on the uploaded information and may also use the information stored from older credit requests. Depending on the rating, the approval can be given automatically or must be delegated to a clerk or supervisor.
  - In case an automated decision is possible, an answer is given immediately to the user without involving any bank employees.

- In case of the non-automatic decision either a clerk or supervisor gets a notification and has to approve or decline the request. The choice of the employee is made on the risk calculated during the rating phase.
- In case of an approval, an offer is created and the customer needs to decide whether to accept or to decline the offer.

Automating the credit approval process in this way has huge benefits for the bank as the process is mostly automated any only requires human interaction if absolutely necessary. Of course, the process needs to be implemented correctly; this will be the topic of some of the following chapters.

3 Automotive Case Study

Much of the research and development costs in the vehicle production is due to the complexity of automotive software, which leads to an increased importance of software engineering in the automotive domain. By nature, automotive software is service-oriented as a modern vehicle consists of many individual parts which need to be orchestrated to perform as a whole. Therefore, there is great potential for service-oriented computing in the automotive world.

A vehicle that leaves the assembly line today is equipped with a multitude of sensors and actuators that provide the driver with services that assist driving the vehicle more safely, for example ABS systems or vehicle stabilisation systems. Driver assistance systems kick in automatically when the vehicle context renders it necessary, and more and more context is taken into account (road condition, vehicle condition, driver condition, weather conditions, traffic conditions etc.). Due to the advances in mobile technology it is possible to take connectivity to the car: telephone and internet access in vehicles are possible today, giving rise to a variety of new services for the automotive domain. The automotive case study is set in this context.

In SENSORIA, we assume a SOA-based software infrastructure such as the one shown in Fig. 1 to be present in vehicles. In the figure, architectural modules of the vehicle are represented as nodes in an UML deployment diagram. This type of diagram has been selected to show the distribution of the components within the different platforms and devices of the vehicle, and those belonging to the vehicle environment.

The vehicle contains sensors and actuators and is able to determine its geographical position. Sensors are used to observe e.g. the vehicle's status. Actuators trigger fully-automatically the on-vehicle (low-level) driving assistance systems like ABS, anti-slipping and stability assistance. Another element of the architecture is the orchestrator of services that is in charge of achieving a goal by means of a composition of services. The discovery selects services based on established criteria. Services can be provided by local or remote service providers; they may be discovered locally or by external discovery services. The driver interface enables communication between driver and vehicle. The driver receives information from the active services and can enter commands to trigger, stop or customize them.

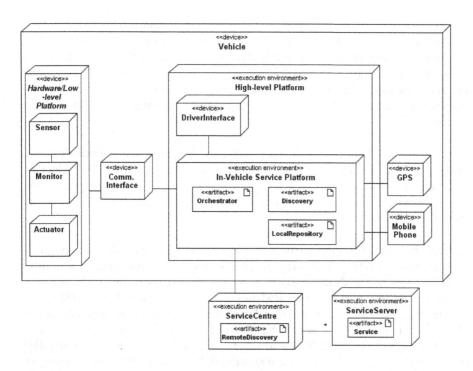

Fig. 1. Architecture of the vehicle in the automotive case study

Several scenarios can be imagined in the context of the architecture defined above. We discuss the ones most used and referred to in the project below.

On Road Assistance. It is also called *On Road Repair* and *Low Oil Level.* In this scenario [3,5] the in-vehicle diagnostic system of the vehicle is triggered by a failure in the car engine, for example, a low oil level and performs an analysis of the sensor values. The diagnostic system reports e.g. a problem with the pressure in one cylinder head, indicating that the driver will not be able to reach the planned destination.

The diagnostic system sends a message to the assistance system, which starts to orchestrate a set of services. Based on availability and the driver's preferences, the service discovery system identifies and selects the appropriate services in the area: repair shops (garage), towing truck and rental car stations. The selection of services takes into account personalized policies and preferences of the driver to find the *best services.* We assume that the owner of the car has to deposit a security payment before being able to order services.

Accident Assistance. This scenario (also know as *Airbag*) is concerned with road traffic accidents and dispatch of medical assistance to crash victims. Drivers interested in such a service must have an in-car GPS location tracking device with communication capabilities and have pre-registered their mobile phone information with the service. If a road traffic accident occurs, the deployment of the car airbag causes the on-board safety system to report the current location (obtained by GPS) to a pre-established accident report endpoint, which in turn attempts to call the registered drivers' mobile phone. If there is no answer to the call then medical assistance is dispatched to the reported location of the car (presuming that the driver has been incapacitated by injuries sustained in the accident).

Route Planning. It is also called *Emergency* [3]. In this scenario a vehicles' navigation system reacts to external events such as a broken car which is blocking the road. For example, two vehicles operating in a convoy mode may be forced to continue in an autonomous way due to the road block; this requires a reconfiguration of goals in both vehicles.

Road Sights. In this scenario, the driver has subscribed to a dynamic landmark service offered by the car company. The vehicles' GPS coordinates are automatically sent to the dynamic sights server at regular intervals, so the vehicles' location is known within a specified radius. Based on the drivers preferences, the dynamic sights server searches a landmark database for appropriate places of interest and displays them on the map of the vehicles' navigation system. The driver clicks on sights he would like to visit which results in more detailed information being displayed about a specific sight (e.g., opening times, guidance to parking etc.).

4   Telecommunication Case Study

The telecommunication case study has focused on the development of applications combining two global computing infrastructures, namely the Internet and next generation telecommunication networks. In this context, telecommunication services and capabilities including call and session control, messaging features, and presence and location features are integrated with the SOA-based computing infrastructure available in computing environments. In particular, issues concerning semantic and dynamic composition as well as orchestration to define, create and execute telecommunication services are addressed. Furthermore, secure and controlled interaction between application components deployed in different domains (e.g., an enterprise domain and a network operator domain) were considered in the case study.

The telecommunication case study mainly addressed issues concerning the evolution of the service infrastructure, not specific telecommunication services. However, some specific services were used in the description to exemplify the infrastructural issues. This case study was carried out during the first two years of the project and was hence used as test bed for the preliminary SENSORIA research results (see [4]).

Telecommunication services, i.e., the services that are provided by a telecommunication infrastructure managed by a public network operator, are evolving by considering several aspects of *convergence*: convergence of media, convergence of terminals, combination of service features, and convergence of telecommunications and Internet worlds. Moreover, the services should be *user-centric*, that is, their behavior should be personalized according to the requirements of single end-users. The possibility of personalisation should be uniform and cover all the features of the service. In particular, the end-users should be seen as single entities even across several different networks, terminals, communication media, and applications.

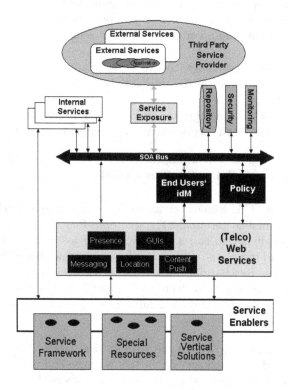

Fig. 2. Horizontal Telco architecture

Most of the current services in the telecommunication area are realized as a set of *vertical platforms*, each of them specialized to provide services involving a specific telecommunication feature and a specific network. Usually, such platforms integrate – in a single system – the service execution environments with the telecommunication features and some supporting functions (e.g., payment, authentication, profiles). Unfortunately, in general, such vertical systems are not connected at all.

This organisation of services introduces several problems in dealing with the realisation of *converged services*. In order to improve this situation, telecommunication services are evolving towards a *horizontal approach* based on the integration of systems for service delivery (see Fig. 2).

In SENSORIA, we have investigated the possibility of evolving telecommunication services according to a horizontal approach with the help of service-oriented architectures. Some of the areas where the SOA approach can be adopted for the evolution of such services are:

- adoption of SOA-based principles and techniques to organize the internal structure of the service layer, and to define the communication bus among the different services and macro-functions;
- evolution of composition mechanisms to create and execute telecommunication services by adopting solutions based on orchestration or choreography and by introducing the possibility to handle semantic and dynamic service compositions;
- adoption of SOA technology to expose telecommunication capabilities to third party applications on the Internet, and to assemble services provided by third parties;
- adoption of SOA technology to introduce a uniform interaction model of services delivered by the service layer and terminal applications.

An interesting setting for evaluating the benefits of SOAs in the telecommunication context is the *Call-And-Pay Taxi* scenario.

Call-and-Pay Taxi. This scenario concerns the retrieval and purchase of goods or services via a mobile terminal. The *Call-and-Pay Taxi service* provides a user with the possibility to call a taxi by sending an SMS to a specific SMS service number and to pay the taxi service by sending another SMS. The service automatically debits the charging amount for the taxi ride to the end-users credit card and transfers the money to the taxi company. From the point of view of the involved human actors (i.e., end-user, call center agent, taxi driver) the service behaves in the following way:

- The end-user sends an SMS to the SMS service number which is associated to the Call-and-Pay Taxi service; in this way the end-user asks to call the taxi company of the town where he is currently located.
- The end-user receives an incoming call on his mobile phone in order to be connected to the call center of the local taxi company.
- The end-user talks to the taxi company agent; the call center agent contacts a taxi driver and confirms to the user the selected taxi number and the expected waiting time.
- The end-user receives an SMS which includes the taxi number and a *call-code* to identify the ride. The taxi driver receives a similar SMS.
- After the taxi ride, the user sends another SMS in order to authorize the payment using the preferred means of payment (stored in the user profile).
- In case of a successful transaction, the taxi driver and the end-user receive a confirmation of the payment with an SMS. In case of failure, an SMS with such an indication is sent to them (and the end-user has to pay in the traditional way).

5   The eUniversity Case Study

The administration of a university is a complicated task. Student applications, enrolment, course management, theses, and examination management all pose individual problems and, in general, a lot of paperwork. Nowadays, many of these tasks can and are being automated using computer systems. As universities are often large organisations with autonomous sub-organisations, a promising approach for this is the use of SOA-based software, in which the individual parts of a university as well as (external) students can work together with respective back- and frontends of a web-based system.

To investigate the problem of developing SOA-based university management systems, we have created a case study based on a set of university scenarios that make use of the specific features of SOAs [2]. In particular, we consider eUniversities, i.e., universities in which at least all of the paperwork, if not the courses themselves, are handled online. Scenarios in such an environment include:

- *Management of curricula*, i.e., providing information on which courses are offered, which requirements and how many credit points each course has, where a course takes place during a certain semester, etc.
- *Management of students*, in particular, enrolment and progress during a course of studies.
- *Thesis management*, i.e., the process of offering, accepting, working on, and submitting bachelor, master, or diploma theses.
- *E-Learning*, i.e., a system which provide students with (additional) training material, and enables the integration (embedding) of courses into other universities to enable students to participate in courses remotely.

During the course of the project, we have investigated the following three scenarios in more detail.

Thesis Management. In this scenario, we have considered the management of a thesis – bachelor, master, or diploma – from the announcement of a thesis topic by a tutor to the final assessment and student notification, including regular updates of the student to the thesis as well as status messages to the tutor, but also considering deadlines imposed by the examination office. This scenario is typical for a service orchestration – a central coordinator service uses several other services in combination to achieve a certain goal, and during this task, needs to be aware of problems, undoing previous work.

Submitting Coursework. We consider services to provide e-learning courses which can be shared between universities and services which enable several universities to jointly provide e-learning courses. Sharing courses in this way enables students to pick from a greatly increased number of courses; however, it also means that the number of students taking part in a course might be rather large. The scenario is that the students inscribed in a class all need to submit their coursework via uploads by the deadline. The question to ask here is how the system scales with respect to increasing student numbers and increasing file sizes.

Student Enrolment. In this scenario, students may apply for a certain course of studies online, providing the necessary documents and certificates via a website. The functionality for handling the enrolment is provided by two service orchestrations which interact with each other and other services to verify the application. The consulted services include the student office, an admission checking service, and a service for the upload of documents. Requirements for this scenario (and for the verification) include that the client and the services should communicate via a secure and reliable connection, that the services are proven to perform as expected up to a certain workload, that messages sent between the services are accountable for, and that no deadlocks occur in the communication.

6   Conclusion

This chapter has introduced the four case studies used in SENSORIA for feeding and steering the foundational research carried out in the project: Three case studies from the industrial domains of finance, automotive, and telecommunications, and one from the academic domain of university management. All case studies have been used extensively in SENSORIA for validating the techniques, methods and languages developed in the project against the requirements discussed in this chapter.

The specification and implementation of demonstrators for the finance, automotive and eUniversity case studies is further discussed in Chapter 7-1. In Chapter 7-2, a detailed overview of the application of the results obtained in SENSORIA (i.e., techniques, methods and languages developed in the technical work packages) to the case studies is be presented.

References

1. Alessandrini, M., Dost, D.: Finance Case Study: Requirements, Specification and Modelling of Selected Scenarios (D8.3.a). Technical report, S&N AG (2007)
2. Hölzl, M.: Distributed E-University Management and E-Learning System: Requirements modelling and analysis of selected scenarios (D8.4.a). Technical report, LMU München (2007)
3. Koch, N., Berndl, D.: Requirements Modelling and Analysis of Selected Scenarios: Automotive Case Study (D8.2.a). Technical report, FAST GmbH (2007)
4. Moiso, C., Ferrari, L., Thuegaz, E., Buscemi, N., Monanari, U., Bertoli, P., Pistore, M., Kazhamiakin, R., Bruni, R., Gnesi, S., ter Beek, M., Petrocchi, M., Mazzanti, F., Fiadeiro, J., Bocchi, L.: Telecommunication Case Study (D8.1.a). Technical report, TILab (2007)
5. Xie, R., Koch, N.: Automotive CASE Study: Demonstrator. Technical report, Cirquent GmbH (2009)

UML Extensions for Service-Oriented Systems*

Howard Foster[1], László Gönczy[2], Nora Koch[3,4], Philip Mayer[3],
Carlo Montangero[5], and Dániel Varró[2]

[1] Imperial College London, UK
[2] Budapest University of Technology and Economics, Hungary
[3] Ludwig-Maximilians-Universität München, Germany
[4] Cirquent GmbH, Germany
[5] Universitá di Pisa, Italy
howard.foster@imperial.ac.uk, {nora.koch,philip.mayer}@pst.ifi.lmu.de,
monta@di.unipi.it, {varro,gonczy}@mit.bme.hu

Abstract. A trend in software engineering is towards model-driven development. Models are used to document requirements, design results, and analysis in early phases of the development process. However, the aim of modeling is very often more ambitious as models are used for automatic generation in so-called model-driven engineering approaches. The relevance of models leads to the need of both, high-level domain specific modeling languages (DSML), and metamodels which are the basis for the definition of model transformations and code generation.

For the service-oriented computing domain we developed within the SENSORIA project a DSML for building and transforming SOA models. This DSML is defined as a family of UML profiles, which complement the SoaML profile for the specification of SOAs structure. Our family of profiles focus on orchestration of services, service-level agreements, non-functional properties of services, implementation of service modes and service deployment.

1 Introduction

A range of domain-specific languages and standards are available for engineering service-oriented architectures (SOAs) such as Web Services Description Language (WSDL), Web Services Business Process Execution Language (WS-BPEL), Web Services Choreography Description Language (WS-CDL), WS-Policy and WS-Security. These languages deal with the various aspects of SOA systems, such as service descriptions, orchestrations, policies and non-functional properties of services at a specification level. However, more systematic and model-driven approaches are needed for the development of service-oriented software. Models of SOAs are required for providing a complete – whenever possible a graphical – picture of the systems represented at a high level of abstraction. Achieving the properties of service-oriented systems mentioned above requires then model elements that ease the understanding of the individual artefacts of a system, and their integration.

---

* This work has been partially sponsored by the project SENSORIA, IST-2 005-016004.

M. Wirsing and M. Hölzl (Eds.): SENSORIA Project, LNCS 6582, pp. 35–60, 2011.
© Springer-Verlag Berlin Heidelberg 2011

Within the SENSORIA project, we have created ways of modeling these different aspects with the help of the Unified Modeling Language (UML)[24]. The UML is accepted as lingua franca in the development of software systems. It is the most mature language used for modeling. However, plain UML is not expressive enough for the specification of structural and behavioral aspects of services. Service modeling introduces a new set of key distinguishing concepts, for example partner services, message passing among requester and provider of services, compensation of long-running transactions, modes, and policies associated to services. Without specific support for those concepts in the modeling language, diagrams quickly get overloaded with technical constructs, degrading their readability.

Several attempts have been made to add service functionality to the UML. Most notably, SoaML [25] is an upcoming standard UML profile of the OMG for specification of service-oriented architectures, which does only cover structural aspects. Our own contribution to the field of UML service modeling complements SoaML, and consists in introducing more service-specific model elements mainly for the behavioral aspects of services-oriented software. In a first step, metamodels are defined as a conservative extension of the UML metamodel, i.e. they do not imply any adjustment in the UML metamodel. In a second step, UML profiles are created for these metamodels using the UML extension mechanisms provided by mapping stereotypes to the metaclasses. The result is the SENSORIA family of UML profiles for the development of SOAs.

The use of the UML for modeling has many advantages when compared to the use of proprietary modeling techniques. These advantages are (1) to be able to use existing CASE tool support, which is provided by commercial and open source tools; (2) to avoid the definition from scratch of a new modeling language, which would require an own project to detail their syntax, semantics and provide user-friendly tool support. These metamodels and the corresponding UML profiles constitute the basis for model transformations and code generation defining a model-driven development process. In particular, the MDD4SOA (Model-Driven Development for SOA) transformers – also developed within the scope of the SENSORIA project – are model transformations implemented as Eclipse plug-ins. They automatically transform service orchestrations specified with our UML4SOA profile to executable code, such as BPEL/WSDL, Java and Jolie.

In the following sections, we will discuss the individual UML extensions which form our SENSORIA family of profiles for SOA development and the SoaML profile (section 3), which are jointly used to model the different aspects of service-oriented software. The SENSORIA family of profiles comprise UML4SOA, a profile for service orchestration (section 4), for non-functional properties of services (section 5), business policies (section 6), for implementation modes of SOAs (section 7), and service deployment (section 8). These UML profiles can be used separately or in combination, depending on the software requirements and the decisions of the service engineer. The running example belongs to the case study from the automotive domain, which is detailed in section 2. Finally, in section 9 we present some related work and conclude in section 10.

2 Case Study

The SENSORIA family of profiles that are presented in the following sections are illustrated by models of the *On Road Assistance* scenario of the automotive case study [15,29]. In this scenario, the diagnostic system reports a failure in the car engine, for example, the vehicle's oil lamp reports a low oil level. This triggers the in-vehicle diagnostic system to perform an analysis of the sensor values. The diagnostic system reports e.g. a problem with the pressure in one cylinder head, and therefore the driver will not be able to reach the planned destination. The diagnostic system sends a message for starting the assistance system, which orchestrates a set of services.

Based on availability and the driver's preferences, the service discovery system identifies and selects the appropriate services in the area: repair shops (garage) and rental car stations. The selection of services takes into account personalized policies and preferences of the driver to find these "best services". We assume that the owner of the car has to deposit a security payment before being able to order services. In order to keep the scenario simple, we limit the involved services, but they could be easily extended e.g. to identify as well a towing service, providing the GPS data of the stranded vehicle in case the vehicle is no longer drivable. In such a case, the driver makes an appointment with the towing service, and the vehicle will be towed to the shop.

The *On Road Assistance* scenario is complemented with the *Emergency* scenario [15] that is needed when the damaged car blocks the route and a convoy behaviour is required from other cars. It is used to illustrate the reconfiguration issues of a service-oriented system. In case of an emergency, the vehicles that are driven in a default mode are reconfigured to be driven in a convoy mode guided by the Highway Emergency System. The master vehicle is then followed by the other vehicles of the convoy. In the *Emergency* scenario the car navigation system is able to react to events which cause the switching between the modes specified in the different architecture configurations.

3 Modeling Structural Aspects of SOAs

The basic structure of a software system is the ground layer on which other specifications are based – this holds true not only for traditional architectures, but also for the SOA-based systems we have considered in SENSORIA. Although the UML does include mechanisms for modeling structural aspects of software, the specific requirements of SOA systems – for example, the central concept of a service and the separation of requested and provided services – cannot be expressed in a concise way, as services and service providers are not first level citizens of the UML.

We therefore need an extension of the UML to be able to express these ideas. In SENSORIA, we have chosen to use the existing profile SoaML, which is currently in a beta 2 phase and on its way to becoming an OMG standard. We feel that we can adequately express our ideas of structural aspects of services in SoaML, and have therefore sought to integrate our own specific profiles presented in later sections with SoaML.

In this section, we introduce some of the basic concepts specified in SoaML which we need for modeling our case study and as a basis for defining our profiles. For the complete description, please refer to the SoaML specification [25].

Structural service modeling employs the basic UML mechanisms for modeling composite structures, enhanced with stereotypes from the SoaML profile – ≪participant≫, ≪servicePoint≫, ≪requestPoint≫, ≪serviceInterface≫ and ≪messageType≫ (listed in Table 1). The basic unit for implementing service functionality is a service participant, modeled as a class with the stereotype ≪participant≫. A participant may provide or request services through ports, which are stereotyped with ≪requestPoint≫ or ≪servicePoint≫, respectively. Each port has a type, which is a ≪serviceInterface≫ implementing or using operations as defined in a standard UML interface definition.

Table 1. SoaML metaclasses and stereotypes (excerpt)

Metaclass	Stereotype	UML Metaclass	Description
Participant	≪participant≫	Class	Represents some (possibly concrete) entity or component that provides and/or consumes services
ServicePoint	≪servicePoint≫	Port	Is the offer of a service by one participant to others using well defined terms, conditions and interfaces. It defines the connection point through which a participant provides a service to clients
RequestPoint	≪requestPoint≫	Port	Models the use of a service by a participant and defines the connection point through which a participant makes requests and uses or consumes services
ServiceInterface	≪serviceInterface≫	Class	Is the type of a ≪servicePoint≫ or ≪requestPoint≫ specifying provided and required operations.
MessageType	≪messageType≫	DataType, Class	Is the specification of information exchanged between service requesters and providers

As an example for using these stereotypes, we present the structural diagram for the scenario introduced in the previous section (see Fig. 1). As can be seen from the figure, the central orchestration of the case study – i.e., the component which coordinates the actions of all the services – is modeled as a ≪participant≫. The *OnRoadAssistant* participant has seven ports, six of which are ≪RequestPoint≫s, indicating that a certain service is requested. The last port is a ≪ServicePoint≫, indicating that a certain service is provided.

As mentioned above, each ≪RequestPoint≫ and ≪ServicePoint≫ is typed with a ≪ServiceInterface≫ which defines, though interface realizations and usage associations, the operations required or provided at the given port. In our case, the orchestration provides, through the ≪ServiceInterface≫ *ClientInterface*, the operation *startAssistant* to clients. In the other direction, it requires e.g. the operation *selectBestGarage* from another service, which is indicated through the ≪ServiceInterface≫ *SelectBestInterface* which is the type of the ≪RequestPoint≫ *selectBestGarage*.

With the basic structure of service-based systems and our case study specified using SoaML, we can move on to define profiles for additional aspects of SOA systems.

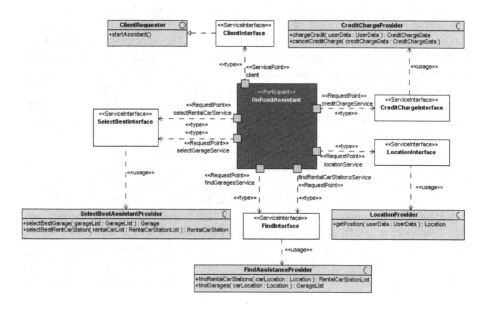

Fig. 1. SoaML structural diagram of the On Road Assistance scenario

4   Service Orchestrations

A key aspect of service-orientation is the ability to compose existing services, i.e. creating a description of the interaction of several services, which has come to be known as an *orchestration*. An orchestration is a behavioral specification of a service component, or ≪Participant≫ in SoaML. As with structural aspects, the UML does contain mechanisms for specifying behavior – for example, as activity or sequence diagrams – but does not contain specific support for constructs used in service orchestrations such as message passing, compensation, event handling, and the combination of these.

To enable developers to model service orchestration behavior in an easy and concise way, we have created UML4SOA, a profile for UML which defines a high-level domain specific modeling language (DSML) for behavioral service specifications. UML4SOA was first introduced in [19] and described in more detail in [20]. It has been used as the central language for the specification of the SENSORIA case studies and enjoys the support of several formalisms and formal tools.

4.1   Metamodel

An excerpt of the UML4SOA metamodel is shown in Fig. 2, which includes the main concepts of our DSML and the relationships among these concepts. For example, we introduce elements such as *ServiceSendAction* for modeling the asynchronous invocation of a service, i.e. without waiting for a reply from the external partner. Another specific concept of the service-oriented domain is the compensation of long-running transactions. Therefore we define model elements such as *CompensationAction* and *CompensationEdge*. For each non-abstract class of the metamodel we defined a stereotype with the objective of producing semantically enriched and increased readable models of service-oriented systems, e.g. a stereotype ≪sendAction≫ for the *ServiceSendAction* metaclass, and a stereotype ≪compensate≫ for the *CompensateAction* metaclass. Table 2 provides an overview of the elements of the metamodel, the stereotypes that are defined for these metamodel elements (they comprise the profile UML4SOA), the UML metaclasses they extend, and a brief description. For further details on UML4SOA, including the full metamodel, the reader is referred to [18].

UML4SOA proposes the use of UML activity diagrams for modeling service behavior, in particular for modeling orchestrations which coordinate other services. We assume that business modelers are most familiar with this kind of notation to show dynamic behavior of business workflows. An UML4SOA ≪ServiceActivity≫, as noted above, can be directly attached as the behavior of a ≪Participant≫.

4.2   Example

As an example for modeling a service-oriented system in UML4SOA, we show the implementation of the *On Road Assistance* scenario defined in Fig. 1.

The process *On Road Assistance* is modeled as a UML4SOA orchestration (see Fig. 3) . It illustrates how the assistance process interacts with its client and its partners through ports. It starts with a receipt (≪receive≫) of the call *startAssistant* through the *client* port, receiving the request to start the assistance. Note that the initial call to *startAssistant* starts the complete activity – a convention we chose to make the workflow more explicit. Furthermore, note that the port is given in the ≪lnk≫ pin, while the operation is denoted in the main body of the action.

Table 2. UML4SOA metaclasses and stereotypes

Metaclass	Stereotype	UML Metaclass	Description
ServiceActivity Node	«serviceActivity»	Activity, StructuredActivityNode	Represents a special activity for service behavior or a grouping element for service-related actions
ServiceSendAction	«send»	CallOperationAction	Is an action that invokes an operation of a target service asynchronously, i.e. without waiting for a reply. The argument values are data to be transmitted as parameters of the operation call. There is no return value
ServiceReceiveAction	«receive»	AcceptCallAction	Is an accept call action representing the receipt of an operation call from an external partner. No answer is given to the external partner
ServiceSend&Receive	«send&receive»	CallOperationAction	Is a shorthand for a sequential order of send and receive actions
ServiceReplyAction	«reply»	ReplyAction	Is an action that accepts a return value and a value containing return information produced by a previous ServiceReceiveAction action
CompensationEdge	«compensation»	ActivityEdge	Is an edge which connects an orchestration element to be compensated with the one specifying a compensation. It is used to associate compensation handlers to activities and scopes
EventEdge	«event»	ActivityEdge	Is an edge connecting event handlers with an orchestration element during which the event may occur. The event handler attached must contain a receive or a timed event at the beginning.
CompensateAction	«compensate»	Action	Triggers the execution of the compensation defined for a certain named service activity (can only be inserted in compensation or exception handlers)
CompensateAllAction	«compensateAll»	Action	Triggers compensation of all nested service activities from the service activity attached to the current compensation or exception handler. The nested service activities are compensated in reverse order of completion.
LinkPin	«lnk»	InputPin	Holds a reference to the partner service by indicating the corresponding service point or request point involved in the interaction
SendPin	«snd»	InputPin	Is used in send actions to denote the data to be sent to an external service
ReceivePin	«rcv»	OutputPin	Is used in receive actions to denote the data to be received from an external service

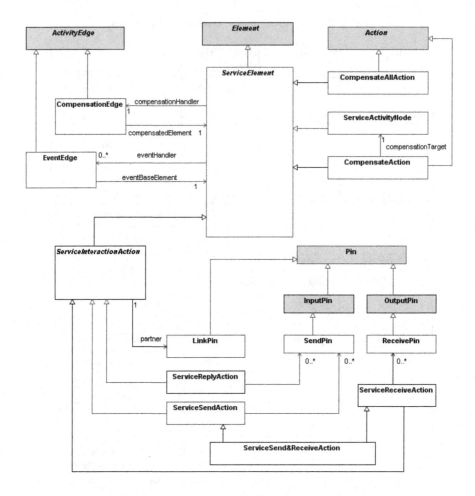

Fig. 2. Excerpt of the UML4SOA metamodel (includes some highlighted UML meta-classes)

Once the initial request has been received, the process goes on to interact with partner services. The process first charges the credit card of the user to ensure that payment is available for later actions. This is done with the help of a ≪send&receive≫ action, invoking the operation ≪chargeCredit≫ on the service attached to the ≪RequestPoint≫ *creditChargeService*. The ≪send&receive≫ action also uses a ≪snd≫ pin for denoting the information to be sent (the variable *userData*, in this case) and the variable in which the return information will be stored (*creditChargeData*, defined in the ≪receive≫ pin). A similar call is placed to retrieve the position of car using the *locationService* port.

Once this initial setup phase has completed, the process enters the *findAssistance* service activity. Here, it simultaneously interacts with two external services available through the *findGaragesService* and *findRentalCarStationsService*

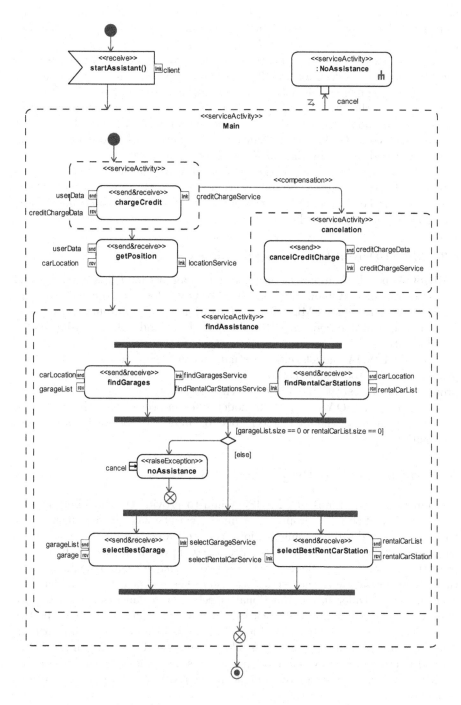

Fig. 3. UML4SOA activity diagram showing the OnRoadAssistance participant

ports. If the process finds both a garage and a rental car station, it continues to retrieve the nearest one. If it is not able to find at least one garage and one rental car station, an exception is thrown.

Note that there is a standard UML exception handler attached to the service activity. Inside the exception handler, the process invokes a ≪compensateAll≫ action. The meaning of this action is to undo previously and successfully completed work. In this case, the process refers of course to the credit card charge. To be able to undo this operation, a compensation handler is attached to that action, which consists of an action canceling the charge with another service call to the service identified by the *CreditChargeInterface* port.

As can be seen from Fig. 3, the behavioral specification of this process is concise and very readable. The specification also directly uses elements defined in the structural diagram in Fig. 1, thus exploiting the information defined there, not repeating it unnecessarily.

4.3 Model-Driven Development Support

UML4SOA specifications can be used for more than just modeling to understand the semantics of a system. With the MDD4SOA (Model-Driven Development for SOA) transformers, UML4SOA orchestrations can be automatically transformed to executable code in BPEL/WSDL, Java, and Jolie by using model transformations.

Also, UML4SOA models enjoy formal methods support – the SENSORIA project includes tools and methods for checking qualitative and quantitative properties of orchestrations, as well as checking protocol compliance of an orchestration. UML4SOA was used to model different scenarios of the SENSORIA case studies. We refer the interested reader to Chapter 7-1 of this book for more information.

5   Non-functional Properties of Services

Non-functional extensions of UML4SOA aim to provide the modeling of arbitrary "quality of service" properties defined for a particular given client-server pair. Since in real service configurations, service properties can vary for different classes of clients, we follow a contract-based approach, where non-functional properties of services are defined between two *participant* components, namely, the *service provider* and the *service requester*. These contracts are modeled by ≪nfContracts≫. Different non-functional aspects (performance, security, etc.) are modeled in corresponding ≪nfCharacteristics≫ which group different properties in ≪nfDimensions≫ (where a ≪runTimeValue≫ is associated to each dimension). The reason for creating separate classes for these instead of storing in properties is to correlate real SLAs where most parameters are typically bound to a range of allowed values. Moreover, concepts like average values, deviation, etc. need to be modeled in a uniform way.

During a negotiation process, participants create an agreed contract of the provider and requester. Finally, properties of services need to be monitored at runtime (modeled as ≪monitor≫) either by the participating parties or by involving a separate entity.

5.1 Metamodel

A metamodel of UML4SOA-NFP is shown in Fig. 4. The profile was motivated by the UML 2.0 Profile for QoS & Fault Tolerance [23]. However, we followed a more simple way of defining a general framework for QoS, which then can be "instantiated" by defining concrete aspects such as performance, security, etc. Table 3 shows the usage of the stereotypes.

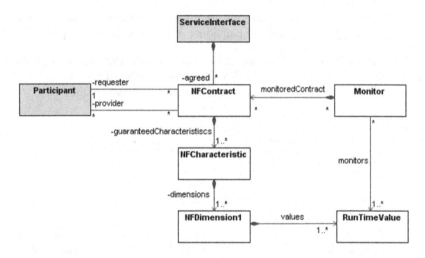

Fig. 4. Metamodel of non-functional extensions (includes some highlighted SoaML metaclasses

Table 3. UML4SOA-NFP metaclasses and stereotypes

Metaclass	Stereotype	UML Metaclass	Description
NFContract	≪nfContract≫	Class	Represents a non-functional contract between a service provider and a service requester
NFCharacteristic	≪nfCharacteristic≫	Class	Represents a non-functional aspect such as performance, security, reliable messaging, etc.
NFDimension	≪nfDimension≫	Class	Groups non-functional properties within a non-functional aspect (characteristics)
RunTimeValue	≪runTimeValue≫	Attribute	An actual non-functional property
Monitor	≪monitor≫	Class	A run-time service to monitor a contract (not used in the paper)

5.2   Examples

In the *On Road Assistance* scenario, several QoS requirements can be formed
on service connections. To illustrate the use of UML4SOA-NFP, we modeled
(part of) a contract between *OnRoadAsssistant* (the orchestrator component)
and *CreditChargeProvider*. First we show a brief textual specification of non-
functional requirements:

- All communications between these services must be secure, e.g. message
  content must be encrypted and digitally signed.
- All messages from the orchestrator component to the credit card manager
  must be acknowledged when received.
- As all succesful scenarios pass this step, the throughput of the service must
  be high enough (1000 requests per hour) with a reasonable response time.

Fig. 5 shows an excerpt of a concrete contract. Note that the class diagram
corresponds to a template which is filled (instantiated as object diagram). This
will include concrete values for encrypting methods, response time, etc.

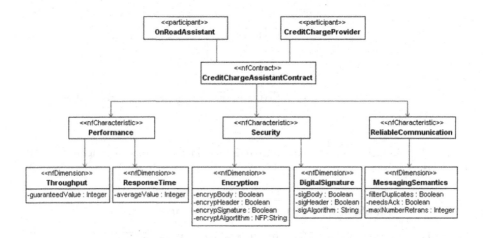

Fig. 5. Non-functional paramaters in (part of) the On Road Assistance scenario

5.3   Model-Driven Development Support

As this profile may describe arbitrary types of requirements (logging, security,
performance, etc.), the development support for different aspects obviously vary
for different development phases (early design/analysis/deplyoment/operation).

   UML4SOA-NFP has support for middleware-level performability analysis as
described in [7] and [9]. This enables the early estimation of a trade-off between
reliability and performance. Evolving model transformations are developed to
support the automated code generation of middleware configuration with QoS

constraints. Details of this technology are described in [6] (modeling), [8] (performability analysis) and [9] (transformations for deployment). These transformations are based on the VIATRA framework, described in details in Chapter 6-2 of this book.

Also a transformation-based technique is currently under development, which will help to create simple transformations on UML4SOA-NFP models extended with additional information on their intended usage (e.g. security analysis) and/ or target platform (e.g. Apache stack). These models and transformations give a flexible tool to support the quickly changing WS-* platforms in every phase of service engineering. This transformation set will include validation steps to check both modeling errors and domain specific requirements.

6   Business Policies Support

This part of the UML4SOA profile deals with the connection of services and business policies, in the context of STPOWLA [10]. The goal of STPOWLA is to define the business process so that the business stakeholder can easily adapt it to the current state of affairs, by controlling the resources used by the basic tasks in the workflows. To this purpose, the stakeholders issue *policy* definitions, which constrain the resource usage as a function of the state of the workflow when a task is needed.

Here we show how to define business workflows in terms of *taskSpecifications*, that is, interfaces of ServicePoints as from SoaML, enriched with information on the ranges of variability in the use of resources (*service level dimensions*).

We note that the profile we present here does not cover policies explicitly. This is why it is called Business Policies *Support* profile. Indeed, policies are better expressed as tables than as UML models. In another chapter of this book (Chapter 1-3) it is shown how to integrate workflows and policies in a SOA, to support flexible workflow enactment.

6.1   Metamodel

The metamodel for business policies support consists of a series of related elements, relationships, and a number of constraints. Not all the concepts are new, since we exploit the *NFDimension* concept from the NF-UML4SOA profile, (cfr. Section 5). We deal first with the elements devoted to the basic tasks in (Fig. 6):

– *ServiceInterface* specifies the interface of the service point a Task connects to at enaction time. Constraint: just one operation specified.
– *Requires* is used to link a TaskSpecification to its ServiceInterface.
– *TaskSpecification* specifies a Task, identifying (via Requires) the ServiceInterface. It also specifies (via Dim) the non-fuctional dimensions that characterize the service to invoke.
– *TaskSpecification* owns an operation called main, with the same parameters and return type of the required service. Indeed, main triggers the search and invocation of a suitable service, and returns the computed result. The search identifies a service implementation that satisfies the current policies.

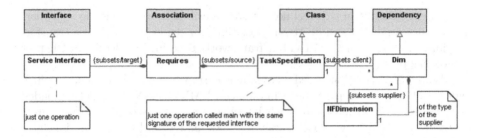

Fig. 6. Metamodel for business policies support: Task specification (includes some highlighted UML classes)

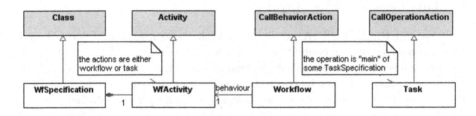

Fig. 7. Metamodel for business policies support: Workflow specification (includes some highlighted UML classes)

- *Dim* allows specifying the relevant service level dimensions in a TaskSpecification, by linking to ≪nfDimension≫ from NF-UML4SOA. It also defines a default value, which is used to select the service provider, when no policy with specific requirements for the target dimension is in place.

The next concepts are depicted in Fig. 7:

- *WfSpecification* defines a workflow, specifying its attributes and internal behavior. The formers can be used to express conditions in the policies. The behavior is specified by the owned WfActivity.
- *Workflow* is an activity action that calls the specified behavior, i.e., a lower level workflow.
- *Task* is an activity action that calls the specified main operation.
- *WfActivity* defines the behavior of a workflow. Constraint: an owned action is either a Workflow or a Task.

All the concepts above are rendered as stereotypes in the UML profile shown in Table 4. The defaultValues are rendered as tagged values of the ≪dim≫ dependency: the tag is defaultValue, and the type is given by the target dimension.

Table 4. Business policies support metaclasses and stereotypes

Metaclass	Stereotype	UML Metaclass	Description
ServiceInterface	«serviceInterface»	Interface	Specifies the interface of the service point a Task connects to at enaction time
Requires	«Requires»	Association	Associates a TaskSpecification to the signature of the services that implement it
TaskSpecification	«taskSpecification»	Class	Specifies a Task, functionally via Requires, and non-functionally via Dim. The latter identifies the QoS dimensions that characterize the service to invoke. It owns a main operation, with the same parameters and return type of the required service, whose behavior is to trigger the search and invocation of a suitable service (i.e., one whose QoS characteristics satisfy the current policies), and to return the computed result
Dim	«Dim»	Dependency	Allows specifying the relevant service level dimensions in a TaskSpecification, by linking to «nfDimension» from UML4SOA-NFP
WfSpecification	«WfSpecification»	Class	Defines a workflow, specifying its attributes and internal behavior. The latter is specified by the owned WfActivity
WfActivity	«WfActivity»	Activity	Defines the behavior of a workflow. Constraint: an owned action is either a Workflow or a Task
Workflow	«Workflow»	CallBehaviorAction	Calls the specified behavior, namely, a lower level Workflow
Task	«Task»	CallOperationAction	Calls the specified main operation

6.2   Examples

To show how STPOWLA supports flexibility in the *On Road Assistance* scenario, we consider, within the general OnRoadAssistance workflow, a single task, namely the one that selects the best garage, and a policy that allows the driver to choose directly the repairing services which he knows and trusts, in his own town:

If the car fault happens in the driver's town, then let him select the services to be used. Otherwise choose the services automatically.

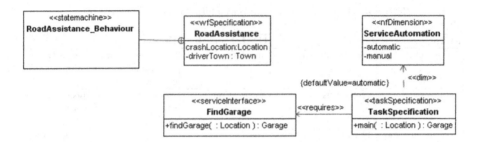

Fig. 8. Fragments of the On Road Assistance model

Fig. 8 shows an excerpt from the model of the scenario just outlined, exemplifying the use of the concepts both at the workflow and at the task level. To formalize the policies, the modeler needs to define, for the workflow, the attributes that specify the driver's home town and the car crash location, as detected by the embedded car GPS. Indeed, they are needed to express the conditions in the policy. So, the ≪wfSpecification≫ RoadAssistance, at the top-centre of the figure, lists the two attributes crashLocation and driverTown. The relevant part of the related ≪wfActivity≫ is shown to the left: the actions appear as shown: here, the task invokes the main operation of FindGarage, whose ≪taskSpecification≫ appears to the right (bottom). The name of the node is of little importance, being useful only to distinguish two nodes in the same workflow, when they use the same ≪taskSpecification≫.

Moreover, ≪taskSpecification≫ FindGarage requires the findGarage service (at its left), and declares the main operation accordingly. The modeler here has to introduce a suitable ≪nfDimension≫ to express the choice between the service that searches for a garage nearby the crash location, and the service that interacts with the driver to contact his own choice. This is AutomationLevel (top-right). The default value is fixed as automatic, via the tagged value for ≪dim≫.

7   Service Modes for Adaptive Service Brokering

In this section we describe a part of the SENSORIA family of profiles that addresses service adaptation and reconfiguration based upon operational states of the service system being described. The Service Modes profile complements the UML4SOA profile for orchestration by providing an abstraction of service system adaptation through architecture, behavior and constraints. Service Modes are an extension of Software Architecture Modes.

Software Architecture Modes are an abstraction of a specific set of services that must interact for the completion of a specific subsystem task, i.e., a mode will determine the structural constraints that rule a (sub)system configuration at runtime [13]. Therefore, passing from one mode to another and interactions among different modes formalize the evolution constraints that a system must satisfy: the properties that reconfiguration must satisfy to obtain a valid transition between two modes which determine the structural constraints imposed to the corresponding architectural instances. A Service Mode represents a Software Architecture Mode scenario of a service system. It combines a service architecture with behavior and policy specifications for service components within the service system and is intended to be evolved as new requirements are desired from the system. In this section we detail the specification of service modes by way of a Service Modes profile in the UML notation.

7.1   Metamodel

A metamodel for service modes (illustrated in Fig. 9) extends and constrains a number of UML core elements. As an overview, a *ModeModel* defines a package which contains a number of service architecture scenarios (as *Mode* packages) and components and also contains a *ModeModelActivity* to define how to switch between different service scenarios. Each scenario is defined in a *Mode* package which is a container for a *ModeCollaboration* and describes the role that each component plays within the scenario (e.g. a service requester and/or a provider). Each *ModeCollaboration* holds a *ModeActivity* which describes the process in which the mode orchestration is fulfilled. Each *ModeCollaboration* also refines the components of the *Mode* for additional service adaptation requirements (such as the constraints for service brokering). A *ModeConstraint* specifies a constraint on adaptation of ModeCollaborations. These constraints can also specify Quality-Of-Service (QoS) attributes for service components, and we reuse the *QoSRequired* and *QoSProvided* stereotypes related to the QoS Profile (as discussed in section 5.1). We now elaborate on service mode architecture, behaviour and adaptation relationships through examples.

7.2   Examples

A **Service Modes Architecture** consists of specifying the service components, their requirements and capabilities and interface specifications. A high-level architecture configuration is given in UML to represent the component specifications and their relationships. Each component will offer services to its clients, each such service is a component contract. A component specification defines a contract between clients requiring services, and implementers providing services. The contract is made up of two parts. The static part, or usage contract, specifies what clients must know in order to use provided services. The usage contract is defined by interfaces provided by a component, and required interfaces that specify what the component needs in order to function. The interfaces contain the available operations, their input and output parameters, exceptions they might raise, preconditions that must be met before a client can invoke the operation, and post conditions that clients can expect after invocation. These operations represent features and obligations that constitute a coherent offered or required service. At this level, the components are defined and connected in a static way, or in other words, the view of the component architecture represents

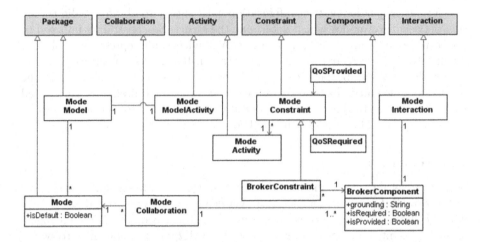

Fig. 9. Metamodel for service modes and service brokering specification (includes some highlighted UML classes)

a complete description disregarding the necessary state of collaboration for a given goal. Even if the designer wishes to restrict the component diagram to only those components which do collaborate, the necessary behavior and constraints are not explicit to be able to determine how, in a given situation, the components should interact. An example composite structure diagram for a service modes architecture is illustrated in Fig. 10 for the Emergency scenario of the Automotive Case Study (discussed in section 2). Note that the architecture represents both local services (via a localDiscovery component) and remote services (remoteDiscovery via a Vehicle Services Gateway).

Service Mode Behavior specification is a local coordinated process of service interactions and events for mode changes. The behavior is similar to that of service orchestrations, for which orchestrations languages such as WS-BPEL are widely adopted. Service mode behavior may be formed as described in section 4. At design time however, the activities for mode orchestration consist of two concepts. Firstly, orchestrating the *default* composition of services required and provided in the specified mode architecture. Secondly, the orchestration should also be able to react to events which cause mode changes, or in other words cater for the switching between the modes specified in the different architecture configurations. To specify mode changes, the engineer adds event handlers (and follow on activities) to react to certain events which cause a mode change. An example Service Mode Behavior is illustrated in Fig. 11. Note the events that lead to mode changes, for example receiving notification of an accident from an highway emergency service leads to a mode switch to a detour mode configuration.

Service Dynamism and Adaptation focuses on constraining changes to architecture and services, identifying both functional and non-functional variants

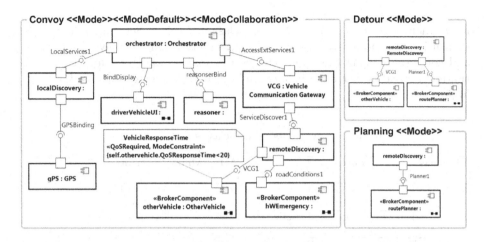

Fig. 10. Emergency service brokering architecture with Modes profile

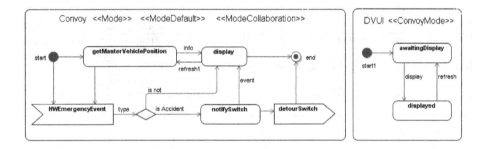

Fig. 11. Convoy service mode behavior specified in an activity diagram

on the specification. Using the Service Modes Profile we identify ModeCollabora-tions (composite structure diagrams) with *ModeConstraints* (UML constraints) which are categorised further by a constraint stereotype. Additionally, architec-tural constraints may be specified in the Object Constraint Language (OCL) or another constraint based language. The constraint language adopted becomes an implementation-dependent aspect of analysing models in UML. The ModeCon-straint is itself extended to support a specific kind of adaptation, that for service brokering. A *BrokerComponent* defines a service component which is included in service brokering specifications and can be used to identify the role of the brokered component (either requested or provided), and holds a specification for the service profile. Additionally, one or more (*BrokerConstraints*) can be associ-ated with a BrokerComponent, to identify the QoS either requested or provided by the service. An example constraint applied to a BrokerComponent is also illustrated in Fig. 10, in this case for the requirement that a *QoSResponseTime* should be offered less than 20ms by the other vehicle service.

As a summary of the semantics for the Service Modes profile, we list each profile metaclass, stereotype and UML metaclass in Table 5. Service Mode models built using the specification described in this section can be analysed for safety and correctness using the approach described in [3] and used for generating runtime service broker requirements and capability specifications as described in [5].

Table 5. Service Modes metaclasses and stereotypes

Metaclass	Stereotype	UML Meta-class	Description
ModeModel	≪ModeModel≫	Package	A Model containing Mode packages
ModeModelActivity	≪ModeModelActivity≫	Activity	The process flow for a Mode-Model (policy)
ModeCollaboration	≪ModeCollaboration≫	Collaboration	Contains composite structure and interactions
ModeActivity	≪ModeActivity≫	Activity	The process flow for a Mode (orchestration)
ModeConstraint	≪ModeConstraint≫	Constraint	Constraints on mode service or activity action
ModeInteraction	≪ModeInteraction≫	Interaction	Interaction protocol between Mode components
BrokerComponent	≪BrokerComponent≫	Component	Service component to be brokered within a Mode
BrokerConstraint	≪BrokerConstraint≫	ModeConstraint	A constraint on a Broker-Component

8   Service Deployment

In this section we describe a part of the SENSORIA family of profiles that addresses describing service composition deployment and more specifically, how service orchestrations are configured with appropriate infrastructure nodes and resources. A Service Deployment profile complements the UML4SOA profile for orchestration by providing an abstraction of service composition deployment through infrastructure nodes such as web server and servlets.

Service compositions, implemented as web services using BPEL or other execution languages, are executed by a specialist container, sometimes called a service composition engine or run-time environment. These containers use various system resources depending on the activities specified in the composition. BPEL engines will, for example upon receiving a SOAP message to start a BPEL process, instantiate this process and execute it in a separate thread concurrently with other ongoing BPEL processes. Again BPEL engines typically have configurable database connections and thread pools and they would delay the start of a BPEL process until they can assign a thread from a pool. Both Web service and BPEL containers typically map these threads efficiently to a set of operating system threads. The amount of operating system threads however, is finite due to the finite amount of memory required to handle the stack segment of the thread. Administrators must therefore carefully configure the thread pools to avoid exhaustion of the operating system resources. A Service Deployment model of the architecture can describe the characteristics of the host server and orchestration, and can be used to analyze such configurations for safety and correctness.

8.1 Metamodel

The Service Deployment metamodel (illustrated in Fig. 12) focuses on modeling the deployment architecture nodes (Servlet, WebServer) and deployment artifacts (ServiceOrchestration and Resource). One or more service orchestrations (of type ServiceOrchestration) are modeled as artifacts which are deployed on to servlet nodes. A service orchestration can only be deployed to one servlet instance. Servlets are hosted on web server nodes (a web server is a web container which manages the creation and deletion of servlet instances). A servlet also has predefined resource allocations, which are modeled as one or more objects of type Resource artifact. Resource is a general object for any finite system allocation object, however in this example we also illustrate a ThreadPool type of Resource.

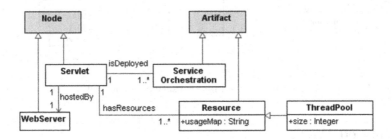

Fig. 12. Metamodel for service composition deployment and resources (includes some highlighted UML classes)

Table 6. Service Deployment metaclasses and stereotypes

Metaclass	Stereotype	UML Metaclass	Description
ServiceOrchestration	≪ServiceOrchestration≫	Artifact	A reference to a service orchestration process
Servlet	≪Servlet≫	Node	An execution container for orchestration processes
WebServer	≪WebServer≫	Node	A host for servlet containers
Resource	≪Resource≫	Artifact	A type of resource used by a Servlet or Webserver
ThreadPool	≪ThreadPool≫	Resource	A resource collection of threads

Semantics. The metamodel for service deployment consists of a series of related elements, relationships and a number of constraints. For each element we list each profile metaclass, stereotype and UML metaclass in Table 6.

8.2 Examples

A deployment model using the Service Deployment profile is illustrated in Fig. 13. Two service orchestrations (RoadAssitance and RoutePlanning) are deployed to a single servlet artifact. The servlet artifact manages a collection of threads in a ThreadPool. The servlet is also hosted by a WebServer. The example can be used to model check that the collaborating service orchestrations, along with the management of thread acquisition and release, is safe and correct.

For a more complete example of using the Service Deployment profile, along with detailed analysis of the model, the reader is invited to refer to [4].

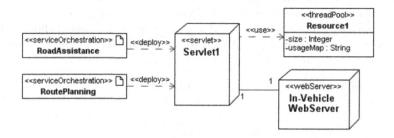

Fig. 13. Example: Deployment model for two service orchestrations and one servlet

9   Related Work

Several other attempts exist to define UML extensions for service-oriented systems. Most, however, do not cover aspects such structural, behavioral and non-functional aspects of SOAs. For example the UML2 profile for software services [14,17] provides an extension for the specification of services addressing only their structural aspects. The UML extension for service-oriented architectures described by Baresi et al. [1] focuses mainly on modeling SOAs by refining business-oriented architectures. The extension is also limited to stereotypes for the structural specification of services. Other modeling approaches require very detailed UML diagrams from designers trying to force service-oriented languages (like BPEL) on top of UML in order to facilitate automated transformation from UML to BPEL [11]. The approach lacks an appropriate UML profile preventing building models at a high level of abstraction; thus producing overloaded diagrams. Some other extensions, conversely to UML4SOA, do not cover vital parts of service orchestrations such as compensation handling, e.g. the UML profile described in [2]. Our UML4SOA approach tries to fill this gap providing a UML profile for service orchestrations.

The OMG also started an effort to standardize a UML profile and metamodel for services (SoaML) [25]. The current beta version focus on structural aspects of services, such as service components, service specifications, service interfaces and contracts for services. We see our family of UML profiles as a complementary set to the profile SoaML.

With respect to business policies, we have already mentioned that several of the stereotypes introduced here bear some relationships to SoaML ones. For instance, a ≪wfSpecification≫ is a ≪capability≫, which can ≪use≫ only (the capabilities offered by) other ≪workflow≫'s and ≪task≫'s. Similarly, a ≪taskSpecification≫ is also a ≪capability≫ , whose ≪contract≫'s can only span the space defined by the ≪NFDimension≫'s indentified via the ≪dim≫ dependencies. In either cases, the ≪serviceInterface≫ is a simple SoaML ≪serviceInterface≫, i.e. a plain UML interface. Finally, the ≪partecipant≫'s that implement these capabilities can be actually invoked only if they fulfill the current contract, as idenfified by the policies in place. Therefore, from the business policies perspective, the Business Policies profile could be seen as a specialization of SoaML, to address the concerns of a large share of the stakeholders, explicitly.

A few words are needed in relation to another widely known standard specification, namely Web Services Policy [28]. In fact, this is a machine-readable language to represent the capabilities and requirements, the *policies*, of a Web service. As such, the standard addresses low level issues, related to the automation of service selection, and will help in the implementation of STPOWLA .

As for non-functional properties, the UML Profile for QoS and Fault Tolerance [23] and UML Profile for Schedulability and Time [12] were considered during the development of UML4SOA-NFP. As our profile is general purpose (i.e., not bound to any specific aspect like security or performance), it can be extended to describe typical patterns for SLAs which is an ongoing work.

What is generally missing from the existing profile approaches is the ability to identify the requirements and capabilities of services and then to elaborate on the dynamic changes anticipated for adaptation or self-management. For the design of service compositions the dynamic composition of services has largely focused on planning techniques, such as in [26,21], generally with the specification of a guiding policy with some goals of service state. Runtime service brokering also plays an important role in being able to adapt component configurations [22] between requesters and providers yet there is little detail on providing analysis of requirements for brokering. *Software Architecture Modes* were perhaps first introduced in [13], in which they identify a mode as an abstraction of a specific set of services that must interact for the completion of a specific subsystem task. Hirsch's introduction to modes included architectural configuration but did not elaborate on component behavioral change as part of mode adaptation. Consequently, the concept of mode architectures has been extended with behavioral adaptation in [16], focusing on modes as behavioral specifications relating to architecture specification albeit indirectly. We provide a UML profile for service modes.

10   Conclusions

As service-oriented computing continues to gain support in the area of enterprise software development, approaches for handling SOA artefacts and their integration on a high level of abstraction while keeping a semantic link to their implementation become imperative. In this paper, we have focused on a UML-based domain specific modeling language for the specification of service-oriented software. Such a modeling language is the basis for the definition and use of model transformers to generate code in executable target SOA languages like BPEL and WSDL, in a model-driven development process.

Our main contribution are a set of UML profiles for modeling of services that comprise modeling of service orchestration, business policies and non-functional properties of services, service modes for adaptive service brokering and service deployment. Each profile provides a small set of model elements that allow the service engineer to produce diagrams which visualize services and their functionality in a simple fashion.

These are profiles for separate purposes, which share some basic concepts (e.g. service, participant, etc.). It is the service engineer who decides which profiles to use as they cover different steps of the development lifecycle, e.g. QoS parameters bound to an *SLA* could be transformed to the input of *Modes* while they can be also used in *St-Powla*. The policy support profile depends on UML4SOA-NFP, insofar as it imports *NFDimension* to characterize the QoS of the services subjected to the policies.

Further details on the profiles and tools discussed in this paper are available on the SENSORIA project website [27].

References

1. Baresi, L., Heckel, R., Thöne, S., Varró, D.: Style-Based Modeling and Refinement of Service-Oriented Architectures. Journal of Software and Systems Modeling (SOSYM) 5(2), 187–200 (2005)
2. Ermagan, V., Krüger, I.: A UML2 Profile for Service Modeling. In: Engels, G., Opdyke, B., Schmidt, D.C., Weil, F. (eds.) MODELS 2007. LNCS, vol. 4735, pp. 360–374. Springer, Heidelberg (2007)
3. Foster, H.: Architecture and Behaviour Analysis for Engineering Service Modes. In: Proceedings of the 2nd Workshop on Principles of Engineering Service Oriented Systems (PESOS 2009), Vancouver, Canada (2009)
4. Foster, H., Emmerich, W., Kramer, J., Magee, J., Rosenblum, D., Uchitel, S.: Model Checking Service Compositions under Resource Constraints. In: ESEC-FSE 2007: Proceedings of the the 6th joint meeting of the European Software Engineering Conference and the ACM SIGSOFT Symposium on the foundations of Software Engineering, pp. 225–234. ACM, New York (2007)
5. Foster, H., Uchitel, S., Magee, J., Kramer, J.: Leveraging Modes and UML2 for Service Brokering Specifications. In: Proceedings of the 4th Model-Driven Web Engineering Workshop (MDWE 2008), Toulouse, France (2008)
6. Gilmore, S., Gönczy, L., Koch, N., Mayer, P., Varró, D.: Non-Functional Properties in the Model-Driven Development of Service-Oriented Systems. Journal of Software and Systems Modeling (2010) (accepted for publication)

7. Gönczy, L., Déri, Z., Varró, D.: Model Driven Performability Analysis of Service Configurations with Reliable Messaging. In: Proc. of Model Driven Web Engineering Workshop, MDWE 2008 (2008)
8. Gönczy, L., Déri, Z., Varró, D.: Model Transformations for Performability Analysis of Service Configurations, pp. 153–166. Springer-Verlag, Heidelberg (2009)
9. Gönczy, L., Varró, D.: Developing Effective Service Oriented Architectures: Concepts and Applications in Service Level Agreements, Quality of Service and Reliability. In: Engineering Service Oriented Applications with Reliability and Security Requirements. IGI Global (2010) (to be published)
10. Gorton, S., Montangero, C., Reiff-Marganiec, S., Semini, L.: StPowla: SOA, Policies and Workflows. In: Di Nitto, E., Ripeanu, M. (eds.) ICSOC 2007. LNCS, vol. 4907, pp. 351–362. Springer, Heidelberg (2009)
11. Gronmo, R., Skogan, D., Solheim, I., Oldevik, J.: Style-Based Modeling and Refinement of Service-Oriented Architectures. In: Eighth IEEE International Enterprise Distributed Object Computing Conference (EDOC 2004), pp. 47–57. IEEE, Los Alamitos (2004)
12. O.M.Group. UML Profile for Schedulability, Performance and Time Specification (2005) ,
    http://www.omg.org/technology/documents/formal/schedulability.htm
13. Hirsch, D., Kramer, J., Magee, J., Uchitel, S.: Modes for software architectures. In: Gruhn, V., Oquendo, F. (eds.) EWSA 2006. LNCS, vol. 4344, pp. 113–126. Springer, Heidelberg (2006)
14. Johnston, S.: UML 2.0 Profile for Software Services (2005),
    http://www-128.ibm.com/developerworks/rational/library/05/419soa
    request For Proposal - AD/02-01/07
15. Koch, N., Berndl, D.: Requirements Modelling and Analysis of Selected Scenarios: Automotive CASE Study. Technical Report D8.2a, SENSORIA Deliverable (2007)
16. Kofroň, J., Plášil, F., Šerý, O.: Modes in Component Behavior Specification via EBP and their application in Product Lines. Information and Software Technology 51(1), 31–41 (2009)
17. Machado, R.J., Fernandes, J.M., Monteiro, P., Rodrigues, H.: Transformation of UML Models for Service-Oriented Software Architectures. In: Proceedings of the 12th IEEE International Conference and Workshops on Engineering of Computer-Based Systems, Washington, DC, USA, pp. 173–182 (2005)
18. Mayer, P., Koch, N., Schroeder, A.: The UML4SOA Profile. Technical report, Ludwig-Maximilians-Universität München (July 2009)
19. Mayer, P., Schroeder, A., Koch, N.: A Model-Driven Approach to Service Orchestration. In: Proceedings of the 2008 IEEE International Conference on Services Computing (SCC 2008), vol. 2, pp. 533–536. IEEE Computer Society Press, Los Alamitos (2008)
20. Mayer, P., Schroeder, A., Koch, N.: MDD4SOA: Model-Driven Service Orchestration. In: The 12th IEEE International EDOC Conference (EDOC 2008), Munich, Germany, pp. 203–212. IEEE Computer Society Press, Los Alamitos (2008)
21. Medjahed, B., Bouguettaya, A., Elmagarmid, A.: Composing Web Services on the Semantic Web. VLDB Journal, 333–351 (2003)
22. Mukhija, A., Dingwall-Smith, A., Rosenblum, D.S.: QoS-Aware Service Composition in Dino. In: ECOWS 2007: Proceedings of the Fifth European Conference on Web Services, Halle, Germany, pp. 3–12. IEEE Computer Society, Los Alamitos (2007)
23. OMG. UML for Modeling Quality of Service and Fault Tolerance Characteristics and Mechanisms, v1.1 (2008), http://www.omg.org/spec/QFTP/1.1/

24. OMG. Unified Modeling Language: Superstructure, version 2.2. Technical Report formal/2009-02-02, Object Management Group (2009)
25. OMG. Service oriented architecture Modeling Language (SoaML) - Specification for the UML Profile and Metamodel for Services (UPMS), revised submission. Specification, Object Management Group (2010),
    http://www.omg.org/spec/SoaML/1.0/Beta2/ (last visited: 22.07.2010)
26. Pistore, M., Marconi, A., Bertoli, P., Traverso, P.: Automated Composition of Web Services by Planning at the Knowledge Level. In: Proceedings of the International Joint Conference on Artificial Intelligence, IJCAI (2005)
27. SENSORIA. Software Engineering for Service-Oriented Overlay Computers,
    http://www.sensoria-ist.eu/ (last visited 15.03.2010)
28. W3C Working Group. Web Services Policy 1.5 - Primer,
    http://www.w3.org/TR/ws-policy-primer (last visit 22.10.2009)
29. Xie, R., Koch, N.: Automotive CASE Study: Demonstrator (Tutorial). Technical report, Cirquent GmbH (2009), http://www.sensoria-ist.eu/ (last visited 15.03.2010)

The Sensoria Reference Modelling Language[*]

José Fiadeiro[1], Antónia Lopes[2], Laura Bocchi[1], and João Abreu[3]

[1] Department of Computer Science, University of Leicester, UK
{jose,bocchi}@mcs.le.ac.uk
[2] Department of Informatics, Faculty of Sciences, University of Lisbon, Portugal
mal@di.fc.ul.pt
[3] Altitude Software, Algés, Portugal
Joao.Abreu@altitude.com

Abstract. This chapter provides an overview of SRML — the Sensoria Reference Modelling Language. Our focus will be on the language primitives that SRML offers for modelling business services and activities, the methodological approach that SRML supports, and the mathematical semantics the underpins the modelling approach, including techniques for qualitative and quantitative analysis.

1 Introduction

This chapter provides an overview of the modelling language — SRML — that we developed in Sensoria. We present the language primitives that SRML offers for modelling business services and activities, and discuss the methodological approach that SRML supports, which includes the use of the UMC model-checker (developed at CNR-ISTI) for qualitative analysis and of the Markovian process algebra PEPA (developed at the University of Edinburgh) for quantitative analysis of timing properties. Only some elements of the mathematical semantics that we developed for the approach are provided in this chapter; full details can be found in [4,6,29,32,30,33].

Our approach addresses *Service-Oriented Computing* (SOC) as a new computational paradigm in which interactions are no longer based on fixed or programmed exchanges between specific parties — what is known as clientship in object-oriented programming — but on the provisioning of *services* by external providers that are procured on the fly subject to a negotiation of service level agreements (SLAs). In SOC, the processes of discovery and selection of services are not coded (at design time) as part of the applications that implement business activities, but performed by the middleware according to functional and non-functional requirements (SLAs). We set ourselves to address the challenge raised on software engineering methodology by the need of declaring such requirements as part of the models of service-oriented applications, reflecting the business context in which services and activities are designed.

---

[*] This work has been partially sponsored by the project Sensoria, IST-2005-016004.

M. Wirsing and M. Hölzl (Eds.): Sensoria Project, LNCS 6582, pp. 61–114, 2011.
© Springer-Verlag Berlin Heidelberg 2011

A number of research initiatives have been proposing formal approaches that address different aspects of SOC independently of the specific languages that organisations such as OASIS (www.oasis-open.org) and W3C (www.w3.org) are making available for Web Services. For example, as presented in Chapter 2-1, several calculi have been developed in SENSORIA that address operational foundations of SOC (in the sense of how services compute) by providing a mathematical semantics for the mechanisms that support 'choreography' or 'orchestration' — sessions, message/event correlation, compensation, inter alia. Whereas such calculi address the need for specialised language primitives for *programming* in this new paradigm, they are not abstract enough to understand the *engineering* foundations of SOC, i.e. those aspects (both technical and methodological) that concern the way applications can be developed to provide business solutions, independently of the languages in which services are programmed.

This is why, in defining SRML, we used as a source of inspiration the Service Component Architecture (SCA) [2]. SCA makes available a general assembly model and binding mechanisms for service components and clients that may have been programmed in possibly many different languages, e.g. Java, C++, BPEL, or PHP. However, where SCA supports bottom-up low-level design, our aim for SRML was, instead, to address top-down high-level design. More specifically, our aim was to develop models and mechanisms that support the design of complex services from business requirements, and analysis techniques through which designers can verify or validate properties of composite services that can then be put together from (heterogeneous) service components using assembly and binding techniques such as the ones provided by SCA. This shift of emphasis from programming to (business) modelling, from component interoperability to business integration, implies that we will be discussing SOC at a level of abstraction that is different from most other work on Web services (e.g. [10,43]) or Grid computing (e.g. [34]).

Having this in mind, the chapter proceeds as follows. In Section 2, we provide an overview of the engineering architecture and processes that we see supporting SOC in Global Computing. In Section 3, we provide a brief overview of how we support the transition from business requirements to high-level design models using a (service-oriented) extension of use-case diagrams. In Section 4, we put forward the coordination model on which SRML is based. In Section 5, we present the modelling primitives of SRML. In Section 6, we discuss our model of configuration management. In Section 7, we discuss the use of model-checking techniques for analysing functional properties of complex services. Finally, in Section 8, we discuss the use of the Markovian process algebra PEPA for analysing timing properties. As a running example, we will use a mortgage-brokerage service that is part of the financial case study developed in SENSORIA (cf. Chapter 7-4). Although our approach is formal, in the sense that a mathematical semantics is available for all the primitives of the language [4,29,30], the paper is mostly mathematics-free with the exception of Sections 4.3, 6, 7.1 and 8.

2   Engineering Software for Service-Overlay Computers

The term 'service' is being used in a wide variety of contexts, often with different meanings. In SENSORIA, we set ourselves to address the notion of 'service-overlay computer', by which we mean the development of highly-distributed loosely-coupled applications over 'global computers' (GC) — "computational infrastructures available globally and able to provide uniform services with variable guarantees for communication, cooperation and mobility, resource usage, security policies and mechanisms" [1].

In this setting, there is a need to rethink the way we engineer software applications, moving from the typical 'static' scenario in which components are assembled to build a (more or less complex) system that is delivered to a customer, to a more 'dynamic' scenario in which (smaller) applications are developed to run on such global computers and respond to business needs by interacting with services and resources that are globally available. In this latter setting, there is much more scope for flexibility in the way business is supported: business processes can be viewed globally as emerging from a varying collection of loosely-coupled applications that can take advantage of the availability of services procured on the fly when they are needed.

In this context, the notion of 'system' itself, as it applies to software, also needs to be revisited. If we take one of the accepted meanings of system — *a combination of related elements organised into a complex whole* — we can see why it is not directly applicable to SOC/GC: services get combined at run time and redefine the way they are organised as they execute; no 'whole' is given *a priori* and services do not compute within a fixed configuration of a 'universe'. In a sense, we are seeing reflected in software engineering the trend for 'globalisation' that is now driving the economy.

SOC brings to the front many aspects that have already been discussed about component-based development (CBD), for instance in [23]. Given that different people have different perceptions of what SOC and CBD are, we will simply say that, in this paper, we will take CBD to be associated with what we called the static engineering approach. For instance, starting from a universe of (software) components as structural entities, Broy et al view a service as a way of orchestrating interactions among a subset of components in order to obtain some required functionality — "services coordinate the interplay of components to accomplish specific tasks" [16]. As an example, we can imagine that a bank will have available a collection of software components that implement core functionalities such as computing interests or charging commissions, which can be used in different products such as savings or loans.

SOC differs from this view in that there is no such fixed system of components that services are programmed to draw from but, rather, an evolving universe of software applications that service providers publish so that they can be discovered by (and bound to) business activities as they execute. For instance, if documents need to be exchanged as part of a loan application, the bank may rely on an external courier service instead of imposing a fixed one. In this case, a courier service would be discovered for each loan application that is processed, possibly taking into account the address to which the documents need to be sent, speed of delivery, reliability, and so on. However, the added flexibility provided through SOC comes at a price — dynamic interactions impose the overhead of selecting the co-party at each invocation — which means that the choice between invoking a service and calling a component is a decision that needs to be taken according to given business goals. This is why SRML makes provision for both SOC and CBD types of interaction (through *requires* and *uses* interfaces as discussed in Section 3).

To summarise, the impact that we see SOC to have on software engineering methodology stems from the fact that applications are built without knowing who will provide services that may be required, and that the discovery and selection of such services is performed, on the fly, by dedicated middleware components. This means that application developers cannot rely on the fact that someone will interact with them to implement the services that may be required so as to satisfy their requirements. Therefore, service-oriented 'clientship' needs to be based on shared ontologies of data and service provision. Likewise, service development is not the same as developing software applications to a costumer's set of requirements: it is a separate business that, again, has to rely on shared ontologies of data and service provision so that providers can see their services discovered and selected.

This view is summarised in Fig. 1, where we elaborate beyond the basic Service-Oriented Architecture [8] to make explicit the different stakeholders and the way they interact, which is important for understanding the formal model that we are proposing. In this model, we distinguish between 'business activities' and 'services' as software applications that pertain to different stakeholders (see [35] for a wider discussion on the stakeholders of service-oriented systems):

- *Activities* correspond to applications developed according to requirements provided by a business organisation, e.g. the applications that, in a bank, implement the financial products that are made available to the public. The *activity repository* provides a means for a run-time engine to trigger such applications when the corresponding requests are published, say when a client of the bank requests a loan at a counter or through on-line banking. Activities may be implemented over given components (for instance, a component for computing and charging interests) in a traditional CBD way, but they can also rely on services that will be procured on the fly using SOC (for instance, an insurance for protecting the customer in case he/she is temporarily prevented from re-paying the loan due to illness or job loss). In SRML, activities are modelled through *activity modules*. As discussed in Section 3, these identify the components that activities need to be bound to when they are launched and the services (types) that they may require as they execute. Activity modules also include a specification of the workflow that orchestrates the interactions among all the parties involved in the activity and a number of SLA constraints used for negotiating service provision from external parties.

- *Services* differ from activities in that they are not developed to satisfy specific business requirements of a given organisation but to be published (in service repositories) in ways that allow them to be discovered when a request for an external service is published in the run-time environment. As such, they are classified according to generic service descriptions — what in Section 5.1 we call 'business protocols' — that are organised in a hierarchical ontology to facilitate discovery. Services are typed by *service modules*, which, like activity modules, identify the components and additional services that may be required together with a specification of the workflow that orchestrates the interactions among them so as to deliver the properties declared in the service descriptions — their 'provides-interfaces'. Service modules also specify service-level agreements that need to be negotiated during matchmaking and selection.
- The *configuration management* unit (discussed in Section 6) is responsible for the binding of the new components and connectors that derive from the instantiation of new activities or services. A formal model can be found in [30].
- The *ontology* unit is responsible for organising both data and service descriptions. In this paper, we do not discuss the classification and retrieval mechanisms per se. See, for instance, [38,44] for some of the aspects involved when addressing such issues.

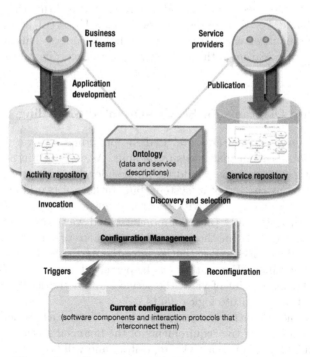

Fig. 1. Overall 'engineering' architecture and processes

Notice that the 'business IT teams' and the 'service providers' can be totally independent and unrelated: the former are interested in supporting the business of their companies or organisations, whereas the latter run a business of their own. They can also belong to the same organisation, as illustrated in our case study. In both cases, they share the ontology component of the architecture so that they can do business together.

3   From Use-Case Diagrams to SRML Modules

Before we introduce the modelling primitives that SRML offers for high-level (business) design, it is important to show how traditional use-case diagrams can be extended so as to support the engineering approach that we described in Section 2. In order to illustrate our approach, we consider the (simplified) case of a financial services organisation that wants to offer a mortgage-brokerage service GETMORTGAGE. This service involves the following steps:

— Proposing the best mortgage deal to the customer that invoked the service;
— Taking out the loan if the customer accepts the proposal;
— Opening a bank account associated with the loan if the lender does not provide one;
— Getting insurance if required by either the customer or the lender.

In our example, the selection of a lender is restricted to firms that are considered to be reliable. For this reason, we consider an UPDATEREGISTRY activity supporting the management of a registry of reliable lenders. This activity relies on an external certification authority that may vary according to the identity of the lender.

3.1   Use-Case Diagrams for Service-Oriented Modelling

Traditionally, use-case diagrams are used for providing an overview of usage requirements for a system that needs to be built. As discussed in Section 2, and reporting to Fig. 1, our aim is to address a novel development process that does not aim at the construction of a 'system' but, rather, of two kinds of software applications — services and activities — that can be bound to other software components either statically (in a component-based way) or dynamically (in a service-oriented way). The methodological implications of this view are twofold. On the one hand, services and activities have the particularity that each has a single usage requirement. Hence, they can be perceived as use cases. On the other hand, from a business point of view, the services and activities to be developed by an organisation constitute logical units.

In our example, UPDATEREGISTRY should be treated as an activity in the sense that it is driven by the requirements of the financial services organisation itself — it will be stored in an activity repository and will be invoked by internal applications (e.g., a web interface). On the other hand, GETMORTGAGE is meant to be placed in a service repository for being discovered and bound to activities running 'globally', i.e. not necessarily in the financial services organisation.

Both UPDATEREGISTRY and GETMORTGAGE can be seen to operate as part of a same business unit and, hence, it makes sense to group them in the same use-case diagram — use-case diagrams are useful for structuring usage requirements of units of business logic. In order to reflect the methodological implications of our approach, we propose a number of extensions to the standard notation of use cases. Fig. 2 uses the mortgage example to illustrate our proposal: the diagram represents a business logical unit with the two use cases identified before. The rectangle around the use cases, which in traditional use-case diagrams indicates the boundary of the system at hand, is used to indicate the scope of the business unit. Anything within the box represents functionality that is in scope and anything outside the box is considered not to be in scope.

For the UPDATEREGISTRY activity, the primary actor is *Registry Manager*; its goal is to control the way a registry of trusted lenders is updated. The registry itself is regarded as a supporting actor. The *Certification Authority* on which UPDATEREGISTRY relies is also considered a supporting actor in the use case because it is an external service that needs to be discovered based on the nature of the lender being considered.

In the GETMORTGAGE service, the primary actor is a *Customer* that wants to obtain a mortgage. The use case has four supporting actors: *Lender, Bank, Insurance* and *Registry*. The *Lender* represents the organisation (e.g., a bank or building society) that lends the money to the customer. Because only reliable firms can be considered for the selection of the lender, the use case involves communication with *Registry*. When the lender does not provide a bank account, the use case involves an external *Bank* for opening a new account. Similarly, the use case involves interaction with an *Insurance* provider for situations where the lender requires insurance or the customer decides to get one.

As in traditional use cases, we view an actor as any entity that is external to the business unit and interacts with at least one of its elements in order to perform a task. As motivated above, we can distinguish between different kinds of actors, which led us to customise the traditional icons as depicted in Fig. 2. These allow us to discriminate between *user/requester* and *resource/service* actors. *User-actors* and *requester-actors* are similar to primary actors in traditional use-case diagrams in the sense that they represent entities that initiate the use case and whose goals are fulfilled through the successful completion of the use case. The difference between them is that a *user-actor* is a role played by an entity that interacts with the activity, while a *requester-actor* is a role played by one or more software components operating as part of the activity that triggers the discovery of the service.

For instance, the user-actor *Registry Manager* represents an interface for an employee of the business organisation that is running *Mortgage Finder* whereas the requester-actor *Customer* represents an interface for a service requester that can come from any external organisation. A requester-actor can be regarded as an interface to an abstract user of the functionality that is exposed as a service;

it represents the range of potential customers of the service and the requirements typically derive from standard service descriptions stored in service repositories such as the UDDI. In SRML, and reporting to Fig. 1, these descriptions are given by business protocols (discussed in Section 5.1) and organised in a shared ontology, which facilitates and makes the discovery of business partners more effective. The identification of requester-actors may take advantage of existing descriptions in the ontology or it may identify new business opportunities. In this case, the ontology would be extended with new business protocols corresponding to the new types of service.

Resource-actors and service-actors of a use case are similar to supporting actors in traditional use-case diagrams in the sense that they represent entities to rely on in order to achieve the underlying business goal. The difference is that a service-actor represents an outsourced functionality to be procured on the fly and, hence, will typically vary from one instance of the use case to another, whereas a resource-actor is an entity that is statically bound and, hence, is the same for all instances of the use case. Resource-actors are typically persistent

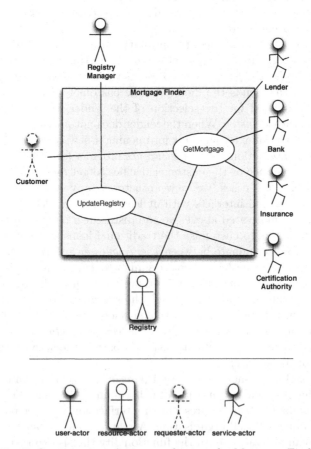

Fig. 2. Service-oriented use-case diagram for Mortgage Finder

sources/repositories of information. In general, they are components that are already available to be shared within a business organisation.

The user- and resource-actors, which we represent at the top and bottom of our specialised use-case diagrams, respectively, correspond in fact to the actors that are presented on the left and right-hand side in traditional use-case diagrams, respectively. In contrast, the horizontal dimension of the new diagrams, comprising requester-and service-actors, captures the types of interactions that are specific to SOC.

We assume that every use case corresponds to a service-oriented artefact and that the association between a primary actor and a use case represents an instantiation/invocation. For this reason, in this context, we constrain every use case to be associated with only one primary actor (either a requester or a user).

3.2   Deriving the Structure of SRML Modules

The proposed specialisations of use-case diagrams allow us to identify and derive a number of aspects of the structure of SRML modules — the main modelling primitives that we use for services and activities. Each use case, representing either a service or an activity, gives rise to a SRML service module or activity module, respectively. Fig. 3 presents the structure of the modules derived from the use-case diagram in Fig. 2.

A SRML module provides a formal model of a service or activity in terms of a configuration of 'interfaces' (formal specifications) to the parties involved. In the case of activity modules:

- A *serves-interface* (at the top-end of the module) identifies the interactions that should be maintained between the activity and the rest of the system in which it will operate. This interface results from the user-actor of the corresponding use case.
- *Uses-interfaces* (at the bottom-end of the module) are defined for those (persistent) components of the underlying configuration that the activity will need to interact with once instantiated. These interfaces result from the resource-actors of the corresponding use case and provide formal descriptions of the behaviour required of the actual interfaces that need to be set up for the activity to interact with components that correspond to (persistent) business entities.
- *Requires-interfaces* (on the right-hand boundary of the module) are defined for services that the activity will have to procure from external providers if and when needed. Typically, these reflect the structure of the business domain itself in the sense that they reflect the existence of business services provided outside the scope of the local context in which the activity will operate. These interfaces result from the service-actors of the corresponding use case.
- *Component* and *wire-interfaces* (inside the module) are defined for orchestrating all these entities (actors) in ways that will deliver stated user requirements through the serves-interface. These interfaces are not derived

from the use-case diagram but from the description of the corresponding business requirements, i.e. they result from a design step. Typically, a designer will choose pre-defined patterns of orchestration that reflect business components that will be created in support of the activity or chosen from a portfolio of components already available for reuse within the business organisation. The choice of the internal architecture of the module (components and wires) should also reflect the nature of the business communication and distribution network over which the activity will run.

In the case of a service module, a similar diagrammatic notation is used except that a *provides-interface* is used instead of a serves-interface:

– The provides-interface should be chosen from the hierarchy of standard business protocols because the purpose here is to make the service available to the wider market, not to a specific client. It derives from the requester-actor of the corresponding use case.

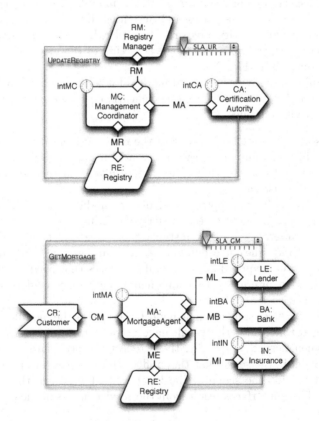

Fig. 3. The SRML modules for the activity UPDATEREGISTRY and the service GET-MORTGAGE

- Some of the component interfaces will correspond to standard components that are part of the provider's portfolio. For instance, these may be application-domain dependent components that correspond to typical entities of the business domain in which the service provider specialises.
- Uses-interfaces should be used for those components that the service provider has for insuring persistence of certain effects of the services that it offers.

In addition, both activity and service modules include:

- An internal configuration policy (indicated by the symbol ⏺), which identifies the triggers of the external service discovery process as well as the initialisation and termination conditions of the components that instantiate the component-interfaces.
- An external configuration policy (indicated by the symbol ▨▭▭▭), which consists of the variables and constraints that determine the quality profile of the activity to which the discovered services need to adhere.

The language primitives that are used in SRML for defining all these interfaces as well as the configuration policies are detailed in Section 5. A summary of the graphical notation can be found in Appendix A at the end of the paper.

4   The Coordination Model

The interfaces of a SRML module identified through a use-case diagram reflect business dependencies of services or activities, not the interfaces that software components offer to be interconnected: modules are not models of components but of business processes. In this section, we detail the coordination model that SRML adopts for component interconnection, i.e. we address the nature of the interfaces that components offer and the way wires interconnect them. We also outline a formalisation of this model, full details of which are available from [4,29].

4.1   Conversational Interactions

Typically, in CBD, one organises component interfaces (what they offer to and expect from the rest of the system) in ports, which include the protocols that regulate message exchange at those ports. In SRML, we have fixed the nature of the interactions and protocols followed by components and wires. We distinguish the following types of interactions:

r&s	The interaction is initiated by the co-party, which expects a reply. The co-party does not block while waiting for the reply.
s&r	The interaction is initiated by the party and expects a reply from its co-party. While waiting for the reply, the party does not block.
rcv	The co-party initiates the interaction and does not expect a reply.
snd	The party initiates the interaction and does not expect a reply.
ask	The party synchronises with the co-party to obtain data.
rpl	The party synchronises with the co-party to transmit data.
tll	The party requests the co-party to perform an operation and blocks.
prf	The party performs an operation and frees the co-party that requested it.

Interactions involve two parties and are described from the point of view of the party in which they are declared, i.e. 'receive' means invocations received by the party and sent by the co-party, and 'send' means invocations made by the party. Interactions can be synchronous, implying that the party waits for the co-party to reply or complete, or asynchronous, in which case the party does not block. Typically, synchronous (blocking) interactions (i.e., ask, rpl, tll and prf) occur with persistent components, reflecting interconnections based on the exchange of *products* (clientship as in OO). The interactions among the components responsible for the orchestration and those involving external services are typically asynchronous (non-blocking, i.e., r&s, s&r, snd and rcv) so that the parties can engage in multiple, concurrent conversations. Interactions of type r&s and s&r are conversational (what we call 2-way), i.e. they involve a number of events exchanged between the two parties:

interaction⌂	The event of initiating *interaction*.
interaction⊠	The reply-event of *interaction*.
interaction✓	The commit-event of *interaction*.
interaction✗	The cancel-event of *interaction*.
interaction⇧	The revoke-event of *interaction*.

The initiation-event is the only event that can be associated with 1-way asynchronous interaction types (snd,rcv). The reply-event is sent by the co-party, offering a deal or declining to offer one; in the first case, the party that initiated the conversation may either commit to the deal or cancel the interaction; after committing, the party can still revoke the deal, triggering a compensation mechanism. See Fig. 4 for some of the possible scenarios (explained further below).

All interactions can have parameters for transmitting data when they are initiated — declared as ⌂. Conversational interactions can also have parameters for carrying a reply — declared as ⊠ — or for carrying data if there is a commit, a cancel or a revoke — declared as ✓, ✗ and ⇧, respectively. In particular, every reply-event *interaction*⊠ has two distinguished parameters:

- *Reply* is a Boolean parameter that indicates whether the reply is positive, meaning that the co-party is ready to proceed. The value of *interaction.Reply*

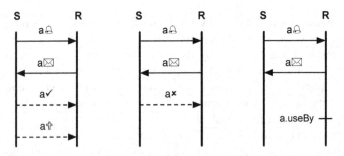

Fig. 4. The protocol of 2-way interactions when the reply is positive

is *False* if, for some reason related with the business logic, the request *interaction*⊖ cannot be fulfilled.

- *UseBy* is a parameter that, in the case of a positive reply, indicates the deadline for receiving the commit and cancel events. The value of this parameter is an expiration time (including the value $+\infty$) obtained by adding the value of the configuration variable (non-functional attribute) *interaction*●* to the instant at which *interaction*⊠ is sent. As discussed in Section 5.2, configuration variables can be subject to negotiation during the discovery/selection process.

Interactions can be seen as ports in the traditional CBD sense, the associated events representing the interface of the components. The sequence diagrams in Fig. 4 illustrate the protocol that is associated with every interaction for which the reply is positive. In the case on the left, the initiator commits to the deal; a revoke may occur later on, compensating the effects of the commit-event *interaction*✓ (this can however be constrained by the business logic, for instance, by defining a deadline for compensation). In the middle, there is a cancellation; in this situation, a revoke is not available. In the case on the right, the expiration time occurs without a commit or cancel having occurred; this implies that no further events for that interaction will occur. In Section 5, we give examples of the intended usage of these primitives.

Events occur during state transitions in both parties involved in the interaction: we use *event!* in order to refer to the publication of event in the life of the initiating party, and *event?* (resp. *event¿*) for its execution (resp. being discarded) by the party that receives it. The occurrences of *event!* and *event?* (or *event¿*) may not coincide in time: we consider that there may exist a delay between publishing and delivering an event. The value of this delay is given by the configuration variable *Delay* associated with the wire through which the events are transmitted (see Fig. 5). In Section 8, we explore timing aspects of service provision in more detail, including the use of PEPA [36] for stochastic analysis.

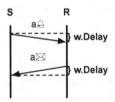

Fig. 5. The intuitive semantics of delays

4.2 Deriving Interactions from Message Sequence Diagrams

One of the ways that we have found useful for identifying the interactions that are relevant for defining a given activity or service module is to draw message sequence diagrams that characterise the interconnections required between the different parties. For instance, the message sequence diagram in Fig. 6 depicts the workflow that is initiated by the initial request received by GETMORTGAGE from the customer *CR*.

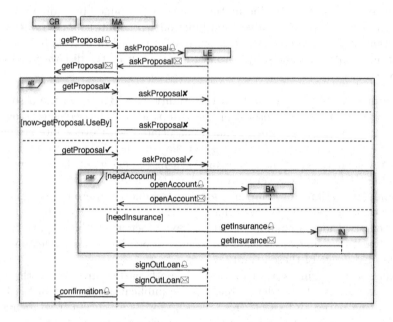

Fig. 6. Identifying interactions within GETMORTGAGE

4.3   A Formal Model

The overall coordination model of SRML can be summarised as follows (see [4,29] for details). We work over configurations of global computers defined by a set **COMP** of components (applications deployed over execution platforms) linked through wires (e.g. interconnections between components over a given communication network), the set of which we denote by **WIRE**.

A *state* consists of:

- The set *PND* of the events that are pending in the wires, i.e. the events that have been published but not yet delivered by the wires to the corresponding co-parties;
- The set *INV* of the events that have been invoked, i.e. those that were delivered by the wires and are stored locally by the components that received them, waiting to be processed;
- The time at that state;
- A record of all events that have been published (!), delivered (¡), executed (?) or discarded (¿);
- The values of all event parameters and configuration attributes.

In this model, state transitions are characterised by what we call a *computation step*, consisting of:

- An ordered pair of states SRC (source) and TRG (target);
- A subset DLV of PND^{SRC} consisting of the events that are pending in the source state and selected for delivery during that step;
- A set PRC that selects from INV^{SRC} one event for every component that has events waiting to be processed;
- A subset EXC of PRC consisting of the events that are actually executed (the others are discarded);
- A set PUB of the events that are published during that step together with a function that assigns a value to the parameters of each such event.

These elements are subject to the following constraints:

- The set INV^{TRG} of the events in the target state that have been invoked consists of the events in DLV (i.e. those that are delivered during the step) together with those already in INV^{SRC} that have not been selected by PRC to be processed;
- The set PND^{TRG} of the events that are pending at the target state consists of the events in PUB (i.e. those that are published during the step) together with the events in PND^{SRC} that have not been selected by DLV to be delivered.

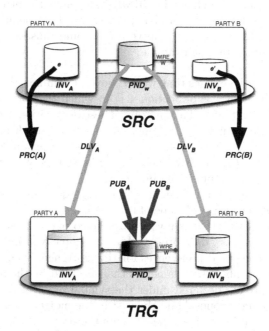

Fig. 7. Graphical representation of event flow from the point of view of a wire w between parties A and B

That is, the set of events that are pending in wires is updated during each computation step by removing the events that the wire delivers during that step — *DLV* — and adding the events that each component publishes — *PUB*. We assume that all the events that are selected by *DLV* are actually delivered to the receiving component, i.e. each wire is reliable — see [4,29] for a model that considers unreliable wires.

At each step, components may select one of the events waiting to be processed; this is captured by the function *PRC*. The fact each component can only process one event at a time is justified by the assumption that the internal state of the components is not necessarily distributed and therefore no concurrent changes can be made to their states.

The set of events that are waiting to be processed by every component is updated in each step by removing the event that is processed and adding the events that are actually delivered to that component. Fig. 7 is a graphical representation of the flow of events that takes place during a computation step from the point of view of components *A* and *B* connected by a wire *w*.

5   The Modelling Primitives of SRML

5.1   Behaviour Specification Languages

The entities involved in service and activity modules — component interfaces, requires-interfaces, provides-interfaces, uses-interfaces, serves-interfaces and wire-interfaces — can be defined in SRML independently of one another as design-time reusable resources. For that purpose, we have defined a number of different but related languages, which we present and illustrate in this section using fragments of our running example.

Signatures. All the languages that we use have in common the declaration of the interactions (in the sense of Section 4.1) in which the corresponding entity can be involved — what we call a *signature*. These declarations are strictly local to the entity, i.e. we cannot rely on global names to establish interconnections between entities — that is the role of the wires. As an example, consider the component-interface *MA*, which we declared to be of type *MortgageAgent*. The corresponding signature is presented in Fig. 8.

Interactions are classified according to the types defined in Section 4.1. For instance, *getProposal* is declared to be of type **r&s**, i.e. as being an asynchronous conversational interaction that is invoked by the co-party. This interaction has three parameters that carry data produced by the co-party at invocation time — the user profile, income and preferences for the mortgage. Such parameters are declared under the symbol ⌂. Parameters that are used by the mortgage agent for sending the reply are declared under the symbol ⊠ — in the case at hand, the details of mortgage proposal and the cost of the mortgage-brokerage service for taking out the loan if the customer accepts the proposal.

The co-party of the mortgage agent in this interaction is not named (the same applies to all other interactions, as discussed in Section 4.1). This makes it possible to specify the behaviour that can be assumed of the mortgage agent at the interface, independently of the way it is instantiated within any given system.

The signature of *MortgageAgent* includes six additional interactions, all of which are self-initiated. While *askProposal, getInsurance, openAccount* and *signoutLoan* are conversational and asynchronous (i.e. of type **s&r** or **snd**), the interactions *getLenders* and *regContract* are synchronous. In the case of *getLenders*, the mortgage agent has to synchronise with the co-party to obtain data (the identification of the lenders that meet the user preferences for the mortgage) while, in the case of *regContract*, the party requests the co-party to perform an operation (register a loan contract) and blocks until the operation is completed.

Business roles. In SRML, interfaces of service components are typed by *business roles*. A business role is specified by defining the way in which the interactions declared in the signature are orchestrated. For that purpose, we offer a textual declarative language based on states and transitions that is general enough to support languages and notations that are typically used for orchestrating workflows such as BPEL and UML statecharts.

In a typical business role, a set of variables provides an abstract view of the state of the component and a set of transitions models the activities performed

```
INTERACTIONS
    r&s getProposal
        ⌂ idData:usrdata,
          income:moneyvalue,
          preferences:prefdata,
        ⊠ proposal:mortgageproposal
          cost:moneyvalue
    s&r askProposal
        ⌂ idData:usrdata,
          income:moneyvalue,
        ⊠ proposal:mortgageproposal
          loanData:loandata,
          accountIncluded:bool,
          insuranceRequired:bool
    s&r getInsurance
        ⌂ idData:usrdata,
          loanData:loandata,
        ⊠ insuranceData:insurancedata
    s&r openAccount
        ⌂ idData:usrdata,
          loanData:loandata,
        ⊠ accountData:accountdata
    s&r signOutLoan
        ⌂ insuranceData:insurancedata,
          accountData:accountdata,
        ⊠ contract:loancontract
    snd confirmation
        ⌂ contract:loancontract
    ask getLenders(prefdata):setids
    tll regContract(loandata,loancontract)
```

Fig. 8. The signature of *MortgageAgent*

by the component, including the way it interacts with its co-parties. For instance, the local state of a mortgage agent is defined as presented in Fig. 9.

Typically, we use a variable (s in our example) to model control flow, including the way the component reacts to triggers. The other state variables are used for storing data that is needed at different stages of the orchestration.

Each transition has an optional name and a number of possible features. See Fig. 10 for an example.

- A trigger is either the processing of an event, like in the example above, or a state condition. The former means that the transition is triggered when the component processes the event, and the latter when the condition changes from false to true.
- A guard is a condition that identifies the states in which the transition can take place — in *GetClientRequest*, the state *INITIAL*. If the trigger is an event and the guard is false, the event is processed but not executed (it is discarded).
- A sentence specifies the effects of the transition in the local state. Given a state variable *var*, we use *var'* to denote the value that *var* takes after the transition. In the case illustrated in Fig. 10, we change the value of s and store the identification of the lenders that match the users-preferences. This data is obtained from a co-party through the synchronous interaction *getLenders*. As already mentioned, this co-party is not identified in the business role: we will see that, because of the way components are wired, the co-party in this interaction within the module GETMORTGAGE is *RE* of type *Registry* — the interface of a persistent component.

Another sentence specifies the events that are published during the transition, including the values taken by their parameters. In this sentence, we use variables and

```
local     s:[INITIAL, WAIT_PROPOSAL, WAIT_DECISION,
              PROPOSAL_ACCEPTED, SIGNING, FINAL],
          lenders:setids,
          needAccount, needInsurance:bool,
          insuranceData:insurancedata, accountData:accountdata
```

Fig. 9. Local state of the *MortgageAgent*

```
transition GetClientRequest
    triggeredBy getProposal⌂
    guardedBy s=INITIAL
    effects s'=WAIT_PROPOSAL
        ∧ lenders'= getLenders(prefdata)
        ∧ ¬empty(lenders') ⊃ s'=WAIT_PROPOSAL
        ∧ empty(lender') ⊃ s'=FINAL
    sends ¬empty(lenders') ⊃ askProposal⌂
            ∧ askProposal.idData=getProposal.idData
            ∧ askProposal.income=getProposal.income
        ∧ empty(lenders') ⊃ getProposal⌧
            ∧ getProposal.Reply=false
```

Fig. 10. Transition *GetClientRequest*

primed variables as in the 'effects'-section. In the example, if there is at least one lender that matches the user-preferences, the interaction *askProposal* is initiated in order to get a mortgage proposal from a lender. Once again, the corresponding co-party is not named: we will see that, within the module GETMORTGAGE, this is an external service provided by a bank or building society that needs to be discovered and bound to the mortgage agent. If no lenders are found that match the user-preferences, a negative reply to *getProposal* is published.

Another example of a transition is *GetLenderProposal* presented in Fig. 11. In this case, the transition is triggered by the processing of the reply to *askProposal* and the effect is to send a reply to *getProposal* (the parameter *Reply* of *askProposal* and the proposal received in proposal are both transmitted by the reply-event). The transition also defines the cost of the mortgage-brokerage service for taking out the loan if the customer accepts the proposal.

Specifications may also declare configuration variables, which are discussed in Section 5.2. These variables are instantiated at run time, when a new session of the service starts, possibly as a result of the negotiation process involved in the discovery of the service. In the case of *MortgageAgent*, we declare the configuration variable CHARGE that determines an additional charge over the base price of the mortgage-brokerage service. In Section 5.2 we will see that, in the module GETMORTGAGE, this extra-charge relates to the period of validity of the loan proposal offered by the service, which is also subject to negotiation.

Notice that, through business roles, SRML offers a very flexible way for modelling control flow because transitions are decoupled from interactions and changes to state variables, which offers a declarative style of defining orchestrations. For instance, the transition *TimeoutProposal* defined below is triggered once the reply to *getProposal* expires; in this situation, the component informs the lender that the proposal was not accepted and moves to the final state.

```
transition GetLenderProposal
    triggeredBy askProposal⊠
    guardedBy s=WAIT_PROPOSAL
    effects needAccount'=askProposal.accountIncluded
        ∧ needInsurance'=askProposal.insuranceRequired
        ∧ askProposal.Reply ⊃ s'=WAIT_DECISION
        ∧ ¬askProposal.Reply ⊃ s'=FINAL
    sends getProposal⊠
        ∧ getProposal.Reply=askProposal.Reply
        ∧ getProposal.proposal=askProposal.proposal
        ∧ getProposal.cost=(CHARGE/100+1)*750
```

Fig. 11. Transition *GetLenderProposal*

```
transition TimeoutProposal
    triggeredBy now>getProposal.UseBy
    guardedBy s=WAIT_DECISION
    effects s'=FINAL
    sends askProposalˣ
```

Fig. 12. Transition *TimeOutProposal*

Other aspects of this declarative style include the possibility of leaving certain aspects under-specified that can be refined at later stages of the development process. This is why the various aspects of a transition are specified as sentences using a logical notation.

More traditional (control-oriented) notations can be used instead for defining orchestrations. In Fig. 13 we show how part of the orchestration of *MortgageAgent* can be defined using a UML statechart. Because statecharts focus only on control flow, we would need to provide a separate specification for the data flow. In [14], we have also shown how BPEL can be encoded in our language.

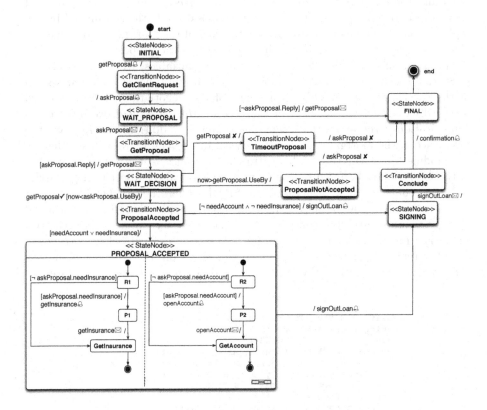

Fig. 13. Using UML statecharts for defining orchestrations in business roles

Business protocols. In SRML, a module may declare a number of requires-interfaces, each of which provides an abstraction (type) for a service that will have to be procured from external providers, if and when needed — what, in SCA, corresponds to an "External Service". In the case of a service module, a provides-interface is also declared for describing the service that is offered by the module, corresponding to what in SCA is called an "Entry Point".

Both types of external interfaces are typed with what we call business protocols, or just protocols if it is clear from the context what kind of protocols we are addressing. Like business roles, protocols include a signature. The difference is that, instead of an orchestration, we provide a set of properties. In the case of a requires-interface, these are the properties required of the external service that needs to be procured. In the case of a provides-interface, we specify the properties offered by the service orchestrated by the module.

In the case of business protocols used for specifying the required services, we declare the interactions in which the external entity (to be procured) must be able to be involved as a (co-)party and we specify the protocol that it has to adhere to. For instance, the service GETMORTGAGE expects the behaviour from a lender described in Fig. 14.

```
BUSINESS PROTOCOL Lender is
    INTERACTIONS
        r&s requestMortgage
            ⌂ idData:usrdata,
              income:moneyvalue,
            ⊠ proposal:mortgageproposal
              loanData:loandata,
              accountIncluded:bool,
              insuranceRequired:bool
        r&s requestSignOut
            ⌂ insuranceData:insurancedata,
              accountData:accountdata,
            ⊠ contract:loancontract
    BEHAVIOUR
        initiallyEnabled requestMortgage⌂?
        requestMortgage✓? enables requestSignOut⌂?
```

Fig. 14. The specification of business protocol *Lender*

Notice that the interactions are again named from the point of view of the party concerned — the lender in the case at hand. The specified properties require the following:

- In the initial state, the lender is ready to engage in *requestMortgage*.
- After receiving the commitment to the mortgage proposal, the lender becomes ready to engage in *requestSignOut*.

The language in which these properties are expressed uses a set of patterns that capture commonly occurring requirements in the context of service-oriented interactions. In Section 7.1, we present their semantics in terms of formulas of the temporal logic UCTL [50]. Intuitively, they correspond to traces of the form depicted in Fig. 15.

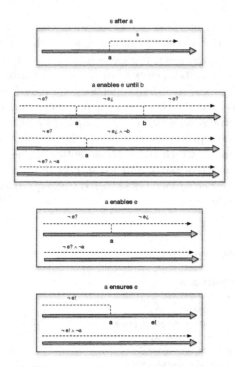

Fig. 15. The traces that correspond to the patterns

The intuitive semantics of these patterns is as follows:

- **initiallyEnabled** e: The event e is enabled (cannot be discarded) in the initial state and remains so until it is executed.
- s **after** a: the state condition s holds forever after the action condition a becomes true.
- a **enables** e **until** b: The event e cannot be executed before a holds and remains enabled after a becomes true until it is either executed or b becomes true (if ever).
- a **enables** e: The event e cannot be executed before a holds and remains enabled after a becomes true until it is executed. It is easy to see that this pattern is equivalent to a **enables** e **until** *false*.
- a **ensures** e: The event e cannot be published before a holds, and is published sometime after a becomes true.

Business protocols are also used for modelling the behaviour that users can expect from a service. This subsumes what, in [8], are called external specifications:

In particular, a trend that is gathering momentum is that of including, as part of the service description, not only the service interface, but also the business protocol supported by the service, i.e. the specification of which message exchange sequences are supported by the service, for example expressed in terms of constraints on the order in which service operations should be invoked.

For instance, the provides-interface of GETMORTGAGE is typed by the business protocol presented in Fig. 16.

This business protocol specifies that the service offered by GETMORTGAGE relies on two asynchronous interactions — *getProposal* and *confirmation*. The properties offered by the service are:

- A request for *getProposal* is enabled when the service is activated.
- The service brokerage has a base price that can be subject to an extra charge, subject to negotiation.
- A confirmation carrying the loan contract will be issued upon receipt of the commit to *getProposal*.

Layer protocols. A module in SRML may also declare one or more uses-interfaces. These provide abstractions of components corresponding to resource actors as discussed in Section 3.1 — the components with which the service needs to interact in order to ensure persistent effects.

Uses-interfaces are specified through what we call layer protocols. Like business protocols, layer protocols are defined by a signature and a set of properties. However, where the interactions used in business protocols are asynchronous, those declared in a layer protocol can be synchronous and blocking.

As an example, consider the specification of the layer protocol fulfilled by a registry as shown in Fig. 17. It defines that a registry can be queried — through the interaction *getLenders* — about the registered lenders that meet given users preferences, and is able to register a new contract through the operation *registerContract*.

The properties of synchronous interactions are typically in the style of pre/post-condition specifications of methods.

```
BUSINESS PROTOCOL Customer is
    INTERACTIONS
        r&s getProposal
            ⌂ idData:usrdata,
              income:moneyvalue,
              preferences:prefdata,
            ⊠ proposal:mortgageproposal
              cost:moneyvalue
        snd confirmation
            ⌂ contract:loancontract
    SLA VARIABLES
        CHARGE:[0..100]
    BEHAVIOUR
        initiallyEnabled getProposal⌂?
        getProposal.cost≤750*(CHARGE/100+1) after
              (getProposal⊠! ∧ getProposal.Reply)
        getProposal✓? ensures confirmation⌂!
```

Fig. 16. The specification of business protocol *Customer*

Interaction protocols. A module consists of a number of interfaces connected through wires. Wires are labelled by connectors that coordinate the interactions in which the parties are jointly involved. In SRML, we model the interaction protocols involved in these connectors as separate, reusable entities.

Just like business roles and protocols, an interaction protocol is specified in terms of a number of interactions. Because interaction protocols establish a relationshipbetween two parties, the interactions in which they are involved are divided in two subsets called roles — A and B. The semantics of the protocol is provided through a collection of sentences — what we call interaction glue — that establish how the interactions are coordinated.

As an example, consider the protocol depicted in Fig. 18, which is used in the wire that connects *MortgageAgent* and *Insurance*. This is a 'straight' protocol that connects directly two entities over two conversational interactions that have two ⌂-parameters and one ⊠-parameter. The property $S_1 \equiv R_1$ establishes that the events associated with each interaction are the same, e.g. that S_1 is the same as R_1.

The names used in interaction protocols are generic to facilitate reuse. In fact, the specification itself is parameterised by the data sorts involved in the interactions. Parameterisation (which is also available for business roles and protocols) provides the means for defining families of specifications. The parameters are instantiated at design time when the specifications are used in the definition of a module. This can be seen at the end of this Section.

Two other families of straight protocols are presented below. These families define the connection of two synchronous interactions with two parameters; in

---

```
LAYER PROTOCOL Registry is

    INTERACTIONS
        rpl getLenders(prefdata):setids
        prf registerContract(loandata,loancontract)
    BEHAVIOUR
```

Fig. 17. The specification of layer protocol *Registry*

```
INTERACTION PROTOCOL Straight.I(d₁,d₂)O(d₃) is

    ROLE A
        s&r S₁
            ⌂  i₁:d₁,  i₂:d₂
            ⊠  o₁:d₃
    ROLE B
        r&s R₁
            ⌂  i₁:d₁,  i₂:d₂
            ⊠  o₁:d₃
    COORDINATION
        S₁ ≡ R₁
        S₁.i₁=R₁.i₁
        S₁.i₂=R₁.i₂
        S₁.o₁=R₁.o₁
```

Fig. 18. The specification of an interaction protocol

the first protocol, the interaction involves a return value. The first interaction protocol establishes that the values returned by the synchronous interaction are the same, while the second protocol synchronises the two operations without any conversion of data.

Interaction protocols are first-class objects that can be (re)used to assign properties to wires, which reflect constraints on the underlying run-time environment. These may concern data transmission, synchronous/asynchronous connectivity, distribution, and other non-functional properties such as security. In such cases, the specifications are not as simple as those of straight protocols.

Connectors. After having chosen the protocols that coordinate the interactions between two parties, we use them as the 'glue' (in the sense of [47]) of the connectors that label the wires that link the corresponding parties. In a connector, the interaction protocol is bound to the parties via 'attachments': these are mappings from the roles to the signatures of the parties identifying which interactions of the parties perform which roles in the protocol. The use of attachments allows us to separate the definition of the interaction protocols from their use in the wires, which promotes reuse: typically, one defines a connector by choosing from a repository of (types of) protocols that have proved to be useful in other situations.

Summarising, connectors are triples $\langle \mu_A, P, \mu_B \rangle$ where:

- P is an interaction protocol. We use $roleA_P$ and $roleB_P$ to designate its roles and $glue_P$ for the role.
- μ_A and μ_B are attachments that connect the roles of the protocol to the signatures of the entities (business roles, business protocols or layer protocols) being interconnected.

```
INTERACTION PROTOCOL Straight.A(d₁,d₂)R(d₃) is
    ROLE A
        ask S₁(d₁,d₂):d₃
    ROLE B
        rpl R₁(d₁,d₂):d₃
    COORDINATION
        S₁(d₁,d₂)=R₁(d₁,d₂)


INTERACTION PROTOCOL Straight.T(d₁,d₂) is
    ROLE A
        tll S₁(d₁,d₂)
    ROLE B
        prf R₁(d₁,d₂)
    COORDINATION
        S₁(d₁,d₂)=R₁(d₁,d₂)
```

Fig. 19. Another two specifications of interaction protocols

For instance, both *Straight.A(prefdata)R(setids)* and *Straight.T(loandata, loan-contract)* are used in the wire *ME* to connect different interactions between *MortgageAgent* and *Registry* as depicted in Fig. 20.

Each row describes one connector. The first two columns define the attachment between *roleA* of the interaction protocol (specified in the middle column) and the signature of *MortgageAgent*. In the same way, the last two columns define the attachment between *roleB* of the interaction protocol and the signature of *Registry*.

We use the same notation for specifying the wires that connect module components to requires-interfaces. However, the specification of these wires is subject to an additional correctness condition that restricts the signature of the requires-interfaces to the interaction used in the corresponding wires. This is to ensure that all the interactions of the services that are bound to the module through the requires-interface have a corresponding co-party.

For instance, the only wire that connects *LE* in GETMORTGAGE is *ML* (with *MA*). Its specification is presented in Fig. 21. The correctness condition is satisfied because the signature of *Lender* is isomorphic to the sum of the interactions of the roles connected to it, i.e. all the interactions of *Lender* are mapped to a port.

The specification of the wires that connect module components to the provides-interface of the module uses a slightly different syntax. This is because what we need to declare is the set of interactions that the components make available to the customer of the service, and the protocols through which the corresponding events are transmitted. In this sense, we do not model the customer proper,

MA MortgageAgent	c_4	ME	d_4	RE Registry
ask getLenders	S_1	Straight. A(prefdata)R(setids)	R_1	**rpl** getLenders
tll regContract	S_1	Straight. T(loandata,loancontract)	R_1	**prf** registerContract

Fig. 20. The specification of the connectors involved in wire *ME*

MA MortgageAgent	c_1	ML	d_1	LE Lender
s&r askProposal	S_1	Straight. I(usrdata, moneyvalue) O(mortgageproposal, loandata, bool,bool)	R_1	**r&s** requestMortgage
⌂idData	i_1		i_1	⌂ idData
income	i_2		i_2	income
⌧proposal	o_1		o_1	⌧proposal
loanData	o_2		o_2	loanData
accountIncluded	o_3		o_3	accountIncluded
insuranceRequired	o_4		o_4	insuranceRequired
r&s signOutLoan	S_1	Straight I(insurancedata, accountdata) O(loancontract)	R_1	**s&r** requestSignOut
⌂ insuranceData	i_1		i_1	⌂ insuranceData
accountData	i_2		i_2	accountData
⌧contract	o_1		o_1	⌧contract

Fig. 21. The specification of the connectors involved in wire *ML*

which in SRML is reflected by omitting the corresponding column of the table that defines the wire.

For instance, the wire *CM* that interconnects *Customer* and *MortgageAgent* in GetMortgage is specified as presented in Fig. 22. In this case, each row also describes one connector whose interaction protocol is specified in the second column. The difference is that the entities that will be connected to the *roleA* of their interaction protocols are unknown (these will belong to the services that will bind to GetMortgage). As before, the last two columns define the attachment between *roleB* of the interaction protocol and the signature of *MortgageAgent*.

5.2   Configuration Policies

Whereas business roles, business protocols, layer protocols and interaction protocols deal with functional aspects of the behaviour of a (complex) service or activity, configuration policies address aspects that relate to processes of discovery, selection and instantiation of services. In SRML, we distinguish between internal and external configuration policies. The former concern aspects related with service instantiation such as the initialization of service components and the triggering of the discovery of required services. The latter address aspects related with the selection of partner services and negotiation of contracts.

Internal configuration policy. The internal configuration policy of a service module concerns the triggering of the discovery and selection process associated with its requires-interfaces, and the instantiation of its component and wire interfaces.

A trigger is usually associated with the occurrence of one or more events and additional conditions on the state of the components in which the events occur. For instance, GetMortgage defines that the lender has to be discovered as soon as *getProposal*$\triangle$ is executed (by the workflow). There is a *default* trigger condition: the publication of the initiation event of the first interaction connected to the requires-interface. In our example, this is the case of the bank and insurance external services.

c_1	**CM**	d_1	**MA** MortgageAgent
S_1 i_1 i_2 i_3 o_1 o_2	Straight. I(usrdata, moneyvalue,prefdata) O(mortageproposal, moneyvalue)	R_1 i_1 i_2 i_3 o_1 o_2	**r&s** getProposal $\triangle$ idData income preferences $\boxtimes$ proposal cost
R_1 i_1	Straight O(loancontract)	S_1 i_1	**snd** confirmation $\triangle$ contract

Fig. 22. The specification of the connectors involved in wire *CM*

In a module, each service component has an associated initialisation condition, which is guaranteed to hold when the component is instantiated, and a termination condition, which determines when the component stops executing and interacting with the rest of the components (in which case it can be removed from the state configuration to which it belongs). Typically, both conditions relate to the state variables of the component, but they can also include the publication of given events. For instance, in the case of *MortgageAgent*, these conditions are defined only in terms of the local variable s (see Fig. 24).

Notice that these conditions can be underspecified, leaving room for further refinement. For instance, we may force the termination of the component after a certain date without specifying exactly when.

External policies. The external policy concerns the way the module relates to external parties: it declares the set of variables that can be used for negotiation and establishing a service level agreement (SLA), and a set of constraints that have to be taken into account during discovery and selection.

SLA variables include all the configuration variables declared in the specifications (except in the provides-interface). For instance, in GETMORTGAGE, *MortgageAgent* declares the configuration variable CHARGE. These variables are local to the interfaces to which they are attached and instantiated when the corresponding component is created. Because constraints apply to the module as a whole, we refer to these variables by preceding them with the name of the entity to which they belong. Hence, in GETMORTGAGE, we refer to *MA*.CHARGE.

SRML also provides a set of standard configuration variables — availability, response time, message reliability, service identification, inter alia. Some of them, e.g. response time, are associated with requires or provides-interfaces, and other, e.g. message reliability, apply to the wires.

The standard configuration variables used in GETMORTGAGE are:

- *interaction*♠*, for every interaction of type r&s; its value is the length of time the reply is valid after *interaction* is issued.
- *wire.Delay*, for every wire; it defines the maximum delivery delay for events sent over that wire.

```
LE: Lender
        intLE⬤trigger: getproposal◟?
BA: Bank
        intBA⬤trigger: default
IN: Insurance
        intIN⬤trigger: default
```

Fig. 23. Trigger conditions in GETMORTGAGE

```
MA: MortgageAgent
        intMA⬤init: s=INITIAL
        intMA⬤term: s=FINAL
```

Fig. 24. Initialization and termination conditions in GETMORTGAGE

- *ServiceId*, for every external-interface; it represents the identification of the service that is bound to that interface (for instance, a URI).

Notice that although these variables are standard they need to be declared in a module if the designer wants them to be involved in the service discovery negotiation process. For instance, their declaration in GETMORTGAGE is presented in Fig. 25.

The approach that we adopt in SRML for SLA negotiation (see also Chapter 3-1) is based on the constraint satisfaction and optimization framework presented in [11] in which constraint systems are defined in terms of c-semirings. As explained therein, this framework is quite general and allows us to work with constraints of different kinds — both hard and 'soft', the latter in many grades (fuzzy, weighted, and so on). The c-semiring approach also supports selection based on a characterisation of 'best solution' supported by multi-dimensional criteria, e.g. minimizing the cost of a resource while maximizing the work it supports.

In this framework:

- A c-semiring is a semiring $\langle A, +, \times, 0, 1 \rangle$ in which A represents a space of degrees of satisfaction, e.g. the set $\{0, 1\}$ for yes/no or the interval $[0, 1]$ for intermediate degrees of satisfaction. The operations $\times$ and $+$ are used for composition and choice, respectively. Composition is commutative, choice is idempotent and 1 is an absorbing element (i.e. there is no better choice than 1). That is, a c-semiring is an algebra of degrees of satisfaction. Notice that every c-semiring S induces a partial order $\leq_S$ (of satisfaction) over A as follows: $a \leq_S b$ iff $a + b = b$. That is, b is better than a iff the choice between a and b is b.
- A constraint system is a triple $\langle S, D, V \rangle$ where S is a c-semiring, V is a totally ordered set (of configuration variables), and D is a finite set (domain of possible elements taken by the variables).
- A constraint consists of a selected subset con of variables and a mapping $def : D^{|con|} \rightarrow S$ that assigns a degree of satisfaction to each tuple of values taken by the variables involved in the constraint.

The external configuration policy of a module involves a constraint system based on a fixed c-semiring and a set of constraints over this constraint system. Because we want to handle constraints that involve different degrees of satisfaction, it makes sense that we work with the c-semiring $\langle [0..1], max, min, 0, 1 \rangle$ of soft fuzzy constraints [11]. In this c-semiring, the preference level is between 0 (worst) and 1 (best).

SLA VARIABLES
CHARGE:[0..100]

Fig. 25. Declaration of SLA variables in GETMORTGAGE

For instance, the external configuration policy of GETMORTGAGE includes the following constraints:

$C_1 : \{MA.\text{CHARGE}, \ MA.getProposal\text{\textbullet}^*\}$,

$$def(c,t) = \begin{cases} 1 & if\ t \leq 10 \cdot c \\ 1 + 2 \cdot c - 0.2 \cdot t & if\ 10 \cdot c < t \leq 5 + 10 \cdot c \end{cases}$$

That is, the more CHARGE is applied to the base price of the brokerage service the longer is the interval during which the proposal is valid.

$$C_2 : \{LE.ServiceId\}, \ def(s) = \begin{cases} 1 & if\ s \in MA.lenders \\ 0 & otherwise \end{cases}$$

That is, the choice of the lender is constrained by the service identifier, which must belong to the set *MA.lenders* (recall that, according to the orchestration of *MortgageAgent*, this set contains the identification of the services provided by trusted lenders that were found to be appropriate for the request at hand).

$C_3 : \{MA.getProposal\text{\textbullet}^*, LE.requestMortgage\text{\textbullet}^*\}$,

$$def(t_1, t_2) = \begin{cases} 1 & if\ t_2 > t_1 + CM.Delay + ML.Delay \\ 0 & otherwise \end{cases}$$

That is, the choice of the lender is also constrained by the period of validity associated with its loan proposals. This period must be greater than the sum of the validity period offered by the brokerage service to its clients and the possible delays that may affect the transmission through the wires involved (notice that *CM.Delay* and *ML.Delay* are not declared as SLA variables and, hence, they are used like constants).

$$C_4 : \{LE.COST, LE.requestMortgage\text{\textbullet}^*\}, \ def(c,t) = \begin{cases} \frac{1}{c} + \frac{t}{100} & if\ c < 500 \\ 0 & otherwise \end{cases}$$

That is, the cost to be paid by the brokerage service to the lender must be less than 500, and the preference between lenders charging the same value will take into account the validity period of the loan proposals.

The value of SLA variables is negotiated during service discovery/binding. Details on negotiation of constraints and SLAs are further discussed in Section 6.3.

5.3 Module Declaration

SRML makes available a textual language for defining modules, which involves the specification of the module external interfaces, service components, wires and policies, as discussed in the previous sections.

In the case of a service module, we also have to map the interactions and SLA variables of the provides-interface to corresponding interactions and variables of the entities that provide the service. This is because the business protocol that labels the provides-interface represents the service that is offered by the module (behavioural properties and negotiable SLA variables), not the activity to which the service will be bound. In the case of GETMORTGAGE, only *MA* is connected to *CR*, so the mapping is actually an identity. This is specified as presented in Fig. 26.

PROVIDES	
CR: Customer	
CR	**MA**
Customer	MortgageAgent
r&s getProposal	**r&s** getProposal
⌂ idData	⌂ idData
income	income
preferences	preferences
⊠ proposal	⊠ proposal
cost	cost
snd confirmation	**snd** confirmation
⌂ contract	⌂ contract
SLA VARIABLES	**SLA** VARIABLES
CHARGE	CHARGE

Fig. 26. Specification of the mapping between *CR* and *MA* in GETMORTGAGE

6 The Configuration-Management Model

6.1 Layered State Configurations of Global Computers

As already mentioned, we take SOC to be about applications that can bind to other applications discovered at run time in a universe of resources that is not fixed a priori. As a result, there is no structure or 'architecture' that one can fix at design-time for an application; rather, there is an underlying notion of configuration of a global computer that keeps being redefined as applications execute and get bound to other applications that offer required services. As is often the case (e.g. [47]), by 'configuration' we mean a graph of components (applications deployed over a given execution platform)linked through wires (e.g. interconnections between components over a given communication network) in a given state of execution. Typically, wires deal with the heterogeneity of partners involved in the provision of the service, performing data (or, more, generally, semantic) integration. See Fig. 27 for an example, over which we will later recognise three business activities (instances).

Summarising, a *state configuration* $\mathcal{F}$ consists of:

- A simple graph $\mathcal{G}$, i.e. a set *nodes($\mathcal{F}$)* and a set *edges($\mathcal{F}$)*; each edge e is associated with a (unordered) pair $n \leftrightarrow m$ of nodes. We take *nodes($\mathcal{F}$)* $\subseteq$ **COMP** (i.e. nodes are components) and *edges($\mathcal{F}$)* $\subseteq$ **WIRE** (i.e. edges are wires).
- A (configuration) state $\mathcal{S}$ as defined in Section 4.3.

Every state configuration $\langle \mathcal{G}, \mathcal{S} \rangle$ can change because either the state $\mathcal{S}$ or the graph $\mathcal{G}$ changes. Changes to the state result from computations executed by components and the coordination activities performed by the wires that connect them as defined in 4.3. However, the essence of SOC as we see it it is not captured at the level of state changes (which is basically a distributed view of computation), but at the level of the changes that operate on configuration graphs: in SOC, changes to the underlying graph of components and wires occur at run time when a component performs an action that triggers the discovery and binding of a service.

An important aspect of our model is the fact that we view SOC as providing an architectural layer that interacts with two other layers (see Fig. 28). This can be noticed in Fig. 27 where shadows are used for indicating that certain components reside in different layers: *AliceRegUI*, *BobEstateUI* and *CarolEstateUI* (three user interfaces) in the top layer, and *MyRegistry* (a database) in the bottom layer. Layers are architectural abstractions that reflect different levels of organisation and change, i.e. one looks at a configuration as a (flat) graph as indicated above but, in order to understand how such configurations evolve, it is useful to distinguish different layers.

In our model, the bottom layer consists of components that are persistent as far as the service layer is concerned, i.e. those that in Section 3 we identified as resource-actors. More precisely, when a new session of a service starts (e.g. a mortgage broker starts putting together a proposal on behalf of a client), the components of the bottom layer are assumed to be available so that, as the service executes, they can be used as (shared) 'servers' — for instance the registry, which shared by all sessions of the mortgage broker, or a currency converter. In particular, the bottom layer can be used for making persistent the effects of services as they execute.

The components that execute in the service layer are created when the session of the corresponding service starts, i.e. as fresh instances that last only for the duration of the session — for instance, the workflow that orchestrates the

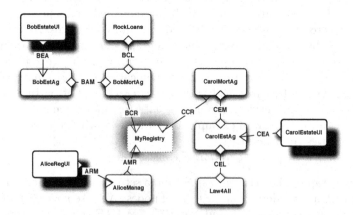

Fig. 27. The graph of a state configuration with 11 components and 10 wires

mortgage-brokerage service for a particular client. In component-based development (CBD) one often says that the bottom layer provides 'services' to the layer above. As we see it in this paper, an important difference between CBD and SOC is precisely in the way such services are procured, which in the case of SOC involves identifying (possibly new) providers and negotiating terms and conditions for each new instance of the activity, e.g. for each new user of a travel agent. SOA middleware supports this service layer by providing the infrastructure for the discovery and negotiation processes to be executed without having to be explicitly programmed as (part of) components.

The top layer is the one responsible for launching business activities in the service layer. The user of a given activity — identified through a user-actor as discussed in Section 3 — resides in the top layer; it can be an interface for human-computer interaction, a software component, or an external system (e.g. a control device equipped with sensors). When the user launches an activity, a component is created in the service layer that starts executing a workflow that may involve the orchestration of services that will be discovered and bound to the workflow at run time.

6.2 Business Activities and Configurations

In our model, state configurations change as a result of the execution of business processes. More precisely, changes to the configuration graph result from the fact that the discovery of a service is triggered and, as a consequence, new components are added and bound to existing ones (and, possibly, other components and wires disappear because they finished executing their computations). The information about the triggers and the constraints that apply to service discovery and binding are not coded in the components themselves: they are properties of the 'business activities' that are active and determine how the configuration evolves. Thus, in order to capture the dynamic aspects of SOC, we need to look beyond the information available in a state. In our approach, we achieve this by making configurations 'business reflective', i.e. by labelling the sub-configurations that correspond to instances of business activities by the corresponding activity module.

For instance, we should be able to recognise an activity in Fig. 27 whose sub-configuration is as depicted in Fig. 29. Intuitively, it corresponds to an instance

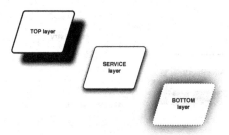

Fig. 28. A 3-layered architecture for configurations

of UPDATEREGISTRY. In order to formalise this notion of typed subconfiguration, we start by providing a formal definition of activity modules. We denote by **BROL** the set of business roles (see 5.1.2), by **BUSP** the set of business protocols (see 5.1.3), by **LAYP** the set of layer protocols (see 5.1.4), and by **CNCT** the set of connectors (see 5.1).

An *activity module M* consist of:

- A graph *graph(M)*.
- A distinguished subset of nodes *requires(M)*⊆*nodes(M)*.
- A distinguished subset of nodes *uses(M)*⊆*nodes(M)*.
- A node *serves(M)*∈ *nodes(M)* distinct from *requires(M)* and *uses(M)*.
- A labelling function $label_M$ such that
    - $label_M(n)$ ∈**BROL** if n ∈*components(M)*, where by *components(M)* we denote the set of *nodes(M)* that are not *serves(M)* nor in *requires(M)* or *uses(M)*.
    - $label_M(n)$ ∈**BUSP** if n ∈*requires(M)*
    - $label_M(n)$ ∈**LAYP** if n ∈*serves(M)*∪*uses(M)*
    - $label_M(e : n \leftrightarrow m)$ ∈**CNCT**.
- An internal configuration policy.
- An external configuration policy.

We denote by *body(M)* the (full) sub-graph of *graph(M)* that forgets the nodes in *requires(M)* and the edges that connect them to the rest of the graph. We can now formalise the typing of state configurations with activity modules that we discussed around Fig. 29, which accounts for the coarser business dimension that is overlaid by services on global computers. That is, we define what corresponds to a state configuration of a service overlay computer, which we call a business configuration. We consider a space $\mathcal{A}$ of business activities to be given, which can be seen to consist of reference numbers (or some other kind of identifier) such as the ones that organisations automatically assign when a service request arrives.

A *business configuration* consists of:

- A state configuration $\mathcal{F}$.

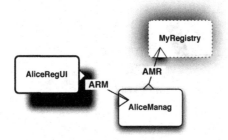

Fig. 29. The sub-configuration corresponding to an instance of UPDATEREGISTRY

- A partial mapping $\mathcal{B}$ that assigns an activity module $\mathcal{B}(a)$ to each activity $a \in \mathcal{A}$ — the workflow being executed by a in $\mathcal{F}$. We say that the activities in the domain of this mapping are those that are active in that state.
- A mapping $\mathcal{C}$ that assigns an homomorphism $\mathcal{C}(a)$ of graphs $body(\mathcal{B}(a)) \rightarrow \mathcal{F}$ to every activity $a \in \mathcal{F}$ that is active in $\mathcal{F}$. We denote by $\mathcal{F}(a)$ the image of $\mathcal{C}(a)$ — the sub-configuration of $\mathcal{F}$ that corresponds to the activity a.

A homomorphism of graphs is just a mapping of nodes to nodes and edges to edges that preserves the end-points of the edges. Therefore, the homomorphism $\mathcal{C}$ of a business configuration $\langle \mathcal{F}, \mathcal{B}, \mathcal{C} \rangle$ types the nodes (components) of $\mathcal{F}(a)$ with business roles or layer protocols — i.e. $\mathcal{C}(a)(n) : label_{\mathcal{B}(a)}(n)$ for every node n — and the edges (wires) with connectors — i.e. $\mathcal{C}(a)(e) : label_{\mathcal{B}(a)}(e)$ for every edge e of the body of the activity. In other words, the homomorphism binds the components and wires of the state configuration to the business elements (interfaces labelled with business roles, layer protocols and connectors) that they fulfil in the activity.

In the example discussed above, we have an activity — that we call *Alice* — such that $\mathcal{B}$*(Alice)* is UPDATEREGISTRY (as in Fig. 3), $\mathcal{F}$*(Alice)* is the sub-configuration in Fig. 29, and $\mathcal{C}$ maps *RM* to *AliceRegUI*, *MC* to *AliceManag*, *RE* to *MyRegistry*, *MR* to *AMR*, and *RM* to *ARM*.

The fact that the homomorphism is defined over the body of the activity module means that business protocols are not used for typing components of the state configuration. Indeed, as discussed above, the purpose of the requires-interfaces is for identifying dependencies that the activity has, in that state, on external services. In particular, this makes requires-interfaces different from uses-interfaces as the latter are indeed mapped through the homomorphism to a component of the state configuration.

In a sense, the homomorphism makes state configurations reflective in the sense of [25] as it adds meta (business) information to the state configuration. This information is used for deciding how the configuration will evolve (namely, how it will react to events that trigger the discovery process). Indeed, reflection has been advocated as a means of making systems adaptable through reconfiguration, which is similar to the mechanisms through which activities evolve in our model.

6.3   Run-Time Discovery and Binding

In order to illustrate how a business configuration evolves through service discovery and binding, we are going to consider another business activity type that supports the purchase of a house. The corresponding module is depicted in Fig. 30.

That is, the orchestration of the purchase of a house is performed by a component EA of type (business role) EstateAgent, which may need to discover and bind to a mortgage dealer *MO* and a lawyer *LA*.

Consider the configuration depicted in Fig. 31, and the business configuration that consists of *Alice* (as defined in Section 6.2) and of the activity *Bob* typed by HouseBuying, which is mapped to the configuration by the homomorphism that associates *GH* with *BobEstateUI*, *EA* with *BobEstateAG* and *HE* with *BEA*. Assume that, in the current state, *intMO*○ **trigger** holds, i.e. that the execution of the workflow associated with *EA* requires the discovery of a mortgage dealer. Let us consider what is necessary for GetMortgage to be selected and bound to HouseBuying as a result of the trigger (see Fig. 32). In our setting, this process involves three steps, outlined as follows:

- **Discovery.** For GetMortgage to be discovered, it is necessary that the properties of its provides-interface *Customer* entail the properties of the requires-interface *Mortgage*, and that the properties of the interaction protocol of *CC* entail those of *EM*.
- **Ranking.** If it is discovered, GetMortgage is ranked among all services that are discovered by calculating the most favourable service-level

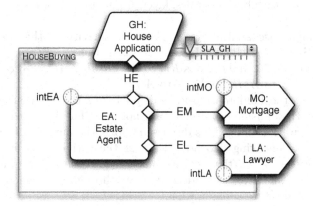

Fig. 30. The HouseBuying activity module

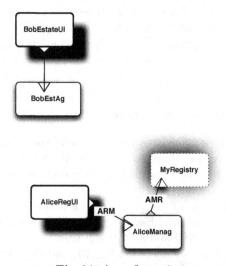

Fig. 31. A configuration

agreement that can be achieved — the contract that will be established between the two parties if GETMORTGAGE is selected. This calculation uses a notion of satisfaction that takes into account the preferences of the activity HOUSEBUYING and the service GETMORTGAGE.

– **Selection.** Finally, GETMORTGAGE can be selected if it is one of the services that maximises the level of satisfaction offered by the corresponding contract.

These steps are formalised in [30]. If GETMORTGAGE is selected then it is unified with HOUSEBUYING, giving rise to another activity module. As depicted in Fig. 33, the resulting activity module is obtained by replacing the requires-interface and corresponding wire of HOUSEBUYING by those that connect the provides-interface of GETMORTGAGE to its body.

At the level of the configuration, we add the new instances of the components of GETMORTGAGE and corresponding wires, making sure that instances of the uses-interfaces are components of the bottom layer (already present in the configuration). This can be witnessed in Fig. 34 where the instance of *RE*

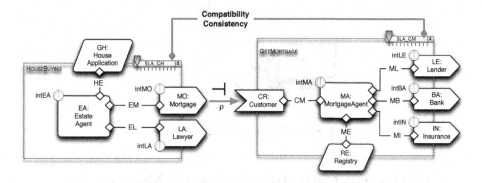

Fig. 32. The elements involved in unification

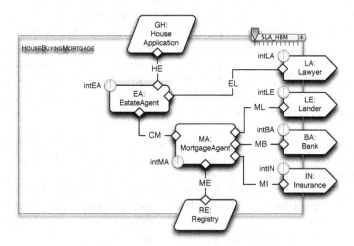

Fig. 33. The result of unification

is the component *MyRegistry*, which is shared with other activities. Notice that
the type of the activity *Bob* is now the activity module in Fig. 34, and that
the homomorphism now maps *MA* to *BobMortBR*, *RE* to *MyRegistry*, *EM* to
BAM and *BE* to *BCR*. It is in this sense that the activity is reconfigured as new
services are discovered and bound to its requires-interfaces. See [30] for a full
formalisation of this process of reconfiguration.

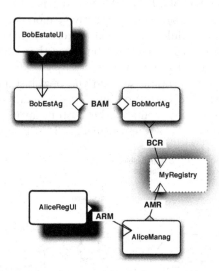

Fig. 34. The result of the binding

7   Checking the Correctness of Service Modules

Service modules are considered to be 'correct' when the properties offered in
their provides-interface are ensured by the orchestration of their components
and the properties specified in their requires-interfaces. Therefore, in order to
prove the correctness of GETMORTGAGE, we would need to check that the properties offered through the business protocol *Customer* — e.g., committing to the
proposal made by *MA* ensures that a confirmation message will be sent conveying
the loan contract — are effectively established by the orchestration performed
by *MA* on the assumption that the properties required of *LE*, *BA* and *IN* are
satisfied.

   In this section, we discuss a model-checking approach that we have developed
for analysing the properties that can emerge from the orchestration of service
behaviour in general, and the correctness of service modules in particular. This
approach is based on the model-checker UMC [39] developed at CNR-ISTI (see
also Chapter 4-2). UMC works over UML state machines and UCTL   [9], a
temporal logic that is interpreted over transition systems in which both states
and transitions are labelled, thus making it easier to express properties of stateful
interactions as required by SRML.

7.1   The UCTL Semantics of Business Protocols

UCTL is a temporal logic that includes both the branching-time action-based logic ACTL [20] and the branching-time state-based logic CTL [24]. The models of UCTL are doubly labelled transition systems (L^2TS for short) which are transition systems whose states are labelled by atomic propositions and whose transitions are labelled by sets of actions [21]. The syntax of UCTL formulas is defined as follows:

$$\phi ::= true \mid p \mid \phi \wedge \phi' \mid \neg\phi \mid E\pi \mid A\pi$$
$$\pi ::= X_\chi \phi \mid \phi_\chi W \phi' \mid \phi_\chi U_{\chi'} \phi' \mid \phi_\chi W \phi' \mid \phi_\chi W_{\chi'} \phi'$$

where p ranges over *state predicates*, χ over *actions*, ϕ over *state formulae*, and π over *path formulae*. E and A are "exists" and "for all" *path quantifiers* respectively. The next operator X says that in the next state of the path, reached by an action satisfying χ, the formula ϕ holds. The intuitive meaning of the doubly-indexed until operator U on a path is that ϕ' holds at some future state of the path reached by a last action satisfying χ', while ϕ has to hold from the current state until that state is reached and all the actions executed in the meanwhile along the path either satisfy χ or τ. Finally, the weak-until operator W holds on a path either if the corresponding strong-until operator holds or if for all states of the path the formula ϕ holds and all the actions of the path either satisfy χ or τ. It is straightforward to derive the well-known temporal logical operators EF ("possibly"), AF ("eventually") and AG ("always") and the diamond and box modalities $<>$ ("possibly") and $[]$ ("necessarily"). In particular, $< \chi > \phi$ stands for $EX_\chi \phi$, meaning that there is transition that satisfies χ which leads to a state that satisfies ϕ; and $[\chi]\phi$ stands for $\neg < \chi > \neg \phi$, meaning that every transition that satisfies χ leads to a state that satisfies ϕ.

To provide the semantics of business protocols in terms of UCTL formulas, we have to consider the declared set of typed interactions and the set of constraints that correlate the events of those interactions. Recall that the types that are associated with each interaction define not only the set of events the external service can engage in as part of that interaction, but also the conversational protocol that the service follows to engage in those events. We will first address the encoding of the patterns that are used to specify behaviour constraints and then we will address the encoding of the conversational protocol that is associated with the interaction types.

The semantics of the behavioural patterns used in business protocols (presented in Section 5.1) is defined in terms of UCTL formulas as follows:

initiallyEnabled e	$A \left(true_{\neg e_i} W_{e?} true \right)$
s **after** a	$AG[a]s$
a **enables** e	$\left(AG[a]\neg EF < e_i > true \right) \wedge \left(A[true_{\neg e?} W_a true] \right)$
a **ensures** e	$\left(AG[a]AF[e!]true \right) \wedge \left(A[true_{\neg e!} W_a true] \right)$

This encoding is justified by the fact that SRML models correspond to L^2TSs in which the actions that label the transitions consist of the several stages of event propagation (publish, deliver, execute or discard), and the state predicates are either pledges (i.e. properties that are ensured by positive replies) or capture the history of events (this is because UCTL does not have past operators).

As already explained, two-way interactions are typed as s&r (send and receive) or r&s (receive and send) to define that the service being specified engages in the interaction as the requester or as the supplier, respectively. Each of these two roles, requester and supplier, has a set of properties associated with it. The following table presents the UCTL encoding of some of these properties.

s&r — Requester	
The reply-event becomes enabled by the publication of the initiation-event and not before.	$i\otimes!$ **enables** $\boxtimes?$
r&s — Supplier	
The reply will be published after and only after the initiation-event was executed	$i\otimes?$ **ensures** $\boxtimes!$
The revoke-event cannot be executed before the execution of the commit-event.	$A[true_{\neg i\Uparrow?} W_{i\checkmark?} true]$

7.2   From SRML Modules to UML State Machines

In order to be able to model-check properties of service behaviour in the context of SRML in general, and the correctness of service modules in particular, we restrict ourselves to those modules in which state machines are used for modelling the internal components, the persistent components, the protocols performed by the wires, and the required behaviour of external services. This is because UMC takes as input a set of communicating state machines with which it associates a L^2TS that represents the possible computations of that system. Model-checking is then performed over this L^2TS.

As discussed in Section 5, using UML state machines for defining workflows is quite standard. However, the cases of wires and requires-interfaces are not as simple. In the case of wires, we need to ensure that event propagation and related phenomena occur according to the rules of the computational model. In the case of requires-interfaces, we need to discuss how the patterns defined in Subsection 5.1 can be represented with state machines.

Encoding requires interfaces. In SRML, requires-interfaces are specified through business protocols with the patterns of temporal logic that we discussed in Subsection 5.1. The proposed encoding associates a state machine with each requires-interface that corresponds to a canonical model of the required behaviour. The strategy of the encoding entails creating a concurrent region for each of the interactions that the external service is required to be involved in — the interaction-regions — and a concurrent region for each of the behaviour constraints – the constraint-regions — except for the constraints defined with the pattern **initiallyEnabled** *e*: as discussed further ahead, these are modelled by the instantiation of a state attribute.

The role of each of the interaction regions is to guarantee that the conversational protocol that is associated with the type of the interaction is respected as discussed before. Events of a given interaction are published, executed and discarded exclusively by the interaction-region that models it. The role of the constraint-regions is to flag, through the use of special state attributes, when events become enabled and when events should be published — the evolution of the interaction-regions, and thus the actual execution, discard and publication of events, is guarded by the value of those flags. Constraint-regions cooperate with interaction-regions to guarantee the correlation of events expressed by the behaviour constraints.

We illustrate this methodology by presenting the encoding of the requires-interface *Lender* in Fig. 35. *Lender* is involved in the two interactions *request-Mortgage* and *requestSignOut*, which are encoded by interaction-regions A and B, respectively; these two interactions are correlated by two behaviour constraints, the second of which originates the constraint-region X. The constraint **initiallyEnabled** *requestMortgage*⊴*?* does not originate a region in the state machine; instead it determines that the flag *requestMortgage*⊴*_enabled* is initially set to *true* and therefore when the event *requestMortgage*⊴ is processed it will be executed (and not discarded) by interaction-region A. When *requestMortgage*⊴ is executed, interaction-region A evolves from state $a1$ to state $a2$ by publishing a positive reply or alternatively from $a1$ to the final state by publishing a negative reply. If the commit-event of *requestMortgage* is processed in state $a2$, it will be executed and therefore the *requestMortgage*✓*_executed* will be set to true. It is at this point that the constraint region X comes into play — this region reacts to the change of value of *requestMortgage*✓*_executed* by setting *requestSignOut*⊴*_enabled* to true. After this happens, region B will be ready to execute the request-event of *requestSignOut* and therefore this two-way interaction can be initiated.

Following our methodology, each interaction declaration and each behaviour constraint encodes part of the final state machine in a compositional way. Associated with each interaction type, there is a particular statechart structure that encodes it. Each of the patterns of behaviour constraints is also associated with a particular statechart structure. A complete mapping from interactions types and behaviour patterns to their associated statechart structure can be found in [4]. Naturally, the encoding we propose for specifications of requires-interfaces is defined in such a way that the transition system that is generated for a service module satisfies the UCTL formulas that are associated with each of the requires-interfaces of that module.

Encoding wires. In SRML wires are responsible for the coordination of the interactions declared locally for each party of the module. For each wire, there is a connector that defines an interaction protocol with two roles and binds the interactions declared in the roles with those of the parties at the two ends of the wire [5]. With our methodology for encoding wires with UML state machines,

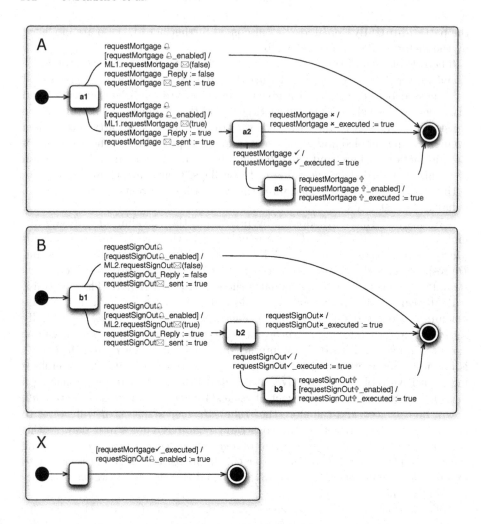

Fig. 35. The UML statechart encoding of the requires-interface *Lender*. *A* and *B* are the interaction-regions and *X* is the constraint-regions.

every connector defines a state machine for each interaction. This state machine is responsible for transmitting the events of that interaction from the sending party to the receiving co-party. Parties publish events by signaling them in the state machine that corresponds to the appropriate connector; this state machine in turn guarantees that these events are delivered by signaling them in the state machine that is associated with the co-party. The relation between parameter values that is specified by the interaction protocol of the connector is ensured operationally by the state machine that encodes that connector – data can be transformed before being forwarded. The statechart contains a single state and as many loops as the number of events that the connector has to forward.

In GETMORTGAGE, two-way interactions are coordinated by straight interaction protocols that bind the names and parameters of *s&r* and *r&s* interaction declarations directly (i.e. events and parameter values are the same from the point of view of the two parties connected). Fig. 36 shows the state machine that encodes this connector for the single interaction that takes place between *MA* and *LE* — there is only one persistent state in which the machine waits to receive events and forward them with the same parameter values.

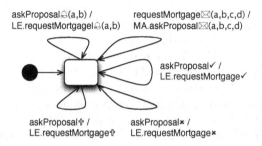

Fig. 36. The UML encoding of the connector that coordinates the single, two-way, interaction between *MA* and *LE* which is named *askProposal* and *requestMortgage* from the point of view of each party respectively

7.3   Model-Checking Service Modules at Work

As mentioned before, our approach to check the correctness of service modules is based on the model-checker UMC [39]. UMC is an on-the-fly model-checker developed for efficient verification of UCTL formulae over a set of communicating UML state machines [42]. A UMC model description consists of a set of UML class definitions and a static set of object instantiations – the actual state machines that form the system under analysis. A UMC model must represent an input-closed system, i.e. the input sources must be modelled as active objects interacting with the rest of the system. Each state machine has a pool that buffers the set of signals that have been received from other machines until they are processed by that machine. According to its class definition, each state machine has at any given time a value for each of its attributes and a set of currently active sub states as specified by the statechart diagram of the class.

In order to illustrate our model-checking approach we will discuss how to model-check the module GETMORTGAGE. First, we have encoded each of its external-required interfaces and each of its connectors using the methodology described in the previous section. Adding the two components that orchestrate the system, we ended up with a set of fourteen communicating UML state machines. Because every input source of a UMC model must also be modelled via an active object, we had to define a machine that initiates the interactions advertised in the provides-interface *Customer*, thus modelling a generic client of the service. Using this system as input to the UMC model-checker, we were able to verify that the doubly labelled transition system that is generated does satisfy the properties associated with the provides-interface *Customer*, shown in Fig. 16. As discussed before, these consists of the properties associated with the types of the declared interactions and those that derive from the patterns of behaviour.

8   Analysing Timing Properties of Complex Services

In this Section, we show how SRML can be extended in order to model the delays involved in the business process through which a service is provided and how time-related properties of service-oriented models can be analysed over such models. For instance, we have in mind the ability to certify that the mortgage-brokerage service satisfies properties of the form *"In at least 80% of the cases, a reply to a request for a mortgage proposal will be sent within 7 seconds"*. Properties of this kind are extremely important in a number of application domains and are usually part of the service level agreements (SLAs) that are negotiated between clients and providers. This approach draws from the work reported in [53].

8.1   Timing Issues in SRML Models

Given two events e_1 and e_2, we denote by $Delay(e_1, e_2)$ the time that separates their occurrences, e.g. $Delay(getProposal\triangle, getProposal\boxtimes)$ in the example above. Because we wish to adopt the PEPA analysis tools [51,19], we assume that such delays follow an exponential distribution of the form $F_{Delay(e_1,e_2)}(t) = 1 - e^{-rt}$. In practical applications, it is rarely the case that it is possible to obtain a complete response-time distribution of all services in the problem under study. It is far more likely that one will only know the average response time. In this setting, it is indeed correct to capture the inherent stochasticity in the system through a *exponential distribution*. The exponential distribution requires only a single parameter, the average response time. Other distributions would require knowledge of higher moments and other parameters which we do not have. We take care not to require too many parameters because finding each one accurately may require careful measurement or estimation. We apply our modelling only in settings where the average response time is a meaningful quantity to use. For example, we do not model systems that have a substantial component requiring a response from a single human participant because the great variance in human response time makes knowledge of the average response time alone insignificant for analysis purposes. This setting connects us to the rich theory of stochastic process including continuous-time Markov chains (CTMC), and a wealth of efficient numerical procedures for their analysis.

In our setting, the rate r is associated with the entity that processes and publishes the events, and used as a modelling primitive in the proposed extension of SRML. Event-based selection of continuations in SRML becomes probabilistic choice in PEPA. We estimate the probability of the relative outcomes and use the resulting probabilities to weight the rates in the PEPA model to ensure the correct distribution across the continuations. In this way all number distributions remain exponential and thus we can achieve probabilistic branching while remaining in the continuous-time Markovian realm.

We report below a number of delays that, according to the computation and coordination model discussed in Section 4.3, can affect service execution. The rates can be negotiated as SLAs with service providers in the constraint systems mentioned in Section 5.2.

Delays in components. Because they may be busy, components store the events they receive in a buffer where they wait until they are processed, at which point they are either executed or discarded. Two kinds of rates are involved in this process:

processingRate. This rate represents the time taken by the component to remove an event from the buffer. Different components may have different processing rates but all events are treated equally by the same component.

executionRate. This represents the time taken by the component to perform the transition triggered by the event, i.e. making changes to the state and publishing events. We assume that discarding an event does not take time. Each transition declared in a business role has its own execution rate, which should be chosen taking into account the specific effects of that transition.

Delays of requires-interfaces. As already mentioned, requires-interfaces represent parties that have to be discovered at run time when the corresponding trigger becomes true. Two kinds of rates are involved in this process:

compositionRate. This rate applies to the run-time discovery, selection and binding processes as performed by the middleware, i.e. (1) the time to connect to a broker, (2) the time for matchmaking, ranking and selection, and (3) the time to bind the selected service. We chose to let different requires-interfaces have different composition rates in order to reflect the fact that different brokers may be involved, depending on the nature of the required external services.

responseRate. These are rates that apply to the responses that the business protocol requires of the external service through statements of the form $e_1 * ensures\ e_2!$. More specifically, we consider a rate $responseRate(e_1, e_2)$ for each such pair of events, which include $responseRate(a\triangle, a\boxtimes)$ for every interaction a of type **r&s** declared in the business protocol.

Delays in wires. Each wire of a module has an associated transfer rate. As mentioned in Section 2, we are considering only interaction protocols that affect a linear transmission from one party to its co-party, and do not involve complex data transformation.

Delays in synchronous communication and resource contention. The interface of a resource consists of a number of synchronous interactions. We define a synchronisation rate for each such interactions and associate it with the

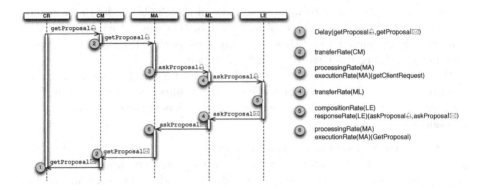

Fig. 37. Cascade of delays in a fragment of *GetMortgage*

events that resolve synchronisation requests by replying to a query or executing an operation.

In summary, we extend every module M with a time policy P that consists of several collections of rates. Each rate is a term of type $\mathbb{R}^+ \cup \{\top\}$, where $\top$ is the passive rate (i.e., the event with a passive rate occurs only in collaboration with another event, when this second event is ready):

- For every requires-interface $n \in requires(M)$
  - $compositionRate(n)$
  - $responseRate(n)(e_1, e_2)$ for every statement ($e_1 *$ **ensures** e_2!)
- For every $w \in edges(M)$, $transferRate(w)$.
- For every $n \in components(M)$
  - $processingRate(n)$
  - $executionRate(n, P)$ for every transition $P \in trans(label_M(n))$
- For every $n \in components(M) \cup serves(M) \cup uses(M)$ and interaction i of type **rpl** and **prf**, $synchronisationRate(n)(i)$.

The sequence diagram in Fig. 37 illustrates how the response time associated with *getProposal◬* depends on the delays associated with the rates discussed in this section. The value of the rates that apply to components and wires to other components or uses-interfaces are fixed when the module is instantiated, i.e. when the interfaces are bound to components or network connections. The rates that involve requires-interfaces are fixed at run time, subject to SLAs.

8.2   Quantitative Analysis of Timing Properties

In this section we discuss the quantitative analysis that we are able to perform on a SRML module by using the PEPA Eclipse Plug-in [51] and IPC [19], components of the SENSORIA Development Environment (see Chapter 6-5).

A SRML module can be coded as a stochastic process so that the timing properties that derive from the timing policy of the module can be analysed using PEPA. This encoding involves several steps. First, the structure of the SRML module is decomposed into a PEPA configuration consisting of a number of PEPA terms. Each PEPA term corresponds to either a node or a wire of the original SRML model. In this way we can easily map the results of the quantitative analysis back to the original SRML specification. Second, the behavioural interface of each entity of the SRML model is encoded into a PEPA term, enabling to analyze the delays due to each single component. See [12] for a detailed account on how to encode a SRML module into PEPA.

Once the SRML module has been encoded into PEPA, we use the PEPA Eclipse Plug-in tool to generate the statespace of the obtained PEPA configuration. We used the static analyser and qualitative analysis capabilites of this tool to determine that the configuration is deadlock free and has no unreachable local states in any component (no "dead code" in the model).

The analysis of a PEPA term encoding a SRML module is inexpensive because the statespace of the model is relatively small, meaning that the number of states of a module grows linearly with respect to the number of nodes. The reason is that the nodes of a SRML module do not execute independently but they wait for one another (i.e., typically not more than one at a time is active).

We performed the passage time analysis of the example illustrated in Fig. 37 encoded into PEPA using the method described in [12]. Our aim was to investigate the probability of each possible delay between $CRgetProposal\triangleleft$ and $CRgetProposal\boxtimes$. We conducted a series of experiments on our PEPA model to determine the answers to the following questions:

1. Is the advertised SLA "80% of requests receive a response within 7 seconds" satisfied by the system at present?
2. What is the bottleneck activity in the system at present (i.e. where is it best to invest effort in making one of the activities more efficient?)

The first question is answered by computing the cumulative distribution function (CDF) for the passage from request to response and determining the value at time $t = 10$. The second question is answered by performing a *sensitivity analysis*. That is, we vary each of the rates used in the model (both up from the true value, and down from it) and evaluate the CDF repeatedly over this range of values. The resulting graphs are shown in Fig. 38 (the plus denotes the coordinate for 7 seconds and 80%).

Each of the graphs is a CDF which plots the probability of having completed the passage of interest by a given time bound. To determine whether the stated SLA is satisfied we need only inspect the value of this probability at the time bound. For the given values of the rates we find that it is the case that this SLA is not satisfied (Fig. 38(a)).

In performing sensitivity analysis we vary each rate through a fixed number of possible values to see if we can identify an improvement which satisfies

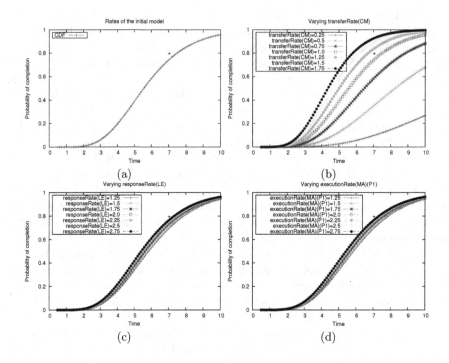

Fig. 38. Sensitivity analysis of response time distributions (from [12])

the SLA. We have begun by considering seven possible values here. Three of these are above the true value (i.e. the activity is being performed faster) and three are below (i.e. the activity is being performed slower). From the sensitivity analysis we determine (from Fig. 38(b)) that variations in rate parameter *transferRate(CM)* have the greatest impact on the passage of interest. Due to the structure of the model this rate controls the entry into the passage from request to response so delays here have a greater impact further through the passage. In contrast variations in rate parameter *responseRate(LE)* (seen in Fig. 38(c)) and *executionRate(MA)(P1)* (seen in Fig. 38(d)) have the least impact overall. Thus if seeking to improve the performance of the system we should invest in improving *coTransferRate* before trying to improve *responseTime(LE)*. Fig. 38(b) illustrates, for example, how the advertised SLA is satisfied by improving the value of *transferRate(CM)* to 1.25. It is entirely possible that the sensitivity analysis will identify several ways in which the SLA can be satisfied. In this case the service stakeholders can evaluate these in terms of implementation cost or time and identify the most cost-effective way to improve the service in order to meet the SLA.

9   Related Approaches

One of the main aspects that distinguishes the approach that we proposed from other work on Web Services (e.g. [8]) and SOC in general (e.g. [2]) is that we address not the middleware architectural layers (or low-level design issues in general), but what we call the 'business level'. For instance, the main concern of the Service Component Architecture (SCA) [2], from which we have borrowed concepts and notations, is to provide an open specification "allowing multiple vendors to implement support for SCA in their development tools and runtime". This is why SCA offers a middleware-independent layer for service composition and specific support for a variety of component implementation and interface types (e.g. BPEL processes with WSDL interfaces, or Java classes with corresponding interfaces). Our work explores a complementary direction: our research aims for a modelling framework supported by a mathematical semantics in which business activities and services can be defined in a way that is independent of the languages and technologies used for programming and deploying the components that will execute them. The fact that the modelling framework is equipped with a formal semantics makes it possible to support the analysis of services, service compositions and activities, a direction that we are pursuing through the use of model-checking [7].

Another architectural approach to SOC has been designed [52] that follows SCA very closely. However, its purpose is to offer a meta-model that covers service-oriented modelling aspects such as interfaces, wires, processes and data. Therefore, as in SCA, interfaces are syntactic and bindings are established at design time, whereas our interfaces are behavioural and binding occurs at run time. Other approaches to service modelling have considered richer interfaces that encompass business protocols, e.g. [10,26,22,45,46], but not the dynamic aspects — discovery and binding — offered by SRML as illustrated in this paper. Indeed, a characteristic that distinguishes our approach from other formal models of services such as [16] is the fact that we address the dynamic aspects of SOC, namely run-time discovery and binding. Formalisms for modelling (web) services tend not to address these. For example, in BPEL, service compositions are created statically and are governed by a centralised engine. This also holds for approaches that focus on choreography (e.g. [18,45]), where it is possible to calculate which are the partners that can properly interact with a service but the actual discovery and binding processes are not considered. Exceptions can be found among some of the process calculi that have been developed for capturing semantic foundations of SOC (e.g. [28,17,37]). However, such process calculi tend not to address dynamic reconfiguration separately from computation, i.e. the process of discovery and binding is handled as part of the computation performed by a service. As far as we know, SRML is the first service-modelling language to separate these two concerns.

Indeed, in our opinion, what makes SOC different from other paradigms is the fact that it concerns run-time, not design-time complexity. This is also the view exposed in [23] — a very clear account of what distinguishes SOC from CBD (Component Based Development). Whereas in CBD component selection is either performed at design time or programmed over a fixed universe of components, SOC provides a means of obtaining functionalities by orchestrating interactions among components that are procured at run time according to given (functional) types and service level constraints.

Another area related to the work that we have presented concerns the non-functional aspects of services, namely the policies and constraints for service level agreement that have to be taken into account in the composition of services. Most of the research developed in this area has been devoted to languages for modelling specific kinds of policies (over specific non-functional features) and of selection algorithms, e.g. SCA Policy [2] among several others [40,41,49,48,27]. These languages have been primarily designed to be part of the technology available for implementing and executing services. As such, they are tailored to the technological infrastructure that is currently enabling web services and are not best placed for being used at high-levels of business modelling.

10 Concluding Remarks

In this chapter, we presented an overview of the formal approach for modelling service-oriented application that we developed within SENSORIAtowards a methodological and mathematical characterisation of the service-oriented computing paradigm [3]. The approach is built around a prototype language called SRML — the SENSORIA Modelling Reference Language — and offers an engineering environment that includes abstraction mappings from workflow languages (such as BPEL [14]) and policy languages (such as StPowla [13]), model-checking techniques that support qualitative analysis, and stochastic analysis techniques for timing properties. SRML is supported by an Eclipse-based editor (available from www.cs.le.ac.uk/srml) that is part of the SENSORIA Development Environment (SDE). A mathematical semantics is available for all aspects of the approach as partially illustrated in the paper (see [4,6,29,32,30,33] for a more comprehensive account).

This methodology has been tested in a number of other domains, including telco [7], travel [6], automotive [15] and procurement [31] scenarios. Tutorials have been given at CONCUR'08, SEFM'08, SFM'09 and DISCOTEC'09. More extended tutorials were given at the Technical University of Valencia (Spain) and the Summer School on Web Engineering held in 2007 in La Plata, Argentina. SRML is also being taught at the University of Leicester to postgraduate students in Computer Science.

Acknowledgments

We would like to thank our colleagues in the SENSORIA project for many useful discussions on the topics covered in this paper. Stefania Gnesi and Franco Mazzanti (CNR-ISTI) contributed directly to the work presented in Section 7, and Stephen Gilmore (Edinburgh), Monika Solanki (Leicester) and Vishnu Vankayala (Leicester) to Section 8. Artur Boronat and Yi Hong (Leicester) contributed directly to the development of the SRML Editor. We are also indebted to Colin Gilmore from Box Tree Mortgage Solutions (Leicester) for taking us through the mortgage-brockerage case study.

References

1. Global computing initiative, http://cordis.europa.eu/ist/fet/gc.htm
2. The open service oriented architecture collaboration, Whitepapers and specifications available from http://www.osoa.org (see also oasis-opencsa.org/sca)
3. Sensoria consortium (2007), White paper available from http://www.sensoria-ist.eu/files/whitePaper.pdf
4. Abreu, J.: Modelling Business Conversations in Service Component Architectures. PhD thesis, University of Leicester (2009)
5. Abreu, J., Bocchi, L., Fiadeiro, J.L., Lopes, A.: Specifying and composing interaction protocols for service-oriented system modelling. In: Derrick, J., Vain, J. (eds.) FORTE 2007. LNCS, vol. 4574, pp. 358–373. Springer, Heidelberg (2007)
6. Abreu, J., Fiadeiro, J.L.: A coordination model for service-oriented interactions. In: Wang, A.H., Tennenholtz, M. (eds.) COORDINATION 2008. LNCS, vol. 5052, pp. 1–16. Springer, Heidelberg (2008)
7. Abreu, J., Mazzanti, F., Fiadeiro, J.L., Gnesi, S.: A model-checking approach for service component architectures. In: Lee, D., Lopes, A., Poetzsch-Heffter, A. (eds.) FMOODS 2009. LNCS, vol. 5522, pp. 219–224. Springer, Heidelberg (2009)
8. Alonso, G., Casati, F., Kuno, H., Machiraju, V.: Web Services. Springer, Heidelberg (2004)
9. Beek, M., Fantechi, A., Gnesi, S., Mazzanti, F.: An action/state-based model-checking approach for the analysis of communication protocols for Service-Oriented Applications. In: Leue, S., Merino, P. (eds.) FMICS 2007. LNCS, vol. 4916, pp. 133–148. Springer, Heidelberg (2008)
10. Benatallah, B., Casati, F., Toumani, F.: Web services conversation modeling: A cornerstone for e-business automation. IEEE Internet Computing 8(1), 46–54 (2004)
11. Bistarelli, S., Montanari, U., Rossi, F.: Semiring-based constraint satisfaction and optimization. Journal of the ACM 44(2), 201–236 (1997)
12. Bocchi, L., Fiadeiro, J., Gilmore, S., Abreu, J., Solanki, M., Vankayala, V.: Analysing time-related properties of service-oriented systems (2010) (submitted), http://www.cs.le.ac.uk/people/jfiadeiro/Papers/SRML-T.pdf
13. Bocchi, L., Gorton, S., Reiff-Marganiec, S.: Engineering service oriented applications: From stPowla processes to SRML models. In: Fiadeiro, J.L., Inverardi, P. (eds.) FASE 2008. LNCS, vol. 4961, pp. 163–178. Springer, Heidelberg (2008)
14. Bocchi, L., Hong, Y., Lopes, A., Fiadeiro, J.: From BPEL to SRML: A formal transformational approach. In: Dumas, M., Heckel, R. (eds.) WS-FM 2007. LNCS, vol. 4937, pp. 92–107. Springer, Heidelberg (2008)
15. Bocchi, L., Fiadeiro, J.L., Lopes, A.: Service-oriented modelling of automotive systems. In: COMPSAC, pp. 1059–1064. IEEE Computer Society, Los Alamitos (2008)
16. Broy, M., Kruger, I., Meisinger, M.: A formal model of services. ACM TOSEM 16(1), 1–40 (2007)
17. Buscemi, M., Montanari, U.: CC-pi: A constraint-based language for specifying service level agreements. In: De Nicola, R. (ed.) ESOP 2007. LNCS, vol. 4421, pp. 18–32. Springer, Heidelberg (2007)

18. Carbone, M., Honda, K., Yoshida, N.: Structured communication-centred programming for web services. In: De Nicola, R. (ed.) ESOP 2007. LNCS, vol. 4421, pp. 2–17. Springer, Heidelberg (2007)

19. Clark, A.: The ipclib PEPA Library. In: Harchol-Balter, M., Kwiatkowska, M., Telek, M. (eds.) Proceedings of the 4th International Conference on the Quantitative Evaluation of SysTems (QEST), pp. 55–56. IEEE, Los Alamitos (2007)

20. De Nicola, R., Vaandrager, F.W.: Action versus state based logics for transition systems. In: Guessarian, I. (ed.) LITP 1990. LNCS, vol. 469, pp. 407–419. Springer, Heidelberg (1990)

21. De Nicola, R., Vaandrager, F.W.: Three logics for branching bisimulation. J. ACM 42(2), 458–487 (1995)

22. Dijkman, R.M., Dumas, M.: Service-oriented design: a multi-viewpoint approach. International Journal of Cooperative Information Systems 13(4), 337–368 (2004)

23. Elfatatry, A.: Dealing with change: components versus services. Communications of the ACM 50(8), 35–39 (2007)

24. Clarke, E.M., Emerson, E.A., Sistla, A.P.: Automatic Verification of Finite State Concurrent Systems using Temporal Logic Specifications. ACM Transactions on Programming Languages and Systems 8(2), 244–263 (1986)

25. Coulson, G., et al.: A generic component model for building systems software. ACM TOCS 26(1), 1–42 (2008)

26. Bordeaux, L., et al.: When are two web services compatible? In: Shan, M.-C., Dayal, U., Hsu, M. (eds.) TES 2004. LNCS, vol. 3324, pp. 15–28. Springer, Heidelberg (2005)

27. Zeng, L., et al.: Qos-aware middleware for web services composition. IEEE Transactions on Software Engineering 30(5), 311–327 (2004)

28. Boreale, M., et al.: Scc: a service centered calculus. In: Bravetti, M., Núñez, M., Tennenholtz, M. (eds.) WS-FM 2006. LNCS, vol. 4184, pp. 38–57. Springer, Heidelberg (2006)

29. Fiadeiro, J.L., Lopes, A., Abreu, J.: A formal model for service-oriented interactions (2010), http://www.cs.le.ac.uk/srml

30. Fiadeiro, J.L., Lopes, A., Bocchi, L.: An abstract semantics of service discovery and binding. In: Formal Aspects of Computing (to appear)

31. Fiadeiro, J.L., Lopes, A., Bocchi, L.: A formal approach to service-oriented architecture. In: Bravetti, M., Núñez, M., Tennenholtz, M. (eds.) WS-FM 2006. LNCS, vol. 4184, pp. 193–213. Springer, Heidelberg (2006)

32. Fiadeiro, J.L., Lopes, A., Bocchi, L.: Algebraic semantics of service component modules. In: Fiadeiro, J.L., Schobbens, P.-Y. (eds.) WADT 2006. LNCS, vol. 4409, pp. 37–55. Springer, Heidelberg (2007)

33. Fiadeiro, J.L., Schmitt, V.: Structured co-spans: An algebra of interaction protocols. In: Mossakowski, T., Montanari, U., Haveraaen, M. (eds.) CALCO 2007. LNCS, vol. 4624, pp. 194–209. Springer, Heidelberg (2007)

34. Foster, I., Kesselman, C. (eds.): The Grid 2: Blueprint for a New Computing Infrastructure. Morgan Kaufmann, San Francisco (2004)

35. Gu, Q., Lago, P.: A stakeholder-driven service life-cycle model for soa. In: IW-SOSWE 2007, pp. 1–7 (2007)

36. Hillston, J.: A Compositional Approach to Performance Modelling (1996)

37. Lapadula, A., Pugliese, R., Tiezzi, F.: A calculus for orchestration of web services. In: De Nicola, R. (ed.) ESOP 2007. LNCS, vol. 4421, pp. 33–47. Springer, Heidelberg (2007)

38. Mayer, P., Koch, N., Schroder, A.: A model-driven approach to service orchestration. In: Proceedings of IEEE International Conference on Services Computing, SCC 2008 (2008)
39. Mazzanti, F.: UMC User Guide v3.3. Technical Report 2006-TR-33, Istituto di Scienza e Tecnologie dell'Informazione "A. Faedo", CNR (2006), http://fmt.isti.cnr.it/WEBPAPER/UMC-UG33.pdf
40. Mukhi, N., Plebani, P., Silva-Lepe, I., Mikalsen, T.: Supporting policy-driven behaviours in web services: experiences and issues. In: Proceedings ICSOC 2004, pp. 322–328 (2004)
41. Mukhija, A., Dingwall-Smith, A., Rosenblum, D.: Qos-aware service composition in dino. In: ECOWS 2007, pp. 3–12. ACM Press, New York (2007)
42. Object Management Group. Unified Modeling Language, http://www.uml.org/
43. Peltz, C.: Web services orchestration and choreography. IEEE Computer 36(10), 46–52 (2003)
44. Rao, J., Su, X.: A survey of automated web service composition methods. In: Cardoso, J., Sheth, A.P. (eds.) SWSWPC 2004. LNCS, vol. 3387, pp. 43–54. Springer, Heidelberg (2005)
45. Reisig, W.: Modeling- and analysis techniques for web services and business processes. In: Steffen, M., Tennenholtz, M. (eds.) FMOODS 2005. LNCS, vol. 3535, pp. 243–258. Springer, Heidelberg (2005)
46. Reisig, W.: Towards a theory of services. In: UNISCON 2008, pp. 271–281 (2008)
47. Shaw, M., Garlan, D.: Software Architecture: Perspectives on an Emerging Discipline (1996)
48. Lin, K.-J., Yu, T.: A broker-based framework for qos-aware web service composition. In: Proc. of the Intl. Conf. on e-Technology, e-Commerce and e-Service, pp. 22–29. IEEE Computer Society, Los Alamitos (2005)
49. OASIS WSBPEL TC. Web services business process execution language, Version 2.0. Technical report, OASIS (2007)
50. ter Beek, M.H., Fantechi, A., Gnesi, S., Mazzanti, F.: An action/State-based model-checking approach for the analysis of communication protocols for service-oriented applications. In: Leue, S., Merino, P. (eds.) FMICS 2007. LNCS, vol. 4916, pp. 133–148. Springer, Heidelberg (2008)
51. Tribastone, M.: The PEPA Plug-in Project. In: Quantitative Evaluation of Systems, pp. 53–54. IEEE, Los Alamitos (2007)
52. van der Aalst, W., Beisiegel, M., van Hee, K., Konig, D.: An soa-based architecture framework. Journal of Business Process Integration and Management 2(2), 91–101 (2007)
53. Vankayala, V.: Business process modelling using SRML (Advanced System Design - Project Dissertation) (2008)

Appendix A — The Iconography

icon	represents	type
name: type	component interface (instantiated when a new session starts; the lifetime is that of the session)	business role (orchestration of inter-actions)
name: type	requires-interface (bound during service execution after discovery)	business protocol (properties required of external services)
name: type	provides-interface (bound when a new session starts)	business protocol (properties offered by the service)
name: type	uses/serves-interface (bound to a component in the bottom/top layer when a new session starts)	layer protocol (properties assumed of the components in the bottom or top layer)
name: type	wire interface (instantiated together with the second party)	connector (interaction protocol and attachments)
constraints	external configuration policy	constraint system
conditions	internal configuration policy	state conditions

Model-Driven Development of Adaptable Service-Oriented Business Processes*

Carlo Montangero[1], Stephan Reiff-Marganiec[2], and Laura Semini[1]

[1] Dipartimento di Informatica, Università di Pisa
{monta,semini}@di.unipi.it
[2] Department of Computer Science, University of Leicester
srm13@le.ac.uk

Abstract. Businesses typically structure their activities with workflows, which are often implemented in a rather static fashion in their IT systems. Nowadays, system requirements change rapidly as businesses try to maintain their competitive edge, calling for similar agility of the IT systems. To this end, we present STPOWLA, an approach that marries service oriented architecture, policies and workflows to support the agile execution of business workflows. In STPOWLA, the business is modelled by workflows, whose tasks are eventually carried out by services. Adapatation is obtained by allowing the stakeholders to define policies that establish the quality levels required of the services. The prototype STPOWLA support architecture comprizes the transformation of the workflow model into executable WS–BPEL to be deployed in the ODE–BPEL execution engine, the generation of default policies from the model, and the enactment of the policies by the APPEL policy server. The SENSORIA Finance Case Study is used throughout the paper.

1 Introduction

It is common practice, to reduce time-to-market, that enterprises federate their operations by networking via Web services, and these federations can change to follow evolving business goals. On a smaller scale, processes may need to adapt to temporary shortage of resources by simplifying, or even skipping, some steps. These environmental changes need to be supported while the software system is operating. The integration of Business Process Management (BPM) and Service Oriented Architecture (SOA) has been recognized as a promising approach in this respect [17].

However, the integration of BPM and SOA still requires large efforts by highly skilled personnel. Currently, the business rules introduced by business roles like sales or technical managers need to be mediated by business analysts who, thanks to their knowledge of the business processes, transforms them into directives to the programmers for updating the workflows, e.g. in WS-BPEL.

---

* This work has been partially sponsored by the project SENSORIA, IST-2005-016004. The authors would also like to thank Hong Qing (Harry) Yu for his contributions towards the implementation of the approach and his input to a draft of section 4.

M. Wirsing and M. Hölzl (Eds.): SENSORIA Project, LNCS 6582, pp. 115–132, 2011.

Charfi and Mezini [10] discussed the integration of rule–based languages and process–based service composition, considering either "to adapt one of the languages to be more compatible with the other by extending e.g., the rule-based language with process-oriented features, or the other way around", or "to enhance one of the languages with an interface to the other language, so that the features of the latter can be used in programs written in the former". They concluded that both approaches suffer from the lack of seamless integration due to the paradigm mismatch which the programmer is confronted with, and privilege an Aspect Oriented approach [11].

In the Service-Targeted Policy-Oriented WorkfLow Approach (StPowla – to be read like "Saint Paula") [12], we have integrated the two paradigms seamlessly, via the SOA: the workflow composes coarse–grain business tasks, and the policies control the fine–grain variations in the service level of each task. The integration occurs at the conceptual level and in the supporting environment, rather than at the linguistic level.

Being policy based, the approach naturally distinguishes between a *core* description of the process and its *variations*, which can be specified by declarative rules, and can be dynamically deployed or removed. This fosters Business Process flexibility, by raising the abstraction level at which the variations are specified, while at the same time providing an efficient implementation technique.

In the approach, business tasks are ultimately carried out by *services*, i.e. computational entities that are characterized by two series of parameters: the *invocation* parameters (related to their functionalities), and the *Service Level* (SL) parameters, related to the resources they exploit to carry out their job: Stakeholders can adapt the core workflows by requiring higher or lower quality of service (QoS), therefore consuming more or less resources.

The kind and granularity of the 'resources' that are identified in the business domain are often more abstract than bandwidth and power, i.e. those usually addressed in service level agreements. For instance, a task of a given type may need higher levels of authorization in given circumstances, and lower levels in others. In StPowla, the authorizing business roles are seen as resources, ordered along an *AuthorizationLevel* dimension: the identification of these *dimensions* is a key design activity in the approach.

The combination of workflows, SOA, and policies can be exploited at its best, if a coherent design strategy is adopted to foster flexibility. In a nutshell, such a strategy is to find the best balance between (i) keeping the workflows simple, i.e. without explicit choices that depend on the quantity/quality of resources available to the tasks, and (ii) providing large and foreseeing ranges of choices to the policies, to support modelling the business rules as they emerge.

In this paper we present the embodiments of the StPowla concepts in UML4SOA [18], the UML profile that introduces stereotypes for the relevant concepts (workflow, tasks, service level, etc.) in the standard framework of UML (classes, interfaces, activities, etc). The main contribution of the paper is the design of an environment to model, deploy, and run StPowla business processes. Note that, besides supporting the use of services with different service levels in the business process, the environment itself is based on a service oriented architecture, orchestrating a workflow engine, a policy server and a service broker.

2 The Modelling Concepts

STPOWLA is a workflow based approach to business process modelling that integrates:

- a standard graphical notation, to ease the presentation of the core business process;
- policies, to provide the desired adaptation to the varied expectations of all the business stakeholders;
- the SOA, to coordinate the available services in a business process.

More specifically, workflows are used in STPOWLA to define the business process core as the composition of building blocks called *tasks*, à la BPMN. Each task performs a meaningful step in the business, whose purpose is well understood at an abstract level by the stakeholders. That is, a task is understood as to its effects in the business, regardless of the many details that need to be fixed in its actual enactment.

Policies are used to express finer details of the business process, by defining Service Level (SL) requirements of task *executions*. The added value is that policies can be updated dynamically, to adapt the core workflow to the changing needs of the stakeholders.

Tasks are the STPOWLA units where BPM, SOA and policies converge, and adaptation occurs: the intuitive notion of task is revisited to offer the novel combination of services and policies.

When the control reaches the task, a service is looked for, bound and invoked, to perform the main functionality of the task. Functional requirements of the task are described in the task specification. Conversely, service invocation is always local to task execution, i.e., a service is invoked to satisfy the requirements of a task, not to satisfy some overarching business requirement.

A task can be associated to a policy. Indeed, the principal means to adapt a workflow to the needs of a stakeholder, is by intervening on the behaviour of the tasks using policies. To define a policy STPOWLA users can refer to the state of the execution of the workflow, as described by task and workflow specification.

In the following, terms in "guillemets" are the UML4SOA stereotypes for the STPOWLA concepts: A ≪workflow≫ is an activity action that calls the specified behavior, i.e., a lower level workflow; A ≪Task≫ is an activity action that calls the specified main operation.

Next, we present the STPOWLA concepts with the support of a *loan negotiation* process, part of the *Finance Portal* case study (Chapter 0-3).

2.1   Model Specification

In StPOWLA a ≪Task≫ is characterized by a ≪Taskspecification≫ via a *name*, a *description*, an *interface*, and a set of service level *dimensions*. The name and description convey the purpose of the ≪Task≫: in well established domains, they identify precise, even if informal, functional requirements for the task. The interface provides the formal signature of the operation carried out by the task. As already mentioned, a task is actually carried out by a service: the interface includes an operation called main, with the same parameters and return type of the required service.

The ≪Taskspecification≫ can specify a number of *service level dimensions* (≪NFDimension≫) that specify the non-functional dimensions that character-ize the service to invoke. Besides specifying the type of each dimension, the designer can define:

- the ranges within which the service level can vary. In the case study the non functional dimensions are specified as enumerations, and the ranges are the enumeration literals: manual and automatic; supervisor and branchManager (see Fig. 1).
- a default value. For instance, manual and supervisor in Fig. 1.

Then, the stakeholders can specify the service levels they require along each dimension, by installing *policies* for a given task, overriding the default value, as discussed below.

Finally, a ≪Taskspecification≫ can have *attributes*: they define properties of a ≪Task≫ that depend on the state of the workflow, and can be used in the policies to access the execution state and select the most appropriate service levels when the ≪Task≫ is activated. Attributes are specified at design–time and bound at run–time, e.g. on task/workflow entry, as a function of the inputs, and of the other attributes.

To sum up, from a behavioural perspective, when the control reaches the task, operation main is executed. The execution of main triggers the search and invocation of a suitable service, and returns the computed result. The search identifies a service implementation that satisfies the current policies, i.e., the policies to be applied in the current state of the workflow, or the default values for the service level, when not overridden.

Just like tasks, ≪workflow≫s have a ≪WfSpecification≫ defining their at-tributes and signature. Moreover, differently from tasks, their behaviour is de-fined explicitly, via an associated UML activity, whose nodes are either tasks or workflows.

2.2   Case Study: Loan Approval

In this scenario, a customer uses a web portal to request a loan from a bank. The request is forwarded to and handled by the *local branch*, i.e. the closest one to the customer's residence. At the local branch, to process the loan request, and

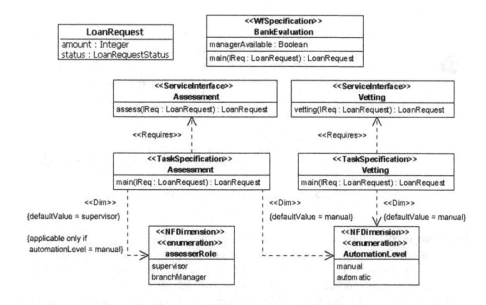

Fig. 1. The specification of BankEvaluation

before a contract proposal is sent to the customer, there are two necessary steps: a preliminary evaluation (*vetting*), to ensure that the customer is credible, and a subsequent step (*assessment*), where the contract proposal can be approved or rejected.

We concentrate on an inner workflow of the *LoanApproval* business process, *Bank Evaluation*. The diagrams in Figures 1 and 2 specify this workflow. As indicated by the main operation in the ≪WfSpecification≫, the *Bank Evaluation* workflow processes a *LoanRequest*, that is, the document collecting all the information on the loan being worked on . The actual process is in Figure 2, and shows the steps to accept or reject the request. The attribute managerAvailable reflects part of the state of the bank's branch enacting the workflow, and can be used to state the business policies.

Let us now have a look at ≪Taskspecification≫ *Assessment*, which characterizes the second step of this workflow. Its ≪ServiceInterface≫ identified by the ≪requires≫ association specifies that this task needs a service able to transform a LoanRequest[1]. This ≪ServiceInterface≫ is implemented by a service invoked by the task and can be adapted along two dimensions: AutomationLevel and AssesserRole. The former is a standard dimension that roughly distinguishes two kinds of implementations: those that exploit only machine resources, automatic, and

---

[1] The description of the transformation is not shown in the diagram, but should appear in the report containing it, or in a suitable pane in the supporting environment (for instance, in the *property* pane in the IBM Rational Software Architect –RSA– where the figure comes from).

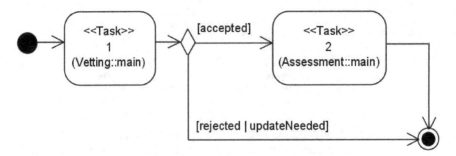

Fig. 2. The BankEvaluation activity

those that need human resources, manual. The second dimension may vary from one ≪Taskspecification≫ to another, since it classifies the different roles that, in different situations, can be involved in the ≪Task≫. Here, we have two such roles, branchManager and supervisor, defined as the default.

To deal with service levels, another stereotype has been introduced, ≪Dim≫, with a tagged value default to specify the default level. In the figure it is shown how the default values can be set in the model. Two dimensions of the same ≪Taskspecification≫ need not be independent: for instance, in our example, AssesserRole makes sense only if AutomationLevel is set to manual.

Besides its ≪Taskspecification≫, a ≪Task≫ also has a *name*, which is only used to distinguish different occurrences of the same task type in the same workflow. Therefore, we simply use integers as names for ≪Task≫s. The BankEvaluation workflow simply states that the request is first subject to Vetting and then, if accepted, to Assessment. In either step, the request may be rejected; after Vetting, more information may be requested from the applicant. The default service levels imply that a supervisor will perform Assessment. Similarly, a clerk will vet the request by default – not shown here. Variations can be specified by policies, as shown next.

2.3   Policies

A task may have associated policies, which come in two flavours: those that adapt the workflow by constraining the task behaviour along its SL dimensions, and those that modify the workflow structure, adding and/or deleting tasks. The latters are discussed in [7]; here we concentrate on the formers, and call them simply policies. For instance, the generic *BankEvaluation* process can be adapted to specific situations via policies, like:

P1: In case of loans of small amount, both vetting and assessment are performed automatically.

P2: In a small branch, the branch manager has to approve all applications.

P3: If the branch manager of a small branch is out of office, loan applications are approved by the manager's representative.

In STPOWLA, the policies act on the process by specifying the requested service levels as a function of the state of execution as expressed in the attributes. To this purpose, we use is APPEL [36]. Developed in the context of telecommunications, APPEL is a general language for expressing policies in a variety of application domains: It is conceived with a clear separation between the *core* language and its specialization for concrete *domains*, a separation which turns out very useful for our purposes.

In APPEL a *policy* consists of a number of *policy rules*, grouped using a number of operators (**sequential**, **par**allel, **g**uarded and **u**nguarded choice). A policy rule has the following syntax

$$[\textbf{when } trigger] \ [\textbf{if } condition] \ \textbf{do } action \tag{1}$$

The core language defines the structure but not the details of these parts, which are defined in specific application domains. Base triggers and actions are domain-specific atoms. An atomic condition is either a domain-specific or a more generic (e.g. time) predicate. This allows the core language to be used for different purposes.

The applicability of a rule depends on whether its trigger has occurred and whether its conditions are satisfied. Triggers are caused by external events. Triggers may be combined using **or**, with the obvious meaning that either is sufficient to apply the rule. Conditions may be negated as well as combined with **and** and **or** with the expected meaning. A condition expresses properties of the state and of the trigger parameters. Finally, actions have an effect on the system in which the policies are applied. A few operators (**and**, **andthen**, **or** and **orelse**) have been defined to create composite actions.

In STPOWLA, to specify tasks, we specialize APPEL. In this paper we only consider the specializations relevant to refinement policies, additional extensions exists for reconfiguration policies and they are introduced in [7]. The only possible trigger of a policy is the activation of the associated task (reconfiguration policies allow for a number of other triggers). To deal with services, we introduce a special action, req(-, -, -), for service discovery and invocation. The semantics of this action is to *find* a service as described by the first and third arguments (specifying service type and SLA constraints), *bind* it, and *invoke* it with the values in the second argument (the invocation parameters).

A *default* policy is associated with each task. It states that when the control reaches the task, a service is looked for, bound and invoked, to perform the functionality of the task (denoted by **main**):

```
when taskEntry(<args>)
  do req(main, <args>, [])
```

where **taskEntry** denotes the policy trigger, whose arguments are the task parameters, if any. Adaptation occurs by overriding the default policy. For instance, to satisfy the requirements expressed by policy P2, we associate the following policy to task Assessment:

```
P2: when taskEntry([]) if thisWF.branchSize = small
       do req(main, [], [AutomationLevel = manual,
                         AssessorRole = branchManager])
```

To ease the policy designer task, policies can also be defined by tables, whose structure is derived from the UML4SOA model of the workflow. A default table is automatically derived, which corresponds to the default policy: no discriminator appears, and the default value is assigned to each SL, as in Table 1. Then, the designer can redefine the default policy, by adding discriminators and SL values. For each new discriminator, the table is automatically extended, by building the decision tree, and by assigning the default value to the SLs. Finally, the designer can override any SL with the intended value. An example, relative to ≪Task≫ 2 of the *BankEvaluation* workflow, is given in Table 2, which reflects the informal policies P1 and P2 of Section 2. In a policy, task and workflow attributes are accessed by name, while the usual OO dot notation allows accessing the attributes of the task data, like in *lReq.amount*. The left side columns encode a decision tree, for the two discriminators $lReq.amount < 5000$ and $branchSize = small$: each row on the right side lists the required service level for each dimension (one per column on the right). For instance, if neither condition holds, the default values are requested for the service levels. The policy names are there for traceability, and the stars denote the only parts of the table that are input by the stakeholders.

Table 1. The policy table for task 2 – automatically derived from the workflow model

Policies for BankEvaluation.2: Assessment	
Requested SLs	
Automation level	AssesserRole
default: manual	default: supervisor

Table 2. The policy table for task 2 – interactively extended by the designer

Policies for BankEvaluation.2: Assessment			
Discriminators		Requested SLs	
iReqAmount<5000 ⋆	*branchSize=small* ⋆	Automation level	AssesserRole
true	true	P1: automatic ⋆	N/A
true	false	P1: automatic ⋆	N/A
false	true	default: manual	P2: branchManager ⋆
false	false	default: manual	default:supervisor

3   Design and Deployment

We distinguish two roles in the design of a system integrating BPM and SOA: the *BP Designer* dealing with workflow and policy specification, and the *Service Producer*, who is in charge of designing, implementing, and registering the services. We can also distinguish between *Workflow* and *Policy Designer*, since they deal with different aspects of the business process. However, we note that they normally work in the same organization, they both specify the requirements from a business point of view, they share the modelling of the task types like the one in Figure 1, and often they are the same person, namely the Business Analyst.

In this section we describe the process to apply the STPOWLA approach, and the tools we propose to support the designers job.

3.1   Workflow Design

The Workflow Designer defines the task types and orchestrates different tasks into an executable process to achieve a business goal which is requested by the end-users. To do that, he uses the UML4SOA profile as notation and the IBM Rational Software Architect (RSA) as editor. Once the workflow model is created (or updated), it is transformed into executable WS-BPEL [29] and deployed in the ODE BPEL execution engine [25]. Besides, policy tables templates, with the adaptable service levels and the default values are automatically derived from the workflow model, as discussed in the last part of the previous sections. The policy definition is also supported by RSA, which has been extended via the *PolicyDesign* plug–in, This way the designer is naturally offered the context for policy definition, that is task types definitions, including attributes and service level dimensions. Once specified and deployed, the policies affect all subsequent workflow enactments.

3.2   Service Design

For the moment being, STPOWLA makes a sort of "closed world" assumption: whenever a new task or dimension is introduced, new refinement services need be designed, implemented and deployed. The discussion that follows describes a method to specify these services.

Any service refining a ≪Taskspecification≫ implements the same ≪ServiceInterface≫ interface, but offers a specific kind of QoS, defined in an associated *capability document* (capDoc). For instance, an "automatic" implementation, and one that involves the BranchManager can be specified as shown in Figure 3 for *Assessment*. The ≪ServiceInterface≫ interface of the ≪Taskspecification≫ is refined respectively by the interfaces *AutomaticAssessment* and *BranchManager-ManalAssessment*. The capDoc tag of ≪TaskRefinement≫ specifies the capDoc describing which service levels the implementation must offer, that is it constrains the possible implementations. For instance, Table 3 shows the two documents referred to in Figure 3. So, the implementer has all the information he needs: functionality from domain knowledge and enterprise standards, service ≪ServiceInterface≫, and capabilities from the capDoc.

Note that the scenario we assume in STPOWLA entails a strict co-operation between task specifier, policy specifier and service implementer: this is possible since they all share the same UML4SOA model of the business.

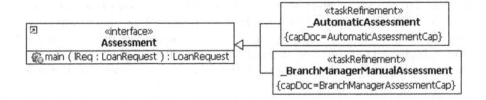

Fig. 3. Service specifications to refine ≪Task≫ 2: Assessment

Table 3. Service capabilities

```
<capDoc name="AutomaticAssessmentCap" serviceType="Assessment"> <and>
  <qos name="AutomationLevel" enum="automatic" confidence="1"/>
</and> </capDoc>
<capDoc name="BranchManagerAssessmentCap" serviceType="Assessment"> <and>
  <qos name="AutomationLevel" enum="manual" confidence="1"/>
  <qos name="AssesserRole" enum="BranchManager" confidence="1"/>
</and> </capDoc>
```

3.3 Deployment

The workflow and policy deployment targets three components of the run–time support, namely the three rightmost ones in Figure 4. Steps 1 to 3 occur when a new UML model is deployed: The BPEL representation of the workflow is generated by the central deployment service, the StPowlaDeployEngine, and downloaded to the workflow engine: We currently use Apache ODE (Orchestration Director Engine) [25] to execute WS-BPEL [29] representations of the workflows. Also, the StPowlaDeployEngine generates the policy tables templates and stores them back into the RSA. Thereafter, whenever a new table instance is deployed, the XML representation of the policy is generated and loaded into the APPEL Policy Engine [36,32]. The last component affected by deployment is the StPowlaEngine, that is, the core of the run–time environment. For each policy, it is loaded with the paths it will use to access the run–time values needed to evaluate the policy itself (more details in Section 4).

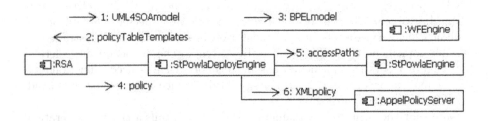

Fig. 4. Workflow and policy deployment

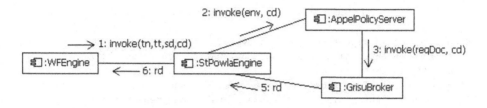

Fig. 5. Runtime STPOWLA choreography

4   Run–Time Environment

In this section we describe the tools we propose to implement the STPOWLA approach. There are four cooperating services and six steps in the run-time environment to complete a task (see Figure 5). The WFEngine interacts with the StPowlaEngine, which coordinates the AppelPolicyServer and the GrisuBroker to select a refinement per each task in the workflow, according to the current state and policies, and invoke it. The AppelPolicyServer selects the requirements for service discovery, and the GrisuBroker performs both discovery and invocation.

The **WFEngine** is the interpreter of the business process. All the tasks have the same BPEL behaviour: they invoke the StPowlaEngine, to detect and invoke the task refinement that best suits the current requirements. The StPowlaEngine receives the *task name (tn)*, *task type (tt)*, *state data (sd)*, and *call data (cd)*. The latter is the data for the invocation of the chosen service, while *sd* carries the relevant information on the state of the workflow enactment, i.e., the current values of the task and workflow attributes. In our example, the second task of Figure 2, the WFEngine will pass as arguments "2" , "Assessment", the current values of the workflow and task attributes (branchSize and managerAvailable), and the loan request, that is, the input argument to the task.

Then, the **StPowlaEngine** builds and sends the environment for policy evaluation to the AppelPolicyEngine. The environment has bindings for the task name and type, and for all the information in the call data and attributes that are used in the policies currently deployed for the task. In the example, the domain of the environment will be {taskName, taskSpecification} united with {branchSize, lReq.amount} or {managerAvailable} according to the deployed policy (P1 or P2, respectively). Remember that, to allow the StPowlaEngine to build such an environment at run–time, whenever a new policy is deployed, the relevant information is stored in the StPowlaEngine itself (step 5 in Figure 4)). To understand how this is done, we need to point out that i) call data are represented in XML, according to schemas that are derived from the UML4SOA model, and ii) state data are also represented in XML in a standard format, shared among the WFEngine, the StPowlaEngine, and the StPowlaDeployEnv. So, the StPowlaEngine knows which data to retrieve from the state and call data, and pairs them to the paths while building the environment.

Table 4. The reqDocs for policies P1 and P2

```
<reqDoc> <serviceType>Assessment</serviceType> <and>
   <qos name="AutomationLevel" enum="automatic" confidence="1"/>
</and> </reqDoc>
<reqDoc> <serviceType>Assessment</serviceType> <and>
    <qos name="AutomationLevel" enum="manual" confidence="1"/>
    <qos name="AssesserRole" enum="branchManager" confidence="1"/>
</and> </reqDoc>
```

The **AppelPolicyServer** determines the requirements of the task refinement service to call, in the current state of workflow enactment, and according to the policies currently installed in the policy engine. We are using the APPEL policy engine [36,32] to reap the benefits of its architecture. Indeed APPEL neatly distinguishes between the core mechanisms for policy evaluation and the extensions mechanisms that allow tailoring the engine to particular domains. Tailoring is done by defining the relevant triggers, predicates and actions: for STPOWLA, we defined i) the trigger related to task entry, which reacts to the invocation from the StPowlaEngine, and ii) the action that builds and returns a specific requirements document (reqDoc) for the service broker. For instance, when policy P2 above is triggered, the policy server returns the upper reqDoc in Table 4. Similarly, the policy server generates the lower document for P1.

The **GrisuBroker** uses the input reqDoc to discover a matching service, i.e. one of the correct ≪Taskspecification≫ and offering service levels that match the request. The discovered endpoint is used to invoke the main operation, with the call data as argument. The data returned by the service is then passed back to the workflow engine, which carries on with the workflow. Note that the lack of a matching service denotes a flaw in the design/deploy process. Indeed, due to STPOWLA's "closed world" assumption, whenever a new service is deployed the needed data access paths are stored in the StPowlaEngine.

For the two policies in our example, Grisu would discover respectively the capDocs shown in Table 3. Grisu can discover these services by comparing reqDocs (like the one in Table 4) and capDocs: no other information is needed. The format of reqDoc and capDoc is taken from the service broker DINO[26]: For this reason, our service broker is called Grisu[2].

5   Barbed Model Driven Development

When thinking of model driven development, the immediate understanding is that models drive software development, in the sense that the software is constructed by transforming models from higher levels of abstraction to the point where we reach a model which is executable with the desired degree of quality characteristics. What tends to be less evident, is that, precisely in order to

---

[2] Grisu is a popular Italian cartoon character, a small dragon: since DINO is a dinosaur, we see Grisu as DINO's child.

reach the desired quality, many other models are used in the verification and assessment of the solutions under consideration at the various stages of development. That is, looking at the development process, besides a spine of model transformations moving from highly abstract, domain related models down to concrete platform related models (programs), we can see a number of barbs, relating models in the spine to specialized models that permit specific, often very sophisticated, analysis of parts of the software under development, usually in the early stages. We called this approach Barbed Model–Driven Software Development [24].

Within the work on STPOWLA, we applied this idea to address the detection of possible conflicts among policies. Indeed, when several policies are composed (or applied simultaneously) they might contradict each other: a phenomenon referred to as *policy conflict*. Policy conflict has been recognised as a problem [31] and there have been some attempts to address this, mostly in the domain of access or resource control. In the case of end-user policies the problem is significantly increased by a number of factors. To name a few:

– the application domains are much more open and hence more difficult to be modelled,
– there will be many more end-user policies than there are system policies (sheer number of policies),
– end-users are not necessarily aware of the wider consequences of a policy that they formulate.

To provide the user with confidence that the rules are conflict free, we propose to filter his/her input to detect those policies that, if entered in the policy engine, would originate conflicts. The advantages include that we can anticipate conflict detection—traditionally performed at run-time—at design-time. Indeed, the well-known advantages of early verification apply to policies as well. In [20,21], we take a logic–based approach to this end: conflicts are detected by deducing specific formulae in a suitable theory. A translation function has been defined to derive the logical representation of APPEL policies in the temporal logic ΔDSTL(x) [22,23]: as a side effect, this function defines a formal semantics for APPEL, which before was only defined informally, like most of the policy languages. The translation maps a group of policies into a logical theory expressing its meaning. The temporal features of ΔDSTL(x) permit the expression of the dynamics of the rules, the event operator facilitates dealing with the triggers, and the spatial features permit addressing the localization of the policies.

More specifically, the filter maintains a logical theory representing

1. the relevant information on the domain, that is, interesting facts and inference rules valid in the application domain,
2. the set of policies currently *installed*, i.e. contained in the Policy Base,
3. a representation of the state space of the system, restricted to the part accessed when selecting the policies, and
4. the definition of what constitutes a conflict.

Then , it is sufficient to equip the filter also with a deduction engine for the logic in use: before a new policy is added to the Policy Base, its logical representation is added to the filter theory, and then the deduction engine is run: if one of the formulae identifying a conflict is derived, the user is informed and he can resolve the detected conflict.

Taking a similar direction, we designed a barb towards UML state machines to model check whether policies are free of conflicts [5]. To this aim, we have defined a semantics-preserving compositional mapping from APPEL to UML, suitable for model checking with UMC [19,37]. Since UMC operates on UML state machines, the target of the mapping happens to be a subset of UML state machines: policies and policy groups are defined using composite states, i.e. states with structure reflecting the one imposed by the APPEL operators onto policies and actions.

A policy in APPEL is built with triggers, conditions, and actions, just like state machine transitions. Indeed, triggers, conditions and basic map onto the UML triggers, conditions and actions that decorate the machine state transitions, in the natural way. This is fortunate, since they are domain dependent, and we can exploit the flexibility that UML provides w.r.t the language in which to express them, to best fit the domain peculiarities. Some more work is needed to map combination of actions since action combinators are defined in terms of the outcome of the actions under composition. However, this is true in a very broad sense that need not consider the details of the action semantics, but only an abstract notion of *success* and *failure*. Intuitively, these notions entail that an action may complete normally (success) or may abort for some reason (failure). Again, APPEL leaves the specifics of when an action succeeds or fails to the domain, and simply defines the success or failure of a composed action as a combination of the successes and failures of the actions under composition.

UMC is an on-the-fly model checker built to analyze UML state machines for properties expressed in the action- and state-based branching-time temporal logic UCTL [6]. In the case of policies, conflicts arise if a pair of conflicting actions is executed. To prove conflict freeness the full state space must be checked to exclude a path along which both actions are executed (in any order). The approach has been validated with the SENSORIA finance case study.

6   Related Work

Much work has been published in the area of business process specifications, ranging from natural English to structured languages used for expressing processes. BPEL [16] is considered the de–facto standard for SOA-based business processes, despite its initial purpose as a service composition language.

Policies are descriptive and essentially provide information that is used to adapt the behaviour of a system. Most work deals with declarative policies. Notable examples are the formalisms to define access control policies, and to detect conflicts [33,15]; formalisms for modelling the more general notion for usage control [38]; formalisms for SLA, i.e. to specify client requirements and service guarantees, and to *sign* an agreement between them [9,8].

Ideas of introducing flexibility into workflows have been presented by Reichert and Dadam [30] and in the Woklet system by Adams et al [3]. The formers discuss a framework for dynamic process change, but do not include support for changes to the workflow in progress. The latter is based on an extensible repertoire of sub–processes aligned to each task, one of which is chosen at runtime. The difference here is that our adaptation focuses on changing the Service Levels, thus providing guidance in the design phase.

In *AgentWork* [27], rules can be used to drop or add individual tasks to workflows. This is close to our reconfiguration policies [13,14]. However, there is no notion of tasks being linked to services in this work, and the policies are concerned with task replacement rather than task implementation or service selection.

A policy-driven approach is proposed in [34], to extend BPEL definitions with transactional behaviour, as the one offered by WS-Coordination. To actually enforce the coordination behaviour for the BPEL processes, as specified by the policies, a separate middleware system has been integrated in the architecture.

Among the various types of software tools available in the marketplace for BPM support, several business rules management tools (BR tools) became available in recent years. Among the most complete and promising solutions are Blaze Advisor [1] and JRules [2]. Recently BR tools have been including SOA integration features, such as deploying rule services as part of an SOA [28].

It is worthwhile to locate STPOWLA in the grid provided by two popular classification of the BR tools [4,35]. Being aimed at business analysts, STPOWLA falls in the knowledge–based BR tools, and can benefit the people/document intensive processes, which it can support with respect to workflow agility and resource management via its reconfiguration/refinement mechanisms. Historically, the knowledge-based BR tools have been targeted to decision intensive business processes. They foster 'rule–driven programming', with no clear difference between the rules driving the high level behavior of the workflow and those governing the application low level, such as computation and inference rules. In this respect, STPOWLA improves the overall structure of process representation with its distinction between core process and variations along the SL dimensions.

7   Conclusions and Future Work

STPOWLA introduces a novel combination of policies and workflows that allows the designer to capture the essence of a business process as workflow and to express variations in a descriptive way.

In this paper we have only considered *static* QoS requests, which involve no run-time assessment of the resources. Consider now P4: "In a big branch, the request should be vetted and approved by different members of staff". Without introducing cross-task requirements, the reqDoc for *Assessment* cannot be completed at design time, that is, it must be parametric and instantiated at run–time as a function of the identity of the vetter. On the capDocs side, one way is to introduce as many different task refinements as assessors, specify each one statically, and let Grisu make the choice. Alternatively, one should change the ≪ServiceInterface≫ of the ≪TaskRefinement≫, adding as a parameter the needed info (the assessor, for P4). In terms of service level, this amounts to characterize the refinement as being able to use any specific resource of the requested type.

We already mentioned that in STPOWLA we assume a strict co-operation between task specifiers, policy specifiers and service implementers, which share the same UML4SOA model of the business process. Looking for task refinements made available by independent providers, involving e.g. interface adaptation, is left for future work.

References

1. http://www.fico.com/en/Products/DMTools/Pages/
   Fair-Isaac-Blaze-Advisor-System.aspx (last visited: March 2009)
2. http://www.ilog.com/products/businessrules/index.cfm (last visited: March 2009)
3. Adams, M., ter Hofstede, A.H.M., Edmond, D., van der Aalst, W.M.P.: Worklets: A service-oriented implementation of dynamic flexibility in workflows. In: Meersman, R., Tari, Z. (eds.) OTM 2006. LNCS, vol. 4275, pp. 291–308. Springer, Heidelberg (2006)
4. Bajech, M., Krisper, M.: A methodology and tool support for managing business rules in organizations. Information Systems 30, 423–443 (2005)
5. ter Beek, M., Gnesi, S., Montangero, C., Semini, L.: Detecting policy conflicts by model checking UML state machines. In: Reiff-Marganiec, S., Nakamura, M. (eds.) Feature Interactions in Software and Communication System X, pp. 59–74. IOS Press, Amsterdam (2009)
6. ter Beek, M.H., Fantechi, A., Gnesi, S., Mazzanti, F.: An Action/State-Based Model-Checking Approach for the Analysis of Communication Protocols for Service-Oriented Applications. In: Leue, S., Merino, P. (eds.) FMICS 2007. LNCS, vol. 4916, pp. 133–148. Springer, Heidelberg (2008)
7. Bocchi, L., Gorton, S., Reiff-Marganiec, S.: Engineering Service Oriented Applications: From StPowla Processes to SRML Models. In: Fiadeiro, J.L., Inverardi, P. (eds.) FASE 2008. LNCS, vol. 4961, pp. 163–178. Springer, Heidelberg (2008)
8. Buscemi, M.G., Ferrari, L., Moiso, C., Montanari, U.: Constraint-Based Policy Negotiation and Enforcement for Telco Services. In: TASE 2007, pp. 463–472. IEEE Computer Society, Los Alamitos (2007)
9. Buscemi, M.G., Montanari, U.: Cc-pi: A constraint-based language for specifying service level agreements. In: De Nicola, R. (ed.) ESOP 2007. LNCS, vol. 4421, pp. 18–32. Springer, Heidelberg (2007)
10. Charfi, A., Mezini, M.: Hybrid web service composition: business processes meet business rules. In: Aiello, M., Aoyama, M., Curbera, F., Papazoglou, M.P. (eds.) ICSOC, pp. 30–38. ACM, New York (2004)
11. Charfi, A., Mezini, M.: AO4BPEL: An Aspect-oriented Extension to BPEL. In: World Wide Web, pp. 309–344 (2007)
12. Gorton, S., Montangero, C., Reiff-Marganiec, S., Semini, L.: StPowla: SOA, Policies and Workflows. In: Di Nitto, E., Ripeanu, M. (eds.) ICSOC 2007. LNCS, vol. 4907, pp. 351–362. Springer, Heidelberg (2009)

13. Gorton, S., Reiff-Marganiec, S.: Policy support for business-oriented web service management. In: Web Congress. LA-Web 2006. Fourth Latin American, pp. 199–202. IEEE Computer Society, Los Alamitos (2006)
14. Gorton, S., Reiff-Marganiec, S.: Towards a task-oriented, policy-driven business requirements specification for web services. In: Dustdar, S., Fiadeiro, J.L., Sheth, A.P. (eds.) BPM 2006. LNCS, vol. 4102, pp. 465–470. Springer, Heidelberg (2006)
15. Halpern, J.Y., Weissman, V.: Using first-order logic to reason about policies. In: Proceedings of the Computer Security Foundations Workshop (CSFW 2003), pp. 187–201. IEEE Computer Society, Los Alamitos (2003)
16. IBM. BPEL4WS, Business Process Execution Language for Web Services, version 1.1 (2003)
17. Kamoun, F.: A roadmap towards the convergence of business process management and service oriented architecture. Ubiquity 8(14) (2007)
18. Koch, N., Mayer, P., Heckel, R., Gonczy, L., Montangero, C.: UML for service-oriented systems, SENSORIA EU-IST 016004 Deliverable D1.4.a. (2007), http://www.pst.ifi.lmu.de/projekte/Sensoria/del_24/D1.4.a.pdf
19. Mazzanti, F.: UMC User Guide v3.3. Technical Report 2006-TR-33, Istituto di Scienza e Tecnologie dell'Informazione "A. Faedo", CNR (2006)
20. Montangero, C., Reiff-Marganiec, S., Semini, L.: Logic-based detection of conflicts in APPEL policies. In: Arbab, F., Sirjani, M. (eds.) FSEN 2007. LNCS, vol. 4767, pp. 257–271. Springer, Heidelberg (2007)
21. Montangero, C., Reiff-Marganiec, S., Semini, L.: Logic-based conflict detection for distributed policies. Fundamenta Informaticae 89(4), 511–538 (2008)
22. Montangero, C., Semini, L.: Distributed states logic. In: 9th International Symposium on Temporal Representation and Reasoning (TIME 2002), Manchester, UK. IEEE CS Press, Los Alamitos (2002)
23. Montangero, C., Semini, L., Semprini, S.: Logic Based Coordination for Event–Driven Self–Healing Distributed Systems. In: De Nicola, R., Ferrari, G., Meredith, G. (eds.) COORDINATION 2004. LNCS, vol. 2949, pp. 248–262. Springer, Heidelberg (2004)
24. Montangero, C., Semini, L.: Barbed model–driven software development: A case study. Electron. Notes Theor. Comput. Sci. 207, 171–186 (2008)
25. Moser, S., van Lessen, T.: Developing, deploying and running a hello world BPEL process with the Eclipse BPEL designer and Apache ODE, http://people.apache.org/~vanto/helloworld-bpeldesignerandode.pdf
26. Mukhija, A., Rosenblum, D.S., Dingwall-Smith, A.: Dino: Dynamic and adaptive composition of autonomous services (2007), http://www.cs.ucl.ac.uk/research/dino/
27. Müller, R., Greiner, U., Rahm, E.: Agent work: a workflow system supporting rule-based workflow adaptation. Data Knowl. Eng. 51(2), 223–256 (2004)
28. Núñez, S.: ILOG JRules 6.5 brings rules to SOA. InfoWorld: Product Guide: ILOG JRules 2007: Review (2007)
29. Oasis Organization. Web services business process execution language version 2.0. - primer (2007)
30. Reichert, M., Dadam, P.: ADEPT flex -supporting dynamic changes of workflows without losing control. J. Intell. Inf. Syst. 10(2), 93–129 (1998)
31. Reiff-Marganiec, S., Turner, K.J.: Feature interaction in policies. Comput. Networks 45(5), 569–584 (2004)
32. Reiff-Marganiec, S., Turner, K.J., Blair, L.: Appel: The accent project policy environment/language. Technical Report TR-161, University of Stirling (December 2005)

33. Siewe, F., Cau, A., Zedan, H.: A compositional framework for access control policies enforcement. In: FMSE 2003, pp. 32–42. ACM Press, New York (2003)
34. Tai, S.: Composing web services specifications: Experiences in implementing policy-driven transactional processes. In: BTW. LNI, vol. 65, pp. 547–559. GI (2005)
35. Teubner, C.: The Forrester Wave: Human Centric BPM for Java Platforms, Q3 2007 (2007),
    `http://www.forrester.com/Research/Document/`
    `Excerpt/-0,7211,38886,00.html`
36. Turner, K.J., Reiff-Marganiec, S., Blair, L., Pang, J., Gray, T., Perry, P., Ireland, J.: Policy support for call control. Computer Standards and Interfaces 28(6), 635–649 (2006)
37. UMC v3.5., `http://fmt.isti.cnr.it/umc`
38. Zhang, X., Parisi-Presicce, F., Sandhu, R., Park, J.: Formal model and policy specification of usage control. ACM Trans. Inf. Syst. Secur. 8(4), 351–387 (2005)

A Formal Support to Business and Architectural Design for Service-Oriented Systems*

Roberto Bruni[1], Howard Foster[2], Alberto Lluch Lafuente[3],
Ugo Montanari[1], and Emilio Tuosto[4]

[1] Department of Computer Science, University of Pisa, Italy
{bruni,ugo}@di.unipi.it
[2] Imperial College London, UK
howard.foster@imperial.ac.uk
[3] IMT Institute for Advanced Studies Lucca, Italy
alberto.lluch@imtlucca.it
[4] Department of Computer Science, University of Leicester, UK
emilio@mcs.le.ac.uk

Abstract. *Architectural Design Rewriting* (ADR) is an approach for the design of software architectures developed within SENSORIA by reconciling graph transformation and process calculi techniques. The key feature that makes ADR a suitable and expressive framework is the algebraic handling of structured graphs, which improves the support for specification, analysis and verification of service-oriented architectures and applications. We show how ADR is used as a formal ground for high-level modelling languages and approaches developed within SENSORIA.

1 Introduction

The IST-FET Integrated Project SENSORIA aims at developing a comprehensive approach to the engineering of service-oriented software systems where foundational theories, techniques and methods are fully integrated into pragmatic software engineering processes. The development of mathematical foundations and mathematically well-founded engineering techniques for service-oriented computing constitutes a key research activity of SENSORIA.

In this paper we report the outcome of some research efforts within SENSORIA aimed at developing formalisations of high-level modelling languages for service-oriented systems. More precisely, we present *Architectural Design Rewriting* (ADR) [5] and we explain how ADR can be used as a formal model for architectural and business design and how it helps in formalising crucial aspects of the UML4SOA and SRML modelling languages, see Chapter 1-1 (UML Extensions for Service-Oriented Systems) and Chapter 1-2 (The SENSORIA Reference Modelling Language), respectively, as well as the Software Modes approach [9].

ADR has been inspired by the long-term experience of SENSORIA researchers on Graph Transformation Systems, process calculi and software engineering and

---

* This work has been partially sponsored by the project SENSORIA, IST-2005-016004.

M. Wirsing and M. Hölzl (Eds.): SENSORIA Project, LNCS 6582, pp. 133–152, 2011.

has been entirely developed under the SENSORIA project, allowing us to establish interesting links with many other formalisms developed within SENSORIA and making it possible to strengthen the collaboration among different research groups with different expertise within the project.

Synopsis. § 2 explains the motivating principles of ADR. § 3 introduces ADR basics and explains how ADR can be considered as an Architectural Description Language on the basis of a running example. § 4 overviews some key aspects of ADR-based formalisations of UML4SOA, SRML and Sofware Modes.

2   Rationale behind Architectural Design Rewriting

The use of graphs or diagrams of various kinds is pervasive in Computer Science, as they are very handy for describing in a two-dimensional space the logical or topological structure of systems, models, states, behaviours, computations, etc.; the reader might be familiar, for example, with the classical graphical presentations of entity-relationship diagrams, of finite state automata and labelled transition systems, of data-structures (like various kinds of lists and trees), static and behavioural UML diagrams (like class, message sequence and state diagrams), of computational formalisms like Petri nets, and so on. One obvious advantage of using graphs or diagrams lies in their ability to represent in a direct way relevant topological features of the systems or models they describe.

On the one hand, software architectural models are intended to describe the structure of a system in terms of computational components, their interactions, and its composition patterns [12]. Using *plain hypergraphs*, the above perspective can find its realisation by modelling "components" and "connectors" as hyperedges and their interconnecting "ports" as nodes. Moreover, nodes, hyperedges and their tentacles can be *typed* so to discard erroneously linked systems.

On the other hand, in [2] it is argued that structured graphs are the most appropriate ones for service-oriented and global computing systems, where scalable techniques and open-ended specifications are important issues not immediately met by plain hypergraphs alone. Structured graphs offer better support for "understanding" graphs (like parsing and browsing large systems), designing systems (like expressing requirements and specifications, facilitating abstraction and refinement, allowing modularity and seamless composition), supporting automated analysis and verification (like model construction, model conformance, behavioural analysis, assessing sound reconfiguration and refactoring transformations) and last but not least, sound and complete visual encoding of computational systems.

Different kinds of structures can be super-imposed on graphs. The simplest one is enclosing a graph G in some sort of box whose label B implicitly defines some properties of the enclosed graph, i.e., its *style*. For example, Fig. 1 (left) shows some basic examples of "topologically" labelled graphs, that can be written, e.g., $Seq[G]$ and $Star[G']$ (for obvious graphs G, G' derivable from Fig. 1) or, equivalently, as membership annotations $G : Seq$ and $G' : Star$, where Seq can be read as the set of all sequentially-linked graphs, and similarly for $Star$.

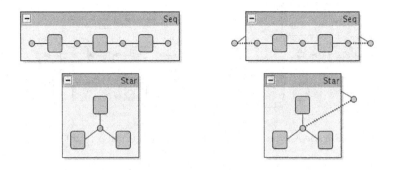

Fig. 1. "Graphs within boxes" (left) and "Graphs within edges" (right)

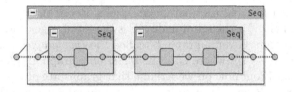

Fig. 2. "Nested graphs"

The natural extension of taking a "graphs within boxes" view is then the "graphs within edges" (or "nested graphs") view, where boxing can be iterated by allowing style labels that are edges themselves (see Fig. 1 (right)). Note that the boxed interfaces are now equipped with tentacles and that dotted lines make explicit the correspondence between inner nodes exposed by interfaces and actual nodes where the module is linked to. When the nodes attached to the tentacles of its (outermost) interface are read as formal parameters, we call it a *design*. This way, boxes can be read as enhanced interfaces allowing for more sophisticated forms of containment, strctured composition, modular specification, logical hierarchies, and node sharing, among others, making such features easily understandable also to non-specialists. For example, Fig. 2 shows that sequential composition of (nested) sequential graphs still yields a sequential graph. Note that if we remove all enclosing boxes from a nested graph then we are left with an *underlying* plain graph, but we loose any information about the conceptual organization of its elements. Thus in a sense, nested graphs can be read as "blueprints" of their underlying graphs.

3   Design Foundations

This section overviews the principles of *Architectural Design Rewriting* (ADR) [5].

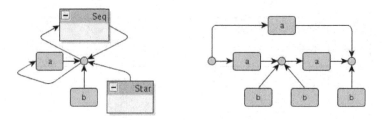

Fig. 3. A type graph (left) and a configuration (right)

3.1 System Configurations

A system configuration in ADR is the underlying graph of a design, representing the architectural units and their interconnections. Recall that a *graph* is a tuple $G = \langle V, E, \theta \rangle$ where V is the set of nodes, E is the set of edges and $\theta : E \to V^*$ is the tentacle function. Given a graph T (called the *type graph*), a *T-typed graph* is a pair $\langle G, t_G : G \to T \rangle$, where G is the *underlying* graph and $t_G : G \to T$ is a graph morphism. From now on we assume that graphs are always typed over a suitable type graph T, even if sometimes it is not described explicitly. Intuitively, a type graph plays the role of an architectural vocabulary and enforces certain tentacles to be connected to nodes of a given type, but note that a type graph T itself cannot impose any sophisticated topological structure on T-typed graphs.

The distinction between refinable components and non-refinable components in software architectures amounts to the distinction between non-terminal and terminal edges in ADR. The underlying idea is the same: a non-terminal edge is an edge intended to be refined (i.e., replaced by an arbitrarily complex graph). Non-terminal edges can appear in designs, representing unspecified parts of a configuration (a refinable component) or in design productions (see later). Terminal edges instead represent parts of a graph that cannot be further refined (non-refinable components).

Fig. 3 shows a type graph (left) and a configuration typed over it (right), where the typing is made explicit by the shapes and labels of nodes and edges. Refinable components are represented as group-boxes, while non-refinable components as plain boxes. The type graph in Fig. 3 includes both kinds of edges, while the configuration is *ground*, in the sense that it consists of terminal edges only.

3.2 Architectural Designs

An architectural *design* is a nested graph representing a structured system configuration. Technically, a *design* is a triple $d = \langle L_d, R_d, i_d \rangle$, where L_d is the interface graph consisting of a single non-terminal edge (the *interface*) whose tentacles are attached to distinct nodes; R_d is the *body graph*; and $i_d : V_{L_d} \to V_{R_d}$ is the (injective) function that maps interface nodes to body nodes.

For example, Fig. 4 shows three designs: the design on the left has a ground body graph that matches the intuition of its interface edge *Star*; the design on the

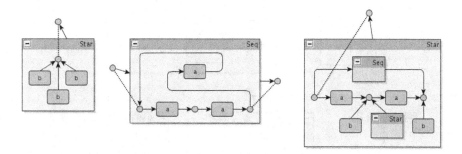

Fig. 4. Three designs

center has a ground body graph shaped as a ring, hence not exactly matching the intended meaning associated with the interface edge *Seq*; the rightmost design has a body graph involving all different kinds of edges and exhibiting little correspondence with the intuitive meaning of its interface edge *Star*.

3.3   Architectural Styles

To avoid the above raised problems, the shape of graphs embedded in a design must be constrained. To this aim architectures are designed inductively by a set of composition operators called *design productions* which enable: (i) top-down refinement, like replacing a refinable components with its (possibly non-ground) realisation, (ii) bottom-up typing, like inferring the "style" of a system configuration, and (iii) well-formed composition, like composing some well-typed architectures together so to guarantee that the result is still well-typed.

Design productions take inspiration from Graph Grammars [7], where hyper-edge replacement rules allow to substitute, in a graph G, a (refinable) edge L with a particular graph R, suitably connected to the nodes of G where L was connected to. Technically, a design production $p = \langle L_p, R_p, i_p \rangle$ is very much like a design but with an order on the non-terminal edges $\{e_1, ..., e_{n_p}\}$ appearing in its body graph (intuitively, the order of the arguments they represent). The *type* of a production p is $A_1 \times A_2 \times ... \times A_{n_p} \to A_p$, where A_k is the non-terminal symbol labelling the k-th non-terminal edge e_k of the body of the production. The functional type means that p can be considered as a function that when applied to a tuple $\langle d_1, d_2, \ldots, d_{n_p} \rangle$ of designs such that $d_i : A_i$, returns a design $d = p(d_1, d_2, \ldots, d_{n_p})$ of type A_p. The definition is obvious: $d = (L_p, R_d, i_p)$, where R_d is obtained from R_p by replacing each non-terminal edge e_k in it with body graph R_{d_k} of d_k respecting its tentacle function i_{d_k}, for $k = 1, \ldots, n_p$.

This view corresponds to a bottom-up design development: a design is constructed by putting together some component designs. However, the dual view is also possible: a production can be seen as a refinement of an abstract component of type A_p as an assembly of concrete and abstract components, the latter being of type $A_1, A_2, \ldots A_{n_p}$.

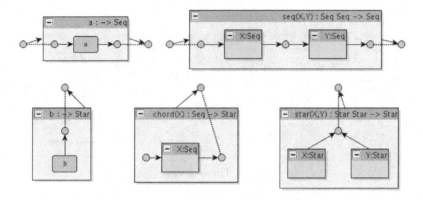

Fig. 5. Architectural styles for sequences and stars

For example, Fig. 5 shows simple design productions for configurations shaped as sequences (*Seq*) and stars (*Star*). Note that, according to the functional flavor described above, the labels of enclosing boxes are enriched with the information about the name of the production, the names of its "arguments", their types and the type of the result. For example, we have constant building blocks a and b (respectively for *Seq* and *Star*) and operation $seq(X, Y)$ that takes two arguments X, Y of style *Seq* and returns a graph of style *Seq* obtained by concatenating the two ends of X and Y to form a sequence and exposing a suitable interface. Another possible reading for the rules is the following: a graph has style *Seq* if it is either a single component a or the sequential composition of two other graphs of styles *Seq*; a graph has style *Star* if it is a single component b or a sequence seen as a chord, or the joint composition of two other graphs of styles *Star*.

3.4   Design Algebra

One key feature of architectural styles is that design productions provide us with a signature for defining graphs. Furthermore, the terms over such a signature do not even need to mention node names or edge names, because the way in which components are connected is entirely embedded in each operation (i.e., in each design production). For example, a term like $star(b, chord(seq(seq(a, a), a)))$ describes a ground configuration, that is conformant to style *Star*: a component b joined with a chord embedding three components a.

In general, it can be the case that different terms denote the same underlying configuration, like $star(b, star(b, b))$ and $star(star(b, b), b)$: they essentially correspond to the graph in Fig. 4 (left). In some cases this distinction can be even desirable, to mark significant design choices no longer recoverable from the configuration itself. In other cases, the distinction can be annoying, because the order in which certain refinement steps are applied is not essential. Often the latter situation can be dealt with at the level of design algebra by imposing suitable structural congruence axioms. All such axioms must be *sound*, in the sense that terms denoting non-isomorphic ground configurations must be kept distinct. However the axiomatization is not required to be *complete*, i.e. terms that are not structurally congruent may still denote the same graph (up to isomorphism). For example, the associativity and commutativity of $star(\cdot, \cdot)$ and the associativity of $seq(\cdot, \cdot)$ are natural axioms for our running example.

3.5 Design Reconfiguration

Software architectures might evolve in different dimensions. First, they might change statically when components are refined or architectures are assembled together. At run-time instead, architectures might evolve due to actions of normal behaviour or reconfigurations. Components leaving or joining the system can require correcting actions that lead the system into a proper state. Sometimes a reconfiguration rule can be described as a direct manipulation of a design or its corresponding term (without variables). However, reconfigurations arise more naturally and in a well-disciplined way at the abstract level of the architecture, i.e., as manipulations of designs. An additional issue that one would like to have in a reconfiguration mechanism is the capacity to give guarantees about the architectural style. For instance, whether it is preserved or not.

Reconfiguration as Graph Rewrites. Since our configurations are represented by graphs, reconfigurations can be defined as graph transformations [7], e.g. based on the single-pushout and double-pushout approaches. Basically the rules come with left- and right-hand side graphs G_L, G_R. Operationally, the rewrite can be applied to any graph G larger than G_L by finding a suitable match (i.e. an occurrence of G_L in G) and the result is the graph obtained from G by removing that instance of G_L and releasing a fresh instance of G_R. There can be items shared by G_L and G_R that are required to trigger the rewrite, but are preserved by the transformation.

This view operates on flat, unstructured graphs, thus disregarding the architectural information and, for instance, not guaranteeing style preservation in the general case. When style preservation is a requirement, we need either ad hoc proofs or a rule format that ensures that any reconfiguration of a well-styled configuration leads to another well-styled configuration. This is not obvious to set-up for graph rewriting techniques as one has to consider all possible contexts where rules are applied.

Synchronised Hyperedge Replacement (SHR) [8] is a graph-based framework for modelling the operational semantics of systems with mobility and multiple synchronisation. Several flavours of SHR semantics exist, but here we focus on a variant without mobility and with Milner dyadic synchronisation, where pairs of complementary transition actions (e.g. read and write) can be synchronised. Since each transition may carry more than one action the synchronisation might involve the whole system. In § 4.2 we shall see that this variant is suitable for defining SRML run-time semantics with ADR. In particular, rewrite rules in that style do not change the interface of components and this is a sufficient condition for the style preservation.

Reconfiguration as Term Rewrites. We have seen that design rules can be given an algebraic formulation in terms of many-sorted operations over a suitable algebra of typed graphs (with interfaces), with terms describing a particular style-proof. Note that in this way it is possible that: (i) the same well-defined architecture can be described by different terms; (ii) the same well-defined architecture can be assigned different classes.

Since style-preserving reconfigurations essentially operate at the level of style-proofs, the algebraic view can be pushed further by term rewriting over (style-) proof terms: a graph transformation rule is seen as a rewrite rule $l \to r$, where l and r are terms of our design algebra with the same type. Typically, both l and r may contain (typed) variables, but they are linear and all the variables in r appear in l. These variables can be instantiated in any way consistent with the types, and both r and l can be freely contextualized in larger contexts. Then, it is possible to apply the rule in any larger architecture $t(l\sigma)$, where σ assigns proof terms to variables and where the type of the hole in $t(\cdot)$ is at the same as the type of l. After the reconfiguration, the architecture $t(r\sigma)$ is obtained.

There is a simple sufficient condition for enforcing style preservation, namely that both the left-hand side l and the right-hand side r of the reconfiguration can be assigned the same proper abstract class. For example, the rewrite rule $chord(seq(a, x)) \to star(b, chord(x))$ can be applied under $star(b, \cdot)$ with substitution $x \mapsto a$ for rewriting $star(b, chord(seq(a, a)))$ to $star(b, star(b, chord(a)))$.

However, it is often the case that a structured architecture can be reconfigured only if all its sub-components are suitably reconfigured first. Stretching the analogy between reconfigurations and rewrite systems the expressiveness of our reconfiguration language is increased by considering conditional labelled rewrite rules, defined inductively over the terms encoding style proofs in SOS style:

$$\frac{x_1 : S_1 \xrightarrow{a_1} x'_1 : S'_1 \quad \dots \quad x_n : S_n \xrightarrow{a_n} x'_n : S'_n}{l(x_1, \dots, x_n) \xrightarrow{a} r(x'_1, \dots, x'_n)}$$

The labels $a, a_1, ..., a_n$ tag the kind of rewrite under consideration. The meaning of such a rule is that, given any assignment σ of concrete architectures to the parameters of l and r, the architecture $l\sigma$ can be reconfigured according to $r\sigma$ only if each $x_i\sigma$ (conformant to style S_i) can be reconfigured to $x'_i\sigma$ (conformant to style S'_i). Obviously, types are not preserved by some of these cases and thus the right- and left-hand sides of the rewriting rule cannot be applied in the same contexts. But this is not a problem because rules are intended to be applied in appropriate (inductively defined) contexts. When no tag labels a rewrite step, then we tacitly assume that its source and target have the same style and that the rewrite step can be applied in any larger context. For example the three SOS rules below account for sequence to star transformation:

$$\frac{}{a \xrightarrow{*} b} \qquad \frac{x : Seq \xrightarrow{*} x' : Star \qquad y : Seq \xrightarrow{*} y' : Star}{seq(x, y) \xrightarrow{*} star(x', y')} \qquad \frac{x : Seq \xrightarrow{*} x' : Star}{chord(x) \to x'}$$

Using them it is possible, e.g., to infer the one-step, unlabelled rewrite leading from $star(b, chord(seq(a, a)))$ to $star(b, star(b, b))$.

We shall exploit SOS style rules in § 4.1 and § 4.3 for modelling reconfigurations in UML4SOA and in software Modes.

4   Formal Support to Business and Architectural Design

We provide in this section a brief overview on the ADR-based formalisation of business and architectural design issues of UML4SOA and SRML.

4.1   UML4SOA Reconfiguration Profile

UML4SOA is a UML profile for designing service-oriented software, defined as a conservative extension of the UML2 metamodel, see Chapter 1-1 (UML Extensions for Service-Oriented Systems). Such a UML profile is the basis for the specification of a model-driven approach for the automated generation of service-oriented software through model transformations. UML4SOA uses extended internal structure and deployment diagrams. The extension for structure diagrams comprises service, service interface and service description. A component may publish several services specified as ports, which are described by service descriptions. Each service may contain a required and a provided interface containing operations. The orchestration of these services defines a new service. The extension for deployment diagrams is restricted to different types of communication paths between the nodes of a distributed system: permanent, temporary and on-the-fly.

UML4SOA profile aims at providing convenient mechanisms to model the inherent dynamic topologies of service-oriented systems: components join and leave the system, and connections are re-arranged. Such dynamic reconfigurations exhibit a number of beneficial features, but require a suitable mechanism to constrain the possible evolutions of system configurations and to avoid ill-formed configurations. In order to express such constraints on topologies, UML4SOA provides ingredients to specify architectural styles, and a methodology for modelling dynamic changes of configurations under architectural styles.

The main idea behind the ADR formalisation is that ⟨⟨fragment⟩⟩-stereotyped components, i.e. configurations, are represented by ADR designs, while the architectural constraints imposed by UML4SOA concepts such as multiplicity or productions are captured by appropriate ADR types and design productions. UML4SOA reconfiguration rules specified as ⟨⟨transformation⟩⟩ packages are represented by ADR rewrite rules. It is worth to recall that the main novel principles of the profile, i.e. style-consistent design-by-refinement and style-preserving, conditional reconfigurations are indeed the quintessence of ADR.

Figure 6 exemplifies how UML4SOA ⟨⟨fragment⟩⟩ components can be mapped to ADR designs: ⟨⟨service⟩⟩ ports are mapped to ADR nodes, while the port type determines the node type (e.g. UML types ChainingPort, CarAcccessPort and StationAcccessPort are represented by node types ●, ○ and ◎, respectively).

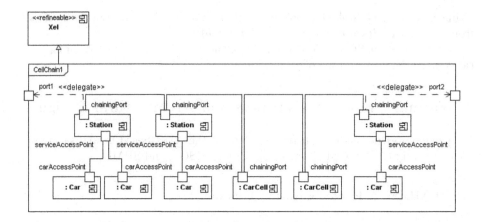

Fig. 6. A configuration of the *On Road Connectivity* scenario

Components are mapped to hyper-edges, where the component type determines the hyper-edge type.

The interface of the design is defined by the ports and the generalisation of the $\langle\langle\text{fragment}\rangle\rangle$ component. The ports of the $\langle\langle\text{fragment}\rangle\rangle$ define the set of interface nodes V_{L_d}, and each $\langle\langle\text{delegates}\rangle\rangle$ edge defines a maplet of the mapping i_d from interface to body nodes V_{R_d}. The type of the graph, as defined by the UML4SOA model, is determined by the generalisation of each $\langle\langle\text{fragment}\rangle\rangle$.

Modelling Architectural Styles in ADR. Refinable components and non-refinable components of UML4SOA specifications are respectively modelled by non-terminal and terminal edges in ADR. Internal structure diagrams and productions are the style definition mechanisms of UML4SOA; they are modelled by ADR design productions. Note however that some of the architectural constraints involved in class diagrams, such as multiplicities, cannot be expressed by type graphs directly. Indeed, type graphs do not impose any multiplicity constraint, i.e. they would amount to a UML $[0..*]$ multiplicity constraint. A suitable way to impose a multiplicity constraint in ADR is by means of design productions. For instance, in ADR the treatment of sets of cars in the UML4SOA specification via multiplicities is dealt with the design productions Car and Cars (see Fig. 7), which respectively allow to refine a generic set of cars as an empty set, a single car or the union of two other sets. In this way, UML4SOA productions are directly mapped into ADR design productions.

Modelling Reconfigurations under Architectural Styles. We just recall here that one of the advantages of ADR reconfigurations over other graph-based approaches is style-preservation, which is guaranteed by rewrites that do not change the overall type (they can actually change the type of certain sub-parts in the rule derivation of the overall reconfiguration).

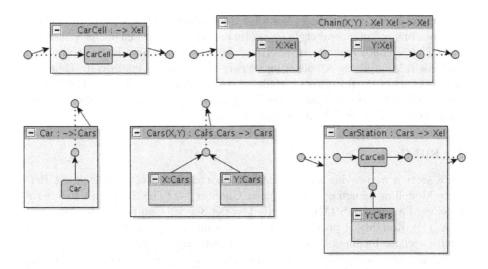

Fig. 7. Design productions for *On Road Connectivity* scenario

Translating UML4SOA reconfiguration rules to ADR in the general case is done by translating the precondition rules, the ⟨⟨transforms⟩⟩ left- and right-hand sides of the rule conclusion, and translating transformation labels into their respective counterparts in ADR. In this process, ⟨⟨pattern⟩⟩ components are translated to ADR designs by first producing ADR design graphs (replacing components with [0..∗] multiplicities by the corresponding non-terminal hyperedge, as done in the example with Cars) and then parsing the result using the ADR productions generated from the UML4SOA productions.

We show now a simple example of an ad-hoc network reconfiguration, which is modelled with inductive reconfiguration rules in SOS style. The base reconfiguration involves a single car:

$$\mathsf{CarToCell} : \ \mathsf{Car} \xrightarrow{\mathrm{tocell}} \mathsf{CarCell}$$

The inductive case we consider is when the union of two collections of cars is reconfigured as the concatenation of the respective reconfigured cells:

$$\mathsf{CarsToCellChain} : \ \frac{x_1 \xrightarrow{\mathrm{tocell}} x_1' \qquad x_2 \xrightarrow{\mathrm{tocell}} x_2'}{\mathsf{Cars}(x_1, x_2) \xrightarrow{\mathrm{tocell}} \mathsf{Chain}(x_1', x_2')}$$

Finally, the cell with the station shutting down is reconfigured by:

$$\mathsf{CellToChain} : \ \frac{x \xrightarrow{\mathrm{tocell}} x'}{\mathsf{CarStation}(x) \longrightarrow x'}$$

Obviously, types are not preserved by CarToCell and CarsToCellChain and thus the right- and left-hand sides of the rewriting rule cannot be applied in the same contexts. Type changing allows for the modelling of reconfigurations that lead from one architectural style to another. The last rule CellToChain, instead, is given as a conditional term rewrite rule, where the premise is in its turn a rewrite rule requiring a collection of cars to become a chain cell, while the conclusion actually transforms a chain of cells into a chain of cells. The type is preserved and the silent label makes it applicable in any larger context (unlike style-changing rewrites labelled `tocell`).

4.2 SRML

In this section we provide a formalisation of some aspects of the SENSORIA Reference Modelling Language (SRML), see Chapter 1-2 (The SENSORIA Reference Modelling Language). SRML is inspired by the Service Component Architecture (SCA [11]). Roughly, it provides primitives for modelling composite services and activities whose business logic involves the orchestration of interactions among more elementary components and the invocation of services provided by external parties.

In [4] we presented a formalisation of the design and reconfiguration aspects of SRML based on ADR. The main idea was to define an ADR architectural style of *correct* SRML diagrams and set of ADR reconfiguration rules correctly modelling the internalisation of services that occurs in SRML, both at design-time (static module composition) and at run-time (dynamic service binding). After recalling the work in [4], this section mainly outlines a formal semantics of the behaviour of SRML specifications based on ADR rules in the form of Synchronised Hyperedge Replacement (SHR).

More precisely, given a SRML specification, first we exploit the translation given in [4] to derive a corresponding ADR design term that evaluates to a particular design, and then we consider the application of SHR rules directly over the design and not over the design term as in the case of reconfiguration.

Binding-time reconfigurations in SRML. We consider a scenario that involves an activity OnRoadRepair that takes place in a software system embedded in a vehicle to handle engine failures detected by a sensor. When the activity is triggered, the system determines the current location of the car by using a GPS device, searches for the closest garage that can ensure minimal levels of repair and call a tow truck, and contacts a car rental service near the garage.

Some architectural elements of SRML are drawn in Fig. 8 and include service modules, service components, wires and interfaces. A module is specified in terms of a number of entities and the way they are interconnected. For example, the activity module shown in Fig. 8 (top-left) involves the following software entities: OR (the orchestrator that coordinates the interactions with the external services) and IM (the component that manages the interactions with the driver). These entities are interconnected through wires, each of which defines an interaction protocol between two entities. Typically, wires deal with the heterogeneity of partners involved in the activity by performing data integration. The activity OnRoadRepair relies on a number of external services that will be discovered on

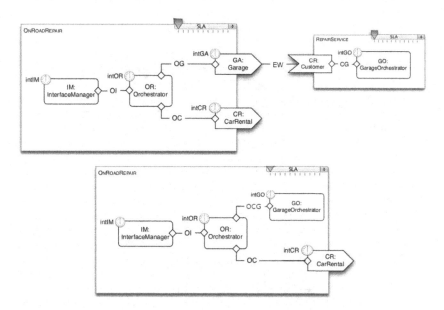

Fig. 8. An SRML diagram before (top) and after (bottom) composition

the fly: (1) the service for booking a garage and calling a tow-truck, and (2) the service for booking a rental car. This dependency is made explicit through the *requires-interfaces* GA and CR, respectively. As illustrated, every activity module declares interfaces of various kind: one and only one *provides-interface* that binds the activity to the application that triggered its execution (e.g., CR in module RepairService), and a number of *requires-interfaces* (possibly none) that bind the activity to services that are procured externally when certain conditions become true (e.g., GA in module OnRoadRepair). Service modules such as RepairService in Fig. 8 provide a service to the external environment and can be dynamically discovered and invoked (instead of being launched directly by users).

The graphical notation of SRML is inspired by the traditional boxes-and-lines or component-and-connectors notations and elements are shaped as in SCA. The structural constraints, in turn, require modules to be interconnected via external wires such that one of the require interfaces of a module is connected to the provide interface of another one. Inside a module, components and interfaces are connected via internal wires. An SRML architecture is given at the highest level of abstraction by an *assembly of modules* with possibly some discovered but not yet bound service modules (i.e., they are still connected via external wires). Figure 8 (top) shows the architecture of our scenario with the service module OnRoadRepair, where one of the two required services (namely RepairService, corresponding to the interface GA) has been discovered and connected via an external wire (EW).

An example of a reconfiguration in SRML is the *composition* of (already discovered) interconnected modules into a single module. SRML provides a

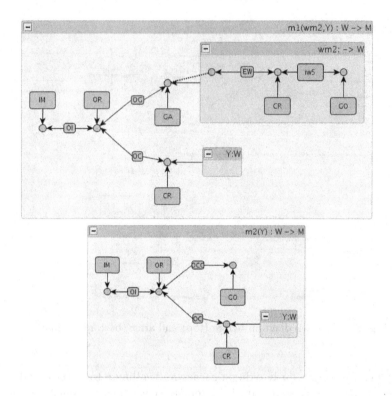

Fig. 9. ADR-view of SRML binding (top) and composition (bottom)

mechanism to achieve this static reconfiguration, by means of an algorithm that manipulates SRML specifications. As an example, the assembly of Fig. 8 (top) can be composed into the service module depicted in Fig. 8 (bottom), where the wire OCG is derived according to certain composition rules. Such reconfigurations require a proof of correctness w.r.t. style preservation.

The formalization of SRML in ADR given in [4] introduces suitable architectural elements for representing service components, internal wires, external wires, provide interface specifications, require interface specifications as terminal edges and activity modules, service modules, wrapped modules and their bodies as non-terminal edges. While the interested reader is referred to [4] for full details, we sketch here the basic idea of the modelling. Figure 9 (top) shows the ADR service module and wrapped module corresponding to the SRML diagram in Fig. 8 (top). When a binding is performed, then the wrapped module is plugged-in the service module. SRML composition is then realised via conditional rewrite rules that synthesize a suitable wiring out of the specifications of the require interface and provide interface of the composed modules, according to the internal and external wiring connecting them. The result is shown in Fig. 9 (bottom), where the internal wiring OCG is synthesized out of OG, GA, EW, CR, and CG.

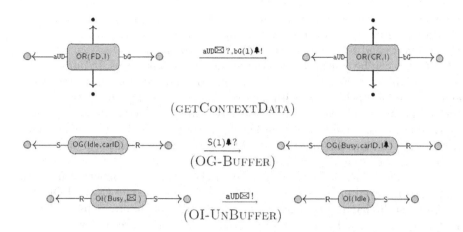

(GETCONTEXTDATA)

(OG-BUFFER)

(OI-UNBUFFER)

Fig. 10. Some operational rules modelling SRML behaviour

Operational Semantics for SRML. To illustrate the SHR modelling of ordinary computational aspects of SRML, let us consider the automotive scenario where the service execution is at the point in which a garage service has been discovered and bound (see Fig. 9 (bottom). The new configuration includes the components and the top/bottom layer interfaces of OnRoadRepair and those of RepairService. The representation of a configuration does not include the external provide/require interfaces because external interfaces do not describe an executable process. Note that Fig. 9 presents a simplified form of the actual graphs, where we just decorate the edges with the component and connector names, while additional information such as the type and state of components or the name of interactions are abstracted away. We shall explicitly represent some of those details when needed.

We continue our illustration with the representation of a transition GETCONTEXTDATA of the business role Orchestrator (to retrieves the data of the driver, for example from InterfaceManager) as a rule in SHR style (see Fig. 10): the transition label witnesses that the component is ready to receive (?) a reply event (⊠) on interaction askUsrDetails (aUD) and simultaneously send (!) an initiation event (♠) on interaction bookGarage (bG), while changing state from FD (FAILURE_DETECTED) to CR (CONTEXT_RECEIVED).

Note that the graphical representation of the rules is simplified for the sake of readability. For instance, not all interactions (represented here as labelled tentacles) are drawn. We put state information (local state, variables) as edge labels in tuples, and we neglect some of the parameters of the interactions. The type of interactions is drawn using different node types, so to forbid any mismatched connection: e.g. we use • for s&r and ∘ for r&s.

Observe that the various events involved in the transition (i.e. the trigger and the events to be sent) are put on the rule label. In this particular case the transition guard is implicit in the edge label (containing the state of the component). In general, guards are modelled as side conditions. Effects, instead, are just the resulting edge label. Transitions are thus given an atomic semantics: trigger, effects and sends are executed simultaneously.

SHR rules can be synchronised together using different styles. In our case, we follow the Milner style, where rule synchronisation requires an action being sent on a node to be synchronised with a corresponding co-action on the same node. Note that since a rule can involve actions of more than one node among those attached to an edge, multiple synchronisations are possible. In our example, rule GETCONTEXTDATA can only be fired if the surrounding connectors are able to perform the corresponding co-actions.

For instance, in the surroundings of the orchestrator component we find two connectors involved in transition GETCONTEXTDATA, namely OG and OI. The binding is such that the bookGarage and askUserDetails interactions of the orchestrator are assigned to roles S of connectors OG and OI, respectively.

All the rules that we need are such that the left-hand side and the right-hand side differ only in the label of the edge, meaning that only the state is changed, but neither the interface nor its bindings, i.e. the type is preserved. This condition is enough to guarantee that the overall design term is not affected by the application of operational rules. Part of the behaviour of the connectors include rules to buffer and unbuffer events (see Fig. 10). For instance, consider the rule to buffer the init event: it changes the state of the connector from Idle to Busy (buffered), and the received parameter I is enqueued (it is just part of the edge label).

A straightforward ternary synchronisation allow us to derive the rewrite

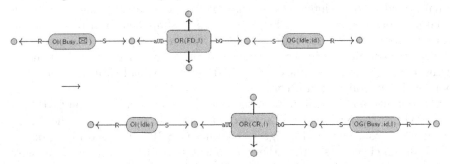

out from rules GETCONTEXTDATA, IO-UNBUFFER and OG-BUFFER. Such derivation synchronises a component with two of its attached connectors. In some cases, connectors might synchronise with both parties such that complex synchronisations involving multiple components and connectors are possible.

4.3   Software Modes

In this section, we consider the ADR modelling of Software Architecture Modes, as presented in [9]. There, a mode abstracts away a specific set of services that must interact for the completion of a specific subsystem task. Modes are first-class architectural ingredients that govern the architecural constraints and reconfiguration mechanisms of a software system.

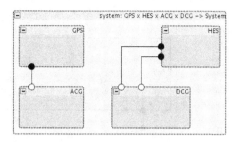

Fig. 11. The RPS subsytem production

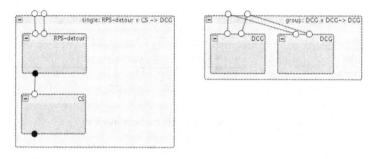

Fig. 12. Building detour convoy groups

Service Modes extend the concept of Software Architecture Modes with that of behaviour and policy specifications for service adaptation and dynamic reconfiguration. Service Modes are specifically aimed at specifying "operational adaptation" for a service-oriented system. They are based upon an evolving set of scenarios describing service component architecture, behaviour and events which trigger reconfiguration, whilst upholding quiescence in service operation.

We illustrate the ADR formalisation of modes with a road assistance scenario of the automotive case study. In the scenario, cars are equipped with navigation systems connected to a road assistance service platform. The focus of our example is on the Route Planning Subsystem (RPS) which is in charge of providing guiding indications to the driver. The RPS has three modes of operation: *Autonomous*, i.e. connected to the GPS to establish the route, *Convoy*, i.e. following another car, *Detour*, i.e. following indications from the Highway Emergency system (HES).

The components that form the RPS subsystem are the Global Positioning System (GPS) the Highway Emergency System (HES), the Route Planning Subsystem (RPS), the Planner (P), the User Interface (UI), and the User Prompt (UP). Some of these (sub)components can be in a different mode. For instance, P can be in modes P-*Master* or P-*Slave*, while the user interface UI and prompt UP can be in modes *Enable* or *Disable*.

Informally, the main architectural constraints require that an RPS must be composed of a P, an UI and an UP. The mode of the RPS depends on the modes

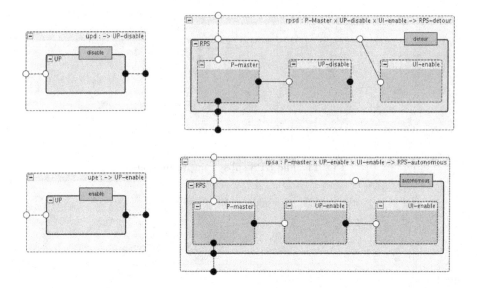

Fig. 13. Building RPSs in various modes

of its constituents. Convoys are formed by a leader RPS followed by RPSs in convoy mode. Leaders can be either in autonomous or detour mode. Autonomous RPSs are connected to the GPS. Detour RPSs are connected to the HES.

The main idea of the formalisation with ADR is to encode a software class as a type T and its various modes as subsorts T-M of T. Additional types can stand for complex constructions (shapes, styles, patterns) such as sequences, sets or trees. Such types can be used to define composition operations that determine the valid configurations. Mode types play a relevant role in reconfigurations.

Structural constraints are captured by a set of ADR design productions that build conformant configurations. For instance, we use productions to build systems (see Fig. 11) and Detour Convoy Groups (DCG) either as a single RPS in detour mode followed by a sequence of RPSs in convoy mode (Fig. 12, left) or two DCGs (Fig. 12, right). Dotted lines between ports denote interface exposure and not binding of actual ports (denoted by straight lines). The figures are drawn according to Darwin notation, but the correspondence with our designs is immediate (ports are nodes, boxes are edges and the flattening axioms apply if the contour of a box is dotted), except for the fact that each port binding actually corresponds to a terminal edge b. Whenever necessary (i.e., not implied by flattening axioms), we assume the expected properties for the operations to hold (commutativity, associativity, etc.). Similar operations are used to build Autonomous Convoy Groups (ACG): they can be built from an RPS in autonomous mode (RPS-autonomous) followed by a sequence of RPSs in convoy mode (CS) or from two ACGs. Productions are also used to build a CS as single RPS in convoy mode or as the concatenation of CSs.

There are also productions to build RPSs in various modes (see Fig. 13 for the productions needed in the examples that concludes this section). An RPS in autonomous mode is a composite component with a P in master mode, an UP in enable mode and an UI in enabled mode. An RPS in detour mode is a composite component with a P in master mode, an UP in disable mode and an UI in enabled mode. An RPS in convoy mode is a composite component with a P in slave mode, an UP in enable mode and an UI in enabled mode. Basically, each pair (component type,mode) has a corresponding constructor and ADR type. Constructors for HES and GPS are similar.

The allowed RPS reconfigurations are from Detour to Autonomous mode (and back) and from Convoy to Autonomous and Detour mode (and back). However, RPS components should not reconfigure independently: their constituents and contexts should reconfigure such that architectural constraints are respected.

For instance, a single RPS in detour mode is moved from the group of RPSs in detour mode to the group of convoys if that RPS reconfigures itself from mode detour to mode autonomous, i.e. if its UP reconfigures from disable to enable mode. Exploiting our design algebra, the corresponding rules can be written as the following (labelled) conditional term rewrite rules:

$$
\frac{\mathit{Xupd} \xrightarrow{d2e} \mathit{Xupe}}{}
$$

$$
\frac{}{\mathit{upd} \xrightarrow{d2e} \mathit{upe}} \qquad \frac{\mathit{Xupd} \xrightarrow{d2e} \mathit{Xupe}}{\mathrm{rpsd}(\mathit{Xpm}, \mathit{Xupd}, \mathit{Xuie}) \xrightarrow{d2a} \mathrm{rpsa}(\mathit{Xpm}, \mathit{Xupe}, \mathit{Xuie})}
$$

$$
\frac{\mathit{Xrpsd} \xrightarrow{d2a} \mathit{Xrpsa}}{\mathrm{system}(\mathit{Xgps}, \mathit{Xhes}, \mathit{Xacg}, \mathrm{group}(\mathrm{single}(\mathit{Xrpsd}, \mathit{Xcs}), \mathit{Xdcg}))}
$$

$$
\longrightarrow \mathrm{system}(\mathit{Xgps}, \mathit{Xhes}, \mathrm{group}(\mathit{Xacg}, \mathrm{single}(\mathit{Xrpsd}, \mathit{Xcs})), \mathit{Xdcg})
$$

5   Conclusion

This chapter collects results from [1,3,4,5,6]. In particular, we have provided an overview of main ADR features and the ADR representation of UML4SOA, SRML and Software Modes; the latter being original to this contribution. The formal semantics prepares the ground towards tool support for analysis and verification from the very early stages of modeling. Thus, ADR offers a comprehensive and pragmatic yet theoretically well founded approach to software engineering for service-oriented systems. Our current efforts are aimed at completing our tool support. First, by automatising the translation of high-level specifications in the considered languages, possibly by means of Maude-supported, MOF-based model transformations. Second, by upgrading the prototypical implementation of ADR into a tool that can be used to formally analyse ADR models either specified directly or transformed from other models.

In fact, ADR specifications can be exploited to perform formal specification and verification based on techniques developed, e.g. for term rewrite systems and graph transformation systems. For instance, ADR specifications can be encoded into Rewriting Logic [10] and benefit from Maude's built-in tools.

References

1. Bruni, R., Hölzl, M., Koch, N., Lluch Lafuente, A., Mayer, P., Montanari, U., Schroeder, A., Wirsing, M.: A service-oriented UML profile with formal support. In: Baresi, L., Chi, C.-H., Suzuki, J. (eds.) ICSOC-ServiceWave 2009. LNCS, vol. 5900, pp. 455–469. Springer, Heidelberg (2009)
2. Bruni, R., Lluch Lafuente, A.: Ten virtues of structured graphs. In: Boronat, A., Heckel, R. (eds.) Proceedings of the 8th International Workhshop on Graph Transformation and Visual Modeling Technique (GT-VMT 2009). Electronic Communications of the EASST, vol. 18 (2009)
3. Bruni, R., Lluch Lafuente, A., Montanari, U.: Hierarchical design rewriting with Maude. In: Rosu, G. (ed.) Proceedings of the 7th International Workshop on Rewriting Logic and its Applications (WRLA 2008). Electronic Notes in Theoretical Computer Science, vol. 238 (3), pp. 45–62. Elsevier, Amsterdam (2009)
4. Bruni, R., Lluch Lafuente, A., Montanari, U., Tuosto, E.: Service-oriented architectural design. In: Barthe, G., Fournet, C. (eds.) TGC 2007. LNCS, vol. 4912, pp. 186–203. Springer, Heidelberg (2008)
5. Bruni, R., Lluch Lafuente, A., Montanari, U., Tuosto, E.: Style Based Architectural Reconfigurations. Bulletin of the European Association for Theoretical Computer Science (EATCS) 94, 161–180 (2008)
6. Bucchiarone, A., Bruni, R., Gnesi, S., Lluch Lafuente, A.: Graph-Based Design and Analysis of Dynamic Software Architectures. In: Degano, P., De Nicola, R., Bevilacqua, V. (eds.) Concurrency, Graphs and Models. Essays Dedicated to Ugo Montanari on the Occasion of His 65th Birthday. LNCS, vol. 5065, pp. 37–56. Springer, Heidelberg (2008)
7. Corradini, A., Montanari, U., Rossi, F., Ehrig, H., Heckel, R., Löwe, M.: Algebraic Approaches to Graph Transformation - Part I: Basic Concepts and Double Pushout Approach. In: Rozenberg, G. (ed.) Handbook of Graph Grammars and Computing by Graph Transformation, pp. 163–246. World Scientific, Singapore (1997)
8. Ferrari, G.L., Hirsch, D., Lanese, I., Montanari, U., Tuosto, E.: Synchronised hyperedge replacement as a model for service-oriented computing. In: de Boer, F.S., Bonsangue, M.M., Graf, S., de Roever, W.-P. (eds.) FMCO 2005. LNCS, vol. 4111, pp. 22–43. Springer, Heidelberg (2006)
9. Hirsch, D., Kramer, J., Magee, J., Uchitel, S.: Modes for software architectures. In: Gruhn, V., Oquendo, F. (eds.) EWSA 2006. LNCS, vol. 4344, pp. 113–126. Springer, Heidelberg (2006)
10. Meseguer, J., Rosu, G.: The rewriting logic semantics project. Theoretical Computer Science 373(3), 213–237 (2007)
11. Service Component Architecture, http://osoa.org
12. Shaw, M., Garlan, D.: Software architecture: Perspectives on an emerging discipline. Prentice Hall, USA (1996)

Core Calculi for Service-Oriented Computing[*]

Luís Caires[1], Rocco De Nicola[2], Rosario Pugliese[2],
Vasco T. Vasconcelos[3], and Gianluigi Zavattaro[4]

[1] CITI and Dept. de Informática, FCT, Universidade Nova de Lisboa, Portugal
luis.caires@di.fct.unl.pt
[2] Dipartimento di Sistemi e Informatica, Università di Firenze, Italy
rocco.denicola@unifi.it, rosario.pugliese@unifi.it
[3] LaSIGE and Dept. Informática, Faculdade Ciências Lisboa, Portugal
vv@di.fc.ul.pt
[4] Dipartimento di Scienze dell'Informazione, Università di Bolona, Italy
zavattar@cs.unibo.it

Abstract. Core calculi have been adopted in the SENSORIA project with three main aims. First of all, they have been used to clarify and formally define the basic concepts that characterize the SENSORIA approach to the modeling of service-oriented applications. In second place, they are formal models on which the SENSORIA analysis techniques have been developed. Finally, they have been used to drive the implementation of the prototypes of the SENSORIA languages for programming actual service-based systems. This chapter reports about the SENSORIA core calculi presenting their syntax and intuitive semantics, and describing their main features by means of a common running example, namely a Credit Request scenario taken from the SENSORIA Finance case study.

1 Introduction

The objective of the SENSORIA project [Sen] was to develop a novel, comprehensive approach to the engineering of software systems for service-oriented overlay computers where theories, techniques and methods are fully integrated in a pragmatic software engineering approach. Specifically, SENSORIA focused on methods and tools for the development of global services that are context adaptive, personalisable and deployable on significatively different platforms over a global computer. A central role in this context is played by the linguistic primitives and the associated semantic models. They are needed both to describe, discover and compose systems and to prove that their behavior is consistent with the expectation of the designer.

In this chapter we report on the work for providing a foundational understanding of the Service-Oriented Computing (SOC) paradigm and for developing calculi for service specifications that allow for modular description of services and support dynamic, ad-hoc, "just-in-time" composition. We used process algebras as our starting point and added primitives for manipulating semi-structured data (e.g. pattern-matching), mechanisms for describing safe client-service interaction (e.g. sessions), operators for composing (possibly unreliable) services, and techniques for services discovery. The outcome was not a single core language but a few calculi differentiated by the chosen

---

[*] This work has been partially sponsored by the project SENSORIA, IST-2005-016004.

M. Wirsing and M. Hölzl (Eds.): SENSORIA Project, LNCS 6582, pp. 153–188, 2011.

level of abstraction, the chosen interaction/coordination mechanisms, the chosen primitives for orchestration. Indeed, process calculi are natural candidates as frameworks for the formal investigation and experimentation of new programming primitives and have indeed already been used in the area of concurrent and distributed programming to understand the different mechanisms for modeling processes interactions.

In the design and definition of the Sensoria core calculi, we started with the selection and classification of the basic mechanisms usually considered in the literature for the specification and development of service-oriented applications. The common basic concepts that we have identified are that of *service caller* and *service callee*. Upon service invocation, differently from what usually happens in traditional client-server paradigms, the caller and the callee can engage in a conversation during which they exchange the information needed to complete all the activities related to the specific service. For instance, a client of an airplane ticket reservation service usually interacts several times with the service before selecting the specific flight to be reserved.

In the service-oriented computing literature, two main approaches are considered to maintain the link between the caller and the callee.

Sessions: A private channel is implicitly instantiated when calling a service: it binds caller and callee and is used for their future communication [HVK98].

Correlations: The link between partners (caller and callee) is determined by correlation values. Those values are explicitly included in the exchanged messages and only messages containing the 'right' correlation values are processed by the partner [OAS07].

In order to investigate session-based service invocation and conversation, we developed the SCC calculus [BBC+06] following a minimalistic approach that can be synthesized with the *"everything is a service"* slogan. After experimentation of the calculus through the modeling of the Sensoria case studies, we noticed that a primitive for inter-session communication was lacking. In fact, if two distinct sessions need to interact in order to complete their activities, the only possibility in SCC is to open a new sub-session. But, the communication sessions and their sub-sessions is limited to the possibility for the sub-session to produce (a sequence of) return values. Due to this limitation, we have decided to investigate a number of different inter-session communication mechanisms to be added to SCC:

Dataflow communication: Different session can be combined using pipelines that implicitly direct the data returned by the sessions connected to the source of the pipelines to the sessions connected to the target.

Stream-based communication: Several named streams can be constructed among sessions, and the processes running in one session can explicitly indicate the stream from which they intend to receive messages.

Conversation-based communication: A single session, although initially established between a caller and callee, is allowed to progressively accommodate and dismiss participants, thus the concept of "conversation" is introduced which mitigates the need of always resorting to sub-sessions.

The extension of SCC with the three inter-session communication mechanisms outlined above lead to the three new calculi CaSPiS [BBDL08], SSCC [LVMR07a], and CC [VCS08], respectively.

As far as correlation-based service invocation and conversation is concerned, we have identified two possible techniques for implementing correlation sets. The first one follows more tightly the tradition of process calculi, adding a sophisticated pattern-matching mechanism on top of a π-calculus like communication. The second one, more tightly related to actual service-oriented programming languages such as WS-BPEL [OAS07], introduces the notion of state. More precisely, we have considered the following two forms of correlation-based service interaction.

Stateless correlation: In order to direct a message to the correct partner, the *most instantiated input* is selected. More precisely, an input operation selects via pattern matching the message to receive, and in case a message matches several input patterns, the one that requires less substitutions is selected.

Stateful correlation: Every process has a corresponding state consisting of valued variables. Given the *correlation variables* (i.e. those variables explicitly indicated as those driving the correlation), a message is directed to a process that contains in its correlation variables the same correlation values included in the message.

The modeling of these two forms of correlation-based service invocation and conversation generated the two process calculi COWS [LPT07a] and SOCK [BGG+06].

In the remaining sections we shall briefly describe the session-based and the correlation-based calculi introduced above. To enable the reader to appreciate the differences between the used formalisms, we will show how they can be used to model a a common running example, namely a Credit Request scenario taken from the SENSORIA Finance case study (see Chapter 0-3).

There are several parties that are involved in this scenario:

- the *client* that asks for a credit;
- the *supervisors* and *employees* that can be asked to review the request;
- the *portal* that interfaces clients, employees and supervisors with the services;
- the *orchestration process* that coordinates the whole procedure;
- some auxiliary services, like the *ratingService*, that are invoked by the orchestrator to assist during the request evaluation.

A Client that wants to submit a credit request has to first log into the system. If the login is successful then he will be asked for some credit data (e.g. the amount) and for some balance and security guarantees. Then the request review phase starts. A rating is computed for the client: either the credit is immediately granted (rating "*AAA*") or the intervention of either an employee or a supervisor is required (rating "*BBB*" and "*CCC*"). The decision (*refuse* or *accept*) is then communicated to the client. In case of *accept*, the client can decide to either *agree* or *decline*. In case of *decline*, the client can ask to submit an updated request. The client can withdraw from the request procedure at any time.

2 Session-Based Core Calculi

An important group of calculi for modeling and proving properties of services is the one based on the explicit notion of session. A session corresponds to a private channel that is instantiated when calling a service: it binds caller and callee and is used for their communication. Our first proposal has been the core calculus SCC that has been influenced by Cook and Misra's Orc [MC07], a basic programming model for structured orchestration of services, and by π-calculus [MPW92] the by now classical representative of name passing calculi. Indeed one could say that SCC combines the service-oriented flavour of Orc with the name passing communication mechanism of π-calculus.

Orc has been appealing to us because of its simplicity and yet great generality. Indeed, its three basic composition operators can be used to model the most common workflow patterns, identified in [vdAtKB03]. We have been aiming at a session based process calculus with a descriptive power similar to that of Orc but with the mathematical cleanness of π-calculus.

SCC supports explicit modeling of sessions that are rendered as private bi-directional channels created upon services invocation and used to bind caller and callee. The interaction is programmed by two communication protocols installed at each side of the bi-directional channel. This session mechanism permits describing and reasoning about interaction patterns that are more structured than the classical *one-way* and *request-response* pattern. SCC could be thus defined as a name passing process calculus with explicit notions of *service definition*, *service invocation* and *bi-directional sessioning*.

Within SCC, services are seen as interacting functions (and even stream processing functions) that can be invoked by clients. Service definitions take the form $s \Rightarrow (x)P$, where s is the service name, x is a formal parameter, and P is the actual implementation of the service. For instance, $\text{succ} \Rightarrow (x)x + 1$ models a service that, received an integer, returns its successor. Service invocations are written as $s\{(x)P\} \Leftarrow Q$: each new value v produced by the client Q will trigger a new invocation of service s; for each invocation, an instance of the process P, with x bound to the actual invocation value v, implements the client-side protocol for interacting with the new instance of s. As an example, a client for the simple service described above will be written in SCC as $\text{succ}\{(x)(y)\text{return }y\} \Leftarrow 5$: after the invocation, x is bound to the argument 5, the client waits for a value from the server and the received value is substituted for y and hence returned as the result of the service invocation.

A service invocation causes activation of a new session. A pair of dual fresh names, r and $\bar{r}$, identifies the two sides of the session. Client and service protocols are instantiated each at the proper side of the session. For instance, interaction of the client and of the service described above triggers the session

$$(vr)(r \triangleright 5 + 1 \mid \bar{r} \triangleright (y)\text{return }y)$$

(in this case, the client side makes no use of the formal parameter). The value 6 is computed on the service-side and then received at the client side, that reduces first to $\bar{r} \triangleright \text{return } 6$ and then to $6 \mid \bar{r} \triangleright \mathbf{0}$ (where $\mathbf{0}$ denotes the nil process).

More generally, within sessions communication is bi-directional, in the sense that the interacting protocols can exchange data in both directions. Values returned outside the session to the enclosing environment can be used for invoking other services. For instance, what follows is a client that invokes the service succ and then prints the obtained result:

$$\text{print}\{(z)\mathbf{0}\} \Leftarrow (\text{ succ}\{(x)(y)\text{return }y\} \Leftarrow 5).$$

(in this case, the service print is invoked with vacuous protocol $(z)\mathbf{0}$).

A protocol, both on client-side and on service-side, can be interrupted (e.g. due to the occurrence of an unexpected event), and interruption can be notified to the environment. More generally, the keyword close can be used to terminate a protocol on one side and to notify the termination status to a suitable handler at the partner site. For example, the above client is extended below for exploiting a suitable service fault that can handle printer failures:

$$\text{print}\{(z)\mathbf{0}\} \Leftarrow_{\text{fault}} (\text{ succ}\{(x)(y)\text{return } y\} \Leftarrow 5).$$

The original proposal of SCC was somehow unsatisfactory with respect to the handling of inter-session communications, thus variants of SCC that make use of different communication mechanisms have been put forward. In the next sections we shall analyze in sequences three of the variants of SCC that have been studied during the project.

2.1 CaSPiS: A Dataflow Service Centered Calculus

CaSPiS [BBDL08] is a variant of SCC that is *dataflow* oriented and makes use of a pipelining operator (*à la* ORC) to model the passage of information between sessions. A *return* operator is used by sessions for passing values to the environment and a new policy for handling (unexpected or programmed) *session closures* is introduced. Specific care is devoted to formal semantics and minimality of the operators.

Like in [HVK98], a session is a chain of dyadic interactions whose collection constitutes a program. Services are seen as passive objects that can be invoked by clients and service definitions can be seen as specific instances of input prefixed processes. The two endpoints of the same session can communicate by exchanging messages. A fresh shared name is used to guarantee that messages are exchanged only between partners of the same session, so that two instances of the same persistent service (that was invoked from two different sessions) run separately and cannot interfere. The central role assigned to sessions and the direct use of operators for modeling sessions interaction renders the logical structure of programs more clear and leads to a well disciplined service specification language that enable us to guarantee proper handling of session closures and in general simplifies reasoning on the specified services.

A gentle introduction to CaSPiS. Within CaSPiS, service definitions are rendered as

$$s.P$$

where s is the service name and P is the *body* defining the service behaviour. P can be seen as a process that receives/sends values from/to the client side and then activates the corresponding computational activities. For instance,

$$\text{succ.}(?x)\langle x + 1 \rangle$$

models a service that receives an integer and returns its successor.

Service invocations can be seen as specific instances of output prefixed processes and are rendered as

$$\overline{s}.P$$

where s is the name of the service to invoke while P is the process implementing the client-side protocol for interacting with the new instance of s. As an example, a client for the simple service described above will be written in CaSPiS as

$$\overline{\text{succ}}.\langle 5 \rangle (?y)\langle y \rangle^\uparrow$$

After succ is invoked, argument 5 is passed on to the service side and the client waits for a value from the server: the received value will be substituted for y and returned as the overall result of the service invocation.

A service definition $s.P$ and a service invocation $\overline{s}.Q$ running in parallel can synchronize with each other: in doing so, they must agree on a fresh session name r. As a result, a new, private session r will be created. The session has two ends, one at client's side where protocol Q is running and one at service's side where protocol P is running. For instance, the interaction of the client and of the service described above triggers the session

$$(vr)(r \triangleright \langle 5 + 1 \rangle \,|\, r \triangleright (?y)\langle y \rangle^\uparrow)$$

Values produced by a *concretion* ($\langle V \rangle P$) at one side of a session are consumed by an *abstraction* ($(F)P$) at the other side. A concretion $\langle V \rangle P$ can evolve to P by sending value V over the session. An abstraction $(F)P$ is a form of guarded command that relies on pattern-matching: $(F)P$ can evolve to $P\sigma$ retrieving a value V matching the pattern F with substitution σ ($match(F, V) = \sigma$). Here, the pattern-matching function *match* is defined as expected: $match(F, V) = \sigma$, if σ is the (only) substitution such that $\text{dom}(\sigma) = \text{bn}(F)$ and $F\sigma = V$.

In the example above, value 6 is computed at the service-side and then received at the client side; the remaining activity is then performed by the client-side of the session

$$r \triangleright \langle 6 \rangle^\uparrow$$

that emits the value 6 outside of the session and becomes

$$r \triangleright \mathbf{0}$$

where $\mathbf{0}$ denotes the empty process. Indeed, the return primitive $\langle V \rangle^\uparrow P$ can be used to return a value *outside* the current session, if the enclosing environment is capable of consuming it.

Values returned outside of the session (to the enclosing environment) with the return operator $\langle \cdot \rangle^\uparrow$ can be used for invoking other services. Indeed, processes can be composed by using the *pipeline* operator

$$P > Q.$$

A new instance of process Q is activated in correspondence of each of the values produced by P that Q can receive. For instance, what follows is a client that invokes the service succ and then prints the obtained result:

$$\langle 5 \rangle > (?x)\overline{\text{succ}}.\langle x \rangle (?y)\langle y \rangle^\uparrow > (?z)\overline{\text{print}}.\langle z \rangle$$

To improve usability, structured values are permitted; services are invoked using structured values that drive usage of the exchanged information. Using this approach, each service can provide different *methods* corresponding to the exposed activities. For instance:

$$\texttt{calculator.} (\text{"sum"}, ?x, ?y)\langle\text{"result"}, x + y\rangle$$
$$+ (\text{"sub"}, ?x, ?y)\langle\text{"result"}, x - y\rangle$$
$$+ (\text{"mul"}, ?x, ?y)\langle\text{"result"}, x * y\rangle$$
$$+ (\text{"div"}, ?x, ?y)\langle\text{"result"}, x/y\rangle$$

models a service `calculator` that exposes the methods for computing the basic arithmetic operations. This service can be invoked as follows:

$$\overline{\texttt{calculator.}}\langle\text{"sum"}, 2, 4\rangle(\text{"result"}, ?y)\langle y\rangle^{\uparrow}.$$

A similar approach is used for session interaction. Indeed, thanks to tags and pattern matching, more sophisticated protocols can be programmed for both the server and client side of a session. For instance, a service-side can reply to a client request with different values denoting the status of the execution:

$$r \rhd (\text{"fail"}, ?x)P_1 + (\text{"result"}, ?y)P_2.$$

Till now, we have seen that CaSPiS permits to define private dyadic sessions between a caller and a callee and that in principle, each side has a protocol to execute and the conversation is concluded when both protocols terminate. On the other hand, if some unexpected event happens on one side, then the session and the corresponding partner would be stuck. This motivates the introduction of suitable primitives for handling the proper closure of a session.

These primitives might be useful to garbage-collect terminated sessions. Most important, one might want to explicitly program session termination, or to manage abnormal events, or timeouts. Being sessions units of client-server cooperation, their termination must be programmed carefully. At least, one should avoid situations where one side of the session is removed abruptly and leaves the other side dangling. CaSPiS comprises a disciplined mechanism for closing sessions following this guidelines:

- a partner can abandon a session at any time, by taking unilateral decision;
- a side cannot force the other one to abandon the session, unless it is willing to;
- if a side abandon a session, then the partner must be informed;
- in case the abandoned session contains nested subsections, then they must be abandoned as well (and their partners must be informed);
- the completion of a session is the default commit, the unexpected abandoning of one side is a failure to be handled by the remaining partner.
- each side must be given the possibility of programming suitable counteractions to be triggered if the partner abandons the session.

The syntax of CaSPiS is reported in Fig. 1. We will call close -free the fragment of the calculus obtained from Fig. 1 by removing close, listeners, signals and terminated sessions. We assume the following disjoint sets

- a countable set of *names* N ranged over by $n, n', ...$
- a countable set of *signal names* $\mathcal{K}$ ranged over by $k, k', ...$
- a signature σ of *constructors* $f, f', ...$, each coming with an integer arity.

$\mathcal{N}$ is assumed to contain two disjoint countable sets $\mathcal{N}_{\text{srv}}$ of *service* names $s, s', \ldots$ and $\mathcal{N}_{\text{sess}}$ of *session* names $r, r' \ldots$, such that $\mathcal{N} \setminus (\mathcal{N}_{\text{srv}} \cup \mathcal{N}_{\text{sess}})$ is infinite. The set $\mathcal{N} \setminus \mathcal{N}_{\text{sess}}$ is ranged over by $x, y, \ldots, u, v \ldots$.

Concerning basic values, note that, for simplicity, we only consider value expressions V built out of constructors in Σ and names $x, y, \ldots, u, v, \ldots$, the latter playing the role of variables or basic values depending on the context. We leave the signature Σ unspecified, but in several examples we shall assume Σ contains tuple constructors $\langle \cdot, \ldots, \cdot \rangle$ of arbitrary arity. Richer languages of expressions, comprising specific data values and evaluation mechanisms, are easy to accommodate. Finally, it is worth to note that session names $r, r', \ldots$ do *not* appear in values or patterns: this implies that they cannot be passed around.

Notice how, in Fig. 1, service and session names are annotated with signal names; such annotations have been introduced to handle the premature closure of sessions. The idea is that upon creation of a session, one associates with the session a pair of names (k_1, k_2), identifying a pair of *termination handlers* services, one for each side ($k_1 \cdot P_1$ specified in the service definition and $k_2 \cdot P_2$ in the service call, respectively). Then: (a) a session side is unilaterally terminated when its protocol executes the command close; (b) the execution of close triggers a signal $\dagger(k)$ sent to the termination-handler service k_i listening at the *opposite* side of the session; (c) at the same time, the session side that has executed close will enter a special closing state denoted $\blacktriangleright P$, where all subsessions of P will be gradually closed. In order to accomplish (b) the name k_i must be known to the current side of the session. To this end, in sessions $r \rhd_k P$ the subscript k refers to the termination handler of the opposite side. To sum up the above discussion, we have that $r \rhd_k (\text{close} \mid P)$ may evolve to $\dagger(k) \mid \blacktriangleright P$. Note that the operator $\blacktriangleright$ should stop any activity *but* invocations $\dagger(k)$ of other handlers. Information about termination handlers to be used is agreed upon by the two sides at invocation time. To this purpose, invocation, $\overline{s}_{k_1}.Q$, mentions a name k_1 at which the termination handler of the client-side is listening. Symmetrically, service definition, $s_{k_2}.P$, mentions a name k_2 at which the termination handler of the service-side is listening. Then $\overline{s}_{k_1}.Q \mid s_{k_2}.P$ can evolve to $(vr)(r \rhd_{k_2} Q \mid r \rhd_{k_1} P)$: in this way, if Q terminates with close, the termination handler k_2 of the callee will be activated, and vice versa.

Note that the simple pattern $(vk)\overline{s}_k.(Q \mid k \cdot \text{close})$ defines a default protocol for closing the own session after receiving the closure signal from the partner. As another example, the encoding of high level transactional constructs, such as compensation pairs $S \div C$, where S is a certain activity to be executed (e.g. a service call) and C is the corresponding compensation, could be encoded in CaSPiS as $(vk)\overline{S}_k.(k \cdot C)$.

As expected, in $(vn)P$, the restriction (vn) binds free occurrences of n in P, while in $(F).P$ any $?x$ in (F) binds free occurrences of name x in P.

In order to simplify the specification of many important patterns for service composition, some CaSPiS derived operators, defined as macros, have been presented in [BBDL08]. Here, we consider some of these macros that will be used in the sequel.

First of all we will abbreviate $\overline{s}.\langle V \rangle (?x)\langle x \rangle^\uparrow$ as $\overline{s}(V)$. This process implements a functional interaction that invokes s, sends value V over the established session, then waits for a value (the result of service invocation) and publishes it locally. $\sum_{i \in I} \tau P_i$ will stand

$$P, Q ::= \sum_{i \in I} \pi_i P_i \quad \text{Guarded Sum} \qquad \pi ::= (F) \qquad \text{Abstraction}$$

$$\begin{array}{llll}
& | \; s_k.P & \text{Service Definition} & \quad | \; \langle V \rangle & \text{Concretion} \\
& | \; \bar{s}_k.P & \text{Service Invocation} & \quad | \; \langle V \rangle^\uparrow & \text{Return} \\
& | \; r_k \triangleright P & \text{Session} & & \\
& | \; P > Q & \text{Pipeline} & \quad V ::= u \, | \, f(\tilde{V}) & \text{Value } (f \in \Sigma) \\
& | \; P|Q & \text{Parallel Composition} & & \\
& | \; (\nu n)P & \text{Restriction} & \quad F ::= \, ?x \, | \, u \, | \, f(\tilde{F}) & \text{Pattern } (f \in \Sigma) \\
& | \; !P & \text{Replication} & & \\
& | \; \text{close} & \text{Close} & & \\
& | \; k \cdot P & \text{Listener} & & \\
& | \; \dagger(k) & \text{Signal} & & \\
& | \; \blacktriangleright P & \text{Terminated Session} & &
\end{array}$$

Fig. 1. Syntax of CaSPiS processes

for $\langle \bullet \rangle^\uparrow > \sum_{i \in I}(?x)P_i$, with $x \notin \bigcup_{i \in I} \text{fn}(P_i)$. We will use also the following abbreviations:

select $F_1, \ldots, F_n$ **from** P **in** Q is a process that waits for the first n values emitted by P matching patterns $F_1, \ldots, F_n$. Once these n values have been collected, process Q is activated.

wait $F_1, \ldots, F_n$ **from** $P_1, \ldots, P_n$ **in** Q is a process that waits for a tuple $(V_1, \ldots, V_n)$, where V_i is the first value emitted by P_i matching F_i, and then activates process Q.

select $?x$ **from** $\bar{s}(V)$ **inif** $(x = F_1)$ **then** P_1 **elseif** $(x = F_2)$ **then** P_2 **elseif** $\cdots$ **else** P_{n+1} is a process that binds to x the first value emitted by the service call $\bar{s}(V)$ and then activates P_i if the ith guard is true. If no-one of the n guards is satisfied then P_{n+1} is activated.

The Credit Request scenario. Here, we will show how the Credit Request Scenario, briefly described in the Introduction, can be specified in CaSPiS.

The scenario is modeled by introducing some simplifications. First, we leave some of the auxiliary services unspecified: below, these services are supposed to receive some data and then send a reply to the invoker, after some internal computations that always terminate (e.g. access to databases). As an example, we specify the service CheckUser, that receives the user's credentials and checks their validity by sending back the result of the evaluation of the internal function **auth**(*user*). Moreover, for the sake of brevity, we omit the parallelism between the requests for balances and for securities and fix an ordering (balances will be demanded first).

Finally, we will merge the behaviour of the *portal* and of the *client* into the *CreditRequester* participant. The orchestration process is modeled by the process *CreditPortal*. The latter offers the service CrReq that can be invoked by clients in order to start the credit request procedure.

For the sake of readability, the main service (the orchestrator) is divided into subprocesses reported below and we have omitted the termination handlers associated to each invocation to the auxiliary services: they are only supposed to close the current session.

CreditPortal offers the CrReq service that is invoked by credit requesters. Once invoked, it installs a termination handler ($k \cdot C$, where the compensation handler C is left unspecified), which handles session closing originating from the caller side, and then proceeds to the conversation with the requester. It receives the user credentials and checks their validity by means of the auxiliary service CheckUser. In case of incorrect login, an error message is sent to the client ($\langle$**excpt**("InvalidLogin")$\rangle$) and the communication is closed. Otherwise an acknowledgment is sent to the requester and the interaction proceeds as specified in process *Creation*.

$$CreditPortal \triangleq !(\nu k)\mathrm{CrReq}_k.(k \cdot C \mid (?id)\textbf{select } ?logged \textbf{ from } \overline{\mathrm{CheckUser}}(id)$$
$$\textbf{inif } logged \textbf{ then } \langle\text{"Valid"}\rangle Creation(id)$$
$$\textbf{else } \langle\textbf{excpt}(\text{"InvalidLogin"})\rangle\text{close})$$

Creation asks the service GetUserData for the user data associated to the given credentials and then proceeds to first receiving the credit data from the requester (($?creditD$)), **then** to creating a new credit request record (by service invocation $\overline{\mathrm{InitCreditData}}(\cdot)$) and then to asking for balances and securities, in this order. An error may occur in the record creation phase: in this case a message is sent to the client ($\langle$**excpt**("InvalidRequest")$\rangle$) and the communication is closed.

$$Creation(id) \triangleq \textbf{select } ?userD \textbf{ from } \overline{\mathrm{GetUserData}}(id)$$
$$\textbf{in } (?creditD)\textbf{select } ?init \textbf{ from } \overline{\mathrm{InitCreditData}}(userD, creditD)$$
$$\textbf{inif } init \textbf{ then } \langle\text{"enterBalances"}\rangle(?bals)\langle\text{"enterSecurities"}\rangle(?secs)$$
$$\textbf{wait } ?ackSec, ?ackBal \textbf{ from}$$
$$\overline{\mathrm{UpdateBalanceRating}}(userD, bals),$$
$$\overline{\mathrm{UpdateSecurityRating}}(userD, secs)$$
$$\textbf{in } Decision(userD, creditD)$$
$$\textbf{else } \langle\textbf{excpt}(\text{"InvalidRequest"})\rangle\text{close}$$

Then the *Decision* phase starts. A rating for the client is computed ($\overline{\mathrm{CalculateRating}}(\cdot)$). The subsequent interaction depends on the result of this computation:

- in case of "AAA", an offer is immediately sent to the client, by continuing as specified in process *Offer*;
- in case of "BBB" (resp. "CCC"), the intervention of an employee (resp. supervisor) is required.

In the latter case, either an offer or a decline document is generated (by either $\overline{\mathrm{GenOffer}}(\cdot)$ or $\overline{\mathrm{GenDecline}}(\cdot)$) and sent to the requester. In case an offer is sent to the client, he can decide to accept or decline; acceptance is registered by the service call $\overline{\mathrm{AcceptOffer}}$. In case of decline, the client can possibly decide to update some of its request data, and this is registered by $\overline{\mathrm{UpdCreditData}}$.

$Decision(user, credit) \stackrel{\Delta}{=}$
    select *?ratingD, ?resp* **from** $\overline{\texttt{CalculateRating}}(user)$
    inif (*resp* = "AAA") **then** *Offer(ratingD, credit)*
          elseif (*resp* = "BBB") **then** *ToClerk(user, ratingD, credit)*
                else *ToSupervisor(user, ratingD, credit)*

$ToClerk(user, rating, credit) \stackrel{\Delta}{=}$ **select** *?approval* **from** $\overline{\texttt{reqClerkApproval}}(user, rating)$
                inif (*approval* = "decline") **then** *Decline(rating, credit)*
                        else *Offer(rating, credit)*

$ToSupervisor(user, rating, credit) \stackrel{\Delta}{=}$ **select** *?approval* **from** $\overline{\texttt{reqSupervisorApproval}}(user, rating)$
                  inif (*approval* = "decline") **then** *Decline(rating, credit)*
                          else *Offer(rating, credit)*

$Offer(rating, credit) \stackrel{\Delta}{=}$ **select** *?offer* **from** $\overline{\texttt{GenOffer}}(rating)$
                in $\langle offer\rangle((\text{true})\texttt{AcceptOffer}.\langle credit\rangle + (\text{false})0)$

$Decline(rating, credit) \stackrel{\Delta}{=}$ **select** *?decline* **from** $\overline{\texttt{GenDecline}}(rating)$
                in $\langle decline\rangle((\text{true})\overline{\texttt{UpdCreditData}}.\langle credit\rangle + (\text{false})0)$

CreditRequester is a recursive client that invokes the CrReq service and then proceeds in the interaction as expected. Notice that, after calling the service CrReq, the client installs a compensation handler ($k' \cdot D$) that is left unspecified. At two points, he can non-deterministically decide to end the conversation (("Valid")close and ⟨"enterBalances"⟩close). Please notice also that acceptance of the offer depends on an internal function **eval**, whose result is sent to the *CreditPortal* ((**eval**(*offer*))). In case the credit request is declined, the user non-deterministically decides either to retry or to abandon. The creation of new credit balances and securities data is rendered here as the creation of new names: ($v\ creditD, bals, secs$). Recursion can be encoded in CaSPiS by combining replication, service definitions and invocations, and pipelines.

$CreditRequester \stackrel{\Delta}{=} (vk')\overline{\texttt{CrReq}}_{k'}.(k' \cdot D \mid \langle id\rangle((\textbf{excpt}(?x))\text{close} + (\text{"Valid"})\text{close} + (\text{"Valid"})CR))$

    $CR \stackrel{\Delta}{=} (vcreditD, bals, secs)\big(\langle creditD\rangle$
              $(\textbf{excpt}(?y))\text{close}$
            + ("enterBalances")close
            + ("enterBalances")$\langle bals\rangle$("enterSecurities")$\langle secs\rangle$
                $((?offer)\langle \textbf{eval}(offer)\rangle + (?decline)(\ \tau.\langle \text{true}\rangle CreditRequester$
                                  $+ \tau.\langle \text{false}\rangle)))\big)$

Process *AuthenticationService* offers the service CheckUser that receives users credentials and returns a boolean value depending on the result of an authentication function, **aut**, that checks the validity of the credentials by accessing some private databases.

$$AuthenticationService \stackrel{\Delta}{=}\ !\texttt{CheckUser}.(?id)\langle \textbf{aut}(id)\rangle$$

The whole system, *Sys*, is given by the parallel composition of all processes:

$$Sys \triangleq (\nu\, id)CreditRequester | (\nu\, \mathsf{CheckUser}, \cdots)(CreditPortal | AuthenticationService | \cdots).$$

2.2   SSCC: Stream-Based Service-Centered Calculus

SSCC (Stream-based Service Centered Calculus [LVMR07a, CLM+08, CLM+07]) captures in a direct way the main activities in service-oriented computations: definition and invocation of services, long-running interactions between the invoker and the provider, and orchestration of complex computations exploiting services as building blocks. SSCC is a variant of SCC that, to better support orchestration, introduces a new construct, called stream, with the aim of collecting the results from some ongoing computations and make them available for new ones. This is the main aspect that differentiates SSCC from CaSPiS [BBDL08], the most direct evolution of SCC. This design choice has been taken in order to simplify static analysis techniques, trying to find a suitable trade-off between expressiveness of the chosen primitives and suitability to analysis. In particular, since stream names can not be communicated, their scope is known statically. An example on how this feature can be exploited while developing a type system can be found in [LVMR07a], where a type system for checking protocol compatibility between invoker and provider of a service is presented. Bisimilarity techniques for proving equivalence of service-oriented systems modeled in SSCC were also studied [CLM+08, CLM+07].

A gentle introduction to SSCC. We present here in detail the stream construct; refer to CaSPiS for the semantics of other primitives (the full syntax of the calculus can be found in Fig. 2). A stream f is declared using a process of the form

$$\mathbf{stream}\, P \,\mathbf{as}\, f \,\mathbf{in}\, Q$$

Here, P and Q are executed *concurrently*, but only P can insert data v in f, by executing

$$\mathbf{feed}\, \langle v \rangle P'$$

Notice that the name of the stream is not explicitly mentioned in the left-hand-side of the construct: the syntactically closest stream is always used. This allows a process to send data to its context, without knowledge of the structure of the context itself, thus enhancing code re-usability. Also, the feed operation is non-blocking, and f acts as a buffer. The context, represented by Q, can read from stream f via a process of the form

$$\mathbf{read}\, f(x) Q'$$

In this case the name of the stream is explicit in the code, allowing a process to acquire data from multiple sources. Also, the read is blocking, allowing the context to wait for the necessary input. A main feature of stream communication is that it is completely orthogonal with respect to the structure of sessions, allowing to easily retrieve data from nested sessions. This reflects in the language the conceptual difference between

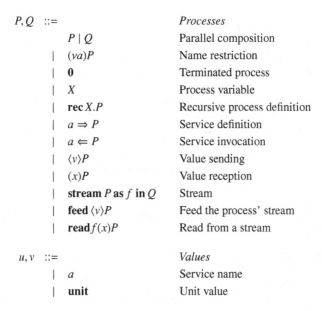

P, Q	::=		*Processes*
		$P \mid Q$	Parallel composition
	|	$(va)P$	Name restriction
	|	**0**	Terminated process
	|	X	Process variable
	|	**rec** $X.P$	Recursive process definition
	|	$a \Rightarrow P$	Service definition
	|	$a \Leftarrow P$	Service invocation
	|	$\langle v \rangle P$	Value sending
	|	$(x)P$	Value reception
	|	**stream** P **as** f **in** Q	Stream
	|	**feed** $\langle v \rangle P$	Feed the process' stream
	|	**read** $f(x)P$	Read from a stream
u, v	::=		*Values*
	|	a	Service name
	|	**unit**	Unit value

Fig. 2. Syntax of SSCC

session communication, based on the network infrastructure, and local communication, based e.g., on shared memory.

A typical situation where streams turn out to be useful is, in our running example, when the *CalculateRating* service needs to obtain various credit ratings from different internal agencies and then chooses one of the ratings based on some criteria. Suppose that the *CalculateRating* service, while aiming at providing better deals for the clients, asks credit ratings to three internal agencies, waits for the first two results to come, and publishes the best rating offer of the two. Calling the services for a given *user* data is as follows.

CreditRating1 $\Leftarrow$ *<user>*(*rating1*) ... |
CreditRating2 $\Leftarrow$ *<user>*(*rating2*) ... |
CreditRating3 $\Leftarrow$ *<user>*(*rating3*) ...

In order to collect the ratings, we use the stream constructor, playing the role of a *service orchestrator*. The various ratings are fed into the stream; a different process reads the stream. We write it as follows.

stream
  CreditRating1 $\Leftarrow$ *<user>*(*rating1*) **feed** *<rating1>* |
  CreditRating2 $\Leftarrow$ *<user>*(*rating2*) **feed** *<rating2>* |
  CreditRating3 $\Leftarrow$ *<user>*(*rating3*) **feed** *<rating3>*
as f **in**
  read $f(x)$ **read** $f(y)$ {*publish−the−most−suitable−rating−between−x−and−y*}

call $a<x1,...,xn>$ $\triangleq a \Leftarrow <x1> ... <xn>(y)$ **feed**$<y>$

$P >^n x1 ... xn > Q$ $\triangleq$ **stream** P **as** f **in read** $f(x1)$ ... **read** $f(xn)$ Q

$a * \Rightarrow P \triangleq$ **rec** $X.\ a \Rightarrow (P|X)$

if b **then** P $\triangleq b \Leftarrow (x)(y)\ x \Leftarrow$ **feed**$<$**unit**$> >^1 > P$

if b **else** P $\triangleq b \Leftarrow (x)(y)\ y \Leftarrow$ **feed**$<$**unit**$> >^1 > P$

if b **then** P **else** Q $\triangleq$ **if** b **then** P | **if** b **else** Q

$true * \Rightarrow (va)(vb) <a><b>\ a \Rightarrow (x)$ **feed**$<x>$

$false * \Rightarrow (va)(vb) <a><b>\ b \Rightarrow (x)$ **feed**$<x>$

Fig. 3. SSCC derived constructs

The above pattern is so common that we provide a special syntax for it, inspired by Orc [MC07].

(**call** *CreditRating1* $<user>$ |
  call *CreditRating2* $<user>$ |
  call *CreditRating3* $<user>$) $>^2$
  $x\ y > \{publish-the-most-suitable-rating-between-x-and-y\}$

The various abbreviations used in this section are summarized in Fig. 3. The first models a synchronous request-response protocol. The second implements sequential composition with value passing from the first process P to the second Q. The third one realizes persistent services, i.e., services that survive multiple invocations. The last five definitions model boolean values (which are not primitive in the calculus) and conditional processes. An implementation in SSCC of the van der Aalst et al. [vdAtKB03] workflow patterns can be found in [LVMR07b].

The Credit Request scenario. We start by modeling a simplified customer that interacts with a *CreditPortal* service. For that, the client identifies itself, and upon successful login provides the requested amount and the guarantee. It then waits for the reply from the Bank and accepts it, regardless of its nature.

creditRequester $\triangleq$ *CreditPortal* $\Leftarrow <id>\ (logged)$
  if *logged* **then** $<amount> <guarantee>\ (reply) <ok>$

The Credit Request Scenario system consists of the following components, among others.

System $\triangleq$ *CreditPortal* | *Decision* | *ToClerk* | *ToSupervisor* | *CalculateRating* | ...

The *CreditPortal* service handles credit requests from customers. The *Decision* service determines the decision level for the credit, returning the appropriate service to be called next: either reply immediately to the customer, hand over to a clerk, or deliver to a supervisor. Services *ToClerk* and *ToSupervisor* handle the approval process by clerks and supervisors. The *CalculateRating* service is used by the *Decision* service and mediates the process of asking ratings to various independent rating agencies. It relies on a *MostSuitableRating* service, chaining the first two answers from the credit rating agencies, and publishing the result m.

CalculateRating $* \Rightarrow (user)$
  (**call** *CreditRating1 <user>* |
   call *CreditRating2 <user>* |
   call *CreditRating3 <user>*) $>^2$
     $x\ y >$ **call** *MostSuitableRating <x,y> $>^1 m > m$*

The *Decision* service, based on the score rating obtained from *CalculateRating*, determines which service should handle the credit decision: directly *Offer* the credit to the client, forward the request *toClerk* or forward the request *ToSupervisor*. We rely on a service *strcmp* to compare strings.

Decision $* \Rightarrow (user) (amount)$ **call** *CalculateRating <user>*
   $>^1 rating > <rating>$. **call** *strcmp<rating, "AAA"> $>^1 b >$*
       if *b* **then** *<Offer>* **else** **call** *strcmp<rating, "BBB"> $>^1 b >$*
       if *b* **then** *<ToClerk>* **else** *<ToSupervisor>*

After receiving its arguments *user* and *amount*, service *Decision* synchronously invokes service *CalculateRating*. The most appropriate rating (following the bank's current policy) provided by this last service is collected in variable *rating*, sent to the invoker, and then the appropriate service to handle the loan approval is determined. One of the three service references, *Offer*, *ToClerk*, or *ToSupervisor*, is returned so that the invoker may use the service to trigger the appropriate approval procedure.

Synchronous interactions are modeled by service invocations followed by a bidirectional session communication, such as the values *user* and *amount* received by the *Decision* service or the interaction with the *CalculateRating* service. Asynchronous interactions instead are modeled by invocations that send the name of services to the invoker (namely, *Offer*, *ToClerk*, and *ToSupervisor*), which should be called by the provider to achieve a result. Notice also that streams (both the explicit ones and the ones hidden inside derived construct *>x>*) can be exploited to synchronize and collect the results of the different activities.

2.3   CC: A Conversation-Oriented Service Centered Calculus

The Conversation Calculus [VCS08, CV09], usually abbreviated as CC, integrates a small set of programming language abstractions for expressing and analyzing service-based systems. Technically, it may be seen as an applied π-calculus that evolved from SCC.

More crucially, the CC introduces the concept of *conversation context*, a notion originally introduced within the SENSORIA project for modeling and analyzing loosely-coupled, multi-party, dynamically evolving service centered interactions. A conversation context is a first-class communication medium where several partners may interact by message passing. In a nutshell, the distinguishing aspects of the CC are:

 – Conversation contexts, and dynamically evolving multi-party conversations.
 – A context sensitive message-passing communication mechanism.

As explained in the introduction, concepts such as sessions [HVK98] and conversations have been used frequently to discuss communication abstractions for service-oriented computing [CHY⁺06, BBC⁺06]. The CC model proposes the technical concept of "conversation" as an extension of the classical concept of binary session, in a precise sense.

Unlike the more specific notion of binary session, which involves exactly two partners (typically, a service provider and a service client), a conversation is a structured, not centrally coordinated, possibly concurrent, collection of interactions between a possibly dynamically varying number of participants. A conversation context may be transparently distributed in many pieces, and processes in any piece may seamlessly talk to processes in the same or any other piece of the same conversation context. Intuitively a conversation context may be seen as a virtual chat room where remote participants exchange messages according to some discipline, while being possibly engaged in some other conversations at the same time. Another advantage of conversations, from a modeling and design viewpoint, is that they prevent the model to be partitioned, sometimes artificially, in a collection of independent binary sessions.

Conversation context identities can be passed around, allowing participants to dynamically join conversations. To join an ongoing conversation, a process may perform a remote conversation access using the conversation context identifier. Then, it becomes able to participate in the conversation to which it has joined, while being able to interact back with the caller context through the access point; all these features are not in the scope of other approaches to multi-party session-based systems, prominently [HYC08]. On the other hand, like a binary session, a conversation may still be implemented using a single private channel identifiers, only known to the current participants. The flexibility in design provided by the notion of conversation as introduced by the CC turns out to be extremely convenient to model and analyze complex service interactions, as we find in real systems, at a very manageable level of abstraction; on the other hand, conversations may also be conveniently disciplined and analyzed by means of typing (see Chapter 2-3).

A gentle introduction to the Conversation Calculus. We informally present the syntax and semantics of the Conversation Calculus, full technical details may be found in [VCS08, CV09]. The syntax of CC is defined in Fig. 4. For simplicity, and without loss of generality, we restrict the current presentation to a monadic version. Essentially, the core CC is an extension of the π-calculus static fragment, obtained by adding the conversation construct $n \blacktriangleleft [P]$, and replacing channel-based communication with context-sensitive message-based communication. A simple mechanism for handling exceptional behavior is also present. The static fragment is defined by the inaction $\mathbf{0}$, parallel composition $P \mid Q$, name restriction $(va)P$ and recursion $\mathbf{rec}\, X.P$. The conversation access construct $n \blacktriangleleft [P]$, allows a process to interact, as specified by P, in conversation n. The distinguished occurrences of a, x, x and X are binding occurrences in $(va)P$, $l^d?(x).P$, $\mathbf{this}(x).P$ and $\mathbf{rec}\, X.P$, respectively.

Conversation Context. A conversation context is a named delimited container where closely related computation and communication happen. In more general terms, a context is a general abstraction that may be used to model locations (*e.g.*, a unit of distribution), service endpoints (e.g., a delimited scope of communication), contexts of

$a, b, c, \ldots \in \Lambda$ *(Names)*

$x, y, z, \ldots \in \mathcal{V}$ *(Variables)*

$n, m, o \ldots \in \Lambda \cup \mathcal{V}$

$l, s \ldots \quad \in \mathcal{L}$ *(Labels)*

$\mathcal{X}, \mathcal{Y}, \ldots \in \chi$ *(Process Vars)*

$d \quad ::= \downarrow \mid \uparrow$ *(Directions)*

$\alpha, \beta ::= l^d\,!(n)$ *(Output)*

     $\mid \quad l^d\,?(x)$ *(Input)*

     $\mid \quad \mathbf{this}(x)$ *(Conversation Awareness)*

$P, Q ::= \mathbf{0}$	*(Inaction)*		$\mid \ \mathbf{rec}\,\mathcal{X}.P$	*(Recursion)*
$\mid \ P \mid Q$	*(Parallel Composition)*		$\mid \ \mathcal{X}$	*(Process Variable)*
$\mid \ (\nu a)P$	*(Name Restriction)*		$\mid \ \Sigma_{i \in I}\,\alpha_i.P_i$	*(Action-Guarded Choice)*
$\mid \ n \blacktriangleleft [\,P\,]$	*(Conversation Access)*			
$\mid \ \mathbf{try}\ P\ \mathbf{catch}\ Q$	*(Handler block)*			
$\mid \ \mathbf{throw}\ P$	*(Throw exception)*			

Fig. 4. Syntax of the Conversation Calculus

conversation (e.g., a correlated set of interacting partners), and other forms of localized interaction. Contexts encapsulate functionality and appear to the surrounding environment as a plain local process, thus allowing system descriptions to abstract away from particular implementation details. We write $n \blacktriangleleft [P]$ to express that process P is inside conversation context names n. Notice that in CC only conversation names (in Λ) may be subject to binding, and freshly generated via $(\nu a)P$.

It is important to stress that if a CC process contains several different sub-terms of the form $n \blacktriangleleft [P_i]$, then all the processes P_i are in the same context, and may transparently interact, so the notation $n \blacktriangleleft [P]$ should *not* be confused with similarly looking notations in different models, such as ambients in the Ambient Calculus [CG98], or even session pieces, such as CaSPiS or SSCC session constructs. In particular, the strong bisimilarity $n \blacktriangleleft [P] \mid n \blacktriangleleft [Q] \sim n \blacktriangleleft [P \mid Q]$ holds (see Chapter 2-2). This equation also allows us to present CC programs modularly, where services published by a site n, modeled by a context $n \blacktriangleleft [P]$, are given in separate program fragments. We will use this in our description below of the Credit Request Scenario.

Communication. In CC, interaction between subsystems (modeled by conversation contexts) is realized by labeled message passing. In general, communication is expressed by the guarded choice construct $\Sigma_{i \in I}\,\alpha_i.P_i$, meaning that the process may select some initial action α_i and then progress as P_i. Communication actions are of two forms: $l^d\,!(n)$ for sending messages and $l^d\,?(x)$ for receiving messages. Message communication is defined by the label l and the direction d. There are two message directions: $\downarrow$ (read "here") meaning that the interaction should take place in the current conversation or $\uparrow$ (read "up") meaning that the interaction should take place in the caller conversation. It is not therefore possible for processes in unrelated different conversations to interact directly. Notice that message labels (from $\mathcal{L}$) are *not* names but free identifiers (cf. record labels, text strings, or XML tags), and therefore are not subject to fresh generation, restriction or binding. To lighten notation we omit the $\downarrow$ in the $\downarrow$-directed messages, without any ambiguity.

Context awareness. A process executing in a given context should be able to dynamically access the identity of such context, in order to correlate its behavior with other partners, and act accordingly. Thus, the CC introduces a context awareness primitive, that binds x to the "current" context name, and proceeds with the continuation as in **this**$(x).P$. Thus, a basic action may also be of the form **this**(x), allowing a process to dynamically access the name of the current conversation.

Service publication and instantiation. Service definitions are published in conversation contexts – seen then as sites or service providers. Published services may be instantiated on clients request, resulting in the creation of a new conversation context split in two pieces. By instantiating a service, a client is able to incorporate in its workflow a new process which, although executing remotely in the server environment, appears to the client as any other of its local subsystems. Access to a newly created conversation may later on be progressively given to other partners, allowing them to join in. Service definition, service instantiation, and conversation join are written respectively

> **def** *ServiceName* $\Rightarrow$ *ServiceBody*
> **new** *ServiceProvider · ServiceName* $\Leftarrow$ *ParticipantProtocol*
> **join** *ServiceProvider · ServiceName* $\Leftarrow$ *ParticipantProtocol*

The **def**, **new** and **join** constructions are idiomatic in CC, encoded using message passing and conversation contexts as follows.

$$\mathbf{def}\ s \Rightarrow P \quad \triangleq s?(x).x \blacktriangleleft [P]$$
$$\mathbf{new}\ n \cdot s \Leftarrow Q \triangleq (vc)(n \blacktriangleleft [s!(c)] \mid c \blacktriangleleft [Q])$$
$$\mathbf{join}\ n \cdot s \Leftarrow Q \triangleq \mathbf{this}(x).(n \blacktriangleleft [s!(x)] \mid Q)$$

Exception handling. Exceptional behavior, in particular fault signaling, fault detection, and resource disposal, are important aspects, orthogonal to communication mechanisms, we therefore provide specific constructions for exception handling, extending the classical **try/throw** primitives. Using these mechanisms, one may define several expressive error recovery mechanisms. For example, in Chapter 3-3 we illustrate how structured compensating transactions, in the style of [BHF04], may be faithfully expressed in the CC.

The Credit Request scenario. We illustrate the expressiveness of the CC by providing a multi-party implementation of the Credit Request scenario. Our CC implementation makes use of all the key features of CC, including multi-party conversations via **join**, (first-class) conversation delegation. In Chapter 2-3 it is also shown how this specific implementation is well-typed, ensuring conversation fidelity and deadlock absence. In Fig. 5 we present a message sequence chart rendering all the interactions in the scenario. While browsing through the example, the reader is invited to notice the following two key aspects.

Dynamic join and leave. The conversation initially established only between client and portal, is later on enlarged by the participation of the bank (to inform the client rate). This illustrates how dynamic multi-party conversations are modeled in CC.

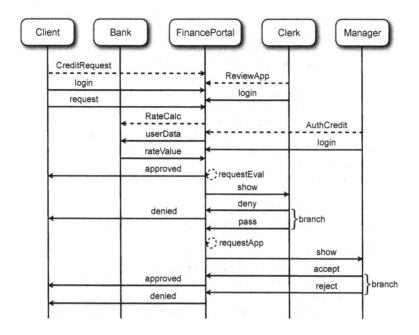

Fig. 5. Credit Request scenario message sequence chart

Partial delegation. In the cases where the portal cannot autonomously decide approval, it postpones the ongoing conversation with the client, by using the portal context as a cache for requests to the clerk (`requestEval`), who may then delegate even further to the manager (`requestApp`). These messages, represented by the traced circles in Fig. 5, contain references to ongoing conversations, which will be later on resumed by the portal, to give the final answer to the client. All this will happen asynchronously with respect to the initial conversation, as effect of independent clerk / manager conversations with the portal. This illustrates how first class delegation of conversation names may be used to conveniently model message correlation, possibly with partial delegation (unlike session delegation in session calculi [HVK98], which is forced to be total). Notice also how the conversation between client, portal and bank, interacts with the conversations between portal and clerk, and portal and manager in a loosely coupled way, by means of context sensitive communication.

We first describe the (sub)conversation between *Client*, *FinancePortal*, and *Bank*, presented in Fig. 6. Interaction starts between the client and the portal by the instantiation of service `CreditRequest`. Under this service instance, the client-portal interaction starts by the exchange of message `login` that authenticates the client in the system. At that point the client places the credit request, transmitting the relevant data in message `request`. Upon reception of the clients request, the portal asks an external service `RateCalc` published by *Bank* to join in the ongoing service conversation, in order to determine the financial rate of the client. To that end messages `userData` and `rateValue` are exchanged in the `CreditRequest` service conversation between the portal and the

FinancePortal ◄ [
   def CreditRequest ⇒
      login$^{\downarrow}$?(*uId*). request$^{\downarrow}$?(*data*).
        join *Bank* · RateCalc ⇐
           userData$^{\downarrow}$!(*data*).
           rateValue$^{\downarrow}$?(*rate*).
           if *rate* = AAA **then** approved$^{\downarrow}$!()
                 else **this**(*clientChat*).
                        requestEval$^{\uparrow}$!(*clientChat, uId, data*)]
|
Bank ◄ [
   def RateCalc ⇒
      userData$^{\downarrow}$?(*data*).
      assessRate$^{\uparrow}$!(*data*).
      rateVal$^{\uparrow}$?(*rate*). rateValue$^{\downarrow}$!(*rate*)]
|
Client ◄ [
   new *FinancePortal* · CreditRequest ⇐
      login$^{\downarrow}$!(*uId*).
      request$^{\downarrow}$!(*data*).
        (approved$^{\downarrow}$?().approved$^{\uparrow}$!() + denied$^{\downarrow}$?().denied$^{\uparrow}$!())]

Fig. 6. Interaction between Client and Finance Portal

bank. So, at this point client, finance portal and bank share a conversation between them. Notice that the finance portal asked bank to join in, via service RateCalc, but while doing so the portal did not lose access to the conversation and actually gets to interact with the bank. After receiving the client rating information the finance portal may either approve the request automatically, if the client rating is very good (triple A), in which case a message approved is sent to the client, or, in case the rating is not high, a bank clerk is asked to review the application. To that end a message requestEval is sent by the CreditRequest service definition code, directed (↑) to the *FinancePortal* conversation, that will be eventually picked up by a service instance that handles interaction between clerks and the portal: service ReviewApp. To allow for the final reply to be issued in the correct CreditRequest service instance conversation, its identity is accessed, via **this**, and is passed along in message requestEval.

Interaction between a bank clerk and the portal, depicted in Fig. 7 is realized by the instantiation of service ReviewApp. Upon service instantiation the clerk authenticates himself by sending message login to the portal. After that, the service definition code specifies the reception of a requestEval message in the (conversation) context of *FinancePortal* (notice the direction is ↑). which originated from some previous interaction between a client and the portal, and that contains the credit request information and also the reference of the conversation in which notification of the final decision on the loan should be sent. Message show is sent to the clerk containing the client data, and the clerk replies back with either a deny message or a pass message. In the former case, the client is immediately notified of the decision: conversation *clientChat* is accessed (*clientChat* was received in message requestEval) and message denied is posted in

FinancePortal ◀ [
  def ReviewApp ⇒
    login$^↓$?(*clerkId*).
    requestEval$^↑$?(*clientChat*, *uId*, *data*).
      show$^↓$!(*uId*, *data*).
      (deny$^↓$?().*clientChat* ◀ [denied$^↓$!()]
      +
      pass$^↓$?().requestApp$^↑$!(*clientChat*, *uId*, *data*))]
  |
Clerk ◀ [
  new *FinancePortal* · ReviewApp ⇐
    login$^↓$!(*clerkId*).
    show$^↓$?(*uId*, *data*).
      printRequest$^↑$!(*uId*, *data*).
      (pass$^↑$?().pass$^↓$!() + deny$^↑$?().deny$^↓$!())]

Fig. 7. Interaction between Clerk and Finance Portal

FinancePortal ◀ [
  def AuthCredit ⇒
    login$^↓$?(*managerId*).
    requestApp$^↑$?(*clientChat*, *uId*, *data*).
      show$^↓$!(*uId*, *data*).
      (accept$^↓$?().*clientChat* ◀ [approved$^↓$!()]
      +
      reject$^↓$?().*clientChat* ◀ [denied$^↓$!()])]
  |
Manager ◀ [
  new *FinancePortal* · AuthCredit ⇐
    login$^↓$!(*managerId*).
    show$^↓$?(*uId*, *data*).
      printRequest$^↑$!(*uId*, *data*).
      (accept$^↑$?().accept$^↓$!() + reject$^↑$?().reject$^↓$!()]

Fig. 8. Interaction between Manager and Finance portal

it. In the latter case, a bank manager is consulted so as to provide a final decision. To that end, message requestApp is posted to the *FinancePortal* context (carrying the *clientChat* reference and the credit request data), for further processing.

The interaction between a bank manager and the finance portal is carried out by an instance of service AuthCredit, and presented in Fig. 8. Interaction in the triggered conversation starts by the exchange of message login. After receiving the login message the service definition code specifies the reception of a requestApp message in the conversation context of *FinancePortal*. The relevant information is then sent to the manager (in message show) who replies with either a message accept or a message reject, after which the client is notified accordingly. Notice that the previously delegated *clientChat* conversation is accessed, and the message approved or a message denied is sent on it.

3   Correlation-Based Core Calculi

Service-oriented computing goes beyond the traditional function invocation (i.e. request-response) pattern introducing stateful interactions also called conversations. The calculi presented so far are based on implicit sessions. In this section, we consider an alternative approach based on *correlation information*, that are data explicitly introduced in part of the exchanged messages in order to route the messages to the correct process instances.

Correlation information is the basis of the Web Services interaction mechanisms which are implemented on top of stateless Internet protocols, such as the hyper-text transfer protocol HTTP. As an example of correlation information, consider the *Internet Cookies* used by web sites in order to relate an HTTP request to a user profile which permits to return, for instance, a customized HTML file.

Correlation information, besides being useful to implement stateful communication on top of stateless protocols, represent also a flexible and user programmable mechanism for managing the relationships among the collaborating partners. For instance, let us consider an orchestrator that must interact in parallel with n different partners. Using binary implicit sessions, the orchestrator activates n different sessions, one for each partner, and in order to exchange data among these sessions the interprocess communication primitives (pipeline, streams or message-exchange) can be exploited. On the contrary, the correlation approach allows the orchestrator to run only one process instance, at the price of including in the exchanged messages, for instance, a process identifier to be used as correlation information.

As an example let us suppose a distributed game scenario where two main services are involved: the master service and the game service. The master service invokes the game service for initiating a game by sending a freshly created game id (gId) that will be used by the latter service for identifying the new game session. When the game is started, the game service waits for two players univocally identified by their ids. Let us assume the players with ids $pId1$ and $pId2$ register themselves to the game. In this case, the game service will add their identifiers to the correlation set of the session game so that the data set formed by gId, $pId1$ and $pId2$ identify the session. From now to the end of the session game, the master service can interact with the service game by exploiting its id gId, whereas the two players can exploit the pairs ($pId1$, gId) and ($pId2$, gId), respectively, assuming that a player can be involved in more than one session game. As shown by this example, correlation set allows for the identification of a service session by means of a set of data which can be partially exploited by other participants for interacting with the right session (e.g. the master service uses only its id without knowing the ids of the players). Moreover, correlation data can be communicated to other services in order to allow them to interact with the right session. In the example above we can imagine that a player leaves the game by communicating its id to a third player which will replace it.

At the programming level, linguistic mechanisms are necessary in order to specify which part of the message contains the correlation information. A typical approach is to declare a *correlation set*, i.e. a set of identifiers of containers for the correlation information.

In order to investigate the impact of the correlation approach in SOC, we have embedded it in *memoryless* and *memoryful* services thus designing two different calculi called COWS and SOCK, respectively. In COWS variables can be assigned only once, and they are replaced with the assigned value; in SOCK, on the contrary, variables can be assigned more than once. The most visible consequence of these two different approaches is that the processes instantiated upon service invocation are explicitly represented in SOCK, while this is not the case in COWS. More precisely, in SOCK, a newly instantiated process P is explicitly associated with its state S using the notation $[P, S]$, while in COWS a newly instantiated process P is simply added in parallel with the other processes.

Another more subtle difference is that in SOCK the correlation information can change during the execution of one process simply by assigning new values to the containers indicated by the correlation set. In this way, for instance, it is possible for a process to dynamically change partners simply by modifying the corresponding correlation information.

The remainder of this section is devoted to the presentation of the two calculi COWS and SOCK. We simply present the syntax and the modeling in the calculi of the Credit Request scenario; the reader interested in the definition of the operational semantics can refer to [LPT07a] and [BGG+06].

3.1 COWS: Calculus for Orchestration of Web Services

COWS (Calculus for Orchestration of Web Services [LPT07a]) is a process calculus for specifying and combining services. It provides a novel combination of primitive constructs and features borrowed from well-known process calculi, such as non-binding receiving activities, asynchronous communication, polyadic synchronization, pattern matching, protection, and delimited receiving and killing activities. As a consequence of its careful design, the calculus makes it easy to model many important aspects of service orchestrations *à la* WS-BPEL [OAS07], such as service instances with shared state, services playing more than one partner role, stateful sessions made by several correlated service interactions, and long-running transactions. In fact, COWS evolved from ws-calculus [LPT06], a process calculus previously introduced to formalize the semantics of WS-BPEL, with the aim to achieve a more foundational and expressive formalism.

In the rest of this section, we report the syntax of COWS, informally explain its semantics and present a specification of the Credit Request scenario. We refer the interested reader to [Lap08, Tie09] for a formal account of COWS's semantics and some analysis techniques, for several examples illustrating peculiarities and expressiveness of the calculus, and for comparisons with other process-based and orchestration formalisms. COWS's basic primitives for termination and for error and compensation handling are specifically described in Chapter 3-3. The specification presented in this section results from a simplification of a COWS specification of the Sensoria Finance case study described and analyzed in Chapter 7-4.

A gentle introduction to COWS. The syntax of COWS is presented in Fig. 9. It is parameterized by three countable and pairwise disjoint sets: the set of *(killer) labels* (ranged over by $k, k', \ldots$), the set of *values* (ranged over by $v, v', \ldots$) and the set of 'write once' *variables* (ranged over by $x, y, \ldots$). The set of values is left unspecified;

$$s ::= u \cdot u'!\bar{\epsilon} \quad | \quad g \qquad\qquad \text{(invoke, receive-guarded choice)}$$
$$| \quad [e] s \quad | \quad s | s \quad | \quad * s \qquad \text{(delimitation, parallel composition, replication)}$$
$$| \quad \mathbf{kill}(k) \quad | \quad \{|s|\} \qquad\qquad \text{(kill, protection)}$$
$$g ::= \mathbf{0} \quad | \quad p \cdot o?\bar{w}.s \quad | \quad g + g \qquad \text{(empty, receive prefixing, choice)}$$

Fig. 9. Syntax of COWS

however, we assume that it includes the set of *names*, ranged over by $n, m, o, p, \ldots$, mainly used to represent partners and operations. The syntax of *expressions*, ranged over by ϵ, is deliberately omitted; we just assume that they contain, at least, values and variables, but do not include killer labels (that, hence, can *not* be communicated).

We use w to range over values and variables, u to range over names and variables, and e to range over *elements*, i.e. killer labels, names and variables. The *bar* $^-$ denotes tuples (ordered sequences) of homogeneous elements, e.g. $\bar{x}$ is a compact notation for denoting a tuple of variables as $\langle x_1, \ldots, x_n \rangle$. We assume that variables in the same tuple are pairwise distinct. We adopt the following conventions for operators' precedence: monadic operators bind more tightly than parallel, and prefixing more tightly than choice. We omit trailing occurrences of $\mathbf{0}$ and write $[e_1, \ldots, e_n] s$ in place of $[e_1] \ldots [e_n] s$. Finally, we write $I \stackrel{\triangle}{=} s$ to assign a name I to the term s.

Services are structured activities built from basic activities, i.e. invoke, receive and kill, by means of choice, parallel composition, delimitation, protection and replication.

Invoke and *receive* are the basic communication activities provided by COWS. Besides input parameters and sent values, both activities indicate an *endpoint*, i.e. a pair composed of a partner name p and of an operation name o, through which communication should occur. An endpoint $p \cdot o$ can be interpreted as a specific implementation of operation o provided by the service identified by the logic name p. An invoke $p \cdot o!\bar{\epsilon}$ can proceed as soon as the evaluation of the expressions $\bar{\epsilon}$ in its argument returns the corresponding values. A receive $p \cdot o?\bar{w}.s$ offers an invocable operation o along a given partner name p. Execution of a receive within a *choice* operator permits to take a decision between alternative behaviours. Partner and operation names are dealt with as values and, as such, can be exchanged in communication, although dynamically received names cannot form the endpoints used to receive further invocations. This permits to easily model many service interaction and reconfiguration patterns.

The *delimitation* operator is the *only* binder of the calculus: $[e] s$ binds e in the scope s. The scope of names and variables can be extended while that of killer labels cannot (in fact, they are not communicable values). Besides for generating 'fresh' private names (as 'restriction' in π-calculus [MPW92]), delimitation can be used for introducing a named scope for grouping certain activities. It is then possible to associate suitable termination activities to such a scope, as well as ad hoc fault and compensation handlers, thus laying the foundation for guaranteeing *transactional properties* in spite of services' loose coupling. This can be conveniently done by relying on the *kill* activity $\mathbf{kill}(k)$, that causes immediate termination of all concurrent activities inside the enclosing $[k]$ (which stops the killing effect), and the *protection* operator $\{|s|\}$, that preserves intact a critical activity s also when one of its enclosing scopes is abruptly terminated.

Delimitation can also be used to regulate the range of application of the substitution generated by an inter-service communication. This takes place when the arguments of a receive and of a concurrent invoke along the same endpoint match and causes each variable argument of the receive to be replaced by the corresponding value argument of the invoke within the whole scope of variable's declaration. In fact, to enable parallel terms to share the state (or part of it), receive activities in COWS do *not* bind variables, which is different from most process calculi.

Execution of concurrent terms is interleaved, but when a kill activity or a communication can be performed. Indeed, the *parallel* operator is equipped with a priority mechanism which allows some actions to take precedence over others. Kill activities are assigned greatest priority so that they pre-empt all other activities inside the enclosing killer label's delimitation. In other words, kill activities are executed *eagerly*, this way ensuring that, when a fault arises in a scope, (some of) the remaining activities of the enclosing scope are terminated before starting execution of the relative fault handler. In fact, activities forcing immediate termination of other concurrent activities are usually used for modeling fault handling. The same mechanism, of course, can also be used for compensation handling. Additionally, receive activities are assigned priority values which depend on the messages available so that, in presence of concurrent matching receives, only a receive using a more defined pattern (i.e. having greater priority) can proceed. This way, service definitions and service instances are represented as processes running concurrently, but service instances take precedence over the corresponding service definition when both can process the same message, thus preventing creation of wrong new instances. In the end, this permits to correlate different service communications, thus implicitly creating interaction sessions.

Finally, the *replication* operator $* s$ permits to spawn in parallel as many copies of s as necessary. This, for example, is exploited to model persistent services, i.e. services which can create multiple instances to serve several requests simultaneously.

The Credit Request scenario. The scenario includes several terms composed in parallel and possibly sharing some private names. It can be modeled by a term of the form

$$Portal \mid \ldots \mid [customerManagement, \ldots] \, (CreditRequest \mid CustomerManagement \mid \ldots)$$

Hereafter we only focus on the service orchestrator *CreditRequest*.

$CreditRequest \triangleq$
   $* [x_{Id}, x_{Name}, x_{Password}]$
      $creditReq \cdot initialize?\langle x_{Id}, x_{Name}, x_{Password} \rangle \cdot$
      $(\, customerManagement \cdot checkUser!\langle x_{Id}, x_{Name}, x_{Password} \rangle$
      $\mid [x_{UserOK}, x_{CustomerData}] \, creditReq \cdot checkUser?\langle x_{Id}, x_{UserOK}, x_{CustomerData} \rangle \cdot$
        $(\, portal \cdot initialize!\langle x_{Id}, x_{UserOK} \rangle$
          $\mid [if, then] \, (\, if \cdot then!\langle x_{UserOK} \rangle$
            $\mid if \cdot then?\langle true \rangle .$

            $[raise] \, (\, [k] \, (\, Creation \mid creditReq \cdot cancel?\langle Id \rangle .$
                     $(\, \mathbf{kill}(k) \mid \{\!\mid raise \cdot abort!\langle \rangle \mid\!\} \,)$
              $\mid raise \cdot abort?\langle \rangle . \, CompensateAll \,)\,)\,)\,)$

Whenever prompted by a customer request, *CreditRequest* creates an instance to serve that specific request and is immediately ready to concurrently serve other requests.

Each interaction with the service starts with a receive activity of the form *creditReq*·
initialize?$\langle x_{Id}, x_{Name}, x_{Password} \rangle$ corresponding to reception of a request emitted by *Portal*
on behalf of a customer. The receive activity creates a new service instance and initial-
izes the variables x_{Id}, x_{Name} and $x_{Password}$, declared local to the instance by the delimitation operator, with data provided by a customer. In particular, variable x_{Id} is used to
store a fresh identifier, generated by *Portal*, univocally identifying a session of the process (which, in COWS, coincides with an instance of the service). The identifier allows
CreditRequest to safely communicate with the involved services. In fact, in each interaction among them, the identifier is used as a correlation datum, i.e. it appears within
each message. Pattern-matching permits locating such identifier in the messages and,
therefore, delivering the messages to the instances identified by the same identifier.

Once created, a *CreditRequest*'s instance requires *CustomerManagement* to check
the customer login data, by invoking the operation *checkUser* provided by the 'internal'
partner name *customerManagement* through the invoke activity *customerManagement*·
checkUser!$\langle x_{Id}, x_{Name}, x_{Password} \rangle$, and waits for a reply. The answer is forwarded to the
customer by means of the invoke activity *portal*·*initialize*!$\langle x_{Id}, x_{UserOK} \rangle$. Concurrently,
by exploiting the private names *if* and *then*, the instance can check the answer. In case
of a positive answer, the service instance activates a 'scope' activity named k which
associates an event and a fault handler to the term *Creation*. When the scope starts, the
handlers are enabled. The event handler is activated by an invocation of the operation
cancel, corresponding to reception of a withdrawal of the credit request emitted by the
Portal on behalf of the customer. This forces the immediate termination of all (unprotected) activities representing the normal behaviour of the scope, by means of activity
kill(k), and the execution of activity *raise*·*abort*!$\langle\rangle$, which activates the fault handler.
To guarantee eventual execution of this invoke, it is protected by the protection operator
$\{\_\}$ that prevents it to be canceled due to an abrupt termination of its enclosing scope k.
The fault handler, in its turn, activates all installed compensation handlers.

Creation $\overset{\Delta}{=}$ $[x_{CreditAmount}, x_{CreditType}, x_{MonthlyInstalment}]$
$\quad$ *crediReq*·*createNewCreditRequest*?$\langle x_{Id}, x_{CreditAmount}, x_{CreditType}, x_{MonthlyInstalment} \rangle$·
$\quad\quad$ (*creditManagement*·*initCreditData*!$\langle x_{Id}, x_{CreditAmount}, x_{CreditType}, x_{MonthlyInstalment} \rangle$
$\quad\quad$ | *HandleBalanceAndSecurityData* | *CreationCH*)

After the data for a new credit request have been received, the service forwards them
to the credit management service, activates the term *HandleBalanceAndSecurityData*,
and installs the compensation handler *CreationCH* for undoing the activities previously
performed along the operation *initCreditData*.

HandleBalanceAndSecurityData $\overset{\Delta}{=}$ $[flow, end]$
$\quad$ ($[x_{BalancePackage}]$ *creditReq*·*enterBalanceData*?$\langle x_{Id}, x_{BalancePackage} \rangle$·
$\quad\quad\quad$ (*balance*·*updateBalanceRating*!$\langle x_{Id}, x_{CustomerData}, x_{BalancePackage} \rangle$
$\quad\quad\quad$ | *creditReq*·*updateBalanceRating*?$\langle x_{Id} \rangle$. *flow*·*end*!$\langle\rangle$))

$\quad$ | $[x_{SecurityPackage}]$ *creditReq*·*enterSecurityData*?$\langle x_{Id}, x_{SecurityPackage} \rangle$·
$\quad\quad\quad$ (*security*·*updateSecurityRating*!$\langle x_{Id}, x_{CustomerData}, x_{SecurityPackage} \rangle$
$\quad\quad\quad$ | *creditReq*·*updateSecurityRating*?$\langle x_{Id} \rangle$. *flow*·*end*!$\langle\rangle$))
$\quad$ | *flow*·*end*?$\langle\rangle$. *flow*·*end*?$\langle\rangle$. (*Decision* | *HandleBalAndSecCH*))

It receives (in parallel) the customer's balance and security data and, then, sends them to the *balance* and *security* services that store such data and, when requested, will compute the corresponding ratings. When the parallel computation ends, i.e. after that two signals along *flow · end* have been consumed, the term *Decision* is activated and the compensation handler *HandleBalAndSecCH* for undoing the already executed activities is installed.

$$Decision \triangleq$$
$$rating \cdot calculateRating!\langle x_{Id}, x_{LoginName}, x_{FirstName}, x_{LastName} \rangle$$
$$\mid [x_{Result}, x_{RatingData}] \; creditReq \cdot calculateRating?\langle x_{Id}, x_{Result}, x_{RatingData} \rangle.$$
$$[if, then] \, (\, if \cdot then!\langle x_{Result} \rangle$$
$$\mid if \cdot then?\langle AAA \rangle. \, Accept$$
$$+ \; if \cdot then?\langle BBB \rangle. \, ClerkApproval$$
$$+ \; if \cdot then?\langle CCC \rangle. \, SupervisorApproval \,)$$

It invokes the service *rating* for getting the rating of the customer request. The returned answer is then used to make a conditional choice. If the answer is *AAA*, the request is accepted without further evaluations and the term *Accept* is activated. Instead, if the answer is either *BBB* or *CCC*, the credit request needs to be further evaluated by a clerk or a supervisor, thus either *ClerkApproval* or *SupervisorApproval* is activated, respectively.

$$ClerkApproval \triangleq$$
$$portal \cdot requestClerkApproval!\langle x_{Id}, x_{RatingData} \rangle$$
$$\mid [x_{ManualAcceptance}] \; creditReq \cdot approvalResult?\langle x_{Id}, x_{ManualAcceptance} \rangle.$$
$$[if, then] \, (\, if \cdot then!\langle x_{ManualAcceptance} \rangle \; \mid \; if \cdot then?\langle true \rangle. \, Accept$$
$$+ \; if \cdot then?\langle false \rangle. \, Decline \,)$$

It requests a clerk approval and, according to the received answer, activates either the term *Accept* or *Decline* (*SupervisorApproval* is similar).

$$Accept \triangleq$$
$$creditManagement \cdot generateOffer!\langle x_{Id}, x_{RatingData} \rangle$$
$$\mid [x_{AgreementData}] \; creditReq \cdot generateOffer?\langle x_{Id}, x_{AgreementData} \rangle.$$
$$(\, portal \cdot offerToClient!\langle x_{Id}, x_{AgreementData} \rangle$$
$$\mid [x_{Accepted}] \; creditReq \cdot offerToClient?\langle x_{Id}, x_{Accepted} \rangle.$$
$$(\, creditManagement \cdot acceptOffer!\langle x_{Id}, x_{Accepted} \rangle$$
$$\mid portal \cdot goodbye!\langle x_{Id} \rangle \,) \,)$$

It requires the credit management service to generate the offer data and forwards them to the customer. The customer will reply by indicating if he accepts or not the offer, and such an answer is then sent to the credit management service. The invoke activity *portal · goodbye!*$\langle x_{Id} \rangle$ simply informs the customer that the process is concluded.

$Decline \triangleq$
  $portal \cdot declineToClient!\langle x_{Id} \rangle$
  $| \; [x_{UpdateDesired}] \; creditReq \cdot declineToClient?\langle x_{Id}, x_{UpdateDesired} \rangle.$
    $[if, then] \; (\; if \cdot then!\langle x_{UpdateDesired} \rangle$
      $| \; if \cdot then?\langle true \rangle. \; updatingManagement \cdot init!\langle x_{Id} \rangle$
      $+ if \cdot then?\langle false \rangle. \; portal \cdot goodbye!\langle x_{Id} \rangle \;)$

It behaves similarly to the previous term, except for the fact that a decline is sent to the customer instead of an offer. The customer will reply by indicating if he desires or not to perform a data update. In the positive case, the service *updatingManagement* is invoked, otherwise a *goodbye* message is sent to the customer.

3.2 SOCK: Service-Oriented Computing Kernel

Differently from COWS, the SOCK [BGG+06] calculus was developed not only taking inspiration, but also trying to be more strongly related to the current Web Services technology. In particular, the following aspects have been extracted:

- the *interaction modalities*: they directly deal with the communication patterns defined by the WSDL specification [WSD01] (e.g. one-way and request-response);
- the *workflow composition model*: it deals with the emerging trend to compose services by means of workflows experienced not only with WS-BPEL but also with more abstract notations such as BPMN [Obj06];
- the *execution modality*: it deals with the possibility to execute service sessions in a concurrent or in a sequential way;
- the *correlated sessions*: they cope with the characteristic of some Web Services to manage different sessions related to different participants by means of the correlation set mechanism;
- the *service state*: it consists of execution state of the service, which can be a shared state among all the service sessions or a session state that expires when the session terminates.

A gentle introduction to SOCK. SOCK organizes the previous mentioned SOC features in a stack of layers: the *service behaviour layer*, the *service engine layer* and the *services system layer*. The first one allows for the design of service behaviours by supplying computation and external communication primitives inspired to Web Services operations and workflow operators (e.g. sequence, parallel and choice). The service engine layer is built on top of the former and allows for the specification of the service declaration where it is possible to design in an orthogonal way three main features: *execution modality*, *persistent state* flag and *correlation sets*. The execution modality deals with the possibility to execute service sessions in a sequential order or concurrently. The persistent state flag allows to declare if each session (of the service engine) has its own independent state or if the state is shared among all the sessions of the same service engine. Since the interaction model is stateless the correlation sets is a mechanism for distinguishing sessions initiated by different invokers by means of the values received within some specified variables. The services system layer allows for the definition and

$$P, Q, \ldots ::= \qquad\qquad\qquad\qquad \text{processes}$$

	$\mathbf{0}$	null process
	$\bar{\epsilon}$	output
	$x := e$	assignment
	$\chi?P : Q$	if then else
	$P; P$	sequence
	$P\|P$	parallel
	$\sum_{i \in W} \epsilon_i; P_i$	non-det. choice
	$\chi \rightleftharpoons P$	iteration
$\bar{\epsilon}$ ::=		output
	$\bar{s}$	output signal
	$\bar{o}@c(x)$	notification
	$\bar{o}_r@c(x, y)$	solicit-Response
ϵ ::=		input
	s	input signal
	$o(x)$	one-way
	$o_r(x, y, P)$	request-response

Fig. 10. Syntax of SOCK processes

for the reasoning on the behaviour of the whole system (i.e. all the services involved in the application).

Service behaviour. In the following we present the syntax of the service behaviour layer which provides the basic communication primitives, the operators to modify the state and the workflow operators. Let *Loc* be a set of locations on which services can run. Let O be a set of operations used for inter-service interactions. Let *Signals* be a set of signal names exploited for synchronizing intra-service processes. Let *Var* be a set of variables ranged over by x, y, z and *Val*, ranged over by v, be a generic set of values. We exploit the notations $x = \langle x_0, x_1, \ldots, x_i \rangle$ and $v = \langle v_0, v_1, \ldots, v_i \rangle$ for representing tuples of variables and values respectively. Let c ranges over $Var \cup Loc$ where $Var \cap Loc = \emptyset$. For the sake of brevity, we do not present the syntax for representing expressions and logical conditions which are ranged over by e and χ, respectively; here we assume that they include all the arithmetic and logic operators, values in *Val* and variables.

We denote with SC the set of all possible processes ranged over by P and Q. $\mathbf{0}$ is the null process. Outputs can be a signal $\bar{s}$, a notification $\bar{o}@c(x)$ or a solicit-response $\bar{o}_r@c(x, y)$ where $s \in Signals, o \in O, c \in Var \cup Loc$, x is the array of the variables which contain the information to send and y is the array of variables where, in the case of the solicit-response, the received information will be stored. Dually, inputs can be an input signal s, a one-way $o(x)$ or a request-response $o_r(x, y, P)$ where $s \in Signals, o \in O$, x is the array of variables where the received information are stored whereas y is the array of variables which contain the information to send in the case of the request-response; finally P is the process that has to be executed between the request message and the response message in a request-response. Signals are used for synchronizing parallel threads within a service behaviour whereas one-way, notification, request-response and solicit-response are exploited for external communication. $x := e$ assigns the result of the expression e to the variable x. $\chi?P : Q$ is the *if_then_else* process, where χ is a logic condition; P is executed only if the condition χ is satisfied; otherwise Q is executed. $P; Q, P \mid Q$ represent sequential and parallel composition respectively, whereas $\sum_{i \in W} \epsilon_i; P_i$ is the non-deterministic choice guarded on inputs. Such a restriction is due to the fact that we are not interested to model internal non-determinism guarded on output processes because they do not actually model any relevant real language construct. Finally, $\chi \rightleftharpoons P$ is the construct to model guarded iterations. It is worth noting that simple input primitives can be programmed by considering a choice with a single branch having empty continuation (i.e. where the process P_i is the process $\mathbf{0}$).

SOCK has been recently extended with mechanisms for fault and compensation handling [GLMZ08]. The main distinguishing feature is that SOCK allows for sophisticated dynamic installation and updating of such handlers. The main principles are:

- the distinction between fault handlers and termination/compensation handlers (the compensation handler is implicitly defined as the latest installed termination handler);
- the possibility to associate handlers to any portion of code using the scope construct;
- the possibility to dynamically define and update handlers;
- the occurrence of a fault inside a request-response pattern triggers the corresponding fault on the client side.

Correspondingly, the syntax is extended as follows:

$$P, Q \quad ::= \quad \dots \quad \mid \quad \mathrm{inst}(\mathcal{H}) \quad \mid \quad \{P : \mathcal{H}\}_q \quad \mid \quad \mathrm{throw}(f) \quad \mid \quad \mathrm{comp}(q) \quad \mid \quad cH$$

We use $\mathcal{H}$ to denote a function from the (disjoint) domains of *Faults* and *Scopes* names to processes.

We consider two kinds of handlers: *fault handlers* to deal with an internal fault and *termination/compensation handlers* to deal with compensations of an activity in case of an external fault. Handlers are installed by the primitive $\mathrm{inst}(\mathcal{H})$ where $\mathcal{H}$ is a partial function from faults and scope names to processes. The construct $\{P : \mathcal{H}\}_q$ defines a process P that runs within a scope named q, with $\mathcal{H}$ defining the currently installed handlers. Commands $\mathrm{throw}(f)$ and $\mathrm{comp}(q)$ respectively raise fault f and ask to compensate scope q. Finally, cH allows to refer to the previously installed handler in the expressions for handler updates.

To illustrate the expressiveness of the dynamic installation of handlers, consider the process $P \equiv \{\mathrm{true} \rightleftharpoons \overline{o}_r @z(\mathbf{y}, \mathbf{x}); \mathrm{inst}([q \mapsto C|cH]) : \mathcal{H}_0\}_q$, where $\mathcal{H}_0$ is a function undefined on all fault names and defined as $\mathbf{0}$ for all scope names. The process P repeatedly invokes the service o_r (using the request-response modality) and installs as many compensations C as the calls to o_r. As soon as the first fault is raised by o_r, all the installed C are executed in parallel. Such a dynamic mechanism is difficult to encode in classical frameworks, where handlers are allocated statically.

Service engine. The second layer, called *service engine layer*, deals with all the aspects that come into play when a behaviour is executed within a service engine. When a service is invoked a particular instance of a service behaviour, called *session*, is created and executed within the corresponding service engine. Since multiple invocations can be concurrently done by different clients, it is important to define how the several sessions are executed: they could be performed sequentially or concurrently. Such a feature is called *execution modality*. Moreover, for each created session, it should be defined how the service state is managed. A session state could expire when the session terminates or a it could remain available and accessible by other sessions. In the former case the state is *not persistent* whereas in the latter case the state is *persistent*. We call this feature *state persistence*. Depending on the execution modality and the state persistence, four service categories are distinguished and summarized below:

1. *concurrent/not persistent*: services which concurrently execute their sessions, each one equipped with its own state that expires when the session is terminated. Usually, WS-BPEL processes belong to this category.
2. *concurrent/persistent*: services which concurrently execute their sessions. Sessions share a common state which does not expire. Services which access to a database could belong to this category.
3. *sequential/not persistent*: services whose sessions are forced to be executed following a sequential order, where each session is equipped with its own state that expires when the session is terminated. For example, a video game is accessed sequentially by each player and each session of the game has its own ephemeral state.
4. *sequential/persistent*: services whose sessions are forced to be executed following a sequential order, where the state does not expire after a session termination. A cash teller machine could be considered as an example of service belonging to this category.

Another issue which is strongly related to the service engine layer is *message correlation*. This deals with the session identification within a service engine. In the case of multiple service invocations that generate a set of sessions, we need to program the engine in such a way that messages are delivered to the right session instance. These aspects are usually in charge of the service execution engines which provide mechanisms for managing with these details. In general, message correlation provides an application level mechanism for supporting session identification independently from the underlying executing framework.

The syntax of the service engine layer is composed of a service declaration and a service execution environment. Within the service declaration it is possible to specify the service behaviour, the state persistence, the correlation set and the execution modality whereas in the service execution environment all the initiated service sessions will be executed. Namely, the service declaration is defined as follows:

$$U ::= P_\times \mid P_\bullet \qquad W ::= c \triangleright U \qquad D ::= !W \mid W^*$$

where $P \in X_{SC}$ is a service behaviour, flag $\times$ denotes that P is equipped with a not persistent state and flag $\bullet$ denotes that P is equipped with a persistent one. c is the correlation set which guards the execution of the sessions, $!W$ denotes a concurrent execution of the sessions and W^* denotes the fact that sessions are executed in a sequential order. D is a service declaration. Hence, a service engine is defined as follows:

$$Y ::= D[H] \qquad H ::= P_S \mid H \mid H \qquad P_S ::= (P, S)$$

where Y is service engine and it is composed of a service declaration D and an execution environment H. H can be a service behaviour coupled with a state (P_S) or the parallel composition of them $(H \mid H)$.

Services system. The services system layer allows for the composition of different engines into a system. The service engines are composed in parallel and they are equipped with a location that allows us to univocally distinguish them in the system. Namely, the syntax of systems is as follows:

$$E ::= Y_l \mid E \parallel E$$

A service engine system E can be a located service engine Y_l, where l is a location, or a parallel composition of engines. A message can be exchanged between two service engines only if an input operation and an output operation on the same operation can be executed by the two service engines.

The Credit Request scenario. We now present part of orchestrator for the credit request scenario modeled with SOCK.

WorkFlow	::= *login(credentials, response, CheckLogin);*
	enterCredit(credit);
	enterBalances(balances);
	enterSecurities(securities);
	$\{Decision\}_{dec}$
CheckLogin	::= *checkLogin@AccountService(credentials,response)*
Decision	::= *calculateRating@RatingService(⟨ balances, securities, credit ⟩,rating);*
	(rating=="AAA"? 0: Employee);Offer
Employee	::= *rating=="BBB"? ToClerk: ToSupervisor*
ToClerk	::= *inst([denyFault ↦ DeclineCk]);*
	requestApproval@ClerkService(⟨ balances, securities, credit ⟩, ⟨⟩)
ToSupervisor	::= *inst([denyFault↦ DeclineSv]);*
	requestApproval@SupervisorService(⟨ balances, securities, credit ⟩, ⟨⟩)
DeclineCk	::= *genDeclineCk@DeclineService(⟨ balances, securities, credit ⟩, decline);*
	sendDecline@Customer(decline)
DeclineSv	::= *genDeclineSv@DeclineService(⟨ balances, securities, credit ⟩, decline);*
	sendDecline@Customer(decline)
Offer	::= *genOffer@OfferService(⟨ balances, securities, credit ⟩,offer);*
	sendOffer@Customer(offer)

The process *WorkFlow* describes the behaviour of the orchestrator responsible for receiving the customer's request and then replying her/him after having invoked the *RatingService* and, in case it is necessary, the *ClerkService* or the *SupervisorService*. The customer initially invokes the *login, enterCredit, enterBalences*, and *enterSecurities* operations. Note that *login* is a request-response operation that invokes a remote *AccountService* to check the credentials, while the other operations are one-way. After receiving the needed information, the orchestrator starts the scope *Decision_{dec}* responsible for sending the reply to the customer. Reply can be sent either to the *sendOffer* or to the *sendDecline* operations of the *Customer*. We assume that *sendDecline* is generated by a fault handler of the orchestrator activated by the fault *denyFault*. This fault is not raised internally by the orchestrator, but by the external *ClerkService* or *SupervisorService* while they are processing the *requestApproval* operation.[1] We assume that those services raise *denyFault* in case their evaluation of the customer's request is negative. As *denyFault* is raised while processing a request-response operation invoked by the orchestrator, the SOCK semantics guarantees that *denyFault* is transparently sent back to the orchestrator thus activating the corresponding fault handler. On the orchestration side, the *inst* primitive is used to dynamically install the correct fault handler that invokes either *genDeclineCk* or *genDeclineSv* in order to generate the expected decline message (in which we assume that there is also indication of who decided to decline the offer). This decline message is then sent back to the customer through its *sendDecline* operation. In case no *denyFault* is raised, an offer generated by an external *OfferService* is sent back to the customer through its *sendOffer* operation.

JOLIE: Java Orchestration Language Interpreter Engine. One of the features that mainly distinguishes SOCK from the other Sensoria calculi is that it is closer to real programming languages. On the one hand, this makes SOCK syntax richer of constructs and details (such as, e.g., the three layers definition) but, on the other hand, this makes SOCK also closer to actual service orchestration languages. This feature of SOCK is witnessed by the fact that JOLIE, a fully fledged programming language, has been developed simply extending the calculus with primitives for data manipulation and by adding the support for interoperability with network protocols (such as SOAP and https). JOLIE (Java Orchestration Language Interpreter Engine) [MGZ07, GMLZ07] is an opensource project released under the LGPL license and publicly available for consultation and use [JOL]. The syntax of JOLIE resembles that of C. This is in contrast with the most credited Web Services orchestration languages, such as XLANG [Tha01] and WS-BPEL, which are based upon XML. The interpretation of JOLIE programs is done via inspection of their abstract syntax tree, and the correspondence with the operational semantics of the SOCK calculus is guaranteed by the fact that each node in the abstract syntax tree simply implements the SOS rules of the corresponding construct.

4   Conclusion

We have reported the main activities conducted on the development of new linguistic tools for services specification and verification. To enable the reader to appreciate the differences between the used formalisms, we considered a simple case study as a running example. The presented formalisms have been the basis for developing new techniques for qualitative and quantitative analysis of services as well as for the formal investigation of patterns and good practices for the composition and orchestration of services. Results on these aspects are reported in other chapters of this volume or have been published elsewhere.

---

[1] Due to space limitation we do not report the specification of the behaviour of the external services invoked by the orchestrator.

A type systems for guaranteeing safe interaction of CaSPiS processes in presented in Chapter 2-3 while a markovian variant of CaSPiS and an associated stochastic logic is introduced in Chapter 5-1 for assessing quantitative aspects of services. A type system for checking protocol compatibility between invokers and service providers in SSCC is presented in [LVMR07a]; moreover, SSCC is endowed with bisimilarity techniques used for proving equivalence of service-oriented systems [CLM+08, LVMR07b].

In Chapter 2-3, a type system has been introduced for ensuring conversation fidelity and deadlock absence of CC specifications; a synopsis of the associated behavioral theory is studied in Chapter 2-2. A summary of encoding techniques that guarantee a faithful representation of compensable transactions in CC, may be found in Chapter 3-3 while a model-checking tools for CC is presented in Chapter 4-3.

Several analysis techniques have been developed for COWS. A Flow Logic for checking information flow properties is presented in [BNNP08], a stochastic extension of COWS that enables verification of quantitative properties is presented in Chapter 5-5, and a few observational semantics for checking interchangeability of COWS terms and conformance against service specifications are briefly presented in Chapter 2-2. A temporal logic and the associated model checker for functional properties are presented in Chapter 4-2, while a type system for guaranteeing confidentiality properties is presented in [LPT07b]. The application of the last two techniques to the analysis of the Finance case study is reported in Chapter 7-4.

As described in Chapter 3-3 the core calculus SOCK allowed us to investigate problems deriving from the combination of failure recovery techniques with bidirectional service invocations, and to formally verify a correct implementation in the orchestration language JOLIE of the SAGAS model for programming long running transactions.

Acknowledgements. This paper is the result of a collaborative effort of many researchers not just of those mentioned in the list of authors. The names of the contributors can be inferred from the list of published papers on the specific core calculi listed in the references. Nevertheless, here we would like to specifically thank some of our colleagues. Lucia Acciai and Francesco Tiezzi contributed to the formalization of the case study that we used as a running example. Francisco Martins wrote the case study in SSCC. Hugo T. Vieira is one of the main co-author of CC and of the associated conversation-type theory. Claudio Guidi contributed to the modeling of the case study in SOCK and to the description of the JOLIE language. Finally, we would like to thank Mariangiola Dezani and Emilio Tuosto for the careful reading of the paper and the many useful suggestions.

References

[BBC+06]   Boreale, M., Bruni, R., Caires, L., De Nicola, R., Lanese, I., Loreti, M., Martins, F., Montanari, U., Ravara, A., Sangiorgi, D., Vasconcelos, V., Zavattaro, G.: SCC: a service centered calculus. In: Bravetti, M., Núñez, M., Tennenholtz, M. (eds.) WS-FM 2006. LNCS, vol. 4184, pp. 38–57. Springer, Heidelberg (2006)

[BBDL08]   Boreale, M., Bruni, R., De Nicola, R., Loreti, M.: Sessions and pipelines for structured service programming. In: Barthe, G., de Boer, F.S. (eds.) FMOODS 2008. LNCS, vol. 5051, pp. 19–38. Springer, Heidelberg (2008)

[BGG⁺06]   Busi, N., Gorrieri, R., Guidi, C., Lucchi, R., Zavattaro, G.: SOCK: a calculus for service oriented computing. In: Dan, A., Lamersdorf, W. (eds.) ICSOC 2006. LNCS, vol. 4294, pp. 63–81. Springer, Heidelberg (2006)

[BHF04]   Butler, M.J., Hoare, C.A.R., Ferreira, C.: A trace semantics for long-running transactions. In: Abdallah, A.E., Jones, C.B., Sanders, J.W. (eds.) CSP 2005. LNCS, vol. 3525, pp. 133–150. Springer, Heidelberg (2005)

[BNNP08]   Bauer, J., Nielson, F., Nielson, H.R., Pilegaard, H.: Relational Analysis of Correlation. In: Alpuente, M., Vidal, G. (eds.) SAS 2008. LNCS, vol. 5079, pp. 32–46. Springer, Heidelberg (2008)

[CG98]   Cardelli, L., Gordon, A.D.: Mobile ambients. In: Nivat, M. (ed.) FOSSACS 1998. LNCS, vol. 1378, pp. 140–155. Springer, Heidelberg (1998)

[CHY⁺06]   Carbone, M., Honda, K., Yoshida, N., Milner, R., Brown, G., Ross-Talbot, S.: A Theoretical Basis of Communication–Centred Concurrent Programming. Technical report, WCDL-Working Note (2006)

[CLM⁺07]   Cruz-Filipe, L., Lanese, I., Martins, F., Ravara, A., Vasconcelos, V.T.: Bisimulations in SSCC. DI/FCUL TR 07–37, Department of Informatics, University of Lisbon (December 2007)

[CLM⁺08]   Cruz-Filipe, L., Lanese, I., Martins, F., Ravara, A., Vasconcelos, V.T.: Behavioural theory at work: program transformations in a service-centred calculus. In: Barthe, G., de Boer, F.S. (eds.) FMOODS 2008. LNCS, vol. 5051, pp. 59–77. Springer, Heidelberg (2008)

[CV09]   Caires, L., Vieira, H.T.: Conversation Types. In: Castagna, G. (ed.) ESOP 2009. LNCS, vol. 5502, pp. 285–300. Springer, Heidelberg (2009)

[GLMZ08]   Guidi, C., Lanese, I., Montesi, F., Zavattaro, G.: On the interplay between fault handling and request-response service invocations. In: ACSD 2008, pp. 190–198. IEEE, Los Alamitos (2008)

[GMLZ07]   Guidi, C., Montesi, F., Lanese, I., Zavattaro, G.: Dynamic fault handling for service oriented applications. In: ECOWS 2008, pp. 225–234. IEEE, Los Alamitos (2007)

[HVK98]   Honda, K., Vasconcelos, V.T., Kubo, M.: Language primitives and type discipline for structured communication-based programming. In: Hankin, C. (ed.) ESOP 1998. LNCS, vol. 1381, pp. 122–138. Springer, Heidelberg (1998)

[HYC08]   Honda, K., Yoshida, N., Carbone, M.: Multiparty Asynchronous Session Types. In: POPL 2008, pp. 273–284. ACM, New York (2008)

[JOL]   JOLIE: website, http://www.jolie-lang.org

[Lap08]   Lapadula, A.: A Formal Account of Web Services Orchestration. PhD thesis, Dipartimento di Sistemi e Informatica, Università degli Studi di Firenze (2008)

[LPT06]   Lapadula, A., Pugliese, R., Tiezzi, F.: A WSDL-based type system for WS-BPEL. In: Ciancarini, P., Wiklicky, H. (eds.) COORDINATION 2006. LNCS, vol. 4038, pp. 145–163. Springer, Heidelberg (2006)

[LPT07a]   Lapadula, A., Pugliese, R., Tiezzi, F.: A Calculus for Orchestration of Web Services. In: De Nicola, R. (ed.) ESOP 2007. LNCS, vol. 4421, pp. 33–47. Springer, Heidelberg (2007), http://rap.dsi.unifi.it/cows

[LPT07b]   Lapadula, A., Pugliese, R., Tiezzi, F.: Regulating data exchange in service oriented applications. In: Arbab, F., Sirjani, M. (eds.) FSEN 2007. LNCS, vol. 4767, pp. 223–239. Springer, Heidelberg (2007)

[LVMR07a]   Lanese, I., Vasconcelos, V.T., Martins, F., Ravara, A.: Disciplining Orchestration and Conversation in Service-Oriented Computing. In: SEFM 2007, pp. 305–314. IEEE, Los Alamitos (2007)

[LVMR07b]   Lanese, I., Vasconcelos, V.T., Martins, F., Ravara, A.: Disciplining orchestration and conversation in service-oriented computing. DI/FCUL TR 07–2, DIFCUL (March 2007)

[MC07]   Misra, J., Cook, W.R.: Computation orchestration: A basis for wide-area computing. Journal of Software and Systems Modeling 6(1), 83–110 (2007)

[MGZ07]   Montesi, F., Guidi, C., Zavattaro, G.: Composing services with jolie. In: ECOWS 2007, pp. 13–22. IEEE, Los Alamitos (2007)

[MPW92]   Milner, R., Parrow, J., Walker, J.: A Calculus of Mobile Processes, I and II. Information and Computation 100(1), 1–40, 41–77 (1992)

[OAS07]   OASIS WSBPEL TC. Web Services Business Process Execution Language Version 2.0. Technical report, OASIS (April 2007)

[Obj06]   Object Management Group (OMG). Business Process Modeling Notation (BPMN) Specification (February 2006)

[Sen]   Sensoria Project. Public web site, http://sensoria.fast.de/

[Tha01]   Thatte, S.: XLANG: Web Services for Business Process Design (2001)

[Tie09]   Tiezzi, F.: Specification and Analysis of Service-Oriented Applications. PhD thesis, Dipartimento di Sistemi e Informatica, Università degli Studi di Firenze (2009)

[VCS08]   Vieira, H.T., Caires, L., Seco, J.C.: The Conversation Calculus: A Model of Service Oriented Computation. In: Gairing, M. (ed.) ESOP 2008. LNCS, vol. 4960, pp. 269–283. Springer, Heidelberg (2008)

[vdAtKB03] van der Aalst, W.M.P., ter Hofstede, A.H.M., Kiepuszewski, B., Barros, A.P.: Workflow patterns. Distributed and Parallel Databases 14(1), 5–51 (2003)

[WSD01]   Web Services Description Language (WSDL). World Wide Web Consortium (2001)

Behavioral Theory for Session-Oriented Calculi[*]

Ivan Lanese[1], Antonio Ravara[2], and Hugo Torres Vieira[2]

[1] Focus Team, Università di Bologna/INRIA, Italy
lanese@cs.unibo.it
[2] CITI and Dep. of Informatics, FCT, Univ. Nova de Lisboa, Portugal
{aravara,htv}@fct.unl.pt

Abstract. This chapter presents the behavioral theory of some of the SENSORIA core calculi. We consider SSCC, μse and CC as representatives of the session-based approach and COWS as representative of the correlation-based one.

For SSCC, μse and CC the main point is the structure that the session/conversation mechanism creates in programs. We show how the differences between binary sessions, multiparty sessions and dynamic conversations are captured by different behavioral laws. We also exploit those laws for proving the correctness of program transformations.

For COWS the main point is that communication is prioritized (the best matching input captures the output), and this has a strong influence on the behavioral theory of COWS. In particular, we show that communication in COWS is neither purely synchronous nor purely asynchronous.

1   Introduction

In most formal languages, it is common to have several terms denoting the same computational process. To understand when this situation occurs, the language needs to be equipped with a notion of equivalence. This notion relies on an underlying description of the behavior of such process.

In process calculi the behavior of systems is usually defined in terms of either a reduction relation or of a labeled transition relation (also called labeled transition system, or LTS). The former describes the possible evolutions of a process in isolation; the latter allows to describe also the potential interactions with the environment (usually, the latter relation includes the former).

The most natural notion of term equivalence is behavioral indistinguishability in any possible context the term may occur in. In fact, it should be possible to replace one equivalent process for another without changing the observable behavior of the system (or part of it). Then, such a relation guarantees the correctness of program transformations developed for, e.g., improving the global performance or to increase fault tolerance. In service-oriented computing, equivalent services can serve the same purpose in a complex orchestration, thus the choice can be driven by their non-functional properties such as cost or performance. Such a notion is called a *contextual* equivalence, and distinguishability

---

[*] This work has been partially sponsored by the project SENSORIA, IST-2005-016004.

M. Wirsing and M. Hölzl (Eds.): SENSORIA Project, LNCS 6582, pp. 189–213, 2011.

is based on a notion of observation. In sequential settings, one may define as observables the values produced by a computation, or even simply termination; in concurrent settings the observables are usually descriptions of a process interaction potential.

Contextual equivalences are, however, difficult to use. They require an universal quantification over possible contexts (normally infinitely many), thus lacking a practical proof technique. A typical solution is to look for a co-inductive congruence relation which characterizes it.

In the realm of process algebras, one can find a myriad of behavioral equivalence notions (van Glabbeek presents an overview, interrelating several notions, in [11]). Different equivalences (or pre-orders) take into account different ways of observing the behavior of processes. Considering the most significant notions, trace equivalence [12] looks at the sequence of observable actions, (labeled) bisimilarity [17] takes into account also points of choice, and testing equivalences [10] consider the interactions between the process and an observer.

Different equivalences can be useful for different purposes; however, two criteria are important: being a congruence, and, in particular, coinciding with the contextual equivalence (which is a congruence by definition). The former result means that given two equivalent processes, placing them in a language context will produce two processes that are again equivalent, thus allowing substituting "equals for equals" in context, not changing the global behavior. The congruence result also testifies that all the constructs of a calculus may be soundly interpreted as compositional semantic operators on bisimilarity equivalence classes. If an equivalence coincides with a given contextual equivalence, it captures exactly the abstract semantics given by the chosen observables.

In mobile process calculi like the π-calculus [21], standard contextual equivalences are barbed congruence [18] and barbed bisimilarity [13] (the basic observables are called barbs). Their co-inductive characterization is based on the notion of *bisimilarity*. For instance, for barbed congruence, it is *full bisimilarity* (the substitution-closed ground bisimilarity) over a(n early) LTS. Bisimilarity is the largest bisimulation, the latter being a relation $\mathcal{R}$ such that if $(P, Q) \in \mathcal{R}$ then for each action of P there is a corresponding action of Q and the two actions lead to processes P' and Q' such that $(P', Q') \in \mathcal{R}$. Bisimilarity is a good tool for proving process equivalence, since it is naturally equipped with a proof technique: to prove that two processes P and Q are bisimilar it is enough to exhibit a bisimulation including the pair (P, Q). There are, in general, two notions of bisimulation: a strong one, taking into account also internal actions, and a weak one, abstracting them away. The latter is particularly interesting, since it allows to prove correctness of program optimizations (in fact equivalent processes need not perform the same number of internal actions).

In this chapter we apply bisimilarity notions to some of the SENSORIA core calculi, namely SSCC, μse, CC and COWS (see Chapter 2-1 for a description of SSCC, CC and COWS, and [6] for μse). The different features of the calculi have a strong impact on their behavioral theory.

For the session-based calculi, standard notions of equivalence can be used, and the main point is the characterization of the communication structure of the processes. In fact, the different notions of binary session (for SSCC), multiparty session (for μse) and dynamic conversation (for CC) are captured by different behavioral equations. We discuss those laws, and exploit them to prove the correctness of different kinds of program transformations. For CC we also prove a normal form result.

Communication in COWS is based on the correlation set mechanism, which provides prioritized communication (the best matching input captures the output). The corresponding barbed bisimilarity is captured by a more complex form of bisimilarity with respect to the ones for the other calculi, and shows that communication in COWS is neither purely synchronous nor purely asynchronous.

2   Behavioral Theory for SSCC

In this section we study the behavioral theory of SSCC (Stream-based Service Centred Calculus [15]), and we apply it to prove the correctness of some program transformations.

We recall that SSCC is a calculus for modelling service-oriented systems based on the concepts of services, binary sessions, and streams. The (static) syntax of SSCC has been defined in Chapter 2-1. We refer to this chapter also for an informal description of the operators, while presenting here the LTS semantics and the behavioral theory. We need as auxiliary operators to define the semantics also $r \lhd P$ for client-side session, $r \rhd P$ for service-side session, $(\nu r)P$ for session name restriction and stream P as $f = v$ in Q for stream with stored values. Processes are herein written in this extended (called run-time) syntax, and considered up to the structural congruence relation inductively defined by the rules in Fig. 1. Note that structural congruence is included in bisimilarity (forthcoming Lemma 2).

Operational Semantics. The semantics of SSCC is defined using an LTS in the early style. This LTS is slightly different, but equivalent to its original presentation in [15]. We require processes to have no free process variables.

$$P|\mathbf{0} \;\equiv\; P \qquad P|Q \;\equiv\; Q|P \qquad (P|Q)|R \;\equiv\; P|(Q|R)$$

$$(\nu n)P|Q \;\equiv\; (\nu n)(P|Q) \quad \text{if } n \notin \text{fn}(Q) \qquad r \rhd (\nu a)P \;\equiv\; (\nu a)(r \rhd P)$$

$$\text{stream } (\nu a)P \text{ as } f = v \text{ in } Q \;\equiv\; (\nu a)(\text{stream } P \text{ as } f = v \text{ in } Q) \quad \text{if } a \notin \text{fn}(Q) \cup \{v\}$$

$$\text{stream } P \text{ as } f = v \text{ in } (\nu a)Q \;\equiv\; (\nu a)(\text{stream } P \text{ as } f = v \text{ in } Q) \quad \text{if } a \notin \text{fn}(P) \cup \{v\}$$

$$(\nu n)(\nu m)P \;\equiv\; (\nu m)(\nu n)P \qquad (\nu a)\mathbf{0} \;\equiv\; \mathbf{0} \qquad \text{rec } X.P \;\equiv\; P[\text{rec } X.P/X]$$

Fig. 1. Structural congruence

Definition 1 (SSCC Labeled Transition System). *The rules in Fig. 2, to-gether with the symmetric version of rules* L-PAR, L-PAR-CLOSE, *and* L-SESS-COM-CLOSE, *inductively define the LTS on processes.*

The LTS uses μ as a metavariable for labels. The bound names in labels are r in service definition activation and service invocation and a in extrusion labels (conventionally, they are all in parenthesis). Label $\uparrow v$ denotes sending value v. Dually, label $\downarrow v$ is receiving value v. We use $\updownarrow v$ to denote one of $\uparrow v$ or $\downarrow v$, and we assume that when multiple $\updownarrow v$ appear in the same rule they are instantiated in the same direction, and that $\overline{\updownarrow} v$ denotes the opposite direction. We use similar conventions for other labels.

Continuing with the labels, $a \Leftarrow (r)$ and $a \Rightarrow (r)$ denote respectively the request and the activation of a service, where a is the name of the service, and r is the name of the new session to be created. We use $a \Leftrightarrow (r)$ to denote one of $a \Leftarrow (r)$ or $a \Rightarrow (r)$. Furthermore, label $\Uparrow v$ denotes the feeding of value v into a stream, while label $f \Downarrow v$ reads value v from stream f. When an input or an output label crosses a session construct (rule L-SESS-VAL), we add to the label the name of the session and whether it is a server or a client session (for example, $\downarrow v$ may become $r \lhd \downarrow v$).

The label denoting a conversation step in a free session r is $r\tau$, and if the value passed in the session channel is private, it remains private in the resulting process. A label τ is obtained only when r is restricted (rule L-SESS-RES). Thus a τ action can be obtained in four cases: a communication inside a restricted session, a service invocation, a feed or a read from a stream. Note also that we have two contexts causing interaction: parallel composition and stream. Finally, bound actions, $(a)\mu$, represent the extrusion of a in their respective free counterparts μ.

Some processes, such as $r \lhd r \lhd P$, can be written using the run-time syntax, but they are not reachable from processes in the static syntax. We consider these processes ill-formed, and will not consider them anymore.

Bisimilarity. We study the usual notions of strong and weak bisimilarity. Both are non-input congruences in the class of SSCC processes. One can get a congruence by considering (strong or weak) full bisimilarity, i.e., by closing bisimilarity with respect to service name substitutions (there is no reason to close with respect to session or stream names, since no substitutions are performed on them). Although the general strategy is the same as for the π-calculus, the proof techniques themselves differ significantly. Herein we only present the main results. Detailed proofs can be found in [8].

To define weak bisimilarity we introduce some abbreviations: let $P \overset{\tau}{\Rightarrow} Q$ denote $P(\overset{\tau}{\rightarrow})^n Q$ (with $n \geq 0$, i.e., zero or more transitions) and let $P \overset{\alpha}{\Rightarrow} Q$ denote $P \overset{\tau}{\Rightarrow} \overset{\alpha}{\rightarrow} \overset{\tau}{\Rightarrow} Q$ for $\alpha \neq \tau$.

Definition 2 (Strong and Weak Bisimilarity). *A symmetric binary relation $\mathcal{R}$ on processes is a* (strong) *bisimulation if, for any processes P, Q such that $P\mathcal{R}Q$, if $P \overset{\alpha}{\rightarrow} P'$ with $\mathrm{bn}(\alpha) \cap \mathrm{fn}(Q) = \emptyset$, then there exists Q' such that $Q \overset{\alpha}{\rightarrow} Q'$*

$$v.P \xrightarrow{\Uparrow v} P \qquad (x)P \xrightarrow{\Downarrow v} P[v/x] \qquad \text{feed}\, v.P \xrightarrow{\Uparrow v} P \qquad f(x).P \xrightarrow{f \Downarrow v} P[v/x]$$
$$\text{(L-SEND, L-RECEIVE, L-FEED, L-READ)}$$

$$\frac{P \xrightarrow{\mu} P' \quad \mu \neq \Uparrow v \quad \mathrm{bn}(\mu) \cap (\mathrm{fn}(Q) \cup \{w\}) = \emptyset}{\text{stream}\, P \,\text{as}\, f = w \,\text{in}\, Q \xrightarrow{\mu} \text{stream}\, P' \,\text{as}\, f = w \,\text{in}\, Q} \qquad \text{(L-STREAM-PASS-P)}$$

$$\frac{Q \xrightarrow{\mu} Q' \quad \mu \neq f \Downarrow v \quad \mathrm{bn}(\mu) \cap (\mathrm{fn}(P) \cup \{w\}) = \emptyset}{\text{stream}\, P \,\text{as}\, f = w \,\text{in}\, Q \xrightarrow{\mu} \text{stream}\, P \,\text{as}\, f = w \,\text{in}\, Q'} \qquad \text{(L-STREAM-PASS-Q)}$$

$$\frac{P \xrightarrow{\Uparrow v} P'}{\text{stream}\, P \,\text{as}\, f = w \,\text{in}\, Q \xrightarrow{\tau} \text{stream}\, P' \,\text{as}\, f = v :: w \,\text{in}\, Q} \qquad \text{(L-STREAM-FEED)}$$

$$\frac{Q \xrightarrow{f \Downarrow v} Q'}{\text{stream}\, P \,\text{as}\, f = w :: v \,\text{in}\, Q \xrightarrow{\tau} \text{stream}\, P \,\text{as}\, f = w \,\text{in}\, Q'} \qquad \text{(L-STREAM-CONS)}$$

$$\frac{r \notin \mathrm{fn}(P)}{a \Leftarrow P \xrightarrow{a \Leftarrow (r)} r \triangleleft P} \qquad \frac{r \notin \mathrm{fn}(P)}{a \Rightarrow P \xrightarrow{a \Rightarrow (r)} r \triangleright P} \qquad \text{(L-CALL, L-DEF)}$$

$$\frac{P \xrightarrow{\mu} P' \quad \mathrm{bn}(\mu) \cap \mathrm{fn}(Q) = \emptyset}{P|Q \xrightarrow{\mu} P'|Q} \qquad \frac{P \xrightarrow{\Uparrow v} P'}{r \bowtie P \xrightarrow{r \bowtie \Uparrow v} r \bowtie P'}$$
$$\text{(L-PAR, L-SESS-VAL)}$$

$$\frac{P[\text{rec}\, X.P/X] \xrightarrow{\mu} P'}{\text{rec}\, X.P \xrightarrow{\mu} P'} \qquad \frac{P \xrightarrow{r \bowtie \Uparrow v} P' \quad Q \xrightarrow{r \bowtie \Downarrow v} Q'}{\text{stream}\, P \,\text{as}\, f = w \,\text{in}\, Q \xrightarrow{\tau\tau} \text{stream}\, P' \,\text{as}\, f = w \,\text{in}\, Q'}$$
$$\text{(L-REC, L-SESS-COM-STREAM)}$$

$$\frac{P \xrightarrow{a \Leftrightarrow (r)} P' \quad Q \xrightarrow{a \overline{\Leftrightarrow} (r)} Q'}{\text{stream}\, P \,\text{as}\, f = w \,\text{in}\, Q \xrightarrow{\tau} (\nu r)\text{stream}\, P' \,\text{as}\, f = w \,\text{in}\, Q'} \qquad \text{(L-SERV-COM-STREAM)}$$

$$\frac{P \xrightarrow{r \bowtie \Uparrow v} P' \quad Q \xrightarrow{r \bowtie \Downarrow v} Q'}{P|Q \xrightarrow{\tau\tau} P'|Q'} \qquad \frac{P \xrightarrow{a \Leftrightarrow (r)} P' \quad Q \xrightarrow{a \overline{\Leftrightarrow} (r)} Q'}{P|Q \xrightarrow{\tau} (\nu r)(P'|Q')}$$
$$\text{(L-SESS-COM-PAR, L-SERV-COM-PAR)}$$

$$\frac{P \xrightarrow{\mu} P' \quad n \notin \mathrm{n}(\mu)}{(\nu n)P \xrightarrow{\mu} (\nu n)P'} \qquad \frac{P \xrightarrow{\tau\tau} P'}{(\nu r)P \xrightarrow{\tau} (\nu r)P'} \qquad \frac{P \xrightarrow{\mu} P' \quad \mu \neq \updownarrow v \quad r \notin \mathrm{bn}(\mu)}{r \bowtie P \xrightarrow{\mu} r \bowtie P'}$$
$$\text{(L-RES, L-SESS-RES, L-SESS-PASS)}$$

$$\frac{P \xrightarrow{r \bowtie (v) \Uparrow v} P' \quad Q \xrightarrow{r \bowtie \Downarrow v} Q' \quad v \notin \mathrm{fn}(Q)}{P|Q \xrightarrow{\tau\tau} (\nu v)(P'|Q')} \qquad \frac{P \xrightarrow{\mu} P' \quad \mu \in \{\uparrow a, r \bowtie \uparrow a, \Uparrow a\}}{(\nu a)P \xrightarrow{(a)\mu} P'}$$
$$\text{(L-PAR-CLOSE, L-EXTR)}$$

$$\frac{P \xrightarrow{r \bowtie (v) \Uparrow v} P' \quad Q \xrightarrow{r \bowtie \Downarrow v} Q' \quad v \notin \mathrm{fn}(Q) \cup \{w\}}{\text{stream}\, P \,\text{as}\, f = w \,\text{in}\, Q \xrightarrow{\tau\tau} (\nu v)\text{stream}\, P' \,\text{as}\, f = w \,\text{in}\, Q'} \qquad \text{(L-SESS-COM-CLOSE)}$$

$$\frac{P \xrightarrow{(v) \Uparrow v} P' \quad v \notin \mathrm{fn}(Q) \cup \{w\}}{\text{stream}\, P \,\text{as}\, f = w \,\text{in}\, Q \xrightarrow{\tau} (\nu v)\text{stream}\, P' \,\text{as}\, f = v :: w \,\text{in}\, Q} \qquad \text{(L-FEED-CLOSE)}$$

Fig. 2. SSCC labeled transition system

and $P' \mathrel{\mathcal{R}} Q'$. *(Strong) bisimilarity $\sim$ is the largest bisimulation. Two processes P and Q are (strong) bisimilar if $P \sim Q$.*

Weak bisimilarity $\approx$ is like the strong version, but using weak transitions $P \overset{\alpha}{\Rightarrow} Q$ instead of strong transitions $P \overset{\alpha}{\rightarrow} Q$.

Also, a full strong (resp. weak) bisimulation is a strong (resp. weak) bisimulation closed under service name substitutions, and we call full strong (resp. weak) bisimilarity $\sim_f$ (resp. $\approx_f$) the largest full strong (resp. weak) bisimulation.

Note that bisimilarity (respectively full bisimilarity) can be obtained as the union of all bisimulations (respectively full bisimulations). Moreover, as desired, structurally congruent processes (cf. Fig. 1) are strong bisimilar.

Lemma 1 (Harmony Lemma). *Let P and Q be processes with $P \equiv Q$. If $P \overset{\alpha}{\rightarrow} P'$, then $Q \overset{\alpha}{\rightarrow} Q'$ with $P' \equiv Q'$, and vice-versa.*

Lemma 2. *Structurally congruent processes are full bisimilar.*

As in the π-calculus, strong and weak full bisimilarity are congruences, i.e., they are closed under arbitrary contexts.

Theorem 1. *Strong and weak full bisimilarity are congruences.*

Useful Axioms. Even if presenting a complete axiomatization for such a complex calculus is out of the scope of this chapter, we present here some axioms (equational laws correct with respect to strong/weak full bisimilarity) that capture key facts about the behavior of processes. Some of them are useful to prove the correctness of the transformations presented in the following. To show the axioms we need to define contexts.

An n-ary context is a process where n subterms have been replaced by symbols $\bullet_1, \ldots, \bullet_n$. The application $\mathcal{C}[\![P_1, \ldots, P_n]\!]$ of context $\mathcal{C}[\![\bullet_1, \ldots, \bullet_n]\!]$ to processes $P_1, \ldots, P_n$ is the process obtained by replacing $\bullet_i$ with P_i.

The correctness of the axioms below can be proved by considering as full bisimulation all the instances of the equations together with the identity.

Session Garbage Collection

$$(\nu r)\mathcal{D}[\![r \rhd \mathbf{0}, r \lhd \mathbf{0}]\!] \sim_f \mathcal{D}[\![\mathbf{0}, \mathbf{0}]\!] \qquad \text{where } \mathcal{D} \text{ does not bind } r \qquad (1)$$

Stream Garbage Collection

$$\mathsf{stream}\, \mathbf{0} \,\mathsf{as}\, f \,\mathsf{in}\, P \sim_f P \qquad \text{if } f \text{ does not occur in } P \qquad (2)$$

Session Independence

$$r \bowtie Q \mid s \bowtie P \sim_f r \bowtie (s \bowtie Q \mid P) \qquad \text{if } s \neq r \qquad (3)$$

The same holds if the two sessions have opposite polarities.

Stream Independence

stream P as f in (stream P' as g in Q) $\sim_f$

stream P' as g in (stream P as f in Q)   if $f \neq g$ (4)

Streams are Orthogonal to Sessions

$$r \bowtie (\text{feed } v \mid P) \sim_f \text{feed } v \mid r \bowtie P \qquad (5)$$

Stream Locality

stream P as f in $(Q \mid Q') \sim_f (\text{stream } P$ as f in $Q) \mid Q'$ if $f \notin \text{fn}(Q')$ (6)

Parallel Composition Versus Streams

stream P as f in $Q \sim_f P \mid Q$ if $f \notin \text{fn}(Q)$ and P does not contain feed   (7)

Interestingly the Session Independence law is strongly dependent on the available operators, and fails in similar calculi such as [5,4]. This captures the fact that in SSCC session nesting is immaterial.

From Object-Oriented to Service-Oriented Models. We apply now the behavioral theory developed so far to bridge the gap between traditional object-oriented and SENSORIA service-oriented models, so to allow the reuse of existing tools and techniques. We detail a model transformation procedure from a common object-oriented communication pattern into a session-based, service-oriented one, and prove it correct with respect to weak full bisimilarity. Since we have also proved that weak full bisimilarity is a congruence, the behavior of every composition built exploiting these services remains unchanged when moving from the original programs into their transformed versions.

UML Sequence Diagrams [2] (SDs) describe the exchange of messages among the components in a complex system. We present here a typical SD and show how it can be implemented in SSCC by exploiting suitable macros. We then show how subsessions can be used to simplify the implementation.

Object-Oriented View. The SD on the left of Fig. 3 describes a common pattern appearing in scenarios involving (at least) three partners. The description of the communication pattern is as follows.

> Object B receives from object A the value w and forwards it (or a value computed from it) to object C. After receiving the value, object C answers with a value w'. Object B replies with v and finally object C replies with value v'. Then, object B forwards it to object A.

Note that "Object B receives from object A the value w" means that object A invokes a method in object B passing the value w. We can imagine for instance that A is the user of the credit portal in the financial case study (see Chapter 0-3), which invokes the credit portal itself (B). The credit portal then interacts with the rating system (C), possibly exchanging different pieces of information. The final answer is then sent back to the user.

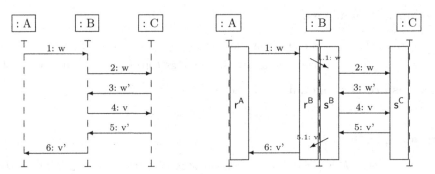

Fig. 3. Sequence diagram communication pattern: object-oriented and session-oriented view

Session-Oriented View. We want to move to a scenario where components are clients and servers of a service-oriented architecture, and where communication happens via sessions. We refine the diagram by incorporating information about the running sessions, in the diagram on the right of Fig. 3, where the slanted arrows mean message passing between sessions. An instance of the credit portal B (let us call these instances *participants*) has a session r running with an instance of client A and another session s running with an instance of the rating system service C. Since sessions involve two partners, a session r between instances of A and B has two sides—called endpoints, r^A at the instance of A and r^B at the instance of B.

In addition to the normal constructs in SSCC, to model object-oriented systems (that do not follow the laws of session communication), it is useful to have two constructs enabling arbitrary message passing. These can be expressed by exploiting fresh auxiliary services.

$$b \Uparrow \langle v_1, ..., v_n \rangle.P \triangleq \text{stream } b \Leftarrow v_1...v_n.\text{feed unit as } f \text{ in } f(v).P$$
$$b \Downarrow (x_1, ..., x_n)P \triangleq \text{stream } b \Rightarrow (z_1)...(z_n).\text{feed } z_1...\text{feed } z_n \text{ as } f$$
$$\text{in } f(x_1)...f(x_n).P$$

where name v and stream f are not used in P and unit is a value used for synchronization.

The diagram on the right of Fig. 3 is directly implemented in SSCC as

$$\text{SC} \triangleq (\nu b, c) \ (\text{A} \mid \text{B} \mid \text{C})$$

where

$$\text{A} \triangleq b \Leftarrow w.(y)P, \ \text{B} \triangleq (\nu b_1, b_2) \ (\text{B}_1 \mid \text{B}_2), \text{ and } \text{C} \triangleq c \Rightarrow (x)w'.(y)v'.S,$$

$$\text{B}_1 \triangleq b \Rightarrow (x)b_1 \Uparrow x.b_2 \Downarrow (y)y.Q, \text{ and } \text{B}_2 \triangleq c \Leftarrow b_1 \Downarrow (x)x.(z)v.(y)b_2 \Uparrow y.R.$$

It is easy to check that the behavior of the process SC above reflects the one described on the right of Fig. 3.

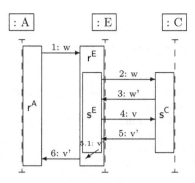

Fig. 4. Sequence diagram: using a subsession

An Optimization. When the credit portal B has the value sent by client A, it may immediately send it to the rating system C, calling it (and thus opening a subsession). One simply has to perform a "local" transformation on B. The resulting diagram is in Fig. 4, and it is implemented in SSCC as process SC′, where we denote by E the new instance of B.

$$SC' \triangleq (\nu b, c) \ (\ A \mid E \mid C \ ) \qquad \text{where}$$

$$E \triangleq b \Rightarrow (x)(\nu b_1)(c \Leftarrow x.(z)v.(y)b_1 \Uparrow y.R \mid b_1 \Downarrow (y)y.Q)$$

Naturally, one asks whether the transformation of SC into SC′ is correct, not changing the observable behavior of processes. Indeed, this is the case, and this can be proved using the definition of full weak bisimilarity and the axioms presented before.

The correctness of the transformation, i.e., SC $\approx_f$ SC′, follows from closure under contexts from the following equation.

$$(\nu c)(B \mid C) \ \approx_f \ (\nu c)(E \mid C) \tag{8}$$

We sketch the correctness proof, while referring to [9] for more details and for other examples of transformations, e.g. replacing auxiliary services with stream-based communications.

Proof (of Equation 8). The proof can be obtained by exhibiting a bisimulation including the two processes. The two processes can mimic each other even if the first one is nondeterministic, since the nondeterminism comes from τ steps, whose order is not important, since the processes are confluent. Garbage collection Equations 1 and 2 are used in the proof. After some steps, the two processes have evolved to:

$$(\nu s)(r \triangleright Q[w/x][v'/y] \mid s \triangleleft R[w/x][w'/z][v'/y] \mid s \triangleright S[w/x][v/y])$$

$$(\nu s)(r \triangleright (s \triangleleft R[w/x][w'/z][v'/y]) \mid Q[w/x][v'/y] \mid s \triangleright S[w/x][v/y])$$

respectively. These processes can be proved equivalent using structural congruence (which is included in full bisimilarity, according to Lemma 2), session independence (Equation 3) and closure under contexts.

$S, T ::=$	$l :: a \Rightarrow P$	Service definition	$\mid \ l :: P$	Located process
$\mid$	$S \mid T$	Composition of systems	$\mid \ (\nu n) S$	New name

$P, Q ::=$	$\mathbf{0}$	Empty process		
$\mid$	$\overline{x} w.P$	Intra-session output	$\mid \ x(y).P$	Intra-session input
$\mid$	$x!w.P$	Intra-location output	$\mid \ x?(y).P$	Intra-location input
$\mid$	$\mathsf{install}[a \Rightarrow P].Q$	Service installation	$\mid \ \mathsf{invoke}\ a.P$	Service invocation
$\mid$	$\mathsf{merge}^p\ e.P$	Entry point	$\mid \ r \triangleright P$	Endpoint
$\mid$	$P \mid Q$	Parallel composition	$\mid \ (\nu n) P$	New name
$\mid$	$\mathsf{rec}\ X.P$	Recursive process	$\mid \ X$	Recursive call

Fig. 5. Syntax of μse systems and processes

3   From Binary to Multiparty Sessions

In this section we apply the notions of bisimilarity from Definition 2 to μse, a name passing calculus for programming dynamic multiparty sessions proposed in [6]. Multiparty sessions extend the idea of sessions to multiparty communications, and have been recently object of deep study in the field of service-oriented computing [3,7,14], since they provide a natural framework to describe the complex interactions among services. The distinctive feature of μse is its ability to dynamically create sessions and merging different existing sessions.

We describe now the syntax and the operational semantics of μse, so to allow to apply bisimilarity in this setting. μse is a calculus featuring names for:

- multiparty sessions (ranged by $r, s, \dots$),
- services (ranged by $a, b, \dots$), able to enter sessions upon invocation,
- channels (ranged by $x, y, \dots$), to route messages inside sessions,
- entry points (ranged by $e, f, \dots$), allowing to merge running sessions,
- locations (ranged by $l, \dots$), where services and sessions are located.

Channels, services and entry points are *communicable values* (ranged over by $v, w, \dots$) while sessions and locations cannot be communicated. We let $n, m, \dots$ range over all names but locations.

The syntax of μse is defined in Fig. 5. Systems (ranged over by $S, T, \dots$) are parallel compositions of *locations* where services are published and processes executed. A location where a service a is defined is meant to be the domain into which all instances of a are executed.

A μse process can be the empty process, a process prefixed by an action, a process running in a session (endpoint), the parallel composition of processes, a process under a name restriction, a recursive process or a recursive invocation.

Processes (ranged over by $P, Q, \dots$) communicate via channels according to two modalities: *intra-session* and *intra-location*. Intra-session communications are used to let different endpoints of the same session to interact regardless their running locations. Conversely, intra-location communications allow endpoints

$$\mathcal{A}|\mathcal{A}' \equiv \mathcal{A}'|\mathcal{A} \qquad \mathcal{A}|\mathbf{0} \equiv \mathcal{A} \qquad (\mathcal{A}|\mathcal{A}')|\mathcal{A}'' \equiv \mathcal{A}|(\mathcal{A}'|\mathcal{A}'')$$

$$(\nu n)(\mathcal{A}|\mathcal{A}'') \equiv \mathcal{A}|(\nu n)\mathcal{A}'', \text{ if } n \notin \text{fn}(\mathcal{A})$$

$$(\nu n)(\nu m)\mathcal{A} \equiv (\nu m)(\nu n)\mathcal{A} \qquad (\nu n)\mathcal{A} \equiv \mathcal{A}, \text{ if } n \notin \text{fn}(\mathcal{A})$$

$$l :: P|l :: Q \equiv l :: (P|Q) \qquad l :: (\nu n)P \equiv (\nu n)(l :: P)$$

$$r \triangleright (\nu n)P \equiv (\nu n)(r \triangleright P), \text{ if } n \neq r \qquad \text{rec } X.P \equiv P\{\text{rec } X.P/X\}$$

$$r \doteq r \equiv \mathbf{0} \qquad (\nu r)(r \doteq s) \equiv \mathbf{0} \qquad r \doteq s|P \equiv r \doteq s|P\{r/s\} \qquad r \doteq s \equiv s \doteq r$$

$$r \triangleright (s \doteq t|P) \equiv s \doteq t|r \triangleright P \qquad l :: (r \doteq s|P) \equiv r \doteq s|l :: P$$

Fig. 6. μse structural congruence

(of possibly different sessions) to communicate, provided that they are running in the same location. This is used to model local communications and replaces SSCC streams.

Processes can install new service definitions in their running locations. Service invocations enable processes to activate new endpoints on the service location. Service invocation requires only the service name, not its location, thus if many services with the same name are available one of them is chosen nondeterministically. Finally, the prefix merge^p e is a mechanism for merging existing sessions.

The operational semantics of μse requires a structural congruence relation and an extended syntax, namely *explicit substitutions* $r \doteq s$ of sessions. Let $\mathcal{A}, \mathcal{B}$ range over systems (including explicit substitutions) and processes. The structural congruence relation is defined in Fig. 6. This exploits the usual notions of free and bound names: the occurrences of y and n are bound in $x(y).P$, $x?(y).P$, $(\nu n)P$ and $(\nu n)S$. Bound names can be safely alpha renamed.

Structural congruence $\equiv$ includes associativity, commutativity and identity over $\mathbf{0}$ for parallel composition and rules for scope extrusion. Also, $\equiv$ gives the semantics of recursion and $r \doteq s$ in terms of substitutions. Note that any explicit substitution $r \doteq s$ is persistent and can freely "float" in the term structure, unless a restriction on r or s forbids its movements.

The operational semantics of μse is specified through an LTS defined on terms up to structural congruence (thus lemmas corresponding to Lemmas 1 and 2 hold by definition). We use α to range over labels. Bound variables occurring in labels are in round parentheses.

Definition 3 (μse Labeled Transition System). *The μse LTS is the least relation generated by the rules in Fig. 7, closed under structural congruence.*

The rules for prefixes simply execute them, moving the information to the transition label. As usual for early semantics, input prefixes guess the actual value and immediately substitute it for the formal variable. Sessions are transparent to most of the actions, while a session name is added to the label in case of session-dependent actions (intra-session communications, invoke and merge). Only the

$$\overline{x}v.P \xrightarrow{\overline{x}v} P \qquad x!v.P \xrightarrow{x!v} P \qquad x(y).P \xrightarrow{xv} P\{v/y\} \qquad x?(y).P \xrightarrow{x?v} P\{v/y\}$$

$$l :: a \Rightarrow P \xrightarrow{r \top a} l :: r \triangleright P \qquad \text{invoke } a.P \xrightarrow{\perp a} P \qquad \text{install}[a \Rightarrow R].P \xrightarrow{a[R]} P$$

$$\text{merge}^p e.P \xrightarrow{e^p} P$$

$$\frac{P \xrightarrow{\alpha} Q \quad \alpha \in \{\perp a, xv, \overline{x}v, e^p\}}{r \triangleright P \xrightarrow{r \ \alpha} r \triangleright Q} \qquad \frac{P \xrightarrow{\alpha} Q \quad \alpha \notin \{\perp a, xv, \overline{x}v, e^p\}}{r \triangleright P \xrightarrow{\alpha} r \triangleright Q}$$

$$\frac{P \xrightarrow{a[R]} Q}{l :: P \xrightarrow{\tau} l :: Q \,|\, l :: a \Rightarrow R} \qquad \frac{P \xrightarrow{\alpha} Q \quad \alpha \notin \{a[R], x?(v), x!v\}}{l :: P \xrightarrow{\alpha} l :: Q}$$

$$\frac{P \xrightarrow{x!v} P' \quad Q \xrightarrow{x?v} Q'}{P|Q \xrightarrow{\tau} P'|Q'} \qquad \frac{\mathcal{A} \xrightarrow{\alpha} \mathcal{A}' \quad \text{bn}(\alpha) \cap \text{fn}(\mathcal{B}) = \emptyset}{\mathcal{A}|\mathcal{B} \xrightarrow{\alpha} \mathcal{A}'|\mathcal{B}} \qquad \frac{\mathcal{A} \xrightarrow{r \ \overline{x}v} \mathcal{A}' \quad \mathcal{B} \xrightarrow{r \ xv} \mathcal{B}'}{\mathcal{A}|\mathcal{B} \xrightarrow{\tau} \mathcal{A}'|\mathcal{B}'}$$

$$\frac{\mathcal{A} \xrightarrow{re^+} \mathcal{A}' \quad \mathcal{B} \xrightarrow{se^-} \mathcal{B}'}{\mathcal{A}|\mathcal{B} \xrightarrow{\tau} \mathcal{A}'|\mathcal{B}'|s = r} \qquad \frac{S \xrightarrow{r \top a} S' \quad T \xrightarrow{r \perp a} T'}{S|T \xrightarrow{\tau} S'|T'}$$

$$\frac{\mathcal{A} \xrightarrow{\alpha} \mathcal{A}' \quad n \notin \text{n}(\alpha)}{(\nu n)\mathcal{A} \xrightarrow{\alpha} (\nu n)\mathcal{A}'} \qquad \frac{\mathcal{A} \xrightarrow{\alpha} \mathcal{A}' \quad \alpha \in \{\overline{x}w, x!w, r\,\overline{x}w, r\,x!w\}}{(\nu w)\mathcal{A} \xrightarrow{(w)\alpha} \mathcal{A}'}$$

Fig. 7. μse operational semantics

name of the innermost session is added. Service definitions can produce sessions, and the session name is guessed in the early style. Install requests are executed when the level of locations is reached. Observe that locations are transparent to all actions but install and intra-location communications. Also, most of the synchronization rules can be applied both at the process and at the system level. The only exceptions are (i) intra-location communication, which is meaningful only at the process level, and (ii) service invocation, which can be stated only at the system level since definitions are always at the top level. Finally, restriction is dealt with using structural congruence, but the rule for extrusions is necessary for interactions with the environment (and notably for bisimulation).

To prove equivalences of μse processes we use the notion of weak bisimilarity, defined as for SSCC (see Definition 2), but using μse LTS. It is not easy to prove that μse bisimilarity is a congruence, since service installation makes it a (partially) higher order calculus, and proving congruence for higher-order calculi is a hard problem. However, standard techniques can be used to show that full bisimilarity is closed under parallel composition, which is the most used composition operation.

As for SSCC, we show here a few axioms for reasoning on μse processes.

Session Garbage Collection

$$r \triangleright \mathbf{0} \sim_f \mathbf{0} \tag{9}$$

Session Independence

$$r \rhd Q \mid s \rhd P \sim_f r \rhd (s \rhd Q \mid P) \tag{10}$$

Location Garbage Collection

$$l :: 0 \mid \mathcal{A} \sim_f \mathcal{A} \tag{11}$$

Intra-Session Communication is Orthogonal w.r.t. Locations

$$l :: \overline{x}w \sim_f l' :: \overline{x}w \tag{12}$$

Intra-Location Communication is Orthogonal w.r.t. Sessions

$$r \rhd x!w \sim_f r' \rhd x!w \tag{13}$$

The axioms concerning sessions are simpler than in SSCC since there is no need to preserve the invariant that sessions have exactly two partners. Note that also in μse session independence hold, i.e. session nesting is immaterial.

We show here how to use bisimilarity to analyze properties of services and multiparty sessions, in particular to prove that an implementation of a service is compliant (i.e., bisimilar) to a more abstract specification.

Let us consider the service *CalculateRating* from the credit request scenario. We can write the specification in μse as:

$$l :: *CalculateRating \Rightarrow P \quad \text{with } P = data(user).some\_comp.\overline{ret}\, rating \tag{14}$$

The symbol $*$ preceding the service definition means that the service is persistent (this can be programmed using recursion). Also, *some_comp* in P denotes some sequence of actions computing the actual rating, e.g. interacting with some local database.

This service is deterministic: once invoked, it waits until receiving a value in channel *data*, then performs *some_comp*, and finally, it sends the *rating* on channel *ret*. *CalculateRating* may be computationally expensive, so different requests can be served using replicated services. The following implementation asks another service $Calc_i$ nondeterministically chosen from a pool $Calc_1, \ldots, Calc_n$ to do the job:

$$l :: (\nu Calc_1 \ldots Calc_n)\big((\nu av)\big(\prod_{i=1}^{n} \text{rec}\, X.av!Calc_i.X \mid$$

$$* CalculateRating \Rightarrow av?(u).\text{invoke}\, u\big) \mid \prod_{i=1}^{n} *Calc_i \Rightarrow P\big)$$

Instead of directly computing the rating, upon invocation the service receives (through an intra-location communication on the private channel av) the name of the "private" local service $Calc_i$ that actually computes the rating. The proof that this implementation is weak bisimilar to system (14) is a simple application of the behavioral theory developed so far. Note that, removing e.g., the restriction on av breaks the bisimilarity, since the implementation of $CalculateRating$ could then interact with another channel av in the environment, while the specification does not allow this interaction.

This implementation exploits multiparty sessions. In fact, the invoker and services $CalculateRating$ and $Calc_i$ are three endpoints of the same session. Note that $Calc_i$ has been added dynamically by $CalculateRating$, however it can interact directly also with the other endpoint. Programming the same behavior in SSCC would require two binary sessions and some auxiliary communications.

Another way to create a ternary session is by using the merge primitive, as shown below. For simplicity, we consider just one such session:

$$(\nu e)l :: CalculateRating \Rightarrow \text{rec } Y.(\text{merge}^+ \ e.\text{install}[CalculateRating \Rightarrow Y]) \ | $$
$$\text{rec } X.(\nu r)r \rhd \text{merge}^- \ e.(P|X).$$

In this case, the invocation in the specification is simulated by the invocation in the implementation plus the merge. Note that e should be bound to avoid interference, and that the merge has to be completed before $CalculateRating$ can be made available again. Similarly, r is restricted to avoid different recursive calls to interfere. We prove now the correctness of the transformation, which exploits the axioms presented before.

Proof (Correctness of the transformation). Upon invocation of $CalculateRating$, system 14 becomes:

$$l :: *CalculateRating \Rightarrow P \ | \ l :: r' \rhd P \tag{15}$$

Its implementation can execute the same transition, and reduce via a sequence of internal actions (merge and install) to:

$$(\nu e)l :: CalculateRating \Rightarrow \text{rec } Y.(\text{merge}^+ \ e.\text{install}[CalculateRating \Rightarrow Y]) \ | $$
$$l :: (\nu r'')r' \rhd \mathbf{0} \ | \ r'' \rhd (P|\text{rec } X.(\nu r)r \rhd \text{merge}^- \ e.(P|X)) \ | \ r' \doteq r''$$

We can use Equation 9 to remove $r' \rhd \mathbf{0}$ and structural congruence to apply and remove the explicit substitution, obtaining:

$$(\nu e)l :: CalculateRating \Rightarrow \text{rec } Y.(\text{merge}^+ \ e.\text{install}[CalculateRating \Rightarrow Y]) \ | $$
$$l :: r' \rhd (P|\text{rec } X.(\nu r)r \rhd \text{merge}^- \ e.(P|X))$$

By unfolding recursion we get:

$$(\nu e)l :: CalculateRating \Rightarrow \text{rec } Y.(\text{merge}^+ \ e.\text{install}[CalculateRating \Rightarrow Y]) \ | $$
$$l :: r' \rhd (P|(\nu r)r \rhd \text{merge}^- \ e.(P|\text{rec } X.(\nu r)r \rhd \text{merge}^- \ e.(P|X)))$$

and using structural congruence and Equation 10 we get:

$$(\nu e)l :: CalculateRating \Rightarrow \text{rec } Y.(\text{merge}^+ \ e.\text{install}[CalculateRating \Rightarrow Y]) \ | $$
$$l :: r' \rhd P \ | \ (\nu r)r \rhd \text{merge}^- \ e.(P|\text{rec } X.(\nu r)r \rhd \text{merge}^- \ e.(P|X))$$

Using again structural congruence, and in particular folding again the recursion we go back to the original system, with an additional $r' \rhd P$ parallel component. This is exactly what happens for the specification, thus one can use closure under parallel composition to prove by co-induction the correctness of the transformation.

4   Dynamic Conversations

In this section we define the behavioral semantics of the Conversation Calculus (CC) [22] (see also Chapter 2-1) and report results that: (1) corroborate our syntactically chosen constructs at the semantic level; and (2) provide further insight on the communication model of the CC. The operational semantics of the core CC is defined by a labeled transition system, which definition relies on the following notions of transition labels and actions.

Definition 4. *Transition labels and actions are defined as follows:*

$$\sigma ::= \tau \mid l^d!(a) \mid l^d?(a) \mid \texttt{this} \qquad \text{(Actions)}$$
$$\lambda ::= c\,\sigma \mid \sigma \mid (\nu a)\lambda \qquad \text{(Transition Labels)}$$

An action τ denotes an internal communication, actions $l^d!(a)$ and $l^d?(a)$ represent communications with the environment, and $\texttt{this}$ represents a conversation identity access. To capture the observational semantics of processes, transition labels need to register not only the action but also the conversation where the action takes place. So, a transition label λ containing $c\,\sigma$ is said to be *located at* conversation c (or just *located*), otherwise is said to be *unlocated*. In $(\nu a)\lambda$ the distinguished occurrence of a is bound with scope λ (cf. the π-calculus bound output actions). For a communication label λ we denote by $\overline{\lambda}$ the dual matching label obtained by swapping inputs with outputs, such that, e.g., $\overline{l^d!(a)} = l^d?(a)$ and $\overline{l^d?(a)} = l^d!(a)$. The $\texttt{this}$ transition label represents a conversation identity access. Processes can explicitly access the identity of the conversation in which they are located (which is captured by a $\texttt{this}$ label), and synchronizations between processes may also require such contextual information.

We may now define the labeled transition system. For the sake of presentation, we split the presentation into two sets of rules, one (in Fig. 8) containing the rules for the basic operators, which are essentially identical to the corresponding ones in the π-calculus, and the other (in Fig. 9) grouping the rules specific to the Conversation Calculus.

Definition 5 (CC Labeled Transition System). *The rules in Fig. 8 and in Fig. 9 inductively define the LTS on processes.*

Transition rules presented in Fig. 8 should be fairly clear to a reader familiar with mobile process calculi. We discuss the intuitions behind the rules shown in Fig. 9. In rule (*Here*) an $\uparrow$ directed message (to the enclosing conversation) becomes $\downarrow$ (in the current conversation), after passing through the conversation

$$l^d!(a).P \xrightarrow{l^d!(a)} P \ (Out) \qquad l^d?(x).P \xrightarrow{l^d?(a)} P\{a/x\} \ (In) \qquad \frac{\alpha_j.P_j \xrightarrow{\lambda} Q \quad j \in I}{\Sigma_{i \in I} \ \alpha_i.P_i \xrightarrow{\lambda} Q}(Sum)$$

$$\frac{P \xrightarrow{\lambda} Q \quad a \in out(\lambda)}{(\nu a)P \xrightarrow{(\nu a)\lambda} Q}(Open) \qquad \frac{P \xrightarrow{\lambda} Q \quad a \notin na(\lambda)}{(\nu a)P \xrightarrow{\lambda} (\nu a)Q}(Res)$$

$$\frac{P \xrightarrow{\lambda} Q \quad bn(\lambda) \,\#\, fn(R)}{P \mid R \xrightarrow{\lambda} Q \mid R}(Par\text{-}l) \qquad \frac{P \xrightarrow{\lambda} P' \quad Q \xrightarrow{\overline{\lambda}} Q'}{P \mid Q \xrightarrow{\tau} P' \mid Q'}(Comm)$$

$$\frac{P \xrightarrow{(\nu a)\overline{\lambda}} P' \quad Q \xrightarrow{\lambda} Q' \quad a \notin fn(Q)}{P \mid Q \xrightarrow{\tau} (\nu a)(P' \mid Q')}(Close\text{-}l) \qquad \frac{P\{rec\, \mathcal{X}.P/\mathcal{X}\} \xrightarrow{\lambda} Q}{rec\, \mathcal{X}.P \xrightarrow{\lambda} Q}(Rec)$$

Fig. 8. CC LTS - Basic operators (π-calculus like)

access boundary. In rule (*Loc*) an unlocated ↓ message (in the current conversation) gets explicitly located at the conversation c in which it originates. In rule (*Through*) an already located communication label transparently crosses some other conversation boundary, and likewise for a τ label in rule (*Tau*). In rule (*This*) a this label reads the current conversation identity, and originates a c this label. A c this labeled transition may only progress inside the c conversation, as expressed by the rule (*ThisLoc*), where a this label matches the enclosing conversation. In rules (*ThisComm-r*) and (*ThisClose-r*) an unlocated communication matches a communication located at c, originating a c this label, thus ensuring the interaction occurs in the given conversation c.

Building on the notion of observation over processes captured by the labeled transition system of the CC, we characterize the CC semantic object by an observational equivalence, expressed in terms of standard notions of strong and weak bisimilarity defined as for SSCC (cf. Definition 2). We prove the expected properties of strong and weak bisimilarity: they are equivalence relations and they are preserved under a standard set of structural laws (cf. π-calculus structural congruence [21]). Then we prove that strong bisimilarity and weak bisimilarity are congruences.

Theorem 2. *Strong bisimilarity and weak bisimilarity are congruences.*

Next, we show other interesting behavioral equations, that confirm basic intuitions about our conversation-based communication model.

Given processes P and Q, the following axioms hold:

Conversation Split

$$n \blacktriangleleft [P] \mid n \blacktriangleleft [Q] \sim n \blacktriangleleft [P \mid Q] \tag{16}$$

Conversation Nesting

$$m \blacktriangleleft [n \blacktriangleleft [o \blacktriangleleft [P]]] \sim n \blacktriangleleft [o \blacktriangleleft [P]] \tag{17}$$

$$\frac{P \xrightarrow{\lambda^\uparrow} Q}{c \blacktriangleleft [P] \xrightarrow{\lambda^\downarrow} c \blacktriangleleft [Q]} (Here) \qquad \frac{P \xrightarrow{\lambda^\downarrow} Q}{c \blacktriangleleft [P] \xrightarrow{c \cdot \lambda^\downarrow} c \blacktriangleleft [Q]} (Loc)$$

$$\frac{P \xrightarrow{a\,\lambda^\downarrow} Q}{c \blacktriangleleft [P] \xrightarrow{a\,\lambda^\downarrow} c \blacktriangleleft [Q]} (Through) \qquad \frac{P \xrightarrow{\tau} Q}{c \blacktriangleleft [P] \xrightarrow{\tau} c \blacktriangleleft [Q]} (Tau)$$

$$\mathsf{this}(x).P \xrightarrow{c\ \mathsf{this}} P\{c/x\} \ (This) \qquad \frac{P \xrightarrow{c\ \mathsf{this}} Q}{c \blacktriangleleft [P] \xrightarrow{\tau} c \blacktriangleleft [Q]} (ThisLoc)$$

$$\frac{P \xrightarrow{\sigma} P' \quad Q \xrightarrow{c\ \bar{\sigma}} Q'}{P \mid Q \xrightarrow{c\ \mathsf{this}} P' \mid Q'} (ThisComm\text{-}r) \qquad \frac{P \xrightarrow{\sigma} P' \quad Q \xrightarrow{(\nu a)c\ \bar{\sigma}} Q'}{P \mid Q \xrightarrow{c\ \mathsf{this}} (\nu a)(P' \mid Q')} (ThisClose\text{-}r)$$

Fig. 9. CC LTS - Conversation operators

Output Nested Up — Output Here

$$n \blacktriangleleft [l^\uparrow!(\tilde{n}).P] \sim l^\downarrow!(\tilde{n}).n \blacktriangleleft [P] \tag{18}$$

Input Nested Up — Input Here

$$n \blacktriangleleft [l^\uparrow?(\tilde{x}).P] \sim l^\downarrow?(\tilde{x}).n \blacktriangleleft [P] \quad (n \notin \tilde{x}) \tag{19}$$

Output Nested Here

$$m \blacktriangleleft [n \blacktriangleleft [l^\downarrow!(\tilde{n}).P]] \sim n \blacktriangleleft [l^\downarrow!(\tilde{n}).m \blacktriangleleft [n \blacktriangleleft [P]]] \tag{20}$$

Input Nested Here

$$m \blacktriangleleft [n \blacktriangleleft [l^\downarrow?(\tilde{x}).P]] \sim n \blacktriangleleft [l^\downarrow?(\tilde{x}).m \blacktriangleleft [n \blacktriangleleft [P]]] \quad (\{m,n\} \# \tilde{x}) \tag{21}$$

Equation 16 captures the notion of conversation context as a single medium accessible through distinct pieces. Equation 17 expresses the fact that processes may only interact in the conversation in which they are located and in the enclosing one (via $\uparrow$ communications). Notice however that there are processes P and Q such that:

$$n \blacktriangleleft [m \blacktriangleleft [P] \mid Q] \not\sim m \blacktriangleleft [P] \mid n \blacktriangleleft [Q] \tag{22}$$

For instance, consider processes R_1 and R_2 defined as follows:

$$R_1 \triangleq c \blacktriangleleft [b \blacktriangleleft [l^\uparrow!(a)] \mid l^\downarrow?(x)] \qquad R_2 \triangleq b \blacktriangleleft [l^\uparrow!(a)] \mid c \blacktriangleleft [l^\downarrow?(x)]$$

Since R_1 exhibits a τ transition and R_2 does not, we have that $R_1 \not\sim R_2$. The inequation (22) contrasts with Equation 16: the relation between a conversation and its caller must be preserved. Equations 18-19 illustrate the notion of enclosing conversation: a $\uparrow$ message prefix located in a nested conversation behaves the same as a $\downarrow$ message prefix in the current conversation. Equations 20-21 show that a here ($\downarrow$) message prefix together with the respective conversation can be pulled up to top level in the conversation nesting.

The behavioral laws shown above hint on the abstract spatial model of CC processes, and pave the way for establishing a normal form result: we prove that any CC process is behaviorally equivalent to a process in normal form—considering the depth of a process is the number of enclosing conversation access pieces, we say a process is in normal form if all its active communication prefixes are of (at most) depth two (see [22]).

To conclude this section, we show an example derivation that uses Theorem 2 and the equational laws above. We consider a system where a *Client* and a *FinancePortal* exchange a `login` message in conversation *CreditChat*, each party holding a distinct piece of the conversation. In Fig. 10 we show that such system behaviorally coincides with a system where such message exchange takes place in a single conversation piece. Such behavioral reconfigurations suggest an alternative characterization of the operational semantics of the CC based on a notion of reduction: we may describe the evolution of the basic representatives of the behavioral equivalence classes, and then close the reduction relation under such equivalence classes.

$$FinancePortal \blacktriangleleft [\, CreditChat \blacktriangleleft [\, \texttt{login}^{\downarrow}?(uId).ServiceProtocol \,]\,]$$
$$|$$
$$Client \blacktriangleleft [\, CreditChat \blacktriangleleft [\, \texttt{login}^{\downarrow}!(uId).ClientProtocol \,]\,]$$

$$\sim \quad \text{(Theorem 2 and Equation 21)}$$

$$CreditChat \blacktriangleleft [\, \texttt{login}^{\downarrow}?(uId).FinancePortal \blacktriangleleft [\, CreditChat \blacktriangleleft [\, ServiceProtocol \,]\,]\,]$$
$$|$$
$$Client \blacktriangleleft [\, CreditChat \blacktriangleleft [\, \texttt{login}^{\downarrow}!(uId).ClientProtocol \,]\,]$$

$$\sim \quad \text{(Theorem 2 and Equation 20)}$$

$$CreditChat \blacktriangleleft [\, \texttt{login}^{\downarrow}?(uId).FinancePortal \blacktriangleleft [\, CreditChat \blacktriangleleft [\, ServiceProtocol \,]\,]\,]$$
$$|$$
$$CreditChat \blacktriangleleft [\, \texttt{login}^{\downarrow}!(uId).Client \blacktriangleleft [\, CreditChat \blacktriangleleft [\, ClientProtocol \,]\,]\,]$$

$$\sim \quad \text{(Equation 16)}$$

$$CreditChat \blacktriangleleft [\, \texttt{login}^{\downarrow}?(uId).FinancePortal \blacktriangleleft [\, CreditChat \blacktriangleleft [\, ServiceProtocol \,]\,]$$
$$|$$
$$\texttt{login}^{\downarrow}!(uId).Client \blacktriangleleft [\, CreditChat \blacktriangleleft [\, ClientProtocol \,]\,]\,]$$

Fig. 10. Credit request system behavioral reconfiguration

$$g + 0 \equiv g \qquad g_1 + g_2 \equiv g_2 + g_1 \qquad (g_1 + g_2) + g_3 \equiv g_1 + (g_2 + g_3)$$

$$s \mid 0 \equiv s \qquad s_1 \mid s_2 \equiv s_2 \mid s_1 \qquad (s_1 \mid s_2) \mid s_3 \equiv s_1 \mid (s_2 \mid s_3)$$

$$* 0 \equiv 0 \qquad * s \equiv s \mid * s$$

$$\{\!|0|\!\} \equiv 0 \qquad \{\!|\, \{\!|s|\!\}\, |\!\} \equiv \{\!|s|\!\} \qquad\qquad \{\!|[e]\, s|\!\} \equiv [e]\, \{\!|s|\!\}$$

$$[e]\, 0 \equiv 0 \qquad [e_1]\, [e_2]\, s \equiv [e_2]\, [e_1]\, s \qquad s_1 \mid [e]\, s_2 \equiv [e]\, (s_1 \mid s_2) \text{ if } e \notin \mathrm{fe}(s_1) \cup \mathrm{fk}(s_2)$$

Fig. 11. COWS structural congruence

5   Behavioral Semantics for COWS

In this section, we present the operational semantics of COWS (Calculus for Orchestration of Web-Services [16]), together with some bisimulation-based observational semantics. The syntax of COWS is presented in Chapter 2-1.

Operational Semantics. The operational semantics of COWS is defined using an LTS in the 'late' style only for *closed* services, i.e. services without free variables and killer labels (of course, closed services may contain free names). To simplify the rules, we exploit a relation of structural congruence, written $\equiv$. It is defined as the least congruence relation induced by the equational laws shown in Fig. 11.

To define the labeled transition relation, we use a few auxiliary functions. As a matter of notation, we shall use $\mathbf{n}$ to range over endpoints that do not contain variables (e.g. $p \bullet o$), and $\mathbf{u}$ to range over endpoints that may contain variables (e.g. $u \bullet u'$). Firstly, we use the function $[\![\_]\!]$ for evaluating *closed* expressions (i.e. expressions without variables): it takes a closed expression and returns a value. It is not explicitly defined since the exact syntax of expressions is deliberately not specified. Secondly, we use the partial function $\mathcal{M}(\_,\_)$ for performing *pattern-matching* on semi-structured data and, thus, determining if a receive and an invoke over the same endpoint can synchronize. Two tuples match if they have the same number of fields and corresponding fields have matching values/variables. Variables match any value, and two values match only if they are identical. When tuples $\bar{w}$ and $\bar{v}$ do match, $\mathcal{M}(\bar{w}, \bar{v})$ returns a substitution for the variables in $\bar{w}$; otherwise, it is undefined. Here substitutions (ranged over by σ) are written as collections of pairs of the form $x \mapsto v$. Application of substitution σ to s is written $s \cdot \sigma$. This may require a preventive α-conversion. In fact, we identify services up to the services' equivalence classes induced by α-conversion, also when this is not explicitly mentioned. We use $\emptyset$ to denote the empty substitution, $|\sigma|$ to denote the number of pairs in σ, and $\sigma_1 \uplus \sigma_2$ to denote the union of σ_1 and σ_2 when they have disjoint domains. Thirdly, we define a function, named $halt(\_)$, that takes a service s as an argument and returns the service obtained by only retaining the protected activities inside s. Function $halt(\_)$ is defined inductively on the syntax of services. The most significant case is $halt(\{\!|s|\!\}) = \{\!|s|\!\}$. In the other cases, $halt(\_)$ returns 0, except for parallel composition, delimitation and replication operators, for which it acts as an homomorphism. Finally, we use two predicates: $\mathrm{noKill}(s, e)$ holds true if either e is not a killer label or $e = k$ and s cannot immediately perform a free activity $\mathbf{kill}(k)$; $\mathrm{noConf}(s, \mathbf{n}, \bar{v}, \ell)$, with ℓ natural number, holds true if s does not produce communication *conflicts*, i.e. s

$$\frac{\llbracket \bar\epsilon \rrbracket = \bar v}{n!\bar\epsilon \xrightarrow{\;n \lhd \bar v\;} 0} \qquad n?\bar w.s \xrightarrow{\;n \rhd \bar w\;} s \qquad \frac{g \xrightarrow{\;\alpha\;} s}{g+g' \xrightarrow{\;\alpha\;} s} \qquad \frac{s \equiv \xrightarrow{\;\alpha\;} \equiv s'}{s \xrightarrow{\;\alpha\;} s'}$$

$$\frac{s \xrightarrow{\;n \lhd [\bar m]\bar v\;} s' \quad n \in \bar v \quad n \notin (\mathbf{n} \cup \bar m)}{[n]\, s \xrightarrow{\;n \lhd [n,\bar m]\bar v\;} s'} \qquad\qquad \frac{s \xrightarrow{\;\sigma \uplus \{x \mapsto v\}\;} s'}{[x]\, s \xrightarrow{\;\sigma\;} s' \cdot \{x \mapsto v\}}$$

$$\frac{s \xrightarrow{\;n \rhd [\bar y]\bar w\;} s' \quad x \in \bar w \quad x \notin \bar y}{[x]\, s \xrightarrow{\;n \rhd [x,\bar y]\bar w\;} s'} \qquad\qquad \frac{s \xrightarrow{\;n \sigma \uplus \{x \mapsto v\}\, \ell\, \bar v\;} s'}{[x]\, s \xrightarrow{\;n \sigma \ell \bar v\;} s' \cdot \{x \mapsto v\}}$$

$$\frac{s_1 \xrightarrow{\;n \rhd \bar v\;} s_1' \quad s_2 \xrightarrow{\;n \lhd \bar v\;} s_2'}{s_1 \mid s_2 \xrightarrow{\;\emptyset\;} s_1' \mid s_2'} \qquad\qquad \frac{s \xrightarrow{\;n \sigma \ell \bar v\;} s' \quad n \in \mathbf{n}}{[n]\, s \xrightarrow{\;\sigma\;} [n]\, s'}$$

$$\frac{s_1 \xrightarrow{\;n \rhd \bar w\;} s_1' \quad s_2 \xrightarrow{\;n \lhd \bar v\;} s_2' \quad \mathcal{M}(\bar w, \bar v) = \sigma \quad |\sigma| \geq 1 \quad noConf(s_1 \mid s_2, \mathbf{n}, \bar v, |\sigma|)}{s_1 \mid s_2 \xrightarrow{\;n \sigma |\sigma| \bar v\;} s_1' \mid s_2'}$$

$$\frac{s_1 \xrightarrow{\;\alpha\;} s_1' \quad \alpha \neq k, n\sigma\ell\bar v}{s_1 \mid s_2 \xrightarrow{\;\alpha\;} s_1' \mid s_2} \qquad\qquad \frac{s_1 \xrightarrow{\;n \sigma \ell \bar v\;} s_1' \quad noConf(s_2, \mathbf{n}, \bar v, \ell)}{s_1 \mid s_2 \xrightarrow{\;n \sigma \ell \bar v\;} s_1' \mid s_2}$$

$$kill(k) \xrightarrow{\;k\;} 0 \qquad\qquad \frac{s \xrightarrow{\;\alpha\;} s' \quad e \notin (e(\alpha) \cup ce(\alpha)) \quad \alpha \neq k, \dagger \quad noKill(s,e)}{[e]\, s \xrightarrow{\;\alpha\;} [e]\, s'}$$

$$\frac{s \xrightarrow{\;k\;} s'}{[k]\, s \xrightarrow{\;\dagger\;} [k]\, s'} \qquad \frac{s \xrightarrow{\;k\;} s' \quad k \neq e}{[e]\, s \xrightarrow{\;k\;} [e]\, s'} \qquad \frac{s \xrightarrow{\;\dagger\;} s'}{[e]\, s \xrightarrow{\;\dagger\;} [e]\, s'}$$

$$\frac{s_1 \xrightarrow{\;k\;} s_1'}{s_1 \mid s_2 \xrightarrow{\;k\;} s_1' \mid halt(s_2)} \qquad\qquad \frac{s \xrightarrow{\;\alpha\;} s'}{\{\!|s|\!\} \xrightarrow{\;\alpha\;} \{\!|s'|\!\}}$$

Fig. 12. COWS operational semantics

cannot immediately perform a receive activity matching $\bar v$ over the endpoint n that generates a substitution with fewer pairs than ℓ. Their inductive definitions can be found in [16].

Definition 6 (COWS Labeled Transition System). *The rules in Fig. 12 inductively define the LTS on processes. Labels α are generated by the following grammar:*

$$\alpha \quad ::= \quad n \lhd [\bar n]\bar v \quad | \quad n \rhd [\bar x]\bar w \quad | \quad \sigma \quad | \quad n\sigma\ell\bar v \quad | \quad k \quad | \quad \dagger$$

The meaning of labels is as follows: $n \lhd [\bar n]\bar v$ and $n \rhd [\bar x]\bar w$ denote execution of invoke and receive activities over the endpoint n with arguments $\bar v$ and $\bar w$, respectively, of which $\bar n$ and $\bar x$ are bound; σ denotes execution of a communication, not subject to priority check, with generated substitution σ to be still applied; $n\sigma\ell\bar v$ denotes execution of a communication, subject to priority check, over n with matching values $\bar v$, generated substitution having ℓ pairs, and substitution

σ to be still applied; k denotes execution of a request for terminating a term from within the delimitation $[k]$, and $\dagger$ denotes taking place of forced termination. In particular, the empty substitution $\emptyset$ and labels of the form $n\,\emptyset\,\ell\,\bar{v}$ denote *computational steps* corresponding to taking place of communication without pending substitutions, while $\dagger$ denotes a computational step corresponding to taking place of forced termination. We will use $bu(\alpha)$ to denote the set of names/variables that occur bound in α, $e(\alpha)$ to denote the set of elements (i.e. names, variables and killer labels) occurring in α, except for $\alpha = n\,\sigma\,\ell\,\bar{v}$ for which we let $e(n\,\sigma\,\ell\,\bar{v}) = e(\sigma)$, and $ce(\alpha)$ to denote the names composing the endpoint in case α denotes execution of a communication.

Observational Semantics. We now define natural notions of barbed bisimilarities for COWS and prove their coincidence with more manageable characterizations in terms of (labeled) bisimilarities. We want to define a notion of *barbed bisimilarity* for the calculus along the line of [13,20]. To this aim, since communication is asynchronous, we consider as *basic observable* only the output capabilities of terms, like for asynchronous π-calculus [1]. The intuition is that an asynchronous observer cannot directly observe the receipt of data that he has sent.

Definition 7 (Basic observable). *Let s be a* COWS *closed term. Predicate* $s \downarrow_n$ *holds true if there exist s', $\bar{n}$ and $\bar{v}$ such that $s \xrightarrow{\;n\,\lhd\,[\bar{n}]\,\bar{v}\;} s'$.*

Definition 8 (Barbed bisimilarity for COWS). *A symmetric binary relation $\mathcal{R}$ on* COWS *closed terms is a* barbed bisimulation *if it is barb preserving, and computation and context closed. Two closed terms s_1 and s_2 are* barbed bisimilar*, written $s_1 \simeq s_2$, if $s_1 \mathcal{R} s_2$ for some barbed bisimulation $\mathcal{R}$. $\simeq$ is called* barbed bisimilarity.

Context closure condition enables compositional reasoning, since it implies that $\simeq$ is a congruence on COWS closed terms, but requires considering all possible language contexts. To avoid this universal quantification, we provide a purely co-inductive notion of bisimulation that only requires considering transitions of the LTS defining the semantics of the terms under analysis. Because in COWS only the output capability of names can be exported, we define a COWS bisimulation as a family of relations indexed with sets of names corresponding to the names that cannot be used by contexts (to test) for reception since they are dynamically exported private names.

Definition 9 (Names-indexed family of relations). *A* names-indexed family $\mathcal{F}$ *of relations is a set of symmetric binary relations $\mathcal{R}_\mathcal{N}$ on* COWS *closed terms, one for each set of names $\mathcal{N}$, i.e. $\mathcal{F} = \{\mathcal{R}_\mathcal{N}\}_\mathcal{N}$.*

To be a congruence, bisimilarity must explicitly take care of the terms resulting from application of function $halt(\_)$, that gets the same effect as of plunging its argument term within the context $[k]\,(\mathbf{kill}(k) \mid [\![\cdot]\!])$.

Definition 10 (COWS bisimilarity). *A* names-indexed family of relations $\{\mathcal{R}_\mathcal{N}\}_\mathcal{N}$ *is a* COWS bisimilarity *if, whenever $s_1 \mathcal{R}_\mathcal{N} s_2$ then the following two conditions hold:*

a. $halt(s_1) \mathcal{R}_\mathcal{N} halt(s_2)$ *and*

b. *if* $s_1 \xrightarrow{\alpha} s_1'$, *where* $bu(\alpha)$ *are fresh, then:*

   1. if $\alpha = \mathbf{n} \triangleright [\bar{x}] \, \bar{w}$ *then one of the following holds:*

     (a) $\exists s_2' : s_2 \xrightarrow{\mathbf{n} \triangleright [\bar{x}] \, \bar{w}} s_2'$ *and*

        $\forall \bar{v}$ *s.t.* $\mathcal{M}(\bar{x}, \bar{v}) = \sigma$ *and* $noConf(s_2, \mathbf{n}, \bar{w}\sigma, |\bar{x}|)$: $s_1'\sigma \, \mathcal{R}_\mathcal{N} \, s_2'\sigma$

     (b) $|\bar{x}| = |\bar{w}|$ *and* $\exists s_2' : s_2 \xrightarrow{\emptyset} s_2'$ *and* $\forall \bar{v}$ *s.t.* $\mathcal{M}(\bar{x}, \bar{v}) = \sigma$ *and*

        $noConf(s_2, \mathbf{n}, \bar{w}\cdot\sigma, |\bar{x}|)$: $s_1'\cdot\sigma \, \mathcal{R}_\mathcal{N} \, (s_2' \mid \mathbf{n}!\bar{v})$ *or* $s_1'\cdot\sigma \, \mathcal{R}_\mathcal{N} \, (s_2' \mid$

        $\{\mathbf{n}!\bar{v}\})$

   2. if $\alpha = \mathbf{n} \, \emptyset \, \ell \, \bar{v}$ *and* $\ell = |\bar{v}|$ *then one of the following holds:*

     (a) $\exists s_2' : s_2 \xrightarrow{\mathbf{n} \, \emptyset \, \ell \, \bar{v}} s_2'$ *and* $s_1' \mathcal{R}_\mathcal{N} s_2'$ *(b)* $\exists s_2' : s_2 \xrightarrow{\emptyset} s_2'$

     and $s_1' \mathcal{R}_\mathcal{N} s_2'$

   3. if $\alpha = \mathbf{n} \triangleleft [\bar{n}] \, \bar{v}$ *where* $\mathbf{n} \notin \mathcal{N}$ *then* $\exists s_2' : s_2 \xrightarrow{\mathbf{n} \triangleleft [\bar{n}] \, \bar{v}} s_2'$ *and* $s_1' \mathcal{R}_{\mathcal{N} \cup \bar{n}} s_2'$

   4. if $\alpha = \emptyset$, $\alpha = \dagger$ *or* $\alpha = \mathbf{n} \, \emptyset \, \ell \, \bar{v}$ *with* $\ell \neq |\bar{v}|$, *then* $\exists s_2' : s_2 \xrightarrow{\alpha} s_2'$ *and*

     $s_1' \mathcal{R}_\mathcal{N} s_2'$

Two closed terms s_1 and s_2 are $\mathcal{N}$-bisimilar, written $s_1 \sim^\mathcal{N} s_2$, if $s_1 \mathcal{R}_\mathcal{N} s_2$ for some $\mathcal{R}_\mathcal{N}$ in a COWS bisimulation. They are COWS bisimilar, written $s_1 \sim s_2$, if they are $\emptyset$-bisimilar. $\sim^\mathcal{N}$ is called $\mathcal{N}$-bisimilarity, while $\sim$ is called COWS bisimilarity.

This definition is more complex than Definition 2, since it has to account for priority of COWS communication, kill, and asynchrony. Our main results prove that COWS bisimilarity $\sim$ is a congruence for COWS and is *sound* and *complete* with respect to barbed bisimilarity.

Theorem 3 (Congruence). $\sim$ *is a congruence for COWS closed terms.*

Theorem 4 (Soundness and completeness of $\sim$ w.r.t. $\simeq$). *Given two COWS closed terms s_1 and s_2, $s_1 \sim s_2$ if and only if $s_1 \simeq s_2$.*

Our semantic theories extend in a standard way to the weak case so that results of congruence and coincidence still hold. We refer the interested reader to the extended version of [19] for the exact definitions and a full account of the proofs.

Examples. We show now that, differently from asynchronous π-calculus, in COWS it is not true that receive activities are always unobservable. To illustrate this, we consider a tailored version of the input absorption law characterizing asynchronous bisimulation in asynchronous π-calculus (i.e., the equation $a(b). \bar{a}b + \tau = \tau$ presented in [1]):

$$[x] \, (\emptyset + \mathbf{n}?\langle x, v \rangle. \mathbf{n}!\langle x, v \rangle) = \emptyset \tag{23}$$

where, for the sake of presentation, we exploit the context $\emptyset + [\cdot] \triangleq [\mathbf{m}] \, (\mathbf{m}!\langle\rangle \mid \mathbf{m}?\langle\rangle + [\cdot])$ and the term $\emptyset \triangleq [\mathbf{m}] \, (\mathbf{m}!\langle\rangle \mid \mathbf{m}?\langle\rangle)$. Communication along the private endpoint $\mathbf{m}$ models the τ action of π-calculus, while activities $\mathbf{n}?\langle x, v \rangle$ and $\mathbf{n}!\langle x, v \rangle$

recall the π-calculus actions $a(b)$ and $\bar{a}b$, respectively. Intuitively, the equality means that a service that emits the data it has received behaves as a service that simply performs an unobservable action, which means that receive activities cannot be observed. In COWS, however, the context $\mathbb{C} \triangleq [y, z]\, \mathbf{n}?\langle y, z\rangle.\, \mathbf{m}!\langle\rangle \mid \mathbf{n}!\langle v', v\rangle \mid [\![\cdot]\!]$ can tell the two terms above apart. In fact, we have

$$\mathbb{C}[\![\emptyset]\!] \xrightarrow{\ \mathbf{n}\,\emptyset\,2\,\langle v', v\rangle\ } \mathbf{m}!\langle\rangle \mid \emptyset$$

where the term $(\mathbf{m}!\langle\rangle \mid \emptyset)$ satisfies the predicate $\downarrow_{\mathbf{m}}$. Instead, the other term cannot properly reply because the receive $\mathbf{n}?\langle x, v\rangle$ has higher priority than $\mathbf{n}?\langle y, z\rangle$ when synchronizing with the invocation $\mathbf{n}!\langle v', v\rangle$. Thus, $\mathbb{C}[\![\,[x]\,(\,\emptyset + \mathbf{n}?\langle x, v\rangle.\, \mathbf{n}!\langle x, v\rangle\,)]\!]$ can only evolve to terms that cannot immediately satisfy the predicate $\downarrow_{\mathbf{m}}$. From this, we have

$$[x]\,(\,\emptyset + \mathbf{n}?\langle x, v\rangle.\, \mathbf{n}!\langle x, v\rangle\,) \not\simeq \emptyset$$

Indeed, in COWS receive activities that exercise a priority (i.e. receives whose arguments contain some values) can be detected by an interacting observer.

Now, consider the term $[x, x']\,(\,\emptyset + \mathbf{n}?\langle x, x'\rangle.\, \mathbf{n}!\langle x, x'\rangle\,)$. Since $\mathbf{n}?\langle x, x'\rangle$ does not exercise any priority on parallel terms, we have that

$$[x, x']\,(\,\emptyset + \mathbf{n}?\langle x, x'\rangle.\, \mathbf{n}!\langle x, x'\rangle\,) \simeq \emptyset \qquad \mathbb{C}[\![\,[x, x']\,(\,\emptyset + \mathbf{n}?\langle x, x'\rangle.\, \mathbf{n}!\langle x, x'\rangle\,)]\!] \simeq \mathbb{C}[\![\emptyset]\!]$$

Similarly, taken $\mathbb{D} \triangleq \mathbf{n}?\langle\rangle.\, \mathbf{m}!\langle\rangle \mid \mathbf{n}!\langle\rangle \mid [\![\cdot]\!]$, we have that

$$\emptyset + \mathbf{n}?\langle\rangle.\, \mathbf{n}!\langle\rangle \simeq \emptyset \qquad \mathbb{D}[\![\emptyset + \mathbf{n}?\langle\rangle.\, \mathbf{n}!\langle\rangle]\!] \simeq \mathbb{D}[\![\emptyset]\!]$$

Therefore, communication in COWS is neither purely asynchronous nor purely synchronous. Indeed, receives having the smallest priority (i.e. whose arguments are, possible empty, tuples of variables) cannot be observed, while, by exploiting proper contexts, the other receives can be detected.

6 Conclusion

In this chapter we have studied behavioral equivalences in the context of different SENSORIA calculi.

For the session-based calculi, SSCC, μse and CC, we have presented a few axioms, and then applied them to prove the correctness of different kinds of program transformations. Observing the behavioral identities characterized for the three calculi one may find similarities. For instance, we may notice that, in some sense, feeding streams, intra-site communication and communication to the caller context are disconnected from the particular subsidiary session or conversation—this is reflected in (5), (13) and (18). On the other hand, the fact that interaction under a session or conversation is independent from the location or caller context is reflected by (12) and (20). However, the presented models also present quite clear distinctions in the behavioral identities shown. For example, (3) and (10) contrast with (22): in CC the relation between caller context and subsidiary conversation must, in general, be preserved, since processes interacting in a subsidiary conversation may also continuously interact in their caller contexts. However, distinct sessions may be nested in μse and SSCC without any consequence to the behavior of processes, as they either interact in the session or interact under the location (μse)/feed streams (SSCC), that can be accessed regardless of session nesting. Another distinction may be noticed at the level of the split rule for CC systems shown in Equation 16, which may not be reproduced in either SSCC or μse.

For the correlation-based calculus COWS instead, the priority mechanism required by correlation has a strong impact on the classical behavioral theory. In particular, we have shown that a particular notion of labeled bisimilarity is needed to capture barbed bisimilarity, and that communication is neither purely synchronous nor purely asynchronous.

Acknowledgments. The work reported herein is the result of a collaborative effort of many researchers, not just of the authors. Special thanks to Rosario Pugliese and Francesco Tiezzi, who wrote the section on COWS.

António Ravara was partially supported by the Security and Quantum Information Group, Instituto de Telecomunicações, Portugal.

References

1. Amadio, R.M., Castellani, I., Sangiorgi, D.: On bisimulations for the asynchronous pi-calculus. Theoretical Computer Science 195(2), 291–324 (1998)
2. Ambler, S.W.: The Object Primer: Agile Model-Driven Development with UML 2.0. Cambridge University Press, Cambridge (2004)
3. Bonelli, E., Compagnoni, A.: Multipoint session types for a distributed calculus. In: Barthe, G., Fournet, C. (eds.) TGC 2007. LNCS, vol. 4912, pp. 240–256. Springer, Heidelberg (2008)
4. Boreale, M., Bruni, R., De Nicola, R., Loreti, M.: Sessions and pipelines for structured service programming. In: Barthe, G., de Boer, F.S. (eds.) FMOODS 2008. LNCS, vol. 5051, pp. 19–38. Springer, Heidelberg (2008)
5. Boreale, M., et al.: SCC: a Service Centered Calculus. In: Bravetti, M., Núñez, M., Tennenholtz, M. (eds.) WS-FM 2006. LNCS, vol. 4184, pp. 38–57. Springer, Heidelberg (2006)
6. Bruni, R., Lanese, I., Melgratti, H., Tuosto, E.: Multiparty sessions in SOC. In: Wang, A.H., Tennenholtz, M. (eds.) COORDINATION 2008. LNCS, vol. 5052, pp. 67–82. Springer, Heidelberg (2008)
7. Carbone, M., Honda, K., Yoshida, N.: Structured communication-centred programming for web services. In: De Nicola, R. (ed.) ESOP 2007. LNCS, vol. 4421, pp. 2–17. Springer, Heidelberg (2007)
8. Cruz-Filipe, L., Lanese, I., Martins, F., Ravara, A., Vasconcelos, V.T.: Bisimulations in SSCC. DI/FCUL TR 07-37, Department of Informatics, Faculty of Sciences, University of Lisbon (2007)
9. Cruz-Filipe, L., Lanese, I., Martins, F., Ravara, A., Vasconcelos, V.T.: Behavioural theory at work: Program transformations in a service-centred calculus. In: Barthe, G., de Boer, F.S. (eds.) FMOODS 2008. LNCS, vol. 5051, pp. 59–77. Springer, Heidelberg (2008)
10. De Nicola, R., Hennessy, M.: Testing equivalences for processes. Theoretical Computer Science 34, 83–133 (1984)

11. van Glabbeek, R.J.: The linear time – branching time spectrum I; the semantics of concrete, sequential processes. In: Handbook of Process Algebra, ch. 1, pp. 3–99. Elsevier, Amsterdam (2001), http://boole.stanford.edu/pub/spectrum1.ps.gz
12. Hoare, C.A.R.: Communicating Sequential Processes. Prentice-Hall, Englewood Cliffs (1985)
13. Honda, K., Yoshida, N.: On reduction-based process semantics. Theoretical Computer Science 151(2), 437–486 (1995)
14. Honda, K., Yoshida, N., Carbone, M.: Multiparty asynchronous session types. In: Proc. of POPL 2008, pp. 273–284. ACM Press, New York (2008)
15. Lanese, I., Martins, F., Vasconcelos, V.T., Ravara, A.: Disciplining orchestration and conversation in service-oriented computing. In: Proc. of SEFM 2007, pp. 305–314. IEEE Computer Society Press, Los Alamitos (2007)
16. Lapadula, A., Pugliese, R., Tiezzi, F.: A calculus for orchestration of web services. In: De Nicola, R. (ed.) ESOP 2007. LNCS, vol. 4421, pp. 33–47. Springer, Heidelberg (2007), http://rap.dsi.unifi.it/cows/papers/cows-esop07-full.pdf
17. Milner, R.: Communication and Concurrency. Prentice Hall, Englewood Cliffs (1989)
18. Milner, R., Sangiorgi, D.: Barbed bisimulation. In: Kuich, W. (ed.) ICALP 1992. LNCS, vol. 623, pp. 685–695. Springer, Heidelberg (1992)
19. Pugliese, R., Tiezzi, F., Yoshida, N.: On observing dynamic prioritised actions in soc. In: Albers, S., Marchetti-Spaccamela, A., Matias, Y., Nikoletseas, S., Thomas, W. (eds.) ICALP 2009. LNCS, vol. 5556, pp. 558–570. Springer, Heidelberg (2009), http://rap.dsi.unifi.it/cows/papers/bis4cows-full.pdf
20. Sangiorgi, D., Walker, D.: On barbed equivalences in pi-calculus. In: Larsen, K.G., Nielsen, M. (eds.) CONCUR 2001. LNCS, vol. 2154, pp. 292–304. Springer, Heidelberg (2001)
21. Sangiorgi, D., Walker, D.: Pi-Calculus: A Theory of Mobile Processes. Cambridge University Press, Cambridge (2001)
22. Vieira, H.T., Caires, L., Seco, J.C.: The conversation calculus: A model of service-oriented computation. In: Gairing, M. (ed.) ESOP 2008. LNCS, vol. 4960, pp. 269–283. Springer, Heidelberg (2008)

Static Analysis Techniques for Session-Oriented Calculi*

Lucia Acciai[1], Chiara Bodei[2], Michele Boreale[1],
Roberto Bruni[2], and Hugo Torres Vieira[3]

[1] Dipartimento di Sistemi e Informatica, Università di Firenze, Italy
{lacciai,boreale}@dsi.unifi.it
[2] Dipartimento di Informatica, Università di Pisa, Italy
{chiara,bruni}@di.unipi.it
[3] CITI/Departamento de Informática, FCT Universidade Nova de Lisboa, Portugal
htv@fct.unl.pt

Abstract. In the SENSORIA project, core calculi have been adopted as a linguistic means to model and analyze service-oriented applications. The present chapter reports about the static analysis techniques developed for the SENSORIA session-oriented core calculi CaSPiS and CC. In particular, it presents a type system for client progress and control flow analysis in CaSPiS and type systems for conversation fidelity and progress in CC. The chapter gives an overview of the these techniques, summarizes the main results and presents the analysis of a common example taken from the SENSORIA financial case-study: the credit request scenario.

1 Introduction

In Chapter 2-1 the core calculi for service specification and analysis developed within SENSORIA have been introduced. These calculi are classified according to the approach adopted to maintain the link between the caller and the callee. We focus here on *session-oriented calculi*, where a private channel is implicitly instantiated upon service invocation between the caller and the callee. Specifically, we report on the static analysis techniques developed within the project for CaSPiS and CC. Recall that in CaSPiS sessions are binary, whereas in CC sessions, also called *conversations*, may dynamically involve multiple parties.

As far as CaSPiS is concerned, we provide contributions towards developing techniques for safe client-service interaction and preventing misuses at the so-called application logic level.

We first introduce a type system providing guarantees of *client progress* [1]. This system ensures that, in a well-typed CaSPiS process and in absence of divergence, any client invoking a service is guaranteed not to deadlock in a conversation with a service. The type system builds upon behavioral types techniques [11], as the behavior of a CaSPiS process is abstracted by means of a simpler ccs-like term. A key point, though, is that types account only for flows of I/O value-types, ignoring the rest. In particular, it is not necessary to equip the language of types with constructs to describe sessions. Indeed, considering the tree describing the nesting of sessions, a service invocation can

---

* This work has been partially sponsored by the project SENSORIA, IST-2005-016004.

M. Wirsing and M. Hölzl (Eds.): SENSORIA Project, LNCS 6582, pp. 214–231, 2011.

produce effects only at the parent level. It is then sufficient to associate to each process a two-level type taking into account just the current-level interactions and the upper-level effects. In order to guarantee progress of the invoker, the system relies on a notion of *compliance* between the client and the service protocols, which is essential to avoid deadlocks.

The second contribution is a Control Flow Analysis for CaSPiS [3] that can detect and prevent certain misuses at the application logic level. The presence of bugs at this level, called *application* or *business logic flaws*, may often lead to undesired behavior or to security attacks. This Control Flow Analysis system statically approximates the behavior of CaSPiS processes, in terms of the possible service and communication synchronizations. More precisely, what the analysis predicts includes everything that may happen, while what the analysis *does not* predict corresponds to something that cannot happen. The session mechanism is particularly valuable for the kind of analysis we use, because it guarantees that sibling sessions established between different instances of the same service and the corresponding clients do not interfere one with the other by leaking information, with two main consequences: first, the analysis can focus on each client-server conversation separately and second, it can focus on the application logic.

We also propose analysis techniques for systems specified in CC, addressing *conversation fidelity* and *progress* [8]. Conversation fidelity captures the fact that all participants in a multiparty conversation follow the protocols of interaction, while progress – differently from client progress discussed above – guarantees absence of deadlocks in the whole system. We introduce two separate but complementary techniques: to discipline multiparty conversations we introduce conversation types, a novel and flexible type structure, able to uniformly describe both the internal and the interface behavior of systems, referred respectively as choreographies and contracts in web-services terminology. To guarantee deadlock freedom we introduce a progress proof system that relies on a notion of ordering of events and, crucially, propagation of orderings in communications.

Structure of the chapter. The chapter is organized in three main sections. Section 2 introduces a type system guaranteeing client progress in CaSPiS; it discusses the main results and proves that client progress is guaranteed in the considered scenario. A simple variation of the scenario is also considered in order to show how the system rules out processes not guaranteeing the client progress property. Section 3 introduces a Control Flow Analysis preventing business logic flaws in CaSPiS, proves that the proposed analysis technique enjoys the subject reduction property and, in order to show how logic flaws are detected, applies this technique to (a variation of) the running example. Section 4 introduces the type system for conversation fidelity and the progress proof system in CC, together with their main properties. Both proposals are then applied to the running example in order to prove that it enjoys conversation fidelity and progress. Finally, Section 5 concludes the chapter.

2   A Type System for Client Progress in CaSPiS

In this section we introduce a type system providing guarantees of client progress. There are three key aspects involved in its design. A first aspect concerns abstraction: types focus on flows of I/O value-types and ignore the rest (actual values, service calls, ...). Specifically, akin to [11], types take the form of ccs-like terms describing I/O flows of processes. In fact, a tiny fragment of ccs, with no synchronization and restriction, is employed, where the role of atomic actions is played by basic types. A second aspect concerns compliance of client protocols with service protocols, which is essential to avoid deadlocks. In the type system, the operational abstractions provided by types are employed to effectively check client-service compliance. To this purpose, types are required to account for process I/O behavior quite precisely. Indeed, approximation might easily result into ignoring potential client-service deadlocks. A final aspect concerns the nesting of sessions. A session at a lower level can exercise effects on the upper level, say the level of any enclosing session. To describe this phenomenon, the system keeps track of the behavior both at the current level and at the level of a (fictitious) enclosing session, along the lines of those in [7,12,13]. This results in type judgments of the form $P : [S]T$, where S is the current-level type and T is the upper-level effect of P. Note that the distinction between types and effects we make here is somehow reminiscent of the type-and-effects systems of [15], with the difference that our effects are very simple (sequences of outputs) and are exercised on an upper level of activity rather than on a shared memory.

2.1 Language Fragment

We consider here a sub-calculus of the close-free fragment of CaSPiS [6], that we call CaSPiS⁻, where return prefixes have always an empty continuation and service protocols do not return any value. From the technical point of view, both limitations are necessary in order to guarantee a two-way operational correspondence between processes and the corresponding types (see [1] for the details). From the practical point of view, the latter limitation means that, once a session is started, for the service there will be no "feedback" of sort as to what is going on inside the session. This is somehow consistent with the idea that services should be stateless entities. Hence, terms of the form $r \triangleright Q$, where Q is a service protocol, cannot produce any visible effect and they might be executed anywhere in the system, not necessarily on the service side. Indeed, under these restrictions, it turns out to be technically convenient to slightly modify the operational semantics so that Q, the service protocol, and P, the client protocol, are both executed at the side of the invoking client. The resulting session will be denoted by $[P\|Q]$. Note that session names, which in the full language are used to locate the two session endpoints, become redundant, as the endpoints now share the same location. Hence session names are discarded right away. To sum up, the set $\mathcal{P}$ of CaSPiS⁻ processes is generated by the following grammar (where F and V are respectively the patterns and values defined in [6] and u can be either a name or a variable)

$$\pi ::= (F) \mid \langle V \rangle \qquad P ::= \sum_{i \in I} \pi_i.P_i \mid \langle V \rangle^\uparrow \mid s.P \mid \overline{u}.P \mid [P\|Q] \mid P > Q \mid P|Q \mid (vs)P \mid !P .$$

Both the structural congruence and the labeled transition relation defined in [6] can be modified as expected to accommodate these changes. In particular, some operational rules must be replaced by the homonymous rules shown in Fig. 1. Notice that upon a synchronization of a service call with the corresponding service definition, the service

$$(\text{Def}) \; \frac{}{s.P \xrightarrow{s\langle P\rangle} \mathbf{0}} \qquad\qquad (\text{Call}) \; \frac{}{\bar{s}.P \xrightarrow{\bar{s}\langle Q\rangle} [P\|Q]}$$

$$(\text{S-Ret}) \; \frac{P \xrightarrow{(v\hat{v})\langle v\rangle^\uparrow} P'}{[P\|Q] \xrightarrow{(v\hat{v})\langle v\rangle} [P'\|Q]} \qquad (\text{Sync}) \; \frac{P \xrightarrow{(v\tilde{n})s\langle R\rangle} P' \quad Q \xrightarrow{\bar{s}\langle R\rangle} Q'}{P\|Q \xrightarrow{\tau} (v\tilde{n})(P'\|Q')}$$

Fig. 1. Labeled semantics

protocol R is sent to the invoker and executed on its side, (S-Sync). Returns are enabled only on the client side of sessions, (S-Ret).

2.2 Proving the Client Progress Property

The client progress property will be defined in terms of an error predicate. Informally, an error occurs when the client protocol of an active session tries to send a value to (or receive from) the service side, but the session as a whole is blocked. This is formalized by the predicate $\to_{\text{ERR}}$ defined below. In the definition, we rely on the standard notion of *contexts*, $C[\cdot], C'[\cdot], \ldots$. We say a context is *static* if its hole is not under the scope of a dynamic operator (input and output prefixes, replication, service definitions and invocations and the right-hand side of a pipeline). In essence, active subterms in a process P are those surrounded by a static context.

Definition 1 (error). $P \to_{\text{ERR}}$ *if and only if whenever* $P \equiv C[[Q\|R]]$, *with* $C[\cdot]$ *static, and* $Q \xrightarrow{\eta}$, *with* $\eta ::= (v) \,|\, (v\hat{v})\langle v\rangle$, *then* $[Q\|R] \xrightarrow{\eta'}\!\!\!\!\!/\,$, *with* $\eta' ::= \tau \,|\, \bar{s}(P')$.

Note that "pending" returns are not taken into account in this definition. Indeed, a return is seen as an output at the upper level, (S-Ret), and the error, if any, is detected in the parent session, if it exists.

A process guarantees client progress if it is error-free at run-time.

Definition 2 (client progress). *Let* $P \in \mathcal{P}$. *We say* P *guarantees client progress if and only if whenever* $P \to^* P'$ *then* $P' \not\to_{\text{ERR}}$.

The above definition of error may seem too liberal, as absence of error does not actually guarantee progress of the session if $[Q\|R] \xrightarrow{\bar{s}(P')}$ and service s is not available. In fact, we are interested in processes where such situations do not arise: we call these processes *available*.

Definition 3 (available process). *We let* available *be the largest predicate on processes satisfying the following conditions. If* P *is* available *then* (i) *whenever* $P \equiv (v\hat{s})C[\bar{s}.P']$, *for some static* $C[\cdot]$, *and* $C[\mathbf{0}] \to^* Q$ *then* $Q \to^* \xrightarrow{(v\tilde{n})s\langle R\rangle}$ *for some* $\tilde{n}$ *and* R; *and* (ii) *whenever* $P \to Q'$ *then* Q' *is* available.

Here, clause (i) guarantees that the system (without interacting with service invocation $\bar{s}.Q$) can always reduce into a state where service s is ready to be invoked and clause (ii) guarantees that availability is preserved by reductions.

$$(\text{T-Out}) \dfrac{\Gamma \vdash P : [S]T \quad \Gamma \vdash u : b}{\Gamma \vdash \langle u \rangle.P : [!b.S]T} \qquad (\text{T-Call}) \dfrac{\Gamma \vdash u : V \quad \Gamma \vdash P : [S]T \quad S \propto V}{\Gamma \vdash \overline{u}.P : [T]0}$$

$$(\text{T-Ret}) \dfrac{\Gamma \vdash u : b}{\Gamma \vdash \langle u \rangle^{\uparrow} : [0]!b} \qquad (\text{T-Pipe}) \dfrac{\begin{array}{c} \Gamma \vdash P : [S]T \quad \Gamma \vdash Q : [\sum_{i \in I} ?b_i.U_i]V \\ out(S) \subseteq \bigcup_{i \in I}\{b_i\} \quad NoSum(S) \end{array}}{\Gamma \vdash P > Q : [S \bowtie \sum_{i \in I} ?b_i.U_i](T|S \text{ @ } V)}$$

Fig. 2. Rules of the type system

Types. Types are essentially a fragment of ccs corresponding to BPP processes [9]. We presuppose a set $\mathcal{B}t$ of *base types*, b, b', ... which include name *sorts* $S, S', \ldots$. Moreover, we presuppose a generic base-typing relation, mapping base values and service names to base types, written $v : b$, with the obvious proviso that service names are mapped to sorts and base values are mapped to the remaining base types. The set $\mathcal{T}$ of types is defined by the grammar below.

$$\alpha ::= !b \mid ?b \mid \tau \qquad T, S, U, V ::= \sum_{i \in I} \alpha_i.T_i \mid T \mid T \mid !T$$

Notice that, like in [7,12], we need not nested session types in our system, because in order to check session safety it is sufficient to check local, in-session communications. In what follows we abbreviate with 0 the empty summation type.

The operational semantics of types can be found in [1]. It is worth to recall that input and output prefixes, ?b and !b, cannot synchronize with each other – we only have interleaving in this fragment of ccs.

The basic requirement for ensuring client progress is *type compliance* between client and service protocols involved in sessions. In the following, we indicate with $\overline{\lambda}$ the *coaction* of λ: $\overline{?b} = !b$ and $\overline{!b} = ?b$. This notation is extended to sets of actions as expected. Moreover, we indicate with $I(S)$ the set of initial actions S can perform: $I(S) = \{\lambda \neq \tau \mid \exists S' : S \xrightarrow{\lambda} S'\}$. Type compliance is defined co-inductively and guarantees that, given two compliant types S (the client's protocol) and T (the service's protocol), at any stage of a computation either S is stuck or there is at least one (weak) action from S matched by a (weak) coaction from T.

Definition 4 (type compliance). *Let be* $S, T \in \mathcal{T}$. *Type compliance is the largest relation on types such that whenever S is compliant with T, written* $S \propto T$, *it holds that*

- *either* $I(S) = \emptyset$ *and* $S \xrightarrow{\tau}{\not\!\!\!\rightarrow}$
- *or (a) either* $S \xrightarrow{\tau}$, *or* $T \xrightarrow{\tau}$, *or* $I(S) \cap \overline{I(T)} \neq \emptyset$; *and (b) the following holds true:*
  1. *for each* S' *such that* $S \xrightarrow{\tau} S'$ *it holds that* $S' \propto T$;
  2. *for each* T' *such that* $T \xrightarrow{\tau} T'$ *it holds that* $S \propto T'$;
  3. *for each* S' *and* T' *such that* $S \xrightarrow{\lambda} S'$ *and* $T \xrightarrow{\overline{\lambda}} T'$ *it holds that* $S' \propto T'$.

Type system and results. The type system is along the lines of those in [7,12]; the most interesting rules are reported in Fig. 2 (the missing ones can be found in [1]). We presuppose a mapping *ob* from sorts $\{S, S', \ldots\}$ to types $\mathcal{T}$, with the intended meaning that if $ob(S) = T$ then names of sort S represent services whose abstract protocol is T. We take $s : T$ as an abbreviation of $s : S$ and $ob(S) = T$ for some S. A *context* Γ is a finite partial mapping from types to variables. For u a service name, a base value or a variable, we take $\Gamma \vdash u : b$ (resp. $\Gamma \vdash u : T$) to mean either that $u = v : b$ (resp. $u = s : T$) or $u = x \in \text{dom}(\Gamma)$ and $\Gamma(x) = b$ (resp. $\Gamma(x) = T$). In the process syntax, we attach type annotations to input variables as expected. Type judgments are of the form $\Gamma \vdash P : [S]T$, where Γ is a context, P is a possibly open process with $\text{fv}(P) \subseteq \text{dom}(\Gamma)$ and S and T are types. Informally, S and T represent respectively the *in-session*, or *internal*, and the *external* types of P. The first one describes the actions P can perform at the current session level (see (T-OUT)), while the second one represents the outputs P can perform at the parent level (see (T-RET)). Notice how, in (T-CALL), the premises ensure compliance between client and service internal types. Rule (T-PIPE) deserves some explanations. We impose some limitations on the types of the pipeline operands. First, the right-hand process is a summation of input-prefixed processes. Second, we make sure that the left-hand type does not contain any summation. Third, we make sure, through $\text{out}(S) \subseteq \bigcup_{i \in I} b_i$, that each (type of) output on left-hand side of a pipeline can be matched by (the type of) an input on the other one. Formally, $\text{out}(S)$ corresponds to the set of all bs that occur in output prefixes (!b) in S. The auxiliary functions $\bowtie$ and @ are used to build respectively the internal and the external type of $P > Q$ starting from the types of P and Q. In essence, both $S \bowtie U$ and $S @ V$ spawn a new copy of type U and V, respectively, in correspondence of each output prefix in S. The main difference is that in @ inputs and silent prefixes in S are discarded, while in $\bowtie$ they are preserved. Both $\bowtie$ and @ are defined by induction on the structure of types, the case of output prefixes is described below, definitions for the omitted cases can be found in [1].

$$!b.S \bowtie \sum_{i \in I} \alpha_i.U_i = \sum_{i \in I} \tau.(U_i | S \bowtie \sum_{i \in I} \alpha_i.U_i) \qquad !b.S @ U = U | (S @ U)$$

The first step towards proving that well-typed processes guarantee client progress is establishing the usual subject reduction property (Proposition 1). Then, we prove a type safety result (Theorem 1), stating that a well typed process cannot immediately generate an error. These are sufficient to conclude that in well-typed and available processes sessions never stuck, unless the client has terminated its protocol, Corollary 1. The proofs follow the lines of those in [1] and are omitted.

Proposition 1 (subject reduction). *Suppose* $\emptyset \vdash P : [S]T$. *Then whenever* $P \xrightarrow{\tau} P'$ *then either* $\emptyset \vdash P' : [S]T$ *or* $S \xrightarrow{\tau} S'$ *and* $\emptyset \vdash P' : [S']T$.

Theorem 1 (type safety). *Suppose* P *is well typed. Then* $P \not\rightarrow_{\text{ERR}}$.

Corollary 1 (client progress). *Suppose* P *is well typed. Then* P *guarantees client progress.*

2.3   Client Progress in the Credit Request Scenario

We reconsider the CaSPiS specification of the Credit Request Scenario (see Chapter 0-3) introduced in Chapter 2-1. Here we add typing annotations for input variables and ignore termination handling, which is not dealt with by the type system. So, termination handlers are discarded and close actions are replaced by the empty process. E.g., *CreditPortal* becomes

$$CreditPortal \triangleq \ !CrReq.(?id : id)\textbf{select}\ (?logged : bool)\ \textbf{from}\ \overline{CheckUser}(id)$$
$$\textbf{in if}\ logged\ \textbf{then}\ \langle\text{"Valid"}\rangle Creation(id)$$
$$\textbf{else}\ \langle\textbf{excpt}(\text{"InvalidLogin"})\rangle$$

We assume that values of the form **excpt**("string") are of base type **exception**. Moreover, we assume that each name has associated a homonymous sort, e.g. *creditD* : creditD. Finally, we assume that each call to an auxiliary service in the system is well typed and returns either boolean values or strings as expected. Suppose now CrReq : T_{CrReq}, where:

$$T_{CrReq} \triangleq \ ?id.\Big(\ \tau.!exception$$
$$+ \tau.!string.?creditD.(\ \tau.!exception$$
$$+ \tau.!string.?bals.!string.?secs.$$
$$(\tau.!(offer).(?bool+?bool) + \tau.S_{eval} + \tau.S_{eval})))$$
$$S_{eval} \triangleq \tau.!(offer).(?bool+?bool) + \tau.!(decline).(?bool+?bool)\,.$$

Then, the whole system *Sys* is well typed, indeed the client protocol has type

$$U_{ClPr} \triangleq !id.(?exception+?string+?string.!creditD.$$
$$(?exception+?string+?string.!bals.?string.!secs.$$
$$(?(offer).!(bool)\quad +$$
$$?(decline).(\tau.!bool + \tau.!bool))))$$

and it is easy to check that $U_{ClPr} \propto T_{CrReq}$. Therefore, client progress is guaranteed. Notice that service CrReq is persistent therefore, assuming that all auxiliary services are persistent too, *Sys* (see Chapter 2-1) is *available* and this guarantees that *CreditRequester*, the invoker, will never block.

Consider now another client, *CreditRequester'* below, that does not expect an exception after sending its credentials:

$$CreditRequester' \triangleq \overline{CrReq}\langle id\rangle((\text{"Valid"})CR + (\text{"Valid"}))\,.$$

Clearly, if we replace the previous client with this one, the system will not be well typed. Indeed, the client protocol in *CreditRequester'* is well typed under

$$U_{ClPr'} \triangleq !id.(?string+?string.!creditD. \ldots)$$

but $U_{ClPr'} \not\propto T_{CrReq}$.

3   From Discovering Type Errors to Preventing Business Logic Flaws

The type system we have seen in Section 2 gives important guarantees about the overall compatibility of interaction protocols between callers and callees, but cannot prevent application logic flaws.

We have investigated this issue, in [3], by adapting the techniques used in the field of network security (see e.g., [5,4]) to that of services. In particular, we have provided a

Control Flow Analysis of CaSPiS, that is shown able to detect some possible misuses and to help prevent them, by taking appropriate counteractions. The analysis statically approximates the behavior of CaSPiS processes, in terms of the possible service and communication synchronizations. More precisely, what the analysis predicts includes everything that may happen, while what the analysis *does not* predict corresponds to something that cannot happen. The model of attacker we are interested in is a bit different from the classical Dolev-Yao one: the *malicious customer* is an insider or, more precisely, an accredited user of a service that has no control of the communication channels, but that does not follow the intended rules of the application protocol. The analysis implicitly considers the possible behavior of such an attacker.

3.1 Language Fragment

For the sake of brevity, we focus here on a simplified version of the close-free fragment of CaSPiS, where the pipeline construct is rendered as $P > (?\tilde{x})Q$: it spawns a fresh instance $Q[\tilde{v}/\tilde{x}]$ of Q on any value $\tilde{v}$ produced by P. Note that the variables $\tilde{x}$ to be bound after pipeline synchronization are included in a special input $(?\tilde{x})$, called *pipeline input* preceding the right branch process. Moreover, we employ sessions polarities to mark a clear distinction between the two sides involved: $r^- \triangleright P$ and $r^+ \triangleright Q$. To distinguish among different occurrences of the same service, we annotate each of them with a different index, as in $s_{@k}$. The synchronization on the service s, on the occurrences $s_{@k}$ and $\bar{s}_{@m}$, results then in a session, identified by $r^p_{s@m:k}$, where p is the polarity. Similarly, we distinguish each pipeline operator with a different label l, as in $>_l$ and we identify the left branch with a label l_0 and the right branch with l_1. The variables $\tilde{x}$ affected by the pipeline input in the right branch of the pipeline, are also identified by the label l_1, as in $P >_l (?\tilde{x}^{l_1})Q$. Note that these annotations do not affect the semantics, whatsoever.

3.2 The Control Flow Analysis

The analysis over-approximates all the possible behaviors of a CaSPiS process, in terms of communication and service synchronizations. The analysis uses the notion of enclosing scope σ, recording the current scope due to services, sessions or pipelines. The result of analyzing a process P is a pair $(I, \mathcal{R})$, called *estimate* for P. The first component I gives information on the contents of a scope. The second component $\mathcal{R}$ gives information about the set of values to which names can be bound.

A proposed estimate $(I, \mathcal{R})$ is correct, if it satisfies the judgements defined by the axioms and rules in the upper (lower, respectively) part of Fig. 3.

First, we check that $(I, \mathcal{R})$ describes the initial process. This is done in the upper part of Fig. 3, where the clauses amount to a structural traversal of process syntax (we have omitted rules for parallel composition, restriction and replication, on which the analysis is just propagated to the arguments).

The clause for service definition checks that whenever a service $s_{@k}$ is defined in $s_{@k}.P$, then the relative hierarchy position with respect to the enclosing scope must be reflected in I, i.e. $s_{@k} \in I(\sigma)$. Furthermore, when inspecting the content P, the fact that the new enclosing scope is $s_{@k}$ is recorded, as reflected by the judgement $I, \mathcal{R} \models^{s_{@k}} P$. Similarly for service invocation $\bar{x}_{@k}$: the only difference is that when x is a variable,

$$I, \mathcal{R} \models^\sigma s_{@k}.P \qquad \text{iff } s_{@k} \in \mathcal{I}(\sigma) \wedge I, \mathcal{R} \models^{s_{@k}} P$$

$$I, \mathcal{R} \models^\sigma \bar{x}_{@k}.P \qquad \text{iff } \forall s_{@m} \in \mathcal{R}(x) : \bar{s}_{@k} \in \mathcal{I}(\sigma) \wedge I, \mathcal{R} \models^{\bar{s}_{@k}} P$$

$$I, \mathcal{R} \models^\sigma r^p_{s@m:k} \triangleright P \qquad \text{iff } r^p_{s@m:k} \in \mathcal{I}(\sigma) \wedge I, \mathcal{R} \models^{r^p_{s@m:k}} P$$

$$I, \mathcal{R} \models^\sigma \Sigma_{i \in I} \pi_i P_i \qquad \text{iff } \forall i \in I : I, \mathcal{R} \models^\sigma \pi_i P_i$$

$$I, \mathcal{R} \models^\sigma (?\bar{x}).P \qquad \text{iff } (?\bar{x}) \in \mathcal{I}(\sigma) \wedge I, \mathcal{R} \models^\sigma P$$

$$I, \mathcal{R} \models^\sigma \langle \bar{x} \rangle.P \qquad \text{iff } \forall \bar{v} \in \mathcal{R}(\bar{x}) \langle \bar{v} \rangle \in \mathcal{I}(\sigma) \wedge I, \mathcal{R} \models^\sigma P$$

$$I, \mathcal{R} \models^\sigma \langle \bar{x} \rangle^\uparrow.P \qquad \text{iff } \forall \bar{v} \in \mathcal{R}(x) \langle \bar{v} \rangle^\uparrow \in \mathcal{I}(\sigma) \wedge I, \mathcal{R} \models^\sigma P$$

$$I, \mathcal{R} \models^\sigma P >_l (?\bar{x}^{l_1})Q \text{ iff } l_0, l_1, \mathcal{I}(l_0), \mathcal{I}(l_1) \in \mathcal{I}(\sigma) \wedge I, \mathcal{R} \models^{l_0} P \wedge I, \mathcal{R} \models^{l_1} (?\bar{x}')Q$$

$$I, \mathcal{R} \models^{l_0} \langle \bar{x} \rangle.P \qquad \text{iff } \forall \bar{v} \in \mathcal{R}(\bar{x}) \langle \bar{v} \rangle^{l_0} \in \mathcal{I}(l_0) \wedge I, \mathcal{R} \models^{l_0} P$$

$$I, \mathcal{R} \models^{l_1} (?\bar{x}^l).P \qquad \text{iff } (?\bar{x}^l) \in \mathcal{I}(l_1) \wedge I, \mathcal{R} \models^{l_1} P$$

(*Service Synch*) $s_{@m} \in \mathcal{I}(\sigma) \wedge \bar{s}_{@k} \in \mathcal{I}(\sigma')$
$\Rightarrow r^+_{s@m:k} \in \mathcal{I}(\sigma) \wedge \mathcal{I}(s_{@m}) \subseteq \mathcal{I}(r^+_{s@m:k}) \wedge$
$\quad r^-_{s@m:k} \in \mathcal{I}(\sigma') \wedge \mathcal{I}(\bar{s}_{@k}) \subseteq \mathcal{I}(r^-_{s@m:k})$

(*I/O Synch*) $\langle \bar{v} \rangle \in \mathcal{I}(r^p_{s@m:k}) \wedge (?\bar{x}) \in \mathcal{I}(r^p_{s@m:k}) \Rightarrow \bar{v} \in \mathcal{R}(\bar{x})$

(*Ret Synch*) $\langle \bar{v} \rangle^\uparrow \in \mathcal{I}(r^p_{s@m:k}) \wedge r^p_{@m:k} \in \mathcal{I}(r^{p'}_{s'@n:q}) \wedge (?\bar{x}) \in \mathcal{I}(r^{p'}_{s'@n:q})$
$\Rightarrow \bar{v} \in \mathcal{R}(\bar{x})$

(*Pipe I/O Synch*) $\langle \bar{v} \rangle^{l_0} \in \mathcal{I}(l_0) \wedge (?\bar{x}^{l_1}) \in \mathcal{I}(l_1) \Rightarrow \bar{v} \in \mathcal{R}(\bar{x})$

(*Pipe Ret Synch*) $\langle \bar{v} \rangle^\uparrow \in \mathcal{I}(r^p_{s@m:k}) \wedge r^p_{s@m:k} \in \mathcal{I}(l_0)$
$\wedge (?\bar{x}^{l_1}) \in \mathcal{I}(l_1) \Rightarrow \bar{v} \in \mathcal{R}(\bar{x})$

Fig. 3. Analysis for CaSPiS processes

the analysis checks for every actual value s that can be bound to x that $\bar{s}_{@k} \in \mathcal{I}(\sigma)$ and $I, \mathcal{R} \models^{\bar{s}_{@k}} P$. The clauses for input, output and return check that the corresponding prefixes are included in $\mathcal{I}(\sigma)$ and that the analysis of the continuation processes hold as well. There is a special rule for pipeline input prefix, that allows us to distinguish it from the standard input one. Note that the current scope has the same identifier carried by the variables. Similarly, there is a rule for output prefixes occurring inside the scope of a left branch of a pipeline. The corresponding possible outputs are annotated with the label l_0. The rule for session, modeled as the one on service definition and invocation, just checks that the relative hierarchy position of the session identifier $r^p_{s@m:k}$ with respect to the enclosing scope must be reflected in $\mathcal{I}$, i.e. $r^p_{s@m:k} \in \mathcal{I}(\sigma)$. It is used in analyzing the possible continuations of the initial process.

The clause for pipeline deserves a specific comment. It checks that whenever a pipeline $>_l$ is met, then the analysis of the left and the right branches is kept distinct by the introduction of two sub-indexes l_0 for the left one and l_1 for the right one. This allows us to predict possible communication over the two sides of the same pipeline. Furthermore, the analysis contents of the two scopes must be included in the enclosing scope identified by σ. This allows us to predict also the communications due to I/O synchronizations, involving prefixes occurring inside the scope of a pipeline.

In the second phase, we check that $(\mathcal{I}, \mathcal{R})$ also takes into account the dynamics of the process under consideration, i.e. the synchronizations τ due to communications, services and pipelines. This is expressed by the closure conditions in the lower part of Fig. 3 that mimic the semantics, by statically modeling the semantic preconditions and the consequences of the possible actions. More precisely, the precondition checks, in terms of $\mathcal{I}$, for the possible presence of the redexes necessary for an action to be performed. The conclusion imposes the additional requirements on $\mathcal{I}$ and on $\mathcal{R}$, necessary to give a valid prediction of the analyzed action. In the clause for *Service Synch*, we have to make sure that the precondition requirements are satisfied, i.e. that: (i) there exists an occurrence of service definition: $s_{@k} \in \mathcal{I}(\sigma)$; (ii) there exists an occurrence of the corresponding invocation $\overline{s}_{@m} \in \mathcal{I}(\sigma')$. If the precondition requirements are satisfied, then the conclusions of the clause express the consequences of performing the service synchronization. In this case, we have that $\mathcal{I}$ must reflect that there may exist a session identified by $r^+_{s@m:k}$ inside σ and by $r^-_{s@m:k}$ inside σ', such that the contents (scopes, prefixes) of $s_{@m:k}$ and of $\overline{s}_{@m}$ may also be inside $\mathcal{I}(r^+_{s@m:k})$ and $\mathcal{I}(r^-_{s@m:k})$, respectively. Similarly, in the clause for *I/O Synch*, if the following preconditions are satisfied: (i) there exists an occurrence of output in $\mathcal{I}(r^p_{s@m:k})$; (ii) there exists an occurrence of the corresponding input in the sibling session $\mathcal{I}(r^{\overline{p}}_{s@m:k})$, then the values sent can be bound to the corresponding input variables. In other words a possible communication is predicted here. Note that the rule correctly does not consider outputs in the form $\langle \tilde{v} \rangle^{l_0}$, because they possibly occur inside a left branch of a pipeline and therefore they are not available for I/O synchronizations. The other rules are analogous.

Our analysis is correct with respect to the given semantics, i.e. a valid estimate enjoys the following subject reduction property.

Theorem 2 (Subject Reduction). *If $P \xrightarrow{\tau} Q$ and $\mathcal{I}, \mathcal{R} \models^{\sigma} P$ then also $\mathcal{I}, \mathcal{R} \models^{\sigma} Q$.*

In the following, we refer to the version of CaSPiS that includes pattern matching into the input construct. Furthermore, we need to consider the possible presence of the *malicious customer*, that is an *accredited customer of a service* that has no control of the communication channels, apart from the one established by the sessions in which he/she is involved. Nevertheless, our attacker does not necessarily follow the intended rules of the application protocol and can try to use the functions of the service in an unintended way, e.g., by sending messages in the right format, but with contents different from the expected ones. More precisely, he/she has a knowledge made of all the public information and increased by the messages received from the service: the attacker can use his/her knowledge to produce messages to be sent to the server. The presented analysis is part of a more complex analysis, that implicitly considers the possible behavior of such an attacker. The complete analysis takes care of the malicious customer presence, by statically approximating its possible knowledge, represented as a new analysis component $\mathcal{K}$. Intuitively, the clauses acting on $\mathcal{K}$ implicitly take the attacker possible actions into account. The component $\mathcal{K}$ contains all the free names, all the messages that the customer can receive, and all the messages that can be computed from them, e.g., if v and v' belong to $\mathcal{K}$, then also the tuple (v, v') belongs to $\mathcal{K}$ and, vice versa, if (v, v') belongs to $\mathcal{K}$, then also v and v' belong to $\mathcal{K}$. Furthermore, all the messages in $\mathcal{K}$ can be sent by the customer.

3.3   Control Flow Analysis of the Scenario

For brevity, we refer to a quite simplified version of the Credit Request Scenario, leaving aside authentication through the credit portal and approval by supervisor. We also omit

$$Prtl \equiv \mathsf{CrReq}.(?x_{usr}, ?x_{cred}, ?x_{bals}, ?x_{secs})$$
$$(\overline{\mathsf{Upd}}.\langle x_{usr}, x_{bals}, x_{secs}\rangle(?x_{ack})\langle\mathsf{go}\rangle^\uparrow >_l (Dcsn(x_{usr}, x_{cred}) >_{l'} \text{Offer}))$$
$$Dcsn(u,c) \equiv (?x_{go})\overline{\mathsf{Rate}}.\langle u,c\rangle((\mathsf{AAA}, ?x_{offer})\langle\mathsf{true}, x_{offer}\rangle^\uparrow + (\mathsf{BBB}, ?x_{risk})Clerk(x_{usr}, x_{risk}))$$
$$Clerk(u,r) \equiv \overline{\mathsf{ReqCk}}.\langle u,r\rangle(?w_{response}, ?w_{offer})\langle w_{response}, w_{offer}\rangle^\uparrow >_{l''}$$
$$(?u_{response}, ?u_{offer})\langle u_{response}, u_{offer}\rangle^\uparrow$$
$$\text{Offer} \equiv (?z_{response}, ?z_{offer})\langle z_{response}, z_{offer}\rangle((\mathsf{true}, ?z_{cred}) + (\mathsf{false}, ?z_{decline}))$$
$$CR(usr) \equiv \overline{\mathsf{CrReq}}.(v\mathsf{cred}, \mathsf{bals}, \mathsf{secs})\langle usr, \mathsf{cred}, \mathsf{bals}, \mathsf{secs}\rangle$$
$$(\mathsf{true}, ?y_{offer})\langle\mathbf{eval}(y_{offer}, \mathsf{cred})\rangle$$
$$\mathcal{I}(*) \ni \mathsf{CrReq}, \overline{\mathsf{CrReq}}, r^+_{\mathsf{CrReq}}, r^-_{\mathsf{CrReq}}$$
$$\mathcal{I}(\mathsf{CrReq}) \ni (?x_{usr}, ?x_{cred}, ?x_{bals}, ?x_{secs}), l_0, l_1, \mathcal{I}(l_0), \mathcal{I}(l_1)$$
$$\mathcal{I}(r^+_{\mathsf{CrReq}}) \ni r^-_{Upd}, r^-_{Rate}, r^-_{ReqCk}$$
$$\mathcal{R}(x_{usr}) \ni usr, \mathcal{R}(x_{cred}) \ni \mathsf{cred}, \mathcal{R}(x_{bals}) \ni \mathsf{bals}, \mathcal{R}(x_{secs}) \ni \mathsf{secs}$$
$$\mathcal{I}(l_0) \ni \overline{\mathsf{Upd}}$$
$$\mathcal{I}(\overline{\mathsf{Upd}}) \ni \langle usr, \mathsf{bals}, \mathsf{secs}\rangle, (?x_{ack}), \langle\mathsf{go}\rangle^\uparrow$$
$$\mathcal{I}(l_1) \ni l'_0, l'_1, \mathcal{I}(l'_0), \mathcal{I}(l'_1)$$
$$\mathcal{I}(l'_0) \ni (?x_{go}), \overline{\mathsf{Rate}}$$
$$\mathcal{I}(\overline{\mathsf{Rate}}) \ni \langle usr, \mathsf{cred}\rangle((\mathsf{AAA}, ?x_{offer}), \langle\mathsf{true}, \mathsf{offer}\rangle^\uparrow, \mathcal{I}(l''_0) \ni \overline{\mathsf{ReqCk}}$$
$$\mathcal{I}(l'_1) \ni (?u_{response}, ?u_{offer})\langle\mathsf{response}, \mathsf{offer}\rangle^\uparrow (\mathsf{BBB}, ?x_{risk}), \overline{\mathsf{ReqCk}}, l''_0, l''_1, \mathcal{I}(l''_0), \mathcal{I}(l''_1)$$
$$\mathcal{I}(\overline{\mathsf{ReqCk}}) \ni \langle usr, \mathsf{risk}\rangle, (?w_{response}, ?w_{offer}), \langle\mathsf{response}, \mathsf{offer}\rangle^\uparrow$$
$$\mathcal{I}(l'_1) \ni (?z_{response}, ?z_{offer}), \langle\mathsf{response}, \mathsf{offer}\rangle, (\mathsf{true}, ?z_{cred}), (\mathsf{false}, ?z_{decline})$$
$$\mathcal{I}(\overline{\mathsf{CrReq}}) \ni \langle usr, \mathsf{cred}, \mathsf{bals}, \mathsf{secs}\rangle, (\mathsf{true}, ?y_{offer}), \langle\mathsf{offer}, \mathsf{cred}\rangle, \langle\mathsf{offer}, \underline{\mathsf{cred'}}\rangle, \langle\mathsf{false}, \mathsf{decline}\rangle$$

Fig. 4. Specification of our scenario and some entries of its analysis

some service counterparts, whose specification is trivial. In this particular toy example, the application logic flaw has been introduced on purpose, in order to illustrate our methodology. Still, we think it is representative of analogous flaws, reported in the literature, as the price modification one [14], handled in [3].

The introduced application logic flaw is related to the handling of requested amount of credit, here not considered for the outcome of the clerk approval request. Note that, as in the original specification, the evaluation of the clerk is not dependent on the requested amount of credit.

The scenario specification and some of the main entries of the analysis are reported in Fig.4, where $*$ identifies the ideal outermost scope in which the system top-level service scopes are. We assume $\mathbf{eval}(o, c)$ either evaluates to $(\mathsf{false}, \mathsf{decline})$ (the conditions offered by the bank are not convenient) or to (true, c) where c is the amount for which the credit is requested. The analysis directly considers the resulting values for $\mathbf{eval}$.

Note that the variable $?z_{credit}$ in *Offer* may be bound to any value the costumer sends, in particular to any credit value $\mathsf{cred'}$, possibly higher than cred. This is reflected by the analysis, because if $\mathsf{cred'} \in \mathcal{K}$, we also have that $\langle\mathsf{offer}, \mathsf{cred'}\rangle$ belongs to $\mathcal{I}(\overline{\mathsf{CrReq}})$. This application flaw depends on the fact that there is no pattern matching on the values received; more generally, no control on this part of input is made. To avoid this problem, we can modify the specification of *Offer*, by assuming it expects to receive a specific value c on the critical input, in our example the value cred initially bound to x_{cred}:

$$\text{Offer}'(c) \equiv (?z_{response}, ?z_{offer})\langle z_{response}, z_{offer}\rangle((\mathsf{true}, c) + (\mathsf{false}, \mathsf{decline})).$$

4   Conversation Types

In the previous sections we have focused our analysis on the interaction between two parties, typically a client and a server. However, service-oriented applications often rely on collaborations between several partners, usually established dynamically and without centralized control. A central concern in the development of service-oriented systems is thus the design of interaction protocols that allow for the decentralized and dynamic collaboration between several parties in a reliable way. Within the Sensoria project we have developed a novel type-based approach that copes with such challenging scenarios involving dynamically established multiparty collaborations [8].

In the remainder of this section we discuss the analysis techniques introduced in [8] that support the verification of key properties, namely conversation fidelity and progress, addressing scenarios where multiple parties interact in a conversation, even when some of them are dynamically called in to participate, and where parties interleave their participation in several of such collaborations, even in the dynamically established ones. Such challenging scenarios are of interest as they can be found in realistic service-oriented applications, and fall out of scope of previous approaches—namely the works on multiparty session types [10,2]. Our techniques, although independent, may be viewed as complementary. In fact, it is their combined use that allows us to prove the progress property.

4.1   Analyzing Multiparty Protocols with Conversation Types

In [8] we introduced a type theory for analyzing concurrent multiparty interactions as found in service-oriented computing based on the notion of conversation (see Chapter 2-1). A conversation is a structured, not centrally coordinated, possibly concurrent, set of interactions between several participants. The notion of conversation builds on the fundamental concept of session, but generalizes it along directions. In particular, conversation types discipline interactions in conversations while accounting for dynamical join and leave of an unanticipated number of participants.

Our type system combines techniques from linear, behavioral, session and spatial types (see [8] for references): the type structure features prefix $M.B$, parallel composition $B_1 \mid B_2$ (to represent concurrent behavior), and also choice and branch types that capture alternative behavior: the former characterizes processes that can perform one of the $M_i.B_i$ choices, and the latter characterizes processes that can perform either one of the $M_i.B_i$ branches. Messages M describe external (receive ? / send !) exchanges in two views (d): with the *enclosing* ($\uparrow$) and *current* conversations ($\downarrow$). They also describe internal message exchanges (τ). The type language is shown in Fig. 5. Notice that conversation types mix, at the same level in the type language, internal/global specifications (τ message exchanges) with interface/local specifications (output ! and input ? types).

Key technical ingredients in our approach to conversation types are the amalgamation of global types and of local types (in the general sense of [10]) in the same type language, and the definition of a merge relation ensuring, by construction, that participants typed by the projected views of a type will behave well under composition. Merge subsumes duality, in the sense that for each τ-free B there are types $\overline{B}, B'$ such that $B \bowtie \overline{B} = \tau(B')$, so dyadic sessions are special cases of conversations. But merge

$$B ::= B_1 \mid B_2 \mid \mathbf{0} \mid \operatorname{rec} \mathcal{X}.B \mid \mathcal{X} \mid \oplus_{i \in I}\{M_i.B_i\} \mid \&_{i \in I}\{M_i.B_i\} \qquad \text{(Behavioral)}$$

$$M ::= p\, l^d([B]) \quad \text{(Message)} \qquad\qquad\qquad p ::= ! \mid ? \mid \tau \quad \text{(Polarity)}$$

$$L ::= n : [B] \mid L_1 \mid L_2 \mid \mathbf{0} \quad \text{(Located)} \qquad\qquad T ::= L \mid B \qquad \text{(Process)}$$

Fig. 5. Conversation types syntax

$$\frac{\forall_{i \in I}(B_i = B_i^- \bowtie B_i^+)}{\oplus_{i \in I}\{\tau\, l_i^{\downarrow}(C).B_i\} = \oplus_{i \in I}\{!\, l_i^{\downarrow}(C_i).B_i^+\} \bowtie \&_{i \in I}\{?\, l_i^{\downarrow}(C_i).B_i^-\}}(Plain)$$

$$\frac{M_1 \# M_2.B_2 \qquad B_1' \mid B_2' = B_1 \bowtie M_2.B_2}{M_1.B_1' \mid B_2' = M_1.B_1 \bowtie M_2.B_2}(Shuffle) \qquad\qquad \frac{B_1 \# B_2}{B_1 \mid B_2 = B_1 \bowtie B_2}(Apart)$$

Fig. 6. Behavioral type merge relation selected rules

of types allows for extra flexibility on the manipulation of projections of conversation types, in an open-ended way. In particular, our approach allows fragments of a conversation type (e.g., a choreography) to be dynamically distributed among participants, while statically ensuring that interactions follow the prescribed discipline.

Building on the capability to mix local and global specifications, we are able to describe, via the merge relation, arbitrary decompositions of the protocol in the roles of one or more parties. This allows, in particular, for a single participant to be initially typed with a fragment of the protocol that will be dynamically delegated away, which is crucial to support conversation join. We write $B = B_1 \bowtie B_2$ to say that B is a particular (in general not unique) behavioral combination of the types B_1 and B_2. The merge of two independent types (measured up to *apartness* # which determines if the types have distinct message alphabets) yields the independent composition of the two types. However, when the types specify behaviors that may synchronize, then the merge relation introduces an internal message exchange τ in the type to represent such synchronization potential. Thus, the merge of two behaviors is defined not only in terms of spatial separation, but also, and crucially, in terms of merging behavioral "traces". Fig. 6 shows a selection of the merge relation rules.

We may then characterize the behavior of CC systems by means of conversation types. Our type system singles out CC processes that enjoy some safety properties, namely that are free from a certain kind of runtime errors, and also that their processes, at runtime, follow the protocols prescribed by the types. The behavioral types capture the protocols of interaction in a single conversation. Since processes, in general, may interact in several conversations, characterizing a CC system involves describing the several protocols the process has in each conversation. Then, the typing judgment: $P ::$ $B \mid n : [B_n] \mid m : [B_m] \mid o : [B_o] \mid \ldots$ specifies that the behavior of process P in conversations $n, m, \ldots$ is captured by behavioral types $B_n, B_m, \ldots$, respectively. Notice that, since CC processes may interact in the current and enclosing conversations, the typing judgment considers an unlocated behavioral type B. Such a typing judgement $P :: T$ intuitively says that if process P is placed in a context where a process that behaves like T is expected then we obtain a safe system.

$$\frac{P :: T_1 \quad Q :: T_2}{P \mid Q :: T_1 \bowtie T_2}(Par) \qquad \frac{P :: L \mid B}{l^d !(n).P :: (L \bowtie n : C) \mid \oplus\{ ! \; l^d(C).B; \tilde{B}\}}(Output)$$

$$\frac{P :: T \mid a : [B] \quad (closed(B))}{(va)P :: T}(Res) \qquad \frac{P :: L \mid B}{n \blacktriangleleft [P] :: (L \bowtie n : [\downarrow B]) \mid loc(\uparrow B)}(Piece)$$

Fig. 7. Selected typing rules

We show a selection of the rules of our type system in Fig. 7. Rule (*Par*) says that the composition is well typed under the merge of the types of the branches. Recall the merge explains the composition of two processes by synchronizing behavioral traces. Rule (*Res*) types the name restriction by checking if the behavioral type of the restricted conversation is closed, in such case eliding it in the conclusion of the rule. Closed behavioral types characterize processes that have matching receives for all sends—roughly, a closed type is defined exclusively on messages of polarity τ. The type associated to a process only describes the behaviors in the visible conversations, and the closed condition avoids hiding a conversation where there are unmatched communications.

The premise of rule (*Output*) specifies that the continuation process P defines some located behavior L and some unlocated behavior B. Then, the output prefix is typed by the merge of the delegated conversation fragment $n : C$ with the located behavior L, along with a choice type that includes the output action specified in the prefix with respective continuation. Notice that the conversation fragment piece that is delegated away is actually a separate $\bowtie$ view of conversation n, which means that the type being sent may actually be some separate part of the type of the conversation. This mechanism is crucial to allow external partners to join in on ongoing conversations in a disciplined way. The behavioral interface of the output prefixed process is a choice type, as the process can choose the specified action from any set of choices that contains it.

We may now state our type safety results. To describe how typings are preserved under process reduction we introduce a notion of type reduction which is a reflexive relation obtained by the closure under static contexts of rule $\tau \, l^d(C).B \rightarrow B$: hence, synchronizations in the process are explained by τ message types. We may then precisely characterize the preservation of typing by means of type reduction.

Theorem 3 (Subject Reduction). *Let process P be such that $P :: T$. If $P \rightarrow Q$ then there is $T \rightarrow T'$ such that $Q :: T'$.*

Subject reduction thus guarantees that well-typedness is invariant under process reduction. Moreover, each reduction in a process is explained by a reduction in the type. Reflexivity in the type reduction relation is required since it allows us to abstract away from message synchronizations that occur at the level of restricted conversations.

Our type safety result asserts that certain error processes are unreachable from well-typed processes. Error processes are configurations where there is an active race on a (linear) message, which means two processes are willing to send or waiting to receive the same message. Thus, a process is not an error only if for each possible immediate interaction in a message there is at most a single sender and a single receiver. We prove well-typed systems are error free, and thus are error free throughout their evolution.

Proposition 2. *If P is a well-typed process then P is not an error process.*

Corollary 2 (Type Safety). *Let P be a well-typed process. If there is Q such that P $\stackrel{*}{\rightarrow}$ Q, then Q is not an error process.*

Our type safety result ensures that, in any reduction sequence arising from a well-typed process, for each message ready to communicate there is always at most a unique input/output outstanding synchronization. Subject reduction also entails that any message exchange in the process must be explained by a τM prefix in the related conversation type, implying conversation fidelity: all conversations follow the prescribed protocols.

4.2 Proving Progress of Conversations

In this section we present the progress proof system, introduced in [8], which allows us to verify that systems enjoy a progress property. While the conversation type system allows us to guarantee that conversations follow the prescribed protocols, it is not enough to guarantee that the systems do not get stuck, due to, e.g., communication dependencies between distinct conversations. As most traditional deadlock detection methods (see [8] for references), we build on the construction of a well-founded ordering on events. Roughly, we must check that the events specified in the continuation of a prefix are of greater rank with respect to the event relative to the prefix itself.

The challenge is how to statically account for the orderings of events on conversations which will only be dynamically instantiated. To solve this problem we attach to our events a notion of prescribed ordering: the ordering that captures the event ordering expected by the receiving process, that the emitted name will have to comply to. In such way, we are able to statically determine the orderings followed by the processes at "runtime", through propagation of orderings in the analysis of message exchanges that carry conversation identifiers. Technically, we proceed by developing a notion of event and of event ordering that allow us to verify that CC processes can be ordered in a well-founded way, including when conversation references are passed around.

Definition 5 (Event orderings and Events). *We say relation Γ between events is an event ordering if it is a well-founded partial order of events. We denote by $(x)\Gamma$ an event ordering parameterized by x. Events, noted e, are defined as $e, e_1, \ldots ::= n.l.(x)\Gamma$.*

Event orderings capture the overall ordering of events. Parameterized event orderings are used to capture the prescribed ordering of conversation fragments that are passed in messages. Events describe a message exchange by identifying the name of the conversation, the label of the message, and the parameterized event ordering.

We may then characterize the event ordering in CC systems by means of a proof system that associates CC systems to event orderings. The proof system is presented by means of judgments of the form $\Gamma \vdash_\ell P$, which state that the communications of process P follow a well determined order, given by event ordering Γ, where ℓ keeps track of the identities of the current and enclosing conversations of P.

We show the rule that orders the output prefix process:

$$\frac{(\ell(d).l.(x)\Gamma' \perp \Gamma) \vdash_\ell P \quad \Gamma'\{x \leftarrow n\} \subseteq (\ell(d).l.(x)\Gamma' \perp \Gamma)}{\Gamma \vdash_\ell l^d!(n).P}(Output)$$

In rule (*Output*), we take the event associated to the prefix $(\ell(d).l.(x)\Gamma'$ where $\ell(d)$ identifies the conversation, l is the message label and $(x)\Gamma'$ specifies the prescribed ordering
for the conversation reference passed in the message) and verify that the continuation is
ordered by events greater than $\ell(d).l.(x)\Gamma'$. Also, and crucially, we check that the name
being passed in the output complies with the ordering prescribed in the event $(x)\Gamma'$ by
verifying that such prescribed ordering, where the variable x is replaced by the name to
be sent n, is contained in the ordering of events greater than $\ell(d).l.(x)\Gamma'$. In such way,
we ensure the overall ordering is still respected after the name passing.

We may now present our progress results. First, we prove orderings are preserved
under process reduction. Then, we present our main progress result, where we exclude
processes that are stuck. We distinguish stuck processes from finished processes, which,
intuitively, can be viewed as collections of service definitions, where there are no pending service calls, neither linear protocols to be fulfilled. We then consider finished processes to be in a stable state, despite the fact they have no reductions.

Theorem 4 (Preservation of Event Ordering). *Let process P be such that* $\Gamma \vdash_\ell P$. *If*
$P \to Q$ *then* $\Gamma \vdash_\ell Q$.

Theorem 5 (Progress). *Let P be a process such that* $P :: T$, *where* $closed(T)$, *and*
$\Gamma \vdash_\ell P$. *If* $P \xrightarrow{*} Q$ *then either Q is a finished process or there is* $Q \to Q'$.

Theorem 5 thus ensures that in systems that get past our rules, services are always available upon request and protocols involving interleaving conversations never get stuck.

4.3 Typing the Credit Request Scenario

In this section we show the typing for the credit request scenario CC implementation
given in Chapter 2-1. The CC code for the credit request, the *CreditRequestSystem*,
presents a challenging scenario for analysis techniques as it involves collaborations
between multiple parties established in a dynamic way and where parties interleave their
participation in several conversations, including ones to which they have dynamically
gained access to. The typing judgment for the entire system is shown in Fig. 8, where we
focus on the typing of the Finance Portal conversation, along with the definitions of the
abbreviations introduced for the service types (e.g., acsT for AuthCreditServiceType).

The typing of the *FinancePortal* conversation captures the interactions in services
CreditRequest, ReviewApp and AuthCredit, along with the messages requestApp
and requestEval which are exchanged between the service instances, each identifying in the argument type the conversation fragment delegated in the communications.
For instance, the (first) argument type of messages requestEval and requestApp is
$\oplus\{!\ \text{approved}^\downarrow(); !\ \text{denied}^\downarrow()\}$, which captures the client conversation fragment delegated from the CreditRequest instance to the ReviewApp service instance, and from
the ReviewApp service instance to the AuthCredit service instance, respectively, allowing for the reply to the client to originate in the other service instances.

The conversation types for each service interaction are obtained by merging service
provider and service user behaviors. For instance, the interaction between the client and

CreditRequestSystem ::

    FinancePortal : [

        τ CreditRequest([crsT]) | τ ReviewApp([rasT]) | τ AuthCredit([acsT])

        | τ requestApp([$\oplus${! approved$^\downarrow$(); ! denied$^\downarrow$()}], *idT*, *dataT*)

        | τ requestEval([$\oplus${! approved$^\downarrow$(); ! denied$^\downarrow$()}], *idT*, *dataT*)]

      | *Bank* : [τ RateCalc([rcsT]) | ...]

      | *Client* : [...] | *Clerk* : [...] | *Manager* : [...]

crsT $\triangleq$? login$^\downarrow$(*idT*).? request$^\downarrow$(*dataT*).τ userData$^\downarrow$(*dataT*).

               τ rateValue$^\downarrow$(*rateT*).$\oplus${! approved$^\downarrow$() ; ! denied$^\downarrow$()}

rasT $\triangleq$? login$^\downarrow$(*idT*).! show$^\downarrow$(*idT*, *dataT*).&{? pass$^\downarrow$() ; ? deny$^\downarrow$()}

acsT $\triangleq$? login$^\downarrow$(*idT*).! show$^\downarrow$(*idT*, *dataT*).&{? accept$^\downarrow$() ; ? reject$^\downarrow$()}

rcsT $\triangleq$? userData$^\downarrow$(*dataT*).! rateValue$^\downarrow$(*rateT*)

Fig. 8. Typing the credit request scenario CC Implementation

the finance portal is captured by the merge of the CreditRequest service type (crsT) with the client role in the service conversation:

    τ login$^\downarrow$(*idT*).τ request$^\downarrow$(*dataT*).τ userData$^\downarrow$(*dataT*).

             τ rateValue$^\downarrow$(*rateT*).$\oplus${τ approved$^\downarrow$() ; τ denied$^\downarrow$()}

    =

    ? login$^\downarrow$(*idT*).? request$^\downarrow$(*dataT*).τ userData$^\downarrow$(*dataT*).

             τ rateValue$^\downarrow$(*rateT*).$\oplus${! approved$^\downarrow$() ; ! denied$^\downarrow$()}

    $\bowtie$

    ! login$^\downarrow$(*idT*).! request$^\downarrow$(*dataT*).&{? approved$^\downarrow$() ; ? denied$^\downarrow$()}

Notice that the merge yields a closed type: hence, all communications are matched. Notice also that the CreditRequest service type (crsT) still refers some internal communications (τ message types in messages userData and rateValue). This is crucial to support the dynamic join of the RateCalc service to the CreditRequest service conversation, as it allows for the *CreditRequest* code to further along delegate a conversation fragment to RateCalc, while ensuring that the overall protocol is followed.

    We may also show that the events in the *CreditRequestSystem* are well ordered, and thus ensure that the *CreditRequestSystem* enjoys some fundamental properties.

Corollary 3. *The CreditRequestSystem enjoys conversation fidelity and progress.*

5 Conclusion

We have reported on the static analysis techniques developed for CaSPiS and CC, two session oriented calculi developed within the Sensoria project [1,3,8]. Each technique aims at guaranteeing a specific property one would expect from service-oriented applications. Our models and techniques may be complementary used and combined in order to provide provide as many guarantees as possible on the correctness of services' behavior.

The most relevant related works have been discussed throughout the chapter. More extensive discussions on related techniques and possible extensions can be found in the original papers introducing the approaches reported here [1,3,8].

References

1. Acciai, L., Boreale, M.: A type system for client progress in a service-oriented calculus. In: Degano, P., De Nicola, R., Bevilacqua, V. (eds.) CGM 2008. LNCS, vol. 5065, pp. 642–658. Springer, Heidelberg (2008)
2. Bettini, L., Coppo, M., D'Antoni, L., De Luca, M., Dezani-Ciancaglini, M., Yoshida, N.: Global Progress in Dynamically Interleaved Multiparty Sessions. In: van Breugel, F., Chechik, M. (eds.) CONCUR 2008. LNCS, vol. 5201, pp. 418–433. Springer, Heidelberg (2008)
3. Bodei, C., Brodo, L., Bruni, R.: Static detection of logic flaws in service-oriented applications. In: Degano, P., Viganò, L. (eds.) ARSPA-WITS 2009. LNCS, vol. 5511, pp. 70–87. Springer, Heidelberg (2009)
4. Bodei, C., Brodo, L., Degano, P., Gao, H.: Detecting and preventing type flaws at static time. Journal of Computer Security 18(2), 229–264 (2010)
5. Bodei, C., Buchholtz, M., Degano, P., Nielson, F., Nielson, H.R.: Static validation of security protocols. Journal of Computer Security 13(3), 347–390 (2005)
6. Boreale, M., Bruni, R., De Nicola, R., Loreti, M.: Sessions and pipelines for structured service programming. In: Barthe, G., de Boer, F.S. (eds.) FMOODS 2008. LNCS, vol. 5051, pp. 19–38. Springer, Heidelberg (2008)
7. Bruni, R., Mezzina, L.G.: Types and deadlock freedom in a calculus of services, sessions and pipelines. In: Meseguer, J., Rosu, G. (eds.) AMAST 2008. LNCS, vol. 5140, pp. 100–115. Springer, Heidelberg (2008)
8. Caires, L., Vieira, H.: Conversation Types. In: Castagna, G. (ed.) ESOP 2009. LNCS, vol. 5502, pp. 285–300. Springer, Heidelberg (2009)
9. Christensen, S., Hirshfeld, Y., Moller, F.: Bisimulation equivalence is decidable for basic parallel processes. In: Best, E. (ed.) CONCUR 1993. LNCS, vol. 715, pp. 143–157. Springer, Heidelberg (1993)
10. Honda, K., Yoshida, N., Carbone, M.: Multiparty Asynchronous Session Types. In: Necula, G.C., Wadler, P. (eds.) POPL 2008, pp. 273–284. ACM Press, New York (2008)
11. Igarashi, A., Kobayashi, N.: A Generic Type System for the π-Calculus. Theoretical Computer Science 311(1-3), 121–163 (2004)
12. Lanese, I., Martins, F., Vasconcelos, V.T., Ravara, A.: Disciplining orchestration and conversation in service-oriented computing. In: SEFM, pp. 305–314. IEEE Computer Society, Los Alamitos (2007)
13. Mezzina, L.: Typing Services. Phd thesis in computer science, IMT Institute for Advanced Studies, Lucca (2009)
14. Neohapsis Archives. Price modification possible in CyberOffice Shopping Cart, http://archives.neohapsis.com/archives/bugtraq/2000-10/0011.html
15. Talpin, J.-P., Jouvelot, P.: The type and effect discipline. Inf. Comput. 111(2), 245–296 (1994)

Call-by-Contract for Service
Discovery, Orchestration and Recovery*

Massimo Bartoletti[1], Pierpaolo Degano[2],
Gian Luigi Ferrari[2], and Roberto Zunino[3]

[1] Dipartimento di Matematica e Informatica, Università degli Studi di Cagliari, Italy
bart@unica.it
[2] Dipartimento di Informatica, Università di Pisa, Italy
degano@di.unipi.it, giangi@di.unipi.it
[3] Dipartimento di Ingegneria e Scienza dell'Informazione, Università di Trento, Italy
zunino@disi.unitn.it

Abstract. We present a framework for designing and composing services in a "call-by-contract" fashion, i.e. according to their behavior. We discuss how to correctly plan service compositions in some relevant classes of services and behavioral properties. To this aim, we propose both a core functional calculus for services, and a graphical design language. The core calculus features primitives for selecting and invoking services that respect given behavioral requirements, typically safety properties on the service execution history. A type and effect system over-approximates the actual run-time behavior of services. A further static analysis step finds the viable plans that drive the selection of those services matching the behavioral requirements on demand.

1 Introduction

The so-called *Service-oriented Architectures* provide state-of-the-art software engineering methods supporting the design of open-ended, heterogenous distributed applications. Service-orientation enables an evolutionary design style where applications are built by gluing together suitable software units called *services*. Services can be published, bound, and invoked by other services using standard internet-based protocols. Moreover applications can dynamically replace the services they use with other services. Finally, services are executed on heterogeneous systems and no assumptions can be taken on their running platforms. The Web service protocol stack (WSDL, UDDI, SOAP, WSBPEL) is the best illustrative example of this approach. Web services have been extremely valuable to highlight the key innovative features of service-orientation. However, experience has singled out several limiting factors of the service protocol stack, mainly because of the purely "syntactic" nature of standards. This has lead to the idea of extending the Web service stack with higher level, "semantic" functionalities. For instance, the design and exploitation of service ontologies is an attempt to address these concerns.

---

* This work has been partially sponsored by the project SENSORIA , IST-2005-016004.

M. Wirsing and M. Hölzl (Eds.): SENSORIA Project, LNCS 6582, pp. 232–261, 2011.

A key issue of the service approach is given by its compositional nature. Services are pluggable entities obtained by combining existing elementary or complex services. Composite services in turn offer themselves as new services. The activities underlying the assembling of services requires coordinating the behavior and managing the interactions of the the component services. Two different approaches are usually adopted to assemble services: *orchestration* and *choreography*. In the first, an intermediate entity, namely the orchestrator, arranges service activities according to the business process. The service choreography, instead, involves all parties and their associated interactions providing a global view of the system. Relevant standard technologies are the Business Process Execution Language (BPEL) [38], for the orchestration, and Web Service Choreography Description Language (WS-CDL) [43], for the choreography.

This chapter focuses on the problem of properly selecting and configuring services so to guarantee that their orchestration enjoys some desirable properties. These properties may involve *functional* aspects, and also *non-functional* aspects, like e.g. security, availability, performance, transactionality, etc. [39]. This poses significant theoretical and technical challenges. In particular, the ability to orchestrate services while guaranteeing certain properties requires a novel view of the interplay between local vs. global properties of services. For instance, the components of a service may locally enjoy a non-functional property (e.g. a security property) while their orchestration globally does not.

In this chapter we survey a semantics-based framework for modelling and orchestrating services in the presence of both functional and non-functional constraints. The formal foundation of our work is λ^{req} [9,10,15]. This is a core calculus that extends the λ-calculus with primitive constructs to describe and invoke services in a *call-by-contract* fashion. Services are modeled as functions with side effects. These side effects represent the actions of accessing resources, and they are logged into *histories*. A run-time monitor may inspect histories, and forbids those executions that would violate the prescribed policies.

Unlike standard discovery mechanisms that match syntactic signatures only, ours also implements a matchmaking algorithm based on service behavior. This algorithm exploits static analysis techniques to resolve the call-by-contract involved in a service orchestration. The published interface of a service takes the form of an annotated type, which represents both the signature of the service (i.e. its input-output information à la WSDL) and a suitable semantic abstraction of the service behavior. In our call-by-contract selection, the client is required to know neither the service name nor its location. Operationally, the service registry is searched for a service with a functional type (the signature) matching the request type; also, the semantic abstraction (the annotation) must respect the non-functional constraints imposed by the request. Our orchestration machinery constructs a *plan* for the execution of services, i.e. a binding between requests and service locations, that are only known to the orchestrator, which guarantees that the properties on demand are always satisfied.

We envisage the impact of our approach on the service protocol stack as follows. First, it requires extending services description languages: besides the standard WSDL attributes, service description should include semantic information about the behavior. Moreover, call-by-contract adds a further layer to the standard service protocol stack: the *planning* layer. This layer provides the orchestrator with the plans guaranteeing that the orchestrated services always respect the required properties. Hence, before starting the execution of the orchestration, the orchestrator engine collects the relevant service plans by inquiring the planning layer. These plans enable the orchestration engine to resolve all the requests in the initiator service, as well as those in the invoked services. Additionally, re-planning can be done at run-time, according to some strategies that will be discussed later on. Summing up, our approach therefore extends the standard notion of orchestrator, by making it to coordinate the composition of services so to ensure the correct execution of call-by-contract invocations.

1.1   Service Interfaces and Contracts

In our approach, the interface of a service is an annotated functional type, of the form $\tau_1 \xrightarrow{H} \tau_2$. When supplied with an argument of type τ_1, the service evaluates to something of type τ_2. The annotation H is a *history expression*, a sort of context-free grammar that abstractly describes the possible run-time histories of the service. Thus, H will be exploited to guide the selection of those services that respect the requested properties about security or other non-functional aspects. Since service interfaces are crucial in the implementation of the call-by-contract primitive, they have to be *certified* by a trusted party, which guarantees that the abstract behavior is a sound over-approximation of the actual behavior.

A *contract* φ is a regular property of execution histories. We express contracts as languages accepted by finite state automata. To select a service matching a given contract φ, and with functional type $\tau_1 \to \tau_2$, a client issues a request of the form $\mathtt{req}\,(\tau_1 \xrightarrow{\varphi} \tau_2)$. The call-by-contract mechanism ensures that the selected service, with interface $\tau_1 \xrightarrow{H} \tau_2$, will always respect the contract φ, i.e. that all the histories represented by H are recognized by the automaton defining φ.

Since service interactions may be complex, it might be the case that a local choice for a service is unsafe in a broader, "global" context. For instance, choosing a low-security e-mail provider might prevent you from using a home-banking service that exchanges confidential data through e-mail. In this case, you should have planned the selection of the e-mail and bank services so to ensure their compatibility. To cope with this kind of issues, we define a static machinery that determines the *viable plans* for selecting services that respect all the contracts, both locally and globally. A plan resolves a call-by-contract into a standard service call, and it is formalized as a mapping from requests to services.

1.2   Planning Service Composition

Our planning technique acts as a *trusted orchestrator* of services. It provides a client with the viable plans guaranteeing that the invoked services always respect the required properties. In our framework the only trusted entity is the orchestrator, and neither clients nor services need to be such. In particular, the orchestrator infers the functional and behavioral type of each service, and it is responsible for certifying the service code and for publishing its interface. We also assume that, whenever a service wants to change its code, it resubmits the code to the orchestrator, so to obtain a new certification. When an application is injected in the network, the orchestrator provides it with a viable plan (if any), constructed by composing and analysing the certified interfaces of the available services. The trustworthiness of the orchestrator relies upon formal grounds, i.e. the soundness of our type and effect system, and the correctness of the subsequent static analysis and model-checking phases that infer viable plans.

As noted above, finding viable plans is not a trivial task, because the effect of selecting a given service for a request is not always confined to the execution of that service. Since each service selection may affect the *whole* execution, we cannot simply devise a viable plan by selecting services that satisfy the constraints imposed by the requests, only. We have then devised a two-stage construction for extracting viable plans from a history expression. Let H be the history expression inferred for a client. A first transformation of H, called *linearization*, lifts all the service choices to the top-level of H. This isolates from H the possible plans, that will be considered one by one in the second stage: model-checking for validity. Projecting the history expression H on a given plan π gives rise to another history expression H', where all the service choices have been resolved according to π. Validity of H' guarantees that the chosen plan π will drive executions that never go wrong at run-time (thus making run-time monitoring unneeded). To verify the validity of H', we first smoothly transform it into Basic Process Algebra (BPA) process. We then model-check this process with a finite state automaton that recognizes validity. At the end, only some (sub-)history expressions within H will be certified, and the plans singling them out are those leading to runs obeying the policies in force. The correctness of all these steps (type safety, linearization, model-checking) has been formally proved in [10].

1.3 Contributions

We briefly summarize the key features of our approach.

1. *Taxonomy of behavioral aspects.* We discuss some design choices that affect behavioral composition of services. These choices address rather general properties of systems: whether services maintain a state across invocations; whether they trust each other; whether they can pass back and forth mobile code; and whether different threads may share part of their state or not. Each of these choices deeply impacts the expressivity of the enforceable properties, as well as the compositionality of planning techniques.

2. *Design Methodology.* We present a formal, UML-like modelling language for designing services. Besides the usual workflow operators, we can express activities subject to non-functional constraints. The awareness of these constraints from the early stages of development is crucial to all the subsequent

phases of software production. Our diagrams have a formal operational semantics, that specifies the dynamic behavior of services. Also, they can be
statically analysed, to infer the contracts satisfied by a service. Our design
methodology allows for a fine-grained characterization of the design choices
that affect to the non-functional properties of interest.

3. *Core calculus for services.* We present an extension of the λ-calculus, with
   primitives for selecting and invoking services that respect given requirements. Service invocation is implemented in a call-by-contract fashion, i.e.
   you choose a service for its behavior, neither for its name nor for the location hosting it. The policies we consider are arbitrary safety properties on
   execution histories; policies can have a local scope.
4. *Planning.* We outlined above the three-step static analysis: typing, linearization and model-checking. These steps are completely mechanizable, so making call-by-contract composition feasible. Studying the output of the model-
   checker may highlight design flaws, suggesting how to revise the contracts
   and the services.
5. *Recovering strategies.* We identify several cases where designers need to take a
   decision before proceeding with the execution. For instance, when a planned
   service disappears unexpectedly, one can choose to replan, so to adapt to
   the new network configuration. Different tactics are possible, depending on
   the boundary conditions and on past experience.

1.4   Our Work within the Context

Our work contributes to a research theme that has been intensively investigated.
Below we briefly survey related work and refer the reader to the relevant sections
of our recent papers for a more detailed discussion.

Our local policies were first introduced in [7], where a block of code B could
be sandboxed by a policy φ, so to require that φ must hold through the execution of B. The definition of policies has since then been revised several times,
so to make them more expressive. In the original formulation, policies could
only inspect sequences of actions, neglecting resources. In [12,15] policies can
be parametrized over a single resource, and resources can be dynamically created; [13] deals with the general case of an arbitrary number of parameters; [3]
adds guards to constrain state transitions in policy automata. Our LocUsT model
checker [44] implements the verification techniques for resource usage described
in the papers cited above; it supports all the extensions studied in the theory.
Recent extensions allowing for a more precise analisys are in [21].

In the papers cited above, policies were exploited to define static enforcement
mechanisms. Actually, dynamic monitoring is in order when static verification
happens to fail. In [4], the security mechanism of Java is extended with our
policies. In this case, a policy may monitor each sequence of method invocations.
In [5] we also proposed a way of instrumenting code so to insert checks when
compliance to a policy cannot be established at static time.

The theory underlying our call-by-contract invocation mechanism was originally introduced in [6]. There, a type and effect system and a model-checker

were exploited to define a call-by-contract orchestrator. In [9] the orchestrator was enhanced, by making it output a set of possible plans that safely drive service compositions. In [11] the planning problem was further explored, by devising several strategies to adopt when services become unavailable. In [14] a design methodology was proposed for services, based on our call-by-contract technique.

Process calculi techniques have been used to study the foundation of services. The main goal of some of these proposals, e.g. [23,17,26,31,20,19] is to formalize various aspects of standards for the description, execution, orchestration and choreography of services. A whole chapter of this book (Chapter 2-1: Core Calculi for Service-Oriented Computing) is devoted to the core calculi introduced within the SENSORIA project. As a matter of fact, our λ^{req} builds over the standard service infrastructure the above calculi formalize. Indeed, our call-by-contract supersedes standard invocation mechanisms and allows for verified planning. Another approach to planning has been proposed in [32], where the problem of achieving a given composition is expressed as a constraint satisfaction problem.

From a technical point of view, the work of Skalka and Smith [36] is the closest to this paper. We share with them the use of a type and effect system and that of model checking validity of effects. In [36], a static approach to history-based access control is proposed. The λ-calculus is enriched with access events and local checks on the past event history. Local checks make validity a regular property, so regularization is unneeded. The programming model and the type system of [36] allow for access events parametrized by constants, and for let-polymorphism. We have omitted these features for simplicity, but they can be easily recovered by using similar techniques.

A related line of research addresses the issue of modelling and analysing resource usage. Igarashi and Kobayashi [28] introduce a type systems to check whether a program accesses resources according to a user-defined policy. A main limitation of this approach is that they do not provide a verification procedure to check resource usages. Our model is less general than the framework of [28], however a generalization of the techniques presented here provides a static verification machinery to verify resource usage policies [15].

Increasing attention has been devoted to express service contracts as behavioral (or session) types. These synthetize the essential aspects of the interaction behavior of services, while allowing for efficient static verification of properties of composed systems. Session types [27] have been exploited to formalize compatibility of components [40] and to describe adaptation of web services [18]. Security issues have been recently considered in terms of session types, e.g. in [16], which proves the decidability of type-checking in an extension of the π-calculus with session types and correspondence assertions [42].

2   A Taxonomy of Behavioral Aspects in Web Services

Service composition heavily depends on which information about a service is made public, on how to choose those services that match the user requirements, and on their actual run-time behavior. Security makes service composition even harder. Services may be offered by different providers, which only partially trust each other. On the one hand, providers have to guarantee that the delivered service respects a given security policy, in any interaction with the operational environment, and regardless of who actually called the service. On the other hand, clients may want to protect their sensitive data from the services invoked.

In the *history-based* approach to security, the run-time permissions depend on a suitable abstraction of the history of all the pieces of code (possibly partially) executed so far. This approach has been receiving major attention, at both levels of foundations [2,24,36] and of language design/implementation [1,22].

The observations of critical activities, e.g. reading and writing files, accessing resources, are called *events*. Sequences of events are called *histories*. The class of policies we consider is that of *safety* properties of histories, i.e. properties that are expressible through finite state automata. The typical run-time mechanisms for enforcing history-based policies are *reference monitors*, which observe program executions and abort them whenever about to violate the given policy. Reference monitors enforce exactly the class of safety properties [35].

Since histories are the main ingredient of our model, our taxonomy focusses on how histories are handled and manipulated by services.

Stateless / stateful services. A stateless service does not preserve its state (i.e. its history) across distinct invocations. Instead, a stateful service keeps the histories of all the past invocations. Stateful services allow for more expressive policies, e.g. they can bound the number of invocations on a per-client basis.

Local / global histories. Local histories only record the events generated by a service on its own site. Instead, a global history may span over multiple services. Local histories are the most prudent choice when services do not trust other services, in particular the histories they generate. In this case, a service only trusts its own history — but it cannot constrain the past history of its callers, e.g. to prevent that its client has visited a malicious site. Global histories instead require some trust relation among services: if a service A trusts B, then the history of A may comprise that of B, and so A may check policies on the behavior of B.

First order / higher order service requests. A request type can be viewed as a functional type taking the the type τ as input and yielding a result of type τ'. A request type is first order when both τ and τ' are base types (*Int*, *Bool*, ...). Instead, if τ or τ' are functional types, the request is higher order. In particular, if the parameter (of type τ) is a function, then the client passes some code to be possibly executed by the requested service. Symmetrically, if τ' is a function type, then the service returns back some code to the caller. Mobility of code impacts the way histories are generated, and demands for particular mechanisms to enforce behavioral policies on the site where the code is run. A typical protection mechanism is *sandboxing*, that consists in wrapping code within an execution monitor enforcing the given policy. When there is no mobile code, more efficient mechanisms can be devised, e.g. local checks on critical operations.

Dependent / independent threads. In a network of services, several threads may run concurrently and compete for services. Independent threads keep histories separated, while dependent threads may share parts of their histories. Therefore, dependent threads may influence each other when using the same service, while independent threads cannot. For instance, consider a one-shot service that can be invoked only one time. If threads are independent, the one-shot service has no way to enforce single use. It can only check that no thread uses it more than once, because each thread keeps its own history. Dependent threads are necessary to correctly implement the one-shot service.

3   A Call-by-Contract Design Methodology for Services

In this section, we discuss the main ingredients of our design methodology. We present the methodology exploiting a *graphical notation* that abstracts from all low level details and focusses only on the key issues. Our notation is related to other graphical design languages for services (e.g. BPMN [29], UML4SOA [30]). Indeed, we envision that our methodology can be incorporated into these languages as well. The main motivation behind using our abstract notation is that our focus here is not on the overall structure of the service architecture, but on how to design the skeleton structure of the service orchestration, taking into account the specific policies and the service contracts on demand. We refer to [14] for a comprehensive presentation of the methodology.

The basic entity is that of *services*. A service is represented as a box containing its code (Fig. 1). The four corners of the box are decorated with information about the service interface and behavior. The label $\ell : \tau$ indicates the *location* ℓ where the service is made available, and its certified published *interface* τ. We assume that each published service has a distinct location ℓ. The other labels instead are used to represent the state of a service at run-time.

The label $\eta = \alpha_1 \cdots \alpha_k$ is an abstraction of the service execution *history*. We are concerned with the sequence of relevant events α_i happened sometimes in the past, in the spirit of history-based security [1]. The label (m, Φ) is a pair, where the first element is a flag m representing the on/off status of the execution monitor, and the second element is the sequence $\varphi_1 \cdots \varphi_k$ of active *policies*. When the flag is on, the monitor checks that the service history η adheres to the policy φ_i (written $\eta \models \varphi_i$) for each $i \in 1..k$.

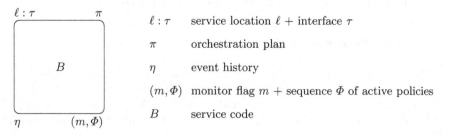

$\ell : \tau$	service location ℓ + interface τ
π	orchestration plan
η	event history
(m, Φ)	monitor flag m + sequence Φ of active policies
B	service code

Fig. 1. Execution state of a service

The block B inside the box is an abstraction of the service code. Formally, it is a sort of control flow graph [34] with nodes modelling activities, blocks enclosing sets of nodes, and arrows modelling intra-procedural flow.

Nodes can be of two kinds, i.e. *events* or *requests*. Events $\alpha, \beta, \ldots$ abstract from critical operations. An event can be parametrized, e.g. $\alpha_w(foo)$ for writing the file foo, $sgn(\ell)$ for a certificate signed by ℓ, etc. A service request has the form $\mathsf{req}_r\tau$. The label r uniquely identifies the request; the type τ is defined as:

$$\tau \ ::= \ b \ | \ \tau \xrightarrow{\varphi} \tau$$

where b is a base type (*Int, Bool*, ...). The annotation φ on the arrow is the query pattern (or *"contract"*) to be matched by the invoked service. Indeed, the property φ acts as a *contract* the called service has to respect. For instance, the request type $\tau \xrightarrow{\varphi} \tau'$ matches services with functional type $\tau \to \tau'$, and whose behavior respects the policy φ.

The label π is the *plan* used for resolving future service choices. A plan formalises how a call-by-contract $\mathsf{req}_r\tau$ is transformed into a standard service call, and takes the form of a function from request identifiers r to service locations ℓ.

Definition 1. Syntax of plans

$\pi, \pi' ::=$	0	empty
	$r[\ell]$	service choice
	$\pi \mid \pi'$	composition

The plan 0 is empty; the plan $r[\ell]$ associates the service published at site ℓ with the request labelled r. Composition $\mid$ on plans is associative, commutative and idempotent, and its identity is the empty plan 0. We require here plans to have a single choice for each request, i.e. $r[\ell] \mid r[\ell']$ implies $\ell = \ell'$. More general notions of plans are possible, we refer to [8] for the details.

Blocks can be of two kinds: (*i*) *safety blocks* $\varphi[B]$ enforce the policy φ on B, i.e. the history must respect φ at each step of the evaluation of B; (*ii*) *planning blocks* $\{B\}$ construct a plan for the execution of B (see Section 6 for a discussion on some planning strategies). Blocks can be nested, and they determine the scope of policies (hence called *local* policies [7]) and of planning.

3.1   A Car Repair Scenario

To illustrate some of the features and design facilities of our framework, we consider the SENSORIA car repair scenario [41], where a car may break and then request assistance from a tow-truck and a garage. We assume a car equipped with a diagnostic system that continuously reports on the status of the vehicle. When a major failure occurs, the in-car emergency service is invoked to select the appropriate tow-truck and garage services. The selection may take into account suitable policies, e.g. the tow-truck should be close enough to reach both the location where the car is stuck and the chosen garage.

The system is composed of three kinds of services: the CAR-EMERGENCY service, that tries to arrange for a car tow-trucking and repair, the TOW-TRUCK service, that picks the damaged car to a garage, and the GARAGE service, that repairs the car. We assume that all the involved services trust each other's history, and so we assume a shared global history, with independent threads. We also design all the services to be stateful, so that, e.g. the driver can personalize the choice of garages, according to past experiences.

We start by modelling the CAR-EMERGENCY service handling the car faults. This service is invoked by the embedded diagnosis system, each time a fault is reported. The actual kind of fault, and the geographic location where the car is stuck, are passed as parameters — named *flt* and *loc*. The diagram of the CAR-EMERGENCY service is displayed on the left-hand side of Fig. 2.

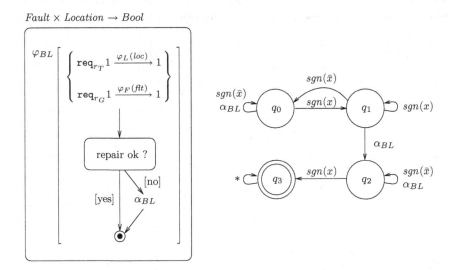

Fig. 2. The CAR-EMERGENCY service and the black-listing policy φ_{BL}

The outer policy φ_{BL} (black-list) has the role of enforcing a sort of "quality of service" constraint. The CAR-EMERGENCY service records in its history the list of all the garages used in past repair requests. When the selected garage ℓ_G completes repairing a car, it appends to the history its own signature $sgn(\ell_G)$. When the user is not satisfied with the quality (or the bill!) of the garage, the garage is black-listed (event α_{BL}). The policy φ_{BL} ensures that a black-listed garage (marked by a signature $sgn(\ell_G)$ followed by a black-listing tag α_{BL}) cannot be selected for future emergencies. The black-listing policy φ_{BL} is formally defined by the *usage automaton* [12] in Fig. 2, right-hand side. Note that some labels in φ_{BL} are parametric: $sgn(x)$ and $sgn(\bar{x})$ stands respectively for "the signature of garage x" and "a signature of any garage different from x", where x can be replaced by an arbitrary garage identifier. If, starting from the state q_0, a garage signature $sgn(x)$ is immediately followed by a black-listing tag α_{BL}, then you reach the state q_2. From q_2, an attempt to generate again $sgn(x)$ will result in a transition to the non-accepting sink state q_3. For instance, the history $sgn(\ell_1)sgn(\ell_2)\alpha_{BL} \cdots sgn(\ell_2)$ violates the policy φ_{BL}.

The crucial part of the design is the planning block. It contains two requests: r_T (for the tow-truck) and r_G (for the garage), to be planned together. The contract $\varphi_L(loc)$ requires that the tow-truck is able to serve the location loc where the car is broken down. The contract $\varphi_F(flt)$ selects the garages that can repair the kind of faults flt. In the requests we simply use the void type 1 for the inputs and outputs of the garage and tow-truck services, hence neglecting them.

The planning block has the role of determining the orchestration plan for both the requests. In this case, it makes little sense to continue executing with an incomplete plan or with sandboxing: you should perhaps look for a car rental service, if either the tow-truck or the garage are unavailable. Therefore, a meaningful planning strategy is trying to find a couple of services matching both r_T and r_G, and wait until both the services are available.

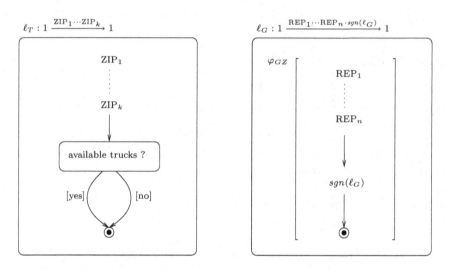

Fig. 3. The TOW-TRUCK (left) and GARAGE (right) services

The diagram of the TOW-TRUCK service is displayed in Fig. 3, on the left. The service will first expose the list of geographic locations $ZIP_1, \ldots, ZIP_k$ it can reach. Each zip code ZIP_i is modeled as an event. The contract $\varphi_T(loc)$ imposed by the CAR-EMERGENCY service ensures that the location loc is covered by the truck service. Formally, $\varphi_T(loc)$ checks if the zip code loc is contained in the interface of the tow-truck service (we omit the automaton for $\varphi_T(loc)$ here). Then, the TOW-TRUCK may perform some internal activities (irrelevant in our model), possibly invoking other internal services. The exposed interface is of the form $1 \xrightarrow{ZIP_1 \cdots ZIP_k} 1$, where 1 is the void type.

The GARAGE service (Fig. 3, right) exposes the kinds of faults $REP_1, \ldots,$ REP_n the garage can repair, e.g. tyres, engine, etc. The request contract $\varphi_G(\mathit{flt})$ ensures that the garage can repair the kind of fault flt experienced by the car. The GARAGE service may perform some internal bookkeeping activities to handle the request (not shown in the figure), possibly using internal services from its local repository. After the car repair has been completed, the garage ℓ_G signs a receipt, through the event $sgn(\ell_G)$. This signature can be used by the CAR-EMERGENCY service to implement its black-listing policy.

The GARAGE service exploits the policy φ_{GZ} (for Garage-Zip) to ensure that the tow-truck can reach the garage address. If the garage is located in the area identified by ZIP_G, the policy φ_{GZ} checks that the tow-truck has exposed the event ZIP_G among the locations it can reach. When both the contract $\varphi_T(\mathit{loc})$ and the policy φ_{GZ} are satisfied, we have the guarantee that the tow-truck can pick the car and deposit it at the garage.

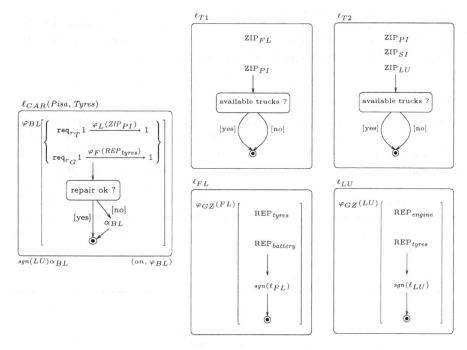

Fig. 4. The CAR-EMERGENCY client (ℓ_{CAR}), two tow-truck services (ℓ_{T1}, ℓ_{T2}), and two garages (ℓ_{FL}, ℓ_{LU})

In Fig. 4, we show a system composed by one car ℓ_{CAR}, two TOW-TRUCK services ℓ_{T1} and ℓ_{T2}, and two GARAGE services ℓ_{FL} and ℓ_{LU}. The car has experienced a flat tyre accident in Pisa (ZIP_{PI}), and it has black-listed the garage in Lucca, as recorded in the history $sgn(LU)\,\alpha_{BL}$. The tow-truck service ℓ_{T1} can reach Florence and Pisa, while ℓ_{T2} covers three zones: Pisa, Siena and Lucca.

The garage ℓ_{FL} is located in Florence, and it can repair tyres and batteries; the garage ℓ_{LU} is in Lucca, and repairs engines and tyres.

We now discuss all the possible orchestrations:

- the plan $r_T[\ell_{T1}] \mid r_G[\ell_{LU}]$ is not viable, because it violates the policy $\varphi_{GZ}(LU)$. Indeed, the tow-truck can serve Florence and Pisa, but the garage is in Lucca.
- similarly, the plan $r_T[\ell_{T2}] \mid r_G[\ell_{FL}]$ violates $\varphi_{GZ}(FL)$.
- the plan $r_T[\ell_{T2}] \mid r_G[\ell_{LU}]$ is not viable, because it violates the black-listing policy φ_{BL}. Indeed, it would give rise to a history $sgn(LU)\,\alpha_{BL}\cdots sgn(LU)$, not accepted by the automaton in Fig. 2.
- finally, the plan $r_T[\ell_{T1}] \mid r_G[\ell_{FL}]$ is viable. The tow-truck can reach both the car, located in Pisa, and the garage in Florence, which is not black-listed.

4 A Core Calculus for Services

In this section we review λ^{req}, in a version with stateless services, local histories, non parameterized events, higher-order requests, and independent threads. We refer to [10,14] for a more detailed presentation.

4.1 Services

A service is modeled as an expression in a λ-calculus enriched with primitives for events and service requests. Events are rendered as side-effects in the calculus. Roughly speaking, λ^{req} services e implement the specification of blocks B in the graphical notation. Note that λ^{req} augments the features of the design language with recursion (instead of loops), parameter passing and higher-order functions.

The abstract syntax of services follows. To enhance readability, our calculus comprises conditional expressions and named abstractions (the variable z in $e' = \lambda_z x.\,e$ stands for e' itself within e, so allowing for explicit recursion). We assume as given the language for guards in conditionals, and we omit its definition here.

Definition 2. Syntax of services

$e, e' ::=$	x	variable
	α	event
	if b then e else e	conditional
	$\lambda_z x.\,e$	abstraction
	$e\,e'$	application
	$\varphi[e]$	safety framing
	$\{e\}$	planning
	$\mathsf{req}_r\tau$	service request
	$\mathsf{wait}\,\ell$	wait reply
	N/A	unavailable

The values v of our calculus are the variables, the abstractions, and the requests. We write $*$ for a distinguished value, and $\lambda.\, e$ for $\lambda x.\, e$, for x not free in e. We also write $e; e'$ for $(\lambda.\, e')\, e$, and $\mathtt{let}\ x\ =\ e\ \mathtt{in}\ e'$ for $(\lambda x.\, e')\, e$. Without loss of generality, we assume that framings include at least one event, possibly dummy.

The stand-alone evaluation of a service is much alike the call-by-value semantics of the λ-calculus; additionally, it enforces all the policies within their framings. Since here services are considered in isolation, the semantics of requests is deferred to Section 4.2. The configurations are triples η, m, e. A transition $\eta, m, e \to \eta', m', e'$ means that, starting from a history η and a monitor flag m, the service e evolves to e', extends η to η', and sets the flag to m'. We assume as given a total function $\mathcal{B}$ that evaluates the guards in conditionals.

Definition 3. Service semantics (stand-alone)

$\eta, m, (\lambda_z x.\, e) v \to \eta, m, e\{v/x, \lambda_z x.\, e/z\}$

$\eta, m, \alpha \to \eta\alpha, m, *$

$\eta, m, \mathtt{if}\ b\ \mathtt{then}\ e_{tt}\ \mathtt{else}\ e_{f\!f} \to \eta, m, e_{\mathcal{B}(b)}$

$\eta, m, \mathcal{C}(e) \to \eta', m', \mathcal{C}(e')$ if $\eta, m, e \to \eta', m', e'$ and $m' = \mathit{off} \vee \eta' \models \varPhi(\mathcal{C})$

$\eta, m, \mathcal{C}(\varphi[v]) \to \eta, m, \mathcal{C}(v)$ if $m = \mathit{off} \vee \eta \models \varphi$

where $\mathcal{C}$ is an *evaluation context* with a hole $\bullet$, of the following form:

$\mathcal{C} \ ::= \ \bullet \mid \mathcal{C}\, e \mid v\, \mathcal{C} \mid \varphi[\mathcal{C}]$

and $\varPhi(\mathcal{C})$ is the set of *active policies* of $\mathcal{C}$, defined as follows:

$\varPhi(\mathcal{C}\, e) = \varPhi(v\, \mathcal{C}) = \varPhi(\mathcal{C})$ $\varPhi(\varphi[\mathcal{C}]) = \{\varphi\} \cup \varPhi(\mathcal{C})$

The first rule implements β-reduction (as usual $\{v/x\}$ denotes substitution). The evaluation of an event α consists in appending α to the current history, and producing the no-operation value $*$. A conditional $\mathtt{if}\ b\ \mathtt{then}\ e_{tt}\ \mathtt{else}\ e_{f\!f}$ evaluates to e_{tt} (resp. $e_{f\!f}$) if b evaluates to true (resp. false). The form of contexts implies call-by-value evaluation; as usual, functions are not reduced within their bodies. To evaluate a redex enclosed in a set of active policies $\varPhi(\mathcal{C})$, the history η' must obey each $\varphi \in \varPhi(\mathcal{C})$, when the execution monitor is on. A value can leave the scope of a framing φ if the current history satisfies φ. When the monitor is on and the history is not going to respect an active policy φ, evaluation gets stuck.

4.2   Networks

A service e is plugged into a network by publishing it at a site ℓ, together with its interface τ. Hereafter, $\ell\langle e : \tau\rangle$ denotes such a *published service*. Labels ℓ can be seen as Uniform Resource Identifiers, and they are only known by the orchestrator. We assume that each site publishes a single service, and that interfaces are certified, i.e. they are inferred by the type system presented later. As usual, we assume that services cannot invoke each other circularly. A *client* is a special published service $\ell\langle e : 1 \rangle$, where 1 is the unit type. A *network* is a set of clients and published services.

The *state* of a published service $\ell\langle e : \tau \rangle$ is denoted by:

$$\ell\langle e : \tau \rangle : \pi \triangleright \eta, m, e'$$

where π is the plan used by the current instantiation of the service, η is the history generated so far, m is the monitor flag, and e' models the code in execution. When unambiguous, we simply write ℓ for $\ell\langle e : \tau \rangle$ in states.

The syntax and the operational semantics of networks follows; the operator $\|$ is associative and commutative. Given a network $\{\ell_i\langle e_i : \tau_i \rangle\}_{i \in 1..k}$, a *network configuration* N has the form:

$$\{\ell_i : \pi_i \triangleright \eta_i, m_i, e'_i\}_{i \in 1..k} = \ell_1 : \pi_1 \triangleright \eta_1, m_1, e'_1 \| \cdots \| \ell_k : \pi_k \triangleright \eta_k, m_k, e'_k.$$

To trigger a computation of the network, we single out a set of clients, and fix the plans π_i for each of them. We name these clients *initiators*. We associate the empty plan to the other services. Then, for all $i \in 1..k$, the initial configuration has $\eta_i = \varepsilon$, $m_i = off$, and $e'_i = *$ if ℓ_i is a service, while $e'_i = e_i$ if ℓ_i is an initiator.

We now comment on the semantic rules of networks in Definition 4. A transition of a stand-alone service is localized at site ℓ (rule STA), regardless of a plan π. The rule NET specifies the asynchronous behavior of the network: a transition of a sub-network becomes a transition of the whole network. Rule PUB inserts a new service in the network, by publishing its interface τ, certified by the type and effect system. The rules DOWN/UP make an idle service unavailable/available. The rules REQ and RET model successful requests and replies. A request r, resolved by the current plan with the service ℓ', can be served if the service is available, i.e. it is in the state $\ell' : 0 \triangleright \varepsilon, *$. In this case, a new activation of the service starts: e is applied to the received argument v, under the plan π', received as well from the invoker. The special event σ signals that the service has started. The invoker waits until ℓ' has produced a value. When this happens, the service becomes idle again. Since we follow here the *stateless* approach, we clear the history of a service at each activation (indeed, statefullness could be easily obtained by maintaining the history η' at ℓ' in the last rule). Rule UNRES triggers the construction of a new plan, in case of an unresolved choice. The rules PLN and FAIL apply a planning/failing strategy to obtain a plan in case of a planned expression $\{e\}$ and of a chosen service which has become unavailable. Several safe strategies are possible, also exploiting the static semantics of networks. We will present some possible strategies in Sect. 6 and 7.

Finally, note that each service has a single instance in network configurations. We could easily model replication of services, by creating a new instance for each request. This change would have no practical impact on our results.

Definition 4. Network semantics

[STA]
$$\frac{\eta, m, e \to \eta', m', e'}{\ell : \pi \rhd \eta, m, e \to \ell : \pi \rhd \eta', m', e'}$$

[NET]
$$\frac{N_1 \to N_1'}{N_1 \parallel N_2 \to N_1' \parallel N_2}$$

[PUB] $N \to N \parallel \ell \langle e : \tau \rangle : 0 \rhd \varepsilon, \mathit{off}, *$ if ℓ fresh and $\vdash_\ell e : \tau$

[DOWN] $\ell \langle e : \tau \rangle : 0 \rhd \varepsilon, m, * \to \ell \langle e : \tau \rangle : 0 \rhd \varepsilon, m, \mathsf{N/A}$

[UP] $\ell \langle e : \tau \rangle : 0 \rhd \varepsilon, m, \mathsf{N/A} \to \ell \langle e : \tau \rangle : 0 \rhd \varepsilon, m, *$

[REQ] $\ell : (r[\ell'] \mid \pi) \rhd \eta, m, \mathcal{C}(\mathsf{req}_r \rho\, v) \parallel \ell' \langle e : \tau \rangle : 0 \rhd \varepsilon, m', * \to$
$\qquad \ell : (r[\ell'] \mid \pi) \rhd \eta, m, \mathcal{C}(\mathsf{wait}\, \ell') \parallel \ell' \langle e : \tau \rangle : (r[\ell'] \mid \pi) \rhd \sigma, m, e\, v$

[RET] $\ell : \pi \rhd \eta, m, \mathcal{C}(\mathsf{wait}\, \ell') \parallel \ell' : \pi' \rhd \eta', m', v \to \ell : \pi \rhd \eta, m', \mathcal{C}(v) \parallel \ell' : 0 \rhd \varepsilon, m', *$

[UNRES] $\ell : (r[?] \mid \pi) \rhd \eta, m, \mathcal{C}(\mathsf{req}_r \rho\, v) \to \ell : (r[?] \mid \pi) \rhd \eta, m, \mathcal{C}(\{\mathsf{req}_r \rho\, v\})$

[PLN] $\ell : \pi \rhd \eta, m, \mathcal{C}(\{e\}) \to \ell : \pi' \rhd \eta, m', \mathcal{C}(e)$ if $(\pi', m') = plan(\pi, m, e)$

[FAIL]
$$\ell : (r[\ell'] \mid \pi) \rhd \eta, m, \mathcal{C}(\mathsf{req}_r \rho\, v) \parallel \ell' \langle e : \tau \rangle : 0 \rhd \varepsilon, m'', \mathsf{N/A} \to$$
$$\ell : \pi' \rhd \eta, m', \mathcal{C}(\mathsf{req}_r \rho\, v) \parallel \ell' \langle e : \tau \rangle : 0 \rhd \varepsilon, m'', \mathsf{N/A}$$
$$\text{if } (\pi', m') = fail(r[\ell'] \mid \pi, m, \mathsf{req}_r \rho)$$

The auxiliary functions *plan* and *fail* will be discussed in Sect. 6.

5   Static Semantics

In this section we define a static analysis for our core calculus. The analysis takes the form of a type and effect system [25,33,37] where the effects, called *history expressions*, represent all the possible behavior of services, while the types extend those of the λ-calculus.

5.1   History Expressions

The syntax of types and history expressions is in Definition 5. History expressions are a sort of context-free grammars. They include the empty history ε, events α, $H \cdot H'$ for sequentialization of code, $H + H'$ for conditionals and branching, security blocks $\varphi[H]$, recursion $\mu h.H$ (where μ binds the occurrences of the variable h in H), localization $\ell : H$, and planned selection $\{\pi_1 \rhd H_1 \cdots \pi_k \rhd H_k\}$.

A history expression represents a set of histories η, possibly carrying security annotations in the form $\varphi[\eta]$. The *denotational semantics* of a history expression

Definition 5. History expressions

H, H'	$::=$		history expressions
	ε		empty
	h		variable
	α		access event
	$H \cdot H'$		sequence
	$H + H'$		choice
	$\varphi[H]$		security block
	$\mu h.H$		recursion
	$\ell : H$		localization
	$\{\pi_1 \triangleright H_1 \cdots \pi_k \triangleright H_k\}$		planned selection

is a set, written $(\ell_i : \mathcal{H}_i)_{i \in I}$. The intended meaning is that the behavior of the service at location ℓ_i is approximated by the set of histories $\mathcal{H}_i$ (I is a finite set of indexes). The *stateless* semantics $\langle\!\langle H \rangle\!\rangle^\pi$ of a closed history expression H depends on the given evaluation plan π, and is defined in two steps. In the first, we define the *stateful* semantics $[\![H]\!]_\theta^\pi$ (in an environment θ binding variables), i.e. a semantics in which services keep track of the histories generated by all the past invocations. A simple transformation then yields $\langle\!\langle H \rangle\!\rangle^\pi$, in which each invocation is instead independent of the previous ones, i.e. it always starts with the empty history. We now briefly comment some peculiar semantic rules.

The meaning of an event α is the pair $(? : \{!, \alpha!, \alpha\})$, where the dummy location ? will be bound to the actual location by the rule for $\ell : H$. The three histories $!, \alpha!, \alpha$ represent the three possible states of a computation: in $!$, the event α has still to be generated; in $\alpha!$, the event has been generated and the computation may still proceed; in α, the computation has terminated. In general, we write $\eta!$ to denote a non-maximal history, i.e. a history which operationally corresponds to a non-terminated computation. While non-maximal histories have to be considered for a smooth semantic treatment, for simplicity we shall always neglect them in our examples.

The semantics of a recursion $\mu h. H$ is the usual fixed point construction. For instance, the semantics of $\mu h. (\gamma + \alpha \cdot h \cdot \beta)$ comprises all the maximal histories of the form $\alpha^n \gamma \beta^n$, for $n \geq 0$ (i.e. $\gamma, \alpha\gamma\beta, \alpha\alpha\gamma\beta\beta, \ldots$).

The history expression $\ell : H$ localizes the behavior H to the site ℓ. For instance, $\ell : \alpha \cdot (\ell' : \alpha') \cdot \beta$ denotes both $\alpha\beta$ occurring at location ℓ, and α' occurring at location ℓ'.

A planned selection abstracts from the behavior of service requests. Given a plan π, a planned selection $\{\pi_1 \triangleright H_1 \cdots \pi_k \triangleright H_k\}$ chooses those H_i such that π includes π_i. For instance, the history expression $H = \{r[\ell_1] \triangleright H_1, r[\ell_2] \triangleright H_2\}$ is associated with a request $\mathbf{req}_r \tau$ that can be resolved into either ℓ_1 or ℓ_2. The histories denoted by H depend on the given plan π: if π chooses ℓ_1 (resp. ℓ_2) for r, then H denotes one of the histories represented by H_1 (resp. H_2). If π does not choose either ℓ_1 or ℓ_2, then H denotes no histories.

Definition 6. Semantics of history expressions

$$\langle\!\langle H \rangle\!\rangle^\pi = \{\, \ell : \{\, \langle\!\langle \eta \rangle\!\rangle \mid \eta \in \mathcal{H} \,\} \mid \ell : \mathcal{H} \in [\![H]\!]_\emptyset^\pi \,\}, \quad \langle\!\langle \eta \rangle\!\rangle = \begin{cases} \eta & \text{if } \sigma \notin \eta \\ \langle\!\langle \eta_0 \rangle\!\rangle \cup \langle\!\langle \eta_1 \rangle\!\rangle & \text{if } \eta = \eta_0 \, \sigma \, \eta_1 \end{cases}$$

$$[\![\varepsilon]\!]_\theta^\pi = (? : \{!, \varepsilon\}) \qquad [\![\alpha]\!]_\theta^\pi = (? : \{!, \alpha!, \alpha\}) \qquad [\![\ell : H]\!]_\theta^\pi = [\![H]\!]_\theta^\pi \{\ell/?\}$$

$$[\![\varphi[H]]\!]_\theta^\pi = \varphi[[\![H]\!]_\theta^\pi] \qquad [\![H \cdot H']\!]_\theta^\pi = [\![H]\!]_\theta^\pi \odot [\![H']\!]_\theta^\pi \qquad [\![H + H']\!]_\theta^\pi = [\![H]\!]_\theta^\pi \oplus [\![H']\!]_\theta^\pi$$

$$[\![h]\!]_\theta^\pi = \theta(h) \qquad [\![\mu h.H]\!]_\theta^\pi = \bigcup_{n>0} f^n(\{\ell_i : \{!\}\}_i) \ \text{ where } f(X) = [\![H]\!]_{\theta\{X/h\}}^\pi$$

$$[\![\{\pi_1 \triangleright H_1 \cdots \pi_k \triangleright H_k\}]\!]_\rho^\pi = \bigoplus_{i \in 1..k} [\![\{\pi_i \triangleright H_i\}]\!]_\rho^\pi \qquad [\![\{0 \triangleright H\}]\!]_\rho^\pi = [\![H]\!]_\rho^\pi$$

$$[\![\{\pi_0 \mid \pi_1 \triangleright H\}]\!]_\rho^\pi = [\![\{\pi_0 \triangleright H\}]\!]_\rho^\pi \oplus [\![\{\pi_1 \triangleright H\}]\!]_\rho^\pi$$

$$[\![\{r[\ell] \triangleright H\}]\!]_\rho^\pi = \begin{cases} [\![H]\!]_\rho^\pi & \text{if } \pi = r[\ell] \mid \pi' \\ (? : \bot) & \text{otherwise} \end{cases}$$

The auxiliary operators $\odot$ and $\oplus$ are introduced in Def. 7. The sequentialization $\odot$ of $(\ell_i : \mathcal{H}_i)_{i \in I}$ and $(\ell_j : \mathcal{H}_j')_{j \in J}$ comprises $\ell_i : \mathcal{H}_i \mathcal{H}_j'$ for all $i = j$, as well as $\ell_i : \mathcal{H}_i$ and $\ell_j : \mathcal{H}_j'$ for all $i \notin J$ and $j \notin I$. As an example, $(\ell_0 : \{\alpha_0\}, \ell_1 : \{\alpha_1, \beta_1\}) \odot (\ell_1 : \{\gamma_1\}, \ell_2 : \{\alpha_2\}) = (\ell_0 : \{\alpha_0\}, \ell_1 : \{\alpha_1\gamma_1, \beta_1\gamma_1\}, \ell_2 : \{\alpha_2\})$. The choice $\oplus$ is pretty the same, except that union replaces language concatenation. For example, $(\ell_0 : \{\alpha_0\}) \oplus (\ell_0 : \{\beta_0\}, \ell_1 : \{\beta_1\}) = (\ell_0 : \{\alpha_0, \beta_0\}, \ell_1 : \{\beta_1\})$.

Example 1. Consider the history expression:

$$H = \ell_0 : \alpha_0 \cdot \{r[\ell_1] \triangleright \ell_1 : \sigma \cdot \alpha_1, r[\ell_2] \triangleright \ell_2 : \sigma \cdot \alpha_2\} \cdot \beta_0$$

The maximal histores of the stateful semantics of H under plan $\pi = r[\ell_1]$ are:

$$[\![\alpha_0 \cdot \{r[\ell_1] \triangleright \ell_1 : \sigma \cdot \alpha_1, r[\ell_2] \triangleright \ell_2 : \sigma \cdot \alpha_2\} \cdot \beta_0]\!]^\pi \{\ell_0/?\} = (\ell_0 : \{\alpha_0\beta_0\}, \ell_1 : \{\sigma\alpha_1\})$$

In this case, the stateless semantics just removes the event σ, i.e.:

$$\langle\!\langle H \rangle\!\rangle^\pi = (\ell_0 : \{\alpha_0\beta_0\}, \ell_1 : \{\alpha_1\}) \qquad \square$$

Example 2. Consider the following history expression. It represents a service ℓ_0 that recursively generates α_0 and raises a request r (to be served by ℓ_1 only).

$$H = \ell_0 : (\mu h. \beta_0 + \alpha_0 \cdot \{r[\ell_1] \triangleright \ell_1 : \sigma \cdot \alpha_1\} \cdot h)$$

The maximal histories of the stateless semantics $\langle\!\langle H \rangle\!\rangle^\pi$ under plan $\pi = r[\ell_1]$ are:

$$(\ell_0 : \{\beta_0, \alpha_0\beta_0, \alpha_0\alpha_0\beta_0, \ldots\}, \ell_1 : \{\alpha_1\}) \qquad \square$$

Definition 7. Auxiliary operators $\odot$ and $\oplus$

$$x\,\mathcal{H} = \begin{cases} \{x\eta \mid \eta \in \mathcal{H}\} & \text{if } x \neq\,! \\ \{x\} & \text{if } x =\,! \end{cases} \quad (a_1 \cdots a_n)\mathcal{H} = a_1 \cdots (a_n\mathcal{H}) \quad \mathcal{H}\mathcal{H}' = \{\eta\mathcal{H}' \mid \eta \in \mathcal{H}\}$$

$$\{\ell_i : \mathcal{H}_i\}_I \odot (? : \bot) = (? : \bot) = (? : \bot) \odot \{\ell_i : \mathcal{H}_i\}_I$$

$$\{\ell_i : \mathcal{H}_i\}_I \oplus (? : \bot) = (? : \bot) = (? : \bot) \oplus \{\ell_i : \mathcal{H}_i\}_I$$

$$\{\ell_i : \mathcal{H}_i\}_I \odot \{\ell_j : \mathcal{H}'_j\}_J = \{\ell_i : \mathcal{H}_i\mathcal{H}'_i\}_{I \cap J} \cup \{\ell_i : \mathcal{H}_i\}_{I \setminus J} \cup \{\ell_j : \mathcal{H}'_j\}_{J \setminus I}$$

$$\{\ell_i : \mathcal{H}_i\}_I \oplus \{\ell_j : \mathcal{H}'_j\}_J = \{\ell_i : \mathcal{H}_i \cup \mathcal{H}'_i\}_{I \cap J} \cup \{\ell_i : \mathcal{H}_i \cup \{\varepsilon\}\}_{I \setminus J} \cup \{\ell_j : \mathcal{H}'_j \cup \{\varepsilon\}\}_{J \setminus I}$$

5.2 Validity

We now define when histories are valid, i.e. they arise from viable computations that do not violate any security constraint. Consider $\eta_0 = \alpha_w \alpha_r \varphi[\alpha_w]$, where φ requires that no write α_w occurs after a read α_r. Then, η_0 is *not* valid according to our intended meaning, because the rightmost α_w occurs within a framing enforcing φ, and $\alpha_w\alpha_r\alpha_w$ does not obey φ. A valid history η must obey all the policies within their scopes, determined by the framing events in η.

We formally define validity through the notion of *safe set*. Intuitively, a safe set contains all the prefixes of a history that should be checked against a policy. Consider again $\eta_0 = \alpha_w \alpha_r \varphi[\alpha_w]$. The prefix α_w is not to be checked, since no policy is active after α_w is performed. Instead, upon entering φ we need to check the past, i.e. the prefix $\alpha_w\alpha_r$, so we include it in the safe set. Of course, the next α_w is performed when the policy is still active, so we include $\alpha_w\alpha_r\alpha_w$ in the safe set as well. Concluding, the safe set of η_0 above is $\varphi[\{\alpha_w\alpha_r, \alpha_w\alpha_r\alpha_w\}]$. For each safe set $\varphi[\mathcal{H}]$, validity requires that *all* the histories in $\mathcal{H}$ obey φ.

Some notation is now needed. Let $\eta^\flat$ be the history obtained from η by erasing all the markers of security blocks $\varphi[\ldots]$, and let η^∂ be the set of all the prefixes of η, including the empty history ε. For example, if $\eta_0 = \alpha_w\alpha_r\varphi[\alpha_w]$, then $(\eta_0^\flat)^\partial = \{\varepsilon, \alpha_w, \alpha_w\alpha_r, \alpha_w\alpha_r\alpha_w\}$. Then, the safe set $S(\eta)$ and validity of histories and of history expressions are defined as in Def. 8.

Note that validity of a history expression is parametric with the given evaluation plan π, and it is defined location-wise on its semantics. If the plan contains unresolved choices for requests mentioned in H, then H is not π-valid.

Example 3. The safe sets of the history expression $H = \varphi[\alpha_0 \cdot \{r[\ell_1] \triangleright \alpha_1, r[\ell_2] \triangleright \varphi'[\alpha_2]\}] \cdot \alpha_3$, with respect to plans $r[\ell_1]$ and $r[\ell_2]$, are:

$$S(\langle\!\langle H \rangle\!\rangle^{r[\ell_1]}) = \{\ \varphi[\{\varepsilon, \alpha_0, \alpha_0\alpha_1\}]\ \}$$

$$S(\langle\!\langle H \rangle\!\rangle^{r[\ell_2]}) = \{\ \varphi[\{\varepsilon, \alpha_0, \alpha_0\alpha_2\}], \varphi'[\{\alpha_0, \alpha_0\alpha_2\}]\ \}$$

Definition 8. Safe sets and validity

The *safe sets* $S(\eta)$ of a history η are defined as:

$$S(\varepsilon) = \emptyset \qquad S(\eta \, \alpha) = S(\eta) \qquad S(\eta_0 \, \varphi[\eta_1]) = S(\eta_0 \, \eta_1) \cup \varphi[\eta_0^\flat \, (\eta_1^\flat)^\partial]$$

A history η is *valid* ($\models \eta$ in symbols) when:

$$\varphi[\mathcal{H}] \in S(\eta) \implies \forall \eta' \in \mathcal{H} \; : \; \eta' \models \varphi$$

A history expression H is π-*valid* when:

$$\forall \ell \; : \; \forall \eta \in \langle\!\langle H \rangle\!\rangle^\pi @ \ell \; : \; \models \eta \qquad \text{where } @ \text{ is defined as } (\ell_i : \mathcal{H}_i)_{i \in I} @ \ell_j \;=\; \mathcal{H}_j$$

Let φ require "never α_3", and let φ' require "never α_2". Then, H is $r[\ell_1]$-valid, because the histories ε, α_0, and $\alpha_0 \alpha_1$ obey φ. Instead, H is not $r[\ell_2]$-valid, because the history $\alpha_0 \alpha_2$ in the safe set $\varphi'[\{\alpha_0, \alpha_0 \alpha_2\}]$ does not obey φ'. □

5.3 A Type and Effect System for Services

We now introduce a type and effect system for our calculus, building upon [6,10]. Types and type environments, ranged over by τ and Γ, are mostly standard and are defined in the following table. The history expression H in the functional type $\tau \xrightarrow{H} \tau'$ describes the latent effect associated with an abstraction, i.e. one of the histories represented by H is generated when a value is applied to an abstraction with that type.

For notational convenience, we assume that the request type ρ in $\mathtt{req}_r \rho$ is a special type. E.g. we use $1 \xrightarrow{\varphi[\varepsilon]} (1 \xrightarrow{\varphi'[\varepsilon]} 1)$ for the request type of a service obeying φ and returning a function subject to the policy φ'. Additionally, we put some restrictions on request types. First, only functional types are allowed: this

Definition 9. Types and Type Environments

$\tau, \tau' ::= 1 \mid \tau \xrightarrow{H} \tau'$	types
$\Gamma ::= \emptyset \mid \Gamma; x : \tau \quad (x \notin dom(\Gamma))$	type environments
$\Gamma, H \vdash e : \tau$	type judgements
$\Gamma, H \vdash_\ell e : \tau$	localized type judgements

models services being considered as remote procedures (instead, initiators have type 1, so they cannot be invoked). Second, no constraints should be imposed over ρ_0 in a request type $\rho_0 \xrightarrow{\varphi} \rho_1$, i.e. in ρ_0 there are no annotations. This is because the constraints on the selected service should not affect its argument.

Types, type environments and typing judgements are defined in Def. 9. A typing judgment $\Gamma, H \vdash e : \tau$ means that the service e evaluates to a value of type τ, and produces a history denoted by the effect H. The localized typing judgment $\Gamma, H \vdash_\ell e : \tau$ is defined as the least relation closed under the typing rules in Def. 10, and we write $\Gamma, (\ell : H) \vdash e : \tau$ when the service e at ℓ is typed by $\Gamma, H \vdash_\ell e : \tau$. We only comment the most peculiar rules. The rule [T-LOC] allows to drop the localization from a typing judgement, by suitably tagging the history expression. The effects in the rule [T-APP] are concatenated according to the evaluation order of the call-by-value semantics (function, argument, latent effect). In rule [T-ABS], the actual effect of an abstraction is the empty history expression, while the latent effect is equal to the actual effect of the function body. Note that [T-ABS] constraints the premise to equate the actual and latent effects, up to associativity, commutativity, idempotency and zero of $+$, associativity and zero of $\cdot$, α-conversion, and elimination of vacuous μ-binders. Our type system does not assign any type to $\mathtt{wait}$ expressions: indeed, waits are only needed in configurations, and not in service code.

We stipulated that the services provided by the network have certified types. Consequently, the typing relation is parametrized by the set W of services $\ell\langle e : \tau \rangle$ such that $\emptyset, \varepsilon \vdash_\ell e : \tau$. We assume W to be fixed, and we write $\vdash_\ell$ instead of $\vdash_{\ell,W}$. To enforce non-circular service composition, we require W to be partially ordered by $\prec$, where $\ell \prec \ell'$ if ℓ can invoke ℓ'; initiators are obviously the least elements of $\prec$, and they are not related to each other. Note that the up-wards cone of $\prec$ of an initiator represents the (partial) knowledge it has of the network.

Example 4. Consider the following λ^{req} expression:

$$e = \text{if } b \text{ then } \lambda_z x. \alpha \text{ else } \lambda_z x. \alpha'$$

Let $\tau = 1$, and $\Gamma = \{z : \tau \xrightarrow{\alpha + \alpha'} \tau; x : \tau\}$. Then, the following typing derivation is possible:

$$\cfrac{\cfrac{\cfrac{\Gamma, \alpha \vdash \alpha : \tau}{\Gamma, \alpha + \alpha' \vdash \alpha : \tau}}{\emptyset, \varepsilon \vdash \lambda_z x. \alpha : \tau \xrightarrow{\alpha + \alpha'} \tau} \qquad \cfrac{\cfrac{\Gamma, \alpha' \vdash \alpha' : \tau}{\Gamma, \alpha' + \alpha \vdash \alpha' : \tau}}{\emptyset, \varepsilon \vdash \lambda_z x. \alpha' : \tau \xrightarrow{\alpha' + \alpha} \tau}}{\emptyset, \varepsilon \vdash \text{if } b \text{ then } \lambda_z x. \alpha \text{ else } \lambda_z x. \alpha' : \tau \xrightarrow{\alpha + \alpha'} \tau}$$

Note that we can equate the history expressions $\alpha + \alpha'$ and $\alpha' + \alpha$, because $+$ is commutative. The typing derivation above shows the use of the weakening rule to unify the latent effects on arrow types. Let now:

$$e' = \lambda_w x. \text{if } b' \text{ then } * \text{ else } w(e\, x)$$

Definition 10. Typing services

$$\Gamma, \varepsilon \vdash_\ell x : \Gamma(x) \quad \text{[T-Var]} \qquad \Gamma, \alpha \vdash_\ell \alpha : 1 \quad \text{[T-Ev]} \qquad \frac{\Gamma, H \vdash_\ell e : \tau \quad \Gamma, H \vdash_\ell e' : \tau}{\Gamma, H \vdash_\ell \text{if } b \text{ then } e \text{ else } e' : \tau} \quad \text{[T-If]}$$

$$\frac{\Gamma; x : \tau; z : \tau \xrightarrow{H} \tau', H \vdash_\ell e : \tau'}{\Gamma, \varepsilon \vdash_\ell \lambda_z x.\, e : \tau \xrightarrow{H} \tau'} \quad \text{[T-Abs]} \qquad \frac{\Gamma, H \vdash_\ell e : \tau \xrightarrow{H''} \tau' \quad \Gamma, H' \vdash_\ell e' : \tau}{\Gamma, H \cdot H' \cdot H'' \vdash_\ell e\, e' : \tau'} \quad \text{[T-App]}$$

$$\frac{\Gamma, H \vdash_\ell e : \tau}{\Gamma, \varphi[H] \vdash_\ell \varphi[e] : \tau} \quad \text{[T-Sec]} \qquad \frac{\Gamma, H \vdash_\ell e : \tau}{\Gamma, H \vdash_\ell \{e\} : \tau} \quad \text{[T-Pln]} \qquad \Gamma, \varepsilon \vdash_\ell * : 1 \quad \text{[T-Unit]}$$

$$\frac{\tau = \biguplus \{\, \rho \boxplus_{r[\ell']} \tau' \mid \emptyset, \varepsilon \vdash_{\ell'} e : \tau' \quad \ell \prec \ell' \langle e : \tau' \rangle \quad \rho \approx \tau' \,\}}{\Gamma, \varepsilon \vdash_\ell \mathbf{req}_r \rho : \tau} \quad \text{[T-Req]}$$

$$\frac{\Gamma, H \vdash_\ell e : \tau}{\Gamma, H + H' \vdash_\ell e : \tau} \quad \text{[T-Wkn]} \qquad \frac{\Gamma, H \vdash_\ell e : \tau}{\Gamma, \ell : H \vdash e : \tau} \quad \text{if } e \text{ is published at } \ell \quad \text{[T-Loc]}$$

Let $\Gamma = \{w : \tau \xrightarrow{H} \tau, x : \tau\}$, where H is left undefined. Then, recalling that $\varepsilon \cdot H' = H' = H' \cdot \varepsilon$ for any history expression H', we have:

$$\Gamma, \varepsilon \vdash * : \tau \quad \frac{\Gamma, \varepsilon \vdash w : \tau \xrightarrow{H} \tau \quad \dfrac{\Gamma, \varepsilon \vdash e : \tau \xrightarrow{\alpha + \alpha'} \tau \quad \Gamma, \varepsilon \vdash x : \tau}{\Gamma, \alpha + \alpha' \vdash e\, x : \tau}}{\dfrac{\Gamma, (\alpha + \alpha') \cdot H \vdash w(e\, x) : \tau}{\dfrac{\Gamma, \varphi[(\alpha + \alpha') \cdot H] \vdash \varphi[w(e\, x)] : \tau}{\Gamma, \varepsilon + \varphi[(\alpha + \alpha') \cdot H] \vdash \text{if } b' \text{ then } * \text{ else } \varphi[w(e\, x)] : \tau}}}$$

To apply the typing rule for abstractions, the constraint $H = \varepsilon + \varphi[(\alpha + \alpha') \cdot H]$ must be solved. Let $H = \mu h.\, \varepsilon + \varphi[(\alpha + \alpha') \cdot h]$. It is easy to prove that:

$$\llbracket H \rrbracket = \llbracket \varepsilon + \varphi[(\alpha + \alpha') \cdot h] \rrbracket_{\{\llbracket H \rrbracket / h\}} = \{\varepsilon\} \cup \varphi[(\alpha + \alpha') \cdot \llbracket H \rrbracket]$$

We have then found a solution to the constraint above, so we can conclude that:

$$\emptyset, \varepsilon \vdash e' : \tau \xrightarrow{\mu h.\, \varepsilon + \varphi[(\alpha + \alpha') \cdot h]} \tau \qquad \square$$

A service invocation $\mathbf{req}_r \rho$ has an empty actual effect, and a functional type τ, whose latent effect is a planned selection that picks from the network those services known by ℓ and matching the request type ρ.

To give a type to requests, the auxiliary operators $\approx$, $\boxplus$ and $\uplus$ are introduced with the help of a running example. We write $\rho \approx \tau$, and say ρ, τ *compatible*, whenever, omitting the annotations on the arrows, ρ and τ are equal.

Let $\rho = (\tau \rightarrow \tau) \xrightarrow{\varphi} (\tau \rightarrow \tau)$, with $\tau = 1$, be the request type in $\mathtt{req}_r \rho$, and consider two services $\ell_i \langle e_i : \tau_i \rangle$ with $\tau_i = (\tau \xrightarrow{h_i} \tau) \xrightarrow{\alpha_i \cdot h_i} (\tau \xrightarrow{\beta_i} \tau)$, for $i \in 1..2$. We have that $\tau_1 \approx \rho \approx \tau_2$, i.e. both services are compatible with the request r.

The operator $\boxplus_{r[\ell]}$ combines a request type ρ and a type τ, if compatible. The request type ρ is composed with the service types τ_1 and τ_2 as follows:

$$\hat{\tau}_1 = (\tau \xrightarrow{h_1} \tau) \xrightarrow{\{r[\ell_1] \triangleright \ell_1 : \varphi[\sigma \cdot \alpha_1 \cdot h_1]\}} (\tau \xrightarrow{\{r[\ell_1] \triangleright \beta_1\}} \tau)$$

$$\hat{\tau}_2 = (\tau \xrightarrow{h_2} \tau) \xrightarrow{\{r[\ell_2] \triangleright \ell_2 : \varphi[\sigma \cdot \alpha_2 \cdot h_2]\}} (\tau \xrightarrow{\{r[\ell_2] \triangleright \beta_2\}} \tau)$$

where $\hat{\tau}_1 = \rho \boxplus_{r[\ell_1]} \tau_1$ and $\hat{\tau}_2 = \rho \boxplus_{r[\ell_2]} \tau_2$.

The top-level arrow carries a planned selection $\{r[\ell] \triangleright \ell : \varphi[\sigma \cdot H]\}$, meaning that, if the service at ℓ is chosen for r, then it generates (at location ℓ, and prefixed by σ) the behavior H, subject to the policy φ. Note that the service at ℓ_1 returns a function whose (latent) effect $\{r[\ell_1] \triangleright \beta_1\}$ means that β_1 occurs in the location where the function will be actually applied.

Finally, the operator $\uplus$ unifies the types obtained by combining the request type with the service types. To conclude our running example, we now unify the combination of the request type ρ with the service types, obtaining:

$$\tau' = (\tau \xrightarrow{h} \tau) \xrightarrow{\{r[\ell_1] \triangleright \ell_1 : \varphi[\sigma \cdot \alpha_1 \cdot h], \ r[\ell_2] \triangleright \ell_2 : \varphi[\sigma \cdot \alpha_2 \cdot h]\}} (\tau \xrightarrow{\{r[\ell_1] \triangleright \beta_1, \ r[\ell_2] \triangleright \beta_2\}} \tau)$$

5.4 Type Safety

We now discuss the main properties of our type and effect system. We shall restrict our attention to the case where (i) services never become unavailable, and (ii) planning is only performed at start-up of execution, i.e. there is no dynamic replanning.

A first result is a theorem stating that our type and effect system correctly over-approximates the actual run-time histories. The formal statement is in [11]. Here we illustrate type correctness through an example.

Example 5. Consider an initiator $e_0 = \alpha_0; (\mathtt{req}_r \rho)*$ at site ℓ_0, with $\rho = 1 \rightarrow 1$, and a single service $e_1 = \lambda. \alpha_1; \varphi[\mathtt{if}\ b\ \mathtt{then}\ \alpha_2\ \mathtt{else}\ \alpha_3]$ at site ℓ_1, with φ requiring "never α_3". Assume that the guard b always evaluates to true, and that the execution monitor is off (we therefore omit it from configurations). Then, under the plan $\pi_0 = r[\ell_1]$, we have the following computation:

$$\ell_0 : \pi_0 \rhd \varepsilon, e_0 \parallel \ell_1 : 0 \rhd \varepsilon, *$$
$$\to \ell_0 : \pi_0 \rhd \alpha_0, \mathtt{req}_r \rho * \parallel \ell_1 : 0 \rhd \varepsilon, *$$
$$\to \ell_0 : \pi_0 \rhd \alpha_0, \mathtt{wait}\, \ell_1 \parallel \ell_1 : 0 \rhd \sigma, e_1 *$$
$$\to \ell_0 : \pi_0 \rhd \alpha_0, \mathtt{wait}\, \ell_1 \parallel \ell_1 : 0 \rhd \sigma\alpha_1, \varphi[\mathtt{if}\cdots]$$
$$\to \ell_0 : \pi_0 \rhd \alpha_0, \mathtt{wait}\, \ell_1 \parallel \ell_1 : 0 \rhd \sigma\alpha_1, \varphi[\alpha_2]$$
$$\to \ell_0 : \pi_0 \rhd \alpha_0, \mathtt{wait}\, \ell_1 \parallel \ell_1 : 0 \rhd \sigma\alpha_1\alpha_2, \varphi[*]$$
$$\to \ell_0 : \pi_0 \rhd \alpha_0, \mathtt{wait}\, \ell_1 \parallel \ell_1 : 0 \rhd \sigma\alpha_1\alpha_2, *$$
$$\to \ell_0 : \pi_0 \rhd \alpha_0, * \parallel \ell_1 : 0 \rhd \varepsilon, *$$

The history expression H_0 extracted from e_0 is:

$$\ell_0 : \alpha_0 \cdot \{r[\ell_1] \rhd \ell_1 : \sigma \cdot \alpha_1 \cdot \varphi[\alpha_2 + \alpha_3]\}$$

Then, the run-time histories generated at ℓ_1 are contained in $(\sigma \langle\!\langle H_0 \rangle\!\rangle^{\pi_0} @\ell_1)^{b\partial} \supseteq \{\varepsilon, \sigma, \sigma\alpha_1, \sigma\alpha_1\alpha_2, \sigma\alpha_1\alpha_3\}$, as predicted by the type correctness theorem.   □

We now state the type safety property. We say that a plan π is *viable* for e at ℓ when the evolution of e within a network, under plan π, does not go wrong at ℓ, i.e. it never reaches a configuration whose state at ℓ is stuck. A state $\ell : \pi \rhd \eta, e$ is *not stuck* if either $e = v$, or $e = (\mathtt{req}_r\rho)v$, or $e = \mathtt{wait}\, \ell'$, or $\ell : \pi \rhd \eta, e \to \ell : \pi \rhd \eta', e'$.

Theorem 1 (Type Safety). *Let $\{\ell_i \langle e_i : \tau_i \rangle\}_{i \in I}$ be a network of services, typed as $\emptyset, H_i \vdash e_i : \tau_i$. If H_i is π_i-valid, then π_i is viable for e_i at ℓ_i.*

6 Planning

Once extracted a history expression H from a service e through the type and effect system, we have to analyse H to find viable plans for executing e. Each service selection may potentially affect the *whole* execution of a program, as shown in Example 6 below. So, we cannot simply devise a viable plan by selecting services that satisfy the constraints imposed by the requests, only.

The first step of our planning technique, called *linearization*, consists in lifting all the service choices $r[\ell]$ to the top-level of H. This semantic-preserving transformation results in effects of the form $\{\pi_1 \rhd H_1 \cdots \pi_n \rhd H_n\}$, where each H_i is free of further planned selection. Its intuitive meaning is that, under the plan π_i, the effect of the overall service composition e is H_i.

Example 6. Let $e = (\lambda x. (\mathtt{req}_{r_2} \rho_2)x)((\mathtt{req}_{r_1}\rho_1)*)$ be an initiator, located at ℓ_0, and let $\rho_1 = \tau \to (\tau \to \tau)$ and $\rho_2 = (\tau \to \tau) \xrightarrow{\varphi} \tau$, where $\tau = 1$ and the contract φ requires "never γ after β". Intuitively, the service selected upon the request r_1

returns a function, which is then passed as an argument to the service selected upon r_2. Assume the network comprises exactly the following four services:

$$\ell_1\langle e_{\ell_1} : \tau \xrightarrow{\alpha} (\tau \xrightarrow{\beta} \tau)\rangle \qquad \ell_2\langle e_{\ell_2} : (\tau \xrightarrow{h} \tau) \xrightarrow{h\cdot\gamma} \tau\rangle$$

$$\ell_1'\langle e_{\ell_1'} : \tau \xrightarrow{\alpha'} (\tau \xrightarrow{\beta'} \tau)\rangle \qquad \ell_2'\langle e_{\ell_2'} : (\tau \xrightarrow{h} \tau) \xrightarrow{\varphi'[h]} \tau\rangle$$

where φ' requires "never β'". Since the request type ρ_1 matches the types of e_{ℓ_1} and $e_{\ell_1'}$, both these services can be selected for the request r_1. Similarly, both e_{ℓ_2} and $e_{\ell_2'}$ can be chosen for r_2. Therefore, we have to consider four possible plans when evaluating the history expression H of e:

$$\begin{aligned}
H = &\{r_1[\ell_1] \rhd \ell_1 : \sigma \cdot \alpha, r_1[\ell_1'] \rhd \ell_1' : \sigma \cdot \alpha'\} \cdot \\
&\{r_2[\ell_2] \rhd \ell_2 : \varphi[\sigma \cdot \{\underline{r_1[\ell_1]} \rhd \beta, \underline{r_1[\ell_1']} \rhd \beta'\} \cdot \gamma], \\
&\quad r_2[\ell_2'] \rhd \ell_2' : \varphi[\sigma \cdot \varphi'[\{\underline{r_1[\ell_1]} \rhd \beta, \underline{r_1[\ell_1']} \rhd \beta'\}]]\}
\end{aligned}$$

Consider first H under the plan $\pi_1 = r_1[\ell_1] \mid r_2[\ell_2]$, yielding $\langle\!\langle H \rangle\!\rangle^{\pi_1} = (\ell_0 : \emptyset, \ell_1 : \{\alpha\}, \ell_2 : \{\varphi[\beta\gamma]\})$. Then, H is not π_1-valid, because the policy φ is violated at ℓ_2. Consider now $\pi_2 = r_1[\ell_1'] \mid r_2[\ell_2']$, yielding $\langle\!\langle H \rangle\!\rangle^{\pi_2} = (\ell_0 : \emptyset, \ell_1' : \{\alpha'\}, \ell_2 : \{\varphi[\varphi'[\beta']]\})$. Then, H is not π_2-valid, because the policy φ' is violated. Instead, the remaining two plans, $r_1[\ell_1] \mid r_2[\ell_2']$ and $r_1[\ell_1'] \mid r_2[\ell_2]$ are viable for e.   □

As shown above, the tree-shaped structure of planned selections makes it difficult to determine the plans π under which a history expression is valid. Things become easier if we "linearize" such a tree structure into a set of history expressions, forming an equivalent planned selection $\{\pi_1 \rhd H_1 \cdots \pi_k \rhd H_k\}$, where no H_i has further selections. E.g., the linearization of H in Example 6 is:

$$\begin{aligned}
\{&r_1[\ell_1] \mid r_2[\ell_2] \rhd \ell_1 : \sigma \cdot \alpha \cdot (\ell_2 : \varphi[\sigma \cdot \beta \cdot \gamma]), \\
&r_1[\ell_1] \mid r_2[\ell_2'] \rhd \ell_1 : \sigma \cdot \alpha \cdot (\ell_2' : \varphi[\sigma \cdot \varphi'[\beta]]), \\
&r_1[\ell_1'] \mid r_2[\ell_2] \rhd \ell_1' : \sigma \cdot \alpha' \cdot (\ell_2 : \varphi[\sigma \cdot \beta' \cdot \gamma]), \\
&r_1[\ell_1'] \mid r_2[\ell_2'] \rhd \ell_1' : \sigma \cdot \alpha' \cdot (\ell_2' : \varphi[\sigma \cdot \varphi'[\beta']])\}
\end{aligned}$$

Finally, we verify the validity of history expressions that, like the H_i produced by linearization, have no planned selections. Our technique is based on model checking Basic Process Algebras (BPAs) with Finite State Automata (FSA). This task is accomplished by our LocUsT model checker [44].

Summing up, we extract from an expression e a history expression H, we linearize it into $\{\pi_1 \rhd H_1 \cdots \pi_k \rhd H_k\}$, and if some H_i is valid, then we can deduce that H is π_i-valid. Type-safety ensures that the plan π_i safely drives the execution of e, without resorting to any run-time monitor. To verify the validity of an history expressions that, like the H_i above, has no planned selections, we regularize H_i to remove redundant framings, we transform H_i into a BPA $BPA(H_i)$, and we model-check $BPA(H_i)$ against the policies on demand.

7 Recovery

We now focus on the case where services may become unavailable, and planning may be performed at run-time. In [14], we devised four main classes of strategies:

Greyfriars Bobby. Follow loyally a former plan. If a service becomes unavailable, just wait until it comes back again. This strategy is always safe, although it might obviously block the execution for an arbitrarily long time — possibly forever.

Patch. Try to reuse as much as possible the current plan. Replace the unavailable services with available ones, possibly newly discovered. The new services must be verified for compatibility with the rest of the plan.

Sandbox. Try to proceed with the execution monitor turned on. The new plan only respects a weak form of compatibility on types ignoring the effect H, but it does not guarantee that contracts and security policies are always respected. Turning on the execution monitor ensures that there will not be security violations, but execution might get stuck later on, because of attempted insecure actions.

Replan. Try to reconstruct the whole plan, possibly exploiting newly discovered services. If a viable plan is found, then you may proceed running with the execution monitor turned off. A complete plan guarantees that contracts and security policies will be always respected, provided than none of the services mentioned in the plan disappear.

To keep our presentation short, we only consider below the Greyfriars Bobby strategy. We complete in Def. 11 the definition of the PLN and FAIL rules of the operational semantics of networks, by implementing the functions *plan* and *fail*.

Suppose one wants to replan an expression e, when the current plan is π and the current state of the monitor flag is m. Our strategy constructs a new plan π' which is coherent with π on the choices already taken in the past. We first update the global history expression (i.e. that used to compute the starting plan) with all the information about the newly discovered services, possibly discarding the services now unavailable. The result of this step is then model checked for viable plans. If a viable plan is found, then it is substituted for the old plan, and the execution proceeds with the execution monitor turned off. If no viable plan is found, the service repository is searched for services that fulfill the "syntactical" requirements of requests, i.e. for each $\mathtt{req}_r\rho$ to replan, the contract type ρ is compatible with the type of the chosen service. The execution then continues with the so-constructed plan π', but the monitor is now turned on, because there is no guarantee that the selected services will obey the imposed constraints. If there are no services in the repository that obey this weaker condition, we try to proceed with an *incomplete* plan $\bar{\pi}|\pi_?$ with unresolved choices (written $r[?]$), keeping the execution monitor on, and planning "on demand" future requests.

Example 7. Consider the following initiator service at location ℓ_0:

$$e_0 = \varphi[(\mathtt{let}\ f = \mathtt{req}_r 1 \to (1 \to 1)\ \mathtt{in}\ f\,*); \{\mathtt{let}\ g = \mathtt{req}_{r'} 1 \to (1 \to 1)\ \mathtt{in}\ g\,*\}]$$

Definition 11. Planning and recovering strategies

Let $\bar{\pi}$ be the sub-plan of π containing all the already resolved choices.
Let H be the history expression of the initiator of the computation.
Let L be the set of newly-discovered available services.
Let H_L be the update of H with the information about the services in L.
Let $\pi' = \bar{\pi} \mid \pi''$ be a plan coherent with π on the already resolved choices.

Then:

$$plan(\pi, m, e) = \begin{cases} (\pi', off) & \text{if } H_L \text{ is } \pi'\text{-valid} \\ (\pi', on) & \text{if } \forall \mathsf{req}_r \rho \in e \ : \ r[\ell'] \in \pi' \wedge \ell' : \tau \implies \rho \approx \tau \\ (\bar{\pi} \mid \pi_?, on) & \text{otherwise, where } \pi_? \text{ maps each } r \notin \bar{\pi} \text{ to } ? \end{cases}$$

$$fail(\pi, m, e) = (\pi, m) \qquad \text{(Greyfriars Bobby)}$$

The service obtains a function f through the first request r, applies it. Then it asks for a plan to get a second function g through r' and apply it. The policy φ requires that neither $\alpha\alpha$ nor $\beta\beta$ are performed at ℓ_0. Suppose the network repository consists just of the following two services, located at ℓ_1 and ℓ_2:

$$\ell_1\langle \lambda x.\lambda y.\, \alpha : 1 \rightarrow (1 \xrightarrow{\alpha} 1)\rangle \qquad \ell_2\langle \lambda x.\lambda y.\, \beta : 1 \rightarrow (1 \xrightarrow{\beta} 1)\rangle$$

The history expression of the initiator service is:

$$H = \ell_0 : \varphi[\{r[\ell_1] \rhd \alpha, r[\ell_2] \rhd \beta\} \cdot \{r'[\ell_1] \rhd \alpha, r'[\ell_2] \rhd \beta\}]$$

Assume that the execution starts with the viable plan $\pi = r[\ell_1] \mid r'[\ell_2]$, which would generate the history $\alpha\beta$ at ℓ_0, so obeying the policy φ.

$$\ell_0 : \pi \rhd \varepsilon, off, e_0 \parallel \ell_1 \rhd \varepsilon, \lambda x.\lambda y.\, \alpha \parallel \ell_2 \rhd \varepsilon, \lambda x.\lambda y.\, \beta$$
$$\rightarrow^* \ell_0 : \pi \rhd \alpha, off, \{\mathtt{let}\ g = \mathsf{req}_{r'} 1 \rightarrow (1 \rightarrow 1)\ \mathtt{in}\ g * \}$$
$$\parallel \ell_1 \rhd \varepsilon, \lambda x.\lambda y.\, \alpha \parallel \ell_2 \rhd \varepsilon, \lambda x.\lambda y.\, \beta$$

Just after the function f has been applied, the service at ℓ_2 becomes unavailable:

$$\rightarrow^* \ell_0 : \pi \rhd \alpha, off, \{\mathtt{let}\ g = \mathsf{req}_{r'} 1 \rightarrow (1 \rightarrow 1)\ \mathtt{in}\ g * \}$$
$$\parallel \ell_1 \rhd \varepsilon, \lambda x.\lambda y.\, \alpha \parallel \ell_2 \rhd \varepsilon, \mathsf{N/A}$$

Assume now that a new service is discovered at ℓ_3, with type $1 \rightarrow (1 \xrightarrow{\beta} 1)$:

$$\rightarrow^* \ell_0 : \pi \rhd \alpha, off, \{\mathtt{let}\ g = \mathsf{req}_{r'} 1 \rightarrow (1 \rightarrow 1)\ \mathtt{in}\ g * \}$$
$$\parallel \ell_1 \rhd \varepsilon, \lambda x.\lambda y.\, \alpha \parallel \ell_2 \rhd \varepsilon, \mathsf{N/A} \parallel \ell_3 \rhd \varepsilon, \lambda x.\lambda y.\, \beta$$

The planning strategy determines that the plan $\pi' = r[\ell_1] \mid r'[\ell_3]$ is viable, and so the execution can safely proceed with π' and with the monitor turned off.

Observe that the plan $\pi'' = r[\ell_3] \mid r'[\ell_1]$ is also viable, but it changes the choice already made for the request r. Using π'' instead of π' would lead to a violation of the policy φ, because of the history $\alpha\alpha$ generated at ℓ_0. $\qquad\square$

It is possible to extend the type safety result in the more general case that also the rules PLN, FAIL and UNRES can be applied. As before, as long as none of the selected services disappear and the initial plan is complete, we have the same static guarantees: starting from a viable plan will drive secure computations that never go wrong, so making the execution monitor unneeded. The same property also holds when the dynamic plan obtained through the rule PLN is a complete one, and the monitor is off.

Instead, when the new plan is not complete, we get a weaker property. The execution monitor guarantees that security will never be violated, but now there is no liveness guarantee: the execution may get stuck because of an attempted unsecure action, or because we are unable to find a suitable service for an unresolved request.

8   Conclusions

We have described a formal framework for designing service-oriented applications, featuring a graphical modelling language, a core calculus with a call-by-contract invocation mechanism, as well as a system verification machinery, deployed as a SENSORIA tool described in Chapter 4-3 (Tools and Verification). All the above items contribute to achieving static guarantees about planning, and graceful degradation when services disappear.

As usual, a prototype can help in the design phase, because one can perform early tests on the system, e.g. by providing as input selected data, one can observe whether the outputs are indeed the intended ones. The call-by-contract mechanism makes this standard testing practice even more effective, e.g. one can perform a request with a given policy φ and observe the resulting plans. The system must then consider *all* the services that satisfy φ, and the observed effect is similar to running a *class* of tests. For instance, a designer of an online bookshop can specify a policy such as "order a book without paying" and then inspect the generated plans: the presence of viable plans could point out an unwanted behavior, e.g. due to an unpredicted interaction between different special offers. As a matter of facts, standard testing techniques are yet not sophisticated enough to spot such kind of bugs. Thus, a designer may find the λ^{req} prototype useful to check the system, since unintended plans provide him with a clear description of the unwanted interactions between services.

References

1. Abadi, M., Fournet, C.: Access control based on execution history. In: Proc. 10th Annual Network and Distributed System Security Symposium (2003)
2. Banerjee, A., Naumann, D.A.: History-based access control and secure information flow. In: Workshop on Construction and Analysis of Safe, Secure and Interoperable Smart Cards, CASSIS (2004)

3. Bartoletti, M.: Usage automata. In: Degano, P., Viganò, L. (eds.) ARSPA-WITS 2009. LNCS, vol. 5511, pp. 52–69. Springer, Heidelberg (2009)
4. Bartoletti, M., Costa, G., Degano, P., Martinelli, F., Zunino, R.: Securing Java with local policies. Journal of Object Technology 8(4) (2009)
5. Bartoletti, M., Degano, P., Ferrari, G.L.: Checking risky events is enough for local policies. In: Coppo, M., Lodi, E., Pinna, G.M. (eds.) ICTCS 2005. LNCS, vol. 3701, pp. 97–112. Springer, Heidelberg (2005)
6. Bartoletti, M., Degano, P., Ferrari, G.L.: Enforcing secure service composition. In: Proc. 18th Computer Security Foundations Workshop (CSFW) (2005)
7. Bartoletti, M., Degano, P., Ferrari, G.L.: History-based access control with local policies. In: Sassone, V. (ed.) FOSSACS 2005. LNCS, vol. 3441, pp. 316–332. Springer, Heidelberg (2005)
8. Bartoletti, M., Degano, P., Ferrari, G.L.: Plans for service composition. In: Workshop on Issues in the Theory of Security (WITS) (2006)
9. Bartoletti, M., Degano, P., Ferrari, G.L.: Types and effects for secure service orchestration. In: Proc. 19th Computer Security Foundations Workshop (CSFW) (2006)
10. Bartoletti, M., Degano, P., Ferrari, G.L.: Planning and verifying service composition. Journal of Computer Security 17(5) (2009)
11. Bartoletti, M., Degano, P., Ferrari, G.L., Zunino, R.: Secure service orchestration. In: Aldini, A., Gorrieri, R. (eds.) FOSAD 2007. LNCS, vol. 4677, pp. 24–74. Springer, Heidelberg (2007)
12. Bartoletti, M., Degano, P., Ferrari, G.-L., Zunino, R.: Types and effects for resource usage analysis. In: Seidl, H. (ed.) FOSSACS 2007. LNCS, vol. 4423, pp. 32–47. Springer, Heidelberg (2007)
13. Bartoletti, M., Degano, P., Ferrari, G.L., Zunino, R.: Model checking usage policies. In: Kaklamanis, C., Nielson, F. (eds.) TGC 2008. LNCS, vol. 5474, pp. 19–35. Springer, Heidelberg (2009)
14. Bartoletti, M., Degano, P., Ferrari, G.L., Zunino, R.: Semantics-based design for secure web services. IEEE Trans. Software Eng. 34(1), 33–49 (2008)
15. Bartoletti, M., Degano, P., Ferrari, G.L., Zunino, R.: Local policies for resource usage analysis. ACM Trans. Program. Lang. Syst. 31(6) (2009)
16. Bonelli, E., Compagnoni, A., Gunter, E.: Typechecking safe process synchronization. In: Proc. Foundations of Global Ubiquitous Computing. ENTCS, vol. 138(1) (2005)
17. Boreale, M., et al.: SCC: A service centered calculus. In: Bravetti, M., Núñez, M., Tennenholtz, M. (eds.) WS-FM 2006. LNCS, vol. 4184, pp. 38–57. Springer, Heidelberg (2006)
18. Brogi, A., Canal, C., Pimentel, E.: Behavioural types and component adaptation. In: Rattray, C., Maharaj, S., Shankland, C. (eds.) AMAST 2004. LNCS, vol. 3116, pp. 42–56. Springer, Heidelberg (2004)
19. Buscemi, M.G., Montanari, U.: CC-pi: A constraint-based language for specifying service level agreements. In: De Nicola, R. (ed.) ESOP 2007. LNCS, vol. 4421, pp. 18–32. Springer, Heidelberg (2007)
20. Carbone, M., Honda, K., Yoshida, N.: Structured global programming for communicating behaviour. In: De Nicola, R. (ed.) ESOP 2007. LNCS, vol. 4421, pp. 2–17. Springer, Heidelberg (2007)
21. Costa, G., Degano, P., Martinelli, F.: Secure service composition with symbolic effects. In: Proc. SEEFM. IEEE Computer Society, Los Alamitos (2009)
22. Edjlali, G., Acharya, A., Chaudhary, V.: History-based access control for mobile code. In: Ryan, M. (ed.) Secure Internet Programming. LNCS, vol. 1603. Springer, Heidelberg (1999)

23. Ferrari, G.L., Guanciale, R., Strollo, D.: JSCL: A middleware for service coordination. In: Najm, E., Pradat-Peyre, J.-F., Donzeau-Gouge, V.V. (eds.) FORTE 2006. LNCS, vol. 4229, pp. 46–60. Springer, Heidelberg (2006)
24. Fong, P.W.: Access control by tracking shallow execution history. In: IEEE Symposium on Security and Privacy (2004)
25. Gifford, D.K., Lucassen, J.M.: Integrating functional and imperative programming. In: ACM Conference on LISP and Functional Programming (1986)
26. Guidi, C., Lucchi, R., Gorrieri, R., Busi, N., Zavattaro, G.: SOCK: A calculus for service oriented computing. In: Dan, A., Lamersdorf, W. (eds.) ICSOC 2006. LNCS, vol. 4294, pp. 327–338. Springer, Heidelberg (2006)
27. Honda, K., Vansconcelos, V., Kubo, M.: Language primitives and type discipline for structured communication-based programming. In: Hankin, C. (ed.) ESOP 1998. LNCS, vol. 1381, p. 122. Springer, Heidelberg (1998)
28. Igarashi, A., Kobayashi, N.: Resource usage analysis. In: Proc. 29th ACM SIGPLAN-SIGACT Symposium on Principles of Programming Languages (POPL) (2002)
29. Object Management Group. Business Process Management Initiative. Business Process Modeling Notation. OMG (2009), http://www.bpmn.org
30. Koch, N., Mayer, P., Foster, H., Montangero, C., Varro, D., Gonczy, L.: UML extensions for service-oriented systems. In: Wirsing, M., Hölzl, M. (eds.) SENSORIA. LNCS, vol. 6582, pp. 35–60. Springer, Heidelberg (2011)
31. Lapadula, A., Pugliese, R., Tiezzi, F.: A calculus for orchestration of web services. In: De Nicola, R. (ed.) ESOP 2007. LNCS, vol. 4421, pp. 33–47. Springer, Heidelberg (2007)
32. Lazovik, A., Aiello, M., Gennari, R.: Encoding requests to web service compositions as constraints. In: van Beek, P. (ed.) CP 2005. LNCS, vol. 3709, pp. 782–786. Springer, Heidelberg (2005)
33. Nielson, F., Nielson, H.R.: Type and effect systems. In: Olderog, E.-R., Steffen, B. (eds.) Correct System Design. LNCS, vol. 1710, p. 114. Springer, Heidelberg (1999)
34. Nielson, F., Nielson, H.R., Hankin, C.: Principles of Program Analysis. Springer, Heidelberg (1999)
35. Schneider, F.B.: Enforceable security policies. ACM Transactions on Information and System Security (TISSEC) 3(1) (2000)
36. Skalka, C., Smith, S.: History effects and verification. In: Chin, W.-N. (ed.) APLAS 2004. LNCS, vol. 3302, pp. 107–128. Springer, Heidelberg (2004)
37. Talpin, J.P., Jouvelot, P.: The type and effect discipline. Information and Computation 2(111) (1994)
38. OASIS TC. Business process execution language for web services version 2.0, http://docs.oasis-open.org/wsbpel/2.0/CS01/wsbpel-v2.0-CS01.html
39. Toma, I., Foxvog, D.: Non-functional properties in Web Services. WSMO Deliverable (2006)
40. Vallecillo, A., Vansconcelos, V., Ravara, A.: Typing the behaviours of objects and components using session types. In: Proc. of FOCLASA (2002)
41. Wirsing, M., et al.: Semantic-based development of service-oriented systems. In: Najm, E., Pradat-Peyre, J.-F., Donzeau-Gouge, V.V. (eds.) FORTE 2006. LNCS, vol. 4229, pp. 24–45. Springer, Heidelberg (2006)
42. Woo, T.Y.C., Lam, S.S.: A semantic model for authentication protocols. In: IEEE Symposium on Security and Privacy (1993)
43. Web services choreography description language. W3C Candidate Recommendation (November 9, 2005), http://www.w3.org/TR/ws-cdl-10/
44. Zunino, R.: LocUsT: a tool for checking usage policies. Technical Report TR-08-07, Dip. Informatica, Univ. Pisa (2008)

CC-Pi: A Constraint Language for Service Negotiation and Composition*

Maria Grazia Buscemi[1] and Ugo Montanari[2]

[1] IMT Lucca Institute for Advanced Studies, Italy
m.buscemi@imtlucca.it
[2] Dipartimento di Informatica, University of Pisa, Italy
ugo@di.unipi.it

Abstract. We overview the cc-pi calculus, a model for specifying QoS negotiations in service composition that also allows to study mechanisms for resource allocation and for joining different QoS parameters. Our language combines a synchronous channel-based communication mechanism with a set of primitives for constraint handling. We also illustrated a variant of the calculus in which the standard non-deterministic choice is replaced by a prioritised guarded choice that follows a static form of priority favouring its left over its right argument. We show how both versions of the calculus work by considering two case studies of the SENSORIA Project taken from the Telecommunication and Finance domains. Specifically, we apply the original cc-pi calculus for specifying Telco QoS policies and for enforcing them at execution time, and we formalise in the prioritised cc-pi a QoS-aware negotiation of a credit request service.

1 Introduction

Service Oriented Computing offers a promising solution for providing applications in open dynamic environments, namely systems in which services may appear and disappear unpredictably and run-time changes like those on resource availability frequently take place. The features of such systems call for a mechanism of service composition that is not only concerned with integrating business applications but also dynamically handles service selection. Services may expose both functional properties (i.e. what they do) and non-functional properties (i.e. the way they are supplied). Non-functional properties focus on the Quality of Service (QoS) and typically include performance, availability, and cost. QoS parameters play an important role in service composition and, specifically, in dynamic discovery and binding. Indeed, a service requester may have minimal QoS requirements below which a service is not considered useful. Moreover, multiple services that meet the functional requirements of a requester can still be differentiated according to their non-functional properties.

A QoS contract is a contract, usually between a service requester and a service provider, that records non-funtional properties about a service. The QoS values

---

* This work has been partially sponsored by the project SENSORIA, IST-2005-016004.

M. Wirsing and M. Hölzl (Eds.): SENSORIA Project, LNCS 6582, pp. 262–281, 2011.

appearing in a contract can be negotiated among the contracting parties prior to service binding. If the QoS negotiation succeeds, the two parties can conclude a contract. In the simplest case, one of the two parties exposes a contract template that the other party can fill in with values in a given range. However, in general the two parties may need a real negotiation in which they place arbitrary complex policies. Moreover, if the parties fail to reach an agreement, they may decide to increase their QoS offers or to weaken their requirements.

In this chapter we present a simple calculus, called *cc-pi calculus*, for modeling processes able to specify QoS requirements and to conclude QoS contracts. Our approach combines basic features of name-passing calculi and of concurrent constraint programming. Name-passing calculi, such as the pi-calculus [12], are a key paradigm of computation whose interaction mechanism may dynamically change the communication topology. Since the introduction of name-passing calculi, the notion of *names* has been recognised as crucial in theories of mobile systems. The name-passing calculus we start with is the *explicit fusion calculus* [20], a variant of the pi-calculus [12] whose input prefix is not binder. As a consequence, the synchronisation mechanism yields *explicit fusions*, i.e. simple constraints expressing name equalities, instead of binding formal names to actual names. For example, consider two processes $\overline{u}\langle v\rangle.P$ and $u\langle x\rangle.Q$, that are ready to make an output and an input on u, respectively (note that neither v nor x are bound). The interaction between these processes results in placing the explicit fusion of v and x in parallel rather than applying the substitution $[v/x]$. This fusion will also affect any further process R running in parallel: $R\,|\,\overline{u}\langle v\rangle.P\,|\,u\langle x\rangle.Q \rightarrow R\,|\,P\,|\,Q\,|\,x = v$. The restriction operator (x) can be used to limit the scope of a fusion, e.g.: $R\,|\,(x)(\,\overline{u}\langle v\rangle.P\,|\,u\langle x\rangle.Q) \rightarrow R\,|(x)(\,P\,|\,Q\,|\,x = v)$.

The cc-pi calculus extends the explicit fusion calculus by generalising explicit fusions like $x = v$ to *named constraints* and by adding primitives for handling such constraints. While the informal concept of constraint is widely used in a variety of different fields, a very general, formal notion of constraint system has been introduced in the concurrent constraint programming paradigm [18]. Concurrent constraint programming is a simple and powerful computing model based on a shared store of constraints that provides partial information about possible values that variables can take. Concurrent agents can act on this store by performing either a `tell` action (for adding a constraint, if the resulting store is *consistent*) or an `ask` action (for checking if a constraint is *entailed* by the store). As computation proceeds, more and more information are accumulated, thus the store is *monotonically refined*.

Unlike classical concurrent constraint programming, our calculus features a `retract` construct, whose effect is to erase a previously told constraint, thus allowing to model the allocation and deallocation of *the same* resource. A further novelty of the cc-pi calculus is that its constraint system relies on the notion of c-semiring [3]. Roughly, a c-semiring consists of a set equipped with two binary operations, the sum $+$ and the product $\times$, such that $+$ is associative, *commutative* and *idempotent*, $\times$ is associative and commutative and $\times$ distributes over $+$. The sum $a + b$ chooses the worst constraint better than a and b, while the product $a \times b$ combines two constraints. A c-semiring is automatically equipped with a partial ordering $a \le b$, which means that a is more constrained than b, or, more interestingly, that a entails b.

Remarkably, our c-semirings are quite adequate for modeling the so-called *soft* constraints, i.e. constraints which do not return only true or false, but more informative values instead. In fact, it is easy to define c-semirings expressing fuzzy, hierarchical, or probabilistic values. Also, optimization algorithms work on the c-semiring consisting of the reals plus infinity with the operations of sum as $\times$ and min as $+$. The last difference with respect to [18] is that we handle variables, or rather names, differently. Indeed, our *named* constraints are based on c-semirings equipped with the notion of permutation algebras, which allows characterising the set of relevant, i.e. *free*, names of a constraint.

As a motivating example, consider a service offering computing resources (e.g. units of CPUs of a given power) and suppose the service provider and a client want to reach a QoS contract. The provider P_N, with N available resources and the client C_n requiring at least n resources can be specified in our framework as follows, being max the maximum number of resources that can be allocated to each client. The graph representation of the constraint system resulting from the above negotiation is depicted below. Each node represents a variable, and each constraint is modelled by a hyperedge connecting the variables involved in the constraint.

$$P_N = (x_0)\,(\texttt{tell}\ (x_0 = N).Q(x_0))$$
$$Q(x) = (v)\,(x')\,(\texttt{tell}\ (x' = x - v).\,\texttt{tell}\ (v \le \textsf{max}).\,v\langle.\rangle\,Q(x'))$$
$$C_n = (y)\,(\texttt{tell}\ (y \ge n).\,\bar{c}\langle y\rangle.\,\tau.\,\texttt{retract}\ (y \ge n).\,\texttt{tell}\ (y = 0)\,).$$

In words, P_N first sets the initial number of resources to N and evolves to Q. Process Q creates a name v representing the resources available to a client and a name x' representing a non-negative integer counting the resources left after concluding a contract with the client; Q then adds the constraints $x' = x - v$ for setting the value of x' and $v \le \textsf{max}$ for imposing the bound max on v. Finally, Q signs the contract, i.e. it synchronises on a channel c with a client and, if the synchronisation succeeds, Q becomes ready to accept a new request. On the other side, C_n initially creates a local name y representing the required resources and places the constraint $y \ge n$. Next, C_n tries to synchronise on a public port c with a server. In case of success, C_n makes some calculation involving the obtained resources, which is modelled as a silent action τ. Then, C_n releases the allocated resources by removing the above constraint on y (retract $(y \ge n)$) and by setting y to 0 (tell $(y = 0)$). Hence, a negotiation between P_N and C_n begins with the two parties placing their constraints. P_N and C_n can then synchronise (thus yielding the fusion of names v and y), if the resulting constraint system is consistent, i.e. if $n \le min(N, \textsf{max})$, as shown by the graph representation below.

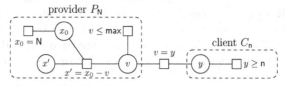

In this work we also present a variant of the cc-pi calculus in which non-deterministic choice is replaced by a form of prioritised guarded choice à la [9], which features a static priority that favours its left over its right argument. We claim that this version is more suited to model the protocol followed by a negotiating partner who usually has a given order of preference between its possible alternatives. The underlying idea is that in a choice $\sum_i \pi_i.P_i$ the branch P_i is selected if i is the minimum index such that the guard π_i is *enabled*. For instance, if $c \times d$ is consistent the process $d \,|\, (\texttt{tell } c.P + \texttt{tell } c'.Q)$ can make a $\texttt{tell } c$ action and evolve as P while the second branch cannot be chosen as $\texttt{tell } c'$ has not the minimum index among the other alternatives. Consequently, the synchronisation mechanism needs to be changed. As an example, composing a process in parallel with an input/output action might enable a guard, thus blocking the execution of a branch with greater index.

The present prioritised version of the cc-pi calculus decreases the level of non-determinism. However, the non-determinism that is removed concerns alternative branches of a choice while the calculus keeps the degree of non-determinism arising from the possible interleavings of processes in parallel. For instance, if there are two choice operators running in parallel, the prioritised transition semantics accounts for selecting an alternative within every choice but, in case both of them have enabled guards, any possible interleaving is allowed.

To show how both the un-prioritised and prioritised versions of the cc-pi work, we consider two case studies of the SENSORIA Project taken from the Telecommunication and Finance domains, which are described in Chapter 0-3. In the first case, we apply the original cc-pi calculus for specifying Telco QoS policies and for enforcing them at execution time. In the second case, we consider a credit request service and we formalise in the prioritised cc-pi a QoS-aware service negotiation.

Synopsis. In §2 we recall the basic concepts about c-semirings and named c-semirings. In §3 we overview the cc-pi calculus by describing its syntax and semantics. In §4 we apply cc-pi for specifying negotiations of Telco policies. In §5 we present a prioritised variant of the cc-pi calculus and in §6 we show an example of QoS negotiation taken from a financial domain. In §7 we draw some conclusions and compare our contribution to related work in the literature.

Several results have been proved for both versions of the calculus. Such contributions are technical and go beyond the scope of the present chapter. We refer the interested reader to [6,7,5,8]. Specifically, in [6] the expressiveness of the un-prioritised calculus is studied by giving reduction-preserving translations of the explicit fusion calculus and of concurrent constraint programming into cc-pi. [7] proposes a labelled semantics of cc-pi along with a notion of open bisimulation much like in pi-calculus. [8] introduces a version of prioritised cc-pi calculus that is a generalisation with dynamic priority of the calculus presented in §5: in [8] we have exploited the presence of constraints in order to allow for dynamic priorities that depend on the store of constraints and we have proved that dynamic priorities are strictly more expressive than static priorities. Finally, the examples shown in sections §4 and §6 are mainly based on [5] and [8], respectively.

2   Named Constraints

Let $\mathcal{N}$ be an infinite, countable set of *names* and let $x, y, z \ldots$ range over names. We define *(name) fusions* as total equivalence relations on $\mathcal{N}$ with only finitely many non-singular equivalence classes. By $x = y$ we denote the fusion with a unique non-singular equivalence class containing x and y. A *substitution* is a function $\sigma : \mathcal{N} \to \mathcal{N}$. We denote by $[y/x]$ the substitution that maps x into y. A *permutation* ρ is a bijective substitution. The *kernel* $K(\rho)$ of a permutation ρ is the set of names that are changed by ρ. A *permutation algebra* A is defined by a carrier set and by a function defining how states are transformed by the finite-kernel permutations. In our case, A characterises the set of 'relevant' names of each element c of the c-semiring as the support $\text{supp}(c)$ in A. Note that the notion of support associated with permutation algebras recalls the concept of free names in process calculi.

We now introduce the basic concepts about c-semirings and named c-semirings. The interested reader is referred to [16,3,2,6] for a more detailed treatment.

2.1   C-semirings

Definition 1. *A* commutative semiring *is a tuple* $\langle A, +, \times, 0, 1 \rangle$ *such that: (i) A is a set and $0, 1 \in A$, and $+, \times : A \times A \to A$ are binary operators making the triples $\langle A, \times, 1 \rangle$ and $\langle A, +, 0 \rangle$ commutative monoids (semigroups with identity), satisfying the following axioms.*

$$a \times (b + c) = (a \times b) + (a \times c) \ \ \forall a, b, c \in A \qquad a \times 0 = 0 \ \ \forall a \in A$$

Definition 2 (c-semiring). *A* constraint semiring *(c-semiring)* $\langle A, +, \times, 0, 1 \rangle$ *is a commutative semiring such that $+$ is idempotent and $a + 1 = 1$ for all $a \in A$ (i.e. with top element).*

Typical examples are the c-semiring for classical constraint satisfaction problems CSPs $\langle \{\mathsf{False}, \mathsf{True}\}, \vee, \wedge, \mathsf{False}, \mathsf{True} \rangle$, the c-semiring for fuzzy CSPs $\langle [0, 1], \max, \min, 0, 1 \rangle$, and the c-semiring of weighted CSPs $\langle \mathbb{R}^+ \cup \{+\infty\}, \min, +, +\infty, 0 \rangle$. Note that the Cartesian product of two c-semirings is a c-semiring, hence this framework is also suited to model multicriteria optimization.

Commutative semirings with top element are also known in the literature as *absorptive*. Next, we briefly overview some classical notions and results on absorptive semirings that are outlined in [16] and that we rephrase below for c-semirings.

Let $\preceq$ be a relation over A such that $a \preceq b$ iff $a + b = b$. This relation gives us a way to compare semiring values and constraints. Assume a c-semiring $S = \langle A, +, \times, 0, 1 \rangle$. Then: (i) $\preceq$ is a partial order; (ii) $+$ and $\times$ are monotone on $\preceq$; (iii) $a \times b \preceq a, b$, for all a, b; (iv) 0 is its minimum and 1 its maximum; and (v) for all $a, b \in A$, $a + b$ is the least upper bound of a and b. Moreover, if $\times$ is idempotent, $a \times b$ is the greatest lower bound of a and b. S is *invertible* if there exists an element $c \in A$ such that $b \times c = a$ for all elements $a, b \in A$ such that $a \preceq b$; S is *complete* if it is closed with respect to infinite sums, and the distributivity law holds also for an infinite number of summands. It can be proved that if S is complete then the set $\{x \in A \mid b \times x \preceq a\}$ admits a maximum for all elements $a, b \in A$, denoted $a \div b$. Note that the idempotency of $\times$ implies that the invertibility property holds. However, for the purpose of this chapter, we simply require invertibility and completeness while not imposing idempotency of $\times$.

2.2   Named C-semirings

A named c-semiring is a complete and invertible c-semiring enriched with a notion of name fusions, a permutation algebra A and a hiding operator $\nu x. c$ that makes a name x local in c. Note that in certain named c-semirings the hiding operator coincides with the homologous operator $\exists x$ defined in concurrent constraint programming. Formally:

Definition 3. *A* named c-semiring $\mathcal{C} = \langle C, +, \times, \nu x., \rho, 0, 1 \rangle$ *is a tuple where:*
(i) $x{=}y \in C$ *for all x and y in $\mathcal{N}$; (ii)* $\langle C, +, \times, 0, 1 \rangle$ *is a complete and invertible c-semiring; (iii)* $\langle C, \rho \rangle$ *is a finite-support permutation algebra such that every permutation ρ distributes over $\times$ and $+$ and is inactive on 0 and 1 ; (iv)* $\forall x$, $\nu x.$: $C \to C$ *is a unary operation; (v) for all* $c, d \in C$ *and for all ρ the following axioms hold.*

$$
\begin{array}{llll}
x{=}y \times c &=& x{=}y \times [y/x]\, c & \qquad \rho\,(\nu x.\,c) = \nu x.\,(\rho\, c) \text{ if } x \notin K(\rho) \\
\nu x.\, 1 = 1 & \nu x.\nu y.\, c = \nu y.\nu x.\, c & & \nu x.\, c = \nu y.\,[y/x]\, c \quad \text{if } y \notin \mathrm{supp}(c) \\
\nu x.\,(c \times d) = c \times \nu x.\, d & \text{if } x \notin \mathrm{supp}(c) & & \nu x.\,(c + d) = c + \nu x.\, d \quad \text{if } x \notin \mathrm{supp}(c)
\end{array}
$$

The top left axiom above accounts for combining fusions and generic elements of c-semirings. According to the top right axiom, the order of ρ and ν can be changed if x is not affected by ρ. The remaining axioms rule how the ν operation interacts with the operations of the c-semiring and they are inspired by the analogous structural congruence axioms for restriction in process calculi. Given $\mathcal{C} = \langle A, +, \times, \rho, \nu x., 0, 1 \rangle$, a *(named) constraint* c is an element of A. For $C \subseteq A$, C is *consistent* if $(\times C) \neq 0$; for $c \in A$, C *entails* c, written $C \vdash c$, if $(\times C) \preceq c$. Moreover, by $c \prec d$ we abbreviate $c \preceq d$ and $c \neq d$.

Soft constraints. Given a domain D of interpretation for the set of names $\mathcal{N}$ and a c-semiring $S = \langle A, +, \times, 0, 1 \rangle$, a *soft* constraint c can be represented as a function $c = (\mathcal{N} \to D) \to A$ associating to each variable assignment $\eta = \mathcal{N} \to D$ (i.e. instantiation of the variables occurring in the constraint) a value in A, which can be interpreted e.g. as a set of preference values or costs. Soft constraints can be combined by means of the operators of S. Assume $\mathcal{C}_{\mathrm{soft}}$ is the tuple $\mathcal{C}_{\mathrm{soft}} = \langle C, +', \times', \nu x., \rho, 0', 1' \rangle$ such that: (i) C is the set of all soft constraints over $\mathcal{N}$, D and S; (ii) name equalities $x = y$ are defined as $(x = y)\eta = 1$ if $\eta(x) = \eta(y)$, $(x = y)\eta = 0$ otherwise; (iii) $(c_1 +' c_2)\eta = c_1\eta + c_2\eta$; (iv) $(c_1 \times' c_2)\eta = c_1\eta \times c_2\eta$; (v) $(\nu x.c)\eta = \sum_{d \in D} (c\eta[d/x])$, where $\sum_{d \in D}$ denotes the c-semiring sum operator and the assignment $\eta[d/x]$ is defined, as usual, as

$\eta[d/x](y) = d$ if $x = y$, $\eta(y)$ otherwise; (vi) $(\rho c)\eta = c\overline{\eta}$ with $\overline{\eta}(x) = \eta(\rho(x))$; (vii) $0'\eta = 0$ and $1'\eta = 1$ for all η. It is possible to prove that $\mathcal{C}_{\mathsf{soft}}$ is indeed a named c-semiring and that the product $\times'$ is invertible and complete provided that $\times$ is so. Remark that for $S = \langle\{\mathsf{False},\mathsf{True}\}, \vee, \wedge, \mathsf{False}, \mathsf{True}\rangle$, the named constraints of $\mathcal{C}_{\mathsf{soft}}$ leads to solutions consisting of the set of tuples of legal domain values. In this case, for instance, the interpretation of the constraint $c = x \leq \mathsf{a} \times \mathsf{b} \leq y$, where x, y are names in $\mathcal{N}$, a, b are domain values in D, and $\leq$ has the usual meaning of "less than or equal" on integers, is that c is the function $(\mathcal{N} \to D) \to \{\mathsf{False}, \mathsf{True}\}$, with the assignment η such that $c\eta = \mathsf{True}$ if $\eta(x) \leq \mathsf{a}$ and $\mathsf{b} \leq \eta(y)$, while $c\eta = \mathsf{False}$ otherwise. For instance, we write $y \leq 2$ to abbreviate a constraint such that for each η that assigns to y a value smaller than or equal to 2 holds True, otherwise holds False. By varying the structure of the underlying c-semiring, we can model *soft* constraints, i.e. constraints that return more informative values than just Booleans. As an example, if we consider two constraints c_1 and c_2 defined over the c-semiring for Fuzzy CSPs $\langle[0,1], \max, \min, 0, 1\rangle$, the product $c_1 \times c_2$ is the minimum between the preference values of c_1 and c_2.

3   The cc-pi Calculus

3.1   Syntax

We assume the countable set of names $\mathcal{N}$ and a set of process identifiers, ranged over by I. We let c range over constraints of an arbitrary named c-semiring $\mathcal{C}$.

Definition 4. *The sets of* prefixes *and* cc-pi processes *are defined as follows:*

PREFIXES $\pi ::= \tau \mid \overline{x}\langle\tilde{y}\rangle \mid x\langle\tilde{y}\rangle \mid \mathtt{tell}\ c \mid \mathtt{ask}\ c \mid \mathtt{retract}\ c \mid \mathtt{check}\ c$

UNCONSTRAINED $U ::= \mathbf{0} \mid U|U \mid \sum_i \pi_i.U_i \mid (x)U \mid I(\tilde{y})$
PROCESSES

CONSTRAINED $P ::= U \mid c \mid P|P \mid (x)P$
PROCESSES

Hereafter, by $\tilde{y}$ we denote a tuple of names. The τ prefix stands for a silent action, the output prefix $\overline{x}\langle\tilde{y}\rangle$ for emitting over the port x the message $\tilde{y}$ and the input prefix $x\langle\tilde{y}\rangle$ for receiving over x a message and fusing it to $\tilde{y}$. Prefix $\mathtt{tell}\ c$ generates a constraint c and puts it in parallel with the other constraints, if the resulting parallel composition of constraints is consistent; $\mathtt{tell}\ c$ is not enabled otherwise. Prefix $\mathtt{ask}\ c$ is enabled if c is entailed by the set of constraints in parallel. Prefix $\mathtt{retract}\ c$ removes a constraint c, if c is present. Prefix $\mathtt{check}\ c$ is enabled if c is consistent with the set of constraints in parallel. *Unconstrained processes* U are essentially processes that can only contain constraints c in prefixes $\mathtt{tell}\ c$, $\mathtt{ask}\ c$, $\mathtt{retract}\ c$, and $\mathtt{check}\ c$. As usual, $\mathbf{0}$ stands for the inert process and $U|U$ for the parallel composition. $\sum_i \pi_i.U_i$ denotes an external choice in which some guarded unconstrained process U_i is chosen when the corresponding guard π_i is enabled. Restriction $(x)U$ makes the name x local in U.

$I(\tilde{y})$ denotes a definition call where a defining equation for the process identifier I is of the form $I(\tilde{x}) \stackrel{\text{def}}{=} U$ with $|\tilde{x}| = |\tilde{y}|$. *Constrained processes* P are defined like unconstrained processes U but for the fact that P may have constraints c in parallel with processes. We simply write processes to refer to constrained processes.

We extend the usual notion of *free names* of a process by stating that the set of free names of a constraint c is the support $\text{supp}(c)$ defined in the previous section. Formally, the set $\text{fn}(P)$ is inductively defined as follows:

$$\text{fn}(\mathbf{0}) = \emptyset \quad \text{fn}(\tau.U) = \text{fn}(U) \quad \text{fn}(\overline{x}\langle\tilde{y}\rangle.U) = \{x, \tilde{y}\} \cup \text{fn}(U) \quad \text{fn}(x\langle\tilde{y}\rangle.U) = \{x, \tilde{y}\} \cup \text{fn}(U)$$

$$\text{fn}(\pi.U) = \text{supp}(c) \cup \text{fn}(U) \quad \text{if } \pi = \texttt{tell } c, \texttt{ ask } c, \texttt{ retract } c, \texttt{ check } c$$

$$\text{fn}(\textstyle\sum_i \pi_i.U_i) = \cup_i \text{fn}(\pi_i.U_i) \quad \text{fn}(I(\tilde{x})) = \text{fn}(U) \quad \text{if } I(\tilde{x}) \stackrel{\text{def}}{=} U$$

$$\text{fn}(c) = \text{supp}(c) \quad \text{fn}(P \,|\, Q) = \text{fn}(P) \cup \text{fn}(Q) \quad \text{fn}((x)\,P) = \text{fn}(P) \setminus \{x\}$$

We write $\text{n}(P)$ for the set of *names* of a process P and $\text{bn}(P) = \text{n}(P) \setminus \text{fn}(P)$ for the set of *bound names*; the usual notion of α-conversion on bound names holds. By σP we denote the process obtained from P by simultaneously substituting each free occurrence of z in P by $\sigma(z)$, possibly α-converting bound names.

3.2 Operational Semantics

The reduction semantics, as usual, is given in two steps: the definition of a *structural congruence*, which rearranges processes into adjacent positions, and a notion of *reduction relation* that captures computations.

Definition 5. *We let* structural congruence, $\equiv$, *be the least congruence over processes closed with respect to α-conversion and satisfying the following rules.*

(Ax-Par) $P|\mathbf{0} \equiv P \qquad P|Q \equiv Q|P \qquad (P|Q)|R \equiv P|(Q|R)$

(Ax-Sum) $P+\mathbf{0} \equiv P \qquad P+Q \equiv Q+P \qquad (P+Q)+R \equiv P+(Q+R)$

(Ax-Res) $(x)\mathbf{0} \equiv \mathbf{0} \quad (x)(y)P \equiv (y)(x)P \quad P|(x)Q \equiv (x)(P|Q) \quad \text{if } x \notin \text{fn}(P)$

(Ax-Rec) $I(\tilde{y}) \equiv [\tilde{y}/\tilde{x}]U \quad \text{if } I(\tilde{x}) \stackrel{\text{def}}{=} U$

These axioms can be applied for reducing every process P into a normal form $(x_1) \ldots (x_n)\,(C \,|\, U)$, where C is a parallel composition of constraints and U is an unconstrained process. Specifically, the axioms are applied from left to right in the following order: (Ax-Res) for moving forward restrictions, and (Ax-Par) for grouping constraints together, and (Ax-Rec). The normal form of a process is unique up to commutativity of parallel composition. In the sequel we write $P\equiv_{\text{nf}} Q$ to mean that Q is the normal form of P.

Definition 6. *The* reduction relation *over processes* $\rightarrow$ *is the least relation satisfying the inference rules in Table 1. We use the following notations: C stands for the parallel composition of constraints $c_1 \,|\, \ldots \,|\, c_n$; C consistent means $(c_1 \times \ldots \times c_n) \neq 0$; $C \vdash c$ if $(c_1 \times \ldots \times c_n) \preceq c$; $C - c$ stands for $c_1 \,|\, \ldots \,|\, c_{i-1} \,|\, c_{i+1} \,|\, \ldots \,|\, c_n$ if $c = c_i$ for some i, while $C - c = C$ otherwise.*

Table 1. Reduction semantics for cc-pi

(TAU) $C \mid \tau.U \rightarrow C \mid U$ (TELL) $C \mid \mathbf{tell}\ c.U \rightarrow C \mid c \mid U$ if $C \mid c$ consistent

(ASK) $C \mid \mathbf{ask}\ c.U \rightarrow C \mid U$ if $C \vdash c$ (RETRACT) $C \mid \mathbf{retract}\ c.U \rightarrow (C-\ c) \mid U$

(CHECK) $C \mid \mathbf{check}\ c.U \rightarrow C \mid U$ if $C \mid c$ consistent

(COM) $C \mid (\overline{x}\langle\widetilde{y}\rangle.U + \sum_i \pi_i.U_i) \mid (z\langle\widetilde{w}\rangle.V + \sum_j \pi'_j.V_j) \quad \longrightarrow \quad C \mid \widetilde{y} = \widetilde{w} \mid U \mid V$
   if $|\widetilde{y}| = |\widetilde{w}|$, $C \mid \widetilde{y} = \widetilde{w}$ consistent and $C \vdash x = z$

$$(\text{SUM}) \quad \frac{C \mid \pi_i.U_i \rightarrow P}{C \mid \sum_i \pi_i.U_i \rightarrow P} \qquad\qquad (\text{PAR}) \quad \frac{P \rightarrow P'}{P \mid U \rightarrow P' \mid U}$$

$$(\text{RES}) \quad \frac{P \rightarrow P'}{(x)\,P \rightarrow (x)\,P'} \qquad (\text{STRUCT}) \quad \frac{P \equiv P' \quad P' \rightarrow Q' \quad Q' \equiv Q}{P \rightarrow Q}$$

The idea behind this reduction relation is to proceed as follows. First, rearranging processes into the normal form $(x_1) \ldots (x_n)(C \mid U)$ by means of rule (STRUCT). Next, applying the rules (TELL), (ASK), (RETRACT), and (CHECK) for primitives on constraints, the rule (SUM) for selecting a branch, and the rule (COM) for synchronising processes. Finally, closing with respect to parallel composition and restriction ((PAR), (RES)). More in detail, rule (TELL) states that if $C \mid c$ is consistent then a process can place c in parallel with C, the process is stuck otherwise. Rules (ASK) and (CHECK) specify that a process starting with an $\mathbf{ask}\ c$ or, respectively, $\mathbf{check}\ c$ prefix evolves to its continuation if c is entailed by C or, respectively, if $c \mid C$ is consistent, and that the process is stuck otherwise. By rule (RETRACT) a process can remove c if c is among the syntactic constraints in C; e.g., the process $x=y \mid y = z \mid \mathbf{retract}\ x = z.U$ does not affect $x=y \mid y = z$. In rules (COM), we write $\widetilde{y} = \widetilde{w}$ to denote the parallel composition of fusions $y_1 = w_1 \mid \ldots, \mid y_n = w_n$. Intuitively, two processes $\overline{x}\langle\widetilde{y}\rangle.P$ and $z\langle\widetilde{w}\rangle.Q$ can synchronise if the equality of the names x and z is entailed by C and if the parallel composition $C \mid \widetilde{y} = \widetilde{w}$ is consistent. Note that it is legal to treat fusions as constraints c over C, because we only require named c-semirings to include name fusions, as noted in § 2. Rule (PAR) allows for closure with respect to unconstrained processes in parallel. This rule imposes to take into account all constraints in parallel when applying the rules for constraints and synchronisation.

The present semantics does not specify how to solve at each step the constraint system given by the parallel composition of constraints C. However, in [14] it is shown how to apply dynamic programming to solve a CSP by solving its subproblems and then by combining solutions to obtain the solution of the whole problem.

Below we consider a slightly more complex scenario of the one given in the introduction with one provider P_N and three clients C_{n_1}, C_{n_2}, and C_{n_3}. The graph representation of the constraint system resulting from the negotiation among the parties is depicted below.

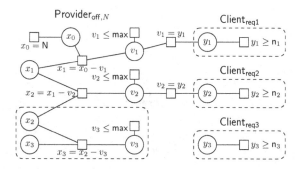

Suppose that P_N has allocated the resources y_1 and y_2, with $y_i \geq n_i$ for $i = 1, 2$, to C_{n_1} and C_{n_2}, respectively. If C_{n_3} makes a request $y_3 \geq n_3$ that P_N is not able to satisfy because $n_1 + n_2 + n_3 \geq N$, the synchronisation between P_N and C_{n_3} cannot take place until some resources $\{y_i\}_i$, with $(\sum_i y_i) \geq n_1 + n_2 + n_3 - N$, are released.

4   A Telecommunication Case Study

In this section we analyse a case study borrowed from the Telecommunication area, described in Chapter 0-3. We show how to apply the cc-pi calculus for specifying, negotiating, and enforcing policies for Telco services. We start by introducing a service scenario called CallBySms.

The CallBySms service allows a mobile phone user to activate a voice call by sending an SMS message to a specific service number. The SMS message must contain a nickname of the person the user wishes to call. The service is able to automatically find the number associated with the nickname and to set up a party call between the user and the callee. In order to keep privacy, the service does not know actual phone numbers, but only opaque-id representing users. The service in turn uses two services, ThirdPartyCall and ShortMessaging, for specifying the operations respectively necessary to set-up and control calls and to receive/send short messages. Figure 1 depicts a possible service scenario in which John wishes to call Mary and he knows that Mary's nickname is "sunshine".

1. The Third Party application subscribes the services that are used by the CallBySms service and signs a QoS contract with the Network Operator;
2. The CallBySMS service is activated and the Third Party application receives a service number, e.g. 11111;
3. Mary sends an SMS "REGISTER sunshine" to the service number 11111;
4. The service associates "sunshine" to the opaque-id of Mary;
5. John sends an SMS "CALL sunshine" to the service number 11111;
6. The service retrieves the opaque-id associated to "sunshine" and set-up a call;
7. John's phone rings; John answers and gets the ringing tone;
8. Mary's phone rings; Mary answers;
9. John and Mary are connected.

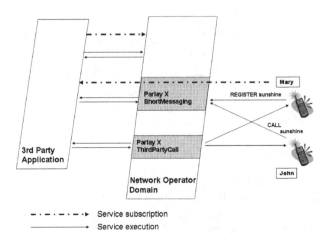

- · — · — · — ·▶ Service subscription
———————▶ Service execution

Fig. 1. CallBySms Service Scenario

Policies as constraints. We now focus on specifying and ensuring *time* policies. In [5] we address modelling and enforcement of other policies such as policies on *frequency*. For simplicity, hereafter we take the reference constraint system to be a classical constraint satisfaction problem by considering the named c-semiring of Boolean values. However, such constraint system can be easily generalised to soft constraint satisfaction problems by replacing the underlying c-semiring with an arbitrary c-semiring.

The constraint $c_{\text{time}}(i, f) = (7 \leq i \leq 9) \times (15 \leq f \leq 18)$ specifies the initial and final time ranges within which calls can be set up by end users. Similarly, $d_{\text{time}}(i, f) = (6 \leq i \leq 8) \times (17 \leq f \leq 19)$ states the time requirements of the third party. The result of combining these policies is the intersection of the initial and final time ranges, which is expressed by the c-semiring product $e_{\text{time}}(i, f) = c_{\text{time}}(i, f) \times d_{\text{time}}(i, f) = (7 \leq i \leq 8) \times (17 \leq f \leq 18)$. Note that the constraint e_{time} is part of the QoS contract among the network operator and the third party application and it is validated by the operator domain once a call request from a end user is received. Other policies might depend on some network operator parameter while being related to the agreement of the third party with every end-user.

Cc-pi specification. We now show the main steps of the formalisation in cc-pi calculus of the policy negotiation and service execution scenario of CallBySms. We refer to [5] for a complete description of the specification.

The negotiation phase between the third party application and the network operator consists of the two parties placing their own constraints and trying to synchronise on port x in order to export their local parameters. If the set of all such constraints induced by the synchronisation is consistent, the two parties have concluded a contract, which is expressed by the c-semiring product of all constraints:

$$\text{NetOp\_Neg}(x, z) = (i, f)\,(\texttt{tell}\ c_{\text{time}}(i, f)).\,x\langle i, f\rangle$$

$$\text{3rdPA\_Neg}(x) = (i', f')\,(\texttt{tell}\ d_{\text{time}}(i', f')).\overline{x}\langle i', f'\rangle$$

The process Clock_T is meant to simulate the actual time by increasing of time unit a variable t starting from its present value T. We assume this $+$ operation automatically resets the clock by the end of the day:

$$\text{Clock}_\mathsf{T}(t) = \texttt{retract}\ (t = \mathsf{T}).\,\texttt{tell}\ (t = \mathsf{T} + 1).\,\text{Clock}_{\mathsf{T}+1}(t)$$

After a service activation request by the third party application, the network operator is ready to accept registration requests from end-users and to forward them to the third party application. An end-user intending to register to Call-BySms tries to synchronise with the network operator on z with its private identity *mary* and nickname *sunshine* as parameters. The network operator forwards this request to the third party application by sending on x the nickname, though not revealing the user's identity:

$$\text{Regist\_User}(z, sunshine) = (mary)\,(\overline{z}\langle mary, sunshine\rangle.\,\text{Wait\_Calls}(mary))$$

$$\text{NetOp\_Acpt\_Reqst}(x, z, i, f, t) = (id, nn)(z\langle id, nn\rangle.\overline{x}\langle nn\rangle.($$
$$\text{NetOp\_Acpt\_Reqst}(x, z, i, f, t)$$
$$|\,\text{NetOp\_Acpt\_Call}(i, f, t, id, nn)))$$

$$\text{3rdPA\_Acpt\_Reqst}(x) = (nn')\,(x\langle nn'\rangle.(\text{3rdPA\_Acpt\_Reqst}(x))$$

A user who wants to call Mary but only knows her nickname is specified by a process sending its private name *john* on the public port *sunshine* and then waiting to be connected with *sunshine* on port *john*. The network operator verifies that the call request is within the legal time range. In case of success, the network operator forwards the name *john* to the private port *mary* in order to connect the two users:

$$\text{Wait\_Calls}(mary) = (cal')\,(mary\langle cal'\rangle.cal'\langle\rangle.\text{Wait\_Calls}(mary))$$

$$\text{Caller}(sunshine) = (john)\overline{sunshine}\langle john\rangle.\overline{john}\langle\rangle$$

$$\text{NetOp\_Acpt\_Call}(i, f, t, id, nn) = (cal)\,nn\langle cal\rangle.(\texttt{check}\ (i \leq t \leq f).\overline{id}\langle cal\rangle.$$
$$\text{NetOp\_Acpt\_Call}(i, f, t, id, nn))$$

The whole system S is given by the parallel composition of the two users, the clock and the processes specifying the policy negotiation followed by the processes modelling the service execution:

$$S = \text{Regist\_User}(z, sunshine)\,|\,\text{Caller}(sunshine)\,|\,\texttt{tell}\ (t = 0).\,\text{Clock}_0(t))$$
$$|\ \text{NetOp\_Neg}(x).\text{NetOp\_Acpt\_Reqst}(x, z, i, f, t)$$
$$|\ \text{3rdPA\_Neg}(x).\text{3rdPA\_Acpt\_Reqst}(x)$$

where the above notation $P.Q$ is shorthand for the process that after completing the execution of P behaves as Q.

Note that our framework can be employed to model more complex negotiation scenarios, e.g. in which there is an arbitrary number of end-users or in which the third party application and the network operator may want to *retract* their initial policies and replace them with weaker constraints, in order to reach an agreement.

5   The Prioritised cc-pi Calculus

We now present a prioritised variant of the cc-pi. The main novelty of the prioritised cc-pi calculus with respect to the original cc-pi calculus concerns the choice operation. First, following [9], we prevent output prefixes from appearing as guards. The main reason behind this restriction is to avoid processes like $(\overline{x}\langle\rangle + y\langle\rangle) \mid (\overline{y}\langle\rangle + x\langle\rangle)$, in which we have to decide which synchronisation take precedence over the other one. Second, the branch $\pi_i.U_i$ of a choice $\sum_i \pi_i.U_i$ is chosen if not only the corresponding guard π_i is enabled but also there is no guard π_j with $j \leq i$ that is enabled. Consequently, we remove axiom (Ax-Sum) from the structural congruence given in Definition 5.

Before introducing the reduction semantics for the prioritised calculus, we formally define the notions of enabled guard and maximal enabled guard. For C the parallel composition of constraints $c_1 \mid \ldots \mid c_n$, we adopt the same abbreviations introduced in Definition 10 plus the following:

- $C \times d$ to mean $c_1 \times \ldots \times c_n \times d$;
- $C \div d$ to mean $(c_1 \times \ldots \times c_n) \div d$.

Definition 7. *Given a process* $P \equiv_{nf} C \mid U \mid \sum_i \pi_i.V_i$, *a guard* π_j *is enabled in* P *if:* (i) $\pi_j = \tau$ *or* (ii) $\pi_j = \texttt{tell } c, \texttt{check } c$ *and* $C \mid c$ *consistent or* (iii) $\pi_j = \texttt{ask } c$ *and* $C \vdash c$ *or* (iv) $\pi_j = z\langle\widetilde{w}\rangle$ *and* $U = U_1 \mid \ldots \mid U_n$ *and there exists* k *with* $1 \leq k \leq n$ *such that* $U_k = \overline{x}\langle\widetilde{y}\rangle.U'$ *and* $|\widetilde{y}| = |\widetilde{w}|$ *and* $C \mid \widetilde{y} = \widetilde{w}$ *consistent and* $C \vdash x = z$, *for some* $x, \widetilde{y}, U'$.

A guard π_j *is a maximal enabled guard in* $P \equiv_{nf} C \mid U \mid \sum_i \pi_i.V_i$ *if* π_j *is enabled in* P *and there is no guard* π_k *of* $\sum_i \pi_i.V_i$ *that is enabled in* P *and such that* $k < j$.

Roughly, a guard is a maximal enabled guard if it is a left-most enabled guard among the alternatives. Note that if more than one branch can be selected in different choices running in parallel, then the choice is performed non-deterministically.

Definition 8 (acceptance set). *Given a process* $P \equiv_{nf} C \mid U$ *with* $U \equiv_{nf} U_1 \mid \ldots \mid U_n$, *the acceptance set of* P, $\mathsf{AS}(P)$, *is defined as follows.*

$$\mathsf{AS}(P) = \{y\langle x\rangle \mid \exists\, m \text{ with } 1 \leq m \leq n \text{ such that } U_m = \sum_{i=1}^{r} \pi_i.V_i \text{ and}$$
$$\pi_j = y\langle x\rangle \text{ not enabled in } P \text{ and } \nexists\, k \text{ with } 1 \leq k \leq r$$
$$\text{s.t. } k < j \text{ and } \pi_k \text{ an enabled guard}\}.$$

Definition 9 (ready set). *Given a process* $P \equiv_{\mathsf{nf}} C \,|\, U$, *with* $U \equiv_{\mathsf{nf}}$ $U_1 \,|\, \dots \,|\, U_n$, *the ready set of* U, $\mathsf{RS}(U)$, *is defined as follows.*

$$\mathsf{RS}(U) = \{\overline{x}\langle w\rangle \,|\, \exists\, m \text{ with } 1 \leq m \leq n \text{ such that } U_m = \overline{x}\langle w\rangle.V_m\}.$$

Roughly, the acceptance set contains all the input prefixes that are not enabled and such that there is no further enabled guard with smaller index. Similarly, the ready set contains the output prefixes that are ready to synchronise, i.e. that are not under another prefix. Given a set of input prefixes X and a set of output prefixes Y, and a parallel composition of constraints C, we say that C *entails* $X \cap Y = \emptyset$, written $C \vdash X \cap Y = \emptyset$, if for every pair $x\langle z\rangle$ in X and $\overline{y}\langle w\rangle$ in Y, either $C \not\vdash x = y$ or $C \times z = w$ is inconsistent. As an example, consider the process $P \equiv_{\mathsf{nf}} C \,|\, (x\langle y\rangle.U_1 + \tau.U_2) \,|\, (z\langle w\rangle.V_1 + \tau.V_2)$. Then, $\mathsf{AS}(P) = \{x\langle y\rangle, z\langle w\rangle\}$. Let U be the process $U = \overline{u}\langle v\rangle \,|\, \sum_i c_i' : \pi_i'.U_i'$. The ready set $\mathsf{RS}(U) = \{\overline{u}\langle v\rangle\}$. For $C = (x = u)$ we have that $C \not\vdash \mathsf{AS}(P) \cap \mathsf{RS}(U) = \emptyset$, because the equality of the channel names x and u is entailed by the store and $C \times y = v$ is consistent.

Definition 10 (Reduction Semantics). *The* prioritised reduction relation *over processes* $\to$ *is the least relation satisfying the inference rules in Table 1 where rules* (SUM), (COM), *and* (PAR) *are replaced by their omologous rules in Table 2.*

Table 2. Novel reduction rules for prioritised cc-pi

$$(\text{PR-SUM}) \quad \frac{C \,|\, \pi_j.U_j \to P \qquad (\star)}{C \,|\, \sum_i \pi_i.U_i \to P}$$

$$(\text{PR-COM}) \quad C \,|\, (\overline{x}\langle \widetilde{y}\rangle.U) \,|\, (\pi_1.V_1 + \dots + z\langle \widetilde{w}\rangle.V_j + \dots + \pi_n.V_n)$$
$$\longrightarrow \; C \,|\, \widetilde{y} = \widetilde{w} \,|\, U \,|\, V_j \qquad (\star\star)$$

$$(\text{PR-PAR}) \quad \frac{P \to P' \qquad (\star\star\star)}{P \,|\, U \to P' \,|\, U}$$

$(\star)$ π_j maximal enabled guard in $C \,|\, (\sum_{i=1}^{n} \pi_i.U_i)$.

$(\star\star)$ $z\langle \widetilde{w}\rangle$ maximal enabled guard in $C \,|\, (\overline{x}\langle \widetilde{y}\rangle.U) \,|\, (\sum_{i=1}^{n} \pi_i.V_i)$.

$(\star\star\star)$ If $P \equiv_{\mathsf{nf}} C \,|\, V$ and $C \vdash \mathsf{AS}(P) \cap \mathsf{RS}(U) = \emptyset$

Rule (PR-SUM) and rule (PR-COM) achieve a form of priority over actions. Rule (PR-SUM) states that the branch $\pi_i.U_i$ is selected if π_i is a maximal enabled guard in the list of alternatives. For instance, $P \equiv_{\mathsf{nf}} x = z \,|\, (\mathsf{ask}\ (x = y).U + \tau.V)$ has only a transition $P \to x = z \,|\, V$ since $\mathsf{ask}\ (x = y)$ is not enabled; on the other side, $Q \equiv_{\mathsf{nf}} x = y \,|\, P$ can only reduce as $Q \to x = y \,|\, x = z \,|\, U$. According to rule (PR-COM), two processes $\overline{x}\langle \widetilde{y}\rangle.U$ and $\sum_i \pi_i.V_i$ can synchronise if there is a maximal enabled guard $z\langle \widetilde{w}\rangle$ in $\overline{x}\langle \widetilde{y}\rangle.U \,|\, \sum_i \pi_i.V_i$. For example, let

$$P \equiv_{\mathsf{nf}} x \neq y \,|\, (z\langle y\rangle.U + \mathtt{retract}\ x \neq y.V) \qquad Q \equiv_{\mathsf{nf}} \overline{z}\langle k\rangle.$$

The parallel composition $P \mid Q$ has a single transition $P \mid Q \rightarrow x \neq y \mid y = k \mid U$. Conversely, if we take $Q' \equiv \overline{z}\langle x \rangle$ then the input prefix $z\langle y \rangle$ cannot successfully synchronize and hence $P \mid Q'$ only has a transition $P \mid Q' \rightarrow V \mid Q'$. Side condition $(\star\star\star)$ of rule (PR-PAR) guarantees that every maximal enabled guard in P is preserved in $P \mid U$. For instance, consider again the processes P, Q, and Q' above. The parallel composition $P \mid Q \mid Q'$ should not execute $\mathtt{retract}$ $x \neq y$, since it is not a maximal enabled guard. Indeed, the only transition of $P \mid Q \mid Q'$ can be obtained by first applying rule (PR-COM) to $P \mid Q$ and, then, rule (PR-PAR) with $U = Q'$. Hence, the action performed is the synchronisation between $z\langle y \rangle$ and $\overline{z}\langle k \rangle$. In [8] we give a formal proof that side condition $(\star\star\star)$ indeed guarantees that the composition with an unconstrained process U does not activate any additional synchronisation that could enable a guard $x\langle y \rangle$ whose index is smaller than the index of a maximal enabled guard.

6   A Finance Case Study

In this section we apply the prioritised cc-pi calculus for specifying QoS negotiations. Consider a credit bank scenario in which a customer requests a mortgage from a bank. This scenario is inspired by a Finance case study presented in Chapter . The detailed interaction process is as follows:

Step I: The customer starts a credit request application and uploads her balances and a certain amount of money.

Step II: As soon as the data are uploaded, they are forwarded to a third party application which analyses them and returns to the bank a profile of the customer.

Step III: Depending of the produced profile, the bank can either reject the application or make an offer. If the customer receives an offer, she can decide whether to accept or reject it. In this last case, the bank may decide for an alternative offer.

The services involved in the above scenario are the *credit request service* invoked by the customer to obtain a mortgage from the bank, and a *financial service* provided by a third party application and that is in turn requested by the bank in order to obtain a customer profile as a result of analysing her data.

The parameters we focus on are: (i) the time taken by each service in order to complete its task (*response time*, for short) and the *cost* of each service. The negotiations are as follows:

1. The first negotiation is between a customer and the bank: the customer specifies a maximum response time while she does not specify a cost because we assume this service is free for him (she will possibly be charged if she obtaines the mortgage).

2. Upon reception of a credit request, the bank starts a second negotiation on the quality of service of a financial service. As the maximum response time for the financial service the bank requests the same response time that it has

to ensure to the customer for the credit service. Therefore, the bank will be able to respect the contract with the customer, provided a financial service will in turn respect its contract with the bank. As for the cost of the service, the bank initially offers a given price. If a financial service satisfying the cost and response time requirements are found, an agreement will be reached and, consequently, the negotiation (1) will be concluded successfully. By contrast, if there is no such financial service, the bank will offer a higher price for the same service. The negotiation will go on until either a suitable financial service is found or a maximum price threshold imposed by the bank is exceeded.

Specification in prioritised cc-pi. We assume that customers and banks negotiate over the channel n the response time, while banks and the third party application providing the financial service negotiate over m the cost of the financial service and the response time. The constant rt stands for the maximal response time accepted by the customer, while oc and max represent the initial and the maximum price offered by the bank for the financial service, where we assume oc $\leq$ max. Moreover, the third party application fixes a minimum cost rc and a minimum response time ot for the offered service. In Table 3, we specify in the prioritised cc-pi calculus a system describing the behaviour of customer, bank, and third party application. We model QoS requirements and guarantees in terms of CSPs (see §2). For the sake of simplicity, we initially consider crisp constraints by taking the c-semiring of classical CSPs: in this case, we recall that the product operation $\times$ is interpreted as a logical $\wedge$ and a composition of constraints is consistent if there exists a legal assignment of the variables. The customer starts by fixing a constraint about the maximum allowed response time, then she communicates on channel n with the bank by sending her QoS request and a channel name ca that will be used to receive the acknowledgement from the bank that the negotiation succeded. Afterwards, the bank sends a request to a third party application over channel m with the response time constraint required by the customer and with an initial maximal price oc. On the other side, the third party application fixes a minimum cost rc for the service and a minimum response time ot that can be guaranteed. If the constraints

Table 3. Credit request: cc-pi specification

$$\text{Customer}_{\text{rt}}(n) = (ctime, ca)\,(\texttt{tell } ctime \leq \text{rt}.\overline{n}\langle ctime, ca \rangle.ca\langle\rangle)$$

$$\text{Bank}_{\text{oc,max}}(n, m) = (btime, bcost, a)\, n\langle btime, a \rangle.$$
$$\text{Req}_{\text{oc,max}}(n, bcost, btime, m, a)$$

$$\text{Req}_{\text{c,max}}(n, bcost, btime, m, a) = \texttt{tell } bcost \leq \text{c}.(m\langle bcost, btime \rangle.\overline{a}\langle\rangle$$
$$+ \text{Neg}_{\text{c,max}}(n, bcost, btime, m, a))$$

$$\text{Neg}_{\text{c,max}}(n, bcost, btime, m, a)) = \texttt{retract } bcost \leq \text{c}.(\texttt{tell } (\text{max} < \text{c} + 50).\overline{fail}\langle\rangle$$
$$+ \text{Req}_{\text{c+50,max}}(n, bcost, btime, m, a))$$

$$\text{3rd\_PA}_{\text{rc,ot}}(m) = (vcost, vtime)\,(\texttt{tell } (vcost \geq \text{rc} \times vtime \geq \text{ot}).$$
$$\overline{m}\langle vcost, vtime \rangle$$

placed by the three entities are consistent, i.e. there is a legal assignment of the names, the bank and the third party application will be able to reach an agreement, and consequently the bank and the customer as well. Such agreements are modelled as successful synchronisations over the channels m and a, respectively. Conversely, if the synchronisation on m cannot take place, the bank retracts its offer and checks whether the maximum max would been exceeded by an higher offer (action tell max $<$ oc $+ 50$). If this is the case the process fails, otherwise the bank starts making a new offer.

As an example, consider the following system composed of a customer, a bank and two third party applications.

$$S \equiv (n, m)(\mathsf{Customer}_{50}(n) \mid \mathsf{Bank}_{150,300}(n, m) \mid \mathsf{3rd\_PA}_{200,40}(m)$$
$$\mid \mathsf{3rd\_PA}_{100,60}(m))$$

The customer requests a maximum response time of 50 time units and the bank starts by offering 150 Euros with a maximal offer of 300 Euros. On the other side, the two third party applications offer minimum response time of 40 and 60 for a minimum price of 200 and 100 Euros respectively. It is clear that the response time offered by the second third party application does not satisfy the request by the customer: in fact, the synchronisation with the bank is never possible as it would yield an inconsistent constraint ($50 \geq 60$). On the other side, the negotiation with the first third party application can take place after the bank has increased its offer once. Formally, the system reduces as follows. For the sake of brevity, we disregard the restricted names, the set of free names of each process definition, and the second provider as it does not take part to the interactions. Moreover, by $\rightarrow^*$ we refer to a sequence of reduction steps $\rightarrow$. First the customer places her own constraint and comunicates with the bank:

$$S \rightarrow^* ((ctime \leq 50) \mid (ctime = btime) \mid (ca = a)$$
$$\mid \ ca\langle\rangle \mid \mathsf{Req}_{150,300} \mid \mathsf{3rd\_PA}_{200,40}) \equiv S'.$$

Next, the bank makes its first offer of 150 Euros to the third party application that, in turn, places its time and cost constraints. The synchronisation on m cannot take place as it would yield an inconsistent constraint ($150 \geq 200$). Hence, the bank removes the initial offer (retract action) and checks whether the maximum would be exceeded by making a bigger offer. Since this limit is respected, the process $\mathsf{Req}_{150+50,300}$ is activated.

$$S' \rightarrow^* (ctime \leq 50) \mid (ctime = btime) \mid (ca = a) \mid (vcost \geq 200 \ \times \ vtime \geq 40)$$
$$\mid \ ca\langle\rangle \mid \mathsf{Req}_{150+50,300} \mid \overline{m}\langle vtime, vcost\rangle.$$

Now, an agreement can be reached with price 200 Euros and response time ranging between 40 and 50 time units.

Let us add to the above system S a third party application $\mathsf{3rd\_PA}_{150,40}$. In this case, once the constraints ($vcost \geq 150$) and ($vtime \geq 40$) have been placed, the minimal enabled guard is $m\langle btime, bcost\rangle$ rather than retract. Hence, the prioritised reduction semantics ensures that the bank will reach an agreement only with this additional provider rather than with $\mathsf{3rd\_PA}_{200E,40}$.

We can also slightly vary the negotiation scenario and allow each party to specify QoS requests and guarantees as soft constraints by changing the underlying named c-semiring while keeping the same process specification. For instance, consider the c-semiring of Fuzzy CSPs and assume the constraint $ctime \leq 50$ of the customer is replaced by the following fuzzy constraint (cost is a meta-variable over the set of non-negative integers):

$$
x \mapsto \text{cost} = \begin{cases} 1 & \text{if } 0 \leq \text{cost} \leq 25 \\ .5 & \text{if } 26 \leq \text{cost} \leq 50 \\ .1 & \text{if } 51 \leq \text{cost} \leq 60 \\ 0 & \text{if } 61 \leq \text{cost} \end{cases}
$$

while the other constraints are translated to trivial fuzzy constraints (i.e. taking only values 0 or 1). Of course, this change in the underlying setting leads to different solutions as, for instance, a negotiation with the third party application $3rd\_PA_{100E,60}$ would now be successful in absence of more convenient agreements.

7   Conclusions and Related Work

In this work we have illustrated the cc-pi calculus, a constraint-based model of QoS negotiations in service composition. Cc-pi features synchronous communications along with explicit primitives for handling constraints. Moreover, cc-pi is parametric with respect to the choice of the underlying named c-semiring structure. We have shown the applicability of the cc-pi by employing the calculus for specification and enforcement of Telco policies. We have also outlined a prioritised variant of the calculus in which the alternatives in a choice rather than being selected non-deterministically are assigned a static priority. We have argued that this prioritised version is more suited to model the protocol followed by a negotiating partner who usually has a given order of preference by employing. To substantiate this claim, we have applied the prioritised cc-pi to model a scenario involving three parties that negotiate their QoS requirements/guarantees about a service meant for financial purposes.

Bistarelli and Santini [4] have presented a constraint-based model for Service Level Agreements as an extension of *soft* concurrent constraint programming. The proposed model includes operations quite different from those of the cc-pi calculus, such as those for relaxing the constraints involving a given set of variables and then adding a new constraint, and for checking if a constraint is not entailed by the store. Coppo and Dezani-Ciancaglini [11] have proposed a calculus of contracts by combining the basic primitives of the cc-pi calculus with the notion of sessions and session types to design communication protocols which assure safe and reliable communication sequences. Bacciu *et al.* [1] have developed a formalism for specifying the service guarantees and requester requirements on QoS and the negotiation mechanism. Unlike our model, their approach relies on fuzzy sets rather than on c-semirings. Mukhija *et al.* [15] have proposed a QoS-aware approach to dynamic service composition by providing a specification language for QoS values and a broker that allows for service provider selection based both on functional and QoS parameters. However, the key contribution of [15] is the algorithm that allows choosing the offer that best matches a given request while we are more interested in specifying the dynamics of the system during the negotiation. Furthermore, none of the above languages allows modelling complex negotiations, i.e. interactions in which QoS requirements may be weakened if an agreement cannot be reached.

We know of no other attempt to assign priorities to the alternatives of a choice operator in a constrained-based paradigm. However, a number of approaches have been proposed for taking into account different aspects of priority using process calculi (see e.g. [9,19], and [10] for a survey on this topic). Most of the contributions within this branch of research assign priority values to actions and can be classified according to two main criteria: dynamic/static priority (referring to the fact that action priorities may or may not change during computations) and global/local pre-emption (meaning that an action with higher priority may or may not pre-empt another action out its scope, hence modelling centralised or distributed system behaviours). We adapt to our constraint-based model the approach in [9] in which a prioritised choice is introduced rather than assigning priorities to actions. Moreover, we differ from models like that in [19] in which the only possible synchronisations are those between processes with the same priorities as this mechanism does not fit the negotiation scenarios we need to model.

Within the SENSORIA project, several process calculi have been designed for modelling interactions in SOC scenarios (see Chapter 2-1). Among those calculi, COWS proposes a communication mechanism featuring dynamic priorities and local pre-emption. Unlike our prioritised calculus, in COWS processes running in parallel are assigned different priorities as a consequence of the fact that receive actions have higher priorities if they have more defined patterns. In fact, the goal of this mechanism is to ensure that service instances take precedence over service definitions, thus preventing creation of wrong new instances.

References

1. Bacciu, A., Botta, A., Melgratti, H.: A fuzzy approach for negotiating quality of services. In: Montanari, U., Sannella, D., Bruni, R. (eds.) TGC 2006. LNCS, vol. 4661, pp. 200–217. Springer, Heidelberg (2007)
2. Bistarelli, S., Gadducci, F.: Enhancing constraints manipulation in semiring-based formalisms. In: ECAI, pp. 63–67. IOS Press, Amsterdam (2006)
3. Bistarelli, S., Montanari, U., Rossi, F.: Semiring-based constraint satisfaction and optimization. Journal of the ACM 44(2), 201–236 (1997)
4. Bistarelli, S., Santini, F.: A nonmonotonic soft concurrent constraint language for sla negotiation. Electr. Notes Theor. Comput. Sci. 236, 147–162 (2009)
5. Buscemi, M.G., Ferrari, L., Moiso, C., Montanari, U.: Constraint-based policy negotiation and enforcement for telco services. In: Proc. TASE, pp. 463–472. IEEE Computer Society, Los Alamitos (2007)
6. Buscemi, M.G., Montanari, U.: Cc-pi: A constraint-based language for specifying service level agreements. In: De Nicola, R. (ed.) ESOP 2007. LNCS, vol. 4421, pp. 18–32. Springer, Heidelberg (2007)

7. Buscemi, M.G., Montanari, U.: Open bisimulation for the concurrent constraint pi-calculus. In: Gairing, M. (ed.) ESOP 2008. LNCS, vol. 4960, pp. 254–268. Springer, Heidelberg (2008)

8. Buscemi, M.G., Montanari, U.: A contraint-based language for Qos negotiation in service composition. Technical report, Dipartimento di Informatica, University of Pisa (2009)

9. Camilleri, J., Winskel, G.: CCS with priority choice. Inform. and Comput. 116, 26–37 (1995)

10. Cleaveland, R., Luttgen, G., Natarajan, V.: Priority in process algebras. Technical report, NASA/CR-1999-208979 ICASE-99-3 (1999)

11. Coppo, M., Dezani-Ciancaglini, M.: Structured communications with concurrent constraints. In: Kaklamanis, C., Nielson, F. (eds.) TGC 2008. LNCS, vol. 5474, pp. 104–125. Springer, Heidelberg (2009)

12. Milner, R., Parrow, J., Walker, D.: A calculus of mobile processes, I and II. Inform. and Comput. 100(1), 1–40, 41–77 (1992)

13. Montanari, U., Pistore, M.: Structured coalgebras and minimal hd-automata for the pi-calculus. Theoret. Comput. Sci 340(3), 539–576 (2005)

14. Montanari, U., Rossi, F.: Constraint relaxation may be perfect. Artif. Intell. 48(2), 143–170 (1991)

15. Mukhija, A., Dingwall-Smith, A., Rosenblum, D.S.: QoS-aware service composition in dino. In: Proc. ECOWS, pp. 3–12. IEEE Comp. Society, Los Alamitos (2007)

16. Rudeanu, S., Vaida, D.: Semirings in operations research and computer science. Fundam. Inf. 61(1), 61–85 (2004)

17. Saraswat, V., Lincoln, P.: Higher-order linear concurrent constraint programming, Technical Report, Xerox Parc (1992)

18. Saraswat, V., Rinard, M.: Concurrent constraint programming. In: Proc. POPL. ACM Press, New York (1990)

19. Versari, C.: A core calculus for a comparative analysis of bio-inspired calculi. In: De Nicola, R. (ed.) ESOP 2007. LNCS, vol. 4421, pp. 411–425. Springer, Heidelberg (2007)

20. Wischik, L., Gardner, P.: Explicit fusions. Theoret. Comput. Sci. 340(3), 606–630 (2005)

Advanced Mechanisms for Service Composition, Query and Discovery*

Michele Boreale[1] and Mario Bravetti[2]

[1] Dip. di Sistemi e Informatica, Università di Firenze, Italy
boreale@dsi.unifi.it
[2] Dip. Scienze dell'Informazione, Università di Bologna, Italy
bravetti@cs.unibo.it

Abstract. One of the ultimate goals of Service Oriented Computing (SOC) is to provide support for the automatic on-demand discovery of basic functionalities that, once combined, correctly compute a user defined task. To this aim, it is necessary for services to come equipped with a computer-understandable interface that allow applications to match the provided functionalities with the user needs. In this context, a prominent issue concerns the compliance between the operations invoked by the client – the client protocol – and the operations executed by the service – the service protocol. Process calculi, the theoretical tools investigated in the Work Package 2 of SENSORIA, can contribute to the solution of this problem. The idea we present in this chapter is to describe the externally observable message-passing behaviour of services as process calculi expressions; following recently adopted terminology, we call this description the *service contract*. We show how, in certain cases, service contracts can be automatically extracted out of service behaviour, and how they can be used to formally check the compliance among the communication protocols of interacting services.

1 Introduction

Service Oriented Computing (SOC) is based on services, intended as autonomous and heterogeneous components that can be published and discovered via standard interface languages and publish/discovery protocols. Web Services is the most prominent service oriented technology: Web Services publish their interface expressed in the Web Service Description Language (WSDL); they are discovered through the UDDI protocol, and they are invoked using SOAP. Even if one of the declared goal of Web Services is to support the automatic discovery of services, this is not yet practically achieved. In SENSORIA, we have addressed this problem by considering how to: (a) actually extracting a manageable description of the service interface (contract) out of a reasonably detailed service specification, and (b) guaranteeing that the services retrieved from a repository behave correctly according to the needs of the user and of the other retrieved

---

* This work has been partially sponsored by the project SENSORIA, IST-2005-016004.

M. Wirsing and M. Hölzl (Eds.): SENSORIA Project, LNCS 6582, pp. 282–301, 2011.

services. In other terms, the retrieved services and the client invocation protocol should be compliant/complementary. For instance, it should be possible to check whether the overall composition of the client protocol with the invoked services is stuck-free.

In order to be able to perform this kind of checks, it is necessary for the services to expose in their interface also the description of their expected behaviour. In general, a service interface description language can expose both *static* and *dynamic* information. The former deals with the signature (name and type of the parameters) of the invocable operations; the latter deals with the correct order of invocation of the provided operations in order to correctly complete a session of interaction. The WSDL, which is the standard Web Services interface description language is basically concerned just with static information.

The aim of this paper is to report about process-algebraic techniques that could be effectively exploited in order to describe also the dynamic part of service interfaces. The choice of process-algebraic techniques for service interface descriptions is a natural one, as demonstrated also by other work by Fournet et al. [11] and Carpineti et al. [6]. The former introduces the notion of *contract* as "interface that specify the externally visible message passing behaviour" of processes, the latter refines this notion of contract considering a more specific client-service scenario.

Following the terminology adopted in this book, we call *service contract* the dynamic part of the service interface. More precisely, the service contract should describe the sequence of input/output operations that the service intends to execute within a session of interaction with other services. Let us consider two major aspects that must be addressed before service contracts become an effective technique for service publication, discovery and composition.

1. **Contract as abstraction.** As reported above, a contract is informally defined as the externally visible message passing behaviour of a service. We formally define, using a process algebraic approach, how to extract the externally observable behaviour from the description of the actual behaviour of a service. The technique that we report is based on the notion of *abstraction context*, which indicates how to statically associate to service events the corresponding observation tags. The achieved abstraction should be enough informative to enable proofs of certain properties (e.g. safety ones) of the actual service.

2. **Contract-based service composition.** One of the most important aspect that the service contract technology should be able to address is *correctness of composition*: given any set of services, it should be possible to prove that their composition is correct knowing only their contracts, i.e. in the absence of complete knowledge about (the internal details of) the services behaviour. We formalize the notion of correct composition, and show which kind of information should be exposed by a service in the corresponding contract, in order to enable proofs of service composition correctness. The notion of correctness that we consider requires that all computations in a service composition may be extended in order to reach a final state in which all services

have successfully completed their activities. In other terms, it is not possible for a service to wait indefinitely for another service to send or receive a message.

Even if the two above contract-based techniques are strictly related, they are concerned with two different levels of abstractions of the service behaviour. In the first case, in order to extract an appropriate contract from a service, it is necessary to start from a detailed description of its behaviour. In the second case, it is possible to abstract away from the values actually exchanged between the service(s) and the client; indeed, only the order of invocations is relevant. These two different levels of abstractions justify the use of two different calculi for service behaviour description. In order to investigate the *contract as abstraction* concept, we start from a Pi-calculus description, while in order to investigate *contract-based service composition*, we abstract away from value passing and we consider a CCS-like process calculus.

This chapter is structured as follows. Sections 2 and 3 discuss, respectively, the two basic aspects: *contract as abstraction* and *contract-based service composition*. Section 4 contain some concluding remarks. Details of the techniques reported in this chapter can be found in [1] as far as Section 2 is concerned, and in [3,5,4] as far as Section 3 is concerned.

2   Contract as Abstraction

According to the Service Oriented Computing paradigm, services can be seen as processes that provide a set of functionalities. A client can invoke a given functionality by sending an appropriate message to the corresponding operation/channel on the service side, and then waiting for a reply message, containing the computed results. More sophisticated schemes that involve complex conversations between the invoker and the service, and between the service and third parties, are also possible. When considering a system composed by several parties, be them clients or services, one is often interested in describing a *choreography*. This is the overall behaviour of the system in terms of, say, invoked service operations together with their argument types, allowable orderings among such operations, and so on. In any case, since services interact via message-passing, they can be seen as processes of some "first-order" calculus, such as Pi- or Join-calculus. Approximating a first-order (Pi, Join) process by a simpler propositional (CCS, BPP, Petri nets,...) model, not explicitly featuring message-passing, can be understood as the operation of extracting a *contract* out of a service. We consider methods to perform such approximations statically. Specifically, we describe a type system to associate Pi-calculus processes with restriction-free CCS types; such types can be thought of as contracts. A process is shown to be in simulation relation with its types, hence safety properties that hold of the types also hold of the process.

2.1   The Asynchronous Pi-Calculus

Processes. Let $\mathcal{N}$, ranged over by $a, b, c, \ldots, x, y, \ldots$, be a countable set of *names* and *Tag*, ranged over by $\alpha, \beta, \ldots$, be a set of *tags* disjoint from $\mathcal{N}$; we assume *Tag* also contains a distinct "unit" tag (). The set $\mathcal{P}$ of processes $P, Q, \ldots$ is defined as the set of terms generated by the following grammar:

$$P, Q ::= \overline{a}\langle b\rangle \mid \sum_{i \in I} a_i(b).P_i \mid \sum_{i \in I} \tau.P_i \mid \text{if } a = b \text{ then } P \text{ else } P \mid !a(b).P \mid (\nu a : \alpha)P \mid P|P.$$

This language is a variation on the asynchronous Pi-calculus. Please note that the restriction operator $(\nu a : \alpha)P$ creates a new restricted name a with initial scope P *and* assigns it a tag α.

In an output action $\overline{a}\langle b\rangle$, name a is the *subject* and b the *object* of the action. Similarly, in a replicated input prefix $!a(b).P$ and in $\sum_{i \in I} a_i(b).P_i$, the names a and a_i for $i \in I$ are said to occur in *input subject position*. Binders and alpha-equivalence arise as expected and processes are identified up to alpha-equivalence of names. Substitution of a with b in an expression e is denoted by $e[b/a]$. In what follows, **0** stands for the empty summation $\sum_{i \in \emptyset} \tau.P_i$. We shall sometimes omit the object parts of input and output actions, when not relevant for the discussion; e.g. $\overline{a}$ stands for an output action with subject a and an object left unspecified. Similarly, we shall omit tag annotations, writing e.g. $(\nu a)P$ instead of $(\nu a : \alpha)P$, when the identity of the tag is not relevant.

Operational semantics. The (early-style) semantics of processes is given by the labelled transition system in Table 1. We let $\ell, \ell', \ldots$ represent generic elements of $\mathcal{N} \cup \textit{Tag}$. A transitions label μ can be a free output, $\overline{a}\langle b\rangle$, a bound output, $(\nu b : \alpha)\overline{a}\langle b\rangle$, an input, $a(b)$, or a silent move, $\tau\langle \ell, \ell'\rangle$. We assume a distinct tag ι for decorating *internal* transitions (arising from conditional and internal chioce; see Table 1) and often abbreviate $\tau\langle \iota, \iota\rangle$ simply as τ. In the following we indicate by $n(\mu)$ the set of all names in μ and by $fn(\mu)$, the set of free names of μ, defined as expected. The rules are standard, except for the extra book-keeping required by tag annotation of bound output and internal actions. In particular, in (RES-TAU) bound names involved in a synchronization are hidden from the observer and replaced by the corresponding tags. Note that if we erase the tag annotation from labels we get exactly the usual labelled semantics of asynchronous Pi-calculus.

2.2 Γ-Abstractions of Processes

A *context* Γ is a finite partial function from names to tags, written $\Gamma = \{a_1 : \alpha_1, \cdots, a_n : \alpha_n\}$, with distinct a_i. In what follows $\Gamma \vdash a : \alpha$ means that $a : \alpha \in \Gamma$. A *tag sorting system* $\mathcal{E}$ is a finite subset of $\{\alpha[\beta] \mid \alpha, \beta \text{ are tags and } \alpha \neq ()\}$. Informally, $\alpha[\beta] \in \mathcal{E}$ means that subject names associated with tag α can carry object names associated with tag β. In what follows, if $\alpha[\beta_1], \cdots, \alpha[\beta_n]$ are the only elements of $\mathcal{E}$ with subject α, we write $\alpha[\beta_1, \cdots, \beta_n] \subset \mathcal{E}$.

Table 1. Operational semantics of Pi-calculus processes. Symmetric rules not shown.

$$(\text{OUT}) \ \ \overline{a}\langle b \rangle \ \xrightarrow{\overline{a}\langle b \rangle} \ 0$$

$$(\text{G-SUM}) \ \textstyle\sum_{i \in I} a_i(b_i).P_i \ \xrightarrow{a_j(c)} \ P_j[c\!/b_j], \ j \in I \qquad (\text{I-SUM}) \ \textstyle\sum_{i \in I} \tau.P_i \ \xrightarrow{\tau} \ P_j, \ j \in I$$

$$(\text{REP}) \ !a(c).P \ \xrightarrow{a(b)} \ P[b\!/c] \,|\, !a(c).P \qquad (\text{COM}) \ \frac{P \ \xrightarrow{\overline{a}\langle b \rangle} \ P' \quad Q \ \xrightarrow{a(b)} \ Q'}{P \,|\, Q \ \xrightarrow{\tau\langle a,b \rangle} \ P' \,|\, Q'}$$

$$(\text{CLOSE}) \ \frac{P \ \xrightarrow{(\nu b:\beta)\overline{a}\langle b \rangle} \ P' \quad Q \ \xrightarrow{a(b)} \ Q'}{P \,|\, Q \ \xrightarrow{\tau\langle a,\beta \rangle} \ (\nu b:\beta)(P' \,|\, Q')} \qquad (\text{OPEN}) \ \frac{P \ \xrightarrow{\overline{b}\langle a \rangle} \ P' \quad b \neq a}{(\nu a:\alpha)P \ \xrightarrow{(\nu a:\alpha)\overline{b}\langle a \rangle} \ P'}$$

$$(\text{IF-F}) \ \text{if } a = b \text{ then } P \text{ else } Q \ \xrightarrow{\tau} \ Q, \ a \neq b \qquad (\text{IF-T}) \ \text{if } a = a \text{ then } P \text{ else } Q \ \xrightarrow{\tau} \ P$$

$$(\text{PAR}) \ \frac{P \ \xrightarrow{\mu} \ P' \quad \text{bn}(\mu) \cap \text{fn}(Q) = \emptyset}{P \,|\, Q \ \xrightarrow{\mu} \ P' \,|\, Q} \qquad (\text{RES}) \ \frac{P \ \xrightarrow{\mu} \ P' \quad a \notin \text{n}(\mu)}{(\nu a:\alpha)P \ \xrightarrow{\mu} \ (\nu a:\alpha)P'}$$

$$(\text{RES-TAU}) \ \frac{P \ \xrightarrow{\tau\langle \ell_1,\ell_2 \rangle} \ P' \quad a \in \{\ell_1, \ell_2\} \quad \ell = \ell_1[\alpha\!/a] \quad \ell' = \ell_2[\alpha\!/a]}{(\nu a:\alpha)P \ \xrightarrow{\tau\langle \ell,\ell' \rangle} \ (\nu a:\alpha)P'}$$

A triple $(P, \Gamma, \mathcal{E})$, written $P_{\Gamma;\mathcal{E}}$, is called Γ-*abstraction* of P under $\mathcal{E}$. In what follows, we shall consider a fixed sorting system $\mathcal{E}$, and keep $\mathcal{E}$ implicit by writing P_Γ instead of $P_{\Gamma;\mathcal{E}}$. Next, we define a labeled transition system with process abstractions as states and transition labels λ, which can be output, $\overline{a}\langle \beta \rangle$, input, $\alpha\langle \beta \rangle$ or annotated silent action, $\tau\langle \alpha, \beta \rangle$. The set of labels generated by this grammar is denoted by Λ. The labeled transition system is defined by the rules below. Here, μ_Γ denotes the result of substituting each $a \in \text{fn}(\mu) \cap \text{dom}(\Gamma)$ by $\Gamma(a)$ in μ. Informally, P_Γ represents the abstract behavior of P, once each concrete action μ has been mapped to an abstract action λ. Note that in both rule (A-OUT_N) and rule (A-INP_N) the context Γ grows with a new association $b : \beta$. In rule (A-INP_N), a tag for b is chosen among the possible tags specified in $\mathcal{E}$. Note that no type checking is performed by these rules, in particular (A-OUT_N) does not look up $\mathcal{E}$ to check that β can be carried by α.

$$(\text{A-OLD}) \ \frac{P \ \xrightarrow{\mu} \ P' \quad \mu ::= \tau\langle \ell,\ell' \rangle | a(b) | \overline{a}\langle b \rangle \quad \text{n}(\mu) \subseteq \text{dom}(\Gamma) \quad \lambda = \mu_\Gamma}{P_\Gamma \ \xrightarrow{\lambda} \ P'_\Gamma}$$

$$(\text{A-OUT}_\text{N}) \ \frac{P \ \xrightarrow{(\nu b:\beta)\overline{a}\langle b \rangle} \ P' \quad \Gamma \vdash a : \alpha}{P_\Gamma \ \xrightarrow{\overline{\alpha}\langle \beta \rangle} \ P'_{\Gamma,b:\beta}} \qquad (\text{A-INP}_\text{N}) \ \frac{P \ \xrightarrow{a(b)} \ P' \quad \Gamma \vdash a : \alpha \quad \alpha[\beta] \in \mathcal{E} \quad b \notin \text{dom}(\Gamma)}{P_\Gamma \ \xrightarrow{\alpha\langle \beta \rangle} \ P'_{\Gamma,b:\beta}}$$

Simulation, bisimulation and modal logic. Given a labelled transition system T with labels in Λ, *strong bisimulation* $\sim$ and simulation $\precsim$ over states of T are defined as expected. The *closed* versions of simulation and bisimulation, written $\precsim^c$ and $\sim^c$, respectively, are defined in a similar manner, but limited to silent transitions, i.e. transitions carrying labels of the kind $\tau\langle \alpha, \beta \rangle$. In the rest of the paper, we will sometimes make use of simple action-based modal logic formulae

$\phi, \psi, \ldots$ taken from modal mu-calculus [19] to formulate concisely properties of types or processes. In particular, a state s of T satisfies $\langle A \rangle \phi$, written $s \vDash \langle A \rangle \phi$, if there is a transition $s \xrightarrow{\lambda} s'$ with $\lambda \in A$ and $s' \vDash \phi$. The interpretation of modality $\langle\!\langle A \rangle\!\rangle \phi$ is similar, but the phrase "a transition $s \xrightarrow{\lambda} s'$ with $\lambda \in A$" is changed into "a sequence of transitions $s \xrightarrow{\sigma} s'$ with $\sigma \in A^*$".

2.3 ccs⁻ Types

In the type system we propose, types are essentially CCS expressions whose behavior over-approximate the (abstract) process behavior.

The set $\mathcal{T}_{\mathrm{CCS}}$ of types, ranged over by $\mathsf{T}, \mathsf{S}, \ldots$, is defined by the following syntax:

$$\mathsf{T} ::= \overline{\alpha}\langle \beta \rangle \ \Big| \ \sum_{i \in I} \alpha_i \langle \beta_i \rangle.\mathsf{T}_i \ \Big| \ \sum_{i \in I} \tau.\mathsf{T}_i \ \Big| \ !\alpha\langle \beta \rangle.\mathsf{T} \ \Big| \ \mathsf{T}|\mathsf{T}$$

where $\alpha, \alpha_i \neq ()$. The empty summation $\sum_{i \in \emptyset} \tau.\mathsf{T}_i$ will be often denoted by nil, and $\mathsf{T}_1 \mid \cdots \mid \mathsf{T}_n$ will be often written as $\prod_{i \in \{1, \cdots, n\}} \mathsf{T}_i$. As usual, we shall sometimes omit the object part of actions when not relevant for the discussion or equal to the unit tag (), writing e.g. $\overline{\alpha}$ and $\tau\langle \alpha \rangle$ instead of $\overline{\alpha}\langle \beta \rangle$ and $\tau\langle \alpha, \beta \rangle$.Types are essentially asynchronous, restriction-free CCS processes over the alphabet of actions Λ. The standard operational semantics of CCS, giving rise to a labelled transition system with labels in Λ, is assumed (see [1]).

The typing rules. We let $\mathcal{E}$ be a fixed tag sorting system and Γ a context. Judgements of the type system are of the form $\Gamma \vdash_{\mathcal{E}} P : \mathsf{T}$. The rules of the type system are presented in Table 2. Notice that rule (T-INP) has been introduced with the sake of improving the readability of the system; indeed expanding (T-SUM) would result in a much longer and more complex rule.

A brief explanation of some typing rules follows. In rule (T-OUT), the output process $\overline{a}\langle b \rangle$ gives rise to the action $\overline{a}\langle b \rangle_{\Gamma} = \overline{\alpha}\langle \beta \rangle$, provided this action is expected by the tag sorting system $\mathcal{E}$. The type T of an input process depends on $\mathcal{E}$: in (T-INP) all tags which can be carried by α, the tag associated with the action's subject, contribute to the definition of the summation in T as expected. In the case of (T-REP), summation is replaced by a parallel composition of replicated types, which is behaviorally – up to strong bisimulation – the same as a replicated summation. The subtyping relation $\lesssim$ is the simulation preorder over $\mathcal{E}$, (T-SUB). The rest of the rules should be self-explanatory.

Results. The subject reduction theorem below establishes an operational correspondence between the abstract behavior P_{Γ} and any type T that can be assigned to P under Γ.

Theorem 1 (subject reduction). $\Gamma \vdash_{\mathcal{E}} P : \mathsf{T}$ *and* $P_{\Gamma} \xrightarrow{\lambda} P'_{\Gamma'}$ *imply that there is* T' *such that* $\mathsf{T} \xrightarrow{\lambda} \mathsf{T}'$ *and* $\Gamma' \vdash_{\mathcal{E}} P' : \mathsf{T}'$.

As a corollary, we obtain that T simulates P_{Γ}: thanks to Theorem 1, it is easy to see that the relation $\mathcal{R} = \{(P_{\Gamma}, \mathsf{T}) \mid \Gamma \vdash_{\mathcal{E}} P : \mathsf{T}\}$ is a simulation relation.

Table 2. Typing rules for ccs⁻ types

$$(\text{T-INP}) \quad \frac{\Gamma \vdash a : \alpha \quad \alpha[\beta_1, \cdots, \beta_n] \in \mathcal{E} \quad \forall i \in \{1, \cdots, n\} : \Gamma, b : \beta_i \vdash_{\mathcal{E}} P : \mathsf{T}_i}{\Gamma \vdash_{\mathcal{E}} a(b).P : \sum_{i \in \{1, \cdots, n\}} \alpha \langle \beta_i \rangle . \mathsf{T}_i}$$

$$(\text{T-REP}) \quad \frac{\Gamma \vdash a : \alpha \quad \alpha[\beta_1, \cdots, \beta_n] \in \mathcal{E} \quad \forall i \in \{1, \cdots, n\} : \Gamma, b : \beta_i \vdash_{\mathcal{E}} P : \mathsf{T}_i}{\Gamma \vdash_{\mathcal{E}} !a(b).P : \prod_{i \in \{1, \cdots, n\}} !\alpha \langle \beta_i \rangle . \mathsf{T}_i}$$

$$(\text{T-GSUM}) \quad \frac{|I| \neq 1 \quad \forall i \in I : \Gamma \vdash_{\mathcal{E}} a_i(b_i).P_i : \sum_{j \in J_i} \alpha_i \langle \beta_j \rangle . \mathsf{T}_{ij}}{\Gamma \vdash_{\mathcal{E}} \sum_{i \in I} a_i(b_i).P_i : \sum_{i \in I, j \in J_i} \alpha_i \langle \beta_j \rangle \mathsf{T}_{ij}}$$

$$(\text{T-OUT}) \quad \frac{\Gamma \vdash a : \alpha \quad \alpha[\beta] \in \mathcal{E} \quad \Gamma \vdash b : \beta}{\Gamma \vdash_{\mathcal{E}} \overline{a}\langle b \rangle : \overline{\alpha}\langle \beta \rangle} \qquad (\text{T-ISUM}) \quad \frac{\forall i \in I : \Gamma \vdash_{\mathcal{E}} P_i : \mathsf{T}_i}{\Gamma \vdash_{\mathcal{E}} \sum_{i \in I} \tau.P_i : \sum_{i \in I} \tau.\mathsf{T}_i}$$

$$(\text{T-PAR}) \quad \frac{\Gamma \vdash_{\mathcal{E}} P : \mathsf{T} \quad \Gamma \vdash_{\mathcal{E}} Q : \mathsf{S}}{\Gamma \vdash_{\mathcal{E}} P|Q : \mathsf{T}|\mathsf{S}} \qquad (\text{T-RES}) \quad \frac{\Gamma, a : \alpha \vdash_{\mathcal{E}} P : \mathsf{T}}{\Gamma \vdash_{\mathcal{E}} (\nu a : \alpha)P : \mathsf{T}}$$

$$(\text{T-IF}) \quad \frac{\Gamma \vdash_{\mathcal{E}} P : \mathsf{T} \quad \Gamma \vdash_{\mathcal{E}} Q : \mathsf{S}}{\Gamma \vdash_{\mathcal{E}} \text{if } a = b \text{ then } P \text{ else } Q : \tau.\mathsf{T} + \tau.\mathsf{S}} \qquad (\text{T-SUB}) \quad \frac{\Gamma \vdash_{\mathcal{E}} P : \mathsf{T} \quad \mathsf{T} \lesssim \mathsf{S}}{\Gamma \vdash_{\mathcal{E}} P : \mathsf{S}}$$

Corollary 1. *Suppose $\Gamma \vdash_{\mathcal{E}} P : \mathsf{T}$. Then $P_\Gamma \lesssim \mathsf{T}$.*

A consequence of the previous result is that safety properties satisfied by a type are also satisfied by the processes that inhabit that type – or, more precisely, by their Γ-abstract versions. Consider the small logic defined in Section 2.2: let us say that $\phi \in \mathcal{L}$ is a *safety* formula if every occurrence of $\langle A \rangle$ and $\langle\!\langle A \rangle\!\rangle$ in ϕ is underneath an odd number of negations. The following proposition, follows from Corollary 1 and first principles.

Proposition 1. *Suppose $\Gamma \vdash_{\mathcal{E}} P : \mathsf{T}$ and ϕ is a safety formula, with $\mathsf{T} \vDash \phi$. Then $P_\Gamma \vDash \phi$.*

As a final remark on the type system, consider taking out rule (T-SUB): the new system can be viewed as a (partial) function that for any P computes a minimal type for P, that is, a subtype of all types of P (just read the rules bottom-up).

2.4 An Example

A simple printing system is considered, where users are required to authenticate themselves before being allowed to print. For simplicity, only two levels of privileges are considered for users, authorized and non-authorized. Correspondingly, two sets of credentials are given: $\{c_i \mid i \in I\}$ (also written $\tilde{c}_i$) for authorized users and $\{c_j \mid j \in J\}$ (also written $\tilde{c}_j$) for non-authorized users, with $\tilde{c}_i \cap \tilde{c}_j = \emptyset$. Process A is an authentication server that receives from any client a credential

c, a private return channel r and an error channel e, and then sends both r and e to a credential-handling process T. If the client is not authorized, T will raise an error on channel e, otherwise T establishes a private connection between the client and the printer by creating a new communication link k and passing it to the client. Process C describes the cumulative behavior of all clients: C tries nondeterministically to authenticate using a credential c_l, $l \in I \cup J$, and then waits for a link to the printer on the private channel r, or for an error, on the private channel e. After printing or receiving an error, C's execution restarts. One expects that every printing request accompanied by authorized credentials will be satisfied, and that every print is preceded by an authentication request.

$$Sys \triangleq (\nu a : aut, \ \tilde{c}_i : ok, \ \tilde{c}_j : nok, \ M : (), \ print : pr)(T \mid C \mid A \mid !print(d))$$

$$T \triangleq \textstyle\prod_{i \in I} !c_i(x, e).(\nu k : key)(\overline{x}\langle k \rangle \mid k(d).\overline{print}\langle d \rangle) \mid \prod_{j \in J} !c_j(x, e).\overline{e}$$

$$A \triangleq !a(c, r, e).\overline{c}\langle r, e \rangle$$

$$C \triangleq (\nu i : iter)\Big(\overline{i} \mid !i.(\nu r : ret, \ e : err)\big(\textstyle\sum_{l \in I \cup J} \tau.\overline{a}\langle c_l, r, e \rangle \mid r(z).((\overline{z}\langle M \rangle \mid \overline{i}) + e.\overline{i})\big)\Big)$$

Below, we analyze this system using CCS types. To ease the notation, we shall omit the unit tag () involved in inputs and outputs and write e.g. $\overline{\alpha}$ instead of $\alpha[()]$. We shall consider a calculus enriched with polyadic communication and values: these extensions are easy to accommodate. Consider the tag sorting system

$$\mathcal{E} = \{\, aut[ok, ret, err], \ aut[nok, ret, err], \ ok[ret, err],$$

$$nok[ret, err], \ ret[key], \ pr[()], \ err[], \ key[()], \ iter[]\,\} \ .$$

It is easy to prove that $\emptyset \vdash_{\mathcal{E}} Sys : \mathsf{T}_T \mid \mathsf{T}_A \mid \mathsf{T}_C \mid !pr = \mathsf{T}$, where

$$\mathsf{T}_T \triangleq !ok\langle ret, err \rangle.(\overline{ret}\langle key \rangle \mid key.\overline{pr}) \mid !nok\langle ret, err \rangle.\overline{err}$$

$$\mathsf{T}_A \triangleq !aut\langle ok, ret, err \rangle.\overline{ok}\langle ret, err \rangle \mid !aut\langle nok, ret, err \rangle.\overline{nok}\langle ret, err \rangle$$

$$\mathsf{T}_C \triangleq \overline{iter} \mid !iter.((\tau.\overline{aut}\langle ok, ret, err \rangle + \tau.\overline{aut}\langle nok, ret, err \rangle) \mid (ret\langle key \rangle.(\overline{key} \mid \overline{iter}) + err.\overline{iter})).$$

Furthermore, it holds that

$$\mathsf{T} \vDash \phi \triangleq \neg \langle\!\langle \Lambda - \{nok\langle ret, err \rangle, aut\langle nok, ret, err \rangle, \tau\langle aut, nok, ret, err \rangle\}\rangle\!\rangle \ \langle\overline{err}\rangle$$

$$\mathsf{T} \vDash \psi \triangleq \neg \langle\!\langle \Lambda - \{ok\langle ret, err \rangle, aut\langle ok, ret, err \rangle, \tau\langle aut, ok, ret, err \rangle\}\rangle\!\rangle \ \langle\overline{pr}\rangle$$

that is, *error* only arises from an authentication request containing non authorized credentials, and every print pr action is preceded by a successful authentication request. Both formulas express safety properties, hence Proposition 1 ensures that are both satisfied by the abstract process $Sys_\emptyset$.

2.5   Extensions

We discuss here the other type systems presented in [1]. We just outline the most relevant aspects and refer the interested reader to [1] for full details. Choreographies are generated by specific compositions of several actors, be them clients or services. In [1] the type system reported here is adapted to choreographies, also called global or closed systems, to contrast them with the CCS⁻ types applicable to *open processes*. In the closed case, types are BPP processes. Sufficient conditions are given under which a minimal BPP type can be computed that is bisimilar to a given process. For closed systems, it is possible to get rid of synchronization in types, obtaining a more direct and precise approximation of the behavior of P_Γ. Roughly, this is achieved by first associating each input prefix $a(b).P$ in the considered process with a labelled rewrite rule $\alpha[\beta] \xrightarrow{\alpha[\beta]} \alpha_1[\beta_1], ..., \alpha_n[\beta_n]$. Here, $\alpha[\beta]$ is the tag-representation of $a(b)$, according to Γ. The right-hand side of the rule is the multiset of observable outputs that can be triggered by a reduction involving the considered input prefix, according to Γ. An output action $\overline{a}\langle b\rangle$ of P is associated with a symbol $\alpha[\beta]$, that can be rewritten according to the rules. Types we obtain in this way are precisely Basic Parallel Processes (BPP, [7]). Results similar to the open case holds for the closed case. Furthermore, by restricting one's attention to (a generalization of) uniform receptive processes [18], it is possible to show that a bisimulation relation relates processes and their types: in this case, processes and their types satisfy the same abstract properties.

It is possible to partially extend the treatment of closed behaviour to the case of Join processes [10] (the Join open case requires additional care and we leave it for future work). The essential step one has to take, at the level of types, is moving from BPP to place/transition Petri nets (PN). Technically, this step is somehow forced by the presence of the join pattern construct in the calculus, which expresses multi-synchronization. In the context of infinite states transition systems [9,13], moving from BPP to PN corresponds precisely to moving from rewrite rules with a single nonterminal on the LHS (BPP) to rules with multisets of nonterminals on the LHS (PN).

3 Contract-Based Service Composition

After having discussed, in the previous section, a general technique to extract a contract from service behaviours, we consider the problem of the exploitation of contracts in order to check the correctness of service compositions. In particular, in this section we take, as a starting point, services described by means of a calculus without value passing, similar to (a distributed version of) the CCS based language used in the previous section as the contract language. We express such services in the form of "plain" (language independent) contracts, i.e. finite labeled transition systems (obtained e.g. as the semantics of service terms), in order to check whether a service can be correctly introduced in a specific service composition. Service compositions, also called *choreographies*, are specified as a set of communicating contracts, in execution at specific locations, also called *roles* in choreographies. Thus, checking whether a service can be correctly introduced in a service composition coincides with checking whether its contract *refines* a contract sitting at a given location in the context of a choreography.

The remainder of this section is devoted to the formal definition of this refinement relation called *subcontract* relation. We first give a declarative definition of the subcontract relation induced by the properties that we want the refinement to satisfy. Then, we provide a testing based procedure to verify whether two contracts are in subcontract relation.

3.1   Behavioural Contracts

Definition 1. *A finite connected labeled transition system (LTS) with termination transitions is a tuple* $\mathcal{T} = (S, \mathcal{L}, \longrightarrow, s_h, s_0)$ *where S is a finite set of states, L is a set of labels, the transition relation $\longrightarrow$ is a finite subset of* $(S - \{s_h\}) \times (\mathcal{L} \cup \{\sqrt{}\}) \times S$ *such that* $(s, \sqrt{}, s') \in \longrightarrow$ *implies* $s' = s_h$, $s_h \in S$ *represents a halt state, $s_0 \in S$ represents the initial state, and it holds that every state in S is reachable (according to $\longrightarrow$) from s_0.*

In a finite connected LTS with termination transitions we use $\sqrt{}$ transitions (leading to the halt state s_h) to represent successful termination. On the contrary, if we get (via a transition different from $\sqrt{}$) into a state with no outgoing transitions (like, e.g., s_h) then we represent an internal failure or a deadlock.

We assume a denumerable set of action names $\mathcal{N}$, ranged over by $a, b, c, \ldots$. We use $\tau \notin \mathcal{N}$ to denote an internal (unsynchronizable) computation. We consider a denumerable set Loc of location names, ranged over by $l, l', l_1, l_2, \cdots$. In contracts the possible transition labels are the typical internal τ action and the input/output actions $a, \bar{a}$, where the outputs (as we will see when composing contracts) are directed to a destination address denoted by a location $l \in Loc$.

Definition 2. *A contract is a finite connected LTS with termination transitions, that is a tuple* $(S, \mathcal{L}, \longrightarrow, s_h, s_0)$, *where* $\mathcal{L} = \{a, \bar{a}_l, \tau \mid a \in \mathcal{N} \wedge l \in Loc\}$.

In the following we introduce a process algebraic representation for contracts by using a simple extension of basic CCS [12] with successful termination **1**.

Definition 3. *We consider a denumerable set of contract variables Var ranged over by $X, Y, \cdots$. The syntax of contracts is defined by the following grammar*

$$C ::= \mathbf{0} \mid \mathbf{1} \mid \alpha.C \mid C{+}C \mid X \mid recX.C$$

$$\alpha ::= \tau \mid a \mid \bar{a}_l$$

where $recX.\_$ is a binder for the process variable X. The set of the contracts C in which all process variables are bound, i.e. C is a closed term, is denoted by $\mathcal{P}_{con}$. In the following we will often omit trailing "1" when writing contracts.

The operational semantics of contracts is defined in terms of a transition system labeled by $\mathcal{L} = \{a, \bar{a}_l, \tau \mid a \in \mathcal{N} \wedge l \in Loc\}$ obtained by the rules in Table 3 (plus symmetric rule for choice), where we take λ to range over $\mathcal{L} \cup \{\sqrt{}\}$. In particular the semantics of a contract $C \in \mathcal{P}_{con}$ gives rise to a finite connected LTS with

Table 3. Semantic rules for contracts (symmetric rules omitted)

$$1 \xrightarrow{\checkmark} 0 \qquad\qquad \alpha.C \xrightarrow{\alpha} C$$

$$\frac{C \xrightarrow{\lambda} C'}{C+D \xrightarrow{\lambda} C'} \qquad\qquad \frac{C\{recX.C/X\} \xrightarrow{\lambda} C'}{recX.C \xrightarrow{\lambda} C'}$$

termination transitions $(S, \mathcal{L}, \longrightarrow, \mathbf{0}, C)$ where S is the set of states reachable from C and $\longrightarrow$ includes only transitions between states of S.

In [4] we formalize the correspondence between contracts and terms of $\mathcal{P}_{con}$ by showing how to obtain from a contract $\mathcal{T} = (S, \mathcal{L}, \longrightarrow, s_h, s_0)$ a corresponding $C \in \mathcal{P}_{con}$ such that there exists a (surjective) homomorphism from the operational semantics of C to $\mathcal{T}$ itself.

In the following we use $C \xrightarrow{\lambda}$ to mean $\exists C' : C \xrightarrow{\lambda} C'$ and, given a string of labels $w \in \mathcal{L}^*$, that is $w = \lambda_1 \lambda_2 \cdots \lambda_{n-1} \lambda_n$ (possibly empty, i.e., $w = \varepsilon$), we use $C \xrightarrow{w} C'$ to denote the sequence of transitions $C \xrightarrow{\lambda_1} C_1 \xrightarrow{\lambda_2} \cdots \xrightarrow{\lambda_{n-1}} C_{n-1} \xrightarrow{\lambda_n} C'$ (in case of $w = \varepsilon$ we have $C' = C$, i.e., $C \xrightarrow{\varepsilon} C$).

Definition 4 (Output persistence). *A contract $C \in \mathcal{P}_{con}$ is output persistent if, given $C \xrightarrow{w} C'$ with $C' \xrightarrow{\bar{a}_l}$, then: $C' \not\xrightarrow{\checkmark}$ and if $C' \xrightarrow{\alpha} C''$ with $\alpha \neq \bar{a}_l$ then also $C'' \xrightarrow{\bar{a}_l}$.*

The output persistence property states that once a contract decides to execute an output, its actual execution is mandatory in order to successfully complete the execution of the contract. This property typically hold in languages for the description of service behaviours or for service orchestrations (see e.g. WS-BPEL) in which output actions cannot be used as guards in external choices (see e.g. the `pick` operator of WS-BPEL which is an external choice guarded on input actions). In these languages, when a process instance or an internal thread decides to execute an output actions, it will have to complete such action before ending successfully. In the context of service descriptions expressed by means of process algebra with parallel composition, a syntactical characterization that guarantees output persistence will be presented in the next section.

The actual impact of output persistence (in turn coming from an asymmetric treatment of inputs and outputs) in our theory is the existence of a maximal independent refinement (see Section 3.4), i.e. a maximal refinement pre-order that makes it possible to independently refine different contracts of an initial coreography (see [3] for a counter-example showing the necessity of output persistence).

3.2   An Example of Service Language

The service language that we consider in this section, that is aimed to modeling choreographies, can be seen as a distributed version of (a slightly modified version of) the CCS$^-$ language considered for contracts in the previous section, where we also distinguish between successful and unsuccessful termination. Other differences also come from the fact that we adopt operators which are closer to choreography languages such as abstract WS-BPEL [16]. For instance, here we consider sequential composition $\_;\_$ instead of the prefix operator $\_.\_$, we use a repetition construct $\_^*$ to program unbounded computations instead of recursive definitions, and we assume that the decision to execute an output operation is taken locally, thus all outputs are of the form $\tau; \bar{b}$ (where τ is the typical internal acion of CCS and $\bar{b}$ is an output action on the name b). An important consequence of this form of output operation is that it is not possible to use output actions as guards of branches in a choice; for instance, we cannot write $a + \bar{b}$, but we have to write $a + (\tau; \bar{b})$ where performing the τ action represents the decision to perform the action $\bar{b}$: once the decision is taken we have to perform $\bar{b}$ to reach success. Contracts arising from services with such a syntax are obviously output persistent. Notice that, as long as output finite persistent contracts are derived from services (here finiteness is guaranteed by usage of the Kleene-star repetition operator instead of general recursion), our contract theory is totally independent from the particular service language considered.

Definition 5 (Services). *The syntax of services is*

$$S ::= \mathbf{0} \quad | \quad \mathbf{1} \quad | \quad \tau \quad | \quad a \quad | \quad \tau; \bar{a}_l \quad | \quad S; S \quad | \quad S + S \quad | \quad S | S \quad | \quad S^*$$

In the following we will omit trailing "$\mathbf{1}$" when writing services.

The operational semantics of services, giving rise to a contract in the form of a finite connected LTS with termination transitions for every S, is quite standard; see [5] for a formal definition.

3.3   Composing Services via Their Contract

Definition 6 (Systems). *The syntax of systems (contract compositions) is*

$$P \quad ::= \quad [C]_l \quad | \quad P \| P \quad | \quad P \backslash L$$

where $L \subseteq \{a_l, \bar{a}_l \mid a \in \mathcal{N} \wedge l \in Loc\}$. A system P is well-formed if: (i) every contract subterm $[C]_l$ occurs in P at a different location l and (ii) no output action with destination l is syntactically included inside a contract subterm occurring in P at the same location l, i.e. actions $\bar{a}_l$ cannot occur inside a subterm $[C]_l$ of P. The set of all well-formed systems P is denoted by $\mathcal{P}$. In the following we will just consider well-formed systems and, we will call them just systems.

The operational semantics of systems is defined by the rules in Table 4 plus symmetric rules. We take λ to range over the set of transition labels $\mathcal{L}_{sys} = \{a_l, \bar{a}_l, \tau, \sqrt{} \mid a \in \mathcal{N} \wedge l \in Loc\}$.

*Example 1 (**Travel Agency Service**).* As a running example, we consider a travel agency service which, upon invocation, sends parellcl invocations to an

Table 4. Semantic rules for contract compositions (symmetric rules omitted)

$$\frac{C \xrightarrow{a} C'}{[C]_l \xrightarrow{a_l} [C']_l} \qquad \frac{C \xrightarrow{\lambda} C' \quad \lambda = \bar{a}_{l'}, \tau, \sqrt{}}{[C]_l \xrightarrow{\lambda} [C']_l} \qquad \frac{P \xrightarrow{\lambda} P' \quad \lambda \neq \sqrt{}}{P\|Q \xrightarrow{\lambda} P'\|Q}$$

$$\frac{P \xrightarrow{a_l} P' \quad Q \xrightarrow{\bar{a}_l} Q'}{P\|Q \xrightarrow{\tau} P'\|Q'} \qquad \frac{P \xrightarrow{\sqrt{}} P' \quad Q \xrightarrow{\sqrt{}} Q'}{P\|Q \xrightarrow{\sqrt{}} P'\|Q'} \qquad \frac{P \xrightarrow{\lambda} P' \quad \lambda \notin L}{P\backslash L \xrightarrow{\lambda} P'\backslash L}$$

airplane reservation service and a hotel reservation service in order to complete the overall organization of a trip. The travel agency service can be defined as:

$$[Reservation; (\ \tau; \overline{Reserve}_{AirCompany}; ConfirmFlight\ |$$
$$\tau; \overline{Reserve}_{Hotel}; ConfirmRoom\ );$$
$$\tau; \overline{Confirmation}_{Client}]_{TravelAgency}$$

A possible client for this service can be as follows:

$$[\tau; \overline{Reservation}_{TravelAgency}; Confirmation]_{Client}$$

while the two reservation services could be:

$$[Reserve; \tau; \overline{ConfirmFlight}_{TravelAgency}]_{AirCompany}$$
$$[Reserve; \tau; \overline{ConfirmRoom}_{TravelAgency}]_{Hotel}$$

3.4   Subcontract Relation

Intuitively, a system composed of contracts is correct if all possible computations may guarantee completion; this means that the system is both deadlock and livelock free (there can be an infinite computation, but given any possible prefix of this infinite computation, it must be possible to extend it to reach a successfully completed computation).

Definition 7 (Correct contract composition). *A system P is a correct contract composition, denoted $P\downarrow$, if for every P' such that $P \xrightarrow{\tau}^* P'$ there exists P'' such that $P' \xrightarrow{\tau}^* P'' \xrightarrow{\sqrt{}}$.*

We are now ready to formalize the notion of pre-order allowing for the refinement of contracts preserving the correctness of contract compositions. We call these class of pre-orders *Independent Subcontracts*. Given a contract $C \in \mathcal{P}_{con}$, we use $oloc(C) \subset Loc$ to denote the set of the locations of the destinations of all the output actions occurring inside C.

Definition 8 (Independent Subcontract pre-order). *A pre-order $\leq$ over $\mathcal{P}_{con}$ is an independent subcontract pre-order if, for any $n \geq 1$, contracts $C_1, \ldots, C_n \in \mathcal{P}_{con}$ and $C_1', \ldots, C_n' \in \mathcal{P}_{con}$ such that $\forall i. C_i' \leq C_i$, and distinguished location names $l_1, \ldots, l_n \in Loc$ such that $\forall i. l_i \notin oloc(C_i) \cup oloc(C_i')$, we have*

$$([C_1]_{l_1} \parallel \ldots \parallel [C_n]_{l_n}) \downarrow \quad \Rightarrow \quad ([C_1']_{l_1} \parallel \ldots \parallel [C_n']_{l_n}) \downarrow$$

We will show that the maximal independent subcontract pre-order can be achieved defining a coarser form of refinement in which, given any system composed of a set of contracts, refinement is applied to one contract only (thus leaving the other unchanged). We call this form of refinement *singular subcontract pre-order*.

Intuitively a pre-order $\leq$ over $\mathcal{P}_{con}$ is a singular subcontract pre-order whenever the correctness of systems is preserved by refining just one of the contracts. More precisely, for any $n \geq 1$, contracts $C_1, \ldots, C_n \in \mathcal{P}_{con}$, $1 \leq i \leq n$, $C_i' \in \mathcal{P}_{con}$ such that $C_i' \leq C_i$, and distinguished location names $l_1, \ldots, l_n \in Loc$ such that $\forall k \neq i. l_k \notin oloc(C_k)$ and $l_i \notin oloc(C_i) \cup oloc(C_i')$, we require

$$([C_1]_{l_1} \parallel \ldots \parallel [C_i]_{l_i} \parallel \ldots \parallel [C_n]_{l_n}) \downarrow \quad \Rightarrow \quad ([C_1]_{l_1} \parallel \ldots \parallel [C_i']_{l_i} \parallel \ldots \parallel [C_n]_{l_n}) \downarrow$$

By exploiting commutativity and associativity of parallel composition we can group the contracts which are not being refined and get the following cleaner definition. We let $\mathcal{P}_{conpar}$ denote the set of systems of the form $[C_1]_{l_1} \parallel \ldots \parallel [C_n]_{l_n}$, with $C_i \in \mathcal{P}_{con}$, for all $i \in \{1, \ldots, n\}$.

Definition 9 (Singular subcontract pre-order). *A pre-order $\leq$ over $\mathcal{P}_{con}$ is a singular subcontract pre-order if, for any $C, C' \in \mathcal{P}_{con}$ such that $C' \leq C$, $P \in \mathcal{P}_{conpar}$, $l \in Loc$ such that $l \notin oloc(C) \cup oloc(C') \cup loc(P)$, we have $([C]_l \| P) \downarrow$ implies $([C']_l \| P) \downarrow$.*

From the simple structure of their definition we can easily deduce that singular subcontract pre-order have maximum, i.e. there exists a singular subcontract pre-order that includes all the other singular subcontract pre-orders.

Definition 10 (Subcontract relation). *A contract C' is a subcontract of a contract C denoted $C' \preceq C$, if and only if for all $P \in \mathcal{P}_{conpar}$, $l \in Loc$ such that $l \notin oloc(C) \cup oloc(C') \cup loc(P)$, we have $([C]_l \| P) \downarrow$ implies $([C']_l \| P) \downarrow$.*

It is trivial to verify that the pre-order $\preceq$ is a singular subcontract pre-order and is the maximum of all the singular subcontract pre-orders.

Theorem 2. *A pre-order $\leq$ is an independent subcontract pre-order if and only if $\leq$ is a singular subcontract pre-order.*

We can, therefore, conclude that there exists a maximal independent subcontract pre-order and it corresponds to "$\preceq$".

Example 2. It is not difficult to see that the parallel composition of the contracts of services *TravelAgency*, *Client*, *AirCompany* and *Hotel* defined in the Example 1 is a correct composition according to the Definition 7. It is also interesting to observe that the travel agency service could invoke sequentially the service without breaking the correctness of the system:

$$[\, Reservation; \tau; \overline{Reserve}_{AirCompany}; ConfirmFlight;$$

$$\tau; \overline{Reserve}_{Hotel}; ConfirmRoom; \tau; \overline{Confirmation}_{Client} \,]_{TravelAgency}$$

Nevertheless, the contract of this new service is not in general a subcontract of the one of the travel agency service proposed in Example 1 because there exist context in which it cannot be a correctness preserving substitute. Consider, for instance, the two following interacting reservation services:

$$[Reserve; HotelConfirm; \tau; \overline{ConfirmFlight}_{TravelAgency}]_{AirCompany}$$

$$[Reserve; \tau; \overline{ConfirmRoom}_{TravelAgency}; \tau; \overline{HotelConfirm}_{AirCompany}]_{Hotel}$$

In this case, the confirmation of the hotel reservation service is always sent to the travel agency before the confirmation of the airplane company; this is not problematic for the travel agency in the Example 1 that performs the invocation in parallel, while the above sequential invocation deadlocks.

3.5   Subcontract Relation Characterization

The definition of the subcontract relation reported in Definition 10 cannot be directly used to check whether two contracts are in relation due to the universal quantification on all possible locations l and contexts P. In this section we first prove that it is not necessary to range over all possible contexts P in order to check whether a contract C' is in subcontract relation with a contract C, but it is sufficient to consider a *restricted class of relevant contexts* in which all input and output operations are performed on channels on which the contract C can perform outputs or inputs, respectively. Then we present an actual procedure, achieved resorting to the theory of *should-testing* [17], that can be used to prove that two contracts are in subcontract relation.

To characterize the restricted class of relevant contexts we have to introduce a subcontract relation parameterized on the set of inputs and outputs executable by the context. In the following we use $\mathcal{N}_{loc} = \{a_l \mid a \in \mathcal{N}, l \in Loc\}$ to denote the set of located action names and we assume that, given $I \subset \mathcal{N}_{loc}, \overline{I} = \{\overline{a}_l \mid a_l \in I\}$.

Definition 11 (Input and Output sets). *Given $C \in \mathcal{P}_{con}$, we define $I(C)$ (resp. $O(C)$) as the subset of $\mathcal{N}$ (resp. $\mathcal{N}_{loc}$) of the potential input (resp. output) actions of C. Formally, we define $I(C)$ as follows ($O(C)$ is defined similarly):*

$$I(\mathbf{0}) = I(\mathbf{1}) = I(X) = \emptyset \qquad I(\tau.C) = I(\overline{a}_l.C) = I(recX.C) = I(C)$$

$$I(a.C) = \{a\} \cup I(C) \qquad I(C+C') = I(C) \cup I(C')$$

Given the system P, we define $I(P)$ (resp. $O(P)$) as the subset of $\mathcal{N}_{loc}$ of the potential input (resp. output) actions of P. Formally, we define $I(P)$ as follows ($O(P)$ is defined similarly):

$$I([C]_l) = \{a_l \mid a \in I(C)\} \qquad I(P\|P') = I(P) \cup I(P') \qquad I(P\backslash L) = I(P) - L$$

We have now to consider slightly more complex contexts than $\mathcal{P}_{conpar}$ systems. We let $\mathcal{P}_{conpres}$ denote the set of systems of the form $([C_1]_{l_1} \| \ldots \| [C_n]_{l_n}) \backslash L$ with $C_i \in \mathcal{P}_{con}$ for all $i \in \{1, \ldots, n\}$ and $L \in \{a_l, \bar{a}_l \mid a \in \mathcal{N} \wedge l \in Loc\}$. Note that, given $P = ([C_1]_{l_1} \| \ldots \| [C_n]_{l_n}) \backslash I \cup \overline{O} \in \mathcal{P}_{conpres}$, we have $I(P) = (\bigcup_{1 \le i \le n} I([C_i]_{l_i})) - I$ and $O(P) = (\bigcup_{1 \le i \le n} O([C_i]_{l_i})) - O$. In the following we let $\mathcal{P}_{conpres,I,O}$, with $I, O \subseteq \mathcal{N}_{loc}$, denote the subset of systems of $\mathcal{P}_{conpres}$ such that $I(P) \subseteq I$ and $O(P) \subseteq O$.

Definition 12 (Input-Output Subcontract relation). *A contract C' is a subcontract of a contract C with respect to a set of input located names $I \subseteq \mathcal{N}_{loc}$ and output located names $O \subseteq \mathcal{N}_{loc}$, denoted $C' \preceq_{I,O} C$, if and only if for all $P \in \mathcal{P}_{conpres,I,O}$, $l \in Loc$ such that $l \notin oloc(C) \cup oloc(C') \cup loc(P)$, we have $([C]_l \| P) \downarrow$ implies $([C']_l \| P) \downarrow$*

It is not difficult to see, looking at Definition 10, that $\preceq = \preceq_{\mathcal{N}_{loc}, \mathcal{N}_{loc}}$. Moreover, notice that, given $\preceq_{I',O'}$, and larger sets I and O (i.e. $I' \subseteq I$ and $O' \subseteq O$) we obtain a smaller pre-order $\preceq_{I,O}$ (i.e. $\preceq_{I,O} \subseteq \preceq_{I',O'}$). This follows from the fact that extending the sets of input and output actions means considering a larger set of discriminating contexts.

The following Proposition shows conditions on the input and output sets under which also the opposite direction holds; more precisely, the set of potential inputs and outputs of the other contracts in the system (as long as it includes those needed to interact with the contract) is an information that does not influence the subcontract relation.

Proposition 2. *Let $C \in \mathcal{P}_{con}$ be contracts, $I, I' \subseteq \mathcal{N}_{loc}$ be two sets of located input names such that $O(C) \subseteq I, I'$ and $O, O' \subseteq \mathcal{N}_{loc}$ be two sets of located output names such that for every $l \in Loc$ we have $I([C]_l) \subseteq O, O'$. We have that for every contract $C' \in \mathcal{P}_{con}$,*

$$C' \preceq_{I,O} C \quad \Longleftrightarrow \quad C' \preceq_{I',O} C \Longleftrightarrow \quad C' \preceq_{I,O'} C$$

It is interesting to note that the above results depend on the systems being output persistent. Consider, e.g., the trivially correct system $[a]_{l_1} \| [\tau.\bar{a}_{l_1}]_{l_2}$. We have that the contract a could be replaced by $a + c.\mathbf{0}$ as well as the contract $\tau.\bar{a}_{l_1}$ that could be replaced by $\tau.\bar{a}_{l_1} + c.\mathbf{0}$; this because it is easy to see that

$$a + c.\mathbf{0} \preceq_{\emptyset, \{a_l, c_l \mid l \in Loc\}} a \quad \text{and} \quad \tau.\bar{a}_{l_1} + c.\mathbf{0} \preceq_{\{a_{l_1}\}, \{c_l \mid l \in Loc\}} \tau.\bar{a}_{l_1}$$

thus, as a consequence of the last two propositions and the fact that $\preceq = \preceq_{\mathcal{N}_{loc}, \mathcal{N}_{loc}}$, we have that

$$a + c.\mathbf{0} \preceq a \quad \text{and} \quad \tau.\bar{a}_{l_1} + c.\mathbf{0} \preceq \tau.\bar{a}_{l_1}$$

But these two examples of subcontracts are not correct if we can write output operations without a previous internal τ action. In fact, the two correct systems $[a]_{l_1} \| [\bar{a}_{l_1} + \bar{c}_{l_1}]_{l_2}$ and $[a + \bar{c}_{l_2}]_{l_1} \| [\bar{a}_{l_1}]_{l_2}$, are no longer correct if we replace the contracts a and $\bar{a}_{l_1}$ with their abovely discussed subcontracts.

The above example show that a subcontract may contain additional inputs (see the additional input on channel c). This property is formalized by the following Lemma that is a direct consequence of the fact that $C' \preceq_{\mathcal{N}_{loc}, \bigcup_{l \in Loc} I([C]_l)} C$ if and only if $C' \preceq C$ as stated by Proposition 2. In the Lemma (and in the following) we use the abuse of notation "$C \backslash M$" to stand for the contract "$C\{0/a | a \in M\}$" achieved replacing all input actions in the set $M \in \mathcal{N}$ with the failed process $\mathbf{0}$.

Lemma 1. *Let* $C, C' \in \mathcal{P}_{con}$ *be contracts. We have*

$$C' \backslash (I(C') - I(C)) \preceq C \quad \Leftrightarrow \quad C' \preceq C$$

The remainder of this subsection is devoted to the definition of an actual procedure for proving that two contracts are in subcontract relation. This is achieved resorting to the theory of *should-testing* [17]. We denote with $\preceq_{test}$ the *should-testing* pre-order defined in [17] where we consider the set of actions used by terms as being $\Lambda = \mathcal{L}_{sys} \cup \{a, \bar{a} \mid a \in \mathcal{N}\}$ (i.e. we consider located and unlocated input and output actions and $\sqrt{}$ is included in the set of actions of terms under testing as any other action). We denote here with $\sqrt{}'$ the special action for the success of the test (denoted by $\sqrt{}$ in [17]). Should testing is a variant of must testing which ensures correctness under a fairness assumption, similarly as for our correct contract compositions. Given two processes P and P', $P' \preceq_{test} P$ iff for every test t, P **shd** t implies P' **shd** t, where Q **shd** t iff

$$\forall w \in \Lambda^*, Q'. \quad Q\|_{\Lambda - \{\tau\}} t \xrightarrow{w} Q' \quad \Rightarrow \quad \exists v \in \Lambda^*, Q'' : Q' \xrightarrow{v} Q'' \xrightarrow{\sqrt{}'}$$

where $\|_S$ is the CSP parallel operator: in $R\|_S R'$ transitions of R and R' with the same label $\lambda \in S$ must synchronize and yield a λ transition.

In order to resort to the theory of [17], we just have to consider "normal form" terms $\mathcal{NF}(C)$, where $\mathcal{NF}(C)$ is obtained from contract terms C by replacing $\sqrt{}.\mathbf{0}$ for $\mathbf{1}$ and by using the notation for prefix and recursion used in [17].

Theorem 3. *Let* $C, C' \in \mathcal{P}_{con}$ *be two contracts. We have*

$$\mathcal{NF}(C' \backslash I(C') - I(C)) \preceq_{test} \mathcal{NF}(C) \quad \Rightarrow \quad C' \preceq C$$

Note that the opposite implication

$$C' \preceq C \Rightarrow \mathcal{NF}(C' \backslash I(C') - I(C)) \preceq_{test} \mathcal{NF}(C)$$

does not hold in general. For example if we take contracts $C = a + a.c$ and $C' = b + b.c$ we have that $C' \preceq C$ (and $C \preceq C'$) (there is no location l and context P such that $([C]_l\|P)\downarrow$ or $([C']_l\|P)\downarrow$), but obviously $\mathcal{NF}(C'\backslash\{b\}) \preceq_{test} \mathcal{NF}(C)$ (and $\mathcal{NF}(C\backslash\{a\}) \preceq_{test} \mathcal{NF}(C')$) does not hold.

In [17] it is proved that, for finite transition systems like our contracts, *should-testing* preorder is decidable and an actual verification algorithm is presented. This algorithm, in the light of our Theorem 3, represents a sound approach to prove also our subcontract relation.

Example 3. We complete the analysis of our running example, showing a subcontract of the original travel agency service. For instance, the following alternative travel agency gives rise to a subcontract of the one proposed in the Example 1:

$$[Reservation; (\ \tau; \overline{Reserve}_{AirCompany}; ConfirmFlight \ |$$
$$\tau; \overline{Reserve}_{Hotel}; (ConfirmRoom + CancelRoom)\ );$$
$$\tau; \overline{Confirmation}_{Client}]_{TravelAgency}$$

as it simply differs for an additional input on the $CancelRoom$ channel, modelling the possibility for the hotel reservation to fail.

4 Conclusion

We have reported an overview of mechanisms that paves the way for service publication, discovery and composition based on the notion of *service contract*, that is an abstract description of the message-passing behaviour of the service. These mechanisms have been developed also in the light of applications to the core calculi described in Chapter 2-1. Also related to service publication, discovery and composition are 2-4 and 3-1. In Chapter 2-4 the authors present a framework for designing and composing services in a "call-by-contract" fashion, i.e. according to their behaviour and show how to correctly plan service compositions in some relevant classes of services and behavioural properties. They propose a core functional calculus for services and a type and effect system over-approximating the actual run-time behaviour of services. A further static analysis step finds the plan that drive the selection of services matching the behavioural requirements on demand. In Chapter 3-1 the authors overview the CC-pi calculus, a model for specifying QoS negotiations in service composition that also allows to study mechanisms for resource allocation and for joining different QoS parameters.

Concerning related work, Igarashi and Kobayashi's work [14] on generic type systems is the first instance of the processes-as-types approach. The work [1] is mostly inspired by [14], with a few important differences. In particular, [1] considers an asynchronous version of the pi-calculus, and types account for a *tag*-wise, rather than *channel*-wise, view of the behaviour of processes. On one hand, this simplification leads to some loss of information, which prevents one from capturing certain liveness properties such as race- and deadlock-freedom. On the other hand, it allows one to make the connection between different kinds of behavior (open/closed) and different type models (CCS/BPP) direct and explicit. As an example, in the case of BPP [1] spells out reasonably simple conditions under which the type analysis is "precise" (Γ-uniform receptiveness). Also, this approach naturally carries over to the Join calculus, by moving to Petri nets types. The paradigm type-as-abstraction is also the subject of [2]. There, sufficient conditions are given under which certain liveness and safety properties, expressed in a simple spatial logic, can be transferred from types to the inhabiting processes.

Another work strongly related to our concept of type-as-abstraction is [15], where the generic type system of Igarashi and Kobayashi is extended in order to guarantee certain safety properties in a resource-access scenario. A pi-calculus enriched with resources and related access primitives is introduced; resources are decorated with access policies formulated as regular languages. CCS types are used to check the behaviour of processes against those policies. The main result ensures that no well-typed process violates at runtime the prescribed policies.

As far as contract-based service composition is concerned, it is important to say that, even if we have characterized our notion of compliance resorting to the theory of testing, there are some relevant differences between our form of testing and the traditional one proposed by De Nicola-Hennessy [8]. The most relevant difference is that, besides requiring the success of the test, we impose also that the tested process should successfully complete its execution. This further requirement has important consequences; for instance, we do not distinguish between the always unsuccessful process 0 and other processes, such as $a.1 + a.b.1$, for which there are no guarantees of successful completion in any possible context. Another relevant difference is in the treatment of divergence: we do not follow the traditional catastrophic approach, but the fair approach introduced by the theory of should-testing of Rensink-Vogler [17]. In fact, we do not impose that all computations must succeed, but that all computations can always be extended in order to reach success.

Contracts have been investigated also by Fournet et al. [11] and Carpineti et al. [6]. In [11] contracts are CCS-like processes; a generic process P is defined as compliant to a contract C if, for every tuple of names $\tilde{a}$ and process Q, whenever $(\nu\tilde{a})(C|Q)$ is stuck-free then also $(\nu\tilde{a})(P|Q)$ is. Our notion of contract refinement differs from stuck-free conformance mainly because we consider a different notion of stuckness. In [11] a process state is stuck (on a tuple of channel names $\tilde{a}$) if it has no internal moves (but it can execute at least one action on one of the channels in $\tilde{a}$). In our approach, an end-state different from successful termination is stuck (independently of any tuple $\tilde{a}$). Thus, we distinguish between internal deadlock and successful completion while this is not the case in [11]. Another difference follows from the exploitation of the restriction $(\nu\tilde{a})$; this is used in [11] to explicitly indicate the local channels of communication used between the contract C and the process Q. In our context we can make a stronger *closed-world* assumption (corresponding to a restriction on all channel names) because service contracts do not describe the entire behaviour of a service, but the flow of execution of its operations inside one session of communication.

The closed-world assumption is considered also in [6] where, as in our case, a service oriented scenario is considered. In particular, in [6] a theory of contracts is defined for investigating the compatibility between one client and one service. Our paper consider multi-party composition where several services are composed in a peer-to-peer manner. Moreover, we impose service substitutability as a mandatory property for our notion of refinement; this does not hold in [6] where it is not in general possible to substitute a service exposing one contract with another one exposing a subcontract. Another, related, significant difference is that contracts in [6] comprise also mixed choices.

References

1. Acciai, L., Boreale, M.: Type abstractions of name-passing processes. In: Arbab, F., Sirjani, M. (eds.) FSEN 2007. LNCS, vol. 4767, pp. 302–317. Springer, Heidelberg (2007)
2. Acciai, L., Boreale, M.: Spatial and Behavioral Types in the Pi-Calculus. In: van Breugel, F., Chechik, M. (eds.) CONCUR 2008. LNCS, vol. 5201, pp. 372–386. Springer, Heidelberg (2008)
3. Bravetti, M., Zavattaro, G.: A Foundational Theory of Contracts for Multi-party Service Composition. Fundamenta Informaticae 89(4), 451–478 (2008)
4. Bravetti, M., Zavattaro, G.: Contract-Based Discovery and Composition of Web Services. In: Bernardo, M., Padovani, L., Zavattaro, G. (eds.) SFM 2009. LNCS, vol. 5569, pp. 261–295. Springer, Heidelberg (2009)
5. Bravetti, M., Zavattaro, G.: Towards a Unifying Theory for Choreography Conformance and Contract Compliance. In: Lumpe, M., Vanderperren, W. (eds.) SC 2007. LNCS, vol. 4829, pp. 34–50. Springer, Heidelberg (2007), http://www.cs.unibo.it/~bravetti/html/techreports.html
6. Carpineti, S., Castagna, G., Laneve, C., Padovani, L.: A Formal Account of Contracts for Web Services. In: Bravetti, M., Núñez, M., Tennenholtz, M. (eds.) WS-FM 2006. LNCS, vol. 4184, pp. 148–162. Springer, Heidelberg (2006)
7. Christensen, S., Hirshfeld, Y., Moller, F.: Bisimulation equivalence is decidable for basic parallel processes. In: Best, E. (ed.) CONCUR 1993. LNCS, vol. 715, pp. 143–157. Springer, Heidelberg (1993)
8. De Nicola, R., Hennessy, M.: Testing Equivalences for Processes. Theoretical Computer Science 34, 83–133 (1984)
9. Esparza, J.: More Infinite Results. In: Current trends in Theoretical Computer Science: entering the 21st century, pp. 480–503 (2001)
10. Fournet, C., Gouthier, G.: The Reflexive Chemical Abstract Machine and the Join Calculus. In: Proc. of POPL 1996, pp. 372–385. ACM Press, New York (1996)
11. Fournet, C., Hoare, C.A.R., Rajamani, S.K., Rehof, J.: Stuck-Free Conformance. In: Alur, R., Peled, D.A. (eds.) CAV 2004. LNCS, vol. 3114, pp. 242–254. Springer, Heidelberg (2004)
12. Milner, R.: A complete axiomatization for observational congruence of finite-state behaviours. Information and Computation 81, 227–247 (1989)
13. Hirshfeld, Y., Moller, F.: Decidability Results in Automata and Process theory. In: Moller, F., Birtwistle, G. (eds.) Logics for Concurrency. LNCS, vol. 1043, pp. 102–148. Springer, Heidelberg (1996)
14. Igarashi, A., Kobayashi, N.: A Generic Type System for the Pi-Calculus. In: Proc. of POPL, pp. 128–141. ACM Press, New York (2001); Full version appeared in Theoretical Computer Science 311(1-3), 121–163 (2004)
15. Kobayashi, N., Suenaga, K., Wischik, L.: Resource Usage Analysis for the Pi-Calculus. In: Emerson, E.A., Namjoshi, K.S. (eds.) VMCAI 2006. LNCS, vol. 3855, pp. 298–312. Springer, Heidelberg (2006)
16. OASIS. Web Services Business Process Execution Language Version 2.0
17. Rensink, A., Vogler, W.: Fair testing. Information and Computation 205(2), 125–198 (2007)
18. Sangiorgi, D.: The name discipline of uniform receptiveness. In: Degano, P., Gorrieri, R., Marchetti-Spaccamela, A. (eds.) ICALP 1997. LNCS, vol. 1256. Springer, Heidelberg (1997); Theoretical Computer Science 221(1-2), 457–493 (1999)
19. Stirling, C.: Modal Logics for Communicating Systems. Theoretical Computer Science 49(2-3), 311–347 (1987)

Advanced Mechanisms for
Service Combination and Transactions[*]

Carla Ferreira[2], Ivan Lanese[1], Antonio Ravara[2],
Hugo Torres Vieira[2], and Gianluigi Zavattaro[1]

[1] Focus Team, Università di Bologna/INRIA, Italy
{lanese,zavattar}@cs.unibo.it
[2] CITI and Departamento de Informática, Faculdade de Ciências e Tecnologia,
Universidade Nova de Lisboa, Portugal
{carla.ferreira,aravara,htv}@fct.unl.pt

Abstract. Languages and models for service-oriented applications usually include primitives and constructs for *exception* and *compensation*
handling. Exception handling is used to react to unexpected events while
compensation handling is used to undo previously completed activities.
In this chapter we investigate the impact of exception and compensation handling in message-based process calculi and the related theories
developed within SENSORIA.

1 Introduction

Long-running transactions (henceforth LRTs) are computer activities that may
last long periods of time. These kinds of activities are particularly common
in systems composed by loosely coupled components communicating by message passing, like most distributed systems and, in particular, service-oriented
systems.

Due to the nature of these systems and to the time duration of the activities, it
is not feasible to lock (non-local) resources, and thus, LRTs do not enjoy some of
the usual ACID properties of database transactions (namely isolation, since the
execution of a single LRT is not intended to block the whole system). Therefore,
to recover from partial executions of LRTs (due to their abortion because of
system failures like unreachability of a partner or time-out of communication, or
to some other unexpected event), it is necessary to foresee special activities to
regain system consistency, i.e., to *compensate* the fact that the transaction has
been aborted. These activities should be triggered in case of transaction failure,
and need to be programmed *a priori*. Note that, in general, the execution of a
compensation does not exactly "undo" the activities already performed by the
LRT (what is, in general, impossible).

1.1 Content of the Chapter

Programming or specification languages provide these days two kinds of recovery
mechanisms: *exception handling* and *compensation handling*. The former uses

[*] This work has been partially sponsored by the project SENSORIA, IST-2005-016004.

M. Wirsing and M. Hölzl (Eds.): SENSORIA Project, LNCS 6582, pp. 302–325, 2011.

primitives like throw to raise failure signals and try-catch to manage them. The latter uses primitives to install and activate dedicated compensation activities. This chapter presents linguistic primitives and associated semantic models for dealing with transaction failure. The main features under inspection are the mechanisms to deal with:

1. failures: *exceptions* or *compensations*;
2. non-interruptable units of process execution: *protection operator*;
3. nested computations: *nested transactions* and *nested failures*.

The models are either based on (mobile) process calculi, or on the service-oriented core calculi developed within SENSORIA. We address three questions:

1. What is the relative expressive power of the mechanisms proposed?
   Section 2 is dedicated to basic linguistic primitives for exception and compensation handling. We present: (1) a study of the expressive power of two well-known exception handling mechanisms, in the context of the Calculus of Communicating Systems, CCS [28]; and (2) compensation handling mechanisms and their relative expressiveness, in the context of mobile process calculi.
2. How can these recovery mechanisms be used in the context of Service-Oriented Computing (SOC)?
   Section 3 presents the application of the mechanisms in some of the SENSORIA calculi.
3. How can one ensure that the compensation activities implement a particular recovery policy?
   Section 4 presents three different models to reason about the compensation activities: two of them use abstract descriptions of the desired behavior, in BPEL and SAGAs respectively, and the last one defines a state-based compensation model to reason about the correctness of the activities.

1.2 Overview of Process Calculi Approaches

In process calculi there are several approaches toward the formalization of LRTs, whose proposals differ with respect to the mechanisms to recover from transaction failure. Table 1 presents a summary of the use of compensation handling mechanisms in different message-based calculi, which we group in three families: π-calculus [29,34] based, session-based and correlation-based. Compensation handling has been investigated also in the context of event-based communication: this is the subject of Chapter 3-4 where compensation handling is investigated in the context of the Signal Calculus SC [14].

π-calculus Based Calculi. The πt-calculus is an extension of asynchronous polyadic π-calculus [34] with the notion of transaction [2]. The compensation mechanism is static, and transaction abort triggers the execution of the compensations of all terminated subtransactions. The cJoin calculus [7] extends the Join calculus [15] with primitives for representing transactions with static compensations.

Table 1. Features of message-based calculi with compensation handling

	communication mechanism	compensation definition	nested vs non-nested	protection operator
πt [2]	π-based	static	nested	no
c-join [7]	π-based	static	nested	no
webπ [24]	π-based	static	non-nested	implementable
webπ_∞ [27]	π-based	static	non-nested	implementable
dcπ [36]	π-based	parallel	nested	yes
CaSPiS [3]	sessions	static	nested	no
CC [37]	sessions	static	nested	no
COWS [26]	correlation	static	nested	yes
SOCK [18]	correlation	dynamic	nested	implementable

Transactions can however dynamically merge, thus merging their compensations. Laneve and Zavattaro defined webπ [24], which is an extension of asynchronous polyadic π-calculus with a timed transaction construct. An untimed version of webπ, called webπ_∞, was proposed by Mazzara and Lanese [27]. Both webπ and webπ_∞ support a non-nested static compensation mechanism. The dcπ calculus [36] is also based on the asynchronous polyadic π-calculus, extended with primitives for representing nested transactions and dynamic compensations. This is obtained by adding information about compensation update to input prefix. Compensation items are composed in parallel. Section 2 presents in more detail the compensation handling mechanisms of webπ_∞ and dcπ.

Session-Based Calculi. The coordinated handling of exceptions of several parties involved in a service conversation is of particular importance, since an exception local to a party must be somehow propagated to all other parties involved in the service task.

CaSPiS [3] includes primitives for compensating aborted sessions (see Section 3 for more details). The Conversation Calculus, CC [37], supports error recovery with two exception primitives: try-catch and throw. Section 4.3 presents in more detail the exception handling mechanism and the soundness model of CC. In the approach of Carbone et al. [13], as in SCC [4] and CaSPiS [3], such error propagation is modeled internally to the semantics of the exception handling primitives. CC considers a different approach, by providing the exception handling primitives with a standard "local" semantics, leaving to the programmer the task of coordinating the exception handling activities. The approach of Carbone et al. [13] already aims at a typed exception handling model, allowing to prove safety and liveness results.

Correlation-Based Calculi. COWS [26] provides a primitive to kill processes within a scope. We show in Section 4.1 how these primitives can be used to encode a BPEL-style scope construct (BPEL [32] is a language for service orchestration which provides static nested compensations). SOCK [18] includes also explicit primitives for dynamic handler update and automatic failure notification to remote partners. Section 3 presents in more detail the compensation handling mechanisms of SOCK. An implementation of SOCK, the language JOLIE [21], inherits its fault handling capabilities.

2   Basic Mechanisms

In this section we focus on different basic linguistic primitives that have been proposed for programming long-running transactions (LRTs), inter-relating them. We leave to the next section their application to service-oriented systems.

2.1   Exception Handling

Here we present and compare with respect to expressiveness two well established mechanisms, the first taken from the tradition of process calculi—the interrupt operator of CSP [20]; the second from popular programming languages—the try-catch operator of languages such as C++ or Java.

Interrupt Versus Try-catch. The interrupt operator $P \triangle Q$ executes P until Q executes its first action; when Q starts executing, the process P is interrupted. The try P catch Q operator executes P, but if P performs a throw action it is interrupted and Q is executed instead. We have found these operators particularly useful because, even if very simple, they are the basic building blocks to model the typical operators for programming LRTs.

These two operators are apparently very similar as they both allow for the combination of two processes P and Q, where the first one executes until the second one performs its first action. Nevertheless, there is an interesting distinguishing feature, as shown by the following example.

Consider for instance a bank payment activity PAY, which may set a variable res to false in case of failure. Failure management can be performed quite simply using try-catch:

try PAY; if $res = $ F then throw else 0; ... catch manageFault

The interrupt operator, instead, needs some help from an external process.

PAY; if $res = $ F then *throw* else 0; ...$\triangle(f.$ manageFault$) \mid \overline{throw}.\overline{f}$

where we assume that *throw* synchronizes with $\overline{throw}$ and f with $\overline{f}$. Here in case of failure the external process is called, and then it enables the compensation. When the compensation starts, the main activity is interrupted. Note however that the interruption is not atomic as in previous case.

As seen in the examples, the main difference is that in the try-catch operator, the decision to interrupt the execution of P is taken inside P itself (by means of the execution of the throw action), while in the interrupt operator $P \triangle Q$ such decision is taken from Q (by executing any initial action). Another difference

Table 2. Interrupt vs try-catch

	interrupt	try-catch
	$\text{CCS}_!^{\triangle}$	$\text{CCS}_!^{\text{tc}}$
replication	existential termination undecidable	existential termination undecidable
	universal termination decidable	universal termination decidable
	$\text{CCS}_{rec}^{\triangle}$	$\text{CCS}_{rec}^{\text{tc}}$
recursion	existential termination undecidable	existential termination undecidable
	universal termination decidable	universal termination undecidable

between the try-catch and the interrupt operators is that the former includes an implicit scoping mechanism which has no counterpart in the interrupt operator. More precisely, the try-catch operator defines a new scope for the special throw action which is bound to a specific instance of exception handler.

Starting from these intuitive and informal evaluations of the differences between such operators, a more rigorous and formal investigation has been performed [5]. To this aim, two restriction-free fragments of CCS [28] have been considered, one with replication and one with restriction, and they have been both extended with either the interrupt or the try-catch operator thus obtaining four different calculi: $\text{CCS}_!^{\triangle}$, $\text{CCS}_!^{\text{tc}}$, $\text{CCS}_{rec}^{\triangle}$, and $\text{CCS}_{rec}^{\text{tc}}$ as depicted in Table 2. Calculi without restriction, the standard explicit binder operator of CCS, have been considered in order to be able to observe the impact of the implicit binder of try-catch. Moreover, replication and recursion have been considered separately because in CCS there is an interesting interplay between these operators and binders [9]: in the case of replication it is possible to compute, given a process P, an upper bound to the nesting depth of binders for all derivatives of P (i.e. those processes that can be reached from P after a sequence of transitions). In CCS with recursion, on the contrary, this upper bound cannot be computed in general.

For these four calculi, the decidability of the following termination problems has been investigated: *existential termination* (i.e., there exists a terminating computation) and *universal termination* (i.e., all computations terminate). The obtained results are depicted in Table 2.

These results about the decidability of existential/universal termination in the considered calculi establish two interesting discrimination results:

- **Basic mechanisms for interruption cannot be in general encoded using only communication primitives.** In CCS without restriction, existential termination is decidable [5], while it turns out to be undecidable when either the interrupt or the try-catch operators are also considered.
- **The try-catch mechanism cannot be in general encoded using communication primitives and the interrupt operator.** In the considered calculus with recursion, universal termination is decidable in the presence of the interrupt operator, while this is not the case for try-catch.

2.2   Compensation Handling

The operators above offer a local approach to error handling and compensations: the trigger of the fault, the executing process and the compensation are all defined inside P and Q. However, in a concurrent and distributed system, fault triggers may also arise from other processes running concurrently.

Static Compensations. Such an aspect has been tackled first by webπ [24] and its untimed version webπ_∞ [27]. There, web transactions, i.e., long-running transactions involving web applications, have been considered, and modeled by adding a workunit construct to the asynchronous π-calculus. We concentrate here on the untimed version proposed by [27], since time introduces a degree of expressive power which is orthogonal to the one represented by compensation primitives we investigate here.

A workunit $\langle P \; ; \; Q \rangle_t$ executes process P until a message $\bar{t}$ (without parameters) is received on channel t. After that, process P is killed and compensation Q is executed. Thus message $\bar{t}$ acts as throw in the case of the try-catch operator. However, here message $\bar{t}$ may come both from inside P, as for throw in try-catch, or from parallel processes. Also, the message may be directed to a specific workunit, instead of being forced to kill the nearest enclosing workunit.

Thus the above example of bank payment can be written in webπ_∞ as:

$$\langle \; \texttt{PAY.if } res = \texttt{F then } \bar{t} \texttt{ else 0.... ; manageFault} \rangle_t$$

where we used prefixing instead of sequential composition (simply because this is the control flow mechanism provided by webπ_∞). However, the example can be simply modified to allow for an external activity to interrupt the transaction. Assume that in parallel some checks on the payment are done. If the checks do not succeed, the transaction can also be interrupted by the parallel process:

$$\langle \; \texttt{PAY.if } res = \texttt{F then } \bar{t} \texttt{ ; manageFault} \rangle_t \; | \; ....\texttt{if } checkRes = \texttt{F then } \bar{t}...$$

Since now the failure signal may also come from outside, it is necessary to define when a workunit has terminated, thus to avoid interrupting and compensating terminated transactions. In webπ_∞ the transaction is considered terminated, and thus discarded, when its body P becomes $\mathbf{0}$. A few other aspects have to be considered for killing and termination. First, since webπ_∞ is asynchronous, messages are considered sent as soon as they become enabled. Thus they can freely float out of workunits. Moreover, they are not deleted when the workunit is interrupted. Another important aspect is transaction nesting. Two approaches exist in the literature: *nested failure* and *non-nested failure*. In the nested failure approach, when a transaction is killed all its subtransactions are killed too. In the non-nested failure approach instead, subtransactions are preserved and continue their regular execution. Suppose for instance that the payment workunit described above is part of a more complex transaction with body Q:

$$\langle\langle \; \texttt{PAY.... ; manageFault} \rangle_t \, | \, Q \; ; \; \texttt{manageLargerFault} \rangle_s$$

With the nested failure approach in case of failure of s also t is killed. However this is not the behavior of $\mathsf{web}\pi_\infty$, which follows the non-nested failure approach. In $\mathsf{web}\pi_\infty$ this behavior can be obtained by adding an explicit kill of t as part of the management of the larger fault, e.g., by replacing the compensation with the process $\bar{t}\,|\,\mathtt{manageLargerFault}$.

The $\mathsf{web}\pi_\infty$ calculus is equipped with a reduction semantics formally describing the behavior of systems based on web transactions, and with a labeled transition system supporting the standard observational equivalence—weak barbed congruence [30]. Furthermore, weak asynchronous bisimilarity [1], adapted to the $\mathsf{web}\pi_\infty$ setting, where transaction kill has to be explicitly considered, characterizes weak barbed congruence. Therefore, transformations of $\mathsf{web}\pi_\infty$ processes can be coinductively proved correct (with respect to weak asynchronous bisimilarity, and thus, with respect to weak barbed congruence).

While referring to the paper [27] for the technical details, we present here a sample law, illustrating handlers reducibility:

$$\langle\!\langle P\ ;\ Q\rangle\!\rangle_x = (x'x'')(\langle\!\langle P\ ;\ \overline{x'}\,\rangle\!\rangle_x\,|\,\langle\!\langle x'.Q\ ;\ \mathbf{0}\rangle\!\rangle_{x''})$$

for each $x', x'' \notin \mathrm{fn}(P) \cup \mathrm{fn}(Q), x' \neq x'' \neq x$. In other words, it is not necessary to have a generic process Q as compensation of a workunit, but it is enough to have a simple output message $\overline{x'}$. In fact, it is enough to put the compensation in another workunit, guarded by an input on the name x'. Note that both the name x' and the name x'' of the auxiliary workunit need to be private (this is done by the restriction operator $(x'x'')$) to avoid interferences.

Dynamic Compensations. In $\mathsf{web}\pi_\infty$, the compensation of each workunit is static, i.e., in a workunit $\langle\!\langle P\ ;\ Q\rangle\!\rangle_x$, P is not allowed to update Q. Assume that P is a complex activity, e.g., executing a sequence of bank payments. If a failure occurs before any bank payment, then no particular error recovery is needed (possibly just some garbage collection or error notification). Instead, if a few bank payments have been completed and an error requires to abort the transaction, then the already completed bank payments have to be annulled. In $\mathsf{web}\pi_\infty$ this can be done for instance by keeping track of the performed bank payments, and by having the compensation Q checking which of them have been completed to annul them. Another solution, suggested by the law above, is to put the compensation in a different workunit to be replaced with an updated one each time a new payment is completed. However, both the solutions are complex and error-prone [19]. In general, one may want to adapt the compensation of a complex transaction to the evolving state of its process P. This kind of problems has been tackled by dcπ [36], by compensable processes [22], and by SOCK [18]. The three approaches differ in a few technical decisions, but they all share the idea that a compensation can be dynamically updated. We present here the general approach in the framework of π-calculus [36,22], leaving to next section the discussion of the interplay with service-oriented features.

Parallel Recovery. The simplest proposal is the one of dcπ. There, scopes (similar to $\mathsf{web}\pi_\infty$ workunits) have the form $t[P]$ where P is the executing process and

t the scope name. Inputs in P may install compensations. For instance, assume that a message $\overline{payConf}\langle v \rangle$ confirms that a payment has been completed, and that v contains the data of the payment. In dcπ such a message can be received by an input $payConf(x)\%\overline{Annul}\langle x \rangle.Q$ that after receiving the message $\overline{payConf}\langle v \rangle$ installs in the nearest enclosing scope a new compensation item $\overline{Annul}\langle v \rangle$ and continues as $Q\{v/x\}$. When a scope is killed, all the installed compensation items are executed in parallel. This form of recovery is called *parallel recovery*. Note that input and compensation update form a unique atomic primitive. This is important since it should never be the case that the state of the transaction is changed (because of the received input), and the compensation has not been changed accordingly. In our example this would cause a performed payment not to be annulled. It would be difficult to ensure this atomicity property if compensation update has to be mimicked as described above.

General Recovery Policies. As shown, dcπ allows to dynamically add new compensation items in parallel. However, it may be handy to have more control on the order of execution of compensation items, and to be able to remove compensation items when they are no more useful. A more general approach has been proposed in the framework of SOCK[18], and analyzed in the framework of π-calculus [22]. We describe here the latter, where compensable processes are defined. Compensable processes define a scope construct $t[P,Q]$ similar to the workunit $\langle\!\langle P \; ; \; Q \rangle\!\rangle_t$ of webπ_∞. However compensable processes provide in addition a compensation update primitive $\mathsf{inst}\lfloor\lambda X.Q'\rfloor.R$ that replaces the current compensation Q in the nearest enclosing scope with the new compensation $Q'\{Q/x\}$. This allows for instance to add a new compensation item in parallel, by choosing $Q' = Q'' \mid X$ where X does not occur in Q'', mimicking dcπ parallel recovery. However, many other options are available. For instance one may execute compensations of different activities in reverse order of completion (this policy is called *backward* recovery [16]). In compensable processes such behavior is obtained by using compensations of the form $\lambda X.(finished)(Q' \mid finished.X)$ where the actual compensation Q' signals its termination with an output on the private channel $finished$. Moreover, the compensation can be deleted by installing $\lambda X.\mathbf{0}$, or replaced with a new compensation by installing $\lambda X.NewComp$ where $NewComp$ does not contain X.

Consider the following scenario: a few bank payments are executed by sending messages to the banks in charge of them. If something goes wrong in one of the payments, all of the performed payments have to be annulled. At the end a final check is performed, and if it succeeds then annul is no more possible. This can be implemented in compensable processes as follows:

$$t[PAY_1.\,\mathsf{inst}\lfloor\lambda X.ANNUL_1.X\rfloor.\ldots.PAY_n.\,\mathsf{inst}\lfloor\lambda X.ANNUL_n.X\rfloor.$$
$$CHECK.\ \texttt{if}\ check = \texttt{ok}\ \texttt{then}\ \mathsf{inst}\lfloor\lambda X.\mathbf{0}\rfloor\ \texttt{else}\ \overline{t},\mathbf{0}]$$

where $PAY_1, \ldots, PAY_n$ are activities executing the payments, $ANNUL_1, \ldots,$ $ANNUL_n$ the corresponding annul activities and $CHECK$ performs the final verification putting the result in $check$.

Differently from webπ_∞, compensable processes have been given both a nested failure semantics and a non-nested failure one, while dcπ follows the nested failure approach. However both compensable processes and dcπ provide a protection operator $\langle P \rangle$ that executes P in a protected way and that can be used to avoid undesired external kills. The non-nested failure approach can thus be mimicked by enclosing each transaction in a protected block.

Another difference between webπ_∞ and compensable processes is that compensable processes scopes never commit. However, webπ_∞ commit behavior can be easily recovered since a scope $(t)t[\mathbf{0}, \mathbf{0}]$ with a restricted name, no body and no compensation is equivalent to $\mathbf{0}$. Note that "no compensation" can be forced in compensable processes with a suitable compensation update, while the same is not possible for webπ_∞.

The definition of the semantics of compensation update requires a bit of care. As said above, in fact, it should never be the case that a state change requiring a compensation update has been performed, and the corresponding compensation update has not been executed. For instance in:

$$t[PAY_1.\,\mathsf{inst}\lfloor \lambda X.ANNUL_1.X \rfloor. \ldots]$$

if the transaction is killed after PAY_1 has been completed but before the compensation has been updated, no annul is performed. For this reason, compensation update has priority w.r.t. other actions. Thus a compensation update is executed as soon as it becomes enabled. This feature comes for free in dcπ, since the input and the compensation update are composed in a unique primitive.

The expressive powers of static recovery, parallel recovery, backward recovery and dynamic recovery have been compared in [22]. There the existence/non existence of suitable encodings (compositional [17], preserving testing equivalence [33], and not introducing divergency) has been discussed. Two main results were achieved:

- **An encoding of parallel recovery into static recovery which satisfies the conditions above and preserves also weak bisimilarity.** The existence of such an encoding proves that parallel recovery and static recovery have the same expressive power. The encoding stores the dynamically created compensation items in the running process protected by protected blocks, and exploits suitable messages to enable them only when needed.
- **A separation result proving that no encoding satisfying the properties above exists from backward recovery to static recovery neither from compensable processes to static recovery.**

The results above, together with the ones presented at the beginning of the section, prove that primitives for interruption and compensation are an important feature of languages, since they can not be encoded in an easy way, and that also the choice of the exact kind of primitives may change the expressive power of the language. Thus a careful choice is needed to decide which of these primitives have to be included in a language. Next section shows how these primitives can be applied to service-oriented systems.

3   Exploiting the Mechanisms in SOC

In this section we show how the mechanisms introduced in the previous sections to deal with failures and compensations can be exploited in service-oriented computing models and languages, where an application is composed by orchestrating different services. Service instances interact giving rise to sessions involving possibly many partners. Thus errors may be both internal to a single session, and in this case the techniques described in the previous section may be applied directly, or may involve different services. The first case has been considered for instance in the Conversation Calculus [37] (see also Chapter 2-1), where a conversation is a set of related interactions that take place in a dedicated medium—a conversation context—which may be accessed from several distributed conversation access pieces (cf. endpoints), each one held by a different party. The Conversation Calculus manages errors by using the try-catch operator discussed in the previous section. As we show in Section 4.3, this is enough to model cCSP [11].

Different approaches were chosen in various other SENSORIA calculi. We explain these approaches below.

3.1   Static Compensation Policies

We present the compensation mechanisms of COWS and of CaSPiS.

Killing Activities. COWS [26] includes primitives used to force immediate termination of concurrent threads. The syntax of COWS and an informal explanation of its semantics are presented in Chapter 2-1. Besides allowing generation of 'fresh' private names (as 'restriction' in π-calculus [29]), the delimitation operator of COWS provides a means for modeling a named scope for grouping certain activities. A named scope $[k]\,s$ can be then equipped with suitable termination activities, as well as ad hoc fault and compensation handlers, thus laying the foundation for guaranteeing transactional properties in spite of services' loose coupling. This can be conveniently done by relying on the *kill* activity $\text{kill}(k)$, that causes immediate termination of all concurrent activities inside the enclosing $[k]$ (which stops the killing effect), and the *protection* operator $\{|s|\}$, that preserves intact a critical activity s also when one of its enclosing scopes is abruptly terminated.

Failure management operators can be programmed and assembled in COWS by simply exploiting these basic operators. For example, the *try-catch* block used for the bank payment activity can be written as follows:

$$PAY \mid [\mathit{if}, \mathit{then}, k]\,(\,\mathit{if} \bullet \mathit{then}?\langle\mathrm{false}\rangle.(\,\text{kill}(k) \mid \{\!|\,\mathit{manageFault}\,|\!\}\,)\,\mid$$
$$\mathit{if} \bullet \mathit{then}?\langle\mathrm{true}\rangle.s\,)$$

Suppose that the result of the payment transaction is provided by the process PAY through the invoke activity $\mathit{if} \bullet \mathit{then}!\langle x_{res}\rangle$ and by setting the variable x_{res} to communicate the success (x_{res} = true) or failure (x_{res} = false) of the transaction. The delimitation of the killer label k confines the transaction, otherwise uncontrolled faults can jeopardize service composition. Suppose that the failure is risen by the activity $if \cdot then!\langle false \rangle$. The management of the corresponding fault can be activated while the activity $if \cdot then?\langle true \rangle.s$ is abruptly terminated by means of the activity $\mathbf{kill}(k)$. To ensure a proper execution order in the above transaction, i.e. the management of the fault should not be performed before the termination of the killing effect of $\mathbf{kill}(k)$, kill activities in COWS have higher priority than other activities.

Finally, restriction and protection operators implicitly provide embedded mechanisms for handling nested failures. The following simple example illustrates the effect of executing a kill activity within a nested protection block:

$$[k] (\{|s_1| \; [k'] \; \{|s_2| \; \mathbf{kill}(k')|\} \; | \; \mathbf{kill}(k)|\} \; | \; s_3) \; | \; s_4$$

evolves to

$$[k, k'] \; \{|s_2| \; \mathbf{kill}(k')|\} \; | \; s_4$$

For simplicity, we assume that s_1 and s_3 do not contain protected activities. In essence, $\mathbf{kill}(k)$ terminates all parallel services inside delimitation $[k]$ (i.e. s_1 and s_3), except those that are protected at the same nesting level of the kill activity (i.e. $s_2 \; | \; \mathbf{kill}(k')$).

Closing Sessions. The Service Centered Calculus (SCC) [4] and its evolution CaSPiS [3] propose another approach. As shown in Chapter 2-1, conversations in CaSPiS are structured as binary sessions involving a client and a service instance, dynamically created during service invocation. CaSPiS features primitives for session closure. Recall that, using close, a partner can leave a session at any time; the semantics will then guarantee that the other party is informed and that nested sessions are closed as well. In terms of transactions, completing and abandoning a session may be understood respectively as commit and failure. CaSPiS compensation handling can be classified as *static*, indeed compensations are programmed once and for all by means of listeners, $k \cdot P$, at design time.

Below, we briefly illustrate the use of session-closing primitives for programming compensations by means of a simple example. Further details can be found in [3], while the (similar) approach proposed by SCC is described in [4].

Consider another version of the bank example, where the bank (process B below) offers a service pay that, after receiving the amount to be paid and the user's credentials, invokes an auxiliary service, checkAmt, in order to check the client's available funds. A client (process C below) invokes this service and requires the payment of an amount a. The example contains three listeners. In B, upon invocation, the listener of the service definition $\mathbf{pay}_k$, $k \cdot \mathbf{close}$, closes the current session and notifies the closure to the invoker, while the listener of service invocation, $\overline{\mathbf{checkAmt}}_{k'}$, also closes the enclosing session by spawning $\dagger(k)$. The listener of service invocation $\overline{\mathbf{pay}}_{k''}$, $k'' \cdot payNotAllowed$, is activated in case of failure in the payment process on the service side: *payNotAllowed* encodes the execution of appropriate recovery actions

$$B \triangleq (\nu\, k)\mathsf{pay}_k.(k \cdot \mathsf{close}$$
$$|\,(?amt, ?id)\mathbf{select}\ ?go$$
$$\mathbf{from}\ (\nu\, k')\overline{\mathsf{checkAmt}}_{k'}.(k' \cdot (\mathsf{close}|\dagger(k)))\,|$$
$$\langle amt, id\rangle(?rep)\langle rep\rangle^{\uparrow})$$
$$\mathbf{inif}\ go\ \mathbf{then}\ \cdots\ \mathbf{else}\ \mathsf{close})$$
$$C \triangleq (\nu\, k'', a, id)\overline{\mathsf{pay}}_{k''}.(k'' \cdot payNotAllowed\,|\,\langle a, id\rangle \cdots)\ .$$

Consider the system $S \triangleq B\,|\,C$. The session installed between the client and the bank can be terminated unexpectedly in two cases: when the auxiliary service closes the interaction unexpectedly or when the checkAmt service answers negatively. After the synchronization of service definition and invocation and the first intra-session communication for sending the amount and the id, the system becomes S' below.

$$S' \triangleq (\nu\, r, k, k'', a, id)$$
$$\Big(r \rhd_{k''} (k \cdot \mathsf{close}\,|\,\mathbf{select}\ ?go$$
$$\mathbf{from}\ (\nu\, k')\overline{\mathsf{checkAmt}}_{k'}.(k' \cdot (\mathsf{close}|\dagger(k)))\,|$$
$$\langle a, id\rangle(?rep)\langle rep\rangle^{\uparrow})$$
$$\mathbf{inif}\ go\ \mathbf{then}\ \cdots\ \mathbf{else}\ \mathsf{close})$$
$$|\,r \rhd_k \big(k'' \cdot payNotAllowed\,|\,\cdots\big)\Big)$$

If the service call $\overline{\mathsf{checkAmt}}$ returns false, S' reduces to S'' and (omitting the terminated session originated by the service invocation $\overline{\mathsf{checkAmt}}_{k'}$.) we have

$$S'' \triangleq (\nu\, r, k, k'', a, id)\Big(r \rhd_{k''} (k \cdot \mathsf{close}\,|\,\mathsf{close})\,|\,r \rhd_k \big(k'' \cdot payNotAllowed\,|\,\cdots\big)\Big)$$
$$\longrightarrow$$
$$(\nu\, r, k, k'', a, id)\Big(\blacktriangleright (k \cdot \mathsf{close}\,|\,\dagger(k''))\,|\,r \rhd_k \big(k'' \cdot payNotAllowed\,|\,\cdots\big)\Big)$$
$$\longrightarrow$$
$$(\nu\, r, k, k'', a, id)\Big(\blacktriangleright (k \cdot \mathsf{close})\,|\,r \rhd_k \big(payNotAllowed\,|\,\cdots\big)\Big) \triangleq S'''\ .$$

In S''', the client proceeds by taking appropriate recovery actions (defined in $payNotAllowed$).

In case the closure is originated by service checkAmt, the signal $\dagger(k)$ will be captured by the listener $k \cdot \mathsf{close}$ and the session closure protocol will proceed similarly.

3.2 Dynamic Compensation Policies

The last approach we consider is the one of the Service Oriented Computing Kernel (SOCK) [10]. As described in Chapter 2-1, SOCK is a calculus for service-oriented computing that has been inspired by the main technologies in the field, in particular WSDL [38], the standard for defining web service interfaces, and WS-BPEL [32], the de-facto standard for web services composition. SOCK allows the definition of services exploiting the one-way and request-response patterns provided by WSDL.

From a compensation point of view, SOCK has been extended in [18] with mechanisms that integrate the WS-BPEL concepts of scope, termination and compensation with the dynamic approach to error recovery described in the previous section.

A scope in SOCK is a process container denoted by a name and able to manage faults. Faults are thrown by the primitive $\mathtt{throw}(f)$ where f is the name of the fault. Inside a scope, three different kinds of handler can be defined. A fault handler f specifies the recovery code to be executed when fault f is thrown inside the scope. A termination handler, which has the name of the scope containing it, specifies how to smoothly terminate the scope when it is reached by an external fault. Finally, compensation handler q specifies how to undo the activities of the finished scope q if required during error recovery inside an outer scope. For instance

$$\{\mathtt{PAY} : [f \to \mathtt{manageFault}, q \to \mathtt{manageExternalFault}]\}_q$$

is a scope that executes activity PAY, executes code $\mathtt{manageFault}$ in case PAY throws fault f and executes code $\mathtt{manageExternalFault}$ in case of external failure.[1]

Assume that activity PAY throws fault f, e.g. since $PAY = PAY' \,|\, \mathtt{throw}(f)$. First, all the activities inside PAY' are terminated, including subscopes. Termination handlers of those subscopes are executed. Then the fault handler for f is looked for inside q. Since it is available then it is executed, handling fault f. If no fault handler was found, the fault would be rethrown to the enclosing scope, let us call it q', while q terminates with a failure. Error handling would continue in q', and the fault would be recursively thrown to the nearest enclosing scope until a handler is found. Both termination handler $\mathtt{manageExternalFault}$ and fault handler $\mathtt{manageFault}$ may use the primitive $\mathtt{comp}(q_1)$ to execute the compensation handler of some subscope q_1 of q to undo its activity. This is available only if q_1 has terminated with success.

Up to here, this is the error recovery policy used also by WS-BPEL. However, in WS-BPEL handlers are defined statically inside the scope. SOCK allows to update them at runtime, thus following the dynamic approach. Consider the scope q above. SOCK provides a compensation update primitive, $\mathtt{inst}([f \to \mathtt{newHandler}])$, similar to the one of compensable processes, to replace the old handler $\mathtt{manageFault}$ with the new handler $\mathtt{newHandler}$. Differently from compensable processes, now the name of the handler(s) to be updated has to be specified. Like in compensable processes, the old handler may not be discarded. In fact, one can use the placeholder cH inside the handler update primitive to recover the old handler. For instance, $\mathtt{inst}([f \to \mathtt{newHandler}; cH])$, adds the new handler $\mathtt{newHandler}$ before the old handler $\mathtt{manageFault}$ (here ; is sequential

---

[1] The actual syntax is slightly more complex, cfr. [18].

composition), producing the new handler `newHandler;manageFault`. Both fault and termination handlers can be updated in this way. A compensation handler instead is just the last defined termination handler when the scope terminates. This is justified by the fact that intuitively the behavior of a service should be the same if the fault occurs just before or just after its termination. Anyway, the ability of dynamically updating the handlers allows to redefine termination handler just before termination if a different behavior is desired for compensation handler. Notice that the update primitive is executed with priority w.r.t. other instructions, so to ensure that the state of the error handlers always matches the state of the computation.

Until now we have managed errors involving just one service instance. As already said, services in SOCK may interact using two modalities: one-way $\overline{o}@z(\boldsymbol{y})$ and request-response $\overline{o}_r@z(\boldsymbol{y}, \boldsymbol{x})$. With the one-way, a service invokes another service o located at z and does not care about the result. This is a loosely coupled interaction pattern, thus does not poses particular problems from an error handling point of view. With the request-response instead a client invokes a service o_r located at z and waits for an answer. This interaction pattern may be spoiled by errors both on client side and on service side. Assume for instance that the invoked service fails because of some fault f, either from the service code or from the service environment. In WS-BPEL such a service will not send back any answer, and the client would wait undefinitely. Vice versa, if the client fails (because of some fault in a parallel process), the answer from the service may be lost. Consider our example of bank payment. Now the payment may be required by a process

$$\{\overline{pay}_r@bank(\boldsymbol{y}, \boldsymbol{x}) \mid Q : [f \rightarrow \texttt{manageFault}, g \rightarrow \texttt{manageRemoteFault}]\}_q$$

Suppose that after the pay_r service has been invoked Q throws fault f. Thus the client will not know whether the operation has been successful (and money has been taken from the account) or not. Clearly the two scenarios require different compensation policies on the client side.

To answer these problems SOCK proposes an approach based on automatic error notification and allows to exploit those notifications during error recovery. In particular, if the server pay_r above fails because of fault g, a faulty answer is automatically sent to the waiting client, where it is considered as a local fault. This has a double aim: on the one side the client will not be stuck waiting for a response that will not arrive, on the other side the client may specify a suitable handler for g allowing to recover locally from the remote error. For instance the handler `manageRemoteFault` may notify the user or look for other payment methods.

Furthermore, if the client fails while waiting for the answer of the request-response operation (the fault comes from Q), the answer from pay_r is waited for before error recovery is started. Also, a non-faulty answer may update the error-handler on the client side requiring for instance to undo the remote activity. This can be obtained by modifying the request-response above into

$$\overline{pay}_r@bank(\boldsymbol{y}, \boldsymbol{x}, [f \rightarrow \texttt{annulPay}; cH])$$

Now, upon successful answer from pay_r, the fault handler for f is updated specifying that in case of such a fault (that, we assume, makes the whole transaction fail) the pay operation should be undone. The compensation update is performed only if the remote operation has been successful, and even if there has been a local fault in the meanwhile.

The proposed approach has been validated (see [18] for details) in different ways. First, by formally proving that the formalism satisfies some expected high-level properties such as "each request-response receives an answer, either a normal one or a faulty one" or "it is never the case that a fault is managed by an handler that has not been updated". Second, SOCK error handling primitives have been used to program error handling for the automotive case study (see Chapter 0-3). Third, SOCK primitives have been introduced in the language JOLIE [31,21], a full-fledged language to program service-oriented applications inspired by SOCK, and used to program real applications.

4   Models of Compensations

In the previous sections we have presented different mechanisms for defining long-running transactions and compensations. However those mechanisms are not all at the same abstraction level. They range from some low level mechanisms, such as the ones of COWS [26] providing basic operators such as kill and protection, to more complex mechanisms such as the ones of SOCK [19] and WS-BPEL [32]. In the literature there are also abstract descriptions of the desired behavior that compensated activities should have, such as the one provided by SAGAs calculi [8]. Also, some approaches aiming at proving the correctness of compensations are emerging [12,35].

In this section we present three comparisons between approaches at different levels of abstraction. These can be exploited with different aims. On one side they provide a way to assess the expressive power of languages, showing that they are able to implement some abstract behavior. On the other side they help the programmer of the application, who can specify the desired recovery strategy at the high level of abstraction and exploit an automatic translation to derive an implementation which is correct by construction. Finally, techniques and strategies developed at one abstraction level can be exported to other levels.

4.1   Encoding BPEL Scopes in COWS

The first encoding that we present shows how COWS basic mechanisms are powerful enough to implement WS-BPEL [32] scope construct.

Consider the following version of the WS-BPEL scope activity:

$$[s : \mathbf{catch}(\phi_1)\{s_1\} : \ldots : \mathbf{catch}(\phi_n)\{s_n\} : s_c]_i$$

This construct permits explicitly grouping activities together[2]. The declaration of a scope activity contains a unique scope identifier i, a service s representing the normal behavior, an optional list of fault handlers $s_1, \ldots, s_n$, and a compensation handler s_c. The fault generator activity **throw**(ϕ) can be used by a service to rise a fault signal ϕ. This signal will trigger execution of activity s', if a construct of the form **catch**$(\phi)\{s'\}$ exists within the same scope. The compensate activity **compensate**(i) can be used to invoke a compensation handler of an inner scope named i that has already completed with success. Compensation can only be invoked from within a fault or a compensation handler. Here, we fix two syntactic constraints: handlers do not contain scope activities and, as in WS-BPEL (see [32]), for each **compensate**(i) occurring in a service there exists at least an inner scope i. Notably, an activity $[s : \textbf{catch}(\phi_1)\{s_1\} : \ldots : \textbf{catch}(\phi_n)\{s_n\} : s_c]_i$ acts as a binder for $\phi_1, \ldots, \phi_n$; in this way, a scope can only catch and handle faults coming from its enclosed activities.

Now we show that this version of fault and compensation handling can be easily encoded in COWS. The most interesting cases of the encoding are the following:

$$\langle\!\langle [s : \textbf{catch}(\phi_1)\{s_1\} : \ldots : \textbf{catch}(\phi_n)\{s_n\} : s_c]_i \rangle\!\rangle_k =$$
$$[\phi_1, \ldots, \phi_n] \, (\, \langle\!\langle \textbf{catch}(\phi_1)\{s_1\} \rangle\!\rangle_k \mid \ldots \mid \langle\!\langle \textbf{catch}(\phi_n)\{s_n\} \rangle\!\rangle_k$$
$$\mid [k_i] \, \langle\!\langle s \rangle\!\rangle_{k_i} \, ; \, (\, x_{done} \bullet o_{done}!\langle\rangle \mid [k'] \, \{\!| make \bullet undo?\langle i\rangle.\langle\!\langle s_c \rangle\!\rangle_{k'} \}\!| \,) \,)$$

$$\langle\!\langle \textbf{catch}(\phi)\{s\} \rangle\!\rangle_k = raise \bullet throw?\langle\phi\rangle.[k'] \, \langle\!\langle s \rangle\!\rangle_{k'}$$

$$\langle\!\langle \textbf{compensate}(i) \rangle\!\rangle_k = make \bullet undo!\langle i\rangle \mid x_{done} \bullet o_{done}!\langle\rangle$$

$$\langle\!\langle \textbf{throw}(\phi) \rangle\!\rangle_k = \{\!| raise \bullet throw!\langle\phi\rangle \}\!| \mid kill(k)$$

The two distinguished endpoints $raise \bullet throw$ and $make \bullet undo$ are used for exchanging fault and compensation signals, respectively. Each scope identifier i or fault signal ϕ can be used to activate scope compensation or fault handling, respectively.

The encoding $\langle\!\langle \cdot \rangle\!\rangle_k$ is parametrized by the label k that identifies the closest enclosing scope, if any. The parameter is used when encoding a fault generator, to launch a kill activity that forces termination of all the remaining activities of the enclosing scope, and when encoding a scope, to delimit the field of action of inner kill activities. The compensation handler s_c of scope i is installed when the normal behavior s successfully completes, but it is activated only when signal $make \bullet undo!\langle i\rangle$ occurs. Similarly, if during normal execution a fault ϕ occurs, a signal $raise \bullet throw!\langle\phi\rangle$ triggers execution of the corresponding fault handler (if any). Installed compensation handlers are protected from killing by means of $\{\!|_-\}\!|$. Notably, the compensate activity can immediately terminate (thus enabling possible sequential compositions by signaling its completion through the endpoint $x_{done} \bullet o_{done}$); this, of course, does not mean that the corresponding handler is terminated.

---

[2] This version only permits to compensate specified inner scopes and does not provide an automatic compensation mechanism à la SAGAs. This latter mechanism, however, can be implemented in COWS by relying on 'queues' (we refer the interested reader to [25] for further details).

4.2   SAGAs in SOCK

The next encoding that we present is from the SAGAs calculi [8] to SOCK [18]. SAGAs calculi are based on the composition of basic activities. An activity A may either terminate with success, or with failure. An activity A may have an associated compensation activity B whose aim is to compensate the activity A in case of failure of the transaction. Activities can be composed using sequential and parallel composition, and grouped into subtransactions. For instance a SAGA executing two payment requests and annulling them in case of failure can be written as:

$$\{[PAY_1\%ANNUL_1; PAY_2\%ANNUL_2]\}$$

Different recovery policies are defined, specifying how to compose compensations and when to execute them. The general idea is that sequential activities are compensated in backward order while parallel activities are compensated in parallel. SAGAs calculi provide different policies, depending on whether parallel activities are stopped in case of fault, and on whether compensations are executed in a centralized or distributed way. We concentrate here on "coordinated interruption", where parallel branches are stopped when a flow aborts, and compensations are handled in a centralized way.

This policy has been implemented using SOCK mechanisms in [23]. SAGA activities have been implemented by SOCK services, invoked using the request-response interaction pattern. For instance, the activity PAY_1 above is implemented by a service PAY_1 located at location l_{PAY_1} and invoked by a request-response $PAY_1@l_{PAY_1}$ (parameters are not considered since they are not important from a failure point of view).

If the activity PAY_1 succeeds, then it sends back an answer (values sent in the answer are not important too). If it fails, then it generates a specific fault c. Through the automatic fault notification mechanism of SOCK, this fault is notified to the caller, where it is raised signaling that the current SAGA is aborting and has to be compensated.

Abortion of a SAGA is managed by using SOCK fault and compensation handlers. Each activity invocation is inside a dedicated scope. If the activity successfully finishes, then its compensation is installed as compensation handler for the scope. At the SAGA level, a fault handler for c is installed, invoking the compensations of the different inner activities in the required order, which is extracted from the structure of the term. For instance, the SAGA of the example above is modeled by a scope of the form

$$\{\mathsf{inst}([c \rightarrow \mathsf{comp}(pay_2); \mathsf{comp}(pay_1)]; \ldots); \{\ldots\}_{pay_1}; \{\ldots\}_{pay_2}\}_u$$

Since compensation handlers are available only after the corresponding activity successfully ends, then only those activities are compensated, as required.

Assume now that the compensating activity $ANNUL_1$ is executed as part of the recovery. As specified by the compensation handler for PAY_1, this is executed with a different handler w.r.t. normal activities. In particular, in case of failure, the fault c is caught, and a fault f (for fail) is raised instead. Fault f is never caught and makes the whole SAGA fail, according to the SAGA idea that failure is a catastrophic event.

The translation outlined above has been described in detail and proved correct in [23]. We outline here also the correctness result. SAGA behavior is defined in terms of a big-step LTS semantics, with rules of the form $\Gamma \vdash S \xrightarrow{\alpha} \square$ where S is a SAGA, Γ a function that specifies for each activity in S whether it succeeds or it fails, α an observation of the computation, specifying the composition of successful activities executed (the composition contains sequential and parallel operators) and $\square$ may be either success, abort (i.e., success of the compensation) or failure. For instance the SAGA above has a big-step transition of the form

$$PAY_1 \mapsto \boxdot, PAY_2 \mapsto \boxtimes, ANNUL_1 \mapsto \boxdot \vdash$$

$$\{[PAY_1\%ANNUL_1; PAY_2\%ANNUL_2]\} \xrightarrow{PAY_1;ANNUL_1} \boxtimes$$

specifying that the SAGA aborts if activities PAY_1 and $ANNUL_1$ succeed and PAY_2 aborts.

SOCK instead has a small step semantics, including different observations such as service invocations and replies, uncaught faults and others. Thus the correctness is expressed in terms of an abstraction of the possible SOCK computation containing only the events corresponding to successful answers from request responses.

The correctness result can be stated as follows (see [23] for a more formal statement).

Theorem 1. Let S be a SAGA. $\Gamma \vdash S \xrightarrow{\alpha} \square$ iff for each observation o which is a linearization[3] of α one of the following happens:

- $\square$ is success and there is a computation starting from the translation of S that does not contain uncaught faults whose abstracted observation is o;
- $\square$ is abort and there is a computation starting from the translation of S whose abstracted observation is o and which terminates with an uncaught fault c which is the only uncaught fault;
- $\square$ is failure and there is a computation starting from the translation of S whose abstracted observation is o and which terminates with an uncaught fault f which is the only uncaught fault.

For the SAGA above the theorem guarantees that the translation of the SAGA has a computation whose abstracted observation is $PAY_1; ANNUL_1$ and which has a unique uncaught fault, c.

4.3   Analysis of Compensations in the Conversation Calculus

In this section we show how the Conversation Calculus (CC) [37] (see also Chapter 2-1) may be used to model and reason about structured compensating transactions, following the techniques detailed in [12]. To reason about compensations

---

[3] A linearization is obtained by taking an actual interleaving for parallel activities.

in an abstract way, independently from a particular language implementation, we introduce a general model of stateful compensating transactions. We then take the core language for structured compensations introduced in [11], the compensating CSP calculus (cCSP), but reinterpret its semantics in our generic compensating model framework and prove the fundamental property expected in any compensation model, namely atomicity of transactions (Theorem 2). Lastly, we present an embedding of cCSP transactions in the Conversation Calculus, which is proven correct since it induces a stateful model of compensating transactions (Theorem 3). In the remainder of this section we describe the main ideas that are at the basis of our development.

In our model, the most elementary program is a *primitive action*, similar to a SAGA activity. A primitive action enjoys the following atomicity property: it either executes successfully to completion, or it aborts. In case of abortion, a primitive action is required not to perform any relevant observable behavior, except signaling abortion by throwing an exception. A transaction, which may involve several primitive actions, must also enjoy the atomicity property: it either executes successfully to completion, or it aborts leaving the system in a state equivalent to the one right before the transaction started executing. An aborted transaction must not have any visible effect on the state of the system, so any actions that were executed up to the point of the abortion must be in some way reverted. Compensations provide a means to achieve this reversibility: if we attach to every action a compensation that reverts the effect of the action, then by executing all compensations of the previously executed actions (in the reverse order) we end up in a state that should be in some sense equivalent to the state right before the transaction started executing.

We define an abstract notion of compensating model, leaving open the intended notion of "similarity" ($\bowtie$) between states, up to to which reversibility is to be measured. The definition is also independent of the concrete underlying operational model.

Definition 1 (Compensation Model). *A compensation model is a pair* $(\mathcal{S}, \mathcal{D})$ *where* $\mathcal{S}$ *gives its static structure and* $\mathcal{D}$ *gives its dynamic structure. The static structure* $\mathcal{S} = (S, \mid, \#, \bowtie)$ *is defined such that:*

- S *is a set of (abstract) states*
- $\mid$ *is a partial composition operation on states*
- $\#$ *is an apartness relation on states*
- $\bowtie$ *is an equivalence relation on* S

The dynamic structure $\mathcal{D} = (\Sigma, \xrightarrow{a})$ *is defined such that:*

- Σ *is a set of primitive actions*
- $\xrightarrow{a}$ *is a labeled (by elements of* Σ*) transition system between states.*

On the one hand, the compensation model describes the static structure which consists in a set of states S, a composition operation over states (defined only when such states are independent/apart $\#$) and an equivalence relation that introduces flexibility at the level of measuring the cancellation effect of compensations: since compensations, in general, may not be able to leave the system in exactly the same state, we must consider a flexible notion of equivalence that allows us to capture that the compensations produce an "equivalent enough" state. On the other hand, the dynamic structure of the compensation model is described by a labeled transition system between the states.

Using this abstract notion of compensation model we proceed by equipping the cCSP with a semantics defined in terms of interpretations of a compensation model. The semantics captures the effects and final status of cCSP programs—the states in which the system is left after executing the program, and a signal that indicates that the program successfully completed or aborted. cCSP programs are split in two categories: basic programs and compensable programs. The simplest compensable program is a pair $P \div Q$ where P and Q are atomic actions and action Q is the compensation of action P. Thus action Q intended to undo the effect of the P action, leading to a $\bowtie$-equivalent state to the state right before P was executed. Complex structured compensable programs may then be defined by composition under various control operators: sequential composition $T; R$, parallel composition $T \mid R$, and others. An arbitrary compensable program T may then be encapsulated as a basic program, by means of the operator $\langle T \rangle$.

The compensation model already allows us to state conditions on basic actions precise enough to derive general properties, namely the following atomicity result, that may then be reused in each particular application of the model.

Theorem 2 (Atomicity). *Let R be a $\bowtie$-consistent compensable program. Then* $\langle R \rangle \sqsubseteq R^+ \oplus throw$.

Theorem 2 guarantees that the behavior of transactions implemented over $\bowtie$-consistent compensable programs approximate atomicity: a transaction either aborts (*throw*) doing "nothing", or ($\oplus$) terminates successfully after executing all of its forward actions (R^+) (P is the forward action in $P \div Q$). The $\bowtie$-consistent condition ensures that for each compensation pair $P \div Q$ in the program, action Q reverts the effect of P up to $\bowtie$.

We now present our provably correct embedding of the cCSP language for structured compensating transactions in the Conversation Calculus. We consider that primitive actions are implemented by CC processes conforming to the following behavior: after some interactions with the environment it either sends (only once) the message $ok^{\downarrow}!$ in the current conversation context without any further action, or aborts, by throwing an exception. If the outcome is abortion, the system should be left in the "same" state (up to $\bowtie$) as it was before the primitive action started executing.

We show a selection of our encoding in Fig. 1. We use $[\, P \,] \triangleq (\nu n)(n \blacktriangleleft [\, P \,])$ as an abbreviation to represent an anonymous (restricted) context (useful to frame local computations). We denote by $[\![P]\!]_{ok}$ the encoding of a basic program P (namely structured compensating transactions) into a conversation calculus process. The ok index represents the message label that signals the successful completion of the basic program, while abortion is signaled by throwing an exception. The encoding of compensable transaction T is denoted by $[\![T]\!]_{ok,ab,cm,cb}$. The encoding of T will either issue a single message $ok^{\downarrow}$ to signal successful completion (and the implicit installation of compensation handlers)

$$[\![\langle T\rangle]\!]_{ok} \quad\triangleq\quad [\,[\![T]\!]_{ok,ab,cm,cb} \mid ab?.\mathbf{throw}\ 0 \mid ok?.ok^\uparrow!\,]$$

$$[\![P \div Q]\!]_{ok,ab,cm,cb} \triangleq [\,\mathbf{try}\ [\![P]\!]_{ok}\ \mathbf{catch}\ ab^\uparrow! \mid$$
$$ok?.ok^\uparrow!.(cm^\uparrow?.[\![Q]\!]_{cb} \mid cb?.cb^\uparrow!)\,]$$

$$[\![T_1; T_2]\!]_{ok,ab,cm,cb} \triangleq [\,[\![T_1]\!]_{ok_1,ab_1,cm_1,cb} \mid ab_1?.ab^\uparrow! \mid$$
$$ok_1?.[\![T_2]\!]_{ok,ab,cm,cm_1} \mid ab?.cm_1!.cb?.ab^\uparrow! \mid$$
$$ok?.ok^\uparrow!.cm^\uparrow?.cm!.cb?.cb^\uparrow!\,]$$

$$[\![T_1 \mid T_2]\!]_{ok,ab,cm,cb} \triangleq [\,[\![T_1]\!]_{ok_1,ab,cm_1,cb_1} \mid [\![T_2]\!]_{ok_2,ab,cm_2,cb_2} \mid$$
$$ok_1?.ok_2?.ok^\uparrow!.cm^\uparrow?.(cm_1! \mid cm_2! \mid cb_1?.cb_2?.cb^\uparrow!) \mid$$
$$ab?.(ok_1?.cm_1!.cb_1?.ab^\uparrow! \mid ok_2?.cm_2!.cb_1?.ab^\uparrow! \mid ab?.ab^\uparrow!)\,]$$

Fig. 1. Encoding of structured compensating transactions in the CC (selected cases)

or (in exclusive alternative) a single message $ab^\downarrow$ to signal abortion. After successful completion, reception of a single message $cm^\downarrow$ ("compensate me") by the residual will trigger the compensation process. When compensation terminates, a single message $cb^\downarrow$ ("compensate back") will be issued, to trigger compensation of previous successfully terminated activities.

We prove that our encoding is correct, by showing that it induces a compensation model in the sense of Definition 1 and with respect to the cCSP semantics (see [12]).

Theorem 3 (Correctness). *Let* $\mathcal{S} = (S, \mid, \#, \bowtie)$ *and* $\mathcal{D} = (\Sigma, \xrightarrow{a})$ *define a CC compensating model* $\mathcal{M} = (\mathcal{S}, \mathcal{D})$. *If* $\langle T\rangle$ *is a* $\bowtie$-*consistent CC program over* Σ, *then* $[\![\langle T\rangle]\!]_{ok}$ *is a CC atomic activity, that either behaves as* T^+, *or aborts without any observable behavior modulo* $\bowtie$.

Theorem 3 states that the mapping $[\![-]\!]_{ok}$ yields a sound embedding of arbitrary ($\bowtie$-consistent) structured compensating transactions in any CC compensating model. By showing that our encoding is an instance of the cCSP semantics, we directly recover the property stated in Theorem 2 to any CC compensation model.

Our framework naturally supports distributed transactions since primitive actions may be realized by calls to remote services. For example, let us consider a cCSP specification of a compensable transaction, which captures a credit request operation between a client and a bank, where the financial ranking of the client is updated according to the credit request operation, e.g., so as to indicate his financial status is less reliable.

$$\langle StartCreditRequest \div AbandonData; UpdateRate \div RestoreRate; ClientAccept \div skip\rangle$$

Whenever a credit request operation starts, some data is created and the client's financial rate is updated. Then either the client accepts or otherwise the transaction is aborted. In the latter case, the client rate is restored and the data of the operation is cleared. Primitive actions such as *UpdateRate* and *RestoreRate* may be implemented via calls to services that realize the expected tasks, for instance:

$UpdateRate \triangleq$ **new** $Bank \cdot$ **UpdateRate** $\Leftarrow$ **lowerClientRate!.(ok?.ok**$^\uparrow$**! + ko?.throw)**

$RestoreRate \triangleq$ **new** $Bank \cdot$ **RestoreRate** $\Leftarrow$ **raiseClientRate!.ok?.ok**$^\uparrow$**!**

Notice that these CC programs either send a single *ok* message or abort by throwing an exception, and hence fit in our previous description of primitive actions. We may then directly obtain a CC implementation of the cCSP transaction specified above, via such implementations of the primitive actions and via the developed embedding of the cCSP compensation operators in CC.

5 Conclusion

In this chapter we have summarized the main results of the SENSORIA project concerning fault and compensation handling in message-based calculi. They concern different aspects. On one side, we have studied different primitives for modeling long-running transactions and compensations, adapting also them to the particular needs of service-oriented computing. In particular, the idea of dynamic handlers is new, and has been studied in details. On the other side, we have analyzed the expressive power of the different primitives, proving some interesting separation results. Finally, we have exploited these mechanisms by inserting them into calculi and languages for service-oriented computing, such as CaSPiS [3], COWS [26], the Conversation Calculus [37], SOCK [10] and Jolie [31]. Similar results for event-based calculi are presented in Chapter 3-4. For instance, a mapping of SAGAs into the Signal Calculus [14] has been presented in [6].

While we have today a huge toolbox of primitives able to deal with the challenges of service-oriented computing, the understanding of the relationships among them is still far. A few works [22,23,12] have appeared analyzing encodings and separation results, but many pieces are missing, and the whole picture is still quite obscure. Keep also in mind that the problem is made hard since the expressive power depends not only on the chosen primitives for fault and compensation handling, but also on the underlying language. Another important stream for future work is the proof of correctness of compensation strategies. For long-running transactions one cannot require, as can be done for ACID transactions instead, that in case of failure the system goes back to the starting state, since recovery is not perfect. A few approaches are emerging here too. The previous section presented a framework for reasoning about the correct recovery, measured up to some particular behavioral equivalence parametrically defined in the framework. An alternative approach is to examine observations: a relation between performed activities and executed compensations is required, based again on some user-defined pattern [35].

Acknowledgments. The work reported herein is the result of a collaborative effort of many researchers, not just of the authors. Special thanks to Lucia Acciai for the contribution on CaSPiS in Section 3, and to Rosario Pugliese and Francesco Tiezzi for the contribution on COWS in the same section.

António Ravara was partially supported by the Security and Quantum Information Group, Instituto de Telecomunicações, Portugal.

References

1. Amadio, R.M., Castellani, I., Sangiorgi, D.: On bisimulations for the asynchronous pi-calculus. Theoretical Computer Science 195(2), 291–324 (1998)
2. Bocchi, L., Laneve, C., Zavattaro, G.: A calculus for long-running transactions. In: Najm, E., Nestmann, U., Stevens, P. (eds.) FMOODS 2003. LNCS, vol. 2884, pp. 124–138. Springer, Heidelberg (2003)
3. Boreale, M., Bruni, R., De Nicola, R., Loreti, M.: Sessions and pipelines for structured service programming. In: Barthe, G., de Boer, F.S. (eds.) FMOODS 2008. LNCS, vol. 5051, pp. 19–38. Springer, Heidelberg (2008)
4. Boreale, M., et al.: SCC: a Service Centered Calculus. In: Bravetti, M., Núñez, M., Tennenholtz, M. (eds.) WS-FM 2006. LNCS, vol. 4184, pp. 38–57. Springer, Heidelberg (2006)
5. Bravetti, M., Zavattaro, G.: On the expressive power of process interruption and compensation. Mathematical Structures in Computer Science 19(3) (2009)
6. Bruni, R., Ferrari, G.L., Melgratti, H.C., Montanari, U., Strollo, D., Tuosto, E.: From theory to practice in transactional composition of web services. In: Bravetti, M., Kloul, L., Tennenholtz, M. (eds.) EPEW/WS-FM 2005. LNCS, vol. 3670, pp. 272–286. Springer, Heidelberg (2005)
7. Bruni, R., Melgratti, H., Montanari, U.: Nested commits for mobile calculi: Extending join. In: Proc. of IFIP TCS 2004, pp. 563–576. Kluwer, Dordrecht (2004)
8. Bruni, R., Melgratti, H., Montanari, U.: Theoretical foundations for compensations in flow composition languages. In: Proc. of POPL 2005, pp. 209–220. ACM Press, New York (2005)
9. Busi, N., Gabbrielli, M., Zavattaro, G.: Replication vs. recursive definitions in channel based calculi. In: Baeten, J.C.M., Lenstra, J.K., Parrow, J., Woeginger, G.J. (eds.) ICALP 2003. LNCS, vol. 2719, pp. 133–144. Springer, Heidelberg (2003)
10. Busi, N., Gorrieri, R., Guidi, C., Lucchi, R., Zavattaro, G.: SOCK: A calculus for service oriented computing. In: Dan, A., Lamersdorf, W. (eds.) ICSOC 2006. LNCS, vol. 4294, pp. 327–338. Springer, Heidelberg (2006)
11. Butler, M.J., Hoare, C.A.R., Ferreira, C.: A trace semantics for long-running transactions. In: Abdallah, A.E., Jones, C.B., Sanders, J.W. (eds.) Communicating Sequential Processes. The First 25 Years. LNCS, vol. 3525, pp. 133–150. Springer, Heidelberg (2005)
12. Caires, L., Ferreira, C., Vieira, H.T.: A process calculus analysis of compensations. In: Kaklamanis, C., Nielson, F. (eds.) TGC 2008. LNCS, vol. 5474, pp. 87–103. Springer, Heidelberg (2009)
13. Carbone, M., Honda, K., Yoshida, N.: Structured interactional exceptions for session types. In: van Breugel, F., Chechik, M. (eds.) CONCUR 2008. LNCS, vol. 5201, pp. 402–417. Springer, Heidelberg (2008)
14. Ferrari, G.L., Guanciale, R., Strollo, D.: JSCL: A middleware for service coordination. In: Najm, E., Pradat-Peyre, J.-F., Donzeau-Gouge, V.V. (eds.) FORTE 2006. LNCS, vol. 4229, pp. 46–60. Springer, Heidelberg (2006)
15. Fournet, C., Gonthier, G.: The join calculus: A language for distributed mobile programming. In: Barthe, G., Dybjer, P., Pinto, L., Saraiva, J. (eds.) APPSEM 2000. LNCS, vol. 2395, pp. 268–332. Springer, Heidelberg (2002)
16. Garcia-Molina, H., Gawlick, D., Klein, J., Kleissner, K., Salem, K.: Coordinating multi-transaction activities. Technical Report Report No. UMIACS-TR-90-24, Univ. of Maryland Institute for Advanced Computer Studies (1990)

17. Gorla, D.: Towards a unified approach to encodability and separation results for process calculi. In: van Breugel, F., Chechik, M. (eds.) CONCUR 2008. LNCS, vol. 5201, pp. 492–507. Springer, Heidelberg (2008)
18. Guidi, C., Lanese, I., Montesi, F., Zavattaro, G.: On the interplay between fault handling and request-response service invocations. In: Proc. of ACSD 2008, pp. 190–199. IEEE Computer Society Press, Los Alamitos (2008)
19. Guidi, C., Lanese, I., Montesi, F., Zavattaro, G.: Dynamic error handling in service oriented applications. Fundamenta Informaticae 95(1), 73–102 (2009)
20. Hoare, C.A.R.: Communicating Sequential Processes. Prentice-Hall, Englewood Cliffs (1985)
21. Jolie website, http://www.jolie-lang.org/
22. Lanese, I., Vaz, C., Ferreira, C.: On the expressive power of primitives for compensation handling. In: Gordon, A.D. (ed.) ESOP 2010. LNCS, vol. 6012, pp. 366–386. Springer, Heidelberg (2010)
23. Lanese, I., Zavattaro, G.: Programming sagas in SOCK. In: Proc. of SEFM 2009, pp. 189–198. IEEE Computer Society Press, Los Alamitos (2009)
24. Laneve, C., Zavattaro, G.: Foundations of web transactions. In: Sassone, V. (ed.) FOSSACS 2005. LNCS, vol. 3441, pp. 282–298. Springer, Heidelberg (2005)
25. Lapadula, A.: A Formal Account of Web Services Orchestration. PhD thesis, Dipartimento di Sistemi e Informatica, Università degli Studi di Firenze (2008), http://rap.dsi.unifi.it/cows
26. Lapadula, A., Pugliese, R., Tiezzi, F.: A calculus for orchestration of web services. In: De Nicola, R. (ed.) ESOP 2007. LNCS, vol. 4421, pp. 33–47. Springer, Heidelberg (2007)
27. Mazzara, M., Lanese, I.: Towards a unifying theory for web services composition. In: Bravetti, M., Núñez, M., Tennenholtz, M. (eds.) WS-FM 2006. LNCS, vol. 4184, pp. 257–272. Springer, Heidelberg (2006)
28. Milner, R.: Communication and Concurrency. Prentice-Hall, Englewood Cliffs (1989)
29. Milner, R., Parrow, J., Walker, D.: A calculus of mobile processes, part I/II. Information and Computation 100, 1–77 (1992)
30. Milner, R., Sangiorgi, D.: Barbed bisimulation. In: Kuich, W. (ed.) ICALP 1992. LNCS, vol. 623, pp. 685–695. Springer, Heidelberg (1992)
31. Montesi, F., Guidi, C., Zavattaro, G.: Composing services with JOLIE. In: Proc. of ECOWS 2007, pp. 13–22. IEEE Computer Society Press, Los Alamitos (2007)
32. Oasis. Web Services Business Process Execution Language Version 2.0 (2007), http://docs.oasis-open.org/wsbpel/2.0/OS/wsbpel-v2.0-OS.html
33. Rensink, A., Vogler, W.: Fair testing. Information and Computation 205(2), 125–198 (2007)
34. Sangiorgi, D., Walker, D.: Pi-Calculus: A Theory of Mobile Processes. Cambridge University Press, Cambridge (2001)
35. Vaz, C., Ferreira, C.: Towards compensation correctness in interactive systems. In: Laneve, C., Su, J. (eds.) WS-FM 2009. LNCS, vol. 6194, pp. 161–177. Springer, Heidelberg (2010)
36. Vaz, C., Ferreira, C., Ravara, A.: Dynamic recovering of long running transactions. In: Kaklamanis, C., Nielson, F. (eds.) TGC 2008. LNCS, vol. 5474, pp. 201–215. Springer, Heidelberg (2009)
37. Vieira, H.T., Caires, L., Seco, J.C.: The conversation calculus: A model of service-oriented computation. In: Gairing, M. (ed.) ESOP 2008. LNCS, vol. 4960, pp. 269–283. Springer, Heidelberg (2008)
38. World Wide Web Consortium. Web Services Description Language (WSDL) 1.1 (2001), http://www.w3.org/TR/wsdl

Model-Driven Development of Long Running Transactions*

Vincenzo Ciancia[1], Gianluigi Ferrari[1], Roberto Guanciale[1],
Daniele Strollo[1], and Emilio Tuosto[2]

[1] Dipartimento di Informatica,
Università degli Studi di Pisa, Italy
{ciancia,giangi,guancio,strollo}@di.unipi.it
[2] University of Leicester, Computer Science Department
University Road, LE17RH, Leicester, UK
et52@mcs.le.ac.uk

Abstract. The management of Long Running Transactions is a crucial aspect in the field of Service Oriented Architectures. This chapter reports on the usage of the ESC middleware in the design and implementation of long running transactions. The middleware has been formally defined as a process calculus and supports a model-driven methodology which clearly separates the development stages of long running transactions.

1 Introduction

Service Oriented Computing (SOC) envisages systems as combination of basic computational entities, called services, whose interfaces can be dynamically published and bound. The main methodologies for composing services are *orchestration* and *choreography*. Services are orchestrated when their execution work-flow is described through an "external" process, called *orchestrator*. A *choreography*, instead, is a design that yields the architecture of the system by specifying how services should be connected and interact to accomplish their tasks within the given choreography. Roughly, choreographies yield an abstract global view of SOC systems that must eventually be "projected" on the distributed components. Both orchestration and choreography can benefit from *model driven development* (MDD, for short) and *refactoring* [1] whereby (models of) systems are repeatedly transformed so that specific concerns are confined at different stages. MDD methodologies typically start from a (semi-)formal specification that focuses on the core *business process* and neglects other aspects (e.g., communication mechanisms or distribution) tackled by subsequent transformations.

An important concern of SOC applications is to guarantee transactional behaviors. Classically transactions are thought of as a sequence of actions to be executed atomically. Namely, if some failure happens at any stage of the sequence, the computation must be reverted to the previous stable state. Such

---

* This work has been partially sponsored by the project SENSORIA, IST-2005-016004.

M. Wirsing and M. Hölzl (Eds.): SENSORIA Project, LNCS 6582, pp. 326–348, 2011.

kind of transactions are referred to as *ACID* (after atomicity, consistency, isolation and durability) [8]. ACID transactions have been recognized as being not suitable for SOC (see e.g.[12]). Indeed, being inherently loosely coupled, SOC systems govern the affairs of transactional behaviors possibly spanning over long temporal intervals.

Long Running Transactions (LRTs) avoid locks over resources and rely on *compensations* as mechanism to recover and deal with failures, aborts and other unexpected dangerous events. Compensations are executed if a failure occurs: a failing activity informs its invokers about the anomalous execution triggering their compensations as well.

The main goal of this chapter is to present a programming middleware developed within SENSORIA which supports a MDD methodology dedicated to manage LRT. Our proposal can be summarized as follows: (i) the designer adopts a *specification language* to model the transactional requirements of the system, (ii) the resulting model is transformed into a *coordination language* for services, (iii) the developer refines the model to add lower abstract details, (iv) the resulting model is transformed to obtain a runnable process. A distinguished feature of our proposal is that any language involved in the development methodology has a formal definition, thus allowing formal reasoning techniques.

The overall architecture of our framework is illustrated in Fig. 1. From left to right, we distinguish three main blocks, the ESC platform, the *SC* process calculus, and the *NCP*, choreography model.

The Signal Calculus [5,4] (*SC*) is an asynchronous process calculus designed with the aim of providing the conceptual counterpart of a programming middleware supporting the development of policies coordinating the behaviour of distributed services. Differently from other SENSORIA approaches (see the chapter), *SC* does not rely on unicast channels to coordinate services. Indeed, service coordination policies (orchestration and choreography) are specified by relying on multicast notification only. Remarkably, the calculus does not assume any centralized mechanism for publishing, subscribing and notifying events. Being a programming middleware, *SC* just supplies a set of basic primitive constructs: higher level constructs can be automatically compiled over the basic primitives. For instance, in Section 3, we report on the transformation rules mapping SAGA LRT [7,2] into *SC*. This leads to a transactional layer on top of *SC* (called Saga in Fig. 1. Notice that in our framework the *SC* calculus plays the key role of intermediate meta-model with the respect to the other two layers.

The Network Coordination Policies [3] (*NCP*) equips our framework with a choreography model. Coordination policies take the form of processes that represent the behavior as observed from a *global* point of view, namely by observing all the public interactions taking place on the network infrastructure. Hence, an *NCP* process describes the interactions that are expected to happen and how these are interleaved.

SC and *NCP* lay at two different levels of abstraction. The former is tailored to support the (formal) design of services, the latter is the specification language to declare the coordination policies. Indeed, certain features can be described at both levels: the *NCP* specification declares *what* is expected from the service network infrastructure, the *SC* design specifies *how* to implement it.

The gap between the local and global abstraction levels has been formally filled [3,10]. It has been proved that for each SC design, there exists an NCP choreography that reflects all the properties of the design. The conformance of an SC design with respect to an NCP specification is formally proved by checking weak asynchronous bisimilarity between them. This notion of conformance has the main benefit of supporting the development of systems in a model driven development fashion. The conformance of each model with respect to an NCP specification allows the designer to choose the required level of abstraction, so that one can focus on coordination of services, without considering the implementation details, or focus on service design, just trying to match the abstract policies. We refer to [10] for a more comprehensive analysis of *SC* and *NCP*. Finally, in Fig. 1, the connections between the *SC* blocks and *NCP* block represent the conformance checking.

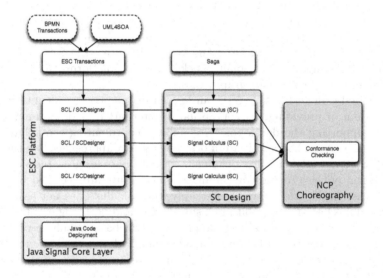

Fig. 1. ESC architecture

At implementation level we find two distinct layers: the Java Signal Core Layer (JSCL) middleware and the Event-based Service Coordination (ESC). JSCL consists of a prototypical middleware reflecting the structure and the programming model of the Signal Calculus. JSCLtakes the form of a set of Java API for programming distributed components interacting by notifying multicast events. JSCL is indeed the run-time support for executing *SC* networks of services. The ESC platform consists of a user-friendly interface in the form of a set of Eclipse plug-ins supplying a graphical and a textual representation of *SC* networks called *Signal Core Language* (SCL). The graphical representation provides the global view of the choreography by considering the components and their interconnections, without detailing their internal logics. The textual notation, instead, provides a closer view of services allowing designers to focus on the behavioral aspects. One can easily pass from the graphical to the textual representation and to automatically generate the runnable JSCL code as well. The ESC platform supplies a set of model transformation tools that, starting from the high level specifications, automatically build their corresponding representation in the SCL representation. In Section 4.1 we discuss how, starting from the SC coding of transactional primitives, it is possible to obtain the actual program at the ESC level. A more comprehensive discussion on the features of the ESC framework can be found in [14].

In summary, the ESC framework goes all the way from a foundational process calculus, the Signal Calculus, and its choreography model, Network Coordination Policy, over a Java middleware, JSCL. In this chapter, the usefulness of the ESC framework will be illustrated by tackling the problem of designing, implementing and refining long running transactions.

2   Beyond Message Passing Coordination for Services

The Signal Calculus is a process calculus designed to specify coordination of services distributed over a network. SC follows the event notification paradigm: communications are performed by the rising and the handling of events. This section reviews the main features of the calculus. Moreover, we present the language, *Signa Core Language* (SCL), extending Java to support SC programming model.

2.1   The Signal Calculus

We now introduce the main syntactic categories of the Signal Calculus, together with some notational machineries. We assume an infinite set $\mathcal{T}$ of *names* ranged by $\tau, \tau', r, s, \ldots$, and a infinite set $\mathcal{A}$ of *component names* ranged by $a, b, c \ldots$. We use $\boldsymbol{a}$ to denote the set of names $a_1, \ldots, a_n$.

SC is centered around the notion of *component*. A component $a[B]_F^R$ is a service identified by a unique name a, the public address of the service. The active computations, called *behaviors* (B), are wrapped and confined inside components. Each SC component specifies (i) the *reaction* (R) to be activated upon reception of notifications to events and (ii) the set of *flows* (F), namely the collection of component names each emitted event will be delivered to. Hence, while reactions define the interacting behavior of the component, flows define the component view of the coordination policies. *Reactions* and *flows* have to be thought of as the middleware interface of components.

Components interact by issuing *events* raised during their internal computations. Classes of homogeneous events are grouped into *topics*. We use the term *topic* to represent the "class" of events (e.g. *ClickMouse*) and *event* to denote

Table 1. *SC* syntax to handle sessions

$R ::= 0 \mid \tau \, \lambda \, s \vartriangleright B \mid \tau \circledcirc s \vartriangleright B \mid R \otimes R'$ 　　　　$F ::= 0 \mid \tau \rightsquigarrow a \mid F \oplus F'$

(a) Reactions 　　　　　　　　　　　　(b) Flows

$B ::= 0 \mid \epsilon; B \mid \mathbf{out}\langle \tau \circledcirc s \rangle; B \mid \mathbf{rupd}\,(R)\,; B \mid \mathbf{fupd}\,(F)\,B; B \mid B \mid B \mid (\nu\tau)B$

(c) Behaviors

$N ::= \emptyset \mid a\,[B]^R_F \mid N \parallel N \mid \langle \tau \circledcirc s \rangle @ a \mid (\nu n)N \quad where\; n \in \mathcal{A} \cup \mathcal{T}$

(d) Networks

---

how its "instance" (e.g. the happening of a mouse click at a well precise position and time) is locally represented by publishers.

Additionally, events come equipped with a session, allowing to distinguish the work-flow instance in which the events of a certain topic occur. Therefore, events are represented as pairs $\tau \circledcirc s$, where the first element is the *topic* and the second element is the *session* identifier [1]. A *session* determines a sort of "virtual communication link" among publishers and subscribers and can be established despite the fact that they do not need to know each other's names. Intuitively, a *session* identifies the scope within which an event is significant: partners that are not in this scope cannot react to events related to such session.

The delivering of events is demanded to the network infrastructure, which encapsulates them inside *envelopes*. An envelope consists of the event itself decorated with the information needed to allow the proper routing within the network infrastructure. Notice that this information is *mandatory* in our approach to achieve decentralization (since we rely on a non-brokered solution [11]).

The syntax of reactions (R) is displayed in Table 1a. A reaction is a (possibly empty) multi-set of unit reactions. A unit reaction $(\alpha \vartriangleright B)$ is composed of a *signature* α and a body B (the behavior of the reaction). The signature α can be either a *check* $(\tau \circledcirc s)$ or a *lambda* $(\tau \lambda s)$ prefix. Again, τ and s denote the event topic and the session, respectively. *Lambda reactions* are activated independently from the session, while *check reactions* handle notification to events belonging to a well defined session. Furthermore, lambda reactions, once installed, remain persistent in the component interface, while check reactions, once executed, are removed from the component interface. A lambda reaction $\tau \lambda s$ acts as a binder for s, i.e. s is the formal name of the session. When notification occurs, s is bound to the actual session. Unit reactions can be empty and can be composed $(R_1 \otimes R_2)$.

---

[1] Even though names $\tau, \tau', \ldots$ and $s, r, \ldots$ belong to the same domain of names $\mathcal{T}$, in order to gain readability, we use these two different notations to denote topic names (τ) and session identifiers (s), respectively.

Flows (F) are described in Table 1b. A flow is a set (possibly empty) of unit flows. A unit flow $\tau \rightsquigarrow a$ expresses the subscription of a set of component names a for the topic τ. Since flows are defined on the component interface, their configuration is locally maintained by each component. We freely use the notation $\tau \rightsquigarrow a$ to denote a flow having a single end point a. Notice that flows allows to filer events only on their topics. In fact, the reactions are demanded to regulate the handling of events according to their sessions. Flows composition, $F \oplus F'$, allows composition of subscriptions.

The syntax of component behaviors is reported in Table 1c. The SC primitives allow one to *dynamically* reconfigure the structure of the coordination policies by adding new flows and reactions. The rule `rupd` (*reaction update*) describes the reconfiguration of the reaction part of the component interface.. In a similar way, the `fupd` (*flow update*) modifies the component flows. An asynchronous *emission*, $\mathsf{out}\langle \tau @ s \rangle; B$, spawns into the network a multicast notification according to the flows. Differently from the π-calculus, we observe that the SC output operation (emission) is not presented as *bare output*. As will be clarified by the semantic rules `out` in Table 2, the continuation B of an output operation is activated without waiting for the consumption of the envelopes from the receivers.

All the SC actions have been presented in the prefixed form $act.B$, with act ranging over atomic actions (i.e. $\{\epsilon, rupd(R), fupd(F), \mathsf{out}\langle \tau @ s \rangle\}$). Once the atomic step act terminates, its continuation B is activated. When it is clear from the context, we will omit the empty behavior, writing act instead of $act.0$. Topics and sessions can be dynamically created by using the primitive $(\nu\tau)B$. Finally, behaviors can be composed in parallel and embody concurrent computations taking place on the same service (e.g. for handling simultaneous notifications received from several partners).

The SC components describe locations on which the current computations are taking place. Components are structured to build a *network* of services whose syntax is reported in Table 1d. In the following, we use capital letters $N, M, ... \in \mathcal{N}$ to denote *networks*. Notice that networks are flat, namely there is no hierarchy of components. A network provides the facility to transport *envelopes* encapsulating the events exchanged among components. This feature is at the core of the SC asynchronous communication. Envelopes $\langle \tau @ s \rangle @ a$ represent the network facility to transport event notifications: they yield the emitted event having topic τ in the session s related to the subscribed component a. The restriction primitive over networks hides a subset of the components to some of the other participants. Notice that behaviors cannot restrict component names, since SC does not allow nested components and hierarchical network structures.

Free (fn) and bound (bn) names are defined in the standard way. Since *lambda reaction* $\tau \lambda s \triangleright B$ and restriction $(\nu\tau)B$ act as binders for s and τ, respectively, hereafter, we report only these rules:

$$fn((\nu\tau)B) = fn(B) \setminus \{\tau\} \qquad bn((\nu\tau)B) = bn(B) \cup \{\tau\}$$

$$fn(\tau \lambda s \triangleright B) = fn(B) \setminus \{s\} \cup \{\tau\} \quad bn(\tau \lambda s \triangleright B) = bn(B) \cup \{s\}$$

$$fn((\nu n)N) = fn(N) \setminus \{n\} \qquad bn((\nu n)N) = bn(N) \cup \{n\}$$

Table 2. SC semantic rules

$$a\,[\mathbf{out}\langle\tau\circledcirc s\rangle.B \mid B']^R_F \;\;\rightarrow\;\; a\,[B \mid B']^R_F \;\|\; \prod_{b\in(F)\downarrow_\tau} \langle\tau\circledcirc s\rangle@b \quad (\mathbf{out})$$

$$\langle\tau\circledcirc s\rangle@a \;\|\; a\,[B]^{\tau\circledcirc s\,\triangleright\,B'\otimes R}_F \;\;\rightarrow\;\; a\,[B|B']^R_F \quad (\mathbf{check})$$

$$\langle\tau\circledcirc s\rangle@a \;\|\; a\,[B]^{\tau\,\lambda\,s'\,\triangleright\,B'\otimes R}_F \;\;\rightarrow\;\; a\,[B|\{s/s'\}B']^R_F \quad (\mathbf{lam})$$

$$a\,[\mathbf{rupd}\,(R')\,.B]^R_F \rightarrow a\,[B]^{R\otimes R'}_F \quad (\mathbf{rupd}) \qquad a\,[\mathbf{fupd}\,(F')\,.B]^R_F \rightarrow a\,[B]^R_{F\oplus F'} \quad (\mathbf{fupd})$$

$$\frac{N\rightarrow N'}{N\parallel M\rightarrow N'\parallel M}\;(\mathbf{npar}) \qquad \frac{N\rightarrow N_1}{(\nu n)N\rightarrow(\nu n)N_1}\;(\mathbf{new})$$

In the following we assume that networks are *well formed*: component names are not replicated and for any $N_1 \parallel N_2, fn(N_1)\cap bn(N_2)=\emptyset$.

SC reactions, flows, behaviors and networks are defined up to a structural congruence relation $\equiv$. We assume that $(R,\otimes,0)$, $(F,\oplus,0)$, $(B,\mid,0)$ and $(N,\parallel,\emptyset)$ are commutative monoids, allowing us to freely rearrange SC terms. Also, we assume the standard scope extrusion rules:

$$a\,[(\nu\tau)B_1 \mid B_2]^R_F \equiv a\,[(\nu\tau)(B_1 \mid B_2)]^R_F\; if\; \tau\notin fn(B_2)$$
$$a\,[(\nu\tau)B]^R_F \equiv (\nu\tau)a\,[B]^R_F \qquad\qquad if\; \tau\notin fn(F)\cup fn(R)$$
$$((\nu n)N_1)\parallel N_2 \equiv (\nu n)(N_1\parallel N_2) \qquad if\; n\notin fn(N_1)\cup fn(N_2)$$

The SC reduction semantics is dispalyed in Table 2. The reduction rules exploit the auxiliary operator $(F)\downarrow_\tau$, that yields the set of components that are subscribed to the topic τ. This operator, called *flow projection*, is inductively defined as follows:

$$(\emptyset_F)\downarrow_\tau=\emptyset \qquad (\tau\rightsquigarrow a)\downarrow_{\tau'}=\begin{cases} a\; if\; \tau'=\tau \\ \emptyset\; otherwise \end{cases} \qquad (F\oplus F')\downarrow_\tau=(F)\downarrow_\tau\cup(F')\downarrow_\tau$$

Rules check and lam describe the activation of check reactions (that require the exact match of the session identifier) and of lambda reactions (receiving the session identifier as argument). Notice that check reactions are consumed, while lambda reactions are persistent. A lambda reaction can be used to publish a public interface that establishes a session with the client. Instead, a check reaction permits a service to handle only events that belong to a given session. For example, if the session is used to identify an instance of a work-flow, this mechanism allows the service to specialize its behavior for each instance and to track the progress of the control flow. Notice that if several reactions can handle the event notification, one of them is non-deterministically selected. This is performed by rearranging the component reactions using the structural congruence.

The rule out introduces in the network a set of envelopes, i.e. an envelope for each of the subscriber components. The subscribed components b are retrieved through the flow projection operator $(b \in (F)\downarrow_\tau)$. Rules rupd and fupd update reactions and flows, respectively. Rules npar and new are the usual rules of process calculi.

2.2 Signal Core Language

The *Signal Core Language* (SCL) is Java implementation of the *SC* programming model. SCL has been implemented as a textual plug-in for the Eclipse environment.

```
 1  restricted: s1,s2;
 2  global: t1, t2, t3;
 3  component a {
 4    local: lt1, lt2;
 5    flows: [t1->a], [lt1->b];
 6    knows: s1,b;
 7    reaction lambda (t1@ws){
 8      addFlow ([ws->b]);
 9      addReaction (
10        reaction check (lt1@lt2){
11          emit (t1@lt1);
12        }
13      );
14      nop;
15      do {/*behavior*/} or {/*behavior*/}
16      split {/*behavior*/} || {/*behavior*/}
17      with (nlt1){/*behavior*/}
18      skip;
19    }
20  }
21  protected component b {
22    knows: s1;
23    main {
24      // behavior
25    }
26  }
```

Code 1.1. SCL language through an example

A typical representation of an SCL network is given in Code 1.1. The example shows a network consisting of two components a and b, defined in the LINES

3-20 and 21-26, respectively. Topic names are declared as `global` and shared among components as shown in LINE 2. Moreover, topics can be declared in a private scope of a component using the primitive `local` (LINE 4) or during the computation through the primitive `with` (LINE 17). Topic names can be private names shared among several components via the primitive `restricted` (LINE 1). Similarly, component names can be declared restricted by tagging components with the `protected` clause (LINE 21). Components can insert restricted names inside their scope (with the exception of the names declared with *local* and *with* clauses) by using the `knows` primitive (LINES 6 and 22).

Components are uniquely identified by a name (e.g. *a*) and declared with the `component` keyword. Components contain a set of local topics, a set of flows and a set of reactions declaring the topics that can be handled and the tasks to perform.

Events are couples $t_1 @ t_2$, where t_1 is the event topic and t_2 is the work-flow session in which it has been declared. Sessions identifiers and topics are freely interchangeable, as show in LINES 7-8 where the session *ws* received by the lambda reaction is afterwards used as topic name for connecting the component *a* to the component *b*. Components declare their entry points by installing reactions. Two kinds of reactions can be defined: the `reaction lambda` (see LINE 7) that is activated regardless its session, and `reaction check` (see LINE 10) that triggers behaviour within a specific session. `Flows` and `reactions` can be defined at initialization phase (LINES 5 and 7, respectively) or added at run-time if required (LINES 8 and 9-13, respectively).

The computational steps described inside reactions, declare their *behaviors*. The basic behavioral instructions are: `emit` (LINE 11), used to send out notification for an occurred event, `addFlow` and `addReaction` previously described, and `nop` (LINE 14) to indicate a block of code externally defined through the host language instructions that do not interfere the coordination patterns (e.g. the access to the database). The `skip` (LINE 18) represents the empty action (the *SC* silent action). Furthermore, behaviors can be composed in sequence (using, as usual the semicolon) or with `do-or` (LINE 15) and `split` (LINE 16) constructs. The former constructs is used to implement the non deterministic execution of two branches. The latter construct allows the parallel composition of two behavioral activities.

Notice that component *b* declares a `main` block (LINES 23-25). The `main` block controls the activation of a component.

3   Experimenting Long Running Transactions

To facilitate the mangement of LRT we equip the ESC framework with suitable facilities for handling the graphical design of LRT. In particular, BPMN [9] and UML4SOA (see Chapter 1-1) have been considered as modelling languages for long running transactions. Furthermore, the Signal Calculus has been exploited to formally drive the implementation of the LRT designs expressed in the graphical notation.

3.1   A Graphical Notation for LRTs

We now introduce a simple graphical notation for specifying business processes. Our main goal here is not to provide a novel graphical modeling language, but rather focussing on the common concepts underlying the treatment of LRT in the existing approaches. In particular, the graphical design notation is intended to describe the work-flow of a service-oriented system by a global point of view. Hence, designers can abstract from service distribution, the communication infrastructure and the technologies that will implement each service. Therefore, the basic elements of the graphical notation are *compensable activities*, namely pairs of main activities and compensations that can be composed sequentially or in parallel. Fig. 2 depicts the designs of sequential (a) and parallel (b) composition of compensable activities adopting the BPMN [9] notation.

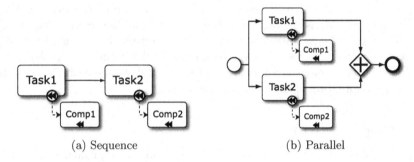

(a) Sequence   (b) Parallel

Fig. 2. Composition of compensable activities

Main activities and their related compensations are represented as boxes linked by dashed arrows. The main activity `Task1` has a "compensation" entry point connecting its compensation `Comp1`. The sequential composition is performed by linking together the main activities (cf. Fig. 2a), while the parallel composition makes use of "fork" and "join" operators. Fig. 2b illustrates the parallel composition of two transactional activities. The two circles represent the *start* event and the *termination* event of the whole business process, while the diamond with the plus operation represents the join of the two parallel activities. The fork operation is implicit in the multiple connections on the start event. Compensable activities, and their compositions, can be enclosed inside transactional boundaries as shown in Fig. 3.

Business processes are built by composing compensable activities. Notice that the mechanisms used to implement the operation logic of compensable activities and the interactions needed to coordinate the whole business process are not specified. Finally, it should be remarked that our graphical modelling language corresponds indeed to Naive Sagas as presented in [2].

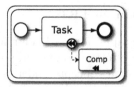

Fig. 3. Transactional boundaries

3.2   From the Graphical Notation to SC (informally)

This section aims at illustrating the way SC is used as an intermediate language to express coordination patterns for services. In particular, we described the mapping from high level transactional primitives into concrete coordination patterns expressed as SC behaviors. We illustrate the SC encoding of the high level transactional primitives by taking advantage of the event notification paradigm. We distinguish two groups of observable events: *i)* the results obtained during the execution of internal steps and *ii)* the results observed by the external activities. Two distinguished event topics f and r are globally used (after Sagas terminology for forward and rollback flow, respectively) to notify successful termination of compensable activities.

Compensable Activity

A compensable activity is expressed by the SC component, called *transactional component*, illustrated in Code 1.2, where *Task* and *Comp*, respectively, represent the main activity and the compensation of the compensable activity, and *next* and *prev* represent the forward and the backward flows.

$$
\begin{aligned}
TC(a, Task, Comp, prev, next) &= (\nu ok, ex)\left(a[0]^{f \wedge s \gg Task \mid \mathbf{rupd}(R_{res})}_{ok \rightsquigarrow a \oplus ex \rightsquigarrow a \oplus f \rightsquigarrow next \oplus r \rightsquigarrow prev}\right)\\
R_{res} &= ok_{\copyright}s \gg \Big(\mathbf{rupd}(r_{\copyright}s \gg Comp)|\mathbf{out}(f_{\copyright}s)\Big) \otimes \\
&\quad\; ex_{\copyright}s \gg \mathbf{out}(r_{\copyright}s)\\
Task &= \epsilon.\mathbf{out}(ok_{\copyright}s) + \epsilon.\mathbf{out}(ex_{\copyright}s)\\
Comp &= \epsilon.\mathbf{out}(r_{\copyright}s)
\end{aligned}
$$

Code 1.2. SC coding of LRT: compensable activity

Main activities and compensations make use of the internal action ϵ to represent a behaviour not observable at SC level. This internal behaviour has to be specified at the implementation level. However, we assume that the implementation of internal behaviour does not alter the structure of the coordination. In other words, the direct access to SC primitives to implement internal behaviour is not allowed since they can invalidate the overall protocol verified at the higher level of abstraction.

Sequence

The sequential composition of SC transactional components is obtained by simply rearranging their interconnections. Namely, given two transactional components TC_a and TC_b of the form:

$$TC_a \triangleq TC(a, Task_a, Comp_a, prev_a, -)$$
$$TC_b \triangleq TC(b, Task_b, Comp_b, -, next_b)$$

the corresponding sequential composition is given by the SC term:

$$TC_a; TC_b \triangleq TC(a, Task_a, Comp_a, prev_a, b) \parallel TC(b, Task_b, Comp_b, a, next_b)$$

The component a on the left side of the composition is connected for forward flows to the component b on its right and conversely for the backward flows b is connected to a.

Parallel Composition

Parallel composition of SC transactional components requires the introduction of two auxiliary SC components called *dispatcher* and *collector* to model the fork and join entry points of Fig. 2b. Dispatchers collect notifications of the forward flow (events having topic f) and redirect them to the parallel transactional components ($\{a, b\}$). Symmetrically, dispatchers bounce rollback events of topic r when the backward flow is executed. Also, collectors propagates forward and backward flows by sending the events of topic f or r as appropriate. Fig. 4 yields a pictorial representation of how the forward and backward flows of the dispatcher d and collector c of parallel components a and b are coordinated by using the f and r events. Notice that a and b have rollback flows connecting each other; in fact, the semantics of Sagas prescribes that, when the main activity of a parallel component fails, the other components must be notified and start their compensations. The SC coding for c and d components is reported in Code 1.3.

$$d[0]_{f \leadsto \{a,b\} \oplus n \leadsto c \oplus r \leadsto prev}^{f \wedge s \triangleright \left(\text{out}(f \textcircled{c} s) \mid \text{out}(n \textcircled{c} s) \mid \text{rupd}\left(r \textcircled{c} s \triangleright \text{rupd}(r \textcircled{c} s \triangleright \text{out}(r \textcircled{c} s))\right)\right)}$$

$$c[0]_{f \leadsto next \oplus r \leadsto \{a,b\}}^{n \wedge s \triangleright \left(\text{rupd}\left(f \wedge s \triangleright \text{rupd}(f \textcircled{c} s \triangleright \text{out}(f \textcircled{c} s) \mid \text{rupd}(r \textcircled{c} s \triangleright \text{out}(r \textcircled{c} s)))\right)\right)}$$

Code 1.3. SC coding of LRT: parallel composition

A distiguished topic n is internally used for implementing the dispatcher-collector synchronization. Intuitively, this topic implements a sort of "private channel" handling the dispacther-collector interaction. For instance, the dispatcher d communicates via the topic n that a new session s is going to start. The collector after having received through the channel n the work-flow session identifier s, installs the reactions needed to handle the events notified by the parallel stages.

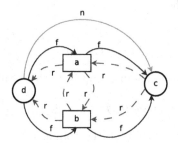

Fig. 4. SC parallel composition

Transactional Enclosure

The intended meaning of transactional enclosure is to avoid that internal failures do affect external activities. To manage transactional enclosures we make full use of dispatcher and collector components. Fig. 5 provides a pictorial representation of the SC encoding. The collector is demanded to receive the notification of forward event (f) of the activty a. Whenever the collector c receives a rollback event, the component a must activate its compensation. Two cases are possible: *i)* a has previously successful terminated, so it has a compensation installed *ii)* a internally failed and no compensations are needed. Also in this case, the topic n is used by the dispatcher d to inform the collector c that a new work-flow instance has been initiated so that the collector can install the proper check reactions to consume two distinct instances of f events coming from a.

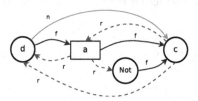

Fig. 5. SC transactional enclosure

The SC coding of transactional enclosures is illustrated in Code 1.4.

$$d[0]_{f \rightsquigarrow a \oplus n \rightsquigarrow c \oplus r \rightsquigarrow prev}^{f \lambda s \rhd \left(\text{out}(n©s) \mid \text{out}(f©s) \mid \text{rupd}\left(r©s \rhd \text{rupd}(r©s \rhd \text{out}(r©s)) \right) \right)}$$

$$not[0]_{f \rightsquigarrow c}^{r \lambda s \rhd \text{out}(f©s)}$$

$$c[0]_{f \rightsquigarrow next \oplus r \rightsquigarrow \{d,a\}}^{n \lambda s \rhd \left(\text{rupd}\left(f©s \rhd \text{out}(f©s) \right) \mid \text{rupd}(r©s \rhd \text{out}(r©s)) \right)}$$

Code 1.4. SC coding of LRT: transaction

4   A Case Study: The Car Repair Scenario

In this section we illustrate how the SENSORIA car repair scenario [15] has been developed by using the ESC framework. Moreover, we will use this scenario to illustrate our model driven development methodology. We start by briefly reviewing the case study. A car manufacturer offers a service that, once a user's car breaks down, the system attempts to locate a garage, a tow truck and a rental car service so that the car is towed to the garage and repaired meanwhile the car owner may continue his travel.

The interdependencies between the service bookings make it necessary to have a coordination with compensations. Before looking for a tow truck, a garage must be found. This poses additional constraints to the candidate tow trucks. If finding a tow truck fails, the garage appointment must be revoked. If renting a car succeeds and finding either a tow truck or a garage appointment fails, the car rental must be redirected to the broken down car's actual location. If the car rental fails, it should not affect the tow truck and garage appointment.

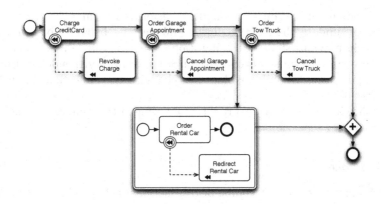

Fig. 6. Car repair scenario: the LRT graphical model

The graphical representation of this scenario is presented in Fig. 6. Notice that the car rental service is a isolated sub-transaction, since it does not affect other activities.

The initial design of the car-repair scenario simply describes the main activities and the transactional aspects of the coordination. In this phase, service distribution or further decomposition of main activities are not relevant issue. Those aspects may be considered at later stages of the development.

4.1   Scl Model Transformation

The Esc framework supplies facilities to transform the abstract initial design into the platform specific Scl model. This model transformation is driven by the *SC* encoding of compensable activities presented above. In the first step the model transformation generates an Scl transactional component for every atomic process (aka an activity and the corresponding compensation). The application of the model transformation to the abstract initial design produces the Scl network depicted in Fig. 7.

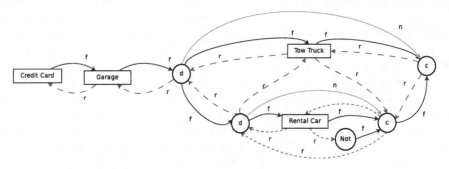

Fig. 7. The generated Scl network

The iterative application of the model transformation can generate *glue* components and update the existing flows, however the behavior of components generated in previous steps of the iteration cannot be altered. This permits to transform a transactional process into an Scl network independently from the context, and reuse it as building block just changing its connections (namely the Scl flows).

The following paragraphs report the Scl coding of the compensable activities of the car repair scenario.

Atomic Process

Code 1.5 illustrates the Scl coding of transactional activity GARAGE.

The component declares two private topics, *ok* and *ex*, (LINE 2) that will be used to check termination of the corresponding main activity. Notice that

```
 1  component garage {
 2    local: ok, ex;
 3    flows: [(ok->garage), (ex->garage),
 4             (r->creditCard), (f->dispatcherPar)];
 5    reaction lambda (f@s) {
 6      split {
 7        /* coding of the main activity */
 8        do {emit <ok@s>;} or {emit <ex@s>;}
 9      } || {
10        addReaction (reaction check (ok@s) {
11          split {
12            emit <f@s>;
13          }||{
14          addReaction (reaction check (r@s) {
15            /* Coding of Compensation.
16               Defined by host language API. */
17            nop;
18            emit <r@s>;
19          });
20        }
21      });
22    } || {
23      addReaction (reaction check (ex@s) {
24        emit <r@s>;
25      });
26    }
27  }
```

Code 1.5. LRT to SCL: compensable activity

all events raised by the component having these topics will be delivered to the component itself (LINE 3). Moreover, these topics are local topics: they are restricted to be within the scope of the component. The component starts its execution by reacting to f (forward) events (BLOCK 5-26). Then, the component bounds (receives) the session identifier s and executes the actual task (LINE 8). We do not implement explicitly this activity, we assume that, in case of successful termination, the ok event will be issued, otherwise the failure event ex will be raised. Concurrently with the main activity, the component installs the reactions to check its termination (BLOCKS 10- 21 and 23-25). A successful execution (LINE 10) has the effect of propagating f event to the next stages of the work-flow (LINE 12). Furthermore, the check reaction for managing rollback notifications is installed (LINE 14-19). When a r event for the session s is received, the compensation is executed (LINE 17) and the rollback event is propagated to the previous stages (LINE 18). For simplicity, the compensation is here expressed by the nop operation. Once compiled into the JSCL code, it will be possible to specify, through the host language API (e.g. Java), the actual code implementing the compensation. If the execution of the activity fails (LINE 23), the handler simply starts the backward flow, raising a rollback event (LINE 24). Since the transformation of an atomic task generates only one SCL component, this component is both the entry point and the exit point of the generated network.

Parallel Composition

The parallel composition of compensable activities relies on the special components collector and dispatcher. Now we describe the SCL code for the dispatcher and the collector generated to implement the parallel composition of the TOWTRUCK and RENTALCAR services.

```
1  component dispatcherPar {
2    flows: [f->towTruck],[f->dispatcherTrans],
3           [r->garage],[n->collectorPar];
4    reaction lambda (f@s) {
5      split {
6        emit (f@s);
7      } || {
8        emit (n@s);
9      } || {
10       addReaction (reaction check (r@s) {
11         addReaction (reaction check (r@s) {
12           emit (r@s);
13         });
14       });
15     }
16   }
17 }
```

Code 1.6. SCL: parallel dispatcher

The dispatcher (c.f. Code 1.6) is the entry point of the parallel branch. Basically, it activates the forward flow of next components, and synchronizes their backward flows. Upon reactions to forward events (LINE 4), the dispatcher emits two events: one having topic f (LINE 6) and the other one having topic n (LINE 8). The former event is delivered to the components in the pool of the parallel activities. The latter event is delivered to the collector. This event is used to communicate the session that will be later used for synchronization purposes.

Similarly, the collector component (in Code 1.7) implements the synchronization mechanism for the forward flows (LINES 4 and 5) and to activate the backward flows of the parallel components when a r event is received (BLOCK 9-11). Notice that the collector exploits the distinguished n event to get information about the session s of the work-flow (LINE 3).

```
1   component collectorPar {
2     flows: [r->towTruck],[r->collectorTrans],[f->...];
3     reaction lambda (n@s) {
4        addReaction check (f@s) {
5          addReaction check (f@s) {
6            split {
7              emit <f@s>;
8            } || {
9              addReaction check (r@s) {
10               emit <r@s>;
11             }
12           }
13         }
14       }
15     }
16  }
```

Code 1.7. SCL: parallel collector

Isolated Transaction

A sub-transaction is compiled into a SCL network that does not effects the computation of tasks performed out of the sub-transaction itself. The transformation makes use of a dispatcher and a collector. The generated SCL code for the sub-transaction containing the RENTALCAR component is provided by three internal components according to the schema given in Fig. 5.

The DISPATCHERTRANS (c.f. Code 1.8) receives from the external activities the forward events (LINE 3), communicates that a new transactional session has been initiated (LINE 4), redirects the forward event to the RENTALCAR (LINE 5) and installs the rollback handler for the current session (BLOCK 6-10). Notice that, the rollback will be sent out (LINE 8) after the reception of two r notifications. The COLLECTORTRANS (c.f. Code 1.8) waits until the dispatcher communicates the new working session (LINE 17). Afterwards, it installs the handler for the f notifications coming from the RENTALCAR (BLOCK 18-23). The received f event is delivered outside (LINE 19) and the handler

5   Scl Model Refactoring

The SCL network obtained directly by the model transformation action over the abstract graphical design only sketches how the overall transaction business process proceeds without making any further assumption on which services implement such components and where they are actually located. In this section, we exploit the SC calculus to formally specify some refactoring rules that supports the refinement of SCL networks in order to include low level details without altering the overall semantics.

```
1   component dispatcherTrans {
2    flows [n->collectorTrans],[f->RentalCar];
3    reaction lambda (f@s) {
4      emit (n@s);
5      emit (f@s);
6      addReaction (reaction check (r@s){
7        addReaction (reaction check (r@s){
8          emit (r@s);
9        });
10     });
11   }
12  }
13
14  component collectorTrans {
15   flows: [f->collectorPar],[r->RentalCar],
16          [r->dispatcherTrans];
17   reaction lambda (n@s) {
18     addReaction( reaction check  (f@s) {
19       emit(f@s);
20       addReaction (reaction check (r@s) {
21         emit (r@s);
22       });
23     });
24   }
25  }
```

Code 1.8. SCL: transactional enclosure

5.1   Refactoring Transactional Components

We have already pointed out that both the main activity and the compensation of a transactional component are embedded into a single *SC* component that manages *ok* and *ex* events in order to propagate forward or backward flows. However, it might be fruitful to assign the compensation task to a different component. For example, the compensation Comp1 in Fig. 2a could run on a different host than Task1, because it involves a remote service. Usually, the actual distribution of services is not tackled in the abstract design of the business process.

The issues of component distribution are naturally faced when the business process is viewed at the abstraction level of SCL networks. For instance, it is possible to allocate components on different hosts by taking advantage of the JSCL facilities.

A simple example of refinement is provided by the delegation refinement where the compensation of a transactional component *a* is switched to the component *b*. This refinement is represented below.

$$DelegatedTC = (\nu b, ex)(C_a \parallel C_b)$$

$$C_a = (\nu ok)a[0]_{ok \rightsquigarrow a \oplus ex \rightsquigarrow b \oplus r \rightsquigarrow b \oplus f \rightsquigarrow next}^{f\lambda s > \left(Task \mid \mathtt{rupd}(R_a) \right)}$$

$$R_a = ok_{\textcircled{s}}s > \left(\mathtt{out}(f_{\textcircled{s}}s) \mid \mathtt{rupd}(r_{\textcircled{s}}s > \mathtt{out}(r_{\textcircled{s}}s)) \right)$$

$$C_b = b\,[0]_{\{r \rightsquigarrow prev\}}^{R_b}$$

$$R_b = ex\lambda s > \mathtt{out}\langle r_{\textcircled{s}}s \rangle \otimes r\lambda s > Comp$$

The refactoring rule relies on the introduction of the restricted component b (where $b \in A$ is fresh). This new component handles the compensation and manages the backward flow. The refactored a component only needs to check the successful termination of its main activity. Indeed, the check reaction R_a propagates the forward flow and activates a listener for the rollback notifications possibly sent by subsequent transactional components. Notice that R_a implicitly delegates the execution of the compensation $Comp$ to the new component b. Once a rollback is captured by a, it is automatically forwarded to the component b.

The initial reactions of b are given by R_b. Intuitively, b waits the notification of an exception from $Task$ or a rollback request coming from subsequent components. In the former case, b simply activates the backward flow (e.g. the reaction migrated from a) while, in the latter case, b executes $Comp$ that, upon termination, starts the backward flow.

5.2   Refactoring Parallel Composition

The model transformation of the parallel composition of two compensable activities relies on two specialized components (*Dispatcher* and *Collector*) that act as the entry and exit point of the whole composition. Fig. 8a illustrates pictorially the shape (in terms of flows and components) of the implementation of the parallel composition of three transactional components. Two distinguished dispatchers (d_1 and d_2) are introduced to manage coordination. Dispatcher d_2 forward the requests to components TC_1 and TC_2 and is externally viewed as the entry point of their parallel composition. The dispatcher d_1 is connected to TC_3 and to d_2 acting as entry point for the whole parallel block. Similar considerations can be used to explain the role played by the exit points c_1 and c_2. The availability of two dispatchers in the coordination lead to examime the strategies for their spatial allocation. For example, the choice of allocating the components d_2, TC_1 and TC_2 permits to reduce the inter-host communications for the forward and backward flow, since the dispatcher receives only one inter-host envelope and then generates two intra-host envelopes for the components TC_1 and TC_2. Instead, if TC_1, TC_2 and TC_3 are constrained to reside on different hosts, then the two dispatchers could be fused together.

We now introduce a refinement pattern for parallel compostion. The proposed transformation tackles two issues:

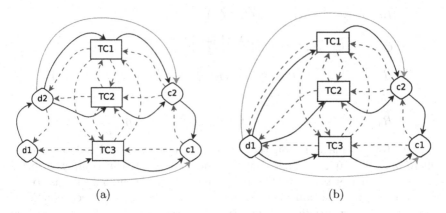

(a)   (b)

Fig. 8. Parallel composition and its refactoring

(i) it can merge two parallel dispatchers into one, thus simplifying the design, (ii) it can split a parallel dispatcher, thus refining the communication hierarchy among hosts.

We discuss the refactoring only for parallel dispatchers. However, the same strategy can be applied to provide a similar refactoring for the collectors.

Let $Sync_n(\tau \textcircled{s}s)(B)$ be the SC process that synchronizes n reception of events $\tau \textcircled{s}s$. This process is specified below.

$$Sync_0(\tau \textcircled{s}s)(B) = B \quad \text{and} \quad Sync_n(\tau \textcircled{s}s)(B) = \mathbf{rupd}\,(\tau \textcircled{s}s > Sync_{n-1}(\tau \textcircled{s}s)(B))$$

Any SC network with a dispatcher d_1 triggering a dispatcher d_2 can be specified as $N_{d_1,d_2} = (\nu d_1)(\nu d_2)(N \parallel D)$, where:

$$D = d_2\,[0]_{\{f \leadsto a_2 \oplus r \leadsto, d_1\}}^{f\ \lambda\ s \rhd Sync_{k_2}(r\textcircled{c}s)(\mathtt{out}\langle r\textcircled{c}s\rangle)\ |\ \mathtt{out}\langle f\textcircled{c}s\rangle}$$

$$\parallel d_1\,[0]_{\{f \leadsto a_1 \cup d_2 \oplus r \leadsto, b\}}^{f\ \lambda\ s \rhd Sync_{k_1}(r\textcircled{c}s)(\mathtt{out}\langle r\textcircled{c}s\rangle)\ |\ \mathtt{out}\langle f\textcircled{c}s\rangle}$$

Below we present the SC process merging two parallel dispatchers (migrating the flows of the component d_2 to the component d_1).

$$N'_{d_1,d_2} = (\nu d_1)\left(\{^{d_1}/_{d_2}\}N \parallel d_1\,[0]_{\{f \leadsto (a_1 \cup a_2) \oplus r \leadsto, b\}}^{f\ \lambda\ s \rhd Sync_{k_1+k_2-1}(r\textcircled{c}s)(\mathtt{out}\langle r\textcircled{c}s\rangle)\ |\ \mathtt{out}\langle f\textcircled{c}s\rangle}\right)$$

The correctness proof of the proposed refinement can be intuitively explained as follow The original system N_{d_1,d_2} consists of dispatchers d_1 and d_2 managing the coordination of a set of components. We use N to denote this set of components. Our refactoring changes only the flows of components in N by migrating all flows towards d_2 onto d_1. The resulting network $\{^{d_1}/_{d_2}\}N$ performs the same actions of the original coordination, but for the notifications to d_2, that are delivered to d_1. We refer to [6,10] for the detailed presentation of the proofs establishing the correctness of the refinements.

6   Concluding Remarks

The size of systems obtained by aggregating services can impose high costs which may not be affordable by small-medium enterprises. Clearly, this may prevent service-oriented technologies to be largely adopted condemning them to fail. To reduce costs and the efforts of adopting service-oriented solutions, it is necessary to allows developers and designers to separately manage the different aspects a system. This goal can be achieved by the adoption of MDD methods. Framework and tools should provide specific formalisms and languages suitable to manage a subset of the whole aspects of an application.

In this chapter we have summarized some results of the SENSORIA project concerning the management of transactional aspects of SOA systems via a MDD methodology. A key feature of our proposal is that any language and technology involved in the stages of the development of long running transactions has formal foundation and specific verification toolkits in the spirit of Barbed Model Driven Development [13]. The general issues related to the Model Driven Engineering of services-based systems and the variety of solutions provided by SENSORIA are discussed in Chapter 6-1. The formal foundations of long running transactions and compensations is the subject of Chapter 3-3 of this volume. Finally, process-calculi techniques have been exploited within SENSORIA to clarify and formally define the basic notions of service, sessions and orchestration. Results on these aspects are reported in other chapters of this volume (see Chapters 2-1 and 2-4).

References

1. Batory, D.: Program refactoring, program synthesis, and model-driven development. In: Goos, G., Harmanis, J., Leeuwen, J. (eds.) CC 2007. LNCS, vol. 4420, pp. 156–171. Springer, Heidelberg (2007)
2. Bruni, R., Melgratti, H., Montanari, U.: Theoretical foundations for compensations in flow composition languages. In: POPL 2005: Proceedings of the 32nd ACM SIGPLAN-SIGACT Symposium on Principles of Programming Languages, pp. 209–220. ACM Press, New York (2005)
3. Ciancia, V., Ferrari, G.L., Guanciale, R., Strollo, D.: Global coordination policies for services. Electr. Notes Theor. Comput. Sci. 260, 73–89 (2010)
4. Ferrari, G., Guanciale, R., Strollo, D., Tuosto, E.: Coordination via types in an event-based framework. In: Derrick, J., Vain, J. (eds.) FORTE 2007. LNCS, vol. 4574, pp. 66–80. Springer, Heidelberg (2007)
5. Ferrari, G.L., Guanciale, R., Strollo, D.: Jscl: A middleware for service coordination. In: Najm, E., Pradat-Peyre, J.-F., Donzeau-Gouge, V.V. (eds.) FORTE 2006. LNCS, vol. 4229, pp. 46–60. Springer, Heidelberg (2006)
6. Ferrari, G.L., Guanciale, R., Strollo, D., Tuosto, E.: Refactoring long running transactions. In: Bruni, R., Wolf, K. (eds.) WS-FM 2008. LNCS, vol. 5387, pp. 127–142. Springer, Heidelberg (2009)
7. Garcia-Molina, H., Salem, K.: Sagas. In: SIGMOD 1987: Proceedings of the 1987 ACM SIGMOD International Conference on Management of Data, pp. 249–259. ACM, New York (1987)

8. Gray, J.: The transaction concept: virtues and limitations (invited paper). In: VLDB 1981: Proceedings of the Seventh International Conference on Very Large Data Bases, pp. 144–154. VLDB Endowment (1981)
9. OMG. Business Process Modeling Notation (2002), http://www.bpmn.org
10. Guanciale, R.: The Signal Calculus: Beyond Message-based Coordination for Service. PhD thesis, Institute for Advanced Studies, IMT, Lucca (2009)
11. Huang, Y., Gannon, D.: A comparative study of web services-based event notification specifications. In: ICPP Workshops, pp. 7–14 (2006)
12. Little, M.: Transactions and web services. Commun. ACM 46(10), 49–54 (2003)
13. Montangero, C., Semini, L.: Barbed model–driven software development: A case study. Electron. Notes Theor. Comput. Sci. 207, 171–186 (2008)
14. Strollo, D.: Designing and Experimenting Coordination Primitives for Service Oriented Computing. PhD thesis, IMT Institute for Advanced Studies, Lucca (2009)
15. Wirsing, M., Clark, A., Gilmore, S., Hölzl, M.M., Knapp, A., Koch, N., Schroeder, A.: Semantic-based development of service-oriented systems. In: Najm, E., Pradat-Peyre, J.-F., Donzeau-Gouge, V.V. (eds.) FORTE 2006. LNCS, vol. 4229, pp. 24–45. Springer, Heidelberg (2006)

Hierarchical Models for Service-Oriented Systems[*]

Roberto Bruni[1], Andrea Corradini[1],
Fabio Gadducci[1], Alberto Lluch Lafuente[2], and Ugo Montanari[1]

[1] Department of Computer Science, University of Pisa, Italy
{bruni,andrea,gadducci,ugo}@di.unipi.it
[2] IMT Institute for Advanced Studies Lucca, Italy
alberto.lluch@imtlucca.it

Abstract. We present our approach to the denotation and representation of hierarchical graphs: a suitable algebra of hierarchical graphs and two domains of interpretations. Each domain of interpretation focuses on a particular perspective of the graph hierarchy: the top view (nested boxes) is based on a notion of embedded graphs while the side view (tree hierarchy) is based on gs-graphs. Our algebra can be understood as a high-level language for describing such graphical models, which are well suited for defining graphical representations of service-oriented systems where nesting (e.g. sessions, transactions, locations) and linking (e.g. shared channels, resources, names) are key aspects.

1 Introduction

As witnessed by a vast literature, graphs offer a convenient ground for the specification and analysis of software systems. As an example, the use of graphs as a suitable domain for the visualisation of a system specified by algebraic means is pursued in various proposals, based on traditional Graph Transformation [15], Bigraphical Reactive Systems [16], and Synchronised Hyperedge Replacement [13].

Despite their expressiveness and flexibility, the use of these formalisms to build a graphical representation for an existing specification language involves two major challenges. First, encoding system configurations (states), guaranteeing that structural equivalence is preserved: i.e. equivalent (e.g. structurally congruent) configurations are mapped into equivalent (e.g. isomorphic) graphs. Second, encoding system dynamics (e.g. behaviour, reconfigurations, model transformations, refactorings), guaranteeing that the original semantics is respected.

Preserving structural equivalence has several advantages. It offers an intuitive normal form representation for systems, and it allows us to reuse results and techniques from graph theory for solving specific problems. In particular, the soundness of the encoding is necessary to use graph transformation approaches [10] to model dynamic aspects since (sub)graph isomorphism is at the base of the rule matching mechanism.

---

[*] This work has been partially sponsored by the project SENSORIA, IST-2005-016004.

M. Wirsing and M. Hölzl (Eds.): SENSORIA Project, LNCS 6582, pp. 349–368, 2011.
© Springer-Verlag Berlin Heidelberg 2011

The encoding of configurations given with an algebraic syntax (e.g. as in process calculi) is facilitated by their structure (i.e. processes are terms) since it can be defined inductively. In absence of an algebraic presentation for the language under consideration, ad-hoc algebraic syntax must be developed if one wants to benefit from structural induction in proofs, transformations or definitions. Still, most graph models are not equipped with algebraic syntax and those that exist require advanced skills to deal with sophisticated models involving set-theoretic definitions of graphs with interfaces (e.g. [15]) or complex type systems (e.g. [7]), hampering definitions and proofs. Moreover, one encounters a severe drawback: namely, the syntax of graph formalisms are often very different from the source language and not provided with suitable primitives to deal with features that commonly arise in algebraic specifications, like names (e.g. references, channels), name restrictions (e.g. hiding, nonce generation) or hierarchical aspects (e.g. ambients, scopes) in the case of process calculi. Identifying the right structure is fundamental to provide scalable techniques.

Our goal is to define a simple flexible syntax for hierarchical models and to develop a technique that simplifies the definition of graphical representations of languages. We think that nesting and linking must be treated as first-class concepts, conveniently represented with a suitable syntax that allows one to express and exploit them. Nesting and linking are two key structural aspects that arise repeatedly in computer systems: consider e.g. the structure of file systems, composite diagrams, networks, membranes, sessions, transactions, locations, structured state machines or XML files. In particular, nesting plays a fundamental role for abstracting the complexity of a system by offering different levels of detail. Various graphical models of nesting and sharing structures already exist but (as we claim in [3,5,4]) none of them offer a simple, intuitive syntax.

Here, the gap between the different levels of abstraction at which algebraic specifications and graphical models reside is filled by a simple algebra that enjoys primitives for dealing with names, restriction, parallel composition and, most importantly, nesting and that is equipped with a (sound and complete) set of axioms equating two terms whenever they represent isomorphic graphs. Besides facilitating the visual specification of configurations, the algebraic structure facilitates definitions, transformations and proofs by induction.

Structure of this chapter. § 2 introduces the algebra of hierarchical graphs. § 3 presents our two models of hierarchical graphs. § 4 shows the expressiveness and flexibility of our design algebra in modelling heterogeneous notations, ranging from workflow languages to sophisticated process calculi.

2   The Syntax of Hierarchical Graphs

We introduce our algebra of hierarchical graphs that we call *designs*. The algebraic presentation of designs is mostly inspired by the graph algebra of [9].

As a matter of notation, we let $\lfloor \overline{x} \rfloor$ denote the set of elements of a list $\overline{x}$ and, conversely, $\lceil X \rceil$ the vector of elements of an ordered set X. We overload $|\cdot|$ to denote both the length of a list and the cardinality of a set.

Definition 1 (design). *A design is a term of sort* $\mathbb{D}$ *generated by the grammar*

$$\mathbb{D} \ ::= \ L_{\overline{x}}[\mathbb{G}] \qquad \mathbb{G} \ ::= \ \mathbf{0} \ \mid \ x \ \mid \ l\langle \overline{x} \rangle \ \mid \ \mathbb{G} \mid \mathbb{G} \ \mid \ (\nu x)\mathbb{G} \ \mid \ \mathbb{D}\langle \overline{x} \rangle$$

where l and L are drawn from vocabularies $\mathcal{E}$ and $\mathcal{D}$ of edge and design labels, respectively, x is taken from a global set $\mathcal{N}$ of nodes and $\overline{x} \in \mathcal{N}^*$ is a list of nodes.

Terms generated by $\mathbb{G}$ and $\mathbb{D}$ are meant to represent (possibly hierarchical) graphs and "edge-encapsulated" hierarchical graphs, respectively. The syntax has the following informal meaning: $\mathbf{0}$ represents the empty graph, x is a discrete graph containing node x only, $l\langle \overline{x} \rangle$ is a graph formed by an l-labelled (hyper)edge attached to nodes $\overline{x}$ (the i-th tentacle to the i-th node in $\overline{x}$, sometimes denoted by $\overline{x}[i]$), $\mathbb{G} \mid \mathbb{H}$ is the graph resulting from the parallel composition of graphs $\mathbb{G}$ and $\mathbb{H}$ (their disjoint union up to shared nodes), $(\nu x)\mathbb{G}$ is the graph $\mathbb{G}$ after making node x not visible from the outside (borrowing nominal calculus jargon we say that the node x is *restricted*), and $\mathbb{D}\langle \overline{x} \rangle$ is a graph formed by attaching design $\mathbb{D}$ to nodes $\overline{x}$ (the i-th node in the interface of $\mathbb{D}$ to the i-th node in $\overline{x}$).

A term $L_{\overline{x}}[\mathbb{G}]$ is a design labelled by L, with body graph $\mathbb{G}$ whose nodes $\overline{x}$ are exposed in the interface. To clarify the exact role of the interface of a design, we can use a programming metaphor: a design $L_{\overline{x}}[\mathbb{G}]$ is like a procedure declaration where $\overline{x}$ is the list of formal parameters. Then, term $L_{\overline{x}}[\mathbb{G}]\langle \overline{y} \rangle$ represents the application of the procedure to the list of actual parameters $\overline{y}$; of course, in this case the lengths of $\overline{x}$ and $\overline{y}$ must be equal (more precisely, the applicability of a design to a list of nodes must satisfy other requirements to be detailed later in the definition of well-formedness). In the following, we shall often write $L[\mathbb{G}]\langle \overline{y} \rangle$ as a shorthand for $L_{\overline{y}}[\mathbb{G}]\langle \overline{y} \rangle$.

Restriction $(\nu x)\mathbb{G}$ acts as a binder for x in $\mathbb{G}$ and similarly $L_{\overline{x}}[\mathbb{G}]$ binds $\overline{x}$ in $\mathbb{G}$. As usual, restrictions and interfaces lead to the notion of *free* nodes.

Definition 2 (free nodes). *The* free *nodes of a design or a graph are denoted by the function $fn(\cdot)$, defined as follows*

$$fn(\mathbf{0}) = \emptyset \qquad\qquad fn(x) = x$$
$$fn(l\langle \overline{x} \rangle) = \lfloor \overline{x} \rfloor \qquad\qquad fn(\mathbb{G} \mid \mathbb{H}) = fn(\mathbb{G}) \cup fn(\mathbb{H})$$
$$fn((\nu x)\mathbb{G}) = fn(\mathbb{G}) \setminus \{x\} \qquad fn(\mathbb{D}\langle \overline{x} \rangle) = fn(\mathbb{D}) \cup \lfloor \overline{x} \rfloor$$
$$fn(L_{\overline{x}}[\mathbb{G}]) = fn(\mathbb{G}) \setminus \lfloor \overline{x} \rfloor$$

Example 1. Let $a, b \in \mathcal{E}$, $A \in \mathcal{D}$, $u, v, w, x, y \in \mathcal{N}$. We write and depict in Fig. 1 some terms of our algebra, where for helping intuition an informal, appealing visual notation is preferred to the formal underlying graphs that will be described in Section 3.1. Nodes are represented by circles, edges by small rounded boxes, and designs by large shaded boxes with a top bar. The first tentacle of an edge is represented by a plain arrow with no head, while the second one is denoted by a normal arrow. In the examples only free nodes are annotated with their identities, while restricted nodes are anonymous (no label). Note how the tentacles of a- and b-labelled boxes attached to x and y do actually cross the interface and are hence denoted by small black boxes in the border of A-labelled designs. This does not happen for tentacles attached to w since it is shared node.

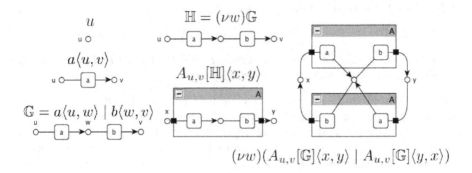

Fig. 1. Some terms of the graph algebra and their informal visual notation

In practice, it is very frequent that one is interested in disciplining the use of edge and design labels so to be attached only to a specific number of nodes (possibly of specific sorts) or to contain graphs of a specific shape. To this aim it is typically the case that: 1) nodes are sorted, in which case their labels take the form $x : s$ for $x \in \mathcal{X}$ the *name* and $s \in S$ the *sort* of the node; 2) each label $l \in \mathcal{E}$ (resp. $L \in \mathcal{D}$) has a fixed rank denoted $ar(l) \in S^*$ (resp. $ar(L) \in S^*$); 3) designs can be partitioned according to their top-level labels (i.e. the set of design labels $\mathcal{D}$ can be seen as the set of sorts, with a membership predicate $\mathbb{D} : L$ that holds whenever $\mathbb{D} = L_{\overline{x}}[\mathbb{G}]$ for some $\overline{x}$ and $\mathbb{G}$).

We say that a design (or a graph) is *well-typed* if for each occurrence of a typed operator $L_{\overline{x}}[\mathbb{G}]$ we have that the (vectors of) types of $\overline{x}$ and L coincide, and similarly for typed operators $\mathbb{D}\langle \overline{x} \rangle$ and $l\langle \overline{x} \rangle$. From now on, we restrict our attention to well-formed designs: all the axioms are going to preserve well-formedness and all the derived operators used for the encodings are well-formed.

Definition 3 (well-formedness). *A well-typed design or graph is* well-formed *if:*

1. *for each occurrence of design $L_{\overline{x}}[\mathbb{G}]$ we have $\lfloor \overline{x} \rfloor \subseteq fn(\mathbb{G})$;*
2. *for each occurrence of graph $L_{\overline{x}}[\mathbb{G}]\langle \overline{y} \rangle$, the substitution $^{\overline{x}}/_{\overline{y}}$ is a function.*

Intuitively, the restriction on the mapping $^{\overline{x}}/_{\overline{y}}$ allows $\overline{x}$ to account for matching of nodes in the interface: distinct nodes in $\overline{y}$ must correspond to distinct nodes in $\overline{x}$ (as the list $\overline{x}$ can contain repetitions).

In order to have a notion of "structurally equivalent" designs, the algebra includes the structural graph axioms of [9] such as associativity and commutativity for | with identity **0** (axioms DA1–DA3 in Definition 4) and name extrusion (DA4–DA6). In addition, it includes axioms to α-rename bound nodes (DA7–DA8), an axiom for making immaterial the addition of a node to a graph where that same node is already free (DA9) and another one ensuring that global names are not localised within hierarchical edges (DA10).

Definition 4 (design axioms). *The structural congruence $\equiv_D$ over well-formed designs and graphs is the least congruence satisfying*

$$
\begin{array}{llll}
\mathbb{G} \mid \mathbb{H} \equiv \mathbb{H} \mid \mathbb{G} & \text{(DA1)} & \mathbb{G} \mid (\nu x)\mathbb{H} \equiv (\nu x)(\mathbb{G} \mid \mathbb{H}) & \text{if } x \notin fn(\mathbb{G}) \quad \text{(DA6)} \\
\mathbb{G} \mid (\mathbb{H} \mid \mathbb{I}) \equiv (\mathbb{G} \mid \mathbb{H}) \mid \mathbb{I} & \text{(DA2)} & L_{\overline{x}}[\mathbb{G}] \equiv L_{\overline{y}}[\mathbb{G}\{\overline{y}/\overline{x}\}] & \text{if } \lfloor \overline{y} \rfloor \cap fn(\mathbb{G}) = \emptyset \;\; \text{(DA7)} \\
\mathbb{G} \mid 0 \equiv \mathbb{G} & \text{(DA3)} & (\nu x)\mathbb{G} \equiv (\nu y)\mathbb{G}\{y/x\} & \text{if } y \notin fn(\mathbb{G}) \quad \text{(DA8)} \\
(\nu x)(\nu y)\mathbb{G} \equiv (\nu y)(\nu x)\mathbb{G} & \text{(DA4)} & x \mid \mathbb{G} \equiv \mathbb{G} & \text{if } x \in fn(\mathbb{G}) \quad \text{(DA9)} \\
(\nu x)0 \equiv 0 & \text{(DA5)} & L_{\overline{x}}[z \mid \mathbb{G}]\langle \overline{y} \rangle \equiv z \mid L_{\overline{x}}[\mathbb{G}]\langle \overline{y} \rangle & \text{if } z \notin \lfloor \overline{x} \rfloor \;\; \text{(DA10)}
\end{array}
$$

where in axiom (DA7) *the substitution is required to be a function (to avoid node coalescing) and to respect the typing (to preserve well-formedness).*

It is immediate to observe that structural congruence respects free nodes, i.e. $\mathbb{G} \equiv_D \mathbb{H}$ implies $fn(\mathbb{G}) = fn(\mathbb{H})$ for any $\mathbb{G}, \mathbb{H}$. Moreover, being $\equiv_D$ a congruence, we remark e.g. that $L_{\overline{x}}[\mathbb{G}] \equiv_D L_{\overline{x}}[\mathbb{H}]$ whenever $\mathbb{G} \equiv_D \mathbb{H}$.

One important aspect of our algebra is allowing the derivation of standard representatives for the equivalence classes induced by $\equiv_D$.

Definition 5 (Normalized form). *A term $\mathbb{G}$ is in normalised form if it is 0 or it has the shape (for some $n + m + p + q \geq 1$ and suitable nodes x_j, z_k and edges $l_h\langle \overline{v}_h \rangle$, $L^i_{\overline{y}_i}[\mathbb{G}_i]\langle \overline{w}_i \rangle$):*

$$
(\nu x_1)\ldots(\nu x_m)(z_1 \mid \ldots \mid z_n \mid l_1\langle \overline{v}_1 \rangle \mid \ldots \mid l_p\langle \overline{v}_p \rangle \mid L^1_{\overline{y}_1}[\mathbb{G}_1]\langle \overline{w}_1 \rangle \mid \ldots \mid L^q_{\overline{y}_q}[\mathbb{G}_q]\langle \overline{w}_q \rangle)
$$

where all terms $\mathbb{G}_i$ are in normalised form, all nodes x_j are pairwise distinct, all nodes z_k are pairwise distinct and letting $X = \{x_1, \ldots, x_m\}$ and $Z = \{z_1, \ldots, z_n\}$ we have $X \subseteq Z$, $fn(\mathbb{G}) = Z \setminus X$ and $fn(L^i_{\overline{y}_i}[\mathbb{G}_i]\langle \overline{w}_i \rangle) = Z$ for all $i = 1...q$.

Proposition 1. *Any term $\mathbb{G}$ admits a $\equiv_D$-equivalent term $norm(\mathbb{G})$ in normalised form.*

Roughly, in $norm(\mathbb{G})$ the top-level restrictions are grouped to the left, and all the global names z_k are made explicit and propagated inside each single component $L^i_{\overline{y}_i}[\mathbb{G}_i]\langle \overline{w}_i \rangle$. Up to α-renaming and to nodes and edges permutation, the normalised form is actually proved to be unique.

3   The Models of Hierarchical Graphs

In this section we present our two models of hierarchical graphs.

3.1   Top-View Model

In [5] we have defined a new, suitable notion of hierarchical graphs with interface: roughly they extend ordinary hyper-graphs with the possibility to embed (recursively) a hierarchical graph within each edge, thus inducing a layered structure of nodes and edges. Notably, the nodes defined in one layer are also visible below in the hierarchy (but not above). The main result of [5] is to show that

the encoding of design terms in hierarchical graphs is surjective and that the
axiomatisation of the design algebra is sound and complete w.r.t. the encoding.
Moreover, in the presence of flattening- or extrusion-axioms (see § 4.1) the encoding can be slightly modified so to extend the validity of main results. The
drawing of hierarchical graphs as defined in [5] is along the informal drawing
seen in Fig. 1: to some extent they illustrate a top view of the system.

We first present the set of *plain* graphs and graph *layers*, upon which we build
our novel notion of *hierarchical* graphs. In the following, $\mathcal{N}$ and $\mathcal{A} = \mathcal{A}_\mathcal{E} \uplus \mathcal{A}_\mathcal{D}$
denote the universe of nodes and edges, respectively, for $\mathcal{A}$ indexed over the
vocabularies $\mathcal{E}$ and $\mathcal{D}$.

Definition 6 (graph layer). *The set $\mathcal{L}$ of graph layers is the set of tuples*
$G = \langle N_G, E_G, t_G, F_G \rangle$ *where $E_G \subseteq \mathcal{A}$ is a (finite) set of edges, $N_G \subseteq \mathcal{N}$ a*
(finite) set of nodes, $t_G : E_G \to N_G^*$ a tentacle function, and $F_G \subseteq N_G$ a set of
free nodes. The set $\mathcal{P}$ of plain graphs contains those graph layers G such that
$E_G \subseteq \mathcal{A}_\mathcal{E}$.

Thus, we just equipped the standard notion of hypergraph with a chosen set of
free nodes, intuitively denoting those nodes that are available to the environment, mimicking free names of our algebra. Next, we build the set of hierarchical
graphs.

Definition 7 (hierarchical graph). *The set $\mathcal{H}$ of hierarchical graphs is the*
smallest set[1] containing all the tuples $G = \langle N_G, E_G, t_G, i_G, x_G, r_G, F_G \rangle$ where

1. $\langle E_G, N_G, t_G, F_G \rangle$ *is a graph layer,*
2. $i_G : E_G \cap \mathcal{A}_\mathcal{D} \to \mathcal{H}$ *is an embedding function (we say $i_G(e)$ is the inner graph*
   of $e \in E_G \cap \mathcal{A}_\mathcal{D}$),
3. $x_G : E_G \cap \mathcal{A}_\mathcal{D} \to \mathcal{N}^*$ *is an exposure function ($x_G(e)$ tells which nodes of*
   $i_G(e)$ are exposed and in which order), such that for all $e \in E_G \cap \mathcal{A}_\mathcal{D}$

   (a) $\lfloor x_G(e) \rfloor \subseteq N_{i_G(e)} \setminus F_{i_G(e)}$, *i.e. free nodes of inner graphs are not exposed;*
   (b) $|x_G(e)| = |t_G(e)|$, *i.e. exposure and tentacle functions have the same*
       arity;[2]
   (c) $\forall n, m \in \mathbb{N}$ *if $x_G(e)[n] = x_G(e)[m]$ then $t_G(e)[n] = t_G(e)[m]$, i.e. it is not*
       possible to expose a node twice without attaching it to the same external
       node.

4. $r_G : E_G \cap \mathcal{A}_\mathcal{D} \to (N_G \hookrightarrow \mathcal{N})$ *is a renaming function ($r_G(e)$ tells how nodes*
   N_G are named in $i_G(e)$), such that for all $e \in E_G \cap \mathcal{A}_\mathcal{D}$ $r_G(e)(N_G) = F_{i_G(e)}$,
   i.e. the nodes of the graph are (after renaming) the free nodes of inner layers.

---

[1] Taking the least set we exclude cyclic dependencies from containment, like a graph
    being embedded in one of its edges.
[2] We shall not put any emphasis on the typing of the graph, but clearly if the set
    of nodes is many sorted an additional requirement should force the exposure and
    tentacle functions to agree on the node types.

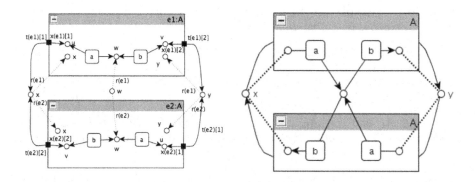

Fig. 2. A hierarchical graph (left) and its simplified representation (right)

Thus, a hierarchical graph G is either a plain graph, or it is equipped with a function associating to each edge in $E_G \cap \mathcal{A}_\mathcal{D}$ another graph. The tuple $\langle N_G, E_G, t_G, i_G \rangle$ recalls the layered model of hierarchical graphs of [11], with i_G being the function that embeds a graph (of a lower layer) inside an edge. Node sharing is introduced by the graph component F_G and the renaming function r_G, inspired by the graphs with (cospan-based) interfaces of [15]. In practice, we shall often assume that $r_G(e)$ (when defined) is the ordinary inclusion: the general case is useful for embedding (and reuse) graphs without renaming their nodes.

Example 2. Consider the last term of Example 1 and its informal graphical representation on Fig. 1 (right). Its actual interpretation as a hierarchical graph appears in Fig. 2 (left) decorated with the most relevant annotations (the tentacle, exposition and renaming functions for the two hierarchical edges). As witnessed by Fig. 2 (right), we can introduce convenient shorthands, such as dotted lines for mapping parameters, node-sharing represented by unique nodes and tentacles crossing the hierarchy levels, dropping the order of tentacles in favour of graphical decorations (missing or different heads and tails) to get a simplified notation that still retains all the relevant information. Note that such a simplified representation is very close to the informal notation shown in Fig. 1.

The above example should highlight that the algebra is providing a simple syntax that hides the complexities of our hierarchical model. The syntax can then be used in definitions, proofs and transformations in a much more friendly way than would be the case when working directly with the actual graphs.

We now present the interpretation of terms as graphs. In the definition below we assume that subscripts refer to the corresponding encoded graph. For instance, $[\![\mathbb{G}]\!] = \langle N_\mathbb{G}, E_\mathbb{G}, t_\mathbb{G}, i_\mathbb{G}, x_\mathbb{G}, r_\mathbb{G}, F_\mathbb{G} \rangle$.

Definition 8 (graph interpretation). *The encoding* $[\![\cdot]\!]$, *mapping well-formed terms into graphs, is the function inductively defined as*

$$[\![x]\!] = \langle \{x\}, \emptyset, \bot, \bot, \bot, \bot, \{x\} \rangle \qquad [\![l\langle \overline{x} \rangle]\!] = \langle \lfloor \overline{x} \rfloor, \{e'\}, e' \mapsto \overline{x}, \bot, \bot, \bot, \lfloor \overline{x} \rfloor \rangle$$
$$[\![G \mid H]\!] = [\![G]\!] \oplus [\![H]\!] \qquad\qquad [\![0]\!] = \langle \emptyset, \emptyset, \bot, \bot, \bot, \bot, \emptyset \rangle$$
$$[\![(\nu x)G]\!] = \langle N_G, E_G, t_G, i_G, x_G, r_G, F_G \setminus \{x\} \rangle$$
$$[\![L_{\overline{x}}[G]\langle \overline{y} \rangle]\!] = \langle N_G, \{e\}, e \mapsto \overline{y}, e \mapsto [\![G]\!] \oplus [\![\lfloor \overline{y} \rfloor]\!], e \mapsto \overline{x}, e \mapsto id_N, (F_G \setminus \lfloor \overline{x} \rfloor) \cup \lfloor \overline{y} \rfloor \rangle$$

where $e' \in \mathcal{A}_{\mathcal{E}}$ *and* $e \in \mathcal{A}_{\mathcal{D}}$, $\bot$ *denotes the empty function, and* $G \oplus H$ *is a graph composition operation that build the disjoint union of* G *and* H *up to their common free nodes (see [5] for the full definition).*

The encoding into (plain) graphs of the empty design, isolated nodes and single edges is trivial. Node restriction consists of removing the restricted node from the set of free nodes. The encoding of the parallel composition is as expected: a disjoint union of the corresponding hierarchical graphs up to common free nodes, plus a possible saturation of the sub-graphs with the nodes now appearing in the top graph layer. A hierarchical edge (last two rows) is basically a graph with a single edge (which is mapped to the corresponding body graph) and a copy of the free nodes of the body graph (properly mapped to the corresponding copies in the body), while adding the names $\lfloor \overline{y} \rfloor$ among the free ones.

The main result in [5] shows that the encoding is sound and complete, meaning that equivalent terms are mapped to isomorphic graph (and vice versa).

Theorem 1 (cf. [5]). *Let* $\mathbb{G}_1$, $\mathbb{G}_2$ *be well-formed terms generated by the design algebra. Then,* $\mathbb{G}_1 \equiv_D \mathbb{G}_2$ *if and only if* $[\![\mathbb{G}_1]\!]$ *is isomorphic to* $[\![\mathbb{G}_2]\!]$.

Moreover, the encoding is surjective.

Proposition 2 (cf. [5]). *Let* G *be a graph. Then, there exists a well-formed term* $\mathbb{G}$ *generated by the design algebra such that* G *is isomorphic to* $[\![\mathbb{G}]\!]$.

3.2   Side-View Model

The graphs-within-edges model corresponds, to some extent, to the top-view of the system. Another possibility is to take a side-view of the system, where containment is traced by dependencies between items in different layers (analogous to the representation of inheritance via arrows in UML class diagrams).

In [3] we have followed the side-view approach to interpret (a slight variation of) the algebra in § 2 over a class of graphs already available in the literature, called gs-graphs [14]. Roughly, gs-graphs are an extension of term-graphs [1] tailored to many-sorted hypersignatures. Moreover, in the formalisation of the model we have exploited the algebraic structure of gs-graph in terms of the so-called gs-monoidal theories [8]. Here we extend [3] to the design algebra of Def. 1 that allows for a more general form of interface.

While we refer the interested reader to [3] for most technical details, the main idea is to take a signature $\Sigma_{\mathcal{D},\mathcal{E}}$ whose sorts correspond to node sorts and whose operators correspond to the labels of edges. One additional sort $\bullet$ is also

$$(\text{op})\ \frac{f \in \Sigma_{u,v}}{f : u \to v} \qquad (\text{id})\ \frac{u \in S^*}{id_u : u \to u} \qquad (\text{bang})\ \frac{u \in S^*}{!_u : u \to \epsilon} \qquad (\text{dup})\ \frac{u \in S^*}{\nabla_u : u \to uu}$$

$$(\text{sym})\ \frac{u, v \in S^*}{\rho_{u,v} : uv \to vu} \qquad (\text{seq})\ \frac{t : u \to v \quad t' : v \to w}{t; t' : u \to w} \qquad (\text{par})\ \frac{t : u \to v \quad t' : u' \to v'}{t \otimes t' : uu' \to vv'}$$

Fig. 3. Inference rules of gs-monoidal theories

introduced to represent "locations" within the hierarchy. Formally, for nodes sorted over S and edges labelled over $\mathcal{D} \cup \mathcal{E}$, we let $S^\bullet = S \cup \{\bullet\}$, assuming that $\bullet \notin S$, and let $\Sigma_{\mathcal{D},\mathcal{E}}$ denote the signature over $S^\bullet$ defined as follows:

$$\Sigma_{\mathcal{D},\mathcal{E}} = \{l : \bullet, ar(l) \to \epsilon \mid l \in \mathcal{E}\} \cup \{L : \bullet, ar(L) \to \bullet, ar(L) \mid L \in \mathcal{D}\} \cup \{\nu_s : \bullet \to s \mid s \in S\}$$

Thus, each hierarchical edge $L \in \mathcal{D}$ defines an operator $L \in \Sigma_{\mathcal{D},\mathcal{E}}$ that takes as arguments a location and the list of actual parameters and returns a location and the list of formal parameters (i.e., it provides the inner graph with the location where to reside and with a local environment). Of course, the type and number of parameters corresponds to the rank of L. Plain edges l provide no result (their co-arity is ϵ, the empty list).

By analogy with the well-known construction that given an ordinary signature allows to define its initial model as the free cartesian category of terms over that signature, starting from $\Sigma_{\mathcal{D},\mathcal{E}}$ we can generate the so-called free gs-monoidal theory $\mathbf{GS}(\Sigma_{\mathcal{D},\mathcal{E}})$, that accounts for all the gs-graphs that can be defined over the signature $\Sigma_{\mathcal{D},\mathcal{E}}$: differently from cartesian categories, gs-monoidal categories account for the sharing of sub-terms/graphs and for the presence of hidden sub-terms/graphs.

The expressions of interest are generated by the rules depicted in Fig. 3: they are obtained from some basic (families of) terms by closing them with respect to *sequential* (seq) and *parallel* (par) *composition*. By rule (op), the basic terms include one generator for each operator of the signature: these can be considered as the elementary bricks of our expressions, and conceptually correspond to the hyperedges of the term graphs. All other basic terms define the wires that can be used to build our graphs: the *identities* (id), the *dischargers* (bang), the *duplicators* (dup) and the *symmetries* (sym).

Note that expressions t are "typed" over pairs of lists of sorts and that their types determine the admissibility of sequential composition. For $t : u \to v$, with respect to our intuitive view of systems, the *source* u expresses the top-interface of t, that must be matched when embedding the expression in a larger context; the *target* v expresses the inner-interface, that constrains the admissible sub-graphs that can be placed below t; sequential composition represents the placing of one system (e.g. $t' : v \to w$) below another (e.g. $t; t'$).

Definition 9 (gs-monoidal theory). *Given a hypersignature Σ over a set of sorts S, the associated* gs-monoidal theory $\mathbf{GS}(\Sigma)$ *is the category whose objects* *are the elements of S^*, and whose arrows are equivalence classes of gs-monoidal terms, i.e., terms generated by the inference rules in Fig. 3 subject to the following conditions*

- *identities and sequential composition satisfy the axioms of categories:*
  [identity] $id_u ; t = t = t ; id_v$ *for all* $t : u \to v;$
  [associativity] $t_1 ; (t_2 ; t_3) = (t_1 ; t_2) ; t_3$ *whenever any side is defined,*
- $\otimes$ *is a monoidal functor with unit* id_ϵ, *i.e. it satisfies:*
  [functoriality] $id_{uv} = id_u \otimes id_v$, *and*
  $(t_1 \otimes t_2) ; (t_1' \otimes t_2') = (t_1 ; t_1') \otimes (t_2 ; t_2')$ *whenever both sides are defined,*
  [monoid] $t \otimes id_\epsilon = t = id_\epsilon \otimes t$ $t_1 \otimes (t_2 \otimes t_3) = (t_1 \otimes t_2) \otimes t_3$
- ρ *is a natural transformation, i.e. it satisfies:*
  [naturality] $(t \otimes t') ; \rho_{v,v'} = \rho_{u,u'} ; (t' \otimes t)$ *for all* $t : u \to v$ *and* $t' : u' \to v'$
  and furthermore it satisfies:
  [symmetry] $(id_u \otimes \rho_{v,w}) ; (\rho_{u,w} \otimes id_v) = \rho_{u \otimes v,w}$ $\rho_{u,v} ; \rho_{v,u} = id_{u \otimes v}$
  $\rho_{\epsilon,u} = \rho_{u,\epsilon} = id_u$
- ∇ *and* ! *satisfy the following axioms:*
  [unit] $!_\epsilon = \nabla_\epsilon = id_\epsilon$
  [duplication] $\nabla_u ; (id_u \otimes \nabla_u) = \nabla_u ; (\nabla_u \otimes id_u)$ $\nabla_u ; (id_u \otimes !_u) = id_u$
  $\nabla_u ; \rho_{u,u} = \nabla_u$
  [monoidality] $\nabla_{uv} ; (id_u \otimes \rho_{v,u} \otimes id_v) = \nabla_u \otimes \nabla_v$ $!_{uv} = !_u \otimes !_v$

We call a *wiring* any arrow of $\mathbf{GS}(\Sigma)$ which is obtained from the rules of Fig. 3 without using rule (op). Notice that the definition of wiring is well-given, because any operator symbol introduced by rule (op) is preserved by all the axioms of the theory. Notably, the wirings of $\mathbf{GS}(\Sigma)$ from u to v are in bijective correspondence with the set of functions $\{k \colon \lfloor u \rfloor \to \lfloor v \rfloor \mid u[k(i)] = v[i]$ for all $1 \le i \le |v|\}$, where for an ordinal $n \in \mathbb{N}$, we write $\underline{n}$ for the set $\{1, \dots, n\}$.

The key consequence is that when drawing gs-graphs, we can abstract away from the way and order in which tentacles cross each other, because the axioms of gs-monoidal theories establish the equivalence of all drawings representing the same (set of) connections.

Then, each term $\mathbb{G}$ is translated to a gs-graph having $\bullet$ followed by (a linearisation of) the sorts of free nodes $fn(\mathbb{G})$ as source interface and the empty list of sorts ϵ as target interface. To fix the set-to-list correspondence between $fn(\mathbb{G})$ and the source interface, we exploit the concept of an *assignment*.

Definition 10 (Assignment). *An assignment is a function* $\sigma \in \bigcup_{n \in \mathbb{N}}\{f \colon \underline{n} \to \mathcal{X} \times S \mid f$ *is injective*$\}$. *An assignment* $\sigma \colon \underline{n} \to \mathcal{X} \times S$ *for a given* $n \in \mathbb{N}$ *is uniquely determined by a list of nodes without repetitions (because it is injective), namely* $\sigma(1), \sigma(2), \dots, \sigma(n)$: *we shall often represent it this way and write* $x : s \in \sigma$ *as a shorthand for* $x : s$ *belonging to* $img(\sigma)$, *the image of* σ.

In the following, by $\tau(\sigma)$ we denote $\tau(\sigma(1), \sigma(2), \dots, \sigma(n))$, i.e., the sequence of sorts of the nodes in $img(\sigma)$. Furthermore, for a given list of nodes $\overline{y} \in (\mathcal{X} \times S)^*$ and an assignment σ such that $|\overline{y}| \subseteq img(\sigma)$, we let $k_{\overline{y}}^\sigma \colon |\overline{y}| \to |\sigma|$ be the function such that $k_{\overline{y}}^\sigma(i) = \sigma^{-1}(\overline{y}|_i)$ for all $0 < i \le |\overline{y}|$.

Definition 11 (GS-graph encoding). *Given an assignment* $\sigma = x_1 : s_1, \ldots, x_n : s_n$ *and a term* $\mathbb{G}$ *with* $fn(\mathbb{G}) \subseteq img(\sigma)$ *such that all its bound variables carry different names[3] (also different from the names in* σ*), we define the gs-graph* $[\![\mathbb{G}]\!]_\sigma : \bullet, \tau(\sigma) \to \epsilon$ *by structural induction as follows (assuming that* $\otimes$ *has conventional precedence over* $;$*):*

- $[\![\mathbf{0}]\!]_\sigma = [\![x : s]\!]_\sigma =\, !_{\bullet, \tau(\sigma)} : \bullet, \tau(\sigma) \to \epsilon$

- $[\![l\langle \overline{y} \rangle]\!]_\sigma = id_\bullet \otimes wir(k_{\overline{y}}^\sigma)$; $l : \bullet, \tau(\sigma) \to \epsilon$, *where the expression* $wir(k_{\overline{y}}^\sigma) : \tau(\sigma) \to ar(l)$ *is the wiring uniquely determined by* $k_{\overline{y}}^\sigma : |ar(b)| \to |\sigma|$.

- $[\![L_{\overline{x}}[\mathbb{G}]\langle \overline{y} \rangle]\!]_\sigma = id_\bullet \otimes \nabla_{\tau(\sigma)}$; $(id_\bullet \otimes wir(k_{\overline{y}}^\sigma)\,;\,L) \otimes id_{\tau(\sigma)}$; $[\![\mathbb{G}]\!]_{\overline{x}, \sigma} : \bullet, \tau(\sigma) \to \epsilon$, *where w.l.o.g. we assume* $\lfloor \overline{x} \rfloor \cap \lfloor \sigma \rfloor = \emptyset$ *and the expression* $wir(k_{\overline{y}}^\sigma) : \tau(\sigma) \to ar(L)$ *is the wiring uniquely determined by* $k_{\overline{y}}^\sigma : |ar(b)| \to |\sigma|$.

- $[\![\mathbb{G}|\mathbb{H}]\!]_\sigma = \nabla_{\bullet, \tau(\sigma)}$; $[\![\mathbb{G}]\!]_\sigma \otimes [\![\mathbb{H}]\!]_\sigma : \bullet, \tau(\sigma) \to \epsilon$

- $[\![(\nu\, x : s)\mathbb{G}]\!]_\sigma = [\![\mathbb{G}]\!]_\sigma : \bullet, \tau(\sigma) \to \epsilon$ *if* $x : s \notin fn(\mathbb{G})$

- $[\![(\nu\, x : s)\mathbb{G}]\!]_\sigma = (\nabla_\bullet\,;\,id_\bullet \otimes \nu_s) \otimes id_{\tau(\sigma)}$; $[\![\mathbb{G}]\!]_{x:s, \sigma} : \bullet, \tau(\sigma) \to \epsilon$ *otherwise, where w.l.o.g. we assume* $x : s \notin \lfloor \sigma \rfloor$.

Note that although $[\![\mathbf{0}]\!]_\sigma$ and $[\![x : s]\!]_\sigma$ are defined in the same way, the first is defined for any σ, while the second one is defined only if $x : s \in \sigma$.

Theorem 2 (cf. [3]). *Let* $\mathbb{G}$ *and* $\mathbb{H}$ *be two terms such that* $\mathbb{G} \equiv_D \mathbb{H}$ *iff for any assignment* σ *we have* $[\![\mathbb{G}]\!]_\sigma = [\![\mathbb{H}]\!]_\sigma$.

Contrary to the encoding in § 3.1 the encoding applies to a restricted class of terms and is not surjective: The crucial fact is that the scoping discipline of restriction restricts the visibility of a localised nodes $x : s$ in such a way that it cannot be used from edges outside the one where $(\nu\, x : s)$ appears, but such a node scoping discipline has no counterpart in gs-graphs. This fact suggests that our algebra can serve to characterise exactly those term graphs with well-scoped references to nodes.

We conclude by sketching in Fig. 4 the gs-graphs corresponding to the two hierarchical graphs in Fig. 1: $A[(\nu w)(a\langle x, w \rangle \mid a\langle w, y \rangle)]\langle x, y \rangle$ on the left, and $(\nu w)(A_{u,v}[\mathbb{G}]\langle x, y \rangle \mid A_{u,v}[\mathbb{G}]\langle y, x \rangle)$ on the right (for $\mathbb{G} = a\langle u, w \rangle \mid a\langle w, v \rangle$). The drawing is decorated with: an external dashed line enclosing the gs-graph and emphasising its interface, the names of free nodes available, some dotted lines suggesting the correspondence between actual and formal parameters of A-labelled edges. Such a decoration is not part of the formal definition and has the only purpose to ease the intuitive correspondence with Fig. 1.

---

[3] This also means that in any occurrence of $L_{\overline{x}}[\mathbb{G}]$ the list $\overline{x}$ has no repetitions.

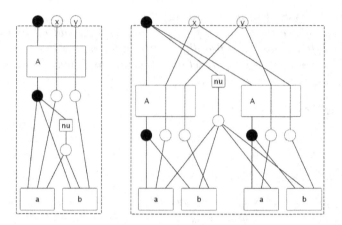

Fig. 4. Hierarchical structure as gs-monoidal terms

4   Applications to Service-Oriented Systems

This section presents one possible application of our approach, namely the graphical encoding of process calculi. We first discuss some methodological aspects and then show two examples, where the emphasis is respectively on the hierarchical nature of transactions and sessions.

4.1   Encoding Methodology

The main idea for defining graphical encoding of process calculi is to interpret process constructors as derived operators of our algebra. In that manner, each process term corresponds to a graph term, and hence to a hierarchical and gs-graph offering both a top and a side view of the same process. Moreover, if the interpretation faithfully captures the structural congruence of the calculus with the axioms of the graph algebra we obtain a nice result: congruent processes uniquely correspond to isomorphic graphs, and vice versa.

Each derived operator defines thus a graph operation that introduces items (nodes and edges). The first step of our methodology is fixing the set of node sorts, edge labels and design labels. Nodes are typically used to represent channels and control points and are sorted accordingly, while plain edges represent constructs such as atomic activities. Instead, inherently hierarchical constructors like session and transaction scopes are represented by designs.

Moreover, other design sorts can be introduced (i.e. one for each syntactical category of the calculus) to play the role of type annotations and constrain the applicability of derived operators, but they must be removed once the graphs are composed. For instance, parallel composition and non-deterministic choices are typically interpreted as graph operations that do not introduce any graph item, thus reflecting the axioms associated to such operations (associativity and commutativity).

The removal of such annotations is done by introducing flattening axioms, which implicitly remove (by performing some kind of hyper-edge replacement [12]) those edges satisfying a specific membership predicate (i.e. being typed with the annotation sorts).

Definition 12 (flattening axiom). *The flattening axiom* flat_L *for a design label* L *is* $L_{\overline{x}}[\mathbb{G}]\langle\overline{y}\rangle \equiv \mathbb{G}\{\overline{y}/\overline{x}\}$.

It is evident that when flat_L is considered, then L-labelled edges are immaterial. Flattening is fundamental in order to characterise classes of graphs by means of derived operators. Indeed, flattening is used in all encondings, where some design labels are used just for the sake of composing various classes of processes and not really to build scopes. So nesting has two roles: as a means to enclose a graph and as a sort of typed interface to enable disciplined graph compositions. The presence of flattening axioms makes the first role immaterial.

Another kind of axioms that are sometimes useful to be included in the structural congruence are *extrusion* axioms.

Definition 13 (extrusion axiom). *The extrusion axiom* extr_L *for a design label* L *is* $L_{\overline{x}}[(\nu z)\mathbb{G}\langle\overline{y}\rangle] \equiv (\nu z)L_{\overline{x}}[\mathbb{G}]\langle\overline{y}\rangle$, *where* $z \notin \lfloor\overline{x}\rfloor \cup \lfloor\overline{y}\rfloor$.

Extrusion axioms are needed to handle those calculi in which name restriction is not localised inside a scope or it is allowed to cross the boundaries of some scopes, as it may happen for some process calculi. Indeed, we shall see in § 4.3 how extrusion axioms are used to capture extrusion for some scope constructs.

Note that the addition of axiom flat_L also implies the validity of axiom extr_L, hence in the following we assume that for each label L exactly one of the following cases applies: either only the extrusion or only the flattening axiom for L is present; or none of flat_L and extr_L is present. Of course the presence of such axioms for a chosen set of labels is often fundamental for the soundness of the encoding.

4.2   Transaction Workflows

We consider in this section the *nested sagas with programmable compensations* of [6], a calculus for long running transactions that aims at providing a core language for composing activities into *sagas* (atomic transactions) or *processes* (non-atomic compensable activities). Formally, the syntax of sagas is as follows.

Definition 14 (sagas syntax). *Let* Λ *be a set of atomic activities ranged over by* a. *The sets* $\mathcal{S}$ *of sagas and* $\mathcal{P}$ *of compensable processes are all the terms generated by* S *and* P *in the grammar below, respectively.*

$$S \ ::= a \mid \{P\} \qquad P \ ::= S\%S \mid P;P \mid P \mid P$$

For the sake of simplicity, with respect to the original presentation we neglect the introduction of nil processes and non-compensable activities. A *saga* is an

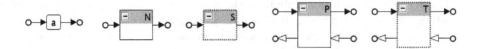

Fig. 5. Type graph for sagas

atomic activity or an arbitrarily complex transaction built out from a compensable processes. A basic process $A\%B$ is built by declaring a saga A as an ordinary flow and equipping it with another saga B as its compensation flow. The calculus provides also primitives for composing processes in sequence and parallel (split&join).

Definition 15 (sagas structural congruence). *The* structural congruence *for sagas is the relation* $\equiv_S \subseteq \mathcal{P} \times \mathcal{P}$, *closed under sagas construction, inductively generated by the following set of axioms (for any* $P, Q, R \in \mathcal{P}$*):*

$$
\begin{aligned}
P ; (Q ; R) &\equiv (P ; Q) ; R & (sA1) \\
P \mid Q &\equiv Q \mid P & (sA2) \\
P \mid (Q \mid R) &\equiv (P \mid Q) \mid R & (sA3)
\end{aligned}
$$

Encoding sagas. We now define the graphical encoding of sagas. As explained, the first step is to interpret syntactical categories of the calculus as suitable design labels and constructors as derived operators over our graph algebra. In this case we decide to introduce design labels N for Nested sagas, S for Sagas, P for compensable Pairs and T (Transactions) for compensable processes. Note that N can be read as a subsort of S, while P as a subsort of T. Figure 5 illustrates the shapes of the nodes and boxes we shall exploit. We have chosen an arity of four tentacles for pairs and transactions to denote the following control points: entry of the ordinary flow (incoming filled arrow), exit of the ordinary flow (outgoing filled arrow), entry of the compensation flow (incoming empty arrow) and exit of the compensation flow (outgoing empty arrow). Activities and sagas are represented by edges with only two tentacles (for the ordinary flow). Note that we have actually a family of activity edges, one for each activity in Λ. Since S and T are just used for composition, we let the flattening axioms flat$_S$ and flat$_T$ hold (whence the dotted borders in Fig. 5).

The encoding is formally defined as follows (cf. Fig. 6).

Definition 16 (sagas encoding). *The interpretation of the sagas operators over the design algebra is given by*

$$
\begin{aligned}
a &\overset{\text{def}}{=} S_{p,q}[a\langle p, q\rangle] \\
\{Q\} &\overset{\text{def}}{=} N_{p,q}[(\nu t)Q\langle p, q, t, q\rangle] \\
A \% B &\overset{\text{def}}{=} P_{p,q,r,s}[A\langle p, q\rangle \mid B\langle r, s\rangle] \\
Q ; R &\overset{\text{def}}{=} T_{p,q,r,s}[(\nu u, v)(Q\langle p, u, v, s\rangle \mid R\langle u, q, r, v\rangle)] \\
Q \mid R &\overset{\text{def}}{=} T_{p,q,r,s}[Q\langle p, q, r, s\rangle \mid R\langle p, q, r, s\rangle]
\end{aligned}
$$

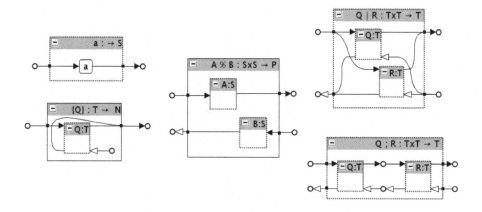

Fig. 6. Graphical interpretation for sagas

Note again that some primitives of the calculus are considered as material in the encoding, i.e. represented by graph items like edges. This is the case of activities as shown in Fig. 5 and also of compensable pairs and nested sagas. Instead, sequencing and parallel composition (see Fig. 6) are immaterial and their associated axioms are captured by the flattening axioms.

The proposed encoding is sound and complete, i.e. equivalent processes and sagas are mapped into isomorphic graphs as shown in [5].

Proposition 3 (cf. [5]). *For any* $Q, R \in \mathcal{P}$ *we have* $Q \equiv_S R$ *iff* $Q \equiv_D R$.

Example 3. Consider the following example, inspired from [6] of the saga

{acceptOrder%refuseOrder ; (updateCredit%refundOrder |
                              prepareOrder%updateStock) |
                              {addPoints%skip}%{substractPoints%skip}) }

The saga is used for modelling a scenario for dealing with purchase orders. The initial activity (*acceptOrder*) handles requests from clients. The next three processes are executed in parallel. The first one (*updateCredit*) charges the amount of the order to the balance of the client. The second one (*prepareOrder*) handles the packaging of the order and updates the stock. The third one deals with point reward activities: it is formed by a nested saga to update the reward balance of a user (part of a program for accumulating points with purchases). All the activities have a corresponding compensation to undo the actions performed by the successful completion of the activities. Note that activity *addPoints* has a vacuous compensation (*skip*) to avoid aborting the purchase when the point accumulation activity aborts due to the absence of a reward account (idem for activity *substractPoints*). The corresponding hierarchical graph is in Fig. 7.

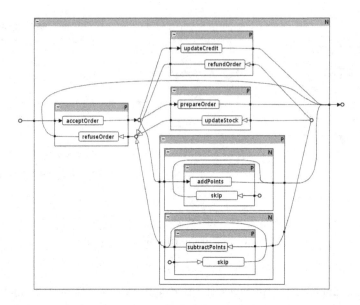

Fig. 7. Graphical encoding of a saga

4.3   Service Sessions

This section sketches the graphical representation of CaSPiS [2], a session-centred calculus developed within SENSORIA. We have chosen this calculus since it represents a non-trivial example of the interplay between nesting and linking introduced by nested sessions, pipelines and communication. We briefly overview CaSPiS and we refer the interested readers to [2] for an exhaustive description. We remark that we focus here on the close-free fragment of the calculus and we present a slightly simplified syntax. Both decisions are for the sake of a convenient and clean presentation and constitute no limitation.

Definition 17 (CaSPiS syntax). *Let $\mathcal{Z}$ be a set of session names, $\mathcal{S}$ a set of service names and $\mathcal{V}$ a set of value names. The set $\mathcal{P}$ of processes consists of all the terms generated by P in the grammar below*

$$P ::= \mathbf{0} \mid r \triangleright P \mid P > Q \mid (\nu w)P \mid P \mid P \mid A.P$$
$$A ::= s \mid \bar{s} \mid (?x) \mid \langle u \rangle \mid \langle u \rangle^\uparrow$$

where $s \in \mathcal{S}$, $r \in \mathcal{Z}$, $u \in \mathcal{V}$, $w \in \mathcal{V} \cup \mathcal{Z}$ and x is a value variable.

Service definitions and invocations are written like input and output prefixes in CCS. Thus $s.P$ defines a service s that can be invoked by $\bar{s}.Q$. Synchronisation of $s.P$ and $\bar{s}.Q$ leads to the creation of a new session, identified by a fresh name r that can be viewed as a private, synchronous channel binding caller and callee. Since client and service may be far apart, a session naturally comes with two sides, written $r \triangleright P$, and $r \triangleright Q$, with r bound somewhere above them by (νr). Rules governing creation and scoping of sessions are based on those of the restriction operator in the π-calculus. Note that nested invocations to services yield separate sessions and thus hierarchies of nested sessions.

When two partner sides $r \triangleright P$ and $r \triangleright Q$ are deployed, intra-session communication is done via input and output actions $\langle u \rangle$ and $(?x)$: values produced by P can be consumed by Q, and vice versa.

Values can be returned outside a session to the enclosing environment using the return operator $\langle \cdot \rangle^\uparrow$. Return values can be consumed by other sessions sides, or used locally to invoke other services, to start new activities. Local consumption is achieved using the pipeline operator $P > Q$. Here, a new instance of process Q is activated each time P emits a value that Q can consume. Notably, the new instance of Q runs within the same session as $P > Q$, not in a fresh one.

Summarising, each CaSPiS process can be thought of as running in an environment providing it different means of communication: one channel for "standard" input, one channel for "standard" output and one channel for returning values one level up.

Example 4. Consider the process $(\nu a)(\nu b)(a \triangleright (P_1|b \triangleright P_2)|a \triangleright P_3|b \triangleright P_4)$. It represents a typical situation where two sessions a and b have been created (e.g. upon two service invocations). Agent $a \triangleright (P_1|b \triangleright P_2)$ participates to sessions a and b (assume P_1 is the protocol for a and P_2 the one for b), with the b side nested in a. The counter-party protocols for a and b are P_3 and P_4, respectively, and they run separately. Notably, values returned one level up by P_2 can be consumed by P_3.

Definition 18 (CaSPiS structural congruence). *The structural congruence for CaSPiS processes is the relation $\equiv_C \subseteq \mathcal{P} \times \mathcal{P}$, closed under process construction, inductively generated by the following set of axioms*

$$
\begin{array}{llll}
P \mid (Q \mid R) \equiv (P \mid Q) \mid R) & \text{(CA1)} & P \mid (\nu n)Q \equiv (\nu n)(P \mid Q) & \text{if } n \notin fn(P) \ \text{(CA6)} \\
P \mid Q \equiv Q \mid P & \text{(CA2)} & ((\nu n)Q) > P \equiv (\nu n)(Q > P) & \text{if } n \notin fn(P) \ \text{(CA7)} \\
P \mid \mathbf{0} \equiv P & \text{(CA3)} & A.(\nu n)P \equiv (\nu n)A.P & \text{if } n \notin A \quad \text{(CA8)} \\
(\nu n)(\nu m)P \equiv (\nu m)(\nu n)P & \text{(CA4)} & r \triangleright (\nu n)P \equiv (\nu n)r \triangleright P & \text{if } n \neq r \quad \text{(CA9)} \\
(\nu n)\mathbf{0} \equiv \mathbf{0} & \text{(CA5)} & (\nu n)P \equiv (\nu m)P\{^m/_n\} & \text{if } m \notin fn(P) \ \text{(CA10)} \\
& & (?x).P \equiv (?y).P\{^y/_x\} & \text{if } y \notin fn(P) \ \text{(CA11)}
\end{array}
$$

Encoding CaSPiS. We first define the alphabets of edge labels and nodes. The set $\mathcal{D}$ of design labels is composed by P, S, D, I, F and T which respectively stand for Parallel processes, Sessions, service Definitions, service Invocations and pipes (From and To). The set $\mathcal{E}$ of edge labels contains def (service definition), inv (service invocation), in (input), out (output) and ret (return). The node sorts considered are $\circ$ (channels), $\bullet$ (control points), $*$ (service names, i.e. $\mathcal{S}$) and $\square$ (values, i.e. $\mathcal{V}$). We assume that for each session name r there is a corresponding channel node.

The graphical representation of each design and edge label and their respective ranks can be found in Fig. 8. For instance, designs of type P are all of the form $P_{p,t,o,i}[\mathbb{G}]$ where p is the control point representing the process start of execution, t is the returning channel, o is the output channel and i is the input channel. Vice

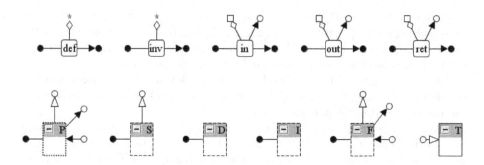

Fig. 8. Type graph for CaSPiS

versa, designs of type D and I only expose the starting point of execution: they are not strictly necessary for the encoding, but can be very useful for visualisation purposes (they enclose the interaction protocols between callers and callees). We let the flattening axiom flat$_P$ hold, together with extrusion axioms extr$_S$, extr$_D$, extr$_I$, extr$_F$. Hence, edges of type P are immaterial (they can be considered as type annotations) and edges of type T define the only *rigid* hierarchy w.r.t. containment and name scoping. Other explicit hierarchies for edge containment are given by session nesting (S), service definition (D), service invocation (I) and pipelining (F). As usual, flattening processes allows for getting rid of the axioms for parallel composition (see [15]). The presence of extrusion axioms is motivated by the structural congruence axioms of CaSPiS, namely CA7 motivates extr$_F$, CA8 motivates both extr$_D$ and extr$_I$, and CA9 motivates extr$_S$. Note that we use dashed border for designs for which the extrusion axiom hold, while designs to be flattened are depicted with dotted borders.

Definition 19 (CaSPiS encoding). *The interpretation of CaSPiS operators over the design algebra is given by*

$$s.Q \stackrel{\text{def}}{=} P_{p,t,o,i}[\,t|o|i|\,D[\,(\nu q,t',o',i')(\text{def}\langle p,s,q\rangle|Q\langle q,t',o',i'\rangle)\,]\langle p\rangle\,]$$

$$\bar{s}.Q \stackrel{\text{def}}{=} P_{p,t,o,i}[\,t|o|i|\,I[\,(\nu q,t',o',i')(\text{inv}\langle p,s,q\rangle|Q\langle q,t',o',i'\rangle)\,]\langle p\rangle\,]$$

$$r \triangleright Q \stackrel{\text{def}}{=} P_{p,t,o,i}[\,t|i|\,S[\,Q\langle p,o,r,r\rangle\,]\langle p,o\rangle\,]$$

$$Q > R \stackrel{\text{def}}{=} P_{p,t,o,i}[\,o\,|\,(\nu m)(\,F[\,Q\langle p,t,m,i\rangle\,]\langle p,t,m,i\rangle\,|$$
$$T[\,(\nu q,t',o')R\langle q,t',o',m\rangle\,]\langle m\rangle\,)\,]$$

$$Q|R \stackrel{\text{def}}{=} P_{p,t,o,i}[\,Q\langle p,t,o,i\rangle|R\langle p,t,o,i\rangle\,]$$

$$(\nu w)Q \stackrel{\text{def}}{=} P_{p,t,o,i}[(\nu w)Q\langle p,t,o,i\rangle]$$

$$0 \stackrel{\text{def}}{=} P_{p,t,o,i}[\,p|t|o|i\,]$$

$$\langle u\rangle.Q \stackrel{\text{def}}{=} P_{p,t,o,i}[\,(\nu q)(\text{out}\langle p,q,u,o\rangle\,|\,Q\langle q,t,o,i\rangle)\,]$$

$$\langle u\rangle^\uparrow.Q \stackrel{\text{def}}{=} P_{p,t,o,i}[\,(\nu q)(\text{ret}\langle p,q,u,t\rangle\,|\,Q\langle q,t,o,i\rangle)\,]$$

$$(?x).Q \stackrel{\text{def}}{=} P_{p,t,o,i}[\,(\nu q,x)(\text{in}\langle p,q,x,i\rangle\,|\,Q\langle q,t,o,i\rangle)\,]$$

Proposition 4 (cf. [5]). *For any $Q, R \in \mathcal{P}$ we have $Q \equiv_{\text{C}} R$ iff $Q \equiv_{\text{D}} R$.*

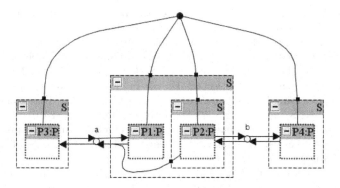

Fig. 9. Example of session nesting

Instead of providing the visualisation of the encoding and a detailed explanation (for which we refer to [4]) we prefer to concentrate on the representation of session nesting with the typical session situation presented before. Figure 9 depicts the graphical representation of our example, where the graph has been further simplified (e.g. fusing nodes, removing isolated nodes and irrelevant tentacles) to focus on the main issues and make immediate the correspondence with the process term. The figure evidences the hierarchy introduced by session nesting and how it is crossed by intra-session communication. It is also worth to note that the graph highlights the fact that the return channel of a nested session is pipelined into the output channel of the enclosing session. More precisely, the return channel of the immediate session where P_2 lives (i.e. b) is connected to the output channel of the session containing it, i.e. the session channel a.

5   Conclusion

This chapter collects results from [3,5,4]. We presented our specification formalism based on a convenient algebra of hierarchical graphs: its features make it well-suited for the specification of systems with inherently hierarchical aspects and in particular, process calculi with notions of scope and containment (like ambients, membranes, sessions and transactions). Some advantages of our approach are due to the graph algebra, whose syntax resembles standard algebraic specifications and, in particular, it is close to the syntax found in nominal calculi. The key point is to exploit the algebraic structure of both designs and graphs when proving properties of an encoding, facilitating proofs by structural induction.

References

1. Barendregt, H., van Eekelen, M., Glauert, J., Kennaway, J., Plasmeijer, M., Sleep, M.: Term graph reduction. In: de Bakker, J.W., Nijman, A.J., Treleaven, P.C. (eds.) PARLE 1987. LNCS, vol. 259, pp. 141–158. Springer, Heidelberg (1987)

2. Boreale, M., Bruni, R., De Nicola, R., Loreti, M.: Sessions and pipelines for structured service programming. In: Barthe, G., de Boer, F.S. (eds.) FMOODS 2008. LNCS, vol. 5051, pp. 19–38. Springer, Heidelberg (2008)
3. Bruni, R., Corradini, A., Gadducci, F., Lluch-Lafuente, A., Montanari, U.: On GS-Monoidal Theories for Graphs with Nesting. In: Engels, G., Lewerentz, C., Schäfer, W., Schürr, A., Westfechtel, B. (eds.) Graph Transformations and Model-Driven Engineering-Essays Dedicated to Manfred Nagl on the Occasion of his 65th Birthday. LNCS, vol. 5765, pp. 59–86. Springer, Heidelberg (2010)
4. Bruni, R., Gadducci, F., Lluch Lafuente, A.: A graph syntax for processes and services. In: Jianwen, S., Laneve, C. (eds.) WS-FM 2009. LNCS, vol. 6194, pp. 46–60. Springer, Heidelberg (2010)
5. Bruni, R., Gadducci, F., Lluch Lafuente, A.: An algebra of hierarchical graphs and its application to structural encoding. Scientific Annals of Computer Science 20, 53–96 (2010)
6. Bruni, R., Melgratti, H.C., Montanari, U.: Theoretical foundations for compensations in flow composition languages. In: Palsberg, J., Abadi, M. (eds.) Proceedings of the 32nd International Symposium on Principles of Programming Languages (POPL 2005), pp. 209–220. ACM, New York (2005)
7. Bundgaard, M., Sassone, V.: Typed polyadic pi-calculus in bigraphs. In: Bossi, A., Maher, M.J. (eds.) Proceedings of the 8th International Symposium on Principles and Practice of Declarative Programming (PPDP 2006), pp. 1–12. ACM, New York (2006)
8. Corradini, A., Gadducci, F.: An algebraic presentation of term graphs, via gs-monoidal categories. Applied Categorical Structures 7(4), 299–331 (1999)
9. Corradini, A., Montanari, U., Rossi, F.: An abstract machine for concurrent modular systems: CHARM. Theoretical Computer Science 122(1-2), 165–200 (1994)
10. Corradini, A., Montanari, U., Rossi, F., Ehrig, H., Heckel, R., Löwe, M.: Algebraic Approaches to Graph Transformation - Part I: Basic Concepts and Double Pushout Approach. In: Rozenberg, G. (ed.) Handbook of Graph Grammars and Computing by Graph Transformation, pp. 163–246. World Scientific, Singapore (1997)
11. Drewes, F., Hoffmann, B., Plump, D.: Hierarchical graph transformation. Journal on Computer and System Sciences 64(2), 249–283 (2002)
12. Drewes, F., Kreowski, H.-J., Habel, A.: Hyperedge replacement, graph grammars. In: Rozenberg, G. (ed.) Handbook of Graph Grammars and Computing by Graph Transformations, Foundations, vol. 1, pp. 95–162. World Scientific, Singapore (1997)
13. Ferrari, G.L., Hirsch, D., Lanese, I., Montanari, U., Tuosto, E.: Synchronised hyperedge replacement as a model for service-oriented computing. In: de Boer, F.S., Bonsangue, M.M., Graf, S., de Roever, W.P. (eds.) FMCO 2005. LNCS, vol. 4111, pp. 22–43. Springer, Heidelberg (2006)
14. Ferrari, G.L., Montanari, U.: Tile formats for located and mobile systems. Information and Computation 156(1-2), 173–235 (2000)
15. Gadducci, F.: Term graph rewriting for the pi-calculus. In: Ohori, A. (ed.) APLAS 2003. LNCS, vol. 2895, pp. 37–54. Springer, Heidelberg (2003)
16. Milner, R.: Pure bigraphs: Structure and dynamics. Information and Computation 204(1), 60–122 (2006)

Analysing Protocol Stacks for Services*

Han Gao, Flemming Nielson, and Hanne Riis Nielson

DTU Informatics, Technical University of Denmark
{hg,nielson,riis}@imm.dtu.dk

Abstract. We show an approach, CaPiTo, to model service-oriented applications using process algebras such that, on the one hand, we can achieve a certain level of abstraction without being overwhelmed by the underlying implementation details and, on the other hand, we respect the concrete industrial standards used for implementing the service-oriented applications. By doing so, we will be able to not only reason about applications at different levels of abstractions, but also to build a bridge between the views of researchers on formal methods and developers in industry. We apply our approach to the financial case study taken from Chapter 0-3. Finally, we develop a static analysis to analyse the security properties as they emerge at the level of concrete industrial protocols.

1 Introduction

Service-oriented systems are becoming the leading edge of IT Systems. The most common implementation of service-oriented systems is protocol-based web services, where security of interactions between clients and services is ensured by means of industrial protocols, e.g. *TLS* [10], *SOAP* [19], HTTP, TCP/IP.

In the service-oriented environment, our view of a system can be divided into different levels; at the abstract level (as is usually the view found in academia), the system is independent of the underlying communication protocols, and at the concrete level (as is usually the view found in industry), the system must be understood in connection with how it makes use of industrial communication protocols. Motivated by this separation of concerns, we present a specification approach called CaPiTo to facilitate modelling systems at both the abstract and the concrete level. To bridge the gap between the two levels, we further define an intermediary level that connects them.

The CaPiTo approach has the advantage that, on the one hand, we can achieve certain level of abstraction without being overwhelmed by the underlying implementation details and, on the other hand, we fully respect the industrial communication protocols used for implementing the service-oriented systems. The main illustration of our approach is by means of the financial Credit Request case study taken from Chapter 0-3. Finally, we apply a protocol analysis tool LySa to the case study and verify it works as expected.

In this paper we introduce the CaPiTo approach of modelling service-oriented applications at different levels in Section 2 (abstract level), Section 3 (protocol

---

* This work has been partially sponsored by the project SENSORIA, IST-2005-016004.

M. Wirsing and M. Hölzl (Eds.): SENSORIA Project, LNCS 6582, pp. 369–389, 2011.

stack plug-in level) and Section 4 (concrete level). The Credit Request example is considered in detail in Section 5 and fully illustrates the use of the three levels of CaPiTo. The static analysis is developed in Section 6. Our conclusion and outlook on further work is presented in Section 7.

2   Abstract Level

The CaPiTo-approach of modelling service-oriented applications involves a total of three levels. At the abstract level, we abstract away from both cryptography and industrial communication protocols, and this allows us to concentrate on the interaction of the services themselves. At the concrete level, the notion of *services* is hidden, while we model both cryptography and the industrial communication protocols used for implementing the service-oriented application. To bridge between these levels, we introduce an intermediary level where the abstract specification is augmented with plug-ins for identifying the industrial protocol stacks to be used.

In the abstract specification, the basic building blocks are values, $v, w \in Val$, which correspond to *closed* expressions, i.e. expressions without free variables. Values are used to represent keys, nonces, messages, etc. Syntactically, they are described by expressions $e \in Expr$. We will use n to range over names, x to range over variables, and e to range over expressions. We use $\vec{v}$ as a short-hand for $v_1, \ldots, v_k$. In addition, we allow the use of functions f (as opposed to the constructors and destructors that will be used in the other levels for modelling cryptography).

Communication is facilitated by means of pattern matching and the binding of values to variables. We distinguish between *defining* occurrences and *applied* occurrences of variables. A defining occurrence is an occurrence where the binding of a variable is performed, while an applied occurrence is an occurrence of a variable where the value bound to it is being requested. We perform this distinction syntactically: the defining occurrence of x is denoted by $?x$, while in the scope of the declaration, the applied occurrences appear as x. Services are built from basic activities, including the service invocation $(\overline{n}[\ ].P)$ and service provision $(n[\ ].P)$, where $n[\ ].P$ defines a service that can be invoked by $\overline{n}[\ ].P$. After a service has been invoked there is a sequence of communication steps taking place. The empty holes $[\ ]$ after the service invocations and responses (e.g. $\overline{n}$ and n) serve as place-holders for plugging in a list of the underlying security protocols to be used to protect the communication steps in the intermediate level (to be presented in the next section). The reader familiar with [7] will notice that our abstract level has been inspired by the CaSPiS process calculus developed in the SENSORIA project. Other activities for building up services include restriction $((\nu\, n)P)$, nondeterministic choice $(P_1 + P_2)$, parallel composition $(P_1 | P_2)$, replication $(!P)$, and service return $(\uparrow \langle \vec{e} \rangle.P)$, where values $\vec{e}$ are returned outside a service to the enclosing environment. The syntax is in Table 1.

Table 1. Syntax of abstract specifications in CaPiTo

$v, w ::= n \mid f(\vec{v})$
$e \quad ::= x \mid n \mid f(\vec{e})$
$p \quad ::= ?x \mid x \mid n$
$P \quad ::= \langle \vec{e} \rangle.P \mid (\vec{p}).P \mid (\nu\, n)P \mid P_1 \mid P_2 \mid !P \mid P_1 + P_2 \mid 0 \mid \overline{n}[\,].P \mid n[\,].P \mid \uparrow \langle \vec{e} \rangle.P$

Table 2. Syntax of plug-in specifications (general) in CaPiTo

$v, w ::= n \mid f(\vec{v})$
$e \quad ::= x \mid n \mid f(\vec{e})$
$p \quad ::= ?x \mid x \mid n$
$P \quad ::= \langle \vec{e} \rangle.P \mid (\vec{p}).P \mid (\nu\, n)P \mid P_1 \mid P_2 \mid !P \mid P_1 + P_2 \mid 0 \mid \overline{n}[ps].P \mid n[ps].P \mid \uparrow \langle \vec{e} \rangle.P$
$ps \quad ::= pi \mid pi; ps$
$pi \quad ::= name, param_1, \cdots, param_k$

3   Protocol Stack Plug-ins

Plug-in Specification. In the abstract modelling of service-oriented applications, certain details are often abstracted away, for example, the underlying industrial protocols to be used to protect the communication steps. From the point of view of the OSI model [20], messages have to pass several layers before reaching the physical link layer and actually being transmitted. Each layer receives information from the layer above, modifies it and passes it down to the next layer. The operation of each layer is controlled by different protocols — hence the layers are said to constitute a protocol stack.

We now introduce an intermediate plug-in level in CaPiTo where we can retain part of the abstract view of service-oriented applications but where we can also begin to be precise about which protocols we intend to use. This takes the form of providing a list of protocols to be placed in the place-holders mentioned above as shown in Table 2. Here *ps* is a protocol stack, which we take to be a non-empty list (separated by semi-colons) of the protocols to be used. Each protocol *pi* is identified by its name and a number of auxiliary parameters ($k \geq 0$).

Transformations of the Plug-in Level. In this section, we shall define a systematic transformation of processes from plug-in level into the concrete level. The transformation is crucial as it works as a bridge between the abstract system model and the industrial realisation and implementation. The primary goal is to remove the service invocation and provision constructs (e.g. $\overline{n}$ and n) and expand away the protocol stack plug-ins by applying each protocol in the protocol stack to all the communication steps that it supposes to protect. This is done in two steps.

The first step is to distinguish between different services as well as different sessions of each service by unique session identifiers. This is taken care of by a transfer function $\mathcal{T}$. The transfer function takes two arguments; the first one

Table 3. The transfer function $\mathcal{T}$

$\mathcal{T}(\overline{s}[ps].P, rl)$	$\triangleq (\nu\, r)\langle r_{env}, s, r\rangle.\overline{r}[ps] \triangleright \mathcal{T}(P, r :: rl)$
$\mathcal{T}(s[ps].P, rl)$	$\triangleq (r_{env}, s, ?r).r[ps] \triangleright \mathcal{T}(P, r :: rl)$
$\mathcal{T}(\langle\vec{e}\rangle.P, r :: rl)$	$\triangleq \langle r, \vec{e}\rangle.\mathcal{T}(P, r :: rl)$
$\mathcal{T}((\vec{p}).P, r :: rl)$	$\triangleq (r, \vec{p}).\mathcal{T}(P, r :: rl)$
$\mathcal{T}(\uparrow \langle\vec{e}\rangle.P, r_1 :: r_2 :: rl)$	$\triangleq \langle r_2, \vec{e}\rangle.\mathcal{T}(P, r_1 :: r_2 :: rl)$
$\mathcal{T}((\nu\, n)P, rl)$	$\triangleq (\nu\, n)\mathcal{T}(P, rl)$
$\mathcal{T}(P_1|P_2, rl)$	$\triangleq \mathcal{T}(P_1, rl)|\mathcal{T}(P_2, rl)$
$\mathcal{T}(P_1 + P_2, rl)$	$\triangleq \mathcal{T}(P_1, rl) + \mathcal{T}(P_2, rl)$
$\mathcal{T}(!P, rl)$	$\triangleq !\mathcal{T}(P, rl)$

Table 4. Syntax of plug-in specifications (session identifer explicit) in CaPiTo, where the rest of syntatical categories remain the same as in Table 2

$$P ::= \langle r, \vec{e}\rangle.P \mid (r, \vec{p}).P \mid (\nu\, n)P \mid P_1|P_2 \mid !P \mid P_1 + P_2 \mid 0 \mid \overline{r}[ps] \triangleright P \mid r[ps] \triangleright P$$

is a plug-in specification to be transferred and the second one is a stack for recording all the session identifiers that are generated along the way, with the topmost identifier being the most recent one. Initially the function is called with *environment*, a special constant, as the second argument, i.e. $\mathcal{T}(P, [r_{env}])$. The result of applying the transfer function is a plug-in specification, of which the syntax is in Table 4. The definition of the transfer function is shown in Table 3. Each service invocation $\overline{s}[ps].P$ leads to the creation of a new session, identified by a fresh session identifier r, that is sent to the corresponding service provider $s[ps].Q$ for synchronisation. At both invocation and provider sides, the identifier r is systematically attached to each communication that belongs to the session, which imposes all the output ($\langle\vec{e}\rangle$) and input operations($(\vec{p})$) to take the form $\langle r, \vec{e}\rangle$ and $(r, \vec{p})$, respectively. Note that in the first two lines, the messages for the communication of r have r_{env} included, e.g. $\langle r_{env}, s, r\rangle$ and $(r_{env}, s, ?r)$. We do this to ensure that a search for matching service invocation and service provider is performed in the entire system (due to the use of r_{env}); it also ensures that outputs and inputs have the required form.

Note that multiple invocations to services will yield separate sessions, as identified by different choice of r, and the hierarchy of nested sessions, which is reflected by the position of each session identifer r in the identifier stack. In fact, when values are returned outside the current session using the return operator, $\uparrow \langle\vec{e}\rangle$, the second topmost identifer in the stack is adopted, which gives $\langle r_2, \vec{e}\rangle$ (see the fifth line of the function definition).

Example 1. Consider $P = \overline{s_1}[pi_1].(\overline{s_2}[pi_2].(\langle A, B\rangle. \uparrow \langle A\rangle.0))$. Applying the transfer function on P, as in $\mathcal{T}(P, [r_{env}])$, gives the following result:

$$(\nu\, r_1)\langle r_{env}, s_1, r_1\rangle.\overline{r_1}[pi_1] \triangleright ($$
$$(\nu\, r_2)\langle r_{env}, s_2, r_2\rangle.\overline{r_2}[pi_2] \triangleright ($$
$$\langle r_2, A, B\rangle.\langle r_1, A\rangle.0))$$

After the transformation, the service s_1 is identified by r_1 and s_2 by r_2. The communication $\langle A, B \rangle$ belongs to the session r_2 hence $\langle r_2, A, B \rangle$. The last message $\uparrow \langle A \rangle$ returns the value A to the session outside r_2, i.e. r_1. This is reflected by its transformation into $\langle r_1, A \rangle$.

The second step is to unfold the protocol stack that is used by each service. When a protocol stack contains a sequence of protocols we first expand away the leftmost (topmost) protocol in the stack and then continue with the subsequent layers. This is formally defined as follows:

$$\overline{r}[pi_1; \ldots ; pi_k] \rhd P \triangleq \overline{r}[pi_k] \rhd (\overline{r}[pi_{k-1}] \rhd (\ldots (\overline{r}[pi_1] \rhd P)))$$
$$r[pi_1; \ldots ; pi_k] \rhd P \triangleq r[pi_k] \rhd (r[pi_{k-1}] \rhd (\ldots (r[pi_1] \rhd P)))$$

The protocol unfolding makes use of protocol definitions which are specified in the concrete level. We shall introduce it in the next section.

4   Concrete Level

Concrete Specifications. At the concrete level of CaPiTo we fully model communication protocols and the use of asymmetric and symmetric cryptography. As defined in Table 5, we write $\mathbf{P}_{v_0^+}(\vec{v})$ for asymmetric encryption and $\mathbf{S}_{v_0^-}(\vec{v})$ for digital signatures; we write $\underline{\mathbf{P}}_{v_0^-}(\vec{v})$ for asymmetric decryption and $\underline{\mathbf{S}}_{v_0^+}(\vec{v})$ for the validation of digital signatures. Symmetric cryptography is modelled as communications through an encrypted tunnel, e.g. $r : e \blacktriangleright P$, with r being the session identifier and e being the symmetric key shared between the sending and receiving principals involved in the communications within P. We also admit a function $\mathbf{H}$ for producing hash values.

Semantics of the Concrete Level. The concrete level semantics consists of a structural congruence and a labelled transition system. The structural congruence $\equiv$ is defined as the least congruence relation induced by the laws in Table 6. The last rule $P_1 \equiv P_2$ if $P_1 \triangleq P_2$ is more general than the usual rule $A \equiv P$ if $A \triangleq P$ for unfolding recursive definitions; this is essential to the CaPiTo approach of unfolding protocol stacks thereby passing from the plug-ing level to the concrete level. We shall provide several examples of this in Section 5.

Let $\xrightarrow{\lambda}$ be the labelled transition relation induced by the rules in Table 7, where $\lambda ::= \tau \mid (r, \vec{v}) \mid \langle r, \vec{v} \rangle \mid \langle r, \mathbf{E}_w(\vec{v}) \rangle \mid (r, \mathbf{E}_w(\vec{v}))$. Here the labels $\langle r, \vec{v} \rangle$ and $(r, \vec{v})$ result from applying rules for output (*out*) and input (*in*), respectively; $\mathbf{E}_w\langle \vec{v} \rangle$ and $\mathbf{E}_w(\vec{v})$ indicate encryption and decryption using the key w; finally, we use τ to denote a silent transaction.

Rules (out) and (in) describe how a list of values $\vec{v}$ is output and how it is then input and matched to a pattern $\vec{p}$ creating new variable bindings recorded in the substitution σ that is then applied to the continuation of the input operation using the following auxiliary definition:

$$\mathcal{M}(\vec{v}, \vec{p}) = \begin{cases} \sigma & \text{if } switch(\vec{p}\sigma) = \vec{v} \text{ and } dom(\sigma) = \mathsf{fv}(\vec{p}) \\ undef & \text{otherwise} \end{cases}$$

Table 5. Syntax of concrete specifications in CaPiTo

$$
\begin{array}{ll}
v, w ::= & n \mid n^+ \mid n^- \mid \mathbf{P}_{n+}(\vec{v}) \mid \mathbf{S}_{n-}(\vec{v}) \mid \mathbf{H}(\vec{v}) \mid f(\vec{v}) \\
e ::= & x \mid n \mid n^+ \mid n^- \mid \mathbf{P}_{n+}(\vec{e}) \mid \mathbf{S}_{n-}(\vec{e}) \mid \mathbf{H}(\vec{e}) \mid f(\vec{e}) \\
p ::= & ?x \mid x \mid n \mid n^+ \mid n^- \mid \underline{\mathbf{P}}_{n-}(\vec{p}) \mid \underline{\mathbf{S}}_{n+}(\vec{p}) \\
P ::= & \langle r, \vec{e} \rangle.P \mid (r, \vec{p}).P \mid (\nu\, n)P \mid\, !P \mid r : e \blacktriangleright P \mid (\nu_\pm\, n)P \mid P_1 + P_2 \mid P_1 | P_2 \mid 0
\end{array}
$$

Table 6. Structural congruence (for all of CaPiTo)

$(\nu\, m)(\nu\, n)P \equiv (\nu\, n)(\nu\, m)P$	$(\nu\, m)0 \equiv 0$
$(\nu_\pm\, m)(\nu_\pm\, n)P \equiv (\nu_\pm\, n)(\nu_\pm\, m)P$	$(\nu_\pm\, m)0 \equiv 0$
$P_1 | (\nu\, m)P_2 \equiv (\nu\, m)(P_1 | P_2) \quad$ if $m \notin \mathsf{fn}(P_1)$	$r : e \blacktriangleright 0 \equiv 0$
$P_1 | (\nu_\pm\, m)P_2 \equiv (\nu_\pm\, m)(P_1 | P_2) \quad$ if $\{m^+, m^-\} \cap \mathsf{fn}(P_1) = \emptyset$	$!P \equiv P | !P$
$r : e \blacktriangleright (\nu\, m)P \equiv (\nu\, m)(r : e \blacktriangleright P) \quad$ if $m \notin \mathsf{fn}(P)$	$P_1 | P_2 \equiv P_2 | P_1$
$r : e \blacktriangleright (\nu_\pm\, m)P \equiv (\nu_\pm\, m)(r : e \blacktriangleright P)$ if $\{m^+, m^-\} \cap \mathsf{fn}(P) = \emptyset$	$P | 0 \equiv P$
$(P_1 | P_2) | P_3 \equiv P_1 | (P_2 | P_3)$	$P_1 \equiv P_2 \ $ if $P_1 \triangleq P_2$

Table 7. Labelled transition systems of the concrete specifications in CaPiTo

(out)	$\langle r, \vec{v} \rangle.P \xrightarrow{\langle r, \vec{v} \rangle} P$	(in)	$\dfrac{\mathcal{M}(\vec{v}, \vec{p}) = \sigma}{(r, \vec{p}).P \xrightarrow{(r, \vec{v})} P\sigma}$
(t-out)	$\dfrac{P \xrightarrow{\langle r, \vec{v} \rangle} P'}{r : w \blacktriangleright P \xrightarrow{\langle r, E_w\langle \vec{v} \rangle \rangle} r : w \blacktriangleright P'}$	(t-in)	$\dfrac{P \xrightarrow{(r, \vec{v})} P'}{r : w \blacktriangleright P \xrightarrow{(r, E_w(\vec{v}))} r : w \blacktriangleright P'}$
(sync)	$\dfrac{P_1 \xrightarrow{\langle r, \vec{v} \rangle} P_1' \quad P_2 \xrightarrow{(r, \vec{v})} P_2'}{P_1 | P_2 \xrightarrow{\tau} P_1' | P_2'}$	(t-sync)	$\dfrac{P_1 \xrightarrow{\langle r, E_w\langle \vec{v} \rangle \rangle} P_1' \quad P_2 \xrightarrow{(r, E_w(\vec{v}))} P_2'}{P_1 | P_2 \xrightarrow{\tau} P_1' | P_2'}$
(r-pass1)	$\dfrac{P \xrightarrow{\lambda} P'}{(\nu\, n)P \xrightarrow{\lambda} (\nu\, n)P'}$ $\;$ if $n \notin \mathsf{n}(\lambda)$	(r-pass2)	$\dfrac{P \xrightarrow{\lambda} P'}{(\nu_\pm\, n)P \xrightarrow{\lambda} (\nu_\pm\, n)P'}$ $\;$ if $\{n^+, n^-\} \cap \mathsf{n}(\lambda) = \emptyset$
(t-pass)	$\dfrac{P \xrightarrow{\lambda} P'}{r : w \blacktriangleright P \xrightarrow{\lambda} r : w \blacktriangleright P'}$ $\lambda ::= \langle r', \vec{v} \rangle | (r', \vec{v})$ $\mid \langle r', E_w\langle \vec{v} \rangle \rangle | (r', E_w(\vec{v})) | \tau$ and $r \neq r'$	(par)	$\dfrac{P \xrightarrow{\lambda} P'}{P | P_1 \xrightarrow{\lambda} P' | P_1}$ if $\mathsf{fn}(P_1) \cap \mathsf{bn}(\lambda) = \emptyset$
(congr)	$\dfrac{P \equiv P' \quad P' \xrightarrow{\lambda} P'' \quad P'' \equiv P'''}{P \xrightarrow{\lambda} P'''}$	(choice)	$\dfrac{P_1 \xrightarrow{\lambda} P_1'}{P_1 + P_2 \xrightarrow{\lambda} P_1'}$

The substitution $\mathcal{M}(\vec{v}, \vec{p}) = \sigma$ resulting from matching $\vec{v}$ against $\vec{p}$ is intended to ensure that $\vec{v}$ and $\vec{p}\sigma$ only differ in their use of asymmetric keys: a public key in one should relate to the corresponding private key in the other. We write $switch(K_A^+) = K_A^-$ and $switch(K_A^-) = K_A^+$.

Rules (t-out) and (t-in) model communications inside a tunnel protected by the symmetric key w. Rule (t-sync) describes the communication inside the tunnel; finally, rule (t-pass) propagates all the activities that are transparent to tunnels. Rules (choice), (par), (r-pass1), (r-pass2) and (congr) are the standard ones for choice, parallel composition, restriction and structural congruence.

Table 8. Transformation of tunnels into LySa

$$
\begin{array}{l}
r : e_0 \blacktriangleright \langle r', \vec{e} \rangle^{l_0}[dest\ \{\vec{l}\}].P \rightsquigarrow \langle r', \{\vec{e}\}^{l_0}_{e_0}[dest\ \{\vec{l}\}]\rangle.r : e_0 \blacktriangleright P \ \text{if } r = r' \\[4pt]
r : e_0 \blacktriangleright \langle r', \vec{e} \rangle^{l_0}[dest\ \{\vec{l}\}].P \rightsquigarrow \langle r', \vec{e} \rangle^{l_0}[dest\ \{\vec{l}\}].r : e_0 \blacktriangleright P \ \text{if } r \neq r' \\[4pt]
r : e_0 \blacktriangleright (r', \vec{p})^{l_0}[orig\ \{\vec{l}\}].P \rightsquigarrow (r', \{\vec{p}\}^{l_0}_{e_0}[orig\ \{\vec{l}\}]).r : e_0 \blacktriangleright P \\
\qquad\qquad \text{if } r = r' \text{ and } \mathsf{fn}(e_0) \cap \cap^k_{i=1}\mathsf{fn}(p_i) = \emptyset \\[4pt]
r : e_0 \blacktriangleright (r', \vec{p})^{l_0}[orig\ \{\vec{l}\}].P \rightsquigarrow (r', \vec{p})^{l_0}[orig\ \{\vec{l}\}].r : e_0 \blacktriangleright P \ \text{if } r \neq r' \\[4pt]
r : e_0 \blacktriangleright (\nu\ n)P \rightsquigarrow (\nu\ n)r : e_0 \blacktriangleright P \ \text{if } n \notin \mathsf{fn}(e_0) \\[4pt]
r : e_0 \blacktriangleright (\nu_{\pm}\ n)P \rightsquigarrow (\nu_{\pm}\ n)r : e_0 \blacktriangleright P \ \text{if } \{n^+, n^-\} \cap \mathsf{fn}(e_0) = \emptyset \\[4pt]
r : e_0 \blacktriangleright\, !P \rightsquigarrow\, !r : e_0 \blacktriangleright P \\[4pt]
r : e_0 \blacktriangleright P_1 \mid P_2 \rightsquigarrow r : e_0 \blacktriangleright P_1 \ \wedge \ r : e_0 \blacktriangleright P_2 \\[4pt]
r : e_0 \blacktriangleright P_1 \,+\, P_2 \rightsquigarrow r : e_0 \blacktriangleright P_1 \ \wedge \ r : e_0 \blacktriangleright P_2 \\[4pt]
r : e_0 \blacktriangleright 0 \rightsquigarrow 0
\end{array}
$$

In Section 6 we will use the protocol analysis tool LySa [6] to analyse concrete specifications in CaPiTo. In order to be syntactically compatible with LySa, there are some issues to be addressed.

Adding Annotations. In order to express our intentions with the protocols, we follow the work of LySa [6] and manually add annotations about the origin and destination of encrypted messages; this modification is performed in the concrete specification of CaPiTo. The idea is that each encryption occurring in a process is annotated with a crypto-point l defining its position as well as a set of crypto-points $\mathcal{L}$ specifying the destination positions where the encryption is intended to be decrypted. Similarly, each decryption is annotated with a crypto-point defining its position as well as a set of crypto-points specifying the potential origins of encrypted messages to be decrypted. For example, consider the process:

$$
r : e \blacktriangleright \langle r, V_1, V_2 \rangle^{l_1}[dest\ \{l_2\}].0 \mid r : e \blacktriangleright (r, V_1, x)^{l_2}[orig\ \{l_1\}].0
$$

Here the first parallel process specifies that the encryption is created at crypto-point l_1 and is intended for decryption at crypto-point l_2, whereas the second parallel process specifies that the message to be decrypted at crypto-point l_2 must come from crypto-point l_1. Similar annotations are made to asymmetric cryptography.

From Tunnels to LySa. The main difference between concrete specifications in CaPiTo and LySa is the way symmetric encryptions and decryptions are handled; LySa has a slightly different syntax and semantics: encryptions (e.g. $\{M\}_K$) and decryptions (e.g. decrypt V as $\{; m\}_K$) are explicitly specified. One way of solving this problem is to transform tunnels into LySa constructs. This is done in an inductive way such that the semantics is preserved. The transformation rules are listed in Table 8.

5   A Service-Oriented Example

To illustrate the use of the CaPiTo approach to specification of service-oriented systems we shall now look at the financial Credit Request case study in Chapter 0-3. In the case study a client C requests a credit from the validation service VS of a bank. Once the bank has obtained the request it will invoke a service at one of two specialised departments, one taking care of smaller enterprises Ser_E and one taking care of larger corporates Ser_C. The overall system is specified as follows at the abstract CaPiTo level. First the client C invokes the service req at the bank by sending its Balance Total Assets (Bta). The validation service VS will handle the request by invoking a validation service val either at Ser_E or at Ser_C. This invocation forwards the balance Bta obtained from the client and the response (recorded in the variable y_r) will tell whether or not the enquiry was valid. Having obtained this answer the validation service VS will send a message back to the client using the construct $\uparrow \langle y_{bta}, y_r \rangle$. The whole system is thus obtained as the parallel composition of the four processes $System \triangleq C \mid VS \mid Ser_C \mid Ser_E$.

$$C \triangleq \, ! \, (\nu \; Bta)\overline{req}[\,].(\langle Bta\rangle.(Bta, ?x_r). \uparrow \langle x_r\rangle.0)$$

$$VS \triangleq \, ! \, req[\,].((?y_{bta}).(\overline{val}[\,].(\langle y_{bta}\rangle.(?y_r). \uparrow \langle y_{bta}, y_r\rangle.0)$$
$$+ \; \overline{val}[\,](\langle y_{bta}\rangle.(?y_r). \uparrow \langle y_{bta}, y_r\rangle.0))$$

$$Ser_E \triangleq \, ! \, val[\,].((?z_{bta}).\langle is\,Valid(z_{bta})\rangle.0)$$

$$Ser_C \triangleq \, ! \, val[\,].((?w_{bta}).\langle is\,Valid(w_{bta})\rangle.0)$$

The case study goes one step further and gives details about the various protocols needed to secure the communication [17] as shown in Fig. 1: The service req provided by the validation service VC and invoked by the client C would be protected by the TLS protocol. The validation service delegates the validation of the balance to the correct service via WS-Security [21] and makes use of a $SOAP$-Mediator (SM) [19] that works as an application level router (using WS-Addressing), and is responsible for invoking the service val offered by the two specialised departments.

$$C \triangleq \, ! \, (\nu \; Bta)\overline{req}[TLS, C, R, CA].(\langle Bta\rangle.(Bta, ?x_r). \uparrow \langle x_r\rangle.0)$$

$$VS \triangleq \, ! \, req[TLS, C, R, CA].((?y_{bta}).($$
$$\overline{val}[P2P^+, S, R; SOAP, VS, SM, Ser_E].(\langle y_{bta}\rangle.(?y_r). \uparrow \langle y_{bta}, y_r\rangle.0)$$
$$+ \; \overline{val}[P2P^+, S, R; SOAP, VS, SM, Ser_C].(\langle y_{bta}\rangle.(?y_r). \uparrow \langle y_{bta}, y_r\rangle.0))$$

$$Ser_E \triangleq \, ! \, val[P2P^+, S, R; SOAP, VS, SM, Ser_E].((?z_{bta}).\langle is\,Valid(z_{bta})\rangle.0)$$

$$Ser_C \triangleq \, ! \, val[P2P^+, S, R; SOAP, VS, SM, Ser_C].((?w_{bta}).\langle is\,Valid(w_{bta})\rangle.0)$$

where $CA = K_{CA}^{\pm}$, $S = (VS, K_{VS}^{\pm})$ and $R = (Ser_E, K_{Ser_E}^{\pm})$. Using the CaPiTo approach we can get a much more modular specification of the scenario than the one given in [17] where all of this is mixed together in a single narration. The idea is simply to specify the relevant plug-ins and then extend the abstract specification with the required information as shown above.

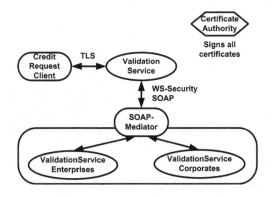

Fig. 1. The credit request case study

Table 9. *TLS* protocol for the service between C and S, where $R = (S, K_S^{\pm})$ and $CA = K_{CA}^{\pm}$

$\bar{r}[TLS, C, R, CA] \triangleright (\langle r, \vec{v}\rangle.P) \triangleq$ $r[TLS, C, R, CA] \triangleright ((r, \vec{p}).P) \triangleq$
$(\nu\, N_C)\langle r, C, S, N_C\rangle.$ $(r, C, S, ?n_C).$
$(r, S, C, ?n_S, \mathbf{S}_{K_{CA}^+}(S, ?x_{ks}))$ $(\nu\, N_S)\langle r, S, C, N_S, \mathbf{S}_{K_{CA}^-}(S, K_S^+)\rangle$
$(\nu\, N)\langle r, C, S, \mathbf{P}_{x_{ks}}(N)\rangle.$ $(r, C, S, \mathbf{P}_{K_S^-}(?n)).$
$r : \mathbf{H}(N_C, n_S, N) \blacktriangleright (\langle r, \vec{v}\rangle.P)$ $r : \mathbf{H}(n_C, N_S, n) \blacktriangleright ((r, \vec{p}).P)$

The *TLS* protocol is used to secure the communication between C and *VS* and the communications between the validation service *VS* and the services Ser_E and Ser_C are to be protected by Web-Service Security (WS-Security) and to be routed by a *SOAP* mediator. Now let us have a closer look at these protocols.

The *TLS* protocol takes place between a client and a server holding a certificate issued by a mutually trusted Certificate Authority. The certificate is then used to prove the identity of the server to the client so that a common master key can be agreed upon; this key is obtained as the hash value of the three nonces exchanged between the client and the server. All further messages are encrypted using this key. The protocol is defined in Table 9.

WS-Security [21] is a communication protocol suite providing security to Web Services, while guaranteeing end-to-end integrity and authenticity. In this case study its use is restricted to signing and encrypting message content, while leaving the message header as plain text, so as to allow *SOAP*-routing. *SOAP* (Simple Object Access Protocol) [19] is used to exchange data in a decentralised distributed scenario and only defines the message format. In this case study, *SOAP* works by incorporating a few additional fields (i.e. sender, receiver) in messages. The protocol stack used in the case study therefore contains WS-Security and *SOAP*. The structure of the stack and what WS-Security (having two variants $P2P$ and $P2P^+$) and *SOAP* do to the messages passing down from the upper layer are illustrated in Fig. 2.

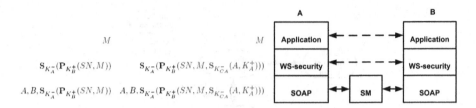

Fig. 2. Protocol stack of the credit request case study

Table 10. Point-to-point protocol for the service s between A and B, where $S = (A, K_A^\pm)$, $R = (B, K_B^\pm)$, and $CA = K_{CA}^\pm$

$$
\begin{aligned}
&\bar{r}[P2P^+, S, R, CA] \triangleright (\langle r, \vec{e}\rangle.P) &\triangleq& (\nu\ SN)\langle r, \mathbf{S}_{K_A^-}(\mathbf{P}_{K_B^+}(SN, \vec{e}, \mathbf{S}_{K_{CA}^-}(A, K_A^+))))\rangle. \\
& & & \bar{r}[P2P, S, R, SN] \triangleright P \\
&\bar{r}[P2P^+, S, R, CA] \triangleright (\langle r', \vec{e}\rangle.P) &\triangleq& \langle r', \vec{e}\rangle.\bar{r}[P2P^+, S, R, CA] \triangleright P \quad \text{if } r \neq r' \\
&r[P2P^+, S, R, CA] \triangleright ((r, \vec{p}).P) &\triangleq& (r, \mathbf{S}_{K_A^+}(\mathbf{P}_{K_B^-}(?sn, \vec{p}, \mathbf{S}_{K_{CA}^+}(A, ?k_a^+)))). \\
& & & r[P2P, (A, k_a^+), R, sn] \triangleright P \\
&r[P2P^+, S, R, CA] \triangleright ((r', \vec{p}).P) &\triangleq& (r', \vec{p}).r[P2P^+, S, R, CA] \triangleright P \quad \text{if } r \neq r' \\
&\bar{r}[P2P, S, R, SN] \triangleright ((r, \vec{p}).P) &\triangleq& (r, \mathbf{S}_{K_A^+}(\mathbf{P}_{K_B^-}(SN, \vec{p}))).\bar{r}[P2P, S, R, SN] \triangleright .P \\
&\bar{r}[P2P, S, R, SN] \triangleright ((r', \vec{p}).P) &\triangleq& (r', \vec{p}).\bar{r}[P2P, S, R, SN] \triangleright P \quad \text{if } r \neq r' \\
&r[P2P, S, R, sn] \triangleright (\langle r, \vec{e}\rangle.P) &\triangleq& \langle r, \mathbf{S}_{K_A^-}(\mathbf{P}_{K_B^+}(sn, \vec{e}))).r[P2P, S, R, sn] \triangleright P \\
&r[P2P, S, R, sn] \triangleright (\langle r', \vec{e}\rangle.P) &\triangleq& \langle r', \vec{e}\rangle.r[P2P, S, R, sn] \triangleright P \quad \text{if } r \neq r'
\end{aligned}
$$

These protocols are modelled as parameters to the service requests and responses. The whole system is defined as

$$System \triangleq (\nu_\pm\ K_{VS})(\nu_\pm\ K_{Ser_E})(\nu_\pm\ K_{Ser_C})\ C|\,VS|SM|Ser_E|Ser_C$$

where the $SOAP$ mediator SM is given by:

$$SM \triangleq\ !\ (?r, ?A, SM, A, ?B, ?M).\langle r, SM, B, A, B, M\rangle$$

and where we assume that the public key of the Certificate Authority CA, $\mathbf{K}_{CA}^+$, is known to all parties involved.

The protocols are defined in Table 10 and Table 11. Protocols $P2P^+$, $P2P$ and $SOAP$ are all defined in an inductive way such that each protocol is able to deal with a sequence of messages. The protocol $P2P^+$ deals with outgoing messages (e.g. $\langle r, \vec{v}\rangle.P$) in the following way: it first generates a sequence number SN for correlating relevant messages, then it encrypts and signs the sequence number SN, the message M and the sender's certificate, using the receiver's public key, and finally it invokes $P2P$ to handle the next message. Reverse actions are taken for incoming messages (e.g. $(r, \vec{p}).P$). Similarly for $P2P$ except that here no sender's certificate is included. The definition of $SOAP$ is parameterised on three principals, R for sender, SM for mediator, and S for receiver. It includes a

Table 11. SOAP protocol for service s between R and S using SM as $SOAP$ Mediator

$$\bar{r}[SOAP, S, SM, R] \rhd (\langle r, \vec{e}\rangle.P) \triangleq \langle r, S, SM, S, R, \vec{e}\rangle.\bar{r}[SOAP, S, SM, R] \rhd P$$
$$\bar{r}[SOAP, S, SM, R] \rhd (\langle r', \vec{e}\rangle.P) \triangleq \langle r', \vec{e}\rangle.\bar{r}[SOAP, S, SM, R] \rhd P \quad \text{if } r \neq r'$$
$$\bar{r}[SOAP, S, SM, R] \rhd ((r, \vec{p}).P) \triangleq (r, SM, S, R, S, \vec{p}).\bar{r}[SOAP, S, SM, R] \rhd P$$
$$\bar{r}[SOAP, S, SM, R] \rhd ((r', \vec{p}).P) \triangleq (r', \vec{p}).\bar{r}[SOAP, S, SM, R] \rhd P \quad \text{if } r \neq r'$$
$$r[SOAP, S, SM, R] \rhd (\langle r, \vec{e}\rangle.P) \triangleq \langle r, R, SM, R, S, \vec{e}\rangle.r[SOAP, S, SM, R] \rhd P$$
$$r[SOAP, S, SM, R] \rhd (\langle r', \vec{e}\rangle.P) \triangleq \langle r', \vec{e}\rangle.r[SOAP, S, SM, R] \rhd P \quad \text{if } r \neq r'$$
$$r[SOAP, S, SM, R] \rhd ((r, \vec{p}).P) \triangleq (r, SM, R, S, R, \vec{p}).r[SOAP, S, SM, R] \rhd P$$
$$r[SOAP, S, SM, R] \rhd ((r', \vec{p}).P) \triangleq (r', \vec{p}).r[SOAP, S, SM, R] \rhd P \quad \text{if } r \neq r'$$

few additional fields to messages for specifying the intended sender and receiver. Here we only show the more relevant entries of the definitions. For complete definitions please see the Appendix.

6 Static Analysis

In this section we specify a static control flow analysis for concrete specifications in CaPiTo. That is we shall focus on the analysis of fully expanded processes, i.e. processes without the use of service invocation ($\bar{s}[ps]$) or service response ($s[ps]$).

6.1 Outline of the LySa Analysis

Instead of developing a new analysis for analysing concrete level specifications, we shall use the protocol analysis tool LySa [6]. The aim of the analysis is to give a safe over-approximation of the protocol behaviour. The control flow analysis describes a protocol behaviour by collecting all the communications that a process may participate in. In particular, the analysis records the tuples that may flow over the network and the values that the variables may be bound to. The information is collected in the following main components:

- $\rho : \mathcal{P}(Var \times Val)$ is a "global" component recording for each variable the set of names it may be bound to.
- $\kappa : \mathcal{P}(Val^*)$ is a "global" component recording all the tuples that have been communicated.
- $\psi : \mathcal{P}(Lab \times Lab)$ is a "local" error component containing an over-approximation of the potential origin/destination violations. If $(l, l') \in \psi$ then something encrypted at crypto-point l might unexpectedly be decrypted at crypto-point l', or something decrypted at l' might have been expected to be encrypted at another place than l.

Formally, the approximation is represented by a triple (ρ, κ, ψ) called an analysis *estimate* of a given process; for an expression a pair (ρ, ϑ) suffices where $\vartheta : \mathcal{P}(Val)$ is an over-approximation of the set of values to which the expression can evaluate.

Table 12. Flattened pattern matching

$$\rho \models_i \epsilon : \hat{V} \triangleright \hat{W} : \psi \qquad \text{iff } \{\vec{v} \in \hat{V} \mid |\vec{v}| = i - 1\} \subseteq \hat{W}$$

$$\rho \models_i n, \vec{p} : \hat{V} \triangleright \hat{W} : \psi \quad \text{iff } \{\vec{v} \in \hat{V} \mid \pi_i(\vec{v}) = n\} \subseteq \hat{V}' \wedge$$
$$\rho \models_{i+1} \vec{p} : \hat{V}' \triangleright \hat{W} : \psi$$

$$\rho \models_i x, \vec{p} : \hat{V} \triangleright \hat{W} : \psi \quad \text{iff } \{\vec{v} \in \hat{V} \mid \pi_i(\vec{v}) \in \rho(x)\} \subseteq \hat{V}' \wedge$$
$$\rho \models_{i+1} \vec{p} : \hat{V}' \triangleright \hat{W} : \psi$$

$$\rho \models_i ?x, \vec{p} : \hat{V} \triangleright \hat{W} : \psi \quad \text{iff } \rho \models_{i+1} \vec{p} : \hat{V} \triangleright \hat{W} : \psi \wedge$$
$$\forall \vec{v} : \vec{v} \in \hat{W} \Rightarrow (\pi_i(\vec{v}) \in \rho(x))$$

$$\rho \models_i \{p_1, \ldots, p_k\}_n^l [orig\ \mathcal{L}], \vec{p} : \hat{V} \triangleright \hat{W} : \psi$$
$$\text{iff } \{v_1, \ldots, v_k \mid \{v_1, \ldots, v_k\}_n^{l'} [dest\ \mathcal{L}'] \in \pi_i(\hat{V})\} \subseteq \hat{V}' \wedge$$
$$\rho \models_1 p_1, \ldots, p_k : \hat{V}' \triangleright \hat{W}' : \psi \wedge$$
$$\{\vec{w} \in \hat{V} \mid \exists \vec{v} \in \hat{W}' : \pi_i(\vec{w}) = \{\vec{v}\}_n\} \subseteq \hat{V}'' \wedge$$
$$\rho \models_{i+1} \vec{p} : \hat{V}'' \triangleright \hat{W} : \psi \wedge$$
$$(l \notin \mathcal{L}' \vee l' \notin \mathcal{L}) \Rightarrow (l, l') \in \psi$$

$$\rho \models_i \underline{\mathbf{P}}_{n-}(p_1, \ldots, p_k)^l [orig\ \mathcal{L}], \vec{p} : \hat{V} \triangleright \hat{W} : \psi$$
$$\text{iff } \{v_1, \ldots, v_k \mid \mathbf{P}_{n+}(v_1, \ldots, v_k)^{l'} [dest\ \mathcal{L}'] \in \pi_i(\hat{V})\} \subseteq \hat{V}' \wedge$$
$$\rho \models_1 p_1, \ldots, p_k : \hat{V}' \triangleright \hat{W}' : \psi \wedge$$
$$\{\vec{w} \in \hat{V} \mid \exists \vec{v} \in \hat{W}' : \pi_i(\vec{w}) = \mathbf{P}_{n+}(\vec{v})\} \subseteq \hat{V}'' \wedge$$
$$\rho \models_{i+1} \vec{p} : \hat{V}'' \triangleright \hat{W} : \psi \wedge$$
$$(l \notin \mathcal{L}' \vee l' \notin \mathcal{L}) \Rightarrow (l, l') \in \psi$$

$$\rho \models_i \underline{\mathbf{S}}_{n+}(p_1, \ldots, p_k)^l [orig\ \mathcal{L}], \vec{p} : \hat{V} \triangleright \hat{W} : \psi$$
$$\text{iff } \{v_1, \ldots, v_k \mid \mathbf{S}_{n-}(v_1, \ldots, v_k)^{l'} [dest\ \mathcal{L}'] \in \pi_i(\hat{V})\} \subseteq \hat{V}' : \psi \wedge$$
$$\rho \models_1 p_1, \ldots, p_k : \hat{V}' \triangleright \hat{W}' : \psi \wedge$$
$$\{\vec{w} \in \hat{V} \mid \exists \vec{v} \in \hat{W}' : \pi_i(\vec{w}) = \mathbf{S}_{n-}(\vec{v})\} \subseteq \hat{V}'' \wedge$$
$$\rho \models_{i+1} \vec{p} : \hat{V}'' \triangleright \hat{W} : \psi$$
$$(l \notin \mathcal{L}' \vee l' \notin \mathcal{L}) \Rightarrow (l, l') \in \psi$$

Before going into details with the analysis rules, we shall introduce an auxiliary function for dealing with pattern matching. We define a judgement for pattern matching, namely $\rho \models_i \vec{p} : \hat{V} \triangleright \hat{W} : \psi$ as shown in Table 12. It traverses the candidate tuple space first in a forward direction, where the tuples in $\hat{V}$ are tested and only tuples satisfying the requirements are carried forward, and then in a backward direction, where the tuples in $\hat{W}$ are those that passed all the requirements. As part of the backward traversal, the judgement also collects *orig*, *dest* annotation violations and records them in the error component ψ as needed.

The judgement for analysing expressions takes the form $\rho \models e : \vartheta$. Basically, the clauses defining the judgement demand that ϑ contains all the values associated with the components of a term, e.g. a name n evaluates to the set ϑ, provided that n belongs to ϑ; similarly for a variable x, provided that ϑ includes the set of values $\rho(x)$ to which x is associated. The judgement for analysing

Table 13. Analysis judgements for expressions and processes

(Name)	$\rho \models n : \vartheta$	iff $n \in \vartheta$
(Pri)	$\rho \models n^- : \vartheta$	iff $n^- \in \vartheta$
(Pub)	$\rho \models n^+ : \vartheta$	iff $n^+ \in \vartheta$
(Var)	$\rho \models x : \vartheta$	iff $\rho(x) \subseteq \vartheta$
(Enc)	$\rho \models \{v_1, \ldots, v_k\}_{v_0}^l[dest\ \mathcal{L}] : \vartheta$	iff $\wedge_{i=0}^k \rho \models v_i : \vartheta_i \wedge$ $\forall w_0, w_1, \ldots, w_k : \wedge_{i=0}^k w_i \in \vartheta_i \Rightarrow$ $\{w_1, \ldots, w_k\}_{w_0}^l[dest\ \mathcal{L}] \in \vartheta$
(AEnc)	$\rho \models \mathbf{P}_{v_0^+}(v_1, \ldots, v_k)^l[dest\ \mathcal{L}] : \vartheta$	iff $\wedge_{i=0}^k \rho \models v_i : \vartheta_i \wedge$ $\forall w_0, w_1, \ldots, w_k : \wedge_{i=0}^k w_i \in \vartheta_i \Rightarrow$ $\mathbf{P}_{w_0^+}(w_1, \ldots, w_k)^l[dest\ \mathcal{L}] \in \vartheta$
(Sig)	$\rho \models \mathbf{S}_{v_0^-}(v_1, \ldots, v_k)^l[dest\ \mathcal{L}] : \vartheta$	iff $\wedge_{i=0}^k \rho \models v_i : \vartheta_i \wedge$ $\forall w_0, w_1, \ldots, w_k : \wedge_{i=0}^k w_i \in \vartheta_i \Rightarrow$ $\mathbf{S}_{w_0^-}(w_1, \ldots, w_k)^l[dest\ \mathcal{L}] \in \vartheta$
(Fun)	$\rho \models f(v_1, \ldots, v_k) : \vartheta$	iff $\wedge_{i=1}^k \rho \models v_i : \vartheta_i \wedge$ $\forall w_1, \ldots, w_k : \wedge_{i=1}^k w_i \in \vartheta_i \Rightarrow$ $f(w_1, \ldots, w_k) \in \vartheta$
(Out)	$\rho, \kappa \models \langle e_1, \ldots, e_k \rangle.P : \psi$	iff $\wedge_{i=1}^k \rho \models e_i : \vartheta_i \wedge$ $\forall w_1, \ldots, w_k : \wedge_{i=1}^k w_i \in \vartheta_i \Rightarrow ($ $\langle w_1, \ldots, w_k \rangle \in \kappa \wedge$ $\rho, \kappa \models P : \psi)$
(Inp)	$\rho, \kappa \models (p_1, \ldots, p_k).P : \psi$	iff $\rho \models_1 p_1, \ldots, p_k : \kappa \triangleright \hat{W} : \psi \wedge$ $\hat{W} \neq \emptyset \Rightarrow \rho, \kappa \models P : \psi$
(New)	$\rho, \kappa \models (\nu\ n)P : \psi$	iff $\rho, \kappa \models P : \psi$
(ANew)	$\rho, \kappa \models (\nu_\pm\ n)P : \psi$	iff $\rho, \kappa \models P : \psi$
(Rep)	$\rho, \kappa \models !P : \psi$	iff $\rho, \kappa \models P : \psi$
(Par)	$\rho, \kappa \models P_1 \mid P_2 : \psi$	iff $\rho, \kappa \models P_1 : \psi \ \wedge \ \rho, \kappa \models P_2 : \psi$
(Chs)	$\rho, \kappa \models P_1 + P_2 : \psi$	iff $\rho, \kappa \models P_1 : \psi \ \wedge \ \rho, \kappa \models P_2 : \psi$
(Nil)	$\rho, \kappa \models 0 : \psi$	iff *true*

processes is $\rho, \kappa \models P : \psi$. For each process P, the analysis mainly collects information into ρ, κ and annotation violations into ψ.

The analysis rules are defined as in Table 13. The (Inp) clause makes use of the auxiliary judgement for pattern matching $\rho \models_i \vec{p} : \hat{V} \triangleright \hat{W}$. It requires that the continuation service P is analysed only when pattern matching returns a non-empty result. The (Out) clause evaluates all the expressions, $e_1, \ldots, e_k$, and requires that all the combinations of these values are recorded in κ. Indeed these are the values that may be communicated. Finally, the continuation service P must be analysed. The rest of the rules are straightforward.

6.2   Properties of the Analysis

We establish the formal correctness of our analysis by showing a subject reduction theorem.

Lemma 1. *If $\rho \models e : \vartheta$ and $v \in \rho(x)$ then $\rho \models e[x \mapsto v] : \vartheta$.*

Proof. By induction on the structure of e.

Lemma 2. *If $\rho, \kappa \models P$ and $v \in \rho(x)$ then $\rho, \kappa \models P[x \mapsto v]$.*

Proof. By applying the induction hypothesis on any subservices and Lemma 1 on any subexpressions.

We define an extended version of substitution. Let σ be an arbitrary substitution, we then define $p \bullet \sigma$ as follows:

$$v \bullet \sigma = v \qquad\qquad (p_1, \ldots, p_k) \bullet \sigma = (p_1 \bullet \sigma, \ldots, p_k \bullet \sigma)$$
$$(?x) \bullet \sigma = \sigma(x) \qquad x \bullet \sigma = \text{undefined}$$

Lemma 3 (Substitution result). $\forall \vec{v}, \vec{p}, \sigma : \mathcal{M}(\vec{v}, \vec{p}) = \sigma$ *iff* $(\vec{v}) = (\vec{p}) \bullet \sigma$.

Proof. By induction on the structure of $\mathcal{M}(\vec{v}, \vec{p})$.

Lemma 4 (Pattern matching result). *If $\mathcal{M}(\vec{v}, \vec{p}) = \sigma$ and $\vec{v} \in \hat{V}$ then there exists $\hat{W}$ such that $\rho \models_1 \vec{p} : \hat{V} \triangleright \hat{W}$ and $\vec{p} \bullet \sigma \in \hat{W}$.*

Proof. By induction on the structure of $\rho \models_1 \vec{p} : \hat{V} \triangleright \hat{W}$.

Lemma 5. *Let P_1 and P_2 be services. The following statements hold:*

(a) if $\rho, \kappa \models P_1$ and $P_1 \xrightarrow{\langle r, \vec{v} \rangle} P_2$ then $\rho, \kappa \models P_2$ and $\langle r, \vec{v} \rangle \in \kappa$
(b) if $\rho, \kappa \models P_1$ and $P_1 \xrightarrow{(r, \vec{v})} P_2$ and $\langle r, \vec{v} \rangle \in \kappa$ then $\rho, \kappa \models P_2$
(c) if $\rho, \kappa \models P_1$ and $P_1 \xrightarrow{\langle r, E_w \langle \vec{v} \rangle \rangle} P_2$ then $\rho, \kappa \models P_2$ and $\langle r, \{\vec{v}\}_w \rangle \in \kappa$
(d) if $\rho, \kappa \models P_1$ and $P_1 \xrightarrow{(r, E_w(\vec{v}))} P_2$ and $\langle r, \{\vec{v}\}_w \rangle \in \kappa$ then $\rho, \kappa \models P_2$

Proof. All four parts of Lemma 5 are proved by induction on the inference tree used to establish the semantics reduction.

We start with the statement (a) by using the analysis rule (Out). Let $\langle r, \vec{v} \rangle.P \xrightarrow{r, \langle \vec{v} \rangle} P$ such that $\rho, \kappa \models \langle r, \vec{v} \rangle.P$, which gives us $\langle r, \vec{v} \rangle \in \kappa$ and $\rho, \kappa \models P$ according to the analysis rule (Out).

When we prove statement (b) of Lemma 5, it suffices to concentrate on the analysis rule (Inp). So assume the following conditions hold

$$\rho, \kappa \models (r, \vec{p}).P \ (1) \qquad (r, \vec{p}).P \xrightarrow{(r, \vec{v})} P\sigma \ (2) \qquad \langle r, \vec{v} \rangle \in \kappa \ (3)$$

Condition (2) gives $\mathcal{M}((r, \vec{v}), (r, \vec{p})) = \sigma$. Applying Lemma 4 to $\mathcal{M}((r, \vec{v}), (r, \vec{p})) = \sigma$ and condition (3), we have $\rho \models_1 (r, \vec{p}) : \kappa \triangleright \hat{W}$ and

$(r, \vec{p})\sigma \in \hat{W}$, which means that $\hat{W} \neq \emptyset$. This together with the analysis rule (Inp) gives us the expected result.

Now we shall prove statement (c). We assume the following conditions hold

$$r : w \blacktriangleright \langle r, \vec{v} \rangle.P \xrightarrow{\langle r, \mathbf{E}_w(\vec{v}) \rangle} r : w \blacktriangleright P \tag{1}$$

$$\rho, \kappa \models r : w \blacktriangleright \langle r, \vec{v} \rangle.P \tag{2}$$

Condition (1) gives $\langle r, \vec{v} \rangle.P \xrightarrow{\langle r, \vec{v} \rangle} P$. According to Table 8, we have

$$r : w \blacktriangleright \langle r, \vec{v} \rangle.P \rightsquigarrow \langle r, \{w\}_{\vec{v}} \rangle.r : w \blacktriangleright P \tag{3}$$

Condition (2) together with (3) give $\rho, \kappa \models \langle r, \{\vec{v}\}_w \rangle.r : w \blacktriangleright P$. Applying the analysis rule (Out) then gives the expected result.

Proving statement (d) is similar.

Theorem 1 (Subject reduction). *If $P_1 \xrightarrow{\lambda} P_2$ and $\rho, \kappa \models P_1$ then $\rho, \kappa \models P_2$.*

Proof. The proof is by induction on the inference of $P_1 \xrightarrow{\lambda} P_2$ and makes use of Lemma 5.

Consider the case (t-sync) and assume the following conditions hold:

$$P_1 \xrightarrow{\langle r, \mathbf{E}_w \langle \vec{v} \rangle \rangle} P_1' \ (4) \qquad P_2 \xrightarrow{(r, \mathbf{E}_w(\vec{v}))} P_2' \ (5) \qquad \rho, \kappa \models P_1 | P_2 \ (6)$$

The assumptions (4) and (5) give $P_1 | P_2 \xrightarrow{\tau} P_1' | P_2'$. Applying the analysis rule (Par) to (6), we get $\rho, \kappa \models P_1$ and $\rho, \kappa \models P_2$. Lemma 5 then gives $\rho, \kappa \models P_1'$ and $\rho, \kappa \models P_2'$. We get the desired result $\rho, \kappa \models P_1' | P_2'$.

The remaining cases are similar or straightforward.

6.3   Modelling the Attacker

Protocols are executed in an environment where there may exist malicious attackers. For most process algebras, this is modelled as $P_{sys} | Q$ with P_{sys} being the implementation of the protocol and Q representing the actual environment, and this is the scenario we consider as well. Following the work of [6], we say that a process P is of type $(\mathcal{N}_f, \mathcal{A}_\kappa, \mathcal{A}_{Enc}, \mathcal{A}_{Enc}^+)$ whenever: (1) it is closed (no free variables), (2) its free names are in $\mathcal{N}_f$, (3) all the arities used for sending or receiving are in $\mathcal{A}_\kappa$, (4) all the arities used for symmetric encryption or decryption are in $\mathcal{A}_{Enc}$, and (5) all the arities used for asymmetric encryption or decryption are in $\mathcal{A}_{Enc}^+$. Clearly one can inspect P_{sys} to find minimal $\mathcal{N}_f, \mathcal{A}_\kappa, \mathcal{A}_{Enc}$ and $\mathcal{A}_{Enc}^+$ such that P_{sys} is of type $(\mathcal{N}_f, \mathcal{A}_\kappa, \mathcal{A}_{Enc}, \mathcal{A}_{Enc}^+)$. We also postulate a new name $n_\bullet$, a new variable $z_\bullet$, and a new crypto-point $l_\bullet$ that are not occurring in P_{sys}. We then define the Dolev-Yao attacker's ability as the conjunction of the 7 components in Table 14.

Table 14. Dolev-Yao attacker's abilities

$$
\begin{array}{ll}
(1) & \bigwedge_{k \in \mathcal{A}_\kappa} \forall \langle v_1, \ldots, v_k \rangle \in \kappa : \ \bigwedge_{i=1}^{k} v_i \in \rho(z_\bullet) \\[4pt]
(2) & \bigwedge_{k \in \mathcal{A}_\kappa} \forall v_1, \ldots, v_k : \ \bigwedge_{i=1}^{k} v_i \in \rho(z_\bullet) \Rightarrow \langle v_1, \ldots, v_k \rangle \in \kappa \\[4pt]
(3) & \bigwedge_{k \in \mathcal{A}_{Enc}} \forall \{v_1, \ldots, v_k\}_{v_0}^l [dest\ \mathcal{L}] \in \rho(z_\bullet) : \\
& \quad v_0 \in \rho(z_\bullet) \Rightarrow (\bigwedge_{i=1}^{k} v_i \in \rho(z_\bullet) \wedge \forall l \in \mathcal{L} : (l, l_\bullet) \in \psi) \\[4pt]
(4) & \bigwedge_{k \in \mathcal{A}_{Enc}} \forall v_0, v_1, \ldots, v_k : \ \bigwedge_{i=0}^{k} v_i \in \rho(z_\bullet) \Rightarrow \{v_1, \ldots, v_k\}_{v_0}^{l_\bullet} [dest\ \{l_\bullet\}] \in \rho(z_\bullet) \\[4pt]
(5) & \bigwedge_{k \in \mathcal{A}_{Enc}^+} \forall (\mathbf{P}_{n^+}(v_1, \ldots, v_k)^l [dest\ \mathcal{L}] \in \rho(z_\bullet) \wedge n^- \in \rho(z_\bullet)) \vee \\
& \quad (\mathbf{S}_{n^-}(v_1, \ldots, v_k)^l [dest\ \mathcal{L}] \in \rho(z_\bullet) \wedge n^+ \in \rho(z_\bullet)) : \\
& \quad \Rightarrow (\bigwedge_{i=1}^{k} v_i \in \rho(z_\bullet) \wedge \forall l \in \mathcal{L} : (l, l_\bullet) \in \psi) \\[4pt]
(6) & \bigwedge_{k \in \mathcal{A}_{Enc}^+} \forall v_1, \ldots, v_k : \ \bigwedge_{i=1}^{k} v_i \in \rho(z_\bullet) \Rightarrow (\\
& \quad (n^+ \in \rho(z_\bullet) \Rightarrow \mathbf{P}_{n^+}(v_1, \ldots, v_k)^{l_\bullet} [dest\ \{l_\bullet\}] \in \rho(z_\bullet)) \wedge \\
& \quad (n^- \in \rho(z_\bullet) \Rightarrow \mathbf{S}_{n^-}(v_1, \ldots, v_k)^{l_\bullet} [dest\ \{l_\bullet\}] \in \rho(z_\bullet))) \\[4pt]
(7) & \{n_\bullet\} \cup \mathcal{N}_f \subseteq \rho(z_\bullet)
\end{array}
$$

6.4 Example Revisited

Let us consider the general scenario that a number of *Clients* may simultaneously request services from *VS* and *Ser$_E$* (or *Ser$_C$*).

$$
((\nu\ K_{VS}^-)(\nu\ K_{Ser_E}^-)(\nu\ K_{Ser_C}^-) \mid_{i=1}^{n} Client_i \mid VS \mid SM \mid Ser_E \mid Ser_C) \mid Attacker
$$

We shall use i to refer to the instance of the protocol where the i'th *Client* is communicating with *VS* and *Ser$_E$*. The index i is added to all variables, cryptopoints and constants thereby allowing the analysis to distinguish between the various instances. This scenario form reflects the fact that *VS*, *SM*, *Ser$_E$* and *Ser$_C$* are ready to interact with legitimate *Clients* as well as the attacker, and the attacker has no knowledge of the principals' private keys. One may also include a dishonest *Client*, who shares long-term keys with the *Certificate Authority*. However such an inside attacker is so powerful in this case study that it is able to interfere with almost all the communications. So for simplicity, we concentrate on the outside attacker. The analysis itself is carried out for $n = 2$, which amounts to partitioning the *infinite* number of *Clients* into two groups, with each group communicating with the rest of the principals. This allows the analysis to see if any two instances of communications can interfere with each other. The concrete level specification is shown in Table 15.

Analysing the case study gives an empty ψ component (i.e. $\psi = \emptyset$) which means that no authentication annotations are violated. For example, one can draw the conclusion that *once the decision has been whether the request has to be validated by the service for enterprises or corporate, it cannot be tricked into being processed by the wrong one*, because $(b4_i, d1_i) \notin \psi$. Inspecting the analysis result more closely, the following entries may be of interest:

$$
\rho(x_{r1}) = \{isValid(Bta_1)\} \quad \rho(x_{r2}) = \{isValid(Bta_2)\}
$$

Table 15. Concrete level specification of credit request case study

---

let $X \subseteq \{1, 2\}$ in

$(|_{i \in X}(\nu_{\pm} \ Kca)(\nu_{\pm} \ K_{Ser_E})(\nu_{\pm} \ Kvs)($

   $/ * \ Client * /$

$((\nu \ Bta_i)(\nu \ r1_i)\langle r_{env}, req, r_1 \rangle.$

  $(\nu \ Nx_i)\langle r_1, C_i, VS, Nx_i \rangle.$

   $(r_1, VS, C_i, ?ny_i, \underline{\mathbf{S}}_{Kca+}(VS, ?kvs) : [\text{at } a1_i \text{ orig } \{b1_i\}]).$

    $(\nu \ N_i)\langle r_1, C_i, VS, \mathbf{P}_{Kvs+}(N_i) : [\text{at } a2_i \text{ dest } \{b2_i\}] \rangle.$

     $r_1 : \mathbf{H}(Nx_i, ny_i, N_i) \blacktriangleright \langle r_1, Bta_i \rangle [\text{at } a3_i \text{ dest } \{b3_i\}].$

      $(r_1, Bta_i, ?xr_i)[\text{at } a4_i \text{ orig } \{b6_i, b9_i\}].\langle r_{env}, xr_i \rangle.0)$

$| \quad / * \ VS * /$

$(r_{env}, req, ?r_1')((r_1', C_i, VS, ?nx_i).(\nu \ Ny_i)$

  $\langle r_1', VS, C_i, Ny_i, \mathbf{S}_{Kca-}(VS, Kvs^+) : [\text{at } b1_i \text{ dest } \{a1_i\}] \rangle.$

   $(r_1', C_i, VS, \underline{\mathbf{P}}_{Kvs-}(?n_i) : [\text{at } b2_i \text{ orig } \{a2_i\}]).$

   $r_1' : \mathbf{H}(nx_i, Ny_i, n_i) \blacktriangleright (r_1', ?bta_i)[\text{at } b3_i \text{ orig } \{a3_i\}].(\nu \ r_2)\langle r_{env}, val, r_2 \rangle.$

    $((\nu \ SN_i)$

    $\langle r_2 VS, SM, VS, Ser_E,$

       $\mathbf{S}_{Kvs-}(\mathbf{P}_{K_{Ser_E}^+}(SN_i, bta, \mathbf{S}_{Kca-}(VS, Kvs^+)) : [\text{at } b4_i \text{ dest } \{c1_i\}]).$

     $(r_2, SM, VS, Ser_E, VS, \underline{\mathbf{S}}_{K_{Ser_E}^+}(\mathbf{P}_{Kvs+}(SN_i, ?vr_i) : [\text{at } b5_i \text{ orig } \{c2_i\}]).$

      $\langle r_1', bta_i, vr_i \rangle [\text{at } b6_i \text{ dest } \{a4_i\}].0+$

    $(\nu \ SN_i)$

    $\langle r_2 VS, SM, VS, Ser_C,$

       $\mathbf{S}_{Kvs-}(\mathbf{P}_{K_{Ser_C}^+}(SN_i, bta, \mathbf{S}_{Kca-}(VS, Kvs^+)) : [\text{at } b7_i \text{ dest } \{d1_i\}]).$

     $(r_2, SM, VS, Ser_C, VS, \underline{\mathbf{S}}_{K_{Ser_C}^+}(\mathbf{P}_{Kvs+}(SN_i, ?vr_i) : [\text{at } b8_i \text{ orig } \{d2_i\}]).$

      $\langle r_1', bta_i, vr_i \rangle : [\text{at } b9_i \text{ dest } \{a4_i\}].0)$

$| \quad / * \ SM * /$

$(?r, VS, SM, VS, ?ser, ?x1).\langle r, SM, ser, VS, ser, x1 \rangle.$

  $(?r', ?ser, SM, ser, VS, ?x2).\langle r', SM, ser, VS, x2 \rangle.0$

$| \quad / * \ Ser_E * /$

$(r_{env}, val, ?r_2').$

$(r_2', SM, Ser_E, VS, Ser_E,$

$\underline{\mathbf{S}}_{Kvs+}(\mathbf{P}_{K_{Ser_E}^-}(?sn_i, ?btas_i, \underline{\mathbf{S}}_{Kca+}(VS, ?kvs)) : [\text{at } c1_i \text{ orig } \{b4_i\}]).$

$\langle r_2', Ser_E, SM, Ser_E, VS, \mathbf{S}_{K_{Ser_E}^-}(\mathbf{P}_{kvs+}(sn_i, isValid(btas_i)) : [\text{at } c2_i \text{ dest } \{b5_i\}]).0$

$| \quad / * \ Ser_C * /$

$(r_{env}, val, ?r_2').$

$(r_2', SM, Ser_C, VS, Ser_C,$

$\underline{\mathbf{S}}_{Kvs+}(\mathbf{P}_{K_{Ser_C}^-}(?sn_i, ?btas_i, \underline{\mathbf{S}}_{Kca+}(VS, ?kvs)) : [\text{at } d1_i \text{ orig } \{b7_i\}]).$

$\langle r_2', Ser_C, SM, Ser_C, VS, \mathbf{S}_{K_{Ser_C}^-}(\mathbf{P}_{kvs+}(sn_i, isValid(btas_i)) : [\text{at } d2_i \text{ dest } \{b8_i\}]).0))$

This confirms that the evaluation results of the form $isValid(Bta_i)$ are correctly returned back from Ser_E to *Client*, via VS and SM. Furthermore, the analysis results also suggest that no sensitive data is leaked to the attacker, i.e. the attacker's knowledge $\rho(z_{\bullet})$ does not contain any important information (recall that $z_\bullet$ is the variable used by the attacker). In summary, both authentication and confidentiality hold in this case study.

7 Conclusion

In this paper, we presented the CaPiTo approach, which is able to model service-oriented systems at different levels of abstractions, e.g. with or without taking the underlying protocol stack into consideration. To the best of our knowledge this is a novel contribution.

We formally developed the abstract, the plug-in and the concrete levels of CaPiTo together with the semantics of the concrete level and showed how to transform the plug-in level to the concrete level. Throughout the paper we illustrated our approach on the Credit Request case study. In our view the main contribution of the CaPiTo approach, compared to that of other service-oriented calculi (e.g. CaSPiS [7]), is that the CaPiTo-approach, on the one hand, allows to perform an abstract modelling of service-oriented applications and, on the other hand, facilitates dealing with existing industrial protocols. It is due to this ability that we believe CaPiTo overcomes a shortcoming identified in SENSORIA— that there is some gap between the level of models and analyses performed by the academic partners and the realisations and implementations performed by the industrial partners.

From a more theoretical perspective we could equip the abstract level of CaPiTo with a semantics in the same style as the one given to CaSPiS [7] and we could then study equivalences between specifications at the various levels of CaPiTo. Similarly we could develop static analyses at several levels of CaPiTo and compare their relative precision. However, in our view this is not what the industrial partners are likely to benefit from; rather we believe that an analysis performed as close as possible to the concrete specification level is more valuable in practice. (Indeed, it reduces the risks of attacks at the level below the level of formalisation.)

Acknowledgement. This work is inspired by earlier discussion with Chiara Bodei about analysis of service-oriented calculi, in particular CaSPiS [7].

References

1. Abadi, M., Gordon, A.D.: A Calculus for Cryptographic Protocols: The Spi Calculus. Information and Computation 148(1), 1–70 (1999)
2. Armando, A., Carbone, T., Compagna, L.: LTL model checking for security protocols. In: Proc. 20th CSFW (2007)
3. Armando, A., Carbone, T., Compagna, L., Cuellar, J., Tobarra, L.: Formal analysis of SAML 2.0 web browser single sign-on: breaking the SAML-based sign on for Google appa. In: Proc. 6th ACM Workshop on Formal Methods in Security Engineering (2008)
4. Bella, G., Longo, C., Paulson, L.: Verifying second-level security protocols. In: Theorem Proving in Higher Order Logics (2003)

5. Broadfoot, P., Lowe, G.: On distributed security transactions that use secure transport protocols. In: Proc. 16th CSFW (2003)
6. Bodei, C., Buchholtz, M., Degano, P., Nielson, F., Nielson, H.R.: Static Validation of Security Protocols. Journal of Computer Security 13(3), 347–390 (2005)
7. Boreale, M., Bruni, R., De Nicola, R., Loreti, M.: Sessions and Pipelines for Structured Service Programming. In: Barthe, G., de Boer, F.S. (eds.) FMOODS 2008. LNCS, vol. 5051, pp. 19–38. Springer, Heidelberg (2008)
8. Boyd, C.: Security architectures using formal methods. IEEE Journal on Selected Areas in Communications 11(5) (1993)
9. Bugliesi, M., Focardi, R.: Language based secure communication. In: Proc. 21st CSFS (2008)
10. Dierks, T., Allen, C.: The TLS protocol version 1.0. RFC 2246, Internet Engineering Task Force (January 1999)
11. Dilloway, C., Lowe, G.: Specifying secure channels. In: Proc. 21st CSFS (2008)
12. Dilloway, C.: On the Specification and Analysis of Secure Transport Protocols. PhD Thesis, Oxford University (2008)
13. Dolev, D., Yao, A.C.: On the Security of Public Key Protocols. IEEE TIT IT-29(12), 198–208 (1983)
14. Hansen, S., Skriver, J., Riis Nielson, H.: Using static analysis to validate the SAML Single Sign-On protocol. In: Proceedings of Workshop on Issues in the Theory of Security (WITS 2005) (2005)
15. Maurer, U., Schmid, P.: A Calculus for secure channel establishment in open networks. In: Gollmann, D. (ed.) ESORICS 1994. LNCS, vol. 875. Springer, Heidelberg (1994)
16. Milner, R.: Communicating and mobile systems: the π-calculus. Cambridge University Press, Cambridge (1999)
17. Nielsen, C.R., Alessandrini, M., Pollmeier, M., Nielson, H.R.: Formalising the S&N Credit Request. Confidential SENSORIAinternal report (Only for use within the Consultion) (2007)
18. Organization for the Advancement of Structured Information Standards, http://www.oasis-open.org/
19. Simple Object Access Protocol (SOAP). W3C, http://www.w3.org/TR/soap/
20. X.200 : Information technology - Open Systems Interconnection - Basic Reference Model: The basic model
21. OASIS Web Services Security (WSS) TC, http://www.oasis-open.org/

A   Complete Protocol Definitions of *SOAP*

Table 16. SOAP protocol for service s between R and responder S using SM as $SOAP$ Mediator

$$\bar{r}[SOAP, S, SM, R] \rhd (\langle r, \vec{e}\rangle.P) \triangleq \langle r, S, SM, S, R, \vec{e}\rangle.\bar{r}[SOAP, S, SM, R] \rhd P$$

$$\bar{r}[SOAP, S, SM, R] \rhd (\langle r', \vec{e}\rangle.P) \triangleq \langle r', \vec{e}\rangle.\bar{r}[SOAP, S, SM, R] \rhd P \text{ if } r \neq r'$$

$$\bar{r}[SOAP, S, SM, R] \rhd ((r, \vec{p}).P) \triangleq (r, SM, S, R, S, \vec{p}).\bar{r}[SOAP, S, SM, R] \rhd P$$

$$\bar{r}[SOAP, S, SM, R] \rhd ((r', \vec{p}).P) \triangleq (r', \vec{p}).\bar{r}[SOAP, S, SM, R] \rhd P \text{ if } r \neq r'$$

$$\bar{r}[SOAP, S, SM, R] \rhd ((\nu\ n)P) \triangleq (\nu\ n)\bar{r}[SOAP, S, SM, R] \rhd P$$

$$\bar{r}[SOAP, S, SM, R] \rhd (P_1 + P_2) \triangleq (\bar{r}[SOAP, S, SM, R] \rhd P_1) + (\bar{r}[SOAP, S, SM, R] \rhd P_2)$$

$$\bar{r}[SOAP, S, SM, R] \rhd (P_1|P_2) \triangleq (\bar{r}[SOAP, S, SM, R] \rhd P_1)| (\bar{r}[SOAP, S, SM, R] \rhd P_2)$$

$$\bar{r}[SOAP, S, SM, R] \rhd (!P) \triangleq !(\bar{r}[SOAP, S, SM, R] \rhd P)$$

$$\bar{r}[SOAP, S, SM, R] \rhd 0 \triangleq 0$$

$$r[SOAP, S, SM, R] \rhd (\langle r, \vec{e}\rangle.P) \triangleq \langle r, R, SM, R, S, \vec{e}\rangle.r[SOAP, S, SM, R] \rhd P$$

$$r[SOAP, S, SM, R] \rhd (\langle r', \vec{e}\rangle.P) \triangleq \langle r', \vec{e}\rangle.r[SOAP, S, SM, R] \rhd P \text{ if } r \neq r'$$

$$r[SOAP, S, SM, R] \rhd ((r, \vec{p}).P) \triangleq (r, SM, R, S, R, \vec{p}).r[SOAP, S, SM, R] \rhd P$$

$$r[SOAP, S, SM, R] \rhd ((r', \vec{p}).P) \triangleq (r', \vec{p}).r[SOAP, S, SM, R] \rhd P \text{ if } r \neq r'$$

$$r[SOAP, S, SM, R] \rhd ((\nu\ n)P) \triangleq (\nu\ n)r[SOAP, S, SM, R] \rhd P$$

$$r[SOAP, S, SM, R] \rhd (P_1 + P_2) \triangleq (r[SOAP, S, SM, R] \rhd P_1) + (r[SOAP, S, SM, R] \rhd P_2)$$

$$r[SOAP, S, SM, R] \rhd (P_1|P_2) \triangleq (r[SOAP, S, SM, R] \rhd P_1)| (r[SOAP, S, SM, R] \rhd P_2)$$

$$r[SOAP, S, SM, R] \rhd (!P) \triangleq !(r[SOAP, S, SM, R] \rhd P)$$

$$r[SOAP, S, SM, R] \rhd 0 \triangleq 0$$

B   Complete Protocol Definitions of $P2P^+$ and $P2P$

Table 17. Point-to-point protocol for the service s between A and B, where $S = (A, K_A^{\pm})$, $R = (B, K_B^{\pm})$, and $CA = K_{CA}^{\pm}$

$$\overline{r}[P2P^+, S, R, CA] \rhd (\langle r, \vec{e}\rangle.P) \triangleq (\nu\ SN)\langle r, \mathbf{S}_{K_A^-}(\mathbf{P}_{K_B^+}(SN, \vec{e}, \mathbf{S}_{K_{CA}^-}(A, K_A^+))))\rangle.$$
$$\overline{r}[P2P, S, R, SN] \rhd P$$
$$\overline{r}[P2P^+, S, R, CA] \rhd (\langle r', \vec{e}\rangle.P) \triangleq \langle r', \vec{e}\rangle.\overline{r}[P2P^+, S, R, CA] \rhd P \ \text{ if } r \neq r'$$
$$\overline{r}[P2P^+, S, R, CA] \rhd ((\nu\ n)P) \triangleq (\nu\ n)\overline{r}[P2P^+, S, R, CA] \rhd P$$
$$\overline{r}[P2P^+, S, R, CA] \rhd (P_1 + P_2) \triangleq (\overline{r}[P2P^+, S, R, CA] \rhd P_1) + (\overline{r}[P2P^+, S, R, CA] \rhd P_2)$$
$$\overline{r}[P2P^+, S, R, CA] \rhd (P_1 | P_2) \triangleq (\overline{r}[P2P^+, S, R, CA] \rhd P_1)|(\overline{r}[P2P^+, S, R, CA] \rhd P_2)$$
$$\overline{r}[P2P^+, S, R, CA] \rhd (!P) \triangleq !(\overline{r}[P2P^+, S, R, CA] \rhd P)$$
$$\overline{r}[P2P^+, S, R, CA] \rhd 0 \triangleq 0$$

$$r[P2P^+, S, R, CA] \rhd ((r, \vec{p}).P) \triangleq (r, \underline{\mathbf{S}}_{K_A^+}(\underline{\mathbf{P}}_{K_B^-}(?sn, \vec{p}, \underline{\mathbf{S}}_{K_{CA}^+}(A, ?k_a^+)))).$$
$$r[P2P, (A, k_a^+), R, sn] \rhd P$$
$$r[P2P^+, S, R, CA] \rhd ((r', \vec{p}).P) \triangleq (r', \vec{p}).r[P2P^+, S, R, CA] \rhd P \ \text{ if } r \neq r'$$
$$r[P2P^+, S, R, CA] \rhd ((\nu\ n)P) \triangleq (\nu\ n)r[P2P^+, S, R, CA] \rhd P$$
$$r[P2P^+, S, R, CA] \rhd (P_1 + P_2) \triangleq (r[P2P^+, S, R, CA] \rhd P_1) + (r[P2P^+, S, R, CA] \rhd P_2)$$
$$r[P2P^+, S, R, CA] \rhd (P_1 | P_2) \triangleq (r[P2P^+, S, R, CA] \rhd P_1)|(r[P2P^+, S, R, CA] \rhd P_2)$$
$$r[P2P^+, S, R, CA] \rhd (!P) \triangleq !(r[P2P^+, S, R, CA] \rhd P)$$
$$r[P2P^+, S, R, CA] \rhd 0 \triangleq 0$$

$$\overline{r}[P2P, L, M, SN] \rhd (\langle r, \vec{e}\rangle.P) \triangleq \langle r, \mathbf{S}_{K_A^-}(\mathbf{P}_{K_B^+}(SN, \vec{e}))\rangle.\overline{r}[P2P, L, M, SN] \rhd P$$
$$\overline{r}[P2P, L, M, SN] \rhd (\langle r', \vec{e}\rangle.P) \triangleq \langle r', \vec{e}\rangle.\overline{r}[P2P, L, M, SN] \rhd P \ \text{ if } r \neq r'$$
$$\overline{r}[P2P, L, M, SN] \rhd ((r, \vec{p}).P) \triangleq (r, \underline{\mathbf{S}}_{K_A^+}(\underline{\mathbf{P}}_{K_B^-}(SN, \vec{p}))).\overline{r}[P2P, L, M, SN] \rhd .P$$
$$\overline{r}[P2P, L, M, SN] \rhd ((r', \vec{p}).P) \triangleq (r', \vec{p}).\overline{r}[P2P, L, M, SN] \rhd P \ \text{ if } r \neq r'$$
$$\overline{r}[P2P, L, M, SN] \rhd ((\nu\ n)P) \triangleq (\nu\ n)\overline{r}[P2P, L, M, SN] \rhd P$$
$$\overline{r}[P2P, L, M, SN] \rhd (P_1 + P_2) \triangleq (\overline{r}[P2P, L, M, SN] \rhd P_1) + (\overline{r}[P2P, L, M, SN] \rhd P_2)$$
$$\overline{r}[P2P, L, M, SN] \rhd (P_1 | P_2) \triangleq (\overline{r}[P2P, L, M, SN] \rhd P_1)|(\overline{r}[P2P, L, M, SN] \rhd P_2)$$
$$\overline{r}[P2P, L, M, SN] \rhd (!P) \triangleq !(\overline{r}[P2P, L, M, SN] \rhd P)$$
$$\overline{r}[P2P, L, M, SN] \rhd 0 \triangleq 0$$

$$r[P2P, L, M, sn] \rhd (\langle r, \vec{e}\rangle.P) \triangleq \langle r, \mathbf{S}_{K_A^-}(\mathbf{P}_{K_B^+}(sn, \vec{e}))\rangle.r[P2P, L, M, sn] \rhd P$$
$$r[P2P, L, M, sn] \rhd (\langle r', \vec{e}\rangle.P) \triangleq \langle r', \vec{e}\rangle.r[P2P, L, M, sn] \rhd P \ \text{ if } r \neq r'$$
$$r[P2P, L, M, sn] \rhd ((r, \vec{p}).P) \triangleq (r, \underline{\mathbf{S}}_{K_A^+}(\underline{\mathbf{P}}_{K_B^-}(sn, \vec{p}))).r[P2P, L, M, sn] \rhd P$$
$$r[P2P, L, M, sn] \rhd ((r', \vec{p}).P) \triangleq (r', \vec{p}).r[P2P, L, M, sn] \rhd P \ \text{ if } r \neq r'$$
$$r[P2P, L, M, sn] \rhd ((\nu\ n)P) \triangleq (\nu\ n)r[P2P, L, M, sn] \rhd P$$
$$r[P2P, L, M, sn] \rhd (P_1 + P_2) \triangleq (r[P2P, L, M, sn] \rhd P_1) + (r[P2P, L, M, sn] \rhd P_2)$$
$$r[P2P, L, M, sn] \rhd (P_1 | P_2) \triangleq (r[P2P, L, M, sn] \rhd P_1)|(r[P2P, L, M, sn] \rhd P_2)$$
$$r[P2P, L, M, sn] \rhd (!P) \triangleq !(r[P2P, L, M, sn] \rhd P)$$
$$r[P2P, L, M, sn] \rhd 0 \triangleq 0$$

An Abstract, on the Fly Framework for the Verification of Service-Oriented Systems*

Stefania Gnesi and Franco Mazzanti

Istituto di Scienza e Tecnologia dell'Informazione "A. Faedo" - CNR

Abstract. In this chapter we present (some of) the design principles which have inspired the development of the CMC/UMC verification framework. The first of these is the need of an abstraction mechanism which allows to observe a model in terms of an abstract L^2TS, therefore hiding all the unnecessary underlying details of the concrete computational model, while revealing only the details which might be important to understand the system behavior. The second of these is the need a Service-Oriented Logic (SocL) which is an event and state based, branching-time, efficiently verifiable, parametric temporal logic, for the formal encoding of service-oriented properties. The third principle is the usefulness of an on-the-fly, bounded model-checking approach for an efficient, interactive analysis of service-oriented systems which starts from the early stages of the incremental system design.

1 Introduction

CMC (COWS Model Checker) and UMC (UML Model Checker) [22,16] are two prototypical instantiations of a common logical verification framework for the verification of functional properties of service-oriented systems. They differ just for the underlying computational models which are built out from COWS [14,13] specifications in the case of CMC, and out from UML [9] statecharts in the case of UMC.

For verification of service-oriented models we do not intend just the final "validation" step of a completed architecture design, but rather a formal support during all the steps of the incremental design phase (hence when running designs are still likely to be incomplete and with high probability to contain mistakes).

Indeed CMC/UMC have been developed having in mind the requirements of the system designer which intends to take advantage of formal approaches to achieve an early validation of the system requirements and an early detection of design errors. From this point of view the design of UMC/CMC has been driven by the desire to achieve the following goals, (or at least, to experiment in the following directions):

- To support a good user experience in the computer-aided application of formal methods.
- The support of abstraction mechanisms allowing to observe the system at an high level of abstraction hiding all the unrelevant and unnecessary computational details.

---

* This work has been partially sponsored by the project Sensoria, IST-2005-016004.

M. Wirsing and M. Hölzl (Eds.): Sensoria Project, LNCS 6582, pp. 390–407, 2011.

- The possibility to manually explore the possible system evolutions and the possibility to generate a "summary" of system behavior in terms of minimal abstract traces.
- The possibility to investigate detailed and complex system properties using a parametric branching time temporal logic supported by an on-the-fly model checker.
- And, in this last case, the possibility of obtaining an understandable explanation of the model-checking results.

In this chapter we present in detail the way in which three of the above design principles, those which actually constitute the foundations of our framework, have been put into practice. These are: the abstraction mechanism, the SocL specification logic, and its on the fly verification approach.

2   Abstraction Mechanisms

In our context, services are considered as entities which have some kind of abstract internal state and which are capable of supporting abstract interactions with their clients, like for example accepting requests, delivering corresponding responses and, on-demand, canceling requests.

On the other side, we have (more then one) concrete operational models, with a specific concrete operational semantics, which describe in detail according to their language the structure of the system states and their possible evolution steps. This means that an abstraction mechanism needs to be applied to the system state description and to the system evolutions information, which allows to extract from the operational semantics of the specific computational model the relevant aspects we want to observe.

In our tools this abstraction step is achieved through the definition of a list of parametric rules which allow to specify which state properties and which transition events we want to observe, and which allow to present them as structured actions of the form $mainlabel(flag, flag, ..)$. When this abstraction step is performed, the semantic model of a service-oriented system can be seen as a doubly labelled transitions system (L^2TS), where both the states and the edges are labelled with sets of the above described structured actions. This abstract L^2TS associated to the operational semantics of the system will constitute the reference structure used by the logic as interpretation domain and by the full-trace minimization algorithms to generate and display the abstract minimized views of the system.

CMC is the instantiation of our verification framework with respect to the COWS process calculus. COWS ha been explicitly defined for the specification and orchestration of services and combines in an original way constructs and well known features like asynchronous communication, polyadic synchronization, pattern matching, protection, delimited receiving and killing activities. The abstraction rules of CMC allow to "intercept" the communication actions occurring between two COWS processes and present them as request/response events in the context of some client-server interaction. The corresponding abstract labels will therefore appear on the edges of the L^2TS as they represent the abstract events occurred during an evolution step. The CMC abstraction rules moreover allow to observe the willingness of a COWS term to participate to a communication synchronization (e.g. to their willingness to perform the input side of the synchronization) and present it as a state property reflecting the willingness of a service to accept operation requests. In this case this abstract property will appear as a abstract label associated to some states of the L^2TS. In Fig. 1 we show an example of such rules: lines starting with the **Action** keyword identify rules which give rise to the abstract labels on the L^2TS edges, and lines starting with the **State** keyword identify rules which give rise to the abstract labels associated to the L^2TS states. Notice that the "*" and the "$i" in the left part of the rules allow to apply a pattern matching schema to the corresponding COWS events or actions, in order to extract the relevant details from the synchronizations and export them into the desired abstract labels.

```
Abstractions {
  Action charge<*,*,*,$1>   -> request(bankcharge,$1)
  Action chargeOK<$1>       -> response(bankcharge,$1)
  Action chargeFail<$1>     -> fail(bankcharge,$1)
  State charge?             -> accepting_request(bankcharge)
}
```

Fig. 1. CMC Abstraction rules for COWS

UMC is instead the instantiation of our verification framework with respect to UML statecharts. These have a standard presentation and semantics as defined by the OMG [9]. The communication events which can be observed in this case are based on the notion of message passing and indeed we can distinguish the event of sending an operation request (on the client side) from the event of accepting that request (on the server side). Moreover UML statecharts are built over the concept of local attribute of objects, and during the execution of a system transition (beyond multiple communication actions) several update whether of the local object attributes can be executed. The abstraction rules of UMC allow to observe all these events (acceptance of a message, sending of an event, update of a local attribute) as abstract events representing relevant aspects of the service-oriented behavior of the system, and represent them as abstract labels associated to the L^2TS edges. Other abstraction rules of UMC allow instead to observe the specific value of selected object attributes, and wether or not an object is in a specific state, and present these information as abstract state predicates labeling the states of the L^2TS.

```
Abstractions {
  Action $1:requestCardCharge($*) -> request(bankcharge,$1)
  Action $1.chargeResponseFail    -> fail(bankcharge,$1)
  Action $1.chargeResponseOK      -> response(bankcharge,$1)
  --
  State inState(bank1.s1) -> accepting_request(bankcharge)
}
```

Fig. 2. UMC Abstraction rules for UML Statecharts

In Fig. 2 we show an example of such rules (and we refer to [17] for a complete presentation of them): as in the previous case lines starting with the **Action** keyword identify rules which give rise to the abstract labels on the L^2TS edges, and lines starting with the **State** keyword identify rules which give rise to the abstract labels associated the L^2TS states. Also in this case the "*" and the "i" in the left part of the rules allow to apply a pattern matching schema to the corresponding UMC events or state structures, in order to extract the relevant details from the underlying communication mechanism and export them into the desired abstract labels.

In Fig 3 we show an example of what could be the abstract L^2TS resulting from a model specified in COWS or UMC. Actually the shown L^2TS is just a minimized version of the L^2TS obtained in the case of the SENSORIA automotive case study (of which only two kinds of interactions and no state properties are observed).

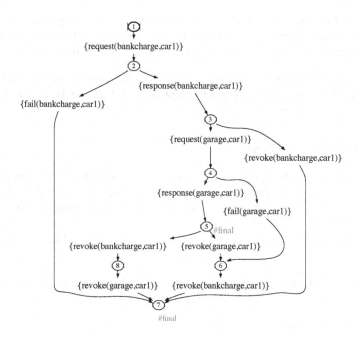

Fig. 3. A minimized version of the automotive L^2TS

The really important fact of our approach is that, independently from the details of the underlying selected computational model, it is just this abstract L^2TS associated to the operational semantics of the system what will constitute the reference structure used by the SocL logic (described in the next section) as interpretation domain.

3   The Logic SocL

SocL [6] is a service-oriented temporal logic derived from UCTL [19,8,7] which has the following characteristics:

- It is a branching time logic, built over the classical intuitive "eventually", "always", "until", "next" temporal operators drawn from mainstream logics like CTL [3], ACTL [4] and ACTLW [18]. The evaluation of this logic is known [1] to be achievable with a computational complexity which is linear with respect to the size of the formula and the size of the model.
- It is an event and state based logic. Being its interpretation domain our abstract state/event based L^2TS structures, SocL allows to directly express state predicates to be evaluated over the abstract labels associated to the states of the L^2TS, and action expressions to be evaluated over the abstract labels associated to the edges of the L^2TS.
- It is a parametric temporal logic, in which the values of the arguments of an abstract event occurring during a transition can be used to dynamically instantiate a parametric subformula to be evaluated in the target state of the transition itself.

In this section, we first introduce some preliminary definitions, then formally define syntax and semantics of SocL and finally show how the logic can be used to formalize typical service properties.

3.1   Preliminary Definitions

In this section we report the definitions of the semantic structures which the logic rely on. They permit to characterize a service in terms of states and predicates that are true over them, and of state changes and actions performed when moving from one state to another.

Let Act be a set of elements called *observable actions*. We will use η to range over 2^{Act}.

Definition 1 ([Labelled Transition System]). *A Labelled Transition System (LTS) over the set of observable actions Act is a quadruple $\langle Q, q_0, Act, R \rangle$, where:*

- *Q is a set of states;*
- *$q_0 \in Q$ is the initial state;*
- *$R \subseteq Q \times 2^{Act} \times Q$ is the transition relation.*

Now, if we extend an LTS with a labeling function from states to sets of atomic propositions we get a system with also labels over states, namely a *Doubly Labelled Transition System*.

Definition 2 ([Doubly Labelled Transition System]). *A Doubly Labelled Transition System (L^2TS) over the set of observable actions Act and the set of atomic propositions AP is a tuple $\langle Q, q_0, Act, R, AP, L \rangle$, where:*

- *Q is a set of states;*
- *$q_0 \in Q$ is the initial state;*
- *$R \subseteq Q \times 2^{Act} \times Q$ is the transition relation*
- *$L : Q \longrightarrow 2^{AP}$ is the labeling function.*

The main difference between the above definitions and the usual ones (as found e.g. in [5]) is that transitions are labelled by a set of actions rather than by a single action. Those transitions labelled by the empty set, i.e. $\emptyset$, correspond to execution of 'unobservable' internal actions. In the sequel, as a matter of notation, instead of $(q, \eta, q') \in R$ we may write $q \xrightarrow{\eta} q'$.

3.2   SocL Syntax and Semantics

We start introducing the set of observable actions which SocL is based upon. As we said in the Introduction, the actions of the logic should correspond to the actions performed by service providers and service consumers, and are characterized by three attributes: type, interaction name, and correlation data[1]. Moreover, to enable capturing correlation data used to link together actions executed as part of the same interaction, they may also contain variables, that we call *correlation variables*. In the sequel, we will usually write *val* to denote a generic *correlation value* and *var* to denote a generic correlation variable. For a given correlation variable *var*, its binding occurrence will be denoted by *var*; all remaining occurrences, that are called *free*, will be denoted by *var*.

Definition 3 ([SocL Actions]). *SocL Actions have the form $t(i, c)$, where t is the type of the action, i is the name of the interaction which the action is part of, and c is a tuple of correlation values and variables identifying the interaction (i and c can be omitted whenever they do not play any role). We assume that variables in the same tuple are pairwise distinct. We will say that an action is closed if it does not contain variables. We will use Act^v to denote the set of all actions, $\underline{\alpha}$ as a generic element of Act^v (notation : emphasizes the fact that the action may contain variable binders), and α as a generic action without variable binders. We will use Act to denote the subset of Act^v that only contains closed actions (i.e. actions without variables) and η as a generic subset of Act.*

Example 1. Action *request*(*charge*, 1234, 1) could stand for an action of type *request* starting an (instance of the) interaction *charge* which will be identified through the correlation tuple $\langle 1234, 1 \rangle$. A *response* action corresponding to the request above, for example, could be written as *response*(*charge*, 1234, 1). Moreover, if some correlation value is unknown at design time, e.g. the identifier 1, a (binder for a) correlation variable *id* can be used instead, as in the action *request*(*charge*, 1234, *id*). A corresponding response action could be written as *response*(*charge*, 1234, *id*), where the (free) occurrence of the correlation variable *id* indicates the connection with the action where the variable is bound.

To define the syntax of SocL we rely on an auxiliary logic of actions.

---

[1] Notice that correlation data are simply regarded as literals and, for such data, the logic supports the equality test only. In fact, we do not need to deal with data types.

Definition 4 (**[Action formulae]**). *The language $\mathcal{AF}(Act^v)$ of the action formulae on Act^v is defined as follows:*

$$\gamma ::= \underline{\alpha} \mid \chi \qquad\qquad \chi ::= tt \mid \alpha \mid \tau \mid \neg\chi \mid \chi \wedge \chi$$

As usual, we will use *ff* to abbreviate $\neg tt$ and $\chi \vee \chi'$ to abbreviate $\neg(\neg\chi \wedge \neg\chi')$.

According to the syntax above, an action formula γ can be either an action $\underline{\alpha}$, which may contain variable binders, or an action formula χ, which is a boolean composition of unobservable internal actions τ and observable actions α without variable binders. As we shall also clarify later, the distinction between action formulae γ and χ is motivated by two reasons: (1) some logical operators can accept as argument only action formulae without variable binders, and (2) actions containing variable binders cannot be composed.

Satisfaction of an action formula is determined with respect to a set of closed actions that represent the observable actions actually executed by the service under analysis. Therefore, since action formulae may contain variables, to define their semantics we introduce the notion of *substitution* and the partial function match that checks matching between an action and a closed action and, if it is defined, returns a substitution.

Definition 5 (**[Substitutions]**). *Substitutions, ranged over by ρ, are functions mapping correlation variables to values and are written as collections of pairs of the form var/val. The empty substitution is denoted by $\emptyset$. Application of substitution ρ to a formula ϕ, written $\phi\rho$, has the effect of replacing every free occurrence of var in ϕ with val, for each var/val $\in \rho$.*

Definition 6 (**[Matching function]**). *The partial function match from $Act^v \times Act$ to substitutions is defined by structural induction by means of auxiliary partial functions defined over syntactic subcategories of Act^v through the following rules:*

$$match(t(i, c), t(i, c')) = match_c(c, c')$$
$$match_c((e_1, c_1), (e_2, c_2)) = match_e(e_1, e_2) \cup match_c(c_1, c_2)$$
$$match_c(\langle\rangle, \langle\rangle) = \emptyset$$
$$match_e(\underline{var}, val) = \{var/val\}$$
$$match_e(val, val) = \emptyset$$

where (e, c) stands for a tuple with first element e, and $\langle\rangle$ stands for the empty tuple. Notably, an action containing free variable occurrences cannot match any closed action.

Example 2. Let us consider again the actions introduced in Example 1. Then, we have $match(response(charge, 1234, 1), response(charge, 1234, 1)) = \emptyset$ and also $match(request(charge, 1234, \underline{id}), request(charge, 1234, 1)) = \{id/1\}$. Instead $match(request(charge, 1234, \underline{id}), response(charge, 1234, 1))$ is not defined since the actions have different types.

Definition 7 (**[Action formulae semantics]**)
The satisfaction relation for action formulae is defined over a set of closed actions and a substitution.

- $\eta \models \underline{\alpha} \blacktriangleright \rho$ *iff* $\exists \alpha' \in \eta$ *such that* $\mathsf{match}(\underline{\alpha}, \alpha') = \rho$;
- $\eta \models \chi \blacktriangleright \emptyset$ *iff* $\eta \models \chi$, *where the relation* $\eta \models \chi$ *is defined as follows:*
  - $\eta \models tt$ *holds always;*
  - $\eta \models \alpha$ *iff* $\alpha \in \eta$;
  - $\eta \models \tau$ *iff* $\eta = \emptyset$;
  - $\eta \models \neg\chi$ *iff not* $\eta \models \chi$;
  - $\eta \models \chi \wedge \chi'$ *iff* $\eta \models \chi$ *and* $\eta \models \chi'$.

Notation $\eta \models \gamma \blacktriangleright \rho$ means: the formula γ is satisfied over the set of closed actions η under substitution ρ. Since the matching function is undefined when its first argument contains free variables, the semantics of actions containing free occurrences of correlation variables is undefined as well. Notice also that a non-empty substitution ρ can be generated only in the first case of the above definition, because the remaining cases only deal with formulae that do not contain variable binders. Finally, the action formula τ is satisfied over the empty set only, which corresponds to the execution of unobservable internal actions.

The last ingredient we need to define the syntax of the logic is the set of atomic propositions. They correspond to the properties that can be true over the states of services.

Definition 8 ([Atomic propositions]). *SocL atomic propositions have the form* $p(i, c)$, *where* p *is the name,* i *is an interaction name, and* c *is a tuple of correlation values and free variables identifying* i *(i and c can be omitted whenever they do not play any role). We will use AP to denote the set of all atomic propositions and* π *as generic element of AP.*

Notably, atomic propositions cannot contain variable binders.

Example 3. Proposition $accepting\_request(charge)$ indicates that a state can accept requests for interaction $charge$, while proposition $accepting\_cancel(charge, 1234, 1)$ indicates that a state permits to cancel those requests for interaction $charge$ identified by the correlation tuple $\langle 1234, 1 \rangle$.

Definition 9 ([SocL syntax]). *The syntax of SocL formulae is defined as follows:*

$$
\begin{aligned}
(state\ formulae)\quad \phi &::= true \mid \pi \mid \neg\phi \mid \phi \wedge \phi' \mid E\Psi \mid A\Psi \\
(path\ formulae)\quad \Psi &::= X_\gamma \phi \mid \phi_\chi U_\gamma \phi' \mid \phi_\chi W_\gamma \phi'
\end{aligned}
$$

E and A are existential and universal (resp.) *path quantifiers.* X, U and W are the *next,* (*strong*) *until* and *weak until* operators drawn from those firstly introduced in [4] and subsequently elaborated in [18]. Intuitively, the formula $X_\gamma \phi$ says that in the next state of the path, reached by an action satisfying γ, the formula ϕ holds.

The formula $\phi_\chi U_\gamma \phi'$ says that ϕ' holds at some future state of the path reached by a last action satisfying γ, while ϕ holds from the current state until that state is reached and all the actions executed in the meanwhile along the path satisfying χ.

The formula $\phi_\chi W_\gamma \phi'$ holds on a path either if the corresponding strong until operator holds or if for all the states of the path the formula ϕ holds and all the actions of the path satisfy χ.

Notice that the weak until operator (also called *unless*) is not derivable from the until operator since disjunction or conjunction of path formulae is not expressible in the syntax of SocL, similarly to any other pure branching-time temporal logic.

The interpretation domain of SocL formulae are L^2TS over the set of actions Act and the set of atomic propositions AP. The semantics of SocL formulae is only defined for *closed* formulae, namely those formulae where any free occurrence of a correlation variable is syntactically preceded by its binding occurrence. Given the formulae $X_\gamma\phi'$, $\phi \, _\chi U_\gamma \, \phi'$ and $\phi \, _\chi W_\gamma \, \phi'$, variables occurring in γ *syntactically precede* the variables occurring in ϕ'.

Paths within L^2TSs represent service computations and are defined as follows:

Definition 10 ([Path]). *Let $\langle Q, q_0, Act, R, AP, L \rangle$ be an L^2TS and $q \in Q$.*

- σ *is a path from q if σ is a (non empty, possibly infinite) sequence $(q_0, \eta_1, q_1)(q_1, \eta_2, q_2) \cdots$ with $q_0 = q$ and $(q_{i-1}, \eta_i, q_i) \in R$ for all $i > 0$.*
- *If $\sigma = (q_0, \eta_1, q_1)(q_1, \eta_2, q_2) \cdots$ then q_i is denoted by $\sigma(i)$ for all $i >= 0$, and η_i is denoted by $\sigma\{i\}$ for all $i >= 1$.*
- *We write $path(q)$ for the set of all paths from q.*

Definition 11 ([SocL semantics]). *Let $\langle Q, q_0, Act, R, AP, L \rangle$ be an L^2TS, $q \in Q$, and $\sigma \in path(q')$ for some $q' \in Q$. The satisfaction relation of closed SocL formulae is defined as follows:*

- $q \models true$ *holds always;*
- $q \models \pi$ *iff $\pi \in L(q)$;*
- $q \models \neg\phi$ *iff not $q \models \phi$;*
- $q \models \phi \wedge \phi'$ *iff $q \models \phi$ and $q \models \phi'$;*
- $q \models E\Psi$ *iff $\exists \sigma \in path(q) : \sigma \models \Psi$;*
- $q \models A\Psi$ *iff $\forall \sigma \in path(q) : \sigma \models \Psi$;*
- $\sigma \models X_\gamma\phi$ *iff $\exists \rho : \sigma\{1\} \models \gamma \blacktriangleright \rho$ and $\sigma(1) \models \phi\rho$;*
- $\sigma \models \phi \, _\chi U_\gamma\phi'$ *iff there exists $j > 0$ such that*
  for all $0 <= i < j : \sigma(i) \models \phi$,
  for all $0 < i < j : \sigma\{i\} \models \chi$,
  $\exists \rho : \sigma\{j\} \models \gamma \blacktriangleright \rho$ *and $\sigma(j) \models \phi\rho$;*
- $\sigma \models \phi \, _\chi W_\gamma\phi'$ *iff either $\sigma \models \phi \, _\chi U_\gamma\phi'$ or*
  for all $j >= 0 : \sigma(j) \models \phi$ and $\sigma\{j+1\} \models \chi$

Other useful logic operators can be derived as usual. In particular, the ones that we use in the sequel are:

- *false* stands for $\neg true$.
- $<\gamma>\phi$ stands for $EX_\gamma\phi$; this is the *diamond* operator introduced in [10] and, intuitively, states that it is *possible* to perform an action satisfying γ and thereby reaching a state satisfy formula ϕ.
- $[\gamma]\phi$ stands for $\neg<\gamma>\neg\phi$; this is the *box* operator introduced in [10] and states that no matter how a process performs an action satisfying γ, the state it reaches in doing so will *necessarily* satisfy the formula ϕ.

- Variants of until operators, which do not specify the last action leading to the state at which the formula on the right hand side holds, can be defined as follows:
  - $E(\phi_{\chi}U\,\phi')$ stands for $\phi' \vee E(\phi_{\chi}U_{\chi}\,\phi')$;
  - $A(\phi_{\chi}U\,\phi')$ stands for $\phi' \vee A(\phi_{\chi}U_{\chi}\,\phi')$;
  - $E(\phi_{\chi}W\,\phi')$ stands for $\phi' \vee E(\phi_{\chi}W_{\chi}\,\phi')$;
  - $A(\phi_{\chi}W\,\phi')$ stands for $\phi' \vee A(\phi_{\chi}W_{\chi}\,\phi')$.
- $EF\phi$ stands for $E(true\,_{tt}\,U\phi)$ and means that there is some path that leads to a state at which ϕ holds; that is, ϕ *potentially* holds.
- $EF_{\gamma}\,\phi$ stands for $E(true_{tt}\,U_{\gamma}\,\phi)$ and means that there is some path that leads to a state at which ϕ holds reached by a last action satisfying γ; if ϕ is *true*, we say that an action satisfying γ will *eventually* be performed.
- $AF_{\gamma}\,\phi$ stands for $A(true_{tt}\,U_{\gamma}\,\phi)$ and means that an action satisfying γ will be performed in the future along every path and at the reached states ϕ holds; if ϕ is *true*, we say that an action satisfying γ is *inevitable*.
- $AG\,\phi$ stands for $\neg\,EF\,\neg\,\phi$ and states that ϕ holds at every state on every path; that is, ϕ holds *globally*.

3.3 A Few Patterns of Service Properties

First we characterize the set of actions Act^{v} and the set of atomic propositions AP which the logic is based upon. This characterization formalizes the intuitive abstract events and predicates we conceptually need in order to express the service-oriented properties shown below, that we later want to verify.

- Act^{v} contains (at least) the following five types of actions: *request*, *responseOk*, *responseFail*, *cancel* and *undo*. The intended meaning of the actions is: *request*(i,c) indicates that the action performed by the service starts the interaction i which is identified by the correlation tuple c; similarly, *responseOk*(i,c), *responseFail*(i,c), and *cancel*(i,c) correspond to actions that provide a successful response, an unsuccessful response, a cancellation, respectively, of the interaction i identified by c; *undo*(i,c) corresponds to an action that unmakes the effects of a previous request.
- AP contains (at least) the atomic propositions *accepting_request*(i,c), *accepting_cancel*(i,c) and *accepting_undo*(i,c), whose meaning is obvious.

Now we show how several typical service-oriented properties can be expressed as formulae in SocL.

1. - - *Available* service - -

   $AG\,(accepting\_request(i))$.
   This formula means that in every state the service may accept a request. A weaker interpretation of service availability, meaning that the service accepts a request infinitely often, is given by the formula $AG\,AF\,(accepting\_request(i))$.
2. - - *Parallel* service - -

   $AG\,[request(i,\underline{var})]$
   $E(true_{\neg\,(responseOk(i,var)\vee responseFail(i,var))}U\,accepting\_request(i))$.

This formula means that the service can serve several requests simultaneously. Indeed, in every state, if a request is accepted then, in some future state, a further request for the same interaction can be accepted before giving a response to the first accepted request. Notably, the responses belong to the same interaction i of the accepted request and they are correlated by the variable var.

This is a clear example of the usefulness of the combined approach based on both actions and propositions. In fact the action $request(i, \underline{var})$ corresponds to the acceptance of a request sent by a client, while the proposition $accepting\_request(i)$ indicates that in the current state the service is able to accept a request from some client (but it has not received such request yet). In this way, SocL can easily deal with both performed and potential actions.

3. - - *Sequential* service - -

$$AG \, [request(i, \underline{var})]$$
$$A(\neg \, accepting\_request(i) \, {}_{tt}U_{responseOk(i,var) \lor responseFail(i,var)} true).$$

In this case, the service can serve at most one request at a time. Indeed, after accepting a request, it cannot accept further requests for the same interaction before replying to the accepted request.

4. - - *One − shot* service - -

$$AG \, [request(i)] \, AG \, \neg \, accepting\_request(i).$$

This formula states that the service is not persistent because, after accepting a request, in all future states, it cannot accept any further request.

5. - - *Off − line* service - -

$$AG \, [request(i, \underline{var})] \, AF_{responseFail(i,var)} \, true.$$

This formula states that whenever the service accept a request, it always eventually provides an unsuccessful response.

6. - - *Cancelable* service - -

$$AG \, [request(i, \underline{var})]$$
$$A(accepting\_cancel(i, var) \, {}_{tt}W_{responseOk(i,var) \lor responseFail(i,var)} true).$$

This formula means that the service is ready to accept a cancellation required by the client (fairness towards the client) before possibly providing a response to the accepted request. A different formulation is given by the formula

$$AG \, [responseOk(i, \underline{var})] \, \neg EF \, <cancel(i, var)> true$$

meaning that the service cannot accept a cancellation after responding to a request (fairness towards the service).

7. - - *Revocable* service - -

$$EF_{responseOk(i,\underline{var})} \, EF(accepting\_undo(i, var))$$

Again, we can have two interpretations. While the previous formula expresses a sort of weak revocability (i.e., after a successful response has been provided, the service can eventually accept an undo of the corresponding request), the following one corresponds to a stronger interpretation

$$AG \, [responseOk(i, \underline{var})] \, A(accepting\_undo(i, var) \, {}_{tt}W_{undo(i,var)} true)$$

since it guarantees that the service can always accept an undo of the request after providing the response.

8. - - *Responsive* service - -

$$AG \, [request(i, \underline{var})] \, AF_{responseOk(i,var) \lor responseFail(i,var)} \, true.$$

The formula states that whenever the service accepts a request, it always eventually provides at least a (successful or unsuccessful) response.

9. - - *Single – response* service - -

$$AG\ [request(i, \underline{var})]$$
$$\neg EF_{responseOk(i,var)\lor responseFail(i,var)}\ EF_{responseOk(i,var)\lor responseFail(i,var)}\ true.$$

The formula means that whenever the service accepts a request, it cannot provide two or more correlated (successful or unsuccessful) responses, i.e. it can only provide at most a single response.

10. - - *Multiple – response* service - -

$$AG\ [request(i, \underline{var})]$$
$$AF_{responseOk(i,var)\lor responseFail(i,var)}\ AF_{responseOk(i,var)\lor responseFail(i,var)}\ true.$$

Differently from the previous formula, here the service always eventually provides two or more responses.

11. - - *No – response* service - -

$$AG\ [request(i, \underline{var})]\ \neg EF_{responseOk(i,var)\lor responseFail(i,var)}\ true.$$

This formula means that the service never provides a (successful or unsuccessful) response to any accepted request.

12. - - *Reliable* service - -

$$AG\ [request(i, \underline{var})]\ AF_{responseOk(i,var)}\ true.$$

This formula guarantees that the service always eventually provides a successful response to each accepted request.

The SocL formulation of the above properties is instructive in that it witnesses that the natural language descriptions of the properties can sometimes be interpreted in different ways: therefore, formalization within the logic enforces a choice among different interpretations. Notably, the formulation is given in terms of abstract actions and state predicates thus, rather than specific properties, the properties we have considered so far represent sorts of generic patterns or classes of properties.

4   The On-the-Fly Verification Approach

The CMC/UMC framework adopts an "on-the-fly" approach to generate the L^2TS from a UML specification, meaning that the L^2TS corresponding to the model is generated "on-demand", following either the interactive requests of a user while exploring the system, or the needs of the logical verification engine. The set of generated system configurations and (possibly) their immediate "next-step" evolutions are incrementally saved into a "Configurations" database and their abstract view is computed. The overall structure of the framework is shown in Fig. 4.

The logical verification engine is the part that best exploits the on-the-fly approach of the L^2TS generator. It maintains an archive of computation fragments; this is not only useful to avoid unnecessary duplications in the evaluation of subformulae, but necessary to deal with recursion in the evaluation of a formula arising from the presence of loops in L^2TSs. Computation fragments have the form:

$$\langle\mathtt{subformula, rootstate, curstate}\rangle \rightarrow \mathtt{computationprogress}$$

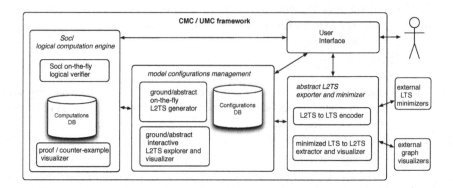

Fig. 4. The architecture of the CMC/UMC framework

and associate a `subformula` to the state in which its recursive evaluation has started (`rootstate`), to the current state in which it is being evaluated (`curstate`) and to its current computation status (`computationprogress`): this last item will in the end be the final `True` or `False` value. To each computation fragment is also associated a reference to a further set of subcomputation fragments which serve to explain the final result.

In general, given a state of an L^2TS, the validity of a SocL formula in that state is evaluated by analyzing the transitions allowed in that state, and by analyzing the validity of the necessary subformulae possibly in some of the necessary next reachable states, all this in a recursive "depth-first" way.

In case of infinite state spaces, the above approach may fail to produce a result even when a result could actually be deduced in a finite number of steps. This is a consequence of the algorithm's "depth-first" recursive structure. The solution taken to solve this problem consists of adopting a bounded model-checking approach [2], i.e. the evaluation is started assuming a certain value as limit of the maximum depth of the evaluation. In this case, if the evaluation of a formula reaches a result within the requested depth, the result holds for the whole system; otherwise the maximum depth is increased and the evaluation is subsequently retried (preserving all useful subresults already found). This approach, initially introduced in CMC/UMC to address infinite state spaces, happens to be quite useful also for another reason: by setting a small initial maximum depth and a small automatic increment of this bound at each re-evaluation failure, once we finally find a result then we also have a reasonable (almost minimal) explanation for it. This is very useful also in case of finite state spaces.

We show in Figure 5 a simplified schema of the algorithm for the evaluation of the 'universally quantified next', i.e. formulae of the form $AX_\gamma\phi$. This is a particularly simple logic operator since it does not involve the complexity induced by recursion; it is however sufficient to give an idea of how the on-the-fly approach of the evaluation mechanism behaves.

```
Evaluate(AXγ φ, StartState, CurrentState) is
   if we have already done this computation and its result is available,
      i.e. <AXγ φ, StartState, CurrentState> → Result
      has already been computed then
         return the already known Result
   end
   if there are no outgoing transitions from CurrentState then
      set <AXγ φ, StartState, CurrentState> → False
      return False
   end
   Result := True
   foreach Transition in OutgoingTransitions(CurrentState) do
      if Satisfies(Transition.Label, γ) then
         TargetState := Transition.TargetState
         Θ := TransitionBindings(Transition.Label, γ)
         TmpResult := False
         foreach substitution ρ in Θ do
            φ' := ApplySubstitution(φ, ρ)
            TmpResult := Evaluate(φ', TargetState, TargetState)
            if TmpResult = True then
               exit
            end
         end loop
         if TmpResult = False then
            Result := False
            exit
         end
      else
         Result := False
         exit
      end
   end loop
   set <AXγ φ, StartState, CurrentState> → Result
   return Result
end Evaluate;
```

Fig. 5. Evaluation process for $AX_\gamma \phi$ formula

In Figure 6 we present instead a simplified schema of the algorithm for the evaluation of the *existentially quantified until* operator, i.e. formulae of the form $E(\phi \,_\chi U_\gamma \, \phi')$, which shows how recursive operators are handled.

The above two schemas illustrate how the on-the-fly approach deals with the compositional structure of SocL formulae and with the on-demand generation of the model in order to minimize the number of subformulae that need to be evaluated. The shown schemas are actually simplified because they do not show neither the data-collection

```
Evaluate(E φ₁ χ U γ φ₂, StartState, CurrentState) is
```
    if *we have already done this computation and its definitive result is available,*
      i.e. `<E φ₁ U γ φ₂, StartState, CurrentState>` → `Result`
    has already been computed **then**
      return *the already known* `Result`
  end
  if *we have already started this computation which is still in progress*
    i.e. `<E φ₁ χ U γ φ₂, StartState, CurrentState>` → `InProgress` **then**
    return `False`   *-- according to the min fixpoint semantics of until*
  end
  `set <E φ₁ χ U γ φ₂, StartState, CurrentState>` → `InProgress`
  if *there are no outgoing transitions from* `CurrentState` **then**
    `set <E φ₁ χ U γ φ₂, StartState, CurrentState>` → `False`
    return `False`
  end
  `Result := Evaluate(φ₁, CurrentState, CurrentState)`
  if `Result := False` **then**
    `set <E φ₁ χ U γ φ₂, StartState, CurrentState>` → `False`
    return `False`
  end
  -- check for possible structural induction
  `Result := False`
  foreach `Transition` **in** `OutgoingTransitions(CurrentState)` **do**
    if `Satisfies(Transition.Label, γ)` **then**
      `TargetState := Transition.TargetState`
      `Θ := TransitionBindings(Transition.Label, γ)`
      foreach *substitution* `ρ` **in** `Θ` **do**
        `φ' := ApplySubstitution(φ₂, ρ)`
        `Result := Evaluate(φ', TargetState, TargetState)`
        if `Result = True` **then**
          `set <E φ₁ χ U γ φ₂, StartState, CurrentState>` → `True`
          return `True`
        end
      end loop
    end
  end loop
  -- check for possible continuation of recursion
  foreach `Transition` **in** `OutgoingTransitions(CurrentState)` **do**
    if `Satisfies(Transition.Label, χ)` **then**
      `TargetState := Transition.TargetState`
      `Result := Evaluate(E φ₁ χ U γ φ₂, TargetState, TargetState)`
      if `Result = True` **then**
        `set <E φ₁ U γ φ₂, StartState, CurrentState>` → `True`
        return `True`
      end
    end
  end loop
  `set <E φ₁ χ U γ φ₂, StartState, CurrentState>` → `False`
  return `False`
end `Evaluate;`

Fig. 6. Evaluation process for $E(\phi \,_\chi U_\gamma\, \phi')$ formula

```
Evaluate(AXγ φ, StartState, CurrentState, Depth) is
   if Depth = MaxDepth then
      return Aborted
   end
   if we have already done this computation and its result is available,
      i.e. <AXγ φ, StartState, CurrentState> → Result
      has already been computed then
         return the already known Result
   end
   if there are no outgoing transitions from CurrentState then
      set <AXγ φ, StartState, CurrentState> → False
      return False
   end
   Result := True
   foreach Transition in OutgoingTransitions(CurrentState) do
      if Satisfies(Transition.Label, γ) then
         TargetState := Transition.TargetState
         Θ := TransitionBindings(Transition.Label, γ)
         TmpResult := False
         foreach substitution ρ in Θ do
            φ' := ApplySubstitution(φ, ρ)
            TmpResult := Evaluate(φ', TargetState, TargetState, Depth+1)
            add_subcomputation
               <AXγ φ, StartState, CurrentState> →
                  (Transition.Label,<φ', TargetState, TargetState>)
            if TmpResult = True then
               exit
            end
            if TmpResult = Aborted then
               Result := Aborted
               continue the analysis in case we can still prove a failure
            end
         end loop
         if TmpResult = False then
            set_unique_subcomputation
            <AXγ φ, StartState, CurrentState> →
               (Transition.Label,<φ', TargetState, TargetState>)
            Result := False
            exit
         end
      else
         set_unique_subcomputation
            <AXγ φ, StartState, CurrentState> →
               (Transition.Label,<>)
         Result := False
         exit
      end
   end loop
   set <AXγ φ, StartState, CurrentState> → Result
   return Result
end Evaluate;
```

Fig. 7. Complete evaluation process for $AX_\gamma \phi$ formula

activities needed to produce at the end of the evaluation process a clear and detailed explanation of the returned results (e.g. a *counterexample*), nor the additional complexity introduced by the *bounded* approach.

In Figure 7 we finally present a more detailed schema of the algorithm for the evaluation of the formula $AX_\gamma\phi$ that shows also the activities we have omitted in the previous schemas. With respect to the simplified version shown in Figure 5, an `Aborted` result can be returned if the current maximal depth for the evaluation is reached. If such a value is returned by the top level evaluation procedure, then all aborted computations are discarded and evaluation is called again with an increased maximal depth (while preserving all already successfully completed subcomputations). In case a subcomputation returns an `Aborted` value, such value is not immediately returned as definitive but the iterations on the possible subevolutions still continue to find a negative result. Finally, when an outgoing transition that does not satisfy the required subformula is found, that negative subcomputation replaces all partial subcomputations recorded up to that point. The explanation of the final result, in fact, does no longer depend on the subcomputations performed in the previous steps.

5 Conclusions

The design and development of our framework has greatly taken advantage from the early experiences gained through its application to the Sensoria case studies. The first of these applications has been the use of UMC for the analysis of communication protocols for service-oriented applications ([19,21]). Subsequently the Sensoria automotive case study has been the stimulus for the first experimentations with the SocL logics and the COWS language [6]. The same case study has also been specified in terms of UML statecharts and verified with UMC [20], thus experimenting with the Sensoria UML profile for SOA [12,15]. Finally both COWS/CMC and UML/UMC have been applied for the formalization and verification of the Sensoria "credit portal" case study [11].

The experience gained so far by the application of our framework to the Sensoria case studies has allowed us to fully confirm the soundness of our approach, to a level even beyond the initial expectations and we really believe that abstract L^2TS as semantic models, state and event based parametric logics, and on the fly model checking constitutes an extremely flexible though powerful approach to system verification.

References

1. Bhat, G., Cleaveland, R., Grumberg, O.: Efficient on-the-fly model checking for CTL*. In: LICS, pp. 388–397. IEEE Computer Society, Los Alamitos (1995)
2. Biere, A., Cimatti, A., Clarke, E., Zhu, Y.: Symbolic model checking without bdds. In: Cleaveland, W.R. (ed.) TACAS 1999. LNCS, vol. 1579, pp. 193–207. Springer, Heidelberg (1999)
3. Clarke, E., Emerson, E.: Design and synthesis of synchronization skeletons using branching-time temporal logic. In: Kozen, D. (ed.) Logic of Programs 1981. LNCS, vol. 131, pp. 52–71. Springer, Heidelberg (1982)
4. De Nicola, R., Vaandrager, F.: Action versus state based logics for transition systems. In: Guessarian, I. (ed.) LITP 1990. LNCS, vol. 469, pp. 407–419. Springer, Heidelberg (1990)

5. De Nicola, R., Vaandrager, F.: Three logics for branching bisimulation. J. ACM 42(2), 458–487 (1995)
6. Fantechi, A., Gnesi, S., Lapadula, A., Mazzanti, F., Pugliese, R., Tiezzi, F.: A model checking approach for verifying COWS specifications. In: Fiadeiro, J.L., Inverardi, P. (eds.) FASE 2008. LNCS, vol. 4961, pp. 230–245. Springer, Heidelberg (2008)
7. Gnesi, S., Mazzanti, F.: On the fly model checking of communicating UML state machines. In: Proc. of SERA 2004, pp. 331–338. ACIS (2004)
8. Gnesi, S., Mazzanti, F.: A model checking verification environment for UML statecharts. In: Proc. of XLIII Annual Italian Conference AICA. AICA (2005)
9. OMG (Object Management Group). Unified Modeling Language, http://www.uml.org/
10. Hennessy, M., Milner, R.: Algebraic laws for nondeterminism and concurrency. J. ACM 32(1), 137–161 (1985)
11. Koch, N., et al.: Relations among case studies and theme 3 results. SENSORIA Deliverable D8.7 (section: credit portal) (2008)
12. Koch, N., Mayer, P., Heckel, R., Gönczy, L., Montangero, C.: UML for Service-Oriented Systems, Sensoria deliverable D1.4a (2007)
13. Lapadula, A., Pugliese, R., Tiezzi, F.: A Calculus for Orchestration of Web Services (full version). Technical report, Dipartimento di Sistemi e Informatica, Univ. Firenze (2007), http://rap.dsi.unifi.it/cows
14. Lapadula, A., Pugliese, R., Tiezzi, F.: A calculus for orchestration of web services. Technical Report, DSI, Università di Firenze (2008),
http://rap.dsi.unifi.it/cows/papers/cows-esop07-full.pdf;
An extended abstract appeared in De Nicola, R. (ed.): ESOP 2007. LNCS, vol. 4421, pp. 33–47. Springer, Heidelberg (2007)
15. Mayer, P., Schroeder, A., Koch, N.: Mdd4soa: Model-driven service orchestration. In: EDOC, pp. 203–212. IEEE Computer Society, Los Alamitos (2008)
16. Mazzanti, F.: UMC User Guide v3.3. Technical report, Technical Report 2006-TR-33, Istituto di Scienza e Tecnologie dell'Informazione "A. Faedo", CNR (2006),
http://fmt.isti.cnr.it/WEBPAPER/UMC-UG33.pdf
17. Mazzanti, F.: Designing uml models with umc. Technical report, Technical Report 2009-TR-43, Istituto di Scienza e Tecnologie dell'Informazione "A. Faedo", CNR (2009)
18. Meolic, R., Kapus, T., Brezocnik, Z.: ACTLW - an action-based computation tree logic with unless operator. Elsevier Information Sciences 178(6), 1542–1557 (2008)
19. ter Beek, M., Fantechi, A., Gnesi, S., Mazzanti, F.: An action/state-based model-checking approach for the analysis of communication protocols for service-oriented applications. In: Leue, S., Merino, P. (eds.) FMICS 2007. LNCS, vol. 4916, pp. 133–148. Springer, Heidelberg (2008)
20. ter Beek, M., Gnesi, S., Koch, N., Mazzanti, F.: Formal verification of an automotive scenario in service-oriented computing. In: Proc. of ICSE 2008, pp. 613–622. ACM Press, New York (2008)
21. ter Beek, M., Gnesi, S., Mazzanti, F., Moiso, C.: Formal modelling and verification of an asynchronous extension of soap. In: Proc. of ECOWS 2006, pp. 287–296. IEEE Computer Society, Los Alamitos (2006)
22. ter Beek, M., Mazzanti, F., Gnesi, S.: Cmc-umc: A framework for the verification of abstract service-oriented properties. In: Proc. of the 24th Annual ACM Symposium on Applied Computing (SAC 2009), pp. 2111–2117. ACM Press, New York (2009)

Tools and Verification[*]

Massimo Bartoletti[1], Luís Caires[2], Ivan Lanese[3], Franco Mazzanti[4],
Davide Sangiorgi[3], Hugo Torres Vieira[2], and Roberto Zunino[5]

[1] Dipartimento di Matematica e Informatica, Università degli Studi di Cagliari, Italy
bart@unica.it
[2] CITI and Dep. de Informatica, FCT, Universidade Nova de Lisboa, Portugal
luis.caires@di.fct.unl.pt, htv@fct.unl.pt
[3] Focus Team, Università di Bologna/INRIA, Italy
{lanese,davide.sangiorgi}@cs.unibo.it
[4] ISTI-CNR, Pisa, Italy
franco.mazzanti@isti.cnr.it
[5] Dipartimento di Ingegneria e Scienza dell'Informazione, Università di Trento, Italy
zunino@disi.unitn.it

Abstract. This chapter presents different tools that have been developed inside the SENSORIA project. SENSORIA studied qualitative analysis techniques for verifying properties of service implementations with respect to their formal specifications. The tools presented in this chapter have been developed to carry out the analysis in an automated, or semi-automated, way.

We present four different tools, all developed during the SENSORIA project, exploiting new techniques and calculi from the SENSORIA project itself.

1   Introduction

This chapter presents a set of tools that have been developed inside the SENSORIA project for analysis and verification of service-oriented systems. The tools allow the application of novel analysis techniques for service-oriented systems that have been studied inside the project. Those tools are (partly) based on calculi and models described in Chapter 2-1. Also, they have been validated by applying them to the SENSORIA case studies (described in Chapter 0-3), as illustrated in Chapter 7-4 for the COWS Model Checker (CMC). This experimentation has provided useful feedback for improving the tools themselves.

We describe four different tools in detail, all developed within the SENSORIA project and based on new techniques and calculi introduced in the project itself. While referring to the next sections and to the publications in the bibliography for a more detailed description of the tools and of the underlying theory, we give here a short outline of each of them.

---

[*] This work has been partially sponsored by the project SENSORIA, IST-2005-016004.

M. Wirsing and M. Hölzl (Eds.): SENSORIA Project, LNCS 6582, pp. 408–427, 2011.
© Springer-Verlag Berlin Heidelberg 2011

CMC and UMC model checkers: CMC (COWS Model Checker) and UMC (UML Model Checker) are two prototypical instantiations of a common logical verification framework for the analysis of functional properties of service-oriented systems. Both tools have the goal of model-checking properties specified in Socl (the Service Oriented Computing Logic), and they differ just for the underlying computational models, which are built out from COWS (see Chapter 2-1) specifications in the case of CMC, and UML statecharts in the case of UMC. In both cases, the specifications are mapped onto Doubly Labeled Transition Systems, in which transitions are labeled by sets of observable events. The on-the-fly model checking technique is used to avoid statespace explosion. In this chapter we describe the tools themselves, while the underlying logic and the algorithms exploited by them have been described in Chapter 4-2.

ChorSLMC: ChorSLMC (Choreography Spatial Logic Model Checker) is a verification tool for service-based systems implemented as an extension to SLMC, a framework for model checking distributed systems against properties expressible in dynamic-spatial logic. Descriptions of participants may be specified either in the Conversation Calculus [29] (see also Chapter 2-1), a core calculus for service-oriented computing developed within the SENSORIA project, or in a fragment of WS-BPEL [1], while choreographic descriptions may be specified in an abstract version of WS-CDL [33]. The tool may also be used on service-based systems to check other interesting properties of typical distributed systems, using the core dynamic-spatial logic available in SLMC.

LocUsT: the LocUsT tool is a model checker for *usages*, abstract descriptions of the behavior of services. Usages are expressed in a simple process calculus. They over-approximate all the possible execution traces of a service, focusing on resource creation and access. *Usage policies* are then used to express constraints on the use of resources, by identifying the forbidden patterns. A policy is represented through a finite state automaton parametrized over resources. LocUsT takes as input a usage and a policy, and decides whether a trace of the usage that violates some instantiation of the policy exists.

The CMC and UMC tools are strongly related, just differing on the format of the description of the model of the system to be analyzed, and concentrate on verifying behavioral properties expressed in Socl logic. ChorSLMC also concentrates on behavioral properties, but they are verified by checking conformance to a choreographic description. LocUsT instead tackles a different problem, concentrating more on the security aspects, and allowing to check that resources are used according to a specified policy.

2   CMC-UMC Verification of Service-Oriented Models

CMC (COWS Model Checker) and UMC (UML Model Checker) [23, 27] are two prototypical instantiations of a common logical verification framework for the verification of functional properties of service-oriented systems. They differ just for the underlying computational models which are built out from COWS [20, 21] specifications in the case of CMC, and out from UML [28] statecharts in the case of UMC. For verification of service-oriented models we do not intend just the final "validation" step of a completed architecture design, but rather a formal support during all the steps of the incremental design phase (hence when running designs are still likely to be incomplete and with high probability to contain mistakes). Indeed CMC/UMC have been developed having in mind the needs of a system designer which intends to take advantage of formal approaches to achieve an early validation of the system requirements and an early detection of design errors. From this point of view the design of CMC/UMC has been driven by the desire to achieve the following goals (or, at least, to experiment in the following directions):

- The support of a good user experience (easiness of use) in the computer-aided application of formal methods.
- The support of abstraction mechanisms allowing to observe the system at an high level of abstraction, hiding all the irrelevant and unnecessary computational details.
- The possibility to explore step by step the possible system evolutions and the possibility to generate a "summary" of system behavior in terms of minimal abstract traces.
- The possibility to investigate detailed and complex system properties using a parametric branching time temporal logic supported by an on-the-fly model checker.
- The possibility of obtaining an understandable explanation of the model-checking results.

In the following we will briefly present the achieved results with respect to the above five points.

User Experience. Several kinds of user interfaces have been experimented in the attempt to make possible the access to verification facilities also by non technical people. This without losing the possibility to tune and control the verification environment in a more advanced way. In particular:

- CMC/UMC are accessible as web applications to allow their experimentation and use without any kind of local installation, and exploiting the friendliness and flexibility of hypertextual documents to support the interactions with the user.
- CMC/UMC are usable with a simple, platform independent, java-based, graphical interface to achieve offline model exploration and verification.
- CMC/UMC are available as binary, platform-specific, command line oriented applications (for Mac, Windows, Linux and Sun systems) to exploit the simplest, most efficient, and finest level of interaction and control of the system verification and exploration.
- Models can be edited as simple textual documents.

- UML Statechart models can also be edited through a dedicated graphical interface.
- UML Statechart models can be extracted from standard UML XMI documents.

Abstraction Mechanisms. In our context, services are considered as entities which have some kind of abstract internal state and which are capable of supporting abstract interactions with their clients, like for example accepting requests, delivering corresponding responses and, on-demand, canceling requests. Moreover, concrete operational models, with a specific concrete operational semantics, are used to describe the details of the system states and their possible evolution steps. This means that an abstraction mechanism needs to be applied to the system state description and to the system evolution information. This mechanism allows to extract from the operational semantics of the specific computational model the relevant aspects we want to observe. In our tools this abstraction step is achieved via a list of pattern matching rules which allow to specify which state properties and which transition events we want to observe. These rules are presented as structured actions of the form "mainlabel(flag,flag,..)". When this abstraction step is performed, the semantic model of a service-oriented system can be seen as a doubly labeled transitions system (L^2TS), where both the states and the edges are labeled with sets of the above described structured actions. This abstract L^2TS induced by the operational semantics of the system will constitute the reference structure used by the logic as interpretation domain and by the full-trace minimization algorithm to generate and display the abstract minimized views of the system.

CMC is the instantiation of our verification framework with respect to the COWS process calculus. COWS ha been explicitly defined for the specification and orchestration of services and combines in an original way constructs and well known features like asynchronous communication, polyadic synchronization, pattern matching, protection, delimited receiving and killing activities. The abstraction rules of CMC allow to "intercept" the communication actions occurring between two COWS processes and present them as request/response events in the context of some client-server interaction. The corresponding abstract labels will therefore appear on the edges of the L^2TS as they represent the abstract events occurred during an evolution step. The CMC abstraction rules moreover allow to observe the willingness of a COWS term to participate to a communication synchronization (e.g., its willingness to perform the input side of the synchronization) and present it as a state property reflecting the willingness of a service to accept operation requests. In this case this abstract property will appear as an abstract label associated to some states of the L^2TS.

UMC is instead the instantiation of our verification framework with respect to UML statecharts. These have a standard presentation and semantics as defined by the OMG (Object Management Group). The communication events which can be observed in this case are based on the notion of message passing. Indeed, we can distinguish the event of sending an operation request (on the client side) from the event of accepting that request (on the server side). Moreover UML

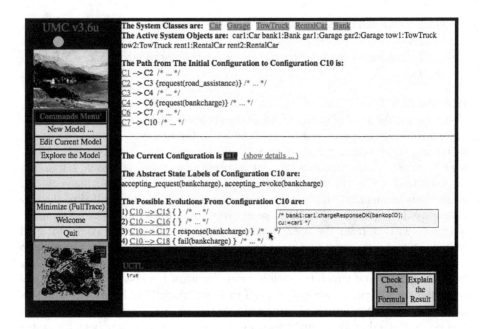

Fig. 1. UMC manual model exploration page

statecharts are built over the concept of local attribute of objects, and during the execution of a system transition (beyond multiple communication actions) several updates of the local object attributes can be executed. The abstraction rules of UMC allow to observe all these events (acceptance of a message, sending of a message, update of a local attribute) as abstract events representing relevant aspects of the service-oriented behavior of the system, and represent them as abstract labels associated to the L^2TS edges. Other abstraction rules of UMC allow instead to observe the specific value of selected object attributes, and whether or not an object in a specific state, and present this information as abstract state predicates labeling the states of the L^2TS.

Step by Step Exploration. The first and simpler way to explore a CMC/UMC model is to manually navigate through its L^2TS structure, observing at each step the set of possible immediate evolutions, the set of abstract events occurring during these evolutions, the set of abstract properties holding in the current state and, if desired, also all the ground details of the underlying computational model with respect to the current state structure and evolutions. The web application interface (shown in Fig. 1), thanks to the use of tooltips, colors and hyperlinks, makes this exploration experience more immediate.

Abstract Minimized Traces. The possibility of selecting a small set of abstract events of interest and, starting from them, compute and observe the minimized full-trace abstract view of the system is an extremely powerful way of checking whether the system behavior matches the intended requirements. This works even in the case in which the requirements themselves are not fully clear or well formalized. Let us consider, for example, the automotive case study described in [25]. This is formalized as a collection of UMC statecharts, which is a model constituted by several hundreds of states. Suppose we are interested in observing only the "bank" related events and the "garage" related events. Using the appropriate abstractions and using UMC to build the minimized model with respect to them we obtain the L^2TS shown in Fig. 2, which summarizes all the possible system traces with respect to the observed set of events. It is extremely easy to become confident of the correctness of the model just looking at the L^2TS, without being forced to identify a priori a *complete* set of requirements and formalize them in terms of logic formulas for being separately model checked. Unfortunately the abstract minimization approach to system verification has also some drawbacks:

- It is computationally expensive: for very large models it might be too much resource consuming to compute its abstract, minimal full-trace view.
- If the L^2TS is not finite, it is not even a matter of available computing resources. Building the abstraction is not possible.
- The abstract view completely lost the connection with the original "concrete" computational model. If the system behavior is not the expected one, no immediate way is available to reconstruct unexpected computations in the concrete model.
- If the resulting chart is rather complex, relying on just the intuition to assess its correctness is unreliable and lacks of concrete formal evidence.

Socl Model Checking. To overcome the drawbacks of the previous approach, as well as to directly formalize and check *specific* functional / safety / liveness requirements of a system, a verification technique based on *on-the-fly, bounded model checking of Socl formulas* is considered. This approach also permits to reduce the average verification time and, at the same time, performing some verification also in the case of non finite-state systems. Socl [15] is a service-oriented temporal logic derived from UCTL [16, 17, 24] of which we recall here the most important characteristics:

- It is a branching time logic, built over the classical intuitive "eventually" (F), "always" (G), "until" (U), "next" (X) temporal operators. The evaluation of this logic is known [7] to be achievable with a computational complexity which is linear with respect to the size of the formula and the size of the model.
- It is an event and state based logic. Being its interpretation domain our abstract state/event based L^2TS structures, Socl allows to directly express state predicates to be evaluated over the abstract labels associated to the states of the L^2TS, and action expressions to be evaluated over the abstract labels associated to the edges of the L^2TS.

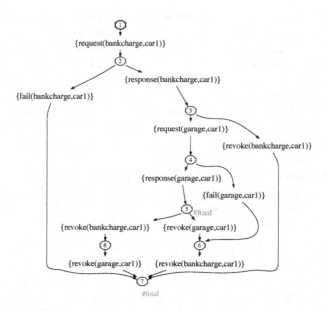

Fig. 2. An abstract view of the automotive case study

- It is a parametric temporal logic, in which the values of the arguments of an abstract event occurring during a transition can be used to dynamically instantiate a parametric subformula to be evaluated in the target state of the transition itself.

Socl is supported in CMC/UMC by an on-the-fly model checking algorithm which generates the model statespace *on demand* according to the flow of the evaluation. The UCTL formula is evaluated adopting a top-down traversal of the structure of the formula itself minimizing the need of the model statespace generation (which is explored in a depth-first way); a *bounded* [8] model checking approach is also used to try to produce an evaluation result also in the case of infinite state models.

The Socl verification engine is exactly the same in both CMC and UMC since it is based on the abstract L^2TS computed from the models, and not on the specific concrete computational models defined by input model specification languages. In the following we show some examples of Socl formulas, just to give an intuition of its structure, referring to [15] for the details of its definition and for its formal presentation. These examples are written with respect to the same abstraction rules used to generate the abstract minimized traces shown in Fig. 2. With respect to the above scenario we can check, for example, that: "*It is always true (AG) that an unsuccessful response from the garage to a client is always eventually (AF) followed by a revoke operation to the bank, on behalf of the same client*". This property can be formalized in Socl (following the CMC/UMC syntax) as:

```
AG [fail(garage, $client)] AF{revoke(bankcharge,%client)} true.
```

Another general property that we can check with respect to the same scenario is that: "*It is always true (AG) that a request for an operation is always followed (AF) either by a successful response to that operation or by a failure notification*". In this case the property can be formalized as:

```
AG [request($operation,$client)]
      AF {response(%operation,%client)
          or fail (%operation,%client)}.
```

Proofs and Counterexamples. It is well known that providing a counterexample for a given temporal logic formula is quite easy in the case of linear time logics and quite complex in the case of branching time logics. The problems to be solved for the generation of useful proofs/counterexamples are essentially three:

- The proof/counterexample is not (in general) based on a single execution path of the system, but may be based on a subgraph of the L^2TS modeling the system.
- Not all the L^2TS states needed by the proof/counterexample are in general "useful" from the point of view of the user.
- The information on the set of L^2TS states needed by the proof/counterexample is sometimes not sufficient to produce usable feedback to the user. We might need to provide feedback also on which subformula was being evaluated when the L^2TS states have been explored.

Let us consider, for example, a simple formula of the kind: "*(AG predicate1) or (AG predicate2)*". If this formula does not hold, its counterexample has the form of a pair of paths, one leading to a state in which *predicate1* does not hold, and another leading to a state in which *predicate2* does not hold.

Let us consider, moreover, the formula: "*EF predicate*". If this formula does not hold, its counterexample would coincide with the full system statespace, however it would be completely pointless to provide the user with an exhaustive list of all the states for which the *predicate* does not hold. On the contrary, if the formula holds the user might be interested in the sequence of steps which would prove it.

Let us consider, as third example, the formula "*EF AG predicate*". If the formula holds for a certain system, the user might be interested in the proof for the first part of the formula, showing an execution path which, starting from the initial state would lead to an intermediate state for which the subformula "*AG predicate*" holds; once identified that intermediate state all the other states reachable from it belonging to the proof of the subformula "*AG predicate*" would probably add only irrelevant noise and complexity to the original information. The "useful" part of the proof, would be constituted by a fragment of the full proof. CMC/UMC tries to convey to the user what is supposed to be the "useful" part of a proof or counterexample, but only more experience might consolidate the identification of the "best" reasonable behavior.

Application to the Case Studies. The design and development of the prototypes has greatly taken advantage from the early experiences gained through their application to the SENSORIA case studies. The first of these applications has been the use of UMC for the analysis of communication protocols for service-oriented applications [24, 26]. Subsequently the SENSORIA automotive case study has been the stimulus for the first experimentations with the Socl logic and the COWS language [15]. The same case study has also been specified in terms of UML statecharts and verified with UMC [25], thus experimenting with the SENSORIA UML profile for SOA [19, 22]. Finally both COWS/CMC and UML/UMC have been applied for the formalization and verification of the SENSORIA Credit Portal case study (see Chapter 0-3).

3   Model-Checking Service Conversations with ChorSLMC

A service-based system is a decentralized coordinated distributed system, where independent partners interact by message passing. It is then useful to consider the extension of automated verification techniques, based on model-checking, to service-oriented models, able to certify the general "standard properties" of concurrent distributed systems, such as reachability, termination, liveness, race-freedom, just to refer a few. We may also be interested in domain specific invariants. This class of properties is easily expressible in some kind of temporal logic. Adding to these, it is well known that to describe interactions among partners in a service relationship two viewpoints are considered particularly useful: orchestration and choreography.

"Orchestration" focuses on the coordination of several partners from the local viewpoint of a single participant, for the purpose of providing a new functionality or service to the external world, "choreography" describes the global behavior of a system that emerges from the interaction of several independent participants. An orchestration can be seen as the description of a workflow process, with its own control flow graph, while a choreography, just like a message sequence chart, describes the message exchanges between a group of partners involved in a complex transaction. Orchestration specification languages are programming languages, with a definite operational semantics (cf. WS-BPEL [1] and various service-oriented calculi described in Chapter 2-1), while choreography languages (cf. WS-CDL [33] and the calculus of [13]) define global behaviors of composite systems "without a single point of control", and are not intended to be "executable". Therefore, in addition to common behavioral-temporal properties, an important analysis problem in service-oriented computing is to check conformance of local descriptions (orchestrations) with respect to choreographies (cf. [9, 14]). Specifying (and checking) conformance of localized process interactions against choreographies requires a specification language able to talk about the internal spatial structure of a concurrent system, and its dynamic evolution. Such expressiveness falls out of the scope of extensional behavioral logics such as Hennessy-Milner logic and variants (and supporting tools).

We have developed a fairly simple, yet powerful, technique, building on dynamic-spatial logics and model-checking [10, 11], particularly appropriate for this class of analysis problems. We have also implemented a supporting tool ChorSLMC, which is an extension of SLMC, a dynamic-spatial logic model-checker. The tool may be used to check not only choreography conformance, but many other key properties of service-oriented systems, such as race-freedom and deadlock absence, and system invariants, that may be easily expressed in the underlying logical framework.

Approach. Our approach to the choreographic analysis problem relies on language translations, and on the reuse of previously developed model-checking techniques for spatial logic and related tools. More concretely, we have developed provably correct encodings, allowing local descriptions of partner sites, expressed in a service-oriented calculus, to be adequately translated into a lower level analysis language (a dialect of the π-calculus), and global descriptions (choreographies), to be adequately translated into dynamic-spatial logic formulas. The correctness of our translation ensures that a system *System*, expressed in the core Conversation Calculus [29] (described in Chapter 2-1 and referred below by CC) or, alternatively, in a simple dialect of WS-BPEL, conforms to a choreography *Choreography*, expressed in a WS-CDL dialect, if and only if its π-calculus translation satisfies the corresponding dynamic-spatial logic formula.

$$[\![System]\!] \models [\![Choreography]\!]$$

The correctness of the translation between the source language (either CC or WS-BPEL) is obtained by observing that for model-checking purposes, we don't really need full abstraction but just some suitable operational correspondence. The encoding of choreographies in the logic is supported by the structural observational power of spatial logics, that allow observation of internal message exchanges, unobservable by purely behavioral logics such as those supported by other existing model checking tools. Choreography conformance of service-oriented systems is then reduced to a model-checking problem that may be easily handled by existing tools, namely the Spatial Logic Model Checker (SLMC) [31, 32] (started to be developed in Global Computing 1 Project Profundis, and extended during Global Computing 2 Project SENSORIA). The structural observation power of spatial logics turns out to be essential in this application to choreographic verification, since, e.g., the message exchanges mentioned in a choreographic description are not observable by traditional process logics invariant under behavioral equivalences. Thus, general process logics and tools that cannot observe internal message exchanges in a system would not be appropriate for the service verification problem we consider here. Both local descriptions of services, expressed in suitable orchestration languages, and the global choreographic descriptions, expressed in a WS-CDL dialect, are translated by ChorSLMC into π-calculus / dynamic-spatial logic specifications, respectively, which are directly fed to the SLMC verification engine.

Input Specification Languages. The ChorSLMC tool supports two modeling languages for defining the behavior of partners in a service collaboration: a core fragment of the Conversation Calculus, obtained by removing exception handling primitives, and a fragment of WS-BPEL. The specification syntax is depicted below, and includes the basic constructors presented in Chapter 2-1. Both the CC model and the WS-BPEL model are detailed in [30].

$$
\begin{array}{lll}
\alpha ::= & LABEL!(\tilde{o}) & \text{(send here)} \\
\mid & LABEL?(\tilde{i}) & \text{(receive here)} \\
\mid & LABEL\hat{}\,!(\tilde{o}) & \text{(send up)} \\
\mid & LABEL\hat{}\,?(\tilde{i}) & \text{(receive up)} \\
\end{array}
$$

$$
\begin{array}{lll}
P ::= & \mathsf{end} & \text{(inaction)} \\
\mid & \mathsf{context}\; n\; \{P\} & \text{(site)} \\
\mid & \alpha.P & \text{(action)} \\
\mid & \mathsf{switch}\; \{\alpha_1.P_1; \ldots; \alpha_k.P_k\} & \text{(select)} \\
\mid & \mathsf{def}\; LABEL \Rightarrow P & \text{(service definition)} \\
\mid & \mathsf{new}\; n.LABEL \Leftarrow P & \text{(service instantiation)} \\
\mid & \mathsf{join}\; n.LABEL \Leftarrow P & \text{(conversation join)} \\
\mid & P_1 \mid P_2 & \text{(parallel)} \\
\mid & Id & \text{(process identifier)} \\
\mid & \mathsf{if}\; (bool\; expr)\; \mathsf{then}\; P_1\; \mathsf{else}\; P_2 & \text{(conditional)} \\
\end{array}
$$

To describe choreographies, a fairly simplified version of the WS-CDL language is also considered, defined as an extension of the dynamic-spatial logic available in SLMC with specialized choreography operators as shown below. In such a way, it is possible to freely mix choreography operators with propositional and first order name quantification, spatial operators and fixpoint operators. The choreography fragment is close to the languages of global types introduced by [13, 18], and is also processed directly by the ChorSLMC tool.

$$
\begin{array}{lll}
A ::= & \mathsf{end} & \text{(no action)} \\
\mid & \mathsf{exchange}(n, LABEL, A) & \text{(may interaction in conversation } n) \\
\mid & \mathsf{exchanges}(n, LABEL, arg, A) & \text{(may interaction in conversation } n) \\
\mid & \mathsf{aexchange}(n, LABEL, A) & \text{(all interaction in conversation } n) \\
\mid & \mathsf{aexchanges}(n, LABEL, arg, A) & \text{(all interaction in conversation } n) \\
\mid & \mathsf{parallel}(A', A'') & \text{(parallel activities)} \\
\mid & \mathsf{choice}(A', A'') & \text{(choice)} \\
\mid & F & \text{(spatial logic formulae)} \\
\end{array}
$$

The language contains constructs to express parallel / choice flow and primitives to express message exchanges: $\mathsf{exchange}(n, LABEL, A)$ asserts that there is a message interaction on label $LABEL$ between two partners in conversation n and A specifies the behavior of the continuation; $\mathsf{exchanges}(n, LABEL, arg, A)$ specifies an extra argument arg which captures the conversation name exchanged in the communication; $\mathsf{aexchange}(n, LABEL, A)$ asserts that after all interactions on label $LABEL$ in conversation n the continuation satisfies behavior A. We

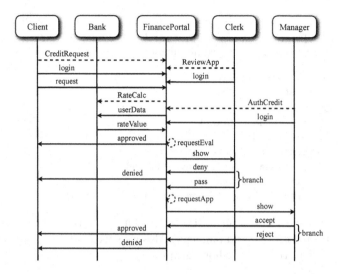

Fig. 3. Credit request message sequence chart

refer to [30] for a detailed explanation of our orchestration and choreography description language semantics, and the formal specification of their translation into the π-calculus and logic understood by the SLMC framework.

Simple Examples. We now illustrate the usage of the specification languages and of our tool. Consider the credit request scenario from the SENSORIA Financial Case Study described in Chapter 0-3, whose choreographic specification may be graphically depicted by the message sequence chart in Fig. 3. We specify the part of the choreography related to the interaction between the client, the finance portal and the bank as follows, using the basic choreographic language for CC systems (actually the input syntax for ChorSLMC).

```
defprop clientInteraction =
   maxfix Loop.
   hidden clientConv.
     exchanges(financePortal, creditRequest, clientConv,
     exchange(clientConv, login,
     exchange(clientConv, request,
     exchanges(bank, rateCalc, clientConv,
     exchange(clientConv, userData,
     exchange(clientConv, rateValue,
     choice(
        exchange(clientConv, approved, exchange(client,approved,Loop)),
        may_tau(clerkInteraction(clientConv,Loop)))))))))));
```

Notice that the exchange specification may be used not only to specify "regular" message exchanges, but also conversation initiation (`creditRequest`) and conversation join (`rateCalc`) messages (see [12]). The behavior of each partner / role is then specified using the appropriate modeling language. We show the code for the *creditRequest* service definition:

```
defproc cc FinancePortalSpec1 =
  context financePortal {
    def creditRequest => (
      login?(uid).request?(data).
        join bank.rateCalc <= (
          userData!(data).rateValue?(rate).
          if (rate=aaa) then approved!().end
          else this(clientChat).
              requestEval^!(clientChat,uid,data).end))};
```

We specify the whole system as the composition of the roles of the finance portal, bank, client, clerk and manager. Also we specify that *clientInteraction* is the entry point of the global choreography.

```
defproc cc System = FinancePortalSpec1 | BankSpec | BankSpec2
          | ClientSpec | FinancePortalSpec2 | ClerkSpec
          | FinancePortalSpec3 | ManagerSpec;
defprop chor = clientInteraction;
```

After all definitions have been loaded into the ChorSLMC tool we may verify that the CC credit request system conforms to the prescribed choreography.

```
check System(up,here) |= chor;
Processing...
* Process System(up,here) satisfies the formula chor *
```

Notice that the tool may be used to automatically verify (for finite state models) not only choreographic conformance of composite service systems, but also common safety and liveness properties, such as invariant satisfaction, race and deadlock absence. For example:

```
check System(up,here) |= eventually(exchange(bank,rateCalc,true));
Processing...
* Process System(up,here) satisfies the formula
eventually (exchange(bank,rateCalc,true)) *
```

To conclude, the ChorSLMC tool provides a very flexible and powerful instrument to analyze general structural safety and liveness properties of service-oriented systems, expressed in languages which are familiar to software engineers, while building in solid process calculi and specification logic based foundations.

4   The LocUsT Tool

A fundamental concern of service-oriented applications is to ensure that resources are used correctly. Devising expressive, flexible and efficient mechanisms to control resource usages is therefore a major issue in the design and implementation of languages for services. In [6], a comprehensive framework has been proposed for safely protecting code with usage policies, within a linguistic setting. Resource usage control is made feasible by suitably extending and integrating techniques from type theory and model-checking.

The LocUsT tool is the verification core of our framework. It takes as input a usage policy and a program abstraction (called a *usage*), and statically checks whether the abstraction complies with the policy. More precisely, LocUsT decides in polynomial time whether a trace of the given usage exists that violates the policy [5].

Usage Policies. Usage policies define safety properties on sequences of resource accesses and creations. We will define below our usage policies, and the compliance of a trace with a policy. First, we introduce some basic notions.

Resources are denoted with $r, r', \ldots \in$ Res, and they can be accessed through *actions* $\alpha, \alpha', \ldots \in$ Act. An *event* $\alpha(r_1, \ldots, r_k) \in$ Ev models the action α (with arity $|\alpha| = k$) being fired on the target resources $r_1, \ldots, r_k$. The special action **new** represents the creation of a resource. *Traces* $\eta, \eta', \ldots \in$ Ev* are finite sequences of events.

Usage policies are an extension of finite state automata. Their edges have the form $\alpha(\boldsymbol{\rho})$, where $\boldsymbol{\rho} \in$ (Res $\cup$ Var)$^{|\alpha|}$. We use final states to represent policy violations: a trace leading to a final state suffices to produce a violation. Two examples of usage policies are in Fig. 4.

Formally, a usage policy φ is a 5-tuple $\langle S, Q, q_0, F, E \rangle$, where:

- $S \subseteq$ Act $\times$ (Res $\cup$ Var)* is the input alphabet,
- Q is a finite set of states,
- $q_0 \in Q \setminus F$ is the start state,
- $F \subset Q$ is the set of final "offending" states,
- $E \subseteq Q \times S \times Q$ is a finite set of edges, written $q \xrightarrow{\alpha(\boldsymbol{\rho})} q'$

Each usage policy φ denotes a set of traces, i.e. the traces that obey φ. The semantics of φ considers all the possible instantiations of its variables to actual resources: a trace η respects φ when η leads no instantiations of φ (on the resources in η) to an offending state.

Usage policies were first introduced in [3], where a block of code B could be sandboxed by a policy φ, so to require that φ must hold through the execution of B. The definition of policies has since then been revised several times, so to make them more expressive. In the original formulation, policies could only inspect sequences of actions, neglecting resources. In [4] policies can be parametrized over a single resource, and resources can be dynamically created; [5] deals with the general case of an arbitrary number of parameters.

Examples. Consider a Web application that allows for editing documents, storing them on a remote site, and sharing them with other users. The editor is implemented as an applet run by a local browser. The user can tag any of her documents as *private*. To avoid direct information flows, the policy requires that private files cannot be sent to the server in plain text, yet they can be sent encrypted. This policy is modeled by $\varphi_{\mathsf{IF}}(x)$ below. After having tagged the file x as private (edge from q_0 to q_1), if x was to be sent to the server (edge from q_1 to q_2), then the policy would be violated: the double circle around q_2 marks it as an offending state. Instead, if x is encrypted (edge from q_1 to q_3), then x can be freely transmitted: indeed, the absence of paths from q_3 to an offending state indicates that once state q_3 is reached, the policy will not be violated on file x. A further policy is applied to our editor, to avoid information flow due to covert channels. It requires that, after reading a private file, any other file must be encrypted before it can be transmitted. This is modeled by $\varphi_{\mathsf{CC}}(x,y)$ below. A violation occurs if after some private file x is read (path from q_0' to q_2'), then some other file y is sent (edge from q_2' to the offending state q_4').

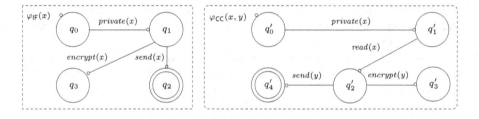

Fig. 4. The information flow policy $\varphi_{\mathsf{IF}}(x)$ and the covert channels policy $\varphi_{\mathsf{CC}}(x,y)$

Here is how the policies $\varphi_{\mathsf{IF}}(x)$ and $\varphi_{\mathsf{CC}}(x,y)$ are expressed in the LocUsT syntax. The field tagged **name** defines the name of the policy. The remaining fields describe the logic of the automaton. The tag **states** is for the set of states, **start** is for the initial state, and **final** is for the list of the final (offending) states. The tag **trans** preludes to the transition relation of the automaton.

```
name: phi_IF                    name: phi_CC
states: q0 q1 q2 q3             states: q0 q1 q2 q3 q4
start: q0                       start: q0
final: q2                       final: q4
trans:                          trans:
q0 -- private(x) --> q1         q0 -- private(x) --> q1
q1 -- encrypt(x) --> q3         q1 -- read(x)    --> q2
q1 -- send(x)    --> q2         q2 -- send(y)    --> q4
                                q2 -- encrypt(y) --> q3
```

Usages. Usages are program abstractions, expressed in a simple process calculus. They over-approximate all the patterns of resource accesses and creations of the service itself. Formally, usages have the following syntax:

$$U, U' ::= 0 \qquad \qquad \text{empty}$$

$\alpha(\boldsymbol{\rho})$	event $(\boldsymbol{\rho} \in \mathsf{Res}^{|\alpha|})$
nu n.U	resource creation
U . U'	sequence
U + U'	choice
$\varphi[U]$	policy framing
mu h.U	recursion
h	recursion variable

The usage 0 represents a computation not affecting resources. The usage $\alpha(\boldsymbol{\rho})$ is for a computation that executes the action α on the resources mentioned in $\boldsymbol{\rho}$. The usage nu n.U represents the creation of a resource n, which can then be used in U with the requirement that the first action on n must be a new(n) event. The operators . and + denote sequentialization and non-deterministic choice of usages, respectively. The usage $\varphi[U]$ represents the fact that the policy φ has to be enforced on the usage U. The usage mu h.U stands for a recursion; the recursion variable h may occur in U.

For instance, consider the following usage:

phi_IF[nu n. new(n).private(n).(send(n)+encrypt(n))]

This usage will be rejected by the LocUsT model-checker, because a send(n) may occur in a trace after a private(n), so violating the policy φ_{IF}.

The following usage will instead pass the model-checking, because the action send is not fired on a private document.

phi_IF[nu n. nu f. new(n).new(f).private(n).read(n).send(f)]

The following usage is rejected by the model-checker, because it violates the policy φ_{CC}. Note in fact that a file f is sent unencrypted after the private file n has been read.

phi_CC[nu n. nu f. new(n).new(f).private(n).read(n).send(f)]

The following trace is detected to attempt a violation of the policy φ_{CC}.

nu n. new(n).private(n).nu f. new(f).
    (mu h. phi_CC[send(f)] + read(n) . h)

After having read the private file n an arbitrary number of times, it may activate the policy φ_{CC}, within which sending the unencrypted file f is no longer permitted.

Finally, the following usage passes the model-checking, since the file f can only be sent after it has been encrypted:

nu n. new(n).private(n).nu f. new(f).
    (mu h. phi_CC[send(f) . h] + read(n) . encrypt(f) . h)

Service Call-by-Contract. So far, we have shown how LocUsT can verify that an abstraction of the service behavior does not violate a given policy. This technique can serve as a foundation for a service composition framework, where services are orchestrated according to their behavioral properties.

In our framework, each service publishes the abstraction of its behavior (i.e. its usage) in a repository. Then, a client can ask for a service that respects a given property (expressed as a usage policy). This is done by querying the repository with that usage policy. Upon such request, the repository matches the given policy against the usages of the registered services. This task can be accomplished by the LocUsT tool. When LocUsT finds that the property requested by the client matches the usage of a service, the name of that service is forwarded to the client, which can then invoke the service using standard mechanisms.

Summing up, our technique allows for defining a call-by-contract invocation mechanism, which allows clients to abstract from the actual service names, and just consider the properties these services have to offer.

The theory underlying our call-by-contract invocation mechanism was originally introduced in [2]. There, a type and effect system and a model-checker were exploited to define a call-by-contract orchestrator. Call-by-contract is described in detail in Chapter 2-4.

Verification Technique. We now briefly recap the verification technique described in detail in [5], which is the one implemented in the LocUsT tool. Our algorithm is composed of several phases, summarized below.

1. **Regularization.** First, the usage is *regularized*, i.e. transformed so that in no trace a policy framing $\varphi[-]$ is entered twice: for instance $\varphi[U \cdot \varphi[U']]$ becomes $\varphi[U \cdot U']$. Particular care must be exercised when handling recursive usages such as $\mathtt{mu}\ h.\ \varphi[h + U]$.

2. **Conversion into BPA.** The usage is transformed in a process of Basic Process Algebras. Dynamic creation caused by $\mathtt{nu}\ n$ is handled by instantiating n with a finite number of static witnesses. Note that this transformation restricts the resources to be considered by the model-checker from an infinite to a finite set. Yet, this phase is correct, as shown in [5]. Some spurious traces might however be introduced by this transformation, so invalidating completeness. For instance, in some trace of the BPA associated to $\mathtt{nu}\ n.U \cdot (\mathtt{nu}\ m.U')$ the same witness might be chosen for both n and m. This would cause the model-checker to report a violation, so over-approximating the predicted behavior. The "Weak Until" phase described below will allow for recovering completeness.

3. **Framing the Policy.** The policy is duplicated in two layers, so that the first layer handles the transitions made by the usage when *outside* the policy framing, and the second handles them when *inside* the policy framing. Thanks to the regularization phase, this phase only needs to consider two layers.

4. **Instantiating the Policy.** The usage policies are instantiated, by non-deterministically assigning to each variable some known resource, including the witnesses generated in the "Conversion into BPA" phase.

5. **Weak Until.** Policies are adapted so to correctly handle traces where the same witness # happens to be generated twice, i.e. those having a double new(#) event. As noticed above, these traces do not correspond to any trace of the original usage, so they must never trigger a policy violation. In [5] this is proved enough to guarantee the completeness of model checking, while preserving its correctness.

6. **Model-Checking.** Finally, the traces of the BPA generated at phase 2 are matched against all the policies obtained after phase 5. Our model-checking algorithm decides whether there exists a policy violated by some BPA trace. Our model-checking procedure is complete, and it always terminates even though the BPA may have an infinite number of traces, possibly of infinite length (for instance, `mu h. c + h.h + a.h.b`).

The complexity of our model-checking algorithm is polynomial in the size of the usage and on the size of the policy. There is an exponential factor in the number of policy parameters, only. From a pragmatic point of view, we expect the number of parameters to be very small in practice. This exponential factor is mainly due to the policy instantiation step above, which is non-deterministic.

5   Conclusion

We have reported on four tools that have been developed within the SENSO-RIA project, providing practical support for the application of SENSORIA techniques to service-oriented systems, including the SENSORIA case studies. The tools tackle, in particular, the problems of model checking service-oriented systems, including multiparty systems, of checking conformance of orchestrations with respect to choreographic descriptions, and of ensuring that systems access resources according to specified policies.

The tools are at different stages of development. The CMC/UMC framework is more mature, and has been integrated in the SENSORIA Development Environment (see Chapter 6-5), thus allowing to use it in an integrated way inside the software development process. The other tools are less mature, and their integration is part of our future plans. However all the tools are publicly available: CMC and UMC at `http://fmt.isti.cnr.it/cmc` and `http://fmt.isti.cnr.it/umc` respectively, ChorSLMC at `http://ctp.di.fct.unl.pt/SLMC/` and Lo-cUsT at `http://www.di.unipi.it/~zunino/software/locust`.

References

1. Alves, A., et al.: Web Services Business Process Execution Language Version 2.0. Technical report, OASIS (2006)
2. Bartoletti, M., Degano, P., Ferrari, G.L.: Enforcing secure service composition. In: Proc. of CSFW-18 2005, pp. 211–223. IEEE Computer Society, Los Alamitos (2005)
3. Bartoletti, M., Degano, P., Ferrari, G.L.: History-based access control with local policies. In: Sassone, V. (ed.) FOSSACS 2005. LNCS, vol. 3441, pp. 316–332. Springer, Heidelberg (2005)

4. Bartoletti, M., Degano, P., Ferrari, G.L., Zunino, R.: Types and effects for resource usage analysis. In: Seidl, H. (ed.) FOSSACS 2007. LNCS, vol. 4423, pp. 32–47. Springer, Heidelberg (2007)
5. Bartoletti, M., Degano, P., Ferrari, G.L., Zunino, R.: Model checking usage policies. In: Kaklamanis, C., Nielson, F. (eds.) TGC 2008. LNCS, vol. 5474, pp. 19–35. Springer, Heidelberg (2009)
6. Bartoletti, M., Degano, P., Ferrari, G.L., Zunino, R.: Local policies for resource usage analysis. ACM Trans. Program. Lang. Syst. 31(6) (2009)
7. Bhat, G., Cleaveland, R., Grumberg, O.: Efficient on-the-fly model checking for CTL*. In: Proc. of LICS 1995, pp. 388–397. IEEE Computer Society, Los Alamitos (1995)
8. Biere, A., Cimatti, A., Clarke, E., Zhu, Y.: Symbolic model checking without bdds. In: Cleaveland, W.R. (ed.) TACAS 1999. LNCS, vol. 1579, pp. 193–207. Springer, Heidelberg (1999)
9. Bravetti, M., Zavattaro, G.: Towards a unifying theory for choreography conformance and contract compliance. In: Lumpe, M., Vanderperren, W. (eds.) SC 2007. LNCS, vol. 4829, pp. 34–50. Springer, Heidelberg (2007)
10. Caires, L.: Behavioral and spatial observations in a logic for the pi-calculus. In: Walukiewicz, I. (ed.) FOSSACS 2004. LNCS, vol. 2987, pp. 72–89. Springer, Heidelberg (2004)
11. Caires, L., Cardelli, L.: A Spatial Logic for Concurrency (Part I). Information and Computation 186(2), 194–235 (2003)
12. Caires, L., Vieira, H.T.: Conversation types. In: Castagna, G. (ed.) ESOP 2009. LNCS, vol. 5502, pp. 285–300. Springer, Heidelberg (2009)
13. Carbone, M., Honda, K., Yoshida, N.: Structured communication-centred programming for web services. In: De Nicola, R. (ed.) ESOP 2007. LNCS, vol. 4421, pp. 2–17. Springer, Heidelberg (2007)
14. Carbone, M., Honda, K., Yoshida, N., Milner, R., Brown, G., Ross-Talbot, S.: A theoretical basis of communication–centred concurrent programming. Technical report, W3C (2006)
15. Fantechi, A., Gnesi, S., Lapadula, A., Mazzanti, F., Pugliese, R., Tiezzi, F.: A model checking approach for verifying COWS specifications. In: Fiadeiro, J.L., Inverardi, P. (eds.) FASE 2008. LNCS, vol. 4961, pp. 230–245. Springer, Heidelberg (2008)
16. Gnesi, S., Mazzanti, F.: On the fly model checking of communicating UML state machines. In: Proc. of SERA 2004, pp. 331–338. ACIS (2004)
17. Gnesi, S., Mazzanti, F.: A model checking verification environment for UML statecharts. In: Proc. of XLIII Annual Italian Conference AICA. AICA (2005)
18. Honda, K., Yoshida, N., Carbone, M.: Multiparty asynchronous session types. In: Proc. of POPL 2008, pp. 273–284. ACM, New York (2008)
19. Koch, N., Mayer, P., Heckel, R., Gönczy, L., Montangero, C.: UML for Service-Oriented Systems. SENSORIADeliverable 1.4a (September 2007)
20. Lapadula, A., Pugliese, R., Tiezzi, F.: A calculus for orchestration of web services. In: De Nicola, R. (ed.) ESOP 2007. LNCS, vol. 4421, pp. 33–47. Springer, Heidelberg (2007)
21. Lapadula, A., Pugliese, R., Tiezzi, F.: A Calculus for Orchestration of Web Services (full version). Technical report, Dipartimento di Sistemi e Informatica, Univ. Firenze (2007), http://rap.dsi.unifi.it/cows
22. Mayer, P., Schroeder, A., Koch, N.: Mdd4soa: Model-driven service orchestration. In: Proc. of EDOC 2008, pp. 203–212. IEEE Computer Society, Los Alamitos (2008)

23. Mazzanti, F.: UMC User Guide v3.3. Technical Report 2006-TR-33, Istituto di Scienza e Tecnologie dell'Informazione "A. Faedo". CNR (2006), http://fmt.isti.cnr.it/WEBPAPER/UMC-UG33.pdf

24. ter Beek, M.H., Fantechi, A., Gnesi, S., Mazzanti, F.: An action/state-based model-checking approach for the analysis of communication protocols for service-oriented applications. In: Leue, S., Merino, P. (eds.) FMICS 2007. LNCS, vol. 4916, pp. 133–148. Springer, Heidelberg (2008)

25. ter Beek, M.H., Gnesi, S., Koch, N., Mazzanti, F.: Formal verification of an automotive scenario in service-oriented computing. In: Proc. of ICSE 2008, pp. 613–622. ACM Press, New York (2008)

26. ter Beek, M.H., Gnesi, S., Mazzanti, F., Moiso, C.: Formal modelling and verification of an asynchronous extension of soap. In: Proc. of ECOWS 2006, pp. 287–296. IEEE Computer Society, Los Alamitos (2006)

27. ter Beek, M.H., Mazzanti, F., Gnesi, S.: CMC-UMC: A framework for the verification of abstract service-oriented properties. In: Proc. of SAC 2009, pp. 2111–2117. ACM Press, New York (2009)

28. Unified Modeling Language, http://www.uml.org/

29. Vieira, H.T., Caires, L., Seco, J.C.: The conversation calculus: A model of service oriented computation. In: Gairing, M. (ed.) ESOP 2008. LNCS, vol. 4960, pp. 269–283. Springer, Heidelberg (2008)

30. Vieira, H.T., Caires, L., Sousa, D.: Checking Services Conformance Based on Spatial Logic Model-Checking (revised). Technical Report TR-DI/FCT/UNL-04/2009, Departamento de Informática, Universidade Nova de Lisboa (2009)

31. Vieira, H.T., Caires, L., Viegas, R.: The Spatial Logic Model Checker, http://ctp.di.fct.unl.pt/SLMC/

32. Vieira, H.T., Caires, L., Viegas, R.: The Spatial Logic Model Checker User's Manual v1.0. Technical Report TR-DI/FCT/UNL-05/2005, Departamento de Informática, Universidade Nova de Lisboa (2005)

33. Web Services Choreography Working Group WCDL. Web Services Choreography Description Language: Primer (2006), http://www.w3.org/TR/2006/WD-ws-cdl-10-primer-20060619/

Specification and Analysis of Dynamically-Reconfigurable Service Architectures[*]

Howard Foster[1], Arun Mukhija[2],
David S. Rosenblum[2], and Sebastian Uchitel[1]

[1] London Software Systems, Dept. of Computing, Imperial College London,
180 Queen's Gate, London SW7 2BZ, UK
{hf1,su2}@doc.ic.ac.uk
[2] London Software Systems, Dept. of Computer Science, University College London,
Gower Street, London WC1E 6BT, UK
{a.mukhija,d.rosenblum}@cs.ucl.ac.uk

Abstract. A Service-Oriented Computing (SoC) architecture consists of a number of collaborating services to achieve one or more goals. Traditionally, the focus of developing services (as software components) has been on the static binding of these services within a single context and constrained in an individual manner. However, service architectures should be dynamic, where service binding and context changes with environmental changes. The task of designing and analysing such architectures becomes very complex. In this chapter we discuss a specification profile and analysis framework for service modes. A service mode provides an encapsulation of both specification and adaptation in different service scenarios. The approach is implemented as a tool suite and integrated into the Eclipse IDE.

1   Introduction

A service mode abstracts a set of services, and their states, that collaborate towards a common service system goal [3]. In Service-Oriented Computing (SOC), a mode can be used to identify which services are required in a service composition and assist in specifying orchestration and choreography requirements through service component state changes. They are specifically aimed towards addressing reconfiguration management within a self-managed service system. The need for such management is highly desirable as we increasingly rely on distributed networks of interrelated systems through the extensive growth and use of the Internet. One highly practical application of modes is to describe the requirements and capabilities for dynamic service brokers in an Service-Oriented Architecture (SOA), detailing specifications of both required and provided service characteristics in a particular system state. Modes also define an operating environment by way of component behaviour and architectural constraints. In the SOA pattern for example, a dynamic service brokering solution needs

---

[*] This work has been partially sponsored by the project SENSORIA, IST-2005-016004.

M. Wirsing and M. Hölzl (Eds.): SENSORIA Project, LNCS 6582, pp. 428–446, 2011.

to address issues of how to specify the Quality-of-Service (QoS) requirements and capabilities, and how to select the most appropriate functionally-equivalent service based on the QoS required and offered. To assist service engineers in modelling service-oriented software systems we describe a modelling profile for Service Modes which captures the specification of collaborating components and services, and provides a mechanism to describe how service adaptation is specified in different modes of operation of the system.

Once the specifications are constructed, they can be analysed for interesting properties of service architecture reconfigurations. For example, in the profile there is a specification of behaviour at three levels for adaptation; 1) the mode composition level, 2) the service mode level and 3) the service component level. Ensuring that the behaviour across these levels is safe and consistent becomes complex without formal and mechanical techniques. We define three properties of analysis which assist service engineers in assessing the suitability of service architecture configurations and provide feedback to improve their quality and reliability. Our work described in this chapter aims to integrate service modelling, self-management concepts and dynamic service brokering to enhance service engineering to cater for change, adaptive and extendible service solutions.

The remainder of this chapter is structured as follows. Section 2 provides a background to software architecture modes and discusses the requirements for dynamic and adaptive service brokering. Section 3 presents a case study which has been used to drive the profile and analysis for service modes. Section 4 details the modelling profile and illustrates a specification with an example from the case study. Section 5 describes the mappings of models built using the profile to formal models in Darwin and the Finite State Processes notation, whilst section 6 discusses the properties and techniques for analysis of these formal models. Section 7 presents an implementation of these techniques and discusses limitations of the current approach. Section 8 concludes the paper with a summary and a view on future work.

2   Background and Related Work

Self-management of software systems is typically described as a combination of self-assembly, self-healing and self-optimisation. Self-management of systems is not a new idea, with ideas from both the cybernetics [17] and system theory [16] worlds. As discussed in [15] however, one of the main existing problems in self-management is to understand the relationship between the system and its subsystems: can we predict a system's behaviour and can we design a system with behaviour specified for all situations?

2.1   Software Architecture Modes

Software Architecture Modes [5] have been proposed as an abstraction to assist in specifying and analysing dynamic and adaptive software component configurations. Software Architecture Modes are an abstraction of a specific set of services that must interact for the completion of a specific subsystem task, i.e., a mode will determine the structural constraints that rule a (sub)system configuration at runtime. Therefore, passing from one mode to another and interactions among different modes formalise the evolution constraints that a system must satisfy: the properties that reconfiguration must satisfy to obtain a valid transition between two modes which determine the structural constraints imposed to the corresponding architectural instances. At a high-level view, a Software Architecture Mode as defined by Hirsch covers four areas of model specification using the Darwin Architecture Description Language (ADL):

Component Models. Darwin supports a hierarchical model, is tractable, and is accompanied by a corresponding graphical notation. The central abstractions managed by Darwin are components and ports. Ports are the means by which components interact. Ports represent services that components either provide to or require from other components. A port is associated with a type: the interface of the service it provides or requires.

Behavioural Specifications. The behaviour of components in Darwin is specified both graphically as a Labelled Transition System (LTS) and textually using the Finite State Processes (FSP) notation. The behaviour of an architecture in Darwin is the composition of the behaviours of its individual component constituents, i.e. the parallel composition of the respective LTSs. The resulting LTS can be checked for such properties as the preservation of system invariants or the existence of deadlocks.

Dynamism and Adaptation. Darwin's concern in supporting dynamic structures is to capture as much as possible of the structure of the evolving system while maintaining its purely declarative form. Architectural modifications at runtime may cause disruption to behavioural aspects of the system such as triggering a deadlock. Changes to a system's structure may only be performed when it is not in the process of exchanging application messages with its environment (quiescent state).

Mode Extensions. A mode is specified by adding a new attribute to components that indicates the mode in which the component is in the corresponding architectural instance. In the case of basic components, the mode identifies the state of the component. For composite ones, the mode for a composite component is directly related with the modes of its constituents. The assumption is that each component is in one mode at a time. Interface ports are either enabled or disabled for binding to other components.

Hirsch's introduction to modes included architectural configuration but did not elaborate on component behavioural change as part of mode adaptation. Consequently, the concept of mode architectures has been extended with behavioural adaptation in [8], focusing on modes as behavioural specifications relating to architecture specification albeit indirectly. The concept of modes complements that of Architectural Design Rewriting (ADR), which has been described in Chapter 1-4. ADR is based on term-rewriting and formalises the development and reconfiguration of style-consistent software architectures. In ADR an architectural style consists of a set of architectural elements and operations called productions which define the well-formed compositions of architectures. Broadly, a term built out of such ingredients constitutes the proof that a design was constructed according to the style, and the value of the term is the constructed software architecture. In this sense, a Mode is an architectural style whose productions are focused on architectural reconfiguration and behavioural correctness.

2.2   Service Modeling and Composition

Related work towards dynamic service architecture and adaptation falls in to two categories, service modelling and service composition. Whilst there have been several Unified Modeling Language (UML) profiles proposed for modelling requirements of services and SOA [6,9], these profiles generally provide a set of stereotypes that focus only on static service artefacts, including a service specifications (interfaces), gateway (ports) and orchestrated collaboration (behaviour specifications). What is generally missing from these existing profile approaches is the ability to identify the requirements and capabilities of services and then to elaborate on the dynamic changes anticipated for adaptation or self-management. For the design of service compositions the dynamic composition of services has largely focused on planning techniques, such as in [14,10] with the specification of a guiding policy with some goals of service state. However, runtime service brokering also plays an important role in SOC being able to adapt component configurations between requesters and providers, yet there has been little coverage on providing analysis of requirements for brokering.

As an example of dynamic service brokering and adaptation the Dino Service Broker project [11] provides a runtime infrastructure and specification language for specifying service requirements including both functional and QoS properties. The Dino brokers are responsible for service discovery, selection, binding, delivery, monitoring and adaptation. Consequently, every service provided needs to specify its service capability (including both functional and QoS offerings) in the language provided by Dino. A service requester forwards its requirements specification document to a Dino broker at runtime, and thereby delegates the task of service discovery and selection to the broker. A shared understanding of the semantics of functional and QoS properties specified by service requesters and providers is achieved by referring to common ontologies.

To leverage the benefits of software architecture modes and service-oriented systems we proposed in [4] an integration of service modelling, self-management techniques and dynamic service brokering (for adaptation). In this chapter we focus on the specification, analysis and tool support of such architectures.

3   Case Study

Our work has been guided by the challenging requirements of service architecture and behaviour adaptation of the Automotive Case Study in SENSORIA. For details of this case study please refer to Part 7, Chapter 1. Our role is to support the service behavioural adaptation and deployment aspects of this case study and in particular, to provide a self-management approach. In this case study are a number of scenarios relating to a In-Vehicle Services Platform and the interactions, events and constraints that are posed on this services architecture. One particular scenario focuses upon Driving Assistance and a navigation system which undertakes route planning and user-interface assistance to a vehicle driver. Within this scenario are a number of events which change the operating mode of the navigation systems. For example, two vehicles are configured where one is a master and another is a slave. Events received by each vehicle service platform, for example an accident happens between vehicles, requires that the system adapts and changes mode to recover from the event. In a more complex example, the vehicles get separated on the highway (because, say, one of the drivers had to pull over), the master vehicle switches to planning mode and the slave vehicle to convoy. However, if an accident occurs behind the master and in front of the slave vehicle, meaning only the slave needs to detour it must somehow re-join the master vehicle route planning. The slave navigation system could firstly change to a detour mode (to avoid the accident), then switch to planning mode (to reach a point in range of the master vehicle), and finally switch to convoy mode when close enough to the master vehicle.

4   Service Modes

4.1   Overview

A Service Mode represents a scenario of a service system. It combines a service architecture with behaviour and policy specifications for service components within the service system and is intended to be evolved as new requirements are desired from the system. In this section we detail the specification of service modes by way of a Service Modes Profile in the UML2 notation.

4.2   Specification

A metamodel for service modes (illustrated in Fig. 1) extends and constrains a number of UML2 core elements. As an overview, a *ModeModel* defines a package which contains a number of service architecture scenarios (as *Mode* packages) and components and also contains a *ModeModelActivity* to define how to switch between different service scenarios. Each scenario is defined in a *Mode* package which is a container for a *ModeCollaboration* and describes the role that each component plays within the scenario (e.g. a service requester and/or a provider). Each *ModeCollaboration* holds a *ModeActivity* which describes the process in which the mode orchestration is fulfilled. Each *ModeCollaboration* also refines the components of the *Mode* for additional service adaptation requirements (such as the constraints for service brokering). We now elaborate on service mode architecture, behaviour and adaptation relationships.

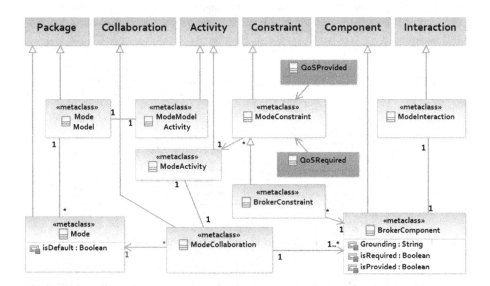

Fig. 1. A MetaModel for service modes and service brokering specification

A **Service Modes Architecture** consists of specifying the service components, their requirements and capabilities and interface specifications. A high-level architecture configuration is given in UML to represent the component specifications and their relationships. Each component will offer services to its clients, each such service is a component contract. A component specification defines a contract between clients requiring services, and implementers providing services. The contract is made up of two parts. The static part, or usage contract, specifies what clients must know in order to use provided services. The usage contract is defined by interfaces provided by a component, and required interfaces that specify what the component needs in order to function. The interfaces contain the available operations, their input and output parameters, exceptions they might raise, preconditions that must be met before a client can invoke the operation, and post conditions that clients can expect after invocation. These operations represent features and obligations that constitute a coherent offered or required service. At this level, the components are defined and connected in a static way, or in other words, the view of the component architecture represents a complete description disregarding the necessary state of collaboration for a given goal. Even if the designer wishes to restrict the component diagram to only those components which do collaborate, the necessary behaviour and constraints are not explicit to be able to determine how, in a given situation, the components should interact. An example composite structure diagram for a service modes architecture is illustrated in Fig. 2 for an In-Vehicle Service composition. Note that the architecture represents both local services (via a localDiscovery component) and remote services (remoteDiscovery via a Vehicle Services Gateway).

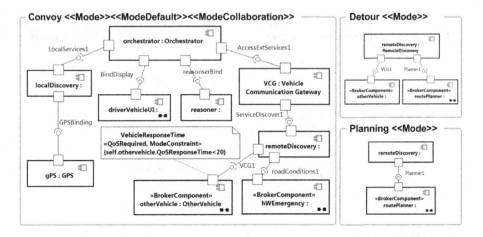

Fig. 2. In-Vehicle service brokering architecture with Modes MetaModel

Service Mode Behaviour specification is a local coordinated process of service interactions and events for mode changes. The behaviour is similar to that of service orchestrations, for which orchestrations languages such as the Web Service Business Process Execution Language (WS-BPEL) are widely adopted. Our work aligns closely with that of the SENSORIA UML4SOA [7] work which has developed UML Activity Diagram to WS-BPEL transformation routines. At design time however, the activities for mode orchestration consist of two concepts. Firstly, orchestrating the *default* composition of services required and provided in the specified mode architecture. Secondly, the orchestration should also be able to react to events which cause mode changes, or in other words cater for the switching between the modes specified in the different architecture configurations. To specify mode changes, the engineer adds event handlers (and follow on activities) to react to certain events which cause a mode change. An example Service Mode Behaviour is illustrated in Figure 3. Note the events that lead to mode changes, for example receiving notification of an accident from an Highway Emergency Service leads to a mode switch to a Detour mode configuration.

Service Dynamism and Adaptation focuses on constraining changes to architecture and services, identifying both functional and non-functional variants on the specification. Using the Service Modes Profile we identify ModeCollaborations (composite structure diagrams) with ModeConstraints (UML constraints) which are categorised further by a constraint stereotype. Alternatively, in the domain of Quality-Of-Service (QoS) a QoS Profile can be used to describe the required QoS when connecting a particular service partner (of a particular type and offering similar specifications of usage). A good example profile is based

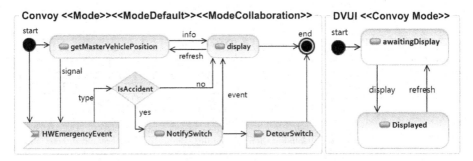

Fig. 3. Convoy service mode behaviour specified in activity diagram

upon a recommendation to the Object Management Group (OMG) in [12]. Additionally, architectural constraints may be specified in the Object Constraint Language (OCL) or another constraint based language. The constraint language adopted becomes an implementation-dependent aspect of analysing models in UML2. The ModeConstraint is itself extended to support a specific kind of adaptation, that for Service Brokering. A *BrokerComponent* defines a service component which is included in service brokering specifications and can be used to identify the role of the brokered component (either requested or provided), and holds a specification for the service profile. Additionally, one or more (*BrokerConstraints*) can be associated with a BrokerComponent, to identify the QoS either requested or provided by the service. An example constraint applied to a BrokerComponent is also illustrated in Fig. 2, in this case for the requirement that a *QoSResponseTime* should be offered less than 20ms by the OtherVehicle service.

As a summary of the semantics for the Service Modes profile, we list each stereotype and their constraints in Table 1.

5   Formal Models

Whilst the UML Service Modes Profile provides an easily accessible form of specifying service mode architecture models, they are more appropriate to visually clarify requirements than to mechanically analyse them. In addition, existing notations (such as Darwin and FSP) have good analyser tool support and are built on mathematical foundations. To build these models for analysis we provide a mapping between the elements of profile specifications and those in the formal notations.

5.1   Architecture Models

A Darwin model is a set of loosely coupled, context-independent software components, which communicate to achieve an overall goal. Components interact by accessing services. Each inter-component interaction is represented by a binding between a required service and a provided service. Our UML2toDarwin mapping

Table 1. Service mode profile semantics for UML2

Stereotype	Type	Element	Description
ModeModel	*extends*	Package	A Model containing Mode packages
	constraints	*self*	Only one Mode can have isDefault as *True*
ModeModelActivity	*extends*	Activity	The process flow for a ModeModel (policy)
	constraints	*self*	May only be associated with one ModeModel
Mode	*extends*	Package	A scenario for service collaborations
	property	isDefault	[Boolean] *True*: identifies a mode as a default mode
	constraints	*self*	Mode must be associated with a ModeModel
ModeCollaboration	*extends*	Collaboration	Contains composite structure and interactions
	constraints	*self*	Must be associated with one and only one Mode.
ModeActivity	*extends*	Activity	The process flow for a Mode (orchestration)
	constraints	*self*	May only be associated with one ModeCollaboration
ModeConstraint	*extends*	Constraint	Constraints on mode service or activity action
	constraints	*self*	Expressions specified in the Object Constraint Language.
ModeInteraction	*extends*	Interaction	Interaction protocol between Mode components
	constraints	*self*	Must be associated with one and only one ModeCollaboration
BrokerComponent	*extends*	Component	Service component to be brokered within a Mode
	property	isRequired	[Boolean] *True*: a requested service component for brokering
	property	isProvided	[Boolean] *True*: a provided service component for brokering
	property	Grounding	[String] the OWL-S document for service matching
BrokerConstraint	*extends*	ModeConstraint	A constraint on a BrokerComponent
	constraints	*self*	Expressions with QoS Ontology references.

extracts various elements of the UML2 Model to construct a Darwin specification. The process is as follows. Given an input of a UML Model, each of the packages in the model are scanned for ModeCollaborations, and a list is created. For each collaboration in the list, the set of elements is analysed for component structure diagrams and a set of components is generated in the Darwin specification. For each component connector within a ModeCollaboration, a series of Darwin *portals* are created to represent required and provided services in the ModeCollaboration, and instances of components in the relationship. An example mapping from a UML ModeBinding to a Darwin model representation is illustrated in Fig. 4.

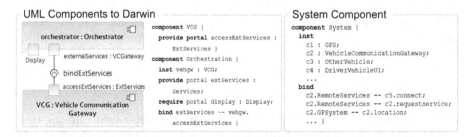

Fig. 4. Partial convoy mode architecture to Darwin ADL component

Additionally, a System component is added to the Darwin model to represent the architecture service composition by declaring instantiations of each service component in the architecture and by representing bindings between these service instances.

5.2   Behaviour Models

To build the behaviour models in the approach the FSP notation is used to formally describing the sequences of behaviour processes specified at both the ModeModel and ModeCollaboration levels of the service mode configurations. To facilitate this we have built several transformations which take either activity diagram, state machine or sequence charts and translate the process flow to corresponding FSP process statements. The fine detail around these translators is not the purpose of this chapter, however for context we provide a brief summary of each transformation. For complete details of transformation, the reader is invited to refer to [3].

A UML Activity Diagram consists of *activities, activityNodes, Edges, Guards* and *Weights*. An activityNode may be one of several types including Action, DataStore, DecisionNode, FlowNode, ForkNode, Event etc. For the purpose of our initial analysis we only consider the simple behaviour node types of Action, DecisionNode and ForkNode. For each mode architecture specified, one or more composition activity diagrams are located in the architecture package. To begin with the transformation identifies an initial (pseudo) node and locates any corresponding first actions by following the initial node edges. Depending on the type of action it encounters it produces a different FSP model. For example, if it encounters a DecisionNode then a guarded FSP process is created, which provides a choice of sequence progress in the FSP model depending on the value of an FSP variable. To represent a choice, an enumerated variable is created to provide alternative paths of execution. If however, the transformer encounters a ForkNode then a parallel process composition is created in the FSP model. Each path from the ForkNode is composed in this parallel process (representing a concurrent transition between the different activity paths in the diagram). Additionally, we represent Events (and their signals) as additional sequence processes in the FSP model. The FSP built from the transformation can be compiled as an LTS, for which an example of the Convoy Service Mode Behaviour is illustrated in Figure 5.

State Machine Transformation takes each of the state machines for each service and builds a corresponding FSP process composition. UML state machine diagrams depict the various states that an object may be in and the transitions between those states. A state machine consists of a series of *regions, states* and *transitions*. Regions include states and transitions. To begin with the transformation identifies an initial (pseudo) state and locates any corresponding first states by following the initial state transitions. If there is more than one transition from a state, then this is modelled as a choice (as the actual runtime may trigger these transitions in any order or not at all). Each transition builds a corresponding FSP sequential process which are composed when the traversal and

transformation of the entire state machine is completed. The result of building
processes and composing them generates an LTS. An LTS example for the DVUI
State Machine given earlier in this section is illustrated in Fig. 5.

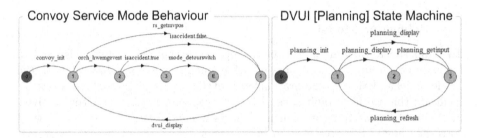

Fig. 5. LTS models of convoy service mode activity (left) and DriverVehicleUI [Planning] state machine (right)

5.3   Combined Models

Darwin ADL specifications and component behaviour models can be translated
to FSP process models using the mechanism discussed in [1]. Their approach
is aimed towards dynamic plug-ins and architecture analysis. The approach in
our work expands on theirs by considering evolving and dynamic models of service architecture whilst maintaining different configurations using the concept of
modes. Firstly, each service behaviour model is composed to build an architecture model. This represents a combined behaviour model of all service behaviour
linked in to a single architecture behaviour model. The transformation creates
an *ArchitectureBehaviour* process which consists of a parallel composition process of all the named service behaviour models created from the state machines
previously. Each state machine model has an initial and end state, and therefore they are composed and synchronised on these states. Secondly, the Service
Mode Behaviour model (transformed from the activity diagram) is included in
a *SystemBehaviour* process. The SystemBehaviour process is aligned with the
System component created in the earlier transformation from architecture to
Darwin ADL. Depending on the analysis required, different models are used as
analysis source, as described in section 6.mBehaviour process is aligned with
the System component created in the earlier transformation from architecture
to Darwin ADL.

6   Service Mode Analysis

It was mentioned at the beginning of this chapter three types of analysis for
a service modes architecture being protocol compatibility, behaviour reachability and modes composition analysis. These types of analysis effectively analyse
lower-level to higher-level aspects of a service modes architecture but others are
considered in future work.

Service *Protocol Compatibility* analyses the expected provided and required service interactions between services in each mode composition. This includes both the ordering of interactions in which services expect their methods to be called, but also the order that they call other service's methods. The process of analysis takes as input the architecture model produced in section 5.1 and analyses each mode service protocol with that of the other services in the architecture configuration. To achieve this an additional FSP process is created selecting only those services in a particular mode configuration (e.g. Convoy Mode) and composes these with both component architecture configuration instances and bindings (from the Darwin model) and service behaviour (from the service FSP model). The property for analysis is described as FSP in Figure 6, where interfaces are represented as variables (set), the || symbol defines a parallel composition, and each service is named from c1...cX. Relabelling using the FSP / operator binds the interfaces of different service components.

Mode *Behaviour Reachability* analyses the expected service composition behaviour with that which is offered by the services in the mode configuration. The goal is to take the behaviour model of the System and compare it to that of the Architecture (on analysis of the combined System and Architecture model described in section 5.3). To achieve this an additional FSP process is specified composing the combined model with that of a new process specification for the System behaviour model. This defines a new property to specify that the System behaviour model is used as the specification against that of the architecture model behaviour (i.e. with that of each of the service's provided behaviour). A deadlock occurs if the System behaviour process is not achievable given the service behaviour required and provided. Sample FSP for analysis is also listed in Fig. 6.

Protocol Compatibility

```
// Interfaces
set Display = {display, ...}
set RemoteServices = {connect, ...}
set Orchestrator = {display, ...}
// DVUI Interface Protocol
DVUI = (c3.init->DVUI_DISP),
DVUI_DISP = (c3.display->DVUI_DISP2),
// Architecture composition
||ConvoyModeArch = {
   c1:GPS||c2:VCG||c3:DVUI||...)
   /{c2.RemoteServices/c5.connect,
     c3.display/c4.display ... }
// Property for analysis
||Property = (ConvoyModeArch).
```

Behaviour Reachability

```
// reuse ConvoyModeArch Model
||Arch = {ConvoyModeArch}.
// FSP for Service Behaviour
GPS = (c1.default->GPS).
VCG = (c2.default->VCG).
DVUI = (c3.init->DVUI_DISP),
DVUI_DISP = (c3.display->DVUI_DISP2),
DVUI_DISP2 = (c3.refresh->DVUI_DISP).
// FSP for Mode Behaviour
MODEB = (c1.getMVehPosition->MODEB2),
MODEB2 = (c3.display->MODEB3), ...
||MODE = (Arch || MODEB).
// property for analysis
||Property = (MODE).
```

Fig. 6. FSP models for service protocol and behaviour analysis

The third type of analysis considered is that of *Modes Composition Analysis*. This analyses the composition of system behaviour specified in all the modes given in the Modes architecture specification. The goal is to ensure that *quiescence* (consistency of system state before and after changes) is upheld. For example, in the switch example from Convoy to Detour (given in Fig. 3) an event received by the composition activity for a HighwayEmergency eventually leads to a notification of architectural change to a Detour Mode. Using analysis through model-checking the service engineer can check whether the behaviour specified in this is compatible through the Detour Mode service composition behaviour receiving this notification. At runtime it would be expected that a coordinator agent manages the events and runtime architecture changes (e.g. swapping in and out different service composition processes).

7   Modes Tool Suite

The Modes Tool Suite provides a set of features to describe, extract, transform and analyse service architecture configurations based upon the specification and models described in earlier sections of this chapter. A prototype implementation of the Modes Tool Suite includes a Modes Model Parser for UML2, Modes Broker Extract for Service Broker Runtime artifacts and extensions to the LTSA Eclipse WS-Engineer tool (and plug-ins). In this section we detail each of these parts. The integrated tool suite is illustrated in Fig. 7, and is available from **http://www.ws-engineer.net**.

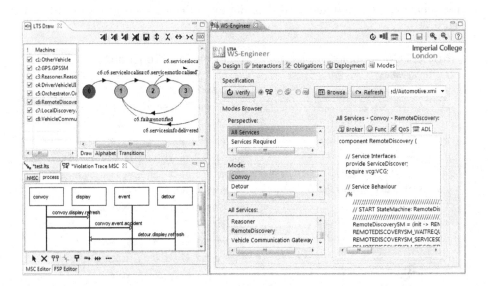

Fig. 7. LTSA WS-Engineer and service mode analysis

7.1   Modes Model Parser

The UMLModesParser component consists of a number of classes (illustrated in Fig. 8). The UMLModesParser component provides extract routines given a source UMLModesModel document. A UMLModesModel extends a UMLModel (inherited from the Eclipse Modeling Framework (EMF) for UML [2]) by providing utility functions for accessing and locating various Mode elements. A UMLModesModel consists of a series of elements of type Mode, ModeCollaboration, ModeConstraint and ModeActivity. A UMLModesModel identifies different modes by its UML package identification (ID) and provides an API to retrieve a package by id or by name. A list of mode names can also be retrieved using a helper function. Using core model traversing routines from the standard EMF packages, a UMLModelParser class provides routines to build a UML Model object of UML elements, types and relationships from the model supplied through the setModel operation. The build action is initiated by calling the parse operation. We extend this class with a UMLModesParser class which provides a parseModePackages operation. The operation initially parses the UML model and then builds a ModesModel object containing a list of each of the Modes located in the UMLModesModel.

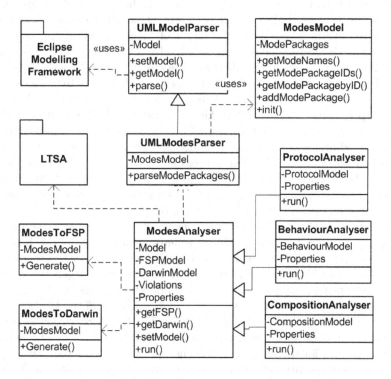

Fig. 8. Core mode parser and analyser classes in the modes tool suite

7.2   Modes Model Analyser

The ModesAnalyser class provides an encapsulation of the analysis techniques described in section 6. The class uses the functionality provided by the UMLModesParser component to transform a UMLModesModel document into formal models, in both FSP and Darwin ADL. A ModesToFSP class provides the transformation routines necessary for behavioural modelling of the ModesModel whilst the ModesToDarwin class provides transformation routines necessary for the interface and relationship modelling of the mode components in the model. The ModesAnalyser class also provides mechanisms to specify bespoke properties (e.g. fluents) to check against these models. The core ModesAnalyser component is extended into three further analysis components representing the *Protocol, Behaviour* and *Composition* analysis techniques described previously. The ModesAnalyser class uses the Labelled Transition System Analyser (LTSA) tool package to compile and check the properties once the ModesModel is transformed to FSP and Darwin.

7.3   Broker Extract Process

The Broker Extract process provides a process to build a set of modes and services for representing broker service requirements and capabilities. The process is illustrated in Fig. 9. For each Mode a set of ModeCollaboration elements are located. In each ModeCollaboration is defined a set of Components. A Component is identified as a candidate brokered service if it has either a stereotype of ServiceRequester or it has a UML Connector which relates the component to another component of type ServiceProvider. If a Service is identified then the service Operations, Ports and Interfaces are extracted. If a Port or Interface contains a child element of type ModeConstraint then this is also extracted. The extracted artifacts for the service are then used to create a Service, which is added to the ModesModel. The process is repeated for each component in a ModeCollaboration, and then for each Mode in the source model. At the end of the parse process, a ModesModel represents a series of Modes containing each of the extracted elements described previously.

The ModesBrokerExtract component consists of several classes to support this process. Firstly a list of BrokerModes is built, which contain the BrokerServices, and provides utility operations to assist retrieving these services for a given mode. The ModesBrokerExtract class inherits from a generic ModesExtract class which simply provides an access operation to the Modes in a model (using the UMLModesParser class). Each Service in each of the BrokerModes is implemented as a class of type BrokerService. The BrokerService class provides attributes for Operations, Constraints, a provide indicator IsProvider and a list of QoS attributes for the service. A QoS class provides an abstract data type for the attributes of Quality of Service aspects in brokering by service matchmaking. The components and classes are illustrated in Fig. 10.

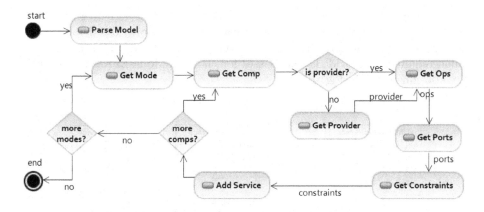

Fig. 9. Activity Diagram of ModesBrokerExtract class

7.4   Modes Browser

The Modes Browser Component and classes (also illustrated in Fig. 10) provide a useful helper component to navigate through modes, retrieving required and provided services and to assist in generating requirement and capability specifications for dynamic service brokering. The generic component does not generate any requirements or capabilities (as this is broker specific). The navigation through modes uses the results of the Modes Broker Extract Component (described in section 7.3). The API for the browser provides operations to changeMode (which switches the list of services to those identified in a particular ModePackage), getRequiredServices (retrieves a list of services that request Provided Services in the current mode), getProvidedServices (retrieves a list of services that offer a Service in the current mode), getQoS which retrieves a list of QoS elements for each service in the current mode, and getConstraints which retrieves a list of ModeContraints for the current mode.

7.5   Dino Service Broker Runtime Artifacts

The Modes Tool Suite also includes an example extension (DinoModesBrowser) specifically aimed at generating artifacts for the Dino Service Broker runtime. For each service a selection of two service deployment artefacts are available. The first is a functional specification. This document provides a functional description of the service. The functionality of a required or provided service is defined using OWL-S [13], which is an OWL-based ontology for Web services and is an emerging standard for the semantic specification of the functionality of services. An OWL-S description of a service has three parts: profile, process model and grounding. A profile describes the capability of a service operation in terms of its input, output, preconditions and effects; a process model describes details of service operations in terms of atomic, simple and composite processes and a grounding describes details of how to invoke a service operation, and is usually mapped to the service interface description of the service operation. Secondly, a non-functional specification is available, which provides details of the constraints for service brokering with a service identification, QoS attribute and value required or provided. The classes for the DinoModesBrowser extensions are also illustrated in Fig. 10.

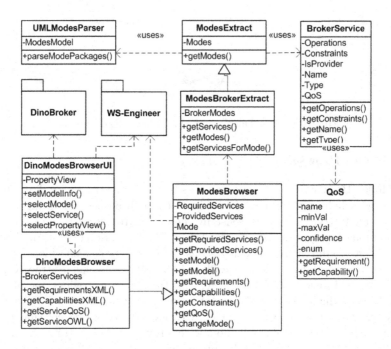

Fig. 10. Mode Broker and Extract Classes in the Modes Tool Suite

7.6   Limitations

The modelling and analysis currently only considers the structural elements of the architecture combined with behaviour specification. In practice there should also be a higher-level policy, which in addition to the service constraints, governs when mode switches can occur and how the coordination should be realised across a distributed services architecture. This policy may take many forms, but is likely to be in a distributed management specification (such as the PONDER2 language) or also include behavioural specification in the form of the Web Service Choreography Description Language (WS-CDL).

8   Conclusions and Future Work

This chapter presented an introduction to the concepts of Service Mode Architectures, and more specifically their specification, analysis and tool support.

Our contribution is aimed at providing easily accessible and practical tools for service engineers to develop adaptive and evolving service architectures and we believe the concept of service modes provides a practical level of abstraction for them to achieve this. We have focused on one case study of SENSORIA for validation, that being the Automotive Case Study. We have suggested modes as an alternative way of addressing operational adaptation, yet modes can also be applied to other domains where adaptation and reconfiguration are needed. Using model checking techniques, we have shown some analysis of service mode models produced from the specifications of these architectures.

Future work will continue to examine efficient transformation routines, enhancing the interpretation of different constructs within service architecture specifications and enabling different notations to be used. In particular we wish to extend the analysis to consider service mode policies and their constraints against architecture specifications. The concept of generating alternative modes is also possible using other architecture analysis tools and analysing this with an overall service adaptation policy specification.

References

1. Chatley, R., Eisenbach, S., Kramer, J., Magee, J., Uchitel, S.: Predictable dynamic plugin systems. In: 7th International Conference on Fundamental Approaches to Software Engineering, Barcelona, Spain (2004)
2. EMF. EMF: The eclipse modeling framework (2008), http://www-.eclipse.org/EMF
3. Foster, H.: Architecture and behaviour analysis for engineering service modes. In: Proceedings of the 2nd Workshop on Principles of Engineering Service Oriented Systems (PESOS) at ICSE 2009, Vancouver, Canada (2009)
4. Foster, H., Uchitel, S., Kramer, J., Magee, J.: Towards self-management in service-oriented computing with modes. In: Di Nitto, E., Ripeanu, M. (eds.) ICSOC 2007. LNCS, vol. 4907, pp. 338–350. Springer, Heidelberg (2009)
5. Hirsch, D., Kramer, J., Magee, J., Uchitel, S.: Modes for software architectures. In: Gruhn, V., Oquendo, F. (eds.) EWSA 2006. LNCS, vol. 4344, pp. 113–126. Springer, Heidelberg (2006)
6. Johnston, S.: UML 2.0 profile for software services. Request For Proposal - AD/02-01/07 (2005), http://www-128.ibm.com/developerworks/rational/library/05/419soa
7. Koch, N., Mayer, P., Heckel, R., Gönczy, L., Montangero, C.: D1.4b: UML for service-oriented systems. Technical Report (October 2007)
8. Kofroň, J., Plášil, F., Šerý, O.: Modes in component behavior specification via EBP and their application in product lines. Information and Software Technology 51(1), 31–41 (2009)
9. Machado, R.J., Fernandes, J.M., Monteiro, P., Rodrigues, H.: Transformation of UML models for service-oriented software architectures. In: Proceedings of the 12th IEEE International Conference and Workshops on Engineering of Computer-Based Systems, Washington, DC, USA, pp. 173–182 (2005)
10. Medjahed, B., Bouguettaya, A., Elmagarmid, A.: Composing web services on the semantic web. VLDB Journal, 333–351 (2003)

11. Mukhija, A., Dingwall-Smith, A., Rosenblum, D.S.: QoS-aware service composition in dino. In: ECOWS 2007: Proceedings of the Fifth European Conference on Web Services, Halle, Germany, pp. 3–12. IEEE Computer Society, Los Alamitos (2007)

12. OMG. UML profile for modeling quality of service and fault tolerance characteristics and mechanisms. *Request For Proposal - AD/02-01/07* (2002)

13. OWL-S. OWL-based web service ontology, version 1.1. The DARPA Program for DAML (November 2004), http://www-.daml.org/services/owl-s/

14. Pistore, M., Marconi, A., Bertoli, P., Traverso, P.: Automated composition of web services by planning at the knowledge level. In: Proceedings of the International Joint Conference on Artificial Intelligence, IJCAI (2005)

15. Roy, P.V.: Self management and the future of software design. In: Formal Aspects of Component Software (FACS 2006), Prague, Czech Republic (2006)

16. Von Bertalanffy, L.: General System Theory: Foundations, Development, Applications. George Braziller, New York (1969)

17. Wiener, N.: Cybernetics, or Control and Communication in the Animal and the Machine. MIT Press, Cambridge (1948)

SoSL: A Service-Oriented Stochastic Logic[*]

Rocco De Nicola[1], Diego Latella[2], Michele Loreti[1], and Mieke Massink[2]

[1] Dipartimento di Sistemi e Informatica - Università di Firenze
{rocco.denicola,michele.loreti}@unifi.it
[2] Istituto di Scienza e Tecnologie dell'Informazione "A. Faedo"- CNR
{diego.latella,mieke.massink}@isti.cnr.it

Abstract. The Temporal *M*obile *S*tochastic *L*ogic (MoSL) has been introduced in previous works by the authors for formulating properties of systems specified in STOKLAIM, a Markovian extension of KLAIM. The main purpose of MoSL is addressing key functional aspects of network aware programming such as distribution awareness, mobility and security and to guarantee their integration with performance and dependability guarantees. In this paper we present SoSL, a variant of MoSL, designed for dealing with specific features of Service-Oriented Computing (SOC). We also show how SoSL formulae can be model-checked against systems descriptions expressed with MarCaSPiS, a process calculus designed for addressing quantitative aspects of SOC. In order to perform actual model checking, we rely on a dedicated front-end that uses existing state-based stochastic model-checkers, like e.g. the Markov Reward Model Checker (MRMC).

1 Introduction

Important features of services are compositionality, context-independence, encapsulation and re-usability. To support the formal design and analysis of SOC applications recently a number of Service-Oriented Calculi have been proposed, see e.g. Chapter 2-1 in this volume.

Most of the proposed calculi are based on process algebras enriched with primitives specific to service-orientation such as operators for manipulating semi-structured data, mechanisms for describing safe client-service interactions, constructors for composing possibly unreliable services and techniques for query and discovery of services.

These calculi provide clean mathematical foundations for modeling typical aspects of SOC like safe service composition, service interaction and service orchestration.

Besides qualitative aspects of service-oriented systems it is also important that phenomena related to performance and dependability are addressed to deal with issues related to quality of service. These aspects are particularly relevant for this class of systems because often the latter rely on components interacting

---

[*] This work has been partially sponsored by the project SENSORIA, IST-2005-016004.

M. Wirsing and M. Hölzl (Eds.): SENSORIA Project, LNCS 6582, pp. 447–466, 2011.

over networks where failures are likely and congestion may cause unpredictable delays.

Traditional performance modeling techniques such as queuing networks and stochastic variants of Petri nets are widely adopted to describe performance and dependability models. Their lack of compositionality, however, hinders their usability when considering systems with many components: it is generally difficult, if not impossible, to "glue" components specifications together to obtain a global model of the system. These considerations have led to the development of stochastic extensions of *process algebras* (see e.g. [5]), since these formalisms assign great importance to compositionality. Different methods have then been devised to associate Continuous Time Markov Chains (CTMC) to terms of process algebras and tools inspired by the process algebras community have been developed to analyze the resulting models. Performance and dependability *guarantees*, have thus been described as temporal logic formulae, and verified in a fully automated manner by using stochastic model checking.

With stochastic model-checking, one can automatically check whether a performance or dependability requirement is fulfilled by a specific system model. Moreover, model-checking tools not only provide a *yes/no* answer, but do provide *also* the values of the probabilities of interest. In this sense, stochastic model-checkers incorporate also the functionality of traditional Markov Chain analysis tools. Also, functional properties of behavior, usually expressed by temporal logics like CTL [8], can be often characterized by formulae of *stochastic* temporal logics, where the degenerate probability values 0 and 1 are used. This means that stochastic logics permit formulating and automatically checking *both* functional *and* non-functional properties of system behavior in an *integrated* way, *within the same* formalism.

One of the most widely used stochastic logic for CTMCs, is CSL (Continuous Stochastic Logic) [2,3], a stochastic extension of CTL that, together with qualitative properties, permits specifying time-bounded probabilistic reachability properties, such as "the likelihood to reach a goal state within t time units while visiting only legal states is at least 0.92". Several software tools have been developed for supporting verification of CSL formulae; here, we just mention PRISM [23] and MRMC [22].

In this work, we provide

- a stochastic (Markovian) extension for one of the service-oriented calculi considered in the SENSORIA Project
- a stochastic logic to reason over the terms of the introduced calculus.

The calculus we consider is CASPIS, a *Calculus of Sessions and Pipelines* [4] that relies on *sessions* and *pipelines* as natural constructors for structuring client-service interaction and service orchestration. To associate a Continuous Time Markov Chain (CTMC) to each CASPIS terms, we take advantage of a versatile technique for the definition of structured operational semantics (SOS) of stochastic process languages which solves in an elegant way the problem of transition multiplicity and is well suited for dealing with two-party CCS-like interaction paradigm which is typical for service-oriented approaches [12] and has been already exploited for providing elegant and uniform semantics of a number of stochastic extensions of process calculi [11].

We adapt the apparent rate approach proposed for a process algebra with multi-party (CSP-like) synchronization by Hillston [21] to a calculus with *two-party* (CCS-like) synchronization while guaranteeing *associativity and commutativity* of parallel composition with respect to a bisimulation-based behavioral equivalence on MarCaSPiS terms that induces the same equalities as those obtained via Strong Markovian Equivalence, as discussed in [12]. According to our approach, the transition relation associates each pair of MarCaSPiS terms and actions to a *function* from MarCaSPiS terms to transition rates that maps each MarCaSPiS term into the rate with which it can be reached from the term at the source of the transition, via the action.

The logic we consider is a variant of MoSL (*Mobile Stochastic Logic*) [9], a logic that allows one to refer to the spatial structure of the network for the specification of properties for STOKLAIM models. Our starting-point was an action-based variant of CSL (as first proposed in [20]), that fits well with the action-based nature of KLAIM. The distinguishing features of MoSL, with respect to CSL, are:

- atomic propositions may refer to the sites where data and processes reside,
- actions are generalized to *action specifiers* that act as patterns to characterize sets of actions, and
- logical variables are incorporated to refer to dynamically created sites.

The logic we introduce in this work is SoSL, a variant of MoSL [9], specifically designed for dealing with specific features of Service-Oriented Computing. SoSL is a *temporal logic* that permits describing the dynamic evolution of the system and it is both *action*- and *state*-based and it is equipped with primitives that permit the use of real-time bounds in the logical characterization of the behaviors of interest. Moreover, SoSL is a *probabilistic logic* that permits expressing not only functional properties, but also properties related to performance and dependability aspects. Finally, SoSL is a *resource oriented logic*, which permits addressing openendedness of SOC. Indeed, SoSL provides modal operators that can be used for specifying how a system is able to react to an *external stimulus*. These allow the verification of assumptions on resources and processes in a system at the logical level, i.e. without having to change the model to investigate the effect of each assumption on the system behaviour.

We also have developed ways for model-checking SoSL formulae against MarCaSPiS specifications by exploiting existing state-based stochastic model-checkers, like e.g. the Markov Reward Model Checker (MRMC). We use techniques similar to those presented in [20] and a front-end for MarCaSPiS, named SoSL-MC, embedding MRMC as a component of the SoSL model-checking algorithm.

2   Preliminaries

We let $\mathbb{N}_{\geq 0}$ ($\mathbb{R}_{\geq 0}$, respectively) denote the set $\{n \in \mathbb{N} \mid n \geq 0\}$ ($\{x \in \mathbb{R} \mid x \geq 0\}$, respectively) and, similarly, $\mathbb{N}_{>0}$ ($\mathbb{R}_{>0}$, respectively) denote the set $\{n \in \mathbb{N} \mid n > 0\}$ ($\{x \in \mathbb{R} \mid x > 0\}$, respectively). For set S we let 2^S denote the power-set of S and 2^S_{fin} the set of *finite* subsets of S. In function definitions as well as application *Currying* will be used whenever convenient.

Definition 1 (Negative Exponential Distributions). *A random variable X has a* negative exponential distribution *with rate $\lambda \in \mathbb{R}_{>0}$ if and only if $\mathbb{P}\{X \leq t\} = 1 - e^{-\lambda \cdot t}$ for $t > 0$ and 0 otherwise.* •

The expected value of an exponentially distributed *random variable* (r.v.) with rate λ is λ^{-1} while its variance is λ^{-2}. The MIN of exponentially distributed independent r.v. $X_1, \dots, X_n$ with rates $\lambda_1, \dots, \lambda_n$ respectively is an exponentially distributed r.v. with rate $\lambda_1 + \dots + \lambda_n$ while the probability that X_j is the MIN is $\frac{\lambda_j}{\lambda_1 + \dots + \lambda_n}$. The MAX of exponentially distributed r.v. is not exponentially distributed.

For countable non-empty set S, we consider the set $S \to \mathbb{R}_{\geq 0}$ of total functions from S to $\mathbb{R}_{\geq 0}$. We let $\mathscr{P}, \mathscr{Q}, \mathscr{R}, \dots$ range over $S \to \mathbb{R}_{\geq 0}$. We let $[]$ denote the 0 constant function in $S \to \mathbb{R}_{\geq 0}$, i.e. $[]\, s \;=_{\text{def}}\; 0$ for all $s \in S$; moreover given $s_1, \dots, s_n \in S$ and, $\lambda_1, \dots, \lambda_n \in \mathbb{R}_{>0}$ we let $[s_1 \mapsto \lambda_1, \dots, s_n \mapsto \lambda_n]$ denote the function in $S \to \mathbb{R}_{\geq 0}$ which maps s_1 to $\lambda_1, \dots, s_n$ to λ_n and any $s \in S \setminus \{s_1, \dots, s_n\}$ to 0. The following definition characterizes *Rate Transition Systems* [12].

Definition 2 (Rate Transition Systems). *A* Rate Transition System *(RTS) is a tuple $(S, A, \rightarrowtail)$ where S is a countable* non-empty *set of states, A is a countable non-empty set of labels and $\rightarrowtail \subseteq S \times A \times (S \to \mathbb{R}_{\geq 0})$ is the transition relation.*

In the sequel RTSs will be denoted by $\mathcal{R}, \mathcal{R}_1, \mathcal{R}', \dots$ As usual, we let $s \overset{\alpha}{\rightarrowtail} \mathscr{P}$ denote $(s, \alpha, \mathscr{P}) \in \rightarrowtail$. Intuitively, $s_1 \overset{\alpha}{\rightarrowtail} \mathscr{P}$ and $(\mathscr{P}\, s_2) = \lambda \neq 0$ means that s_2 is reachable from s_1 via the execution of α and that the duration of such an execution is characterized by a random variable whose distribution function is negative exponential with rate λ. On the other hand, $(\mathscr{P}\, s_2) = 0$ means that s_2 is not reachable from s_1 via α.

Definition 3 (Σ_S). *Σ_S denotes the subset of $S \to \mathbb{R}_{\geq 0}$ including only all functions expressible using the $[\dots]$ notation, i.e. $\mathscr{P} \in \Sigma_S$ if and only if $\mathscr{P} = []$ or there exist $n > 0$, $s_1, \dots, s_n \in S$ and $\lambda_1, \dots, \lambda_n \in \mathbb{R}_{>0}$ such that $\mathscr{P} = [s_1 \mapsto \lambda_1, \dots, s_n \mapsto \lambda_n]$.* •

We equip Σ_S with a few useful operations, i.e. $+ : \Sigma_S \times \Sigma_S \to (S \to \mathbb{R}_{\geq 0})$ with $(\mathscr{P} + \mathscr{Q})\, s \;=_{\text{def}}\; (\mathscr{P}\, s) + (\mathscr{Q}\, s)$ and $\bigoplus : \Sigma_S \to 2^S \to \mathbb{R}_{\geq 0}$ with $\bigoplus \mathscr{P}\, C \;=_{\text{def}}\; \sum_{s \in C}(\mathscr{P}\, s)$, for $C \subseteq S$, and we use the shorthand $\oplus \mathscr{P}$ for $\bigoplus \mathscr{P}\, S$. The proposition below trivially follows from the relevant definitions:

Proposition 1. *(i) All functions in Σ_S yield zero almost everywhere, i.e. for all $\mathscr{P} \in \Sigma_S$ the set $\{s \in S \mid (\mathscr{P}\, s) \neq 0\}$ is finite; (ii) Σ_S is closed under $+$, i.e. $+ : \Sigma_S \to \Sigma_S \to \Sigma_S$.* $\qquad\qquad\square$

Proposition 1(i) above guarantees that $\bigoplus$ is well defined.

Definition 4. *Let $\mathcal{R} = (S, A, \rightarrowtail)$ be an RTS, then: (i) $\mathcal{R}$ is total if for all $s \in S$ and $\alpha \in A$ there exists $\mathscr{P} \in (S \to \mathbb{R}_{\geq 0})$ such that $s \xrightarrow{\alpha} \mathscr{P}$; (ii) $\mathcal{R}$ is functional [1] if for all $s \in S$, $\alpha \in A$, and $\mathscr{P}, \mathscr{Q} \in (S \to \mathbb{R}_{\geq 0})$ we have: $s \xrightarrow{\alpha} \mathscr{P}, s \xrightarrow{\alpha} \mathscr{Q} \implies \mathscr{P} = \mathscr{Q}$; (iii) $\mathcal{R}$ is a Σ_S-RTS if $\rightarrowtail \subseteq S \times A \times \Sigma_S$.* $\qquad\bullet$

In the sequel we consider only *functional Σ_S-RTS*.

2.1   Paths and Probability Measures

For the class of functional Σ_S-RTS we can easily associate a measure to computations (paths) following the same approach proposed in [3].

Definition 5. *If $\mathcal{R} = (S, A, \rightarrowtail)$ is a functional Σ_S-RTS and $A' \subseteq A$, we let:*

- $\mathcal{X} : S \times A \to \Sigma_S$ *be such that* $\mathcal{X}[s, \alpha] = \mathscr{P}$ *if and only if* $s \xrightarrow{\alpha} \mathscr{P}$;
- $\mathbf{E}^{A'}[s] = \sum_{\alpha \in A'} \oplus \mathcal{X}[s, \alpha]$;
- $\mathbf{R}^{A'}[s_1, \alpha, s_2] = \frac{\mathcal{X}[s_1, \alpha](s_2)}{\mathbf{E}^{A'}[s_1]}$.

A path π in $\mathcal{R} = (S, A, \rightarrowtail)$ with actions in $A' \subset A$ is a non-empty sequence of the form $s_0(\alpha_0, t_0)s_1(\alpha_1, t_1) \cdots$ where, for each $i \geq 0$: $s_i \in S$, $\alpha_i \in A'$, $t_i \in \mathbb{R}_{>0}$ and $\mathcal{X}[s_i, \alpha_i](s_{i+1}) > 0$. We say that π is *maximal* if and only if π is infinite or there exists j such that s_j is *absorbing*, i.e. $\mathcal{X}[s_j, \alpha] = []$ for all α.

For path $\pi = s_0\,(\alpha_0, t_0)\,s_1\,(\alpha_1, t_1) \cdots$, natural number j and $t \in \mathbb{R}_{\geq 0}$:

$$\mathsf{len}(\pi) \quad =_{\text{def}} \begin{cases} \infty \text{ if } \pi \text{ is infinite} \\ l \quad otherwise,\ \text{where } s_l \text{ is the absorbing state of } \pi \end{cases}$$

$$\mathsf{st}(\pi, j) \quad =_{\text{def}} \begin{cases} s_j \qquad \text{if } 0 \leq j \leq \mathsf{len}(\pi) \\ \text{undefined } otherwise \end{cases}$$

$$\mathsf{ac}(\pi, j) \quad =_{\text{def}} \begin{cases} \alpha_j \qquad \text{if } 0 \leq j < \mathsf{len}(\pi) \\ \text{undefined } otherwise \end{cases}$$

$$\mathsf{dl}(\pi, j) \quad =_{\text{def}} \begin{cases} t_j \qquad \text{if } 0 \leq j < \mathsf{len}(\pi) \\ \infty \qquad \text{if } j = \mathsf{len}(\pi) \\ \text{undefined } otherwise \end{cases}$$

$$\pi(t) \quad =_{\text{def}} \begin{cases} \mathsf{st}(\pi, \mathsf{len}(\pi)) \text{ if } t > \sum_{j=0}^{\mathsf{len}(\pi)-1} t_j \\ \mathsf{st}(\pi, m) \qquad otherwise,\ \text{where } m = \text{MIN}\{j \mid t \leq \sum_{k=0}^{j} t_k\} \end{cases}$$

---

[1] *Fully-stochastic according to the terminology used in [12].*

For each $s \in S$ and $A' \subseteq A$, $Paths_s^{A'}$ denotes the set of paths with actions in A' starting from s. We also let I, $I_0 \ldots$ denote *non-empty* intervals in $\mathbb{R}_{\geq 0}$ where we use $\inf I$ and $\sup I$ to denote lower and upper bound of I respectively.

The probability measure $\mathbb{P}_s^{A'}$ over $Path_s^{A'}$ can be defined by considering the smallest σ-algebra on $Prob_s^{A'}$ containing all the cylinder sets

$$C(s_0, (\alpha_0, I_0), \ldots, (\alpha_{n-1}, I_{n-1}), s_n)$$

that contain all the paths $s_0'(\alpha_0', t_0')s_1'(\alpha_1', t_1') \cdots s_i = s_i'$, $\alpha_i' = \alpha_i$ and $t_i \in I_i$ for $i : 0 \leq i \leq n$. The probability measure is defined inductively as follows:

- $\mathbb{P}_{s_0}^{A'}(C(s_0)) = 1$;
- $\mathbb{P}_{s_0}^{A'}(C(s_0, (\alpha_0, I_0), \ldots, s_n, (\alpha_n, I_n), s_{n+1})) =$

$$\mathbb{P}_{s_0}^{A'}(C(s_0, (\alpha_0, t_0), \ldots, s_n)) \cdot \mathbf{R}^{A'}[s_n, \alpha_n, s_{n+1}] \cdot \left(e^{-\inf I_n \cdot \mathbf{E}^{A'}[s_n]} - e^{-\sup I_n \cdot \mathbf{E}^{A'}[s_n]} \right)$$

3   MarCaSPiS: Markovian CaSPiS

In this section we recall a Markovian extension of CaSPiS (called MarCaSPiS) already presented in [10]. In MarCaSPiS, each *output activity* (service invocation, concretion and return) is equipped with a parameter (a *rate*, $\lambda \in \mathbb{R}_{>0}$) characterizing a random variable with a negative exponential distribution, modeling the duration of the activity. Furthermore, each *input activity* (service definition and abstractions) is annotated with a *weight* ($\omega \in \mathbb{N}_{>0}$): a positive integer that will be used for determining the probability that the specific input is selected when a complementary output is executed.

The stochastic operational semantics of MarCaSPiS is defined by means of RTS. Detailed discussions on MarCaSPiS and motivations on the proposed semantics can be found in [10].

3.1   Syntax and Stochastic Semantics of MarCaSPiS

The syntax of MarCaSPiS is presented in Fig. 1, where operators are listed in decreasing order of precedence while $\tilde{V}$ and $\tilde{F}$ denote a sequence of values and patterns respectively.

Let $\mathcal{N}$ be a countable set of *names* ranged over by $n, n', \ldots$. Set $\mathcal{N}$ contains two disjoint countable sets $\mathcal{N}_{\text{srv}}$ of *service* names $s, s', \ldots$ and $\mathcal{N}_{\text{sess}}$ of *session* names $r, r' \ldots$, such that $\mathcal{N} \setminus (\mathcal{N}_{\text{srv}} \cup \mathcal{N}_{\text{sess}})$ is infinite. The set $\mathcal{N} \setminus \mathcal{N}_{\text{sess}}$ is ranged over by $x, y, \ldots, u, v \ldots$.

The syntax of MarCaSPiS is similar to that of CaSPiS except for CaSPiS output activities, which are enriched with the rates of exponential distributions, and input activities, which are enriched with weights. We shall also assume that for each process **rec** $X.P$, variable X is not bound in P and occurs only guarded, i.e. prefixed by π, s^{ω} or $\overline{s}^{\lambda}$. Moreover, for each process P we assume that each session name r occurs in P at most twice and that for each process $r \triangleright Q$, r does not occur in Q. The set of all MarCaSPiS processes will be denoted by $\mathcal{C}$.

$$P, Q ::= A \qquad \text{Guarded Sum} \qquad\qquad \pi ::= (F)_\omega \quad \text{Abstraction}$$
$$| \; D \qquad\quad \text{Service Definitions} \qquad | \; \langle V \rangle_\lambda \quad \text{Concretion}$$
$$| \; I \qquad\quad\;\; \text{Service Invocations} \qquad | \; \langle V \rangle_\lambda^\uparrow \quad \text{Return}$$
$$| \; r \triangleright P \qquad \text{Session} \qquad\qquad\qquad A ::= \pi P \, | \, A + A$$
$$| \; P > Q \qquad \text{Pipeline} \qquad\qquad\quad D ::= s^\omega . P \, | \, D + D$$
$$| \; P | Q \qquad\; \text{Parallel Composition} \quad I ::= \bar{s}^\lambda . P \, | \, I + I$$
$$| \; (\nu n) P \qquad \text{Restriction}$$
$$| \; \mathbf{rec} \; X.P \quad \text{Recursion}$$
$$| \; X \qquad\quad\; \text{Process Variable}$$
$$V ::= u \, | \, f(\tilde{V}) \;\; (f \in \Sigma) \qquad\qquad F ::= \, ?x \, | \, u \, | \, f(\tilde{F}) \;\; (f \in \Sigma)$$

Fig. 1. Syntax of MarCaSPiS processes

$$P | (\nu n) Q \equiv (\nu n)(P | Q) \text{ if } n \notin \mathrm{fn}(P)$$
$$(\nu n)(\nu m) P \equiv (\nu m)(\nu n) P$$
$$((\nu n) Q) > P \equiv (\nu n)(Q > P) \text{ if } n \notin \mathrm{fn}(P)$$
$$r \triangleright (\nu n) P \equiv (\nu n)(r \triangleright P) \text{ if } r \neq n$$
$$(\nu m) P \equiv (\nu n) P[n/m] \text{ if } n \notin \mathrm{fn}(P)$$

Fig. 2. Structural congruence laws

Structural congruence $\equiv$ is defined as the least congruence relation induced by the laws in Fig. 2. This set of laws contains the structural rules for restriction from the π-calculus, plus the obvious extension of the restriction's scope extrusion law to pipelines and sessions. For each $P \in \mathcal{C}$ we let $[P]$ denote its structural congruence class and $rep([P])$ the associated representative while $\mathcal{C}_\equiv$ denotes the set of representatives of the elements in $\mathcal{C}$. We abstract from the particular definition of $rep([P])$. We usually write $rep[P]$ or even P instead of $rep([P])$, the intended meaning being clear from the context.

In order to define the RTS associated to MarCaSPiS processes we will use the labelled transition relation defined by the rules of Table 1 and Table 2.

We find it convenient to introduce the following notations and operations on next state functions.

Definition 6. *For each $\mathscr{P}, \mathscr{Q} : \mathcal{C} \to \mathbb{R}_{\geq 0}$ and $P, Q \in \mathcal{C}$, $C \subseteq \mathcal{C}$, we let:*

- $(\mathscr{P} + \mathscr{Q}) P = (\mathscr{P} P) + (\mathscr{Q} P)$
- $(\mathscr{P} | \mathscr{Q}) R = \mathbf{if} \; R = P | Q \; \mathbf{then} \; (\mathscr{P} P) \cdot (\mathscr{Q} Q) \; \mathbf{else} \; 0$
- $\left(\frac{\mathscr{P} \cdot \omega_1}{\omega_2} \right) P = \mathbf{if} \; \omega_2 \neq 0 \; \mathbf{then} \; \frac{(\mathscr{P} P) \cdot \omega_1}{\omega_2} \; \mathbf{else} \; 0, \; \text{where } \omega_1, \omega_2 \in \mathbb{R}_{\geq 0}$
- $\mathscr{P}_{/\equiv} P = \mathbf{if} \; P = rep[P] \; \mathbf{then} \; \bigoplus \mathscr{P} \, [P] \; \mathbf{else} \; 0$
- $\mathscr{P}[Q/X](R) = \sum_{\{P : P[Q/X] = R\}} \mathscr{P}(P).$

We let $\mathcal{A}$ be the set of transition labels α having the following syntax and names:

$$
\begin{aligned}
\alpha ::=\quad & \mu && \text{(interactions with environment)} \\
& \mid \gamma && \text{(internal interactions)} \\
& \mid \overleftrightarrow{r} && \text{(session interactions)} \\
& \mid (\nu n)\alpha && \text{(open)} \\
\mu ::=\quad & s(r) \mid \bar{s}(r) && \text{(service definition/invocation)} \\
& \mid \quad (V) \mid \langle V \rangle && \text{(value consumption/production)} \\
& \mid r : (V) \mid r : \langle V \rangle && \text{(consumption/production within session } r) \\
& \mid \uparrow V && \text{(value return)} \\
\gamma ::=\quad & \overleftrightarrow{s} && \text{(service synchronisation)} \\
& \mid \tau && \text{(silent step)}
\end{aligned}
$$

Labels μ identify the interactions of a process with the environment, labels γ identify internal synchronisations, while $\overleftrightarrow{r}$ and $(\nu n)\alpha$ identify an interaction over session r and the exection of action α under the scope of private name n.

We define names $n(\alpha)$, free names $fn(\alpha)$ and bound names $bn(\alpha)$ as expected; in particular $bn(s(r)) = bn(\bar{s}(r)) = \{r\}$ while $bn((\nu \tilde{n})\alpha) = \{\tilde{n}\} \cup bn(\alpha)$. In the sequel we also use $\tilde{\cdot}$ to denote sequence of elements.

Definition 7. *The operational semantics of* MarCaSPiS *processes is defined by means of an RTS* $\mathcal{R}_{MC} = (\mathcal{C}_\equiv, \mathcal{A}, \rightarrowtail_{/\equiv})$ *where:*

$$
rep([P]) \stackrel{\alpha}{\rightarrowtail}_\equiv \mathscr{P} \Leftrightarrow \exists Q \in [P] : Q \stackrel{\alpha}{\rightarrowtail} \mathscr{Q} \wedge \mathscr{P} = \mathscr{Q}_\equiv
$$

Rules OUT, IN, RET, INV and DEF describe the behavior of concretion, abstraction, return, service definition and service invocation. For instance, rule OUT states that expression $\langle V \rangle_\lambda P$ evolves to process P with rate λ, while IN states that if $\sigma = match(V, F)$ then $(F)_\omega P$ evolves to $P\sigma$ with weight ω.

Rule SUM states that $P + Q$ can behave either like P or like Q. Moreover, rates/weights of each transition are added to take multiplicity into account. For instance:

$$
\cfrac{\cfrac{}{\langle 3 \rangle_{.5}\mathbf{nil} \stackrel{\langle 3 \rangle}{\rightarrowtail} [\mathbf{nil} \mapsto .5]}\text{OUT} \quad \cfrac{}{\langle 3 \rangle_{.75}\mathbf{nil} \stackrel{\langle 3 \rangle}{\rightarrowtail} [\mathbf{nil} \mapsto .75]}\text{OUT}}{\langle 3 \rangle_{.5}\mathbf{nil} + \langle 3 \rangle_{.75}\mathbf{nil} \stackrel{\langle 3 \rangle}{\rightarrowtail} [\mathbf{nil} \mapsto 1.25]}\text{SUM}
$$

Rules S-OUT, S-IN and S-RET respectively state that each output ($\langle V \rangle$), input ((V)) and return ($\uparrow V$) performed within a session becomes a session output ($r : \langle V \rangle$), a session input ($r : (V)$) and an output.

Rule S-PASS states that if P performs a transition labelled α leading to $\mathscr{P}$ and α is not an input, an output or a return, and does not contain name r, the same transition is performed by $r \triangleright P$ leading to $r \triangleright \mathscr{P}$. Rule P-PASS behaves similarly.

Table 1. Stochastic Labelled Transition Relation (Part 1)

$$\frac{}{\langle V \rangle_\lambda P \overset{\langle V \rangle}{\rightharpoonup} [P \mapsto \lambda]} \ \text{Out} \qquad\qquad \frac{\sigma = match(V, F)}{(F)_\omega P \overset{\langle V \rangle}{\rightharpoonup} [P\sigma \mapsto \omega]} \ \text{In}$$

$$\frac{}{\langle V \rangle_\lambda^\uparrow P \overset{\uparrow V}{\rightharpoonup} [P \mapsto \lambda]} \ \text{Ret} \qquad\qquad \frac{r \notin \text{fn}(P)}{\overline{s}^\lambda.P \overset{\overline{s}(r)}{\rightharpoonup} [r \triangleright P \mapsto \lambda]} \ \text{Inv}$$

$$\frac{r \notin \text{fn}(P)}{s^\omega.P \overset{s(r)}{\rightharpoonup} [r \triangleright P \mapsto \omega]} \ \text{Def} \qquad\qquad \frac{P \overset{\alpha}{\rightharpoonup} \mathscr{P} \quad Q \overset{\alpha}{\rightharpoonup} \mathscr{Q}}{P + Q \overset{\alpha}{\rightharpoonup} \mathscr{P} + \mathscr{Q}} \ \text{Sum}$$

$$\frac{P \overset{\langle V \rangle}{\rightharpoonup} \mathscr{P}}{r \triangleright P \overset{r:\langle V \rangle}{\rightharpoonup} r \triangleright \mathscr{P}} \ \text{S-Out} \qquad\qquad \frac{P \overset{\langle V \rangle}{\rightharpoonup} \mathscr{P}}{r \triangleright P \overset{r:(V)}{\rightharpoonup} r \triangleright \mathscr{P}} \ \text{S-In}$$

$$\frac{P \overset{\uparrow V}{\rightharpoonup} \mathscr{P}}{r \triangleright P \overset{\langle V \rangle}{\rightharpoonup} r \triangleright \mathscr{P}} \ \text{S-Ret} \qquad\qquad \frac{P \overset{\alpha}{\rightharpoonup} \mathscr{P} \quad \alpha \neq \langle V \rangle, (V), \uparrow V \quad r \notin \text{fn}(\alpha)}{r \triangleright P \overset{\alpha}{\rightharpoonup} r \triangleright \mathscr{P}} \ \text{S-Pass}$$

$$\frac{P \overset{\alpha}{\rightharpoonup} \mathscr{P} \quad \alpha \neq \langle V \rangle, \tau}{P > Q \overset{\alpha}{\rightharpoonup} \mathscr{P} > Q} \ \text{P-Pass} \qquad\qquad \frac{P \overset{\tau}{\rightharpoonup} \mathscr{P} \quad \forall V. \left(P \overset{\langle V \rangle}{\rightharpoonup} \mathscr{P}_V, Q \overset{(V)}{\rightharpoonup} \mathscr{Q}_V \right)}{P > Q \overset{\tau}{\rightharpoonup} (\mathscr{P} > Q) + \Sigma_V \frac{(\mathscr{P}_V > Q) | \mathscr{Q}_V}{\oplus \mathscr{Q}_V}} \ \text{P-Sync}$$

$$\frac{P \overset{\alpha}{\rightharpoonup} \mathscr{P} \quad Q \overset{\alpha}{\rightharpoonup} \mathscr{Q} \quad \alpha \neq \overleftrightarrow{s}, \overleftrightarrow{r}, (\nu n)\alpha'}{P | Q \overset{\alpha}{\rightharpoonup} \mathscr{P} | Q + P | \mathscr{Q}} \ \text{Par}$$

$$\frac{P \overset{\overleftrightarrow{s}}{\rightharpoonup} \mathscr{P} \quad P \overset{s(r)}{\rightharpoonup} \mathscr{P}_d \quad P \overset{\overline{s}(r)}{\rightharpoonup} \mathscr{P}_i \quad Q \overset{\overleftrightarrow{s}}{\rightharpoonup} \mathscr{Q} \quad Q \overset{\overline{s}(r)}{\rightharpoonup} \mathscr{Q}_i \quad Q \overset{s(r)}{\rightharpoonup} \mathscr{Q}_d}{P | Q \overset{\overleftrightarrow{s}}{\rightharpoonup} \frac{\mathscr{P} | Q \cdot \oplus \mathscr{P}_d}{\oplus (\mathscr{P}_d + \mathscr{Q}_d)} + \frac{P | \mathscr{Q} \cdot \oplus \mathscr{Q}_d}{\oplus (\mathscr{P}_d + \mathscr{Q}_d)} + \frac{(\nu r)(\mathscr{P}_d | \mathscr{Q}_i)}{\oplus (\mathscr{P}_d + \mathscr{Q}_d)} + \frac{(\nu r)(\mathscr{P}_i | \mathscr{Q}_d)}{\oplus (\mathscr{P}_d + \mathscr{Q}_d)}} \ \text{Call}$$

$$\frac{P \overset{\overleftrightarrow{r}}{\rightharpoonup} \mathscr{P} \quad Q \overset{\overleftrightarrow{r}}{\rightharpoonup} \mathscr{Q} \quad \forall V. \left(P \overset{r:\langle V \rangle}{\rightharpoonup} \mathscr{P}_{\langle V \rangle} \quad P \overset{r:(V)}{\rightharpoonup} \mathscr{P}_{(V)} \quad Q \overset{r:\langle V \rangle}{\rightharpoonup} \mathscr{Q}_{\langle V \rangle} \quad Q \overset{r:(V)}{\rightharpoonup} \mathscr{Q}_{(V)} \right)}{P | Q \overset{\overleftrightarrow{r}}{\rightharpoonup} \mathscr{P} | Q + P | \mathscr{Q} + \Sigma_V \frac{\mathscr{P}_{\langle V \rangle} | \mathscr{Q}_{(V)}}{\oplus \mathscr{Q}_{(V)}} + \Sigma_V \frac{\mathscr{P}_{(V)} | \mathscr{Q}_{\langle V \rangle}}{\oplus \mathscr{P}_{(V)}}} \ \text{S-Sync}$$

$$\frac{P \overset{\alpha}{\rightharpoonup} \mathscr{P} \quad n \notin \text{n}(\alpha) \quad \alpha \neq \tau}{(\nu n)P \overset{\alpha}{\rightharpoonup} (\nu n)\mathscr{P}} \ \text{R-Pass} \qquad\qquad \frac{P \overset{\overleftrightarrow{n}}{\rightharpoonup} \mathscr{P}_n \quad P \overset{\tau}{\rightharpoonup} \mathscr{P}}{(\nu n)P \overset{\tau}{\rightharpoonup} (\nu n)(\mathscr{P}_n + \mathscr{P})} \ \text{Hide}$$

$$\frac{P \overset{\alpha}{\rightharpoonup} \mathscr{P} \quad \alpha = (\nu\tilde{n})\langle V \rangle, (\nu\tilde{n}) \uparrow V, (\nu\tilde{n})r : \langle V \rangle \quad n \notin \{\tilde{n}\} \quad n \in \text{fn}(V)}{(\nu n)P \overset{(\nu n)\alpha}{\rightharpoonup} \mathscr{P}} \ \text{Open}$$

$$\frac{P[\textbf{rec } X.P/X] \overset{\alpha}{\rightharpoonup} \mathscr{P}}{\textbf{rec } X.P \overset{\alpha}{\rightharpoonup} \mathscr{P}} \ \text{Rec} \qquad\qquad \frac{P \equiv Q \quad Q \overset{\alpha}{\rightharpoonup} \mathscr{P}}{P \overset{\alpha}{\rightharpoonup} \mathscr{P}_{/\equiv}} \ \text{Struct}$$

Table 2. Stochastic Labelled Transition Relation (Part 2)

$$\frac{\alpha \neq \langle V \rangle \quad bn(\alpha) \cap fn(\langle V \rangle_\lambda P) = \varnothing}{\langle V \rangle_\lambda P \overset{\alpha}{\rightarrowtail} []} \text{ F-Out} \qquad \frac{\alpha \neq \uparrow V \quad bn(\alpha) \cap fn(\langle V \rangle_\lambda P) = \varnothing}{\langle V \rangle^\uparrow_\lambda P \overset{\alpha}{\rightarrowtail} []} \text{ F-Ret}$$

$$\frac{\alpha = (V) \to \neg match(V, F) \quad bn(\alpha) \cap fn(\langle V \rangle_\lambda P) = \varnothing}{(F)_\omega P \overset{\alpha}{\rightarrowtail} []} \text{ F-In}$$

$$\frac{\alpha \neq \overline{s}(r) \quad bn(\alpha) \cap fn(\overline{s}^\lambda.P) = \varnothing}{\overline{s}^\lambda.P \overset{\alpha}{\rightarrowtail} []} \text{ F-Inv} \qquad \frac{\alpha \neq s(r) \quad bn(\alpha) \cap fn(s^\omega.P) = \varnothing}{s^\omega.P \overset{\alpha}{\rightarrowtail} []} \text{ F-Def}$$

$$\frac{}{\mathbf{nil} \overset{\alpha}{\rightarrowtail} []} \text{ Nil} \qquad\qquad \frac{}{(\nu n)P \overset{\overleftrightarrow{n}}{\rightarrowtail} []} \text{ F-Res}$$

Rule P-Sync governs synchronization within pipelines. A state R can be reached from $P > Q$, P evolves with τ to P' and $R = P' > Q$ or P produces a value V (leading to P') that Q can consume (leading to Q') and $R = (P' > Q)|Q'$. All the transitions not involving communication along the pipe are captured by $P \overset{\tau}{\rightarrowtail} \mathscr{P}$ while the other ones are determined by considering, for each value V, $\mathscr{P}_V$ and $\mathscr{Q}_V$ such that $P \overset{\langle V \rangle}{\rightarrowtail} \mathscr{P}_V$ and $Q \overset{(V)}{\rightarrowtail} \mathscr{Q}_V$. Hence, $(\mathscr{P}_V > Q)|\mathscr{Q}_V$ characterizes all the processes reachable from $P > Q$ after a synchronization on value V while $\oplus \mathscr{Q}_V$ is the total weight of input of V in Q. Thus, $\frac{(\mathscr{P}_V > Q)|\mathscr{Q}_V}{\oplus(\mathscr{Q}_V)}$ characterizes the synchronization rates on V. The complete synchronization rate is finally obtained by considering all possible values V that P can generate as an output: $\Sigma_V \frac{(\mathscr{P}_V > Q)|\mathscr{Q}_V}{\oplus(\mathscr{Q}_V)}$. This value is finite and computable.

Indeed, for each process P the set of values V such that $P \overset{\langle V \rangle}{\rightarrowtail} \mathscr{P}$ and $\mathscr{P} \neq []$ is finite.

Rule Par states that if α is not a synchronization action ($\overleftrightarrow{s}$ or $\overleftrightarrow{r}$), the states reachable from $P|Q$ via α are those reachable from P composed in parallel with Q, and the states reachable from Q, composed in parallel with P. Notice that it is crucial to have specific rules for proving the $[]$ derivation when one side of the parallel composition is not able to perform a given action; the rules defined in Table 2 are introduced for modeling the impossibility of a process to perform a given action. They state that no process is reachable from concretions, abstractions, returns, service definitions and service invocations by a transition that is not labelled by one of the following: $\langle V \rangle$, (V), $\uparrow V$, $s(r)$ or $\overline{s}(r)$ respectively. Rule Nil states that process **nil** cannot evolve to any other process while rule F-Res states that no synchronization on n can occur in $(\nu n)P$. It is easy to show that the operational semantics rules guarantee that for each $P \in \mathcal{C}$ and for each transition label α, if $fn(P) \cap bn(\alpha) = \varnothing$, then there exists $\mathscr{P}$ such that $P \overset{\alpha}{\rightarrowtail} \mathscr{P}$. Moreover, side conditions on free names permit avoiding unexpected binding by bound names in α.

Rules CALL and S-SYNC model synchronization of parallel components. These rules are similar to P-SYNC, but they have to take into account local synchronizations occurring in P and Q in order to build the global next state function. Let us consider CALL for the activation of service s. We first consider the simplified scenario in which no activation of service s can be performed by P or Q alone, i.e. $P \overset{\overrightarrow{s}}{\rightarrowtail} []$ and $Q \overset{\overrightarrow{s}}{\rightarrowtail} []$. In this case, we get the rule below:

$$\frac{P \overset{s(r)}{\rightarrowtail} \mathscr{P}_d \quad P \overset{\overline{s}(r)}{\rightarrowtail} \mathscr{P}_i \quad Q \overset{\overline{s}(r)}{\rightarrowtail} \mathscr{Q}_i \quad Q \overset{s(r)}{\rightarrowtail} \mathscr{Q}_d}{P|Q \overset{\overrightarrow{s}}{\rightarrowtail} \frac{(\nu r)(\mathscr{P}_d|\mathscr{Q}_i)+(\nu r)(\mathscr{P}_i|\mathscr{Q}_d)}{\oplus(\mathscr{P}_d+\mathscr{Q}_d)}}$$

Notice that in the above rule the probabilities obtained from the weights associated to the specific synchronisations (i.e. $\mathscr{P}_d$ and $\mathscr{Q}_d$) and the total weight of the definitions for service s (i.e. $\oplus(\mathscr{P}_d + \mathscr{Q}_d)$), are combined with the relevant rates in the resulting next state function $\frac{(\nu r)(\mathscr{P}_d|\mathscr{Q}_i)+(\nu r)(\mathscr{P}_i|\mathscr{Q}_d)}{\oplus(\mathscr{P}_d+\mathscr{Q}_d)}$.

In the general case, when activation of service s can also be performed (locally) by P, i.e. $P \overset{\overrightarrow{s}}{\rightarrowtail} \mathscr{P} \neq []$, or by Q, i.e. $Q \overset{\overrightarrow{s}}{\rightarrowtail} \mathscr{Q} \neq []$, the *total* weight to be used for computing transition probabilities, *including* those modeling activations of service s local to P (Q respectively), is $\oplus(\mathscr{P}_d + \mathscr{Q}_d)$. This implies that the next state function for such local activation of service s, namely $\mathscr{P}|Q$ ($P|\mathscr{Q}$, respectively) must be first "cleaned up" of (total) weight $\oplus(\mathscr{P}_d)$ ($\oplus(\mathscr{Q}_d)$, respectively), relative to P (Q, respectively) alone.

Rule S-SYNC is similar. However, local synchronizations over session r within P (resp. within Q) cannot take place. Rules R-PASS, HIDE, and OPEN handle name restrictions. The first rule states that if α does not contain the restricted name, then the next state function of $(\nu n)P$ is obtained as the *restriction* of the next state function of P. Rule HIDE handles synchronizations in the presence of a private name while OPEN handles extrusion of private names. Finally, rules REC and STRUCT are standard rules for recursion and for handling structural equivalent terms, where $\mathscr{P}/\equiv$ is the next state function obtained by summation of the rates of structurally congruent terms.

Theorem 1. $\mathcal{R}_{MC}$ *is a functional* Σ_S-*RTS*.

4   SoSL: Service-Oriented Stochastic Logic

In order to enable the specification of performance and dependability properties of MarCaSPiS processes, we propose to use a temporal logic. This logic is both action- and state-based, as opposed to only state-based logics, such as LTL and CTL, and only action based logics, such as ACTL. This entails that modal operators such as until are equipped with sets of actions. To be able to refer to the service-oriented and open character of the specified systems, the logic has some constructs to refer to the ability of the system to react to *external events*, like for instance the invocation of a service, triggering the execution of some activities. These operators are inspired by the logic MoMo [14].

The action/SOC ingredients are embedded into the (action-based variant of the) real-time probabilistic logic CSL. This results in a logic with the following key features:

- it is a *temporal logic* that permits describing the dynamic evolution of the system;
- it is both *action-* and *state-*based;
- it is a *real-time* logic that permits the use of real-time bounds in the logical characterization of the behaviors of interest;
- it is a *probabilistic logic* that permits expressing not only functional properties, but also properties related to performance and dependability aspects; and, finally
- it is a *resource oriented logic*, which permits addressing open-endedness of SOC.

We start by presenting the syntax and semantics of SoSL and then we consider the more practical issue of model-checking properties expressed in the logic.

4.1   Syntax

Basic state formulae. Basic state formulae permit specifying properties concerning:

- the ability of a system to react to external interactions;
- the ability of a system to react to the creation/deletion of components;
- the use of *private* names (services).

To describe the ability of a system to react to external *interactions*, modal operator $\langle \mu \int_{\bowtie p} \Phi$ is used. A process P satisfies $\langle \mu \int_{\bowtie p} \Phi$ if the relative probability of satisfying Φ after a μ transition is $\bowtie p$, where $\bowtie \in \{<, \leq, \geq, >\}$.

For instance, one could be interested in specifying that a process is ready to receive an invocation on service s and, after that, property Φ is satisfied with probability that is greater than 0.75:

$$\langle s(r) \int_{>0.75} \Phi$$

In Φ session name r will be used to *control* the protocol of the considered service.

To verify how a given system reacts to the deletion/creation of new/existing components, variants of the MoMo *consumption* ($\rightarrow$) and *production* ($\leftarrow$) operators are used. Production and consumption operators permit formalizing properties concerning the availability of resources (i.e. services and processes) and system's reactions to placement of new resources in a state.

A consumption formula has the following syntax:

$$Q \rightarrow \Phi$$

This formula is satisfied by a process P whenever $P \equiv P'|Q$ and P' satisfies Φ. Similarly, a production formula has the following syntax:

$$Q \leftarrow \Phi$$

This formula is satisfied by any process P such that $P|Q$ satisfies Φ.

Production and consumption formulae are very useful for context-system specifications. For instance, given a net P, one could be interested in studying the reaction of the system to the addition of a new component.

Finally, operators $\nabla x.\Phi$ and $\Phi\mathbb{R}s$, already introduced in [7], are used to specify properties regarding the use of (new) names. A process P satisfies $\nabla x.\Phi$ if and only if there exists a (new) name n, that does not occur free neither in P nor in Φ, such that P satisfies $\Phi[n/x]$. A process satisfies $\Phi\mathbb{R}s$ if and only if $P \equiv (\nu s)Q$ and Q satisfies Φ. Notice that, only *service names* can be revealed. Indeed, we let communications occurring among the two participants of a session be unobservable.

We can summarise the grammar for basic state formulae as follows:

$$\rho ::= Q \rightarrow \Phi \mid Q \leftarrow \Phi \mid \langle\mu\int_{\bowtie p}\Phi \mid \nabla x.\Phi \mid \Phi\mathbb{R}s$$

Action specifiers and action sets. As in the branching-time temporal logic CTL, also in SoSL we distinguish between two classes of formulae, namely, *state* formulae $\Phi, \Phi', \Phi_1, \ldots$ and *path* formulae $\varphi, \varphi', \varphi_1, \ldots$. As we deal with a combined state- and action-based model it is useful to be able to refer to these actions in the logic, in much the same vein as in action-based CTL [15]. In fact, the actions are specified by sets of *action specifiers*. In the case of MarCaSPiS, where *sessions* are private names that cannot be discovered, the only actions we consider are those related to internal synchronisations γ (τ and $\overleftrightarrow{s}$). Action specifiers Ξ are built using the grammar:

$$\Omega, \Xi \quad ::= \quad \top \mid \Xi \cup \Omega \mid \Xi - \Omega \mid \tau \mid \overleftrightarrow{s} \mid \overleftrightarrow{?x}$$

Here, $\top$ stands for "any set" and can be used when no requirement on actions is imposed. $\Xi \cup \Omega$ identifies the set of actions satisfying Ξ or Ω while $\Xi - \Omega$ is satisfied by all the actions that satisfy Ξ but do not satisfy Ω. The meaning of the other action specifiers is now self-explanatory.

Path formulae. The basic format of a path formula is the CTL *until* formula $\Phi\ \mathcal{U}\ \Psi$. In order to be able to refer also to actions executed along a path, we in fact use the variant of the *until* operator as originally proposed in action-based CTL [15]. To that end, the until-operator is parametrized with two action sets. A path satisfies $\Phi\ _\Xi\mathcal{U}_\Omega\ \Psi$ whenever eventually a state satisfying Ψ—in the sequel, a Ψ-state—is reached via a Φ-path—i.e. a path composed only of Φ-states—*and*, in addition, while evolving between Φ states, actions are performed satisfying Ξ and the Ψ-state is entered via an action satisfying Ω. Finally, we add a time constraint on path formulae. This is done by adding time parameter t—in much the same way as in timed CTL [1]—which is either a real number or may be infinite. In addition to the requirements described just above, it is now imposed that a Ψ-state should be reached within t time units. If $t = \infty$, this time constraint is vacuously true, and the until from action based CTL is obtained. Similarly, a path satisfies $\Phi\ _\Xi\mathcal{U}^{<t}\ \Psi$ if the initial state satisfies Ψ (at time 0) or eventually a Ψ state will be reached in the path, by time t via a Φ-path, and, in

addition, while evolving between Φ-states, actions are performed satisfying Ξ. Accordingly, the syntax of path formulae is:

$$\varphi \quad ::= \quad \Phi \ _{\Xi}\mathcal{U}_{\Omega}^{\leq t}\,\Psi \mid \Phi \ _{\Xi}\mathcal{U}^{<t}\,\Psi$$

Note that the only difference between the two until-operators is the absence or presence of the right-hand subscript, i.e., the action set specifying the constraints on the action which must be executed for entering the Ψ-state. We emphasize that $\Phi \ _{\Xi}\mathcal{U}^{<t}\,\Psi$ is *not* equivalent to $\Phi \ _{\Xi}\mathcal{U}_{\top}^{\leq t}\,\Psi$, because the latter formula requires that at least *one* transition is performed to reach a Ψ state, whereas this is not required in the former. The precise difference between the two until-formulae will become apparent when defining the semantics (cf. Sect. 4.2). Finally, notice that the above interpretation of the until-operators adheres to the standard interpretation of temporal logics. As we have seen, this entails that a formula $\Phi \ _{\Xi}\mathcal{U}^{<t}\,\Psi$ holds for a path whenever, e.g., the initial state satisfies Ψ. This should not be confused with "first passage" (and is also not meant to model this) where a transition into a Ψ-state is needed.

Obviously, variables may occur in formulae and are replaced by the associated values via the substitutions generated by action specifier pattern-matching. For example, TRUE $_{\top}\mathcal{U}_{?x}^{\leq\infty} \nabla y. \,\wr x(y) \,\int_{<=0}$ TRUE states that a service x will eventually be invoked afterwards we reach a state where it is not available.

State formulae. Properties about states are formulated as state formulae. Basically, there are three categories of state formulae. The first category includes formulae in propositional logic, where the atomic propositions are TRUE and the basic state formulae introduced in Sect. 4.1. The second category includes statements about the likelihood of paths satisfying a property. Finally there are the so-called long-run properties. Of course, in general, a formula can be composed of sub-formulae of different categories. Let us be a bit more precise about the probabilistic path properties. Let φ be a property imposed on paths. A process P satisfies the property $\mathcal{P}_{\bowtie p}(\varphi)$ whenever the total probability mass for all paths starting in P that satisfy φ meets the bound $\bowtie p$. For instance, the property $\mathcal{P}_{>0.99}(\rho_1 \ _{\top}\mathcal{U}_{\top}^{\leq 31.2} \rho_2)$ states that the probability to reach a ρ_2-state within 31.2 time units, via a path of ρ_1-states only, and with at least one transition, exceeds 0.99. The following formula refers to the *news server* model and states that the probability that the server **news** is invoked within 72.04 time-units is at least 0.85:

$$\mathcal{P}_{\geq 0.85}(\text{TRUE} \ _{\top}\mathcal{U}_{\overrightarrow{news}}^{<72.04} \text{TRUE})$$

Long-run properties refer to the system when it has reached an equilibrium. A state P satisfies $\mathcal{S}_{\bowtie p}(\Phi)$ if, when starting from P, the probability of reaching a state which satisfies Φ in the long run is $\bowtie p$. For instance, the formula

$$\mathcal{S}_{\geq 0.2}(\wr\overline{\texttt{emailMe}}(r) \,\int_{\geq 1} \text{TRUE})$$

states that, in the long run, the probability to find the system ready to invoke service **emailMe** is at least 0.2.

Interesting complex properties can be built by means of nesting the above operators.

In summary, state-formulae are built according to the grammar:

$$\varPhi ::= \text{TRUE} \mid \rho \mid \neg\varPhi \mid \varPhi \vee \varPhi \mid \mathcal{P}_{\bowtie p}(\varphi) \mid \mathcal{S}_{\bowtie p}(\varPhi)$$

4.2 Semantics

In the following sections, we will discuss the satisfaction relation $\models$ for state formulae and path formulae. The latter will need the satisfaction relation defined also for action specifiers.

Table 3. Satisfaction relation for state formulae

$P \models \text{TRUE}$	
$P \models \neg\varPhi$	iff $P \models \varPhi$ does not hold
$P \models \varPhi_1 \vee \varPhi_2$	iff $P \models \varPhi_1$ or $P \models \varPhi_2$
$P \models \mathcal{S}_{\bowtie p}(\varPhi)$	iff $\lim_{t\to\infty} \mathbb{P}\{\pi \in Paths_P^{\mathcal{A}_S} \mid \pi(t) \models \varPhi\} \bowtie p$
$P \models \mathcal{P}_{\bowtie p}(\varphi)$	iff $\mathbb{P}\{\pi \in Paths_P^{\mathcal{A}_S} \mid \pi \models \varphi\} \bowtie p$
$P \models {}^?\mu \int_{\bowtie p} \varPhi$	iff $P \xrightarrow{\mu} \mathscr{P}$ and $\sum_{Q \models \varPhi} \frac{\mathscr{P}(Q)}{\oplus \mathscr{P}} \bowtie p$
$P \models Q \to \varPhi$	iff $P \equiv P'\|Q$ and $P' \models \varPhi$
$P \models Q \leftarrow \varPhi$	iff $P\|Q \models \varPhi$
$P \models \nabla x.\varPhi$	iff $\exists n \notin \text{fn}(P) \cup \text{fn}(\varPhi) : P \models \varPhi[n/x]$
$P \models \varPhi\textcircled{R}s$	iff $\exists Q : P \equiv (\nu s)Q$ and $Q \models \varPhi$

State formulae. Table 3 gives the definition of the satisfaction relation for SoSL formulae. For deciding whether a process P satisfies formula $\mathcal{S}_{\bowtie p}(\varPhi)$ the limit for $t \to \infty$ of the probability mass of the set of all those paths π starting from P (containing only synchronization actions) and satisfying $\varPhi$ at time t (i.e. $\pi(t) \models \varPhi$) must be computed and it must be checked whether it respects bound $\bowtie p$. Process P satisfies $\mathcal{P}_{\bowtie p}(\varphi)$ if the probability mass of the set of paths starting from P (containing only synchronisation actions) which satisfy φ is $\bowtie$ p. To compute the probability measure associated with a set of paths starting from a process P, only internal synchronisation actions are considered. For this reason, we consider the set $Paths_P^{\mathcal{A}_S}$ where $\mathcal{A}_S$ is the set of synchronisation labels γ defined in Section 3.

In order for a process P to satisfy $Q \to \varPsi$ it must be of the form $P'\|Q$ (up to associativity and commutativity of parallel composition), for some P', and P' must satisfy $\varPsi$. On the contrary, P satisfies $Q \leftarrow \varPsi$ if and only if $P\|Q$ satisfies $\varPsi$.

A process P satisfies $\langle\mu\rangle\int_{\bowtie p}\Psi$ if and only if P can perform transition μ. Moreover, the relative probability of satisfying Ψ after this transition is $\bowtie p$. Such a probability is computed in the following way:

$$\sum_{Q\models\Psi}\frac{\mathscr{P}(Q)}{\oplus\mathscr{P}}\bowtie p$$

Notice that the counter part of the considered actions could not be in the considered system. Hence, the standard stochastic operators, that only consider synchronizations, are not able to specify this kind of properties.

The definition of the satisfaction relation for the other kinds of state formulae is straightforward.

Table 4. Satisfaction relation for action specifiers

$[]$,	γ	$\models$	$\top$	
δ,	γ	$\models$	$\varXi\cup\varOmega$	iff $\delta,\gamma\models\varXi$ or $\delta,\gamma\models\varOmega$
δ,	γ	$\models$	$\varXi-\varOmega$	iff $\delta,\gamma\models\varXi$ and $\exists\delta':\delta',\gamma\not\models\varOmega$
$[]$,	τ	$\models$	τ	
$[]$,	$\overleftrightarrow{s}$	$\models$	$\overleftrightarrow{s}$	
$[s/x]$,	$\overleftrightarrow{s}$	$\models$	$\overleftrightarrow{?x}$	

Sets of action specifiers. Table 4 gives the definition of the satisfaction relation for action specifiers and sets thereof. The concept behind the definition of the satisfaction relation for action specifiers is that an action γ satisfies an action specifier $\varXi$ if and only if the action *matches* the specifier.

Path formulae. The definition of the satisfaction relation for path formulae, given in Table 5, formalizes the meaning of the until operators, as discussed in Sect. 4.1.

Derived operators. Some frequently used operators can be derived from those of SoSL. The first set of derived operators, given on the left-hand-side of Table 6, shows how the standard until-operators from both action-based CTL and plain CTL are obtained, the next operator, and the modalities from Hennessy-Milner logic. The second set, given on the right-hand-side of the table, includes the eventually ($\Diamond$) and always ($\Box$) operators.

Table 5. Satisfaction relation for path formulae

$\pi \models \Phi \;_\Xi\mathcal{U}_\Omega^{\leq t} \Psi$ iff there exists k, $0 < k \leq (\text{len }\pi)$ s.t. the following *three* conditions hold:
   1) $t > \sum_{j=0}^{k-1} \mathsf{dl}(\pi, j)$
   2)   there exists δ s.t. the following *three* conditions hold:
      2.1) $\mathsf{st}(\pi, k-1) \models \Phi$
      2.2) $\delta, \mathsf{ac}(\pi, k-1) \models \Omega$
      2.3) $\mathsf{st}(\pi, k) \models \Psi\delta$
   3)   if $k > 1$ then there exist $\delta_0, \ldots, \delta_{k-2}$ s.t.
      for all j, $0 \leq j \leq k-2$ the following *two* conditions hold:
      3.1) $\mathsf{st}(\pi, j) \models \Phi$
      3.2) $\delta_j, \mathsf{ac}(\pi, j) \models \Xi$

$\pi \models \Phi \;_\Xi\mathcal{U}^{<t} \Psi$ iff $\mathsf{st}(\pi, 0) \models \Psi$ or
there exists k, $0 < k \leq (\text{len }\pi)$ s.t. the following *three* conditions hold:
   1) $t > \sum_{j=0}^{k-1} \mathsf{dl}(\pi, j)$
   2) $\mathsf{st}(\pi, k) \models \Psi$
   3)   there exist $\delta_0, \ldots, \delta_{k-1}$ s.t.
      for all j, $0 \leq j \leq k-1$ the following *two* conditions hold:
      3.1) $\mathsf{st}(\pi, j) \models \Phi$
      3.2) $\delta_j, \mathsf{ac}(\pi, j) \models \Xi$

Table 6. Derived operators

$\Phi \;_\Xi\mathcal{U}_\Omega \Psi =_{\text{def}} \Phi \;_\Xi\mathcal{U}_\Omega^{\leq\infty} \Psi$	$\mathcal{P}_{\bowtie p}(_\Xi\Diamond_{\Xi'}^{\leq t} \Phi) =_{\text{def}} \mathcal{P}_{\bowtie p}(\text{TRUE} \;_\Xi\mathcal{U}_{\Xi'}^{\leq t} \Phi)$
$\Phi \;\mathcal{U} \Psi =_{\text{def}} \Phi \;_\top\mathcal{U} \Psi$	$\mathcal{P}_{\bowtie p}(_\Xi\Box_{\Xi'}^{\leq t} \Phi) =_{\text{def}} \neg\mathcal{P}_{\bowtie p}(_\Xi\Diamond_{\Xi'}^{\leq t} \neg\Phi)$
$\mathbf{X}_\Xi^{\leq t} \Phi =_{\text{def}} \text{TRUE} \;_\varnothing\mathcal{U}_\Xi^{\leq t} \Phi$	$\mathcal{P}_{\bowtie p}(_\Xi\Diamond^{<t} \Phi) =_{\text{def}} \mathcal{P}_{\bowtie p}(\text{TRUE} \;_\Xi\mathcal{U}^{<t} \Phi)$
$\langle\Xi\rangle \Phi =_{\text{def}} \mathcal{P}_{>0}(\mathbf{X}_\Xi \Phi)$	$\mathcal{P}_{\bowtie p}(_\Xi\Box^{<t} \Phi) =_{\text{def}} \neg\mathcal{P}_{\bowtie p}(_\Xi\Diamond^{<t} \neg\Phi)$
$[\Xi] \Phi =_{\text{def}} \neg\langle\Xi\rangle\neg\Phi$	

4.3   Model Checking SoSL

Following the same approach proposed in [9], we can verify whether a given MarCaSPiS specification satisfies or not a SoSL formulae. The idea is to use existing state-based stochastic model-checkers, like e.g. the Markov Reward Model Checker (MRMC), and wrapping them in the SoSL model-checking algorithm and using techniques similar to those presented in [20].

SoSL-MC, which is implemented in OCAML, permits analyzing the execution of MarCaSPiS programs and generating their reachability graphs. Moreover, after loading a MarCaSPiS specification and a formula, it verifies, by means of one or more calls to the MRMC model checker, the satisfaction of the formula by the specification.

Examples of analysis performed with SoSL-MC can be found in Chapter 5-5 and Chapter 7-3 where two of the SENSORIA case studies are taken into account.

5   Conclusions and Related Work

We have presented the Service-Oriented Stochastic Logic, SoSL, that permits describing both action and state-based properties of service-oriented systems. The logic is instrumental for the formal specification of performance and dependability properties of systems modeled with MarCaSPiS, a stochastic calculus that permits an integrated analysis of both qualitative and quantitative aspects of formal specifications of services.

The proposed logic permits describing properties of the dynamic evolution of the system. It is both *action-* and *state-*based and has operators that permit modelling real-time bounds in the logical characterization of the behaviors of interest. Moreover, SoSL is a *probabilistic logic* that permits expressing not only functional properties, but also properties related to performance and dependability aspects. Furthermore, the *open-endness* operators of SoSL, namely $\mathcal{l}\mu \int_{\bowtie p} \Phi, Q \rightarrow \Phi, Q \leftarrow \Phi$, can be used for specifying, *at the logic level* (i.e. without modification of the underlying model), how a system reacts to *external stimuli* or to the *inclusion* or *removal of entities* (e.g. services or their clients). MarCaSPiS and the proposed logic have been used in Chapter 5-5 and Chapter 7-3 for specifying and verifying quantitative aspects of two of the SENSORIA case studies.

Several (temporal) logics have been proposed which aim at describing properties of systems related either to mobility ([13,6,7,17,24] among others) or to probabilistic/stochastic behavior (e.g. [18,19,2,3,20]), or to SOC (e.g. [16]). To the best of our knowledge, [9] is the first approach towards a probabilistic logic for mobility, and we are not aware of any logic which addresses all the above mentioned important features of SOC, dealt with in SoSL.

References

1. Alur, R., Dill, D.: A theory of timed automata. Theoret. Comput. Sci. 126, 183–235 (1994)
2. Aziz, A., Sanwal, K., Singhal, V., Brayton, R.: Model checking Continuous Time Markov Chains. ACM Transactions on Computational Logic 1(1), 162–170 (2000)
3. Baier, C., Haverkort, B., Hermanns, H., Katoen, J.-P.: Model-Checking Algorithms for Continuous-Time Markov Chains. IEEE Transactions on Software Engineering 29(6), 524–541 (2003)
4. Boreale, M., Bruni, R., De Nicola, R., Loreti, M.: Sessions and pipelines for structured service programming. In: Barthe, G., de Boer, F.S. (eds.) FMOODS 2008. LNCS, vol. 5051, pp. 19–38. Springer, Heidelberg (2008)

5. Brinksma, E., Hermanns, H.: Process Algebra and Markov Chains. In: Brinksma, E., Hermanns, H., Katoen, J.-P. (eds.) EEF School 2000 and FMPA 2000. LNCS, vol. 2090, pp. 183–231. Springer, Heidelberg (2001)
6. Caires, L., Cardelli, L.: A spatial logic for concurrency (part I). Information and Computation 186(2), 194–235 (2003)
7. Cardelli, L., Gordon, A.: Anytime, anywhere: modal logics for mobile ambients. In: Twentyseventh Annual ACM Symposium on Principles of Programming Languages, pp. 365–377. ACM, New York (2000)
8. Clarke, E.M., Emerson, E.A.: Design and synthesis of synchronization skeletons using branching-time temporal logic. In: Logic of Programs, pp. 52–71 (1981)
9. De Nicola, R., Katoen, J.P., Latella, D., Loreti, M., Massink, M.: Model checking mobile stochastic logic. Theoretical Computer Science 382(1), 42–70 (2007)
10. De Nicola, R., Latella, D., Loreti, M., Massink, M.: MarCaSPiS: a Markovian Extension of a Calculus for Services. Electronic Notes in Theoretical Computer Science 229(4), 11–26 (2009)
11. De Nicola, R., Latella, D., Loreti, M., Massink, M.: On a Uniform Framework for the Definition of Stochastic Process Languages. In: Alpuente, M., Cook, B., Joubert, C. (eds.) FMICS 2009. LNCS, vol. 5825, pp. 9–25. Springer, Heidelberg (2009)
12. De Nicola, R., Latella, D., Loreti, M., Massink, M.: Rate-Based Transition Systems for Stochastic Process Calculi. In: Albers, S., Marchetti-Spaccamela, A., Matias, Y., Nikoletseas, S., Thomas, W. (eds.) ICALP 2009. LNCS, vol. 5556, pp. 435–446. Springer, Heidelberg (2009)
13. De Nicola, R., Loreti, M.: A modal logic for mobile agents. ACM Transactions on Computational Logic 5(1), 79–128 (2004)
14. De Nicola, R., Loreti, M.: Multiple-Labelled Transition Systems for nominal calculi and their logics. Mathematical Structures in Computer Science 18(1), 107–143 (2008)
15. De Nicola, R., Vaandrager, F.: Action versus state based logics for transition systems. In: Guessarian, I. (ed.) LITP 1990. LNCS, vol. 469, pp. 407–419. Springer, Heidelberg (1990)
16. Fantechi, A., Gnesi, S., Lapadula, A., Mazzanti, F., Pugliese, R., Tiezzi, F.: A model checking approach for verifying cows specifications. In: Fiadeiro, J.L., Inverardi, P. (eds.) FASE 2008. LNCS, vol. 4961, pp. 230–245. Springer, Heidelberg (2008)
17. Ferrari, G., Gnesi, S., Montanari, U., Pistore, M.: A model-checking verification environment for mobile processes. ACM Publications Home Page Transactions on Software Engineering and Methodology 12(4), 440–473 (2003)
18. Hansson, H., Jonsson, B.: A logic for reasoning about time and reliability. Formal Aspects of Computing 6(5), 512–535 (1994)
19. Hart, S., Sharir, M.: Probabilistic Temporal Logics for Finite and Bounded Models. In: De Millo, R. (ed.) 16th Annual ACM Symposium on Theory of Computing, pp. 1–13. ACM, New York (1984) ISBN 0-89791-133-4
20. Hermanns, H., Katoen, J.-P., Meyer-Kayser, J., Siegle, M.: Towards model checking stochastic process algebra. In: Grieskamp, W., Santen, T., Stoddart, B. (eds.) IFM 2000. LNCS, vol. 1945, pp. 420–439. Springer, Heidelberg (2000)
21. Hillston, J.: A compositional approach to performance modelling. Distinguished Dissertation in Computer Science. Cambridge University Press, Cambridge (1996)

22. Katoen, J.-P., Khattri, M., Zapreev, I.: A Markov reward model checker. In: Second International Conference on the Quantitative Evaluation of Systems (QEST 2005), pp. 243–244 (2005) ISBN 0-7695-0418-3
23. Kwiatkowska, M., Norman, G., Parker, D.: Probabilistic Symbolic Model Checking using PRISM: A Hybrid Approach. Software Tools and Technology Transfer 6(2), 128–142 (2004)
24. Merz, S., Wirsing, M., Zappe, J.: A spatio-temporal logic for the specification and refinement of mobile systems. In: Pezzé, M. (ed.) FASE 2003. LNCS, vol. 2621, pp. 87–101. Springer, Heidelberg (2003)

Evaluating Service Level Agreements Using Observational Probes

Allan Clark and Stephen Gilmore

The University of Edinburgh, Scotland

Abstract. We report on our use of quantitative modelling in predicting the success of systems and services in achieving Service Level Agreements (SLAs). We construct models of the systems in the stochastic process algebra PEPA[1], and queries in the language of eXtended Stochastic Probes (XSP[2]). The query and model together are translated into an underlying continuous time Markov chain (CTMC) which is evaluated in order to assess the SLA. This most often requires a passage-time analysis where a passage (sequence of activity observations) is specified and the numerical analysis returns a function mapping the probability of completing the passage against time since the passage was initiated.

1 Introduction

Service Level Agreements (SLAs) underpin the expectation of the performance of a system as seen by a particular client of the service. Most often an SLA will speak about the response-time of the system. It is usually concerned with the time taken between the user initiating some sequence of behaviours and the completion of the goal or end of that sequence of behaviours. Usually this will involve some interaction with the service but may include activities that the client performs on their own. In a more complex setting the client may interact with a set of services in order to complete their task. This set of services may be invoked in series or in parallel and it may be that completion is marked by all services responding, only the fastest responding or a subset of all services responding.

The response-time is concerned with the time taken for a user or client to perform two activities, often called the 'request' and the 'response' although they need not actually be requests and responses. There may be multiple kinds of request and response activities such as successful or failed responses. An occurrence of a request activity begins the passage which we wish to analyse while an occurrence of a response activity completes the passage.

An example SLA is "Ninety percent of all client requests receive some response within ten seconds". Note that this is more precise than a statement about the average response-time. An average response-time does not require any percentage of passages to be below a fixed target time. To evaluate an SLA, passage-time quantiles leading to a cumulative distribution function (CDF) must be computed. A CDF plots the probability of completing the passage within a

M. Wirsing and M. Hölzl (Eds.): SENSORIA Project, LNCS 6582, pp. 467–485, 2011.

given time. The graph in Figure 1 shows four different cumulative distribution functions all which have the same average duration. It is interesting here that two of the distributions succeed in attaining an early SLA while the other two fail, but when the SLA is later with a higher percentage required the successful distributions are swapped with the failed ones.

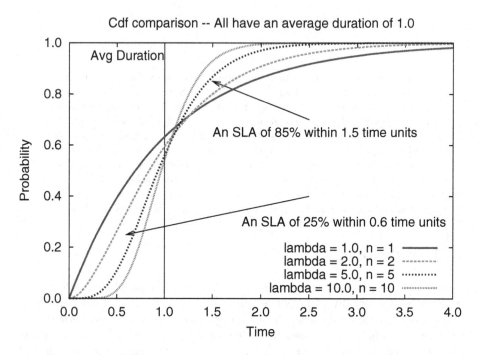

Fig. 1. The passage-time profiles for four distributions all of which share the same average duration. From their associated passage-time CDFs however we see that their ability to satisfy distinct SLAs are quite different.

Many times this will be insufficiently precise because it does not say anything about the kinds of responses possible and their frequency. For example one simple way to increase the likelihood that the service attains the SLA as presented above is to immediately reply to all requests with a failure such as "Service too busy" or "Loan application denied". Therefore we often wish to refine our SLA by adding constraints such as in the following modification to the above SLA: "Ninety percent of all *positive* responses are received within ten seconds" or "Ninety percent of all client requests receive some response within ten seconds and of those eighty-five percent are successful responses". The first talks about only the positive responses which may be a small or large proportion of all responses while the second refinement is concerned with all responses in general but specifies a proportion of acceptably fast responses which must be positive.

The analysis specification of an agreed upon SLA takes two important steps. The first is the specification of the service as it is or will be deployed. This includes the environment in which the service is deployed most notably the clients which interact with the service but also may include other relevant components which may enhance or restrict the system performance. Generally the system is too large or expensive to reproduce for the purposes of analysis. Instead we abstract the parts of the system which we hope are relevant to the analysis into an abstract model which is generally defined in some modelling formalism, but could be simply a computer program designed specifically for the purpose, in this chapter we shall use the process algebra PEPA, which will be described later in this section(see 1.1). The specification of the model is in part an art form, in which the modeller must choose which parts of the real system to abstract away from and which parts to model explicitly. There is usually a trade-off between the accuracy of the results and the complexity of the model. The more complex the model the less it may be understood and often the time taken for numerical analysis will be increased. The less complex the model the easier it is to understand and more efficient it is to evaluate, but the results may lose their relevance to the real system if too many important details are abstracted. In section 2 we will make use of PEPA to model an example service, that of an emergency response service to automobile airbag deployments.

The second part is the specification of the passage of interest within the defined model. In this chapter we will use eXtended Stochastic Probes(XSP)[2] which will be explained in Section 3. Once the analysis specification is complete the calculation of results is fully automated in software, this process is described in the same section as well as our first results for our example model.

In Section 4, we analyse the results produced so far and refine the query specification to obtain more detailed information which could allow hypothetical service engineers to improve the system's performance. As part of our refined analysis we will make use of *sensitivity analysis* in section 4.1. Sensitivity analysis requires that we vary a particular aspect of the model whilst maintaining the remainder of the model constant and perform the same analysis on the resulting set of related models. This highlights the effect that the varied aspect of the model has on the performance of the analysed passage, in other words we learn the sensitivity of the performance of the analysed passage to the varied aspect of the model, hence the term sensitivity analysis. Most often the aspect of a model which we vary is the rate at which a given activity within the model is performed, or the population size of a given component such as the number of server components.

1.1 PEPA

We work with the Markovian process algebra PEPA defined in [1]. Applications of the language are described in [3,4,5]. PEPA is a stochastically-timed process algebra where sequential components are defined using prefix and choice and models require these sequential components to cooperate on some activities, and hide others. Rates are associated with activities performed by each component and the passive rate $\top$ is used to indicate that the component will passively cooperate with another on this activity. In this case the passive component may enable or restrict the activity from being performed by the cooperating component but the rate when enabled is determined by the actively cooperating component. The component $(\alpha, r).P$ performs the activity α at rate r whenever it is not blocked by a cooperating component and becomes the process P. The component $(\alpha, \top).P$ performs the activity α passively to become the process P. It is illegal to have such a passive activity which is not ultimately performed in synchronisation with a component performing α actively. The $\top$ rate may be multiplied by a scalar as in $(\alpha, \top \times 0.3).P$ to affect the probability that this path is taken when two passive occurrences of α are done in competition. Note though that this does not affect the rate at which the activity is performed as the rate is determined by the active component. Sequential components are combined using the synchronisation operator, the component $P \bowtie_{\mathcal{L}} Q$ represents the parallel combination of the two components P and Q which must cooperate over the activities in the set $\mathcal{L}$ and may perform any other activities independently to each other. The component $P \parallel Q$ is a synonym for the component when the synchronisation set is the empty set.

We use the version of PEPA with functional rates [6] ("marking dependent rates", in Petri nets terms) and arrays of components. We write $P[5]$ to denote five copies of the component P which do not cooperate and $P[5][\alpha]$ to denote five copies of the component P which cooperate on the activity α. That is, $P[5]$ is an abbreviation for $P \parallel P \parallel P \parallel P \parallel P$ and $P[5][\alpha]$ is an abbreviation for $P \bowtie_{\{\alpha\}} P \bowtie_{\{\alpha\}} P \bowtie_{\{\alpha\}} P \bowtie_{\{\alpha\}} P$. We also allow the special cooperation $P \bowtie_{*} Q$ to be a synonym for $P \bowtie_{\mathcal{L}} Q$ where $\mathcal{L}$ is the set of activities which both processes P and Q perform. The special component Stop indicates a component which has terminated and can no longer perform any activities. Finally our probe language makes use of immediate actions which are written $\alpha.P$ to mean the process which instantaneously performs the action α to become the process P. These are generally cooperated over such that components can be blocked until another component has entered a state which may perform the appropriate immediate synchronisation.

A PEPA model can be compiled into several different formats for analysis. There are three techniques commonly used to analyse a PEPA model; translation to a continuous time Markov chain (CTMC), a set of ordinary differential equations (ODEs)[7] and the use of stochastic simulation algorithm (SSA)[8,9]. This is summarised in the diagram shown in Figure 2. In this chapter we will focus on analysis by means of translation to the underlying CTMC.

2   Model Specification

The example scenario we will be using is the airbag scenario. In this case car drivers register their car and mobile phone number with an accident service. The car is equiped with sensors which detect when the airbag has been deployed and whether or not this was likely due to a severe accident in which the driver or others may be in need of emergency ambulance assistance. When this happens the car instrument automatically sends a signal to a call centre with some number

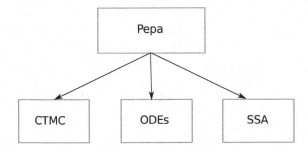

Fig. 2. The compilation strategies for a PEPA model

of operators. The signal includes some diagnostics available from sensors within the car including the speed of the car at the time of the accident and the location as obtained from a GPS device. Upon receiving such a signal a call centre operator will attempt to contact the driver of the car involved in the accident via the registered mobile phone number. If the driver is unhurt they should pick up the phone and can relay whether or not an ambulance is required. However if the driver does not respond then it is assumed that an ambulance is required and one is called for and dispatched to the scene of the accident.

There are several interesting points of analysis for such a system. We would like to ensure that the service has enough call centre operators to service the number of registered drivers, that is we wish to ensure that there are not more simultaneous requests (accident detection signals) than there is capacity to deal with. In this model we take the view that if the call centre services a small enough area then car accidents are infrequent enough for it to be assumed that no two accidents occur at the same time. In this case we need not model the thousands of registered drivers of a system and can model only the interaction between a single client driver and the call centre. In this case we are most interested in how long the call centre operator should wait for the driver to answer before considering the driver to be uncontactable. There is the specific case where two or more registered drivers crash into each other, but we still make the assumption that there are enough call centre operators to deal with this and that calling any one of them will result in an ambulance being dispatched if one is required. The PEPA model in Figure 3 describes the interaction between a single car driver and the call centre.

The car component may perform an *airbag* activity which must be passively observed by the driver of the car. Upon observing the *airbag* activity the driver may remain unhurt and move into the Okay state. In this state the driver may answer their phone or observe that an ambulance has arrived to help them even though they do not require such assistance. This may happen if an ambulance is dispatched for them because they have not answered their phone quick enough. Alternatively upon observing the *airbag* activity the driver may become hurt in which case they are unable to answer their phone and can only observe the aid of an ambulance which has been dispatched to rescue them. When the car

$$
\begin{aligned}
\text{Car} &\stackrel{\text{def}}{=} (airbag, \lambda_{air}).\text{Sending} \\
\text{Sending} &\stackrel{\text{def}}{=} (send, \lambda_{send}).\text{Car} \\[1em]
\text{Driver} &\stackrel{\text{def}}{=} (airbag, \top \times 0.8).\text{Hurt} \\
&\quad + (airbag, \top \times 0.2).\text{Okay} \\
\text{Okay} &\stackrel{\text{def}}{=} (answer, \lambda_{answer}).\text{Driver} \\
&\quad + (rescue, \top).\text{Driver} \\
\text{Hurt} &\stackrel{\text{def}}{=} (rescue, \top).\text{Driver}
\end{aligned}
$$

$$
\begin{aligned}
\text{Service} &\stackrel{\text{def}}{=} (send, \top).\text{Search} \\
\text{Search} &\stackrel{\text{def}}{=} (search, \lambda_{search}).\text{Dial} \\
\text{Dial} &\stackrel{\text{def}}{=} (dial, \lambda_{dial}).\text{Wait} \\
\text{Wait} &\stackrel{\text{def}}{=} (answer, \top).\text{Service} \\
&\quad + (timeout, \lambda_{timeout}).\text{Call} \\
\text{Call} &\stackrel{\text{def}}{=} (ambulance, \lambda_{amb}).\text{Service} \\[1em]
\text{Ambulance} &\stackrel{\text{def}}{=} (ambulance, \top).\text{Rescue} \\
\text{Rescue} &\stackrel{\text{def}}{=} (rescue, \lambda_{rescue}).\text{Ambulance}
\end{aligned}
$$

$$
(\text{Car} \underset{airbag}{\bowtie} \text{Driver}) \underset{\mathcal{L}}{\bowtie} (\text{Service} \underset{ambulance}{\bowtie} \text{Ambulance})
$$
$$
\text{where } \mathcal{L} = \{send, answer, rescue\}
$$

Fig. 3. The PEPA model specifying the behaviour of a single car driver and call centre for the airbag emergency service

component has completed an *airbag* activity they send data to the service, which must then process the data by searching for the registered driver's phone number and dialing, these processes may be automatic or done by a call centre operator.

Part of the reason for producing this model is to determine whether optimising such operations would be beneficial to the service performance. After dialing the service can either perform an *answer* activity in cooperation with the driver, or can independently *timeout*. Notice that the service may *timeout* even if the driver is unhurt, because the driver has not answered their phone fast enough. One question our model should be able to answer is whether or not the *timeout* activity has been set for the correct rate, if the rate is too slow then the service becomes slow and ambulances are not dispatched swiftly enough to injured drivers in need of medical assistance. However if the rate of the *timeout* activity is set too high we risk needlessly calling for many ambulances for drivers who do not require them.

Finally the service, upon failing to contact the driver and performing a *timeout* will call for an ambulance which may then perform with the driver, whether the driver is hurt or not, a shared *rescue* activity. The rate of the *rescue* activity is particularly hard to specify since it depends on how quickly an ambulance can be expected to navigate the traffic of the city and reach the scene of the accident. This clearly depends on many factors such as the size of the city, the time of the crash and the weather. However this activity will be outside of the passages which we wish to analyse since it is not a part of the service offered and therefore not part of a related service level agreement.

As a small aside we briefly explain here why the weights on the two passive observations of the *airbag* activity, performed by the Driver component do not affect the rate at which this activity occurs. There are two ways for the Car $\underset{airbag}{\bowtie}$ Driver component to complete the *airbag* activity. We may have:

$$
\begin{aligned}
&(airbag, \lambda_{air}).\text{Sending} \rightarrow \text{Sending} \\
&(airbag, \top \times 0.8).\text{Hurt} \rightarrow \text{Hurt}
\end{aligned}
\quad \text{or} \quad
\begin{aligned}
&(airbag, \lambda_{air}).\text{Sending} \rightarrow \text{Sending} \\
&(airbag, \top \times 0.2).\text{Driver} \rightarrow \text{Driver}
\end{aligned}
$$

The rates at which both these transitions may occur are computed as per the operational semantics of PEPA. The first is:

$$\frac{\lambda_{air}}{\lambda_{air}} \times \frac{\top \times 0.8}{(\top \times 0.8) + (\top \times 0.2)} \times min(\lambda_{air}, (\top \times 0.8) + (\top \times 0.2)) = 0.8 \times \lambda_{air}$$

The second is:

$$\frac{\lambda_{air}}{\lambda_{air}} \times \frac{\top \times 0.2}{(\top \times 0.8) + (\top \times 0.2)} \times min(\lambda_{air}, (\top \times 0.8) + (\top \times 0.2)) = 0.2 \times \lambda_{air}$$

Therefore the total rate at which the component (Car $\underset{airbag}{\bowtie}$ Driver) performs the *airbag* activity is:

$$(0.8 \times \lambda_{air}) + (0.2 \times \lambda_{air}) = \lambda_{air}$$

Notice that this calculation does not depend on the probabilities used as weights, it is not even necessary for those weights to sum to one. The overall affect is that the passive observations do not affect the rate of the shared activity only the active rates do.

In the next section we consider the specification of the analysis of this model which we would like to perform. As we stated above most commonly for service level agreements we are interested in studying passages within the model generally between some form of request or initiation and some form of response or completion. There are several passages within this model which we could analyse. Ultimately for quality of overall service we would wish to analyse the response-time as observed by the client, this would be the time from when the airbag is deployed until either the driver reports that they are uninjured or until an ambulance arrives at the scene. However since the service in question has no control over how long the ambulance takes to arrive at the scene we wish to measure the responsiveness of the service. Therefore we measure from the airbag activity as performed by the car until either the driver reports that they are well or the service calls to dispatch an ambulance.

A final comment on the model is that of course there are many facets of this problem which are difficult to quantify. Such as the likelihood that a driver who forgot their phone is involved in an accident, the likelihood that an accident occurs when the ambulance service is busy, the cost of unnecessarily calling on the ambulance service etc.

3   Measurement Specification

In order to evaluate the passage in question the PEPA model is translated into a CTMC. This is done by generating the entire state space of the model through depth first search and calculating the rates between states of the CTMC according to the semantics of PEPA. The CTMC analsyer is then given a set of source states and a set of target states and computes the probability of transitioning along some path from one of the source states to one of the target states. This section is concerned with how we specify the sets of source and target states to the CTMC analyser. The user should not need to know about the details of the derived CTMC because it may be rather large and in any case the user should specify the desired analysis at the same level as the specification of the model.

In the previous section we discussed which passages within the model we might wish to analyse. We talked about analysis of passages delineated by occurrences of activities. Note that there is no reference to the states of the system. The addition of the observing stochastic probes allows us to convert a specification which describes observations of performed activities into specifications of the sets of source and target states. The particular passage within the model that we identified as important was initiated by the occurrence of an *airbag* activity and terminated by either an *answer* or an *ambulance* activity. Note that we measure the time taken from after the completion of the source activity (*airbag*), until after the completion of either of the target activities (*answer* or *ambulance*). This is an unusual response-time measurement in that the activities which begin and end the passage are performed solely by two separate components. Usually a response-time query analyses the time taken between one particular component performing each of two sets of activities, the request and the response. Note though that if it were necessary we could have the driver component observe the calling of the ambulance by the service even though this does not match the reality since the driver need not observe this.

In essence we have two distinct passages to measure; the first is that ended by the client answering the phone and the second is that ended by the dispatching of an ambulance. These passages may well have quite different passage-time profiles since we instinctively expect the latter to take longer. Because of this we will not consider our analysis to be complete until we have analysed both kinds of passage in isolation, this avoids one kind of passage having unacceptably poor performance while the other has good enough performance to compensate thus making the general passage appear to have suitable overall performance. In particular we would like to avoid the possibility that the *airbag − answer* passage is fast enough and occurs often enough that the general passage appears to have acceptable performance even though the *airbag − ambulance* passage does not. However we will concern ourselves first of all by combining these two kinds of passages into a single passage begun with an *airbag* activity and ended with either an *answer* or an *ambulance* activity.

In order to evaluate this passage within the model we must translate the model into a CTMC and then specify to the CTMC analyser the set of source states and the set of target states. However we wish that the user need not know about the CTMC derived from the model and that they specify the passage at the same level as the model specification. The most obvious way to do this is to specify the states in a compositional manner, that is by specifying the states of the individual components within the model. In this case there are only four components to specify, where the operator $\models$ means that the named component is in the given local state, we may begin by specifying the first source state as:

Car Component $\models$ Sending
Driver Component $\models$ Driver
Service Component $\models$ Service
Ambulance Component $\models$ Ambulance

This is only one particular source state, in this case there are more source states such as:

Car Component $\models$ Sending
Driver Component $\models$ Hurt
Service Component $\models$ Service
Ambulance Component $\models$ Rescue

These extra source states correspond to the Driver, Service and Ambulance components being in different states, not all are reachable, for example the Service component cannot be in the Dial state, but in general there may be many reachable source states and to specify each separately would be tedious and inefficient. Instead we specify the component states which characterise a source state, by implication any other component may be in any state.

Car Component $\models$ Sending

This will specify a set of states including some which are unreachable but that need not concern us because such states will not be represented in the derived CTMC. Target states may be specified in just the same manner by:

Service Component $\models$ Service

After the occurrence of either the *answer* or the *timeout* which completes a passage we enter the Service state of the service component. Note that a target state may be entered without completing a passage of interest (in fact in this model the initial state is also a target state) but that this does not affect the measurement or analysis.

In general when specifying states we need not specify the name of the component which is in the given local state. So the above can simply be written as Service == 1, which means "there is exactly one component in the local state: Service".

For this particular passage the specification of the states is rather simple in that we need only specify the exact state of one of the components. In general state specifications may make reference to many components and relationships between those components. Figure 4 gives the full grammar for state specifications, it is essentially a language of arithmetic and relational operators. Hence one can specify a passage such as:

Source = Broken > Working
Target = Working > Broken

Which may be relevant for a model with a number of servers some of which may be offline and some online. This particular specification measures a passage which begins when the number of broken/offline servers is greater than the number of working/online servers and ends once the reverse becomes true.

For such measurements which are concerned with the passage between two *situations*, state specifications are a convenient and intuitive method of passage specification. However many passages are delineated by two *events*, the source and target events, where an event is chiefly an occurrence of an activity (though it may be one which occurs when the model is in some state/situation). Specifying such passages via state specifications may be error prone, because the user must identify the states of components after a source or target event occurs. Additionally the specification is non-robust to changes within the model. So that if the modeller makes a modification to their model the specification of the passage is likely to require an analogous update. Finally for many passages which we wish to measure, and in particular for many response-time analyses the source states cannot be readily specified because they are indistinguishable from some other states within the model. We require to add something to the model to distinguish certain states or passages such that they can be more readily analysed. Our solution to these and more analysis specification problems has been the introduction of stochastic probes which in their latest incarnation have been called eXtended Stochastic Probes(XSP)[2].

In the XSP framework passages are described by a language specifying sequences of activity observations. A passage specification written in XSP is then transformed into a PEPA component, which is then added to the model in co-operation over the activities which it observes (we call this the alphabet of the probe). The probe component switches states based on the activities it observes. States of interest, and in particular the source and target states may then be specified (automatically) by reference to the state of the probe component.

The language is similar to the language of regular expressions with the activity observations as the tokens, for instance the following probe specification defines a passage of one 'a' activity followed by one or more sequences of a 'b' followed by a 'c' activity and finally the passage is completed by either a 'd' or 'e' activity.

$$a, (b, c)+, (d|e)$$

By default the source event is taken to be the set of activities which are enabled at the start of the specification, which in the above example is the singleton set $\{a\}$. The target event is taken to the be set of activities which may end the specification, in the above example this is the set $\{d, e\}$. However the user may override this default using the labels start and stop. A label is given using a colon first and attached to the end of a sub-phrase of the probe specification, usually it is simply attached to a single activity. The above example then is equivalent to the following two probe specifications:

a:start, $(b, c)+, (d$:stop$|e$:stop$)$
a:start, $(b, c)+, (d|e)$:stop

In most cases the default for the target event is correct, however in some cases it is useful to specify a sequence of activities which must take place before a source event is observed. At the implementation level the labels are implemented as immediate actions and when the start label is present the source states are taken to be those which result from an immediate start transition, and similarly the target states are taken to be those which result from an immediate stop transition. All of this occurs automatically and need not be known to the user. However as we will see later one can use the fact that labels are immediate actions to communicate events between multiple added stochastic probes.

Recall that in order to evaluate the passage the CTMC analyser must be provided with two sets of states, the source and target states. The PEPA software translates the stochastic probe specification into a sequential PEPA component and then specifies the states in the same manner as we have already done for our unprobed model using a state specification which need only refer to the added probe component. Our passage is specified with the simple probe specification:

$airbag$:start, $(answer \mid ambulance)$:stop

This is automatically translated into the following PEPA component:

$$\text{Probe} \stackrel{def}{=} (airbag, \top).\text{Probe}_1$$
$$\text{Probe}_1 \stackrel{def}{=} start.\text{Probe}_2$$
$$\text{Probe}_2 \stackrel{def}{=} (answer, \top).\text{Probe}_3$$
$$+ (ambulance, \top).\text{Probe}_3$$
$$\text{Probe}_3 \stackrel{def}{=} stop.\text{Probe}$$

This PEPA component is then composed with the entire system in a cooperation of the activities which the probe observes the model performing (ie. the alphabet of the probe) namely the set $\mathcal{P} = \{airbag, answer, ambulance\}$. So that the main cooperation of a probed model has the form:

$$\text{Probe} \bowtie_{\mathcal{P}} \text{System}$$

Notice that the states Probe_1 and Probe_3 are vanishing states since there are immediate transitions from them and since we do not cooperate with any component of the start and stop activities the probe component will never be blocked in these states.

Our software then takes the probed model and derives the entire state space. This is then converted into a CTMC and the set of source states are all those states which are the result of a start transition. Similarly the set of target states are all of those which are the result of a stop transition. The full grammar for eXtended Stochastic Probe specification is given in Figure 5.

The graph in Figure 6 shows both the cumulative distribution and the probability density function of the response-passage we have analysed. The cumulative distribution function (CDF) plots the probability of completing the analysed passage within the given time. As time increases the value of the CDF approaches 1, provided that the passage must always complete (some passages may deadlock without completing). The probability density function (PDF) is a measure of how likely the passage is to complete at any given time after it was begun. Because a time point is infinitesimally small the probability of completing at that exact point is zero, therefore we plot a probability density against time. It is best thought of as the derivative of the CDF, hence when the CDF sharply increases the PDF will be high and when the CDF is relatively flat the PDF will be close to zero. As time goes to the limit the area under the PDF graph will approach one, once again assuming that the passage always completes eventually. For the remainder of this chapter we will be chiefly concerned with the CDF since these help us to answer the queries related to the service level agreements in which

$expr$	:=	$Process$	population
	|	int	constant
	|	$expr\ relop\ expr$	comparison
	|	$expr\ binop\ expr$	arithmetic
$relop$	:=	$=\ \|\ \neq\ \|\ >\ \|\ <$	
	|	$\geq\ \|\ \leq$	relational operators
$binop$	:=	$+\ \|\ -\ \|\ \times\ \|\ \div$	binary operators
$pred$	:=	$\neg pred$	not
	|	$true\ \|\ false$	boolean
	|	if $pred$	
		then $pred$	
		else $pred$	conditional
	|	$pred$ && $pred$	disjunction
	|	$pred\ \|\|\ pred$	conjunction
	|	$expr$	expression

Fig. 4. The full grammar for state specifications

P_{def}	:=	$name :: R$	locally attached probe
	|	R	globally attached probe
R	:=	$activity$	observe action
	|	R_1, R_2	sequence
	|	$R_1\ \|\ R_2$	choice
	|	R:label	labelled
	|	$R/activity$	resetting
	|	(R)	bracketed
	|	$R\ n$	iterate
	|	$R\{m,n\}$	iterate
	|	R^+	one or more
	|	R^*	zero or more
	|	$R^?$	zero or one
R	:=	$\ldots\ \|\ \{pred\}R$	guarded

Fig. 5. The full grammar for eXtended Stochastic Probe specifications

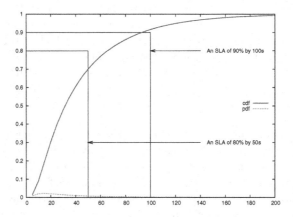

Fig. 6. The cumulative distribution and probability density functions of our first analysis of the response-passage in the airbag call centre model. Shown together with two boxes representing service level agreements.

we are interested. In this particular case we see that the CDF has a similar look to an exponential distribution. This is because our passage in question is made up of one of two activities which have a relatively long average duration (the *timeout* and *answer* activities) together with several activities which have a relatively short average duration. This means that the passage is dominated by these two 'bottleneck' activities and hence the response-profile is similar to that of simply the single activities in question. In the next section we will explore this in more detail.

We can also determine bottleneck activities through the use of sensitivity analysis. Sensitivity analysis allows us to vary the rate at which a particular activity is performed whilst maintaining all other rates constant. This allows us to determine how sensitive the passage is to that particular rate. If the response-profile changes a lot in response to varying a particular rate then that activity has a large affect and hence if we are trying to improve system performance that is a good candidate activity to attempt to optimise. Where the response-profile does not change much then that activity cannot be usefully optimised in the present system configuration. Here we should find that optimising, in other words decreasing the average duration of, the activities *timeout* and *answer* would increase the performance of the system. Clearly here the *answer* activity is outside the control of the system implementors but the *timeout* activity is not. In this instance setting a low *timeout* duration may mean that we needlessly call for the dispatch of an ambulance because the driver did not answer the phone quickly enough.

Finally from the graph we determine whether we would satisfy a simple service level agreement stating a percentage and a time by which the given percentage of requests should be completed. This is shown on the graph by drawing an SLA box by disecting the axes with a horizontal line from the given percentage and a vertical line from the given time. Where the CDF crosses the box along the horizontal line the SLA has been achieved but where it crosses the vertical line it has failed. Shown on the graph are two SLAs one which is satisfied: "Ninety percent of all requests are completed within one hundred seconds" and one which is not: "Eighty percent of all requests are completed within fifty seconds".

4   SLA Analysis

We now wish to split up the measurement of the passage to allow us to separately measure each of the two courses the passage may take. This is to detect the case that one course is particularly fast while the other is particularly slow, causing the slow passage to have unacceptably poor performance while the fast passage happens often enough that the overall passage performance satisfies the given SLA. We need not modify our model in order to analyse the two passages separately, the language of XSP is expressive enough to allow this. We focus first of all in analysing all passages from *airbag* to *ambulance*. We might try the following very simplistic probe:

airbag:start, *ambulance*:stop

Unfortunately this will incorrectly analyse from the occurrence of *any airbag* activity until an eventual *ambulance* activity. This includes *airbag* activities which result in an unhurt driver, who may then answer the phone rather than allow a timeout which will result in the conclusion of the passage with an *ambulance* activity. It may happen that the model loops round several *airbag* − *answer* sequences before eventually the driver is hurt and a *timeout* occurs and finally the *ambulance* activity completes the passage. Clearly this is not analysing the passage we intend, we would like to put a guard on the end of the *airbag* activity to say that the passage should only be started when an *airbag* activity which results in the driver becoming hurt is observed. Unfortunately the language of XSP only allows guards to be put on the front of the activity. We can solve this problem however by adding an activity which is performed after the *airbag* activity, we can then put a guard on the extra activity. Of course in order to leave the behaviour of the model and passage unaffected the extra activity must take zero time, in other words we must use an immediate action. We can add the immediate action with the addition of a labelled probe, which simply observes an *airbag* activity and then performs the immediate action which we will name *signal*. We then add a second probe that waits for a *signal* action to occur but guards this with a state specification on the state after the *airbag* occurrence. The two added probes are then:

airbag : *signal*
{Hurt == 1}*signal* : *start*, *ambulance* : *stop*

Equivalently we can separate out those *airbag* requests which may result in the driver answering the phone by adding the following two probes:

airbag : *signal*
{Okay == 1}*signal* : *start*, (*answer* | *ambulance*) : *stop*

Note that we still allow this second passage to be ended via an *ambulance* activity, this is because even if the airbag activity does not cause the driver to be injured they may still miss the phone call which will result in an ambulance being called unnecessarily. The graphs in Figure 7 depict the CDFs for both passages as well as re-plotting the CDF of the original general passage. The left hand graph is the original model from which we can make several observations; there are as we supposed two distinct passages, the 'hurt passage' and the 'okay passage'. The hurt passage takes longer to complete since there are more activities and a *timeout* is slower than an *answer* activity. The general passage which is the combination of the two takes less time than the hurt passage but more than the okay passage. Notice that the line for the general passage is closer to that of the hurt passage, because this path occurs more often. In this particular model it is easy to see that this passage occurs more often, but this is in general not easy to tell solely from looking at the model, numerical analysis is required.

On the graphs the exponential distributions for the *timeout* and *answer* activities are also plotted. The first thing to notice is that the CDF of the hurt-passage is similar to that of the exponential for the *timeout*. This gives us good evidence that the *timeout* activity is dominating the hurt-passage such that it is the bottleneck. This is similarly the case for the *answer* activity and the okay-passage. There is an important difference, notice that it is never the case that the hurt-passage is more likely to complete than a simple occurrence of the *timeout* activity. This is because all hurt-passages include one *timeout* activity. However as time increases it becomes more likely that the okay-passage is completed than is a single occurrence of its dominating activity the *answer* activity. This is because when the *answer* activity takes a long time the okay-passage may be shortcut by a *timeout* activity, and since after the *timeout* all that is required to complete the passage is the fast *ambulance* activity this means the okay-passage can be faster than the slow occurrences of the *answer* activity. To put this another way, the bottleneck of the okay-passage is the race between the *answer* and *timeout* activities which is faster than a single *answer* activity on its own.

Finally the graph on the right is a reproduction of the graph on the left but for a slightly modified model. In this model we have exchanged the weights on the passive rates at which the Driver component observes the *airbag* activity. This means that the hurt passage will now occur less often than the okay passage. As we can see the two individual passages are unaffected since for those passages the time it takes to complete is not dependent on how often they are begun. However the general passage is now faster since the okay passage which is the faster of the two makes up the majority of those general passage occurrences. The CDF of the general passage is now closer to that of the okay passage.

4.1   Sensitivity Analysis

As we stated previously from our analysis of our model we suspect that the *timeout* and *answer* activities are bottleneck activities whose rates greatly affect the probability of completion of the passage within a given time. This model was particularly amenable to this kind of analysis, specifically done via analysis of

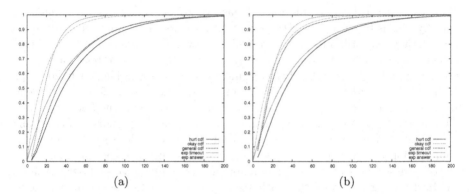

Fig. 7. Two graphs showing the CDFs for the separate passages. We also plot the CDFs for the 'bottleneck' activities *timeout* and *answer*. The graph on the left is for the original model and the graph on the right for a modified model in which the probabilities that the driver is hurt and okay have been swapped, showing that the CDF of the general passage resembles more closely that of the separate passage which occurs more often.

the structure of the model. We are not always so fortunate in the composition of our models and in any case it is important to confirm your conclusions with numerical analysis. To some extent we have done this by noting that the CDF lines of the two distinct passages are similar to those of the exponentials of the suspected bottleneck activities, however for a truer understanding we require what is known as *sensitivity analysis*. Generally speaking sensitivity analysis involves varying one aspect of a model while maintaining the rest of the model as is and performing the same analysis on each of the set of modified models. In our case the aspect of the model which we will vary is the rate of one of the activities. We will show the effect that varying the rates of the two suspected bottleneck activities has on each of the passages.

The graphs in Figure 8 are surface plots representing the sensitivity of the three analysed passages to the rates associated with the activities *timeout* and *answer*. Graphs (a) and (c) analyse the general passage *airbag − (answer | ambulance)* and graphs (b) and (d) respectively analyse the more specific passages; the hurt-passage, when the *airbag* activity causes the driver to be injured and the okay-passage, when the *airbag* activity causes the driver to be unhurt. Graphs (a) and (b) vary the rate associated with the *timeout* activity and graphs (c) and (d) vary the rate associated with the *answer* activity. From graphs (a) and (b) we see that both the general passage and the hurt passage are clearly very much affected by the rate of the *timeout* activity. The hurt passage is affected even more so than the general passage because some of the paths taken for the general passage do not include a *timeout* activity whereas all paths for the hurt-passage do. The difference is not very pronounced, this is because most of the paths taken in the general passage are occurrences of the hurt-passage as these graphs are from the original model in which eighty percent of all airbag occurrences result in an injured driver. Contrast this with the bottom two graphs

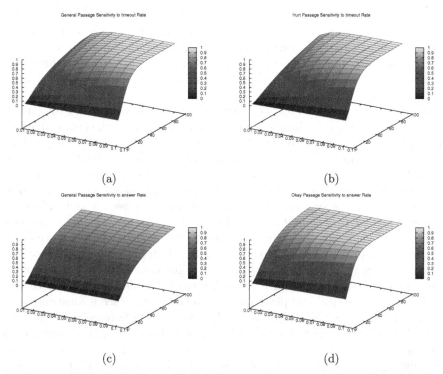

Fig. 8. Sensitivity analysis for the rates associated with the *timeout* (top two graphs) and the *answer* (bottom two graphs) activities. The two graphs on the left analyse the general passage while the graphs on the right analyse the separate 'hurt' (graph b) and 'okay' (graph d) passages showing a large effect on a separate passage is reflected in the general passage if the given separate passage occurs often enough (top two graphs) but not if the separate passage is infrequent relative to the general passage (bottom two graphs).

(c) and (d). In graph (c) varying the rate associated with the *answer* activity does affect the probability of completing the general passage but not by very much, because most such passages do not include an *answer* activity. Graph (d) however shows that varying this rate does have a very large affect on the probability of completing the okay-passage, since the probability of completing the okay-passage is not affected by how often it occurs, but is very much affected the *answer* activity. Notice though that the affect that varying the rate has is less pronounced towards the left hand of the graph when the *answer* rate is small. This is because at low *answer* rates the *answer* activity is often beaten by the *timeout* activity and hence even for the okay-passage many occurrences do not feature an *answer* activity.

From these graphs we can confirm our suspicion from our earlier analysis that the *timeout* activity is indeed a bottleneck activity for both the hurt-passage and the general passage and that optimising this activity will have the most significant improvement for the service of the system in general. Optimising for the *answer* activity will have less affect for the general passage. We have also shown system performance in general is not dependent on a particular passage performing particularly well and often enough to mask the unacceptable performance of an important path through the model. We speculate that in this model the important passage is the hurt-passage, as the penalty for failing to complete this passage in a short enough time may be human life.

Lastly we note that this form of analysis must be coupled with expert analysis of the actual system in question. As modellers we can speculate that the optimisation of certain activities will increase the system performance. However we say nothing as to how such an activity may be optimised, for example it is difficult to see how the *answer* activity, performed by the client may be optimised. Optimising the *timeout* activity, as we mentioned before, has some serious effects for the system's behaviour which have not been modelled here. In particular with a very short *timeout* we risk calling for an ambulance unnecessarily. Such behaviour can easily be added to the model from which we could determine the probability and frequency with which this undesired behaviour occurs. Once again it would then require specialist knowledge, in particular the cost of unnecessarily calling for an ambulance, to then decide upon the correct compromise between system performance and behaviour. Such a constraint may be written as a service level agreement which we then undertake to evaluate, for example: "Less than five percent of airbag deployments in which the driver does not require emergency aid result in the service requesting the dispatchment of an ambulance". Our goal as modellers is simply to provide data for the system designers, it is then their task to present the most efficient/cost effective system based on that and their own information.

5   Conclusions

In this chapter we have used the stochastic process algebra PEPA to model and analyse a sophisticated automotive crash assistance service. The system as deployed is clearly complex involving the traffic system of an entire city but we have been able to identify and model the important parts for system evaluation and abstract those parts about which assumptions must be made. In particular we are unconcerned with how often airbags are deployed and are interested only in the performance of the system from the moment one such registered airbag is deployed and the succesful conclusion of the service. In particular we have assumed that no two cars crash simultaneously in different parts of this city. More performance modelling could be done to conclude whether or not this is a safe assumption and whether or not the service must be therefore increased, ie. more operators added, in order to allow the assumption that any such crash has exclusive use of the service. This makes this service an agreeable one for the purposes of demonstration of the technique for response-time analysis. In general response-time analysis rests on two factors, how available the system is for each request and how long each request takes during its usage. Here we have concentrated on the second part of this since each use can be assumed to have exclusive access to the service.

Since only one client is required here the state space has been low enough to allow precise analysis via the translation of the model into a continuous time Markov chain. This has allowed us to use the well known technique of uniformisation to obtain passage-time quantiles which map the probability of completion of a given passage against time since the passage was initiated. This is exactly the style of analysis that is required to answer the important questions of a service level agreement. However we have also shown that deeper understanding of the passage is often required such that inadequate performance is not masked within an overall acceptable performance rate. Our key technique is the specification of the passages to analyse in the language of eXtended Stochastic Probes. These allow the user to define robust passages which may be used to analyse several similar models and all at an appropriately high level akin to that with which the user must define their model. Of particular note is that the user may specify their passage by the events with which it is intuitively delineated rather than the states resulting from those events.

Acknowledgements. The authors are supported by the EU FET-IST Global Computing 2 project SENSORIA ("Software Engineering for Service-Oriented Overlay Computers" (IST-3-016004-IP-09)). The ipc/Hydra tool chain has been developed in co-operation with Jeremy Bradley, Will Knottenbelt and Nick Dingle of Imperial College, London.

References

1. Hillston, J.: A Compositional Approach to Performance Modelling. Cambridge University Press, Cambridge (1996)
2. Clark, A., Gilmore, S.: State-aware performance analysis with eXtended Stochastic Probes. In: Thomas, N., Juiz, C. (eds.) EPEW 2008. LNCS, vol. 5261, pp. 125–140. Springer, Heidelberg (2008)
3. Hillston, J.: The nature of synchronisation. In: Herzog, U., Rettelbach, M. (eds.) Proceedings of the Second International Workshop on Process Algebras and Performance Modelling, Erlangen, pp. 51–70 (1994)
4. Hillston, J.: Tuning systems: From composition to performance. The Computer Journal 48(4), 385–400 (2005); The Needham Lecture paper
5. Hillston, J.: Process algebras for quantitative analysis. In: Proceedings of the 20th Annual IEEE Symposium on Logic in Computer Science (LICS 2005), Chicago, pp. 239–248. IEEE Computer Society Press, Los Alamitos (2005)
6. Hillston, J., Kloul, L.: An efficient Kronecker representation for PEPA models. In: de Alfaro, L., Gilmore, S. (eds.) PROBMIV 2001, PAPM-PROBMIV 2001, and PAPM 2001. LNCS, vol. 2165, pp. 120–135. Springer, Heidelberg (2001)
7. Hillston, J.: Fluid flow approximation of PEPA models. In: Proceedings of the Second International Conference on the Quantitative Evaluation of Systems, Torino, Italy, pp. 33–43. IEEE Computer Society Press, Los Alamitos (2005)
8. Gillespie, D.: Exact stochastic simulation of coupled chemical reactions. Journal of Physical Chemistry 81(25), 2340–2361 (1977)
9. Bradley, J., Gilmore, S.: Stochastic simulation methods applied to a secure electronic voting model. Electr. Notes Theor. Comput. Sci. 151(3), 5–25 (2006)

Scaling Performance Analysis Using Fluid-Flow Approximation*

Mirco Tribastone and Stephen Gilmore

School of Informatics
The University of Edinburgh, Scotland
{mtribast,stg}@inf.ed.ac.uk

Abstract. The fluid interpretation of the process calculus PEPA provides a very useful tool for the performance evaluation of large-scale systems because the tractability of the numerical solution does not depend upon the population levels of the system under study. This paper offers a tutorial on how to use this technique by analysing a case study of a service-oriented application to support an e-University infrastructure.

1   Introduction

The quantitative analysis of large-scale applications using discrete-state models is fundamentally hampered by the rapid growth of the state space as a function of the number of components in the system (*state-space explosion*). Markov chains—traditionally employed in performance evaluation studies—are no exception, despite much effort aimed at *largeness avoidance*, e.g., by means of aggregation techniques [1] or *largeness tolerance*, e.g., by means of out-of-core solution methods [2]. One radical approach to tackling state-space explosion is to abandon the discrete-state representation in favour of a continuous-state view expressible in terms of a computationally less expensive ordinary differential equation (ODE) model. Here, the performance evaluation is based on the numerical integration of an associated initial-value problem, whose tractability is largely independent from the actual population levels of the system under study. Interestingly, under specific circumstances ODE models may be directly inferred from Markov models, and represent the limiting behaviour of the stochastic process when some system parameter, typically population size, is sufficiently large [3]. In such cases these ODEs shall be referred to as the *fluid-flow approximation* of the associated Markov model.

The stochastic process algebra PEPA gives rise to continuous-time Markov chains (CTMCs) which admit a fluid-flow approximation, therefore it can be used as a scalable analysis tool for the performance evaluation of large systems. There are three main advantages in using a high-level modelling language as opposed to a direct description based on the CTMC representation. First, the language is formal and can be implemented on a computer, thus providing a

---

* This work has been partially sponsored by the project SENSORIA, IST-2005-016004.

M. Wirsing and M. Hölzl (Eds.): SENSORIA Project, LNCS 6582, pp. 486–505, 2011.

general modelling framework. Second, the model may be used to carry out other forms of analysis beyond performance evaluation, e.g., static analysis to verify the well-formedeness of the input model, or model-checking for deadlock detection. Third, in most cases the model description is more compact than its underlying representation, whose fully automated derivation process shields the modeller from typically tedious and error-prone tasks.

The purpose of this paper is to provide a tutorial on how to use PEPA for modelling large-scale systems. After an overview of the language and its stochastic and fluid-flow interpretations in Section 2, the paper presents in Section 3 a model of a service-oriented application for an e-University infrastructure supporting thousands of students. The model is developed according to a more general modelling pattern which captures performance concerns related to resource contention at both the hardware and the software level. Section 4 deals with the analysis of the model from the standpoint of the user-perceived performance, computed as the average response time of the system. This analysis is accompanied by screenshots of a software toolkit for PEPA (the *PEPA Eclipse Plug-in*, one of the formal analysis tools hosted on the SENSORIA *Development Environment*) to show how the results can be practically evaluated. Finally, Section 5 gives concluding remarks.

2   Overview of PEPA

2.1   Language Operators

PEPA is a CSP-like process calculus extended with the notion of exponentially distributed activities [4]. A PEPA model consists of a collection of components (also termed processes) which undertake actions. A component may perform an action autonomously (*independent actions*) or in synchronisation with other components in the system (*shared actions*). The language supports the following operators:

Prefix $(\alpha, r).E$ constitutes the atomic unit of computation of a PEPA model. It denotes a component which may perform an activity (α, r) of type α, subsequently behaving as E, which is said to be a *derivative* of the component. The activity rate r is taken from the domain $\mathbb{R}_{>0} \cup \{\top\}$. If the rate is a positive real then the activity duration is assumed to be drawn from an exponential distribution with mean $1/r$ time units. The symbol $\top$ denotes a form of *passive synchronisation* whereby an activity of type α is to be executed in synchronisation with some other component, which will determine the overall rate of execution of the shared action. The models presented in this paper do not make use of passive synchronisation. The set of action types in a PEPA model is denoted by $\mathcal{A}$, whereas $\mathcal{Act}$ denotes the set of activities.

Choice $E + F$ indicates that a component may behave as E or F. Unlike traditional process calculi in which the choice is non-deterministic, the behaviour in PEPA (and indeed in all other stochastic process calculi) is determined stochastically. For instance, let $r, s > 0$, in the choice $(\alpha, r).E + (\beta, s).F$ the actions α and β are executed with probabilities $r/(r + s)$ and $s/(r + s)$, respectively.

Constant $A \overset{def}{=} E$ is used to model cyclic behaviour. Consider $A \overset{def}{=} (\alpha, r).B$, $B \overset{def}{=} (\beta, s).A$. Here, A is a component with two derivatives which performs sequences of α- and β-activities forever.

Cooperation $E \bowtie_L F$ is the synchronisation operator of PEPA. The components E and F are required to synchronise over the action types in the set L. All the other actions are performed autonomously. For instance, $(\alpha, r).(\beta, s).E \bowtie_{\{\alpha\}} (\alpha, t).(\gamma, u).F$ is a cooperation between two components which may perform a shared activity of type α, with rate $\min(r, t)$, subsequently behaving as $(\beta, s).E \bowtie_{\{\alpha\}} (\gamma, u).F$. Then actions β and γ are carried out autonomously. By contrast, in the cooperation $(\alpha, r).E \bowtie_{\{\alpha\}} (\beta, s).F$ the process $(\alpha, r).E$ does not progress because α is not available in the right hand side of the cooperation. The set of all shared action types between E and F is sometimes denoted by the symbol $*$.

Hiding E/L relabels the activities of E with the *silent action* τ for all types in L. Thus, $\big((\alpha, r_1).E/\{\alpha\}\big) \bowtie_{\{\alpha\}} (\alpha, r_2).F$ does not cooperate over α because the process in the left-hand side of the cooperation performs a transition (τ, r_1) to E. All α-transitions performed by E are similarly hidden.

An interesting class of PEPA models comprises those which can be generated by the following two-level grammar:

$$S ::= (\alpha, r).S \quad | \quad S + S \quad | \quad A_S, \quad A_S \overset{def}{=} S$$

$$C ::= S \quad | \quad C \bowtie_L C \quad | \quad C/L \quad | \quad A_C, \quad A_C \overset{def}{=} C$$

The first production defines *sequential components*, i.e., processes which only exhibit sequential behaviour (by means of the prefix operator), and branching (by means of the choice operator). The second production defines *model components*, in which the interactions between the sequential components are expressed through the cooperation and hiding operators. A model component designated as the *system equation* defines the environment which embraces all of the behaviour of the system under study.

The model shown in Fig. 1 is defined using such a grammar and will be used in the remainder of this section to illustrate the main properties of PEPA. The model may represent a basic client/server scenario. A client is a sequential component which cycles between the two derivatives *Download* and *Think*. Similarly, a server is a two-derivative component with derivatives *Upload* and *Log*. In derivative *Download* the client is able to carry out a shared action *comm* in cooperation with the server's derivative *Upload*. The derivatives *Think* and *Log* model autonomous activities performed by the components. In a distributed application, activities of this kind may be used to denote genuinely local computations or to abstract away interactions with other components with negligible impact on the performance characteristics of the system. The use of a *component*

$$Download \stackrel{def}{=} (comm, r_d).Think$$

$$Think \stackrel{def}{=} (think, r_t).Download$$

$$Upload \stackrel{def}{=} (comm, r_u).Log$$

$$Log \stackrel{def}{=} (log, r_l).Upload$$

$$System \stackrel{def}{=} Download[N_C] \underset{\{comm\}}{\bowtie} Upload[N_S]$$

Fig. 1. Simple PEPA model of a client/server scenario

array $E[N]$ occurs frequently in the modelling of large-scale systems because it characterises a population of N independent and identical sequential components E. More formally, $E[N]$ is a shorthand notation for $\underbrace{E \bowtie_\emptyset E \cdots \bowtie_\emptyset E}_{N}$. Although this notation does not add expressiveness to the language with respect to its stochastic semantics, replicated behaviour in this form is fundamental in the fluid-flow interpretation of PEPA, as shown later in this section.

2.2 Markovian Semantics

The operational semantics of PEPA is shown in Fig. 2. Rule C_2 is the fundamental inference for the characterisation of the dynamic behaviour of a shared action. It implements the semantics of *bounded capacity*: informally, the overall rate of execution of a shared activity is the minimum between the rates of the synchronising components (as a result, since the individual activities are exponentially distributed so is the synchronised action). The rule relies on the notion of *apparent rate* to compute the total capacity of a cooperating component, according to the following definition.

Definition 1. *The* apparent rate *of action* α *in process* E, *denoted by* $r_\alpha(E)$, *indicates the overall rate at which* α *can be performed by* E. *It is recursively defined as follows:*

$$r_\alpha((\beta, r).E) = \begin{cases} r \text{ if } \beta = \alpha \\ 0 \text{ if } \beta \neq \alpha \end{cases}$$

$$r_\alpha(E + F) = r_\alpha(E) + r_\alpha(F)$$

$$r_\alpha\left(E \underset{L}{\bowtie} F\right) = \begin{cases} \min(r_\alpha(E), r_\alpha(F)) \text{ if } \alpha \in L \\ r_\alpha(E) + r_\alpha(F) \quad\quad \text{ if } \alpha \notin L \end{cases}$$

$$r_\alpha(E/L) = \begin{cases} r_\alpha(E) \text{ if } \alpha \notin L \\ 0 \quad\quad \text{ if } \alpha \in L \end{cases}$$

Prefix

$$S_0 : \frac{}{(\alpha, r).E \xrightarrow{(\alpha,r)} E}$$

Choice

$$S_1 : \frac{E \xrightarrow{(\alpha,r)} E'}{E + F \xrightarrow{(\alpha,r)} E' + F} \qquad S_2 : \frac{F \xrightarrow{(\alpha,r)} F'}{E + F \xrightarrow{(\alpha,r)} E + F'}$$

Cooperation

$$C_0 : \frac{E \xrightarrow{(\alpha,r)} E'}{E \bowtie_L F \xrightarrow{(\alpha,r)} E' \bowtie_L F}, \alpha \notin L \qquad C_1 : \frac{F \xrightarrow{(\alpha,r)} F'}{E \bowtie_L F \xrightarrow{(\alpha,r)} E \bowtie_L F'}, \alpha \notin L$$

$$C_2 : \frac{E \xrightarrow{(\alpha,r_1)} E' \quad F \xrightarrow{(\alpha,r_2)} F'}{E \bowtie_L F \xrightarrow{(\alpha,R)} E' \bowtie_L F'}, \alpha \in L \qquad R = \frac{r_1}{r_\alpha(E)} \frac{r_2}{r_\alpha(F)} \min (r_\alpha(E), r_\alpha(F))$$

Hiding

$$H_0 : \frac{E \xrightarrow{(\alpha,r)} E'}{E/L \xrightarrow{(\alpha,r)} E'/L}, \alpha \notin L \qquad H_1 : \frac{E \xrightarrow{(\alpha,r)} E'}{E/L \xrightarrow{(\tau,r)} E'/L}, \alpha \in L$$

Constant

$$A_0 : \frac{E \xrightarrow{(\alpha,r)} E'}{A \xrightarrow{(\alpha,r)} E'}, A \stackrel{def}{=} E$$

Fig. 2. Markovian semantics of PEPA

According to this definition, for the array of sequential components $Download[N_C]$ the apparent rate of $comm$ is

$$r_{comm} (Download[N_C]) = N_C \, r_{comm} (Download) = N_C \times r_d. \qquad (1)$$

Similarly,

$$r_{comm} (Upload[N_S]) = N_S \, r_{comm} (Upload) = N_S \times r_u. \qquad (2)$$

Given a PEPA component E, the operational semantics induces the *derivative set*, denoted by $ds(E)$, which is the set of the possible states reachable from E. A *derivation graph* whose nodes are in $ds(E)$ and arcs in $ds(E) \times \mathcal{A}ct \times ds(E)$ indicates all the transitions between each pair of derivatives of E. Arcs are taken with multiplicity corresponding to the number of distinct inference trees which give the same transition. The derivation graph is ultimately mapped onto a CTMC in which each state corresponds to a derivative in $ds(E)$.

The states reachable from the system equation *System* in Fig. 1 are obtained by constructing derivation trees which begin with the transitions enabled by the constituent sequential components. By rules S_0 and A_0 the following two transitions can be inferred for *Download* and *Upload*:

$$Download \xrightarrow{(comm, r_d)} Think \tag{3}$$

$$Upload \xrightarrow{(comm, r_u)} Log \tag{4}$$

The dynamic behaviour of the leftmost component $Download$ of the array can be collected by $N_C - 1$ applications of rule C_0. The first application has the form:

$$\frac{Download \xrightarrow{(comm, r_d)} Think}{Download \parallel Download \xrightarrow{(comm, r_d)} Think \parallel Download}$$

Then, for $1 \leq i \leq N_C - 2$, the other $N_C - 2$ applications are of type

$$\frac{Download \parallel Download[i] \xrightarrow{(comm, r_d)} Think \parallel Download[i]}{Download \parallel Download[i] \parallel Download \xrightarrow{(comm, r_d)} Think \parallel Download[i] \parallel Download}$$

For $i = N_C - 2$, the conclusion of this rule may be written as

$$Download[N_C] \xrightarrow{(comm, r_d)} Think \parallel Download[N_C - 1] \tag{5}$$

The behaviour of the leftmost component $Upload$ can be collected in a similar way, leading to a transition in the form

$$Upload[N_S] \xrightarrow{(comm, r_u)} Log \parallel Upload[N_S - 1] \tag{6}$$

Finally, by applying rule C_2 to (5) and (6),

$$Download[N_C] \underset{\{comm\}}{\bowtie} Upload[N_S] \xrightarrow{(comm, R)}$$

$$Think \parallel Download[N_C - 1] \underset{\{comm\}}{\bowtie} Log \parallel Upload[N_S - 1] \tag{7}$$

where, by rule C_2 and equations (1) and (2),

$$R = \frac{r_d}{r_{comm}(Download[N_C])} \frac{r_u}{r_{comm}(Upload[N_S])}$$
$$\times \min(r_{comm}(Download[N_C]), r_{comm}(Upload[N_S]))$$
$$= \frac{r_d}{N_C \, r_d} \frac{r_u}{N_S \, r_u} \min(N_C \, r_d, N_S \, r_u) = \frac{1}{N_C} \frac{1}{N_S} \min(N_C \, r_d, N_S \, r_u)$$

The conclusion of (7) is not the only transition enabled by the $System$, because each individual component $Download$ can be paired with each component $Upload$ to carry out action $comm$. Hence, $Download[N_C] \underset{\{comm\}}{\bowtie} Upload[N_S]$ enables $N_C \times N_S$ transitions to distinct states of type

$$\underbrace{Download \parallel \cdots \parallel Download \parallel Think \parallel Download \parallel \cdots \parallel Download}_{N_C \text{ sequential components}}$$

$$\underset{\{comm\}}{\bowtie} \underbrace{Upload \parallel \cdots \parallel Upload \parallel Log \parallel Upload \parallel \cdots \parallel Upload}_{N_S \text{ sequential components}} \tag{8}$$

which only differ in the locations of the components *Think* and *Log*. Since each transition occurs at rate R, the exit rate from $Download[N_C] \bowtie_{\{comm\}} Upload[N_S]$ is $N_C \times N_S \times R = \min(N_C r_d, N_S r_u)$ and the factor $1/(N_C \times N_S)$ is the probability that one specific pair of components makes that transition.

2.3 Markovian Aggregation Techniques

Each of the states of kind (8), say *Think* $\parallel$ *Download*$[N_C - 1] \bowtie_{\{comm\}} Log \parallel$ *Upload*$[N_S - 1]$, has transitions to $(N_C - 1) \times (N_S - 1)$ distinct states in which there are two copies of *Think*, $(N_C - 2)$ copies of *Download*, two copies of *Log*, and $(N_S - 2)$ copies of *Upload*. Similarly, each of such states, say *Think*$[2] \parallel$ *Download*$[N_C - 2] \bowtie_{\{comm\}} Log[2] \parallel Upload[N_S - 2]$, has transitions to $(N_C - 2) \times (N_S - 2)$ distinct states in which there are three copies of *Think*, $(N_C - 3)$ copies of *Download*, three copies of *Log*, and $(N_S - 3)$ copies of *Upload*. Overall, this model will have a state space of cardinality $2^{N_C + N_S}$, clearly unsatisfactory for large-scale models. The reduction technique presented in [5] goes a long way toward alleviating this problem. Using a strong notion of equivalence in PEPA called *isomorphism*, the original states are aggregated in such a way that the location of each sequential component is not recorded, therefore the $N_C \times N_S$ states of kind (8) collapse into the same state of the aggregated chain. The reduction achieved by this algorithm depends on the structure of the model under study. Overall, the exponential growth of the non-aggregated state space of the model in Fig. 1 is simplified to a state space cardinality which is polynomial in N_C and N_S (the state space size is $(N_C + 1) \times (N_S + 1)$).

2.4 Fluid-Flow Approximation

The fundamental limitation of the Markovian approach is that the model dynamics is based on a discrete-state representation. As the number of components increases, more and more of these discrete changes need to be accounted for, leading to a dramatic growth in the state-space. The fluid-flow approximation abandons the traditional Markovian interpretation in favour of an alternative view in which such discrete changes are approximated in a continuous fashion. This section presents the rationale behind this approach by means of the running example in Figure 1. Further details may be found in the papers which have dealt with this analysis more formally [6,7,8,9].

The fluid-flow interpretation deals with populations of identical components. Since one single individual is a sequential component cycling through a number of derivatives, the population behaviour is described by a state representation which counts how many individuals exhibit a particular derivative at any point in time. For instance, the model in Fig. 1 shows two distinct population classes, i.e., N_C components cycling through *Download* and *Think*, and N_S components cycling through *Upload* and *Log*. Based on this, it is possible to define a vector state descriptor, called the *numerical vector form* (NVF), in which each element of the vector is associated with a distinct derivative in the system. The initial state *System* in Fig. 1 can be represented by the NVF $(N_C, 0, N_S, 0)$, using the mapping whereby the elements of the vector, from left to right, are associated with the population levels of *Download*, *Think*, *Upload*, and *Log*. Analogously, the aggregated state for (8) is given the NVF $(N_C-1, 1, N_S-1, 1)$. The transition between these two states may be represented as follows:

$$(N_C, 0, N_S, 0) \xrightarrow{comm, \min(N_C \, r_d, N_S r_u)} (N_C - 1, 1, N_S - 1, 1) \tag{9}$$

A crucial step toward fluid-flow approximation is the generalisation of (9) for an arbitrary NVF ξ, i.e.,

$$\xi = (\xi_1, \xi_2, \xi_3, \xi_4) \xrightarrow{comm, \min(\xi_1 \, r_d, \xi_3 r_u)} \xi' = (\xi_1 - 1, \xi_2 + 1, \xi_3 - 1, \xi_4 + 1) \tag{10}$$

With analogous arguments it is possible to derive generic transitions for the activities *think* and *log*, i.e.,

$$\xi = (\xi_1, \xi_2, \xi_3, \xi_4) \xrightarrow{think, \xi_2 r_t} \xi'' = (\xi_1 + 1, \xi_2 - 1, \xi_3, \xi_4) \tag{11}$$

$$\xi = (\xi_1, \xi_2, \xi_3, \xi_4) \xrightarrow{log, \xi_4 r_l} \xi''' = (\xi_1, \xi_2, \xi_3 + 1, \xi_4 - 1) \tag{12}$$

Such transitions can be interpreted in a continuous manner. For instance, (10) says that there is (on average) a unitary decrease in the number of components *Download* and *Upload* after $1/\min(\xi_1 r_d, \xi_3 r_u)$ time units, to which it corresponds a unitary increase in the components *Think* and *Log*. Letting $x_i(t), 1 \le i \le 4$, be the continuously changing population counts, their variation due to this transition over some finite interval of time Δt may be written as:

$$\begin{aligned}
x_1(t + \Delta t) - x_1(t) &= -\min(x_1(t) r_d, x_3(t) r_u) \Delta t \\
x_2(t + \Delta t) - x_2(t) &= -\min(x_1(t) r_d, x_3(t) r_u) \Delta t \\
x_3(t + \Delta t) - x_2(t) &= +\min(x_1(t) r_d, x_3(t) r_u) \Delta t \\
x_4(t + \Delta t) - x_2(t) &= +\min(x_1(t) r_d, x_3(t) r_u) \Delta t
\end{aligned} \tag{13}$$

Incorporating the contributions of the transitions (11) and (12) into (13) in a similar way leads to the finite-difference equations

$$\begin{aligned}
x_1(t + \Delta t) - x_1(t) &= -\min(x_1(t) r_d, x_3(t) r_u) \Delta t + x_2(t) r_t \Delta t \\
x_2(t + \Delta t) - x_2(t) &= -\min(x_1(t) r_d, x_3(t) r_u) \Delta t - x_2(t) r_t \Delta t \\
x_3(t + \Delta t) - x_2(t) &= +\min(x_1(t) r_d, x_3(t) r_u) \Delta t + x_4(t) r_l \Delta t \\
x_4(t + \Delta t) - x_2(t) &= +\min(x_1(t) r_d, x_3(t) r_u) \Delta t - x_4(t) r_l \Delta t
\end{aligned} \tag{14}$$

which define the following ODE model by dividing (14) by Δt and taking the limit $\Delta t \to 0$:

$$\begin{aligned}
\dot{x}_1 &= -\min(x_1(t) r_d, x_3(t) r_u) + x_2(t) r_t \\
\dot{x}_2 &= -\min(x_1(t) r_d, x_3(t) r_u) - x_2(t) r_t \\
\dot{x}_3 &= +\min(x_1(t) r_d, x_3(t) r_u) + x_4(t) r_l \\
\dot{x}_4 &= +\min(x_1(t) r_d, x_3(t) r_u) - x_4(t) r_l
\end{aligned}$$

Related Work. The topic of deterministic interpretation of process algebra models has received much attention recently. Cardelli has investigated the relationship between the continuous- and the discrete-state representation of the *Chemical Ground Form,* used for the modelling of chemical reactions [10]. A route toward fluid approximation has also been followed in the context of the *stochastic Concurrent Constraint Programming* process algebra [11].

3   e-University Case Study

The model presented in this section is based on the e-University SENSORIA case study (also cfr. Chapter 0-2 and Deliverable 8.4.a [12]). The scenario of interest is the *Course Selection* scenario, where students obtain information about the courses available at their education establishment and may enrol in those for which specific requirements are satisfied.

Although the overall application is intended to be service-oriented, the scenario investigated here is such that the kinds of services available in the system do not to change over the time frame captured by this model. This reflects the fact that a university's course organisation is likely to be fixed before it is offered to students (furthermore, minor changes are likely not to affect the system's behaviour significantly). The model will not consider other services which may be deployed in an actual application (e.g., authentication services) because their impact on performance is assumed to be negligible. The scenario also considers a constant population of students to capture a real-world situation where the university's matriculation process is likely to be completed before the application may be accessed.

3.1   Model

The access point to the system is the *University Portal,* a front-end layer which presents the available services in a coherent way, e.g., by means of a web interface. There are four services in this model: (i) *Course Browsing* allows the user to navigate through the University's course offerings; (ii) *Course Selection* allows the user to submit a tentative course plan which will be validated against the University's requirements and the student's curriculum; (iii) *Student Confirmation* will enforce the student to check relevant personal details; (iv) *Course Registration* will confirm the student's selection. These components make use of an infrastructural *Database* service, which in turn maintains an event log through a separated *Logger* service.

The modelling paradigm adopted here captures the behaviour of a typical multi-threaded multi-processor environment used for the deployment and the execution of the application. The *University Portal* instantiates a pool of threads, each thread dealing with a request from a student for one of the services offered. During the processing of the request the thread cannot be acquired by further incoming requests, but when the request is fulfilled the thread clears its current

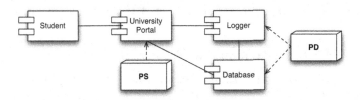

Fig. 3. Deployment diagram of the e-University case study. Solid connectors between components indicate request/reply communication. Dashed lines denote the deployment of services onto processors.

state and becomes available to be acquired again. Analogous multi-threaded behaviour will be given to *Database* and *Logger*. Performance issues may arise from the contention of a limited number of threads by a potentially large population of students. If at some time point all threads are busy, further requests must queue, provoking delays and capacity saturation. This model also proposes another level of contention by explicitly modelling the processors on which the threads execute. Here, delays may occur when many threads try to acquire a limited number of processors available. Furthermore, this may be worsened by running several multi-threaded services on the same multi-processor system, as will be the case in the deployment scenario considered in this model: *University Portal* will run exclusively on multi-processor *PS*, whereas *Logger* and *Database* will share multi-processor *PD* (cfr. Fig. 3).

General modelling patterns. Processing a request involves some computation on the processor on which the service is deployed. Such a computation in the PEPA model is associated with an activity $(type, rate)$, where $type$ uniquely identifies the activity and $rate$ denotes the average execution demand on the processor (i.e., $1/rate$ time units). A single processing unit may be modelled using a two-state sequential component. One state enables an *acquire* activity to grant exclusive access to the resource, while the other state enables all the activities deployed on the processor. Letting n be the number of distinct activities, the following pattern is used for a processor:

$$Processor_1 \stackrel{def}{=} (acquire, r_{acq}).Processor_2$$
$$Processor_2 \stackrel{def}{=} (type_1, r_1).Processor_1$$
$$+ (type_2, r_2).Processor_1 \qquad (15)$$
$$+ \ldots$$
$$+ (type_n, r_n).Processor_1$$

Communication in this model is synchronous and is modelled by a sequence of two activities in the form $(request_{from,to}, r_{req}).(reply_{from,to}, r_{rep})$ where the subscript *from* denotes the service from which the request originates and *to* indicates the service required. A recurring situation is a form of blocking experienced by the service invoking an external request. Let A and B model two distinct inter-acting services, e.g.,

$$A \stackrel{def}{=} (request_{A,B}, r_{reqA}).(reply_{A,B}, r_{repA}).A'$$

$$B \stackrel{def}{=} (request_{A,B}, r_{reqB}).(execute, r).(reply_{A,B}, r_{repB}).B'$$

The communication between A and B will be expressed by means of the cooperation operator $A \bowtie_{L} B$, $L = \{request_{A,B}, reply_{A,B}\}$. According to the operational semantics, A and B may initially progress by executing $request_{A,B}$, subsequently behaving as the process $(reply_{A,B}, r_{repA}).A' \bowtie_{L} (execute, r).(reply_{A,B}, r_{repB}).B'$. Now, although the left-hand side of the cooperation enables $reply_{A,B}$, the activity is not offered by the right-hand side, thus making the left-hand side effectively blocked until $execute$ terminates (i.e., after an average duration of $1/r$ time units). These basic modelling patterns will be used extensively in this case study, as discussed next.

University Portal. A single thread of execution for the application layer *University Portal* is implemented as a sequential component which initially accepts requests for any of the services provided:

$$\begin{aligned}
Portal \stackrel{def}{=}\ & (request_{student,browse}, \nu).Browse \\
& + (request_{student,select}, \nu).Select \\
& + (request_{student,confirm}, \nu).Confirm \\
& + (request_{student,register}, \nu).Register
\end{aligned}$$

The rate ν will be used throughout this model in all the request/reply activities. In the following, the action type $acquire_{ps}$ is used to obtain exclusive access to processor PS.

Course Browsing is implemented as a service which maintains an internal cache. When a request is to be processed, the cache query takes $1/r_{cache}$ time units on average, and is successful with probability 0.95, after which the retrieved data is processed at rate r_{int}. Upon a cache miss, the information is retrieved by the *Database* service, and is subsequently processed at rate r_{ext}:

$$Browse \stackrel{def}{=} (acquire_{ps}, \nu).Cache$$

$$Cache \stackrel{def}{=} (cache, 0.95 r_{cache}).Internal + (cache, 0.05 r_{cache}).External$$

$$Internal \stackrel{def}{=} (acquire_{ps}, \nu).(internal, r_{int}).BrowseRep$$

$$External \stackrel{def}{=} (request_{external,read}, \nu).(reply_{external,read}, \nu).$$
$$(acquire_{ps}, \nu).(external, r_{ext}).BrowseRep$$

$$BrowseRep \stackrel{def}{=} (reply_{student,browse}, \nu).Portal$$

(16)

Course Selection comprises four basic activities. An initial set-up task initialises the necessary data required for further processing (rate r_{prep}). Then, two activities are executed in parallel, and are concerned with validating the selection against the university requirements (rate r_{uni}) and the student's curriculum (rate r_{curr}), respectively. Finally, the outcome of this validation is prepared to be shown to the student (rate r_{disp}). The relative ordering of execution is maintained by considering three distinct sequential components. The first component prepares the data, then forks the two validating processes, waits for their completion, and finally displays the results:

$$Select \stackrel{def}{=} (acquire_{ps}, \nu).(prepare, r_{prep}).ForkPrepare$$

$$ForkPrepare \stackrel{def}{=} (fork, \nu).JoinPrepare$$

$$JoinPrepare \stackrel{def}{=} (join, \nu).Display$$

$$Display \stackrel{def}{=} (acquire_{ps}, \nu).(display, r_{disp}).SelectRep$$

$$SelectRep \stackrel{def}{=} (reply_{student,select}, \nu).Portal$$

The two validating processes are guarded by the fork/join barrier as follows:

$$ValUni \stackrel{def}{=} (fork, \nu).(acquire_{ps}, \nu).(validate_{uni}, r_{uni}).(join, \nu).ValUni$$
$$ValCur \stackrel{def}{=} (fork, \nu).(acquire_{ps}, \nu).(validate_{cur}, r_{cur}).(join, \nu).ValCur$$

$$(17)$$

These components will be arranged as follows in order to obtain a three-way synchronisation:

$$Select \underset{\{fork,join\}}{\bowtie} ValUni \underset{\{fork,join\}}{\bowtie} ValCur$$

Student Confirmation is represented in the PEPA model as an activity performed at rate r_{con}. The service uses *Logger* to register the event:

$$Confirm \stackrel{def}{=} (acquire_{ps}, \nu).(confirm, r_{con}).LogStudent$$

$$LogStudent \stackrel{def}{=} (request_{confirm,log}, \nu).(reply_{confirm,log}, \nu).ReplyConfirm \quad (18)$$

$$ReplyConfirm \stackrel{def}{=} (reply_{student,confirm}, \nu).Portal$$

Finally, *Course Registration* performs some local computation (rate r_{reg}) and then contacts *Database* to store the information:

$$Register \stackrel{def}{=} (acquire_{ps}, \nu).(register, r_{reg}).Store$$

$$Store \stackrel{def}{=} (request_{register,write}, \nu).(reply_{register,write}, \nu).ReplyRegister$$

$$ReplyRegister \stackrel{def}{=} (reply_{student,register}, \nu).Portal$$

$$(19)$$

The general pattern (15) is applied to processor *PS* as follows:

$$PS_1 \stackrel{def}{=} (acquire_{ps}, \nu).PS_2$$
$$PS_2 \stackrel{def}{=} (cache, r_{cache}).PS_1 + (internal, r_{int}).PS_1 + (external, r_{ext}).PS_1$$
$$+ (prepare, r_{prep}).PS_1 + (display, r_{disp}).PS_1 + (validate_{uni}, r_{uni}).PS_1$$
$$+ (validate_{cur}, r_{cur}).PS_1 + (confirm, r_{con}).PS_1 + (register, r_{reg}).PS_1$$

Database. This service exposes two functions for reading and writing data. Reading is a purely local computation, whereas writing additionally uses the *Logger* service. In this model, *Database* is only accessed by the university portal in states *External* and *Store* in equations (16) and (19), respectively. Let *PD* denote the processor on which *Database* is deployed, acquired through action *acquire*$_{pd}$. Similarly to *University Portal*, a single thread of execution for *Database* is:

$$
\begin{aligned}
Database &\stackrel{def}{=} (request_{external,read}, \nu).Read \\
&\quad + (request_{register,write}, \nu).Write \\
Read &\stackrel{def}{=} (acquire_{pd}, \nu).(read, r_{read}).ReadReply \\
ReadReply &\stackrel{def}{=} (reply_{external,read}, \nu).Database \\
Write &\stackrel{def}{=} (acquire_{pd}, \nu).(write, r_{write}).LogWrite \\
LogWrite &\stackrel{def}{=} (request_{database,log}, \nu).(reply_{database,log}, \nu).WriteReply \\
WriteReply &\stackrel{def}{=} (reply_{register,write}, \nu).Database
\end{aligned}
\tag{20}
$$

Logger. This service accepts requests from *Student Confirmation* and *Database*, as described in equations (18) and (20), respectively. It is deployed on the same processor as *Database*, i.e., processor *PD*. Thus, one thread execution may be modelled as follows:

$$
\begin{aligned}
Logger &\stackrel{def}{=} (request_{confirm,log}, \nu).LogConfirm \\
&\quad + (request_{database,log}, \nu).LogDatabase \\
LogConfirm &\stackrel{def}{=} (acquire_{pd}, \nu).(log_{conf}, r_{lgc}).ReplyConfirm \\
ReplyConfirm &\stackrel{def}{=} (reply_{confirm,log}, \nu).Logger \\
LogDatabase &\stackrel{def}{=} (acquire_{pd}, \nu).(log_{db}, r_{lgd}).ReplyDatabase \\
ReplyDatabase &\stackrel{def}{=} (reply_{database,log}, \nu).Logger
\end{aligned}
\tag{21}
$$

Taking together (20) and (21) it is possible to write the sequential component that models the processor *PD*:

$$
\begin{aligned}
PD_1 &\stackrel{def}{=} (acquire_{pd}, \nu).PD_2 \\
PD_2 &\stackrel{def}{=} (read, r_{read}).PD_1 + (write, r_{write}).PD_1 \\
&\quad + (log_{conf}, r_{lgc}).PD_1 + (log_{db}, r_{lgd}).PD_1
\end{aligned}
$$

Student Workload. A student is modelled as a sequential component which interacts with the university portal and cyclically accesses all of the services available:

$$
\begin{aligned}
StdThink &\stackrel{def}{=} (think, r_{think}).StdBrowse \\
StdBrowse &\stackrel{def}{=} (request_{student,browse}, \nu).(reply_{student,browse}, \nu).StdSelect \\
StdSelect &\stackrel{def}{=} (request_{student,select}, \nu).(reply_{student,select}, \nu).StdConfirm \\
StdConfirm &\stackrel{def}{=} (request_{student,confirm}, \nu).(reply_{student,confirm}, \nu).StdRegister \\
StdRegister &\stackrel{def}{=} (request_{student,register}, \nu).(reply_{student,register}, \nu).StdThink
\end{aligned}
$$

System Equation. The multiplicity of threads and processors is captured in the system equation, in which all the sequential components illustrated above are composed with suitable cooperation operators to enforce synchronisation between shared actions. The complete system equation for this model is:

$$StdThink[N_S] \bowtie_* \left(\left(Portal[N_P] \underset{M_1}{\bowtie} ValUni[N_P] \underset{M_1}{\bowtie} ValCur[N_P] \right) \right.$$
$$\left. \underset{M_2}{\bowtie} Database[N_D] \underset{M_3}{\bowtie} Logger[N_L] \right) \bowtie_* \left(PS_1[N_{PS}] \underset{\emptyset}{\bowtie} PD_1[N_{PD}] \right)$$

where

$$M_1 = \{fork, join\}$$
$$M_2 = \{request_{external,read}, reply_{external,read}, request_{register,write},$$
$$reply_{register,write}\}$$
$$M_3 = \{request_{confirm,log}, reply_{confirm,log}, request_{database,log},$$
$$reply_{database,log}\}$$

It is worth pointing out that the separate validating threads *ValUni* and *ValCur* inherit the multiplicity levels of the thread *Portal* which accesses them.

4   Model Evaluation

This section is concerned with the analysis of the e-University case study. The performance metrics of interest are discussed in Section 4.1. Section 4.2 illustrates the difficulties regarding the Markovian interpretation of the model, and Section 4.3 presents the results obtained with fluid-flow approximation.

4.1   Metrics

The system performance will be evaluated with respect to the *average response time* experienced by a student to carry out the complete sequence of operations with the university portal. The thinking time exhibited by the derivative *StdThink* will not be computed as part of this response time. The performance is evaluated for steady-state conditions, i.e., after a sufficiently long time period after which the system's state does not change. Under these conditions, the computation of average response time in PEPA admits a simple formulation based on Little's law [13], as discussed in [14]. Little's law says that in a system in a stationary state, the number of users L in the system is related to the throughput of user arrivals λ and the average response time W by the formula

$$L = \lambda W$$

In this case study, L and λ can be computed in a straightforward way. The number of students in the system is equal to N_S (the total student population) minus the population of students who are thinking. This is directly obtained from

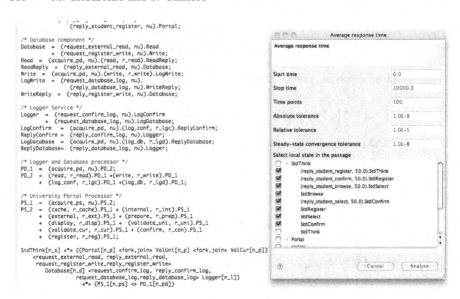

Fig. 4. Screenshot of the PEPA Eclipse Plug-in showing the editor area (left) with an excerpt of the e-University case study and the dialogue box for the calculation of the average response time (right). The modeller is requested to set up the parameters for the ODE numerical integrator (top) and select which derivatives are to be interpreted as the user being in the system (bottom).

the underlying differential equation model, since one coordinate, say $x_{StdThink}(t)$ (whose steady-state value shall be denoted by $x_{StdThink}(\infty)$), is associated with the population count of the sequential component *StdThink*. The throughput of student arrival is given by the number of students performing the *think* action in the steady state. Since one single student carries out that action at rate r_{think}, the total throughput is the product $r_{think}\, x_{StdThink}(\infty)$. The average response time is therefore:

$$W = \frac{N_S - x_{StdThink}(\infty)}{r_{think}\, x_{StdThink}(\infty)}$$

In practice, the average response time is calculated using the *PEPA Eclipse Plug-in*, a software tool which supports Markovian analysis and fluid-flow approximation of PEPA in the Eclipse framework [15]. A screenshot of the tool is shown in Fig. 4.

4.2   Markovian Analysis

As discussed in Section 2, Markovian analysis is fundamentally limited by the rapid growth of the state space as a function of the population levels of the sequential components. Table 1 shows the state-space cardinality for some model configurations. Even for a small system with only ten clients (last row) the state space reaches over five million states; furthermore, there is a dramatic increase as

Table 1. State-space growth of the e-University case study

N_S	N_P	N_D	N_L	N_{PS}	N_{PD}	Size
1	any	any	any	1	any	48
1	any	any	any	≥ 2	any	49
2	1	1	1	1	1	230
3	1	1	1	1	1	680
3	2	2	2	2	2	5540
10	2	2	2	2	2	512116
10	3	2	2	2	2	5075026

a function of N_P (the number of portal threads)—adding one copy may result in an increase by a factor of ten (compare the last two rows). Nevertheless, Markovian analysis is a valuable tool for validating the correctness of the model. In particular, the first two rows of Table 1 give confidence that the model matches the modeller's intended behaviour. Indeed, when there is only one student the state space is fairly small regardless of the multiplicity levels of threads and processors because at most only one of them will be used. Setting N_{PS} to any value greater than one add only one more state because the two activities *ValCur* and *ValUni* of equation (17) may now run in parallel on two distinct processors (instead, when $N_{PS} = 1$ only one of them may access the same processor at a time). Another form of qualitative analysis can be based on visual inspection of the reachability graph, which can be walked through to generate possible trajectories of the system.

Explicit enumeration of the state space of a PEPA model is available in the Eclipse plug-in through a top-level menu item, as shown in Fig. 5. The reachability graph may be iteratively walked using the *Single Step Navigator*, shown in Fig. 6.

4.3   Fluid-Flow Analysis

The model gives rise to a set of 63 coupled ODEs, not shown in this paper for the sake of conciseness. The analysis presented in this section is concerned with establishing a satisfactory system configuration that is able to handle more than 6000 students with acceptable average response time. The parameter space is very large because, in addition to the student population level N_S, there are 20 other parameters in this model: 15 rate parameters and 5 concurrency levels for threads and processors. We will consider the *dimensioning problem*, which is evaluating the overall system performance in different configurations with rates which are fixed (cfr. Table 2).

Figure 7 shows a typical response-time profile as a function of the workload characteristics, with all the other concurrency levels set as follows: $N_P = N_D = N_L = 20, N_{PS} = N_{PD} = 8$. This configuration does not meet the requirements proposed at the beginning of this section if $r_{think} = 0.0010$. Indeed, the average

Fig. 5. State-space exploration with the PEPA Eclipse plug-in. The top-level menu item *Derive* is available for any syntactically correct PEPA model. The *State Space View* (bottom) is updated with a tabular representation of the state space.

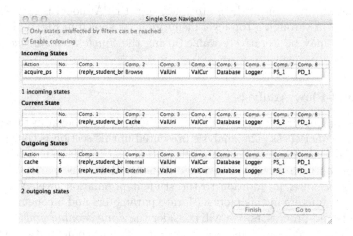

Fig. 6. The *Single Step Navigator* allows the inspection of the reachability graph of a PEPA model. Given a configuration with all population counts set to one, this screenshot presents the neighbourhood of the state when the *cache* activity is being performed, showing that there are two possible outcomes leading to the local state *Internal* and *External*, respectively.

Table 2. Rate parameter set used for fluid-flow analysis

Messages	Portal	Database	Logger
$\nu = 50.0$	$r_{cache} = 10.0$	$r_{read} = 5.0$	$r_{lgc} = 2.0$
	$r_{int} = 2.0$	$r_{write} = 1.0$	$r_{lgd} = 1.5$
	$r_{ext} = 2.0$		
	$r_{prep} = 5.0$		
	$r_{disp} = 8.0$		
	$r_{uni} = 5.0$		
	$r_{cur} = 4.0$		
	$r_{con} = 2.0$		
	$r_{reg} = 2.5$		

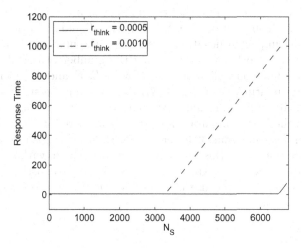

Fig. 7. Response time profile as a function of the student population

response time is constant at 4.79 time units for population levels less than 3300, meaning that there is a high probability of any student accessing the system finding resources available. However, the average response time increases steeply for workload populations greater than 3300, showing a particularly detrimental effect of the delays due to resource contention. Conversely, the configuration is satisfactory when $r_{think} = 0.0005$, since this effect manifests for student populations greater than 6500. However, this may not be an optimal solution, i.e., it may be possible to find configurations consisting of fewer components which yield similar performance.

The results of a possible optimisation study are presented in Table 3. The reference point is the average response time for $N_S = 6650$ of the aforementioned configuration (denoted by A in the table) when $r_{think} = 0.0005$. Decreasing all thread multiplicities to 16 does not have any impact on the response time

Table 3. Average response time for $N_S = 6650$ and different system configurations

Configuration	N_P	N_D	N_L	N_{PS}	N_{PD}	Response time
A	20	20	20	8	8	44.61
B	16	16	16	8	8	44.61
C	16	16	16	7	7	334.38
D	16	8	8	8	8	44.61
E	15	8	8	8	8	100.56
F	14	8	8	8	8	249.47
G	12	8	8	8	8	621.06
H	16	6	6	8	8	44.61
I	16	4	4	8	8	980.38

(compare A and B), however reducing the number of processors available leads to significant delays (compare B and C). Comparing B and D, the user-perceived performance is not impacted negatively by halving the number of database and logger threads. On the other hand, reducing the number of portal threads by one is particularly unfavourable (compare D with E, F, and G). Configuration H shows that the multiplicity levels of N_D and N_L may be still reduced, but further decreases incur a significant performance penalty (configuration I). In conclusion, H is the best configuration of those considered in Table 3, yielding the same performance but using 32 fewer threads than the original configuration. It must be pointed out that this strategy—carried out here without assistance of automatic parameter-space exploration tools—is not exhaustive. However it is not difficult to imagine the use of fluid-flow models in more sophisticated optimisation frameworks.

5 Conclusion

PEPA's ability to provide both discrete- and continuous-state interpretations has been shown to be of practical interest in the modelling of large-scale service-oriented applications. Although Markovian analysis is easily defeated by the very rapid growth of the state space, this paper has shown how it may still be useful for the purposes of model debugging. By considering a *minimal manifestation* of the system obtained by setting unrealistically low population levels, the modeller may obtain a state space of manageable size which may be inspected to gain confidence that the discrete-state transitions exhibited by the model match the intended behaviour. On the other hand, the recently proposed fluid-flow approximation was used to evaluate the performance of the system in a scalable manner, by making the computational cost of the analysis largely independent from the population levels of the system's components. The modelling methodology adopted here is rather general and may be applied to other distributed systems where the main concern is to analyse resource contention due to multi-threading and processor sharing. The software toolkit for PEPA supports all of the forms of analysis considered in this paper for the benefit of other researchers and practitioners.

References

1. Buchholz, P.: Exact and Ordinary Lumpability in Finite Markov Chains. Journal of Applied Probability 31, 59–75 (1994)
2. Deavours, D.D., Sanders, W.H.: An Efficient Disk-Based Tool for Solving Large Markov Models. Perform. Eval. 33, 67–84 (1998)
3. Kurtz, T.G.: Solutions of ordinary differential equations as limits of pure Markov processes. J. Appl. Prob. 7, 49–58 (1970)
4. Hillston, J.: A Compositional Approach to Performance Modelling. Cambridge University Press, Cambridge (1996)
5. Gilmore, S., Hillston, J., Ribaudo, M.: An efficient algorithm for aggregating PEPA models. IEEE Transactions on Software Engineering 27, 449–464 (2001)
6. Hillston, J.: Fluid flow approximation of PEPA models. In: Proceedings of the Second International Conference on the Quantitative Evaluation of Systems, Torino, Italy, pp. 33–43. IEEE Computer Society Press, Los Alamitos (2005)
7. Bradley, J., Gilmore, S., Hillston, J.: Analysing distributed internet worm attacks using continuous state-space approximation of process algebra models. Journal of Computer and System Sciences 74, 1013–1032 (2008)
8. Ding, J., Hillston, J.: Convergence of the Fluid Approximation of PEPA Models. In: Seventh Workshop on Process Algebra and Stochastically Timed Activities (PASTA), Edinburgh, UK (2008)
9. Hayden, R., Bradley, J.T.: Fluid semantics for passive stochastic process algebra cooperation. In: VALUETOOLS 2008 (September 2008)
10. Cardelli, L.: On process rate semantics. Theor. Comput. Sci. 391, 190–215 (2008)
11. Bortolussi, L., Policriti, A.: Stochastic concurrent constraint programming and differential equations. Electr. Notes Theor. Comput. Sci. 190, 27–42 (2007)
12. Hölzl, M.: Requirements Modelling and Analysis of Selected Scenarios. SENSORIA Deliverable 8.4.a (2007)
13. Little, J.: A Proof of the Queuing Formula: $L = \lambda W$. Operations Research 9, 383–387 (1961)
14. Clark, A., Duguid, A., Gilmore, S., Hillston, J.: Espresso, a Little Coffee. In: Process Algebra and Stochastically Timed Activities (PASTA), Edinburgh, UK (2008)
15. Tribastone, M., Duguid, A., Gilmore, S.: The PEPA Eclipse Plug-in. Performance Evaluation Review 36, 28–33 (2009)

Passage-End Analysis for Analysing Robot Movement

Allan Clark, Adam Duguid, and Stephen Gilmore

The University of Edinburgh, Scotland

Abstract. We report on a new style of passage measurement – called passage-end calculations – associated with stochastic probes and their extension to eXtended Stochastic Probes (XSP) [1]. While stochastic probes allow for the analysis of a passage to be split up into several cases depending on the conditions which hold at the start of the passage, even XSP lacks the ability for the same kind of separation depending on conditions at the end of the passage. In particular we would like to separate successful responses to a request from negative responses, timeouts or other failures. This allows us to evaluate refined service level agreements such as: "At least 90 percent of all *successful* requests are responded to within 10 seconds" or "At least 90 percent of all requests are responded to within 10 seconds *and* at least 60 percent of all such requests are successful." We present a case study in the use of passage-end measurements using a robot bowling demonstration used at the ICT 2008 computer fair, one of Europe's leading information technology fairs.

1 Introduction

Quantitative analysis is an important phase in the design of a new computer-based system. We wish to know that the new system will provide the level of service for which it is designed. An important set of measurement queries in the analysis of a system is response-time or, more generally, passage-time analysis. The analysis of a passage is interested in the time profile of paths between a specific set of source states and a specific set of target states. Often both the set of source and target states represent sets of states which result from an occurrence of a particular kind of activity or sequence of activities. For example a common passage is the time taken from a "request" made by a client and the corresponding "response" received by the client. For this reason stochastic probes [2] were developed as a measurement specification language and further enhanced to become the language of *eXtended Stochastic Probes* or XSP [1].

Many systems which are analysed for response-time profiles have more than one way in which the passage in question may terminate. Commonly a "request" from a client may end in a successful completion such that the client received the desired response or service. However, other outcomes are possible. The request may end in a failed service due to a timeout because the client does not meet the criteria set by the service provider. This may even be caused when the service provider is overwhelmed with requests from many clients.

M. Wirsing and M. Hölzl (Eds.): SENSORIA Project, LNCS 6582, pp. 506–521, 2011.

There may also be two or more methods in which the response or service is provided, for example a data retrieval request may be serviced by a cache or not. In these situations we wish to analyse the passage-time profiles for the separate cases of success and failure, or cache and "network" retrieval. It may be for example that the general response-time analysis indicates acceptable performance but that successful requests are serviced too slowly.

We work with the Markovian process algebra PEPA. The PEPA language is defined in [3]. Applications of the language are described in [4,5,6].

PEPA is a stochastically-timed process algebra where sequential components are defined using prefix and choice and models require these sequential components to cooperate on some activities, and hide others. Rates are associated with activities performed by each component and the passive rate $\top$ is used to indicate that the component will passively cooperate with another on this activity. In this case the passive component may enable or restrict the activity from being performed by the cooperating component but the rate when enabled is determined by the actively cooperating component.

In PEPA the component $(a, r).P$ performs the activity a at rate r whenever it is not blocked by a cooperating component and becomes the process P. The component $(a, \top).P$ passively synchronises on the activity a and becomes process P. We use the version of PEPA with functional rates [7] ("marking dependent rates", in Petri net terms) and arrays of components.

We write $P[5]$ to denote five copies of the component P which do not cooperate and $P[5][\alpha]$ to denote five copies of the component P which cooperate on the activity α. That is, $P[5]$ is an abbreviation for $P \parallel P \parallel P \parallel P \parallel P$ and $P[5][\alpha]$ is an abbreviation for $P \underset{\{\alpha\}}{\bowtie} P \underset{\{\alpha\}}{\bowtie} P \underset{\{\alpha\}}{\bowtie} P \underset{\{\alpha\}}{\bowtie} P$.

Finally the probe language which we use makes use of immediate actions which are written $a.P$ to denote the process which instantaneously performs the action a to become the process P. These are generally cooperated over such that components can be blocked until another component has entered the state to make the appropriate immediate synchronisation.

The rest of this paper is structured as follows: in Section 2 we overview the architecture of the stochastic probes framework for query specification. In Section 3 we review how stochastic probes are utilised to provide average response-time calculations ensuring that the "rules of the game" are not violated and in fact amending the model in the case that they are. Similarly in Section 4 passage-time analysis using stochastic probes is reviewed. In Section 5 we define precisely what we have termed "passage-end calculations" and describe the novel machinery used to extract passage-end quantiles from a passage specified using stochastic probes. We then detail the new kinds of analyses and results which can be obtained from a passage-end analysis of a passage within a model. In Section 6 we introduce our case study scenario and the related PEPA model and show some results of the analysis. Finally in Section 7 and 8 we review related work and conclude.

2   Stochastic Probes

A stochastic probe is a passive component added to a model in order to make reasoning about the model more convenient. In the context of PEPA a stochastic probe is a single sequential component which observes the sequences of actions performed by the whole or a part of the model in question. The observations of actions are done by passively cooperating with the model over the activities which the probe wishes to observe. These activities are defined as the alphabet of the probe. As each activity is observed by the probe it changes its own internal state. Therefore the state in which the probe resides acts as a filter on the entire state space of the model. A simple passage probe can distinguish between states within or outside a passage between two activities, for example consider the probe component defined by:

$$\text{Stopped} \stackrel{def}{=} (request, \top).\text{Running}$$
$$\text{Running} \stackrel{def}{=} (response, \top).\text{Stopped}$$

This is attached to the main system equation of the model by:

$$\text{System} \bowtie_{\mathcal{L}} \text{Stopped}$$

where $\mathcal{L}$ is the alphabet of the probe; in this case, $\{request, response\}$. This probe will remain in the Stopped state until it observes, via passive cooperation, the System performing a *request* activity upon which the probe moves into the Running state. Once in the Running state the probe must observe the occurrence of a *response* activity before returning to the Stopped state. When the state space of this entire model is derived those states in which the probe is in the Running state correspond to those states of the model which are in between *request* and *response* activities. Hence the passage in the model between these two activities can be measured using a simple filter which makes reference only to the state of the probe.

2.1   Probe Specification Language

However the above probe is not very robust. In defining the probe specification language we have two golden rules; firstly we demand that the user need not modify their model in order to perform queries upon it – this in turn assists our probe specifications in remaining robust over several versions of the same model. Secondly we insist that the addition of a probe component does not alter the behaviour of the model it is intended to observe. If this is the case then we are failing to analyse the original model. The above probe will block any occurrence of the *response* activity while in the Stopped state and any occurrence of the *request* activity while in the Running state. This is permissible if the model always performs these two activities alternately, but not if we may get two or more of either activity without observing the other. To allow for this we add *self-loops* to the probe, such that the probe may 'ignore' the occurrence of a given activity without blocking its instance. The probe can be modified as such:

$$\text{Stopped} \overset{def}{=} (request, \top).\text{Running}$$
$$+ \underline{(response, \top).\text{Stopped}}$$
$$\text{Running} \overset{def}{=} (response, \top).\text{Stopped}$$
$$+ \underline{(request, \top).\text{Running}}$$

The underlined additions are the self-loops thus in every state of the probe the model may perform any of the activities in the probe alphabet without being blocked by the cooperation with the probe. The model may of course perform other activities not in the alphabet of the probe at any time.

With such a simple probe we can write the PEPA component corresponding to the probe by hand. However for more complicated probes this is tiresome and, in part because of the necessity for the addition of self-loops, error-prone. To alleviate this stochastic probes may be specified in a regular-expression like probe language. The above probe would be specified as simply (*request, response*). More complex probes may be provided such as: $((r, r, r)/s, s)$ which allows us to ask the question: "What is the probability that we are in a state in which three or more 'r' activities have been observed without observing an 's' activity." In a real-world model the activity 'r' may correspond to successful completion of a service and 's' may correspond to a failure. The probe language is converted into PEPA components via a translation to non-deterministic finite automata which are then converted to deterministic finite automata. The self-loops are then added and the resulting DFA is then minimised. The minimised deterministic finite automaton is then already a PEPA sequential component which can be attached to the model. All of the steps in this process are well known transformations providing confidence in our translation and are described in detail in [8].

2.2   Local Probes

Often we do not wish the probe to observe activities performed by the entire model but a sub-portion of it. In particular when analysing response-time we are not interested in the passage between a *request* and a *response* as observed by an external observer because the *response* may be to a different client than the *request* was generated from. Instead we wish to analyse the response-time as observed by a single client. To achieve this we can simply attach the probe to a single client rather than the entire system equation. This involves opening the system equation, attaching the probe component in cooperation with a single client (which may have originally been a part of a client process array), and then re-building the system equation. When this is done it can be convenient to attach multiple probes to separate components and have the local probes communicate with a master probe which is attached to the entire (modified) system equation. The communication between probes must not alter the behaviour of the model and to that end is done with immediate actions. This process is described in greater detail in [9].

Immediate communication signals are attached within the probe language using the colon syntax. We use these to specify the start and end of a passage within a complex probe. So the probe defined by: $((a, a, a)/b)$:start, c:stop describes a passage which is started once a sequence of three 'a' activities uninterrupted by a 'b' activity is observed. The passage is stopped by a single occurrence of a 'c' activity.

For a passage measurement specification a simple master probe is added by default that observes only start and stop signals sent from another user defined attached (possibly local) probe. The master probe has two states, and is always defined by:

$$\text{Stopped} \stackrel{def}{=} \text{start.Running}$$
$$+ \text{ stop.Stopped}$$
$$\text{Running} \stackrel{def}{=} \text{stop.Stopped}$$
$$+ \text{ start.Running}$$

The system equation now becomes

$$(\text{System} \underset{\mathcal{L}}{\bowtie} \text{UserProbe}) \underset{\mathcal{K}}{\bowtie} \text{Stopped}$$

where $\mathcal{L}$ is the alphabet of the user probe and $\mathcal{K}$ is $\{\text{start}, \text{stop}\}$. In general the self-loops added here are not required but they are never harmful. The steady-state probability of being within the specified passage is the sum of the steady-state probabilities of being in any state such that the master probe is in the Running state.

3   Average Response-Time Analysis

In the previous section we have seen that through the use of probes we can determine the states along the passage and hence the steady-state probability of being within the specified passage. Additionally we know all of the actions which commence a passage, it is simply all the transitions labelled as the start action. However immediate transitions cannot be represented in the CTMC. Between state space generation and the translation from the state space to the generator matrix of the CTMC we must remove the vanishing states. The vanishing states are those states which have out-going immediate transitions since those states will no longer be represented in the CTMC. To remove a vanishing state we re-target those transitions into the vanishing state to the states which are the target of the immediate out-going transitions. We repeat this procedure until all vanishing states have been removed or we detect an instantaneous loop.

We have therefore lost the immediate transitions labelled start but can recover this information in one of two ways. Either during the reduction we record which timed transitions have which immediate actions coalesced into them or after the reduction we may select those transitions which move from a state in which the master probe is in the Stopped state to one in which it is in the Running state. The first solution has the advantage of being more general because it then becomes possible to take the throughput of any immediate transitions whether or not they begin a specified passage of interest. The second method has the advantage of working even when the probe is inserted manually with no communication signals. Our implementation chooses the first alternative and allows the user to specify alternative start and stop signals which may be timed transitions or immediate actions because in either case we have the machinery to calculate their throughput.

We now have both steady-state measures required to compute the average response-time (or average time to complete a passage) using Little's Law [10].

4   Passage-Time Quantile Analysis

Sometimes average response-time analysis is too coarse because it does not show us the distribution around the average value. Passage-time quantiles allow us to answer the question: "What is the probability that the specified passage completes at or within a given time t?"

We compute from the specified passage and the Markov chain the probability density function (pdf) and the cumulative distribution function (cdf). The cumulative distribution plots the probability of completing the passage within time t and the probability density is a measure of the probability of completing the passage at exactly time t. This is a probability density because the probability of completing the passage at exactly any given time is zero. The area under the pdf sums to one if we assume that the passage always completes eventually.

To compute passage-time quantiles we must first distinguish the set of source states and the set of target states. The set of target states can be approximated by those states which are not within the passage. More precisely the set of target states are those which can be reached from within the passage states (where the master probe is running) via a single transition. This single transition must be a passage-ending event, in the default case a (coalesced) stop probe communication signal. The set of source states are those states within the passage set which may be reached from outside the passage via a single transition. That transition must be a source event, in the default case a (coalesced) start probe communication signal. The source states can be identified via a *source probe*, defined as:

SourceStopped $=$ start.SourceRunning
$\qquad + (\forall \alpha \neq$ start $\in \mathcal{A})\alpha.$SourceStopped
SourceRunning $= (\forall \alpha \in \mathcal{A})\alpha.$SourceStopped

Where $\mathcal{A}$ is the alphabet of activities performed by the entire model. This transitions into the SourceRunning state whenever a source event is observed and transitions out of the running state on observation of any activity at all. In our implementation this is automatically computed and added to the model.

In order to compute the passage-time quantiles we must discover the distribution of probability mass at the beginning of a passage. This is found by computing the Embedded Markov Chain (EMC) of the generator matrix. The probability of each source state s is given by $\pi_s^e / \sum_{j \in \mathcal{S}} \pi_j^e$ where $\mathcal{S}$ is the set of source states, π^e is the steady-state probability distribution computed as the solution to the EMC, hence $\sum_{j\in\mathcal{S}} \pi_j^e$ is the probability of being in any source state.

The generator matrix Q of our model is then uniformised by dividing through by a rate q larger than the absolute value of any value in Q. Since all the diagonal elements in Q are the negation of the sum of the other row elements this value is given by: $max(\forall i\,|Q_{ii}|)$. We obtain the uniformised chain by $P = (Q/q) + I$ where I is the identity matrix. This gives us a deterministic time Markov chain where each 'hop' has the same mean holding-time.

Using the uniformised Markov chain we can calculate the transient probability distribution for any time t, however in order to calculate passage-time quantiles we modify the uniformised Markov chain. We add an absorbing state whose only out-transition is one to itself. Each of the target states are modified to transition to the absorbing state with probability one. This allows us to calculate the probability of completing the *first* passage and not subsequent passages. That is, we avoid the problem of passing through a target state and looping back around to begin the passage once more.

We then use this modified, uniform Markov chain P' to calculate the probability distribution after each hop π^n where $\pi^n = \pi^{n-1}P'$ and π^0 was calculated above using the EMC. Using this our cdf and pdf values at time t are given respectively by:

$$F_{ij}(t) = \sum_{n=1}^{\infty} \left(\left(1 - e^{-qt} \sum_{k=0}^{n-1} \frac{(qt)^k}{k!}\right) \sum_{k\in j} \pi_k^{(n)} \right)$$

and

$$f_{ij}(t) = \sum_{n=1}^{\infty} \left(\frac{q^n t^{n-1} e^{-qt}}{(n-1)!} \sum_{k\in j} \pi_k^{(n)} \right)$$

Such an infinite sum cannot of course be calculated but we can make some approximation by computing enough hops so that any further computation will not add significant probability to the value at that time. We know when we have calculated enough hops N because either all of the probability is in the absorbing state or the possibility of performing N hops within time t is sufficiently close to zero. The method of uniformisation for passage-time quantiles from a set of source states to a set of target states in a CTMC is described in detail in [11] by the current authors and also in [12,13,14].

5   Passage-End Calculations

In [1] we note that it is common to split up the measurement of a passage for different kinds of runs of the passage. One common way in which to do this is to split the passage up based on the starting conditions. For example we may first of all wish to analyse the response-time of a service as observed by a single client. Once this is known, in order to provide more information on how this may be improved, we may wish to analyse the response-time (as observed by a single client) of all requests that are made when the service is definitely not broken. We would expect this to be better than the more general case of all requests. Conversely we may also analyse the response-time for all requests made when the service certainly is broken and expect this to be worse than for the general case. From this we may determine whether, in order to improve response-time, it is better to repair the server more quickly or make the server more reliable such that it breaks less often.

Although with eXtended Stochastic Probes splitting the measurement of a passage with respect to the starting conditions is convenient it is not clear how one may split-up a passage based on how the passage completes. The novelty in this paper is the use of several absorbing states utilising one absorbing state for each kind of target event. For a passage-end calculation the user must specify a list of target actions. These may be actions performed by the model itself or communication signals sent by user defined probes. During the transient analysis procedure described in the preceding section, rather than modifying all target states to transition to a single absorbing state each target state is modified to transition to the particular absorbing state based on the target event which caused the transition into the target state.

As an example, consider analysing the response-time of a service which may be begun with a *request* but may be concluded with either a *cached* response or a *networked* response. It is not possible to simply measure these two passages with separate runs using a probe such as: *request*:start, *cached*:stop and equivalently so for *networked*. The reason is that this will compute the probability of completing the passage at (or within) time t via a *cached* response *plus* the probability of completing the passage via a *networked* response and then restarting and completing the passage via the *cached* response all at (or within) time t. Indeed you may complete the passage twice, three times or any number of times via the *networked* response before finally completing via the *cached* response.

Using the same algorithm we can calculate the raw pdf and cdf of the passage from the *request* to the *cached* response. In this case the cdf will not tend to one but to the percentage of requests which are ultimately serviced by the cache. Similarly for the area under the pdf and for both functions of the *request* to *networked* passage.

We can normalise these graphs based on the probability of completing at or within the given time t via *any* target event. We will see examples of this in the case study in Section 6.4.

We can instead normalise the raw pdf and cdf by dividing through the probability of completing at (or within) time t by the percentage of all requests which are ultimately serviced by the target event in question. We can know this percentage by calculating enough hops such that sufficiently close to all of the probability mass at π^N is in one of the absorbing states. We may then take the probability of being in the appropriate absorbing state at π^N.

Hence using a passage-end calculation it is possible to calculate:

- The probability of completing a passage by a *cached* response at or within a given time.
- The probability that, assuming the passage completes at or within a given time in some way, that it does so via the *cached* response. This answers such questions as: "What percentage of responses received within 5 seconds are received via the cache/network?"
- The cdf and pdf profiles for all requests which are serviced by the cache.

In the above *cached* may be substituted for *networked* and more generally for any target event – which may be a probe communication signal – of the given passage. The second kind of question is helpful in evaluating some service-level-agreements, particularly for services which may end in success, failure or cancellation. For example the service level agreement may say that ninety percent of requests are responded to within 10 seconds. We may analyse the model and find that this is indeed the case but a passage-end analysis reveals that eighty-nine percent of such requests are rejection/failure responses. Hence we may wish to modify our service-level-agreement by saying that ninety percent of all *successful* requests are responded to within 10 seconds.

Passage-end analysis also allows us to compute the response-time quantiles for sets of passages which begin with the same activity. The only way to do this previously was to modify the model such these passage were begun with distinct starting actions. This violates one of our golden rules that the modeller must not be forced to modify their model in order to make their measurement. In this case it is particularly important because although in some instances making such a modification is quite simple in many cases it is subtly difficult to calculate the respective rates correctly.

Finally note that if the passage must be split based on events which occur before the target events then a probe may be added to distinguish these as different target events using a probe communication signal. For example the following probe: a:start, $(b, d$:viab$)|(c, d$:viac$)$ allows us to split up the passage from 'a' to 'd' depending on whether we first go via a 'b' or a 'c' activity.

6   Case Study: Robot Bowling

As part of our European research project, SENSORIA, we were invited to model a rather unusual application, robot bowling. The project selected a robot bowling competition as a demonstrator for the ICT 2008 computer fair, one of Europe's leading information technology fairs. The SENSORIA project wanted to demonstrate its methods on an unusual and eye-catching example; the robot bowling competition was selected to be this unusual example. The robot bowling concept was developed by our SENSORIA project partners in the School of Management MIP Politecnico di Milano. The robot was built and configured by a team from the Museo Nazionale della Scienza e della Tecnologia Leonardo da Vinci, Milan. The robot is shown in use on the right hand side of Fig. 1.

6.1   Design of the Robot

The design of the Lego robot bowler enables the robot to move as a tracked vehicle. Two motors independently drive the two main wheels, with an additional free-wheel caster at the rear for balance. Each motor can exist in one of three states; forward, reverse and off, with no ability to otherwise vary the voltage beyond the direction of the motor's rotation. This allows forward and reverse motion (both motors operating in the same direction) or clockwise and anti-clockwise rotation on the spot (both motors active but in opposite directions).

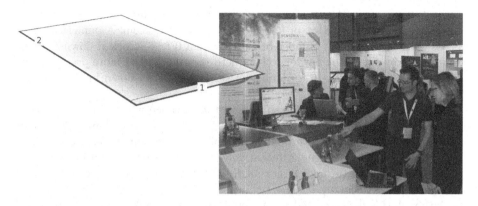

Fig. 1. The gradient of the ramp and the robot bowling competition at the ICT 2008 fair in Lyon

The robot uses a third motor to control the gripper at the front for holding the bowling ball.

The robot has two light sensors, each placed facing downwards in front of one of the main wheels of the robot. These sensors act as the robot's "eyes". It has no other sensors and must navigate solely on the basis of the information received from these sensors. The purpose of the light sensors is to detect the gradient found in the controlled environment that the robot exists in, as can be seen in both sides of Fig. 1. The objective is to reach the darkest point (labelled 1 in the figure) and the robot does this by taking the difference between the two light sensor readings and comparing this against a threshold. If the value is larger than the threshold, the robot will turn, if the difference is below the threshold the robot will move forward.

The user-configurable parameter was the sample rate. This is defined as the duration of either rotating or moving forward. The variation in accuracy (measured by the distance from the darkest point in the environment) is mainly the result of the change in reachable angles. By increasing the length of time that the robot will either move forward or rotate, fine control over positioning is lost and thus precision is reduced overall.

The observed behaviour is for the robot to move from the starting position (labelled 2 in Fig. 1) to a vertically central point before rotating approximately 90 degrees clockwise. This part of the robot's behaviour is based purely on pre-established timings, with no input from the sensors. Once turned roughly towards its objective, the robot relies on the cycle of *sense → rotate/move forward*, with the duration for the rotate or forward motion set as described above. The robot will release the ball once the silver strip is reached.

6.2   Scoring and the Competition Rules

In the bowling competition the parameter settings for the robot were chosen by a user who would try to maximise their score when using the robot to bowl a ball towards a set of six skittles. There are seven possible outcomes, corresponding to missing all of the skittles, or knocking down some of them. A numerical score is assigned based on the number of skittles from 0 to 6 knocked down and the time taken by the robot bowler to complete the run. Stated more precisely, the objective is to maximise the number of skittles knocked down in the shortest time.

A player can control the threshold and the distance which the robot moves forward each time. They can increase their numerical score by having the robot move more slowly and turn through smaller angles. This will increase the robot's accuracy but will take longer. Alternatively they can have the robot move further each time and turn through larger angles. This will improve the robot's speed but decrease its accuracy.

Although this light-hearted, rather entertaining example is quite far removed from our usual domain of computer software, hardware and communications it seemed well-suited to passage-end analysis because the objective is to maximise the score when bowling without unnecessary delay. Hence we proceeded to develop a PEPA model of the problem and carry out passage-end analysis.

6.3   The PEPA Model

The model represents the sampling process and the behaviour of the robot bowler.

Sampling. It is essential to record the number of samples of the light intensity which the robot makes. Because each sample causes the robot to move forward (to re-position for the next sample) only a limited number of samples can be made before the robot has reached its position at the silver strip at the front of the gradient, and must bowl.

We use an array of components to count each sample.

$$SampleSlot \stackrel{def}{=} (sample, \top).Sampled + (restart, \top).SampleSlot$$
$$Sampled \stackrel{def}{=} (restart, \top).SampleSlot$$
$$Samples \stackrel{def}{=} SampleSlot[10][restart]$$

This definition gives rise to the statespace shown in Fig. 2.

Robot. Dynamically, we can interpret the PEPA model as a sequence of events which occur in time. At each stage the robot bowler has two options:

1. to spend more time in calibration in order to improve accuracy (represented as sampling in the model); or
2. to roll the ball now.

The accuracy of the robot bowler improves with increased sampling and is represented by a simple counter which indicates how many pins the robot would be likely to knock down if they bowled the ball now. This counter starts at 0 and increases to 6 (there are six pins in the example).

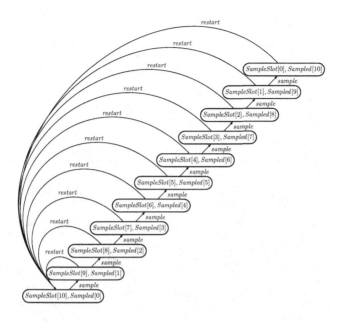

Fig. 2. The statespace of the component $SampleSlot[10][restart]$

A functional rate is used to influence the probability of each outcome. The expression in this functional rate can refer to the global state of the model. In this case it depends only on the number of samples which have been made, that is, how many of the components in the $Samples$ array are in the $Sampled$ state.

$$Robot \stackrel{def}{=} (\ send, \quad send_{rate}).Robot_0$$
$$Robot_X \stackrel{def}{=} (\ sample, \quad sample_{rate}).Robot_X$$
$$+ (\ forward, \quad forward_{rate}).Robot_{X+1}$$
$$Robot_N \stackrel{def}{=} (\ roll_0, \quad f_0(Sampled)).Finished_0$$
$$+ (\ roll_1, \quad f_1(Sampled)).Finished_1$$
$$+ (\ roll_2, \quad f_2(Sampled)).Finished_2$$
$$+ (\ roll_3, \quad f_3(Sampled)).Finished_3$$
$$+ (\ roll_4, \quad f_4(Sampled)).Finished_4$$
$$+ (\ roll_5, \quad f_5(Sampled)).Finished_5$$
$$+ (\ roll_6, \quad f_6(Sampled)).Finished_6$$
$$Finished_i \stackrel{def}{=} (\ restart, \ restart_{rate}).Robot$$

Each of the f_X functions are a functional rate based on the number of samples which have been made. For example $f_0(x) = if\ x < 4\ then\ r_{roll} * 2\ else\ r_{roll}/2$ The seven "finished" states are different merely to allow the passage-end calculations to differentiate the target states, this can also be done with a probe.

System description. It now remains only to compose the robot and the component which counts samples, requiring them to cooperate on the sample activity

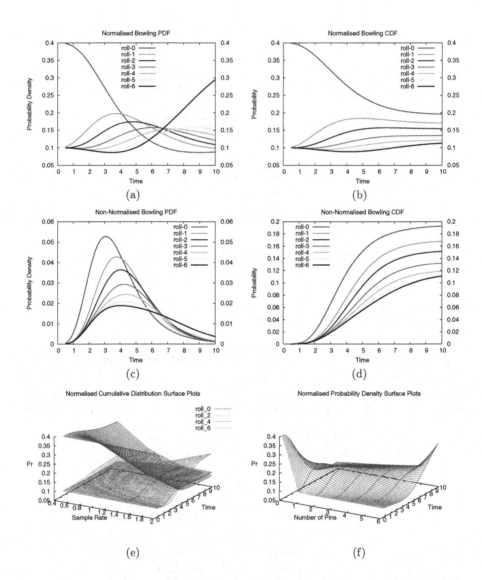

Fig. 3. (a) maps for each of the roll-X the probability that *if* we do finish at that time what is the probability that we do so with roll-X (ie with knocking down that number of pins). (b) is studying the same problem with the CDFs, so this maps time against the probability that *if* we have already finished by time t then we finished via a roll-X action. (c) is the raw probability density of finishing via a roll-X action. (d) is the raw probability that by time t we have finished via a roll-X action. (e) is a surface plot which shows how the cumulative distribution functions for knocking down 0, 2, 4, and 6 pins depend on the sampling rate. (f) is a surface plot of the data from (a).

(to keep the counter in step) and the restart activity (to allow them to return
to the initial state).

$$System \stackrel{def}{=} Robot \underset{\{sample, restart\}}{\bowtie} Samples$$

6.4   Results

We analysed this model using `ipclib` [15], an extension of the IPC tool previously used for computing response-time quantiles from PEPA models [16,17].
The results are presented in Fig. 3. The graphs show the expected result that the
likelihood of knocking down zero pins is highest when little time has been spent
in calibration and with more and more calibration the robot is more and more
likely to knock down more pins. However, they precisely quantify the probability
of each outcome of each type at each point in time.

7   Related Work

Although the PEPA language is often used for modelling software systems (as
in [18,19]) and services (as in [20]) it has also been used for modelling physical
systems such as production cells [21], robot control problems [22], and even lift
systems [23]. Using PEPA as a Markovian process algebra, the authors of [23]
found significant differences between the Markovian results obtained by using
PEPA from the predictions made by control engineers using approximate equation models. The problem of distinguishing a particular client or process for
observation as discussed in Section 2.2 has also been recently considered in
the context of generalised stochastic Petri nets in[24] although distinguishing
the passage based on the terminating conditions is not considered, we feel that
passage-end analysis would fit equally well for Petri nets as with PEPA.

8   Conclusions

We have modified passage-time analysis to allow for distinct passage results.
Thus passage-time analysis has been extended to allow passage-end analysis. We
have done so within the framework of eXtended Stochastic Probes thus ensuring
that our passage-end queries remain robust over model modifications and do not
require that the modeller modify their original model. The set of queries which
can be specified with XSP is therefore extended.

Another bonus which we obtain almost for free is the ability to analyse passages which may never complete at all. This only works for passages in which
there is only one source state, because if the model deadlocks we cannot analyse
the EMC to obtain the distribution of probability to the source states at the beginning of the passage. A passage which may for example result in a deadlocked
situation before it is complete. This allows the modeller to provide a concrete
answer to the question: "How long should I wait for my response?" because we

can now say that a given percentage of all requests which ultimately are successfully serviced are serviced within 10 seconds, hence if you have waited longer than 10 seconds it is likely you will never receive a response and hence can cancel the request yourself.

Acknowledgements

The authors are supported by the EU FET-IST Global Computing 2 project SENSORIA ("Software Engineering for Service-Oriented Overlay Computers" (IST-3-016004-IP-09)). The robot bowling problem was brought to our attention by Paola Fantini and Claudio Palasciano of MIP-Politecnico di Milano.

References

1. Clark, A., Gilmore, S.: State-aware performance analysis with eXtended Stochastic Probes. In: Thomas, N., Juiz, C. (eds.) EPEW 2008. LNCS, vol. 5261, pp. 125–140. Springer, Heidelberg (2008)
2. Argent-Katwala, A., Bradley, J., Dingle, N.: Expressing performance requirements using regular expressions to specify stochastic probes over process algebra models. In: Proceedings of the Fourth International Workshop on Software and Performance, Redwood Shores, California, USA, pp. 49–58. ACM Press, New York (2004)
3. Hillston, J.: A Compositional Approach to Performance Modelling. Cambridge University Press, Cambridge (1996)
4. Hillston, J.: The nature of synchronisation. In: Herzog, U., Rettelbach, M. (eds.) Proceedings of the Second International Workshop on Process Algebras and Performance Modelling, Erlangen, pp. 51–70 (November 1994)
5. Hillston, J.: Tuning systems: From composition to performance. The Computer Journal 48(4), 385–400 (2005); The Needham Lecture paper
6. Hillston, J.: Process algebras for quantitative analysis. In: Proceedings of the 20th Annual IEEE Symposium on Logic in Computer Science (LICS 2005), Chicago, pp. 239–248. IEEE Computer Society Press, Los Alamitos (2005)
7. Hillston, J., Kloul, L.: An efficient Kronecker representation for PEPA models. In: de Luca, L., Gilmore, S. (eds.) PROBMIV 2001, PAPM-PROBMIV 2001, and PAPM 2001. LNCS, vol. 2165, pp. 120–135. Springer, Heidelberg (2001)
8. Clark, A.: A revised PEPA probe implementation. In: Proceedings of the 6th Workshop on Process Algebra and Stochastically Timed Activities (PASTA), Imperial College, London, July 26-27, pp. 5–11 (2007)
9. Argent-Katwala, A., Bradley, J., Clark, A., Gilmore, S.: Location-aware quality of service measurements for service-level agreements. In: Barthe, G., Fournet, C. (eds.) TGC 2007 and FODO 2008. LNCS, vol. 4912, pp. 222–239. Springer, Heidelberg (2008)
10. Little, J.D.C.: A proof of the queueing formula $l = \lambda w$. Operations Research 9, 380–387 (1961)
11. Clark, A., Gilmore, S.: Terminating passage-time calculations on uniformised Markov chains. In: Argent-Katwala, A., Dingle, N.J., Harder, U. (eds.) Proceedings of the Twenty-Fourth annual UK Performance Engineering Workshop, pp. 64–75 (June 2008)

12. Grassmann, W.: Transient solutions in Markovian queueing systems. Computers and Operations Research 4, 47–53 (1977)
13. Gross, D., Miller, D.: The randomization technique as a modelling tool and solution procedure for transient Markov processes. Operations Research 32, 343–361 (1984)
14. Dingle, N.J.: Parallel Computation of Response Time Densities and Quantiles in Large Markov and Semi-Markov Models. PhD thesis, Department of Computing, Imperial College London. University of London (October 2004)
15. Clark, A.: The ipclib PEPA Library. In: Harchol-Balter, M., Kwiatkowska, M., Telek, M. (eds.) Proceedings of the 4th International Conference on the Quantitative Evaluation of SysTems (QEST), pp. 55–56. IEEE, Los Alamitos (2007)
16. Bradley, J., Dingle, N., Gilmore, S., Knottenbelt, W.: Extracting passage times from PEPA models with the HYDRA tool: A case study. In: Jarvis, S. (ed.) Proceedings of the Nineteenth annual UK Performance Engineering Workshop, University of Warwick, pp. 79–90 (July 2003)
17. Bradley, J., Dingle, N., Gilmore, S., Knottenbelt, W.: Derivation of passage-time densities in PEPA models using IPC: The Imperial PEPA Compiler. In: Kotsis, G. (ed.) Proceedings of the 11th IEEE/ACM International Symposium on Modeling, Analysis and Simulation of Computer and Telecommunications Systems, University of Central Florida, pp. 344–351. IEEE Computer Society Press, Los Alamitos (2003)
18. Hillston, J., Kloul, L.: Performance investigation of an on-line auction system. Concurrency and Computation: Practice and Experience 13, 23–41 (2001)
19. Duguid, A.: Coping with the parallelism of BitTorrent: Conversion of PEPA to ODEs in dealing with state space explosion. In: Asarin, E., Bouyer, P. (eds.) FORMATS 2006. LNCS, vol. 4202, pp. 156–170. Springer, Heidelberg (2006)
20. Clark, A., Gilmore, S.: Evaluating quality of service for service level agreements. In: Brim, L., Leucker, M. (eds.) Proceedings of the 11th International Workshop on Formal Methods for Industrial Critical Systems, Bonn, Germany, pp. 172–185 (August 2006)
21. Holton, D.: A PEPA specification of an industrial production cell. In: Gilmore, S., Hillston, J. (eds.) Proceedings of the Third International Workshop on Process Algebras and Performance Modelling, Special Issue of The Computer Journal, vol. 38(7), pp. 542–551 (December 1995)
22. Gilmore, S., Hillston, J., Holton, D., Rettelbach, M.: Specifications in Stochastic Process Algebra for a Robot Control Problem. International Journal of Production Research 34(4), 1065–1080 (1996)
23. El-Rayes, A., Kwiatkowska, M., Minton, S.: Analysing performance of lift systems in PEPA. In: Pooley, R., Hillston, J. (eds.) Proceedings of the Twelfth UK Performance Engineering Workshop, Edinburgh, Scotland, pp. 83–100 (September 1996)
24. Dingle, N.J., Knottenbelt, W.J.: Automated Customer-Centric Performance Analysis of Generalised Stochastic Petri Nets Using Tagged Tokens. In: Third International Workshop on Practical Applications of Stochastic Modelling (PASM 2008), Palma de Mallorca, Spain (August 2008)

Quantitative Analysis of Services*

Igor Cappello[1], Allan Clark[2], Stephen Gilmore[2], Diego Latella[3], Michele Loreti[4], Paola Quaglia[1], and Stefano Schivo[1]

[1] Dipartimento di Ingegneria e Scienza dell'Informazione, Università di Trento
[2] School of Informatics, The University of Edinburgh
[3] Istituto di Scienza e Tecnologie dell'Informazione "A. Faedo"- CNR
[4] Dipartimento di Sistemi e Informatica, Università di Firenze

Abstract. We show a number of applications of the tools which have been developed within the SENSORIA project to perform quantitative analysis of services. These tools are formally grounded on source calculi which allow the description of services at distinct levels of abstraction, and hence pose distinct challenges to both modelling and analysis.

The reported applications refer to (suitable subcomponents of) the Finance Case-Study, and show instances of, respectively, exact model checking of Mar-CaSPiS against the both state-aware and action-aware logic SoSL, exact and statistical model checking of sCOWS against the state-aware logic CSL, querying of PEPA models by terms of the XSP language that expresses both state-aware and action-aware stochastic probes.

1 Introduction

A number of calculi have been defined to formally model services and then analyze their behaviour. Some of them come equipped with quantitative measures and probabilistic/stochastic semantics, and hence allow the description of non-functional aspects of computation like, e.g., performance, resource usage, or dependability.

Based on the above calculi, some tools have been developed within the SENSORIA Project to assist in the verification of the quantitative properties of services. Here we show the applicability of those tools together with a sample of the obtained results. The analysis refers to a credit request scenario. This in turn is part of the specification of a credit portal which is referred to as the SENSORIA Finance Case-Study and is fully illustrated in Chapter 7-4.

The credit portal is a business-to-business (B2B) application where a bank wishes to offer its loan services to business customers. It is important that loan applications are processed efficiently (so that the bank does not lose customers to a rival bank). A high degree of automation is provided to meet this demand for efficient processing. Where human intervention is needed in the decision-making process this too must be driven by a deep sense of urgency in processing the request in a timely manner.

The credit portal is implemented using the JBOSS enterprise Java technology. This is an extensible Web service framework in which traditional web service components

* This work has been partially sponsored by the project SENSORIA, IST-2005-016004.

M. Wirsing and M. Hölzl (Eds.): SENSORIA Project, LNCS 6582, pp. 522–540, 2011.

can be supplemented using flexible rulesets which allow complex business rules to be coded concisely. These rulesets can also be updated quickly in response to changing business policies, regulations, procedures, and governmental or legal requirements. This configuration allows the bank both to respond quickly to changing practices within the financial industry and to gain the greatest advantage from business opportunities by bringing new products and services onto the market ahead of its rivals.

Some businesses which use the services of the bank are long-established customers with a lengthy and well-documented history of financial solidity and probity, together with substantial credit reserves and securities. Modest loan applications from these customers can be directly approved by a *pre-decision* process which validates the content of the loan request and the securities. In such a case it is possible that the decision to lend can be taken entirely by the application of the predefined rules stored on the server and executed by the local rule engine. This is the fastest route to approval of a loan request because it is one which completes entirely without human intervention.

Not all loan requests can be so rapidly approved. Many will require more lengthy scrutiny, evaluation and checking. In these cases a bank clerk will process the credit request. There are several possible next outcomes here. First, the clerk may approve the request but must then forward the credit request to a supervisor who must also approve the request. Second, the clerk may decline the request. Third, the clerk may enter into a negotiation with the customer with the intention of updating the request to reduce the capital requested, or change the terms of repayment. This then initiates another request from the customer which is to be processed in the manner just described.

Quantitative evaluation of this scenario presents technical challenges because there are two distinct timescales in use here. The pre-decision processing is performed on a timescale of seconds whereas the human processing and evaluation proceeds on a timescale of days. Systems where activities proceed at very different rates provide numerical problems for the underlying software routines because they demand more computational effort than models which operate on a single timescale. When rates are separated by several orders of magnitude, as they are here, the problem is often referred to as a *multi-scale problem* and its attendant numerical problem as *stiff* (meaning intractable or computationally expensive). Thus this problem is a good test for the robustness of the quantitative analysis tools developed in the SENSORIA Project.

The rest of the chapter is organized as follows. Section 2, Section 3, and Section 4 present the analysis of the credit request scenario specified in MarCaSPiS, in sCOWS [11,13], and in PEPA [6], respectively. Concluding remarks are reported in Section 5.

The analysis of the MarCaSPiS specification of the scenario is based on a stochastic model checking technique. Properties are described in SoSL (Service-Oriented Stochastic Logic), a stochastic modal logic for service-oriented computing presented in Chapter 5-1. The analysis is then performed by exploiting SoSL-MC, a stochastic model-checker for SoSL which uses MRMC [7] as a component. In particular MRMC is wrapped in the algorithms implemented in SoSL-MC.

Section 3 presents the sCOWS specification of the credit request scenario. The model is analyzed by means of two different techniques: exact model checking and statistical simulation-based model checking. In both cases, the property specification language is CSL [1]. The tool for statistical model checking is a stand-alone application, while the one for exact model checking provides input to PRISM [8], a well-known probabilistic model checker. Comparisons between the results obtained by the two kinds of analysis are also reported.

The applications shown in Section 4 are based on the PEPA specification of the relevant scenario. Stochastic properties of services are obtained by querying the model using the XSP performance language [4]. This is an action-aware language of stochastic probes: once fixed the actions relevant to the sort of analysis that the user wishes to carry on, the tool delivers the probability of completing the passage between them in the given time bound.

2 Analysis in MarCaSPiS

MarCaSPiS is the Markovian extension of CaSPiS [2]. In MarCaSPiS, each *output activity* (service invocation, concretion and return) is equipped with a parameter (a *rate*, $\lambda \in \mathbb{R}^+$) characterising a random variable with a negative exponential distribution, modeling the duration of the activity. Furthermore, each *input activity* (service definition and abstractions) is annotated with a *weight* ($\omega \in \mathbb{N}^+$): a positive integer that will be used for determining the probability that the specific input is selected when a complementary output is executed.

In this section we show how MarCaSPiS can be used for specifying and verifying quantitative aspects of the Finance Case-Study. A MarCaSPiS specification of the Finance Case-Study is obtained from the one in CaSPiS, presented in Chapter 2-1, by adding rates (and weights) to actions.

Parties considered in the specification are:

- the supervisor and clerk that can be asked to review the request;
- the portal that acts as an interface for clients and that coordinates the whole procedure;
- auxiliary services, login and rating, invoked by the portal in order to assist in the request evaluation.

Each of the above parties is rendered as a service that is waiting for an invocation. We let portal, login and rating be replicated services. Hence, they are always able to react to invocations. On the contrary, supervisor and clerk, which describe the behaviour of people involved in the decision process, are not replicated.

A client that wants to submit a credit request has to first log into the system. If the login is successful then he will be asked for some credit data (e.g. the amount) and for some balance and security guarantees. Then the request review phase starts. A rating is computed for the client: either the credit is immediately granted (rating AAA) or the intervention of either a clerk or a supervisor is required (rating BBB and CCC). The decision (decline or accept) is then communicated to the client.

In the analysis proposed in this section we study how system performance is influenced by the client distributions within the three rating categories. The following scenarios are considered:

S1: 50% of clients have rate AAA, 33% rate BBB, and 17% rate CCC.
S2: 25% of clients have rate AAA, 50% rate BBB, and 25% rate CCC.
S3: 17% of clients have rate AAA, 33% rate BBB, and 50% rate CCC.

In the analysis the following properties will be considered:

1. *System performance*, how fast the system is able to handle pending requests;
2. *Supervisor and Clerk workload*, how much time supervisor and clerk spend to review requests;
3. *System reactivity*, how much time a system needs to manage a request.

These properties are specified by means of SoSL (Service-Oriented Stochastic Logic). This is a *temporal logic* that permits describing the dynamic evolution of the system. SoSL is both *action-* and *state*-based and it is equipped with primitives that permits the use of real-time bounds in the logical characterisation of the behaviours of interest. Moreover, SoSL is a *probabilistic logic* that permits expressing not only functional properties, but also properties related to performance and dependability aspects.

In the analysis we assume that, on the average, portal takes a decision every time unit, clerk takes a decision every 5 time units, and supervisor takes a decision every 10 time units. Moreover, we also assume that login and rating handle 10 invocations per time units on the average.

2.1 System Performance

We aim at verifying the capability of the system to handle pending requests. For this reason, we consider a configuration where the credit portal is in parallel with n clients ($n \in \{1, 2, 3\}$). We are interested in determining the probability (p) that all the clients are served within t time units (All the clients are served when the system reaches a deadlock state). This property can be expressed in SoSL by the following formula:

$$\mathcal{P}_{\geqslant p}(\text{TRUE} \; _\top \mathcal{U}^{<t} \; [\top]\text{FALSE})$$

In Figure 1 is shown how the probability p varies as a function of time t. In all the considered cases (1, 2 and 3 clients) the greater is the percentage of clients with rating AAA, the higher is the probability of serving all the requests within t time units.

2.2 Supervisor and Clerk Workload

Besides system performance, it could be also interesting to verify the workload of supervisor and clerk. This analysis could help system designers to evaluate the number of people to engage.

In order to perform this analysis we consider a system where a client continuously contacts the portal. In this case we are interested in studying the probability that services supervisor and clerk are under-used. We say that a service is *under-used* if the probability is less than 0.4 that the service is used within 10 time units. Under-utilization for service s can be rendered in SoSL with formula Φ_s defined as follows:

$$\Phi_s \stackrel{\Delta}{=} \mathcal{P}_{<0.4}(\text{TRUE} \; _\top \mathcal{U}^{\leq 10}_{\overset{\leftrightarrow}{s}} \text{TRUE})$$

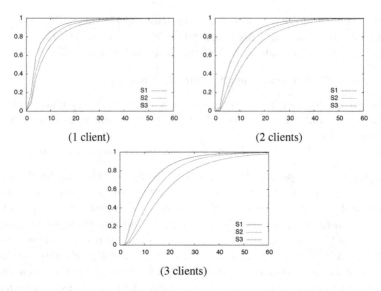

(1 client)   (2 clients)

(3 clients)

Fig. 1. System performance

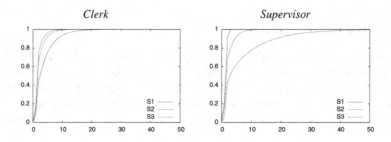

Clerk   *Supervisor*

Fig. 2. Supervisor and Clerk workload

We are interested in those states such that the probability is larger than or equal to p that, by time t, a state is reached where **supervisor** (resp. **clerk**) is *under-used*.

These properties are rendered in SoSL as follows:

$$\mathcal{P}_{\geqslant p}(\text{TRUE }_T\mathcal{U}^{<t}\ \Phi_{\text{supervisor}}) \qquad \mathcal{P}_{\geqslant p}(\text{TRUE }_T\mathcal{U}^{<t}\ \Phi_{\text{clerk}})$$

In Figure 2 is reported the result of the analysis. In the considered specification both the clerk and the supervisor are under-used.

2.3   System Reactivity

In Section 2.2 we have studied a performance measure of the Finance Case-Study. This is expressed in terms of the probability to completely handle a set of clients in a given

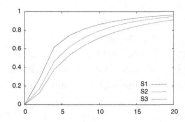

Fig. 3. System reactivity

time with a given probability. However, this measure is also influenced by many aspects that are not under the control of the designer. For instance, the time spent by a client for sending data.

In this section we study *system reactivity*. This aims at measuring the capacity of the system to react to external interactions. In particular, we will consider a property of the form: "if a client contacts the portal and sends the data, then with probility p the portal will send the decision within t time units".

This property can be specified in SoSL as follows:

$$\nabla x. \wr s(x) \cdot x : \langle \text{ID} \rangle \cdot x : \langle \text{AMNT} \rangle \wr_{\geq 1} \mathcal{P}_{\geq p}(\text{TRUE}\ _\top \mathcal{U}^{<t}\ \wr s(x) \cdot x : (\text{DEC}) \wr_{\geq 1} \text{TRUE})$$

In Figure 3 is reported the result of the analysis where, as expected, we have better performance in scenario **S1** while the worst case is scenario **S3**.

3   Analysis in sCOWS

In this section we report on some analysis results obtained by using two tools which have been developed within the SENSORIA Project to verify quantitative properties of services described in a stochastic extension of COWS [9]. The detailed description of the stochastic calculus, named sCOWS, is outside the scope of this paper. Here we just mention that, in the tradition of stochastic process calculi, the main syntactic difference between sCOWS and COWS is in the fact that in sCOWS basic actions are associated with a random variable expressing their rates. Other differences - i.e., the use of service identifiers vs replication, and the adoption of a labelled semantics vs a reduction semantics - are ascribed to meet some technical requirements for the applicability of Markovian techniques. For a detailed description of the sCOWS semantics the interested reader is referred to either [11] (which shows the essence of the stochastic enrichment on the monadic calculus) or [13] (where the extension of the full polyadic calculus is presented).

COWS is a calculus strongly inspired by WS-BPEL which combines primitives of well-known process calculi (like, e.g., the π-calculus [10,12]) with constructs for web services orchestration. Differently from CASPIS, no primitive for opening or ending sessions is explicitly available in COWS. The communication paradigm of the calculus is rather based on a mechanism of *best-matching* of the parameters of complementary invoke (send) and request (receive) activities. Briefly put, when an invoke (request, resp.) can match more than on request (invoke, resp.), only the communications that induce the least number of parameter actualizations are allowed. For instance, using an asynchronous π-calculus like notation and assuming that integer numbers play the role of ground constants, in the following parallel composition

$$\overline{x}\langle x, 7\rangle \mid x(w, 7).P_1 \mid x(y, z).P_2 \mid x(z, 11).P_3$$

one single communication would be allowed: the one between the sending process $\overline{x}\langle x, 7\rangle$ and the receiving process $x(w, 7).P_1$. Precisely, the pairing of $\overline{x}\langle x, 7\rangle$ with $x(z, 11)$ would be made impossible by the mismatch of the ground constants, and the pairing of $\overline{x}\langle x, 7\rangle$ with $x(y, z)$ would instead be prevented by the fact that this is not the best available match for the output action. Indeed, pairing $\overline{x}\langle x, 7\rangle$ with $x(y, z)$ would induce the substitution of both y and z, while pairing $\overline{x}\langle x, 7\rangle$ with $x(w, 7)$ results in substituting w only. The above example simply shows how the mechanism of sessioning is rendered in COWS. Just think of the ground constant 7 as a private session identifier: all the communications reserved for that particular session will not be intercepted by concurrent peers.

3.1 sCOWS Specification of the Scenario

We present below the sCOWS specification of the analyzed scenario. The setting is of a bank credit request service, which can be invoked by customers. The example presents the login phase of the scenario, which is implemented at two distinct levels of abstraction. In the first case, referred to as *fine-grained*, the bank service is composed of a portal service (acting as an interface towards customers) and a login database (which may be thought of as a bank private service). In the second case, called *coarse-grained*, the login database is not explicitly considered: the whole login process is modelled as if it were completely handled by the portal implementation, and the existence of a login database is abstracted away. Indeed, the two specifications interpret the login process as seen by the bank and by the customer, respectively. The services involved in the two cases are, respectively:

- Customer (Table 1) and Portal (Table 2) for the coarse-grained instance;
- Customer (the same as above), Portal', and LoginDB (Table 3) for the fine-grained instance;

where we use strings starting by 'V' to denote variables.

In the coarse-grained specification of the scenario, the login process starts with an invocation by the customer over the portal.customerLogin channel. The customer provides his username (user), his password (pwd), and a private name (initialId), which is used to distinguish among invocations by different customers. The complementary request action is performed by the Portal service, and another instance of Portal is spawned to serve possible invocations from further customers. Since the

Table 1. Definition of Customer for both the coarse- and the fine-grained specifications

```
Customer() = [user] [pwd] [initialId] (
        (portal.customerLogin!<user, pwd, initialId>,1.0)
      | (
            (portal.loginKo?<initialId>,1.0).nil
            + [VmyKey] (portal.loginOk?<initialId, VmyKey>,1.0).(
                (initialId.customerLoginOk!<loginOk>,1.0)
        )   )   )
```

Table 2. Definition of Portal for the coarse-grained specification

```
Portal() = [VtheUser][VthePwd][VtheId] (
        (portal.customerLogin?<VtheUser, VthePwd, VtheId>,1.0).(
        [lkey][ndc] (
            (ndc.ndc!<ndc>,1.0)
          | (
                (ndc.ndc?<ndc>,failRate).
                    (portal.loginKo!<VtheId>,1.0)
                + (ndc.ndc?<ndc>,okRate).
                    (portal.loginOk!<VtheId, lkey>,1.0)
            )   )
        | Portal()
        )   )
```

login database service is not present in the current scenario, the task to decide whether a login attempt is successful or not is fully delegated to the portal. The outcome of the login attempt is abstracted as the mutually exclusive choice between two internal communications over the ndc.ndc channel. In case of successful login, a private name (lkey) is sent to the customer. This private name models a session identifier, which will be persistently used in further interactions between the customer and any additional service provided by the bank. In the definition of Portal, most of the actions are given basic rate 1.0. Here we observe that this is not the case for the two receiving actions on ndc.ndc which are associated with the symbolic values failRate and okRate. As explained below, these values can be eventually instantiated after the generation of both the labelled transition system and the Markov Chain. This feature, which takes advantage of the PRISM built-in facilities, allows us to model check different configurations of the same sCOWS specification re-using the same PRISM model and just tuning the values of symbolic basic rates.

In the fine-grained specification, the decision whether an attempted login is successful or not is taken by Portal' on the basis of the outcome of its interactions with the login database LoginDB. The portal service forwards to LoginDB the credentials received by the Customer, and conversely sends the response back to the relevant customer. As in the coarse-grained instance, the request actions involved in the outcome of the login attempt are associated with symbolic basic rates.

Table 3. Definition of `Portal'` and of `LoginDB` for the fine-grained specification

```
Portal'() = [VtheUser][VthePwd][VtheId](
        (portal.customerLogin? <VtheUser, VthePwd, VtheId>,1.0).(
          [lkey](
              (db.login!<lkey, VtheUser, VthePwd>,1.0)
              | (
                  (db.userKo?<lkey>,1.0).(portal.loginKo!<VtheId>,1.0)
                  + (db.userOk?<lkey>,1.0).(
                      (portal.loginOk!<VtheId, lkey>,1.0)
                      | (portal.creditRequest?<lkey>,1.0)
                        .(portal.createInst!<lkey>,1.0)
              )   )   )
            | Portal'()
          )   )


LoginDB() = [VrespKey][Vusr][Vpwd](db.login?<VrespKey, Vusr, Vpwd>,1.0).(
        [nd1][ch1](
            (nd1.ch1!<ch>,1.0)
            | (
                (nd1.ch1?<ch>,okRate).
                    (db.userOk!<VrespKey>,1.0)
                +(nd1.ch1?<ch>,failRate).
                    (db.userKo!<VrespKey>,1.0)
            )   )
          | LoginDB()
        )
```

3.2 Probabilistic Model Checking in sCOWS

Probabilistic model checking of sCOWS specifications is based on a Java tool called sCOWS_LTS that provides input to PRISM, a probabilistic model checker for the analysis of properties expressed in CSL (Continuous Stochastic Logic).

The developed tool first implements the sCOWS operational semantics to get the Labelled Transition System (LTS) associated with the input service. For instance, for three parallel customers, Figure 4 and Figure 5 show the LTSs of the fine- and of the coarse-grained specifications, respectively. For the sake of readability, the labels associated with transitions are omitted by both the two graphs. Apart from the lower number of nodes in the coarse-grained case, notice that both LTSs have the same number of absorbing states, representing the possible final configurations of the global service that only depend on the number of successfully logged on customers (0, .., 3).

The second computational phase of the developed tool consists in the generation of the Continuous Time Markov Chain (CTMC) in PRISM notation. To ease expressing and checking relevant quantitative properties, PRISM allows the association of CTMC states with variables. In order to take full advantage of this feature, when the LTS is translated into the CTMC, the user can specify which sort of actions are relevant to the

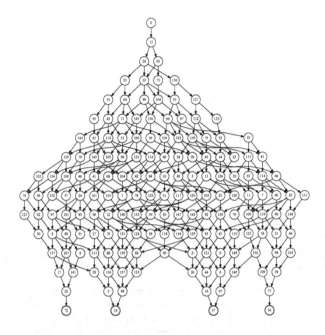

Fig. 4. LTS of the fine-grained specification (labels omitted)

analysis he intends to carry on. For example, the user can choose to associate the communication over a given channel with the increment of an integer PRISM variable. This is indeed what was done for the examples of analysis that are shown below. In those cases we were interested in checking properties depending on the number of successfully logged on customers. Then we used the variable finished to trace the number of communications over the channel portal.loginOk.

Examples of properties against which sCOWS models can be checked are given below. The first one (1) is a property for *transient* analysis, and the second one (2) is a *steady-state* property, namely they refer, respectively, to the transient evolution of the system, and to its behaviour at steady-state. Formally:

$$P_{=?}[\text{true } \mathcal{U}[T, T] \text{ finished} = \text{N}] \tag{1}$$

i.e., "What is the probability that exactly N customers are logged on at time T?", and

$$S_{=?}[\text{finished} = \text{N}] \tag{2}$$

i.e., "What is the long-run probability of being in a state where exactly N customers are logged on?". Relatively to (2), notice that, since in the configuration at hand there is no steady-state, the use of the CSL S operator expresses the long-run probability of reaching one of the final configurations of the system. Also, the results obtained by checking (2) represent the asymptotic view of the results for the transient analysis of (1).

Exploiting the support for symbolic rates, we checked our specifications with two different instances of the pair (okRate, failRate). In particular, we considered the

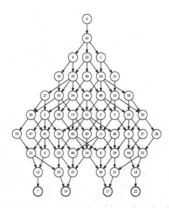

Fig. 5. LTS of the coarse-grained specification (labels omitted)

Table 4. Parametric probabilities to get a particular final configuration (r_{ok} stays for okRate, and r_f stays for okRate)

Logins	0	1	2	3
Probability	$\left(\frac{r_f}{r_{ok}+r_f}\right)^3$	$3\left(\frac{r_{ok}}{r_{ok}+r_f}\right)\left(\frac{r_f}{r_{ok}+r_f}\right)^2$	$3\left(\frac{r_{ok}}{r_{ok}+r_f}\right)^2\left(\frac{r_f}{r_{ok}+r_f}\right)$	$\left(\frac{r_{ok}}{r_{ok}+r_f}\right)^3$

pair (okRate = 4.0, failRate = 2.0) where the two values are much similar, and the pair (okRate = 30.0, failRate = 2.0) in which the okRate is fifteen times bigger than failRate. The results of the analysis are collectively reported in Figure 6. As expected, for both the two instances of the pair (okRate, failRate), the fine-grained specification shows to be slower than the coarse-grained one. Notice however that the additional transitions of the fine-grained model are executed before deciding upon the success or the failure of the login attempt, and hence belong to the transient behaviour of the global system, while property (2) refers to steady-state. For this reason, once fixed specific values for the pair (okRate, failRate), one would expect comparable results for both the coarse- and the fine-grained specifications. In fact, the probability to reach a particular final configuration is driven by a binomial distribution $B\left(3, \frac{\text{okRate}}{\text{okRate}+\text{failRate}}\right)$ which only depends on the values assigned to the symbolic rates (okRate, failRate).

Table 5. Long-run probabilities of being in one of the absorbing states in the different instances of the two specifications

Logins	(okRate = 4.0, failRate = 2.0)			(okRate = 30.0, failRate = 2.0)		
	Fine	Coarse	Analytical	Fine	Coarse	Analytical
0	0.0370369	0.0370370	$0.0\overline{37}$	2.441×10^{-4}	2.441×10^{-4}	$2.44140625 \times 10^{-4}$
1	0.2222216	0.2222220	$0.\overline{2}$	1.09863×10^{-2}	1.09863×10^{-2}	$1.0986328125 \times 10^{-2}$
2	0.4444432	0.4444438	$0.\overline{4}$	0.1647944	0.1647947	0.164794921875
3	0.2962957	0.2962958	$0.\overline{296}$	0.8239731	0.8239734	0.823974609375

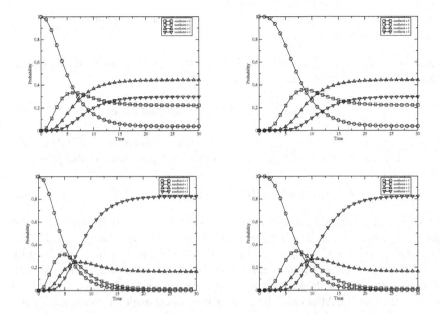

Fig. 6. Long-run probability that N customers are successfully logged on at time T: basic rates (okRate = 4.0, failRate = 2.0) (top) and (okRate = 30.0, failRate = 2.0) (bottom); coarse-grained specification (left) and fine-grained specification (right)

Table 5 sums up the experimental data we obtained when checking (2) and compares them to the theoretical analytical values resulting from the instantiation of the expressions in Table 4. The numerical values obtained by the model checker are approximated to seven digits. There are a few discrepancies (always bound by 10^{-6}) between corresponding experimental and theoretical data. We ascribe this shift to the rounding errors introduced by the model checker computations.

3.3   Approximate Model Checking in sCOWS

Despite of the many optimizations implemented in sCOWS_LTS, on some occasions the state space of a specification can be so big that the generation of the CTMC, as well as the application of numerical algorithms to solve the chain, become really demanding tasks. To face this problem and check properties of sCOWS services without generating their complete transition systems, we also developed a tool for approximate statistical model checking. The tool, called sCOWS_AMC, is based on the generation of simulation traces obtained by running a Monte Carlo algorithm. At high level, given a formula ϕ, its model checking consists in the following steps:

– computation of a number of execution traces obtained by direct simulation of the source sCOWS specification;

- evaluation of ϕ against each of the traces;
- statistical reasoning based both on the number of samples performed and on the desired error threshold.

Our tool currently supports the verification of CSL transient time-bounded path formulas like, for instance, the following ones:

$$P_{\geqslant 0.8}[\texttt{finished} < 2 \ \mathcal{U}[10, 20] \ \texttt{finished} >= 2] \tag{3}$$

i.e., "Is there a probability of at least 80% that in the execution time range $[10, 20]$ the number of logged-on customers varies from a value less than two to a value greater or equal two?",

$$P_?[\texttt{finished} < 2 \ \mathcal{U}[10, 20] \ \texttt{finished} >= 2] \tag{4}$$

i.e., "What is the probability that in the execution time range $[10, 20]$ the number of logged-on customers varies from a value less than two to a value greater or equal two?"

The truth value of CSL probabilistic formulas of the type of (3) is calculated by means of the *sequential probability ratio test* [15] and is inspired by the same approach used Ymer [16]. This method requires to perform a sequence of observations of the hypothesis to be tested. After each observation an error estimation is made, taking into account the results of all the previous observations. When a given error threshold is crossed, the hypothesis is either accepted or rejected. In our case, performing an observation corresponds to testing the formula over an execution trace, which is generated on demand. This approach does not involve the estimation of the probability with which the property is verified: it only checks whether the probability lies below or beyond the given threshold.

Statistical checking of probability estimation formulas, like e.g. (4), requires a different technique which is based on the choice of two parameters: the *approximation parameter* ε, and the *confidence parameter* δ. As in the above case, the analysis is computed on a series of observations on random walks over the LTS. This time, however, the number of observations necessary to obtain the desired approximation level is estimated *before* observations are made. As shown in [5], taking a sample of

$$4 \times \frac{\log \frac{2}{\delta}}{\varepsilon^2}$$

observations, ensures that the probability that the obtained estimation diverges from the real value by more than ε is less than δ. Also, the complexity of this probability estimation method is linearly dependent on the number of observations, and hence on $\log \frac{1}{\delta}$ and on $\frac{1}{\varepsilon^2}$. So the value of the approximation parameter has to be carefully selected. Given the best-matching communication policy of sCOWS, all the possible transitions exiting from a state must be computed on the fly at each step of the simulation. Hence random walks over sCOWS specifications are more costly than over CTMCs. To get a good balance between approximation value and execution time, we carried out our experiments by choosing $\delta = 10^{-1}$ and $\varepsilon = 10^{-2}$, so testing properties over 52042 execution traces.

Table 6. Comparative view of the model checking approach and the statistical checking approach (time expressed in seconds)

Coarse-grained specification				
Customers	State space size	LTS generation time	Model Checking time	Simulation time
2	20	1.4	1.5	417.3
3	55	3.5	1.5	988.7
4	125	25.3	1.4	1,979.5
5	251	287.7	3.4	2,801.0
Fine-grained specification				
Customers	State space size	LTS generation time	Model Checking time	Simulation time
2	44	3.2	1.5	1,125.6
3	164	22.5	1.5	3,271.8
4	494	310.6	7.4	4,958.9
5	1,286	48,420.5	69.5	11,734.3

3.4 Comparison between the CTMC- and the Simulation-Based Approaches

Table 6 shows a comparative view of the results we obtained by applying probabilistic and statistical model checking. Comparison is in terms of execution time. As expected, for the coarse-grained specification the simulation-based method is less efficient than the other. This is due to the fact that the state space is not very large, and thus relatively cheap to build. Conversely, when the number and the complexity of the involved services increase, the method based on the generation of the complete LTS gets outperformed by the approach used in sCOWS_AMC.

4 Analysis in PEPA

We turn now to modelling of the credit request scenario in PEPA [6] and analysis of the model using the PEPA software tools developed within the Sensoria Project [3,14].

We begin with a description of the bank's customers and the process which they follow in order to secure a loan from the bank. This presents the customer's view of the process in terms of activities and choices along the way.

The customer's first action is to initiate a loan (*request*). To carry this through they must enter their balance data and securities (*enterData*) and send this to the credit portal with an XBRL upload (*uploadData*). (XBRL is the eXtensible Business Reporting Language.) The customer then waits to see if the request will be approved or declined (the *approve* and *decline* activities respectively). If the request is approved the customer has no further business and the next waiting customer can be considered. If the request is declined the customer can try again (*reapply*) and will do so with probability t_0. If they do not wish to reapply they can yield to the next customer.

This behaviour is described in PEPA thus. A rate is associated with each activity and a probability is associated to this when the customer is making the decision of what course of action to take next.

$$Customer \overset{def}{=} (request, r_{request}).Entering$$
$$Entering \overset{def}{=} (enterData, r_{enterData}).Upload$$
$$Upload \overset{def}{=} (uploadData, r_{upload}).Wait$$
$$Wait \overset{def}{=} (approve, \top).Customer$$
$$+ (decline, \top).Decide$$
$$Decide \overset{def}{=} (reapply, r_{reapply} \times t_0).Entering$$
$$+ (reapply, r_{reapply} \times t_1).Customer$$

The service is a reactive system. It takes no action until the upload of XBRL data is complete. At this point it validates the data by using a validation web service which determines whether or not the balance data is valid (*validateData*). We are not interested in the processing of invalid data in this scenario and so the next behaviour which we model is passing the valid data to the bank (*sendBank*). The service is then ready to receive the next request.

$$Service \overset{def}{=} (uploadData, \top).Validate$$
$$Validate \overset{def}{=} (validateData, r_{validate}).SendBank$$
$$SendBank \overset{def}{=} (sendBank, r_{sendBank}).Service$$

The relevant business functions of the bank are expressed in the *Bank* component. This documents the "predecision" phase which can have three possible outcomes. Some applications can be immediately approved, and others immediately declined. Some proportion need to be processed by a bank employee who will either decline the loan, or approve it (which requires confirmation, which may or may not be forthcoming).

$$Bank \overset{def}{=} (sendBank, \top).PreDecide$$
$$PreDecide \overset{def}{=} (predecide, r_{predecide} \times p_0).Approve$$
$$+ (predecide, r_{predecide} \times p_1).Decline$$
$$+ (predecide, r_{predecide} \times p_2).Employee$$
$$Employee \overset{def}{=} (decide, r_{decide} \times q_0).Confirm$$
$$+ (decide, r_{decide} \times q_1).Decline$$
$$Confirm \overset{def}{=} (decide, r_{decide} \times s_0).Approve$$
$$+ (decide, r_{decide} \times s_1).Decline$$
$$Approve \overset{def}{=} (approve, r_{inform}).Bank$$
$$Decline \overset{def}{=} (decline, r_{inform}).Bank$$

To complete the model description we need to compose the sequential components defined above and require them to cooperate on their shared activities. This leads to the following model composition, which defines the initial state of the model.

$$Customer \underset{\{uploadData,approve,decline\}}{\bowtie} (Service \underset{\{sendBank\}}{\bowtie} Bank)$$

In order to numerically evaluate this model it is necessary to assign particular values to the rates and probabilities used in the model. These values can be found in Tables 7 and 8. A screenshot of the PEPA Eclipse Plug-in processing the model can be found in Figure 7.

Table 7. Table of rate values used in the model. All rates are expressed at the granularity of minutes. The reciprocal of the rate gives the mean or expected value of the duration of the activity. Thus, the average time for one bank employee to decide on a loan is about 82 minutes ($1/r_{decide}$ = 81.90008).

Customer rates	Service rates	Bank rates
$r_{request}$ = 3.11944	$r_{validate}$ = 1.43141	$r_{predecide}$ = 5.15757
$r_{enterData}$ = 0.04667	$r_{sendBank}$ = 1.53785	r_{decide} = 0.01221
r_{upload} = 0.88424		r_{inform} = 0.45729
$r_{reapply}$ = 0.02036		

Table 8. Table of probability values used in the model. Each column sums to 1.

Predecision	Employee decision	Supervisor decision	Reapplication
p_0 = 0.20907	q_0 = 0.17441	s_0 = 0.56423	t_0 = 0.08970
p_1 = 0.32075	q_1 = 0.82559	s_1 = 0.43577	t_1 = 0.91030
p_2 = 0.47018			

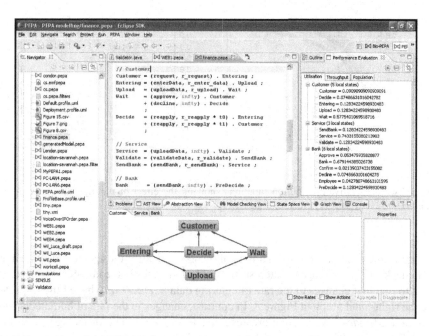

Fig. 7. Screenshot of the PEPA Eclipse Plug-in processing the credit request scenario. The PEPA model is displayed in the editor and the Abstraction view gives a graphical presentation of the *Customer* component. Performance results are shown in the Performance Evaluation view.

The computational difficulty of the problem is compounded as usual in service-oriented computing because we face the problem of being uncertain about which instance of a service centre will be selected at run-time. Because of this we must evaluate the model not just one time but repeatedly, once for each possible binding of rate parameters to rate constants. This *parameter sweep* must consider the full combinatorial potential of rate parameter assignments and the credit portal must satisfy its service-level agreement for every possible parameter assignment.

We queried the model using the XSP performance query language [4]. The query which we applied was the following:

request:start, (*approve* | *decline*):stop

Informally, we can think of this query as starting a clock when a request arrives and stopping this clock when the request is either approved or declined. More formally, this query defines a set of start states (all those states reachable via activity *request*), a set of end states (all those states reachable via activities *approve* or *decline*), and the set of all paths through the model's underlying labelled transition system from start states to end states. The analysis results computed by the PEPA tools deliver the probability of completing the passage from the start states to the end states for any given time bound. We present these results in Figure 8.

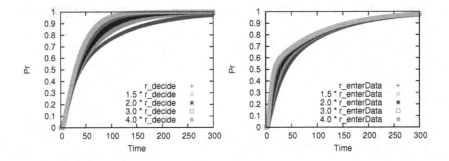

Fig. 8. Two cumulative distribution functions showing the effect of scaling rates *r_decide* and *r_enterData*

One of the uses of these results is to allow us to identify those activities which are bottlenecks for the passage of interest. By varying the rates in the model we can experiment to find that changes to the rate of entering data (*r_enterData*) have little impact—see the right-hand graph in Figure 8. In contrast, changes in the rate of human decision making (*r_decide*) have a much greater impact—compare the left-hand graph in Figure 8. From investigations such as these we can decide where effort would be best spent in improving functions within the entire business process.

5   Concluding Remarks

We presented a number examples of quantitative analysis of scenarios taken from the SENSORIA Finance Case-Study. The shown applications are based on tools developed within the Project for three distinct stochastic process calculi: MarCaSPiS, sCOWS, and PEPA.

The tool SoSL-MC, built around the MRMC model checker, allows checking MarCaSPiS specifications against properties expressed in SoSL, a service oriented stochastic logics. The examples presented in the paper show how the distribution of clients among the three possible rating classes influences system performance.

Relative to sCOWS, two tools have been illustrated. They adopt distinct approaches to the model checking of CSL formulas. The tool sCOWS_LTS generates the transition system corresponding to the given sCOWS specification, then converts it into a CTMC to be used as input for PRISM. In sCOWS_AMC, instead, statistical reasoning is applied to get the wanted results (possibly with a small approximation error) starting from simulations rather than from LTSs. The two tools have been applied to compare the long-run probability of successful login for both different rates in the specifications and different implementation of the login procedure. Also, the range of applicability of the two tools has been briefly commented upon in a comparative way.

The latest kind of analysis reported in the paper was the one carried out using PEPA and the query language XSP of stochastic probes. This setting has been used to perform sensitivity analysis over the basic rates associated to actions embedding the waiting time for loan approval or decline.

References

1. Aziz, A., Sanwal, K., Singhal, V., Brayton, R.: Model-checking continuous-time markov chains. ACM Trans. on Computational Logic 1(1), 162–170 (2000)
2. Boreale, M., Bruni, R., De Nicola, R., Loreti, M.: Sessions and pipelines for structured service programming. In: Barthe, G., de Boer, F.S. (eds.) FMOODS 2008. LNCS, vol. 5051, pp. 19–38. Springer, Heidelberg (2008)
3. Clark, A.: The ipclib PEPA Library. In: Harchol-Balter, M., Kwiatkowska, M., Telek, M. (eds.) Proceedings of the 4th International Conference on the Quantitative Evaluation of SysTems (QEST), pp. 55–56. IEEE, Los Alamitos (2007)
4. Clark, A., Gilmore, S.: State-aware performance analysis with eXtended Stochastic Probes. In: Thomas, N., Juiz, C. (eds.) EPEW 2008. LNCS, vol. 5261, pp. 125–140. Springer, Heidelberg (2008)
5. Hérault, T., Lassaigne, R., Magniette, F., Peyronnet, S.: Approximate probabilistic model checking. In: Steffen, B., Levi, G. (eds.) VMCAI 2004. LNCS, vol. 2937, pp. 307–329. Springer, Heidelberg (2004)
6. Hillston, J.: A Compositional Approach to Performance Modelling. Cambridge University Press, Cambridge (1996)
7. Katoen, J.-P., Khattri, M., Zapreev, I.S.: A Markov reward model checker. In: Quantitative Evaluation of Systems (QEST), pp. 243–244. IEEE CS Press, Los Alamitos (2005)
8. Kwiatkowska, M., Norman, G., Parker, D.: PRISM: Probabilistic Model Checking for Performance and Reliability Analysis. ACM SIGMETRICS Performance Evaluation Review 36(4), 40–45 (2009)

9. Lapadula, A., Pugliese, R., Tiezzi, F.: Calculus for Orchestration of Web Services. In: De Nicola, R. (ed.) ESOP 2007. LNCS, vol. 4421, pp. 33–47. Springer, Heidelberg (2007)
10. Milner, R.: Communicating and mobile systems: the π-calculus. Cambridge Universtity Press, Cambridge (1999)
11. Prandi, D., Quaglia, P.: Stochastic COWS. In: Krämer, B.J., Lin, K.-J., Narasimhan, P. (eds.) ICSOC 2007. LNCS, vol. 4749, pp. 245–256. Springer, Heidelberg (2007)
12. Sangiorgi, D., Walker, D.: The π-calculus: a Theory of Mobile Processes. Cambridge Universtity Press, Cambridge (2001)
13. Schivo, S.: Statistical model checking of Web Services. PhD thesis, Int. Doctorate School in Information and Communication Technologies, University of Trento (2010)
14. Tribastone, M., Duguid, A., Gilmore, S.: The PEPA Eclipse Plug-in. Performance Evaluation Review 36(4), 28–33 (2009)
15. Wald, A.: Sequential tests of statistical hypotheses. The Annals of Mathematical Statistics 16(2), 117–186 (1945)
16. Younes, H.L.S.: Ymer: A statistical model checker. In: Etessami, K., Rajamani, S.K. (eds.) CAV 2005. LNCS, vol. 3576, pp. 429–433. Springer, Heidelberg (2005)

Methodologies for Model-Driven Development and Deployment: An Overview*

László Gönczy, Ábel Hegedüs, and Dániel Varró

Department of Measurement and Information Systems,
Budapest University of Technology and Economics
{gonczy,hegedusa,varro}@mit.bme.hu

Abstract. SENSORIA proposes a model-driven approach for the entire development cycle of services-based applications and infrastructures including the design, formal analysis, deployment and re-engineering of services. This chapter presents the model-driven engineering vision of the project and a summary of achievements to demonstrate the feasibility of the approach. This approach and the challenges in model driven development are illustrated on the example of an end-to-end model transformation chain which bridges BPEL with precise formal model checking technologies and supports the back-annotation of the analysis results directly to the engineering level design model.

1 Introduction

This chapter introduces a model-driven SENSORIA approach for service engineering. The project delivered a comprehensive approach for service modeling, analysis and deployment with novel *modeling languages*, qualitative and quantitative techniques for service *analysis*, automated model driven *deployment* mechanisms and legacy transformations. *Model transformation* served as a key technology for model-driven service engineering. The first part of the chapter first discusses the overall methodology and then briefly overviews some key contributions of the project (Sec. 2). Obviously, these individual contributions are presented from the viewpoint of model-driven development. Most of these are discussed in detail in other chapters of this book or in publications related to the project.

The second part (Sec. 3) presents a selected "end-to-end" example for using model-driven techniques for analyzing services. Here high-level, standard models of business processes and their correctness requirements are translated to a formal model (namely, transition systems and temporal logic formulae) in order to enable exhaustive verification by a model checker, which is a common scenario in the SENSORIA project.

Furthermore, this forward model transformation is also complemented with the back-annotation of analysis results to the original service models. The technique we present enables the easy visualization/simulation of model checker

---

* This work has been partially sponsored by the project SENSORIA, IST-2005-016004.

M. Wirsing and M. Hölzl (Eds.): SENSORIA Project, LNCS 6582, pp. 541–560, 2011.

results right on the original business processes, therefore enabling the service developer to correct design flaws.

The tool support integrated into the SENSORIA Development Environment is briefly discussed in Sec. 3.5. Finally, Section 4 discusses related work and Section 5 concludes the paper.

2   Overview on Model-Driven Methodologies

2.1   The Sensoria Service Engineering Approach

This crosscutting chapter presents the *engineering vision* of the SENSORIA project, which facilitates a model-driven development approach. After a brief conceptual introduction, the chapter presents a high-level overview in order to demonstrate the feasibility of the approach by summarizing selected achievements in the project from a practical, engineering and tool-oriented viewpoint.

Actors in a service-oriented project. A primary goal of the SENSORIA project is to provide support for different stakeholders and actors during the entire project lifecycle for developing service-oriented overlay systems of a justifiable quality. These participants inevitably include the following ones:

- *Domain experts* are responsible for synthesizing requirements from business-related knowledge such as organization-specific roles, typical business scenarios or workflows, or business-critical data. While domain experts are obviously experts in their own application domain, they typically lack general software (and service) engineering skills, thus high-level, easy-to-understand languages are essential for them to record their business knowledge.
- *Service modelers* are in charge of the technical design of service-oriented systems, which has to meet the business-related requirements. Service modelers are typically engineers with skills in modern service-oriented modeling languages and design technologies. However, they are typically less knowledgeable in how to provide guarantees for the proven quality of service.
- *Service certifiers* are frequently a project-independent entity or authority being responsible for assuring the approved quality of services. While today, this role is still restricted to dedicated application areas (such as mission or safety-critical applications), it is expected that the role of dependability (i.e. justifiable quality of services) will drastically increase in traditional business areas. Service certifiers are typically skilled in formal (mathematical)analysis and testing techniques in order to carry out precise analysis of the service, which is currently in the design phase.
- *Service managers* are in charge of the proper deployment and maintenance (e.g. upgrade) of business-critical services. They are experts in the underlying service infrastructures.

SENSORIA proposes a model-driven approach for the entire development cycle of services based applications and infrastructures including the design, the formal

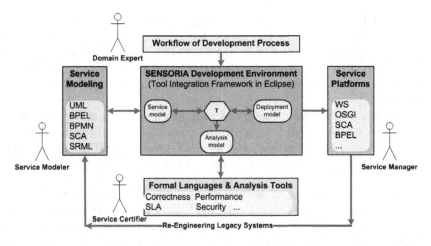

Fig. 1. The SENSORIA engineering approach

analysis, the deployment and re-engineering of services. The core ideas of the SENSORIA engineering approach are illustrated in Fig. 1.

The main contributions of SENSORIA can be summarized from an engineering perspective as follows:

- Precise capturing of domain-specific requirements
- High-level front-end service modeling languages
- Hidden formal analysis of services
- Deep semantic analysis for certification
- Automated deployment of services to various infrastructures
- Customizable orchestrator for tool integration
- Model transformations for bridging models and languages
- Reengineering of legacy services
- Standards-compliant languages and service infrastructure

The current paper provides a brief, high-level overview of selected contributions within each category above.

Experience on using these methods on SENSORIA case studies is collected in Chapter 7-2.

2.2   Contributions of Sensoria

Precise capturing of domain-specific requirements. This work is an enhancement of the Requirement Engineering technique presented previously. Here the emphasis was on Business Process Reengineering where functional and security requirements must be guaranteed during the engineering process. Thus the connections between business processes and requirement models were investigated and the notion of *goal equivalence* was introduced. A framework was defined to support *Goal Equivalent Secure Business Process Reengineering* in [1].

High-level front-end service modeling languages. In order to support service modelers, SENSORIA facilitates the use of high-level front-end service modeling languages. A primary means for that is the definition of a service-oriented UML Profile, thus off-the-shelf UML CASE tools can be used by service engineers to construct service models. UML4SOA is described in detail in Chapter 1-1.

As an alternate solution, SENSORIA proposes a new domain-specific modeling language (called SRML) for a rich semantic definition of components and services. A visual SRML editor, and an EMF-compliant SRML metamodel is developed, the approach is reported in detail in Chapter 1-2.

Hidden formal analysis of services. As a core contribution, SENSORIA facilitates a model-driven, hidden formal analysis of service-oriented overlay systems. Since service modelers typically lack mathematical skills to carry out an in-depth analysis of the system in an early phase of design, we carry out automated model analysis by transforming high-level service models into precise mathematical models in order to carry out quantitative and qualitative analysis. Results of the mathematical analysis are aimed to be back-annotated to the high-level models service engineers, thus hiding the technicalities of the underlying mathematical analysis.

A method was created for *model-based qualitative analysis of services via call by contract.* Here UML models are passed to a static checker by automated model transformations in order to analyze service behavior against security policies [2].

Techniques for *model-based quantitative performance analysis of services* by extracting a performance model from high-level service models captured in UML were also investigated. The performance model is mapped onto a stochastic process of the PEPA framework whose analysis allows the service modeler to obtain quantitative measures such as throughput and utilization (Chapter 5-2 and Chapter 5-3).

We proposed the use of Modes to abstract a selected set of services, and use UML2 models to analyze self-managing and reconfigurable service architectures for consistency and constraints. In addition, coordination processes may be synthesized to manage the changes in architecture as environmental changes occur. The approach is illustrated through the use of the SENSORIA Development Enrivonemnt with collaborating UML2, Darwin and Ponder2 model-transformation to deployment artefacts (see Chapter 4-4).

Recently, we developed novel model-based *analysis methods for service orchestration* designed in UML4SOA. Here we check consistency and protocol conformance of service compositions described as UML activity diagrams and protocols defined by UML state machines. Details of this method are provided in [3].

Finally, we also help service developers to estimate the cost of reliability (in terms of response time overhead) by introducing performability analysis techniques for reliable messaging middleware. UML4SOA models with specifications on non-functional parameters of service communication are transformed into PEPA models according to messaging mode/characteristics and the cost of middleware configuration alternatives can be evaluated by sensitivity analysis (see [4] for details).

Deep semantic analysis for certification. The service-oriented calculi developed in WP2 are intended for deep semantic analysis carried out by service certifiers having in-depth mathematical knowledge. Previously we also demonstrated that a model-driven approach is also applicable here as well by bridging UML models of service orchestrations and sound formal notations. More specifically, a transformation is presented, which maps UML activity diagrams to the saga calculus. This allows a sound formal analysis of the orchestration's control flow based on a simple and formally easily amenable representation.

A transformation has also been developed to map UML4OSA models to Jolie orchestrations, which permits the use of the analysis features provided by SOCK, the formal background of Jolie [5]. This transformation is part of the MDD4SOA toolkit.

Automated deployment of services to standards-compliant service infrastructures. Service managers responsible for deploying and maintaining service-oriented applications need to face the challenge that more and more emphasis is put on the reliability, availability, security, etc. of such services. In order to meet such non-functional requirements, a service needs to be designed for reliability by making design decisions on a high, architectural level. Details of the techniques are presented in [6], where a model-driven approach for the automated deployment of services to standards-compliant service infrastructures is described. Starting from a platform-independent service model enriched by non-functional attributes for reliable messaging, low-level service configuration descriptors are generated by appropriate model transformations for standards-compliant middleware supporting reliable and secure messaging. This year we extended existing model transformations to include the Apache Axis2 platform as target execution environment.

As a "side effect" of these developments, a novel approach is being investigated to facilitate the development of *customizable model transformations*. As illustrated by the above techniques, there are multiple model transformations during analysis and development of service-oriented systems. In these transformations, typically there are steps where a high level system model is parsed in order to generate a subset of the model, which is relevant for a particular analysis method (performance, security, etc) while other steps aim at the creation of deployment artifacts for different platforms (e.g. Web service implementation on Apache/IBM, considering different configuration constraints). These steps all need similar model transformations/translations, which can be "parameterized" by high level engineering models. This approach needs the development of models rather than transformations.

Customizable orchestrator for tool integration. Different application domains and organizations frequently need to customize the overall development process to the specific needs of the domain. However, when new tools are intended to be added to the workflow of the organization, this requires significant efforts in tool integration. In order to bridge the gap between the development process and the development tools (thus reducing the complexity of tool integration), the SENSORIA Development Environment (SDE) is provided, acting as a central orchestrator for individual tools and services. SDE uses Eclipse based de facto standards, such as EMF-based interfaces for models and OSGI services for design, analysis, model transformation and deployment steps.

Advances on the SDE and currently integrated tools are described in Chapter 6-5.

Model transformations for bridging models and languages. The model-driven development, analysis and deployment of services with justifiable quality necessitates that the automated model transformations bridging different languages and tools are precise themselves. SENSORIA builds on modern Eclipse-based model transformation frameworks (such as VIATRA2 [7] and the TIGER EMF Transformer) supporting standards EMF-based interfaces with precise mathematical foundations provided by the paradigm of graph transformation.

Furthermore, we have also investigated innovative ways for accelerating the process of designing model transformations. Model transformation by example is a novel approach in model-driven software engineering to derive model transformation rules from an initial prototypical set of interrelated source and target models, which describe critical cases of the model transformation problem in a purely declarative way.

Recently, we investigated techniques for *incremental, live model transformations*. We adapted the well-known RETE algorithm from the field of rule-based systems to make pattern matching more efficient, therefore reducing execution time of model transformations. We implemented the algorithm for the VIATRA2 model transformation framework. Unlike batch transformations, live transformations are triggered by model changes and they are executed incrementally to synchronize models.

Furthermore, the Moment-GT model transformation engine has been developed to facilitate verifiable model transformations using the Maude rewriting logic engine as formal background. These techniques are presented in Chapter 6-2).

Reengineering of legacy services. In order to support the reengineering and redeployment of existing legacy applications to more modern service-oriented platforms, the reengineering methodology is summarized from the global software engineering view of SENSORIA. Each instantiation of the methodology determines what programming language can be used as input and what concrete platform will the services adhere to. Reengineering is also carried out by model transformations (Chapter 6-4).

Standards-compliant languages and service infrastructure. In order to widen the practical usability of results, interfaces and platforms used within the SENSORIA engineering approach are compliant with standards and/or industrial best practices. For instance, service models are captured in UML, BPEL or using EMF-compliant graphical editors in Eclipse. Target deployment platforms include service infrastructures supporting various WS-* standards on several (IBM, Apache) platforms. Services are deployed by using standard service descriptors such as WSDL, and currently there is an ongoing development to support SCA.

3   From BPEL to SAL and Back: an End-to-End Example on Model-Driven Analysis

The development of a fully-fledged verification tool directed by model-driven analysis necessitates the application of numerous model-based techniques. In this section these techniques are presented through a complex end-to-end example implementation providing design-time verification support for business processes. First the verification approach is described, followed by a short presentation of the challenges in model-driven analysis. Finally the usage of the different techniques are described on the example implementation.

3.1   Practical Design-Time Verification of Business Processes

Motivation. Business processes are often used to coordinate the work of different stakeholders in business-to-business collaborations as well as Enterprise Application Integration. Since these workflows set up the cooperation between actors, their quality is critical to the organization and any malfunction may have a significant negative impact on financial aspects. To minimize the possibility of failures, designers and analysts need powerful tools to guarantee the correctness of business workflows.

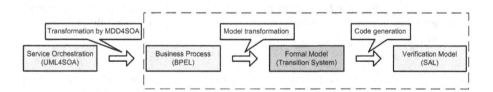

Fig. 2. BPEL verification approach overview

Approach. The main steps of the method presented in [8] are illustrated in Fig. 2. In the current chapter, we restrict our investigations to using BPEL as an input language. However, the SENSORIA toolset offers the higher-level UML4SOA models to capture business processes and derive actual BPEL descriptions by automated model transformation. In the next step, the input BPEL business process description is transformed into a formal model in the form of state transition systems. In the second stage, this transition system is projected into the language of the Symbolic Analysis Laboratory (SAL) [9]. The actual verification is then carried out with symbolic or bounded model checking techniques [10].

Requirements against the business process are captured as the expressions of the Linear Temporal Logic [11]. General (application-independent) requirements and arbitrary business process-specific requirements may be verified with the model checking technique. As a distinctive feature of this verification technique, it provides support for analyzing error propagation between variables.

In the method, model checking is used for verification purposes. The result of model checking is a sequence of actions, which violate the requirement (counter-example). The system satisfies the requirement if a counter-example cannot be found. The counter-example represents an execution of the BPEL process, but deriving and presenting this execution is non-trivial.

Running example. The SENSORIA project incorporates complex case studies from different domains, which are used for demonstration purposes. We selected the Finance Case Study [12] as a running example for our paper. The case study includes a credit request process, which we modeled in BPEL, a simplified version of the process is shown on Fig. 3.

The credit request process starts with a **Login** part where the client logs in the system, if the login is successful, the main part (**Scope**) of the process starts, enabling an **Event handler** executed if the process is canceled and a **Fault handler** for catching errors. Next a cycle is started (**Repeat until**), which repeats as long as the request is not accepted and updates are made. The cycle core starts with **creating a new request**, followed by entering the **Balance** and **Security** data and **Calculating the rating**. If the rating is *AAA* the rating is accepted at once, otherwise *BBB* ratings are approved by a clerk, the rest are approved by a supervisor.

After the approval is returned (**Wait for approval**), the request is accepted if the rating was accepted (**Rating accepted?**). If the request is rejected (**Reject request**), the client can update the request and try again. Finally the process finishes after **logging out**.

Verification example. The implemented running example business process was verified using general requirements. Fig. 3 illustrates a snapshot from the animation of the execution.

The validated requirement stated that the **Update desired** variable is always written during the execution before reading (i.e. no uninitialized reading occurs). Verification revealed that the process does not satisfy this requirement.

Specifically, this variable is only written if the request is rejected and the client wishes to update some of the data to try again (during the **Reject request** part). Therefore, when the request is accepted on the first try (**Accept request**),

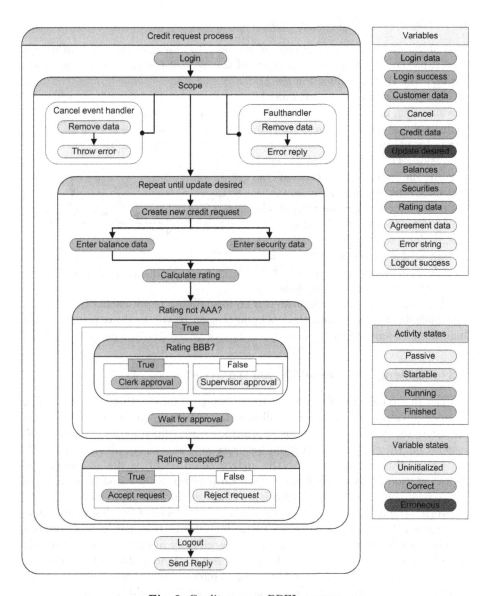

Fig. 3. Credit request BPEL process

the evaluation of the condition for the `Repeat until` activity leads to an uninitialized variable reading error.

This minor error can be corrected multiple ways including: initializing the variable at the beginning of the process, before executing the cycle the first time or updating the variable when accepting the request.

3.2 Methodological Overview

The SENSORIA engineering approach (see Sec. 2.1) includes the usage of hidden formal methods. A more detailed view of this part of the approach is presented through the BPEL verification method.

The general overview of model-driven design is shown on Fig. 4. The high-level system models are used to create formal models by model transformation. The definition of the syntax of the models are created by metamodeling. Model importers are defined for creating instance models conforming to metamodels from external data and code generation is employed for exporting the generated formal model for external analysis tools. Traceability information

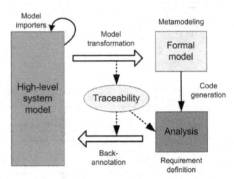

Fig. 4. Methodological overview

created during the transformation is used for defining requirements verified during analysis and for aiding the back-annotation of the analysis results to the high-level system model.

3.3 Challenges in Model-Driven Analysis

Automated model transformations are widely used for creating analysis models from design models for executing validation, verification, qualitative or quantitative analysis. Although numerous approaches were defined for analyzable model generation, they often lack solutions for processing analysis results automatically and thus fail to present them to the analyst in an intuitive, design model level representation. This reverse transformation problem, called *back-annotation* is non-trivial and appears as an additional challenge in most analysis techniques.

Storing the information regarding the correspondence of the design and analysis models is strongly related to back-annotation. *Traceability* is a common requirement in software development and specifically in model transformations. Several aspects of model-based design necessitate traceability information for either automatic execution or aiding user interaction. These aspects include multiple-phased transformations, requirement definition and back-annotation.

Defining requirements for analysis models is a core aspect for numerous analysis techniques. In order to ensure that formal methods remain hidden through the approach, *intuitive requirement definition* support is essential. Instead of assembling a formula manually, the user should be able to define them on a graphical user interface where general requirements can be parameterized based on the actual model and domain-specific ones can be assembled using domain-specific terms.

3.4 Implementation

The implementation of the method requires the application of a combination of MDA techniques. Note that it is possible to start out from a UML4SOA service orchestration by generating the business process with the MDD4SOA toolkit. In order to be able manipulate model instances, first the metamodels for both the BPEL business processes (source) and the transition systems (target) are created using the metamodeling capabilities of VIATRA2. The source model instances are created from the XML format process description files using an importer. The target model is then constructed from the source model with the execution of an automatic model transformation. The transition system description (SAL model) is created using a special transformation, which implements code generation. The analysis is carried out by model checking requirements defined against the business process on the generated model. Back-annotation of the model checking results is provided by another transformation, which uses the traceability information generated during the source-target transformation. The various tools and their input-outputs are illustrated in Fig. 5.

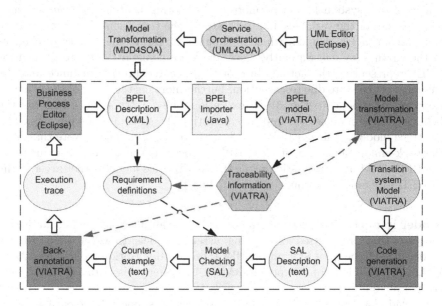

Fig. 5. BPEL verification approach steps

Metamodeling. Metamodels for the source and target models are created using the VIATRA2 Textual Metamodeling Language (VTML). VTML is capable of describing arbitrary model structures including type and containment hierarchy, instantiation and user defined relations. The BPEL metamodel is systematically created using the XML schema definition provided with the standard. The transition systems metamodel is also systematically created, based on the official SAL DTD.

Traceability. An additional supporting metamodel is used during the BPEL2SAL transformation for *storing the traceability information* between the source and target model instance elements (see Fig. 5). It is also called the *static traceability metamodel*, which is used for representing the correspondence between the structure of models. The metamodel is separated from both the source or target models to ensure that arbitrary formal models can be utilized for analysis purposes without having to change the source metamodel. The elements of the metamodel are called *traceability records.*

The results of the analysis represent an execution trace of the business process described as a counter-example in the transition system. Note that the metamodels defined for BPEL and SAL describe only the structure of the language while an execution trace contains both runtime and history information as well. Therefore additional metamodels are required for supporting back-annotation (see Fig. 5).

Counter-example and execution traces. The SAL counter-example is modeled by taking into account two aspects of the language. First the actual state of the transition system has to be modeled by storing *runtime information* such as the values of the variables and the states of the transitions. Then a *execution trace metamodel* is defined, which is capable of storing the history of changes in the runtime model. Similarly, the same kind of metamodels are defined for BPEL representing the actual state of the executed process instance and the changing of the state due to execution. Furthermore, as the steps of the counter-example correspond to the BPEL execution, the correspondence between the behavior of the models is stored by connecting the steps in the source and target trace models. This is called the *dynamic traceability model.* Note that from the back-annotation point of view, BPEL process is the source static model of the BPEL2SAL transformation while the BPEL trace model is the target of the SAL2BPEL transformation.

Model import. The static metamodels define an abstract syntax for BPEL processes that can be used for creating instance models. However these instance models have to be created from the BPEL process description (concrete syntax). Although possible, manual model creation is strongly discouraged due to high error-probability.

Instead, *importers* are implemented to provide support for creating source models automatically from the business process description XML files. The importer utilizes that the metamodel corresponds to the schema of the XML file and creates the model instance using a *generic solution* by retrieving the metamodel elements based on the type of the currently parsed XML element.

It is important to note that BPEL processes created manually can also contain unintentional syntax errors. The MDD4SOA toolset can be used for generating the BPEL description from higher-level UML4SOA models, thus eliminating the possibility of such errors.

Model transformation. The *BPEL2SAL transformation* is the main component of the implementation, which constructs the target model by traversing the source model using complex model transformation rules and patterns. Although BPEL includes numerous element types, which have different semantics it is possible to extract several generic rules to decrease the complexity of the transformation program.

The SAL transition system has separate parts, which are generated at different phases of the transformation. Although the traceability records are created when the *variable declarations* are handled, the variables are needed in both the *variable initialization* and *transition construction* phases. Thus the traceability model is used repeatedly to find the corresponding variables to the relevant BPEL elements (e.g. find the SAL element corresponding to the BPEL variable `Balances`, which is written during the execution of the `Enter balance data` activity). Note that generally transformations can be separated to various phases thus this scenario appears in many cases.

Model export. The model generated by the BPEL2SAL transformation cannot be used for verification as it is. Similarly to the importers, an automatic solution is needed for exporting abstract models to their concrete syntax.

Code generation is used to export the target model to a file in the appropriate format in order to be verifiable by the SAL model checking framework. This transformation traverses the target model using simple rules and patterns, which correspond to the grammar of SAL described in its Data Type Definition.

Requirement definition. The requirements against business process are defined as LTL formulae evaluated through model checking. Note that the requirements, which are *validated against the business process* can be best described using the source model (i.e. the BPEL process itself [13]). However, for realization they have to be *formally specified as an LTL formula* using the formalism of the target model (in this case, the SAL transition system variables). The traceability model can be used to identify which SAL variable should be used for a given BPEL element (e.g. to describe that the `Login` activity always finishes the corresponding SAL variable is needed).

User-guided definition. General requirement patterns can be defined by using the actual BPEL process as a parameter. By creating general requirement templates the effort required to assemble an LTL formula can be removed. For example a requirement template can be the following: $G(< variable > / = onlyRead)$ where $< variable >$ is the parameter selected from the variables of the verifiable BPEL process. Such templates are used to provide a user interface for requirement definition.

Syntax checking. LTL formulae can be tailored to express arbitrary requirements, however it is easy to make syntax errors when this is done manually. Although such errors are recognized by well-formedness checks in the model checking framework, it is advantageous to validate the formula before initializing the framework. A formula parser integrated into the user interface and implementing the grammar of LTL gives instant feedback by pointing out which part of the formula is grammatically incorrect.

Further improvement possibilities. The definition of process-specific requirements has two aspects for which integrated user interface support would be essential. One is the automatic translation of the BPEL process elements to transition system variable names by selecting them in the graphical process developer interface. The other is the introduction of intuitive BPEL-specific requirement building blocks, such as *"happens after"*, *"is in given state"*, *"happens once/never in all/at least one execution"*. The combination of these techniques could result in an effective requirement definition interface.

From counter-example to trace model. The SAL trace model is created automatically from the plain text counter-example returned by the model checking framework. The implementation takes advantage of the built-in generic EMF metamodel and importer of the VIATRA2 framework by generating first an EMF model for the transition system and the counter-example, which can be imported into the VIATRA2 framework.

The imported VIATRA2 EMF model conforms to the EMF metamodel and contains abundant information unnecessary for the back-annotation. Therefore a preprocessing transformation is used for generating the domain-specific SAL trace model from the EMF model. This trace model conforms to the SAL simulation trace metamodel.

Back-annotation transformation. The execution of the business process is represented with a BPEL trace model generated from the SAL trace model by the back-annotation transformation. The back-annotation transformation is implemented as an interface in the sense that it provides the following functions for handling the BPEL trace: (1) *initialize* for creating the dynamic BPEL model and the empty trace; (2) *forward step* for updating the dynamic model according to the next step in the trace, the step is generated based on the corresponding SAL trace step if it does not exist yet; (3) *backwards step* for reverting the dynamic model to the state before the actual step; and (4) *reset* for returning to the start of the trace and the initial state of the dynamic model. After the execution of each function, the state changes of the BPEL elements are exported so that they can be used outside the model transformation framework (e.g. to drive the animation of the BPEL process).

The transformation uses the traceability information (a model instance of the static traceability metamodel, which is one of the assisting metamodels) generated during the BPEL2SAL transformation. Furthermore dynamic traceability information is created whenever a forward step requires the generation of a BPEL step. This information is used for identifying the step in the SAL trace model from which the transformation has to continue.

Exporting model changes. The changes in dynamic model are exported for driving the animation of the business process execution. The changes are described as a pair containing the fully qualified name of the element and its new state. Exporting is implemented by defining a new function for the VIATRA2 framework, which can be used during model transformation.

As the changes have to be stored in memory until the transformation finishes, a service-based *export manager* is implemented that provides two service operations. The first can be used from the transformation function for storing the changes, the second is used for retrieving the changes. By implementing the export manager as a service, the back-annotation transformation and the tool used for presenting the BPEL execution are completely separated and either can be replaced by alternative techniques.

Summary. In this section the challenges and techniques related to model-driven design were described through an end-to-end example providing design-time verification for business processes. The Finance case study is used to illustrate how the verification results are represented with the animation of the BPEL process execution. Among the challenges of model-driven analysis, back-annotation, traceability and requirement definition were described. The model-driven techniques present in the example were detailed from the implementation point of view.

3.5   Overview of Integrated Toolchain

The implemented development tool provides complex functionality including a user interface for verifying business processes with general and user defined requirements and an extension for the Eclipse BPEL Designer [14] graphical business process developer tool. This extension is capable of animating the business process execution derived from the counter-example returned by the model checker. This high-level tool depends on several other tools, which are integrated in order to hide from the user the technical details and the formal methods used.

Tool-integration. Using the SENSORIA *Development Environment* (SDE), the low-level analysis and transformation tools are completely separated from the high-level tool. Fig. 6 shows how the different tools are connected to form the complete verification assistant tool. The functionality of both the VIATRA2 *framework* and the *SAL framework* is available through integration tools developed for the SDE. The *BPEL2SAL Tool* implements functions corresponding to the steps of the method such as transforming a business process, checking certain requirements and exporting the verification results. These tools provide their functionality as services through the SDE.

The verification is carried out by the user through the *Verification User Interface* integrated into the Eclipse framework. The graphical interface is separated from the *Verification Controller*, which contains the business logic for the verification tool. It performs the selected operation by first checking the acceptability

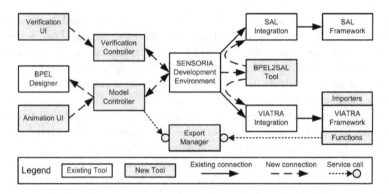

Fig. 6. Integrated tools overview

of the parameters then calling the service of the *BPEL2SAL Tool*, finally the results are displayed on the interface.

The back-annotation is implemented as animation of the BPEL process execution in the *BPEL Designer*. An *Animation User Interface* is used for selecting an exported verification result and controlling the animation. The business logic for this interface is implemented in the *Model Controller* that is responsible for directing the back-annotation transformation and uses the *Export Manager* service for retrieving the changes corresponding to the next step in the execution.

Business process execution animation. The execution derived from the counter-example can be presented on the graphical interface of the BPEL designer tool. Thus the results of the verification are illustrated with the same interface that was used to create the business process. The implementation extends the designer tool non-intrusively (i.e. without modifying the original implementation) with functions accessible from outside the tool. These functions provide support for setting the runtime state of the business process elements. The state is illustrated by coloring the graphical representation of the element (e.g. green for startable activity, red for erroneous variable).

The animation of the execution can be controlled with an easy-to-use interface either in a step-by-step or continuous way. It is possible to step forward and backward in the execution trace and the animation can be reset to the initial state. These functions correspond to the back-annotation transformation (see Sec. 3.4) Furthermore the animation can be toggled for fast stepping when several steps are executed at once.

Traceability visualization. The traceability information generated by the transformations is used for multiple purposes throughout the approach. As these include use cases when the traceability model is handled manually (e.g. domain-specific requirement definition), the visualization of these models is essential for aiding the analysis. The model visualization component[1] of the VIATRA2

---

[1] Additional details of the visualization are found on the website:
http://home.mit.bme.hu/~ujhelyiz/pub/traceabilityvisualization.html

framework was extended with support for domain-specific layouts to visualize traceability models.

Summary. In this section the overview of the integrated toolchain was described. First the existing and new tools and their connections are presented. The implemented graphical user interface is introduced, which provides a frontend for the verification method and animation support for visualizing the results. Finally the traceability information can be visualized using a component of the transformation framework.

As for the integration of this work in the SENSORIA chain, other modeling frontends such as Activity Diagrams in the UML4SOA notations can be easily integrated, however, this would need a modification of the editor to have the same simulation/back-annotation functionality.

4   Related Work

As this overview chapter presented several approaches of SENSORIA, here we cannot detail technical related work to all methods. These are covered in chapters of this book and other publications mentioned in Sec. 2.

It is worth mentioning that the above techniques were combined in several approaches, among others in [15] with a focus on management of non-functional properties in the development of Service-Oriented Systems, or in [16] to achieve advanced composition analysis support. In [17], "patterns" for service engineering were collected.

Business process verification. The verification of business processes has been thoroughly studied in the recent years. The early approaches only dealt with single processes, neglecting effects resulting from the fact that these workflows usually take part in multi party, distributed cooperations.

In [18] a subset of Petri nets was defined that models structurally sound workflows. Several structural properties of business processes could be analyzed. However, the proper utilization of a specific subset (omitting flow links) of the BPEL language can guarantee the soundness of the business process. In [19] an approach is introduced that enables model checking of business processes implemented in BPEL v1.1. The workflow implementation is transformed into Petri nets. The authors report that they have modeled the entire semantics of the language.

Foster et al. [20] propose Finite State Processes and the use of LTSA to verify Web services compositions. They use Message Sequence Charts to specify criteria, which is also one of the intended future research directions. The objective of [21] was to provide an analysis method that is capable of the modeling and verification of the four examples presented in the standard of BPEL v1.1 [22]. Hence event, fault and compensation handlers are not dealt with.

Garcia-Fanjul et al. in [23] describe a similar technique with a different purpose: they use SPIN to generate test cases for given requirements. However, their work aims at finding proper test suites for the implementation of BPEL processes and does not address design flaws. Recent works concerning the semantics of BPEL v1.1 processes, e.g. [24], are based on π-calculus. However, the definition of the requirements which can be checked by using this semantics is very general. To our best knowledge, [25] is one of the few works dealing with the data flow in service compositions.

Traceability. Triple graph grammars [26] (TGG) is a technique where the correspondence between two different types of models is defined in a declaratively, this can be used to define synchronization model transformations. [27] uses TGG for UML model-based tool integration, which supports the synchronization between various languages throughout the development process. [28] defines correspondence models interconnecting the source and target models of the incremental model synchronization also using TGGs.

QVT Relations [29] is an OMG standard with specific focus on bidirectional transformations for incremental model synchronization and defines a formalism similar to TGGs.

[30] includes similar traceability models to synchronize abstract and concrete syntax of domain-specific modeling languages. Live model transformations and synchronization requires precise traceability information although the use cases are often different from ours. The paper also includes a detailed evaluation of the state-of-the-art of traceability aspects.

[31] uses traceability to store the execution trace of the transformation, which generates Alloy models from UML. The back-annotation transformation is automatically generated based on this trace using a QVT-based implementation. However traceability information is only used for automated execution, visualization is not supported.

5   Conclusions

This chapter presented an overview on the SENSORIA engineering approach where model-driven technologies can be connected to develop trustworthy service-oriented systems. These technologies have some common problems (traceability, back-annotation, intuitive requirement definition, etc.) to face in order to be effective for a day-by-day use in engineering process. Such issues and an end-to-end solution were also presented (BPEL2SAL). Please note that this method is extendable, either the input can be an orchestration in UML4SOA (which would need additional transformations) or the analysis infrastructure can be replaced.

We envision that more and more "orchestrations" for service development would be composed in order to meet requirements of different service domains (e.g. automotive or financial systems) using the above techniques and exploiting the benefits of model-driven service engineering.

References

1. López, H.A., Massacci, F., Zannone, N.: Goal-Equivalent Secure Business Process Re-engineering. In: Di Nitto, E., Ripeanu, M. (eds.) ICSOC 2007. LNCS, vol. 4907, pp. 212–223. Springer, Heidelberg (2009); To appear as Springer Verlag book
2. Montangero, C., Reiff-Marganiec, S., Semini, L.: Logic–based detection of conflicts in APPEL policies. In: Arbab, F., Sirjani, M. (eds.) FSEN 2007. LNCS, vol. 4767, pp. 257–271. Springer, Heidelberg (2007)
3. Mayer, P., Schroeder, A., Koch, N.: MDD4SOA: Model-Driven Service Orchestration. In: Proceedings of the 12th IEEE International EDOC Conference. IEEE, Los Alamitos (2008)
4. Gönczy, L., Déri, Z., Varró, D.: Model Transformations for Performability Analysis of Service Configurations, pp. 153–166. Springer, Heidelberg (2009)
5. Guidi, C., Lucchi, R., Gorrieri, R., Busi, N., Zavattaro, G.: SOCK: A calculus for service oriented computing. In: Dan, A., Lamersdorf, W. (eds.) ICSOC 2006. LNCS, vol. 4294, pp. 327–338. Springer, Heidelberg (2006)
6. Gönczy, L., Varró, D.: Engineering Service Oriented Applications with Reliability and Security Requirements. In: Developing Effective Service Oriented Architectures: Concepts and Applications in Service Level Agreements, Quality of Service and Reliability. IGI Global (2010) (to be published)
7. VIATRA2 Framework: Eclipse GMT Subproject, http://www.eclipse.org/gmt/
8. Kovács, M., Varró, D., Gönczy, L.: Formal Analysis of BPEL Workflows with Compensation by Model Checking. IJCSSE 23(5) (November 2008)
9. Shankar, N.: Symbolic Analysis of Transition Systems. In: Gurevich, Y., Kutter, P.W., Vetta, A., Thiele, L. (eds.) ASM 2000. LNCS, vol. 1912, pp. 287–302. Springer, Heidelberg (2000)
10. Sorea, M.: Bounded Model Checking for Timed Automata. Electronic Notes in Theoretical Computer Science 68(5) (2002)
11. Emerson, E.A.: Temporal and Modal Logic. Formal Models and Semantics, vol. B, pp. 995–1072. Elsevier, Amsterdam (1990)
12. Alessandrini, M., Dost, D.: SENSORIA Deliverable D8.3.a: Finance case study: Requirements modelling and analysis of selected scenarios. Technical report, S&N AG (August 2007)
13. Xu, K., Liu, Y., Wu, C.: Bpsl modeler – visual notation language for intuitive business property reasoning. Electron. Notes Theor. Comput. Sci. 211 (2008)
14. Eclipse BPEL Designer: Eclipse Project, http://www.eclipse.org/bpel/
15. Gilmore, S., Gönczy, L., Koch, N., Mayer, P., Varró, D.: Non-Functional Properties in the Model-Driven Development of Service-Oriented Systems. Journal of Software and Systems Modeling (2010) (accepted)
16. Foster, H., Mayer, P.: Leveraging integrated tools for model-based analysis of service compositions. In: ICIW 2008: Proceedings of the 2008 Third International Conference on Internet and Web Applications and Services, pp. 72–77. IEEE Computer Society, Washington (2008)
17. Wirsing, M., Hölzl, M., Acciai, L., Banti, F., Clark, A., Nicola, R.D., Fantechi, A., Gilmore, S., Gnesi, S., Gönczy, L., Koch, N., Lapadula, A., Mayer, P., Mazzanti, F., Pugliese, R., Schroeder, A., Tiezzi, F., Tribastone, M., Varró, D.: SENSORIA patterns: Augmenting service engineering with formal analysis, transformation and dynamicity. In: Proceedings of the 3rd International Symposium on Leveraging Applications of Formal Methods, Verification and Validation (ISoLA 2008) (2008)

18. van der Aalst, W., van Hee, K.: Workflow Management Models, Methods, and Systems. The MIT Press, Cambridge (2002)
19. Hinz, S., Schmidt, K., Stahl, C.: Transforming BPEL to petri nets. In: van der Aalst, W.M.P., Benatallah, B., Casati, F., Curbera, F. (eds.) BPM 2005. LNCS, vol. 3649, pp. 220–235. Springer, Heidelberg (2005)
20. Foster, H.: A Rigorous Approach To Engineering Web Service Composition. PhD thesis, Inperial College London (2006)
21. Nakajima, S.: Model-Checking Behavioral Specification of BPEL Applications. ENTCS 151(2), 89–105 (2006)
22. Andrews, T., Curbera, F., Dholakia, H., Goland, Y., Klein, J., Leymann, F., Liu, K., Roller, D., Smith, D., Thatte, S., Trickovic, I., Weerawarana, S.: Business Process Execution Language for Web Services Version 1.1. IBM, BEA Systems, Microsoft, SAP AG, Siebel Systems (May 2003)
23. García-Fanjul, J., Tuya, J., de la Riva, C.: Generating Test Cases Specifications for Compositions of Web Services. In: Bertolino, A., Polini, A. (eds.) Proc. of WS-MaTe2006, Palermo, Sicily, Italy, June 9, pp. 83–94 (2006)
24. Mazzara, M., Lucchi, R.: A Pi-Calculus Based Semantics for WS-BPEL. Journal of Logic and Algebraic Programming (2006)
25. Kazhamiakin, R., Pistore, M.: Static Verification of Control and Data in Web Service Compositions. In: Proc. of ICWS 2006, pp. 83–90. IEEE Comp. Soc., Washington (2006)
26. Schürr, A.: Specification of Graph Translators with Triple Graph Grammars. In: Mayr, E.W., Schmidt, G., Tinhofer, G. (eds.) WG 1994. LNCS, vol. 903, pp. 151–163. Springer, Heidelberg (1995)
27. Becker, S.M., Haase, T., Westfechtel, B.: Model-based a-posteriori integration of engineering tools for incremental development processes. Software and Systems Modeling 4(2), 123–140 (2005)
28. Giese, H., Wagner, R.: Incremental Model Synchronization with Triple Graph Grammars. Springer, Heidelberg (2006)
29. The Oject Management Group. Meta Object Facility (MOF) 2.0 Query/View/ Transformation, QVT (2008), http://www.omg.org/spec/QVT/
30. Ráth, I., Ökrös, A., Varró, D.: Synchronization of Abstract and Concrete Syntax in Domain-specific Modeling Languages. Journal of Software and Systems Modeling (2009)
31. Shah, S.M.A., Anastasakis, K., Bordbar, B.: From UML to Alloy and back again. In: MoDeVVa 2009: Proceedings of the 6th International Workshop on Model-Driven Engineering, Verification and Validation, pp. 1–10. ACM, New York (2009)

Advances in Model Transformations by Graph Transformation: Specification, Execution and Analysis*

Gábor Bergmann[2], Artur Boronat[1], Reiko Heckel[1], Paolo Torrini[1],
István Ráth[2], and Dániel Varró[2]

[1] Department of Computer Science, University of Leicester
{aboronat,pt95,reiko}@le.ac.uk
[2] Department of Measurement and Information Systems,
Budapest University of Technology and Economics
{bergmann,rath,varro}@mit.bme.hu

Abstract. Model transformations are a core technology of today's model-driven software development processes. *Graph transformations* provide a state-of-the-art formalism to specify and execute such transformations in practice. This was the case in the SENSORIA project, where graph transformations have been used as enabling technology in a number of applications, as well as the basis of research in many topics. In this chapter, we overview the research results that have been achieved in the theory and practice, concentrating on three key areas: (i) the high-level *specification* of transformations, (ii) correctness *analysis* of transformations using formal methods, and (iii) novel event-driven *execution* schemes relying on incremental graph pattern matching technology.

1 Introduction

Model transformations serve a key role in the model-driven development of service-oriented applications. Numerous concrete model transformations have been developed within the scope of the SENSORIA project to support the design, deployment, verification, and code generation for services. The rule and pattern based paradigm of *graph transformations* frequently served as formal background of such transformations. However, in addition to using transformations as an enabling technology for service-oriented computing, valueable research results have been achieved in the theory and practice of model transformations themselves throughout the project. Summarizing such innovative results is the main scope of the current chapter.

First, traditional batch-like transformations have been complemented with *event-driven, live transformations* [1], which immediately react to model changes in an incremental way (Section 2). The efficient execution of such model transformations have been guaranteed by *incremental graph pattern matching techniques* [2] by adapting the well-known RETE algorithm, which enabled to transform models with well over a million model elements within the VIATRA2 model transformation framework [3,4].

---

* This work has been partially sponsored by the project SENSORIA, IST-2005-016004.

M. Wirsing and M. Hölzl (Eds.): SENSORIA Project, LNCS 6582, pp. 561–584, 2011.

In order to ease the *specification of transformations* for non-experts, a novel approach called *model transformation by example* (MTBE) [5] was proposed, which aims at semi-automatically deriving transformation rules from a prototypical set of source and target model pairs (Section 3).

In order to investigate non-functional properties for models exceeding the capabilities of model checkers, *stochastic graph transformation* [6] (Section 4) has been proposed as specification technique where events (rule matches) are associated with general probability distribution imposing generalized semi-Markov schemes.

Finally, to *assure the correctness of model transformations* such as checking invariants or temporal properties, the MOMENT2 framework (Section 5) formalized MOF metamodels with precise algebraic semantics [7]. Furthermore, model transformations themselves were formalized with rewriting logic as provided by the underlying Maude framework [8].

2   Live and Incremental Model Transformations

Traditionally, model transformation tools support the *batch execution* of transformation rules, which means that input is processed "as a whole", and output is either regenerated completely, or, in more advanced approaches, updated using trace information from previous runs. However, in software engineering using multiple domain-specific languages, models are *evolving* and changing continuously. In case of large and complex models used in agile development, batch transformations may not be feasible.

Incremental model transformations are aimed at updating existing target models based on changes in the source models (called *target incrementality* in [9]), and to minimize the parts of the source model that needs to be reexamined by a transformation when the source model is changed (*source incrementality*). To achieve target incrementality, an incremental transformation approach creates "change sets" which are merged with the existing target model instance. In order to efficiently calculate which source element may trigger changes (source incrementality), the *transformation context* has to be maintained, which describes the execution state of the model transformation system (e.g. variable values, partial matches). Depending on whether this is possible or not, there are two main approaches to incremental transformations, as discussed in Fig. 1 (adapted from [10]):

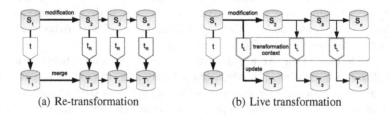

(a) Re-transformation   (b) Live transformation

Fig. 1. Incremental transformation approaches

- Systems employing *re-transformations* lack the capability to maintain the transformation context over multiple execution runs, thus the entire transformation has to be re-run on the modified source models. This approach generates either new output models which must be merged with existing ones, or change sets which can be merged *in-situ*. As noted in [10], since the transformation context is lost, a merging strategy has to be employed. This involves the computation of which model elements are involved in the change, and which elements should be left untouched by the transformation.
- In contrast, *live transformations* maintain the transformation context continuously so that the changes to source models can be instantly mapped to changes in target models. Live transformations are persistent and go through phases of execution whenever a model change occurs. Similarly to re-transformations, the information contained in trace signatures is used in calculating the source elements that require re-transformation. However, as the execution state is available in the transformation context, this re-computation can be far more efficient.

2.1 Demonstrating Example

We demonstrate our approach by the incremental on-the-fly validation of a complex dynamic modeling constraint for user editing events, in the context of the Petri net domain-specific modeling language (Fig. 2(a)). In this use case, the user is editing models using a domain-specific editor which is capable of enforcing static type constraints so that only syntactically correct Petri net graphs can be produced. However, an advanced framework may go beyond this and provide immediate feedback if more dynamic constraints, such as a *capacity constraint* (e.g. the user tries to assign too many tokens to a place), are violated.

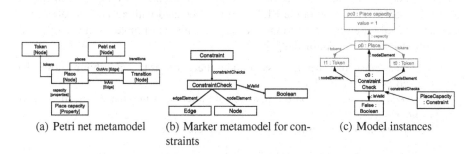

(a) Petri net metamodel   (b) Marker metamodel for constraints   (c) Model instances

Fig. 2. VIATRA metamodels and model instances

In order to provide support for the editor, the modeling environment makes use of a *marker metamodel* which is a special type of trace model depicted in Fig. 2(b). A *Constraint* denotes a particular run-time constraint being enforced within the editor, e.g. "PlaceCapacity". For each constraint, we explicitly mark all the (Petri net) elements, which are required to evaluate the constraint within a given context by a *ConstraintCheck* element. Each evaluation context of a *Constraint* is explicitly marked by a *ConstraintCheck* instance (i.e. separately for each Petri net place and its respective tokens in our case).

The *isValid* relation indicates whether the constraint is valid *currently* for the context defined by the ConstraintCheck instance; the runtime environment makes use of this relationship to indicate graphical feedback to the user. In Fig. 2(c), place *p0* contains two tokens but has a capacity of 1, thus, the associated ConstraintCheck instance indicates that the PlaceCapacity constraint is violated in this context. In our demonstrating example used throughout this section, we aim at providing an incremental evaluation of the capacity constraint in all contexts in response to elementary changes or complex transactions initiated by the user or another transformation.

2.2 Incremental Pattern Matching

Core idea. In case of incremental pattern matching, the occurrences of a pattern are readily available at any time, and they are incrementally updated whenever changes are made. As pattern occurrences are stored, they can be retrieved in constant time[1], making pattern matching a very efficient process. Furthermore, changes of occurrence sets can be treated as events and handled appropriately. Besides memory consumption, the drawback is that these stored result sets have to be continuously maintained, imposing an overhead on update operations.

In this approach, we rely on the incremental pattern matcher component of the VI-ATRA2 framework; it is based on the RETE algorithm [11], which is a well-known technique in the field of rule-based systems. This section is dedicated to giving a brief overview on how we adapted the concepts of RETE networks to implement the rich language features of the VIATRA2 graph transformation framework.

Tuples and Nodes. The main ideas behind the incremental pattern matcher are conceptually similar to relational algebra. Information is represented by a tuple consisting of model elements. Each node in the RETE net is associated with a (partial) pattern and stores the set of tuples that conform to the pattern. This set of tuples is in analogy with the relation concept of relational algebra.

- The *input nodes* are a special class of nodes that serve as the underlying knowledge base representing a model.
- *Intermediate nodes* store partial matches of patterns, or in other terms, matches of partial patterns.
- Finally, *production nodes* represent the complete pattern itself.

Joining. The key component of a RETE is the join node, created as the child of two parent nodes, that each have an outgoing RETE edge leading to the join node. The role of the join node can be best explained with the relational algebra analogy: it performs a natural join on the relations represented by its parent nodes.

Fig. 3(a) shows a simple pattern matcher built for the *sourcePlace* pattern illustrating the use of join nodes. By joining three input nodes, this sample RETE net enforces two entity type constraints and an edge (connectivity) constraint, to find pairs of Places and Transitions connected by an out-arc.

---

[1] Excluding the linear cost induced by the size of the result set itself.

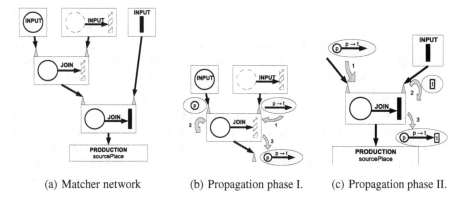

| (a) Matcher network | (b) Propagation phase I. | (c) Propagation phase II. |

Fig. 3. RETE matcher for the sourcePlace pattern

Updates after model changes. The primary goal of the RETE net is to provide incremental pattern matching. To achieve this, input nodes receive notifications about changes on the model, regardless whether the model was changed programmatically (i.e. by executing a transformation) or by user interface events.

Fig. 3(b) shows how the network in Fig. 3(a) reacts on a newly inserted out-arc. The input node for the relation type representing the arc releases an update token. The join node receives this token, and uses an effective index structure to check whether matching tuples (in this case: places) from the other parent node exist. If they do then a new token is propagated on the outgoing edge for each of them, representing a new instance of the partial pattern "place with outgoing arc". Fig. 3(c) shows the update reaching the second update node, which matches the new tuple against those contained by the other parent (in this case: transitions). If matches are found, they are propagated further to the production node.

2.3   Live Transformations Driven by Incremental Pattern Matching

Based on our incremental pattern matching technology introduced in Sec. 2.2, we now propose a novel approach to live model transformations.

Overview of the approach. In our approach, a *model change* is detected by a change in the *match set* of a graph pattern. The match set is defined by the subset of model elements satisfying structural and type constraints described by the pattern. Formally: a subgraph S of the model G is an element of the match set M(P) of pattern P, if S is isomorphic to P.

Changes in the matching set can be tracked using the RETE network. A model change occurs if the match set is expanded by a new match or a previously existing match is lost. Since a graph pattern may contain multiple elements, a change affecting any one of them may result in a change in the match set. The RETE-based incremental pattern matcher keeps track of every constraint prescribed by a pattern, thus it is possible to determine the set of constraints causing a change in the match set.

Our approach can be regarded as an extension of the *fact change* approach [10]. It provides support for the detection of changes of arbitrary complexity; not only atomic and compound model change facts (with simple and complex patterns respectively), but also operations, or sequences of operations can be tracked using this technique (either by representing operations directly in the model graph, or by using reference models).

Explicit specification. In addition to targeting the incremental execution of model synchronization transformations, our approach is intended to support a broader range of live transformations. For this purpose, incremental transformation rules, called *triggers* are explicitly specified by the transformation designer. A trigger is defined in the form of a graph transformation rule: the precondition of its activation is defined in the form of a graph pattern, while the reaction is formulated by arbitrary (declarative or imperative) transformation steps.

In fact, not only tool integration, but many application scenarios can be formulated as incremental transformations, especially, in the context of domain-specific modeling such as (i) model execution (simulation), where triggers may be used to execute the dynamic semantics of a domain-specific language [12]; (ii) constraint management, where incremental transformations are used to check and enforce the validity of a complex constraint [1]; (iii) event-driven code generation [13], where the textual representation of abstract models may be incrementally maintained as the source model changes.

Triggers. In our approach, the basic unit of incremental transformations is the *trigger*. The formal representation of a trigger is based on a simplified version of the graph transformation rule: it consists of a *precondition pattern* and an *action* part consisting of a sequence of VIATRA2 transformation steps (including simple model manipulations as well as the invocation of complex transformations).

```
@Trigger(priority='10', mode='always', sensitivity='rise')
gtrule initPlace() = {
 precondition pattern pre(P) = {
  Place(P);
  Place.Place_Capacity(PC);
  Place.capacity(Cap,P,PC);
  neg pattern placeSet(P) = {
    Constraint.ConstraintCheck(CC);
    Constraint.ConstraintCheck.nodeElement(NE,CC,P);
  }
 }
 action {
  new(Constraint.ConstraintCheck(CC));
  new(Constraint.ConstraintCheck.nodeElement(NE, CC, P));
}}
```

Fig. 4. Place instance initialisation

In Fig. 4, a simple trigger is shown. It is automatically fired after the user creates a new Place and the modeling environment creates (as a complex model change involving multiple elements) an additional Capacity and a ConstraintCheck marker element for the new Place-Place_Capacity pair. As a common technique in graph transformation based approaches, we use a negative application condition to indicate that the action sequence should only be fired for new pairs without a marker element.

This simple example highlights a number of extensions that constitute our additions to the VIATRA2 transformation language: the new `Trigger` annotation is used to indicate that the graph transformation rule should be executed as an event-driven transformation.

Complex change detection. With triggers, more complex model changes (such as the creation of complex structures, deletions, as well as attribute updates) can be specified as preconditions to fire model manipulation sequences. For more details, see [1] and [14].

2.4 Related Work

Incremental updating techniques have been widely used in different fields of computer science. Now we give a brief overview on incremental techniques that are used in the context of graph transformation.

Incremental pattern manipulation. The transformation engine of TefKat [15] performs an SLD resolution based interpretation during which a search space tree is constructed to represent the trace of transformation execution. This tree is maintained incrementally in consecutive steps of transformations as described in [16]. The uniform, incremental handling of model elements and patterns can be considered a unique, advanced feature of the approach.

View updates. In relational databases, materialized views, which explicitly store their content on the disk, can be updated by incremental techniques like Counting and DRed algorithms [17]. As reported in [18], these incremental techniques are also applicable for views that have been defined for graph pattern matching by the database queries of [19].

RETE networks used for graph transformation. RETE networks [11], which stem from rule-based expert systems, have already been used as an incremental graph pattern matching technique in several application scenarios including the recognition of structures in images [20], and the co-operative guidance of multiple uninhabited aerial vehicles in assistant systems as suggested by [21]. Our contribution extends this approach by supporting a more expressive and complex pattern language.

3   Model Transformation by Example

3.1 Motivation

When designing model transformations, transformation designers need to understand not only the transformation problem, i.e. how to map source models to target models, but significant knowledge is required in the transformation language itself to formalize the solution. Unfortunately, many domain experts, who are specialized in the source and target languages, lack such skills in underlying transformation technologies.

Model transformation by example (MTBE) is a novel approach [5, 22] to bridge this conceptual gap in transformation design. The essence of the approach is to derive model transformation rules from an initial prototypical set of interrelated source and target models, which describe critical cases of the model transformation problem in a purely declarative way. A main advantage of the approach is that transformation designers use the concepts of the source and target modeling languages for the specification of the transformation, while the implementation, i.e. the actual model transformation rules are generated (semi-)automatically. In our context, (semi-)automatic rule generation means that transformation designers give hints how source and target models can *potentially* be interconnected in the form of a mapping metamodel. Then the actual contextual conditions used in the transformation rules are derived automatically based upon the prototypical source and target model pairs.

3.2   Overview of Model Transformation by Example

Model transformations by example (MTBE) is defined as a highly iterative and interactive process as illustrated in Fig. 5.

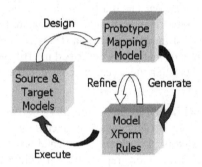

Fig. 5. Model transformation by example: process overview

Step 1: Set-up of prototype mapping models. The transformation designer assembles an initial set of interrelated source and target model pairs, which are called *prototype mapping models* in the rest of the paper. These prototype mapping models typically capture critical situations of the transformation problem by showing how the source and target model elements should be interrelated by appropriate mapping constructs.

Step 2: Automated derivation of rules. Based on the prototype mapping models, the MTBE framework should synthesize a set of model transformation rules, which correctly transform as many prototypical source models into their target equivalents as possible.

Step 3: Manual refinement of rules. The transformation designer can refine the rules manually at any time by adding attribute conditions or providing generalizations of existing rules.

Step 4: Automated execution of rules. The transformation designer validates the correctness of the synthesized rules by executing them on additional source-target model pairs as test cases, which will serve as additional prototype mapping models. Then the development process is started all over again.

The main vision of the "model transformations by example" approach is that the transformation designer mainly uses the concepts of the source and target languages as the "transformation language", which is very intuitive. He or she does not need to learn a new formalism for capturing model transformations.

While certain steps can be partially automated, we regard MTBE as a highly iterative and interactive process. Our experience also shows that it is very rare that the *final* set of transformation rules is derived right from the *initial* set of prototype models. Furthermore, transformation designer can overrule the automatically generated rules at any time, especially, when certain critical abstractions or generalizations are not detected automatically.

Concerning correctness issues, one would expect as a minimum requirement that the derived model transformation rules should correctly transform all prototypical source models into their target equivalent. However, this is not always practical, since over-specification or incorrect specification in prototype mapping models may decrease the chance of deriving a meaningful set of model transformation rules. Since MTBE takes prototype mapping models as specifications, (unintended) omissions in them might easily result in incorrect rules. Therefore, MTBE approaches should ideally tolerate a certain amount of "noise" when processing prototype mapping models.

Steps of automation. From a technical point of view, the process of model transformation by example can be split into the following phases to support the semi-automatic generation of transformation rules:

1. *Set up an initial prototype mapping model.* In the first step, an initial prototype mapping model is set up manually from scratch or by using existing source and target models.
2. *Context analysis.* Then we identify (positive and negative) constraints in the source and target models for the presence of each mapping node. For instance, only top-level classes are related to database tables or a table related to a class always contains a primary key column. For this purpose, we first examine the contexts of all mapped source and target nodes.
3. *Connectivity analysis.* For each edge in the target metamodel, we identify contextual conditions (in the source and mapping models) for the existence of that target edge.
4. *Derive transformation rules for target nodes.* Then we derive transformation rules for all (types of) mapping nodes that derive only target nodes using the information derived during context analysis. Informally, the context of source nodes will identify the precondition of the derived model transformation rules, while the context of target nodes will define the postcondition of model transformation rules. As a result, we create target nodes from source nodes interconnected by a mapping structure (of some type).
5. *Derive transformation rules for target edges.* Finally, we derive transformation rules for each target edge based upon the information gained during connectivity analysis of source and target elements.

6. *Iterative refinement*. The derived rules can be refined at any time by extending the prototype mapping model or manually generalizing the automatically generated rules.

In the scope of the SENSORIA project, we investigated [5] how the MTBE approach can be automated by using inductive logic programming [23] as an underlying framework. Our investigations demonstrated that it is possible to construct relatively small proto-type mapping models for practical problems from which the complete set of model transformation rules can be derived semi-automatically. Furthermore, we also identi-fied critical transformation problems where our approach failed to derive a complete solution, as in case of non-deterministic model transformation problems or counting in transformations.

3.3 Prototype Tool Support

We have implemented a prototypical tool chain (illustrated in Fig. 6) to automate MTBE by integrating an off-the-shelf model transformation tool with an ILP engine using Eclipse as the underlying tool framework.

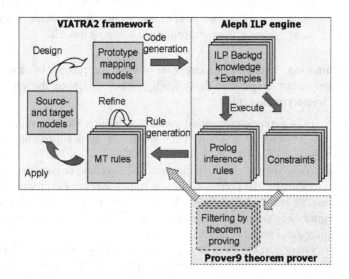

Fig. 6. A prototype tool chain for automating MTBE

- Source and target metamodels and models as well as prototype mapping models are constructed and stored as ordinary models in the VIATRA2 model space.
- Then a first transformation takes prototype mapping models and generates a set of ILP problems.
- These models are fed into the Aleph ILP engine to induce inference rules (for con-text analysis or connectivity analysis) or learn negative constraints. Obviously, this step is hidden from the user, as Aleph runs in the background.

- Ongoing work aims at integrating the Prover9 theorem prover in order to filter redundant constraints.
- Based upon the discovered inference rules, transformation rules are synthesized in the graph transformation based language of the VIATRA2 framework [24].
- These transformation rules are then executed as ordinary transformations within VIATRA2 to complete the lifecycle of our model transformation by example approach.

This initial tool chain was already a great help for us in carrying out our experiments. Since a different ILP problem is submitted to Aleph for each type of mapping node or target edge, their manual derivation was already infeasible in practice.

However, additional future work should be carried out to improve the usability of the tool chain. Probably the most critical issue is that prototype mapping models need to be defined using the abstract syntax of the language, which is frequently too complex notation for domain experts. Ideally, mappings could be defined using the concrete syntax of source and target languages.

3.4 Related Work

While the approach presented here is based on [5, 22], Strommer et al. independently presented a very similar approach for model transformation by example in [25]. The main conceptual difference between the two approaches is that [25] presents an object-based approach which finally derives ATL [26] rules for model transformation, while [22] is graph-based and derives graph transformation rules.

In a recent paper of Strommer [27], their MTBE approach is applied to a model transformation problem in the business process modeling domain and several new MTBE operators used on the concrete syntax were identified. Disregarding the string manipulation (which is obviously out of scope for the current paper), all the rest can be incorporated in our approach. In this sense, our limitations only arise in significantly more complex model transformation problems.

Naturally, the model transformation by example approach shows correspondence to various "by-example" approaches, like

- query-by-example [28] to derive queries for relational data constructed from sample tables
- *programming-by-example* [29, 30] where the programmer demonstrates actions on example data, and the computer records and possibly generalizes these actions or
- XML schema transformer derivation approaches [31, 32, 33, 34], which generate XSLT code to carry out transformations between XML documents.

4 Stochastic Simulation

Non-functional aspects such as performance and reliability play a critical role in concurrent architectures and particularly SOA. In order to formalise, measure, and predict these properties, stochastic methods are needed. At the same time such systems are characterised by a high degree of architectural reconfiguration. Viewing the architecture of a distributed system as a graph, this is naturally modelled as graph transformation. Stochastic graph transformation systems (SGTS) [35] support integrated modelling of architectural reconfiguration and non-functional aspects. In its simplest form a SGTS is a graph transformation system (GTS) where each rule name is associated with a rate of an exponential distribution governing the delay of its application. However, this approach has its limitations.

- Exponential distributions do not always provide the best abstraction. For example, the time it takes to make a phone call or transmit a message is more likely to follow a normal distribution.
- There are situations where the distributions do not only depend on the rules, but also on the graphs and matches they are applied to. For example, the time it takes to deliver a message may depend on the distance it has to travel, which may be an attribute of the connection.

To counter these limitations, *generalised* SGTS [36] allow for general distributions dependent on rule - match pairs (rather than just rule names). Generalised semi-Markov processes provide a semantic model for such systems, supporting stochastic simulation. Rather than model checking, simulations provide a more flexible tradeoff between analysis effort and confidence in the result and so allow to verify soft performance targets in large-scale systems.

In [6] we have presented a tool called GraSS, for <u>Gra</u>ph-based <u>S</u>tochastic <u>S</u>imulation, to enable the analysis of such processes. The tool is developed in Java-Eclipse, extending the VIATRA2 model transformation plugin with a control based on the SSJ library for Stochastic Simulation in Java [37]. The main performance challenge, which essentially consists of finding, at each state of the simulation, all the matches of all rules, is alleviated by VIATRA2's RETE-style incremental pattern-matching approach [38].

4.1 Simulating Stochastic Graph Transformations

The interface between the stochastic control component of the simulation and the graph transformation engine is based on a generic definition of SGTS. Refining [39], a *graph transformation approach* is given by a class of graphs G, a class of rules $\mathcal{R}$, and a $\mathcal{R} \times G$-indexed family of sets of *rule matches* $\mathcal{M}_{r,G}$ for rule r into graph G. Transformation is defined by a family of partial functions $\Rightarrow_{r,m}: G \to G$, such that $\Rightarrow_{r,m}(G)$ is defined if and only if $m \in \mathcal{M}_{r,G}$. This captures the idea that rule application is well-defined and deterministic if m is a match for r in G.

For a set of rules R, $\mathcal{E}_R$ is the set of *events*, i.e., compatible pairs $\langle r, m \rangle$. $\mathcal{S} = \langle R, G_0, F \rangle$ is a *stochastic graph transformation system* with set of rules R, initial graph G_0, and $F : \mathcal{E}_R \to (\mathbf{R} \to [0,1])$ assigning each event a continuous distribution function such that $F(e)(0) = 0$.

We encode SGTS into generalised semi-Markov schemes (GSMS), a generalisation of Markov chains associated with generalised semi-Markov processes [40]. Here transitions are independent of past states, but unlike Markov chains they may depend on the time spent in the current one, i.e., interevent times may be non-exponentially distributed. Formally, a GSMS is a structure

$$\mathcal{P} = \langle S, E, act : S \to \wp(E), trans : S \times E \to S, \delta : E \to (\mathcal{R} \to [0,1]), init : S \rangle$$

where S is a set of states (given by all graphs reachable in S), E is a set of events (the rule matches $\mathcal{E}_R$), *init* is the initial state (graph G_0), *act* gives the set of events (rule matches) enabled in a state (graph), *trans* is the transition function (given by $trans(G, \langle r, m \rangle) = \Rightarrow_{r,m} (G)$), and δ defines the cumulative probability distribution for each event (given by F).

The simulation component uses VIATRA2 as a graph transformation tool to implement the elements of the GSMS that depend on the representation of states and events, notably $S, E, act, trans, init$, i.e., GTSs are represented as VIATRA2 models. Probability distributions are loaded from an XML file, where the type of distribution (either exponential or normal) as well as its parameters (either rate or mean and variance, respectively) can be specified.

Based on this data, a GSMS simulation in GraSS consists of the following steps

1. Initialisation — the simulation time T is initialised to 0 and the set of the enabled matches (active events) is obtained from the graph transformation engine. For each active event, a scheduling time t_e is computed by a random number generator (RNG) based on the probability distribution assigned to the event. Timed events are collected as a list ordered by time (state list).
2. At each simulation step
   (a) the first element $k = (e, t)$ is removed from the state list
   (b) the simulation time is increased to t
   (c) the event e is executed by the graph transformation engine
   (d) the new state list s' is computed, by querying the engine, removing all the elements that have been disabled, adding to the list an event for each newly enabled match m with time $t = T + d$, where d is provided by the RNG depending on $F(m)$, and reordering the list with respect to time

One can specify the number of runs for experiment and their max depth (either by number of steps or simulation time). GT rules with empty postconditions can be used as probes. Statistics about the occurrences of probe rule precondition patterns are computed as SSJ tally-store class reports, giving average values for each run as well as over all of them. GraSS uses the VIATRA2 Eclipse interface, and allows for standard (i.e. automated) simulation execution as well as step-by-step execution with visualisation — useful to debug models.

4.2 Case Study: A P2P Network Model

We illustrate the application of GraSS by the SGTS modelling and simulation of the P2P reconfiguration model presented in [35] — more details to be found in [6]. The GTS below models basic P2P network reconfigurations. Rule *new* on the left adds a new peer, registers it and links it to an existing peer. Rule *kill* deletes a peer with all links attached. Predicate *disconnected* checks if there are exist two nodes that are not connected by a path of links labelled l.

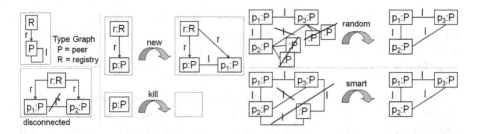

The two rules on the right create redundant links to increase reliability in case a peer is lost. Rule *random* creates a link between *p2* and *p3* unless there is one already or the number of additional connections of either *p2* or *p3* is greater than two. Rule *smart* creates a link if there is no two-hop path between *p2* and *p3* apart from the one via *p1*.

We can consider two families of systems, $SGTS_{random,x}$ and $SGTS_{smart,x}$. The former has rules $\{new, kill, random\}$ and rates $\sigma(new) = \sigma(kill) = 1$ and $\sigma(random) = x$. In the latter, *random* is replaced by *smart* with $\sigma(smart) = x$. In both cases x ranges from 1 to 10,000 to test different ratios between basic and redundancy rules.

Experimental results have confirmed the inverse dependency observed in [35] between the rate of the *smart* rule and the probability of being disconnected, whereas for the *random* rule an increased rate does not lead to any significant change in reliability. The performance (number of simulation steps per sec) is limited by the complexity of pattern *disconnect* which, in a network of n peers, checks for (non-) existence of n^2 paths. This may be hard due to transitive closure. However, given initial models of small size, simulations of 5 runs with a time limit of 10s have always been carried out in less than a minute. Reliance on incremental pattern matching means that — discounting rules that involve full state space search, such as *disconnect* — the size of the model only affects simulation up to number of RNG calls, whereas increase in number and complexity of the rules can add to the cost of graph transformation, too.

5   Analysis and Verification of Graph-Based Model Transformations

Our approach focuses on the formalization of MOF-model transformations in rewriting logic by reusing the theory of graph transformation systems [8]. In this way, MOMENT2 enhances the application of Maude tools reachability analysis and LTL model checking [41] to model transformations (and graph transformation systems). At the same time, MOMENT2 provides the rewriting logic semantics of graph transformations so that the computational semantics of graph rewriting is given by term rewriting, by adding the novel feature of defining production rules as equations.

This approach opens new possibilities to verify properties on model transformations and graph transformation systems based on rewriting logic and Maude, model checking of model transformations with LTL and with the temporal logic of rewriting [42], verification of model-based real-time systems with Real-Time Maude [43], and the verification of model-based probabilistic systems based on PMaude [44], by means of OMG standards such as MOF [7], OCL [45] and QVT.

In this section, we concentrate on presenting the MOMENT2 tool, which brings the model transformation approaches based on graph grammars and informal approaches extending MOF, such as QVT, significantly closer. MOMENT2 provides support for defining model transformations, executing them, and model checking their properties by means of the underlying Maude tool.

Specifically, in MOMENT2 a user can define MOF model transformations in EMF by using QVT and graph-based notions. Transformation rules are similar to SPO production rules where model patterns are specified with QVT syntax, preconditions can be defined as negative model patterns and as OCL conditions, and attribute values can be manipulated with OCL expressions. Distinctive features of MOMENT with respect to graph transformation approaches are that the semantics of containment relations in models is preserved and that production rules can be defined either as equations, to encode deterministic behaviour, or as rewrite rules, to encode non-deterministic behaviour.

A model transformation is automatically compiled into a rewrite theory providing its rewriting logic sematics, which is directly executable in the underlying Maude rewrite engine. In this way, model transformations can be directly executed; and they can be also model checked both for satisfaction of invariants and of linear temporal logic (LTL) properties.

5.1   Specification: Modelling a Distributed MUTEX Algorithm

A distributed mutual exclusion algorithm is used in operating systems and DBMS to ensure that a resource is never used by more than one process at a time. However, each request of a process for a resource must eventually be granted without running into a deadlock.

In our approach, a model represents the state of the system, where all the objects that may be part of the model are instances of the classes that appear in the metamodel in Fig. 7.(a). Fig. 7.(b) provides both a model describing a deadlock state (bottom part of the figure) and its representation in the concrete syntax (top part of the figure) that we use for explaining the transformation: *processes* are drawn as black nodes and *resources* as light boxes. An edge from a process to a resource models a *request*. A solid edge in the opposite direction shows that the resource is currently *held by* the process. A dashed edge from a resource to a process asks the process to *release* the resource.

Fig. 8 provides two sets of production rules describing: (i) the mutual exclusion algorithm (ME) and (ii) the distributed deadlock detection mechanism (DDD).

Mutual exclusion. The system state consists of a cyclic list of processes, where an edge between two processes points to the *next* process, and a collection of resources. For each resource in the system there is a *token*, represented by an edge with a white flag, which is passed from process to process along the ring. If a process wants to use a resource, it waits for the corresponding token. *Mutual exclusion* is ensured because there is only one token for each resource in the system.

Among the ME rules, *pass(p, r)* describes that a process having the token may pass it to the next process in the ring, provided that it does not have a request on the corresponding resource. This negative application condition is visualized by the crossed-out

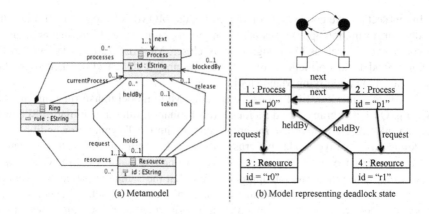

(a) Metamodel   (b) Model representing deadlock state

Fig. 7. (a) Metamodel $\mathcal{M}$. (b) Model representing a deadlock state (bottom) and its representation using concrete syntax (top).

request edge from the process to the resource. If a process wants to use a resource, it may generate a request. This is modeled by the rule *req(p, r)*, which is only applicable if the process does not have any requests yet, and if the particular resource is not used already by this process. If a process receives a token and there is a request for the resource, the process will chose the rule *take(p, r)* replacing the token and the request by a *heldBy* edge from the resource to the process. When it has finished its task, the process may release its resource and give the token to the next process using *rel(p, r)* and *give(p, r)*. This will happen only when there are no pending requests, which is modeled by a negative application condition at *rel(p, r)*.

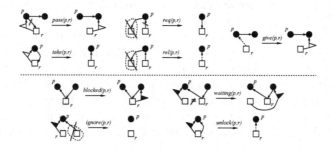

Fig. 8. Algorithm for mutual exclusion

Distributed deadlock detection. In a model representing a state, a deadlock is represented as a cycle of *request* and *heldBy* edges. The *distributed deadlock detection* uses *blocked* messages in order to detect cyclic dependencies. They are represented by edges with a black flag from a resource to a process. In order to detect such cycles in a distributed way, a process holding a resource requested by another process will use the rule *blocked(p, r)* to send a blocked-message to that process. If this process itself blocks another one, it will use the *waiting(p, r)* rule to pass this message on. The inequation in this rule ensures that resource *r* is not the original one. If the process does not hold any resource, it deletes the message with *ignore(p, r)*. Thanks to the mutual exclusion, each resource is held by only one process. Hence, if the message arrives at a process who holds the original resource, this is the original sender of the message. The deadlock thus detected is broken by the *unlock(p, r)* rule which replaces the *heldBy* edge and the blocked message with a *release* edge, asking the ME-rule *give(p, r)* to give the token to the next process.

We use this algorithm to show how model transformations are defined in MOMENT2[2]. In the resulting model transformation, we verify safety and liveness properties. On the one hand, we model check the safety property *MUTEX-safe: a resource cannot be held by two different processes*, by means of reachability analysis of an invariant defined with a model pattern. On the other hand, the liveness property *MUTEX-live: each request of a resource by a process will eventually be granted*, by means of model checking of LTL properties.

Model transformation rules can be defined either as *equations* or as *rewrites* by the respective keywords eq or rl, respectively. A model transformation rule always consists of three elements: a label, a left-hand side (LHS) pattern and a right-hand side (RHS) pattern, where the LHS and RHS patterns correspond to collections of object template patterns in the QVT terminology, or to graph patterns in the graph tranformation terminology. Optionally, we can add a set of (possibly conditional) negative application conditions (NACs) to each model transformation rule and a global condition with the when clause.

A model pattern is a collection of object patterns that are applied over a specific domain model. The LHS model pattern of the *rel(p,r)* model rewrite in Fig. 9 can be applied over a model that conforms to the metamodel in Fig. 7.(a). In this model pattern, an object of type *Process* points to an object of type *Resource* through a *holds* reference. We also match the value of attribute *id* of the *Resource* object with the variable *R1ID* to illustate how attributes can be included in model patterns. This model pattern is shown as a graph pattern in Fig. 9.

5.2   Execution

Model transformations are declared with several parameters, called domains. Each domain may correspond to a different metamodel. To execute a transformation, a user can specify either an input or an output model for each domain of the transformation. Input models are EMF models that are used as input data and output models are paths in the filesystem where the corresponding resulting models are persisted as EMF models. For the example above, there is a single domain in the transformation. Since the simulation for this example is non-terminating, we do not need to specify a value for the output model. This facility enables the use of MOMENT2 for executing model transformations and for analysing them within the EMF as discussed below.

---

[2] More details on the encoding of the transformation can be found in [8].

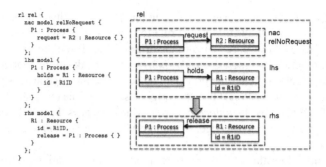

Fig. 9. Rewriting rule in MOMENT2

(Bounded) Model Checking Model-Based Invariants. For $\mathcal{R} = (\Sigma, E \cup A, R)$ a rewrite theory obtained by compiling model equations into corresponding equations E, and model rewrites into rules R, we are interested in cheking *invariants*, that is, predicates that hold of a given initial state and of all states reachable from it by state transitions. The invariants in question can be *graph-based*. This means that if they hold for a state representing a graph with a given choice of names, *they should also hold for any other choice of names which is a permutation* of the original names. This can be guaranteed by construction if we define the *negation* of such a state predicate by means of a pair (P, C), where P is a model pattern (so that the names involved in the pattern P are generic names described by name variables), with P describing potentially "bad" states, and where C is an equational condition (which may involve Boolean OCL expressions) imposing additional semantic restrictions on the graph pattern P. The compilation process then transforms the pair (P, C) into a corresponding pair (t, C'), where t is the term pattern corresponding to P, and C' is a Boolean condition involving the variables of t that expresses C at the term level. The *invariant* $I_{\neg(t,C')}$ defined by (t, C') is then the *complement* of the set of states satisfying (t, C'), that is, the complement of the set of states that are substitution instances of t and satisfy C'.

If the number of states reachable from *init* is infinite, breadth-first search become a *semi-decision procedure* to verify the *violation* of the invariant: if any such violation exists, we are guaranteed to find it. The same search command in Maude provides such a semi-decision procedure.

In the example, we want to verify the mutual exclusion algorithm by ensuring that a resource will never be held by two different processes. This invariant can be verified with the command:

```
search [1, unbounded] =>* domain model {
  p1 : Process { holds = r1 : Resource{} }
  p2 : Process { holds = r1 : Resource{} }
}
```

Model Checking LTL Properties. A model transformation $(\mathcal{M}, \mathcal{T})$ is formalized as a rewrite theory $\mathbb{R}(\mathcal{M}, \mathcal{T})$ specifying a *model transition system* where models $M : \mathcal{M}$ constitute system states and where the application of model rewrites constitute state transitions.

Maude provides support for model checking LTL safety and liveness properties. MO-MENT2 uses Maude's LTL model checker by defining state predicates over models through equations and OCL expressions. In this section, we provide (i) the definition of model predicates, (ii) the notion of model transition system, and (iii) the verification of LTL properties in a model transition systems.

In the example, the equation in Fig. 10(a) indicates when the request(P, R) predicate is satisfied in a given state M, such that $M : \mathcal{M}$, where P and R are string variables. That is, the request(P, R) predicate is satisfied in a state, when there is a process with id P that requests a resource with id R. The parameters of a predicate can be either constants or variables that are bound in a domain pattern.

```
domain model {                          domain model {
   p : Process {                           p : Process {
      id = P,                                 id = P,
      request = r : Resource { id = R }       holds = r : Resource { id = R }
   }                                       }
} |= requests( P, R ) = true .          } |= heldBy( R, P ) = true .
```

Fig. 10. Predicate equations: (a) request - (b) heldBy

It is important to make sure that satisfaction of state predicates is *defined* for all the cases in which a model predicate holds. The cases where a model predicate is not satisfied do not need to be specified. The following equation defines the satisfaction of the state predicate heldBy(R, P), specifying when a resource with id R is held by a process with id P (Fig. 10(b)).

Verification of LTL properties in model transition systems. LTL properties can be defined in MOMENT2 by using Maude's LTL specification and model predicates as defined above. In a LTL formula, model predicates can be used as propositions. In the example, we want to verify that each process that request a resource is always eventually served. This can be specified with the LTL formula requests("p0", "r0") |-> heldBy("r0","p0"), which is equivalent to [] (requests("p0", "r0") -> <> heldBy("r0", "p0")).

MOMENT2 compiles the model predicates and the LTL formula into Maude following the guidelines provided in [41] so that the Maude model checker is used to verify the *MUTEX-live* property in the theory $\mathbb{R}(\mathcal{M}, \mathcal{T}) \cup \mathbb{A}(\mathcal{D})$. The tool generates the following command and executes it in Maude, without user interaction:

```
red modelCheck( mutexAlgorithm(model,0 ),
   requests("p0","r0") |-> heldBy("r0","p0") ) .
```

By using the model in Fig. 7 as initial state, Maude's model checker found a path in which the property cannot be verified. In particular, the two processes *p0* and *p1* request the resource *r0* and the *pass* rule is henceforth applied over the resource *r1*. This is due to the fact that the rules are not applied in a *fair* way, i.e., all rules are not equally applied in all possible paths. In the example, this problem can be solved by forcing the application of the *take* rule. In the metamodel in Fig. 7, we have added the properties *rule* and *currentProcess* to the *Ring* class. The *rule* property indicates which rule has been applied and the *currentProcess* property indicates which process has been activated by the application of a rule. In the model transformation, model rules have to be modified so that each rule updates the *rule* and *currentProcess* in the *Ring* object as in the *take* rule (Fig. 11(a)).

```
rl take {
  lhs model {
    rg : Ring {  }                        domain model { } |= enabled-take( P ) = true [owise]
    r : Resource {                        domain model {
      token = pl : Process {                rg : Ring {
        request = r : Resource { }            rule = "take",
      }                                        currentProcess = pl : Process { id = P }
    }                                        }
  };                                       } |= enabled-take( P ) = false
  rhs model {
    rg : Ring {                           domain model {
      rule = "take",                        rg : Ring {
      currentProcess = pl : Process {}        rule = "take",
    }                                         currentProcess = pl : Process { id = P }
    r : Resource {                          }
      heldBy = pl : Process { }           } |= take( P ) = true
    }
  };
}
```

Fig. 11. (a) Rule *take* - (b) Predicates *enabled-take* and *take*

Two more model predicates (shown in Fig. 11(b)) are needed to check when the *take* rule has not been applied (enabled-take) and when it has been applied (take).

The *MUTEX-live* property can be model checked by encoding the fairness of the *take* rule in the LTL formula as follows:

```
([] <> enabled-take( "p0" ) -> [] <> take( "p0" )) ->
(requests("p0", "r0") |-> heldBy("r0", "p0"))
```

which is verified by Maude's model checker:

```
ModelChecker: Property automaton has 4 states.
ModelCheckerSymbol: Examined 5299 system states.
rewrites: 2253359 in 13756ms cpu (13895ms real) (163803 rewrites/second)
result Bool: true
```

5.3   Related Work

In the formal analysis of dynamically evolving systems, several approaches based on model-checking provide automated procedures for formal verification. On the one hand, model-checking tools with specific support for graph transformations have been implemented. GROOVE [46] is a graph-based analysis tool that provides model checking for LTS whose states are graphs. Augur [47,48] is an analysis tool based on the translation of graph transformations to Petri nets and the application of Petri net analysis techniques. On the other hand, generic model checkers have been used, such as SPIN [49], an on-the-fly model checker that has a CSP-based input language, Promela. In contrast with state space-based approaches, on-the-fly model checking can work without generating full Kripke model. Another generic tool that has been used in this context is Bogor [50], an extensible model-checking framework.

There are other approaches that use Maude for encoding graph transformations. In particular, [51] maps visual graph transformations in Atom3 to rewrite rules in Maude where graphs encoded as collections of objects can be rewritten modulo structural axioms (associativity and commutativity). Reachability analysis with Maude's search command is used to check properties of models in domain-specific languages. However, the approach is not MOF conform (no containment relations are taken into account), there is no support for operations on attributes, and no concept of production rules as equations.

6 Conclusion

In this chapter, we reported on the research progress that has been achieved in graph transformation over the four years of the SENSORIA project. Overall, graph transformation approaches have served well as enablers in a number of case studies and demonstrators (e.g. in UML model transformations, web services deployment generation, and BPEL analysis). The case studies and applications scenarios of SENSORIA have stimulated research in three key areas:

- *Model transformation by example* has provided a novel and intuitive way of transformation specification, by easing the learning curve of transformation languages by allowing the designer to map source and desired target models directly.
- *Live and incremental transformations* have significantly improved the efficiency of transformation execution in a number of crucial scenarios, e.g. in giving a performance boost to WSDL code generation that was part of BUTE's contribution.
- *Graph transformation verification* by rewriting logic has been a pioneering achievement by providing a formal semantics to graph transformations and an efficient tool to execute and verify concrete transformations with respect to structural constraints as well as temporal invariants and properties.
- Finally, *stochastic graph transformations*, based on incremental transformations, provided a novel, cross-over application into the networking simulation domain with promising early results.

In the future, the results of SENSORIA will live on in the form of continued research in all of these areas, since a lot of goals remain to be reached: we need more refined tool support and improved scalability, to be elaborated in more complex experimental scenarios, to all of which the case studies and demonstrators will provide further inspiration.

Acknowledgements. All the work presented in this chapter was supported by the SENSORIA FET-GC2 IP European Union research project (IST-3-016004).

References

1. Ráth, I., Bergmann, G., Ökrös, A., Varró, D.: Live model transformations driven by incremental pattern matching. In: Vallecillo, A., Gray, J., Pierantonio, A. (eds.) ICMT 2008. LNCS, vol. 5063, pp. 107–121. Springer, Heidelberg (2008)
2. Bergmann, G., Ökrös, A., Ráth, I., Varró, D., Varró, G.: Incremental pattern matching in the VIATRA transformation system. In: GRaMoT 2008, 3rd International Workshop on Graph and Model Transformation, 30th International Conference on Software Engineering (2008)
3. VIATRA2 Framework. An Eclipse GMT Subproject, http://www.eclipse.org/gmt/
4. Varró, D., Balogh, A.: The Model Transformation Language of the VIATRA2 Framework. Science of Computer Programming 68(3), 214–234 (2007)
5. Varró, D., Balogh, Z.: Automating model transformation by example using inductive logic programming. In: Cho, Y., Wainwright, R.L., Haddad, H., Shin, S.Y., Koo, Y.W. (eds.) Proceedings of the 2007 ACM Symposium on Applied Computing (SAC), Seoul, Korea, March 11-15, pp. 978–984. ACM, New York (2007)
6. Torrini, P., Heckel, R., Ráth, I.: Stochastic simulation of graph transformation systems. In: Rosenblum, D.S., Taentzer, G. (eds.) FASE 2010. LNCS, vol. 6013, pp. 154–157. Springer, Heidelberg (2010)
7. Boronat, A., Meseguer, J.: An Algebraic Semantics for MOF. In: Fiadeiro, J.L., Inverardi, P. (eds.) FASE 2008. LNCS, vol. 4961, pp. 377–391. Springer, Heidelberg (2008)
8. Boronat, A., Heckel, R., Meseguer, J.: Rewriting logic semantics and verification of model transformations. In: Chechik, M., Wirsing, M. (eds.) FASE 2009. LNCS, vol. 5503, pp. 18–33. Springer, Heidelberg (2009)
9. Czarnecki, K., Helsen, S.: Feature-based survey of model transformation approaches. IBM Systems Journal 45(3), 621–645 (2006)
10. Hearnden, D., Lawley, M., Raymond, K.: Incremental Model Transformation for the Evolution of Model-Driven Systems. In: Wang, J., Whittle, J., Harel, D., Reggio, G. (eds.) MoDELS 2006. LNCS, vol. 4199, pp. 321–335. Springer, Heidelberg (2006)
11. Forgy, C.L.: Rete: A fast algorithm for the many pattern/many object pattern match problem. Artificial Intelligence 19(1), 17–37 (1982)
12. Ráth, I., Vágó, D., Varró, D.: Design-time Simulation of Domain-specific Models By Incremental Pattern Matching. In: 2008 IEEE Symposium on Visual Languages and Human-Centric Computing, VL/HCC (2008)
13. Ráth, I., Varró, G., Varró, D.: Change-driven model transformations. In: Schürr, A., Selic, B. (eds.) MODELS 2009. LNCS, vol. 5795, pp. 342–356. Springer, Heidelberg (2009)
14. Ráth, I., Ökrös, A., Varró, D.: Synchronization of abstract and concrete syntax in domain-specific modeling languages. Journal of Software and Systems Modeling (2009) (accepted)
15. Lawley, M., Steel, J.: Practical declarative model transformation with Tefkat. In: Bézivin, J., Rumpe, B., Schürr, A., Tratt, L. (eds.) Proc. of the International Workshop on Model Transformation in Practice (MTiP 2005) (October 2005), http://sosym.dcs.kcl.ac.uk/events/mtip05/
16. Hearnden, D., Lawley, M., Raymond, K.: Incremental model transformation for the evolution of model-driven systems. In: Nierstrasz, O., Whittle, J., Harel, D., Reggio, G. (eds.) MoDELS 2006. LNCS, vol. 4199, pp. 321–335. Springer, Heidelberg (2006)
17. Gupta, A., Mumick, I.S., Subrahmanian, V.S.: Maintaining views incrementally. In: ACM SIGMOD Proceedings, Washington, D.C., USA, pp. 157–166 (1993)
18. Varró, G., Varró, D.: Graph transformation with incremental updates. In: Heckel, R. (ed.) Proc. of the 4th Workshop on Graph Transformation and Visual Modeling Techniques (GT-VMT 2004), Barcelona, Spain. ENTCS, vol. 109, pp. 71–83. Elsevier, Amsterdam (2004)

19. Varró, G., Friedl, K., Varró, D.: Graph transformation in relational databases. Journal of Software and Systems Modelling 5(3), 313–341 (2006)

20. Bunke, H., Glauser, T., Tran, T.H.: An efficient implementation of graph grammar based on the RETE-matching algorithm. In: Ehrig, H., Kreowski, H.-J., Rozenberg, G. (eds.) Graph Grammars 1990. LNCS, vol. 532, pp. 174–189. Springer, Heidelberg (1991)

21. Matzner, A., Minas, M., Schulte, A.: Efficient graph matching with application to cognitive automation. In: Nagl, M., Schürr, A. (eds.) Proc. of the 3rd International Workshop and Symposium on Applications of Graph Transformation with Industrial Relevance, Kassel, Germany, pp. 293–308 (October 2007)

22. Varró, D.: Model transformation by example. In: Wang, J., Whittle, J., Harel, D., Reggio, G. (eds.) MoDELS 2006. LNCS, vol. 4199, pp. 410–424. Springer, Heidelberg (2006)

23. Muggleton, S., de Raedt, L.: Inductive logic programming: Theory and methods. Journal of Logic Programming 19(20), 629–679 (1994)

24. Balogh, A., Varró, D.: Advanced model transformation language constructs in the VIATRA2 framework. In: ACM Symposium on Applied Computing — Model Transformation Track (SAC 2006), Dijon, France, pp. 1280–1287. ACM Press, New York (2006)

25. Wimmer, M., Strommer, M., Kargl, H., Kramler, G.: Towards model transformation generation by-example. In: Proc. of HICSS-40 Hawaii International Conference on System Sciences, Hawaii, USA (January 2007)

26. Jouault, F., Allilaire, F., Bézivin, J., Kurtev, I.: Atl: A model transformation tool. Sci. Comput. Program 72(1-2), 31–39 (2008)

27. Strommer, M., Murzek, M., Wimmer, M.: Applying Model Transformation By-Example on Business Process Modeling languages. In: Proc. 3rd International Workshop on Foundations and Practices of UML

28. Zloof, M.M.: Query-by-example: the invocation and definition of tables and forms. In: Kerr, D.S. (ed.) VLDB, pp. 1–24. ACM, New York (1975)

29. Cypher, A. (ed.): Watch What I Do: Programming by Demonstration. The MIT Press, Cambridge (1993)

30. Repenning, A., Perrone, C.: Programming by example: programming by analogous examples. Communications of the ACM 43(3), 90–97 (2000)

31. Lechner, S., Schrefl, M.: Defining web schema transformers by example. In: Mařík, V., Retschitzegger, W., Štěpánková, O. (eds.) DEXA 2003. LNCS, vol. 2736, pp. 46–56. Springer, Heidelberg (2003)

32. Ono, K., Koyanagi, T., Abe, M., Hori, M.: XSLT stylesheet generation by example with WYSIWYG editing. In: Proceedings of the 2002 Symposium on Applications and the Internet (SAINT 2002), Washington, DC, USA, pp. 150–161. IEEE Computer Society, Los Alamitos (2002)

33. Yan, L.L., Miller, R.J., Haas, L.M., Fagin, R.: Data-driven understanding and refinement of schema mappings. In: Proc. ACM SIGMOD Conference on Management of Data (2001)

34. Erwig, M.: Toward the automatic derivation of XML transformations. In: Jeusfeld, M.A., Pastor, Ó. (eds.) ER Workshops 2003. LNCS, vol. 2814, pp. 342–354. Springer, Heidelberg (2003)

35. Heckel, R.: Stochastic analysis of graph transformation systems: A case study in P2P networks. In: Van Hung, D., Wirsing, M. (eds.) ICTAC 2005. LNCS, vol. 3722, pp. 53–69. Springer, Heidelberg (2005)

36. Khan, A., Torrini, P., Heckel, R.: Model-based simulation of VoIP network reconfigurations using graph transformation systems. In: Corradini, A., Tuosto, E. (eds.) Intl. Conf. on Graph Transformation (ICGT) 2008 - Doctoral Symposium. Electronic Communications of the EASST, vol. 16 (2009),
http://eceasst.cs.tu-berlin.de/index.php/eceasst/issue/view/26

37. L'Ecuyer, P.L., Meliani, L., Vaucher, J.: SSJ: a framework for stochastic simulation in Java. In: Proceedings of the 2002 Winter Simulation Conference, pp. 234–242 (2002)

38. Bergmann, G., Ökrös, A., Ráth, I., Varró, D., Varró, G.: Incremental pattern matching in the viatra model transformation system. In: GRaMoT 2008: Proceedings of the Third International Workshop on Graph and Model Transformations, pp. 25–32. ACM, New York (2008)

39. Kreowski, H.J., Kuske, S.: On the interleaving semantics of transformation units - a step into GRACE. In: Cuny, J., Engels, G., Ehrig, H., Rozenberg, G. (eds.) Graph Grammars 1994. LNCS, vol. 1073, pp. 89–106. Springer, Heidelberg (1996)

40. D'Argenio, P.R., Katoen, J.P.: A theory of stochastic systems part I: Stochastic automata. Inf. Comput. 203(1), 1–38 (2005)

41. Clavel, M., Durán, F., Eker, S., Meseguer, J., Lincoln, P., Martí-Oliet, N., Talcott, C.: All About Maude - A High-Performance Logical Framework. LNCS, vol. 4350. Springer, Heidelberg (2007)

42. Meseguer, J.: The temporal logic of rewriting. Technical Report UIUCDCS-R-2007-2815, CS Dept., University of Illinois at Urbana-Champaign (February 2007)

43. Ölveczky, P.C., Meseguer, J.: Semantics and pragmatics of Real-Time Maude. Higher-Order and Symbolic Computation 20(1-2), 161–196 (2007)

44. Agha, G.A., Meseguer, J., Sen, K.: Pmaude: Rewrite-based specification language for probabilistic object systems. Electr. Notes Theor. Comput. Sci. 153(2), 213–239 (2006)

45. Boronat, A., Meseguer, J.: Algebraic semantics of OCL-constrained metamodel specifications. In: Oriol, M., Meyer, B. (eds.) TOOLS EUROPE 2009. LNBIP, vol. 33, pp. 96–115. Springer, Heidelberg (2009)

46. Rensink, A.: The GROOVE simulator: A tool for state space generation. In: Pfaltz, J.L., Nagl, M., Böhlen, B. (eds.) AGTIVE 2003. LNCS, vol. 3062, pp. 479–485. Springer, Heidelberg (2004)

47. König, B., Kozioura, V.: Augur—a tool for the analysis of graph transformation systems. EATCS Bulletin 87, 125–137 (2005); Appeared in The Formal Specification Column

48. König, B., Kozioura, V.: AUGUR 2—a new version of a tool for the analysis of graph transformation systems. In: Proceedings of GT-VMT 2006 (Workshop on Graph Transformation and Visual Modeling Techniques). Electronic Notes in TCS (2008)

49. Holzmann, G.J.: The SPIN Model Checker. Addison-Wesley, Reading (2003)

50. Robby, Dwyer, M.B., Hatcliff, J.: Bogor: An extensible and highly-modular model checking framework. In: Proceedings of the Fourth Joint Meeting of the European Software Engineering Conference and ACM SIGSOFT Symposium on the Foundations of Software Engineering, ESEC/FSE 2003 (2003)

51. Rivera, J.E., Guerra, E., de Lara, J., Vallecillo, A.: Analyzing rule-based behavioral semantics of visual modeling languages with maude. In: Gašević, D., Lämmel, R., Van Wyk, E. (eds.) SLE 2008. LNCS, vol. 5452, pp. 54–73. Springer, Heidelberg (2009)

Runtime Support for Dynamic and Adaptive Service Composition *

Arun Mukhija[1], David S. Rosenblum[1], Howard Foster[2], and Sebastian Uchitel[2]

[1] London Software Systems, Dept. of Computer Science, University College London,
Gower Street, London WC1E 6BT, UK
{a.mukhija, d.rosenblum}@cs.ucl.ac.uk
[2] London Software Systems, Dept. of Computing, Imperial College London,
180 Queen's Gate, London SW7 2BZ, UK
{hf1, su2}@doc.ic.ac.uk

Abstract. The ability to dynamically compose autonomous services for optimally satisfying the requirements of different applications is one of the major advantages offered by the service-oriented computing (SOC) paradigm. A dynamic service composition implies that services requesters can be dynamically bound to most appropriate service providers that are available at runtime, in order to optimally satisfy the service requirements. At the same time, the autonomy of services involved in a composition means that the resulting composition may need to be adapted in response to changes in the service capabilities or requirements. Naturally, the infrastructure and technologies for providing runtime support for dynamic and adaptive composition of services form the backbone of the above process. In this chapter, we describe the Dino approach for providing the runtime support for dynamic and adaptive service composition. The Dino approach provides comprehensive support for all stages of a service composition life-cycle, namely: service discovery, selection, binding, delivery, monitoring and adaptation.

1 Introduction

Software systems are already a part of our everyday life, and are destined to become even more pervasive in the coming years. These systems will be increasingly distributed, and operate in dynamic conditions. The high value and efficiency offered by a multitude of software systems comes at a price of high complexity involved in the development and operation of these systems.

The complexity of software systems can be divided into: *computational complexity* and *coordination complexity*. While the efforts to deal with computational complexity have been ongoing for the last several years with considerable success, the focus on managing coordination complexity has been more recent and is mainly driven by the advent of highly distributed software systems.

Service-oriented computing (SOC) offers a promising solution for managing coordination complexity in distributed software systems. SOC builds on the idea

---

* This work has been partially sponsored by the project SENSORIA, IST-2005-016004.

M. Wirsing and M. Hölzl (Eds.): SENSORIA Project, LNCS 6582, pp. 585–603, 2011.

of modeling interactions between distributed software components as services provided and consumed by the components. The notion of services allows loose coupling between software components, as the services can be described and accessed using standard (platform- and implementation language-independent) service description languages and communication protocols. The loose coupling in turn allows reusability of software components, implying that a new software system can be developed by composing many of the existing *independently-deployed* and *readily-accessible* software components, while requiring to implement only a minimal number of new application-specific components to be integrated with the existing components.

The work on SOC so far has been mostly targeted toward enabling integration of business applications – either within an enterprise (i.e. enterprise application integration) or, more commonly, beyond enterprise boundaries (i.e. B2B integration). However, the potential of SOC is immense in enabling collaborations between autonomous service requesters and providers in open dynamic environments. Service composition in open dynamic environments, though building on the foundational techniques for integration of business applications, is significantly more complex and challenging than the latter. Below we discuss some of the major challenges involved in composing services in open dynamic environments.

The earliest applications as well as focus of research on SOC have been toward composing services at design time rather than at runtime. Design time service composition is the preferred approach when service partners are known in advance, for example in restricted business environments. However, design time service composition is not feasible in open dynamic environments where services participating in a composition may not be known in advance, i.e. these services can be discovered and composed only at runtime.

Dynamic service composition implies that all steps related to the composition process i.e. service discovery, selection, binding and delivery are done at runtime and in an entirely automated manner. This, in turn, imposes additional challenges for *rich* description of services and *intelligent* matchmaking. Moreover, since service partners are not known in advance and are discovered only at runtime, the level of trust between partners is typically low. This calls for appropriate *monitoring* of service delivery, and preferably maintaining a *trust rating* for different service providers.

Another challenge is that the current SOC techniques mostly assume a relatively stable execution environment. That is, once a service composition is formed, the composition is assumed to be largely stable for the period of execution, with only a limited fault-tolerance capability provided to deal with any unforeseen changes in the environment. In open dynamic environments, on the other hand, runtime changes in the execution environment are a norm, such as changes in the QoS provided by a service or the availability of the service itself. Runtime changes in the execution environment therefore call for an approach for *self-adaptive* service composition able to deal with such changes.

The above challenges have motivated our work on developing the Dino approach for proving runtime support for dynamic and adaptive composition of autonomous services. This chapter describes the Dino approach, and shows how it helps in meeting the above challenges effectively.

The rest of this chapter is organized as follows. In Section 2, we give an overview of the Dino approach. In Section 3, we provide a detailed description of the design of the Dino runtime infrastructure for enabling dynamic and adaptive composition of autonomous services. This section includes sub-sections describing the runtime support provided by Dino for different stages of a service composition life-cycle. In Section 4, we discuss the implementation of a prototype of the Dino runtime infrastructure. In Section 5, we discuss the related work, and finally in Section 6, we present the concluding discussion.

2 Overview of the Dino Approach

W3C defines a service as "an abstract resource that represents a capability of performing tasks that form a coherent functionality from the point of view of providers entities and requesters entities. To be used, a service must be realized by a concrete provider agent." [18].

In the SOC paradigm, distributed software components interact with each other by providing services to other components and consuming services provided by other components. A software component providing a certain service is called a service provider, and a software component interested in consuming a service provided by another component is called a service requester. The service requester and service provider are just the logical roles played by a software component. In practice, the same software component can – and, in fact, is likely to – play the role of a service provider as well as service requester in a given composition. That is, a component might provide certain services, and at the same time require some services from some other components. Services are provided and consumed by way of message exchanges between a service requester and a service provider. We will simply refer to a software component providing and/or requiring a service as a *service entity* when the role played by the component is not relevant.

The service composition approach of Dino builds on the idea of *rich* specification of service requirements and capabilities to allow automated discovery and selection of services. Dino provides a runtime infrastructure for service composition. The runtime infrastructure consists of a number of Dino brokers, which are responsible for service discovery, selection, binding, delivery, monitoring and adaptation. Detailed description of the various stages of service composition in the Dino approach is given in the next section.

First, we introduce the concept of *modes* of a service entity. A service entity might have alternative modes of operation, only one of which is active at a given time. A change in mode is usually triggered by a change in the execution environment of the service entity, such as a change in the resources available or a change in the user's needs or preferences. A change in mode implies a change in the internal configuration of a service entity. From an external perspective, a change in mode means a change in service requirements or capabilities of the service entity. Hirsch et al. [6] provide an architectural approach, based on the Darwin architecture description language [8], for modeling different modes of a software component in terms of differences in their required and provided interfaces. We build on the foundational work by Hirsch et al. for modeling modes of a service entity at the architecture level, and provide support for the different modes of operation of service entities during service composition. The modeling of the different modes of a service entity is described in Chapter 4-4.

The Dino runtime infrastructure is responsible for service composition. Fig. 1 gives an overview of the service composition process in the Dino approach. Every service requester needs to provide its service requirements to a Dino broker in a standard format. The Dino broker carries out matchmaking between the service requester and potential service providers, based on the specifications of the respective service requirements and capabilities. Once the most appropriate service providers for the given service requirements are determined, the Dino broker establishes bindings between the service requester and service providers. The Dino broker is also responsible for (partially) monitoring the service deliveries, and carrying out an adaptation of the service composition in response to changes in the service capabilities or requirements.

To illustrate the design and operation of Dino in the following section, we consider an example scenario from the Automotive case study, which is briefly described in Chapter 0-3. A service entity called Driving-Assistant provides a route planning service (RPS) for providing route-guiding instructions to a driver. Driving-Assistant, in turn, requires some other services to be able to provide the RPS. The services required by Driving-Assistant depend upon its current mode of operation. That is, a change in mode implies a change in the service requirements of Driving-Assistant. This example will be further elaborated in the following discussion.

3   Design of the Dino Runtime Infrastructure

3.1   Specification of Service Requirements and Capabilities

Specifications of service requirements and capabilities play a very important role in the automated composition of services. Ideally, these specifications should be as unambiguous and comprehensive as possible. A simple syntactic specification of a service interface, such as the one described using industry standard WSDL (Web Services Description Language), does not offer a completely unambiguous solution. Recent work on semantic specification of services, led by OWL-S [12], aims to utilize shared ontologies for avoiding any potential ambiguity in service descriptions.

In Dino, every service requester is required to specify its service requirements in an XML-based document called ReqDoc. Similarly, every service provider is required to specify its service capabilities in an XML-based document called

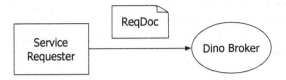

a. ReqDoc sent to a Dino broker

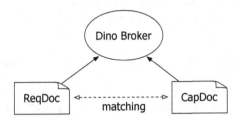

b. Functional and QoS matching

c. Service delivery through the Dino broker

Fig. 1. Service composition in the Dino approach

CapDoc. Both ReqDoc and CapDoc rely on OWL-S [12] for specifying service functionality, which is an OWL-based ontology for the semantic specification of services. In addition, ReqDoc and CapDoc include specifications of the QoS for each required and provided service. Although OWL-S allows extension of its basic specification for describing non-functional properties, it is not expressive enough for describing various QoS policies for automated composition of services. Therefore, we have developed our own language for describing the QoS. The functional and QoS descriptions are maintained separately in ReqDoc and CapDoc for easy manageability. In particular, for every service, the functionality of the service is described in a .owl file and the QoS is described in a .qos file. QoS dimensions described in the .qos file can refer to the service operations described in the .owl file, as required.

Both ReqDoc and CapDoc are divided into mode segments, with each mode segment specifying services required or provided in the corresponding mode. Fig. 2 shows a simplified version of the ReqDoc of Driving-Assistant service entity. Driving-Assistant has three possible modes: *autonomous, convoy* and *detour*. In the autonomous mode, the route is planned autonomously by Driving-Assistant, and it requires only a GPS service and Map service. In the convoy mode, the driver needs to follow another vehicle, and therefore Driving-Assistant requires input from the RPS of the leading vehicle of the convoy. And in the detour mode, the vehicle is guided by an external emergency system (to avoid some problems, such as accident or works in the street), and therefore Driving-Assistant requires highway emergency service (HES).

```
<ReqDoc name="Driving-Assistant">
    <mode name="autonomous">
        <service name="GPS" functional="gps-req.owl" qos="gps-req.qos"/>
        <service name="Map" functional="map-req.owl" qos="map-req.qos"/>
    </mode>
    <mode name="convoy">
        <service name="RPS" functional="rps-req.owl" qos="rps-req.qos"/>
    </mode>
    <mode name="detour">
        <service name="HES" functional="hes-req.owl" qos="hes-req.qos"/>
    </mode>
</ReqDoc>
```

Fig. 2. Requirements document of Driving-Assistant

```
<CapDoc name="Driving-Assistant">
    <mode name="autonomous, convoy, detour">
        <service name="RPS" functional="rps-cap.owl" qos="rps-cap.qos"/>
    </mode>
</CapDoc>
```

Fig. 3. Capabilities document of Driving-Assistant

In Fig. 2, the .owl file referred by the `functional` attribute of a `<service>` element contains the functional description of the service in OWL-S, and the .qos file referred by the `qos` attribute contains the QoS description of the service. The name of a service is used for internal reference only. As mentioned above, maintaining the functional and QoS descriptions separately allows easy manageability. In particular, the QoS description is likely to change more frequently than the functional description. For example, due to a change in the execution environment conditions, a service provider may need to update the QoS it can offer, while continuing to provide the same functionality as before. Maintaining these two descriptions separately allows easily updating one, without interfering with the other. The format of CapDoc is similar to that of ReqDoc, as shown in Fig. 3. The service requirements and capabilities of a service entity can change independently of each other with a change in the mode of the entity. For instance, in the above example, only the service requirements of Driving-Assistant change with a change in mode, while its service capabilities remains the same in all three different modes. The functional description in ReqDoc is more abstract than the one in CapDoc, as explained below.

An OWL-S description of a service consists of three parts: *profile, process model* and *grounding*. A profile describes a service operation in terms of its input, output, preconditions and effects. A process model describes details of service operations in terms of *atomic, simple* and *composite* processes (only atomic process descriptions are used in Dino). And a grounding describes details of how to invoke a service operation, and is usually mapped to the WSDL description of the service operation. The functional specification of a required service contains the corresponding OWL-S profiles only, while that of a provided service contains all three parts of the OWL-S description. The advantage of OWL-S is that the descriptions of the required and provided services can refer to the shared ontologies for the common understanding of the terms used in the descriptions. This helps in removing any ambiguity and allows for automated matchmaking. Another advantage offered by OWL-S is that services can be described following the principle of design-by-contract by including preconditions and effects for every operation, as opposed to a simple interface specification that can be described using WSDL. For more details on OWL-S, please refer to the OWL-S specification [12].

For the QoS specification of services, there are currently no established standards. Although OWL-S allows specifying the non-functional properties of a service as a list of name-value pairs, it is not rich enough for describing complex QoS policies of service requesters and providers. The QoS properties of services are defined using an XML-based specification language provided by Dino. Below we give a brief overview of the QoS specifications in a .qos file. More details of the QoS specifications in Dino can be found in [11].

Similar to the .owl file, the .qos file also contains pointers to the shared ontologies for the common understanding of the terms used in the QoS specifications. The development of a QoS ontology for Web services is a separate and broad area of research. A few independent proposals for defining a QoS ontology have been presented, such as QoSOnt [3], OWL-QoS (formerly DAML-QoS) [20], work by Maximilien and Singh [10] etc. However, none of these proposals is as yet mature enough to be established as a standard. There has also been an initiative to combine the features of different ontologies, with an aim to propose a standard QoS ontology [4].

The QoS dimensions of a service can be domain-independent, such as response time, throughput, availability, security, cost, location, etc., or domain-specific, such as accuracy of results, fidelity of data, etc. The domain-specific dimensions are defined in a domain-specific QoS ontology, while the domain-independent dimensions are defined in a generic QoS ontology. Some QoS dimensions might actually be *aggregate* of other *primitive* QoS dimensions. For example, security is an aggregate of encryption, authentication, authorization, confidentiality etc. Each primitive QoS dimension is specified in a <qos> element in the .qos file. The attributes of a <qos> element refer to the corresponding ontology where these are defined. Each aggregate QoS dimension is specified using an envelope element called <aggregate>, which contains all the constituent <qos> or <aggregate> elements as its sub-elements. The QoS dimensions described in the .qos file can refer to the service operations described in the .owl file, as required.

The attributes of a <qos> element are: name (specifying the unique name of the QoS dimension in the corresponding ontology), operation (reference to the service operation(s) in the associated .owl file that is characterized by this QoS dimension; if no operations are specified then this QoS dimension characterizes all operations specified in the .owl file), unit (unit of measurement), minVal (for numerically quantifiable values only; this is the lowest value of the offered QoS dimension and it appears in CapDoc only), maxVal (opposite of minVal, i.e. the highest value of the offered QoS dimension), mpVal (for numerically quantifiable values only; this is the most preferred value of the required QoS dimension and it appears in ReqDoc only), lpVal (opposite of mpVal, i.e. the least preferred value of the required QoS dimension), enum (comma-separated enumeration of discrete values; the order of enumeration is from the most preferred to least preferred when appearing in ReqDoc, while in CapDoc the order is not important), confidence (confidence level of the service provider in these values), priority (relative priority of this QoS dimension compared to other QoS dimensions; it appears in ReqDoc only). Many of the above attributes are optional in a QoS specification. An example QoS specification for the response time offered by a Map service provider, and that required by Driving-Assistant is shown in Fig. 4. The QoS values specified for a required or offered service can be computed using the quantitative analysis techniques developed within the SENSORIA project, which are described in Chapter 5-5.

```
<qos name="responseTime" operation="localMap" unit="ms"
    minVal="100" maxVal="1100" confidence="0.99"/>
```

a. Response time offered by a Map provider

```
<qos name="responseTime" operation="localMap" unit="ms"
    mpVal="0" lpVal="2000" confidence="0.95" priority="0.8"/>
```

b. Response time required by Driving-Assistant

Fig. 4. QoS specification of response time

Different QoS dimensions are further combined using elements such as <and>, <or>, <xor>, <not>, etc., in order to specify complex QoS policies of the service requesters and providers. These policies are taken into account by Dino brokers during service matching and selection process. For example, a <xor> element can be used by a service provider to indicate different alternative QoS values it can offer, probably at different prices. An <and> element can be used for grouping several different QoS dimensions together within a <xor> element, to present these dimensions collectively as an atomic alternative. Further details of the QoS specifications in Dino can be found in [11].

For the functional specifications, we assume that detailed descriptions of the operations required and provided by service entities are sufficient for automated matchmaking. The preconditions and effects described in the OWL-S specifications of operations provide implicit constraints on the order of invocation of these operations. The conversation logic, i.e. what messages to exchange using these operations, is implemented within the service entities involved in the exchange. The conversation logic can be implemented in a conventional programming language, or a special-purpose service orchestration language like WS-BPEL [16]. However, if the conversation logic is implemented in WS-BPEL, the conventional use of WS-BPEL – which involves static service composition, and execution using a WS-BPEL engine – needs to be changed to take advantage of the Dino runtime infrastructure for dynamic service composition.

The specifications of service requirements and capabilities, as required for dynamic service composition, can be generated directly from the service models. An approach for generating these specifications from the service models is described in a previous paper [5], and is also discussed in Chapter 4-4. Next, we discuss the process of service discovery and selection in Dino.

3.2 Service Discovery and Selection

Once service entities have specified their service requirements and capabilities in the respective ReqDoc and CapDoc documents, they can utilize the Dino runtime infrastructure for collaborating with other service entities by forming a service composition.

The process of service discovery is always initiated by a service requester. A service requester invokes a Dino broker, and passes its ReqDoc to the broker (refer Fig. 1a). Additionally, the service requester provides the broker with an ordered list of modes that it is willing to accept. The list is ordered according to the preference of the service requester. It is possible that the service requester provides only a single mode that it is willing to accept. Providing a list of modes gives more flexibility to the Dino broker such that if the most preferred mode of the service requester cannot be accepted due to unavailability of the required services, then the Dino broker may attempt to satisfy the requirements for the next mode, and so on.

A Dino broker can be located anywhere in the network, e.g. on the same node as a service requester or on a trusted third party node. However, as discussed later, for the better monitorability reasons, it is recommended that a Dino broker be hosted on the same node as a service requester interested in using the broker.

Upon invocation, the Dino broker begins search for the services that can satisfy the service requirements specified in the ReqDoc passed to it. A search for services can be done using a number of different mechanisms, depending on the application domain and environment. The search mechanisms include searching a centralized service registry, local registries of Dino brokers where services can register, a search engine such as a peer-to-peer search engine for services (based on Limewire) developed as a part of the Dino project [2], or simply past records maintained by Dino brokers containing the previous search results. The currently available modes are marked in a CapDoc for the purpose of service discovery and selection. These modes can be changed by the service provider, as and when the capability of the service provider changes.

The search for candidate services is done by matching both the functional and QoS properties specified for the required service and the provided services (refer Fig. 1b). The functional matching is done by matching the OWL-S profiles described in service requirements with the OWL-S specifications in service capabilities descriptions. For the functional matching, a number of matchmakers for OWL-S specifications are available. We have used the OWL-S API developed at MINDSWAP [9] for developing a matchmaker for functional matching. For matching the QoS, we have developed our own matching algorithm. When more than one service match a service requirement – as is likely in a services marketplace envisioned for open dynamic environments – the Dino broker uses a QoS-based selection algorithm for selecting the best match.

The QoS-based selection algorithm takes into account the *relative benefit* offered by a provided service with respect to the QoS criteria specified by the service requester, as well as the *trustworthiness* of the service provider. The QoS-based selection algorithm, along with the language for QoS specifications, is an important constituent of the service composition process in Dino. The details of the QoS-based selection algorithm can be found in [11].

Once the best match for every required service in a given mode is selected, the Dino broker establishes bindings with the selected service providers.

3.3   Service Delivery and Monitoring

Once all the required services are selected and the corresponding bindings have been established, the delivery of services from the selected service providers to the service requester can begin. As mentioned earlier, a service is delivered by exchange of request and response messages between a service requester and a service provider. For invoking a service, the service requester sends a request message to the Dino broker. The Dino broker forwards this message to the corresponding service provider. Similarly, the response from the service provider is sent to the broker, which then forwards this response to the service requester (refer Fig. 1c). The service requester and service provider do not have a direct reference to each other, and interact only through the Dino broker. This is useful in case an adaptation of the service composition is required, in response to a change in the service being delivered. However, Dino provides flexibility to the service requester to opt for a direct delivery of service (i.e. without the involvement of the Dino broker), if required, for example due to hard real-time constraints on the response time etc. The option for direct delivery can be indicated in the ReqDoc. In such a case, the Dino broker simply provides a reference of the service provider to the service requester at the end of the service selection phase, and the service requester and service provider interact with each other directly thereafter. However, the default method of delivery is through a Dino broker.

When a service is delivered through a Dino broker, the broker is able to perform syntactic mapping of the messages exchanged between the service requester and service provider, when these messages have matching semantics but differing syntax. Recall that the matchmaking is performed on the basis of semantic specifications of service requirements and capabilities. However, there might be syntactic incompatibilities between the service requester and service provider, e.g. they might use different names for an operation while assuming the same semantics for the operation. To avoid this problem, the service requester always sends messages using the same nomenclature as in the profile used to specify service requirements in ReqDoc. The Dino broker internally translates these messages into the nomenclature expected by the service provider, using the information available from the service provider's grounding description. This translation is facilitated by the OWL-S API [9].

In addition to supporting delivery of service messages, Dino brokers play an important role in monitoring the service delivery, in particular the QoS being delivered. The actual monitoring is performed by a collaboration between the service requester and Dino broker. This is because only a few QoS dimensions can be monitored independently by the Dino broker (such as availability), while others (such as accuracy of results) can be monitored by the service requester only. For some QoS dimensions, such as response time, even though the precise values can be obtained when monitored by the service requester, reasonably approximate values can be obtained when monitoring is done by the Dino broker, if the broker and the service requester are located on the same network node. Our aim is to maximize the proportion of monitoring done by the Dino broker, to relieve the service requester from the overhead involved in monitoring. For the QoS dimensions that can be monitored by the service requester only, the service requester provides feedback to the Dino broker in case the monitored values deviate from the initially agreed values. The work by Raimondi et al. [13] provides an excellent formal basis, based on timed automata, for monitoring various commonly-used QoS dimensions, such as response time, availability etc.

Next, we discuss the adaptation actions performed by the Dino broker when a service delivery deviates from the initially agreed values and consequently fails to meet the requirements of the service requester.

3.4   Service Recomposition

When a Dino broker discovers that a services delivery has deviated from the initially agreed values (either by monitoring on its own, or by getting feedback from the service requester), and has consequently failed to meet the requirements of the service requester, it initiates adaptation actions. At this stage, we are not concerned with the actual cause behind a deviation of service delivery – be it a hardware failure, mobility of a node, increased load on the service provider, or even malicious behavior of the service provider. The adaptation involves selecting an alternative service provider to replace the current service provider. In addition, the trust rating of the current service provider is lowered whenever a services delivery deviates from the initially agreed values, even if it still continues to meet the requirements of the service requester and hence no adaptation action is taken by the Dino broker. Details of the trust ratings management in Dino can be found in [11].

If more than one service provider had matched successfully during the initial search, the Dino broker need not conduct a new search, and tries to establish a binding with a service provider that had previously matched successfully. Otherwise, the Dino broker needs to search for an alternative service provider, in a similar manner as done initially. The criteria for selecting a service provider from among several candidates remains the same as during the initial selection. It is possible that no alternative service provider is found for a required service. In this case, the service requester can either inform a new mode, or lower its criteria for the selection of the required services in the current mode.

If an alternative service provider is found successfully and a new binding is established, the Dino broker is responsible for managing the handover from the old service provider to the new service provider, ideally in a way transparent to the service requester. In case of stateful services, the handover involves transferring the state of the old service provider to the new service provider, so that the new service provider is able to resume the execution correctly. For the state transfer, we argue for a change in the conventional way of maintaining the persistent state in a service entity (i.e. the state that needs to remain persistent in between invocations). In the conventional way, the state of a software component is its internal matter and is hidden from the external world. Even though some parameters of the state can be queried, the overall state is largely oblivious to other components. We argue that increasingly in SOC, a service requester might be interested in switching its service provider at runtime, especially for long running interactions. At the same time, the service requester would not like to loose the results of its past computations, i.e. its state maintained by the service provider. One option will be for the service requester to maintain a copy of the state relevant to it at all times. However, this is likely to create an unnecessary overhead for the service requester.

This is similar to a real world situation where a patient (i.e. service requester) wants to switch her family physician (i.e. service provider), for example due to relocation. But at the same time, the patient would not want to loose her past medical history records, as these are very important for the patient. The common solution in this case is for the patient's current family physician to send her records to her new family physician. These records are already in the form that any qualified physician will be able to understand and make sense of. The same model of transfer of records can be replicated in adaptive service recomposition, with the state related to the service requester being transferred from the old service provider to the new service provider. This transfer can take place with the Dino broker acting as an intermediary. A fundamental problem with this scheme, however, is that the new service provider should be able to understand and make sense of the state being transferred to it, in order to use the state properly.

A reasonable solution to the above problem is for all the service providers providing similar functionality, i.e. the ones that can potentially replace each other at runtime, to have a common shared understanding of the persistent state to be maintained. This solution can be realized by developing a standardized OWL-based ontology for state representation, similar to the ones used for the semantic specifications of the services themselves. Development of such a standardized ontology would require a group effort by different stakeholders, and is considered a part of the future work.

However, in case of an abrupt loss of a service, the state transfer between service providers may not be possible. The concerned service entities need to implement appropriate recovery mechanisms for such a case.

Once the new service provider is ready, the service requests from the service requester are forwarded to the new service provider instead of the old service provider, even though the service requester itself might be oblivious to a change in the actual service provider. During the time that the new service provider is selected and activated, any service requests from the service requester are queued within the Dino broker, to be forwarded to the new service provider once the new service provider is ready to accept requests.

A runtime change in the mode of a service requester or service provider might result in changes in the corresponding service requirements or capabilities. The concerned Dino brokers are responsible for carrying out recomposition of services accordingly to accommodate these changes. In particular, a change in the service capabilities might result in the adaptation of the service composition as described above, i.e. by replacing the old service provider with a new service provider. Whereas, a change in the service requirements results in the service requester invoking the Dino broker to discover and select new service providers for the newly required services, in a similar manner as done initially, while bindings with any obsolete (no longer required) services can be closed safely.

The dynamic service recomposition ability allows a Dino-managed service-oriented application to continue its execution unhindered even in the wake of unpredictable changes in its execution environment.

4 Implementation of the Dino Runtime Infrastructure

A prototype Dino broker is implemented in Java, and is accessible as a Web service. A partial specification of the DinoBroker interface (showing basic operations) is shown in Fig. 5. A WSDL description is generated from the DinoBroker interface for SOAP access.

The component diagram of the Dino Broker is shown in Fig. 6. The Broker component handles requests from applications for registering ReqDocs and Cap-Docs, changing modes, and invoking services. The Broker component also manages sessions, and coordinates interactions between discovery engines, the invocation engine, and the repository.

Continuing with the Automotive case study used earlier on in the description, we take another example scenario from this case study. A mobile client in a moving vehicle is interested in performing location-sensitive search for restaurants.

```
public interface DinoBroker {
    public String startSession();
    public void quitSession(String sessionId);
    public void registerReqDoc(String sessionId, String reqDocURL);
    public void registerCapDoc(String sessionId, String capDocURL);
    public SelectModeResponse selectMode(String sessionId,
                        String[] requestedModes);
    public InvocationResponse invokeService(String sessionId,
                        String serviceName, Param[] params);
}
```

Fig. 5. Interface of the Dino broker

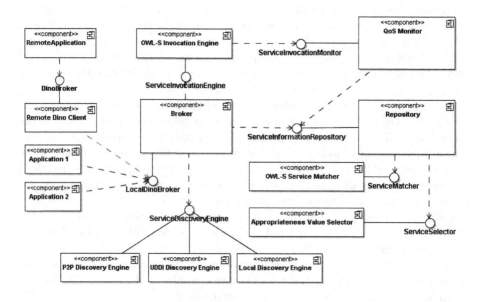

Fig. 6. Component diagram of the Dino broker

There are two modes in which the client can operate. The user-input-location mode requires only the restaurant-search service. This service takes a number of inputs, including the location, which are used to search for restaurants. In this mode, the client needs to ask the user for the current location. In the gps-location mode, two additional services are required. The gps service returns the latitude and longitude at which the client is located. This will be a local service with access to a GPS device. The latlong-to-city service takes a latitude and longitude, and returns the town or city which best corresponds to the location. Generally, the client will ask for gps-location as the preferred mode, and user-input-location as an alternative mode.

To start using the Dino broker, a client must call the startSession method. This method returns a session identifier which must be used for all subsequent communication with the Dino broker. As multiple clients can use the Dino broker simultaneously, and the Dino broker maintains state for each client, session identification is necessary to match the client calls to the existing session state.

Having obtained a session, the client can register a ReqDoc using the `registerReqDoc` method. This requires a URL to be provided from which the Dino broker can retrieve the ReqDoc. Each session has a single ReqDoc, and calling this method again results in an existing ReqDoc being replaced by the new ReqDoc. Similarly, a service provider can register a CapDoc using the `registerCapDoc` method.

Once a ReqDoc has been registered by a client, it must select which mode it wants to use. This will determine what services the Dino broker has to discover. The client provides an array of possible modes that it is willing to accept, in the order of preference. The Dino broker attempts to satisfy the requirements of one of the modes and, if successful, reports which mode it has selected inside a `SelectModeResponse` object. If no mode can be satisfied, a `ServiceDiscoveryException` is thrown. Once a mode has been selected, the client can invoke services which are required in the selected mode, using the `invokeService` method. The parameters passed to this method and returned by it are OWL-S parameters, which are translated by the Dino broker into the appropriate form using the OWL-S API [9] and the OWL-S description of the invoked service.

In the restaurant search scenario, the `gps` service is invoked with no parameters, and returns a parameter representing latitude and longitude. This output in then used as input to the `latlong-to-city` service, which requires latitude and longitude as input and returns the name of a city. This city name is then used as one of the input parameters to the `restaurant-search` service.

As discussed above, a Dino broker performs the functional and QoS matchmaking for every required service, in order to identify candidate service providers. When more than one candidate service provider is found for a required service, the broker selects the most appropriate service provider using the QoS-based service provider selection algorithm. We have carried out the performance evaluation for the functional matching, QoS matching, and QoS-based service provider selection stages for varying numbers of service providers. For each execution, service providers were generated such that half of the total number of service providers satisfied the functional requirements, and half of those also satisfied the QoS requirements (and therefore qualified as candidate service providers). Five QoS dimensions were used for the experiments. The performance of functional matching, QoS matching, and service provider selection was measured for 400 to 8000 service providers in increments of 400. In each case, the matching and selection process was executed 10 times to find the average value. These experiments were carried out on a personal computer running Windows XP with 1GB of RAM and a 3GHz dual-core processor.

The results of the experiments are shown in Fig. 7. These results show the total time taken for service provider selection, and how the different stages contribute to it. It can be seen that all stages in the above process scale linearly with the number of service providers. The total time for service provider selection is only 90 ms for 8000 service providers, and all three stages contribute almost equally to this time.

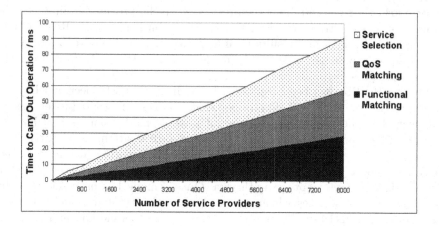

Fig. 7. Time for service matching and selection

5 Related Work

In the last few years, there has been a significant amount of work done in the area of service composition. A large portion of the work on service composition, and in particular the standardization effort so far, has been on providing specification languages for describing service compositions. These languages are used for modeling a service composition as a workflow of service interactions. The interactions between service partners in a service composition can be described either as an *orchestration* or a *choreography*. An orchestration describes a local view of a service composition from the perspective of one service partner and its interactions with other partners. A choreography, on the other hand, describes a global view of a service composition comprising of all service partners and messages exchanged between these partners. A choreography-based approach is, in effect, a *top-down* approach where a choreography is designed and analyzed first, before it is executed by the corresponding service partners. An orchestration-based approach, on the other hand, follows a *bottom-up* approach where each orchestration is designed and implemented individually, while the resulting choreography is formed automatically at runtime by the executions of these orchestrations.

A choreography-based approach presumes that all services participating in a composition are known in advance. This is possible only if the concrete providers for the participating services are also known in advance, because different providers providing the same type of service might have different service requirements. That is, inclusion of different providers for a given service might result in different compositions. Therefore, a global view of a service composition prior to its execution requires the knowledge of concrete service partners forming the composition. This may not be possible in open dynamic environments, where concrete service partners can be discovered and composed only at runtime, rendering choreography-based approaches inappropriate for such environments. Orchestration-based approaches are better suited for open dynamic environments, as here each service partner needs to model only its own interactions with other services, and this can be done at an abstract level without requiring the knowledge of concrete service partners.

An emerging standard for describing a choreography is WS-CDL (Web Services Choreography Description Language) [17], and that for describing orchestrations is WS-BPEL (Web Services Business Process Execution Language) [16]. Both WS-CDL and WS-BPEL are XML-based languages. A service orchestration described in WS-BPEL is like a flow-chart, specifying control logic and flows of interactions between the host service partner (for which the orchestration is described) and other partners involved in the orchestration. A number of execution engines for service orchestrations described in WS-BPEL have been developed, such as ActiveBPEL [1]. These execution engines support only design time service composition. This is because WS-BPEL has been originally designed, and mostly used, in restricted environments where service partners are known in advance, and service requirements and capabilities are not likely to change during execution. However, the execution engines for WS-BPEL can, in principle, be integrated with a Dino broker for allowing dynamic service composition. That is, an execution engine may act as a service requester, and interact with the Dino broker on behalf of the host service partner for which the service orchestration is described.

Sycara et al. [14] propose a broker-based approach where brokers are delegated the task of service composition. This approach is therefore related to our approach, as our approach also relies on the concept of brokers for service composition. However, in contrast to the above approach, our approach provides support for the specification of QoS in the description of service requirements and capabilities, as the QoS plays an important role in selecting a service provider. Moreover, our approach also provides support for automated adaptation of a service composition.

Yu and Lin [19] also propose a broker-based approach for selecting and composing services based on their QoS. However, this approach assumes a choreography view of the service composition to be available, and aims to identify appropriate service partners to be composed together in accordance with this choreography view. Clearly, such an approach is not suitable for the open dynamic environments that our approach targets.

Liu et al. [7] and Wang et al. [15] provide more general approaches for QoS-based service selection, and these approaches can be used for the local selection of a service provider without regard to the choreography view. However, both these approaches compare the QoS offered by a service provider with that of other competing service providers during service selection, but they do not take into account the QoS required by the service requester itself. As we have shown in a previous paper [11], this can lead to sub-optimal solutions, as the QoS required by the service requester should be an important criterion to be taken into account for service selection.

6 Conclusion

In this chapter, we have described the Dino approach for providing runtime support for dynamic and adaptive service composition, which is particularly useful for composing autonomous services in open dynamic environments. The approach is comprehensive in its support for different stages of a service composition life-cycle. The dynamic service composition is facilitated by formalizing the specifications of functional and non-functional service requirements and capabilities. The runtime infrastructure provided by Dino consists of a number of brokers, which are responsible for discovery, selection, binding and delivery of services. In addition, the Dino brokers are responsible for (partially) monitoring the services being delivered, and taking adaptation actions in response to changes in the service capabilities or requirements, thereby enabling self-adaptive service compositions.

References

1. ActiveBPEL Open Source Engine, www.activebpel.org/
2. Ali, F., et al.: Dinowire – A Peer-to-Peer Infrastructure for Service Discovery in Service-Oriented Architectures, Group project report, University College London (2007)
3. Dobson, G., Lock, R., Sommerville, I.: QoSOnt: A QoS Ontology for Service-Centric Systems. In: Proc. of the 31st EUROMICRO Conference on Software Engineering and Advanced Applications (August-September 2005)
4. Dobson, G., Sanchez-Macian, A.: Towards Unified QoS/SLA Ontologies. In: Proc. of the 3rd International Semantic and Dynamic Web Processes Workshop (September 2006)
5. Foster, H., Mukhija, A., Rosenblum, D.S., Uchitel, S.: A Model-Driven Approach to Dynamic and Adaptive Service Brokering using Modes. In: Proc. of the 6th International Conference on Service Oriented Computing (December 2008)
6. Hirsch, D., Kramer, J., Magee, J., Uchitel, S.: Modes for Software Architectures. In: Proc. of the 3rd European Workshop on Software Architecture (September 2006)
7. Liu, Y., Ngu, A., Zeng, L.: QoS Computation and Policing in Dynamic Web Service Selection. In: Proc. of the 13th International World Wide Web Conference (May 2004)
8. Magee, J., Dulay, N., Eisenbach, S., Kramer, J.: Specifying Distributed Software Architectures. In: Proc. of the 5th European Software Engineering Conference (September 1995)
9. Maryland Information and Network Dynamics Lab Semantic Web Agents Project, OWL-S API, http://www.mindswap.org/2004/owl-s/api/
10. Maximilien, E.M., Singh, M.P.: A Framework and Ontology for Dynamic Web Services Selection. IEEE Internet Computing 8(5), 84–93 (2004)
11. Mukhija, A., Dingwall-Smith, A., Rosenblum, D.S.: QoS-Aware Service Composition in Dino. In: Proc. of the 5th IEEE European Conference on Web Services (November 2007)

12. OWL-S: Semantic Markup for Web Services, W3C Member Submission, November 22 (2004), http://www.w3.org/Submission/OWL-S/
13. Raimondi, F., Skene, J., Emmerich, W.: Efficient online monitoring of web-service SLAs. In: Proc. of the ACM International Symposium on Foundations of Software Engineering (November 2008)
14. Sycara, K., Paolucci, M., Soudry, J., Srinivasan, N.: Dynamic Discovery and Coordination of Agent-Based Semantic Web Services. IEEE Internet Computing 8(3), 66–73 (2004)
15. Wang, X., Vitvar, T., Kerrigan, M., Toma, I.: A QoS-Aware Selection Model for Semantic Web Services. In: Proc. of the 4th International Conference on Service Oriented Computing (December 2006)
16. Web Services Business Process Execution Language Version 2.0, OASIS Standard, April 11 (2007), http://docs.oasis-open.org/wsbpel/2.0/wsbpel-v2.0.html
17. Web Services Choreography Description Language Version 1.0, W3C Candidate Recommendation, November 9 (2005), http://www.w3.org/TR/ws-cdl-10/
18. Web Services Glossary, W3C Working Group Note, February 11 (2004), http://www.w3.org/TR/ws-gloss/
19. Yu, T., Lin, K.-J.: A Broker-Based Framework for QoS-Aware Web Service Composition. In: Proc. of the International Conference on e-Technology, e-Commerce and e-Service (March-April 2005)
20. Zhou, C., Chia, L., Lee, B.: DAML-QoS Ontology for Web Services. In: Proc. of the 2nd International Conference on Web Services (July 2004)

Legacy Transformations for Extracting Service Components*

Carlos Matos[1,2] and Reiko Heckel[2]

[1] ATX II Tecnologias de Software S.A.
Rua Saraiva de Carvalho 207C, 1350-300 Lisboa, Portugal
carlos.matos@atxsoftware.com
[2] Department of Computer Science, University of Leicester
University Road, Leicester LE1 7RH, United Kingdom
{cmm22, reiko}@mcs.le.ac.uk

Abstract. This chapter presents an overview of the work on migration of legacy systems towards Service-Oriented Architectures that is taking place within the SENSORIA project. In this context, a general methodology for software reengineering was developed and instantiated in two dimensions to allow service components to be extracted from legacy applications. The main goal of this work is to provide a systematic way of addressing such reengineering projects with a high degree of automation while being largely independent of the programming language. The approach is based on a combination of techniques such as source code analysis, graph transformation, and code transformation. The focus in this text is on the description of the methodology, its dimensions for SOA, a prototype implementation and preliminary results and conclusions.

1   Introduction

This chapter presents an overview of the work done in SENSORIA project for the migration of legacy systems towards Service-Oriented Architectures. This work was motivated by the increasing demand for modernising existing systems, which is driven, amongst other aspects, by the high frequency of change in business requirements and evolution in technology.

SOA is steadily becoming adopted in software engineering practice. Reports show that many newly developed applications and business processes designed nowadays use service-oriented architectures to some extent [1]. It is estimated that by 2011 (with 0.8 probability) more than 80% of existing applications will be at least partly reengineered to participate in service-oriented architectures [2].

With this growth in SOA adoption, the need for a systematic approach towards reengineering for SOA also increases. However, several principles of service-orientation pose major challenges for these efforts:

1. The separation of business from presentation logic
2. The loosely coupled relationship between services
3. The coarse-grained nature of services

---

* This work has been partially sponsored by the project SENSORIA , IST-2005-016004.

M. Wirsing and M. Hölzl (Eds.): SENSORIA Project, LNCS 6582, pp. 604–621, 2011.

As legacy systems were not usually built with these concerns in mind, much effort is needed to accommodate them. Approaches based on wrapping existing applications into web service interfaces do not fully address these principles—a deep restructuring approach is necessary.

This chapter presents a methodology to address migration of legacy software to SOA complying with the above principles while allowing for a high degree of automation, providing support for the full reengineering cycle and having into consideration scalability matters.

Our proposal can be seen as an instance of the horseshoe model [3], a conceptual model for reengineering at different levels, with a focus on transformations at the level of architectural models. In this paper, this goal is achieved by using techniques such as code pattern matching and graph transformation. In order to structure the process, we propose an overall methodology, instantiated in two dimensions to address the technological and the functional evolution. The former is concerned with technical purpose of the code and the latter focuses on its implementation of relevant business-level functionalities.

The remainder of this paper is organized as follows: Section 2 describes in more detail the SOA properties mentioned above and Section 3 presents our general methodology for architectural migration. Next, a summary of the technological dimension in Section 4 is presented and the functional dimension is detailed in Section 5. Section 6 presents a prototype implementation of the methodology, together with initial results from a small case study. Section 7 discusses related work and Section 8 concludes the paper and presents future work.

2   Challenges of SOA to Reengineering

For an approach to successfully support migration to SOA, it is necessary to address the properties discussed in the previous section. These are discussed in more detail in the following subsections.

2.1   The Separation of Business from Presentation Logic

In legacy applications it is common to find, mixed up in a kind of "architectural spaghetti", code fragments concerned with database access, business logic, presentation aspects and exception handling, among others. However, it is not possible to derive services directly while business logic is tightly coupled with presentation logic. Therefore, an appropriate decomposition of the code is required such that business functions are isolated as candidate services or service constituents.

2.2   The Loosely Coupled Relationship between Services

It is common to find a complex network of dependencies between different functionalities in existing systems. However, service-orientation principles state that services must interact without tight, cross-service dependencies [4]. Therefore, a decomposition of different functionalities is required to provide a degree of independence.

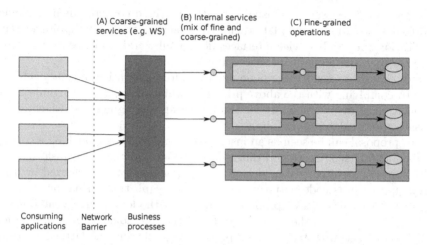

Fig. 1. Service granularity across application tiers

2.3 The Coarse-Grained Nature of Services

Legacy applications typically consist of elements that are of a fine-grained nature, for instance components with operations that represent logical units of work, e.g. reading individual items of data. Object-Oriented (OO) class methods are an example of such fine-grained operations. The notion of service, however, is of a different, more coarse-grained nature. Services represent logical groupings of, possibly fine-grained, operations, work on top of larger data sets, and in general expose a greater range of functionality. In particular, services that are deployed and consumed over a network must exhibit such a property in order to limit the number of remote consumer-to-provider roundtrips and the corresponding processing cycles.

Fig. 1 presents a graphical representation of granularity across different application tiers. In an SOA context, legacy logical units of work have to be appropriately composed and reengineered in order to form services of desired granularity and of adequate support for multi-party business processes.

3 General Methodology of Architectural Migration

This section describes the general methodology proposed for migrating the architecture of applications. Depending on the intended target architecture, changes are required along either the technological or functional dimensions or, as is the case with SOAs, both. Technological restructuring is used in the layering of software systems and may lead to a 3-tiered architecture, separating logic, data, and user interface (UI). This process addresses the principle of separation between business and presentation logic. Functional restructuring separates components which, after having replaced their UI tier with an appropriate interface and

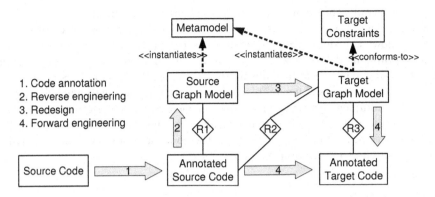

Fig. 2. General methodology

being grouped according to specific parameters, represent services. This dimension addresses the properties of loosely coupled services and their coarse-grained nature.

The general methodology instanced for both technological and functional dimensions is presented in Fig. 2. This consists of the steps described in the next subsections.

3.1 Code Annotation

At this stage, the source code is annotated by code categories. Blocks of source code are labelled according to the different elements of the target architecture they will be mapped to. This process is largely automated but, depending on the source system and the specific dimension, requires some level of input from the developer that is driving the process. This activity can thus be seen as an interleaving of automated and manual code annotations.

The code categories to be used in this step depend on the target architecture. If migrating to a 3-tier system, the categories to consider are UI, Logic and Data, as is described in this paper for the technological dimension. The categories for the functional dimension are related to the contribution of source code to particular services (e.g. managing accounts, customers, etc).

3.2 Reverse Engineering

Based on the information gathered from the annotation process, this step obtains a graph representation of the code. This graph will not have a 1-1 mapping with the source code, and its level of detail depends on the annotation. Structural elements that are annotated as contributing to just one category are represented by a single node. If instead they are fragmented into several categories, each of these fragments has a separate representation in the model. Since, for example, a method completely identified as belonging to the user interface is represented by one node only, this allows the model to be much more succinct than the code, leading to highly scalable solution. Another benefit of a graph representation is that it allows transformations to be described in an intuitive, visual way.

The graph model is based on a metamodel that consists of a type graph that contains: code structure information, its categorization and association to architectural elements. An example is shown later (cf. Section 6) when discussing a prototype implementation. This metamodel is general enough to accommodate both the source and target system, but also intermediate stages of the redesign transformation. Additionally, it contains the code categories that were available throughout the code annotation step.

3.3   Redesign

This step has the goal of producing the target model. For this purpose, it applies graph transformation rules to the source graph. The rules conceptually extend the graph transformation suggested by Mens *et al* in [5] to formalize refactoring [6]. The intended result is expressed by an extra set of constraints over the metamodel, which are satisfied when the transformation is complete. For instance, it is possible to specify a constraint that ensures there are no direct edges from a code fragment of a specific category to another of a specific different category. The code categorization provides the control required to automate the transformation process, limiting the need for user input to the code annotation step. Rule components (left-hand side, right-hand side and negative application conditions), as well as source, target and intermediate graphs are instances of the metamodel. In the technological dimension the rules aim to re-organize the model into a 3-tier architecture, thus complying to the SOA property described in section 2.1. The rules for the functional dimension restructure the model so that services comply to the properties mentioned in sections 2.2 and 2.3.

3.4   Forward Engineering

The final step is the process of obtaining the target code. This can be achieved by keeping a log of the transformations that are applied at model level and use this to drive the code level transformations. The result of this step, the annotated code in relation with a graph model, has the same structure as the input to step 1, thus allowing for several iterations of the whole process.

This is particularly relevant if the reengineering is directed towards service-oriented systems. In this case, the transformation has to address both technological and functional dimensions, i.e., respectively, transformation into a three-tier architecture and decomposition into functional components.

One of the main goals of this methodology is to allow a high degree of automation. Manual intervention, when applicable, is only required in step 1. A more detailed description of the general methodology can be found in [7].

4   Technological Dimension

In this section we summarize the instance of the general methodology for the technological dimension. A more detailed description can be found in [8].

4.1   Code Annotation

The code annotation step of the technological dimension is based on code pattern matching rules. These are used to automatically identify which source code fragments belong to User Interface, Logic and Data access concerns. Rules can be specific to a programming language (e.g. annotating with UI all static method calls to Classes known to deal with presentation aspects), specific to a development paradigm (e.g. assuming OO code) or even technology independent (e.g. rules based on matches from other rules). Although a majority of code patterns can be used in reused for multiple projects, differences in the involved technologies, or unusual coding patterns, may make it necessary to have manual intervention.

Some code statements can be considered to fall within more than one category. An example would be the result of a UI method call being used directly in a Logic operation. Since we can perform the annotation at the abstract syntax tree (AST) [9] level, it is possible to separate the parts that belong to one category from the others. In terms of transformation this example would lead to the direct UI call being replaced by a Controller method call (in the context of a Model-View-Controller pattern). Similar approaches are used for other kinds of mixed category statements.

4.2   Reverse Engineering

The reverse engineering step is fully automated and is achieved by taking the annotated code as input and generating a graph model complying to the specified metamodel. In this representation it is possible to see links between the different architectural concerns and have an overall feel on how the original application is structured.

4.3   Redesign

The redesign step is achieved by executing a set of graph transformation rules over the source graph model. The resulting model, which is achieved automatically, will comply to the specified target constraints and reflect a correct separation between the concerns UI, Logic and Data access. This guarantees, for example, that there are no direct calls from the UI to the Data access layer or calls from Data access to Logic.

4.4   Forward Engineering

In order to obtain the final code, the forward engineering step uses the information gathered in the redesign step to drive code transformations. Regarding object-oriented applications, this can be achieved via code refactorings.

5   Functional Dimension

In this section we describe the instance of the general methodology for the functional dimension. Given that the steps of reverse engineering and forward engineering are equivalent in both dimensions, taking advantage of following the same methodology, these are not described here to avoid repetition.

5.1   Code Annotation

The code annotation phase in the functional dimension presents more challenges than that of the technological dimension given its broader scope. While in the latter there is a big common ground between different applications (especially if they share the choice of technology), the former depends on application features that can come from a number of different domains. This, and the different nature of the two dimensions, also has an effect on the strategy of approach.

The functional code annotation phase consists of two tasks:

1. operation identification
2. grouping of operations into services

In this chapter, *operation* stands for a functionality that is likely to be at a too low granularity to be considered as a service in an SOA context. The categories used in this dimension are not known beforehand. It is during the code annotation step that these will be extracted. The names drawn to identify each category are based in the operation identifier thus, depending on the accuracy of these, it may be necessary to intervene manually so adequate names are used.

The identification of operations in source code is performed by firstly locating their entry points. The techniques used for this purpose include:

- Code belonging to the Logic layer that is invoked by the UI (as depicted in Fig. 3)—Code that is directly called from user interface components typically represent entry points to relevant functionality;
- External API's (e.g. from IDL files) - APIs that are published for external follow well known structures;
- Code that falls into a typical pattern of control/data flow—There are many code patterns that can help to identify entry points to application functionalities (an example is given in Section 6.1);
- Entry point for code that is mapped to more than one operation—Blocks of code that are used by several different application functionalities have entry points that are likely to lead to relevant operations (given that this is a very general approach, granularity of code blocks identified using it may vary greatly). This is represented in the graphical example of Fig. 3 as grey triangles;
- Known feature location techniques as the case of Latent Semantic Indexing (LSI) [10], a static approach, and Scenario Based Probabilistic (SBP) [11], a dynamic technique. There are some feature location techniques that have been tested in different environments, typically to aid in software maintenance tasks, and that presented their effectiveness.

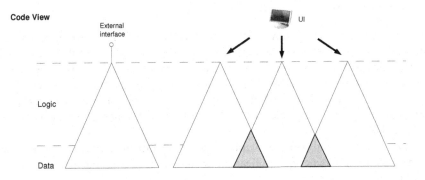

Fig. 3. Identification of operations

The dependencies between each operation entry point and remaining code can be determined using slicing techniques. A list of candidate operations can then be presented to the developer driving the process, allowing human intervention / input either for manual adaptations (supported, for example, by feature location techniques LSI and SBP as mentioned above) or for a new automated round of operation identification.

In the second step of service extraction operations previously obtained are grouped into coherent services. This is an inherently semi-automated task where operations that are related in some manner are grouped together. Automation proposes ranked groupings of operations by using metrics, including:

- overlapping between operations
- actors involved
- information about data accessed (including type of access: read, delete, etc)
- similarity measure (e.g. using LSI)

User input can then be given to decide which grouping to use, either by selecting one from the proposed automatically or by making manual assignments. The result is the source code annotated according to the operations and services that it will be mapped to afterwards to produce the graph model and drive the redesign process.

5.2   Redesign

The graph transformation rules used in this dimension are designed so that operations are grouped into meaningful services (as defined in the annotation step) and so that services have loosely coupled relations, thus complying with the last two SOA properties mentioned in Section 2.

Where in the technological dimension we have mainly rules for decomposing code structures, here there are, additionally, rules that compose/group code structures. The former are used to guarantee loose coupling and the latter to build the adequate granularity of services throughout the system.

6 Prototype

In the context of SENSORIA project, a prototype is being developed to apply the methodology described here. This currently supports the full reengineering cycle, following the steps of code annotation, reverse engineering, redesign and forward engineering. This implementation has as target the migration of Java applications but, as described in the previous sections, following this methodology provides a great degree of independence that is further explored throughout this section.

The following subsections summarize this implementation together with details of its use over an application included in the financial case study of SENSORIA.

6.1 Code Annotation

The code annotation step was implemented using CareStudio (Fig. 4 provides a screenshot of the application). This is an Eclipse plugin based on a tool by ATX (L-CARE) that, amongst other code analysis and reengineering functionalities, allows the specification and execution of code pattern matching rules and storing the resulting markings/annotations in XML format. The code patterns are defined over an XML representation of the AST of the code. Rules for code pattern matching are defined as XPath queries. XPath [12] is a query language that enables the selection of elements from an XML document based on path expressions and conditions. The rules allowed in CareStudio can range from simple XPath expressions to a combination of an arbitrary number of expressions, using the output of expressions ("parameter equation <identifier>") as parameters for others. It is also possible to specify conditions ("condition <identifier>") to the main expression ("main <identifier>"). Next we present two examples of code pattern matching rules that exist in the prototype, the first belonging to the technological dimension and the second one to the functional dimension. Some expressions were simplified for readability.

1. *Attributes that belong to the user interface.* Attributes of types that are known *a priori* to belong to the UI code category can be directly identified as such. The expression used to locate these cases is:

```
parameter equation UI_TYPES{getConst("uitypes")};
main equation ALL{//FieldDeclaration};
condition MAIN_EQ{$ALL[contains($UI_TYPES, concat(";",Type/Name/@value,";"))]};
```

2. *Methods with high Fan-In.* Methods that are called from a variety of locations in source code are likely to have a significant role in an operation (albeit potentially of too low granularity to be alone considered services). A detailed discussion about this technique can be found in [13] where it was used in the context of Aspect Mining. The expression used in CareStudio to locate these situations is (variable N is a parameter for the rule):

```
main equation METHOD{//Method};
condition METHODCALLS{count(//FunctionOp[Name/@value=$METHOD/Name/@value]) >
$N};
```

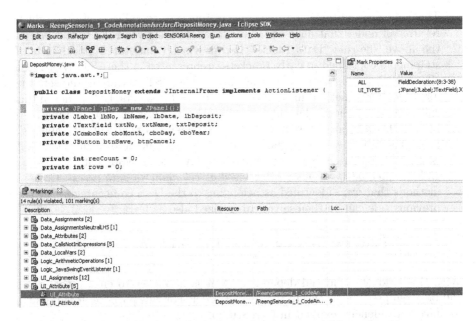

Fig. 4. CareStudio - an Eclipse plugin for code pattern matching - showing one occurrence of an UI attribute declaration (rule UI_Attribute)

One consideration that can take place when analysing these pattern matching rules is that while some have to be programming language specific to some extent, others can be very general as is the case in the second set of examples. Rules of the latter type have a big potential for reuse in multiple projects.

Currently there exist around 40 code annotation rules in this prototype, most of which are programming language independent (approximately two thirds). Additionally, even rules that need to take specific language aspects into consideration can be configured in such a way that they can be easily ported to another context. This is the case of the first rule where the list of a programming language classes that are seen as belonging to the UI is stored in a global variable called "uitypes". This way, all rules that depend on this aspect, can work in other contexts just by having a different configuration file.

Additionally, there are many rules of a higher abstraction level, in the sense that they make use of the result of applying others first. Next we present two examples of this kind of code pattern matching rules that exist in the prototype:

1. *Data access methods.* Methods in which all contents have already been identified as belonging to the Data code category can be categorized as belonging to that category:

```
main equation METHODS{getMarkedNodes("Data_Blocks")/parent::*/parent::Method};
```

This rule and the following make use of function "getMarkedNodes" which returns all nodes that have been annotated with a given rule. In the case of the above, the rule "Data_Blocks" had previously annotated blocks (sets of statements contained in curly brackets - represented in the AST by element "Block") that belonged to the Data layer. The AST in CareStudio sets the main block of a method in the path "Method/Statements/Block" hence this rule selects "Method" elements whose main block was previously annotated by rule "Data_Blocks" ("parent::*" was used instead of "parent::Statements" just for succinctness). "getMarkedNodes" is an example of a function that is available in CareStudio in order to simplify rule development.

2. *Calls to methods previously categorized as belonging to data access.* Calls to methods that were identified as belonging to the Data code category by the previous rule can be themselves categorized also as Data:

```
main equation
CALLS{//FunctionOp[Name/@value=getMarkedNodes("Data_Methods")/Name/@value]
/parent::*};
```

With this kind of sequential dependencies, it is necessary to ensure that rules will be attempted to execute in the correct order. For this purpose, it is possible to make dependencies explicit in CareStudio.

6.2   Reverse Engineering

This step achieves a more abstract representation than the abstract syntax tree, allowing us to describe transformations in a more intuitive way and for these to be programming language independent. Additionally, given that, in these graphs, we only represent the elements required according to the annotation, the model to be transformed is simpler and the transformation process has a better performance. Reducing the model size like this also allows addressing scalability issues which are particularly relevant when migrating large legacy systems.

Given that no tool existed that could take the output from CareStudio and produce a result with the format we need for the next step, a new tool was built specifically for this purpose. This was developed based in the above requirements and, due to the choice of tool for the redesign step, the result is a graph model represented in Eclipse Modeling Framework (EMF) [14]. An example of graph generated by the reverse engineering tool can be seen in Fig. 5.

From the XML we can see some of the characteristics mentioned in subsection 3.2 regarding granularity and succinctness of representation. Class "Deposit-Money" has members that belong to several code categories so it is categorized with the "*" concern. One of its methods, "actionPerformed", was fully categorized as "UI" hence only one node is used to represent it. Another method, "populateArray" consists of code blocks of two categories ("UI" and "Data") so these are represented as well.

```
<?xml version="1.0" encoding="ASCII"?>
<OO:GraphOO xmi:version="2.0" xmlns:xmi="http://www.omg.org/XMI" xmlns:xsi="http://www.w3.org/2001/XMLSchema-instance" xmlns:...
  <structuralElements xsi:type="OO:Component" name="General" componentType="//@codeCategories.0">
    <codeFragments xsi:type="OO:PackageType" name="General" codeCategory="//@codeCategories.0">
      <classes name="DepositMoney" astNodeID="DepositMoney.java.ast.xml#1010" codeCategory="//@codeCategories.0" tgen="//@str...
        <variables name="jpDep" astNodeID="DepositMoney.java.ast.xml#1017" codeCategory="//@codeCategories.1"/>
        <variables name="lbNo" astNodeID="DepositMoney.java.ast.xml#1027" codeCategory="//@codeCategories.1"/>
        (...)
        <methods name="actionPerformed" astNodeID="DepositMoney.java.ast.xml#1925" codeCategory="//@codeCategories.1"/>
        <methods name="populateArray" astNodeID="DepositMoney.java.ast.xml#2050" codeCategory="//@codeCategories.0">
          <codeBlocks name="CodeBlock" astNodeID="DepositMoney.java.ast.xml#2058"
              codeCategory="//@codeCategories.3" index="1"/>
          <codeBlocks name="CodeBlock" astNodeID="DepositMoney.java.ast.xml#2132"
              codeCategory="//@codeCategories.1" index="2"/>
          <codeBlocks name="CodeBlock" astNodeID="DepositMoney.java.ast.xml#2153"
              codeCategory="//@codeCategories.3" index="3"/>
        </methods>
      </codeFragments>
      <codeFragments xsi:type="OO:PackageType" name="External" codeCategory="//@codeCategories.0">
        <classes name="JInternalFrame" astNodeID="DepositMoney.java.ast.xml#1012" codeCategory="//@codeCategories.1" gen="//@st...
      </codeFragments>
  </structuralElements>
  (...)
  <codeCategories xsi:type="OO:ComponentType">
    <concern name="*"/>
  </codeCategories>
  <codeCategories xsi:type="OO:ComponentType">
    <concern name="UI"/>
  </codeCategories>
  (...)
```

Fig. 5. XML representation of graph obtained through the reverse engineering step

6.3 Redesign

Like in the reverse engineering step, redesign transformations are based on a graph metamodel. The prototype is thus using a type graph that can represent object-oriented applications. Fig. 6 presents this type graph that includes both structural information about the code (bottom) but also its categorization and organization in architectural components/connectors(top-right and top-left, respectively).

The graph transformation rules were designed in the Tiger EMF Transformer tool [15]. This is an Eclipse plugin application that allows the definition of rules and generates Java code that is capable of executing them over a graph represented in EMF and that complies to the specified type graph. The rule management features of this tool are graphical based, facilitating the rule development.

An example of graph transformation rule can be seen in Fig. 7. The top indicates the left-hand side of the rule and the bottom refers to the right-hand side. Negative application conditions are not shown for simplicity. This consists of the *Move Method UI* rule whose purpose is to move methods identified in the code annotation step as belonging to the UI code category from generic classes to UI ones. This rule performs one of the necessary activities of the technological dimension to achieve the SOA property of separating UI code from business logic.

The execution of the Java code generated by the tool produces a new graph, after application of the previously specified rules. In order to facilitate the next step, a logging aspect was also added to the generated code (with AspectJ), reporting every transformation made in the model, in order to guide the final step.

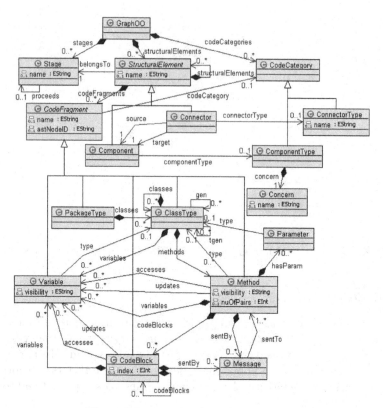

Fig. 6. Type graph for the OO paradigm

6.4   Forward Engineering

The log created by the redesign step includes information on the graph transformation rules that were applied as well as their order and the nodes of the
graph that were affected. The way the forward engineering step works is to map
this log to a sequence of code refactorings that, after applied to the source code,
produce the final, transformed, target code.

The Java application that was built for this purpose uses Eclipse's built-in
refactorings so the work is mainly focused in mapping graph transformation rules
to the right refactorings and dealing with their parametrization. In short, the tool
parses the log from the redesign step, for each executed graph transformation rule
identifies the refactoring, or group of refactorings, to be applied, and executes
the transformation.

The optimal result for this step is code that complies to the service-orientation
principles discussed in the beginning of this chapter. However, in situations in
which not all necessary code annotation rules or graph transformation rules were
specified the result may be incomplete. By analysing this and then reviewing the
prior steps, it is possible to improve on the implementation.

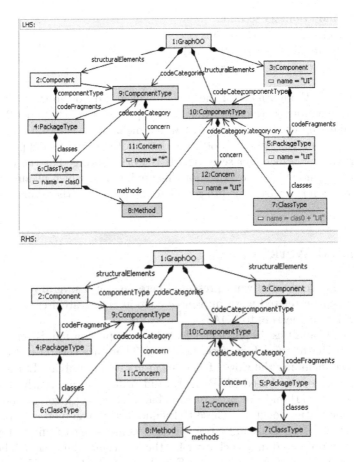

Fig. 7. Move Method UI transformation rule

All the tools used for the prototype were implemented in Eclipse and can be used as plugins to this IDE. The prototype is under development and the main objective is to provide means to evaluate our approach to fully address reengineering projects. Details about future work are given in Section 8.

6.5   Application to Case Study

To validate the implementation of the prototype during its development, we used a Java application that is part of the financial case study in SENSORIA . This consists of a small banking application in Java with 21 classes. This has an UI written in Swing and this code is mixed both with the application logic and data access.

In order to determine the kind of performance an implementation of our methodology can have, we applied the prototype to this application and recorded the time spent for each of its steps:

1. Code annotation: 24 seconds
2. Reverse engineering: 53 seconds
3. Redesign: under 1 second (921 ms)
4. Forward engineering: 35 seconds

Thus, and even though most of the tools involved did not go through an optimization procedure yet, the total time for this process was still under 2 minutes. The redesign step was particularly fast which means that the contribution from the reverse engineering step in producing the smallest graph model possible may prove very valuable in larger scenarios. It is worth noting that the code annotation had around 90% of coverage for this application, which means that after more annotation rules are added to complete the prototype these times may vary slightly.

7   Related Work

Given its wide scope, the work presented here falls into several research areas. Next we describe related work in: source code analysis, architectural transformation and reengineering to SOA.

Source code analysis, in particular feature/concept location, is related to the first step of the methodology described here. There are several techniques for this purpose including the work of Marcus *et al* [10] in applying LSI to concept location, the scenario-based (SBP) feature identification approach of Antoniol and Gueheneuc [11] and the work of Eisenbarth *et al* [16] involving both static and dynamic feature location. These techniques are all candidates to be applied in the context of an SOA migration project, considering the first step of the methodology presented in this chapter for the functional dimension. The ARTI-SAn framework, described by Jakobac, Egyed and Medvidovic in [17], categorizes code using an iterative user-guided method. The categories used are: "processing", "data" and "communication". The approach differs from ours in several aspects. Firstly, the goal of the framework is program understanding and not the creation of a representation that is aimed to be used as input for the transformation part of a reengineering methodology. Another important difference is that in ARTISAn the annotation/categorization process (called "labeling") is based on clues that result in the categorization of classes only. In our approach we need, and support, the method and code block granularity levels.

Work in the area of architecture transformation is diverse and includes examples closely related to our work. Use of graph transformation for reengineering has been suggested previously [18] in a different context (migrating mainframe COBOL to client/server) with similarities to our technological dimension. A model-based technique based on graph transformation for a-posteriori integration of legacy applications into SOA is proposed in [19]. This focuses on generating wrappers and glue code, rather than transforming directly the source code. Ivkovic and Kontogiannis [20] proposed a framework for quality-driven software architecture refactoring using model transformations and semantic annotations.

Fahmy *et al* [21] use graph rewriting to specify architectural transformations at the description level. In our case, we build a graph that models the software but also maps the code to target architectural elements. It is this information that guides the redesign process described in this paper.

Even before the advent of SOAs, approaches for reengineering business applications were proposed, based on the integration of legacy components after separating application logic from presentation [22]. Work in reengineering to SOA is new. It primarily focuses on identifying and extracting services from legacy code and wrapping them for deployment. We name just two examples in this section. Sneed [23] presents a method for wrapping PL/I, COBOL, and C/C++ code behind an XML shell which allows functions within the programs to be offered as web services. A lighter code-independent approach was developed by Canfora *et al* [24], which wraps only the presentation layer of legacy form-based UI as services. Our work is different from other approaches, in that our goal is not just to provide existing functionality as services but to do so while complying to the service-orientation principles described in Section 2.

8   Conclusion

The main contribution of this work is the definition of a methodology and its technological and functional dimensions, that can be used for multiple types of reengineering projects, including migration towards service-oriented architectures, while having a high level of automation. By making use of techniques such as source code pattern matching and graph transformation, and applying those in the technological and functional dimensions, the result is a concrete process of addressing SOA migration projects in a systematic way. In order to achieve that goal, one requirement that is addressed by the approach is of programming language independence. Wherever possible, abstractions take place in order to achieve this. A clear example is of performing transformations in the model level and only when necessary applying them in the source code. Another very important requirement that is taken into consideration is of scalability. By reducing the model to the elements that are absolutely necessary, as was described in the reverse engineering step, the redesign process is more easily applicable in large scenarios, and it also facilitates the use of model analysis techniques.

A prototype is currently being developed to evaluate this approach at a larger scale and an initial version is already being applied to a small case study. The early tests show that this approach can be put into practice with good results.

Future work will consolidate of the code pattern matching rules for both the technological and functional dimension to achieve a more complete coverage of situations that can be found in legacy applications. This is already being done in parallel with overall improvements in the techniques that will be found when testing more situations and with an evaluation on a larger case study.

Acknowledgments

Thanks to Rui Correia (formerly at ATX II Tecnologias de Software S. A., Portugal) and Dr. Mohammad El-Ramly (Cairo University, Egypt, previously at the University of Leicester, U.K.) for their participation.

References

1. Abrams, C., Schulte, R.W.: Service-oriented architecture overview and guide to SOA research. Technical Report G00154463, Gartner Research (January 2008)
2. Natis, Y.V., Pezzini, M., Schulte, R.W., Iijima, K.: Predicts 2007: SOA advances. Technical Report G00144445, Gartner Research (November 2006)
3. Kazman, R., Woods, S., Carrière, J.: Requirements for integrating software architecture and reengineering models: CORUM II. In: Proceedings of Working Conference on Reverse Engineering (WCRE), pp. 154–163. IEEE Computer Society, Washington, DC (1998)
4. Erl, T.: Service-Oriented Architecture: Concepts, Technology, and Design. Prentice Hall PTR, Upper Saddle River (2005)
5. Mens, T., Demeyer, S., Janssens, D.: Formalising behaviour preserving program transformations. In: Corradini, A., Ehrig, H., Kreowski, H.-J., Rozenberg, G. (eds.) ICGT 2002. LNCS, vol. 2505, pp. 286–301. Springer, Heidelberg (2002)
6. Fowler, M.: Refactoring: Improving the Design of Existing Code. Addison-Wesley, Boston (1999)
7. Heckel, R., Correia, R., Matos, C., El-Ramly, M., Koutsoukos, G., Andrade, L.: Architectural Transformations: From Legacy to Three-tier and Services. In: Software Evolution, pp. 139–170. Springer, Heidelberg (2008)
8. Correia, R., Matos, C., Heckel, R., El-Ramly, M.: Architecture migration driven by code categorization. In: Oquendo, F. (ed.) ECSA 2007. LNCS, vol. 4758, pp. 115–122. Springer, Heidelberg (2007)
9. Koschke, R., Girard, J.F.: An intermediate representation for reverse engineering analyses. In: Proceedings of Working Conference on Reverse Engineering (WCRE), pp. 241–250 (1998)
10. Marcus, A., Sergeyev, A., Rajlich, V., Maletic, J.I.: An information retrieval approach to concept location in source code. In: Proceedings of Working Conference on Reverse Engineering (WCRE), pp. 214–223. IEEE Computer Society, Washington (2004)
11. Antoniol, G., Gueheneuc, Y.G.: Feature identification: A novel approach and a case study. In: Proceedings of International Conference Software Maintenance (ICSM), pp. 357–366. IEEE Computer Society, Washington (2005)
12. W3C: XPath specification, http://www.w3.org/TR/xpath
13. Marin, M., van Deursen, A., Moonen, L.: Identifying aspects using fan-in analysis. In: Proceedings of Working Conference on Reverse Engineering (WCRE), pp. 132–141. IEEE Computer Society, Washington (2004)
14. Eclipse: Eclipse Modeling Framework, http://www.eclipse.org/emf/
15. Tiger EMF Transformer, http://tfs.cs.tu-berlin.de/emftrans/
16. Eisenbarth, T., Koschke, R., Simon, D.: Locating features in source code. IEEE Transactions on Software Engineering 29(3), 210–224 (2003)
17. Jakobac, V., Egyed, A., Medvidović, N.: Improving system understanding via interactive, tailorable, source code analysis. In: Cerioli, M. (ed.) FASE 2005. LNCS, vol. 3442, pp. 253–268. Springer, Heidelberg (2005)

18. Cremer, K., Marburger, A., Westfechtel, B.: Graph-based tools for re-engineering. Journal of Software Maintenance 14(4), 257–292 (2002)
19. Haase, T.: Model-driven service development for a-posteriori application integration. In: Proc. of International Conference on e-Business Engineering (ICEBE), pp. 649–656. IEEE Computer Society, Washington (2007)
20. Ivkovic, I., Kontogiannis, K.: A framework for software architecture refactoring using model transformations and semantic annotations. In: Proceedings of European Conference on Software Maintenance and Reengineering (CSMR), pp. 135–144. IEEE Computer Society, Washington (2006)
21. Fahmy, H., Holt, R.C., Cordy, J.R.: Wins and losses of algebraic transformations of software architectures. In: Proceedings of International Conference on Automated Software Engineering (ASE), pp. 51–60. IEEE Computer Society, Washington (2001)
22. Kiesel, N., Klein, P., Nagl, M., Schmidt, V.: Verteilung in betriebswirtschaftlichen anwendungen: Einige bemerkungen von seiten der softwarearchitektur. In: Jhnichen, S. (ed.) Online 1994 Congress VI, pp. C.620.01–C.620.29 (1994)
23. Sneed, H.: Integrating legacy software into a service oriented architecture. In: Proceedings of European Conference on Software Maintenance and Reengineering (CSMR), pp. 3–14. IEEE Computer Society, Los Alamitos (2006)
24. Canfora, G., Fasolino, A.R., Frattolillo, G., Tramontana, P.: Migrating interactive legacy systems to web services. In: Proceedings of European Conference on Software Maintenance and Reengineering (CSMR), pp. 24–36. IEEE Computer Society, Washington (2006)

The Sensoria Development Environment*

Philip Mayer[1] and István Ráth[2]

[1] Ludwig-Maximilians-Universität München, Germany
[2] Budapest University of Technology and Economics, Hungary
mayer@pst.ifi.lmu.de, rath@mit.bme.hu

Abstract. Developing service-oriented software involves dealing with multiple languages, platforms, artefacts, and tools. The tasks carried out during development are varied as well; ranging from modeling to implementation, from analysis to testing. For many of these tasks, the Sensoria project has provided tools aiding developers in their work – with a specific focus on tools based on rigorous formal verification methods, but also including modeling, transformation, and runtime tools. To enable developers to find, use, and combine these tools, we have created a tool integration platform, the Sensoria Development Environment (SDE), which a) gives an overview of available tools and their area of application, b) allows developers to use tools in a homogeneous way, re-arranging tool functionality as required, and c) enables users to stay on a chosen level of abstraction, hiding formal details as much as possible. In this chapter, we give an in-depth review of the SDE, integrated tools, and ways of using tools in combination for developing and verifying service-oriented software systems.

1   Introduction

The success of the Service-Oriented Architecture (SOA) [3] in both industry and research has resulted in a growing need for tool support for developers of services and service-based systems. Specific support for developing SOA systems is beneficial in all phases of the development process, ranging from modeling to runtime, from analysis to implementation.

The Sensoria project [9] has provided tools and techniques for many of the tasks developers are faced with during the development of SOA systems. A key first result of Sensoria in this context is a set of languages for describing SOA systems, like, for example, the UML profile for services (UML4SOA) [5] and accompanying tool support. However, the main consideration in Sensoria was rigorous engineering of service-oriented systems with a specific focus on formal verification. As our verification and validation methods are often directly based on a formal model, tool support had to be created for allowing developers to use these methods while staying on their chosen level of abstraction – for example, UML. To deal with this issue, Sensoria has investigated model transformations, a concept taken from the model-driven architecture (MDA) community, to ease

---

* This work has been partially sponsored by the project Sensoria, IST-2005-016004.

M. Wirsing and M. Hölzl (Eds.): Sensoria Project, LNCS 6582, pp. 622–639, 2011.

the transition between developer-level models of a SOA system and the formal languages required for verification, with the additional benefit of being able to generate executable code as well. Finally, runtime support for services in the form of dynamic discovery mechanisms requires a broker infrastructure and testing tools which should be accessible during development as well.

Altogether, these considerations have led us to develop a tooling platform, the SENSORIA Development Environment (SDE) [4], which integrates the various tools required in the service development process, including modeling, analysis, code generation, and runtime functionality. The SDE:

1. gives an overview of available tools and their area of application,
2. allows developers to use tools in a homogeneous way, re-arranging tool functionality as required, and
3. enables users to stay on a chosen level of abstraction, hiding formal details as much as possible.

In this chapter, we give an in-depth review of the SDE, integrated tools, and ways of using tools in combination for developing and verifying service-oriented software systems. In section 2, we give a high-level overview of the SDE. Section 3 further details design and implementation of our integration platform. In section 4, we give an overview of tools integrated into the SDE. Section 5 shows examples of how tools can be orchestrated to perform in collaboration. Finally, section 6 concludes the chapter.

2   High-Level Overview

The SENSORIA project aims to support developers of service-oriented software systems at various points in the development process. Specific focus is placed on (formal) verification of service artefacts, which includes appropriate modeling support for developers as well as code generation and runtime support. Through various tools, we are thus able to offer functionality which covers the complete model-driven process of service engineering, which is shown in Fig. 1.

After starting with requirements for a SOA-based system, developers advance to the modeling phase. From this phase, various analyzes of the models may be performed, many of them carried out with the help of automated model transformations. Finally, code is generated from the improved models; runtime support is available for executing this code on various platforms. The figure shows the phases which are covered by tools integrated into the SDE – Modeling, Transformation, Analysis, Code Generation, and Runtime. The following functionality is available in each of these phases:

- **Modeling.** Graphical editors for familiar modeling languages such as UML, which allow intuitive modeling at a high abstraction level, and also text- and tree-based editors for formal languages like process calculi.

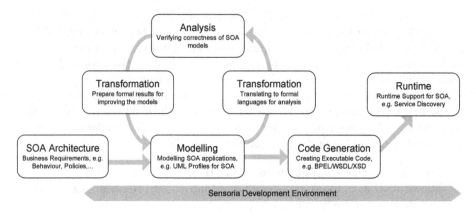

Fig. 1. Development approach

- **Model Transformation Functionality, including Code Generation.**
  Automated model transformations from UML to process calculi and back to
  bridge the gap between these worlds; also, generation of executable code (for
  example, Web Service standards like BPEL).
- **Formal Analysis Functionality.** Model checking and numerical solvers
  for stochastic methods based on process calculi code defined by the user or
  generated by model transformation.
- **Runtime Functionality.** Integration of runtime platforms, for example
  BPEL process engines or the Java runtime as well as runtime support for
  services, for example dynamic service brokering.

The functionality indicated in the previous list is implemented in various tools,
some of which have been developed within SENSORIA, some developed outside
of the project (for a full list of SENSORIA tools, see section 4). The tools are
not only developed at different sites, but are also vastly different with regard to
user interface, functionality, required computing power, execution platform and
programming language. However, all of the tools contribute to the development
process and in many cases deliver artefacts which may serve as input to other
tools.

The SENSORIA Development Environment (SDE) provides this functionality through a carefully designed, lightweight integration architecture. This is
achieved through the following core features:

- **A SOA-based platform.** The SDE itself is based on a Service-Oriented
  Architecture, allowing easy integration of tools and querying the platform
  for available functionality. The tools hosted in the SDE are installed and
  handled as services.
- **A Composition Infrastructure.** As development of services is a highly individual process and may require several steps and iterations, the SDE offers
  a composition infrastructure which allows developers to automate commonly
  used workflows as an orchestration of integrated tools.

- **Hidden Formal Methods.** To allow developers to use formal tools without requiring them to understand the underlying formal semantics, the SDE encourages the use of automated model transformations which translate between high-level models and formal specifications.

As with services in a SOA, tool composition in our integration tool is a lightweight one, i.e., the connection between tools is not a priori fixed and adding additional tools requires only minimal change to the integrated tools. Using the tool-as-a-service metaphor, tools are services, each consisting of functions which can be invoked by the user or other services. Contrary to Web services [8], user interaction is very important for some software development tools. For example, a modeling tool requires a lot of user interaction – ideally, the modeling tool runs on the computer of the user. A model checker, on the other hand, requires a lot of computing power and thus will most likely run on a dedicated server to be accessed remotely with none or only a minimal, generated UI available. Both use cases are supported in the SDE.

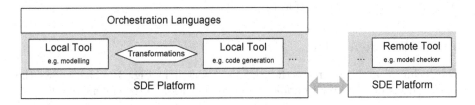

Fig. 2. SDE architecture

By using a SOA-based infrastructure, combining tools into more complex tool chains is straightforward, i.e. possible via dedicated orchestration languages. A typical scenario for tool composition can be found in the analysis and verification of software; for example, model checkers require a certain input format into which most source models first need to be transformed; the same applies to the output. The SDE contains both a textual (JavaScript) and a graphical (UML-based) orchestration language, allowing users to integrate various tools, thereby handling the data flow between these tools. Having encapsulated the integrating steps, they can be run over and over again for performing the same steps with different input and output data.

Finally, the SDE aims at providing formal verification tools to pragmatic developers. This requires, as indicated above, the use of model transformations to allow developers to stay on their chosen level of abstraction while still enjoying the results available through rigorous verification methods. Through tool chaining and the ability to install verification tools remotely, the SDE enables an MDA-like approach to the analysis of service artefacts.

Fig. 2 shows the architecture of the SDE. As discussed previously, the integration platform hosts a number of tools as services. Through its dedicated orchestration infrastructure, the SDE allows developers to orchestrate tools to be used in combination, which includes using model transformations and a remote invocation functionality for invoking tools hosted on different machines.

The next section will introduce the technical details of the SDE implementation.

3   Design and Implementation

The aim of SENSORIA is to support the creation of service-oriented software by augmenting existing development processes and tools. A requirement for the SDE was therefore to integrate with existing tools and platforms for the development of SOA systems. For this reason, the SDE is based on the well-known Eclipse platform [2] and its underlying, service-oriented OSGi [6] framework. OSGI is based on so-called bundles, which are components grouping a set of Java classes and meta-data providing among other things name, description, version, exported and imported packages of the bundle. A bundle may provide arbitrary services to the platform.

3.1   SDE Core and UI

The technical architecture of the SDE is depicted in Fig. 3, which shows the SDE Platform as an OSGi bundle, its dependencies and dependent bundles.

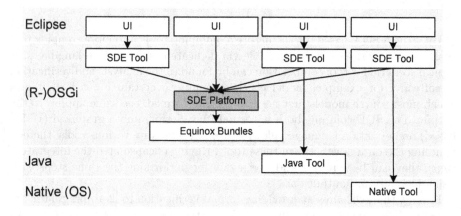

Fig. 3. SDE technical architecture

Fundamentally, all tools are integrated as OSGi bundles which offer certain *functions* for invocation by the platform. As indicated above, the tools integrated into the SDE are vastly different, ranging from user-driven graphical modeling tools to computationally intensive analysis tools with very basic interaction mechanisms. Thus, it is not possible to define a common API for all tools. In the SDE, this problem is solved by using (declarative) OSGi services for each tool. Furthermore, the SDE allows tools to provide their own UI, but also provides a generic invocation mechanism which enables users to invoke arbitrary functions, either directly or through an orchestration. Finally, tool integration requirements should be kept low to ensure integration of as many tools as possible. The SDE re-uses OSGi and Eclipse technology and declarative service descriptions which are generated from Java annotations for a fast and straightforward integration process.

As can be seen in Fig. 3, the SDE platform and the integrated tools are based on (R-)OSGi only (or, more specifically, the Equinox implementation of OSGi [1]). This means that fundamentally, tools must be implemented in Java, although they may wrap native code or remote invocations as they wish. Being only based on OSGi, they can be invoked completely independently from Eclipse. If they additionally choose to provide a UI, this UI is integrated into and based on the Eclipse platform, as is the UI for the SDE platform itself.

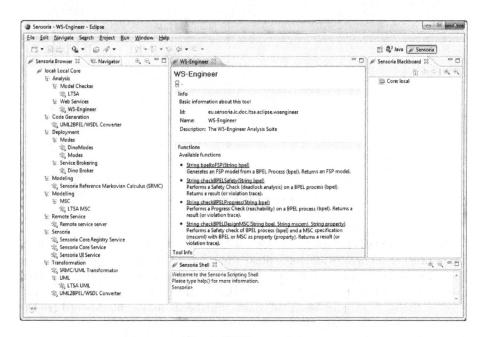

Fig. 4. SDE screenshot

Fig. 4 shows a screenshot of the SDE UI. On the left hand side, the tool browser shows installed tools available for invocation and automation. Tools are grouped by category, allowing quick access by application area. Double-clicking a tool in the browser yields more information about the tool and its functionality. This information is shown in the view in the middle: As an example, an integrated tool for qualitative analysis (WS-Engineer) is shown in more detail. Each tool function displayed here can be invoked by clicking the link and providing the parameters. Finally, on the right, the SENSORIA Blackboard is shown, which is a storage area where tools may place arbitrary objects for later use. Finally, at the bottom, the SENSORIA Shell is displayed, which is a live JavaScript execution environment (see section 3.2).

As an example for a function invocation, clicking on the `bpelToFSP()` function in the WS-Engineer tool yields the following dialogs, where the data for the single parameter (`bpel`) can be selected from various sources (Fig. 5).

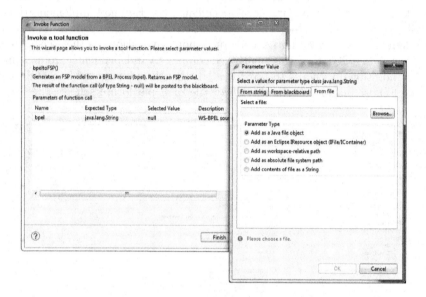

Fig. 5. SDE wizard

Finally, the SDE core integrates with R-OSGi [7] to provide the ability to host tools for external invocation, and connect to remote SDE cores. The tools in the tool view in Fig. 4 (left), for example, are listed under the local core. Further (remote) cores may be added as required, and their tools are then listed and used in the same way as described above. Furthermore, the blackboard (right) also distinguishes between the various cores.

3.2   Composing Tools

The SDE provides the ability to compose new tools out of existing ones, a process known as orchestration in the SOA world. Creating orchestrations is possible using two mechanisms: A textual, JavaScript-based approach, and a graphical, UML-activity-diagram-like workflow approach.

Orchestrating with JavaScript. The ability to use tool APIs directly within JavaScript enables developers to create a workflow by simply invoking tool functions and passing data in-between those functions. To enable the newly created workflow to be usable as a tool in its own right, two things are required: Instead of simply creating a workflow, a JavaScript function definition is required which states a function name and parameters. As each tool, function, parameters, and return types may have descriptions and additional meta-data attached, this meta-data must be specified in some way in the JavaScript source files. Both points have been addressed in the SDE. The first is simple; function definitions are already part of the JavaScript specification. The second was solved by employing a JavaDoc-comment-style approach to meta-data specification. Tags like @description are used to convey meta-data information.

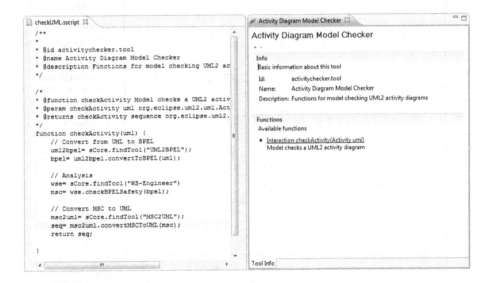

Fig. 6. Orchestration with JavaScript

As an example, Fig. 6 (left) shows a script for converting UML2 activity diagrams to BPEL, then analyzing them using the WS-Engineer tool, and finally converting the result back to UML2 sequence diagrams showing the error trace. Fig. 6 (right) shows the converted tool inside the SDE tool browser. Scripts created like this can be used on any SDE installation which has the required tools installed. No particular deployment is necessary save copying the script and registering it with the core.

For testing purposes, the SDE also contains a JavaScript live execution environment, the SDE Shell (Fig. 4), where JavaScript commands can be executed without compiling a complete script.

Graphical Orchestration. Besides the ability to use JavaScript for orchestration as indicated above, the SDE also contains the ability to orchestrate tools graphically. The syntax used is that of UML2 activity diagrams, where the main focus is on data flow, i.e. the flow of information from pin to pin. An activity in the diagram represents one function in the tool to be generated which has input pins (parameters) and one output pin (return type). Inside the activity, actions represent function calls to arbitrary (installed) tools. These actions have pins themselves; data flow edges model the data transfer.

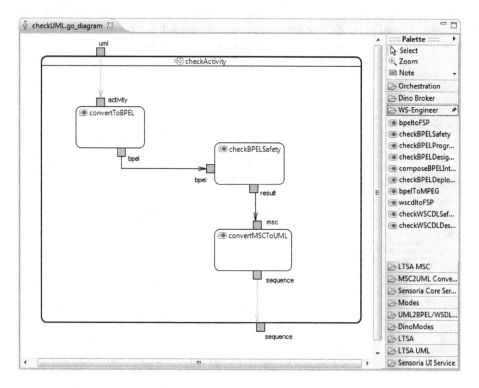

Fig. 7. Graphical orchestration

As an example, consider the screenshot in Fig. 7, which shows the orchestration introduced in the previous paragraph as a graphical workflow, including the editor which supports it. The function checkActivity(uml) is modeled as an UML2 activity, and each call to a particular function of an installed tool is modeled as an action. On the right-hand side, the toolbar shows all available tools and the functions they provide. Once modeled, an orchestration such as the one above is converted to a Java class, compiled in-memory and installed as a tool in the SDE.

3.3   Extending the Platform

The SOA-based architecture of the SDE makes it easy to add new tools – the SDE publishes a core API and an extension point for registering tools. Basically, each tool is an OSGi bundle with some published API and meta-data XML to register the tool with the SDE core. Thus, creating a facade class and registering the class with the SDE extension point enables tool functionality to be immediately available within the SDE, both for manual invocation and automation. Tools within the SDE are loosely coupled, as they are fundamentally independent from each other and interact through their published service interfaces only. They may, of course, require other tools to be installed for them to work. This is defined in a declarative way through the Equinox extension mechanism and checked by the platform prior to tool installation. The SDE core also contains a set of Java 5 annotations, which enable tool developers to define their tools and functions without writing any XML. As an example, consider Fig. 8: On the left-hand side, a tool interface with SDE annotations is shown; on the right-hand side, the corresponding tool view in the SDE.

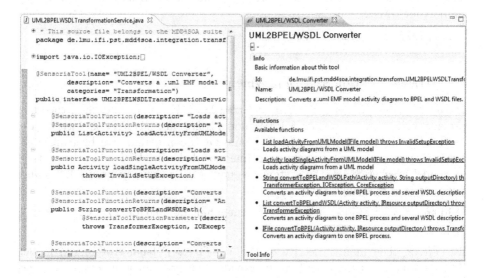

Fig. 8. SDE tool registration

The API defined within the integration tool service bundle provides access to all installed tools. A tool may use this API to verify installation of required tools; search for tools based on meta-data, and invoke functionality as needed. Therefore, it serves as a discovery service which moderates between the tools. Once the connection has been made, communication between tools is done directly.

4   Integrated Tools

This section lists all tools which have been integrated into the SDE platform, sorted by integrated category.

4.1   Modeling

ArgoUML. ArgoUML is an open source UML modeling tool which includes support for all standard UML 1.4 diagrams.

> http://argouml.tigris.org/

Rational Software Architect. Rational Software Architect is a UML modeling tool which supports UML2.0 profiles and is built on the Eclipse platform.

> http://www.ibm.com/software/awdtools/architect/swarchitect/

MagicDraw. MagicDraw is a platform independent UML modeler with profile support for UML2.

> http://www.magicdraw.com/

4.2   Transformation and Deployment

Hugo/RT. Hugo/RT is a UML model translator for model checking, theorem proving, and code generation: A UML model containing active classes with state machines, collaborations, interactions, and OCL constraints can be translated into the system languages of the real-time model checker UPPAAL, the on-the-fly model checker SPIN, the system language of the theorem prover KIV, and into Java and SystemC code.

> http://www.pst.informatik.uni-muenchen.de/projekte/hugo/

VIATRA2. The main objective of the VIATRA2 (VIsual Automated model TRAnsformations) framework is to provide a general-purpose support for the entire life-cycle of engineering model transformations including the specification, design, execution, validation and maintenance of transformations within and between various modeling languages and domains.

> http://wiki.eclipse.org/VIATRA2

SOA2WSDL-Transformation. The SOA2WSDL transformation, written in VIATRA2, takes high level UML models and produces WSDL (Web Services Description language) output.

> http://viatra.inf.mit.bme.hu/

SRMC/UML Bridge. The SRMC/UML bridge offers facilities for meta-model transformation. It translates a subset of UML2 models (Interactions and State Machines) into an SRMC description for performance evaluation. Results are reflected back into the UML model.

http://groups.inf.ed.ac.uk/srmc/

UML2PEPA Transformation. The UML2PEPA transformation, written in VI-ATRA2, takes high level UML models and produces PEPA models used for analysis in the PEPA/SRMC tool.

http://viatra.inf.mit.bme.hu/

Modes Parser and Browser. The Modes Parser and Browser is a WS-Engineer plug-in to parse and extract broker requirements from UML2 Modes Models.

http://www.doc.ic.ac.uk/ltsa/eclipse/wsengineer

4.3   Analysis

LTSA. LTSA is a verification tool for concurrent systems. It checks that the specification of a concurrent system satisfies the properties required of its behavior. In addition, LTSA supports specification animation to facilitate interactive exploration of system behavior.

http://www.doc.ic.ac.uk/ltsa/

WS-Engineer. The LTSA WS-Engineer plug-in is an extension to the LTSA Eclipse Plug-in which allows service models to be described by translation of the service process descriptions, and can be used to perform model-based verification of Web service compositions.

http://www.doc.ic.ac.uk/ltsa/eclipse/wsengineer/

SRMC Core. SRMC (SENSORIA Reference Markovian Calculus) Core provides support for SRMC, an extension to PEPA. It covers steady-state analysis of the underlying Markov chain of SRMC descriptions.

http://groups.inf.ed.ac.uk/srmc/

MDD4SOA Protocol Analysis. The MDD4SOA Protocol Analysis Tool verifies protocol compliance of services modeled in UML4SOA given a protocol state machine. The verification yields a violation graph in case of an error.

http://www.mdd4soa.eu/

SPIN. Spin is a model checker that can be used for the formal verification of distributed software systems.

http://spinroot.com/

UPPAAL. Uppaal is an integrated tool environment for modeling, validation and verification of real-time systems modeled as networks of timed automata, extended with data types (bounded integers, arrays, etc.).

http://www.uppaal.com/

CMC / UMC. CMC and UMC are model checkers and analyzers for systems defined by interacting UML state charts. Both allow on-the-fly model checking of abstract behavioral properties in the Socl branching-time state-action based, parametric temporal logic.

http://fmt.isti.cnr.it/cmc/,http://fmt.isti.cnr.it/umc/

LySa tool. LySa is a static analyzer for security protocols defined in the LYSA process calculus. The tool provides a LYSA editor and analyzer, the latter of which will verify properties related to secrecy and authentication.

http://www2.imm.dtu.dk/cs_LySa/lysatool/

4.4   Deployment and Runtime

MDD4SOA Transformers. The MDD4SOA transformers are a set of EMF transformers for converting UML4SOA models into target languages. Supported are BPEL/WSDL, Java, and Jolie.

http://www.mdd4soa.eu/

UML2AXIS Transformation. The UML2AXIS transformation, written in VIATRA2, takes high level UML models and produces Web service code based on the Apache Axis Java library.

http://viatra.inf.mit.bme.hu/

Dino Broker. The Dino Broker provides dynamic runtime discovery of services which are described in OWL and WSDL documents, thus enabling developers to bind services which correspond to specific criteria.

http://www.cs.ucl.ac.uk/staff/a.mukhija/dino/

5   Tool Applications

The tools listed in the previous section can be combined in various ways to achieve different transformations and analyzes. Fig. 9 lists, non-exhaustively, the links between the tools.

As examples, we provide three scenarios with different tools to give some insights into how tools have been chained together within the SENSORIA project. In the following sections, we use four paragraphs to describe each scenario:

- **Use Case** describes when and why to use a certain tool chain.
- In **Tools Involved**, we list the tools required to perform the functionality of the scenario.
- **Data Flow** shows the individual steps to be executed in the tool chain.
- Finally, **Results** describes the consequences and benefits of the scenario.

The tool chains may be realized manually, i.e. with the user performing one step after another and storing the intermediate objects on disk or on the blackboard, or automatically by employing the JavaScript orchestrator or the graphical orchestration mechanism.

5.1   Checking and Deploying Dervice Orchestrations

Use Case. Using a model-driven approach for developing software has been advocated for some time. SENSORIA addresses this area with a customized UML profile for modeling services and service orchestrations. Besides modeling the orchestration implementation itself, a behavioral protocol can help to assess the external behavior of the orchestration and used to verify the actual implementation. Once a service orchestration has been verified, it needs to be transformed to code in target languages like BPEL or Java to deploy it for execution.

Tools Involved. This tool chain includes a UML modeler with profile support, like MagicDraw or Rational Software Architect. A protocol analysis tool (part of MDD4SOA) is used to report on protocol violations. Finally, model transformers (also part of MDD4SOA) are used to transform the UML specifications to code in executable languages (for example, BPEL and WSDL) for deployment.

Data Flow. The chain starts with the user who employs a UML modeler to design both the orchestration implementation and the service protocol. The resulting diagrams are saved as documents in the XMI format. These files can then be used by the MDD4SOA Protocol Analyzer, which either reports no protocol violations or creates a violation trace. This process is repeated until the process is error-free. Finally, the UML2 models are read by the MDD4SOA Transformers, which generate the appropriate target code, depending on which language has been selected by the user.

Results. Chaining tools together in this fashion enables the developer to quickly react to changes in requirements, as the chain can be run automatically whenever a change has occurred, either informing the user of newly introduced problems in the protocol or, if the protocol is valid, with the new implementation in the selected target language.

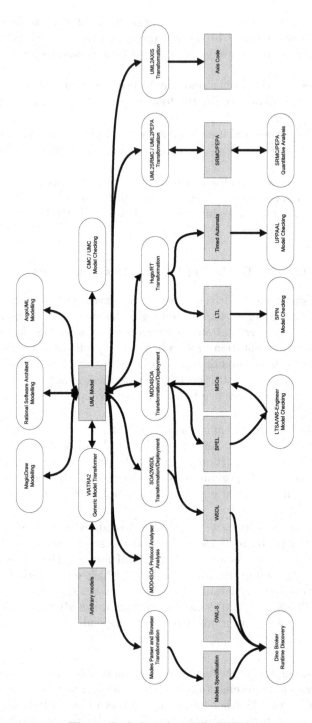

Fig. 9. Tool chaining in the SDE

5.2   Qualitative and Quantitative Analysis

Use Case. Service-oriented software systems are commonly distributed – they make use of a network to combine various individual software components to work in coordination to reach a higher-level goal. In general, a SOA system contains many different threads of execution, which run in parallel and interact with one another in nontrivial ways. This poses a difficult problem to software designers, as the interaction of such threads needs to be analyzed in order to ensure that no undesirable effects (such as deadlocks) occur. Furthermore, it is not always clear how the system time is spent during runtime. Therefore, mechanical checkers are needed to verify whether a certain implementation is free from conditions such as deadlocks, and secondly for assessing the runtime characteristics of the overall system.

Tools Involved. Again, we employ UML modelers like Rational Software Architect or MagicDraw for the modeling of a service-oriented system written in UML. Based on these models, quantitative analysis as well as qualitative analysis is then performed by the SRMC tool and the WS-Engineer tool, respectively. While the former is able to deal with UML directly, the latter requires the BPEL format as input, so we bring in another tool (one of the MDD4SOA transformers) for converting between UML and BPEL.

Data Flow. The chain starts with the user who employs a UML modeler to design a model of communicating systems in UML2. The resulting model, in the format of an UML2 XMI file, can be read directly by the SRMC tool to report on the distribution of time spent in the various states of the process. Using the MDD4SOA transformers, the UML2 model is converted to BPEL to serve as input for WS-Engineer, which is used to verify the required properties (for example, freeness from dead-locks). Finally, the result of the analysis is shown to the user: The quantitative analysis can be directly annotated to the original UML model (or output as graphs), the qualitative analysis – if resulting in an error trace – is shown as Message Sequence Charts (MSCs) or UML2 sequence diagrams.

Results. This tool chain provides the user with a "one-click" verification of the model – instead of requiring the user, as is common in many verification tools, to activate a translation of service implementations, feed the translation through a model parser, compile the model, and invoke a verify option on the model checker. All these single steps are handled by the tool chain and the script used to combine the two different analyzers. Thus, checking becomes less of a hassle and will be executed more often, resulting in higher-quality systems.

5.3   Modes-Based Dynamic Runtime Discovery

Use Case. One of the promises of the Service-Oriented Architecture is the ability to quickly react to changes, for example – on the business level – a change of a business partner, or – on a technical level – network connection problems or server overload. To deal with these problems, the concept of dynamic service discovery and binding has been introduced, which enables developers to specify, on an abstract level, the properties and constraints required of certain services needed by an orchestration. Specification of such properties, the criteria of when to change the service to be used (specified by "modes"), and testing of the resulting runtime behavior are non-trivial issues, and tool support is needed to make such approaches practical.

Tools Involved. The main focus of this tool chain lies on testing of dynamic service discovery, hence the most important tool is the Dino Broker used for service discovery. Serving input to Dino is the Modes Parser and Browser Tool which handles translation of modes from the UML2 models. Dino also requires WSDL and OWL documents for service specification which can, in part, be generated by the VIATRA2 SOA2WSDL transformation tool. Again, the initial mode specification is done in UML2, for which a UML2 modeler is required.

Data Flow. The chain starts with the user who employs a UML modeler to design a model of a SOA system enhanced with mode specifications and the required constraints on services. The Modes Parser and Browser Tool is then used to convert these specifications to input for the Dino Broker. In parallel, the services to be discovered are deployed to the Dino runtime, either from pre-existing OWL/WSDL specifications or from those generated by the SOA2WSDL transformation. Finally, the developer can employ the Dino Broker front-end which is available through the SDE to test-drive the service discovery, and once satisfied, use the generated documents for the final implementation.

Results. The ability to generate input for Dino from UML2 and test-driving the discovery right from within the development environment greatly speeds up the process of finding the right mode and constraint specifications. Automation allows writing test cases for the complete process, thus the user may change the specifications at the beginning of the chain and verify the output stemming from an actual discovery run with the Dino Broker, thus saving time and effort in debugging.

6   Conclusion

In this chapter, we have discussed the need for, requirements of, implementation, and usage of a tool integration platform for the development of service-oriented software systems, the SENSORIA Development Environment (SDE). Based on a service-oriented architecture itself, the SDE contains tools for modeling and analyzing service artefacts as well as generating code and supporting services at runtime, allows remote invocation of tool functionality, and enables composition of tools by a textual and graphical orchestration mechanism. Furthermore, we have discussed integrated tools providing support for the development of SOA software, and have outlined how to use tools in combination on top of the SDE.

We believe that thinking of individual development tools as services and including SOA features like self-describing services, remote invocation, and orchestration into our tooling environment greatly extends the applicability of the integrated tools. By including transformation tools, we ensure that using analysis tools is possible without understanding the details of the underlying formal specifications, thus allowing more developers to profit from rigorous verification of their systems.

The SDE, including the integrated tools, is available for download at our dedicated tooling website, `http://svn.pst.ifi.lmu.de/trac/sct`. The website also contains a tutorial for tool integration and videos demonstrating the SDE in action.

References

1. Eclipse Foundation. Eclipse Equinox - Implementation of the OSGi R4 core framework specification (2009), `http://www.eclipse.org/`
2. Eclipse Foundation. The Eclipse Open Source Community and Java IDE (2009), `http://eclipse.org/equinox/`
3. Erl, T.: Service-Oriented Architecture: Concepts, Technology, and Design. Prentice Hall International, Englewood Cliffs (2005)
4. Mayer, P., Ráth, I., Horváth, Á.: Report on the Sensoria Development Environment - Second Version. Technical report, LMU München (2008)
5. Mayer, P., Schroeder, A., Koch, N.: MDD4SOA: Model-Driven Service Orchestration. In: The 12th IEEE International EDOC Conference (EDOC 2008), Munich, Germany, pp. 203–212. IEEE Computer Society Press, Los Alamitos (2008)
6. OSGi Alliance. Osgi specification release 4 (March 2008), `http://www.osgi.org/Specifications/`
7. Rellermeyer, J.S., Alonso, G., Roscoe, T.: R-OSGi: distributed applications through software modularization. In: Cerqueira, R., Pasquale, F. (eds.) Middleware 2007. LNCS, vol. 4834, pp. 1–20. Springer, Heidelberg (2007)
8. Weerawarana, S., Curbera, F., Leymann, F., Storey, T., Ferguson, D.F.: Web Services Platform Architecture: SOAP, WSDL, WS-Policy, WS-Addressing, WS-BPEL, WS-Reliable Messaging and More. Prentice Hall PTR, Upper Saddle River (2005)
9. Wirsing, M., Bocchi, L., Clark, A., Fiadeiro, J., Gilmore, S., Hölzl, M., Koch, N., Mayer, P., Pugliese, R., Schroeder, A.: Sensoria: Engineering for service-oriented overlay computers. In: Nitto, E.D., Sassen, A.-M., Traverso, P., Zwegers, A. (eds.) At Your Service: Service-Oriented Computing from an EU Perspective, pp. 159–182. MIT Press, Cambridge (2009)

Specification and Implementation of Demonstrators for the Case Studies*

Jannis Elgner[1], Stefania Gnesi[2], Nora Koch[3,4], and Philip Mayer[3]

[1] S & N AG, Germany
jelgner@s-und-n.de
[2] Istituto di Scienza e Tecnologie dell'Informazione "A. Faedo"
ISTI–CNR, Pisa, Italy
gnesi@isti.cnr.it
[3] Ludwig-Maximilians-Universität München, Germany
{kochn,mayer}@pst.ifi.lmu.de
[4] Cirquent GmbH, Germany

Abstract. A main challenge in SENSORIA has been the inclusion of case studies from different industrial and academic application areas, namely finance, automotive, telecommunications, and university administration. The case studies, along with a short description of available scenarios, have already been introduced in Chapter 0-3. In this chapter, we go into more detail, presenting the (graphical) specifications for selected scenarios by using the modeling approaches introduced in SENSORIA. Furthermore, we detail the implementation of demonstrators for some of the case studies.

1 Introduction

The partners of the SENSORIA project have used realistic case studies for feeding and steering the research process according to the expectations of society and its economy, discussing and communicating ideas among partners and communicating research results to and getting feedback from the research community at large. These case studies have already been shortly introduced in Chapter 0-3. Each of the scenarios presented has been employed by different partners with different requirements, methods, and tools as a test bed for demonstrating the feasibility and effectiveness of the use of the SENSORIA results.

In this chapter, we present some of the scenarios in more detail. We select three scenarios from the case studies which have been extensively used in the project with the application of research results and tools. For two of the scenarios, namely finance and eUniversity, we provide an extended description by using the graphical modeling languages used or introduced in SENSORIA, namely the UML extensions UML4SOA [3] and the upcoming OMG standard SoaML [4]. For the automotive case study, we present a demonstrator, i.e., the software resulting

---

* This work has been partially sponsored by the project SENSORIA, IST-2005-016004.

M. Wirsing and M. Hölzl (Eds.): SENSORIA Project, LNCS 6582, pp. 640–654, 2011.

from applying the SENSORIA development approach to the development of a SOA system.

The following three sections each present one of the scenarios; starting with Finance, moving on to Automotive, and finally discussing eUniversity. We conclude in Sect. 5.

2   Finance Case Study: Credit Request Scenario

The *CreditRequest* scenario [1] from the finance domain models the loan approval workflow of a bank: A customer intends to lend some money, i.e. request a credit. During the process of approving or disapproving the credit request process, the customer must provide some input (like balances and securities), and the bank must either automatically or via human intervention approve or decline the request. A *risk rating* determines most of the decisions during this process, for example, whether a credit request is approved at all, and whether it can be approved automatically.

This scenario has been modeled in SENSORIA with a combination of *SoaML* and *UML4SOA* elements, and has been implemented using model transformations to BPEL and WSDL code. In this section, we introduce parts of the model for the *CreditRequest* scenario.

Fig. 1 shows the static system structure of the scenario. The main process, shown in the middle and implemented as an orchestration, is the *CreditRequest*, which provides its services through the *CreditManagementService* port. *Rating* is another orchestration which the *CreditRequest* participant uses to calculate the rating. The services of *Rating* itself are provided through the *RatingService* port (left of the *Rating* participant).

The other participants are atomic services performing tasks like calculating ratings, storing data, and interacting with the user.

– The *Portal* services, both provider and consumer, are services concerned with user interaction. They are implemented as a set of web pages which handle communication with the customer and the bank employees through different frontends.
– The *CustomerManagement* service provides an interface to the customer database for identifying customers.
– For analysing input data from the customer, the two services *SecurityAnalysis* and *BalanceAnalysis* are used.
– Finally, the *RatingCalculator* service is used to calculate the actual risk rating.

The entire workflow implemented in the *CreditRequest* and *Rating* orchestrations has been defined with the help of the UML4SOA UML extension, and used as input to verification tools and for generating code. Due to the size of the process it is not possible to show every part here; we therefore have to content ourself with the overview of the behavior of the *CreditRequest* process as shown in Fig. 2.

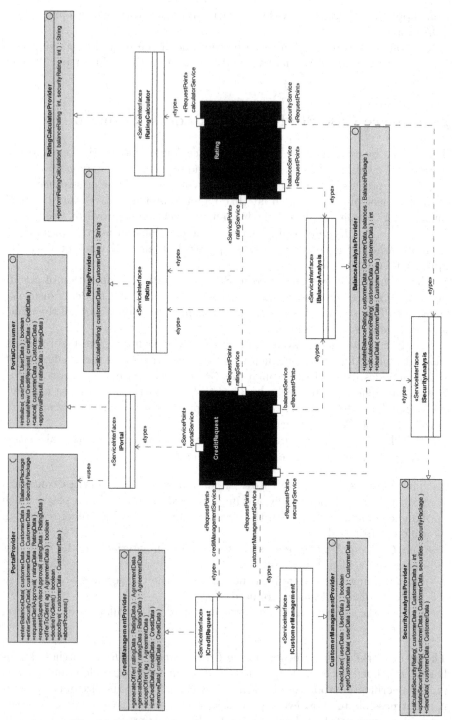

Fig. 1. The Static Structure of the CreditRequestScenario

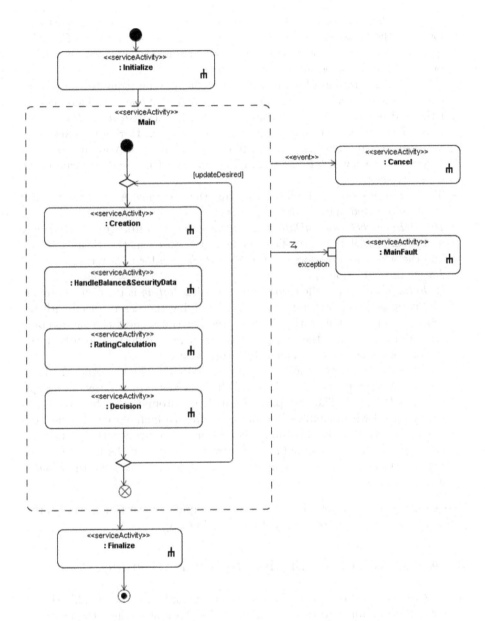

Fig. 2. The behavioral specification of the CreditRequest scenario

The process is further subdivided into individual service activities which we shall describe now.

- The *Initialize* service activity is used to bootstrap the service. A customer logs into the website, which leads to a call from the portal to the *CreditRequest* orchestration. The credentials of the customer are verified and, in the positive case, he is logged in to the system.
- We are then entering a loop in which a credit may be requested more than once by the same user with a changing amount of money or different securities and balances. The loop contains four activities: *Creation*, *HandleBalance&SecurityData*, *RatingCalculation*, and *Decision*. During the execution, an event may occur (*Cancel*), which aborts the process. Also, an exception might be thrown which is handled in *MainFault* and also leads to termination of the process.
- The *Creation* scope deals with initializing the workflow: A request for a new credit is received and the data initialized.
- *HandleBalance&SecurityData* handles the upload and storage of the balances and securities of the user. The balances are stored in the *BalanceService* and the securities are stored in the *SecurityService* for later retrieval by the *Rating* orchestration.
- In *RatingCalculation*, the second orchestration *Rating* is invoked to provide the main workflow with a risk rating, identifying the risk involved with the requested credit. This rating implies whether the request can be accepted automatically. If not, the rating implies whether the decision can be made by a clerk or has to be escalated to a supervisor.
- The *Decision* activity handles the process of deciding first whether the bank accepts the credit request, and second allows the customer to review, accept, or reject the offer. The first part, if not done automatically, involves a call to the portal which enables the corresponding bank employee to review the credit request and give his input. The second also involves the portal; this time the customer is notified and can review an offer on the website.
- If the customer has accepted an offer, or is no longer interested, the *Finalize* activity cleans up and ends the process.

The *CreditRequest* scenario has been used as input for the formal verification tools in SENSORIA. This is described in detail in Chapter 7-4.

3   Automotive Case Study: On Road Assistance

In the *OnRoadAssistance* scenario from the automotive case study [2,5] the vehicle reacts to a failure in the car engine. Such an event triggers the in-vehicle diagnostic system to perform an analysis of the sensor values. The diagnostic system reports e.g. a problem with the pressure in one cylinder head, indicating that the driver will not be able to reach the planned destination. The necessary reactions to this report are handled in a service-oriented way by means of an orchestration.

Like the finance scenario from the last section, the *OnRoadAssistance* scenario has been modeled with a combination of the *SoaML* and *UML4SOA* extensions to the UML. Fig. 3 shows the orchestration of services for the *OnRoadAssistance* participant. See Chapter 1-1 for further details of both the static structure and the dynamic behavior of this scenario, which we will not repeat here. Instead, we discuss the *implementation* of a *demonstrator* for the scenario on the technical basis of web services, which is achieved by means of automated model transformations based on other results of the SENSORIA project.

The main goal of the automotive demonstrator [5] is to show the power of the SENSORIA development approach based on the application of model-driven architecture (MDA) principles in the area of service-oriented computing. Following the model-driven approach, an implementation is created by the construction of models and model transformations. The demonstrator shows how this model-driven development process which automatically generates and deploys a service based on a model of the composition of services works in practice.

The automotive demonstrator for the *OnRoadAssistance* scenario is built as a web application: On the client side, only a fully JavaScript enabled web browser is needed. The business logic, specified as a service orchestration, is deployed on the server side. On the server, the application uses the following three tier architecture (see also Fig. 4).

Presentation Layer. The ViewManager in the presentation layer is a component developed to parse the client request, to call the service orchestration and generate web pages for the client.

Business Logic Layer. The business logic is located in the second layer. The main component is a BPEL process which is in charge of the service orchestration. Several local or remote web services can be called by the BPEL process. A special service is used for the invocation of a broker for dynamically identifying partner services (we use the broker Dino, which has been developed within SENSORIA).

Database Layer. A database lies in the third layer, i.e., the persistence layer. The database contains all data needed by the services.

The Automotive Demonstrator implements the *OnRoadAssistance* scenario [2]. In order to keep the scenario simple, the demonstrator is limited to localizing garage and rental car station services, but this can be easily extended e.g. to identify as well a towing service, providing the GPS data of the stranded vehicle in case the vehicle is no longer drivable.

The services involved in the implementation of the *OnRoadAssistance* are the following:

- A *Position Service* providing the GPS data of the stranded vehicle
- A *Bank Service* for charging a credit card
- *Garage Services* for localizing and selecting garages
- *Rental Car Services* for localizing and selecting car rental stations

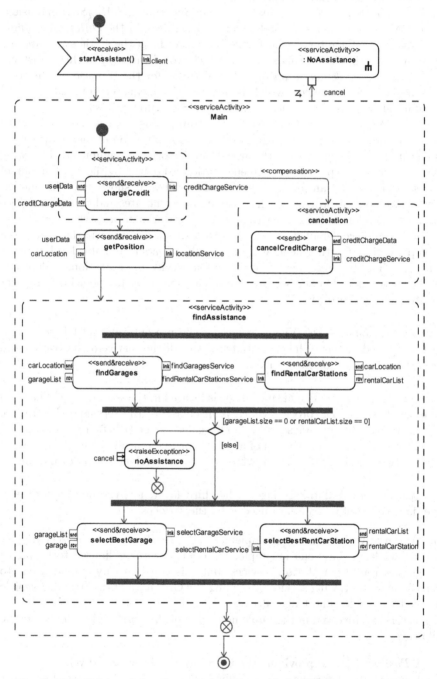

Fig. 3. UML4SOA activity diagram showing the OnRoadAssistance participant

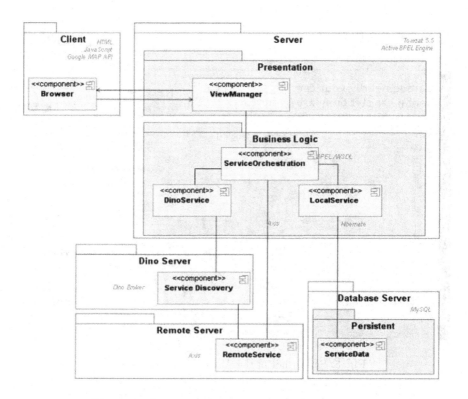

Fig. 4. Architecture of the automotive demonstrator

For demonstration purposes, two models of the same process are built, showing the benefits of the model-driven approach by later switching between them.

The first model is built as the sequential orchestration of the required services for a) determining the car position, b) finding garages in the vicinity of the car and selecting the most convenient garage, and c) finding rental car stations nearby and selecting one. The orchestration process finishes with the credit card charge service. Using a chain of model transformations, the model is transformed to an executable service implemented in BPEL and deployed to an appropriate application server. Model transformations and deployment are performed in a fully automatic way.

The automotive demonstrator is designed in such a way that the invocation of each service is visualized in a web browser and expects a user interaction, almost all just a click on a continue button. In fact, the position of the car, asset of garages and car rentals nearby the car position, and then the selected garage and car rental station are visualized using the Google maps API (see Fig. 5). For the implementation of the interactions and the visualisation, dynamically generated web pages are associated to each service, and the BPEL process is enriched with additional interactive features by a complementary model transformation.

Fig. 5. Screenshot of the Automotive Demonstrator

The power of the model-driven development approach is shown by a second run of the generation that consists of changing the orchestration model shown in Fig. 3. The changes are twofold: First, the credit charge service is invoked at the beginning of the process instead of at the end, and second, the localisation of garages and rental car stations as well as the selection of the most appropriate garage and rental car station are parallelized (see Fig. 5).

The process of generating the automotive demonstrator was implemented using the SENSORIA Development Environment (SDE), which is an Eclipse-based framework for the integration and use of the tools developed in the project for the analysis and development of service-oriented software. The model transformations and deployment are performed automatically with the same tool chain that was implemented for this purpose in the SDE (see Fig. 6). For further details on SDE the reader is referred to Chapter 6-5.

The basic transformation from SoaML and UML4SOA to BPEL and WSDL is performed by using a first transformer from the MDD4SOA suite [3]. Additional model-to-model and model-to-code transformers of MDD4SOA have been introduced to handle user interactions and automatic deployment of a web application onto a web application server. The first additional model transformation is needed to provide BPEL and WSDL code that is executable by a specific BPEL engine (in our case, ActiveBPEL). The second model transformation is needed to allow user interactions and to visualize results step by step during the

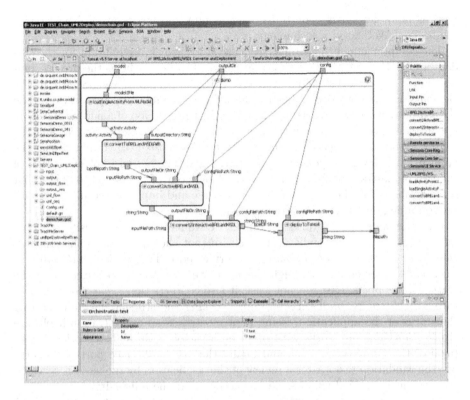

Fig. 6. SDE tool chain for the model-driven development

demonstration. The third one is used to deploy the resulting web application. Note that the model transformations are independent of the scenario, even more they are independent of the BPEL/WSDL application, i.e. they are generic and reusable for other services modeled as orchestration of other services.

4   eUniversity Case Study: Student Application

In the *StudentApplication* scenario of the eUniversity case study, students may apply for a certain course of studies at a university online, providing the necessary documents and certificates via a website. The functionality for handling applications is provided by service orchestrations which make use of a number of atomic services like the student office service, an admission checking service, and a service for the upload of documents to perform their task.

In the following, we detail the model of the *StudentApplication* scenario. Again, we employ the UML modeling language with the additional profiles SoaML [4] and UML4SOA [3] presented in Chapter 1-1. Like the other scenarios presented in the last sections, the student application scenario has been

used as input for verification tools in SENSORIA and has been implemented on
the basis of Web Service technology.

The components of the eUniversity case study which are relevant for the student application scenario are shown in Fig. 7. The figure shows the overall composition of the SOA system modeled as a UML class diagram using SoaML model elements. Each of our two orchestrations offers or requires multiple services: The *ApplicationCreator* is invoked by the client for the creation of a new application, but invokes several other services as well, such as the *ValidationService* and the *StatusService*. The objective of the *ApplicationValidator* is to verify whether the application follows the policies of the university. The actual implementation of the two orchestrations further refines the behaviour of this scenario. The other services, including the client service, are atomic and implemented in a standard programming language (for example, in Java).

Overall, the scenario works as follows: A student uses the website to apply for a certain course of studies. The website (not shown) contacts the *ApplicationCreator* through its *creationService* service port. The *ApplicationCreator*, in turn, calls other entities through the *uploadService*, the *officeService*, and the *statusService* ports. Last but not least, it also contacts the *ApplicationValidator* through the *validationService* port for checking the student data and setting the status of the application. Being implemented as an orchestration itself, the *ApplicationValidator* works with other entities too – through the *officeService* (again), the *admissionService*, and finally the *decisionService* ports – to carry out the validation task. After a review of the application by the various services, the student is notified whether he was accepted at the university.

The two processes *ApplicationCreator* and *ApplicationValidator* from Fig. 7 are modeled as UML4SOA orchestrations. The first one is shown in Fig. 8. It illustrates how the creator interacts with its partners through ports. It starts with a receipt of the call *newApplication* through the *creationService* service port, receiving the application. After the receipt of this call, the *StatusService* and the *UploadService* are initialized, and the initial call is returned. Completing the initialisation phase, the *startValidation* call is sent to the *ApplicationValidator* to request the start of the validation. After having done so, the process waits for another call from the client. The student will either press the button to complete the application, or another one to cancel it.

If a *cancelApplication* call is received, the validation service is instructed to cancel the validation, and the status service is notified that the application has been canceled. If, on the other hand, the student chose to complete the application, the uploaded documents are retrieved from the *uploadService* and a final validation is requested from the *ApplicationValidator*, using the *completeValidation* call. If the result is okay, the student is registered at the *StudentOffice* with *registerStudent*. In any case, the initial call is replied to.

Besides the normal flow of the activity, the diagram also shows a second structured activity node – a compensation handler. The actions defined within *CompensationHandler* are executed if the main activity has been completed successfully, but needs to be undone. This functionality can be triggered externally

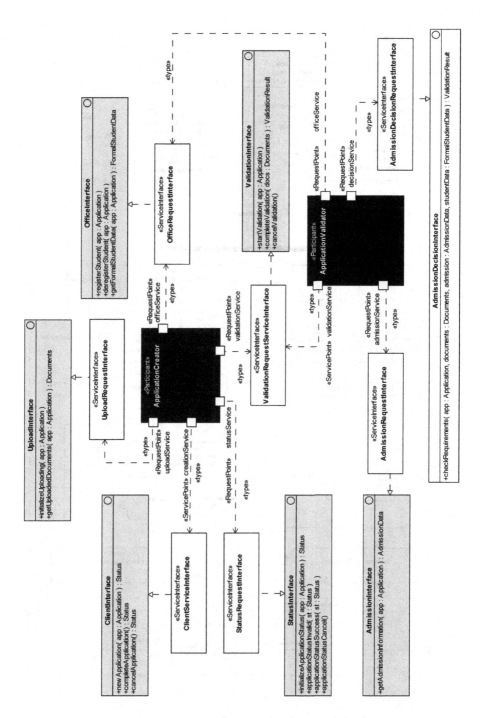

Fig. 7. The eUniversity StudentApplication scenario

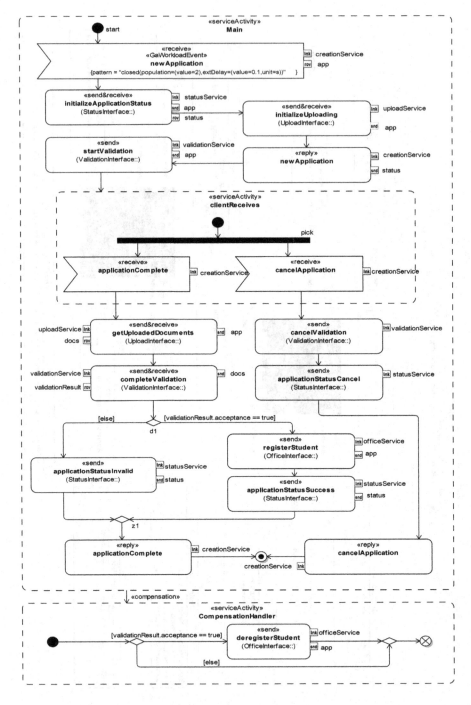

Fig. 8. UML4SOA activity diagram showing the ApplicationCreator

after the orchestration has been completed. If the application has been completed successfully before, the student is removed from the list of applicants by using a *deregisterStudent* call on the *OfficeService*.

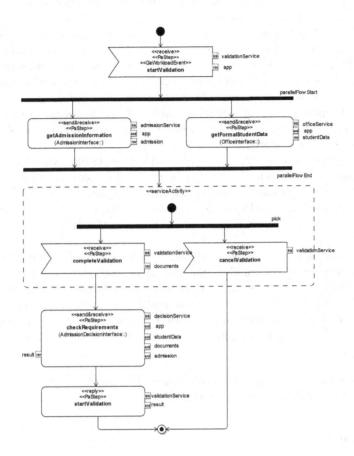

Fig. 9. UML4SOA activity diagram showing the ApplicationValidator

The second activity diagram, modeling the *ApplicationValidator*, is shown in Fig. 9. This service acts as supplier to the creation service, starting with the receipt of the *startValidation* call from the *ApplicationCreator* through the *validationService* port. Afterwards, both the *OfficeService* and the *Admission-Service* are contacted simultaneously to check admission of the student, and to check the student data. Subsequently, the process waits for the *completeValidation* call from the *ApplicationCreator*. After it is received, all the information gathered so far is checked with the help of the *DecisionService*, and the result is returned to the *ApplicationCreator*.

5 Conclusions

This chapter has discussed three of the scenarios of the SENSORIA case studies in detail, presenting graphical models of structure and behavior as well as the implementation of a demonstrator.

Firstly, the *CreditRequest* scenario of the Finance case study has been discussed. This scenario has been used as a test bed for demonstrating the feasibility and effectiveness of the use of the SENSORIA process calculi and some of their related analysis techniques and tools. Moreover, it has been used to provide an effective implementation of (part of) the SENSORIA approach, specifically modeling and formal analysis of service-oriented software based on mathematically founded techniques. Chapter 7-4 further details the use of formal analysis tools on the credit request scenario.

The Automotive case study scenarios and in particular, the *OnRoadAssistance* scenario, have been widely used by the project partners to illustrate the approaches they implemented with easily understandable examples. The demonstrator explained in this chapter has shown how the SENSORIA techniques can be employed for a reaching a fully automated, model-driven approach to SOA development.

Finally, the eUniversity case study has taken concepts from familiar ground for researchers, providing an ideal playground for testing new approaches, methods, and tools for the support of service-oriented architectures. The *StudentApplication* scenario which has been presented in detail in the previous section has been used for qualitative and quantitative analysis integrated with model-driven development and the generation of a running system based on web service technology.

All three case study scenarios are available for download from the SENSORIA web site (http://www.sensoria-ist.eu).

References

1. Alessandrini, M., Dost, D.: Finance Case Study: Requirements, Specification and Modelling of Selected Scenarios (D8.3.a). Technical report, S&N AG (2007)
2. Koch, N., Berndl, D.: Requirements Modelling and Analysis of Selected Scenarios: Automotive Case Study (D8.2.a). Technical report, FAST GmbH (2007)
3. Mayer, P., Schroeder, A., Koch, N.: MDD4SOA: Model-Driven Service Orchestration. In: The 12th IEEE International EDOC Conference (EDOC 2008), Munich, Germany, pp. 203–212. IEEE Computer Society Press, Los Alamitos (2008)
4. OMG. Service Oriented Architecture Modelling Language Beta 1 (2009), http://www.soaml.org/
5. Xie, R., Koch, N.: Automotive CASE Study: Demonstrator. Technical report, Cirquent GmbH (2009)

Sensoria Results Applied to the Case Studies*

Maurice H. ter Beek

ISTI–CNR, Pisa, Italy
terbeek@isti.cnr.it

Abstract. In this chapter we provide an overview of the application
of the results obtained in Sensoria (i.e., techniques, methods and languages developed in the technical work packages WP1-WP7) to case studies from the Automotive, eUniversity, Finance and Telecommunication
domains (developed in work package WP8).

Introduction

We will not describe the case studies in this chapter, since they are introduced
in detail in Chapters 0-3 and 7-1. Likewise we will not describe all details of the
various techniques, methods and languages, which can be found in other chapters
of this book. The scope of this chapter is rather to emphasize the central role of
the case studies in *feeding* and *steering* the research in Sensoria. This is done
by providing a concise overview of the exploitation of Sensoria results in the
case studies. Chapter 7-4 moreover provides an in-depth view of the Sensoria
approach applied to the Finance case study.

This chapter is structured as follows. After this introduction, we summarize
a series of contributions that report on applications of techniques, methods and
languages of WP1-WP7 to the case studies.[1] We describe the experience of
applying a particular technique, method or language to a case study scenario,
but *not* the technique, method or language itself, which are presented in the other
chapters. As such, the goal of this chapter is to answer the following questions:

Aim: besides validating the technique, method or language against requirements of the case study, was there a specific *aim* that triggered the use of
the case study?

Experience: which were the *problems* (if any) faced when applying the technique, method or language to the case study and what are the *results* that
have been obtained?

Benefits: what have been the *advantages* (from the engineering, scientific or
business point of view) of applying the technique, method or language to
the case study?

Feedback: did the application of the technique, method or language to the case
study lead to *improvements* of that technique, method or language?

---

* This work has been partially sponsored by the project Sensoria, IST-2005-016004.
[1] We include applications to the Bowling Robot demonstration described in Chapter 7-3.

M. Wirsing and M. Hölzl (Eds.): Sensoria Project, LNCS 6582, pp. 655–677, 2011.

The contributions are organized according to the three themes of SENSORIA.

The first theme deals with linguistic primitives for services, their interaction and composition. These languages are developed on two levels of abstraction: an *architectural* level (e.g., UML4SOA, SRML) and a *programming* level (e.g., COWS, SOCK/Jolie, CaSPiS). This theme constitutes the work packages WP1, WP2 and WP5.

The second theme, constituting the work packages WP3 and WP4, deals with type systems (e.g., λ^{req}), logics (e.g., SocL, SoSL/MoSL), and extensions of the process calculi developed in Theme 1 (e.g., MarCaSPiS, sCOWS) in order to develop verification techniques (e.g., CMC-UMC, PEPA software toolkit) for the *analysis* of behavioral, performance and QoS properties of services.

The third theme, finally, deals with various engineering aspects of services: *model-driven development* (e.g., MDD4SOA, SDE, VIATRA2), *deployment* (e.g., Modes, Dino, JCaSPiS, Model transformations for deployment) and *reengineering* (e.g., graph transformations). This theme constitutes the work packages WP6 and WP7.

The chapter concludes with a synthetic overview of the case studies to which the SENSORIA techniques, methods and languages have been applied, followed by more detailed analytic overviews of the specific experience/benefits of these applications, organized by theme.

1   Linguistic Primitives

The research in Theme 1 focuses on the development of a generalized concept of service for global computers through the introduction of novel semantically well-founded modeling and programming primitives for services.

1.1   Architectural Level

The UML2 profile UML4SOA is an implementation- and platform independent means of modeling service-oriented systems, in particular *service interactions* and *orchestrations*. It is described in detail in Chapter 1-1. To test its usefulness in practice, all case studies have been described with UML4SOA, and the resulting diagrams have often been used as the starting point for analyzing the case studies with formal verification frameworks (see Sect. 2). This has led to several improvements, among which shortcuts for SOC patterns and specific support for the soaML profile (created by an OMG task force), which allows the modeling of services, provided and required ports, interfaces, and message types in addition to the behavioral specifications in UML4SOA. Moreover, the need for data handling within UML4SOA diagrams was identified, to allow creation, manipulation, and sending/receiving of UML-typed data to and from partners. Finally, the diagrams created for the case studies became quite large, which has led to the inclusion of subscoping in UML4SOA as a means to swap out parts of orchestration processes. The profile has been integrated in a model-driven development process described in Sect. 3.

The Sensoria Reference Modeling Language (SRML) offers primitives for modeling *business services* and *activities*, in which interactions are supported through interfaces. SRML supports a methodological approach that includes the use of the UMC model checker for qualitative analysis and of the Markovian process algebra PEPA for quantitative analysis of timing properties (see Sect. 2). An advantage of SRML that modeling is done at a high level of abstraction, where one can assume that the basic mechanisms of SOAs, like sessions and service discovery/binding, are provided by the middleware and, therefore, need not be part of the models. SRML is described in detail in Chapter 1-2. SRML's primitives and interaction protocols have been validated by modeling scenarios from the Automotive, Finance and Telecommunications case studies [1,2,3,4]. Its application to these case studies also served to validate SRML's three-layered approach (a service layer in between a top and a bottom layer) and the way to define SLAs. The experience with modeling nontrivial interaction protocols has resulted in the addition of key parameters to interactions. The application to the Finance case study served to validate the extension of SRML with timing aspects and the use of PEPA together with SRML to analyze timing properties.

The Service-Targeted Policy-Oriented WorkfLow Approach (StPowla) is a workflow-based approach to *business process modeling* integrating a simple graphical notation, the policy language Appel and the SOA. It is described in detail in Chapter 1-3. To exemplify the approach, StPowla has been applied to a scenario from the Finance case study [5], using UML4SOA to model the workflow. The details of the business process are expressed as compositions of policies written in Appel. Conflicts can be avoided by the analysis techniques of [6,7] (see Sect. 2). An improvement that is the result of specifying this scenario in StPowla is that default templates for the policies are now automatically derived from the workflow, ready to be filled in by the business analyst and converted by the policy server. StPowla has also been applied to the Telecommunications case study [8], in order to assess its impact on the design of business processes.

1.2 Programming Level

Among the core calculi developed in Sensoria and described in Part 2, COWS, SOCK, (Mar)CaSPiS and λ^{req} have been applied to the Automotive and Finance case studies and CC has been applied to the Finance case study.

The Calculus for Orchestration of Web Services (COWS) is a modeling notation for all relevant phases of the life cycle of service-oriented applications, among which publication, discovery, SLA negotiation and orchestration. Besides service interactions and compositions, important aspects like *fault* and *compensation handling* can be modeled in COWS. Extensions moreover allow timed activities, constraints and stochastic reasoning. Application to the case studies has demonstrated the feasibility of modeling service-oriented applications with the specific mechanisms and primitives of COWS [9,10,11]. It has moreover triggered the development of an automatic translation from UML4SOA diagrams into COWS and that of COWS-based verification tools (see Sect. 2). The credit request scenario of the Finance case study has also been modeled in sCOWS (see

Chapter 5-5), which is a stochastic extension of COWS [12], allowing quantitative analyses with its related tools (see Sect. 2). In the tradition of stochastic process calculi, the main syntactic difference from COWS is that in sCOWS basic actions are associated with a random variable expressing their rates. Other differences (i.e., the use of service identifiers versus replication, and the adoption of a labeled semantics versus a reduction semantics) are ascribed to meet some technical requirements for the applicability of Markovian techniques.

The Service-Oriented Computing Kernel (SOCK) is a calculus that closely follows recent technologies, with message routing based on *correlation sets* and *request-response service invocations* in WSDL style as primitives. SOCK can therefore easily be implemented on top of common service platforms. This is exploited in the Java Orchestration Language Interpreter Engine Jolie [13], whose properly extended semantics coincide with SOCK. The Automotive case study has been modeled with SOCK and implemented in Jolie [14], to validate SOCK's primitives and, in particular, its extension to model faults and compensations. This was needed to verify in practice its innovative dynamic handler installation and automatic fault notification, which has led to improved handlers [15].

The service-oriented architecture of the credit request scenario from the Finance case study has been fully implemented in Jolie [16], with the aim of showing that Jolie is a mature technology for developing distributed applications by using a fully implemented *service-oriented programming paradigm*. In Jolie everything is a service. Services can be embedded and aggregated to obtain complex services. Hence, designing a service-oriented architecture in Jolie is simple because a programmer is forced to develop only services. The application to the Finance case study has led to the discovery of a new service-oriented architectural pattern, called SoS (Service of Services), in which a service can be considered a proprietary resource of a client rather than of a session. New service-oriented architectural patterns discovered in Jolie are described in detail in [17].

The Calculus of Services with Pipelines and Sessions (CaSPiS) is a calculus for service-oriented applications based on the notions of *sessions* and of *pipelines*. A session corresponds to a private channel, instantiated upon service invocation, that binds the caller and the callee. Pipelines are used to manage dataflow among sessions. CaSPiS also provides linguistic primitives for handling programmed session closures. CaSPiS is described in detail in Chapter 2-1, which also contains a CaSPiS model of a significant fragment of the credit request scenario from the Finance case study that was used to test the effectiveness of the technique against a concrete and nontrivial example. The credit request scenario and the Bowling Robot case study have also been modeled with MarCaSPiS (see Chapters 5-5 and 7-3), which is a Markovian extension of CaSPiS (see Chapter 2-1), allowing the automatic analysis with its related stochastic logic (see Sect. 2).

The Conversation Calculus (CC) is a minimal typed model for expressing and analyzing *interaction* in service-oriented systems. It is based on a novel notion of *conversation* which extends the notion of session in a novel direction, allowing, in particular, the specification and analysis of dynamically established service collaborations between multiple parties, which is important to support features such as dynamic discovery of services. CC is described in [18] and in Chapter 2-1. Extensions to CC considering exception handling techniques have been studied, showing CC is able to embed *compensable transactions* (see Chapter 3-3). The credit request scenario from the Finance case study has been modeled and typed in CC, thus allowing to verify key properties of the system such as *conversation fidelity*, *progress* and *choreography conformance* (see Sect. 2).

λ^{req} is a core functional calculus for services and service orchestration. It is described in detail in Chapter 2-4. λ^{req} features primitives for selecting and invoking services that respect given behavioral requirements (*call-by-contract*). Services are modeled as functions with side effects representing the action of accessing *security-critical* resources. Security policies are arbitrary safety properties on program executions. A key point is that security policies are applied within a given scope, so-called *local policies*. The design methodology has been applied to the on road assistance scenario from the Automotive case study and to the Finance case study [19,20,21], focusing, respectively, on the design of the workflow of the service orchestration and taking into account the specific driver policies and security service contracts and on policies for resource usage.

CaPiTo is a process calculus for modeling service-oriented applications at both the *abstract* and the *concrete* level, thus achieving a certain level of abstraction without being overwhelmed by the underlying implementation details, but respecting the concrete industrial standards used for implementing the service-oriented applications. It is described in detail in Chapter 4-1. A scenario from the Finance case study has been modeled by CaPiTo [22], showing that CaPiTo is powerful enough to model service-oriented applications, in particular when cryptographic protocols are used to ensure security. It moreover allows the application of the protocol analysis tool LySa to verify the case study (see Sect. 2).

The SENSORIA Reference Markovian Calculus (SRMC) is a stochastic process calculus which explicitly represents *uncertainties* about system configuration in addition to the controlled randomness of an underlying stochastic process [23]. Uncertainty in SOC is understood as different service instances having different performance characteristics due to the inherent heterogeneity of large-scale distributed systems. The expressivity of SRMC was tested by modeling the e-University case study [24] and a novel analysis approach was created to allow precise quantitative statements about such models (see Sect. 2).

The cc-pi calculus is a constraint-based language that supports dynamic selection of services by allowing to specify *QoS negotiations* among service providers and requesters. It combines basic operations of concurrent constraint programming with a symmetric, synchronous mechanism of interaction à la pi-calculus. Chapter 3-1 presents its key features. The cc-pi calculus has been applied to the Telecommunication case study for specifying QoS policies and for enforcing them at execution time [25]. In Chapter 3-1, a variant of the cc-pi calculus that features a choice operator whose branches have a *priority* is proposed, and the credit request scenario from the Finance case study has been modeled in cc-pi, thus allowing for a model of QoS negotiations in which the partners involved have a given order of preference between their possible alternatives.

Architectural Design Rewriting (ADR) is a term-rewriting and graph-based approach to *style-consistent design* and *reconfiguration* of software architectures. It is described in detail in Chapters 1-4 and 3-5. ADR has been applied to scenarios from the Automotive case study [26], to disambiguate the informal specifications of architectural issues by formally modeling architectural constraints and reconfigurations. This has led to an extension of the approach, separating term-rewriting techniques for reconfiguration from those for ordinary behavior, and to specific mechanisms to deal with certain architectural constraints.

A logical specification framework based on *institutions* allows for declarative specifications and modeling of service-oriented architectures. These logics have been applied to the course selection scenario from the eUniversity case study to validate the approach [27]. This has shown that it is useful to separate the description of the behavior of individual services from that of their choreography, which has led to two different logical systems (a local and a global one) formalized as institutions.

2 Qualitative and Quantitative Analysis

The research in Theme 2 focuses on the development of mathematical analysis and verification techniques and tools for system behavior and QoS properties.

2.1 Qualitative Analysis

StPowla's policy language Appel has been applied to the Automotive and Finance case studies. In [6], policies for the on road assistance scenario from the Automotive case study have been defined by *liveness* formulae in a distributed temporal logic and conflicts detected by (semi-) automatic theorem proving. This application has required an extension of the semantics of Appel, which was originally defined only for the non-distributed fragment. In [7], it is shown how to use UMC for the *conflict detection* of policies in a scenario from the Finance case study expressed in UML. This application has required the definition of a correspondence between Appel policies and UML state machines.

CMC and UMC are two prototypical instantiations of a common logical verification framework for the analysis of *functional* properties of service-oriented systems, as described in detail in Chapters 4-2 and 4-3. They only differ with respect to the underlying computational models, which are built from COWS specifications in the case of CMC and from UML statecharts in the case of UMC. The CMC-UMC framework has been used to analyse scenarios from the Automotive, Finance and Telecommunications case studies [9,10,11,28,29,30,31,32] and to the Bowling Robot case study (see Chapter 7-3). This was done by model checking behavioral properties expressed in either the action- and state-based branching-time temporal logic UCTL or its *service-oriented specialization* SocL, for which a set of patterns of service properties was defined. These applications to the case studies have led to a fine-tuning of both the logics and the model-checking approach.

UMC has been integrated in the SRML methodology (see Sect. 1), allowing the model checking of SRML specifications of service compositions based on typical service interaction patterns encoded with UML statecharts [33]. Furthermore, *confidentiality* properties have been verified for the systems modeled in COWS (see Sect. 1) by using its type system, thus showing the feasibility also of type checking. The obtained feedback has steered the development of frameworks allowing service designers to specify service-oriented applications in UML4SOA diagrams and, through an automated translation into either COWS or UML statecharts, to analyse them by means of the CMC-UMC verification framework.

The Verification ENvironment for UML models of Services (VENUS) tool automatically *translates* UML4SOA models of services and natural language statements of service properties into COWS terms and SocL formulae and then checks them using CMC, possibly providing counterexamples. VENUS is described in detail in Chapter 7-4. It has been explicitly developed to *shepherd* the (non-expert) users in writing the behavioral service properties they want to verify. It has been applied to the credit request scenario from the Finance case study in Chapter 7-4.

Both the type system for CaSPiS, developed in [34], and the Control Flow Analysis for CaSPiS, developed in [35], have been applied to the credit request scenario from the Finance case study. The type system aims at statically checking the *client progress* property. This property states that a client-service interaction will not deadlock until the client completes its protocol. The Control Flow Analysis aims instead at detecting and preventing certain *misuses* at the service application logic level. A CaSPiS model of the credit request scenario is reported in Chapter 2-1. Both static techniques and their applications to the scenario are described in Chapter 2-3.

The *static analysis* techniques developed for CC, described in [18] and in Chapter 2-3, single out systems where multiple parties interacting in a conversation follow the prescribed protocols of interaction, even when some of them have dynamically joined the conversation, and systems that are free from deadlocks, even when participants are simultaneously involved in several (even dynamically acquired) conversations. Using the credit request scenario from the Finance case study modeled and typed in CC (see Sect. 1), it has been proven that the multi-party interaction in the credit request system follows *well-defined* protocols of interaction and is *free from deadlocks* (see Chapters 2-1 and 2-3).

The chorSLMC tool has been developed to support the verification of *choreography conformance* by translating CC specifications in a dialect of the π-Calculus and WS-CDL-like choreography descriptions in dynamic spatial logic formulae, which then allows the use of the Spatial Logic Model Checker SLMC [36] to check a system's conformance to the given choreography, among other properties. This is described in detail in Chapter 4-3. The credit request system from the Finance case study has been checked to conform to the prescribed choreography using the chorSLMC tool, based on the CC implementation presented in Chapter 2-1 and on the Conversation Types shown in Chapter 2-3 (see Sect. 1).

The protocol analysis tool LySa [37] has been applied to the CaPiTo model of a scenario from the Finance case study [22] (see Sect. 1 and Chapter 4-1). This analysis suggests that the *authentication* property holds: Once the decision has been made as to whether the request has to be validated by the service, it cannot be tricked into being processed by the wrong one. The analysis moreover suggests that no sensitive data is leaked to the attacker, hence *confidentiality* holds as well. A number of further static analyses have been applied to process-algebraic models of the Automotive case study [38,39,40], with the aim of validating *privacy-related* properties, correct *service delivery* and proper *message correlation*, respectively.

Event-based Service Coordination (ESC) is a middleware supporting the design and implementation of service coordination policies (both *orchestration* and *choreography*). A distinguishing feature of ESC is the facility to manage *long-running transactions*. At the abstract level, the middleware takes the form of the Signal Calculus (SC), an asynchronous process calculus where service interactions are managed by issuing and reacting to suitable (multicast) events. The SC-ESC framework provides a variety of techniques that are mathematically rigorous and pragmatically useful, and which enable the implementation of SOC systems. The framework is described in detail in Chapter 3-4. Scenarios from the Automotive and Finance case studies have been specified and implemented in the SC-ESC framework [41,42,43,44,45]. The management of the case studies has allowed to experiment, evaluate and reason about long-running transactions.

Open Consume-Produce-Read (OCPR) nets are a type of Petri nets that can model the behavior of OWL-S web services through a direct mapping [46]. A compositional notion of equivalence between web services represented as OCPR nets has been applied to several scenarios from the Automotive and Finance case studies [46,47]. It has been employed for checking whether or not a service specification is *equivalent* to a service implementation, and whether or not one (sub)service may *replace* another (sub)service without altering the behavior of the whole application. The need to address the asymmetry of the matching of services (i.e., to check whether a (composition of) service(s) matches a query that specifies the behavior of the desired service (composition) to be found) triggered the introduction of simulation, thus taking into account the chance of satisfying a query with an overspecified service.

The LTSA WS-Engineer tool provides support for a model-based approach to verifying compositions of service architectures, behavior and deployment configurations. The tool supports verification of properties created from design specifications and implementation models to analyze *correctness* and *consistency* of *service compositions*. LTSA WS-Engineer supports verification of service compositions with design (in the form of MSCs), interactions (between multiple services), choreography (in the form of WS-CDL) and deployment models (in the form of xADL2 or UML2). It has been applied to scenarios from the Automotive, Finance and eUniversity case studies [48,49,50] as well as to the Bowling Robot case study (see Chapter 7-3), which has helped greatly to further develop the tool.

2.2   Quantitative Analysis

The Mobile Stochastic Logic (MoSL) has been applied to the accident assistance scenario from the Automotive case study [51,52], with the aim of validating the expression of non-functional, *performance* and *dependability-oriented* properties/requirements of/on services. In particular, a complex *responsiveness* property is developed in detail. The major benefit of using MoSL is the possibility of using arbitrarily nested logical operators: This allows the expression of properties whose formulation would be very difficult and error-prone in natural language. Furthermore, MoSL allows both functional and non-functional requirements to be expressed in an integrated way.

The Service-oriented Stochastic Logic (SoSL), a variant of MoSL, was designed for dealing with specific SOC features. It has been applied to the MarCaSPiS model of the credit request scenario from the Finance case study (see Sect. 1), as described in Chapter 5-1. Three specific aspects have been addressed: system *performance*, supervisor and employee *workload*, and system *reactivity*. The probability for clients to get served as a function of (waiting) time has been studied and such a probability dramatically decreases when the number of clients increases. Supervisor and employee workload has been found rather low, showing that the service is under-used. On the down side, only scenarios with few clients active at the same time could be analyzed due to the size of the state space, a problem that could be tackled with the use of MarCaSPiS discrete simulation or Ordinary Differential Equations semantics. SoSL has also been applied to the MarCaSPiS model of the Bowling Robot case study (see Sect. 1), as described in Chapter 7-3. This latter analysis has focused on the probability of the set of computations that lead to a state satisfying a generic property, showing that the methodology using MarCaSPiS provides both "intuitive" and effective estimations of the robot's behavior (with respect to variations of the model's parameters) as well as a formal basis for reasoning about functional properties of the robot.

λ^{req} is equipped with a formal methodology that makes secure orchestration feasible. An abstraction of the program behavior is first extracted, through a type and effect system. This abstract behavior over-approximates the possible runtime histories of all services involved in an orchestration. The abstract behavior is then model checked to construct the skeleton structure of the orchestrator that securely coordinates the running services. Starting from λ^{req} models of scenarios from the Automotive and Finance case studies (see Sect. 1), it has been shown that the awareness of security from the early stages of development will foster security through all the following phases of software production. In particular, the output of the model checker has been exploited to highlight design flaws, suggesting how to revise the orchestration and the security policies.

Software tools for the well-known stochastic process algebra PEPA have been applied to almost all case studies: *safety*, *response-time* and *passage-end* analyses have been performed on scenarios from the Automotive case study [53,54,55], which has led to a more user-friendly PEPA development environment and to integration with the SDE (see Sect. 3). Passage-end analysis was also applied to the Bowling Robot case study (see Chapters 5-4 and 7-3). Moreover, *response-time* and *sensitivity* analyses have been applied to the credit request scenario from the Finance case study (see Chapter 5-5), with the intention of identifying the bottleneck activity: sensitivity analysis was used to generate a family of cumulative distribution functions detailing the response-time distribution of the credit request process, which identified decision making as the bottleneck activity. Such investigations allow one to decide where effort would be best spent in improving functions within the entire business process. This quantitative analysis was technically particularly challenging because it is a *multi-scale* problem where rates are separated by several orders of magnitude and the attendant numerical problem is *stiff* (i.e., computationally expensive). Finally, the eUniversity case study has been used to illustrate the main theoretical developments of PEPA with respect to its deterministic interpretation. One of these is described in detail in Chapter 5-3: A modeling strategy which may be applied to a variety of distributed applications, including service-oriented ones. This has revealed as one of PEPA's key benefits, its capability of targeting both a stochastic and a deterministic semantics, and it has prompted further work in the area of software tool development.

SRMC can be seen as an extension of PEPA (formally, a superset). The kinds of analysis that can be performed on SRMC models are supported by a suite of software tools that provides tight integration with the PEPA modeling and analysis tools [56]. A number of qualitative analyses have been performed on the SRMC model of the eUniversity case study (see Sect. 1), among which the scalability of the eUniversity system in the presence of increasing numbers of student users and uncertainty about system configuration [24].

Two distinct tools have been developed to assist the quantitative analyses of sCOWS specifications. One of them, called sCOWS_LTS, allows sCOWS probabilistic model checking through the generation of the LTS (Labeled Transition System) corresponding to the specification, and its subsequent translation to a CTMC (Continuous Time Markov Chain) that can be used as input for the PRISM model checker of CSL (Continuous Stochastic Logic) formulae. The second tool, named sCOWS_AMC, implements approximate statistical model checking of sCOWS terms against CSL. It is a stand-alone tool running a Monte Carlo algorithm and hence based on the generation of simulation traces of the computation rather than on the generation of the global LTS of the specification. Both tools have been used to analyze the system performance of the COWS model of the Finance case study's credit request scenario (see Chapter 5-5).

3   Deployment and Development

The research in Theme 3 focuses on model-based development techniques for refining and transforming service specifications, novel techniques for deploying service descriptions, methods for reengineering legacy systems into service-oriented ones, and a software development process for service-oriented systems.

3.1 Deployment and Reengineering

The notion of software architecture Modes in the context of SOC abstracts a set of services, and their states, collaborating towards a common goal. A Mode can be used to identify the services required in a service composition, and assist in specifying *orchestration* and *choreography* requirements through service component state changes. Modes are described in detail in Chapter 4-4. The concept of Modes complements that of ADR (see Sect. 1): A Mode is an architectural style whose productions focus on architectural change and behavioral correctness. Modes have been applied to the route planning scenario from the Automotive case study [57,50], which has led to the development of a UML2 Modes profile. Moreover, the approach has been extended to Service Mode analysis (see Chapter 4-4), including extensions to the WS-Engineer tool (see Sect. 2).

The Dino approach provides runtime support for dynamic and adaptive *service composition*. It does so for all stages of a service composition life cycle: service discovery, selection, binding, delivery, monitoring and adaptation. Dino is described in detail in Chapter 6-3. Dino has been applied to the several scenarios from the Automotive case study [58], in order to provide the requirements, guide the design, and help validate the work done in the Dino project (see Chapter 6-3). This has allowed the design to be validated and improved. The Dino runtime was extended by S&N with an "intelligent" mode, allowing operators to select their priority of matching services, and integrated into the credit request scenario from the Finance case study [59].

JCaSPiS is a Java framework that permits implementing service-oriented applications based on the CaSPiS paradigm [60]. Indeed, JCaSPiS provides a set of classes that implements primitives for publishing and invoking services, for defining protocols used to control the service interactions, and mechanisms for the handling of unexpected behaviors (session closures). Starting from the CaSPiS specification of the credit request scenario from the Finance case study (see Sect. 1), a *real-world* scenario was implemented with JCaSPiS. This allows programmers to use a formal language to model system components and their interactions and, moreover, analyses performed at the level of specification are preserved at the level of implementation. The application to the case study has led to the development of new functionalities.

The Model-Driven Development Approach for SOA (MDD4SOA) is a tool to *transform* UML4SOA orchestration models to abstract code in executable languages (BPEL/WSDL, Java and Jolie). It is described in detail in Chapter 1-1 (see also the section on model-driven development below). The model transformers have been applied to scenarios from all case studies [61,62,63], with the exception of the Bowling Robot case study. The aim was to validate the practicability of the UML4SOA profile and, in particular, the usefulness of the MDD4SOA transformers in practice (by means of a *complete transformation* from an UML4SOA model down to actual code and its execution on a target platform). Obviously, the development of MDD4SOA has gone hand in hand with that of UML4SOA. The transformers have shown their use in SENSORIA for converting UML models to input languages for analysis and for using the converted models as the basis for the implementation of the case studies. These uses have themselves led to improvements of the transformers, among which more readable and precise error reporting.

A general methodology for *architectural migration* based on Graph Transformations (GT) takes a graph model of the source code, after categorizing blocks of source code according to the target architecture, and transforms these into a graph model of the target architecture, through the creation of a metamodel-based representation of the code, and, finally, into the target code. It is described in detail in Chapter 6-4. The methodology has been applied to a scenario from the Finance case study [64]. This scenario has a two-tier architecture (client/server) but presentation, business logic and data access code elements are all mixed in both tiers. By applying the GT rules it was possible to *untangle* these concerns and obtain a well-organized model, following the service-orientation requirement of separation between business and presentation logic. This has led to an improvement of the existing GT rule set and to new GT rules, thus increasing the number of supported situations. The resulting rule set can be used to automate part of the process in projects that involve architecture migration.

The VIATRA2 *model transformation* framework forms the basis of a model-driven method for facilitating the development and deployment of services with security and reliable communication requirements. It is described in detail in Chapters 6-1 and 6-2. *Deployment transformations*, extended with some Java-based template generation, take UML4SOA models as input and produce standards-compliant service descriptors (WSDL files) and configuration descriptors to reliable and secure service middleware of the Apache platform. This method has been tested on scenarios from the Automotive, Finance and eUniversity case studies. This has shown that while the size of these models does not necessarily require a sophisticated model-driven approach, incremental development of services and reusability of components is strongly supported by this method, which is a clear benefit for such projects. Moreover, the time consuming and error-prone task of creating XML descriptors is done automatically.

3.2   Model-Driven Development

The model-driven engineering approach MDD4SOA (described above) is based on model-to-model and model-to-code transformations for *model refinement* and *code generation*, in particular PIM-to-PIM and PIM-to-PSM transformations (where PIM stands for Platform Independent Model and PSM for Platform Specific Model). The particular PIM that is used to transform a UML4SOA model to a PSM is called the Intermediate Orchestration Model (IOM). The transformations have been applied to the thesis management scenario from the eUniversity case study and to the on road assistance scenario from the Automotive case study for testing purposes [62,63]. In particular, the Automotive Demonstrator focuses on the development process of service-oriented software [63], demonstrating how a model-driven process can work. The feedback has led to improvements of the UML4SOA metamodel and profile as well as of MDD4SOA.

Model Transformation By Example (MTBE) is a model-driven software engineering approach to *derive* model transformation rules from an initial prototypical set of interrelated source and target models, which describe critical cases of the transformation in a purely declarative way [65,66]. Its applicability was assessed by trying to reproduce the model transformation rules for the UML2SOA transformation as part of VIATRA (see above). As sample input model the UML component model of the credit request scenario from the Finance case study was used. The sample output model was generated by the original VIATRA transformation (previously developed by hand). Using MTBE, it was possible to derive most transformation rules in the form of graph transformation rules in the VIATRA framework directly from the UML models of the scenario. This has steered research for better guiding the users when an MTBE run does not provide meaningful results so that the training models can be changed appropriately. The VIATRA2 transformation framework was also extended with *incremental pattern matching mechanisms*, helping fast execution of model transformations.

The BPEL2SAL *transformation chain*, which has been implemented in VIATRA2 (see above), facilitates model-driven analysis of service orchestrations. Symbolic Analysis Laboratory (SAL) is a verification framework that is directed at analyzing properties of transition systems by combining tools for program analysis, model checking, and theorem proving [67]. BPEL2SAL is described in detail in Chapter 6-1. As a distinctive feature, the transformations are extended with enhanced traceability techniques which facilitate the visualization of model-checking results directly on the Eclipse BPEL designer tool. The method has been applied on scenarios from the Finance and eUniversity case studies.

The SENSORIA Pattern language describes which problems are addressed by SENSORIA techniques and tools, how they *solve* the *problems* they address, and which *forces* determine whether or not a technique or tool is appropriate for a given *situation*. It moreover does so in a manner accessible to software developers not involved in SENSORIA. The language is described in detail in Chapter 7-5. Each pattern is accompanied by examples taken from the case study application in which the pattern was identified [68], and which have been used to validate the pattern. The pattern catalogue serves to document the advantages and disadvantages of different approaches and to enhance the discussion between SENSORIA partners. Finally, since the patterns are derived from the case studies development, they are strongly influenced by feedback from these case studies.

The SENSORIA Development Environment (SDE) is a *tool integration platform* for the tools developed in SENSORIA, which allows developers to *find*, *use* and *combine* them. To integrate with existing tools and platforms for the development of SOA systems, the SDE is based on the industry-standard Eclipse platform and its underlying, service-oriented OSGi framework. It is described in detail in Chapter 6-5. The orchestration features within the SDE have been employed for combining several integrated tools for the development and analysis of the case studies. The main benefit of the SDE is its integrative nature: all SEN-SORIA tools are available within the SDE with a uniform API description and the ability to take part in larger orchestrations. Creating orchestrations is possible using either a textual, JavaScript-based approach or a graphical, UML-activity-diagram-like workflow approach. The opportunity to integrate tools into the SDE has prompted SENSORIA tool developers to spend time on thinking about the collaboration of individual tools, which benefits the end user. Feedback from applying tools to the case studies, with the SDE as underlying platform for tool invocation, has led to improved SDE interfaces. The resulting wizard-based service call infrastructure has the advantage of always presenting the same interface to developers regardless of the tool or orchestration. The graphical orchestration mechanism is also a direct result of these applications. In [63], a detailed documentation of the implemented Automotive Demonstrator illustrates the use of a set of techniques, methods and tools from the SDE developed within the scope of SENSORIA (e.g. UML4SOA, MDD4SOA, Dino). The use of the SDE for analyzing orchestrations in the eUniversity case study with the help of three integrated tools (WS-Engineer, PEPA, and MDD4SOA) is described in detail in [49].

4   Concluding Overview

In Table 1, we provide a synthetic overview of the case studies to which the SENSORIA techniques, methods and languages have been applied. This table, organized by theme, clearly illustrates the central role of the *industrial* case studies from the Automotive and—in particular—Finance domains, as well as the more specific role of the *academic* eUniversity case study. Note that only few SENSORIA techniques, methods and languages have been applied to the Bowling Robot and Telecommunications case studies. This is due to the following reasons. First, the *industrial* Telecommunications case study has suffered from the fact that Telecom Italia has considerably reduced its effort in SENSORIA rather early on in the project. Second, the Bowling Robot *demonstration* has been introduced rather late in the project, initially as a game scenario to show SENSORIA's software engineering approach at hands-on demonstrations, after which it has evolved into a case study.

In Tables 2-4 we provide more detailed analytic overviews of the specific experience/benefits of having applied the SENSORIA techniques, methods and languages to the case studies, organized in the format of one table per theme. These tables thus contain very brief summaries of the answers to the four questions (aim, experience, benefits, feedback) that we presented in the Introduction as the goal of this chapter. We have compiled these summaries based on the answers provided by the partners that have developed and used the various SENSORIA techniques, methods and languages.

Table 1. Validation of SENSORIA techniques, methods and languages

		Automotive	Finance	eUniversity	Bowling Robot	Telco
THEME 1	UML4SOA	✓	✓	✓	✓	✓
	SRML	✓	✓			✓
	StPowla	✓	✓			✓
	(s)COWS	✓	✓			
	SOCK/Jolie	✓	✓			
	(Mar)CaSPiS	✓	✓		✓	
	CC		✓			
	λ^{req}	✓	✓			
	CaPiTo		✓			
	SRMC			✓		
	cc-pi		✓			✓
	ADR	✓				
	Institutions			✓		
THEME 2	SocL	✓	✓			
	CMC-UMC	✓	✓		✓	✓
	VENUS		✓			
	chorSLMC		✓			
	LySa		✓			
	SC-ESC	✓	✓			
	OCPR	✓	✓			
	WS-Engineer	✓	✓	✓	✓	
	SoSL/MoSL	✓	✓		✓	
	PEPA toolkit	✓	✓	✓	✓	
THEME 3	Modes	✓				
	Dino	✓	✓			
	JCaSPiS		✓			
	MDD4SOA	✓	✓	✓		✓
	GT		✓			
	VIATRA2	✓	✓	✓		
	MTBE		✓			
	Patterns	✓	✓	✓		
	SDE	✓	✓	✓		

Table 2. Theme 1: experience/benefits of Sensoria techniques, methods & languages

Theme 1	Automotive	Finance	eUniversity	Bowling Robot	Telco
UML4SOA	Test usefulness in practice; Provide models for verification; Now short-cuts SOC patterns, support soaML profile, data handling & subscoping				
SRML	Validate primitives, 3-layer approach & definition SLAs; Validate timing extension				Test interactions: add key parameters
StPowla		Validate approach; Now derives policy templates			Assess impact on business process design
COWS sCOWS	Feasibility mechanism + primitives to model SOA & provide stochastic description				
SOCK	Validate primitives & faults + compensations modeling; Verify dynamic handler & automatic fault notification; Now improved handlers				
Jolie	Test programming a SOA; Found new SOA patterns				
CaSPiS MarCaSPiS	Test its effectiveness & its Markovian extension			Feasibility of methodology	
CC		Type to verify key properties			
λ^{req}	Call-by-contract invocation				
CaPiTo		Model SOA especially if crypto protocols for security			
SRMC			Test expressivity; New analysis approach		
cc-pi		Validate prioritized variant			Validate basic primitives
ADR	Disambiguate informal SOA specifications by formal model of reconfigurations & constraints				
Institutions			Validate approach; Useful to separate behavioral description of services from choreography		

Table 3. Theme 2: experience/benefits of SENSORIA techniques, methods & languages

Theme 2	Automotive	Finance	eUniversity	Bowling Robot	Telco
StPowla	Detection of conflicts by theorem proving; Needed extension Appel semantics	Detection of conflicts by UMC; Needed definition correspondence Appel - UML			
SocL	Test expressivity for SOA properties; Defined patterns of service properties				
CMC-UMC	Test & fine-tune model checker; Verify properties; Feasibility type checking with CMC; Now automatic translations from UML4SOA to COWS (VENUS) & UMC			Test & fine-tune model checker; Verify properties; Now automatic translations from UML4SOA to UMC	
VENUS		Assist user to write properties to verify			
CaSPiS		Type system to check progress property; Control flow analysis to detect & prevent misuses			
chorSLMC		Verify multiparty interaction; Proved protocols of interaction well-defined+ deadlock-free			
SC-ESC	Experiment, evaluate & reason about long-running transactions				
LySa		Proved authenticity+confidentiality			
OCPR	Defined compositional notion of service equivalence; Verified service equivalence & replaceability				
WS-Engineer	Analyzed correctness & consistency of service compositions; Helped to further develop the tool	Check interactions between orchestrations for deadlocks		Test & further develop the tool	

continued on next page...

Table 3. (*continued*)

Theme 2	Automotive	Finance	eUniversity	Bowling Robot	Telco
SoSL/MoSL	Test expressivity for SOC features; Verify dependability (workload, reactivity) & performance properties of services: difficult & error-prone in natural language			Show methodology provides intuitive & effective estimations of robot behavior	
λ^{req}	Exploit output of model checker to highlight design flaws, suggesting how to revise the orchestration & security policies				
PEPA toolkit	Passage-end, response-time & safety analysis; Development environment now more user-friendly	Sensitivity & response-time analysis to identify bottleneck activity; technically particularly challenging	Show main developments PEPA wrt deterministic semantics; Key benefit PEPA: target both a deterministic & a stochastic semantics	Passage-end analysis: precisely quantified probability of expected outcome	
SRMC			Test software tool suite; Verify scalability in presence uncertainties		
sCOWS_LTS sCOWS_AMC		Analysis of system performance			

Table 4. Theme 3: experience/benefits of SENSORIA techniques, methods & languages

Theme 3	Automotive	Finance	eUniversity	Bowling Robot	Telco
Modes	Test modeling orchestration+ choreography requirements; Created UML2 profile; Extended analysis & WS-Engineer				
Dino	Provide requirements, guide design & validate Dino; Now improved & extended design				
JCaSPiS		Implement a real scenario; Preserve analysis from modeling to implementation level; Now new functionalities			
MDD4SOA	Validate practicability UML4SOA& usefulness MDD4SOA transformers in practice (by full transformation from UML4SOA to actual code & execution);Transformers now more readable & precise error reporting				Validate approach; Developed hand in hand with UML4SOA
GT		Untangle business & presentation logic; New rule set; Architecture migration now automated			
VIATRA2	Test method; Support incremental service development & reusability; XML descriptors created automatically; Now BPEL2-SAL orchestration analysis back-annotated				
MTBE		Test method; Steered better user guiding			
Patterns	Accompanied by examples from the case study application that identified patterns; Created pattern catalogue documenting (dis)advantages & feedback of approaches				
SDE	Orchestration features employed to combine integrated tools for development & analysis of case studies; Now contains all SENSORIA tools; Now improved SDE interfaces & graphical orchestration mechanism				

Acknowledgments. We thank our partners in the SENSORIA project for their contributions to this chapter.

References

1. Abreu, J., Bocchi, L., Fiadeiro, J.L., Lopes, A.: Specifying and composing interaction protocols for service-oriented system modelling. In: Derrick, J., Vain, J. (eds.) FORTE 2007. LNCS, vol. 4574, pp. 358–373. Springer, Heidelberg (2007)
2. Bocchi, L., Fiadeiro, J.L., Lopes, A.: Service-oriented modelling of automotive systems. In: COMPSAC, pp. 1059–1064. IEEE, Los Alamitos (2008)
3. Bocchi, L., Fiadeiro, J.L., Lopes, A.: A use-case driven approach to formal service-oriented modelling. In: Margaria, T., Steffen, B. (eds.) ISoLA 2008. CCIS, vol. 17, pp. 155–169. Springer, Heidelberg (2008)
4. Bocchi, L., Fiadeiro, J.L., Gilmore, S., Abreu, J., Solanki, M., Vankayala, V.: A formal approach to modelling time properties of service-oriented systems (submitted)
5. Gorton, S., Montangero, C., Reiff-Marganiec, S., Semini, L.: StPowla: SOA, policies and workflows. In: Di Nitto, E., Ripeanu, M. (eds.) ICSOC 2007. LNCS, vol. 4907, pp. 351–362. Springer, Heidelberg (2009)
6. Montangero, C., Reiff-Marganiec, S., Semini, L.: Logic-based detection of conflicts in Appel policies. In: Arbab, F., Sirjani, M. (eds.) FSEN 2007. LNCS, vol. 4767, pp. 257–271. Springer, Heidelberg (2007)
7. ter Beek, M.H., Gnesi, S., Montangero, C., Semini, L.: Detecting policy conflicts by model checking UML state machines. In: ICFI 2009, pp. 59–74. IOS (2009)
8. Fantini, P., Montangero, C., Palasciano, C., Reiff-Marganiec, S., Semini, L.: Supporting user-friendly design of flexible business processes in StPowla. Technical Report PISATR0825, Dipartimento di Informatica, Università di Pisa (2008)
9. Fantechi, A., Gnesi, S., Lapadula, A., Mazzanti, F., Pugliese, R., Tiezzi, F.: A model checking approach for verifying COWS specifications. In: Fiadeiro, J.L., Inverardi, P. (eds.) FASE 2008. LNCS, vol. 4961, pp. 230–245. Springer, Heidelberg (2008)
10. Lapadula, A., Pugliese, R., Tiezzi, F.: Specifying and analysing SOC applications with COWS. In: Degano, P., De Nicola, R., Meseguer, J. (eds.) Concurrency, Graphs and Models. LNCS, vol. 5065, pp. 701–720. Springer, Heidelberg (2008)
11. Gnesi, S., Pugliese, R., Tiezzi, F.: The SENSORIA pattern-based approach applied to the finance case study. SENSORIA Deliverable Th05 (2010)
12. Prandi, D., Quaglia, P.: Stochastic COWS. In: Krämer, B.J., Lin, K.-J., Narasimhan, P. (eds.) ICSOC 2007. LNCS, vol. 4749, pp. 245–256. Springer, Heidelberg (2007)
13. Montesi, F., Guidi, C., Zavattaro, G.: Composing services with JOLIE. In: ECOWS 2007, pp. 13–22. IEEE, Los Alamitos (2007)
14. Guidi, C., Lanese, I., Montesi, F., Zavattaro, G.: On the interplay between fault handling and request-response service invocations. In: ACSD 2008, pp. 190–199. IEEE, Los Alamitos (2008)
15. Montesi, F., Guidi, C., Lanese, I., Zavattaro, G.: Dynamic fault handling mechanisms for service-oriented applications. In: ECOWS 2008, pp. 225–234. IEEE, Los Alamitos (2008)
16. Guidi, C., Montesi, F.: Implementation of the finance case study in Jolie (2009), http://www.jolie-lang.org/

17. Guidi, C., Montesi, F.: Reasoning about a service-oriented programming paradigm. In: ter Beek, M.H. (ed.) YR-SOC 2009. EPTCS, vol. 2, pp. 67–81 (2009)

18. Vieira, H.T.: A Calculus for Modeling and Analyzing Conversations in Service-Oriented Computing. PhD thesis, Universidade Nova de Lisboa (2010)

19. Bartoletti, M., Degano, P., Ferrari, G., Zunino, R.: Secure service orchestration. In: Aldini, A., Gorrieri, R. (eds.) FOSAD 2007. LNCS, vol. 4677, pp. 24–74. Springer, Heidelberg (2007)

20. Bartoletti, M., Degano, P., Ferrari, G., Zunino, R.: Semantics-based design for secure web services. IEEE Transactions on Software Engineering 34, 33–49 (2008)

21. Bartoletti, M., Degano, P., Ferrari, G., Zunino, R.: Local policies for resource usage analysis. ACM Transactions on Programming Languages and Systems 31 (2009)

22. Gao, H., Nielson, F., Nielson, H.R.: Protocol stacks for services. In: FCS (2009)

23. Clark, A., Gilmore, S., Tribastone, M.: Service-level agreements for service-oriented computing. In: Corradini, A., Montanari, U. (eds.) WADT 2008. LNCS, vol. 5486, pp. 21–36. Springer, Heidelberg (2009)

24. Clark, A., Gilmore, S., Tribastone, M.: Scalable analysis of scalable systems. In: Chechik, M., Wirsing, M. (eds.) FASE 2009. LNCS, vol. 5503, pp. 1–17. Springer, Heidelberg (2009)

25. Buscemi, M.G., Ferrari, L., Moiso, C., Montanari, U.: Constraint-based policy negotiation and enforcement for telco services. In: TASE 2007, pp. 463–472. IEEE, Los Alamitos (2007)

26. Bruni, R., Lluch Lafuente, A., Montanari, U., Tuosto, E.: Style-based architectural reconfigurations. Bulletin of the EATCS 94, 161–180 (2008)

27. Knapp, A., Marczyński, G., Wirsing, M., Zawłocki, A.: A heterogeneous approach to service-oriented systems specification. In: SOAP track at SAC 2010. ACM, New York (2010)

28. ter Beek, M.H., Gnesi, S., Mazzanti, F., Moiso, C.: Formal modelling and verification of an asynchronous extension of SOAP. In: ECOWS 2006, pp. 287–296. IEEE, Los Alamitos (2006)

29. ter Beek, M.H., Fantechi, A., Gnesi, S., Mazzanti, F.: An action/state-based model-checking approach for the analysis of communication protocols for service-oriented applications. In: Leue, S., Merino, P. (eds.) FMICS 2007. LNCS, vol. 4916, pp. 133–148. Springer, Heidelberg (2008)

30. ter Beek, M.H., Gnesi, S., Koch, N., Mazzanti, F.: Formal verification of an automotive scenario in service-oriented computing. In: ICSE 2008, pp. 613–622. ACM, New York (2008)

31. ter Beek, M.H., Bucchiarone, A., Gnesi, S.: Dynamic software architecture development: Towards an automated process. In: SEAA 2009, pp. 105–108. IEEE, Los Alamitos (2009)

32. ter Beek, M.H., Mazzanti, F.: Modelling and analysing the finance case study in UMC. Technical Report 2010-TR-007, ISTI-CNR (2010)

33. Abreu, J., Mazzanti, F., Fiadeiro, J.L., Gnesi, S.: A model-checking approach for service component architectures. In: Lee, D., Lopes, A., Poetzsch-Heffter, A. (eds.) FMOODS 2009. LNCS, vol. 5522, pp. 219–224. Springer, Heidelberg (2009)

34. Acciai, L., Boreale, M.: A type system for client progress in a service-oriented calculus. In: Degano, P., De Nicola, R., Meseguer, J. (eds.) Concurrency, Graphs and Models. LNCS, vol. 5065, pp. 642–658. Springer, Heidelberg (2008)

35. Bodei, C., Brodo, L., Bruni, R.: Static detection of logic flaws in service-oriented applications. In: Degano, P., Viganò, L. (eds.) ARSPA-WITS 2009. LNCS, vol. 5511, pp. 70–87. Springer, Heidelberg (2009)

36. Vieira, H.T., Caires, L., Viegas, R.: The Spatial Logic Model Checker v2.01 (November 2009), http://www-ctp.di.fct.unl.pt/SLMC/
37. Buchholtz, M., Nielson, H.R.: LySa tool v2.02 (October 2006), http://www.imm.dtu.dk/English/Research/Language-Based_Technology/Software/LySaTool.aspx
38. Nielson, H.R., Nielson, F.: A flow-sensitive analysis of privacy properties. In: CSF 2007, pp. 249–264. IEEE, Los Alamitos (2007)
39. Nielson, F., Nielson, H.R., Bauer, J., Nielsen, C.R., Pilegaard, H.: Relational analysis for delivery of services. In: Barthe, G., Fournet, C. (eds.) TGC 2007. LNCS, vol. 4912, pp. 73–89. Springer, Heidelberg (2008)
40. Bauer, J., Nielson, F., Nielson, H.R., Pilegaard, H.: Relational analysis of correlation. In: Alpuente, M., Vidal, G. (eds.) SAS 2008. LNCS, vol. 5079, pp. 32–46. Springer, Heidelberg (2008)
41. Ciancia, V., Ferrari, G., Guanciale, R., Strollo, D.: Checking correctness of transactional behaviors. In: Suzuki, K., Higashino, T., Yasumoto, K., El-Fakih, K. (eds.) FORTE 2008. LNCS, vol. 5048, pp. 134–148. Springer, Heidelberg (2008)
42. Ferrari, G., Guanciale, R., Strollo, D., Tuosto, E.: Event-based service coordination. In: Degano, P., De Nicola, R., Meseguer, J. (eds.) Concurrency, Graphs and Models. LNCS, vol. 5065, pp. 312–329. Springer, Heidelberg (2008)
43. Ferrari, G., Guanciale, R., Strollo, D., Tuosto, E.: Refactoring long running transactions. In: Bruni, R., Wolf, K. (eds.) WS-FM 2008. LNCS, vol. 5387, pp. 127–142. Springer, Heidelberg (2009)
44. Strollo, D.: Designing and Experimenting Coordination Primitives for Service Oriented Computing. PhD thesis, IMT Institute for Advanced Studies, Lucca (2009)
45. Guanciale, R.: The Signal Calculus: Beyond Message-based Coordination for Services. PhD thesis, IMT Institute for Advanced Studies, Lucca (2009)
46. Bonchi, F., Brogi, A., Corfini, S., Gadducci, F.: On the use of behavioural equivalences for web services' development. Fundamenta Informaticae 89, 479–510 (2008)
47. Bonchi, F., Brogi, A., Corfini, S., Gadducci, F.: A net-based approach to web services publication and replaceability. Fundamental Informaticae 94, 305–330 (2009)
48. Foster, H., Uchitel, S., Magee, J., Kramer, J.: Tool support for model-based engineering of web service compositions. In: ICWS 2005, pp. 95–102. IEEE, Los Alamitos (2005)
49. Mayer, P., Junker, M., Foster, H., Tribastone, M.: The SDE closeup: Analyzing service-oriented software with the help of formal tools. Technical report, Lehrstuhl PST, Institut für Informatik, Ludwig-Maximilians-Universität München (2008)
50. Foster, H.: Architecture and behaviour analysis for engineering Service Modes. In: PESOS 2009, pp. 1–8. IEEE, Los Alamitos (2009)
51. De Nicola, R., Katoen, J.P., Latella, D., Loreti, M., Massink, M.: Model checking mobile stochastic logic. Theoretical Computer Science 382, 42–70 (2007)
52. De Nicola, R., Katoen, J.P., Latella, D., Loreti, M., Massink, M.: Stochastic logics. SENSORIA Deliverable 4.2a (February 2007)
53. Clark, A., Gilmore, S.: Evaluating quality of service for service level agreements. In: Brim, L., Haverkort, B.R., Leucker, M., van de Pol, J. (eds.) FMICS 2006 and PDMC 2006. LNCS, vol. 4346, pp. 181–194. Springer, Heidelberg (2007)
54. Argent-Katwala, A., Clark, A., Foster, H., Gilmore, S., Mayer, P., Tribastone, M.: Safety and response-time analysis of an automotive accident assistance service. In: Margaria, T., Steffen, B. (eds.) ISoLA 2008. CCIS, vol. 17, pp. 191–205. Springer, Heidelberg (2008)
55. Clark, A., Duguid, A., Gilmore, S.: Passage-end analysis. In: Bradley, J.T. (ed.) EPEW 2009. LNCS, vol. 5652, pp. 110–115. Springer, Heidelberg (2009)

56. Clark, A., Gilmore, S., Tribastone, M.: Quantitative analysis of web services using SRMC. In: Bernardo, M., Padovani, L., Zavattaro, G. (eds.) SFM 2009. LNCS, vol. 5569, pp. 296–339. Springer, Heidelberg (2009)
57. Hirsch, D., Kramer, J., Magee, J., Uchitel, S.: Modes for software architectures. In: Gruhn, V., Oquendo, F. (eds.) EWSA 2006. LNCS, vol. 4344, pp. 113–126. Springer, Heidelberg (2006)
58. Mukhija, A., Dingwall-Smith, A., Rosenblum, D.S.: QoS-aware service composition in Dino. In: ECOWS 2007, pp. 3–12. IEEE, Los Alamitos (2007)
59. Alessandrini, M.: Intelligent Service System. PhD thesis, Westfälische Wilhelms-Universität Münster (2009)
60. Bettini, L., De Nicola, R., Loreti, M.: Implementing session centered calculi. In: Wang, A.H., Tennenholtz, M. (eds.) COORDINATION 2008. LNCS, vol. 5052, pp. 17–32. Springer, Heidelberg (2008)
61. Foster, H., Mayer, P.: Leveraging integrated tools for model-based analysis of service compositions. In: ICIW 2008, pp. 72–77. IEEE, Los Alamitos (2008)
62. Mayer, P., Schroeder, A., Koch, N.: MDD4SOA: Model-driven service orchestration. In: EDOC 2008, pp. 203–212. IEEE, Los Alamitos (2008)
63. Xie, R., Koch, N.: Automotive case study: Demonstrator. Report. Cirquent (2009)
64. Heckel, R., Correia, R., Matos, C.M.P., El-Ramly, M., Koutsoukos, G., Andrade, L.F.: Architectural transformations: From legacy to three-tier and services. In: Software Evolution, pp. 139–170. Springer, Heidelberg (2008)
65. Varró, D.: Model transformation by example. In: Wang, J., Whittle, J., Harel, D., Reggio, G. (eds.) MoDELS 2006. LNCS, vol. 4199, pp. 410–424. Springer, Heidelberg (2006)
66. Balogh, Z., Varró, D.: Model transformation by example using inductive logic programming. Software and System Modeling 8, 347–364 (2009)
67. Shankar, N.: Symbolic analysis of transition systems. In: Gurevich, Y., Kutter, P.W., Vetta, A., Thiele, L. (eds.) ASM 2000. LNCS, vol. 1912, pp. 287–302. Springer, Heidelberg (2000)
68. Wirsing, M., Hölzl, M.M., Acciai, L., Banti, F., Clark, A., Fantechi, A., Gilmore, S., Gnesi, S., Gönczy, L., Koch, N., Lapadula, A., Mayer, P., Mazzanti, F., Pugliese, R., Schroeder, A., Tiezzi, F., Tribastone, M., Varró, D.: SENSORIA patterns: Augmenting service engineering with formal analysis, transformation and dynamicity. In: Margaria, T., Steffen, B. (eds.) ISoLA 2008. CCIS, vol. 17, pp. 170–190. Springer, Heidelberg (2008)

Analysing Robot Movement Using the SENSORIA Methods[*]

Maurice H. ter Beek[1], Alessandro Lapadula[2],
Michele Loreti[2], and Claudio Palasciano[3]

[1] ISTI–CNR, Pisa, Italy
terbeek@isti.cnr.it
[2] DSI, Università di Firenze, Italy
{lapadula,loreti}@dsi.unifi.it
[3] MIP Politecnico di Milano, Italy
palasciano@mip.polimi.it

Abstract. In this paper, we give a recount of the application of SEN-SORIA approaches, languages, and tools to the modeling of movement of the robot that has taken the lead role in SENSORIA demonstrations at the exhibitions ICT 2008 in Lyon and FET 2009 in Prague. The demos were centred around a robot-bowling game that actively involved the visitors in programming a robot that plays bowling, using some of the techniques developed in SENSORIA in order to predict the outcomes of the game according to their design choices. Specifically, the SENSORIA techniques have been used for the analysis of functional and non-functional properties of the system, both in the ex-post analysis of the robot movement during the demo and in the ex-ante analysis of the possible robot configurations during the design of the robot and of the demo itself. This paper presents how the techniques have been applied and to what extent the results of the application match the real robot behavior. The SENSO-RIA modeling and analysis techniques used are the UML4SOA graphical modeling language, the Performance Evaluation Process Algebra PEPA, the UMC model checker and the Markovian process algebra MarCaSPiS.

1 Introduction to the Bowling Robot Case Study

The Bowling Robot case study was at first developed as a robot-bowling game scenario for demonstrating SENSORIA's software engineering approach and tools in a practical way during hands-on demonstration, after which it evolved into a case study, apt to show SENSORIA results applied to the design and development of a real system, the robot that plays bowling itself. Specifically, the Bowling Robot has been used as a showcase for the modeling techniques and tools, in particular qualitative and quantitative modeling, and was not intended to address service composition/orchestration issues.

In fact, initially, the Bowling Robot scenario was developed in order to show in advance to the demo participants, who were asked to make some choices during the programming of the Robot Player, how different control policies and

---

[*] This work has been partially sponsored by the project SENSORIA, IST-2005-016004.

M. Wirsing and M. Hölzl (Eds.): SENSORIA Project, LNCS 6582, pp. 678–697, 2011.
© Springer-Verlag Berlin Heidelberg 2011

parameter choices may affect the robot's performance. This was aimed at allowing the demo participants to reason on the robot's parameters and environment and make sensible choices in order to try to win the robot-bowling game. In this phase, the Robot Player development was meant to be conducted in a traditional spiral approach including design, construction of the robot, program writing, and testing 'on the field'. We would have designed the Robot Player first and then applied SENSORIA results in order to be able to show how SENSORIA would support the visitor in programming the robot during the demo.

During the design of the robot, some complex and interleaved choices were needed concerning the mechanical features, control policies, and possible parameter sets. During testing experiments on the field, unexpected properties of the system under development came out and the necessity to analyze the scenario in more detail appeared clear, in order to ensure proper behavior of the robot while allowing a visitor at the same time to enjoy a nice choice among different control policies and parameter values. Some 'hidden' needs were identified, such as 'the robot must always complete the proper actions and arrive at the end of the lane'. We therefore expressed as design questions desirable properties of the system. During the development of the robot very soon the testing of the overall behavior of the robot program was substituted by experiments planned for the determination of the environment and the robot's 'internal' parameters such as the robot speed. This led us to focus on the usage of different SENSORIA languages and tools, not only during the demo sessions but during the design of the demo itself and, finally, to further analysis after the demo development ended. This process may also be considered as a hint of how a traditional system development approach may change with the availability of SENSORIA.

This paper is organized as follows. In Sect. 2 we describe the context of the robot-bowling game scenario, after which we describe the Bowling Robot case study and its relevance to SENSORIA in Sect. 3. The results of the application of four SENSORIA techniques to the case study are presented in Sect. 4, while we report our conclusions and the lessons learned in Sect. 5.

2   Context Description

The Bowling Robot case study context is a game scenario developed for demonstrating SENSORIA's potential impacts on the software systems development process in a SOA context presented at the ICT exhibit in Lyon, November 2008, and at the FET exhibit in Prague, April 2009.

The Bowling Robot demo scenario is focused on people who want to play bowling on the Internet by means of a so-called 'Virtual Bowling' service. The Virtual Bowling service provides an actual competition performed by a robot, called "Player". The game is personalized according to each virtual player's profile (e.g. her/his gender, depending on whether a red or blue ball is used). This information is provided to the Player by a second robot, called "Coach", that receives from the Virtual Bowling service the gamers' requests including information about the virtual player and communicates them to the Robot Player.

In the Bowling Robot scenario, we imagine that a human player, i.e. one of the exhibit visitors, is to specify the program that determines the behavior of the Robot Player during the game. The Bowling Robot case study is centred around this concept: the visitor, in order to optimize the robot's performance, has to reach the maximum score in the game taking into account the physical characteristics of the robot and of the environment, and in this process s/he is supported by the SENSORIA tools and languages. In particular, SENSORIA modeling approaches facilitate the prediction of robot behavior at design time.

The Bowling Robot demo presented at ICT'08 and FET'09 has four phases:

phase 1 The visitor programs the robot using the standard Lego GUI.

phase 2 The visitor is able to make choices in order to improve her/his Lego program with the support of SENSORIA analysis techniques.

phase 3 The visitor has access to the Virtual Bowling service that activates the bowling-robot game.

phase 4 After the game, a score is computed for each visitor in order to award a daily SENSORIA robot-bowling champion cup.

3   Case Study Description

In the robot-bowling game, the main characteristic of the environment is the floor of the bowling alley, that presents a pattern with a radial geometry, darkening from white to black (see Fig. 1): the maximum black point is in the optimal launching position (2), right in front of the first pin.

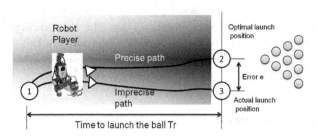

Fig. 1. Bowling Robot scenario

In this context, the Robot Player begins from loading position (1) at the start of the bowling lane (80 cm) and aims to reach the optimal launching position (2). The Robot Player detects the color of the floor by means of two light sensors. The Player, aiming to follow the maximum value of the gradient towards the black, at fixed time intervals T measures the level of white/black on the floor and decides to go forward or turn to correct its path. Finally, due to possible imperfect path finding, the Player may reach the end of the lane in position (3) and launch the ball (actually, drop it on a ramp towards the pins). The Player recognizes the end of the lane as it is marked by a silver ribbon giving the maximum white value on the floor MAX. The computed game score depends on:

1. the number of pins knocked down,
2. the time to arrive at the launching position and drop the ball (Tr), and
3. the distance from the optimal launching position, i.e. error e.

Accordingly, the visitor is asked to program the Robot Player to pull down as many pins as possible in the shortest possible time with the maximum precision (minimize e). For the sake of simplicity, we define as 'precise launches' those with error $e < 10$ cm, evidenced by a green zone 20 cm wide at the end of the lane, centered w.r.t. the optimal launching position. The programming choices available to the visitor are taken from a limited set, in order to allow each visitor to complete the demo in a few minutes.

Having fixed the path dimensions and geometry we decided the mechanical structure of the Player that includes two sensors to measure the color of the path on the floor, two wheels, two motors, and, in front, a simple mechanical hand (served by a third motor) that allows to get and release the ball. Concerning movements, a Player can go forward or turn approximately on its place. In particular, each of the two wheels of the Player is connected to a motor that is powered with a fixed power level during the game. The Player can go forward or turn by switching on and off only one of the two motors (e.g. in order to turn right, the Player switches off the right motor while the left motor is on). In Fig. 2 the Robot Player of ICT'08, based on standard Lego NXT robot kit, is shown.

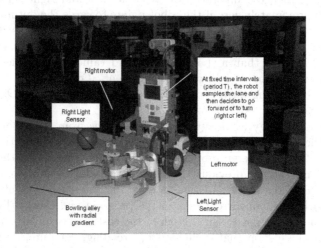

Fig. 2. The Robot Player

In order to assess its position on the path, the robot has two light sensors aimed at the floor, one on each side near each wheel. The sensor readings are numerical values that are higher as the color of the path goes from white to black. The measured radial gradient is 2.66 sensor units/cm.

At fixed time intervals the Robot Player stops, reads the sensors and then, by comparing the readings with a threshold value S, decides to go forward or turn (right or left) for that time interval T. The time interval can be imagined as a sampling period or alternatively its reciprocal is the frequency at which the system is controlled. Finally, when the Player reads maximum value of light reading (MAX), s/he decides that the end of the alley is reached and launches the ball. The overall workflow includes, after reading the sensor values, computing a specific value D depending on the sensors readings, which is to be used afterwards to decide whether the robot is on the correct path (and has to go forward) or not (and has to turn), and in the latter case, in which direction to turn.

During the Lego programming phase of the demo, the visitor builds up the Lego program by completing a pre-defined program flow:

1. choose blocks (tagged with self-explicating titles) from a predefined set and
2. set some program parameters within the program blocks.

During this phase the visitor is asked to choose between two different "Follow the Gradient" strategies, represented by two specific personalized program blocks, and to specify how long is the light sensors' sampling period T, among the set 0.2, 0.5, 0.7 and 1.0 seconds.

The two possible "Follow the Gradient" strategies available to the programmer of the Player are described in Figs. 3 and 4. The first (Strategy #1, Fig. 3) takes into account that, given the geometry on the floor path and the position of the two light sensors (symmetrically positioned with reference to the longitudinal axis of the Player), the difference between the left and right sensor readings should be approximately zero if the robot points towards the optimal launching position (2). Accordingly, at each step, the robot computes the difference D and the sign $SIGN$ between the readings of the right and the left sensor. If the difference D is lower than a specified threshold value S, then the Player goes forward, i.e. the robot is 'following the gradient'. Otherwise, the robot turns right or left depending on the sign of the computed difference D, in order to correct the path.

The second strategy (Strategy #2, Fig. 4) stems from the following consideration: if the robot is correctly 'following the gradient' towards the maximum black point (2), the difference of the reading of one sensor with the reading of the same sensor at the previous time interval should be positive and greater than the threshold value S. In this case we imagine that each of the sensors is controlled by one concurrent task in the program and checks this difference to decide whether or not to turn. Each of the tasks, consequently, as in Fig. 4, executes the main loop that includes stop, reading, compute, decide, and go forward/turn depending on the decision for that interval.

In detail, refering to the task that reads the left sensor, after having read the sensors and computed the difference $leftDelta(t)$ between the current sensor reading $leftData(t)$ and the previous one $leftData(t-1)$, the robot decides to turn if the difference is below the threshold value S and to go forward otherwise. In particular, it can be shown that if the robot aims to the left of the optimal launching position (2), then the $rightDelta(t)$ difference is higher than

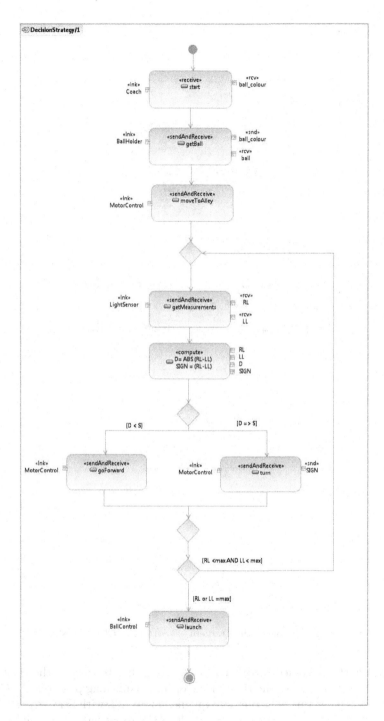

Fig. 3. "Follow the gradient" – Strategy #1

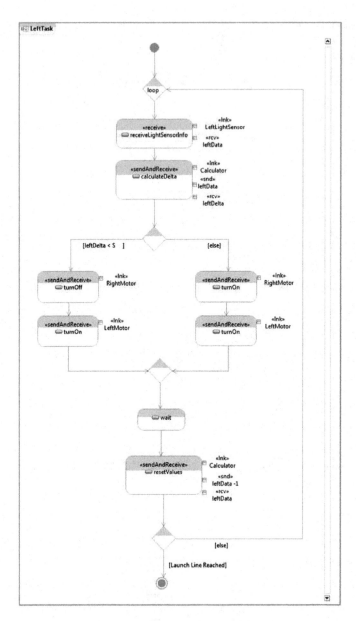

Fig. 4. "Follow the gradient" – Strategy #2, left task

the *leftDelta(t)* difference and therefore the robot has to turn to the right; vice versa if the robot aims to the right of the optimal launching position (2). Consequently, to achieve this behavior, as explained in Sect. 2, with Strategy #2, if the *leftDelta(t)* difference is below the threshold S the robot has to turn right, i.e. it has to turn off the right motor, otherwise the robot switches on both motors. As we will show later, Strategy #2 as presented so far is flawed: it has been devised on purpose in order to allow a positive search for programming errors.

To summarize, sampling period T and threshold value S are the main parameters that can be chosen to determine the robot's behavior and affect its performance, i.e. the time to launch the ball (Tr), the error in reaching the optimal position (e) and, ultimately, the number of knocked down pins. According to that, during the design of the Robot Player, concerning most of all design decisions and in particular the definition of the possible "Follow the Gradient" strategies and of the possible set of parameters T and S, the following 'design questions' arose, more or less explicitly:

DQ1 Does the robot always arrive at the end of the lane, and launch the ball?
DQ2 Does the robot mostly launch the ball within approximately one minute?
DQ3 What is the robot's performance according to different parameter choices?
Are there interesting/unexpected situations that Sensoria might evidence?

4   Use of Sensoria Tools and Results

As shown in the previous sections, Sensoria has been used both during the Robot Player design and development and during the demo. The Bowling Robot scenario has allowed the use of the following Sensoria tools and languages:

- For qualitative analysis, error identification: WS-Engineer/LTSA (see Chapter 4-4) and the UML profile UML4SOA (see Chapter 1-1).
- For qualitative analysis, system properties verification: UML model checker UMC and its logic UCTL (see Chapters 4-2 and 4-3).
- For quantitative analysis, non-functional properties: Performance Evaluation Process Algebra PEPA with IPC compiler (see Chapter 5-4 and references).
- For qualitative/quantitative analysis: both functional and non-functional properties: MarCaSPiS, Markovian extension of the process calculus CaSPiS (see Chapters 2-1 and 5-1).

The first two analyses, performed with UML4SOA and UMC models, allowed us to reply to **DQ1**. The quantitative analysis with PEPA allowed us to ensure robot behavior during the design and to show the visitor during the demo both the answer to **DQ2** and the robot's possible performance depending on different choices of design parameters, specifically parameter T (**DQ3**). Finally, analysis with MarCaSPiS allowed us to reply to **DQ1–3** using a more detailed model of the Robot Player behavior. The Sensoria models have been developed in each specific language as a mirror of the Lego program deployed on the robot.

4.1   Qualitative Analysis, Error Identification (UML4SOA Model)

During the first design activities of the robot we used the WS-Engineer tool to check the Lego programs under development for errors. We used it to perform a qualitative analysis since, being based on LTSA, it allows model checking to be carried out on the UML4SOA model of the robot and to detect deadlocks and verify arbitrary properties stated in the process calculus FSP (see Chapter 4-4 for details). Specifically, the model was written in UML4SOA, which was transformed by means of the SENSORIA MDD4SOA transformation tool (see Chapter 1-1) to generate BPEL code, which was then used as input for WS-Engineer that, in turn, internally converted the BPEL code into FSP.

The following property has been analyzed: if a task starts interacting with motors, both calls to each motor are executed without interruption. This allowed us to tell that Strategy #1 has no error, while Strategy #2 does have one. This error, specifically, is related to an undetermined behavior: as both the left and right task at the same time switch on and off the same robot motor (see Fig. 5), the resulting behavior is that the Player is not able even to move. This allowed the visitors to avoid using the flawed Strategy #2. It was possible to show to the demo visitors that the Player under Strategy #2 would go back and forth on her/his place without moving properly, but only one of them asked to do so.

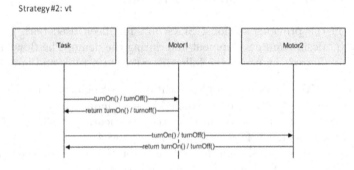

Fig. 5. Violation trace for Strategy #2

4.2   Qualitative Analysis, System Properties Verification (UMC/UCTL Model)

An alternative technique for qualitative analysis is offered by model checking with UMC, which allows the formal verification of the dynamic behavior of UML models. A UMC model of the robot's behavior consists of a description in UML state machines. The robot's desirable properties are then expressed using the UCTL logic, which is essentially the full modal/propositional μ-calculus extended with higher-level CTL/ACTL-like operators and structured action expressions (see Chapters 4-2 and 4-3 for details), and verified with UMC.

UMC enables modeling a Robot Player as a composition of evolving and communicating objects, where objects are class instances (Coach, Light Sensor, Robot Player, etc.), which together perform the desired action sequence. The set of objects and classes which constitute a system can be described in UML by a structure diagram, while the dynamic behavior of the objects can be described by associating a UML statechart diagram to their classes. Each object of the system will therefore behave like a state machine. An excerpt (class Robot) of the UMC model of the Player under Strategy #1 is as follows.

```
Class Robot is
 Signals:
 //signals received from DecisionStrategy component
 start;
 getBall;
 moveToAlley;
 getMeasurements;
 doComputation;
 turn;
 goForward;
 launch;
 //Signals to/from other components
 ballColor(bc:Token);                     //reception of ball color
 receiveBall(b);                          //reception of ball
 moveDone;                                //effected movement signal
 lightVal(rl_val: Token, ll_val: Token);  //reception of light values
 Vars:
 ball_color: Token := null;
 ball: Token := null;
 RL: Token := null;
 LL: Token := null;
 sign:Token := null;
 coachObj: Coach;
 ballHolderObj: BallHolder;
 motorControlObj: MotorControl;
 lightSensorObj: LightSensor;
 ballControlObj: BallControl;
 decisionStrategyObj: DecisionStrategy;
 State top = r0,r1,r2,r3,r4,r5,r6,r7,r8,r9,r10,r11,r12,r13
 Transitions:
 r0 -> r1 {- / decisionStrategyObj.nextAction(self)} //start request
 r1 -> r2 {start / coachObj.requestBallColor(self)} //receives decision strategy and
 r2 -> r3 {ballColor(bc) / ball_color := bc;         //then asks coach for ball color
           decisionStrategyObj.nextAction(self)} //receives ball color
 r3 -> r4 {getBall / ballHolderObj.requestBall(self,ball_color)} //asks ball holder for ball
 r4 -> r5 {receiveBall(b) / ball := b; decisionStrategyObj.nextAction(self)} //receives ball
 r5 -> r6 {moveToAlley / motorControlObj.requestMoveToAlley(self)} //motors to move on alley
 r6 -> r7 {moveDone / decisionStrategyObj.nextAction(self)} //receives movement done signal
 r7 -> r8 {getMeasurements / lightSensorObj.requestLightVal(self)} //asks for light values
 r8 -> r9 {lightVal(rl_val,ll_val) / RL := ll_val; LL := ll_val;
           decisionStrategyObj.nextAction(self)} //receives light values    //computes:
 r9 -> r10 {doComputation / decisionStrategyObj.calcDeltaAndSign(self,LL,RL)} //delta & sign
 r10 -> r11 {goForward / motorControlObj.requestMoveForward(self)} //motor to move forward
 r10 -> r11 {turn / motorControlObj.requestTurn(self)} //motor to turn //first get moveDone,
 r11 -> r12 {moveDone / decisionStrategyObj.decideLaunch(self,LL,RL)} //then launch decision
 r12 -> r8 {getMeasurements / lightSensorObj.requestLightVal(self)} //cycles to r8 for
 r12 -> r13 {launch / ballControlObj.launch} //launches ball       //new measurements
 end Robot;
```

The analysis performed shows that the Robot Player under Strategy #1 is able to complete the actions required for a bowling game, i.e. the sequence of movements up to launching the ball while moving along the alley. Specifically, the following properties (written in UCTL) have been verified true for Strategy #1.

1. The robot always eventually launches the ball: *AF EX {launch} true*
   If this property holds, the system is not effected by deadlock in any possible trace before reaching a state in which the *launch* action can be performed.

2. The next action after a movement request is notifying movement completion:

$$AF\ EX\ \{requestMoveForward\ OR\ requestTurn\ OR\ requestMoveToAlley\}$$
$$AX\ \{moveDone\}\ true$$

If this property holds, the robot performs no other actions after each movement request, until the motor announcing the requested maneuver finished.

3. At least once, the proper action sequence for a bowling game is performed:

$$AF\ EX\ \{start\}\ AF\ EX\ \{getBall\}\ AF\ EX\ \{moveToAlley\}$$
$$AF\ EX\ \{getMeasurements\}\ AF\ (EX\ \{goForward\}\ true\ AND$$
$$EX\ \{turn\}\ true)\ AF\ EX\ \{launch\}\ true$$

The fact that this property holds guarantees that the robot's behavior includes at least once the desired sequence of actions for a bowling game: starting movement, getting the ball, moving to the alley, get measurements and going forward (turning) and, finally, launching the ball.

During the demo we showed that the Robot Player's behavior under Strategy #1 followed the proper sequence of movements up until launching the ball.

4.3 Quantitative Analysis, Non-functional Properties (PEPA Model)

During the Player development a series of experiments had been performed in order to ensure proper behavior of the robot during the demo over a possible set of different design features, such as threshold value, distance between sensors, sampling period. The robot showed satisfactory behavior under the following parameters choices: distance between sensors $d = 9$ cm, threshold value $S = 20$ sensor units and sampling period in the interval from 0.2 to 1 sec. In particular, rather counter-intuitively, the robot behavior experimentally showed that, as the sampling period increases (e.g. from 0.2 sec to 1 sec) the time to roll the ball Tr decreases, i.e. the robot becomes quicker to reach the end of the alley while the frequency at which the system is controlled decreases (see Table 1).

Table 1. Experimental results

Sampling period T (sec)	Time to roll ball Tr (sec)	Distance from optimal launching position = error e (cm)	Precise occurrence (percentage of precise events)
0.2	53	4.3	100%
0.5	24	3.9	100%
0.7	22	6.7	80%
1.0	21	10.7	50%

In fact, the set of experiments performed (approximately 20 samples for each of the sampling period values) reported an overall average Tr of 53 sec for $T = 0.2$

and of 21 sec for $T = 1$ sec. The same experiments reported that the error e (distance from the optimal position (1)) increases from 4 cm to approximately 11 cm on average if the sampling period goes from 0.2 to 1: from this point of view, as it is most likely to be expected, the robot is more imprecise if the frequency at which the system is controlled decreases. In particular, the robot is most likely to be imprecise than precise if T is higher than 1 sec.

This was exactly what we needed for the sake of a game competition: the visitor is asked to choose the value of a control parameter (T) which is related to the trade-off between two performance indicators, i.e. time to launch Tr and precision (related to error e). This leaves her/him freedom to decide, as the information available is not enough to precisely forecast the outcome of their choice on the value of T (they were not allowed to know the rating calculation formula). To show i) on the one hand to the visitors how Sensoria can predict the outcome of programmer's choices concerning the value of sampling period T and ii) on the other hand give an answer to the aforementioned design question **DQ2** concerning the overall time to roll the ball Tr, and specifically to the above mentioned unexpected behavior, we developed the following approximate model of the Robot Player behavior using the PEPA modeling approach (see Fig. 6).

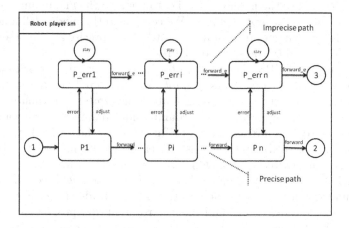

Fig. 6. State machine model of Robot Player

Concurrent systems can be modeled in PEPA as composition of components which undertake actions. In PEPA actions have a duration. Thus, the expression $(\alpha, r).P$ denotes a component which can undertake an action α at a rate r, to evolve into component P. The rate r models a delay of variable duration. Delays are samples from an exponential random variable with parameter r. See Chapter 5-4 and its references for details on PEPA.

We intuitively describe the PEPA model using a state machine model (see Fig. 6). The robot starts its run on the bowling alley in state $P1$ (we did not model the straight line movement from starting position (1) to the beginning of the bowling alley) and completes the run in two possible ways: it follows the 'precise' path indicated by the states from P1 to P n or the imprecise path, related to the states from P_err1 to P_err n. Due to the geometry of the problem, we imagine that after each step the robot is in one of two possible states: pointed towards the position (2) or not. Accordingly, the first situation corresponds to a state P on a precise path and the second to the robot on an imprecise path.

The robot completes its path to the end of the alley (80 cm long) in a total number of n steps, each one corresponding to a single sampling cycle. At each step i, with reference to Fig. 7, if the robot is on the precise path, it can deviate from the optimal path with probability e_prob, going in state P_err i, or, with probability $(1 − e\_prob)$, can assess that it has to go forward straight to position (2) (optimal route) so it goes in state P i+1 on the precise path. The probability e_prob is related to the error that affects the readings of the light sensors (and most likely to mechanical structure imperfection and differences between motors as well). If the robot is on the imprecise path, it has three possibilities: to remain onto the imprecise path without progressing towards the end of the alley (with probability a_prob), to remain onto the imprecise path while anyway progressing towards the end of the lane (with probability fe_prob, or, finally, to go back to the precise path (i.e. to point to the maximum black point) with probability $1 − a\_prob − fe\_prob$. We completed the model defining the rate at which the system goes from state to state on the precise and imprecise paths, forwardrate, related to the speed of the robot.

To perform the PEPA analysis, we observed the robot behavior to assess the values of probabilities e_prob and fe_prob, and measured the robot movements during a single sampling cycle to assess rate forwardrate. To estimate e_prob, for each value of sampling period T, we counted how many times the robot moved from a precise to an imprecise path, i.e. if pointing to the optimal lauch position the Player did not go straight. Likewise, for each T, to estimate the probability of remaining on the imprecise path (fe_prob) we counted how many times the Player remained in the wrong direction if s/he headed in the wrong direction. According to experiments and analysis done on Strategy #1 deadlock-free characteristics, we decided to consider a_prob null (i.e. the robot always progresses towards the end of the alley). Concerning the rate forwardrate, we measured both the linear and the angular speed of the robot, measuring respectively the distance (cm) and the rotation (degrees) over several sampling cycles.

Table 2. Internal robot parameters

Sampling period T (sec)	Distance covered (DC) in a single sampling cycle (cm)	Rotation during sampling period (degrees)	Rotation (radians)	Sampling rate $(1/T)$	# sampling cycles to cover alley (80/DC)
0.2	0.4	2.9	0.05	5.0	200
0.5	2.4	16.6	0.29	2.0	36
0.7	3.4	24.5	0.43	1.43	23
1.0	5.5	46.7	0.81	1.0	14

Table 2 shows, for each sampling period T, the rectilinear distance covered (DC) by the robot during a single sampling cycle, the rotation during sampling period (radians), the corresponding rate at which sampling occurs $(1/T)$ and the number of sampling cycles that are needed for the robot to cover the 80 cm distance to the end of the alley. According to this measurement we defined the parameters of the Player PEPA model (see the code that follows below).

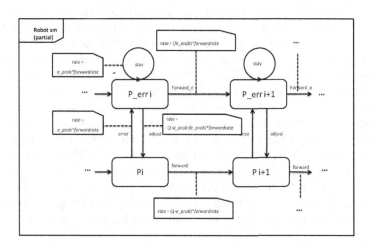

Fig. 7. State machine model of Robot Player: action rates

```
// PEPA model of Robot Player for T = 1 (forwardrate = 1)
n = 14;
// 4 error paths taken if robot is on right path in 49 movements
e_prob = 0.082;
a_prob = 0.00;
// 48 error paths taken if robot is on error path in 49 samples
fe_prob = 0.98;
forwardrate = 1.0;

Step = (forward,infty).StepDone + (start,infty).Step;
StepDone = (stop1,infty).Step + (start, infty).Step;
Steps = Step[n][stop1,start];
Step_e = (forward_e,infty).StepDone_e + (start,infty).Step_e;
StepDone_e = (stop2,infty).Step_e + (start,infty).Step_e;
Steps_e = Step_e[n][stop2,start];
AllSteps = (Steps < > Steps_e);

PlayerStop1 = (start,1.0).Player;
PlayerStop2 = (start,1.0).Player;
Player = (forward,(1-e_prob) * forwardrate).Player          // Precise path
       + (error,e_prob * forwardrate).PlayerError
       + (stop1,(1-e_prob) * forwardrate).PlayerStop1;
PlayerError = (adjust,(1-a_prob-fe_prob) * forwardrate).Player   // Imprecise path
            + (forward_e,fe_prob*forwardrate).PlayerError
            + (stop2,fe_prob * forwardrate).PlayerStop2;
Player < forward,forward_e,start,stop1,stop2 > AllSteps     // System equation
```

In particular, to take into account the effective robot speed, the PEPA calculations have been performed for each T value varying in accordance with the number of steps n of the model. To simplify the modeling, we considered only the linear speed: as one can see in Table 2, for $T = 0.2$ sec, first line of the table, if the robot covers DC $= 0.4$ cm in each step, it needs $n = 200 = 80/0.4$ steps.

It must be said that as the robot deviates from the original straight line with high probability, this approximation leads to computing a total time to launch the ball Tr that is certainly underestimated. Anyway, we had also to take into account the fact that the computation time is a polynomial function of the number n of steps in the model[1], therefore we had to take it as low as possible. Moreover, specifically in the case of $n = 200$ steps, the available computing resources have been not enough to perform the computations, even with that approximation; in fact, we reduced the model to 20 steps, introducing further approximations for the sake of the demo, that we will not discuss here.

We are mainly interested in an intuitive explanation of the results obtained with SENSORIA modeling techniques compared with the experimental findings. The results of PEPA's quantitative analysis are shown in Fig. 8: the cumulative probability functions of the time to roll the ball Tr for the robot ending in the precise path (line labeled stop_1) and for the robot ending out of the precise 'zone' along the imprecise path (line labeled stop_2). The left graph shows Tr for sampling period equal to 0.5 sec; that on the right for sampling period $T = 1$ sec.

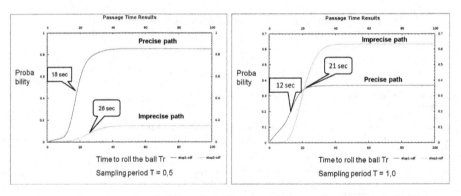

Fig. 8. Cumulative probability distributions of time to launch the ball (Tr)

The graphs show that with sampling period $T = 0.5$ sec the robot is precise in approximately 84% of the cases and on average launches the ball in $Tr = 18$ sec, while in 16% of the cases it is imprecise and launches in $Tr = 26$ sec. Our PEPA model computes $Tr = 20$ sec to roll the ball on average on all launches (precise or imprecise). If the sampling period is $T = 1$ sec the robot is precise in 37% of the cases and on average launches in 12 sec, while it is imprecise in approximately 63% of the cases and launches in 21 sec. The total average Tr is 18 sec.

---

[1] Computational resources increase with space state size, that, in this PEPA model, is proportional to the number of steps n squared.

We can say that the results of the PEPA quantitative analysis intuitively agree with the experiments performed with the real robot. As shown in Table 3, both data series (computed and experimental) with increasing sampling period T, show that time to roll the ball Tr decreases, while the robot is less precise and becomes most likely imprecise if $T = 1$.

Table 3. Comparison of results of PEPA analysis and experimental data

T (sec)	PEPA average time Tr (sec)	PEPA precision (% precise launches)	Experimental average Tr (sec)	Experimental precision (% precise launches)
0.5	20	84%	24	100%
0.7	19	63%	22	80%
1.0	18	37%	21	50%

To summarize, the PEPA quantitative analysis, even if based on an approximate model, has allowed us, while choosing a sensible set of parameter values for the sampling period T according to all design choices made before, to explain the reasons of an unexpected behavior of the system during the system design and development. This led us to decide that the sampling period T, that was related to the unexpected behavior, was the one to be chosen as a programming parameter for the demo. Furthermore, the same analysis have been used to show the demo participants how the robot behavior could be predicted.

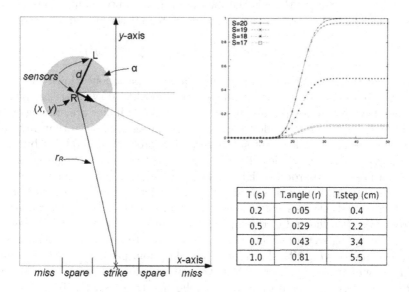

T (s)	T.angle (r)	T.step (cm)
0.2	0.05	0.4
0.5	0.29	2.2
0.7	0.43	3.4
1.0	0.81	5.5

Fig. 9. Some details of the Bowling Robot scenario in MarCaSPiS (left + table) and results of experiments with T equal to 0.5, 0.7, and 1.0 sec (right)

4.4 Qualitative/Quantitative Analysis, Functional and Non-functional Properties (MarCaSPiS Model)

Both qualitative and quantitative aspects of the Bowling Robot scenario are analysed with MarCaSPiS, the stochastic extension of CaSPiS. The analysis concerns the mathematical modeling of the robot behavior in accordance with Strategy #1. The analysis was performed by taking into account the environmental parameters (like the geometry of the path gradient), the internal robot parameters (like robot speed and sensor reading errors) and the programming parameters available in the design (sampling period T and threshold value S).

Figure 9 shows some details of the scenario modeled in MarCaSPiS. Its main parameters are the Cartesian coordinates of the right-sensor $R = (x, y)$ and the angular coordinate of the robot's direction α. These parameters univocally identify the robot's position. Angular and rectilinear movements, denoted by $T.angle$ and $T.step$ respectively, can be defined as functions of the parameter T (see, e.g., values in Fig. 9 for sampling periods $0.5, 0.7,$ and 1 sec). No MarCaSPiS analysis was performed for $T = 0.2$ sec as the model's state space size exceeded the available computation resources. The Cartesian coordinates of the left-sensor can be obtained from R and α by using the following trigonometric functions:

$$L = (x_L, y_L) = (x - d \cdot \sin(\alpha), y + d \cdot \cos(\alpha))$$

A robot decides upon the next action according to the floor gradient. An approximation of the floor gradient is modeled by means of function $L(r)$ defined as $MAX + k \cdot r$, where MAX is the maximum light sensor value, constant k is -2.66 unit/cm and r is one of the following right/left sensor radial coordinates:

$$r_L = \sqrt{(x_L^2 + y_L^2)} \qquad r_R = \sqrt{(x^2 + y^2)}$$

The end of the bowling lane (along the x-axis) is partitioned into three zones w.r.t. the outcomes of a launch: all pins are knocked down (strike), pins are knocked down but some pins are missing (spare), and all pins are missing (miss).

The Robot Player is modeled in MarCaSPiS as a process that invokes a light sensor service. The robot-side interaction protocol is modeled by means of process "robotProcess" described in Fig. 10 (left column). This process sends the robot position to process "lightSensorsProcess" to receive the light-intensity measurements. Measurements permit deciding whether to move forward or turn left or right, or whether or not to launch the ball. This last decision is made when the robot reaches the end of the lane (see also process "lightSensorsProcess").

After receiving measurements rl and ll, process "robotProcess" compares the difference $abs(rl - ll)$ with the value of the threshold parameter S to determine the new robot position. After each movement, the new robot position (denoted by R' and α') is calculated by using the following trigonometric functions:

turn right $R' = (x, y)$ and $\alpha' = \alpha - T.angle$
turn left $R' = (x + d \cdot (\sin(\alpha') - \sin(\alpha)), y + d \cdot (\cos(\alpha) - \cos(\alpha')))$ and $\alpha' = \alpha + T.angle$
go forward $R' = (x + T.step \cdot \cos(\alpha), y + T.step \cdot \sin(\alpha))$ and $\alpha' = \alpha$

```
let robotProcess[ x: float , y: float , a: float ] be      let lightSensorsProcess[] be
  var rl : float;                                            var x : float;
  var ll : float;                                            var y : float;
  send( COORDINATES[x , y , a] ):.7;                         var a : float;
  receive( INTENSITIES[ rl? , ll? ] ):.5;                    receive( COORDINATES[ x? , y? , a? ] ):.5;
  if ( abs(rl-ll) < S ) then # go forward                    if ( (y => 0.0) & (y + d*cos(a) => 0.0 ) ) then
  begin                                                      begin # end of lane not reached
    robotProcess( x+(T.step*cos(a)) ,                          chc # non deterministic choice introduce ERR
                  y+(T.step*sin(a)) ,                          [] tau:.98;send( INTENSITIES[ MAX-k*sqrt(pow(x,2)+pow(y,2)) ,
                  a );                                                MAX-k*sqrt(pow(x-d*sin(a),2)+pow(y+d*cos(a),2))) ] ):.5;
  end                                                                lightSensorsProcess();
  else # turn                                                  [] tau:.1;send( INTENSITIES[ MAX-k*sqrt(pow(x,2)+pow(y,2)) ,
  begin                                                              MAX-k*sqrt(pow(x-d*sin(a),2)+pow(y+d*cos(a),2)))+ERR ] ):.5;
    if ( (rl-ll) > 0.0 ) then # turn right                          lightSensorsProcess();
    begin                                                      [] tau:.1;send( INTENSITIES[ MAX-k*sqrt(pow(x,2)+pow(y,2))+ERR ,
      robotProcess( x ,                                              MAX-k*sqrt(pow(x-d*sin(a),2)+pow(y+d*cos(a),2))) ] ):.5;
                    y ,                                              lightSensorsProcess();
                    a-T.angle );                                 end
    end                                                      end
    else # turn left                                         else # end of lane reached!!
    begin                                                    begin
      robotProcess( x+d*(sin(a+T.angle)-sin(a)) ,              if ( (x - d*sin(a) / 2.0 <= STRK) & (STRK + x - d*sin(a) / 2.0 => 0.0) )
                    y+d*(cos(a)-cos(a+T.angle)) ,              then begin # good shot
                    a+T.angle ) ;                                    strike();
    end                                                            end
  end                                                          else
end                                                            begin
                                                                if ( (x - d*sin(a) / 2.0 <= SPAR) & (SPAR + x - d*sin(a) / 2.0 => 0.0) )
                                                                then begin # spare
                                                                     spare();
                                                                   end
                                                              else
                                                              begin # bad shot
                                                                miss();
                                                              end
                                                            end
                                                          end
                                                        end
```

Fig. 10. MarCaSPiS interaction protocol

Errors can occur in the interaction protocol during light sensors reading, as modeled in Fig. 10 (right column); "lightSensorsProcess" introduces errors through two measurement types: a correct one (evaluated by function $L(r)$ defined above) and an incorrect one (one for each sensor) characterized by error ERR.

After receiving a new robot position, "lightSensorsProcess" controls if the launching line is reached by checking the y-coordinate of each sensor. The outcome of a launch is determined in terms of the robot-midpoint position by checking whether the x-coordinate $x - (d/2) \cdot \sin(\alpha)$ belongs to one of the zones strike, spare, or miss (characterized by constants $STRK$ and $SPAR$).

MarCaSPiS' operational semantics permits characterizing the stochastic behavior of systems, whose properties can be specified with SOSL (Service-Oriented Stochastic Logic, see Chapter 5-1) and automatically checked using SOSL–MC.

We are primarily interested in an intuitive explanation of the results by showing the feasibility of our methodology with MarCaSPiS. We report an analysis based on experiments performed using MarCaSPiS in comparison to experimental results. We focus on the probability of the set of computations that lead to a state satisfying a generic property φ. This can be evaluated by means of the SOSL formula $true \, \{*\} \, U \, \varphi$. When specifying the formula, we use property $\varphi = $ "strike" to identify states of the model which correspond to an outcome "strike"; we use properties $\varphi = $ "spare" and $\varphi = $ "miss" to identify states corresponding to outcomes "spare" and "miss", respectively. Figures 9 (right) and 11 show graphics generated by SOSL–MC illustrating the results of three sample experiments. We assume that the Robot Player is already on the alley and ready to bowl. Initially, the robot position is given by $R = (0\,cm, 80\,cm)$ and $\alpha = \pi$. The common parameters used in all experiments are: $d = 9\,cm$ (distance between sensors), $MAX = 711\,unit$ (max-black intensity), $STRK = 10\,cm$ and $SPAR = STRK + 12.5\,cm$ (strike and spare zones), and error $ERR = 2\,unit$. To display the results, we simulate model computations in the time interval $[0, 50]$.

The first graphic of Fig. 9 (right) permits answering a more general formulation of **DQ2** regarding whether the robot launches the ball within k time units (for a given k occurring in $[0, 50]$) arriving at strike zones and spare or miss zones. The former type of zone corresponds to precise launching, the latter to imprecise launching. The used parameters are: sampling periods $T = 0.5$ sec and $T = 0.7$ sec, and threshold parameter $S = 20\,unit$. This experiment also permits answering a formulation of **DQ1** regarding whether and how a robot arrives at the end of the bowling lane. To comment on some of the results of Fig. 9 (right), it shows that a robot with sampling period $T = 0.5$ sec is more precise (arriving at strike zones) than one with parameter $T = 0.7$ sec (which reaches launching zones more quickly, but can arrive at spare or miss zones) and much more than one with parameter $T = 1$ sec. It furthermore shows that for $T = 0.5$ the robot is most likely to be precise, according to experimental data.

We can say that the results of the MarCaSPiS analysis are intuitively in agreement with the experiments performed with the real robot. As shown in Table 4, both data series (computed and experimental) with increasing sampling period T, show that time to roll the ball Tr decreases, while the robot is less precise and becomes most likely imprecise if $T = 1$.

Table 4. Comparison of results of MarCaSPiS analysis and experimental data

T (sec)	MarCaSPiS average time Tr (sec)	MarCaSPiS precision (% precise launches)	Experimental average Tr (sec)	Experimental precision (% precise launches)
0.5	23.34	100%	24	100%
0.7	20.74	95%	22	80%
1.0	20.67	85%	21	50%

The last experiments are designed to answer questions of type **DQ3** on how robot behaviors change depending on different model parameters. Properties φ are specified to denote *"strike"* or *"spare"* outcomes separately. Figure 11 illustrates the evolving of the probability of a robot launching the ball with parameters $T = 0.5$ sec w.r.t. variations of parameter S from $20\,unit$ to $17\,unit$. In particular, Fig. 11 (left) illustrates the decreasing probability of arriving at a strike zone by reducing the value of S; conversely, Fig. 11 (right) illustrates the increasing probability of arriving at a spare zone by reducing the value of S.

To conclude, our MarCaSPiS methodology provides both 'intuitive' and effective estimations of robot behaviors (w.r.t. variations of model parameters) and a formal basis to reason on other functional properties of the Robot Player.

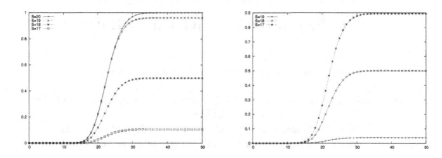

Fig. 11. Results of experiments with $\varphi = $ *"strike"* (left) and $\varphi = $ *"spare"* (right)

5   Conclusions and Lessons Learned

Concerning the demo, the Bowling Robot scenario has been particularly effective both in attracting visitors at the SENSORIA booths and in fostering their interest into the SENSORIA project after first impression. Nearly 200 visitors came to the SENSORIA booths during each exhibit and approximately 30 visitors each day participated in the robot-bowling game. Visitors judged particularly effective the way SENSORIA analysis (both qualitative and quantitative) helped making the choices on the program parameter values and policies, so that each demo session has been performed in a few minutes, as requested by the demo specifications, and time remained for the visitor to ask questions about SENSORIA.

During the development of the robot, on the one hand, very soon the testing of the overall behavior of the robot program was substituted by experiments planned for the determination of the environmental parameters, such as the linear and angular speed of the robot or the probability distribution of the sensor reading errors, showing a hint of how the SENSORIA approach, especially in a SOA concurrent environment, might lead to anticipate during the design phase a more detailed specification of the functional and non-functional aspects of the system and of its components. On the other hand, concerning the analysis with PEPA and MarCaSPiS, we discovered that, depending on the choice of system parameters, it is very easy to incur into a state-space explosion, i.e. the model dimensions grow to the extent that calculations are not possible due to limitation of the computing resources or take too much time for the project purposes or resources. In order to avoid this, it is important to carefully plan the experiments to be done and in particular the possible approximations that might be enacted.

Acknowledgments. This work benefited from discussions with P. Mayer (who wrote the UML4SOA model and did the WS-Engineer analysis) and A. Clark (who helped a lot in writing the PEPA model). Special thanks to A. Fantechi, who reviewed the paper, for his useful suggestions.

The Sensoria Approach
Applied to the Finance Case Study*

Stefania Gnesi[1], Rosario Pugliese[2], and Francesco Tiezzi[2]

[1] Istituto di Scienza e Tecnologie dell'Informazione "A. Faedo", ISTI - CNR, Pisa
stefania.gnesi@isti.cnr.it
[2] Dipartimento di Sistemi e Informatica, Università degli Studi di Firenze
rosario.pugliese@unifi.it, tiezzi@dsi.unifi.it

Abstract. This chapter provides an effective implementation of (part of) the Sensoria approach, specifically *modelling* and *formal analysis* of service-oriented software based on mathematically founded techniques. The 'Finance case study' is used as a test bed for demonstrating the feasibility and effectiveness of the use of the process calculus COWS and some of its related analysis techniques and tools. In particular, we report the results of an application of a temporal logic and its model checker for expressing and checking functional properties of services and a type system for guaranteeing confidentiality properties of services.

1 Introduction

The Sensoria approach encompasses the whole development process of service-oriented software, from systems specified in high-level languages to deployment and re-engineering. In fact, as part of the project the partners have developed a large set of languages, methods, techniques and tools that can be applied during the development of service-oriented applications. Each of these project's outcomes has been designed to solve a certain type of problems and is applicable to some specific situations. It is thus difficult to identify the 'best' technique or tool that solves a particular problem arising in the development process.

To shepherd the prospective user through the selection procedure, as a result of a collaboration among several people involved in the project, a *catalogue of patterns* has recently started to be developed (see Chapter 7-5). Several patterns have been already catalogued that address a broad spectrum of SOA engineering aspects such as modelling, specification, analysis, verification, orchestration, deployment. Besides as an index to Sensoria outcomes, this catalogue serves as a guidance for using them and for better understanding relative advantages and disadvantages.

Since we want to demonstrate the feasibility and effectiveness of the use of the process calculus COWS [LPT07a] (see also Chapter 2-1), we consider relevant to this chapter those patterns involving process calculi as specification formalisms and their related techniques for qualitative and quantitative analysis, and present solutions to these patterns in terms of COWS and its related analysis techniques and tools. As a test bed, we use the 'Finance case study' (its UML4SOA modelling can be found in Chapter 7-1).

---

* This work has been partially sponsored by the project Sensoria, IST-2005-016004.

M. Wirsing and M. Hölzl (Eds.): Sensoria Project, LNCS 6582, pp. 698–718, 2011.

This way the chapter provides an effective implementation of (part of) the Sensoria approach, specifically *modelling* and *formal analysis* of service-oriented software based on mathematically founded techniques.

Hence, this chapter contains the following contributions. Section 2 presents a COWS specification of the Finance case study. Section 3 illustrates a solution to the *Functional Service Verification* pattern, where service behavioural properties are expressed using the temporal logic SocL and verified using the model checker CMC [FGL+08] (see also Chapters 4-3 and 4-2). Section 4 illustrates a solution to the *Service Specification and Analysis* pattern, where confidentiality properties are checked using the type system of [LPT07b]. Section 5 reports on an ongoing effort for devising an integrated approach that can lead to verifiable implementations of service components from abstract architectural models of business activities. To this aim we are developing software tools that can provide access to verification functionalities also to users not familiar with formal methods. Section 6 briefly reviews some feedbacks from an application of COWS and its related analysis techniques to the Finance case study.

2   A COWS Specification of the Finance Case Study

In this section, we present a relevant part of a COWS specification modelling the Finance case study (the whole specification is reported in [Tie09]). We will gently introduce COWS's syntax and semantics in a step-by-step fashion while commenting upon the specification and refer the interested reader to Chapter 2-1 for a presentation of COWS's syntax and an informal explanation of its semantics.

We start with an informal specification of the scenario. The considered service provides a customer company with the possibility to ask for a loan to a bank and then orchestrates the necessary steps for processing the credit request, which may involve an evaluation by either a clerk or a supervisor before a contract proposal is sent to the customer. Initially, the customer logins to the *credit request* service by providing his username and password, then uploads the necessary data for his request. More specifically, he firstly provides the credit data (e.g. the desired amount), then the securities of the loan and his balance. When the request is completely filled by the customer, the service calculates the rating of the customer request, by resorting on a (possibly) external service, and takes a decision on it. The decision can be either to immediately accept the request, if the rating value is "*aaa*", or to accept or decline it according to a clerk or a supervisor evaluation, if the rating value is "*bbb*" or "*ccc*", respectively. In case of a decline, the possibility to update the data and restart the request processing is given to the customer. At any moment the customer may require to abort the process. If this happens, the process terminates and, in case, the request data are deleted. As we will see later on, this requires execution of *compensation activities* to semantically rollback the action of storing the request data performed by the involved services. This prevents such services from maintaining information of already aborted requests.

The COWS term representing the overall scenario is

$$CreditInstitute \mid RatingProvider \mid BalanceAnalysisProvider$$
$$\mid SecurityAnalysisProvider \mid Portal$$

The services above are composed by using the parallel composition operator $\_|\_$ that allows the different components to be concurrently executed and to interact with each other.

CreditInstitute is defined as follows.

$$[customerManagement, creditManagement] \,(CreditRequest$$
$$| \,\, CustomerManagement$$
$$| \,\, CreditManagement\,)$$

The term is the parallel composition of the (considered) subservices of the credit institute. The delimitation operator $[\_]\_$ is used here to declare that *customerManagement* and *creditManagement* are shared partner names known to *CreditRequest*, *CustomerManagement* and *CreditManagement*, and only to them. Basically, this ensures that external services cannot directly interact with *CustomerManagement* and *CreditManagement*, which are indeed 'internal' subservices of *CreditInstitute*. Service *CreditRequest* is publicly invocable and can interact with *Portal* and other external services, other than with the two above internal services.

Hereafter we only focus on service *CreditRequest*, which is defined as follows.

$* [k, raise, x_{Id}, x_{Name}, x_{Password}]$
$\quad creditReq \cdot initialize?\langle x_{Id}, x_{Name}, x_{Password}\rangle.$
$\quad\quad(\, customerManagement \cdot checkUser!\langle x_{Id}, x_{Name}, x_{Password}\rangle$
$\quad\quad\quad | \,[x_{UserOK}] \, creditReq \cdot checkUser?\langle x_{Id}, x_{UserOK}\rangle.$
$\quad\quad\quad\quad(\{ portal \cdot initialize!\langle x_{Id}, x_{UserOK}\rangle \}$
$\quad\quad\quad\quad | \,[if, then]$
$\quad\quad\quad\quad\quad(if \cdot then!\langle x_{UserOK}\rangle$
$\quad\quad\quad\quad\quad | \, if \cdot then?\langle \mathbf{false}\rangle. \,(\mathbf{kill}(k) \,| \, \{ raise \cdot abort!\langle\rangle \} \,)$
$\quad\quad\quad\quad\quad\quad + if \cdot then?\langle \mathbf{true}\rangle.$
$\quad\quad\quad\quad\quad\quad\quad(customerManagement \cdot getCustomerData!\langle x_{Id}, x_{Name}, x_{Password}\rangle$
$\quad\quad\quad\quad\quad\quad\quad | \,[x_{LoginName}, x_{FirstName}, x_{LastName}]$
$\quad\quad\quad\quad\quad\quad\quad\quad creditReq \cdot getCustomerData?\langle x_{Id}, x_{LoginName}, x_{FirstName}, x_{LastName}\rangle.$
$\quad\quad\quad\quad\quad\quad\quad\quad Main \,) \,) \,) \,)$

The replication operator $* \,\_$, that spawns in parallel as many copies of its argument term as necessary, is exploited to model the fact that, whenever prompted by a customer request, *CreditRequest* creates an instance to serve that specific request and is immediately ready to concurrently serve other requests. Each such instance has a private name k, a reserved partner name *raise* to raise fault signals, and its own copies of variables x_{Id}, x_{Name} and $x_{Password}$. Name k introduces a named scope that groups together all the activities of the instance, making it possible to associate with such scope suitable termination activities, as well as ad hoc fault and compensation handlers. Each interaction with the service starts with a receive activity of the form $creditReq \cdot$ $initialize?\langle x_{Id}, x_{Name}, x_{Password}\rangle$ corresponding to reception of a request emitted by *Portal* on behalf of a customer. The receive activity creates a new service instance and initializes the variables x_{Id}, x_{Name} and $x_{Password}$, declared local to the instance by the delimitation operator, with data provided by a customer. In particular, variable x_{Id} is used to store a fresh datum, generated by *Portal*, univocally identifying a session of the process (which, in COWS, coincides with an instance of the service). The identifier allows *CreditRequest* to safely communicate with the involved services. In fact, in each interaction among them, the identifier is used as a correlation datum, i.e. it appears within each message. Pattern-matching permits locating such datum in the messages and, therefore, delivering the messages to the instances identified by the same datum.

Once created, a *CreditRequest*'s instance requires *CustomerManagement* to check the customer login data, by invoking the operation *checkUser* provided by the 'internal' partner name *customerManagement* through the invoke activity *customerManagement·checkUser!$\langle x_{Id}, x_{Name}, x_{Password} \rangle$*, and waits for a reply. The answer is forwarded to the customer by means of the invoke activity *portal · initialize!$\langle x_{Id}, x_{UserOK} \rangle$*. To guarantee eventual execution of this invoke, it is protected by the protection operator $\{\!|\_|\!\}$ that prevents it to be cancelled due to an abrupt termination of its enclosing scope k. Concurrently, by exploiting the receive-guarded choice operator $\_+\_$ and the private names *if* and *then*, the instance can make a conditional choice based on the answer. A negative answer forces the immediate termination of the instance, through the execution of the activity **kill**(k), and the emission of an (internal) fault signal *raise · abort!$\langle \rangle$*. Notice that, in this specific case, the fault signal is not caught and dealt with by any fault handler. In case of a positive answer, the service instance gets the customer data from *CustomerManagement*, by means of a pair of invoke-receive activities over the operation *getCustomerData*, and activates the term *Main*, which is defined as follows.

$[raise, comp]$
$(\, [k_{Main}]$
$\quad (\, [repeat, until, update, desired]$
$\quad\quad (\, repeat \cdot until!\langle \rangle$
$\quad\quad | * repeat \cdot until?\langle \rangle.$
$\quad\quad\quad [k_{loop}]$
$\quad\quad\quad (\, Creation$
$\quad\quad\quad | update \cdot desired?\langle \mathbf{true} \rangle. (\, \mathbf{kill}(k_{loop}) \mid \{\!| repeat \cdot until!\langle \rangle |\!\} \,)$
$\quad\quad\quad + update \cdot desired?\langle \mathbf{false} \rangle. Finalize \,)\,)$
$\quad | creditReq \cdot cancel?\langle x_{Id} \rangle. (\, \mathbf{kill}(k_{Main}) \mid \{\!| raise \cdot abort!\langle \rangle |\!\} \,) \,)$
$\quad | raise \cdot abort?\langle \rangle.$
$\quad [end]$
$\quad (\, comp \cdot creation!\langle creation, end \rangle$
$\quad | comp \cdot end?\langle \rangle.$
$\quad\quad (\, comp \cdot handleBalanceAndSecurityData!\langle handleBalanceAndSecurityData, end \rangle$
$\quad\quad | comp \cdot end?\langle \rangle. portal \cdot abortProcess!\langle x_{Id} \rangle \,)\,)\,)$
$\quad | * [x, y] comp \cdot creation?\langle x, y \rangle. comp \cdot y!\langle \rangle$
$\quad | * [x, y] comp \cdot handleBalanceAndSecurityData?\langle x, y \rangle. comp \cdot y!\langle \rangle \,)$

This term models a 'scope' activity named k_{Main} which is equipped with an event and a fault handler. When the scope starts, the handlers are enabled. The event handler (highlighted by a dark gray background) is activated by an invocation of the operation *cancel*; this forces the immediate termination of all (unprotected) activities representing the normal behaviour of the scope, by means of activity **kill**(k_{Main}), and the execution of activity *raise • abort!⟨⟩*, which activates the fault handler. Then, the fault handler (highlighted by a light gray background) sends two compensation signals along endpoints of the form *comp • scopeName*, where *scopeName* is replaced by *creation* and *handleBalanceAndSecurityData*, and terminates by sending a message notifying the customer that the process has correctly aborted. The private name *end* permits sequentializing the above activities. It is worth noticing that, if no compensation handler has yet been installed, the compensation activities have to immediately terminate without doing nothing. To this aim, the two (replicated) receive activities *comp • scopeName?⟨x, y⟩* catch the compensation signals, only if no compensation handlers are ready to do so[1], and reply with the corresponding termination signals.

The normal behaviour of the scope consists of a repeat-until loop, implemented by using the replication operator together with the private names *repeat* and *until*. At each iterative step, the term *Creation* is executed which upon termination allows a conditional choice to be taken: if the customer has requested an update (i.e. activity *update • desired?⟨true⟩* is executed), the remaining activities of the current iterative step are stopped (by the activity **kill**(k_{loop})) and the loop is restarted (by the signal *repeat • until!⟨⟩*); if no update has been requested (i.e. activity *update • desired?⟨false⟩* is executed), the term *Finalize* is activated.

Finalize is simply the invoke activity

$$portal • goodbye!⟨x_{Id}⟩$$

that informs the portal that the process is concluded.

Creation is defined as follows.

$[x_{CustomerId}, x_{CreditAmount}, x_{CreditType}, x_{MonthlyInstalment}]$
creditReq • createNewCreditRequest?⟨$x_{Id}, x_{CustomerId}, x_{CreditAmount}, x_{CreditType}, x_{MonthlyInstalment}$⟩ •
(*creditManagement • initCreditData!⟨$x_{Id}, x_{CustomerId}, x_{CreditAmount}, x_{CreditType}, x_{MonthlyInstalment}$⟩*
  | *creditReq • initCreditData?⟨x_{Id}⟩.*
   (*portal • createNewCreditRequest!⟨x_{Id}, working⟩*
    | *HandleBalanceAndSecurityData*
    | $[x_{End}]$ ⦃ *comp • creation?⟨creation, x_{End}⟩.*
          (*creditManagement • removeData!⟨x_{Id}⟩*
           | *creditReq • removeData?⟨x_{Id}⟩. comp • x_{End}!⟨⟩*) ⦄)))

After the data for a new credit request have been received, the service forwards them to the credit management service and waits for an acknowledgement. Then, it replies to the portal to notify that the system is working on the request, activates the term *HandleBalanceAndSecurityData*, and installs a compensation handler for undoing the activities previously performed along the operation *initCreditData*. The compensation handler (highlighted by a gray background) is a protected term waiting for a compensation request, i.e. a signal along *comp • creation*. When this signal is received, the compensation handler becomes active and invokes the operation *removeData* provided by *creditManagement*.

---

[1] Indeed, because of the semantics of parallel composition, the receives *comp • scopeName?⟨x, y⟩* are assigned a lower priority than that assigned to the receives *comp • scopeName?⟨scopeName, x_{End}⟩* performed by the compensation handlers.

HandleBalanceAndSecurityData is defined as follows.

$[flow, end]$
$(\ (\ portal \cdot enterBalanceData!\langle x_{Id} \rangle$
$\quad |\ [x_{BalancePackage}]$
$\qquad creditReq \cdot enterBalanceData?\langle x_{Id}, x_{BalancePackage} \rangle \cdot$
$\qquad (\ balance \cdot updateBalanceRating!\langle x_{Id}, x_{LoginName}, x_{FirstName}, x_{LastName}, x_{BalancePackage} \rangle$
$\qquad\quad |\ creditReq \cdot updateBalanceRating?\langle x_{Id} \rangle \cdot flow \cdot end!\langle \rangle\ )\ )$
$\quad |\ (\ portal \cdot enterSecurityData!\langle x_{Id} \rangle$
$\qquad |\ [x_{SecurityPackage}]$
$\qquad\quad creditReq \cdot enterSecurityData?\langle x_{Id}, x_{SecurityPackage} \rangle \cdot$
$\qquad\quad (\ security \cdot updateSecurityRating!\langle x_{Id}, x_{LoginName}, x_{FirstName}, x_{LastName}, x_{SecurityPackage} \rangle$
$\qquad\qquad |\ creditReq \cdot updateSecurityRating?\langle x_{Id} \rangle \cdot flow \cdot end!\langle \rangle\ )\ )$
$|\ flow \cdot end?\langle \rangle.$
$\ \ flow \cdot end?\langle \rangle.$
$\ \ (\ RatingCalculation$
$\quad |\ [x_{End}]$
$\qquad \{\ comp \cdot handleBalanceAndSecurityData?\langle handleBalanceAndSecurityData, x_{End} \rangle.$
$\qquad [completed]$
$\qquad (\ balance \cdot clearData!\langle x_{Id} \rangle\ |\ creditReq \cdot clearData?\langle x_{Id}, b \rangle. comp \cdot completed!\langle \rangle$
$\qquad\quad |\ security \cdot clearData!\langle x_{Id} \rangle\ |\ creditReq \cdot clearData?\langle x_{Id}, s \rangle. comp \cdot completed!\langle \rangle$
$\qquad\quad |\ comp \cdot completed?\langle \rangle. comp \cdot completed?\langle \rangle. comp \cdot x_{End}!\langle \rangle)\ \}\ )\ )$

It requires the customer to enter (in parallel) balance and security data and, then, sends them to the *balance* and *security* services that store such data and, when requested, will compute the corresponding ratings. When the parallel computation ends, i.e. after that two signals along *flow · end* have been consumed, the term *RatingCalculation* is activated and a compensation handler (highlighted by a gray background) for undoing the already executed activities is installed. Notably, since the compensation activities share the same operation name *clearData*, names *b* and *s* are used in the receiving activities to distinguish the responses.

RatingCalculation is defined as follows.

$rating \cdot calculateRating!\langle x_{Id}, x_{LoginName}, x_{FirstName}, x_{LastName} \rangle$
$|\ [x_{Result}, x_{RatingData}]\ creditReq \cdot calculateRating?\langle x_{Id}, x_{Result}, x_{RatingData} \rangle. Decision$

It invokes the service *rating* for getting the rating of the customer request. When an answer is returned, it activates the term *Decision*, which is defined as follows.

$[if, then, end, x_{ManualAcceptance}, x]$
$(\ if \cdot then!\langle x_{Result} \rangle$
$|\ (\ if \cdot then?\langle aaa \rangle.$
$\quad [var, set]\ (\ var \cdot set!\langle undef \rangle\ |\ var \cdot set?\langle x_{ManualAcceptance} \rangle. approval \cdot end!\langle \rangle\ )$
$\quad +\ if \cdot then?\langle x \rangle. Approval\ )$
$|\ approval \cdot end?\langle \rangle.$
$\quad (\ if \cdot then!\langle x_{Result}, x_{ManualAcceptance} \rangle$

$$| [x_1, x_2, x_3, x_4]$$
$$(\ if \cdot then?\langle aaa, x_1 \rangle. \ Accept$$
$$+\ if \cdot then?\langle x_2, \mathbf{true} \rangle. \ Accept$$
$$+\ if \cdot then?\langle x_3, x_4 \rangle. \ Decline \ )))$$

Firstly, it checks the rating result. If it is *aaa*, the service assigns the value *undef* to $x_{ManualAcceptance}$ and skips the approval phase; otherwise, the term *Approval* starts. Then, if the rating result is *aaa* or $x_{ManualAcceptance}$ has been set to **true** (i.e. either $if \cdot then?\langle aaa, x_1 \rangle$ or $if \cdot then?\langle x_2, \mathbf{true} \rangle$ is executed), the term *Accept* is activated; otherwise, *Decline* is executed.

Approval is defined as follows.

$$[if, then, x]$$
$$(\ if \cdot then!\langle x_{Result} \rangle$$
$$| \ (\ if \cdot then?\langle bbb \rangle.$$
$$portal \cdot requestClerkApproval!\langle x_{Id}, x_{RatingData} \rangle$$
$$+\ if \cdot then?\langle x \rangle.$$
$$portal \cdot requestSupervisorApproval!\langle x_{Id}, x_{RatingData} \rangle \ )$$
$$| [x_{ApprovalData}]$$
$$creditReq \cdot approvalResult?\langle x_{Id}, x_{ManualAcceptance}, x_{ApprovalData} \rangle. \ approval \cdot end!\langle \rangle \ )$$

It checks if the rating result is equal to *bbb*. In the positive case, it requests a clerk approval, otherwise a supervisor approval. After a response from either a clerk or a supervisor, it terminates the approval phase by sending the signal $approval \cdot end!\langle \rangle$.

Decline is defined as follows.

$$creditManagement \cdot generateDecline!\langle x_{Id}, x_{RatingData} \rangle$$
$$| [x_{DeclineData}] \ creditReq \cdot generateDecline?\langle x_{Id}, x_{DeclineData} \rangle.$$
$$(\ portal \cdot declineToClient!\langle x_{Id}, x_{DeclineData} \rangle$$
$$| [x_{UpdateDesired}] \ creditReq \cdot declineToClient?\langle x_{Id}, x_{UpdateDesired} \rangle.$$
$$update \cdot desired!\langle x_{UpdateDesired} \rangle \ )$$

It requires the credit management service to generate the decline data and forwards them to the customer. The customer will reply by indicating if he desires or not a data update, and such response will be sent to the main scope (see the definition of the term *Main*) by means of the invoke activity $update \cdot desired!\langle x_{UpdateDesired} \rangle$.

Finally, *Accept* is defined as follows.

$$creditManagement \cdot generateOffer!\langle x_{Id}, x_{RatingData} \rangle$$
$$| [x_{AgreementData}]$$
$$creditReq \cdot generateOffer?\langle x_{Id}, x_{AgreementData} \rangle.$$
$$(\ portal \cdot offerToClient!\langle x_{Id}, x_{AgreementData} \rangle$$
$$| [x_{Accepted}]$$
$$creditReq \cdot offerToClient?\langle x_{Id}, x_{Accepted} \rangle.$$
$$[if, then, end]$$
$$(\ if \cdot then!\langle x_{Accepted} \rangle$$
$$| \ if \cdot then?\langle \mathbf{false} \rangle. \ update \cdot desired!\langle \mathbf{false} \rangle$$
$$+\ if \cdot then?\langle \mathbf{true} \rangle.$$
$$(\ creditManagement \cdot acceptOffer!\langle x_{Id}, x_{Accepted} \rangle$$
$$| \ portal \cdot acceptOffer?\langle x_{Id} \rangle. \ update \cdot desired!\langle \mathbf{false} \rangle \ )))$$

It behaves similarly to the previous term, except for the fact that an offer is generated instead of a decline and, moreover, the acceptance of the offer by the customer is sent to the credit management service. Notice that, whether the customer accepted or not, the activity *update · desired*!⟨**false**⟩ is executed to indicate to the main scope that the data update is not desired.

3   A Logical Methodology for Checking Functional Properties

In this section, we present a solution to the *Functional Service Verification* pattern (see Chapter 7-5), where service behavioural properties are expressed using the action- and state-based, branching-time, temporal logic SocL and verified using the on-the-fly model checker CMC. Both SocL and CMC are part of a methodology for verifying functional properties of services introduced in [FGL⁺08] and also described in Chapters 4-3 and 4-2; there, among many other Sensoria tools, the tool UMC is also described which is based on the same CMC's underlying computational model but uses UML statecharts, rather than COWS, as an input specification language. Here we briefly report the main ingredients of the logic and refer the interested reader to [FGL⁺08] (and Chapter 4-2) for a formal account of the semantics of SocL formulae.

This approach takes an abstract point of view: services are thought of as software entities which may have an internal state and can perform actions, by which they can also interact with each other. A service is thus characterized in terms of states and atomic propositions that are true over them, and of state changes and actions performed when moving from one state to another. Atomic propositions express the potential capability of the service to perform a specific action, i.e. that in a given state the action is enabled.

An action has a *type*, e.g. accept a request, provide a response, etc., and is part of a possibly long-running *interaction* started when a client firstly invokes one of the operations exposed by the service. Thus, according to this view, an interaction identifies a collection of actions, each of them corresponding to a single invocation of a service operation. Since service operations can be independently invoked by several clients, multiple instances of a same interaction can be simultaneously active. To univocally identify an action, *correlation data* are used as a third attribute of service actions.

Correspondingly, the actions of the logic are characterised by three attributes: type, interaction name, and correlation data. They may also contain variables, called *correlation variables*, to enable capturing correlation data used to link together actions executed as part of the same interaction. For a given correlation variable *var*, its binding occurrence is denoted by $\underline{var}$; all remaining occurrences, that are called *free*, are denoted by *var*. Formally, SocL actions have the form $t(i, c)$, where t is the type of the action, i is the name of the interaction which the action is part of, and c is a tuple of correlation values and variables identifying the interaction (i and c can be omitted whenever do not play any role). We use $\underline{\alpha}$ as a generic action (notation $\underline{\cdot}$ emphasises the fact that the action may contain variable binders), and α as a generic action without variable binders. SocL atomic propositions have the form $p(i, c)$, where p is the name, while i and c are as above. We will use π as a generic atomic proposition.

For example, action *request*(cr, 1234, 1) could stand for a *request* action for starting an (instance of the) interaction cr which will be identified through the correlation tuple $\langle 1234, 1 \rangle$. A *response* action corresponding to the request above could be written as, e.g. *response*$(cr, 1234, 1)$. If some correlation value is unknown at design time, e.g. the identifier 1, a (binder for a) correlation variable *id* can be used instead, as in the action *request*$(cr, 1234, \underline{id})$. A corresponding response action could be written as *response*$(cr, 1234, id)$, where the (free) occurrence of the correlation variable *id* indicates the connection with the action where the variable is bound. Similarly, actions like *cancel*$(cr, 1234, id)$, *fail*$(cr, 1234, id)$ and *undo*$(cr, 1234, id)$ could indicate *cancellation*, *failure* and *compensation* notification for the same request. As regards atomic propositions, *accepting_request*$(login)$ indicates that a state can accept requests for interaction *login*, while proposition *accepting_cancel*$(cr, 1234, id)$ indicates that a state permits to cancel those requests for interaction *cr* identified by the correlation tuple $\langle 1234, id \rangle$.

The syntax of SocL formulae is defined as follows:

(*state formulae*) ϕ ::= *true* $\mid \pi \mid \neg\phi \mid \phi \wedge \phi' \mid E\Psi \mid A\Psi$

(*path formulae*) Ψ ::= $X_\gamma \phi \mid \phi_\chi U_\gamma \phi' \mid \phi_\chi W_\gamma \phi'$

(*action formulae*) γ ::= $\underline{\alpha} \mid \chi$ χ ::= *tt* $\mid \alpha \mid \tau \mid \neg\chi \mid \chi \wedge \chi$

where state formulae are the main syntactic category.

We comment on salient points. Action formulae are simply boolean compositions of actions, where *tt* is the action formula always satisfied, τ denotes unobservable actions, $\neg$ and $\wedge$ are the standard logical operators for negation and conjunction, respectively. As usual, we will use *ff* to abbreviate $\neg tt$, $\chi \vee \chi'$ to abbreviate $\neg(\neg\chi \wedge \neg\chi')$ and $\phi_1 \Rightarrow \phi_2$ to abbreviate $\neg\phi_1 \vee \phi_2$. π denotes an *atomic proposition*, that is a property that can be true over the states of services. Atomic propositions have the form $p(i, c)$, where p is the name, i is an interaction name, and c is a tuple of correlation values and variables identifying i (as before, i and c can be omitted whenever do not play any role). E and A are existential and universal (respectively) *path quantifiers*. X and U are the *next* and (*strong*) *until* operators [DV90], while W is the *weak until* operator [MKB08]. Intuitively, the formula $X_\gamma \phi$ says that in the next state of the path, reached by an action satisfying γ, the formula ϕ holds. The formula $\phi_\chi U_\gamma \phi'$ says that ϕ' holds at some future state of the path reached by a last action satisfying γ, while ϕ holds from the current state until that state is reached and all the actions executed in the meanwhile along the path satisfy χ. The formula $\phi_\chi W_\gamma \phi'$ holds on a path either if the corresponding formula with strong until operator holds or if for all the states of the path the formula ϕ holds and all the actions of the path satisfy χ.

Other useful operators can be derived as usual; those that we use in the sequel are:

- $[\gamma]\phi$ stands for $\neg EX_\gamma \neg\phi$ and means that no matter how a process performs an action satisfying γ, the state it reaches in doing so will *necessarily* satisfy ϕ.
- $EF\phi$ stands for $\phi \vee E(true _{tt} U_{tt} \phi)$ and means that there is some path that leads to a state at which ϕ holds; i.e., ϕ *potentially* holds.
- $EF_\gamma \phi$ stands for $E(true _{tt} U_\gamma \phi)$ and means that there is some path that leads to a state at which ϕ holds reached by a last action satisfying γ; if ϕ is *true*, we say that an action satisfying γ will *eventually* be performed.
- $AF_\gamma \phi$ stands for $A(true _{tt} U_\gamma \phi)$ and means that an action satisfying γ will be performed in the future along every path and at the reached states ϕ holds; if ϕ is *true*, we say that an action satisfying γ is *inevitable*.

- $AG\phi$ stands for $\neg EF \neg \phi$ and means that ϕ holds at every state on every path; i.e., ϕ holds *globally*.

Properties of the case study specified with SocL. In [FGL+08] we have singled out many significant classes of desirable properties of the externally observable behaviour of services. Over the COWS specification presented in Section 2, by using the model checker CMC, we have checked the following properties:

Availability:

$AG(accepting\_request(login))$

This formula means that the service *CreditRequest* is *available*, i.e. it is always capable to accept a login request.

Responsiveness:

$AG\,[request(cr,\underline{id})]\,AF_{response(cr,id)\vee cancel(cr,id)}\,true$

This formula means that *CreditRequest* is *responsive*, i.e. it always guarantees an answer (i.e. an offer or a decline, sent by means of action *response(cr, id)*) to each received credit request, unless the customer cancels his own request (by means of action *cancel(cr, id)*). The answer from *CreditRequest* and the request of cancellation from *Portal* belong to the same interaction *cr* of the credit request and are properly *correlated* by variable *id*.

Interruptibility:

$AG\,[request(cr,\underline{id})]\,A(accepting\_cancel(cr,id)\,_{tt}U_{cancel(cr,id)\vee response(cr,id)}\,true)$

The system can accept a cancellation of a credit request, after that the customer has sent his credit request and until he cancels the request or receives an answer.

Compensability:

$AG\,[request(rating,\underline{id})]\,EF_{cancel(cr,id)}\,AF_{undo(cr,id)}\,AF_{undo(cr,id)}\,AF_{undo(cr,id)}\,true$

We want to ensure that if a cancellation is requested after the rating calculation has started, then all compensation activities of services *balance*, *security* and *creditManagement* will be executed. Each such compensation corresponds to performing action *undo(cr, id)*. Thus, by exploiting the fact that any compensation activity can be executed at most once (this can be easily checked separately for each compensation activity), we require all computations after a cancellation to contain three occurrences of *undo(cr, id)*.

Fault handling:

$AG\,(raising\_abort(cr)\;\Rightarrow\;AF_{fail(cr)}\,true)$

Whenever an abort exception is raised (atomic proposition *raising_abort(cr)*), the failure is notified to the customer (by means of action *fail(cr)*).

Model checking SocL *formulae.* The formulae presented in Section 3 are stated in terms of *abstract* actions and atomic propositions, meaning that, e.g., a credit is requested or the system is ready to accept a login. In other words, the properties we want to verify are formalized as SocL formulae in a completely independent way of the service specification. This is a key feature of the verification methodology introduced in [FGL+08]. To perform the verification, these formulae must be tailored to the COWS specification of Section 2 that is expressed in terms of *concrete* actions, i.e. communication of data tuples along endpoints. This is done by defining an appropriate set of *abstraction rules* that relate the actions in the specification to the actions and atomic propositions in the SocL formulae. These rules are provided as an input to CMC, together with the COWS specification and the SocL formula to be checked, and are used by the tool to transform the labels of the Doubly Labelled Transition System (L^2TS) corresponding to the COWS specification during its on-the-fly generation. It is worth noticing that in the L^2TS corresponding to a COWS term, each transition is labelled with the actions performed when moving from the source state to the target one, while each state is labelled with the actions enabled in that state. CMC supports the overall verification process.

The abstraction rules we have used for our analysis are

$$Action\ createNewCreditRequest(\$id, *, *, *, *) \rightarrow request(cr, \$id)$$
$$Action\ offerToClient(\$id, *) \rightarrow response(cr, \$id)$$
$$Action\ declineToClient(\$id, *) \rightarrow response(cr, \$id)$$
$$Action\ cancel(\$id) \rightarrow cancel(cr, \$id)$$
$$Action\ calculateRating(\$id, *, *, *) \rightarrow request(rating, \$id)$$
$$Action\ clearData(\$id) \rightarrow undo(cr, \$id)$$
$$Action\ removeData(\$id) \rightarrow undo(cr, \$id)$$
$$Action\ abortProcess \rightarrow fail(cr)$$
$$State\ abort! \rightarrow raising\_abort(cr)$$
$$State\ initialize? \rightarrow accepting\_request(login)$$
$$State\ cancel?(\$id) \rightarrow accepting\_cancel(cr, \$id)$$

The metavariable "$id" is used to capture the corresponding argument of the operation so that it can be used in the abstract action, while the wildcard "*" is used as a placeholder for any argument.

We comment on some of the rules, the remaining ones can be interpreted similarly. The first rule prescribes that whenever a concrete action involving the operation *createNewCreditRequest* (with any five arguments) occurs in the label of a transition, then it is replaced by the abstract action *request(cr, 1234)* (where we suppose that 1234 is the value passed as the first argument to *createNewCreditRequest*). This way, while the first datum exchanged when executing operation *createNewCreditRequest* is preserved (that is, the session identifier), the other four data are discharged in the 'abstraction process'. Similarly, the second rule prescribes that whenever an action involving the operation *offerToClient* (with any pair of arguments) occurs in the label of a transition, then it is replaced by the abstract action *response(cr, 1234)*. Again, the preserved datum is the session identifier which is used to correlate responses from the contacted *CreditRequest* service. To correlate cancellations to the corresponding credit requests, the fourth rule permits replacing an action involving the operation *cancel* (with one argument) by the abstract action *cancel(cr, 1234)*. The last three rules work similarly, but they relate concrete actions labelling states (rather than transitions) to atomic propositions. The symbols "!" and "?" permit specifying if a rule applies to invoke actions or to receive ones, respectively.

The verification process shows that all the abstract properties we presented in Section 3 do hold for the COWS specification of the Finance case study presented in Section 2, except for the last property. Indeed, if during the login phase *CustomerManagement* replies to *CreditRequest* that the customer username and password are not correct, *CreditRequest* raises a fault that is not caught by any fault handler. Thus, no message is sent to the customer to notify him that the process has been aborted. This can be remedied by associating a fault handler behaving as the *Main*'s fault handler to the activities for initialization performed within the term *CreditReq*.

4 A Type System for Checking Confidentiality Properties

In this section, we present a solution to the *Service Specification and Analysis* (see Chapter 7-5) through the type system for COWS introduced in [LPT07b]. This type system permits expressing and forcing policies regulating the exchange of data among interacting services and ensuring that, in that respect, services do not manifest unexpected behaviours. This enables us to check confidentiality properties, e.g., that critical data such as personal information are shared only with authorized partners.

The types express the policies for data exchange in terms of *regions*, i.e. sets of service partner names attachable to each single datum. Service programmers can thus settle the partners usable to exchange any given datum (and, then, the services that can share it), thus avoiding the datum being accessed (by unwanted services) through unauthorised partners. Then, a type inference system (statically) performs some coherence checks (e.g. the service used in an invocation must belong to the regions of all data occurring in the argument of the invocation) and annotates variable declarations with the minimal regions that ensure consistency of services initial configuration. COWS operational semantics uses these annotations in very efficient checks (i.e. subset inclusions) to authorise or block transitions, in order to guarantee that computations proceed according to them. This property, called *soundness*, can be stated as follows: a service *s* is *sound* if, for any datum *v* in *s* associated to region *r* and for all evolutions of *s*, it holds that *v* can be exchanged only by using services in *r*. As a consequence of the type soundness of the language, it follows that well-typed services always comply with the policies regulating the exchange of data among interacting services.

We illustrate now some relevant properties for the Finance case study. We first consider the point of view of the customer, then that of the service.

From the customer point of view, the service programmer can specify policies stating that the customer's personal information and the credit request data cannot become available to unauthorised users. Thus, for example, the balance data *balancePackage*, communicated by *Portal* to *CreditRequest* and, then, forwarded to service *BalanceAnalysisProvider*, gets annotated with the policy {*creditReq, balance*}, that allows *CreditRequest* and *BalanceAnalysisProvider* to receive the datum but prevents them from transmitting the datum to other services. Other non-critical data, e.g. *customerId*, can be transmitted without an attached policy. The service invocations performed by *Portal* get annotated as follows:

$$creditReq \cdot createNewCreditRequest!\langle id, customerId, \{amount\}_{\{creditReq, x_{creditMng}\}},$$
$$\{mortgage\}_{\{creditReq, x_{creditMng}\}}, \{instalment\}_{\{creditReq, x_{creditMng}\}}\rangle$$

$$creditReq \cdot enterBalanceData!\langle id, \{balancePackage\}_{\{creditReq, balance\}}\rangle$$

$$creditReq \cdot enterSecurityData!\langle id, \{securityPackage\}_{\{creditReq, security\}}\rangle$$

Notice that, while it is perfectly reasonable to assume that the partner names *balance* and *security* are known a priori by *Portal*, the partner name of the credit management service, since it is private, must be communicated by *CreditRequest* to *Portal* at run-time. Indeed, besides policies fixed at design time, the type system permits to express also policies that depend on values discovered at runtime. Thus, in our example, to support communication of the partner name initially unknown, the invoke activity *portal·initialize*!$\langle x_{Id}, x_{UserOK} \rangle$ performed by *CreditRequest*, which notifies the result of the login check to the customer, has to be modified as follows

$$portal \cdot initialize!\langle x_{Id}, x_{UserOK}, customerManagement \rangle$$

The annotations set by programmers are written as a subscript of the datum to which they refer to. Instead, the annotations put by the type inference, to better distinguish them from those put by the programmers, are written as a superscript of the variable declaration to which they refer to. Thus, the syntax of variable delimitation becomes $[\{x\}^r]\,s$, which means that the datum that dynamically will replace x will be used in s at most by the partners belonging to the region r. Hence, for example, once the type inference phase ends, the term *HandleBalanceAndSecurityData* (subterm of *CreditRequest*) gets annotated as follows

[*flow, end*]
((*portal·enterBalanceData*!$\langle x_{Id} \rangle$
   | $[\{x_{BalancePackage}\}^{\{creditReq,balance\}}]$
   creditReq·enterBalanceData?$\langle x_{Id}, x_{BalancePackage} \rangle$.
    (*balance·updateBalanceRating*!$\langle x_{Id}, \{x_{LoginName}\}_{\{balance\}}, \{x_{FirstName}\}_{\{balance\}},$
                             $\{x_{LastName}\}_{\{balance\}}, \{x_{BalancePackage}\}_{\{balance\}} \rangle$
    | *creditReq·updateBalanceRating*?$\langle x_{Id} \rangle$. *flow·end*!$\langle \rangle$))
| (*portal·enterSecurityData*!$\langle x_{Id} \rangle$
   | $[\{x_{SecurityPackage}\}^{\{creditReq,security\}}]$
   creditReq·enterSecurityData?$\langle x_{Id}, x_{SecurityPackage} \rangle$.
    (*security·updateSecurityRating*!$\langle x_{Id}, \{x_{LoginName}\}_{\{security\}}, \{x_{FirstName}\}_{\{security\}},$
                             $\{x_{LastName}\}_{\{security\}}, \{x_{SecurityPackage}\}_{\{security\}} \rangle$
    | *creditReq·updateSecurityRating*?$\langle x_{Id} \rangle$. *flow·end*!$\langle \rangle$))
| *flow·end*?$\langle \rangle$. ...)

Indeed, the annotations inferred for variables $x_{BalancePackage}$ and $x_{SecurityPackage}$ are derived from the use of these variables made by *HandleBalanceAndSecurityData*. Thus, they are assigned regions $\{creditReq, balance\}$ and $\{creditReq, security\}$, respectively, because they are only used in the receives along *creditReq·enterBalanceData* and *creditReq·enterSecurityData*, and in the invokes along *balance·updateBalanceRating* and *security·updateSecurityRating*. Hence, the partner name of such endpoints must belong to the region of the corresponding variables.

Now, *Portal* can safely communicate balance data (respectively, security data) to *CreditRequest*, since the region $\{creditReq, balance\}$ (resprespectively $\{creditReq, security\}$) of the data contains the region of the receiving variable (in fact, they coincide). More in general, the typed version of the credit request service, respects all above defined policies.

Suppose instead that service *CreditRequest* (accidentally or maliciously) attempts to reveal the balance data through some internal operation such as *int·o*!$\langle \{x_{BalancePackage}\}_r \rangle$, for some region r. For *CreditRequest* to successfully complete the type inference phase, we should have $int \in r$. Then, as result of the inference, we would get the annotated variable declaration $[\{x_{BalancePackage}\}^{r'}]$, for some region r' with $r \subseteq r'$. Now, the interaction between the typed terms *Portal* and *CreditRequest* would be blocked by the runtime checks because the datum sent by *Portal* would be annotated as $\{balancePackage\}_{\{creditReq,balance\}}$ while the region r' of the receiving variable $x_{BalancePackage}$ is such that $int \in r \subseteq r' \nsubseteq \{creditReq, balance\}$.

From the *CreditRequest*'s point of view, the service programmer can require the customer not to pass to other services the offer that has been specifically computed for the customer demands. Therefore, the corresponding invocation performed by *CreditRequest* gets annotated as follows:

$$portal \cdot offerToClient!\langle x_{Id}, \{x_{AgreementData}\}_{\{portal\}}\rangle$$

For what concerns the type inference of the involved terms we can reason as before.

5   Automated Verification of UML4SOA Models of Services

Although the logical verification methodology described in Section 3 is effective and automated, people willing to use it are required to be able to understand and deal with algebraic and logical tools, i.e. the process calculus COWS and the temporal logic SocL. Sometimes this may not be the case, especially within industrial contexts. To make the verification of service properties more accessible, we then put forward the idea of exploiting translations of languages at different abstraction levels, i.e. modelling languages and process calculi, as those defined in [BFL⁺09, BPT09]. Here, we report on an ongoing effort for devising an approach that integrates our verification methodology with language translations aiming at obtaining verifiable implementations of service components from abstract architectural models of business activities. To this aim, we are developing two software tools[2]: UStoC, that supports translation from UML4SOA to COWS, and Venus, that, by closely integrating UStoC and CMC, provides access to verification functionalities also to those users not familiar with formal methods.

In Section 2, the UML4SOA activity diagrams specifying the behaviour of the services involved in the Finance case study (presented in Chapters 0-3 and 7-1) are translated 'by hand' into COWS terms to enable a subsequent analysis phase. By accomplishing this task, we have experimented how the specific mechanisms and primitives of COWS are particularly suitable for encoding services specified by UML4SOA activity diagrams. This is not surprising if one considers that both UML4SOA and COWS are inspired by WS-BPEL. To formalize those intuitions and support a more systematic and mathematically well-founded approach to engineering of SOA systems, we have defined a compositional encoding of UML4SOA activity diagrams into COWS terms. This way, developers can concentrate on modelling the high-level behaviour of the system and use the encoding for analysis purposes. Such encoding is implemented by UStoC, a software tool that given a UML4SOA specification, consisting of a set of XMI files [OMG] automatically generated by the UML editor MagicDraw [NMI], returns a COWS term written in the syntax accepted by CMC. UStoC's workflow is graphically depicted in Fig. 1.

---

[2] Both tools are freely downloadable from http://rap.dsi.unifi.it/cows/ and can be redistributed and/or modified under the terms of the GNU General Public License.

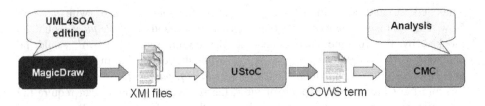

Fig. 1. Verification process of UML4SOA models of services

UStoC works properly with activity diagrams specified by using version 1.2 of the UML4SOA profile. Therefore, to use the tool for translating the Finance case study, we need to specify the case study using the profile mentioned above. For the sake of simplicity, we consider here just an excerpt of the scenario, which is composed of three services: creditRequest that performs the initialization activities and terminates upon receiving the data for a new credit request, customerManagementService that, when invoked, non-deterministically replies either yes or no to every request, and portalService that, if the login succeeds, non-deterministically sends either a credit request or a cancellation request. The UML4SOA diagram modelling service creditRequest is shown in Fig. 2. To analyse this scenario, firstly we generate a file XMI (saved with extension .uml) for each UML4SOA diagram by using MagicDraw. Then, we load the three created files into UStoC (by pushing the 'Add' button on the right-hand side of the graphical interface, a screenshot of which is shown in Fig. 3) and encode them into a COWS term (by pushing the 'Start encoding' button). Finally, we can export the COWS term from UStoC to CMC and start to analyse it exactly as described in Section 3.

The above example shows how UStoC simplifies the modelling phase of the verification process by enabling the use of the abstract modelling language UML4SOA. However, the problem of making more accessible our verification methodology to people without significant expertise on process calculi and logics is not resolved. To remedy this, we are developing Venus, a software tool that integrates UStoC and CMC in order to hide the use of COWS and SocL and, hence, make the verification process as much transparent as possible for developers. The issue of tailoring and reflecting the (low-level) results obtained by the verification of COWS terms to the corresponding (high-level) UML4SOA specifications is tackled by exploiting abstraction rules that permit specifying a 'bridge' between the two specification levels.

Let us see how Venus can be used to analyse the excerpt of the Finance case study previously introduced. First of all, similarly to UStoC, Venus requires the user to provide the XMI files storing the UML4SOA diagrams (Fig. 4). Then, it requires the user to select the properties that he wants to verify out of a list of predefined general properties written in natural language (Fig. 5). Notably, expert users can add in the text area at the bottom of the window further properties directly expressed as SocL formulae. Now, the user has to define the intuitive semantics of the relevant operations of the loaded UML4SOA specification. This is done by specifying the operations representing initial requests, positive responses, negative responses, cancellations, ..., and by

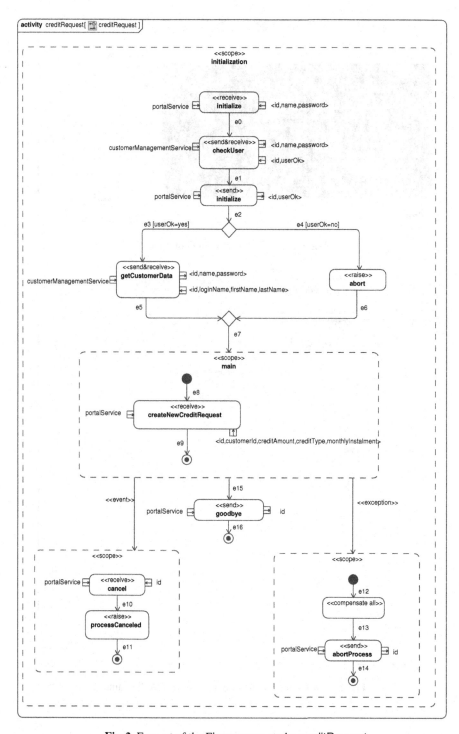

Fig. 2. Excerpt of the Finance case study: creditRequest

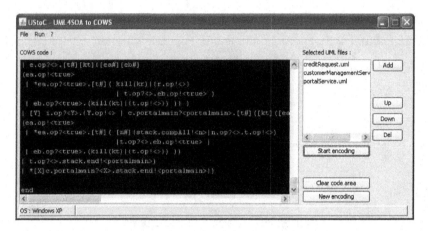

Fig. 3. A screenshot of UStoC interface

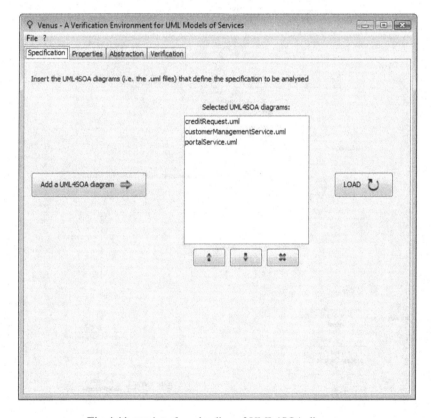

Fig. 4. Venus interface: loading of UML4SOA diagrams

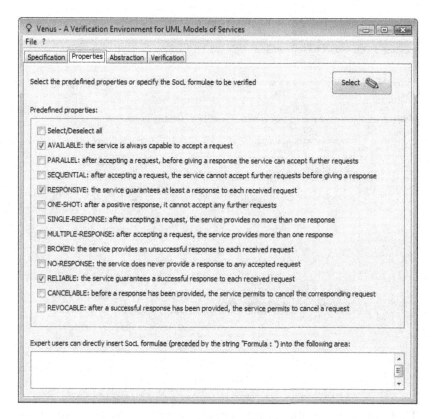

Fig. 5. Venus interface: selection of service properties

possibly indicating the corresponding correlation data (Fig. 6). In our example, we specify that an invocation of operation initialize corresponds to sending an initial request to the service and the value that will be assigned to variable id will be used to correlate positive and negative responses to such request. Notice that Venus requires to specify such operations only for the categories that are needed for checking the properties previously selected (in this case, e.g., initial request, positive response and negative response). Moreover, for each category, more than one operation can be specified by using the associated 'Add' button. The information provided at this step are used, on the one hand, to express the selected general properties as SocL formulae and, on the other hand, to generate the abstraction rules that will be applied to the COWS term resulting from the translation of the UML4SOA diagrams provided at the initial step. Expert users can also provide here custom abstraction rules. Finally, Venus properly arranges all data, loads them into CMC, and allows the user to check the validity of each property and, possibly, to require an explanation in case of a negative result (Fig. 7).

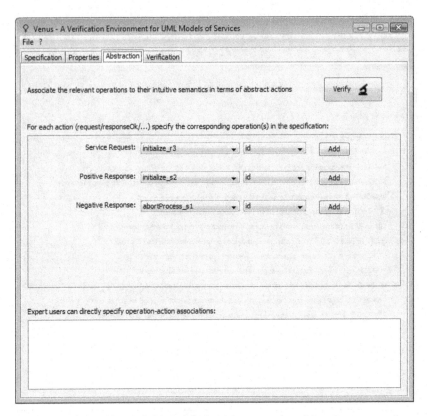

Fig. 6. Venus interface: definition of the intuitive semantics of the relevant operations

6   Concluding Remarks

We have presented a COWS specification of the Finance case study and two analysis techniques, namely a temporal logic and its model checker for expressing and checking functional properties and a type system for guaranteeing confidentiality properties.

The specification of the case study demonstrates that COWS's distinctive features, as e.g. the termination constructs and the correlation mechanism, are effective tools for specifying service-oriented systems. In fact, kill activities are suitable for representing ordinary and exceptional process terminations, while protection permits to naturally represent exception and compensation handlers that are supposed to run after normal computations terminate. Even more crucially, the correlation mechanism permits to automatically correlate messages belonging to the same long-running interaction, preventing to mix messages from different service instances. Also the encoding of UML4SOA in COWS, which is at the basis of the tools UStoC and Venus, has greatly benefitted from COWS's distinctive features. The definition of such an encoding appears to be problematic and less intuitive if one use a different, e.g. session-based, calculus.

There are several requirements and properties concerning to liveness, correctness, and security that an implementation of the Finance case study is expected to fulfill.

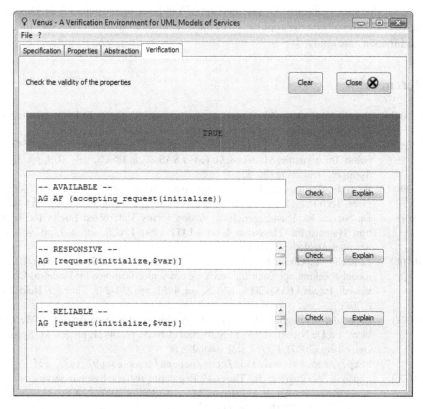

Fig. 7. Venus interface: verification of the service properties

The methodology reported in Section 3, and then exploited by the tools presented in Section 5, has proven to be very effective to check a large spectrum of behavioural properties. With respect to the many other temporal logics proposed in the literature, one important advantage of SocL is that the service properties can be formulated in a way which is independent from individual service domains and specifications. Security properties regarding the exchange of data among service components can be instead insured by means of the type system reported in Section 4. Since it is not realistic to assume complete knowledge of the whole system and access to the internal implementation of all the involved services, a practical implementation of this approach would require services to declare how they use the data they exchange and should rely on a mechanism ensuring that service behaviours do comply with their declaration. The runtime support should also take charge of performing the checks described in Section 4 to authorise or block transitions.

Some other analysis techniques for COWS terms have been developed as a result of the Sensoria project. In particular, a Flow Logic for checking information flow properties is presented in [BNNP08], a stochastic extension of COWS that enables verification of quantitative properties is presented in [PQ07] (see also Chapter 5-5), and a few observational semantics for checking interchangeability of COWS terms and conformance against service specifications are presented in [PTY09] (see also Chapter 2-2). However, we have not yet results on the application of these techniques to the COWS specification of the Finance case study.

References

[BFL+09]   Bocchi, L., Fiadeiro, J.L., Lapadula, A., Pugliese, R., Tiezzi, F.: From Architectural to Behavioural Specification of Services. ENTCS 253, 3–21 (2009)

[BNNP08]   Bauer, J., Nielson, F., Nielson, H.R., Pilegaard, H.: Relational Analysis of Correlation. In: Alpuente, M., Vidal, G. (eds.) SAS 2008. LNCS, vol. 5079, pp. 32–46. Springer, Heidelberg (2008)

[BPT09]   Banti, F., Pugliese, R., Tiezzi, F.: Automated Verification of UML Models of Services, Tech.Rep., DSI, Univ. Firenze (2009), http://rap.dsi.unifi.it/cows

[DV90]   De Nicola, R., Vaandrager, F.W.: Action versus State based Logics for Transition Systems. In: Guessarian, I. (ed.) LITP 1990. LNCS, vol. 469, pp. 407–419. Springer, Heidelberg (1990)

[FGL+08]   Fantechi, A., Gnesi, S., Lapadula, A., Mazzanti, F., Pugliese, R., Tiezzi, F.: A model checking approach for verifying cows specifications. In: Fiadeiro, J.L., Inverardi, P. (eds.) FASE 2008. LNCS, vol. 4961, pp. 230–245. Springer, Heidelberg (2008)

[LPT07a]   Lapadula, A., Pugliese, R., Tiezzi, F.: A Calculus for Orchestration of Web Services. In: De Nicola, R. (ed.) ESOP 2007. LNCS, vol. 4421, pp. 33–47. Springer, Heidelberg (2007), Full version available at http://rap.dsi.unifi.it/cows/papers/cows-esop07-full.pdf

[LPT07b]   Lapadula, A., Pugliese, R., Tiezzi, F.: Regulating data exchange in service oriented applications. In: Arbab, F., Sirjani, M. (eds.) FSEN 2007. LNCS, vol. 4767, pp. 223–239. Springer, Heidelberg (2007)

[MKB08]   Meolic, R., Kapus, T., Brezocnik, Z.: ACTLW - an Action-based Computation Tree Logic With Unless Operator. Elsevier Information Sciences 178(6), 1542–1557 (2008)

[NMI]   No Magic Inc. MagicDraw UML personal edition 16.5, http://www.magicdraw.com/

[OMG]   Object Management Group. XMI Mapping Specification, v2.1.1

[PQ07]   Prandi, D., Quaglia, P.: Stochastic COWS. In: Krämer, B.J., Lin, K.-J., Narasimhan, P. (eds.) ICSOC 2007. LNCS, vol. 4749, pp. 245–256. Springer, Heidelberg (2007)

[PTY09]   Pugliese, R., Tiezzi, F., Yoshida, N.: On observing dynamic prioritised actions in SOC. In: Albers, S., Marchetti-Spaccamela, A., Matias, Y., Nikoletseas, S., Thomas, W. (eds.) ICALP 2009. LNCS, vol. 5556, pp. 701–720. Springer, Heidelberg (2009)

[Tie09]   Tiezzi, F.: A COWS specification of the Finance case study (version 4.6.2). Technical report, DSI, Univ. Firenze (2009), http://rap.dsi.unifi.it/cows/

SENSORIA Patterns

Matthias Hölzl, Nora Koch, Philip Mayer, and Martin Wirsing*

Ludwig-Maximilians-Universität, München, Germany
{hoelzl,koch,mayer,wirsing}@pst.ifi.lmu.de

Abstract. We describe the SENSORIA development approach using a pattern language for augmenting service engineering with formal analysis, transformation and dynamicity. The pattern language is designed to help software developers choose appropriate tools and techniques to develop service-oriented systems with support from formal methods; the full pattern catalog spans the whole development process from the modeling stage to deployment activities. Some of the patterns are specific to SENSORIA; other patterns are extensions or adaptations of patterns presented by other authors.

1 Introduction

The SENSORIA project is investigating a broad range of issues related to engineering service-oriented architectures, ranging from foundational research to practically usable tools. SENSORIA proposes a model-driven approach in which services are first modeled in a platform-independent notation such as UML4SOA [14]; these designs are then transformed into formal models that can be analyzed using tools based on mathematical methods. Afterwards, the design models can be used to generate code for different service platforms.

The research results of SENSORIA are widely disseminated and well known in the broader scientific community. However, scientific publications generally contain little guidance for the practical software developer who seeks to apply them. To make research results available in a way that is useful beyond the scientific community we have developed a pattern catalog that enables software engineers to quickly determine whether SENSORIA tools and techniques exist to address a particular development problem and, in the case of a positive answer, the recommended approach for employing them.

Pattern-based approaches to presenting guidance for software developers has a well-established history in computer science; patterns have been used to describe problems and possible solutions in areas ranging from business processes to software design and low-level implementation methods. Given the wide scope of SENSORIA it is not surprising that the full catalog of SENSORIA patterns also encompasses a wide range of abstraction levels, from implementation-oriented patterns in the spirit of [10] to architectural or process patterns. The pattern language is inspired by the "Pattern Language for Pattern Writing" presented in [15], the pattern language used in [8] and the guidance in [5]. For readers familiar with the pattern community, it should be noted that we use

---

* This work has been partially sponsored by the EU project SENSORIA (IST-2005-016004).

M. Wirsing and M. Hölzl (Eds.): SENSORIA Project, LNCS 6582, pp. 719–736, 2011.

the pattern format as an expository tool; our patterns are not necessarily obtained by "mining" existing applications for patterns.

1.1 Overview of SENSORIA Patterns

The patterns presented in this section can be classified into three different categories:

- Patterns for new activities in the software development process that allow SENSO-RIA methods to be introduced. For example, the pattern *Functional Service Verification* presented in this chapter is of this kind: it introduces the formal verification of services and details the benefits and costs of performing such analysis.
- Patterns that show how SENSORIA techniques change an activity that is commonly performed when developing and deploying service-oriented architectures. The patterns *Service Modeling* and *Generate Implementation* in this chapter are examples of this type of pattern: while all model-driven approaches generate parts of the implementation from models, the benefits and costs of doing so vary significantly when tools based on formal models are employed in the course of software development.
- Adaptations of patterns presented by other authors, in those cases where the tools and techniques developed by SENSORIA contribute novel aspects to the proposed solution or offer new solution possibilities. In these cases we include an extended version of the existing pattern in the SENSORIA pattern language to document the influence of our techniques on the proposed solution and to point developers to the tools that can be employed when realizing the pattern. Tailoring patterns to specific tools or circumstances has a long tradition in the pattern community, see, e.g., [1], which shows how the patterns in [10] can be adapted to a particular programming language.

1.2 The SENSORIA Pattern Language

The pattern language used in this chapter is a slight revision of the one first introduced in [25]; it is based on principles described in [15,5] and similar to the one used in [8].

As usual, each pattern consists of mandatory and optional elements which are presented in a fairly rigid structure to simplify the process of selecting and applying suitable patterns. The elements that have to be present in each pattern are:

- A pattern **name** that provides a short and descriptive way to refer to the pattern.
- A **context** in which the pattern is applicable: most patterns are not "universal" solutions but only apply in certain circumstances which are described by the context.
- A concise **description** of the problem solved by the pattern. This is different from the context in that the problem is the design or implementation challenge that is directly addressed by the pattern whereas the context describes conditions in which the pattern is applicable but which are generally not influenced by an application of the pattern.
- The **forces** that determine whether using the pattern is appropriate.

- The **solution** proposed and the **consequences** resulting from the use of the solution. The solution is the concrete description how the pattern is applied; the consequences show how this influences the resulting system. There is a certain amount of overlap between consequences and forces, but generally the forces are more abstract, concise and less precise than the detailed consequences.
- Furthermore each pattern has to be accompanied by **examples**. In this chapter we mostly refer the reader to other chapters that demonstrate the relevant pattern.

Several optional sections can be used to clarify the pattern, e.g., **related patterns**, example **code** or **models**, or **tools** to support the pattern. For space reasons we have omitted some elements appearing in the full pattern catalog from some of the patterns in this chapter.

This chapter is structured as follows: the following section contains patterns that outline a development process that allows Sensoria techniques to be used to maximum effect. Afterwards, section 3 shows an example how patterns for developing service-oriented architectures from Erl's pattern catalog [8] can be enhanced by making use of Sensoria results. The final sections present related work and conclude.

2   Sensoria Development Patterns

This section uses patterns to describe a development process that makes maximum use of Sensoria results: *Service Modeling* introduces a modeling process using SoaML and UML4SOA; this pattern is a slight revision of the one presented in [25]. Having models in UML is the basis for two more patterns presented in this chapter: *Extract Formal Models* and *Generate Implementation*. Formal models are mainly useful as input for analysis tools; this is described by pattern *Analyze with Formal Methods*. Most development projects extend or replace existing legacy systems. The pattern *Extract Service Model* enables the developer to use Sensoria tools and techniques for these systems as well.

2.1   Service Modeling

Systems built on SOAs add new layers of complexity to software engineering, as many different artifacts must work together to create the sort of loosely coupled, adaptive, fault-tolerant systems envisioned in the service domain. It is therefore important to apply best practices already in use for older programming paradigms to services as well; in particular, modeling of systems on a higher level of abstraction should be used to get a general idea of the solution space. Modeling services should be possible in a language which is both familiar to software architects and thus easy to use, but also contains the necessary elements for describing SOA systems in a straightforward way.

Context. You are designing a system which is based on a SOA. The system is intended to offer services to multiple platforms and makes use of existing services and artifacts on multiple hosts which must be integrated to work together in order to realize the functionality of the system.

Problem. When designing SOA systems, it is easy to get lost in the detail of technical specifications and implementations. Visualizing the planned service oriented architecture is therefore crucial for effective task identification, separation, and communication. Using a familiar, easy-to-understand, and descriptive language is a key success factor in this context.

Forces.

- The amount of specifications and platforms in the SOA domain makes it difficult to get a general idea of the solution space.
- Modeling the whole system in an abstract way gives a good overview of the tasks to be done, but does not directly yield tangible results. For small systems and projects, it is necessary to tailor this modeling task or even to skip it altogether.
- The model must be updated to reflect the architecture if it changes during implementation, or if new requirements appear.
- The model is platform independent, and may be used to generate significant parts of the system. In case the system's target platform is not fixed or may experience changes, the workload involved in system re-implementation can be reduced considerably.
- Having a global architectural view eases the task of understanding the SOA environment. This fact is of major significance if the SOA environment is to be extended by another team of software engineers or at a later date.
- The envisioned target platform(s) and language(s) should be supported by the modeling approach such that code generation may be used.

Solution. Use a specialized (graphical) modeling language to model the system and employ these models as far as possible for generating the system implementation. There are several languages which might be employed for this kind of task. One of the most widespread modeling languages in the software engineering domain is the Unified Modeling Language (UML). As UML itself does not offer specific constructs for modeling service-oriented artifacts, it needs to be extended using its built-in profile mechanism. SoaML [18] and UML4SOA [14] are two such profiles, which together enable modeling of both static and dynamic aspects of service-oriented systems. SoaML allows modeling the static part of SOA systems and features specialized constructs for services, service providers, and message types. UML4SOA complements SoaML with support for the dynamic parts of SOA systems, featuring service interactions, long-running transactions, and event handling. Models designed using SoaML and UML4SOA can be used in a model driven development approach for SOA, MDD4SOA [14], which offers tools for generating code.

Consequences. Pros: A positive result of modeling a service-oriented system in a high-level way is that it gives a better idea of how the individual artifacts fit together. This is of particular importance in larger projects and for communication between developers and/or the customer. By using transformations, the models can also be employed for generating skeletons to fill with the actual implementation. However, the effort involved in creating readable models should not be underestimated. Also, care should be taken to only model aspects relevant on the design level instead of implementing the complete system on the modeling level.

Cons: Often the fully automated generation of implementations is not feasible; instead only implementation fragments can be generated and their implementation has to be completed manually. In this scenario model/implementation divergence may pose a significant problem and special care has to be taken that models are kept consistent with the implementation. This increases the cost of modeling and reduces the benefit of model-driven development.

Tools. The use of a UML profile has the advantage that all UML CASE tools that support the extension mechanisms of the UML can be used, i.e. there is no need for the development of specific and proprietary tools. The SoaML and UML4SOA profiles may be provided already for the UML tool of choice, or may be defined by the means provided by the platform. In the SENSORIA project, the UML4SOA profile was defined for the Rational Software Modeler (RSM) and MagicDraw; SoaML is available for these platforms as well. MDD4SOA provides executable transformations for models from both UML tools to code skeletons of various target platforms, including the Web service platform and the Java platform. The transformers are integrated into the Eclipse environment.

Examples. More detailed descriptions of languages for service modeling and their applications are given in Chapter 1-1 (UML Extensions for Service-Oriented Systems) and Chapter 1-2 (The SENSORIA Reference Modelling Language); a model-driven approach to business processes is introduced in Chapter 1-3 (Model-Driven Development of Adaptable Service-Oriented Business Processes). More detailed examples for models can be found in the chapters on case studies, in particular Chapter 7-4 (The SENSORIA Approach Applied to the Finance Case Study) and Chapter 7-2 (SENSORIA Results Applied to the Case Studies).

Related Patterns. This pattern forms the basis for the approach described in this chapter; it is a requirement for *Extract Formal Models* and *Generate Implementation*.

2.2 Extract Formal Models

Context. You have modeled a part of the system using UML4SOA and want to ensure that the model satisfies certain properties.

Problem. Many properties of models in UML4SOA cannot be directly analyzed. Manually building models for formal analysis has several disadvantages: (1) The manually created models may not faithfully represent the UML4SOA model. (2) Manually building models is a time-intensive process. (3) The model has to be manually kept in sync with changes made to the UML4SOA model.

Forces.

- Extraction of formal models allows the UML4SOA model to be analyzed without manually creating additional models.

– The extracted model faithfully represents the UML4SOA model if the extractor is correct.
– The extracted model may be more complicated than a manually created model and contain details that are unnecessary for the desired analysis. This may significantly increase the complexity of the analysis step.
– The UML4SOA model has to be elaborated in detail to contain enough information for model extraction.

Solution. Use tools to automatically extract formal models from the UML4SOA models. The kind of models that should be extracted depend on the analysis that is to be performed.

Consequences. Pros: Manually building formal models is expensive and not economically feasible for most large systems. Additionally, a manual extraction process may introduce errors not present in the original model, or fail to correctly specify all subtleties of the original model. If a tool that automatically extracts the required models exists, analysis with formal methods becomes more reliable and significantly cheaper. SENSORIA provides a number of model transformations from UML4SOA into process calculi and orchestration languages – for example, the process calculi COWS and PEPA, or the language BPEL. These tools can be integrated into the build process of the system such that the availability of up-to-date formal models is ensured.

Cons: Automatically generated models often contain details that are not relevant to the performed analyses. Since many tools based on formal methods suffer from "state explosion" problems, the increased size of the extracted model can impede analysis efforts.

Tools. SENSORIA provides various tools for transforming UML models (and in particular, SoaML and UML4SOA models). The model transformer Hugo/RT [12] translates UML specifications into input languages for the well-known model checkers UPPAAL and SPIN. The SRMC/UML bridge translates UML4SOA activities into the process calculus PEPA [23]. The VENUS tool allows converting UML4SOA activities into the process calculus COWS [13]. Furthermore, the MDD4SOA transformer suite [14] translates UML4SOA diagrams to Java, the orchestration language Jolie, and WS-BPEL; the latter can be used as input for the verification tool WS-Engineer [9].

Examples. A detailed example of how the pattern *Extract Formal Models* can be used in the software development process can be found in Chapter 6-1 (Methodologies for Model-Driven Development and Deployment: an Overview); more details about transformations is contained in Chapter 6-2 (Advances in Model Transformations by Graph Transformation: Specification, Analysis and Execution).

Related Patterns. The pattern *Extract Formal Models* is closely related to *Analyze with Formal Methods* since model extraction often precedes formal analysis. It is also related to *Generate Implementation* since the additional modeling effort required for formal analysis can better be recouped if the model also serves as input to code generation.

2.3 Analyze with Formal Methods

While models are often at a higher level of abstraction than code, they nevertheless are susceptible to the same problems: they may not satisfy certain properties that the modeler expects them to have; different models may specify the same part of the system in contradictory ways, etc. Unless the models are executable and therefore relatively low-level, these defects may remain undetected until the system is actually implemented. This negates one of the main benefits that modeling is supposed to provide.

Context. You have either extracted or manually specified formal models of the system.

Problem. You want to verify that the formal models satisfy certain properties, e.g., a given service should always be available to accept new requests or the overall system should be free from deadlocks.

Forces.
– Formal models of the components under consideration exist or can be extracted.
– The desired properties can be formally specified.
– Developers have to be qualified to decide which analysis tools are adequate for the given problem, be able to use the tools, and in some cases interpret their output.

Solution. Use tools based on formal methods such as model checkers or the performance analysis tools for Pepa [6,11] to analyze whether the desired properties hold.

Consequences. Pros: Tools based on formal methods can verify that the system satisfies certain properties that are difficult to check otherwise, or that the system exhibits certain performance characteristics. If the tools can be applied at an early stage of system development it is possible to find design and modeling errors long before the system is implemented and therefore reduce the development cost. Furthermore, certain kinds of errors that are well-suited to formal analysis, such as deadlocks or unintended interactions that divulge secret information to third parties, are notoriously difficult to find using traditional approaches.

Cons: On the other hand the use of analysis tools based on formal methods requires a lot of experience on the part of the users: even when using hidden formal methods the user has to be able to determine which properties of the system are amenable to formal analysis, which tools are appropriate, and how the desired properties can be encoded. This can, to a certain extent, be ameliorated by new developments such as Venus [22], but it is unlikely that the use of formal methods will be completely transparent to the developer in the foreseeable future. Furthermore, many tools based on formal methods require a detailed specification of the complete system behavior and therefore necessitate comprehensive models of all system components, even ones that are not directly involved in the behavior under consideration. Related to this last point is another weakness of some formal methods: they cannot work on open systems and results can therefore only be obtained for "closed approximations" of the specified system. This is, in general, not problematic when the existence of undesirable behavior is demonstrated by the formal analysis, e.g., when deadlocks or traces which validate system invariants are found. But it is often not clear that positive results, e.g., the absence of invalid traces, can be transferred from a closed approximation to the open system.

Tools. SENSORIA provides several tools for formal analysis and verification. WS-Engineer [9] is a verification tool for performing model-based verification of web service compositions. The SRMC/PEPA tool [23] covers steady-state analysis of the underlying Markov chain of SRMC descriptions. CMC and UMC are model checkers and analyzers for systems defined by interacting UML statecharts [21]. The sCOWS Model Checker [20] allows to perform statistical model checking on sCOWS, a stochastic extension of COWS. Finally, the LySA tool is a static analyzer for security protocols defined in the LYSA process calculus [4].

Examples. Parts 2, 4 and 5 of this book contain many examples for formal analysis methods; in particular, examples for qualitative analysis techniques can be found in Chapter 2-3 (Static Analysis Techniques for Session-Oriented Calculi), Chapter 4-1 (Analysing the Protocol Stack for Services), Chapter 4-2 (An Abstract, On-The-Fly Framework for the Verification of Service Oriented Systems), Chapter 4-3 (Tools and Verification), and Chapter 4-4 (Specification and Analysis of Dynamically-Reconfigurable Service Architectures); examples for quantitative analysis techniques are given in Chapter 5-1 (SoSL: Service Oriented Stochastic Logics), Chapter 5-2 (Evaluating Service Level Agreements using Observational Probes), Chapter 5-3 (Scaling Performance Analysis using Fluid-Flow Approximation), Chapter 5-4 (Passage-End Analysis for Analysing Robot Movement) and Chapter 5-5 (Quantitative Analysis of Services).

Related Patterns. The formal models for analysis can often be extracted as described in the pattern *Extract Formal Models*. The detailed system model needed for formal analysis often contains many of the same model refinements that are needed to employ the *Generate Implementation* pattern.

2.4 Generate Implementation

Generating implementations from models is the key characteristic of model-driven development. The SENSORIA approach for formally supported software development supports such generation with multiple tools.

Context. You are deciding which development approach to apply to a software system, or you have already developed (UML/UML4SOA) models for the system. You want to implement the system on one or more platforms.

Problem. While UML models are a useful development tool, many models do not specify executable behavior, and even for behavioral models there is no widely used execution platform that can directly operate on UML models.

Forces.

- UML models can be specified at various levels of abstraction ranging from very abstract structural views of a system to detailed behavioral descriptions.
- Even behavioral specifications are often not detailed enough to completely describe the intended behavior of the system.

- The amount of work to fully specify all system behaviors is significant when compared to the commonly used level of abstraction for models.
- Implementations can be obtained in various ways: manual implementation of the model, partial code-generation by a CASE tool, or generation of the complete application.
- Some parts of an application are not easily specified using UML, e.g., user interfaces.

Solution. Fully specify the important behavior of the system (that implements the business process) in the model, generate code from this implementation, and manually implement parts of the code that are difficult to model and verify.

Consequences. *Pros:* By generating the implementation from models, the correctness of the implementation relative to the model depends only on the quality of the transformation from models to code. Once a mature code generator has been developed, the consistency of model and implementation can be assumed. Changes to the model can immediately be reflected in the implementation without incurring additional implementation costs.

Generating implementations for different execution platforms is easy if model transformations into all platforms exist. Only the manually written parts of the code have to be rewritten when supporting an new platform or transitioning to a new platform. Necessary deployment artifacts can automatically generated.

Neutral: By manually implementing those parts of the system which are difficult to express in UML and for which no formal verification is necessary, the modeling effort can be reduced, at the cost of an increase in platform dependencies and implementation costs.

Cons: The required detail of the models increases significantly, thereby making the modeling step more time consuming and increasing the difficulty of changes to the models. If no model transformation into the desired target platform is available it has to be developed, often at significant cost. In some cases, manually generated code can be smaller and more efficient than automatically generated code; in particular if the code generator is not sophisticated enough to perform static analysis and optimization. This may be particularly significant when developing software for embedded or otherwise resource-constrained systems. Furthermore, debugging of generated implementations often has to be performed at the source-code level since no back-translation from code to model elements is available in the debugger. This can make debugging of generated implementations difficult.

Tools. SENSORIA provides both a generic model transformation tool for writing and executing arbitrary transformations and specific tools tailored towards a single use case. The former tool is Viatra2 [24], a framework which provides general-purpose support for the entire life-cycle of engineering model transformations including the specification, design, execution, validation and maintenance of transformations within and between various modeling languages and domains. The latter are provided by multiple tools. The first two are written in VIATRA2: The SOA2WSDL transformation takes high level UML4SOA models and produces WSDL output, whereas the

UML2Axis transformations take high level UML4OA models and produce WSDL, WS-ReliableMessaging, WS-Security and Apache Axis-specific configuration files as output. The tool suite MDD4SOA [14] already mentioned above transforms SoaML and UML4SOA models to BPEL, WSDL, and XSD as well as Java and Jolie. Finally, the Modes Parser and Browser [9] generates broker requirements for Dino from UML2 Modes models.

Examples. The chapters on the SENSORIA case studies contain examples for the generation of implementations, see in particular Chapter 7-4 (The SENSORIA Approach Applied to the Finance Case Study) and Chapter 7-2 (SENSORIA Results Applied to the Case Studies).

Related Patterns. This pattern enjoys a synergistic relationship with *Extract Formal Models*, since a more detailed UML model can enable both extraction of formal models and generating the implementation. This can significantly alter the cost/benefit balance of detailed modeling.

2.5   Extract Service Model

Service-oriented architectures are generally not developed from scratch; in most cases the functionality of existing business-critical legacy systems has to be integrated or replaced. A number of patterns for integrating legacy software into a service-oriented architecture exist, with different trade-offs. For example, in [8] the *Legacy Wrapper* pattern is introduced which wraps the legacy system with a service façade. While this is a relatively quick and cheap solution it often poses difficulties for long-term maintenance and deployment. As SENSORIA has developed the powerful, model-based re-engineering tool *CareStudio* the *Extract Service Model* pattern is a viable alternative with higher up-front investments but better long-term maintainability.

Context. You have a legacy application that performs a vital business function, possibly with complex business logic integrated into the code. You want to integrate the legacy application into a service-oriented infrastructure.

Problem. Often service-oriented systems are introduced to supersede existing legacy technologies. In these cases it is usually not feasible to re-implement the functionality of the legacy system; therefore, its functionality is wrapped by a service binding. If the legacy system is hidden behind a thin service layer, the interface of the wrapper is largely pre-determined by the capabilities and interfaces of the existing solution which are often at the wrong level of abstraction or granularity for a service-oriented architecture. This leads to non-standard service contracts that expose details of the legacy system's implementation and technology. Writing a thick wrapper that exposes a clean service-oriented interface is often difficult as many legacy systems do not expose a clean separation between user interface, domain logic and storage backend.

Forces.

- A legacy application performing vital functionality exists.
- It is not economically feasible or desirable to develop replacements for the legacy systems from scratch. Therefore the legacy application should be integrated into a service-oriented architecture.
- The resulting software is not only supposed to facilitate transition to another system.
- The new system should exhibit clean service contracts between its components to be maintainable and extensible for future requirements.

Solution. Use the SENSORIA re-engineering approach which consists in annotating the original source code, extracting a service model from the annotated source code, and generating a new, service-oriented implementation from the annotated code.

Consequences. Pros: By creating a service model and a truly service-oriented implementation the long-term maintainability and extensibility is ensured. Often integration into a service-oriented architecture can be more seamless than wrapper-based solutions; the extracted service-oriented implementation can make use of standard infrastructure services provided by the environment and therefore profit from enhancements made to the overall system.

Cons: For re-engineering purposes the source code of the legacy system has to be available, which is often not the case. The legacy code has to be annotated which makes it necessary that developers that understand the old code base are available or that developers familiarize themselves with the old code base.

Neutral: The up-front cost of re-engineering can be significantly higher than the cost of wrapping a legacy system, although this will often be offset by reduced deployment and operational costs and better future extensibility of the system.

Tools. This pattern is supported by a set of SENSORIA tools grouped around *CareStudio* [2] which allow transformations to be applied to source code, with a focus on achieving SOA-compliant code. The tool uses a model transformation approach to the migration and includes emitters for source code.

Examples. A comprehensive description of the *Extract Service Model* pattern is contained in Chapter 6-4 (Legacy Transformations for Extracting Service Components).

Related Patterns. When following this pattern, a service model is extracted and then used for code generation. The pattern is therefore closely related to *Service Modeling* and *Generate Implementation*. The extracted model can be used to formally validate properties of the system using patterns *Extract Formal Models* and *Analyze with Formal Methods*.

3   Enhancing SOA Patterns

This section describes how existing patterns for SOA development can be extended with SENSORIA tools and methods, contributing novel aspects to the proposed solution and offering new solution possibilities. We present extensions of two patterns from Thomas Erl's "SOA Design Patterns" [8], *Concurrent Contracts* and *Trusted Subsystem*.

3.1 Concurrent Contracts

Contracts between client and service and interfaces offered by services play an important role in the development of service-oriented architectures. The following pattern shows how techniques developed as part of SENSORIA can help service providers to offer suitable interfaces for different classes of clients, and clients to find and utilize the most appropriate contract offered by a provider. It is an extension of the *Concurrent Contracts* pattern from Thomas Erl's "SOA Design Patterns" [8] with SENSORIA-specific material. The pattern as originally described deals only with contracts; we have extended the pattern to also take into account services that offer multiple interfaces backed by the same implementation.

Context. Services often have to serve different customers which have slightly different needs and permissions, and which may be of unknown provenience and therefore trusted to different degrees. Exposing the same interface and service contract to all clients may therefore not be feasible; on the other hand having different services for closely related and largely overlapping functionality is not desirable.

Problem. Often services are described as exposing a single interface or contract that the service fulfills. This simple view does not adequately reflect the situation encountered when building service-oriented architectures: often different clients have many overlapping requirements but also significant differences. For example, several clients may request personnel data from a company's "personnel service," but there may be differences in that

– they may be trusted to different degrees, e.g., services operated by the company itself may enjoy higher trust than services operated by clients or partners of the company;
– some clients may be allowed to see protected data, e.g. services operated by the accounting department may have access to salary information which is not available to other services;
– some clients may be allowed to issue more powerful queries, e.g., the statistics department may be allowed to issue queries that aggregate data whereas other clients may only be able to query individual employees.

To avoid undue multiplication of services it seems desirable to have a single service that handles all clients; on the other hand the differences in the clients may make it difficult or even impossible to define a single service interface or contract that satisfies the needs of all clients. Furthermore such an interface will expose unneeded complexity to clients that do not need advanced capabilities and the definition of a single policy that covers all the different clients is often difficult and poses governance and administration problems.

Forces.

- The service has to accommodate different types of consumers with important similarities but significant differences. For example, some customers may be less trusted than others.
- It is desirable to limit the number of deployed services and to avoid duplicated functionality in several services.
- Defining a single interface and a single contract that satisfy the needs of all clients is difficult or impossible.
- Exposing several contracts and interfaces for a service may increase the complexity of the system and make it more difficult for clients to choose an appropriate service.

Solution. The same underlying service implementation may expose several different interfaces or contracts. Each exposed interface or contract can be optimized for the needs of one customer or several customers with similar needs and trustworthiness. Each contract can be versioned and governed individually, thereby simplifying deployment and governance of individual contracts; interfaces are generally more closely tied to the service implementation than contracts, but by using a model-driven approach and carefully separating interfaces and implementation during design time a certain degree of independent versioning and governance can be ensured for interfaces as well; in particular it is often possible to maintain backward-compatible interfaces when the implementation of a service is upgraded.

On the other hand, having to provide the functionality for several contracts places additional burden on the implementation and evolution of the service itself. Care has to be taken that changes to the implementation do not violate the guarantees of any exposed interface or contract. This effect can be ameliorated by employing the formal methods developed as part of the SENSORIA project to verify that the implementation is faithful to the guarantees of each exposed interface or contract.

Similar situations exists for consumption and provisioning of the service: By providing multiple interfaces each client has to choose the most appropriate one; this increases the time a developer needs to understand the system and diminishes the positive effect of having specialized interfaces for the needs of several clients. For the service provider, multiplying the number of contracts and interfaces may increase the governance effort and deployment complexity of the whole system, even though they are reduced for each individual service interface. In both cases techniques developed by SENSORIA, in particular "call-by-contract" as provided by λ^{req} and the dynamic selection of available service interfaces and contracts by Dino [16], can help ameliorate these problems.

Consequences. *Pros:* Introducing new interfaces and contracts that are closely matched to the requirements of a group of clients can greatly simplify the development of clients as well as governance and deployment. Providing several interfaces can reduce the need for different services that provide closely related functionality.

Cons: Adding new interfaces to a service has similar governance and management overhead to adding completely new services. Indeterminate application of the *Concurrent Contracts* Pattern can therefore lead to a overly large service inventory that is difficult to use, maintain and develop.

Tools. By using UML4SOA in an early development stage, as for example with the application of the *Service Modeling* pattern, you can simplify the application of *Concurrent Contracts*. Service providers can also use UML4SOA during deployment to formulate the capabilities and potential consumers of each service contract.

When formal methods are used to verify the contracts with respect to their implementation, the model transformations and tools corresponding to the chosen verification method can be used. Particularly applicable tools for this pattern are PEPA or SMRC to analyze whether the performance characteristics of the provided contracts match the needs of the clients, see Chapter 5-3 (Scaling Performance Analysis using Fluid-Flow Approximation) and Chapter 5-5 (Quantitative Analysis of Services). Furthermore, λ^{req} enables requirements-based selection of service contracts, see Chapter 2-4 (Call-by-Contract for Service Discovery, Orchestration and Recovery). Dino can be used to provide semantic matching of services and interfaces at run time, see Chapter 6-3 (Runtime Support for Dynamic and Adaptive Service Composition). Process-calculus based static analysis methods can be used to verify the correctness of the provided contracts with respect to their implementation; see pattern *Analyze with Formal Methods* for more details.

Examples. Examples for the application of the *Concurrent Contracts* pattern can be found in Erl [8]; more detailed examples of the application of the SENSORIA methods are described in the chapters of this volume mentioned in the previous section. In addition Chapter 3-2 (Advanced Mechanisms for Service Composition, Query and Discovery) and Chapter 6-3 (Runtime Support for Dynamic and Adaptive Service Composition) provide information about dynamic discovery of appropriate service contracts.

Related Patterns. For *Concurrent Contracts* to be applied, the service contract itself should ideally be fully decoupled from the underlying service implementation; often a façade that supports multiple contracts without the need for redundant service logic can be used to implement this. See the patterns *Decoupled Contract* and *Service Façade* described in Erl [8] for further information about this topic. Other patterns that support different clients for a service are *Contract Denormalization* and *Validation Abstraction*, also described in Erl [8]. However, when using *Concurrent Contracts* the need for contract denormalization may be reduced since the capabilities required by different clients could be exposed by separate contracts.

Application of the *Concurrent Contracts* pattern can often be simplified by using the *Service Modeling* pattern to model the contracts and the shared implementation artifacts. After the *Concurrent Contracts* pattern has been applied, the *Analyze with Formal Methods* pattern can be used to ensure that the functional and non-functional properties of the resulting service satisfy the requirements of the contracts and interfaces.

3.2   Trusted Subsystem

As more and more critical data is stored in and processed by service-oriented systems, ensuring their availability while securing them against unauthorized access and malicious attacks has become a priority. A large number of tools and techniques have been developed to address these issues. Here we focus on one possible design pattern, the

Trusted Subsystem. Our description is an adaptation and extension of some important points presented in Thomas Erl's "SOA Design Patterns"; the full description of the pattern with examples and discussion of useful technologies can be found there.

Context. You are designing a service-oriented system that processes critical or confidential data. In this system, some services are exposed to clients that do not have access rights. You want to protect the data and make it easy and transparent to grant and revoke authorizations.

Problem. Granting clients direct access to services containing important data poses many security problem and complicates the management of authorizations. Furthermore it poses problems of *transitive trust:* if service A calls service B on behalf of client C, who is responsible for checking that the call is authorized?

Forces.

- Services should be protected from unauthorized access.
- Management of authorizations should be easy and transparent.

Solution. The services containing critical or confidential data can only be accessed via another service that is responsible for verifying the client's authorizations. This trusted front-end service always uses its own credentials to access the protected resources. Client authorizations are not passed on by the front-end to the protected resources, but a client identifier may be included in the calls to the protected resources. The trusted subsystem is responsible for verifying that all accesses to the resources are performed only by authorized clients and that clients cannot pass counterfeit identifiers to services. The front-end service thus establishes a trust boundary. When applying this pattern to several front-end services acting on the same resources it is possible to establish nested or overlapping trust boundaries.

Consequences. *Pros:* The front-end service is responsible for enforcing the trust boundary for the protected subsystems. Therefore there is a single point where access policy can be implemented, monitored and authored. Since credentials are established by the client for complete transactions there is no problem with transitive trust relationships. Services inside the trusted boundary can have very simple security mechanisms since they only have to authenticate the trusted subsystem.

Cons: The trusted subsystem is a single point of failure and also a potential performance bottleneck since it must process every interaction with the protected resources. Security breaches of the front-end can have devastating consequences for the whole system as a compromise of this subsystem can be used to exploit all downstream resources in its trust boundaries. It is therefore a prime target for attackers.

Neutral: SENSORIA methods can achieve a particularly good relationship between cost and effectiveness when they are applied to the trusted subsystem: by validating the security properties of this service using qualitative methods a high degree of trust in the security of the whole system inside the trust boundary can be established; by using qualitative analysis to analyze the performance characteristics of the system bottlenecks can be discovered and prevented during early design stages.

Tools. Essentially, the whole range of SENSORIA modeling and analysis methods can be gainfully employed to model and analyze the trusted subsystem. In particular, λ^{req} can often be used to validate the contracts of the trusted subsystems, and Lysa [3], the corresponding LysaTool [26,4] and CryptoKlaim [17] can be employed to establish the security of the protocols between clients and the trusted service as well as inside the trust boundary. Qualitative analysis of arbitrary properties including security is also supported by the SENSORIA model checkers WS-Engineer [9], CMC and UMC [21], and sCOWS [20]. Finally, the SRMC/PEPA tool [23] covers the performance side of the analysis with steady-state analysis of the underlying Markov chain of SRMC descriptions.

Examples. Examples for trusted subsystems can be found in Erl [8]. Qualitative analysis including verification of security properties is discussed in Chapter 4-2 (An Abstract, On-The-Fly Framework for the Verification of Service Oriented Systems), and Chapter 4-3 (Tools and Verification). See Chapter 4-1 (Analysing the Protocol Stack for Services) for an example of applying the LysaTool. Quantitative, and in particular performance analysis is discussed in Chapter 5-5 (Quantitative Analysis of Services).

Related Patterns. Since the *Trusted Subsystem* pattern identifies services which are particularly worthwhile targets for the SENSORIA tools and methods, it is related to most of the other patterns presented in this section: *Service Modeling* of the trusted subsystem can enable the use of other patterns, such as *Extract Formal Models*, *Analyze with Formal Methods*, or *Generate Implementation*.

4   Related Work

The idea of using patterns to describe common problems in software design and development was popularized by the so-called "Gang of Four" book [10]. Since its publication a wide range of patterns and pattern languages for many areas of software development has been published, see e.g. the Pattern Languages of Programs (PLoP) conferences and the associated Pattern Languages of Program Design volumes, or the LNCS Transactions on Pattern Languages of Programming.

   The area of patterns for SOA has recently gained a lot of attention, and several collections of design patterns for SOA have been published or announced [8,19]. The article [7] provides a short introduction. However, these patterns address more general problems of SOA, while our patterns are focused on the formally supported techniques provided by SENSORIA. Therefore, our patterns can serve as an extension of, rather than as a replacement for, other pattern catalogs.

5   Conclusions and Further Work

In this chapter, we have presented some results of the IST-FET EU project SENSORIA in the form of a pattern language. The patterns address a broad range of issues, such as modeling, specification, analysis, verification, orchestration, and deployment of services. As a final treat, the relationships between the patterns introduced in this chapter are shown in Fig. 1.

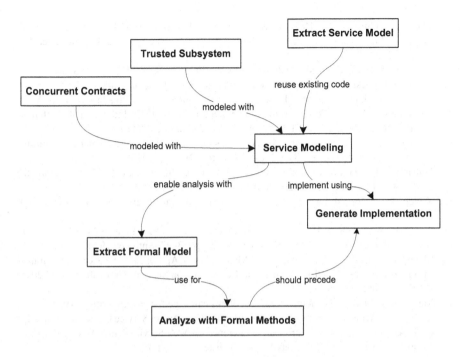

Fig. 1. SENSORIA pattern relationships

We are currently working on systematizing and extending the collection of patterns in these areas, and we will also be developing patterns for areas which are not currently addressed, e.g., business process analysis and modeling.

This pattern catalog is a useful guide to the research results of the SENSORIA project: as already mentioned in the introduction, we are investigating a broad range of subjects and without some guidance it may not be easy for software developers to find the appropriate tools or techniques.

References

1. Alpert, S., Brown, K., Woolf, B.: The Design Patterns Smalltalk Companion. Addison-Wesley Professional, Reading (1998)
2. ATX Technologies. Modernizing Software and Increasing Business Values,
   http://www.atxtechnologies.co.uk/
3. Bodei, C., Degano, P., Gao, H., Nielson, H.: Detecting Replay Attacks by Freshness Annotations. In: Proceedings of WITS 2007, Informatics and Mathematical Modelling, Technical University, Dipartimento di Informatica (April 2007)
4. Buchholtz, M., Nielson, H. R.: LySaTool,
   http://www.imm.dtu.dk/English/Research/LanguageBased_
   Technology/Software/LySaTool/
5. Buschmann, F., Henney, K., Schmidt, D.C.: Pattern Oriented Software Architecture On Patterns and Pattern Languages, vol. 5. Wilcy, Chichester (2007)

6. Clark, A., Gilmore, S., Hillston, J., Tribastone, M.: Stochastic Process Algebras. In: Bernardo, M., Hillston, J. (eds.) SFM 2007. LNCS, vol. 4486, pp. 132–179. Springer, Heidelberg (2007)
7. Erl, T.: Introducing soa design patterns. SOA World Magazine 8(6) (June 2008)
8. Erl, T.: SOA Design Patterns. Prentice Hall/Pearson PTR, London (2008)
9. Foster, H., Uchitel, S., Kramer, J., Magee, J.: WS-Engineer: A Tool for Model-Based Verification of Web Service Compositions and Choreography. In: IEEE International Conference on Software Engineering (ICSE 2006), Shanghai, China (May 2006)
10. Gamma, E., Helm, R., Johnson, R., Vlissides, J.: Design patterns: elements of reusable object-oriented software. Addison-Wesley Co., Inc., Boston (1995)
11. Hillston, J.: Fluid Flow Approximation of PEPA models. In: Proc. 2nd Int. Conf. Quantitative Evaluation of Systems (QEST 2005). IEEE, Los Alamitos (2005)
12. Knapp, A.: A formal approach to object-oriented software engineering. Softwaretechnik-Trends 21(3) (2001)
13. Lapadula, A., Pugliese, R., Tiezzi, F.: A Calculus for Orchestration of Web Services. In: Nicola, R.D. (ed.) ESOP 2007. LNCS, vol. 4421, pp. 33–47. Springer, Heidelberg (2007)
14. Mayer, P., Schroeder, A., Koch, N.: A Model-Driven Approach to Service Orchestration. In: Proceedings of the IEEE International Conference on Services Computing (SCC 2008). IEEE, Los Alamitos (2008)
15. Meszaros, G., Doble, J.: Metapatterns: A pattern language for pattern writing (1996)
16. Mukhija, A., Dingwall-Smith, A., Rosenblum, D.: QoS-Aware Service Composition in Dino. In: Proceedings of the 5th European Conference on Web Services (ECOWS 2007), Halle, Germany. IEEE Computer Society Press, Los Alamitos (2007)
17. Nielsen, C., Nielson, F., Nielson, H.: CryptoKlaim. Work in progress (2006)
18. OMG. Service Oriented Architecture Modelling Language Beta 1,
    http://www.soaml.org
19. Rotem-Gal-Oz, A.: SOA Patterns. Manning (2009) (to appear)
20. Schivo, S.: sCOWS Model Checker,
    http://sites.google.com/site/sschivo/scows-model-checker
21. ter Beek, M.H., Mazzanti, F., Gnesi, S.: Cmc-umc: a framework for the verification of abstract service-oriented properties. In: Shin, S.Y., Ossowski, S. (eds.) SAC, pp. 2111–2117. ACM, New York (2009)
22. Tiezzi, F.: Venus: A Verification ENvironment for UML models of Services,
    http://rap.dsi.unifi.it/cows/
23. Tribastone, M.: The PEPA Plug-in Project. In: Fourth International Conference on the Quantitative Evaluation of Systems, UK, pp. 53–54. IEEE Computer Society Press, Los Alamitos (2007)
24. VIATRA2 Project. VIATRA2 (VIsual Automated model TRansformations),
    http://dev.eclipse.org/viewcvs/indextech.cgi/gmthome/
    subprojects/VIATRA2/index.html
25. Wirsing, M., Hölzl, M.M., Acciai, L., Banti, F., Clark, A., Fantechi, A., Gilmore, S., Gnesi, S., Gönczy, L., Koch, N., Lapadula, A., Mayer, P., Mazzanti, F., Pugliese, R., Schroeder, A., Tiezzi, F., Tribastone, M., Varró, D.: SENSORIA Patterns: Augmenting Service Engineering with Formal Analysis, Transformation and Dynamicity. In: Margaria, T., Steffen, B. (eds.) ISoLA 2008. Communications in Computer and Information Science, vol. 17, pp. 170–190. Springer, Heidelberg (2008)
26. Yüksel, E., Nielson, H., Nielsen, C., Örencik, M.: A Secure Simplification of the PKMv2 Protocol in IEEE 802.16e-2005. In: FCS-ARSPA 2007 Informal Proceedings (2007)

Author Index